ENCYCLOPEDIA YEAR BOOK
1982

GROLIER

This annual has been prepared as a yearbook for general encyclopedias. It is also published as *The Americana Annual.*

Library of Congress Catalog Card Number: 48-171

ISBN: 0-7172-0813-3

ISSN: 0196-0172

Printed in the United States of America

COVER PHOTO CREDITS: (front) Industrialized nations summit conference—UPI; Egyptian leaders—Barry Iverson/Gamma-Liaison; Reagan inauguration, Pope John Paul II, AWACS, royal wedding, baseball strike ends—UPI; French leaders—Gamma-Liaison; (spine) Sandra Day O'Connor—Michael Ging/Black Star; (back) hostages—Gamma-Liaison; space shuttle, David Stockman and Donald Regan—UPI; Northern Ireland hunger strike—Sutton/Liaison; Haig and Gromyko, Lena Horne, air traffic controllers strike—UPI; John McEnroe—Fred Mullane/Sports Photo File; videodisc—Courtesy, Matsushita News Center; Rubik's Cube—Gene Maggio—The New York Times Pictures.

CONTENTS

FEATURE ARTICLES OF THE YEAR

THE ALPHABETICAL SECTION

Separate entries on the continents, the major nations of the world, U.S. states, Canadian provinces, and chief cities will be found under their own alphabetically arranged headings.

ECONOMICS AND INDUSTRY

GOVERNMENT, HUMAN WELFARE, LAW, AND POLITICS

HUMANITIES, ARTS, AND HOBBIES

SCIENCE AND TECHNOLOGY

MISCELLANEOUS

SPECIAL REPORTS

THE YEAR IN REVIEW

By Peter Jennings
Chief Foreign Correspondent
ABC NEWS

*Representatives of 22 nations and the UN attended the North-South conference at Cancún, Mexico, in October.**

How uncomplicated the year would have been if the 1981 baseball strike had been the only disruption in American lives.

Unfortunately, it was also the year when a great many people became convinced that some politicians actually considered "a limited nuclear war" possible. An inflexible, aging Soviet leadership and a new U.S. president determined to reassert American strength (as he saw it) combined to make East-West relations the centerpiece of international attention.

The emphasis of the Ronald Reagan administration on military solutions to what others regarded as political problems alarmed the international community. The reaction in Western Europe was the reinvigoration of campaigns for nuclear disarmament, more specifically a sharp increase in unilateralism. The NATO alliance's 1979 decision to deploy new U.S. cruise and Pershing missiles in Western Europe by 1983 was widely and seriously questioned. A great many Europeans were every bit as concerned about President Reagan's policies and outlook on the world as they were about those of the Soviet Union. The now lengthy Soviet campaign against deploying new missiles in Europe made inroads, particularly among the young. The Soviets convinced many Europeans that Moscow was more interested in negotiating arms reductions than was the new team in Washington. Popular pressure on European governments to reverse their 1979 decisions intensified.

While the superpowers were increasing their military budgets, the rich and poor nations—including the United States but not the Soviet Union—were meeting in Cancún, Mexico. The participants failed to reach any understanding on how urgently solutions were needed for the problems of the very poorest nations. The United States was the most outspoken opponent of global negotiations for a reapportionment of the world's wealth. American prestige was not helped by the view held in many developing countries that the new administration in Washington couldn't visualize what the problems really were in resource-poor, overpopulated regions of the world.

In the United States itself, the most fundamental shift in domestic economic policy since the New Deal began to cut deeply into programs for the less privileged. The president's harshest critics said his policies were turning the war against poverty into a war against the poor. Reaganomics, as it was sometimes called, did mark the first time since the 1930s that the U.S. government hadn't tried to spend its way out of recession. By year's end the administration was backing off its commitments to a balanced budget by 1984. The president's ideological goal was characterized as an attempt to bring about permanent shrinkage in the American economy.

Speaking of possible turning points—America's labor leaders viewed the government's harsh application of law against striking air traffic controllers as a possible turning point in U.S. labor history.

It was a year when those looking for trends seemed more exhausted than usual by their efforts. Establishment politics in a good part of the industrialized world first shifted to the right, with the notable exception of the election in France of a Socialist president. But by year's end, hard pressed by unemployment and high interest rates, the industrial world's electorate was all for a little more Keynes and a little less of the Reagan revolution.

It was a year when contradictions were unusually confusing. The U.S. government cracked down on the nation's air controllers, yes, but it was also the first to support the continuing battle by Poland's independent unions to undermine Soviet influence in the Warsaw Pact. President Reagan's hard-line, anti-Soviet policies were put aside when he lifted the grain embargo applied by the Jimmy Carter administration. The debate over Poland's debt, largely to Western banks, raged on. Was it unwise to ease financial pressure on the Soviets, or was it a humanitarian commitment to Polish citizens seeking a freer life?

Individuals seemed more inclined than ever to take out their personal vengeance on public figures. President Reagan survived an attempt on his life, as did Pope John Paul II. In Iran, high office almost guaranteed an assassination attempt, often successful. In Egypt, President Anwar el-Sadat died at the hands of Muslim extremists trying to ignite a revolution similar to the one in Iran.

Michael Evans/The White House

By year's end a major question was whether President Sadat's bold experiment in peacemaking with Israel would survive him. The Reagan administration had its way with Congress over the sale of AWACS planes to Saudi Arabia, but U.S. foreign policy in the Middle East continued to be uncertain. The Camp David agreements may have almost run their course. Palestinian autonomy talks, an ingredient of those accords, continued to exclude Palestinians living under Israeli control. The Palestine Liberation Organization (PLO) continued to score modest diplomatic victories. An alternate peace plan, proposed by Saudi Arabia, won some support. The Reagan administration clearly would like the AWACS agreement to fit into a wider, successful Middle East diplomacy, but it had difficulty convincing many Arab governments that the Soviet threat was the most important factor in regional destabilization. Libya's mercurial Muammar el-Qaddafi received more than his usual share of attention.

If the United States sometimes seemed bemused by the complexities of the Middle East, the events of 1981 in Central America conspired to make many Americans more aware of their own backyard. The much-beleaguered, U.S.-supported government in El Salvador caused enormous headaches in Washington. The Reagan administration, intent on drawing the line on what it regards as Communist-inspired revolution, was determined to stop another left-wing takeover.

Antigovernment forces were regarded in Washington as terrorists, but Mexico and France, two of America's most important allies, recognized the opposition as a "representative political force." Guatemala was being shaken by political violence, and Nicaragua was ruled by the left-wing Sandinistas. Costa Rica, the only long-standing democracy in the region, was teetering on the brink of bankruptcy.

A pause, you suggest, for something to lighten the heart.

On Inauguration Day, Americans received their best gift of the year. The hostages were released from Iran to a genuine outpouring of national euphoria. The rest of the allied world shared America's relief and relished the possibility that U.S. foreign policy would no longer be paralyzed. By year's end the national nightmare had receded.

Columbia flew successfully. The world's first reusable spacecraft provided at least a temporary psychological boost for a nation beset by doubts as to its own technological prowess. Long-term benefits remained in question.

Prince Charles married Lady Diana. Royalists and sentimentalists the world over were delighted, and it was hard for the rest not to notice. When the media pay as much attention to the problem of international refugees, the world will seem better balanced to some. The UN High Commissioner for Refugees did win the Nobel Prize for Peace.

For many months—and 1981 was not exceptional in this regard—Northern Ireland was anything but peaceful. IRA prisoners resorted to hunger strikes to try to force changes in their prison status. The protest cost ten prisoners' lives, and its success in the short run was questionable. The IRA's long-term goal, evicting the British from Northern Ireland, seemed just as distant. On mainland Britain, a generation of young unemployed and nonwhites, each and sometimes together, resorted to violence to draw attention to the nation's industrial and economic problems. Britain's reputation for civility and tolerance was somewhat tarnished. Canada continued to fight over its national constitution. Greece elected a socialist prime minister, who despite his advance billing, hastened to reassure his NATO partners that Western defenses would not suddenly be crippled. The Chinese image-makers took another crack at the once top billing of Mao Zedong. The new Chinese leadership's promises of greater freedoms looked to be less than ironclad.

The L.A. Dodgers won the World Series.

** Standing, from left: Pres. Krajer (Yugoslavia), Pres. Nyerere (Tanzania), P. M. Thatcher (Britain), P. M. Suzuki (Japan), P. M. Burnham (Guyana), Pres. Mitterrand (France), P. M. Gandhi (India), Pres. Shagari (Nigeria), P. M. Fälldin (Sweden), Pres. Herrera Campíns (Venezuela), Sec. Gen. Waldheim (UN). Seated, from left: Pres. Reagan (U.S.), For. Min. Aké (Ivory Coast), Pres. Sattar (Bangladesh), Pres. Benjedid (Algeria), For. Min. Genscher (W. Ger.), P.M. Trudeau (Canada), Pres. López Portillo (Mex.), Prince Fahd (Saudi Arabia), For. Min. Pahr (Austria), For. Min. Guerreiro (Brazil), P. M. Zhao (China), Pres. Marcos (Philippines).*

Ken Regan/Camera 5

JANUARY

1 Greece officially becomes the tenth member of the European Community.

Premier Abdou Diouf replaces the retiring Léopold Sedar Senghor as president of Senegal.

5 The 97th U.S. Congress convenes in Washington, with the Senate and House controlled by different parties—Republican and Democratic, respectively—for the first time in 49 years.

Prime Minister Margaret Thatcher of Great Britain announces her first cabinet changes since taking office in May 1979.

6 After a four-day visit by Chad's President Goukouni Oueddei, Libya announces that the two countries will merge.

9 U.S. Rep. Raymond F. Lederer (D-PA) is found guilty on charges of bribery and conspiracy relating to the Abscam investigation.

14 In his farewell address to the nation, U.S. President Jimmy Carter focuses on three issues: "The threat of nuclear destruction, our stewardship of the physical resources of our planet, and the preeminence of the basic rights of human beings."

António Ramalho Eanes is sworn in for his second term as president of Portugal. Five days earlier, Prime Minister Francisco Pinto Balsemão and his coalition cabinet had been sworn in.

17 President Ferdinand Marcos of the Philippines calls an end to eight years of martial law and orders the release of 341 prisoners.

18 Canada's Prime Minister Pierre Elliott Trudeau concludes a six-nation, 23-day tour to promote "a revolution in economic development for the world's poor nations."

20 The 52 American hostages in Iran are freed after 444 days of captivity and flown to a U.S. Air Force base in Wiesbaden, West Germany. Their release follows the signing one day earlier of an accord negotiated through Algerian intermediaries. A principal element was the return of $8,000,000,000 in Iranian assets frozen in the United States.

Ronald Wilson Reagan, 69, takes the oath of office as the 40th president of the United States.

Gamma/Liaison

The freed American hostages arrive in Wiesbaden, West Germany, exulting in the end of their ordeal.

UPI

January in Washington was a time of celebration. Fireworks lit the sky over the Lincoln Memorial on the eve of the presidential inauguration. Right, Chief Justice Warren Burger administers the oath of office. The release of the hostages came literally minutes after the swearing-in.

UPI

Flags adorn the south lawn of the White House as the newly-installed president honors the returned hostages with an official reception January 27.

25 Behind quarterback Jim Plunkett, the Oakland Raiders defeat the Philadelphia Eagles, 27–10, in pro football's Super Bowl XV.

Jiang Qing, a member of China's so-called "Gang of Four," and nine other defendants are convicted of crimes committed during the Cultural Revolution. Their sentences range from 16 years in prison to possible death for Jiang.

31 Polish government officials and Solidarity leader Lech Walesa agree on a 40-hour, five-day workweek for the labor union in 1982.

FEBRUARY

3 The U.S. Senate confirms Raymond Donovan as secretary of labor, completing the confirmation process for the Reagan cabinet.

4 Gro Harlem Brundtland becomes the first woman premier of Norway, replacing Odvar Nordli, who resigned January 29.

5 In a televised address to the nation, President Ronald Reagan warns that the United States faces "an economic calamity of tremendous proportions" and urges Congress to cooperate in cutting federal spending and personal income tax.

U.S. Marine Corps Private Robert Garwood is convicted by a military tribunal of collaborating with the enemy and assaulting a fellow soldier while a prisoner of war in Vietnam.

8 Eight persons are killed and at least 200 injured as fire, apparently the result of arson, sweeps through 20 floors of the Las Vegas (NV) Hilton Hotel.

9 In the face of continuing labor unrest, Polish Premier Josef Pinkowski is replaced by the country's defense minister, Gen. Wojciech Jaruzelski, 57.

10 Cynthia Dwyer, an American free-lance journalist, is released by Iran after spending more than nine months in prison for alleged espionage.

11 Chun Doo Hwan, who had assumed power in September 1980, is elected to a full seven-year term as president of South Korea.

13 Australian publishing magnate Rupert Murdoch buys the prestigious daily *Times of London* newspaper for a reported $27 million.

18 In his first State of the Union address, President Reagan presents to Congress an economic recovery program calling for a total reduction of $49,000,000,000 from former President Carter's federal budget for fiscal 1982 and a 10% cut in individual income tax beginning July 1, 1981.

24 Spanish civil guards, led by Lt. Col. Antonio Tejero Molina, end an 18-hour occupation of the parliament building in Madrid. The attempted right-wing coup fails, as the army remains loyal to King Juan Carlos, who opposed the takeover. The cabinet and legislators had been taken hostage while voting on the proposed new government headed by Leopoldo Calvo Sotelo. No one was injured in the assault.

Prince Charles, the 32-year-old heir to the English throne, and Lady Diana Spencer, 19, the daughter of an earl, announce their engagement. A July wedding is expected.

26 Pope John Paul II concludes a 12-day pilgrimage to the Philippines, Guam, and Japan.

27 After posting a deficit of $1,710,000,000 for 1980, the largest annual loss ever for an American company, Chrysler Corp. is granted an additional $400,000,000 in federal loan guarantees.

J. Pavlovsky/Sygma

Spanish legislators are set free after being held overnight in a failed coup.

MARCH

1 British Prime Minister Margaret Thatcher concludes a three-day visit to Washington, during which she discussed economic and strategic issues with U.S. President Reagan.

2 The United States sends 20 additional military advisers and $25,000,000 in new aid to El Salvador after the State Department issued a report (February 23) with "definitive evidence" that several Communist countries, principally Cuba, had been providing arms and military training to leftist rebels in El Salvador.

3 At the conclusion of the 26th Congress of the Communist Party of the Soviet Union, President Leonid Brezhnev announces that the entire Politburo has been reelected to a new five-year term.

5 The city of Atlanta, GA, is promised nearly $1,000,000 in federal aid for child mental health and social programs in the wake of the unsolved murders of at least 22 black children.

11 Gen. Augusto Pinochet declares himself the president of Chile for an eight-year term.

President Reagan ends a two-day visit to Canada, his first trip abroad since taking office.

14 Three Pakistani gunmen who had hijacked a Pakistani airliner March 2 and held hostage its more than 100 passengers and crewmen on an airstrip in Damascus, Syria, since March 9, surrender to authorities. The hijackers freed the hostages after Pakistan agreed to their demands for the release of 54 political prisoners and after Libya reportedly agreed to accept the hijackers. But the Libyans then refused to allow the plane to enter, and the aircraft returned to Damascus.

Michael Evans/The White House

Policeman Thomas Delahanty (foreground) and James Brady, the president's press secretary, lay wounded near a side entrance to the Washington Hilton Hotel, as Secret Service agents hold down the alleged assailant. President Reagan, wounded, has already been rushed away from the scene.

15 President David Dacko of the Central African Republic is reelected.

22 Rate increases approved by the board of governors of the U.S. Postal Service on March 10 take effect. First-class postage rises from 15 to 18 cents for the first ounce.

23 The U.S. Supreme Court rules, 6–3, that a state can make it a criminal offense for a doctor to perform an abortion on a teenage girl without informing her parents (*H.L. v. Matheson*).

24 The White House reports that Vice-President George Bush has been selected by President Reagan to head a special "crisis management" team. Secretary of State Alexander Haig publicly expresses his "lack of enthusiasm."

26 The Social Democratic Party, a new centrist party in Great Britain, officially comes into existence.

Norway and Sweden sign a 20-year energy cooperation agreement.

27 A Los Angeles Superior Court jury rules that the *National Enquirer* had libeled actress Carol Burnett in a 1976 article and orders the magazine to pay her $1,600,000 in damages.

29 Gen. Roberto Eduardo Viola is sworn in as the president of Argentina, replacing the retiring Gen. Jorge R. Videla.

30 President Reagan is shot in the chest outside the Washington Hilton Hotel, undergoes surgery to remove the bullet, and is given an "excellent" chance of complete recovery. Also struck in the barrage of .22-caliber revolver shots is White House Press Secretary James S. Brady, Secret Service agent Timothy J. McCarthy, and District of Columbia policeman Thomas Delahanty. The alleged assailant, 25-year-old John Warnock Hinckley, Jr., is tackled by Secret Service agents at the scene of the shooting and is whisked away in a police car for booking.

A tentative agreement is reached between Polish government negotiators and leaders of the labor union Solidarity, and a general strike threatened for the next day is canceled. The tentative accord comes three days after a four-hour warning strike by most of the country's 13,000,000 industrial workers, the largest organized protest in the history of modern Poland.

Indiana University wins the National Collegiate Athletic Association (NCAA) men's basketball championship by defeating the University of North Carolina, 63–50.

APRIL

3 Thai troops loyal to Prime Minister Prem Tinsulanonda retake government headquarters in Bangkok two days after the buildings were seized in an attempted coup by a group of army officers.

6 Mark Eyskens is sworn in as the prime minister of Belgium, replacing Wilfried Martens, whose government resigned March 31 in a dispute over economic policy.

7 The Warsaw Pact ends three weeks of military maneuvers around Poland, after Soviet President Leonid Brezhnev states that the Polish government would be able to solve its own problems.

In a nationwide plebiscite, voters in the Philippines approve constitutional amendments which would establish a modified form of parliamentary government and permit President Ferdinand Marcos to run for another six-year term.

8 U.S. Secretary of State Alexander Haig ends four days of talks in the Middle East with leaders of Egypt, Israel, Jordan, and Syria.

A federally-funded study by sociologist Dr. James S. Coleman concludes that private and parochial high schools provide a better education than public high schools.

10 A United Nations conference on African refugee problems ends two days of meetings, during which the 85 attending nations pledged $563,000,000 in aid through 1982.

12 Tom Watson wins the 45th Masters golf tournament at the Augusta (GA) National Golf Club.

Joe Louis, whom many consider one of the greatest heavyweight boxing champions of all time, dies in Las Vegas, NV, at age 66.

13 The Parti Québécois (PQ) of provincial Premier René Lévesque is reelected to a five-year term as Quebec's governing party.

14 The U.S. space shuttle Columbia lands safely at Edwards Air Force Base in California 54 hours after lift-off from Cape Canaveral, FL. The 36-orbit mission is considered an overwhelming success.

Mayor Tom Bradley of Los Angeles is elected to his third term.

15 *The Washington Post* announces that it is relinquishing the Pulitzer Prize that had been awarded two days earlier to one of its reporters, Janet Cooke, for a feature story about an eight-year-old heroin addict. Cooke revealed that the story had been fabricated.

NASA

The space shuttle Columbia glides in for an airplane-like landing, ending a successful maiden voyage.

17 The Polish government and members of Rural Solidarity sign an agreement granting the farmers' union official recognition by May 10.

24 U.S. President Reagan lifts the 15-month-old embargo on grain sales to the USSR.

28 In his first major public appearance since being wounded March 30, President Reagan makes a televised address before Congress in which he appeals for passage of his budget program.

Israeli jets shoot down two Syrian helicopters said to have been attacking Lebanese Christian militia in Lebanon. Two Syrians are reported killed in the attack. It is Israel's first aerial intervention in the escalating conflict.

MAY

1 The Japanese government announces that it will voluntarily limit its automobile exports to the United States for at least two years, and possibly a third.

Sen. Harrison J. Williams (D-NJ) is found guilty by a federal jury on nine criminal charges relating to the Abscam investigation.

4 Gov. Edward King of Massachusetts signs a bill providing $9,400,-000 in state funds for Boston's school system, which officially ran out of money April 16.

5 Irish hunger-striker Robert Sands dies in Maze Prison, Belfast. A member of the Irish Republican Army (IRA) who had been elected to Parliament, Sands demanded that IRA inmates be recognized as political prisoners and not common criminals.

6 U.S. diplomat Philip Habib leaves Washington on a special mediation mission to Jerusalem, Beirut, and Damascus. A Soviet official also arrives in Damascus to help mediate the crisis between Israel and Syria over the latter's missiles in Lebanon.

Gamma/Liaison

The presidency of France passed from Valéry Giscard d'Estaing (left) to François Mitterrand (right).

10 François Mitterrand, 64, the leader of France's Socialist Party, defeats incumbent Valéry Giscard d'Estaing in the second round of presidential balloting. Mitterrand will become the nation's first left-wing president since the founding of the Fifth Republic in 1958.

13 Pope John Paul II is shot and wounded in an assassination attempt in a crowded St. Peter's Square. Two bullets strike the pontiff, one in the abdomen, and he is rushed to a hospital for emergency intestinal surgery. Police immediately arrest a Turkish terrorist, Mehmet Ali Agca, who had threatened the pope once before.

14 The Boston Celtics win their 14th National Basketball Association championship by defeating the Houston Rockets, 102–91, in the sixth game of their best-of-seven final play-off series.

16 Japanese Foreign Minister Masayoshi Ito resigns in a dispute with Prime Minister Zenko Suzuki over the country's defense relations with the United States. After two days of talks with U.S. President Reagan in Washington, May 7–8, Suzuki had joined in a communiqué in which he promised to increase Japan's defense forces. Sunao Sonada is quickly named Ito's successor.

21 The U.S. Senate ratifies, 76–20, a $695,450,000,000 compromise budget resolution for fiscal 1982. The House of Representatives approved, 244–155, the administration-endorsed resolution one day earlier.

The New York Islanders win their second straight National Hockey League championship by defeating the Minnesota North Stars, 5–1, in the fifth game of their best-of-seven Stanley Cup play-off series.

A sympathizer of the Irish Republican Army seeks support for the imprisoned IRA hunger strikers.

Sutton/Liaison

22 West German Chancellor Helmut Schmidt ends two days of talks at the White House with President Reagan on the U.S.-Soviet nuclear buildup and the possibility of future arms limitation talks.

Prime Minister Thorbjörn Fälldin of Sweden forms a new minority coalition government, removing the need for national elections. The previous coalition broke up May 4 in a disagreement over tax policy.

In the so-called "Yorkshire Ripper" trial, Peter Sutcliffe is found guilty by a London jury and sentenced to a life term for 13 murders and seven attempted murders.

24 President Jaime Roldós Aguilera of Ecuador is killed in a plane crash near the Peruvian border.

26 A U.S. Marine EA-6B combat jet crashes during an attempted night landing on the deck of the nuclear aircraft carrier *Nimitz*. Fourteen men are killed and 48 others injured in the crash and ensuing fire; three F-14 fighter planes are destroyed and 16 others damaged.

At the end of a two-day meeting in Geneva, 12 of the 13 members of the Organization of Petroleum Exporting Countries (OPEC) agree to freeze crude oil prices and cut production by at least 10%.

30 President Ziaur Rahman of Bangladesh and two aides are slain in an unsuccessful coup attempt by a group of military leaders. Vice-President Abdus Sattar declares a state of emergency and assumes the duties of acting president.

UPI

Elizabeth Taylor won acclaim for her Broadway debut in The Little Foxes.

JUNE

4 Israeli Prime Minister Menahem Begin and Egyptian President Anwar el-Sadat meet in Sharm el-Sheikh in Israeli-occupied Sinai for their first high-level talks since January 1980.

5 Ernest Lefever, President Reagan's nominee for assistant secretary of state for human rights, withdraws from consideration after the Senate Foreign Relations Committee recommends, 13–4, that he be rejected by the full Senate body.

7 Israeli fighter planes attack and destroy the Osirak nuclear reactor near Baghdad, Iraq. The Israeli government claims that the plant was producing an atomic bomb to use against Israel.

8 President José López Portillo of Mexico begins two days of talks with President Reagan in Washington.

UPI

Protestors demonstrate against the docking in Japan of the U.S. aircraft carrier *Midway*. The action comes in the wake of disclosures that American ships armed with nuclear weapons had entered Japanese waters and ports.

8 Two days after ratifying a 40-month contract, striking coal miners begin returning to work in Eastern coal fields. The 72-day strike by 160,000 members of the United Mine Workers union was the second longest in the industry's history.

12 Major league baseball players go on strike in a disagreement with team owners over the issue of free-agent compensation.

13 Several blank pistol cartridges are fired at Queen Elizabeth II of Great Britain as she rides through London on horseback in a ceremony marking her official birthday.

15 After several months of negotiations, the United States agrees to provide Pakistan with $3,000,000,000 in economic and military aid.

16 In Peking, U.S. Secretary of State Alexander Haig announces that the United States has decided to begin selling arms to China.

President Ferdinand Marcos of the Philippines is reelected to a six-year term.

21 In the second stage of elections for France's National Assembly, the Socialist Party wins an absolute majority, giving newly-elected President François Mitterrand solid control of the government. The first round of balloting was held June 14.

22 Abolhassan Bani-Sadr is dismissed as president of Iran by religious ruler Ayatollah Ruhollah Khomeini.

25 The U.S. Supreme Court rules, 6–5, that the exemption of women from having to register for the military draft is not unconstitutional (*Rostker v. Goldberg*).

27 The 50-nation Organization of African Unity concludes a four-day annual summit in Nairobi, Kenya.

The army chief of staff and national commander of Bolivia are placed under arrest after an attempted coup.

28 A bomb explosion at offices of the Islamic Republican Party in Tehran kills 72 Iranian politicians, including Chief Justice Ayatollah Mohammed Beheshti and four cabinet ministers.

29 The Central Committee of the Chinese Community Party names Hu Yaobang, 66, as the successor to Chairman Hua Guofeng.

30 Garret FitzGerald of the Fine Gael Party is elected prime minister of Ireland by the Dáil (lower house of parliament).

David Rubinger/TIME

An Israeli soldier casts his vote in parliamentary elections. The balloting produced no clear winner.

JULY

2 The U.S. Supreme Court rules that Presidents Carter and Reagan had the legal authority to enforce the agreement with Iran that in January led to the release of the American hostages in Iran.

4 John McEnroe wins the men's singles title at Wimbledon. In four sets the American tennis star defeated Björn Borg, who was seeking his sixth consecutive Wimbledon crown. Earlier Chris Evert Lloyd took her third Wimbledon women's singles title.

6 Isabel Martinez de Perón, former president of Argentina, is ordered freed following five years of house arrest in Buenos Aires.

7 President Reagan announces that he will nominate Sandra Day O'Connor, 51-year-old judge on the Arizona Court of Appeals, to the U.S. Supreme Court. The retirement of Justice Potter Stewart caused the court vacancy.

8 Prime Minister Margaret Thatcher pleads for calm as British cities continue to experience outbreaks of violence.

9 Prime Minister Menahem Begin closes Israel's border with Jordan to two-way tourist travel.

11 Italy's Prime Minister Giovanni Spadolini wins a vote of confidence in the Chamber of Deputies. The Senate had approved the new cabinet on July 9.

17 Israeli jets bomb a densely populated area of Beirut, Lebanon, killing some 300 persons. An urgent session of the UN Security Council convenes to discuss the attack.

Wayne B. Williams, a 23-year-old music promoter, is indicted on charges of murdering two black youths in Atlanta.

The UN General Assembly conference on Cambodia concludes with a call for the withdrawal of Vietnamese troops and for UN-supervised elections.

Two walkways suspended above the Hyatt Regency Hotel lobby in Kansas City (MO) collapse, killing at least 111 persons.

A cartoonist's view of the appointment of the first woman, Sandra Day O'Connor, to the U.S. Supreme Court.

David Burnett/Contact

McNamee/"Newsweek"

The new Princess of Wales and her husband, Prince Charles, ride in an open carriage through the streets of London following their July 29 nuptials in St. Paul's Cathedral, right.

18 Stanislaw Kania is reelected chairman of Poland's Communist Party in a historic secret ballot at the party congress.

21 Leaders of seven major industrial democracies conclude their annual economic conference in Ottawa, Canada.

22 Mehmet Ali Agca is found guilty of attempting to murder Pope John Paul II and two American women in St. Peter's Square on May 18. The 23-year-old Turk is sentenced to life in prison.

The Chrysler Corporation announces that it earned $11.6 million in the second quarter of 1981, its first profitable period since the fourth quarter of 1978.

23 Time Inc. announces that its newspaper *The Washington Star* will cease publication on August 7.

24 Israeli and Palestinian forces agree to a cease-fire across the Israel-Lebanon frontier.

27 President Reagan delivers a televised address urging support "for the first real tax cut for everyone in 20 years."

29 Charles, the prince of Wales, and Lady Diana Spencer are married in St. Paul's Cathedral in London.

Abolhassan Bani-Sadr, the deposed president of Iran, is granted political asylum in France. Mohammed Ali Rajai was elected president of Iran on July 24.

31 Omar Torrijos Herrera, 52-year-old Panamanian strongman, is killed in an airplane crash.

AUGUST

1 Gen. Gregorio Alvarez is designated president of Uruguay, effective Sept. 1, 1981.

3 Representatives of Egypt and Israel sign an agreement establishing a 2,500-member peacekeeping force in the Sinai following Israel's withdrawal.

5 The U.S. Federal Aviation Administration begins sending dismissal notices to striking air traffic controllers. Some 13,000 air traffic controllers had gone on strike across the United States on August 3.

Israel's new four-party coalition government, headed by Prime Minister Menahem Begin, wins a vote of confidence in the Knesset (parliament).

President Reagan welcomes Egypt's President Anwar el-Sadat to the White House for talks.

E.I. duPont de Nemours & Company announces that it has acquired a controlling interest in Conoco Inc., the ninth largest U.S. oil company.

9 Major league baseball returns to the U.S.-Canadian scene following a seven-week strike by the players. The National League defeats the American League, 5–4, in the 52d All-Star Game.

10 U.S. Secretary of Defense Caspar W. Weinberger tells reporters that the United States had decided recently to produce neutron weapons.

11 The Canadian Union of Postal Workers accepts a new contract, ending a six-week strike by Canada's postal workers.

13 President Reagan signs into law the Economic Recovery Tax Bill and the Omnibus Budget Reconciliation Bill. According to the president, the tax act "represents $750,000,000,000 in tax cuts over the next five years" and "the budget reduction bill means $130,000,000,000 in savings over the next three years."

14 Polish leaders, including party chairman Stanislaw Kania, and Soviet President Brezhnev begin "a friendly, working visit" in Crimea.

Members of the Professional Air Traffic Controllers Organization (PATCO) went on strike August 3, causing the delay and even the cancellation of many scheduled flights.

Michael Grecco/Picture Group

William Campbell/Sygma

Egypt's President Anwar el-Sadat (right) and Israel's Prime Minister Menahem Begin meet in Alexandria, Egypt, August 25–26. The two heads of state agree to resume Palestinian autonomy talks.

17 The United States announces the end of the suspension of deliveries of F-16s and F-15s to Israel.

19 The United States announces that two navy F-14 jets shot down two Soviet-built Libyan SU-22s about 60 mi (96 km) from the Libyan coast. According to the spokesman, the Navy jets had first been fired on by the Libyan planes. The United States calls the attack "unprovoked" and a matter of "grave concern."

24 The Reagan administration formally informs Congress that it intends to sell five radar planes, known as Airborne Warning and Control Systems (AWACS), and other air-defense equipment to Saudi Arabia. Congress has until October 30 to vote a joint resolution against the sale.

In New York City, Mark David Chapman, who pleaded guilty to the murder of former Beatle John Lennon, is sentenced to 20 years to life in prison.

25 The U.S. Voyager 2 spacecraft sweeps past Saturn, transmitting photos of the planet's rings and moons.

26 Egypt's President Sadat and Israel's Prime Minister Begin conclude their 12th meeting in four years after agreeing to resume the Palestinian autonomy talks.

27 A U.S. State Department spokesman "confirms" that North Korea "fired a missile at a U.S. Air Force plane flying in South Korea and international air space" on August 26.

30 A bomb explodes in an office in Tehran killing Iran's President Mohammed Ali Rajai and Prime Minister Javad Bahonar.

31 The United States vetoes a Security Council resolution condemning South Africa for its raid into Angola. On August 26 South Africa's Prime Minister P. W. Botha acknowledged that South African forces had entered Angola in pursuit of Angolan-based guerrillas who had been fighting for the independence of South-West Africa (Namibia).

SEPTEMBER

2 President David Dacko of the Central African Republic is ousted in a bloodless coup led by army chief of staff Gen. Andre Kolingba, who suspends the constitution and declares himself president.

In Portugal, President António Ramalho Eanes gives his approval to a new three-party coalition government formed by Prime Minister Francisco Pinto Balsemão, who had resigned August 11.

4 France's ambassador to Lebanon, Louis Delamare, is fatally shot by gunmen in West Beirut.

5 In a speech before a special session of the Egyptian parliament, President Anwar el-Sadat lashes out against Muslim fundamentalists, Coptic Christians, and certain nonreligious opponents. Following the arrest of more than 1,500 critics of the government over the previous two days, Sadat announces additional restrictive measures, including the removal of the Coptic pope, Shenuda III.

8 After returning to Washington from a month's vacation at his ranch in California, President Ronald Reagan begins three days of meetings with economic advisers to discuss further cuts in the budget, the problem of high interest rates, and the business community's lack of confidence in his economic recovery program.

9 The French cabinet approves legislation nationalizing 36 banks and several major industrial concerns.

Vernon E. Jordan, Jr., announces that he is resigning as president of the National Urban League, effective Dec. 31, 1981.

10 President Reagan and Israeli Prime Minister Menahem Begin end two days of talks in Washington with an agreement for closer military ties.

11 Queen Beatrix of The Netherlands swears in a new left-of-center coalition government, headed by Prime Minister Andries van Agt of the Christian Democratic Party.

13 John McEnroe defeats Björn Borg to capture his third consecutive U.S. Open tennis championship. Tracy Austin won the women's crown.

14 Prime Minister Margaret Thatcher of Great Britain makes several changes in her cabinet, generally favoring the members who more strongly support her conservative economic and monetary policies.

15 Pakistan formally accepts a six-year, $3,200,000,000 military and economic aid package from the United States.

Ismat Kittani of Iraq is chosen president of the 36th UN General Assembly.

16 In its strongest attack to date on the independent trade union Solidarity, the Polish Communist Party denounces the labor movement as having embarked on a course leading "toward a new national tragedy." The denunciation comes six days after Solidarity openly challenged the Communist regime by calling for free parliamentary elections. That call was made during the union's first national congress, held in Gdansk.

"Sugar Ray" Leonard scores a 14th-round knockout over Thomas Hearns to win the undisputed world welterweight boxing championship.

19 At least a quarter million protesters gather in Washington to participate in a Solidarity Day rally organized by the AFL-CIO. Spokespersons representing the nation's major labor unions, black and Hispanic groups, women, the aged, and the disabled voice their opposition to the policies of the Reagan administration.

21 The tiny British colony of Belize, located in Central America, becomes independent.

Addressing the UN General Assembly, U.S. Secretary of State Haig calls "simply unrealistic" a request by the Third World nations for a large increase in aid from the industrialized West.

24 A day after meetings between Secretary Haig and Soviet Foreign Minister Andrei A. Gromyko at the UN, the United States and the USSR pledge to "spare no effort" in talks, scheduled to begin November 30 in Geneva, on the mutual reduction of medium-range nuclear forces in Europe.

25 Mexico's ruling Institutional Revolutionary Party nominates Miguel de la Madrid Hurtado as its candidate to replace President José López Portillo in December 1982 elections. The party's candidate has won every presidential election in the past 52 years.

Some 250,000 Americans participate in the Solidarity Day rally in Washington.

P. Breese/Gamma-Liaison

Barry Iverson/Gamma-Liaison

Egypt's President Anwar el-Sadat, Vice-President Hosni Mubarak (far left), and Defense Minister Abdel Halim Abu Ghazala participate in a military parade ceremony in a suburb of Cairo, October 6. Moments later the president was assassinated and the vice-president was in charge of the government.

28 In an historic decision, the Canadian Supreme Court rules (7–2) that the federal government's attempt at patriation of the national constitution is legal. At the same time, however, it holds (6–3) that the move "offends the federal principle" by being carried out without the consent of a sufficient number of provinces.

30 The U.S. Postal Service announces that it will raise the price of a first-class domestic stamp to 20¢, effective November 1.

OCTOBER

2 U.S. President Ronald Reagan announces a five-part plan for strengthening and modernizing the country's arsenal of strategic nuclear weapons. The program includes the building of 100 MX missiles—to be deployed in fixed, existing silos rather than proposed mobile bases—as well as 100 B-1 long-range bombers.

3 After seven months and the death of ten men, the hunger strike campaign by Irish republicans in Maze Prison near Belfast, Northern Ireland, is called off. The six living hunger strikers give up "reluctantly," after realizing that their families would not let them die.

4 Participating nations of the European Monetary System (EMS) agree to currency revaluations to bring their divergent rates of inflation in closer line. The values of the West German mark and Dutch guilder are raised, while those of the French franc and Italian lira are lowered.

The body of Lee Harvey Oswald, accused assassin of President John F. Kennedy, is exhumed and positively identified in Fort Worth, TX, disproving the theory of a British author that the coffin contained the body of a Soviet spy.

5 Hojatolislam Mohammed Ali Khamenei, a 42-year-old clergyman, is declared the winner of the Iranian presidential election, held three days earlier.

6 At a military parade near Cairo commemorating Egypt's air attack on Israel in 1973, commandos leap from a truck and storm the reviewing stand, firing machine guns and hurling grenades. Eight government officials and foreign diplomats are killed, including President Anwar el-Sadat. Vice-President Hosni Mubarak immediately assumes control of the government and armed forces.

7 The eight-day Commonwealth Heads of Government Meeting, in which 44 sovereign states took part, concludes in Melbourne, Australia, with a communiqué calling for "global negotiations" on economic development.

10 In Bonn, West Germany, some 250,000 demonstrators express their disapproval of a NATO plan to station additional medium-range nuclear missiles in Western Europe.

Andreas Papandreou (center), the 62-year-old son of former Prime Minister George Papandreou, led his Socialist party to a decisive victory in Greece's October 18 parliamentary elections, ending seven years of pro-Western Conservative government.

Mulhauser/Gamma

14 A new minority Conservative Party government, headed by Kaare Willoch, takes office in Norway.

18 Stanislaw Kania is dismissed as first secretary of the Polish Communist Party amid criticism of his handling of the nation's economic and labor problems. He is replaced by his premier, Wojciech Jaruzelski.

19 President Reagan and French President François Mitterrand take part in ceremonies marking the 200th anniversary of the American victory, with French assistance, in the Battle of Yorktown, the final campaign in the U.S. War of Independence.

21 Andreas Papandreou is sworn in as prime minister of Greece, three days after his Panhellenic Socialist Movement (Pasok) party won a strong majority in parliamentary elections.

A communiqué issued at the end of a two-day meeting of NATO defense ministers in Gleneagle, Scotland, reaffirms the organization's 1979 pledge to deploy U.S. nuclear weapons in Western Europe.

Palestine Liberation Organization (PLO) leader Yasir Arafat concludes a two-week trip to Asia and the Soviet Union, during which he held talks with Japanese Prime Minister Zenko Suzuki and won full diplomatic recognition of the PLO from Moscow.

22 Representatives of 14 developing and 8 industrialized nations attend the opening session of the two-day North-South conference at the Mexican resort of Cancún. President Reagan supports talks between rich and poor countries but insists they be held within the framework of existing international agencies.

27 President Urho Kekkonen, 81, of Finland resigns because of ill health after more than 25 years in office.

28 The U.S. Senate votes (52 to 48) to allow an $8,500,000,000 sale of AWACS (Airborne Warning and Control System) planes and other military equipment to Saudi Arabia. The vote is regarded as a major legislative victory for President Reagan.

The Los Angeles Dodgers defeat the New York Yankees, 9-2, to win baseball's World Series, four games to two.

31 The Caribbean islands of Antigua and Barbuda become a single independent nation at midnight, ending three and a half centuries of British rule.

NOVEMBER

2 After a meeting with King Hussein of Jordan at the White House, President Reagan reaffirms the U.S. commitment to the Camp David peace process for the Middle East. Hussein endorses an alternate plan proposed by Saudi Arabia.

Martin A. Levick/Black Star

Mayor Edward I. Koch of New York City, running with the endorsement of both the Democratic and Republican parties, was elected to a second four-year term with a record 75% of the vote.

3 Highlighting Election Day in the United States, Charles Robb (D) wins the Virginia gubernatorial race, and the mayors of New York, Detroit, Cleveland, Pittsburgh, Seattle, and Phoenix are reelected.

5 The federal government and nine English-speaking provinces of Canada reach a compromise agreement on a new national constitution. French-speaking Quebec is alone in opposing the plan.

6 Sweden releases the Soviet submarine that had run aground in its restricted waters 11 days earlier. Radiation readings suggested that the sub was carrying nuclear warheads. Its captain maintained that foul weather had caused the sub to lose its way.

9 The International Monetary Fund approves a $5,800,000,000 loan to India. It is the largest loan ever granted by the organization.

12 U.S. Budget Director David Stockman is reprimanded by President Reagan for his published expressions of doubt about the administration's budget and tax cuts. Stockman's remarks were made in an interview for the December edition of *Atlantic Monthly*.

President João Baptista Figueiredo of Brazil returns to his post, after a 53-day absence to recuperate from a heart attack.

14 The U.S. space shuttle Columbia ends a shortened, two-day mission with a safe landing at Edwards Air Force Base in California. The shuttle's second flight was cut short by malfunctioning fuel cells.

16 Soviet President Leonid Brezhnev declares that the nation's short supply of food is its "central" economic and political problem.

17 Houston elects its first woman mayor, Kathryn Jean Whitmire, 35.

18 In a speech televised live in Europe, President Reagan calls on the Soviet Union to join in a four-point agenda for controlling the nuclear arms buildup. The major proposal calls for the United States to cancel plans for new medium-range missiles in Europe and for the USSR to dismantle comparable weapons already in place. The official Soviet press rejects the plan as a "propaganda ploy."

20 World Chess Champion Anatoly Karpov of the USSR retains his title by defeating challenger Viktor Korchnoi of Switzerland.

23 President Reagan vetoes a government spending bill and orders the shutdown of all nonessential federal services. Congress later in the day approves current financing levels until December 15, Reagan approves the extension, and the shutdown is ended.

White House Press Secretary James Brady returns home from the hospital nearly eight months after being shot in the head in the assassination attempt against President Reagan.

25 Soviet President Brezhnev ends three days of talks with West German Chancellor Helmut Schmidt in Bonn. Their discussions focused on arms issues, with Brezhnev expressing distrust of Washington.

Only hours after convening, an Arab League meeting in Fez, Morocco, breaks up over Syrian opposition to the Saudi peace plan.

26 In a parliamentary by-election in Crosby, near Liverpool, Social Democrat Shirley Williams upsets the Conservative candidate to become the new party's first member of the British House of Commons.

29 U.S. National Security Adviser Richard Allen announces that he is taking a leave of absence until the Justice Department completes its investigation of his receipt of $1,000 from a Japanese magazine. Allen had been paid the money to help arrange an interview with First Lady Nancy Reagan, put it in a safe, and failed to turn it in. He claimed to have simply forgotten.

Roberto Suazo Córdova is elected president of Honduras. He will head the nation's first civilian administration since 1972.

30 The United States and Soviet Union open talks in Geneva on the reduction of nuclear forces in Europe.

The United States and Israel sign an agreement to strengthen strategic cooperation against Soviet threats to the Middle East.

Democrat James Florio concedes defeat to Thomas H. Kean, 46, in the contested November 3 race for governor of New Jersey.

DECEMBER

4 At a meeting of the Organization of American States (OAS) on St. Lucia, U.S. Secretary of State Alexander Haig calls for regional cooperation in halting the arms buildup and outlines an economic assistance program for Latin America and the Caribbean.

5 The United States and Turkey announce plans for a new joint defense unit to ''enlarge and improve'' military cooperation.

7 Reagan administration officials confirm a budget deficit projection of a record $109,000,000,000 for fiscal 1982, with slow economic growth, rising interest rates, and high unemployment.

John E. Jacob is named president of the National Urban League, to replace the retiring Vernon Jordan.

8 Soviet physicist and dissident Andrei Sakharov, 60, ends his 17-day hunger strike after the Kremlin agrees to grant Lisa Alekseyeva, the wife of his stepson, Alexei Semyonov, an emigration visa to join her husband in the United States.

9 U.S. air traffic controllers who had been fired in August for striking against the government are allowed to apply for any federal employment, except in the Federal Aviation Administration.

10 Citing ''increased risks,'' President Reagan calls on Americans living in Libya to leave immediately and invalidates passports for travel to that country. The appeal comes only a few days after intelligence reports disclose that Libyan leader Muammar el-Qaddafi had dispatched a team of gunmen to assassinate President Reagan.

China and India open talks in Moscow on their longstanding dispute over the Himalayan frontier.

11 Javier Pérez de Cuellar, 61, of Peru, is elected the fifth secretary general of the United Nations, to take office January 1.

West German Chancellor Helmut Schmidt and East German party leader Erich Honecker meet at Biesenthal, East Germany, for the first top-level talks in more than ten years.

President Roberto Viola of Argentina, in office for only eight months, is removed by the ruling military junta. Gen. Leopoldo Galtieri is named as his successor.

13 Polish Prime Minister Wojciech Jaruzelski issues a decree of martial law, restricting civil rights, banning public gatherings, and suspending operation of the Solidarity trade union federation. The decree comes in the wake of a new wave of strikes and a call by Solidarity leaders for a nationwide referendum on the future of Polish government. Union activists react to the ban by urging a general strike. Communications to the West are cut off.

14 Former Belgian Prime Minister Wilfried Martens announces the formation of a center-right government, ending a three-month crisis.

17 U.S. Brig. Gen. James L. Dozier, a high-ranking NATO official, is kidnapped in Verona, Italy, by Red Brigade terrorists.

18 The United States announces that it is ''suspending'' its November 30 agreement with Israel for strategic military cooperation. President Reagan ordered the move because of Israel's formal annexation of the Golan Heights on December 14.

26 Saudi Arabia and Iraq sign an agreement in Baghdad ending their 60-year-old border dispute.

28 The first ''test-tube'' baby in the United States is born.

29 Declaring that ''the Soviet Union bears a heavy and direct responsibility'' for the curtailment of civil and labor rights in Poland, President Reagan announces a series of trade sanctions, including a ban on the sale of high technology equipment, against Moscow.

UPI

Romuald Spasowski, the Polish ambassador to the United States, asked for and was granted political asylum on December 20. The diplomat called his defection an ''expression of solidarity'' with the Polish people in the face of the ''brutality and inhumanity'' of the newly-decreed martial law.

UN

Membership in the United Nations has more than tripled since the organization was founded in 1946, and the political complexion of the General Assembly has undergone a radical change.

MICROSTATES AND THE COMMUNITY OF NATIONS

By PROFESSOR ELMER PLISCHKE
Author, *Microstates in World Affairs*

Like Gulliver, rendered impotent by the Lilliputians, the United States and other major powers are seeing their influence eroded by a proliferation of tiny new countries and the remolding of the international community. A rapid increase in the number of new nations has given rise to basic changes in the conduct of diplomacy and the functioning of international organizations.

Strange New World. Between 1978 and 1981 alone, these nations gained independence: Zimbabwe (formerly Southern Rhodesia) in Africa; Kiribati (Gilbert Islands), the Solomon Islands, Tuvalu (Ellice Islands), and Vanuatu (New Hebrides) in the Pacific; and Dominica, St. Lucia, St. Vincent and the Grenadines, Belize, and Antigua and Barbuda in the Caribbean. These new nations brought to more than 100 the number of additions to the international community since World War II. And in late 1980, the United States signed agreements to establish four Micronesian statelets—the Marshall Islands, the Northern Marianas, the Republic of Belau (Palau Islands), and the Federated States of Micronesia. These islands have a combined population of only 115,000 and occupy a total of 687 sq mi (1 779 km^2)—about the size of Honolulu, HI—dispersed over an expanse of the Pacific Ocean as large as the United States.

This splintering has led to the emergence of some strange creations in recent years: an independent country with fewer than

7,000 inhabitants, occupying an isolated Pacific islet no larger than George Washington's estate at Mount Vernon; a Caribbean republic with a population smaller than that of Columbia, SC, and whose first emissary to the Organization of American States (OAS) was a hired foreign diplomat; and a small Asian kingdom which maintains diplomatic relations with only four other countries and accredits envoys to only two of them.

At formal international gatherings, the United States is now flanked by delegations not only from such major post–World War II countries as India, Indonesia, Nigeria, Pakistan, and the Philippines, but also by representatives from such smaller entities as Bahrain, Djibouti, the Maldives, Nauru, Qatar, Samoa, Surinam, and, were they to be officially recognized, the four South African "homelands" of Transkei, Bophuthatswana, Venda, and Ciskei. In the last decade, the United Nations has granted membership to more than a dozen small island-states, including the Bahamas, Cape Verde, Comoros, Dominica, Grenada, Saõ Tomé and Príncipe, the Seychelles, Belize, and Antigua and Barbuda.

Although the independence of Namibia (South-West Africa) has been widely debated, relatively little attention has been paid to discussions in the UN regarding self-government for such places as Brunei (Northern Borneo), Ifni, and French Polynesia, or for the Cayman, Cocos (Keeling), Virgin, and Wallis-Futuna islands.

The United Nations has also considered decolonization and self-rule for a host of other possible statelets. These include a dozen territories—such as Gibraltar and the Tokelau Islands—that are smaller than the District of Columbia (63 sq mi, or 163 km^2), and more than 15 islands with populations of less than 10,000. Even more curious were the UN discussions regarding self-governance for the 1,600 islanders who populate 4 sq mi (10 km^2) of Pacific coral atolls, and for the fewer than 100 inhabitants of Pitcairn Island, the speck of land made famous by the *Bounty* mutineers in the 18th century.

Belize (formerly British Honduras) gained full independence on Sept. 21, 1981. The Central American country has a population of 160,000. Below, mahogany logs await export at the harbor in Belize City.

Editorial Photocolor Archives

If the United Nations considers Pitcairn and other territories of that size as candidates for self-government and independence, they why not Montserrat, Socotra, and St. Helena—or even Ascension, Norfolk, and the Falkland Islands, each of which has fewer than 2,000 inhabitants? How many settlers are needed on the unpopulated islets of Baker, Howland, Navassa, and Palmyra, or the sub-Antarctic South Sandwich archipelago to qualify them for independence and statehood? Even more fancifully, what is the potential of a manmade coral nodule in the Pacific Ocean or a floating resort-casino anchored beyond territorial waters in the Mediterranean or off the coast of Hawaii (for which plans have already been announced)?

Fragmentation of the Community of Nations. The community of nations has grown from nine recognized states when the United States was born, to about 20 following the Latin American revolutions of the early 19th century, to approximately 45 by 1900, and, following the dissolution of the eastern European empires at the end of World War I, to 67 by 1940. Under the aura of what U.S. President John Kennedy called "a worldwide declaration of independence," the number of independent states increased by approximately 100 in the next 40 years. Thus, the global community nearly quadrupled in the 20th century, growing at a rate of almost 250% during the single generation after World War II.

Decolonization pressures in the United Nations resulted in the liquidation of most of the mid-20th century Belgian, British,

Gamma, Paris

King Baudouin of Belgium (left) is the guest of Congo's (today Zaire's) President Mobutu for observances marking the 10th anniversary of national independence. The African republic became independent in 1960. The worldwide movement toward independence peaked in the 1960s.

Riviere, Gamma/Liaison

In 1980, the Anglo-French Condominium of New Hebrides became the independent nation of Vanuatu. Above, representatives of France and Great Britain join with the nation's new leadership in reviewing the celebrations. The fledgling South Pacific island state was torn by violent political upheaval.

Dutch, French, Italian, Portuguese, and Spanish empires. More than 1,250,000,000 people, occupying more than 14,000,000 sq mi (36 260 000 km^2) of territory were rapidly absorbed into scores of new states. Not counting the secession of those earlier-integrated territories, such as Quebec or Ulster, today fewer than .05% of the world's population, occupying less than .03% of its landed domain, remains nonindependent. The great majority of nonindependent territories are of microstate proportion (have a population of fewer than 300,000).

The independence boom peaked in the 1960s with the birth of 44 new nations, but it continued in the 1970s with the emergence of 28 more. There are a good many other prospects for the 1980s: in addition to Namibia and several South African "homelands," potential new nations include French Guiana, the Caribbean islands of Guadeloupe and the Netherlands Antilles, the four Micronesian republics, and other islands in the Pacific.

As the number of nations has increased, their average size has grown smaller and smaller. In 1940, Luxembourg and Vatican City were the only minute members of the society of nations; more than two thirds of all the countries in the world had populations exceeding 5,000,000. As 1981 drew to a close, more than 80—nearly half—fall below that level. Of these, 40 (23% of independent countries) have fewer than 1,000,000 inhabitants, and 22 are microstates.

Future Proliferation. In 1969, the U.S. State Department projected the emergence of 50 new states, each with a population of fewer than 100,000. Some of these—Antigua and Barbuda, Belize, Dominica, Kiribati, Saõ Tomé and Príncipe, the Seychelles, St. Vincent, Tonga, and Tuvalu—have already gained independence. On the basis of UN decolonization consideration, it is possible to project 50 new states during the last decades of the 20th century.

UN

In Papua-New Guinea, independence came gradually: a House of Assembly was formed in 1964; Australia granted self-governing status in 1973; and absolute sovereignty was achieved in 1975.

All but seven of these possible new nations are microentities, and more than 30 are sub-microentities (have a population of fewer than 100,000).

Should this projection be realized, the world community would increase to more than 200 nations. Of these, all but 86 would have fewer than 5,000,000 people. Three of every five countries would be less populous than metropolitan Chicago, and two of every five would have fewer inhabitants than metropolitan New Orleans (1,000,000). Approximately 65 (nearly 30%) would be microstates—smaller in population than Lancaster, PA—and some 40 submicrostates (19%) would have populations smaller than attendance at the Super Bowl or enrollment at the University of California.

Geographic Changes. The independence boom has also brought significant geographic shifts in the community of nations. At the time of World War II, three fourths of all independent nations lay in Europe and the Western Hemisphere. More than 60 new countries emerged in Africa and Asia, and these areas eventually accounted for more than 40% of the total. But with half of the 50 potential new nations located in the Western Hemisphere and Europe, they, together with Oceania, would embrace 53% of the total.

Another marked change has been the increase of insular countries. Before World War II, there were only seven island-states (one tenth of the society of nations), including Japan and Great Britain. Iceland, Indonesia, the Philippines, and Sri Lanka (Ceylon) gained independence in the 1940s. Since 1960, more than two dozen other island-states were born, increasing the total to 40 (23%).

Changes in North-South Balance. Another major consequence of state proliferation has been the rise of the so-called Third and Fourth worlds and the changing balance in relations between the industrialized North and the developing South. Following World War II, it was presumed that the Western Allies would remain aligned as an anti-Axis aggregation. As the Cold

War developed in the late 1940s, however, three major blocs emerged—the Western, Communist, and neutralist or uncommitted nations. As the Western empires dissolved in the 1960s, the politically nonaligned nations began to recognize common economic interests, paving the way for the development of the Third- and Fourth-world bloc. Continuing to expand during the 1970s, this group voiced strong economic opposition to the Western industrial powers and took on a new designation—the developing or less-developed countries (LDCs).

Because national alignments vary on different issues, it is difficult to specify the number of states in each major bloc. While the Western World embraces some 25 to 30 nations, at least one third of these are developing countries and only about a dozen are regarded as industrialized democracies. The Communist bloc includes some 18 states, most of which are also regarded as developing nations; several of these—such as Albania, Mongolia, and the Southeast Asian countries—are clearly part of the Third- and Fourth-world bloc.

Of the remaining countries in the world—more than 120—all but 30 came into existence during or after World War II, and most of them since 1960. In the North-South and Industrialized-LDC dialogue, this bloc is augmented by at least ten Western and a majority of Communist countries. The Third and Fourth worlds comprise more than 140 nations, so that in international diplomacy they hold a decisive 85% majority.

This growing and potentially dominant bloc of states—some of which have been transformed from dependencies of Western powers to wards of the international community—is gaining con-

St. Lucia in the Windward Islands boasts scenic beauty and a promising economic future. After 176 years of British power, the Caribbean island earned independence in 1979. It became the 40th member state of the Commonwealth and 152d member of the United Nations.

De Wys

siderable influence in the treatment of important economic and social issues in the United Nations and other international forums. This is most apparent in such matters as development aid, seabed and other resources, and the New Economic Order.

Diplomatic and Organizational Changes. A final modification of the community of nations centers on the mutation of the diplomatic process and the functioning of global institutions. State proliferation has produced a relative decline in diplomatic representation. Optimally, every country should accredit an emissary to every other country, which today would mean more than 27,700 diplomatic missions scattered throughout the world.

In 1980, however, the members of the international community acknowledged formal diplomatic relations with only about 45% of their number. Actual diplomatic representation was lower still, amounting to only 35%; thus, many governments claimed regular diplomatic relations without the exchange of envoys. In other words, in the aggregate, states are unrepresented by traditional emissaries in approximately two thirds of the rest of the international community.

Even these figures are inflated; in 1980, there were only about 6,100 diplomatic missions in the capital cities of the world, or only 22% of the potential. As a result, an increasing proportion of international relations must be conducted by other diplomatic processes, including unidirectional representation and the use of such multilateral forums as the United Nations.

Since 1960, membership in the United Nations and other international bodies has been open to almost any independent nation, regardless of its size, population, and resources. Only rarely does a country, such as Switzerland or Vatican City, elect not to join; only a few, such as the Republic of China and the Koreas, are denied membership for political reasons. On the other hand, all of the microstates that apply are granted entry; only a few, such as Nauru and Tonga, have not yet joined. As a result, the United Nations has more than tripled in size since 1946.

Whereas only four countries with populations today of fewer than 5,000,000 (of which Iceland is the only microstate) were members of the United Nations in 1950, there are now 31 members with populations of fewer than 1,000,000, and half of these are microstates.

UN

Representatives of Third World nations have had an increasingly strong voice in the international decision-making process.

William Wisser, Photoreporters

The Conference of Foreign Ministers of Nonaligned Nations was held in New Delhi in February 1981. At its close, the delegates passed a resolution calling for the withdrawal of foreign troops from Afghanistan and Cambodia. India's Foreign Minister Narsimha Rao chaired the conference; Prime Minister Indira Gandhi is seated to his right.

Every tiny newcomer in the UN General Assembly exercises the same voting power as the United States, which is half again as populous as all the small states combined. Dominica, the Seychelles, Saõ Tomé and Príncipe, and St. Vincent—with a combined population of little more than 300,000—can outvote China, India, and the Soviet Union—whose combined population is approximately 1,900,000,000. Since 1946, the voting strength of the original framers of the UN has declined from 1/50th to 1/150th.

Moreover, while the United States contributes 25% to the regular budgets of the United Nations and its specialized agencies—some $400,000,000 to $500,000,000 annually—a Third World microstate pays only about $80,000. At present, 55% of the member nations make the minimum contribution of .02%. These 85 contributors wield a majority of votes and together provide only 1.7% of the UN budget; the 25 Western powers which contribute nearly 70% of the organization's funds wield less than 17% of its votes.

Whether or not the peoples of prospective new nations are entitled to manage their own affairs and to enjoy the rights and privileges of political autonomy is not the central issue. Unrestrained expansion, however, has produced distortions in the global community. The question is whether new states, regardless of size, form of government, degree of self-sufficiency, and ability to contribute, should be given an equal voice in the affairs of the community and an equal vote in its institutions.

Either the proliferation of Lilliputian nations must be checked, or else alternatives for their status and role must be devised. Global agencies such as the United Nations need to examine how unrestrained expansion has affected, and will affect in the future, the international system. Organizational development must be regarded as a central policy issue. The longer action is delayed, the fewer options there will be for a workable solution, and the more difficult it will be to reverse the atomization of the world community.

See also NATIONS OF THE WORLD (pages 566–72).

Michael Evans, Sygma

Ronald Reagan's nomination for the presidency by the Republican Party in 1980, above, was an endorsement of his conservative views. His election victory represented a complete reversal in the public's thinking since 1964, when conservative Barry Goldwater won the party endorsement (facing page, bottom) but lost in a landslide to Lyndon Johnson. It was during the Goldwater campaign that Reagan gained recognition as a potentially successful politician.

U.S. POLITICAL CONSERVATISM
Meanings and Origins

By
Seymour Martin Lipset

Ronald Reagan's landslide victory in the 1980 U.S. presidential election was greeted by political pundits and news media commentators as the culmination of a decade-long shift in the political thinking of the American voter. Sixteen years after coming to political prominence as a supporter of Barry Goldwater, whose overwhelming defeat in the 1964 election was a repudiation of conservatism, Reagan won the presidency. His campaign promises and old-fashioned social values struck the right note with the American public in 1980. "Liberals" were out and the "New

About the author: Seymour Martin Lipset is Professor of Sociology and Political Science, and Senior Fellow, The Hoover Institution on War, Revolution, and Peace, Stanford University. He is the author of numerous books, including *The Politics of Unreason: Right-Wing Extremism in America, 1790–1977* (1978; with Earl Raab) and *The First New Nation: The United States in Historical and Comparative Perspective* (1979). Professor Lipset is a noted neoconservative.

Right" was in. There appeared to be a new conservative consensus in American politics.

With all the attention given this conservative revival, however, a major uncertainty persisted: what does the term "conservative" actually mean? A *New York Times*–CBS News poll in the spring of 1981 was illuminating. Asked to identify "the biggest difference between liberal and conservative views," 52% of the respondents said they couldn't be sure, 15% cited government spending policy, and 12% pointed to differences in mental attitude and temperament.

Two fundamentally different meanings of conservatism are found in common usage. The first focuses on conservatism as a body of ideas used to justify established institutions and to preserve them in the face of assault, regardless of the success or purpose of those institutions. According to this definition, those who resist change in any society, even a postrevolutionary one, can be designated conservative. The second definition views conservatism as a substantive political doctrine originating in the ideas of Edmund Burke and Joseph de Maistre and in opposition to the egalitarian and anticlerical French Revolution. Belief in the beneficial effects of hierarchy, reverence for church and family, and a conviction that property and freedom are inseparably connected are the underlying tenets of the conservative political doctrine.

Conservatism as a coherent political doctrine originated in Europe. European conservative thought, particularly before World

Bettman Archive

As a reasoned philosophy, conservatism has its origins in the thought of British statesman and political theorist Edmund Burke (1729-97). In his "Reflections on the Revolution in France" (1790), Burke set out his political ideology of organic growth as opposed to violent change.

Fred Ward, Black Star

War II, has looked back nostalgically to an idealized image of a cohesive, stable, and cultured preindustrial society characterized by an alliance of the throne and altar—state and church—in which peoples' positions were defined by an interrelated complex of roles, and in which the state, church, and aristocracy fulfilled the values of *noblesse oblige* and took responsibility for the welfare of the average person. There have been national variations in this ideology, related in some degree to varying religious traditions and military resources, but there is a core myth rooted in the shared history of medieval Catholic Europe.

American Conservatism. Conservatism in the United States has generally taken the form of a belief in the need for social and moral continuity rather than an attachment to traditional society. As a number of historians have emphasized, America from its revolutionary beginnings was a liberal, rather than a conservative, society. In addition to lacking the institutional actors of European conservatism—monarchy, aristocracy, established church, and traditional peasantry—the United States lacked the feudal ideals of prerevolutionary Europe that gave conservatism its substance. As a society formed by settlers who rejected the hierarchically organized churches and fixed class system of Europe, and as a nation founded in a revolution that rejected the alliance and dominance of throne and altar, the central ideology of the United States has been antistatist, individualistic, egalitarian, and democratic. Americans, even those responsible for the constitution, have attempted to preserve a continuity with the past, but it is a past dominated by Lockean liberalism, emphasizing individual rights and government by popular consent, allied with a deep-seated optimism and a willingness to innovate. Gunnar Myrdal has noted the paradox involved here: "America is . . . conservative. . . . But the principles conserved are liberal and some, indeed, are radical." The consequences of this were recognized by the English socialist H. G. Wells, writing in 1906: "It is not difficult to show, for example, that the two great political parties in America represent only one English party, the middle-class Liberal Party. . . . The new world [was left] to the Whigs and Nonconformists and to those who became Radicals in England, and Jeffersonians and then Democrats in America. All Americans are, from the English point of view, liberals of one sort or another."

"We are a nation that has a government—not the other way around. . . . Our government has no power except that granted it by the people. It is time to check and reverse the growth of government which shows signs of having grown beyond the consent of the governed."
—Inaugural Address of President Ronald Reagan, Jan. 20, 1981

The Political Philosophy of the American Public

"People who are conservative in their political views are referred to as being right of center and people who are liberal in their political views are referred to as being left of center." From March 13 to March 16, 1981, The Gallup Poll organization questioned a group of Americans regarding their political philosophy. The question asked: "Just your best impression, which one of the following categories best describes your *own* political positions?" The responses included:

	Far left	Substantially left	Moderately left	Slightly left	Middle of the road (Volunteered)	Slightly right	Moderately right	Substantially right	Far right	Don't know
NATIONAL	2%	4%	11%	14%	12%	20%	19%	7%	4%	7%
RACE										
White	2	4	12	14	10	21	20	8	3	6
Nonwhite	5	7	9	8	20	13	15	3	6	14
AGE										
Total under 30	4	9	15	15	6	20	14	5	4	8
18–24 years	5	8	19	15	6	19	12	5	3	8
25–29 years	2	9	10	16	5	21	18	4	7	8
30–49 years	2	2	11	14	14	22	20	8	3	4
50 & older	1	3	9	12	13	18	23	8	5	8
POLITICS										
Republican	1	4	7	10	7	19	30	14	4	4
Democrat	3	5	12	14	14	22	13	4	4	9
Independent	2	4	14	17	12	18	20	5	4	4

Fred A. Conrad, New York Times Pictures

For Americans of every political persuasion, the aristocratic, monarchial, and oligarchic societies of Old Europe were anathema. American conservatives came to recognize that, like it or not, they had to operate within the context of a society in which egalitarian and liberal values were dominant, and in which both the rights of the people to govern, and of the able to succeed, were accepted as inviolable.

The U.S. Political System. This predisposition has been strengthened by the compromise coalition politics characteristic of the American party system. The need to construct coalitions, often involving groups with sharply opposed interests and values, and the development of party ideologies and rhetoric appropriate to keeping such coalitions together, repeatedly undercut the purity of competing political doctrines. In a two-party system, both parties aim at securing a majority. Elections become occasions for the two parties to seek the broadest base of support by convincing divergent groups of their common interests. In contrast to much of Europe, where divergent parties join coalitions and form multiparty cabinets after elections, in the United States the constitutional requirement that executive power be in the hands of an elected president rather than in a cabinet responsive to parliament has meant that divergent factions come together before elections to select presidents or governors. The system encourages compromise and the incorporation into party values of those general elements of liberal consensus upon which the polity rests.

From the 1930s on, the divisions between the two major coalition parties have been identified as a struggle between liberalism and conservatism. Liberalism, linked to the Democratic Party, has emphasized the egalitarian component of the American creed, stressing the role of the state in enhancing equal opportunity for deprived groups. Conservatism, identified with the Republican Party, has put more stress on liberty and individual freedom, opposing a strong state. Both strands, however, continue to adhere to

Conservative intellectual William F. Buckley, Jr., above, is editor-in-chief of the respected monthly, "National Review," which turned 25 in 1980.

Milton Friedman, the foremost conservative economist in the United States and a 1976 Nobel laureate, stands by the somewhat "old-fashioned" theory that economic events are shaped most importantly by the quantity of money in circulation.

Karin Vismara, Black Star

the classic liberal doctrine, as enunciated in the Declaration of Independence, of equality and personal liberty.

Varying Strands. Within the framework provided by the American liberal tradition, conservatism has exhibited a wide diversity. Since 1945 there have been four main streams of conservatism: traditional conservatism, libertarian conservatism, conservative liberalism or neoconservatism, and populist conservatism.

The chief representatives of the traditional conservatism are, in intellectual life, Russell Kirk, Peter Viereck, and William Buckley, and in national politics, senators Barry Goldwater (R-AZ) and John Tower (R-TX). The traditional conservatives have emphasized their links to a major founder of European conservative thought, Edmund Burke. This stream of conservatism is closest to the traditionalist, aristocratic conservatism of Europe in its appeal to the "collective wisdom of our ancestors." It is also similar to European conservatism in its belief in the redemptive qualities of Christianity, which for many traditional conservatives is not liberal Protestantism but a traditionalist Catholicism of a medieval cast. It is therefore not surprising that, as George Nash has noted, a key feature is "its extraordinary orientation toward Europe" with a concomitant "relative lack of interest in the specifically American past." It is on these grounds that such writers as Louis Hartz and Clinton Rossiter have argued that traditional conservatism is out of tune with the essential liberal tradition of American politics.

Unlike traditional conservatism, libertarian conservatism is embedded in the classical liberal tradition. The principal intellectual advocates of this stream of conservatism are Friedrich Hayek, Milton Friedman, and the Chicago school of economists, while politically it is represented by Ronald Reagan. Although the main focus of traditional conservatism is the social and moral fabric of the nation, the major area of concern for libertarian conservatives is the economy. This brand of conservatism asserts the virtues of the free market and limited, instrumental state controls against the dangers inherent in big government. While traditional conservatives emphasize the communal nature of society, libertarian conservatives emphasize the primacy of the individual and individual freedom.

Among the four streams of conservatism, neoconservatism—or "neoliberalism" as its adherents prefer to describe it—is the most deeply rooted in the American tradition of pragmatic individualism. Neoliberals or neoconservatives accept existing welfare institutions and, unlike the other types of conservatives, support efforts to achieve greater egalitarianism in society. The principal proponents of neoconservatism—Daniel Bell, Nathan Glazer, Irving Kristol, Norman Podhoretz, Senators Daniel P. Moynihan (D-NY) and Henry Jackson (D-WA), and the current U.S. ambassador to the UN, Jeane Kirkpatrick, are, with the exception of Kristol, all Democrats. Although neoconservatives have emphasized a substantive doctrine supporting economic growth, meritocracy, and the traditional family, their conservatism lies most squarely in their defense of established institutions against radical attack, especially by the left-wing counterculture. In this light, the

Adam Scull, Black Star

A former academic and U.S. ambassador to the United Nations, Sen. Daniel Patrick Moynihan (D-NY) espouses a theory of "neoconservatism." His first book, "Beyond the Melting Pot" (1963), was a collaboration with another noted neoconservative, Nathan Glazer. Moynihan is regarded as an expert on urban and ethnic minority problems.

neoconservatives may be accurately described as neoliberal, for the roots of their political philosophy are to be found in traditional American liberalism rather than conservatism.

Populist conservatism emphasizes many of the social concerns of traditional conservatism, but in a more authoritarian fashion. It has also been associated with a mass appeal to the less educated and more religiously fundamentalist. Recruiting from strata of society threatened by the more permissive, sexually freer, and secular cosmopolitan values associated with modernization, populist conservatives have attempted to turn back the clock to a more traditional society. Populist conservatism has taken a number of forms in American history, from assorted anti-Masonic groups in the early 19th century, to the mass-based Know-Nothings of the 1850s, the American Protective Association of the 1890s, and the Ku Klux Klan of the 1920s. Populist conservatism reappeared after World War II in the form of Sen. Joseph McCarthy's "crusade" to expose and wipe out the Communist conspiracy which had supposedly infiltrated American government and other major institutions, particularly the opinion-molding and entertainment media. During the 1960s and early 1970s, it was associated with the presidential campaigns of George Wallace, who attacked changes in race relations, sexual behavior, and attitudes toward law and order.

At the beginning of the 1980s, new movements of populist conservatism, based on the efforts of New Right and fundamentalist evangelical organizations, received widespread attention. Tactically more moderate than previous movements of populist conservatism, evangelical political groups, such as the Reverend Jerry Falwell's Moral Majority and the Christian Voice, have supported strongly conservative policies on a long list of domestic and foreign policy issues. The efforts of the evangelical political

Southern populist conservatism was most dramatically represented by former Gov. George Wallace (D-AL). A segregationist, Wallace disregarded a federal injunction in June 1963 by personally barring two blacks from entering the University of Alabama at Tuscaloosa. Below, a staunch Governor Wallace confronts U.S. Deputy Attorney General Nicholas Katzenbach at the door to the school before stepping aside later in the day.

Steve Schapiro, Black Star

Michael Abrahamson, Liaison

Amid a resurgence of evangelical political groups, legalized abortion is one of several social changes that has met new resistance. Above, a group of demonstrators calls for a "right-to-life" constitutional amendment.

organizations are directed chiefly at such moral issues as school prayer, the Equal Rights Amendment, homosexual rights, and legalized abortion. Having a constituency that is disproportionately from the South, rural, and fundamentalist, this movement attempts to resuscitate a traditional society that appears threatened by the spread of modernity and cosmopolitan values.

The resurgent, politically powerful conservatism of the 1980s is a coalition of the four tendencies. Given the differences in values and interests among them, the alliance is an uneasy one. The better-educated traditional conservatives, the libertarian conservatives, and the neoconservatives are all fundamentally concerned with extending personal and group freedom, although the neoconservatives are less interested than the others in freeing business from government control. The populists, on the other hand, are primarily concerned with social issues, such as sexual permissiveness, feminism, and the place of religion in schools and other institutions. Their desire to use federal authority to restrict personal freedom conflicts with the assumption of classic American liberalism, and hence, with the other conservative outlooks. It remains to be seen, therefore, whether the conservative alliance of the 1980s can hold together.

For Further Reading

Buckley, William F., ed., *Did You Ever See a Dream Walking? American Conservative Thought in the Twentieth Century* (1970); **Burke, Edmund,** *Reflections on the Revolution in France* (1955); **Coser, Lewis A. and Howe, Irving,** *The New Conservatives: A Critique from the Left* (1977); **Hartz, Louis,** *The Liberal Tradition in America* (1962); **Kirk, Russell,** *The Conservative Mind* (1954); **Kristol, Irving,** *Two Cheers for Capitalism* (1978); **Maistre, Joseph de,** *Works* (1961); **Nash, George, H.,** *The Conservative Intellectual Movement in America, Since 1945* (1979); **Rossiter, Clinton,** *Conservatism in America* (1955); **Steinfels, Peter,** *The Neoconservatives* (1980); **Wells, H.G.,** *The Future in America* (1906).

Cleveland Museum of Natural History

Donald Johanson (left) and colleague Tim White analyzed some 350 fossil fragments found in Africa and named a new species. The discovery of "Lucy" and the debate over her are recounted in Johanson's and Edey's book.

Simon and Schuster

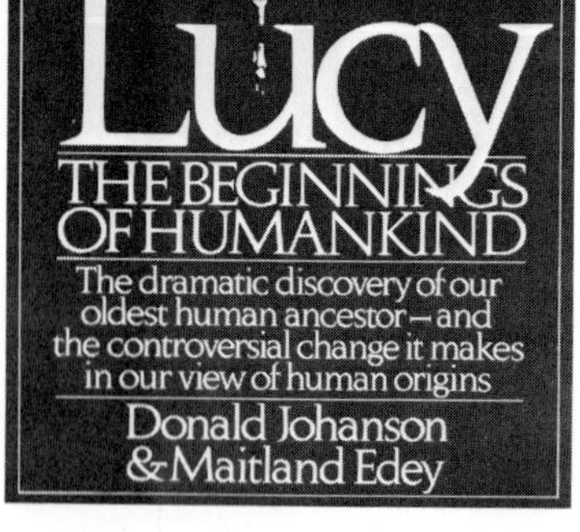

"LUCY"
A Human Ancestor?

BY IAN TATTERSALL
Curator, Department of Anthropology
American Museum of Natural History

In that 110-degree heat we began jumping up and down . . . howling and hugging in the heat-shimmering gravel, the small brown remains of . . . a single hominid skeleton lying all around us.

From "Lucy: The Beginnings of Humankind," by Donald C. Johanson and Maitland A. Edey

With these words, Dr. Donald C. Johanson of the Cleveland Museum of Natural History described his and a colleague's reaction to one of the most remarkable paleoanthropological discoveries of the century. In 1974, at a desert site near Hadar, Ethiopia, he spotted a collection of bones which proved to be more than 3,000,000 years old. A dance of joy in the sizzling heat was not an overreaction, but the fossils, which Johanson named "Lucy," opened the door to one of the most publicized controversies in the annals of physical anthropology. After several years of study, Johanson and Tim White, who joined him in the analysis, labeled the species *Australopithecus afarensis* and proposed a new version of the human family tree. Johanson's book, published in 1981, stirred the interest of the public and widened the debate over the meaning of Lucy.

Background. During the 1950s, the principal hominid (humanlike) fossils up to then discovered fell into three broad, time-successive groups. Earliest were the "australopithecines" of South Africa, which came in two varieties: *Australopithecus* (A.) *africanus,* a lightly-built ("gracile") biped with a brain a little larger than that of an ape, but with a considerably smaller body; and a somewhat similar, but larger and more robust form usually referred to as *A. robustus.* The gracile species was generally regarded as ancestral to later hominids, and the robust one as a dead-end branch on the human family tree. At first, the age of these fossils could only be guessed; all of them had been found in cave-fill sites that could not be fitted into the sequence of geological events. From faunal comparisons with dated sites elsewhere, however, it is now known that the bones date principally from the period between about 3,000,000 and 1,500,000 years ago, the robust forms being the more recent.

The next group of hominids (1,000,000 to 500,000 years ago) consisted of such types as Java and Peking Man, which were assigned to our own genus as *Homo erectus.* These were fully upright hunters who made tools and used fire, but whose skulls differed markedly from ours. At about 1 000 cm^3 (61 cu inches) in volume, their brains were twice the size of those of the australopithecines but substantially smaller than those of modern humans (which average about 1 400 cm^3 or 85 cu inches). The brain was

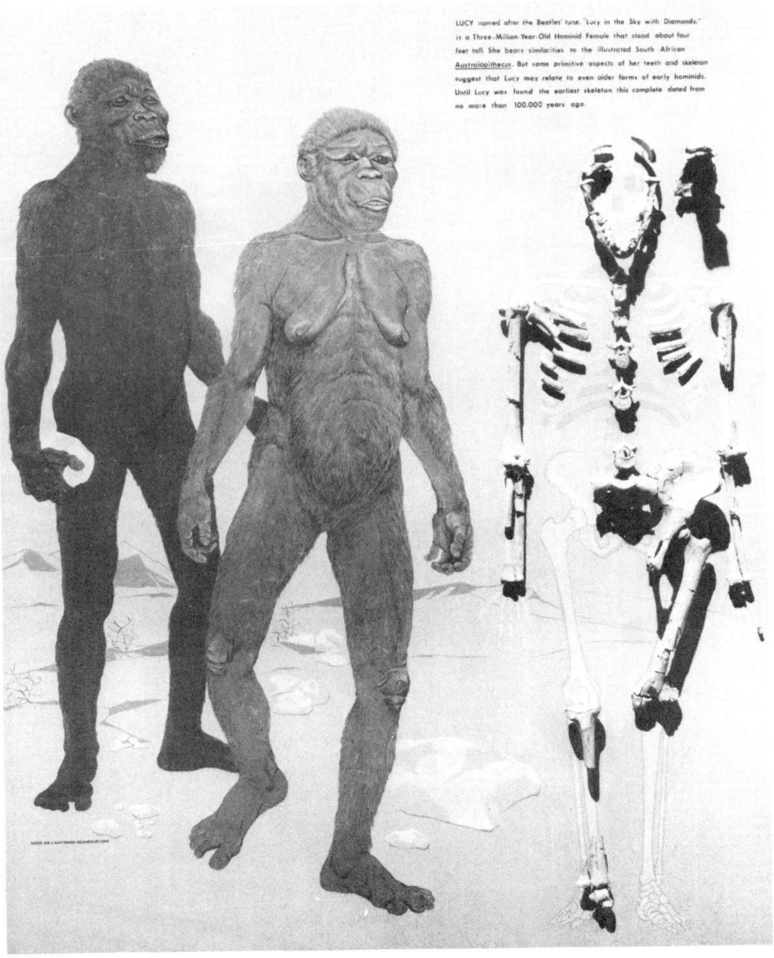

As the caption states, "Lucy, named after the Beatles' tune 'Lucy in the Sky with Diamonds,' is a three-million-year-old hominid female that stood about four feet [1.2 m] tall. She bears similarities to the illustrated South African Australopithecus. But some primitive aspects of her teeth and skeleton suggest that Lucy may relate to even older forms of early hominids. Until Lucy was found, the earliest skeleton this complete dated from no more than 100,000 years ago."

enclosed in a long, low, heavy skull with large brow ridges that overhung a robust and somewhat projecting face.

The final fossil stage was represented by hominids of the middle- to late-Pleistocene epoch. These were generally admitted to the species *Homo sapiens,* albeit as "archaic" types.

The fossil record of mankind had an unprecedented series of additions in the decade before 1970. This golden era of human fossil hunting began in 1959, when Mary and Louis Leakey discovered a robust australopithecine ("Zinjanthropus") at Olduvai Gorge, Tanganyika (Tanzania), in sediments also containing stone tools. In 1961, a new method was used to date the deposits in which the fossil was found. The potassium/argon dating technique, which has since revolutionized paleoanthropology, yielded an astonishing age of about 1,800,000 years for the sediments.

Briefly, potassium/argon dating is a measurement of the breakdown of the radioactive isotope potassium-40 into the rare gas argon-40. Because the breakdown takes place at a constant rate, the amount of argon produced is proportional to time. Potassium-bearing volcanic rocks contain no argon when they crystallize, so they can be dated on the basis of the amount of argon they now contain. The date derived indicates when the rock was laid down and not the age of any particular fossil. (Fossils aren't found in volcanic rocks.) But in a situation where fossil-bearing sedimentary rocks are interspersed, like layers in a cake, with datable volcanic rocks, scientists can extrapolate from the age of a lava flow the age of fossils found in sedimentary rocks just above it or just below.

The year 1961 also saw the recovery at Olduvai, in deposits about 1,850,000 years old, of a more lightly built hominid with a larger brain than "Zinj." Leakey, who for many years had favored the early origin of our own genus in Africa, named his discovery *Homo habilis* ("handy man," because of the stone tools found with him), and claimed that it, not the gracile *Australopithecus* or even *Homo erectus,* was the ancestor of modern man. The main *Homo habilis* fossils consisted of part of a braincase, a lower jaw, and some postcranial bones that included a perfectly bipedal foot. At

UPI

The British husband-and-wife team of Louis and Mary Leakey, after digging and sifting through the fossil-rich Olduvai Gorge in Tanganyika for more than 25 years, in 1959 discovered the remains of a 1.8 million-year-old human ancestor, named "Zinjanthropus." It was one of many important finds by the Leakeys.

Photos Joachim Hampel/University of California at Berkeley

Potassium/argon dating uses sophisticated equipment to analyze argon extracts (below) from rocks. The method allows scientists to determine the age of fossils in the rock.

the time, the naming of this new species was rather skeptically viewed by many anthropologists. In 1972, however, *Homo habilis* seemed to be validated when Leakey's son Richard recovered, near Lake Turkana in Kenya, a skull attributable to the species. This specimen, known simply as ER 1470, had a brain-volume of almost 800 cm^3 (49 cu inches) and was initially believed to be about 2,600,000 years old; it has now, however, been shown to date from around 1,900,000 years ago. Especially as misdated, ER 1470 cast doubts upon prevailing scenarios of human evolution, most of which had until then disregarded *Homo habilis* and instead accepted the basic progression of *A. africanus—Homo erectus—Homo sapiens.*

"Lucy and the "First Family." While the debate over *Homo habilis* continued, a Franco-American paleontological team began work at Hadar, Ethiopia, in sediments even older than those at Lake Turkana. In 1972, some hominid leg bones turned up, notable among them the knee joint (a telltale structure) of an upright biped. The 1974 field season yielded not only several hominid jaws with teeth, but also "Lucy" herself: much of the skeleton of a tiny adult female hominid, who stood over 3½ ft (1.1 m) tall. In early human paleontology, a single fragment of jaw is often cause for rejoicing; this find was unprecedented. Again the bone structure was that of an erect biped. In 1975, the group hit one of the biggest bonanzas in the annals of paleontology: the "First Family." A single patch of sediment produced some 200 separate fossil pieces, representing at least 13 early hominids. One suggestion is that all these individuals had died together, trapped in an arroyo by a flash flood. The Hadar fossils date from between about 4,000,000 and 3,000,000 years ago, Lucy falling in the recent end of the range, and the First Family about in the middle.

At first, Don Johanson, leader of the American contingent and responsible for the study of the hominids, believed that two species were represented in the Hadar fossil sample. Most of the specimens, he felt, belonged to a species of *Homo,* while others, smaller in size (Lucy among them), were allied with *A. africanus.* At about the same time as this analysis found its way into print, Mary Leakey and co-workers were publishing their own view that some jaws and teeth recovered at Laetoli, in Tanzania, and securely dated at about 3,700,000 years, also represented early *Homo.* Most striking of the finds at Laetoli, however, were not teeth or bones, but trails of hominid footprints that showed beyond any doubt that their makers had been striding, upright bipeds just like modern humans in locomotion. Inferences about behavior made from bones are always open to question. Many scientists had felt that although there was evidence to show that early hominids had been bipedal, these early forms had in some way been less "efficient" bipeds than we are today. But the Laetoli footprints told an unequivocal tale: protohumans were up and walking on two legs almost 4,000,000 years ago, well before the hominid brain had expanded to any degree and before stone tools came into use. (The earliest stone tools yet discovered, also from Hadar, date from about 2,500,000 years ago.) Most previous ideas about human bipedalism had it tied in with big brains and toolmaking; now a different adaptive significance had to be sought.

In the most widely accepted human family tree (left) A. africanus *is regarded as the ancestor of both* A. robustus *and* Homo. *Drs. Johanson and White, however, constructed a new diagram (right).* A. afarensis *(Lucy) is given the place of common ancestor to the australopithecines and* Homo. *This view challenges the Leakeys' contention that the australopithecine line was a dead end (not depicted).*

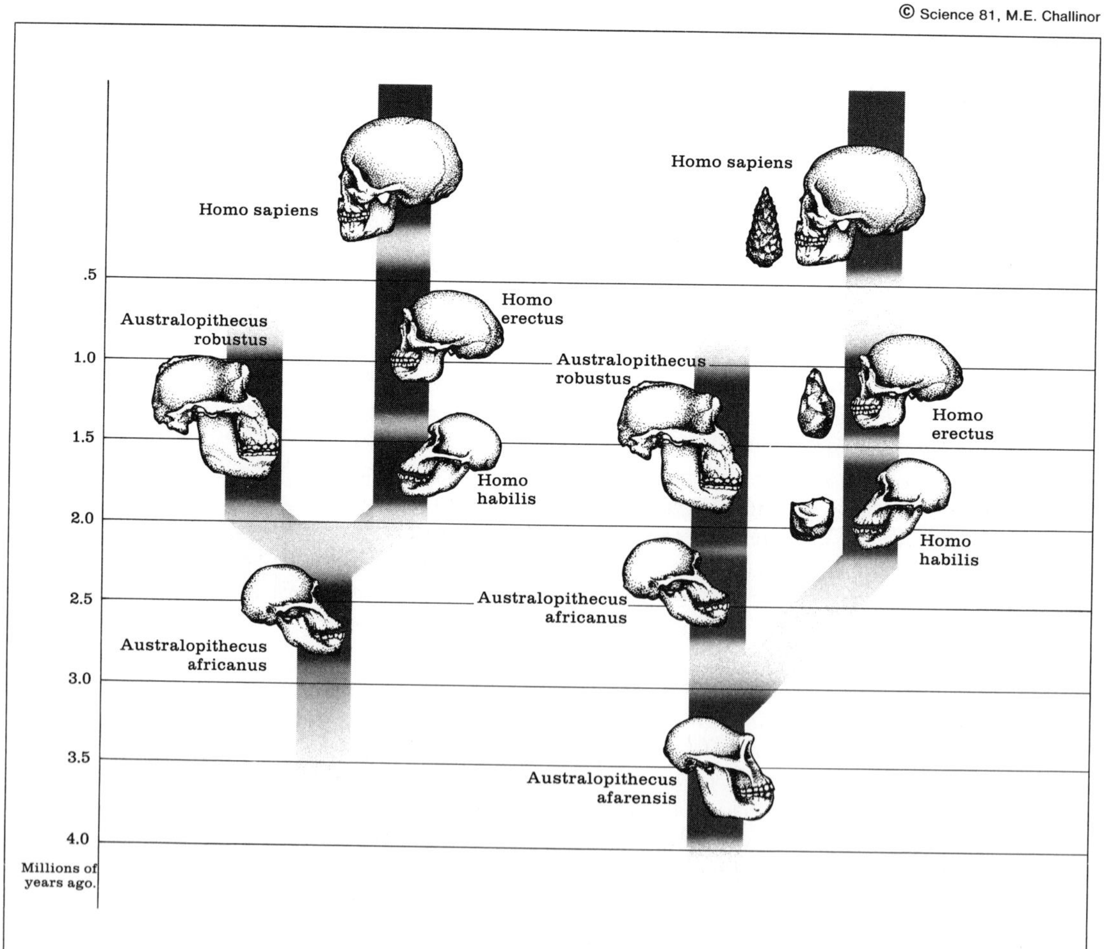

UPI

Richard Leakey, the son of Mary and Louis Leakey, and his wife examine a 1.9 million-year-old femur and skull which he discovered in Kenya in 1972. Known as ER 1470, the skull specimen seemed to confirm the elder Leakeys' theory that Homo habilis *was a key link in the chain of human evolution.*

In this connection, anthropologist Owen Lovejoy has suggested that the reproductive success of these early hominids was enhanced by the development of the nuclear family, which was itself, he believes, made possible by bipedalism. The more mobile males, he proposes, were enabled by their newly-freed hands to carry food home over long distances to a more sedentary mate. Thus relieved of the necessity to forage constantly, the female could cope with more dependent children and produce offspring more frequently. Lovejoy argues that the noncyclical sexual receptiveness characteristic of human females was developed to reinforce the male-female "pair bond" on which the nuclear family is based. This scenario has both its adherents and its detractors, and likely will be a source of argument for some years to come.

In his detailed analysis of the Hadar hominids, Johanson was joined by Tim White, who had been involved with the description of the Laetoli material. Eventually the two decided that the original interpretations of both the Hadar and Laetoli hominid fossils had been incorrect. They now concluded that only one hominid species was represented at both sites. In addition, they maintained that this species was distinct from all previously described *Australopithecus* and *Homo* species. It could, however, be included in the australopithecine genus as *Australopithecus afarensis.* Finally, Johanson and White claimed that *A. afarensis* was a common ancestor both to the *A. africanus—A. robustus* line of evolution (a dead-end) and to the line that led through *Homo habilis* to *Homo erectus* and finally to *Homo sapiens.*

The reception accorded *A. afarensis* and the Johanson-White evolutionary tree reflects the fact that one of the hardest tasks in all of paleontology is the delimiting of species in the fossil record.

Wide World Photos

Footprints discovered in Laetoli, Tanzania, by Mary Leakey in 1978 provided unmistakable evidence that protohumans were on two feet more than 3.5 million years ago. The skull of A. afarensis *(Lucy—right, center) more resembles that of a chimpanzee, top, than that of a modern man, bottom. The Leakeys maintained that the two finds were from different species; Johanson concluded that only one species was represented.*

Members of the same species share a basic resemblance, but physical appearance does vary somewhat among individuals. Speciation (the differentiation of one species from another) can occur without resulting in a great deal of physical difference between the two groups produced, and sometimes it does not occur despite quite extensive differences within a species. In other words, not all species show the same degree of physical variation among their members. Consequently, there can be no hard and fast rules about the amount of variation permissible in a fossil assemblage assigned to a single species. The variation in the Hadar/Laetoli fossil sample is quite large, especially in regard to size, but Johanson and White would claim that this range merely reflects size and size-related differences between the smaller females and larger males. Not surprisingly, many paleoanthropologists disagree.

The Leakeys, for instance, feel that Johanson was right the first time, and that two species, one *Australopithecus* and one *Homo,* are present in the sample. This would fit in with their idea that a very early *Homo* existed in Africa, but that position seems a bit shaky. *Homo habilis* from Olduvai and Lake Turkana is distinguished primarily by its relatively large brain, and there is no evidence of anything from Hadar outside the range of 380 to 450

The Cleveland Museum of Natural History

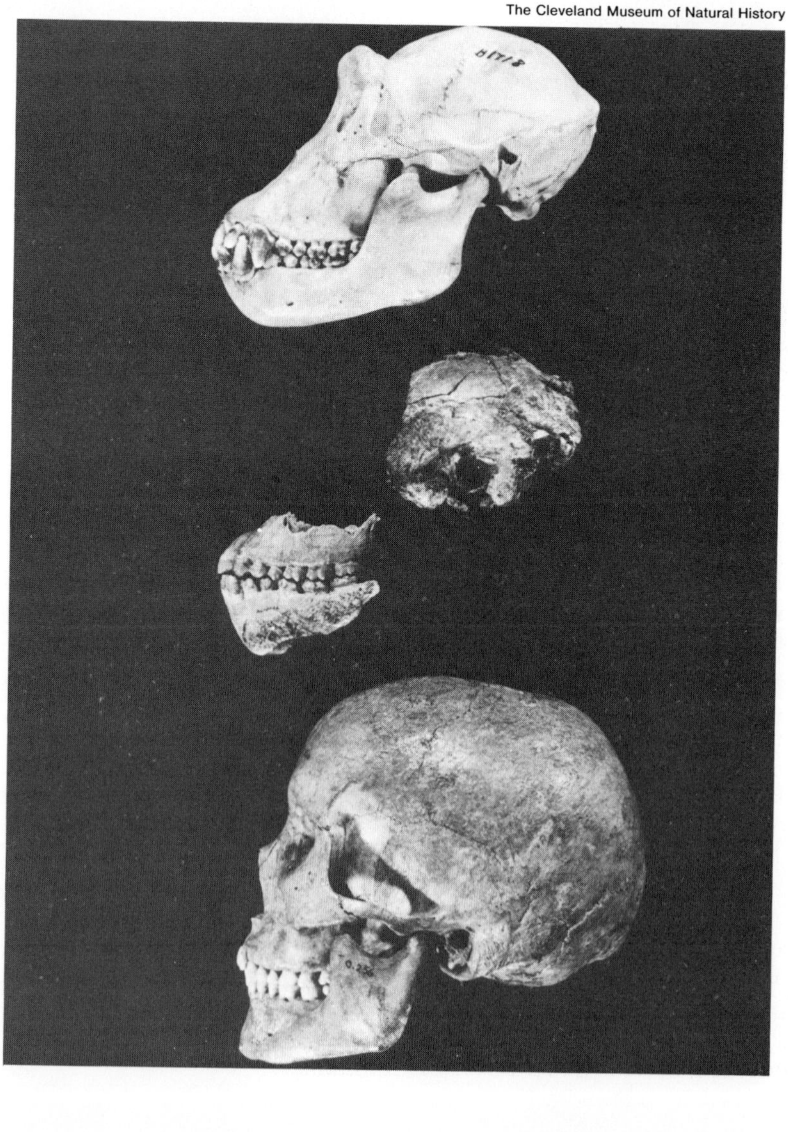

John L. Alexandrowicz, New York Times Pictures

The debate between Donald Johanson (left) and Richard Leakey (right) was often heated.

cm^3 (23 to 27 cu inches); this compares, for instance, with 300 to 400 cm^3 (18 to 24 cu inches) for the larger-bodied chimpanzee.

The eminent paleoanthropologist Phillip Tobias has taken another view. He has argued that the Laetoli and Hadar hominids represent no more than subspecies (local races) of *A. africanus* and merely extend the range of this species farther back in time. Tobias views *A. africanus* as ancestral to both the robust australopithecines and *Homo.* Yet another interpretation has been proposed by Todd Olson. He would allocate the larger Hadar specimens to a species of robust australopithecine ancestral to other hominids of this kind, while placing Lucy and other smaller specimens in *africanus,* which he would transfer to the genus *Homo.*

Obviously, the central problem lies in recognizing how many species are represented at Hadar/Laetoli, and to which other hominid(s) it/they are allied. As noted above, there is no objective way of knowing how many species are represented in any given fossil sample, although some cases are much easier to decide than others. Hadar is clearly one of the tough cases, and the question will, no doubt, be debated for years. It does seem most likely, however, that Johanson and White were correct in allocating the material to a single variable species, and in recognizing this species as separate and new. Whether or not this species is ancestral to two separate *Australopithecus* and *Homo* lineages, however, is another question. Ancestry is impossible to *prove,* and demonstration that relationships of this kind are possible must await more exhaustive anatomical analysis than has so far been possible.

Nonetheless, what Lucy and her relatives from Laetoli have already told us is exciting enough. A hominid species was up on two feet long before the advent of tools or the development of the vaunted big brain. This finding overturns the assumptions of only a few years ago and necessitates a reassessment of the whole question of how humans became humans.

The Moore School of Electrical Engineering

The ENIAC (Electronic Numerical Integrator and Calculator), the first totally electronic digital computer, was built for the U.S. Army and introduced in 1946, marking the start of a new industrial revolution.

THE COMPUTER EXPLOSION

By Colin Norman
Writer, Science Magazine

In 1946, the world's first electronic computer was switched on at the Moore School of Engineering in Pennsylvania. It was an impressive piece of engineering. Called ENIAC (Electronic Numerical Integrator and Calculator), it occupied a large room, contained 18,000 vacuum tubes and miles of wire, and consumed enough power to drive a locomotive. Today, a computer with equivalent capabilities fits on a desk top, costs less than $1,000, and requires about as much electricity as a television set. Such are the dimensions of the computer revolution.

A Second Industrial Revolution. As computers have shrunk in both size and cost, they have proliferated at an astonishing pace. Not only are computers themselves finding their way into growing numbers of offices, schools, and even homes, but computer "intelligence" is being built into a vast array of machines, ranging from children's toys to industrial robots and guided missiles. This computer explosion, says a committee of the National Academy of Sciences, "has ushered in a second industrial revolution. . .; its impact on society could be even greater than that of the original industrial revolution."

The rapid spread of computers and computer technology, which is well under way, will change the way we communicate, store, and process information. It will also radically alter the nature of many industrial processes, a development that will trans-

Lawrence Laboratory, Livermore, CA

During its 35-year history, the electronic computer industry has changed considerably as seen by the "Octopus" (above), the time-sharing computations system at the Lawrence Laboratory in Livermore, CA.

form millions of jobs and change the mix of skills needed in society. And it will have a major impact on personal lives as electronic equipment becomes more widely used in education, entertainment, and everyday tasks.

The technological advances underpinning the computer revolution began just more than three decades ago, but the pace of change increased rapidly in the 1970s and it is still accelerating. It started in 1947, the year after ENIAC made its debut, with the construction of the transistor. The basic building blocks of all modern electronics, transistors consist of semiconductor material—usually silicon—containing microscopic quantities of impurities such as boron and phosphorus. The semiconductor material acts like tiny electronic switches, shuttling electrons around electrical circuits.

The development of the transistor, which is much smaller and less power-hungry than the vacuum tube, quickly began to transform electronic equipment. A little more than a decade later, in 1959, the transformation advanced another major step when scientists at Texas Instruments and at Fairchild Camera and Instrument Company independently developed the integrated circuit. They formed several transistors in a single piece of silicon and joined them together by depositing aluminum conductors on the semiconductor surface. The advent of this novel device not only meant that more components could be crammed into smaller space, but it also eliminated much of the costly process of wiring together individual transistors. By 1962, integrated circuits were being mass produced.

Microelectronic Chips. As the design and construction of integrated circuits improved, the number of transistors that could be packed into a single silicon chip increased exponentially, doubling every year from the early 1960s to the late 1970s. By 1980, the most densely-packed circuits contained nearly 100,000 components in a silicon chip less than one fourth the size of a penny postage stamp. And the process is not over yet. Chips containing more than 250,000 components are expected to be on the market in 1982, and by 1990 the million-component chip should be in production.

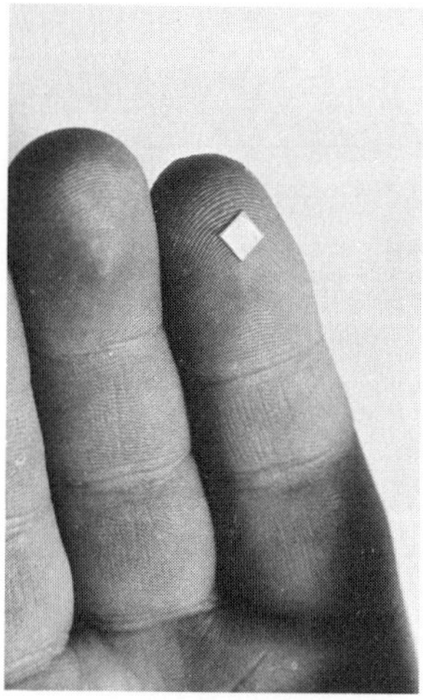

General Automation

The development of microelectronic chips, including the silicon-on-sapphire one, above, has made the computer explosion possible.

These microelectronic chips lie at the heart of the computer explosion. Once a circuit has been designed and etched onto a glass template, called a mask, it can be mass produced for a few dollars a copy by a complex process akin to photoengraving. In other words, a mass of circuitry that once would have filled a room and cost hundreds of thousands of dollars can now be run off like a Xerox copy. This is the reason why electronic equipment has become cheaper, more compact, and more powerful, and why computers have become so ubiquitous.

Integrated circuits are used in virtually all modern electronic goods. Silicon chips known as microprocessors, which are essentially microscopic computers, constitute the electronic "brains" of equipment ranging from calculators to cruise missiles. Integrated circuits, especially designed to store information in a code represented by pulses of electrons, constitute the memory of intelligent machines. And a variety of other specialized chips perform such tasks as operating digital watches and controlling the picture in a television set. Computers themselves employ a cluster of integrated circuits to process and store information.

During the 1970s, the manufacture of microelectronic chips expanded from negligible proportions into a $10,000,000,000-a-year global business. But the economic impact of the development of integrated circuits is far greater than even this figure suggests, for they have transformed and expanded the market for electronic

© Punch/Rothco

Lee Foster/FPG

After children were first introduced to computers in the classroom, they took to computer games. Many such games have merit as educational tools.

equipment—indeed, microelectronics has been described as "the crude oil of the electronics industry." Sales of electronics goods worldwide topped $150,000,000,000 in 1980 and, according to several projections, electronics could rival automaking as the world's largest manufacturing industry within a decade.

Computerized Consumer Goods. One conspicuous aspect of this development has been the advent of a growing array of computerized consumer goods. In the space of less than ten years, the manufacture of pocket calculators, digital watches, electronic games, and computer toys—none of which could have existed before the development of integrated circuits—has mushroomed into a $4,000,000,000-a-year business. Established products are also being transformed as silicon chips replace mechanical or electromechanical parts. Some washing machines, for example, are now equipped with a microprocessor that controls the sequence of wash cycles and water temperatures according to instructions entered through a calculator-style keyboard, and more than half of the microwave ovens sold in the United States in the early 1980s were equipped with microelectronic timing devices.

The automobile industry has also turned to microelectronics in a big way. Computerized engine controls, which are more flexible and can respond more quickly to changing conditions than mechanical systems, are a major component of the designs to improve fuel economy and reduce exhaust emissions. The first such controls were built into American cars in the late 1970s and by 1982 they had become standard equipment. These computer controls are designed mostly to regulate fuel and air intake and ignition timing in response to data fed into a microprocessor from sensors in the engine. Eventually, computer technology will also be applied to braking, clutch control, and virtually every major operation of the engine and drive-train. The passenger compartment is also seeing the impact of the computer revolution, as digital speedometers, clocks, and other electronic dashboard instruments become standard features.

The sheer size of the automobile industry—30 million new cars roll off the world's assembly lines each year—represents a massive market for computer technology. Already, automobile manufacturers are installing more electronic circuitry each year than the computer industry was using a decade ago. In 1980, according to one estimate, the global market for automotive electronics amounted to $1,600,000,000, and it is growing rapidly.

Range and Use. Computers themselves, however, account for the bulk of the integrated circuits produced each year. The revolution in microelectronics has vastly broadened the range and uses of computers. Just a few years ago, computers were large, expensive machines costing hundreds of thousands of dollars apiece and their use was restricted to large institutions such as universities, government agencies, and major corporations. Now, home computers the size of a typewriter can be bought for less than $1,000, and powerful business machines for less than $10,000. These developments have brought computing power to the fingertips of a growing number of people and they have opened the way for an expansion of electronic record keeping, data processing, and information retrieval. They have also blurred the distinction between computers and other office equipment, for computer intel-

The EADAS/NM system in Bell Labs' Network Management System in Columbus, OH, was installed in the late 1970s to help alleviate local network problems. The computer has had an overwhelming effect on the telecommunications industry.

Bell Labs

WANG

Word processors, small computers equipped with the capacity to edit text stored electronically in the machine's memory, have changed the work habits of many writers and editors.

ligence is now being built into typewriters, copiers, telephones, and other office machinery, providing them with the ability to process and transmit information.

Computer manufacturing is the fastest-growing manufacturing industry in the United States. According to an estimate by the Electronic Industries Association, sales of computers and related equipment by American companies amounted to $24,000,000,000 in 1980, with growth rates averaging more than 20% a year for the past few years. Although big machines still account for the bulk of the value of computer sales, small personal computers and office machines are by far the fastest-growing segment of the market. The recent entry into the personal computer market of International Business Machines (IBM), the world's largest computer manufacturer, is expected to accelerate this trend.

The spread of small, relatively cheap computers has had a major impact on offices. Until recently, virtually all computing was confined to central data-processing departments, but now small computers are routinely found in sales departments, stockrooms, planning departments, and accounting units. Many of these machines can also be linked to the company's large computer, which serves as a data bank or is used to perform calculations beyond the capabilities of the smaller machines.

Word processors, which are essentially small computers equipped with the capacity to edit text stored electronically in the machine's memory, are also finding their way into a growing number of offices. Although these machines only came onto the market in the early 1970s, an estimated 400,000 were in use in the United States by 1978 and sales are expected to reach perhaps 200,000 a year by the mid-1980s. The computer revolution has also spawned a host of other "intelligent" office equipment. Facsimile machines, for example, can "read" printed text, convert it to electronic signals, and transmit it over telephone lines to other facsimile machines that reconvert the signals to printed form—a

© Punch/Rothco

"Oh, the alphabet, and programming our microcomputer."

Photos Texas Instruments

Texas Instruments uses industrial robots to assemble their pocket calculators. Introduced in the 1970s, such calculators were an instant success with consumers.

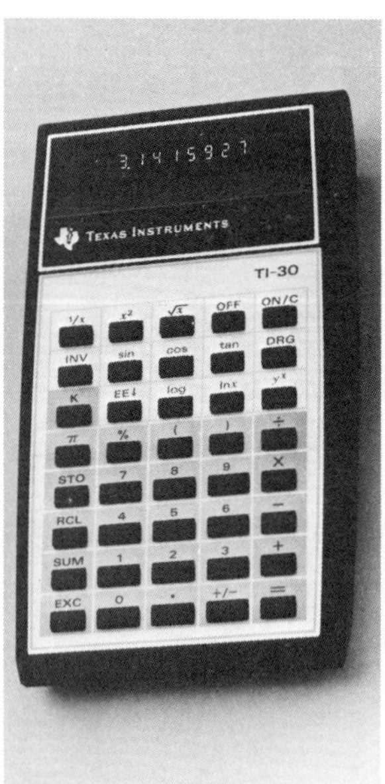

process akin to long-distance photocopying. By 1983, according to a projection by the Stanford Research Institute, some 8,000,000,000 pages of text will be transmitted over telephone lines between facsimile machines in the United States. High-speed computerized printers have also been developed to print the output from word processors at thousands of lines per minute.

This new generation of office equipment is encouraging a shift from paper to electronics as the basic medium for handling information. At present, office communications are largely limited to paper documents that are sent through the mails and filed in bulky filing cabinets. But the growing use of computers and computerized office machines means that more and more information is being converted to electronic signals, sent over telephone lines, and stored in electronic data banks.

As computerized equipment proliferates, it is throwing a strain on the telephone system. Built to carry voice communications, the current generation of telephone switching systems are hard pressed to transmit the digital signals generated by computers at the required speed, and many of them are reaching capacity. Consequently, most industrial countries are in the midst of upgrading their telephone systems by replacing electromechanical exchanges with computerized switching systems. This transformation, equivalent in scope to the earlier replacement of operators with automatic exchanges, will provide a vital link between computerized machines.

New Developments and the Future. Among other developments, the merger between telecommunications and computing will pave the way for an anticipated explosion of electronic transmission of messages and data. Electronic cash registers, for example, may one day be hooked up to bank computers to debit a customer's account directly for each purchase. Computerized supermarket checkout systems can be linked to a central computer that looks after stock control and automatically reorders items that are getting low on the shelves. Home computers, linked to the household television set, can be used to retrieve information from data banks and to receive news services. And the electronic transmission of documents may eventually supplant some traditional mail service. Such developments are not just remote possibilities. They are in limited operation already.

This revolution in information processing and data transmission is already beginning to change the nature of many white-collar jobs. But the computer explosion is making its mark in manufacturing industries as well, for computerized machinery is being incorporated into every state of production, from design shops to assembly lines.

Computer-aided design systems, which enable an engineer to design a part on a computer screen and then use the computer to draw up the specifications for manufacturing it, are already widely used in the automobile, aerospace, and similar heavy industries. They are also the heart of the process for manufacturing computer chips. Sales of such systems have been climbing in the United States by more than 30% a year since the mid-1970s, and they are expected to reach about $2,500,000,000 a year by 1985.

As far as manufacturing processes are concerned, until recently it has not been economical to automate the manufacture of

A 1981 strike by U.S. air traffic controllers focused public attention on the technical complexity of guiding flights. Large airports could not function efficiently without computers.

Federal Aviation Administration

items unless thousands of copies are required, because it has been too difficult to retool and reset machines frequently to perform new tasks. A human operator has been required. But recently, computer controls have been incorporated into a growing number of grinders, lathes, drills, and other machine tools, enabling them to perform new operations simply by changing the computer program or by typing new instructions on a keyboard. These so-called numerically controlled machine tools can be used in conjunction with computer-aided design: the computer used to design a part generates the instructions for the machine that will manufacture it. By 1990, predicts General Motors president E.M. Estes, 90% of the machines bought by the automobile industry will be computer-controlled.

Computer-based automation is also being extended to the assembly stage of production, for a new generation of electronic robots is being developed to perform a wide range of complex tasks. These machines bear little resemblance to the androids of *Star Wars.* They consist essentially of a flexible arm, on the end of which is a tool such as a welder or a paint spray, whose motions are controlled by a small computer.

Although estimates differ, it is generally agreed that about 7,000 industrial robots were in use worldwide in 1981. They are performing mostly heavy, repetitive tasks such as removing cast metal from a furnace or welding car bodies. In Nissan's Zama plant near Tokyo, for example, robots have been conducting some

A U.S. postal employee monitors the processing of mail by automatic equipment which is linked to a computer system.

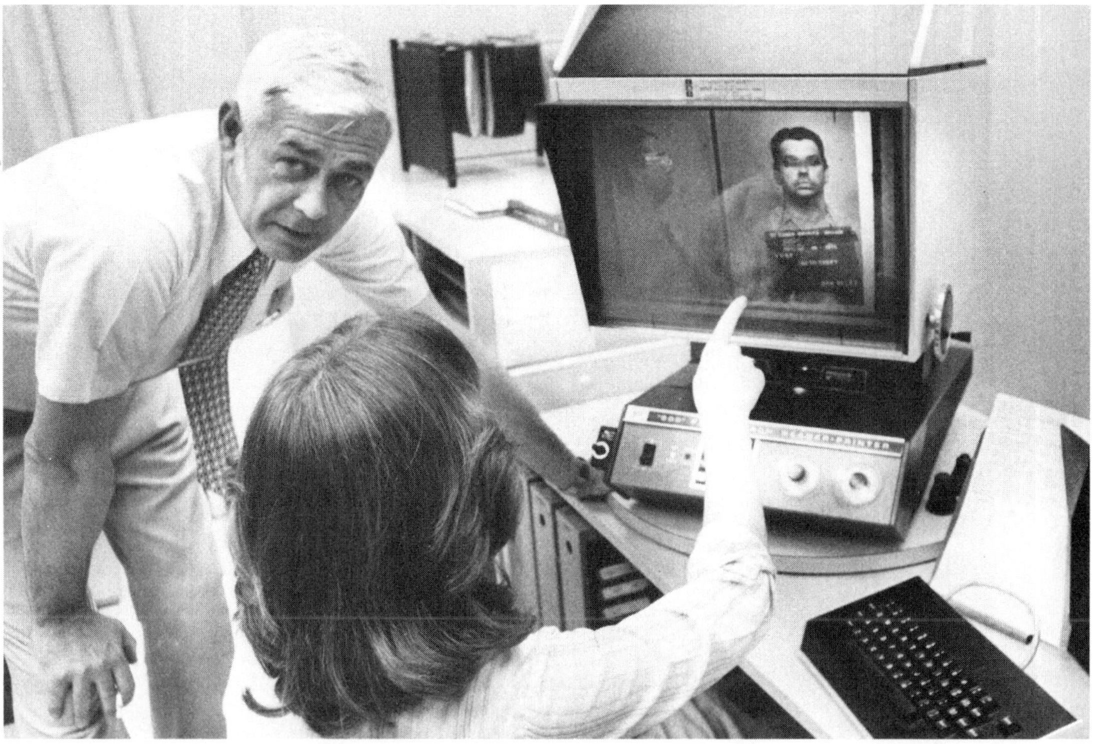

UPI

The Scientific Criminal Identification System responds to descriptive information fed in on a keyboard by displaying color photographs of 29 possible suspects from its memory bank of several thousand previously arrested persons.

96% of the welding since the late 1970s, a level that is currently being matched in the most up-to-date assembly plants in the United States.

The number of working robots is expected to rise sharply during the 1980s, as more manufacturers automate their production lines and as robots themselves become more versatile. One key development, now in the testing stage, is to equip robots with a sense of "vision" by linking them up to a camera and coordinating their movements with the televised image. This would vastly extend their range of uses, for they would no longer require parts to be fed to them at a constant rate and in an unvarying alignment. By 1985, according to one estimate, 8,000 robots could be clanking away in American factories alone.

As this computer revolution sweeps through factories and offices, it will have a fundamental impact on jobs. Experts have predicted that as many as 45% of the jobs in the American economy could be affected by computer-based automation. This does not mean that they will all disappear, but it does mean that the jobs will change in a way that will require new skills. And the introduction of the new machines will generally be accompanied by changes in the way work is organized. This, in turn, will require unprecedented retraining, and it will place new demands on a work force that is already suffering from high levels of unemployment.

The computer explosion, and the advances in microelectronics that have propelled it along, have clearly begun to alter society. "It is not an exaggeration to say that most of the technological achievements of the past decade have depended on microelectronics," says Robert Noyce, chairman of Intel Corporation. Yet, Noyce points out, "the microelectronics revolution is far from having run its course."

Interlochen Photo

THE ECONOMICS OF THE ARTS

BY W. MCNEIL LOWRY

"It's offensive to me that anybody would refer to high art as art for a small audience. . . . While rich folks historically have endowed and supported art, the appreciators of art certainly don't come from the privileged class. It isn't the privileged few who jam the museums, the concert halls, the regional theaters, the off-Broadway theaters. High art is for all the people."

Hal Prince
Broadway Producer-Director

Setting aside the commercial theater and film industries, and the galleries and impresarios who present artists for a fee, the economics of the arts in the United States are the economics of the voluntary nonprofit corporation. On that instrument have depended the extent and quality of American dance, theater, opera, music, and museums of fine art, and in large part the career opportunities of most creative and performing artists.

There are a number of factors intrinsic to the economy of the nonprofit corporation in the arts. The most basic, which is shared with similar institutions in education and health, is that the nonprofit corporation in the arts is labor intensive—from two thirds to three fourths of its expenditures are in personnel. The next is that its economic resources are devoted to the artistic process itself rather than to a single artifact, performance, or production. It is an institution rather than an entrepreneur. These two most basic factors produce the third: the inability to convert to the economics of scale—to increase volume through extensive tours outside the

About the author: W. McNeil Lowry is former vice-president of the Humanities and Arts division of The Ford Foundation. The recipient of several awards for service to the arts, Mr. Lowry is the author of numerous articles and lectures on the arts. He also was editor of *The Performing Arts and American Society,* published by Prentice-Hall in 1978.

Peter L. Gould/FPG

The Stuttgart Ballet

institution's own home and (to date, at least) to extend it through telecommunications. The three factors produce the fourth, shared again with colleges and hospitals, namely a dependency on unearned (contributed) income varying historically from 25 to 50%, and more recently from 35 to 45% among major art fields.

A concentration on quality, on professional standards of training, and on creative repertoire has been the nonprofit artistic institution's chief justification for unearned income. Other justifications—more broadly social, educational, or economic—have been pressed increasingly in a generation of growth and expansion, of the institutions themselves and of their audiences, unequaled in the history of the United States or of any other country. For the purposes of this article, these justifications are irrelevant save as they throw light upon some moderate shifts in the mix of sources for the contributed income.

Funding Sources. Dating the generation under discussion roughly 1955–80, *Giving U.S.A.,* the 1980 annual report of the American Association of Fund-Raising Counsel Inc. (AAFRC) in New York City, found that the most important continuing source was the individual donor, whose contributions to all nonprofit organizations rose from $5,710,000,000 in 1955 to almost $40,000,000,000 in 1980. In the entire period individual contributions remained in a high 75–86% range of all giving from the whole private sector.

In 1980 a little more than 6% of private philanthropy went to the arts and humanities; in volume the increase went from about $200 million in 1955 to $2,960,000,000 in 1980. It was in this gen-

Rallies were held in six U.S. cities in mid-July 1981 "to focus public attention and awareness on the key role that the National Endowment for the Arts has played in fostering the quality, diversity, and distribution of American art." Below, dancers perform during the rally in Lincoln Center Plaza, New York City.

Keith Meyers/New York Times Pictures

WGBH Educational Foundation

Telethons are a prime means of raising funds for U.S. public television. Individual contributions are the number one source of financial support for the arts.

eration that the only real fluctuation in the mix of funding sources occurred. At the outset contributions from individuals continued to dominate the scene almost overwhelmingly. In 1957 the Ford Foundation launched the first philanthropic program in support of the arts on a national scale, with large expenditures beginning in 1962. Strictly in proportion to foundation gifts, though still largest in dollar volume, contributions by individuals declined relatively until about 1970, when the trend among national foundations began to reverse, most noticeably after 1974.

Direct intervention by the federal government in the support of the arts began after the establishment of the National Foundation on the Arts and Humanities in 1965, with significant annual budgets after 1970 and the further development of arts councils in more and more states. A fairly consistent proportion of one-third public to two-thirds private sources of unearned income to the arts has existed during the past few years. Since 1975 the corporate gifts component within the private sector has increased dramatically, though rarely accounting for more than 4 to 5% of operating budgets in a given field. Contributions by individual patrons equaled those from all other sources.

Earned and unearned income to the arts in the period 1970–1980 allowed for the growth of museums and performing-arts groups even with the continued burden of inflation on the operations of labor-intensive enterprises. The results overreached all expectations and occurred amid warnings that nonprofit companies and institutions in the arts were an indeed endangered species.

Various Studies. The most comprehensive economic analysis yet made in the field was *The Finances of the Performing Arts* by the Ford Foundation in New York City in 1974. A survey of 166

WALL FLOWERS

Mazzotta/Rothco

professional nonprofit resident theaters, operas, symphonies, ballets, and modern-dance companies, this study collected uniform expenditure and income data over six seasons beginning with 1965–66. Among a range of assumptions and trend values adopted by the authors of the report was one that posited an inflation rate of 7% per year from 1970–71, the last season of actual data collected, to 1980–81. The "earnings gap" of $335 million thus projected for 1980–81 stuck fast in the minds of most of the organizations' leaders. When published, the operating statements for the 1980–81 season will not use comparable breakdowns except between gross income and expenditure. But nonprofit theater and symphony figures for 1980, compiled for *Theatre Facts 80* by Theatre Communications Group in New York City and by the Research and Reference Department of the American Symphony Orchestra League in Vienna, VA, as well as other tangible data, suggest that the "best case" projections of the Ford Foundation report were met or surpassed. Performing-arts institutions, despite inflation, grew during the 1970s and raised far more money in contributions than all but the most bullish advocates dared to predict. Not publicized by September 1981, except marginally in the orchestra field, was the real growth not visible in operating statements—in capital reserve position, endowment, and plant funds. Here the Ford Foundation's Cash Reserve Program, the National Endowment for the Arts challenge grants, and the corporations' and others' susceptibility to the leverage of matching have played major roles.

Will these trends continue? As for private-sector contributions, the more optimistic advocates in the field agreed with the 1979–84 projections of the Chemical Bank Economic Research Department's report, *Giving and Getting* (New York, 1980). This study assumed an inflation rate of between 7.5 and 9.3%, very restrained annual percentage changes in gross national product (GNP) when adjusted for inflation, and annual percentage changes in nominal dollar personal income of 10 to 11.7%. By December these potential changes appeared overly optimistic. Nevertheless, the study expects contributions to the arts and humanities to exhibit the most rapid rate of growth among all nonprofit beneficiaries of private-sector giving through 1984. Dollar volumes are projected to rise from $2,960,000,000 in 1980 to $5,400,000,000 in 1984, with annual percentages of change between 11.5 and 14.2%. Contributions to all nonprofit fields by individual patrons are predicted to increase by average growth rates above those for the total private sector; corporate contributions also will increase but more slowly and at fluctuating rates; bequests and foundations will rise barely and at a rate below that of inflation. The Chemical Bank study did not attempt a separate forecast for foundation giving to the arts and humanities, which increased sharply in 1979 but nearly leveled off in 1980.

The Reagan Plan. The "renaissance" of expanded opportunity that Chemical Bank found in private-sector prospects for the arts was a conclusion reached before the new Reagan administration in Washington sought to change the existing mix of private and public support for the arts. Under the new directorship of David Stockman, the Office of Management and Budget (OMB) proposed a 50% reduction in the 1982 budget for the National Endowment for the Arts (NEA) that had been prepared by the outgoing Carter administration. On November 4, the Senate and House appropriations subcommittees indeed accepted a figure of $149 million for the NEA, but some threat of a presidential veto of the entire Interior Department appropriations bill appeared possible following the Congressional recess in December.

The impact of the Reagan administration's proposal is, however, more important in its reflection of national policy than in any absolute dollar loss in NEA appropriations. Though the current mix of funding sources has had only a few years to become accepted, a perceived transformation of one component in the pattern can have dynamic effect on the others. An example is the advent of a multimillion dollar national program in the arts from the Ford Foundation, which in the 1960s and 1970s gave new

Actor Charlton Heston, co-chairman of the Presidential Task Force on the Arts and Humanities, testifies before U.S. House of Representatives committee hearings on federal appropriations for the arts.

D. Gorton/New York Times Pictures

stimulus to private sources and helped to speed the intervention of the federal government in the field.

But setting aside political and social factors in favor of the purely economic, the most troublesome aspect of the Reagan administration's approach was that it attempted to rest on two erroneous analyses—that private-sector support of the arts had not increased since the government's intervention, and that federal funds were now the source for first appeal by small or large artistic enterprises.

Even the Presidential Task Force on the Arts and Humanities, appointed by President Reagan in May and chaired by actor Charlton Heston and University of Chicago President Hanna H. Gray, had by August accepted publicly both the historical facts and current data. Many of the task force's members, but perhaps not all, had accepted another reality, that existing corporate sources would continue in their newly-developed patterns and had no intention of picking up whatever funding the federal government might choose to drop. On balance, the question of whether the government ever should have involved itself in the direct support of the arts has been revived, but the direct economic effects of the administration's attempt to shift national policy will come from budget and tax legislation.

Initially those effects appear both mixed and contradictory: The scale of NEA operations will shrink by at least one fifth in 1982. But federal deficits for the ensuing three years of the Reagan administration could make the 1982 level a ceiling through 1984. The momentum of increase in state funding for the arts, if taken as an aggregate, will be arrested. Overall state losses in federal grants and income-tax revenues could affect most state budgets for the arts (with exceptions in New York and elsewhere).

No new ways of administering or disbursing NEA funds can be expected to have a direct effect on private-sector giving to the arts, all components of which have their own course. NEA's use of challenge and matching leverage has peaked. Even changing matching ratios to a 1–4 or 1–5 requirement would only reduce the number of grantees.

In February 1981, Daniel Terra, 70-year-old chemical company executive, was named U.S. ambassador-at-large for cultural affairs, the president's representative at "major national and international cultural events."

Rollin A. Riggs

The tax legislation signed by President Reagan in August can have direct effects on gifts from the private sector. The gains that might come from allowing short-form taxpayers to deduct contributions begin in 1982 under rather spartan ceilings. But the simultaneous decreases in tax rates for personal incomes and in federal inheritance taxes can reduce the motivation for more affluent contributors. One can at least speculate that the new legislation could slow the previously anticipated increase in individual contributions, make for fewer bequests, and for the first time impede the establishment of small private foundations. The proposal made in August by Daniel Terra, U.S. ambassador-at-large for cultural affairs, that contributions above $1,000 be taxed at a lower rate, would meet vociferous opposition in Congress even if the president were to offer such an amendment.

The past five years have witnessed increased stability of earned income, capital assets, and productivity in nonprofit institutions in the arts. Contributed income prospects are positive. In any sector of the economy, nevertheless, the perception of both operators and investors has a role, and late 1981 was too early to know whether a threatened shift in national policy had affected the climate for both.

UPI

The incumbent U.S. president and three of his predecessors meet at the White House. Gerald Ford, Jimmy Carter, and Richard Nixon represented Ronald Reagan at the funeral of Egypt's President Sadat.

THE ALPHABETICAL SECTION

ADVERTISING

Advertising in the United States outpaced inflation by about 4% in 1981, climbing to an estimated $62,000,000,000, some 13% higher than the previous year's outlays. One of the industry's major indicators—new product introductions—ran an astonishing 8% higher than the year before, belying the axiom that advertisers prune big-budget rollouts in recessionary times. In the first nine months of 1981, advertisers introduced 976 products, up from 908 for the same period in 1980.

Laws and Regulations. As the year drew to a close, the Federal Trade Commission (FTC), watchdog of the advertising industry, withdrew from a major dispute with the industry regarding children's advertising. The argument, which had been going on for four years, was whether the FTC had the power to restrict or even ban advertising considered "unfair" (as opposed to "deceptive") to children. Under the Ronald Reagan administration, which is against over-regulation of the industry, the FTC's power as arbiter of "unfair" advertising is expected to be narrowed significantly.

In 1981, the U.S. Supreme Court ruled on several cases involving advertising. In *U.S. Postal Service v. Council of Greenburgh Civic Association,* the justices held, 7-2, that organizations were not allowed to put unstamped leaflets in private mailboxes. And in *Metromedia v. San Diego,* they struck down, 6-3, a city ordinance that banned all billboards except those used for advertising on the premises of commercial establishments.

The new U.S. Supreme Court—eight men and one woman—faces a decision on a Federal Communications Commission (FCC) ruling, upheld by the U.S. Circuit Court of Appeals in New York, to allow cable television operators to rebroadcast local shows out-of-town. Local broadcasters have asked the court to force the FCC to protect their exclusive rights to syndicated programs in their own markets.

Media. The network television ratings race in 1980–81 was complicated by an actors' strike that had delayed much of that season's new programming. When the dust finally settled, CBS repeated its 1979–80 prime time win. New labor problems, this time with directors and writers, also delayed the launch of the 1981–82 season. As cable television increased its penetration to nearly 30% of American households, the networks began experiencing a decline in nightly audience share. Reflecting the ever-increasing popularity of news programs, the three major networks gave thought to expanding their nightly news to a full hour (over the objections of some local affiliates) and to aggressively promoting morning news as well.

Reflecting the social climate of the times, television sponsors felt pressure from groups that objected to shows regarded as containing too much sex, violence, and profanity. The Coalition for Better Television, an organization claiming to represent 400 private groups nationwide, was formed in February. It threatened a boycott of companies which sponsored shows deemed offensive, but canceled the boycott in late June.

In 1981 the number of radio networks continued to burgeon as a result of satellite communications technology. The print media, however, continued to suffer, with some of the country's largest publications, including *TV Guide,* adjusting rate bases downward in an effort to improve profitability. For the first time in history, consumer magazines are generating more revenue from subscribers than from advertisers.

Volume. Advertisers were expected to increase their outlays to $61,600,000,000 in 1981, an increase of 12.8% over the previous year, but only 2.7% greater than the 1980 gain. As in other years, almost one third of the outlay was spent in newspapers ($17,800,000,000), a 14.8% increase. Total television spending increased by 10.5% to $12,600,000,000, including $5,600,000,000 on network (up 9.8%), $3,300,000,000 on local (up 10%), and $3,700,000,000 on national spot (up 12.1%). In terms of year-to-year gains, however, television buys were off 1.3%. Outdoor advertising, at $700,000,000 (up 16.7%), was also a loser compared with the previous year. Direct mail advertising outstripped its 1980 record-setting year, coming in at $8,700,000,000 (up 14.5%). Advertising outlays in magazines were $3,400,-000,000 (up 9.7%); radio, $4,400,000,000 (up 15.8%); business publications, $1,800,000,000 (up 5.9%); and miscellaneous, $12,200,000,000 (up 11%).

Canada. In the Canadian advertising industry, further fragmentation of television audiences, combined with the need to target markets more accurately, is creating rapid growth in the once sluggish magazine business. In 1981, a mixed performance by the advertising industry reflected the nation's general economic difficulties. While total media spending kept pace with inflation by increasing 12.3% (to $3,960,000,000), the growth was uneven. Newspapers accounted for the largest single share—$1,000,000,000—but the increase was only 9% higher than 1980. Television was up 14% to $684,000,000, surpassing radio ($435,000,000, up 12%). General magazines showed outstanding growth—$177,000,-000, up 22%. Business publications were also strong, with a 20% increase to $126,000,000. Weekend supplement growth remained slow, with a 3% increase to $12,000,000, while farm publications showed a surprising leap of 25% to $16,000,000. Directory advertising at $254,000,-000 was up 12%, while outdoor advertising grew 10% to $247,000,000. The remaining moneys spent on advertising in Canada went to a wide variety of miscellaneous media.

EDWARD H. MEYER
President
Grey Advertising Inc.

In New Delhi, India, during the foreign ministers' conference of the nonaligned nations, Afghans demand the withdrawal of Soviet troops from their homeland. A resolution calling for such a withdrawal was adopted at the February meeting.

Teki/Gamma-Liaison

AFGHANISTAN

On the battlefield and in diplomacy the Afghanistan problem remained on dead center.

The Insurgency. During 1981 the insurgency against the Soviet puppet regime became a war of national liberation. The *mujahidin* (freedom fighters), better armed and using more sophisticated tactics, escalated their struggle both in rural areas and in the cities. Soviet response was to adopt new tactics. They minimized their casualties by venturing less from their tanks and forts and surrendered control of the countryside, contenting themselves with mastery over the capital, Kabul, and the main military posts and communications routes. The mujahidin increasingly harried communications and strong points and even principal cities. The Soviets retaliated by destroying crops and villages to starve the guerrillas. They also fomented tribal feuds by paying off competing tribal chiefs.

In the spring of 1981, the Soviets launched an offensive spearheaded by three Afghan army divisions moving out of Kabul, but large-scale Afghan desertions and lack of fighting spirit soon stalled the offensive and the insurgency intensified along classical guerrilla lines. As fighting ebbed in one region it flared up in another. Major Afghan army defections occurred in Kandahar and Ghazni, where entire regiments of the crack 7th Infantry Division deserted and attacked their Soviet supervisors.

The mujahidin developed a fearsome terrorist and psychological warfare capability. Posters and pamphlets in Russian appeared in Kabul and even in Soviet barracks informing Soviet troops who they were really fighting. Between April and June, more than 80 top Afghan officials were killed in Kabul, including the deputy chief of KHAD (the Afghan KGB or secret police), gunned down in front of the Soviet embassy in broad daylight. Soviet troop morale sagged badly. A black market in which Soviet soldiers exchanged weapons and ammunition for drugs and liquor flourished. Looting and rape became common. Soviet dead, formerly shipped home for burial, were now interred in Afghanistan to veil Soviet losses from the Russian people.

In sum, 1981 saw a considerable escalation in the resistance to Soviet occupation, which the USSR was unable or unwilling to match. By year's end, the Soviets controlled only Kabul, parts of other cities, and major military centers, and had only tenuous control of the main supply routes from the USSR to Kabul. The mujahidin controlled nearly 90% of the country and on two occasions occupied the major cities of Herat and Kandahar. They inflicted serious damage to the main Soviet airbase at Bagram and held Gulbahar, astride the main supply route from the USSR, as well as the adjacent Panshir valley.

Arms Supplies. During 1981 the mujahidin performed the astonishing feat of continuing to hold off the Red Army while fighting with antiquated weapons. Their few modern arms were captured from the Soviet army or supplied by Afghan deserters. Western sources hinted about large supplies coming from the West but the mujahidin denied these reports. For example, Sayed Ahmed Gailani, leader of the National Islamic Front, made a spring tour of Western countries, pleading for weapons but was put off with vague replies. U.S. President Ronald Reagan, in a television interview during Gailani's stay in Washington, stated that he would "consider aiding the freedom fighters if they asked for it." Yet for the last two years they have been asking for just that. Many private U.S. foreign affairs organizations, including the prestigious Council on Foreign Relations, joined with Brit-

Alain Guillo/Black Star

Afghan guerrillas control the countryside. Rebel resistance to the Soviets increased in 1981.

ish, French, and German counterparts to point to the linkage between the Afghan resistance and Soviet restraints in Poland and to urge arming the Afghans. Gailani managed to confer with Congressional leaders who tried to obtain a clear statement of support for the rebels from the CIA, to no avail. The only unequivocal statement came from Anwar el-Sadat, who shortly before his death stated publicly that he was sending Soviet-made weapons to the Afghans and the United States was paying for them.

Unified Resistance. In an attempt to provide an umbrella organization for the resistance groups operating in Pakistan, the Islamic Unity of the Mujahidin was formed in July but soon fell apart. Such efforts to achieve a surface unity are cosmetic attempts to court external sources of support and have proved irrelevant in the Afghan situation. The groups based in Pakistan are not truly representative of the fighters within Afghanistan. The real mujahidin are operating in accordance with Afghan cultural patterns, ruled by regionally- and tribally-oriented kinship units. This resistance has an operational unity in the sense that they are all fighting the same enemy for tribal autonomy and out of hatred for the Russian invaders. Their allegiance to the political groups in Pakistan is limited to using them as a source of supplies, money, and external contacts.

Diplomatic Solution. The stalemate on the battlefield was paralleled by the unsuccessful international efforts to find a political solution. Early in the year, Pakistan, alarmed by the increasing number of refugees and the threat of Soviet retaliation, hinted it might be willing to negotiate with Afghanistan but repeated its obligation to the Islamic Conference not to recognize the legitimacy of the Babrak Karmal regime. Pakistan's Foreign Minister Agha Shahi requested UN Secretary-General Kurt Waldheim to appoint a special mediator as recommended in the General Assembly resolution of November 1980. Waldheim appointed a Peruvian diplomat, Xavier Pérez de Cuellar. This coincided with a Soviet diplomatic campaign to obtain international recognition for the Karmal regime. The USSR urged Pakistan and Iran to negotiate directly with the Afghan government. This would confer legitimacy on Karmal and provide international validity to the Soviet invasion. But Pakistan would negotiate only through a UN intermediary and only if the Afghan delegate represented the ruling People's Democratic Party of Afghanistan (PDPA) rather than the Afghan government. Iran refused to negotiate at all unless Soviet troops first withdrew. By the end of the year, Pérez de Cuellar arranged indirect talks between Afghanistan and Pakistan, with Waldheim as the intermediary, but the talks were soon deadlocked. The principal obstacle was the Soviet refusal to withdraw before the survival of the Karmal regime was assured. In May, Soviet President Leonid Brezhnev stated that Soviet withdrawal was contingent "on a guarantee by the United States and Afghanistan's neighbors of complete cessation of all forms of outside interference."

Soviet intransigence also blocked demands for Soviet withdrawal by the Islamic Conference meeting in Saudi Arabia in January and by the foreign ministers of the nonaligned nations meeting in New Delhi in February. Official proposals for a negotiated two-stage settlement were made in June by the Common Market countries and presented in Moscow by British Foreign Minister Lord Carrington in July. Again the Soviets said no. In August the USSR sent Deputy Foreign Minister Nikolai Firyubin to Pakistan to pressure President Mohammed Zia ul-Haq into recognizing the Karmal regime. Zia refused.

The United States, succumbing to European pressure for arms talks and détente, made cautious official approaches to the USSR, suggesting Soviet withdrawal from Afghanistan in return for international guarantees that any new Afghan regime would not be hostile to the Soviet Union. The Soviets rejected these approaches. The U.S. initiative, however, had been weakened by the lifting of the grain embargo in April which had signaled to the USSR the weakness of American economic retaliation. Soviet contempt for the "linkage" principle was demonstrated when, almost immediately after resuming grain purchases from the United States, the USSR announced that it would provide 300 000 t (327,600 T) of wheat to Afghanistan.

During the elaborate 1981 diplomatic dance no one consulted the mujahidin about the kind of political solution they would accept. The hatred against the Russians is so intense in the entire Afghan population that only a total Soviet withdrawal and destruction of the Communist regime might satisfy the mujahidin. Unless the feelings of those who are actually fighting the Soviets are taken into account any diplomatic solution concocted by outsiders is likely to fail.

Internal Developments. During 1981 the Karmal regime, prodded by the USSR, made several attempts to win popular support and broaden its base. It gave government appointments to several Khalqi leaders previously jailed or exiled and even to some supporters of the previous Mohammed Daud government. A conference of the newly formed National Fatherland Front was held in Kabul and loudly advertised as a new form of *Loya Jirgah* (Grand Tribal Council). Most Afghans disregarded it. Land reforms were modified to win support from rural leadership groups, such as landlords and mullahs (often the same persons). Offers to respect land titles of high army officers and refugees were made. All these reconciliation efforts failed. When the government tried to call back into service all former army recruits, the edict was met by major riots and mass flight from the cities.

Meantime the Soviet occupiers continued relentlessly their campaign to "Sovietize" Afghan society. They opened three new technical schools, increased the number of students sent to the USSR from 4,000 to 7,000 per year, and reshaped the central state organs into Soviet patterns. The Revolutionary Council of the PDPA was organized like the Supreme Soviet. The Council of Ministers, the Presidium, and the Politburo all copied Soviet models. Afghan youth and pioneer organizations were formed; the school curricula were reshaped to Russian standards with Communist indoctrination at all levels. Even the electric power grid was integrated with the Soviet system across the border. All information media were placed under strict propaganda guidelines. Russian language study became compulsory in all schools. The Soviet strategy of absorption became clear during 1981: reshape the state machinery in all areas under Soviet control; outside these enclaves, try to get control of the most productive areas and let the resistance starve on what is left until their spirit and the will to resist breaks. Whether this would succeed remained to be seen.

The Economy. The USSR pumped large sums into Afghanistan to keep the economy afloat. No exact figures exist but an Afghan defector, who was top economic adviser to Karmal, estimated economic aid alone is costing the Soviets more than $300 million per year. Since most rural areas are outside of government control and the war has devastated villages and crops, the cities have been deprived of food and are ravaged by inflation. The USSR had to import large amounts of food for the areas it controls. Customs duties, the principal source of government revenue, have declined to almost zero so the entire cost of government, education, and defense has to be subsidized by the USSR. In addition, of course, the cost of military operations is very high. So far the USSR has been willing to support these expenses, about which the Russian people know nothing, but as the insurgency has increased the costs became more onerous. The USSR has tried to share the burden, pressuring its Eastern European satellites to contribute to aid programs. Afghanistan, represented by Soltan Ali Keshtmand, was given observer status at the Council for Mutual Assistance, the Soviet equivalent of the European Common Market. In agriculture, 25 state farms, supported by machinery and tractor stations, were planned in 1981. Afghan farmers refused to participate. Economists estimate that it will be many years after peace is restored before Afghanistan can again reach even the low stage of development that existed before the Soviet invasion.

Refugees. Victims of the war continued to flee to Pakistan and to a lesser extent into Iran. The United Nations High Commissioner for Refugees has stated that the number of refugees is often exaggerated but agrees that the figure is close to two million. In Pakistan, the refugees represent not only an economic burden but a potential political threat since most of them are Pushtuns and, together with the large Pushtun minority already in Pakistan, the refugees add to the separatist tendencies which already exist in the North West Frontier Province where most of them are concentrated. This explains in part Pakistan's anxiety to find a political solution to the problem of the Soviet occupation of Afghanistan. (*See also* REFUGEES.)

A late-in-the-year analysis of the Afghanistan situation by the U.S. State Department concluded that both sides in the conflict are weakened by internal divisions, that, nevertheless, the resistance movement is gaining in effectiveness, and that there is no evidence of other Communist nations helping the regime. At the same time, President Reagan again urged the Soviets to withdraw.

LEON B. POULLADA
Northern Arizona University

AFGHANISTAN • Information Highlights

Official Name: Democratic Republic of Afghanistan.
Location: Central Asia.
Area: 250,000 sq mi (657 497 km²).
Population (1981 est.): 16,400,000.
Chief Cities (1980 est.): Kabul, the capital, 800,000; Kandahar, 230,000; Herat, 150,000.
Government: *Head of state,* Babrak Karmal, president (took power Dec. 1979). *Head of government,* Soltan Ali Keshtmand, prime minister (named June 1981). *Policymaking body*—35-member Revolutionary Council.
Monetary Unit: Afghani (49.33 afghanis equal U.S.$1, May 1981).
Agriculture (major products): Wheat, cotton, fruit and nuts, karakul pelts, wool, mutton.

New York Times Pictures

Refugee camp in Hargeisa, Somalia. The homeless are now a major problem for the African continent.

AFRICA

For Africa, 1981 was a year of frustrating inability to solve problems that have transformed into chronic crises, particularly refugees, food shortages, national debts, and political repression. The most difficult and persistent problem concerned refugees. In a half decade, the number of refugees in Africa has soared from one million to more than five million. Officials of the Office of the United Nations High Commissioner for Refugees claim that one in two refugees in the world is an African. Other informed sources estimate the number of displaced persons in Africa is approaching 13 million. Refugees are concentrated in Somalia, Sudan, Cameroon, Zaire, Burundi, and Tanzania.

This human catastrophe came into sharp focus in April when the United Nations Secretary-General Kurt Waldheim convened the International Conference on Aid to Refugees in Africa (ICARA). In an effort to mobilize assistance, the 85 nations pledged $560 million in emergency aid. The United States, historically the largest contributor to such programs, pledged $285 million. Unfortunately, the pledges amounted to less than half that requested by the Organization of African Unity (OAU). A general consensus prevailed at the conference that the funds will only meet immediate needs and cannot begin to resolve the refugee problem.

Women and children, particularly, have been driven from their homes by combinations of drought, floods, famine, and political repression. One hundred and fifty million Africans in 25 countries are facing food shortages, caused partially by a progressively less favorable ratio between population growth rates and the rate of staple food production. Sub-Saharan Africa, the only region in the world where per capita food production has declined since 1960, is rapidly becoming a chronic food deficit area.

Kenya provides a vivid illustration of the retrogression during the 1970s from food self-sufficiency to food dependency. Sparsely populated Kenya was historically a net exporter of a wide range of food. Today, its exploding population exceeds 16 million, with an annual growth rate of 3.9%, more than double the annual rate of increase in food production, which is crippled by a stagnating agricultural sector. Lacking birth control or family-planning programs, Kenya's population is expected to double within 18 years.

Food and refugee problems are interrelated and act as a time bomb, with potentially catastrophic consequences. Africans tragically lack the expertise and financial resources to deal with the crises. Moreover, the industrialized nations lack the resolve to provide assistance sufficient to offer lasting solutions.

Curiously, African leaders were less preoccupied with refugees than with the liberation of white-controlled Namibia. A United Nations–sponsored Geneva conference failed to open the way for UN-supervised elections that might lead to independence for Africa's last colony. The "contact group" on Namibia (the United States, West Germany, France, Canada, and Britain) was unable to find a formula for avoiding a diplomatic collision with African nations over the Namibian crisis. In Namibia, the Democratic Turnhalle Alliance, a South African–backed multiracial movement, rejected UN assurances of impartial elections. It argued that the UN had compromised its objectivity by recognizing the opposition group, the Soviet-backed South West Africa People's Organization (SWAPO), as the only authentic voice of Namibia's people.

Efforts to break the impasse were set back in August by South Africa's massive attacks on SWAPO bases in southern Angola, along Namibia's border. South Africa fears losing its mineral-rich, illegally held colony to a future SWAPO government. The United States angered African nations by vetoing a subsequent UN Security Council resolution condemning South Africa's raids. But by September the "contact group" had worked out a new timetable for "final negotiations" on the colony's independence. It was questionable whether the parties involved would accept it.

Freedom of the press became another major issue of continental proportions. Government control over the news media increased in many countries. South Africa's *Post* and *Sunday Post,* the nation's largest African papers, closed following the threat of a government ban, and numerous journalists were banned in a crackdown on the African press. Press freedom also came under attack in black-ruled Africa. Zimbabwe nationalized the privately owned Argus Company and replaced it with a tightly controlled government news agency.

In Lesotho, 1981 witnessed the assassination of the prominent editor of *Leselinyana,* the nation's most popular newspaper. The editor was a strident critic of government policies. Across the continent, authorities in Sierra Leone detained several reporters of the *Tablet,* an independently-run biweekly. In Kenya, where an independent press has flourished for decades, President Arap Moi's government arrested the editor of the prestigious *Daily Nation,* for articles on labor unrest. In neighboring Uganda, three employees of the opposition newspaper, *Topic,* were arrested and its editor vanished. By midyear, Ugandan President Milton Obote had closed five weekly papers that had criticized atrocities committed by the army. Not all regimes, however, succeeded in their efforts to muzzle the press. Ghana's Supreme Court ruled in September that President Hilla Limann lacked authority to appoint or remove editors of the state-owned media.

Africa's ruling elites have become increasingly sensitive to criticism, not only by their own citizens but by the international press. Through UNESCO, many Third World governments promoted a proposal for a New World Information Order aimed at greater regulation and licensing of journalists and tighter control over the news releases of international press agencies. Most Western countries, particularly the United States, stoutly resist the effort.

It was not difficult for the world press to dwell on discouraging news in 1981. African countries are progressively weakening under worldwide pressures of persistent inflation and economic stagnation. Diminishing demands for raw minerals and agricultural produce have caused a drastic deterioration in the terms of trade. Even the oil-producing countries, which had hitherto escaped the full impact of global recession, began to feel the effects of an oil glut in world markets. Faced by a wave of canceled contracts, countries such as Nigeria greatly reduced their oil production. Falling world prices for copper and cobalt brought deeper economic problems to Zambia and Zaire. And slumping prices for diamonds hurt Sierra Leone, Angola, and South Africa. All of them rely heavily on minerals for export earnings. The dismal picture repeated itself in many countries exporting commercial crops. By midyear, cocoa and coffee prices had reached the lowest levels since 1976.

Slumping prices for African products spelled a commensurate erosion in purchasing power. With foreign revenue shortfalls, most countries experienced deepening budget deficits and mounting external debt owed to banks, government agencies, and corporations. Everywhere, unpopular austerity measures were taken and development plans curtailed, delayed, or abandoned altogether. Consequently, most countries in 1981 had to contend with frustrated citizens and rising labor unrest. Problems which only a year ago seemed capable of resolution in the foreseeable future were now perceived as intractable.

The 18th annual summit of the Organization of African Unity (OAU) was held in Nairobi, Kenya, in June on a note of anxiety over the rising incidence of intra-African conflict. Nigeria's President Alhaji Shehu Shagari boycotted the meeting in anger over the OAU's refusal to deal with Nigerian-Cameroonian border clashes. Many OAU delegates expressed fear and outrage over South Africa's assaults on Angola and Libya's military presence in Chad.

WESTERN SAHARA: DEADLOCK IN THE DESERT

Warfare sputtered on between the forces of Morocco's King Hassan II and guerrillas of the Polisario Front in this former Spanish territory annexed by Morocco and Mauritania in 1975. In 1981, Mauritania joined Libya and Algeria in recognizing Polisario as the legal representative of the Saharan people. Mauritania also broke diplomatic relations with Morocco. Mauritania accused Morocco of masterminding a foiled coup against it. King Hassan, faced with a costly two-front war, elicited a pledge of fresh military support from the Reagan administration. Polisario is supplied with Soviet armory by the Algerians and Libyans.

Morocco's economy and morale have suffered from this inconclusive desert war of attrition; and at the OAU summit in June, King Hassan agreed to a cease-fire and a referendum on the issue of Moroccan rule in the disputed territory. However, a Polisario attack on a Moroccan garrison in Western Sahara in October threatened to destroy the very fragile peace process.

Wide World Photos

Dawda Jawara is at the British royal wedding; forces in Gambia try to remove him as president.

WEST AFRICA: LABOR UNREST AND LIBYAN ADVENTURISM

On New Year's Day 1981 Abdou Diouf was sworn in as president of Senegal, to complete the term of his predecessor, Leopold Senghor, scheduled to expire in 1983. Senegal is the only nation in black Africa to have a leader, Senghor, who guided his country to independence, governed it constitutionally, and voluntarily relinquished power to a constitutional successor. In 1981, Senegal was also one of the few African countries to strengthen the process of popular democracy. President Diouf and his ruling Socialist Party rewrote the electoral laws to create a genuine multiparty system. Eleven political parties now enjoy a legal existence; collectively, they embody a wide spectrum of political opinion.

Democratic rule was severely shaken in neighboring Gambia by a nearly-successful radical military coup against the government of President Sir Dawda Jawara while he was attending the royal wedding in England. At the eleventh hour, the revolt was crushed by the Senegalese army, called in by the Gambian president. Bilateral talks on the question of a possible confederation between the two countries followed. Tiny Gambia, long considered one of Africa's most democratic states, is English-speaking but surrounded on three sides by Francophone Senegal.

Democracy also came under attack in Nigeria, where it had only recently been restored after years of military rule. The various political factions jockeyed for power and in the process tattered the fragile fabric of national unity. A state governor was impeached, and a bipartisan political accord, which saw the return to civilian rule, was rapidly unraveling.

West Africa was not able to escape the general economic malaise of the subcontinent, or to avoid massive labor unrest which followed in its wake. In May, the huge Nigerian Labor Congress staged a general strike and forced the government to increase substantially the national minimum wage. Sierra Leone, a far poorer country with meager resources and a high inflation rate, faced its first general antigovernment strike in August and September. A major grievance was the high cost of rice, the country's staple. The price of rice is a volatile political issue throughout much of West Africa.

The region was also shaken by Libya's deepening involvement in the internal affairs of sovereign states. It began in 1973 when Libya annexed a mineral-rich piece of northern Chad in return for military assistance to the Muslim faction in Chad's civil war. In December 1980 Libyan troops were dispatched to Chad to help the new government in liquidating its opposition. The 11,000-strong Libyan force stayed on as an army of occupation and initiated a process it hoped would lead to a merger between the two nations. Through French intervention, the Libyan troops withdrew late in the year.

The Libyan dictator, Col. Muammar el-Qaddafi, was subsequently accused by many African states of meddling in other countries' affairs and of fostering Islamic fundamentalism. In December 1980, Nigerian troops dislodged Muslim fanatics from the northern city of Kano, killing more than a thousand in the process. The fundamentalists were led by a Cameroonian fanatic whom the Nigerians alleged received Libyan assistance. The issue of Libyan expansionism was also felt in the Sudan, which clashed with Qaddafi's forces along the Libyan-Sudanese border.

A new consensus was emerging in West Africa on the question of development priorities. Most countries had begun to recognize the urgency of food crop expansion and to place it at the center of their development plans. Since 1974, the Niger Republic has devoted enormous resources to increasing food production. By 1981, it had become one of the few African countries actually to reverse the trend toward greater food dependency. Other nations have become inspired by the Niger miracle.

EAST AFRICA: PAINFUL BELT TIGHTENING

As elsewhere in Africa, the year was marked by stagnant economic conditions and soaring debts. Because East Africa possesses no oil of its own, the economic downturn was particularly painful. In Uganda, Dr. Milton Obote, who had returned to power in December 1980, faced a shattered economy and opposition from many quarters. Armed confrontations multiplied within the army and against guerrillas loyal to Idi Amin, the former dictator. There were attacks on police stations, urban population centers, and isolated villages by forces seeking Obote's overthrow. The situation deteriorated further after June, when the two-year defense pact between Uganda and Tanzania expired and Tanzania's President Julius Nyerere withdrew his peacekeeping forces. As security collapsed nearly everywhere, thousands of Ugandans fled. Obote's popularity fell further after he initiated a program of extreme economic austerity and an attack on corruption and black marketing.

By contrast, President Nyerere's popularity in Tanzania endured and was responsible for political stability in the face of deepening economic depression. Drought and soaring oil import bills brought Tanzania to the verge of bankruptcy and contributed to the failure of an experiment in collective agriculture. Food production dropped, and the country increased imports to avoid massive starvation. Many regions retrogressed into a basic barter economy.

THE HORN OF AFRICA: NO HORN OF PLENTY

The war for the arid Ogaden reached an agonizing stalemate in 1981. Somali-Libyan relations deteriorated after Qaddafi signed a treaty of cooperation and friendship with Ethiopia and Southern Yemen, Somalia's mortal enemies. In Ogaden province, the slow-motion war between the Ethiopian army and the Western Somali Liberation Front continued to generate refugees. By October, approximately 1.4 million displaced persons were crowded into refugee camps in Somalia. Their survival rested precariously on massive infusions of food and medical supplies from the UN Office of the High Commissioner for Refugees, from Africare (a voluntary agency), and from the American Central Mennonite Committee. However, observers reported that the Somali government had diverted substantial quantities of the relief food to the army.

The Ethiopian-Libyan axis and the assassination of Egyptian President Anwar el-Sadat made the Somalis and Sudanese feel less secure. Sudan's President Jaafar al-Nemery, faced with a faltering economy and rising popular discontent along with the threat of Ethiopian-Libyan encirclement, called upon Americans for greater military support. The Horn of Africa and the Upper Nile, though bulging with hungry refugees, are viewed by the great powers as a vital element of Middle East strategy.

CENTRAL AFRICA: BUYING TIME

A military coup in the Central African Republic in September forced the resignation of the newly-elected civilian president, David Dacko.

Niger, a nation seeking to improve its food production, benefits from a CARE soil erosion project.

UPI

This was the second time Dacko had been overthrown. He served as president from independence in 1960 to 1966, when he was overthrown by Col. Jean Bedel Bokassa. This time, Dacko had failed to stem discontent over his inability to deal with the republic's faltering economy.

In Zaire, the International Monetary Fund (IMF) gained greater control over the country's chronic debt repayment problems. The IMF announced in June that it would extend a $1,200,000,000 credit and would reschedule previously rescheduled debts. Zaire's indebtedness exceeds $4,500,000,000, and only massive Western support has kept the nation from total collapse. The June 1981 reprieve came only two months after President Sese Mobutu's unpopular regime was shaken by the resignation and self-imposed exile of its adroit prime minister, Nguza Karl-I-Bond.

Zaire gained world attention in 1981 by becoming the first non-Communist country to sell diamonds on its own (in Kinshasa) rather than through the monopolistic giant De Beers Central Selling Organization. Zaire is the world's leading producer of industrial diamonds. Hitherto, the South African–based De Beers conglomerate marketed more than 85% of the world's diamonds. Zaire hopes to increase its profit margin at a time of sagging world diamond prices.

Neighboring Zambia suffered considerable economic and political unrest in 1981 which almost toppled the 17-year-old government of President Kenneth Kaunda. A soaring foreign exchange deficit created scarcities in imported goods and necessitated factory closures and layoffs. Labor unrest grew and forced reductions in copper and cobalt prices and output. The metals together account for nearly 95% of export earnings. President Kaunda, to strengthen his own faltering position, reorganized the ruling United National Independence Party and expelled from it many top officials of the powerful Zambian Congress of Trade Unions. The move only further alienated Kaunda from his people.

The president's waning popularity was bolstered, if only temporarily, by an excellent maize harvest and massive infusions of loans from Western institutions. A $946 million IMF loan, one of the largest ever extended to an African nation, was complemented by a Euromarket loan of $150 million and by a World Bank loan of $16.9 million for small-scale enterprises. Additional West German and Canadian loans totaling $70 million were earmarked for infrastructure and small industries.

In Angola, civil war continued between the Marxist government and guerrilla forces of UNITA (*União Nacional para Independência Total de Angola*), under the charismatic leadership of Dr. Jonas Savimbi. The Reagan administration, anxious to support anti-Communist forces worldwide, lobbied in Congress for repeal of the 1976 Clark amendment which prohibits military aid to Savimbi. In October, the Senate voted for repeal. But a tough fight was expected in the House. Paradoxically, American trade and investment in Angola were growing.

SOUTHERN AFRICA: WAR AND PEACE

The South African government intensified its search for security in an increasingly hostile racial environment. Military spending for 1981–82 climbed 40% and the police budget rose by 97%. Arms expenditures were expected to reach $2,750,000,000, a historic high.

The year opened with South African commando attacks on African National Congress (ANC) refugee camps in Mozambique. The outlawed ANC was the major guerrilla force; it aimed to overthrow white South African political and economic institutions. ANC attacks within South Africa increased dramatically in 1981. An electric power station outside Durban was sabotaged in April. A month later, ANC bombs extensively damaged a Durban military recruiting center, an East London police station, and rail lines in Durban and Johannesburg.

Christopher S. Wren/New York Times Pictures

Guerrillas with Soviet-made weapons continued to fight to gain control of the Ogaden region from Ethiopia.

ANC bombs in July knocked out electrical transformers in the Transvaal, South Africa's industrial heartland. This was followed by an attack on a military post outside Pretoria, the nation's administrative capital.

South Africa also had to contend with a black labor movement that over the last two years had become militant, politicized, better organized, and more disruptive. In recent years, the government had cautiously attempted to reform and democratize the country's racist and archaic labor laws. But it was also determined to retain sweeping controls over the trade unions. In 1981, it cracked down on more than 250 black political and labor activists, students, and journalists. By midyear, 60 members of the radical South African Allied Workers' Union found themselves in jail.

The government of Prime Minister P. W. Botha tried to fragment its nonwhite opposition by holding out hope of greater political participation to the mixed-race (Coloured) and Asian populations. As a first step, the Senate, largely a ceremonial upper house, was replaced by a 61-member multiracial advisory council. Most Asians and Coloureds boycotted the plan which, because it excluded blacks, further united the nonwhite majority. By contrast, the white population became more polarized. April parliamentary elections, for whites only, assured the continued dominance of the ruling National Party. But they revealed a shift, especially to the right, and a growing fear of black power. In reaction, the government backed away from its efforts to reform the country's racial laws.

White South Africa drew some comfort from a rapprochement with the United States under President Reagan. In a major about-face for the United States, the Reagan administration decided to collaborate more closely with South Africa on military matters. Over the last half decade, trade between the two countries has increased steadily. The United States became South Africa's leading trade partner in 1980 with American exports up 74%, to $2,200,000,000. The United States in turn placed more importance on its imports of South African minerals.

These trends have evoked deep concern and suspicion among black African countries. In March, Mozambique expelled six Americans for allegedly organizing a CIA spy ring. The United States retaliated by cutting off food aid, at a time when Mozambique was experiencing severe economic problems.

In neighboring Lesotho, life also became a little less secure. In 1970, Prime Minister Leabua Jonathan refused to yield power and suspended the constitution after losing a parliamentary election. Since then, the banned Basutoland Congress Party has conducted a low-level guerrilla war against the unpopular regime. Government efforts to crush the resistance movement led to violence. The cycle of violence accelerated in 1981, leaving hundreds of prominent government critics missing or dead and thousands in detention or self-imposed exile.

UPI

South Africa's seat in the UN remains vacant as the General Assembly debates the Namibia issue.

The peaceful conditions in Zimbabwe stood in sharp contrast to the turmoil of South Africa and Lesotho. The levels of violence and political instability were vastly reduced in 1981 as a result of a successful program of general disarmament and a reconciliation between Prime Minister Robert Mugabe and his archrival, Joshua Nkomo. Mugabe also consolidated his control over party and military affairs. Edgar Tekere was dismissed from the cabinet and from his post as secretary-general of the ruling ZANU-PF party. Tekere represented the more radical antiwhite wing within ZANU. Mugabe also removed Peter Walls as military commander-in-chief and replaced him with another, more compliant, white.

The prime minister's policies of economic pragmatism and political conciliation bore some fruit. Though white emigration increased, there was no "white flight." The country suffered from a loss of artisans, but white farmers and businessmen in the key economic sectors shared in the post-independence economic recovery.

Africa ended the year in a condition of deeper poverty, greater political instability, and less certainty about a peaceful and prosperous future. The continent had become less unified and more vulnerable to external global forces beyond its control. At the same time, government leaders were increasingly reliant on international lending institutions and economic aid programs.

RICHARD W. HULL, *New York University*

UPI

A soybean farm in Blooming Prairie, MN. The 1981 U.S. soybean crop was the second largest on record.

AGRICULTURE

Following abnormally hot weather and dry conditions in the South during 1980, the United States had very favorable weather and excellent crops in 1981.

The corn crop of 8,080,000,000 bushels, or 205 million metric tons (t), was the largest on record and 22% greater than the 1980 crop. All feed grain production (corn, oats, barley, and sorghum) was 240 million t, up 21% from the 198 million t of 1980. Also the soybean crop of 2,110,000,000 bushels was the second largest crop on record and 302 million bushels, or 18%, larger than the 1980 crop. The U.S. wheat crop was a record 2,750,000,000 bushels (74.8 million t), 377 million bushels more than in 1980. Cotton production of 14.8 million bales was 33% greater than in 1980. Hay production increased 5% over 1980, while pasture and range conditions were 22% better than in 1980. Due to lower livestock prices during the first half of 1980, the number of hogs raised, the number of cattle fed for beef, and the number of chickens raised were down slightly.

Late in the year, the large crop yields depressed grain prices considerably below the previous year. High interest rates, additional inflation in farming costs, and lower commodity prices caused realized net farm income to decline from 1980. Due to inflation, the purchasing power of income from farming declined to the lowest level of the last decade. The rather rapid inflation in food prices that continued was due to higher processing and marketing costs, rather than to farm commodity prices.

Land price inflation continued, although at a somewhat less rapid rate than in previous years. Dampened farm income, extremely high interest rates, and high farm input prices, along with high rents or prices for land, caused great difficulty for young farmers. Because of the higher costs and investments required, many young people who wish to start their own farms cannot do so. A few states set up trial programs to supply a limited number of young farmers with capital at reduced interest rates.

Even under the partial grain embargo to the Soviet Union, United States grain exports remained at very high levels. About 40% of grain entering world trade came from the United States. The nation exported nearly a third of its total grain production. Large grain exports based on intensive crop production were associated with severe soil erosion across the United States. A report on soil conservation problems, under the Resources Conservation Act (RCA), was to be released early in 1982.

U.S. Agricultural Policy. Secretary of Agriculture John Block, following the general guidelines of President Ronald Reagan's administration, suggested a reduction in federal outlays for farm price support and related programs. High farm price supports for dairy products caused large surpluses of butter to build up and to be held by the government. The U.S. Department of Agriculture offered to sell large amounts of butter to other countries at prices far below the domestic market levels in order to reduce the costs of carrying these stocks. Initially, consideration was given to selling the surplus butter directly to the Soviet Union. But with unfavorable response due to the recent termination of the grain embargo, the butter was sold to other countries, including New Zealand, who then could sell their own butter to the USSR. The farm policy of the Reagan administration emphasized exports, soil conservation, and expanded research for agriculture, with less emphasis on high loan rates or support prices. However, due to large crops, low grain prices and potential budget impacts, the 1981 farm bill maintained many provisions of previous ones. For example, it allowed crop set-asides or supply control to help bolster price levels and commodity loans to reduce marketings in surplus production periods.

During the early fall, David Stockman, director of the Office of Management and Budget, suggested the possibility of a crop set-aside or supply control program for 1982. The purpose of the set-aside, authorized under previous legislation, would be to reduce treasury outlays for grain support prices, more than to increase farm income. Later, Agriculture Secretary Block announced that supply controls (set-asides) would be invoked for wheat in 1982. Later, he announced the likelihood of a set-aside or supply control for corn and other feed grains in 1982. Whereas President Jimmy Carter promoted a vast program of converting grain to alcohol for use in automobiles as a means of increasing grain prices, this program was de-emphasized in the Reagan administration. Brazil, basing the production on sugarcane, remained the only nation using agriculture as a major source of alcohol for liquid fuel purposes.

During his campaign, President Reagan promised to end the partial embargo on grain exports to the USSR that President Carter invoked in response to the Soviets occupying Afghanistan. However, with political tension remaining between the two countries, President Reagan did not revoke the embargo until April 1981. The embargo did not relate to the 8 million t of grain that the United States had contracted to sell annually to the USSR in a five-year agreement signed in October 1975 and ending Sept. 30, 1981. It did relate to amounts greater than the 8 million t that the Soviets wished to buy. The Soviet Union was in the process of acquiring additional quantities from the United States when President Carter announced the embargo. The Soviet Union turned to Argentina and other grain exporting countries for the amounts needed in 1981.

Soviet Grain Production and Needs. Before the embargo, the USSR had planned to import about 37.5 million t of grain. The embargo denied the Soviets about 12 million t, half of which they made up by purchases from other countries at higher prices, and the remainder by reducing the use of grain for livestock feed and by drawing down inventories.

The USSR had a third successive year of crop shortfalls. The 1981 grain crop was only 175 million t, 26% less than planned and below the 189 million t of 1980. The nation experienced extremely hot and dry weather during the growing season and too much moisture during the wheat harvesting season. However, it did not have to reduce livestock production by amounts as large as expected by officials of the Carter administration since it was able to offset reductions in grain imports from the United States by increases in imports from other countries.

The United States and the USSR began new grain bargaining sessions during June. In August 1981, they agreed to extend the five-year grain agreement by one year. The agreement requires the Soviets to purchase 6 million t. However, to buy more than 8 million t, they must obtain special U.S. government approval. Secretary Block indicated that with a large U.S. crop and depressed grain prices in prospect, the United States would be willing to sell them as much as 18 million metric t. The Soviets were reluctant, however, to buy even the amount allowed under the contract extension. By September, they had already purchased 20 million t from other sources. The USSR will need to import about 42 million t of grain in 1982, as compared with 34.5 million t in 1981. They also contracted to buy 52 million t over the next five years from Argentina, Australia, and Canada.

European Conditions. The Polish union, Solidarity, initiated in 1980 as a protest against higher food prices, continued to expand and strengthen in 1981. While the government wanted to quadruple food prices, union strength was able to forestall such large increases. However, bread and flour prices were increased 300%. Food supplies remained tight in Poland and rationing to consumers became increasingly severe. The crop situation in other Eastern Euro-

© Gamble/"Florida Times-Union"

pean countries did not allow them to offset the deficit, and Poland's balance of payments and foreign indebtedness problems hindered it from buying supplies from the United States and other exporting countries. During September the United States announced a special food aid program for Poland. With poor crops in 1980, livestock production in Poland contracted seriously in 1981. Due to poor agricultural performance and pressures of Solidarity, the government agreed to extensive agricultural reforms. Most of these were aimed at improving the potential of private farms, which work 75% of the land. The rest of Eastern Europe had near normal weather. Oilseed and sugar beet output increased, but payment difficulties resulted in lower grain exports than normal and thus restrained livestock production.

Livestock production in Western Europe recovered in 1981, led by a dynamic poultry sector in France and Spain. France increased its meat exports outside the European Community (EC) by a considerable amount. Grain production in Western Europe was somewhat higher than in 1980. Cold, rainy weather caused fruit losses in Germany, Italy, and France and a reduced lamb crop in England. Drought reduced grain production in Spain by about 10% below 1980 levels.

The EC increased prices by 9.6% early in 1981, the largest increase since 1975. Thus the value of farm output increased considerably in 1981 even with a modest gain in output.

Asia. China increased grain imports to a record 15 million tons, due to increased domestic demand and reduced 1980 output. While 1981 production increased, imports still grew because government leaders want to continue to ensure grain rations to urban dwellers. A U.S.-China agreement calls for 6–10 million t of grain to be shipped annually to China.

Weather was favorable in Southeast Asia. Indonesia, Malaysia, and Thailand harvested large rice crops. Since unfavorable weather caused it to suffer a food shortage, South Korea replaced Indonesia as the world's largest rice importer. Monsoon rains were good in India during the summer. The country indexed crop prices to farm input prices. It contracted, at the displeasure of Indian farmers, to import 1.5 million t of grain from the United States as a means of holding down consumer prices.

Other Regions. Canadian grain production recovered to record levels in 1981 due to both a larger acreage and high yields. Wheat exports were at record levels and should continue. Drought carried into 1981 for Australia, and production was depressed considerably from 1980. Exports of both wheat and coarse grains declined. Japan continued to reduce its surplus rice stocks. Stocks were reduced especially through exports to South Korea and use of rice as livestock feed.

Argentina's 1981 grain crop was more than double the 21.4 million t of 1980. Large exports to the USSR and high prices encouraged larger plantings. Devaluation of the peso also encouraged grain exports. Corn and soybean production were at record levels in Brazil. The new plantings of 1974 caused the coffee harvest to increase by nearly 50%.

South Africa and Zimbabwe both had record corn yields and were able to export large amounts in early 1981 to other South African countries experiencing a grain shortage. Black South African countries formed a Conference on the Coordination of Development in South Africa (SADCC) to promote regional food self-sufficiency.

U.S. corn exports to the Middle East and North Africa increased by more than 40% due to increased livestock production in the region and poor grain crops in some countries. Egypt and Israel increased their food trade with each other as part of the Camp David accord.

Commodity Summary. World grain production was generally favored by good weather and advanced considerably over the previous year. Wheat, coarse grain, rice, and total grain production were at record levels. Also, international trade in grains reached new levels.

Increased world production of oilseeds allowed greater production of high protein feeds for livestock. While world export demand for vegetable oils was weak in 1980–81, production also increased in 1981–82. Due to the 1980 drought, the United States raised its import quotas for peanuts. China, India, Sudan, and Argentina filled most of the enlarged quota.

Increased area in some countries and large Soviet and Cuban crops boosted global sugar production in 1981–82. Declining sugar prices early in the year triggered International Sugar Agreement (ISA) import restrictions and export quotas. The world sugar price dropped below 16 cents per pound for five consecutive days in May.

Although Brazil's coffee crop increased by 50%, due to new plantings, total world production declined slightly due to poor crops in some other Latin American, Asian, and African countries. Coffee prices remained low in 1981. World cocoa bean production was up marginally from the previous year. World stocks would likely increase for the fourth consecutive year. Stagnant cocoa consumption and stock buildups caused prices to remain depressed.

World cotton production climbed sharply in the 1981–82 crop year. Global planting increased 2% while yields were exceptionally high in the United States. China, India, and the Soviet Union also had large crops.

From a food and fiber standpoint, 1981 was an exceptional global year, with record crops. Large 1981 production should help maintain favorable consumer prices.

EARL O. HEADY
Iowa State University

(1 metric ton = 1.102 short tons.)

Financial difficulties left the city of Birmingham, AL, without bus service for three months during 1981.

The Birmingham News Company

ALABAMA

Actions of the legislature dominated Alabama news during 1981.

Legislative Politics. The legislature convened in regular session in February. In response to a U.S. Supreme Court decision invalidating a portion of its death penalty law, the legislature passed a new capital punishment bill. However, when the legislature adjourned in May it had not passed an education appropriations bill. Such a measure was approved in a specially called session in August. Public education continued at reduced funding levels during 1981. Tax revenues for several years have not equaled the amounts appropriated to schools and colleges by the legislature.

Also in special session the legislature approved a new congressional redistricting plan. Alabama has seven members of the U.S. House of Representatives, as it had prior to the 1980 census. However, the new districts reflect growth and movement of the population during the 1970s. The state Democratic Party made no concerted effort to try to gerrymander the new districts so as to impair the reelection chances of the three Republican incumbent U.S. representatives. In part this restraint was attributable to the lobbying efforts of the conservative religious group, the Moral Majority.

The legislature convened in special session in late September to consider state legislative reapportionment. The possibility that black representation in the House of Representatives might be reduced if a committee-endorsed plan were adopted led to immediate controversy.

Prison Reform. In response to the state government's continued reluctance to provide prison facilities sufficient to meet federal judicial standards, U.S. District Judge Robert Varner in July ordered the release of 277 inmates from Alabama penal institutions to relieve congested conditions. The severity of overcrowding, in Judge Varner's opinion, amounted to "cruel and unusual punishment" in violation of the U.S. Constitution.

Urban Problems. The city of Mobile returned to federal court in May in defense of its commission form of government. The U.S. Supreme Court had sent the case back for district trial to determine if the municipality's system of at-large elections had the effect and had been specifically constructed in 1911 with the purpose of minimizing the influence of black voters.

During the months of March, April, and May, Birmingham was the largest city in the nation without a functioning mass transit system. An estimated 38,000 regular passengers were forced to rely on makeshift arrangements when, due to financial difficulties, the local transit authority had to discontinue service. Buses rolled again in June—but schedules were further reduced and fares continued to be very high.

Birmingham went even longer without a police chief. Chief Bill Myers resigned in January; subsequently the Jefferson County Personnel Board nominated three candidates from whom Major Richard Arrington was supposed to select a new chief. However, the mayor still had declined to do so by late 1981.

William H. Stewart
The University of Alabama

ALABAMA • Information Highlights

Area: 51,705 sq mi (133 916 km^2).
Population: (1980 census): 3,890,061.
Chief Cities (1980 census): Montgomery, the capital, 178,157; Birmingham, 284,413; Mobile, 200,452; Huntsville, 142,513; Tuscaloosa, 75,143; Dothan, 48,750; Gadsden, 47,565; Decatur, 42,002; Prichard, 39,541; Florence, 37,029.
Government (1981): *Chief Officers*—governor, Forrest H. James, Jr. (D); lt. gov., George McMillan (D). *Legislature*—Senate, 35 members; House of Representatives, 105 members.
State Finances (fiscal year 1980): *Revenues*, $4,154,000,000; *expenditures*, $4,002,000,000.
Personal Income (1980): $29,199,000,000; per capita, $7,488.
Labor Force (July 1981): *Nonagricultural wage and salary earners*, 1,344,500; *unemployed*, 152,500 (9.3% of total force).

ALASKA

Major issues in 1981 included control of the legislature, disposing of billions in oil revenues, and limiting state spending.

Politics. When the legislature convened in Juneau in January, Republicans and Democrats moved jointly to organize control of the state Senate. It was three weeks later before the House of Representatives organized with a slim margin of Democratic control. The Democrats' hold on the House dissolved two weeks before adjournment, when disaffected rural and Anchorage Democrats joined with Republicans and Libertarians to take over. One key issue was the proposed move of the state capital from Juneau. Through much of the session, Anchorage and southcentral delegates maneuvered to circumvent a 1979 initiative that would have the effect of preventing such a move.

Subsistence. Another major divisive question was "subsistence." Under the law, subsistence hunters receive preference when game is limited. The issue may damage relations between whites and natives.

Oil Revenues. Early in the session it appeared that the state would have an enormous surplus of money from oil. After the legislature spent most of the surplus in the last two weeks of the session, it was revealed that a glut of oil would reduce revenues. Declining oil prices reduced revenues and the legislature may have created a shortfall. In response to anticipated revenues, the legislature abolished personal income taxes, relying solely on oil royalties and incidental revenues to support public programs. Many local governments moved to eliminate or suspend sales taxes as well, counting on state funds to provide financing.

Following adjournment, Gov. Jay Hammond called a special session to pass a limit on state spending. Such an amendment was passed and prepared for submission to the voters for ratification in 1982.

Lawyers Penny and Ron Zobel question the constitutionality of Alaska's Permanent Fund Law.

"The Anchorage Times"

Permanent Fund Case. In October, the U.S. Supreme Court heard arguments about the constitutionality of Alaska's Permanent Fund Law. The fund, which receives at least 25% of revenues from oil, was due to begin paying annual dividends to Alaskans of $50.00 for each year of residence. Anchorage attorneys Ron and Penny Zobel challenged the law on the ground that it unconstitutionally penalizes more recent arrivals and violates the constitutional right to travel. The court was expected to rule on the case in 1982.

Offshore Oil Leases. U.S. Secretary of the Interior James Watt agreed to suspend federal plans to lease tracts in Bristol Bay to oil companies. The bay is a prime fishery and there was concern over possible impact of exploratory drilling and potential oil spills on the salmon, which constitute the chief livelihood of the area. The North Slope Borough was less successful in attempts to prevent leasing in the Beaufort Sea, a shallow sea with known oil reserves, which is a migration route for bowhead whales.

Natural Gas Line. Construction of the line to bring natural gas from Prudhoe Bay to the "lower 48" was advanced in late fall when President Ronald Reagan approved waivers to permit companies to bill customers for costs of construction before completion of the line. The line is legally required to be financed privately. Prior to adjourning in December, Congress passed a special financial package for the $43,000,000,000 pipeline. The new act waives provisions of a 1977 law, signed by President Jimmy Carter, under which a consortium would build the pipeline. The new legislation shifts some of the financial risks to users of the natural gas if the line is not completed. In addition, the gas producers will have an equity stake in the pipeline. President Reagan signed the bill into law on December 15.

Petrochemical Study. During the year, much attention centered on a study by a Dow-Shell group to determine whether a petrochemical industry in the state would be feasible. The report listed a number of serious problems confronting

ALASKA • Information Highlights

Area: 591,004 sq mi (1 530 700 km^2).
Population (1980 census): 400,481.
Chief Cities (1980 census): Juneau, the capital, 19,528; Anchorage, 173,017; Fairbanks, 22,645; Sitka, 7,803; Ketchikan, 7,198; Kodiak, 4,756; Kenai, 4,324; Bethel, 3,576; Valdex, 3,079; Petersburg, 2,821.
Government (1981): *Chief Officers*—governor, Jay S. Hammond (R); lt. gov., Terry Miller (R). *Legislature*—Senate, 20 members; House of Representatives, 40 members.
State Finances (fiscal year 1980): *Revenues,* $3,230,000,000; *expenditures,* $2,033,000,000.
Personal Income (1980): $5,136,000,000; per capita, $12,790.
Labor Force (July 1981): *Nonagricultural wage and salary earners,* 190,600; *unemployed,* 17,400 (8.4% of total force).

such an industry, but concluded that, given certain conditions, an industry could be profitable. Controversy surrounded the study, including attacks on the objectivity of the group itself. Many environmentally concerned Alaskans believed that air and water pollution questions were not adequately addressed.

Alaska Railroad. Alaska's senators Ted Stevens and Frank Murkowski, both Republicans, proposed that control of the Alaska Railroad be transferred from the federal to the state government.

Agriculture. In the state's interior, the Delta Barley Project entered its second bad harvest with a heavy, wet snowfall in mid-September. The snowfall caught farmers with less than one third of the crop harvested.

Fisheries. It was another record year for salmon, with significant runs of all varieties. The recent upturn in salmon harvests is credited to the 200-mile limit, which protects anadromous species from overfishing close to shore.

Anchorage Election. In a nonpartisan race, Tony Knowles, a Democrat and restaurant owner, was elected mayor of Anchorage on October 27. Knowles defeated Joe Hayes (R), speaker of the state House of Representatives.

Census. Results of the 1980 census revealed that Alaska's population increased by 32.4% in the 1970s, from 302,583 to 400,481. However, federal redistricting was not required.

Education. The University of Alaska opened in the fall with increased enrollments. At the Fairbanks campus, there were more students than dormitory facilities.

ANDREA R. C. HELMS
University of Alaska, Fairbanks

ALBANIA

The year 1981 marked the 35th anniversary of the People's Socialist Republic of Albania (PSRA) and the 40th of the ruling Albanian Party of Labor (APL).

Politics and Government. At the seventh APL congress, November 1–7, Enver Hoxha, 73, was reelected first secretary. Hoxha, who has held the post since 1941, also has the most seniority among the party leaders. According to the first secretary, APL membership rose from 101,500 to 122,600 between 1976 and 1981.

Three incumbent Politburo members—Haki Toska, Spiro Koleka, and Pilo Peristeri—were not reelected. The five new members elected by the congress—Muho Asllani, Hajredin Celiku, Besnik Bekteshi, Foto Cami, and Prokop Murra—are in their late 40s or early 50s and are apparently being groomed to replace the aging first generation of Communist leaders. There were relatively few changes in the composition of the party's Central Committee, with 70 of the 77 members elected in 1976 retaining their positions. It thus appeared that the purge of the ruling elite launched in 1973 had run its course.

In his report to the APL congress, First Secretary Hoxha declared that there would be no changes in Albania's domestic and foreign policies so long as he remains in power. He reiterated his contention that the PSRA is the only Communist state that has remained loyal to the teachings of Marxism-Leninism. The Albanian party leader pledged to continue his struggle against Soviet, Chinese, and Yugoslav "revisionism" as well as U.S. "imperialism." He also emphasized that he would persevere in his efforts to eliminate all remaining "bourgeois" and "non-Marxist" influences in Albania.

On December 18, Radio Tiranë announced that Prime Minister Mehmet Shehu, 68, had committed suicide. Shehu, who held the office since 1954, had been regarded as the most likely successor to First Secretary Hoxha.

Foreign Affairs. Albanian-Yugoslav relations deteriorated markedly after the outbreak of riots and demonstrations in March and April by ethnic Albanians in the Yugoslav Autonomous Socialist Province of Kosovo. When the PSRA supported demands for a full-fledged Kosovo republic within the Yugoslav federation, Belgrade blamed Albania for the unrest. Despite harsh polemics between the two states, there was no apparent disruption in diplomatic and commercial relations.

Albania refused even to consider a rapprochement with its former allies, the Soviet Union and China. Although Great Britain and West Germany expressed interest in establishing diplomatic relations with Tiranë, the PSRA rejected both overtures. Albanian spokesmen continued to denounce the United States, voicing strong criticism of the domestic and foreign policies of the Reagan administration.

Economy. Albania failed to achieve the economic goals of the 1976–80 five-year plan. Industrial production rose by 34% instead of the projected 41–44%; and agricultural output increased by 21%, about half of the planned level. In the 1981–85 plan, industrial output is scheduled to rise by 36–38% and agricultural production by 30–32%.

NICHOLAS C. PANO
Department of History
Western Illinois University

ALBANIA • Information Highlights

Official Name: People's Socialist Republic of Albania.
Location: Southern Europe, Balkan peninsula.
Area: 11,100 sq mi (28 749 km^2).
Population (1981 est.): 2,800,000.
Chief Cities (1975): Tiranë, the capital, 192,000; Shkodër, 62,400; Dürres, 60,000.
Government: *Head of state,* Haxhi Lleshi, president of the Presidium (took office 1953). *First secretary of the Albanian Party of Labor,* Enver Hoxha (took office 1941). *Legislature* (unicameral)—People's Assembly, 250 members.
Monetary Unit: Lek (7 lekë equal U.S.$1, July 1981—noncommercial rate).
Manufactures (major products): Textiles, timber, construction materials, fuels, semiprocessed minerals.
Agriculture (major products): Corn, sugar beets, wheat, cotton, grapes, potatoes, dairy products.

ALBERTA

Despite soaring interest rates, continued inflation, and high unemployment elsewhere, Alberta experienced uninterrupted prosperity in 1981. The unemployment rate remained under 4% despite the influx of much unskilled labor from other provinces. Labor unrest in the province was minimal, although a long nationwide postal strike caused problems.

Industry and Government. Political activity was characterized by federal-provincial confrontations, one over proposed patriation of the British North America Act, which could severely limit provincial powers. Another controversy concerned both pricing and revenue-sharing of Alberta's gas and oil resources, which are 85% provincially owned. Lack of agreement until late August resulted in a sharp decline in exploratory drilling. It also halted development of an oil sand extraction plant and a heavy oil project in northeastern Alberta, and at year's end, further work on both remained in doubt. The cancellation of oil production cuts by the province was part of the final settlement, relieving the federal government of the necessity of subsidizing the importation of 180,000 barrels of oil per day.

Completion of the southern portion of the planned Alaska gas pipeline opened new U.S. markets for Alberta's surplus gas.

Agriculture and Forestry. Light snow cover and little early spring precipitation threatened drought conditions which later were negated by adequate rainfall. This was followed by extremely hot, dry weather in August and September, ideal for harvesting a crop record-breaking in both size and grade.

A work stoppage in the Thunder Bay terminal elevators threatened to impede delivery of cereals for export, but ended after 16 days.

The hot weather, so beneficial to grain crops, was extremely detrimental to Alberta's forests. Early abundant moisture at first inhibited fires, but by late summer the number of blazes, often set by lightning, exceeded all previous records, ultimately totaling some 1,500.

Social Services and Education. The provincial department of social services was shaken by exposure of a number of irregularities and derelictions of duty, the result of investigative journalism. A rather extensive departmental shake-up followed.

After several years of stable registrations, postsecondary student enrollments began to increase. Rigid limitations on provincial funding, however, continued to place educational institutions at all levels under increasing financial difficulties.

Transportation. Discontinuance of transcontinental railroad passenger (VIA) service through Edmonton proved to be extremely unpopular.

Sports. In Edmonton, to supplement facilities provided for the 1978 Commonwealth Games, work proceeded apace on construction for the 1983 World Student Games. In October, Calgary was awarded the 1988 Winter Olympics. Its promoters were confident that they could be held without deficit.

The Edmonton Eskimos won the Western Conference football pennant for the fifth consecutive year and went on to capture, for the fourth time in a row, the Grey Cup, emblematic of the Canadian title.

JOHN W. CHALMERS
Concordia College, Edmonton

ALBERTA • Information Highlights

Area: 255,285 sq mi (661 189 km^2).
Population (April 1981 est.): 2,153,200.
Chief Cities (1976 census): Edmonton, the capital, 461,-361; Calgary, 469,917.
Government (1981): *Chief Officers*—lt. gov., Frank Lynch-Staunton; premier, Peter Lougheed (Progressive-Conservative): atty. gen., Neil Crawford; chief justice, Court of Appeals, William A. McGillivray; chief justice, Court of Queen's Bench, W. Sinclair. *Legislature*—Legislative Assembly, 79 members.
Education (1981–82 est.): *Enrollment*—elementary and secondary schools, 451,190 pupils; postsecondary, 49,580.
Personal Income (average weekly salary, April 1981): $376.88.
Unemployment Rate (June 1981, seasonally adjusted): 3.4%.
(All monetary figures are in Canadian dollars.)

ALGERIA

President Chadli Benjedid continued to consolidate control over the Algerian government in 1981 by removing from power his major political rivals and continuing a crackdown on corruption. Economic problems resulting from a world oil glut and prolonged negotiations with foreign buyers over the export price of liquefied natural gas (LNG) taxed the government's ambitious development plans. Chadli's pragmatic approach to foreign policy resulted in new initiatives toward Western countries and strengthened relations with African nations.

Politics and Internal Security. Following a July meeting of the central committee of the ruling National Liberation Front (FLN), Chadli continued his countercorruption campaign, begun only months after assuming power in 1979, by suspending four of the committee's members for alleged corruption and embezzlement. The suspended members, Col. Ahmed Bensherif, former national gendarmerie commander, Tayebi Larbi, former agriculture minister, Mahmoud Guennez, former national assembly vice-president, and Mustapha Bouarpha, head of the national information commissariat, were prominent members of the Revolutionary Council under the late President Houari Boumedienne.

Their removal was followed by the dismissals from the FLN politburo of Chadli's two main political rivals—Abdelaziz Bouteflika, a former foreign minister, and Mohamed Salah Yahiaoui, former head of the FLN. After Boumedienne's death, Bouteflika and Yahiaoui had been the two leading candidates to succeed to the

UPI

Chadli Benjedid (extreme right) and Pierre Elliott Trudeau confer in Algiers in May. The Canadian prime minister urged the Algerian president to use his influence to reduce tensions in the Middle East.

presidency. Chadli, the army's compromise candidate, won out after a deadlock between the supporters of the two men. They retained their membership in the FLN central committee.

The politburo was increased in size from 7 to 10 members, with the appointments of 5 government officials to join the 4 others, plus Chadli, on the governing body.

In late September, rioting Islamic fundamentalists took over a mosque at Laghouat, an oasis town 250 mi (400 km) south of Algiers. Members of the illegal Muslim Brotherhood called the town's inhabitants to a holy war against authorities, opposing the "godless materialism" of Algeria's socialist system. The Muslims were evicted from the mosque by police after three days of clashes which left several dead and wounded.

Economy. Although Chadli has shifted the economy's emphasis from heavy industrialization that must rely upon foreign revenue to basic needs such as housing, health, education, agriculture, and infrastructure, a wave of strikes hit Algeria early in 1981. Customs, transport, and oil workers walked off their jobs in salary disputes.

Algeria's heavy dependence on gas and oil exports for nearly 96% of its foreign exchange and government revenue presented problems in 1981 as a world oil glut and unsuccessful negotiations with some foreign buyers over raising the export price of LNG resulted in decreased currency earnings. In late 1981, talks progressed between Sonatrach, the state oil and gas corporation, and three U.S. natural gas companies over the LNG price. The American companies hope to take over LNG imports previously destined for El Paso Gas Co., the largest U.S. importer. Deliveries to the company were halted in 1980, and negotiations ended in February 1981, at a $365 million loss to the American importer.

Discussions with French, Italian, and British LNG importers were continuing as Sonatrach sought to rewrite its contracts, pegging the gas price to that of its oil. Oil production fell off significantly in 1981, and Algeria was seeking, with little success, oil-for-goods barter deals to delay lowering its $40 per barrel price of oil. Foreign companies, including Honda of Japan, said the Algerian price was too high.

Foreign Relations. The Algerian government's successful mediation role in the U.S.-Iranian hostage crisis failed to net concrete results in terms of improving relations with the U.S. government. The United States planned, however, to deliver C-130 transport planes, modifying a long-standing refusal to sell arms to Algeria.

Algeria continued to support the Polisario Front in the Western Saharan war against Morocco. Chadli participated in an Organization of African Unity (OAU)-sponsored meeting in Nairobi in August to work out details for implementation of a cease-fire and referendum to end the war in the disputed territory. The referendum was agreed to at the June OAU summit.

Chadli toured sub-Saharan Africa in March and April, part of a diplomatic initiative to mend fences with some nations and shore up relations with closer allies. He also visited Moscow, although Algeria's relations with the Soviets have been cooler under Chadli than under Boumedienne. A visit to Algiers by the British Foreign Secretary, Lord Carrington, was designed to strengthen trade ties and promote investment in Algeria's development plans.

MARGARET A. NOVICKI, *"Africa Report"*

ALGERIA • Information Highlights

Official Name: Democratic and Popular Republic of Algeria.
Location: North Africa.
Area: 919,595 sq mi (2 381 751 km^2).
Population (1981 est.): 19,300,000.
Chief cities (1980 est.): Algiers, the capital, 2,200,000; Oran, 633,000; Constantine, 384,000.
Government: *Head of state,* Chadli Benjedid, president (took office Feb. 1979). *Head of government,* Mohammed Ben Ahmed Abdelghani, prime minister (took office March 1979).
Monetary Unit: Dinar (4.47 dinars equal U.S.$1, July 1981).
Manufactures (major products): Petroleum, gas, petrochemicals, fertilizer, iron and steel, transportation equipment.
Agriculture (major products): Wheat, barley, oats, wine, fruit, olives, vegetables, livestock.

ANGOLA

Amid expanding oil and diamond output, the People's Republic of Angola faced deepening security problems in the south and worsening relations with the United States.

Domestic Affairs. The single greatest crisis besetting the government was a lingering war against the opposition movement, *União Nacional para Independência Total de Angola* (UNITA), in the southeast. On the losing side of the 1976 civil war, UNITA continued to harry government forces and their Cuban allies. UNITA guerrillas disrupted for another year copper shipments on the Benguela Railway from Zaire and laid waste to agriculture.

In late December 1980, the ruling *Movimento Popular de Libertação de Angola* (MPLA) held an extraordinary congress to examine political, economic, and defense problems. The congress could be seen as a success for consolidating the presidency of José Eduardo dos Santos, who then and in 1981 spoke out against corruption and inefficiency as undermining Angolan production.

Economy. Oil, the mainstay of the economy, rose in output and revenue. More agreements were signed with Western companies to double production by 1985. Diamond production was also up and a state company was formed to represent the government in diamond production. Diamonds, coffee, or maize have yet to reach preindependence levels. Congestion at Luanda's docks brought visits by the president and efforts to open bottlenecks. Scarcity of consumer goods encouraged the formation of a black market. The kwanza was so devalued that some workers were paid partly in kind.

Foreign Affairs. A Central Committee, meeting in June, reported that not since 1976 when South African forces withdrew from the civil war had Pretoria's raids reached such intensity and constancy. Then, in August, South Africa unleashed its largest offensive into southern Angola to uproot guerrilla bases of the South West Africa People's Organization (SWAPO). Angola supports SWAPO's war for independence for South-West Africa (Namibia), allowing it sanctuary.

The Reagan administration in Washington carried on its predecessor's policy of refusing diplomatic relations with Angola because of the presence of 20,000 Cuban troops. But the administration also urged Congress to repeal the Clark amendment that debarred aid to UNITA. Ties between Angola and Cuba and the Soviet Union remained firm despite Luanda's pragmatic approach to doing business with Western companies.

THOMAS H. HENRIKSEN
Hoover Institution on War, Revolution and Peace

ANGOLA • Information Highlights

Official Name: People's Republic of Angola.
Location: Southwestern Africa.
Area: 481,351 sq mi (1 246 700 km^2).
Population (1981 est.): 6,700,000.
Chief Cities (1970 census): Luanda, the capital, 480,613; Huambo, 61,885; Lobito, 59,258.
Government: *Head of state and government,* José Eduardo dos Santos, president (took office 1977).
Monetary Unit: Kwanza (27 kwanzas equal U.S. $1, October 1980).
Manufactures (major products): Cement, textiles, fuel oil.
Agriculture (major products): Manioc, coffee, cotton, sisal, tobacco.

ANTHROPOLOGY

Beyond the continuing controversy between Donald C. Johanson and Richard Leakey over the primacy of their fossil finds in the evolution of *Homo sapiens* (*see* feature article, page 42), anthropology in 1981 saw an increasing interest in medical, symbolic, and politico-legal anthropology; the death of Carleton S. Coon, one of the last great general anthropologists; a reexamination of the place of the fossil *Ramapithecus* in primate evolution; and an interesting report on language use in monkeys.

Directions. At the annual meeting of the American Anthropological Association in Los Angeles, Dec. 3–6, 1981, almost 26% of the sessions were devoted to educational, medical, symbolic, and politico-legal anthropology. Among a number of books published in these fields during the year were Clifford Geertz's *Negara: The Theatre State in Nineteenth Century Bali,* and Michael Harner's *The Way of the Shaman: A Guide to Power and Healing,* examining one aspect of medical practice in non-Western traditions. Closer to home was Alan Harwood's *Ethnicity and Medical Care.*

Language in Monkeys. A group of Rockefeller University researchers studying vervet monkeys in Amboseli National Park, Kenya, have come to the conclusion that warning calls and other sounds made by the animals while feeding could be interpreted as elements of a rudimentary language. The report, written by Robert M. Seyfarth, Dorothy L. Cheney, and Peter Marler and published in *Science* magazine, describes adult vervets as having three acoustically different alarm calls for three different predators—leopards, eagles, and pythons. Each alarm type is associated with a different set of responses by the monkeys. The responses are related to the nature of the hunting behavior of the predators involved. The researchers believe that by attaching acoustically specific alarm calls to certain species, vervet monkeys are actually categorizing the more than 100 animal species in their environment. Furthermore, adult vervets are more selective in giving alarm calls than infants. Infants seem to generalize, giving leopard alarms primarily for terrestrial mammals, eagle alarms for birds, and snake alarms for snakes and other long, thin objects. Thus, it appears that infants distinguish among general predator classes, while adults distinguish among particular predator species within such classes. The infants' ability to classify apparently improves with age and experience. The nature of this categorization and learning process remains to be determined.

Ramapithecus. Duke University anthropologist Richard Kay has offered a new theory on the relationship of an early primate, *Ramapithecus,* to the hominid line of evolution. The ramapithecines were first discovered in India in 1934 and dated at about 14 million years. The major question concerning them has been whether they are ancestors of the human species or merely an evolutionary dead end. Dr. Kay believes that the creature was an arboreal form of hominid that subsisted largely on nuts and hard fruits found in trees and survived until about six million years ago. More importantly, he feels that the ramapithecines are direct ancestors of the australopithecines and therefore of humans. His argument is based largely on their dentition, which exhibits a number of hominid characters. Kay's theory is disputed by Vincent Sarich (University of California at Berkeley), who believes that molecular evolution of blood proteins shows that humans and apes had a common ancestor and diverged from that ancestor four to six million years ago. Thus, for Sarich and his colleagues, Ramapithecus was much too early to be considered a hominid.

Deaths. Among several well-known anthropologists who died were Prince Peter of Greece and Denmark, 71, who worked in Tibet before and after World War II; and Carleton S. Coon, 77, one of the last great generalists. Coon worked in archaeology, physical anthropology, and ethnology. He was primarily interested in the origins of the human species and in the ethnology of the Middle East and North Africa. Among his best-known books are *The Seven Caves* (1957) and *The Origin of Races* (1962).

HERMAN J. JAFFE
Brooklyn College, City University of New York

ANTIGUA AND BARBUDA

Antigua and Barbuda, sister islands in the southeastern Caribbean, became an independent nation at midnight, Oct. 31, 1981, ending nearly 350 years of British rule. Princess Margaret of Great Britain, representing the queen, attended the opening of parliament, the installation of the government of Prime Minister Vere Bird, and other ceremonies in the capital of St. John's on Antigua.

Located in the Windward Islands, Antigua was discovered by Christopher Columbus in 1493. The Spanish and French tried to colonize it but failed, and the British succeeded in 1632. In 1967, the islands became a self-governing state within the West Indies Associated States.

The new nation of Antigua and Barbuda (combined population, about 77,000; area, 170 sq mi—440 km^2) faces serious economic difficulties. Unemployment has been estimated at 20% and per capita annual income at about $1,050. Sugarcane growing and tourism are the major industries. Upon independence, Great Britain granted $18 million in loans and grants over ten years.

In mid-November, Antigua and Barbuda became the 157th member of the United Nations.

ARCHAEOLOGY

In 1981, good fortune offset reduced funding as a remarkable series of archaeological discoveries emerged from fieldwork, laboratory analysis, and the synthesis of information already on hand. Appropriately, 1981 was the 1,000th anniversary of the digging up by Rolf Rødsander and Styrbjorn of a pre-Eskimo house mound in Greenland, the first known excavation in the New World. However, the year was marred by the deaths of an unusual number of premier archaeologists: Ole Klindt-Jensen and Hans Helbaek of Denmark, François Bordes of France, Andrei Almarik of the USSR, and Donald Crabtree, Chester Gorman, and Hugh Hencken of the United States.

EASTERN HEMISPHERE

Early Cultures. Excavations in the Awash Valley, Afar, Ethiopia, in 1977 by French and New Zealand archaeologists produced cobble choppers and sharp flake tools, which overlay directly volcanic tuff now dated by potassium argon to about 2.8 million years. The tools, at about 2.5 million years old, are the oldest known human artifacts. The site is to the west of the famous "Lucy" Australopithecine site, which is almost a million years older (*see* feature article, page 42).

Human-made chopping tools and scrapers were found in a limestone cave near Liège, Belgium, along with bones of horses and other extinct animals that lived during the Mindel glaciation (third from last). It is the northernmost evidence of human life from this extremely cold climatic era.

The long-known and justifiably famous cave occupations at Zhou-K'oudien in northern China, where the "Peking" fossils were found, has finally been given an absolute date by thermoluminescence analysis of hearth remains. The age for this site, also of the Mindel glaciation, came out to ca. 600,000 years.

Study of hand axes and animal bones from the Acheulian site at Olorgesaillie, Kenya, revealed that the tools were used to butcher now-extinct giant gelada baboons, of which 90 had been killed and eaten by early humans ca. 500,000 years ago. Eighty percent of the bones came from juveniles, which would have been easier prey than adults, which were the size of modern female gorillas.

Bronze and Iron Ages. Two boys, ages 9 and 11, while playing on the family farm in Zealand, Denmark, made the largest find in gold-rich Danish prehistory since a farm maiden's discovery in 1639. The boys unearthed two gold bracelets, each weighing 1.3 kg (2.9 lbs), dating from the end of the Northern Bronze Age, ca. 700 B.C. This was a time of poverty, caused by the onset of a cool, rainy climate and the collapse of a lucrative trade in bronze tools and weapons due to the advent of cheaper iron goods.

In Xinjiang Uygur (Chinese Turkestan), an accidental mummy resulted from the desiccation of a body buried under a sand dune. The tall, well-preserved young woman wore shoulder length blonde hair. Even her eyelashes were preserved. The woollen shroud enveloping the body yielded a carbon-14 age of 275 (±105) B.C., an era when Iranic speaking horse-nomads were widespread in central Asia.

Romanized Mediterranean. Rome itself is too built-over to permit insight into the development of ancient Latin cities from simple peasant villages, but Ficana, south of Rome on the Tiber River, provides accessible residues of this process. Originally settled in the Bronze Age, ca. 1300 B.C., it continued in the Iron Age as a village with round wooden houses, until the 6th century B.C., when stone foundations and writing were introduced. Masonry architecture developed during the next century, and for a while the town flourished as part of the fledgling Roman empire. But after Rome built the port of Ostia at the Tiber's mouth, ca. 300 B.C., Ficana rapidly declined and reverted to countryside.

While routinely investigating a third-century synagogue in Israel, American archaeologists uncovered the lid of an ark of the covenant. The half-ton limestone was carved in provincial Roman style with lions flanking a niche.

Tribal Migrations. The tumuli associated with the Megalithic site of Tondidarau (North Mali) were found to be composed of collapsed terra cotta funerary architecture. Radiocarbon tests from ritual fireplaces produced a date of approximately 100 years before the Arab-Islamic invasions of A.D. 734.

Gaining general acceptance was the theory of J. N. L. Myres that the Anglo-Saxons started going to England in force more than 50 years earlier than the semi-folkloric "historical" date of A.D. 450. This date now seems to reflect the point at which the immigrants gained the upper hand over the Romano-British. The new understanding also necessitates revision of palaeolinguistic theories concerning rates of language change.

It had always been difficult to verify archaeologically that Jutes were really among the newcomers to England, since very few graves dating to 400–500 were known in Danish Jutland. In 1981, a large cemetery including many inhumation graves of this era was found near Aalborg in northern Denmark.

At Cutry, France, near the Luxembourg border, a rare sort of cemetery has yielded graves from after the pre-Roman Celtic Iron Age, tombs from Roman times, and finally, Merovingian graves from after the Frankish invasions (beginning A.D. 400). Essentially the same population and its descendants must have persisted there until the present day. One Roman cremation lay next to the inhumation of a Barbary macaque, from Spain or North Africa, which must have been brought back as a pet.

Nearby, at Auden-le-Tiche, hilltop graves of veritable Franks exhibit an aristocracy in the process of becoming Christianized in the 7th century. One warrior had as his grave marker a stone crucifix bearing a paganistic sun symbol, while a rich lady wore a bronze finger ring, engraved with a cross, along with a gold garnet brooch inlaid with jewels and a fossil belemnite, anciently thought to be the tip of one of Thor's thunderbolts.

Viking Products. Vikings of the west Atlantic once harvested seeds of lyme grass (*Elymus arenarius*) to make bread, since this hardy cereal grows even north of the arctic circle. Analysis of the nutritional value of lyme grass shows it to be among the most nutritious cereal grains known, having almost as much protein as beans. Recultivation of this former Viking crop would allow millions of acres in the arctic to be turned into farmland by the year 2000.

WESTERN HEMISPHERE

Norse trade goods from the Viking colonies on Greenland were recovered from three differ-

The "young lady of Loulan," a mummy unearthed in China in 1980, proved to be nearly 6,500 years old.

UPI

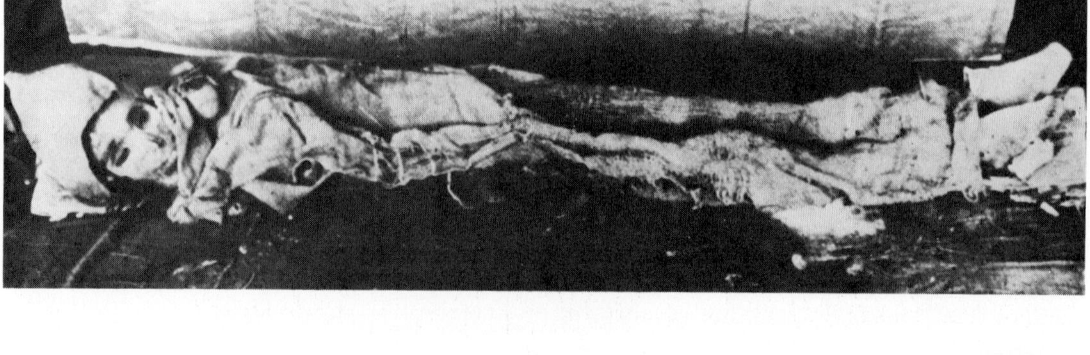

UPI

The first intact ark of the covenant, a chest used to hold the scriptures in ancient synagogues, was discovered in Israel.

ent sites near Ellesmere Island. In the west, the arm of a bronze balance comes from a Thule (Eskimo) campsite, while on Skraeling Island offshore to the east, chain mail, ship's rivets, and cloth were retrieved from the permafrost. An Eskimo-made figurine excavated on the south coast of Baffin Island depicts a Norseman garbed in 13th-century-style hooded clothing.

Early Villagers. The oldest known sedentary village in the Americas, La Paloma on the central Peruvian coast, dates to ca. 5,700 B.C., when the local folk restricted their nomadic movements and made semipermanent dug-out houses roofed with willow poles and covered with grasses and cane. The villagers themselves were buried in and around the houses. Although about half the children died, they ate some of the earliest cultivated peanuts, squash, and peppers, as seen in the preserved stomach contents of burials. Later occupants ate more fish and land animals, as the over-cultivated land was becoming a desert and had to be abandoned about 3,000 B.C.

Excavators from Wichita State University revealed that the Nebo Hill folk of eastern Kansas and Missouri also practiced a rudimentary squash agriculture. They lived in houses based on U-shaped clay foundations and made a simple, fiber-tempered pottery which disintegrates easily. One fragmentary figurine resembles those of the elaborate Poverty Point Group in Louisiana. New thermoluminescence dates of about 1,200 B.C. show that it overlaps with a late phase of Nebo Hill.

Enduring Traditions. The waterlogged Hoko River village site in Washington is 2,800 years old, but it is so clearly in the Northwest Coast tradition that Makah Indians can identify the uses and names of the well-preserved artifacts brought forth by University of Washington archaeologists. Recovered were basketry, wood carving tools, harpoon points, and two conical hats indicating high social status in ethnographic times. Stone microlith tools, previously unrecognized as artifacts, were still in their wooden hafts.

In Voyageur National Park, MN, fabric-impressed pottery was accompanied by phytoliths of wild rice (*Zizania aquatica*) at an Early Woodland campsite. This is the clearest evidence yet of the gathering of this wild grain as early as A.D. 200.

New Culture. An entirely new culture discovered in the northern Bluegrass by Kentucky academic and private archaeologists answered the nagging question of what culture south of the Ohio River was contemporary with the famous Ohio Hopewell. The recently named Newtown Group lived in U-shaped houses set around a central swept plaza, leaving behind their dwellings a ring of refuse. Limestone-tempered pottery and triangular spear points were manufactured ca. A.D. 600.

Maya Ball Games. Cave paintings executed during the Classic Period (ca. A.D. 800) of Maya Civilization were found in Guatemala. Chambers deep in a large cave bore mainly hieroglyphic writing and numbers, but depictions of Mayan rituals were found in one passageway. The tableaux feature scenes of the sacred ball game, showing players outfitted with straw hats, chest armor, knee pads, and large round balls which carom off the sides of the terraced ball court.

RALPH M. ROWLETT
University of Missouri-Columbia

ARCHITECTURE

The year 1981 was one in which the various architectural awards programs reflected the current main concerns of the profession even more closely than in the past. Criteria were based on regard for the environment, for energy conservation, and for building preservation—along with design diversity tailored to the locale and the designers' and clients' personal desires, rather than to strict Modernist disciplines. There was strong recognition of the search for new, more pleasing forms that was becoming more evident in high-rise construction.

The highest award that an architectural firm could receive was given by the American Institute of Architects (AIA) to Hardy Holzman Pfeiffer Associates of New York City. This firm had designed many projects that ranged from the large and new (the corporate headquarters for Best Products in Richmond, VA, and the Boettcher Concert Hall in Denver being among the most recent at the time) to preservation and adaptive reuse (the Saint Louis Art Museum and the Madison, WI, Civic Center). Each is characterized by a stylish verve that combines playfulness, concern for the surroundings, and a love of decorative detail that would have been considered unfashionable only a few years before. The institute's coveted Gold Medal went to Josep Lluis Sert, an architect with deep roots in the modern movement, but one who has always had a very personal design expression.

Individual Projects. Such criteria were very evident in the institute's awards to individual projects. In the new construction category, the jury, chaired by Hugh Stubbins, awarded apartment buildings on New York City's Roosevelt Island, an ensemble by architects Sert, Jackson & Associates that steps up ziggurat-style from the shoreline to reward residents with terraces with panoramic views and to enclose an urban street at the center; the Ramsey County Adult Detention Center in Saint Paul, MN, by Gruzen & Partners, a building that conceals its large and unpleasant presence by being built into a riverside cliff; Saint Mary's Gardens in Oakland, CA, a group of apartments for the elderly designed by architects Peters, Clayberg & Caulfield in house-like varied buildings that alter preconceptions of institutional use; the National Permanent Building in Washington by Hartman-Cox Architects, a speculative office building that honors its historic neighbors with an exposed concrete frame shaped to be reminiscent of them; and Banco de Occidente in Guatemala City, three bank buildings designed by Skidmore, Owings & Merrill with exceptional consideration of local vernacular in the form of courtyards and openness to the street along with responsible security. Also awarded were Thorncrown Chapel in Eureka Springs, AR, by Fay Jones & Associates, a soaring wood frame stretched with glass that recalls historic building forms in nonliteral terms; a residence for Norman Gaffney in Coatesville, PA, designed by Bohlin Powell Larkin Cywinski to be a rustic vertical structure within the foundations of a long-gone barn; and the East Building of the National Gallery of Art in Washington by I. M.

The Madison Civic Center was honored as a "sensitive alternative" to the isolated cultural center.

American Institute of Architects (AIA)

Photos AIA

The Coatesville, PA, home of Norman Gaffney is a "remarkable siting of building within walls of a ruined barn." The AIA cited the "nest of buildings" as creative, and "idiosyncratic on a small budget."

Pei & Partners, which combines monumental proportions with innovative shapes.

The Post-Modernists. While design expression continued to grow in widely divergent directions—from the sleekest to the most rustic—one group of architects, the Post-Modernists, continued to remain the most visible and perhaps influential. Freely borrowing historic forms in unexpected ways, this group—led by architects Michael Graves, Allan Greenberg, Philip Johnson, Robert Kliment, Frances Halsband, Rodolfo Machado, Jorge Silvetti, Charles Moore, Robert Stern, Stanley Tigerman, Robert Venturi, John Rauch, and Denise Scott Brown—was the subject of an exhibition at Smith College in the spring and of a subsequent book, *Speaking a New Classicism,* by Helen Searing and Henry Hope Reed. While directly affecting the design of only a small portion of new buildings, the influence of these architects has been felt in a general softening of hard-edge design approaches, in a more decorative expression of structural elements such as vaults and columns, and in an increasingly varied, muted color palette.

Residences, Other Facilities, Office Buildings. The most design diversity was shown in residences, in which the architects and clients are most free to express their personalities. In contrast to the rustic, AIA-award-winning Gaffney house, notably diverse examples emerged throughout the United States. Among them were the recipients of the Homes for Better Living Awards, sponsored by the AIA and *Housing* magazine. Most remarkable were a new house in eastern Pennsylvania by Hugh Newell Jacobsen, who joined a series of what appeared to be 18th-century facades in ever diminishing sizes; a house in Tampa by Rowe Holmes Associates Architects with a strong regional vernacular stemming from the 19th century; and a matching extension to a neo-Tudor house in Washington by Hartman-Cox. Only one winner, Hoyt Square condominiums in Portland, OR, by Robert S. Leeb Architects, was in the strictly modern style that would have been mandatory only a few years previous.

Venturi, Rauch and Scott Brown designed a house in Bermuda in the local tradition, while other architects, including Gwathmey Siegel & Associates and William Kessler continued to produce notable houses in the Modern style.

More surprisingly, apartment complexes began to show the inroads of individual design expression. Ranging from the 1950s Hollywood style in Florida (Arquitectonica) to the neocolonial in Minneapolis (Frederick Bentz/Milo Thompson & Associates), to the 1920s Modernist in Houston (Taft Architects), these complexes are bound to have an impact on other designers, as they express regional character.

Influential projects for smaller-scale educational, civic, and recreational facilities began to take on a regional flair. Among them were the Green Mountain Valley School in Vermont by

Turner Brooks, Watson Hall for Hotchkiss School in Connecticut by Woollen Associates, a court tennis facility for the casino in Newport by Forbes Hailey Jeas Erneman, and a firehouse in Scranton, PA, by David Leung, David Hemmler, and Alex Camayd.

But the most dramatic and visible design innovation was taking place in office buildings. This field, long dominated by box-like construction, was beginning to sprout a generation of novel forms from both established and young firms. Published in the architectural press in 1981 were plans for a large group of such buildings by Kohn Pedersen Fox and several buildings by Skidmore, Owings & Merrill, long considered masters of corporate architecture. Aside from unusual shapes, the designs explored combined uses in the same buildings, including enclosed urban parks and many-storied atriums that promised to revolutionize both the office space and public use. Another corporation-favored architectural firm, Welton Becket, announced plans for Dravo Tower in Pittsburgh, a 54-story, exposed-steel skyscraper in the form of a nearby historic tower of much smaller scale. Johnson/Burgee went ahead with a 56-story tower in Houston that would have three stepped segments with gable ends like a Netherlands house, and an enormous banking facility at the base in the shape of a Renaissance hall. The Battery Park City Authority announced plans for a major segment of its proposed development for lower Manhattan by Cesar Pelli & Associates to resemble a group of skyscrapers from the 1930s. The $1,000,000,000 project would house offices and apartments behind varied facades that would step up and down the sides of each tower.

Other Awards. British architect James Stirling was named the winner of the third annual Pritzker Architecture Prize, sponsored by the Hyatt Foundation. The 25th R. S. Reynolds Memorial Award went to Hugh Stubbins and Associates for Citicorp Center in New York City, one of the first skyscrapers to break the rectilinear mold. The year's Arnold W. Brunner Memorial Prize in Architecture went to Gunnar Birkerts. And the Reynolds Metals Company was selected to receive a special AIA award. A traveling exhibition of furniture and interior design was mounted to honor Marcel Breuer, who died July 1, 1981.

Preservation. Hand in hand with the search for design diversity—especially as reflected in the restatement of historic styles—went ever-increasing concern for the preservation of existing older structures. It was no longer necessary for the structure to be one of true landmark quality to arouse a desire among architects to preserve it. And there was increasing awareness of the often lower costs in rehabilitation instead of all-new construction. Undoubtedly, the most spectacular ongoing restoration in the United States was that nearing completion by architects of the Ehrenkrantz Group on the elaborate terra cotta facades of the Woolworth Building, designed by Cass Gilbert in New York, and once the tallest building in the world. The AIA awards, which tend to honor more innovative adaptive reuse projects, went to 38 East Schiller in Chicago, a Victorian townhouse converted by architects Chrysalis Corporation with the insertion of a separating mirrored-glass screen wall; the Crocker Art Gallery in Sacramento, a more straightforward restoration effort for a High Victorian house that involved innovative structural stabilization techniques; the Madison Civic Center for which Hardy Holzman Pfeiffer Associates designed complementary additions to a Moorish-style movie theater to furnish a home for the performing arts; the Oaks in Oak Park, IL, two former hotels joined by architects Nagle, Hartray & Associates to form 76 apartments for the aged; the Hall of Languages at Syracuse University, a High Victorian building remodeled by architects Sargent-Webster-Crenshaw & Folley and Architectural Resources Cambridge Inc. to provide a grand new interior space; the Hendley Building in Galveston, TX, remodeled by Taft Architects, as a headquarters for the Historical Foundation; and the Jones Laboratory, a cancer-research center in Cold Spring Harbor, NY, by William H. Grover and Charles W. Moore.

Other notable examples of reuse in 1981 were the conversion of several individual buildings in San Antonio into a museum of art (Cambridge Seven Associates); the revival of the Adolphus Hotel in Dallas by architects Beran & Shelmire; the remodeling of a large complex of industrial buildings in Norwich, CT, into housing for the elderly by Stephen Jacobs & Associates; and the restoration of some of the spectacular period spaces in Stanford White's Villard Houses in Manhattan as public rooms for an adjacent and otherwise ordinary hotel tower.

Among the more interesting outgrowths of the preservation effort was a competition, won by architect Michael Graves, for a library to adjoin the Mission of San Juan Capistrano in California. Another such competition, won by the Design Alliance, was to join two grand turn-of-the-century mansions in Pittsburgh to form a center of the arts.

A large part of the outlook for U.S. architects' continued prosperity involved the economy and the effects of the policies of the new Reagan administration. Contrary to expectations, construction volume remained strong in nonresidential areas, despite high interest rates. New tax laws were regarded as a big boost for industrial construction. Other federal actions, particularly the relaxation of stringent controls, such as the Federal Housing Administration (FHA) Minimum Property Standards, were greeted with enthusiasm.

CHARLES K. HOYT
Associate Editor, "Architectural Record"

Argentines crowd into a financial exchange house in Buenos Aires to exchange their pesos into U.S. dollars. Economic problems, particularly several devaluations of the currency, plagued the South American nation in 1981.

UPI

ARGENTINA

Army Gen. Roberto Viola replaced Gen. Jorge Videla in the presidency on March 29. Viola was chosen for a 1981–84 term by the ruling junta, consisting of heads of the Army, Navy, and Air Force. The Army was represented in the junta by Gen. Leopoldo F. Galtieri. Vice Adm. Jorge Isaac Anaya replaced Adm. Armando Lambruschini in the junta in September. Viola's highest level appointments reflected his disposition to steer the country toward civilian rule. In fact, six civilians were appointed to governorships in the 22 provinces. Late in the year, however, the junta removed Viola from the presidency and named Galtieri as the new chief executive. The action was accomplished without explanation. Galtieri was to remain Army commander.

Government. Guidelines for a statute on political parties were prepared by the junta for Viola, who promised to have the statute ready in 1982. Unofficial sources indicated that the statute would provide for government financing of a multiparty system and that the government would also determine who would lead the parties. Political figures made known their preference for a liberal 1964 statute on political parties and popular elections in 1984. Government officials initiated a dialogue with the principal political forces in September. In order to placate the largest political force, the followers of the late Juan D. Perón, the government on July 9 paroled former President Isabel Martínez de Perón, who had been sentenced to more than eight years in prison on charges of misusing public funds and transferring a public building to the Peronist political party. She had been detained since the 1976 military coup that brought down her government. One of the strongest voices favoring a return to civilian rule in 1984 was that of Ricardo Balbín, 77, leader of the centrist radical party, who died on September 9. Following his death, Gen. (ret.) Albino Harguindeguy, an adviser to and occasional spokesman for the junta, reiterated the hardline military position that the next president would be chosen by the armed forces.

According to a report released in February by the United Nations Human Rights Commission, half of the 13,000 complaints it received about missing persons and political terrorism involved Argentina. The Argentine government admitted in March to holding 900 political prisoners, down from a high of 5,000. Human-rights organizations in Buenos Aires claimed that the number of disappeared persons was at least 12,000. Repression continued against trade unionists, but noticeably shifted to the press. A particular target was the 113-year-old *La Prensa.* By midyear, the regime had withdrawn all of its advertising and announcements from that paper. Right-wing terrorist organizations threatened to censor the daily, and its hard-hitting reporters were being threatened and physically attacked. Editions of other publications were confiscated. When two press photographers were beaten by federal police in October, 200 members of the press corps staged a protest demonstration in front of the presidential palace. An even bigger demonstration had occurred on May 1, when 1,000 persons marched on the presidential palace, demanding information on their missing relatives. Added attention was focused on the denial of human rights in Argentina with the publication of *Prisoner Without a Name, Cell Without a Number* by Jacobo Timerman, a former newspa-

ARGENTINA • Information Highlights

Official Name: Republic of Argentina.
Location: Southern South America.
Area: 1,072,158 sq mi (2 776 889 km^2).
Population (1981 est.): 28,200,000.
Chief Cities (1970 census): Buenos Aires, the capital, 2,972,453; Córdoba, 781,565; Rosario, 750,455.
Government: *Head of state and government,* Gen Leopoldo Galtieri, president (took office Dec. 22, 1981). *Legislature*—Congress (dissolved March 24, 1976); Legislative Advisory Commission established.
Monetary Unit: New Peso (8,225.00 new pesos equal U.S.$1, Nov. 1981).
Manufactures (major products): Processed foods, motor vehicles, textiles, chemicals, metal and metal products, electrical appliances.
Agriculture (major products): Grains, oilseeds, livestock products.

per publisher who was jailed and tortured in Argentina.

Economic Conditions. The country was plagued with a deep recession, increasing unemployment, and high rates of inflation. By early July, after a series of devaluations, the peso, which was being exchanged at 2,000 to the U.S. dollar at the beginning of the year, was going at 8,800 per dollar on the free market. With bank failures and bankruptcies on the rise, unemployment and underemployment had topped 40% in the first quarter. At midyear, inflation was hovering around 100%, threatening a return to the disastrous early months of 1976, when inflation reached 60% per month. Heading up the administration's economic team was Lorenzo Sigaut, who forecast an economic boom resulting from the peso devaluations. Hugo Lamonica, undersecretary of finance, counted on a huge influx of foreign investment capital as a result of a cheaper peso. Because of the peso rate, the government was predicting an influx of tourism receipts. Additional credits were pumped into the agricultural sector to increase the grain harvest in 1982 by 50% over the 24 million t (26.2 million T) harvested in 1981. A trade surplus of U.S.$2,500,000,000 was projected for the latter half of the year.

The economic chaos provoked a rash of illegal strikes and demands for a change of government. Peronist unions called a nationwide "day of protest" on July 22, after having postponed the event for three weeks. It failed to paralyze the country, as only about 20% of the work force joined in. Ten union leaders were jailed. On September 15, 100,000 automobile industry workers stopped working and held assemblies to protest layoffs and some 40,000 firings in that industry. The construction industry reported an 80% decline in activity, idling 300,000 construction workers.

The staggering Viola administration, rumored in July to be on the way out, revived when publicly endorsed by Galtieri who indicated that programs aimed at pressing problems were forthcoming from the junta. In September, Viola commissioned alternate economy recovery plans.

Foreign Relations. Following the inauguration of Ronald Reagan, relations with Washington thawed considerably. On September 30, the U.S. Senate voted to give President Reagan permission to resume arms sales to Argentina, which had been suspended by the Carter administration because of Argentina's human rights record. Earlier, the Reagan administration had instructed its delegates to international development banks to vote for loans to Argentina.

On Dec. 12, 1980, Pope John Paul II issued his mediation decision on the Argentina border dispute with Chile. While Chile accepted the papal ruling, Argentina did not. Deciding to delay the mediation process, Argentina did not respond to the Vatican proposal until March. On April 24, Chile arrested two Argentine officers in Chilean territory for spying. Chile's refusal to release the officers led Argentina to close its 2,600-mile (4 160-km) border with Chile. Six weeks later, the border was reopened and prisoners held by both countries were exchanged. In September, Foreign Minister Oscar H. Camilión suggested a new papal mediation effort.

LARRY L. PIPPIN, *Elbert Covell College*

ARIZONA

The Water Issue. Arizona's booming growth and economy are threatened by the scarcity of water. The underground aquifers that have supplied the southern regions of the state are being consumed at a much faster rate than nature is able to replenish them. Likewise, the burgeoning Phoenix metropolitan area is testing the limits of its Salt River source. In Arizona, water means wealth and power, and those who control water, control Arizona. Conflicts regarding water control have pitted farmers and ranchers against city dwellers, whites against Indians, environmentalists against developers, Phoenix against Tucson, and, of course, Republicans against Democrats.

At the core of these battles is the Central Arizona Project (CAP), the huge canal now under construction which will bring water east from the Colorado River basin to Phoenix and, maybe, Tucson. Controversial because of its expense, the questionable supply estimates of river water upon which it is based, and the past reluctance of the state to adopt groundwater regulations, the project stirred new emotions in 1981. Secretary of the Interior James Watt implied that construction of the Tucson leg of the canal might be conditional upon Democratic Congressman Morris K. Udall's support of construction of the proposed Orme flood control dam east of Phoenix, as well as Udall's future cooperation on other environmental matters. (Udall is chairman of the House Interior Committee.)

The proposed dam would flood approximately two thirds of the Yavapai Indians' Fort McDowell reservation, causing them, against their wishes, to relinquish their ancestral tribal home. The Yavapais were joined in their strug-

ARIZONA • Information Highlights

Area: 114,000 sq mi (295 260 km²).
Population (1980 census): 2,717,866.
Chief Cities (1980 census): Phoenix, the capital, 764,911; Tucson, 330,537; Mesa, 152,453; Tempe, 106,743; Glendale, 96,988; Scottsdale, 88,364; Yuma, 42,433; Flagstaff, 34,641; Chandler, 29,673; Sierra Vista, 25,968.
Government (1981): *Chief Officers*—governor, Bruce E. Babbitt (D); secy. of state, Rose Mofford (D). *Legislature*—Senate, 30 members; House of Representatives, 60 members.
State Finances (fiscal year 1980): *Revenues*, $3,187,000,000; *expenditures*, $2,637,000,000.
Personal Income (1980): $23,951,000,000; per capita, $8,791.
Labor Force (July 1981): *Nonagricultural wage and salary earners*, 995,900; *unemployed*, 74,000 (6.5% of total force).

gle by environmentalists who also objected to the proposed dam's destruction of a scenic portion of the Verde River.

Should this issue be resolved and the canal be extended to Tucson, the related question of how this CAP water will be allocated will once again pit the Indians against the settlers in the sun-drenched Tucson valley. Additional water is essential to sustain Tucson's sun belt prosperity as one of the fastest growing cities in the nation. On the other hand, the Papago Indians, whose bone-dry reservation borders the city, see the same water as fundamental to the economic survival of their impoverished tribe. Udall, once more, is caught in the middle.

Other News. Despite its relatively small population, Arizona continued to enjoy the national political prominence of its public servants. Added to a distinguished list is the first woman to be appointed to the U.S. Supreme Court, former Arizona state senator and Appeals court judge Sandra Day O'Connor. (*See also* BIOGRAPHY.)

After months of legislative bickering, Arizona remained the only state that does not participate in the federal medicaid program.

Both of the state's major universities, the University of Arizona and Arizona State University, were shaken by athletic scandals which resulted in the dismissal of the football coaches and their staffs at the two institutions.

The Arizona lottery, approved by voters in 1980, proved to be a major source of state revenue, as more than 40 million one-dollar tickets were purchased in the first two games.

JAMES W. CLARKE, *University of Arizona*

ARKANSAS

A conservative mood pervaded Arkansas government and politics in 1981. Faced with cuts in federal funds and popular resistance to state and local tax increases, all levels of government reduced services and trimmed public payrolls. Even state water quality standards were lowered.

Charles Bussey became the first black to be elected mayor of Little Rock.

Legislature. The General Assembly in a 66-calendar-day biennial session, the shortest since 1967, authorized voters in each city and county to approve a locally initiated one cent sales tax; reduced the vehicle registration fee; created within the state Education Department independent divisions for vocational-technical and general education; raised the state hourly minimum wage from $2.60 to $2.85; required public schools to teach a Bible-centered theory about the creation of man and the universe (see RELIGION: Survey); and raised to 80,000 lb (36 287 kg) the maximum weight for trucks shipping Arkansas agricultural products.

The movement of people from the eastern to other sections of the state and an 18.8% population increase since 1970 (to 2,285,513) required the state Board of Apportionment—consisting of the governor, a Republican, and the attorney general and secretary of state, both Democrats—to make extensive and vexing changes in state legislative district boundaries. Republicans, including the governor, accused the board of gerrymandering and appealed the reapportionment of the Senate to the state Supreme Court.

Governor. Frank White, the state's second Republican governor since 1874, promoted conservative policies, appointed supporters to the state administration, and campaigned for the 1982 gubernatorial election. Most of the few bills sponsored by him, including budget cuts, were adopted in some form by the Democratic legislature. By emphasizing the dramatic, he blunted Democratic efforts to persuade the public to censure him for not resolving problems, including the Fort Chaffee Cuban refugee issue, for which former Gov. Bill Clinton was blamed during the 1980 campaign.

Governor White warned that the program for the state-sponsored Governors School, a five-week summer school for 250 to 300 academically elite high-school students, should not contain moral "garbage"; he appointed Orval E. Faubus, former six-term Democratic governor who used state troops to block integration of Little Rock Central High School in 1957, head of the Veterans Affairs Department; and he urged implementation of the death sentence in Arkansas.

Administration. Dramatic utility rate increases sparked widespread criticism of the Republican-dominated Public Service Commission and a drive to initiate a constitutional amendment to elect, rather than to let governors appoint, the three commission members. Federal Judge G. Thomas Eisele stated that the 12-year federal court supervision of state prisons could end as constitutional deficiencies were corrected. However, Pulaski County Sheriff Tommy Robinson dramatized the overcrowded conditions at local prison facilities by chaining 19 county prisoners to state prison gates. The U.S. Supreme Court upheld the state's 10% interest ceiling on loans made in the state.

WILLIAM C. NOLAN
Southern Arkansas University

ARKANSAS • Information Highlights

Area: 53,187 sq mi (137 754 km²).
Population (1980 census): 2,285,513.
Chief Cities (1980 census): Little Rock, the capital, 158,461; Fort Smith, 71,384; North Little Rock, 64,419; Pine Bluff, 56,576; Fayetteville, 36,604; Hot Springs, 35,166; Jonesboro, 31,530; West Memphis, 28,138; Jacksonville, 27,589; El Dorado, 26,685.
Government (1981): *Chief Officers*—governor, Frank White (R); lt. gov., Winson Bryant (D). *General Assembly*—Senate, 35 members; House of Representatives, 100 members.
State Finances (fiscal year 1980): *Revenues*, $2,295,000,000; *expenditures*, $2,148,000,000.
Personal Income (1980): $16,651,000,000; per capita, $7,268.
Labor Force (July 1981): *Nonagricultural wage and salary earners*, 745,300; *unemployed*, 83,600 (8.2% of total force).

ART

In 1981 the art market suffered some setbacks, though record sales continued to be made; many noteworthy exhibitions were held, but no single event dominated; and new museums or additions to existing ones opened.

Auctions and the Market. Leading auction houses and many collectors experienced disappointments when, for the first time after a series of record-breaking seasons, a great number of works of art failed to reach expected prices or remained unsold. Even paintings by such famous artists as Murillo and Jan Breugel the Elder, which are rare at auctions and had been expected to go for $700,000 each, did not find buyers. Neither did a Winslow Homer, a Picasso (admittedly badly restored and disowned by the artist), and a rare group of eight paintings by René Magritte, for which the owner had expected $2 million. On the other hand, records continued to be broken: Ribera's "Saint Jerome," for which $250,000 had been expected, went for $340,000, the highest price ever paid for a work by this artist, and a Santi di Tito, estimated at $30,000, sold for $110,000, also a record. A self-portrait by Picasso, signed "Yo" and dated 1901, went to an American collector for $5.3 million, the highest price ever paid for a Picasso or any other 20th-century work. A record was set for Guardi when his "San Giorgio Maggiore" went for $320,000, instead of the expected $40,000. Degas' portrait of his brother sold for $2 million, compared with the 1980 record price for a Degas of $1 million.

The disappointments were attributable to a variety of factors: sellers who set unrealistic prices and buyers who were increasingly value-conscious and more conservative in the face of fluctuating gold and currency markets. In recent years, certain areas have been overpriced, but good quality will always sell. The final results showed Sotheby Parke Bernet, Christie's, and Phillips Son & Neale, the three major auction houses, registering their highest sales. Because of the unfavorable rate of exchange for the British pound, the dollar sum was off, except in the case of Sotheby. Total sales for the New York branches surpassed the totals for the London houses of Sotheby and Christie's, putting New York into first place in art auction sales.

As interest in the art of the 1920s and 1930s is leveling off, the post–World War II period is experiencing a rise in popularity and, consequently, in prices. In 1981, records were set for both major and less well-known artists of the postwar era. During a two-day sale in May, Sotheby sold $3.3 million worth, the highest prices being paid for a Franz Kline ($350,000) and a Mark Rothko ($190,000), both abstracts. Collectors of such works are in general young and new to auctions.

Interest also is increasing in 19th- and early 20th-century American and European bronzes. Realistic animal and figure sculptures of relatively small size, they are often bought for decoration of home or office. The steady rise of value in this field can be measured by the example of Remington's popular "Bronco Buster," casts of which went for $20,000 in 1973, $33,000 in 1977, $45,000 in 1979, $55,000 later in 1979, and $68,000 in 1980. But at some Art Deco and Art Nouveau auctions, only slightly more than half the offerings were sold. Such rare and exceptional pieces as Tiffany lamps and Ruhlmann furniture, however, continued to attract buyers.

Museums and Exhibitions. Much of the museum news of 1981 was made by the Metropolitan Museum of New York. New sections continue to be opened as a result of the ambitious reorganization of the past several years. A decade after Mrs. Vincent Astor first conceived of the reconstruction of an authentic 12th-century

In accordance with Picasso's own terms, his "Guernica" was returned to Spain in 1981.

Museum of Modern Art

The Metropolitan Museum of Art, Gift of the Vincent Astor Foundation

The Metropolitan Museum's new Astor Garden is a reconstruction of a 12th century Chinese garden.

Chinese garden, the Astor Garden was inaugurated. It was the product of close cooperation between the Met and the People's Republic of China, which provided workmen and materials. The Douglas Dillon Galleries of Chinese Painting on three sides of the garden contribute to an impression of ordered nature. Some 80 masterpieces from the Song, Yuan, Ming, and Qing dynasties are displayed. Also opened at the Met was the Raymond and Beverly Sackler Gallery for Assyrian Art, to house the museum's great collection of Assyrian stone sculpture acquired early in the century and in storage for 13 years.

In addition to the welcome return to view of the Met's own treasures, several loan exhibitions introduced art unfamiliar to the American public. One such show was the "German Masters of the Nineteenth Century," on display at the Met in the spring and at the Toronto Art Gallery in the summer. Organized by Stefan Waetzold of the Berlin Museums, it consisted of loans from West German collections. Until recently, only the French art of this period had commanded the attention and respect of art historians and museum visitors. The German show was therefore a revelation. The exhibition was combined with a symposium at the Met, as well as a rich program on the cultural manifestations of 19th-century Germany, held at various other locations in New York City. Among them were stage designs from the Theatermuseum in Munich, held at the Cooper-Hewitt Museum, and the graphic work of German Romantic artists, at the Goethe House.

From an earlier era came the objects in a show called "The Royal Abbey of Saint-Denis in the Time of Abbot Suger." The occasion was the 900th anniversary of the birth of the abbot, who played an influential role in French art and politics of his time. Brought together at the Cloisters in New York were objects made for Saint-Denis, now scattered all over the world. A symposium, attended by art historians from many nations, coincided with the show.

Another international show at the Met, "5000 Years of Korean Art," organized by the National

M.H. deYoung Memorial Museum

"Jack-in-the-Pulpit" vase was part of "The Art of Louis Comfort Tiffany" show at San Francisco's deYoung Museum.

National Gallery of Art

Some of the works of Auguste Rodin, including "The Age of Bronze" (right), were presented at the National Gallery.

Museum of Korea, dazzled visitors with an array of gold objects—crowns, girdles, earrings, bracelets, cups, and bowls—as well as some remarkable sculptures and ceramics. In addition to New York, the show visited San Francisco, Seattle, Chicago, Cleveland, Boston, Kansas City, and Washington, DC. Also non-Western in origin were the pieces in the show "For Spirits and Kings," 150 objects of African art from the Paul and Ruth Tischmann Collection. More comprehensive than the 1980 show of Nigerian art, it demonstrated that stereotypes of African art hold true for only a small minority of works.

The Met's educational activities were assured sufficient funding with a gift of $10 million by Harold D. Uris, a New York real estate developer and philanthropist. Of the total amount, the largest single monetary donation in the Met's history, $3 million will be used to create a new visitor's orientation center, to improve the Junior Museum auditorium and other educational facilities, and to install a multimedia information system. The rest will be placed in an endowment fund to support the education center and its activities in perpetuity.

In the future, New Yorkers will have greater exposure to Far Eastern art, not only at the newly installed galleries at the Met but also at the new Asia Society building. Under construction at Park Avenue and 70th Street for the previous two years, the $16.6 million building, designed by Edward Larrabee Barnes, was inaugurated in April 1981 with a two-and-a-half-month program of events, including concerts, films, symposia, and public-affairs discussions. It houses some 300 objects donated by John D. Rockefeller, which can now be exhibited together and permanently for the first time. They originated in China, Japan, India, and Southeast Asia. The new building also provides space for the society's own collection of Southeast Asian art, and for changing exhibitions, lectures, concerts, and films. In addition, the society intends to expand its educational activities, bringing programs on Asia to schools and into homes via television.

In contrast to the completely new Asia Society edifice, the other "new" museum buildings of the year were additions to, or adaptations of, existing buildings. The San Antonio Art Museum, an adaptation, was praised as both an imaginative piece of urban planning and a stunning display of design virtuosity and adaptability. Built at the beginning of the century as the Lone Star Brewery in the shape of a Romanesque Revival twin tower, the edifice and the neighborhood it overlooks had gradually fallen into decay. At a cost far less than that of a new structure, the brewery was subjected to "adaptive reuse," a concept increasingly popular in contemporary urban planning. The original structure was left essentially intact, but its interior was modernized and provided with extensive skylighting. While the museum's art collection is not to be ranked with those of the major U.S. museums, it was expected to attract more donations to fill the large and impressive quarters. The museum promises to become the cultural center of a truly revitalized area picturesquely located along the banks of the San Antonio River.

An interesting development in museum history occurred in July 1981, when the Whitney Museum of American Art in New York opened a branch in Stamford, the heart of Connecticut's affluent Fairfield County. The satellite gallery is being supported by the Champion International Corporation and housed in the company's downtown headquarters. For the first time, a museum has acknowledged the population flow to the suburbs and is following its audience. This was not, however, the first time the Whitney reached out for an audience beyond the east side of Manhattan; in 1973 it opened a branch in an old police station in the lower Broadway area. In 1982 it is expected to open one on 42d Street to attract potential lunchtime visitors.

In Boston, the major event of 1981 was the inauguration in July of the West Wing of the Museum of Fine Arts. Designed by I. M. Pei, who also designed the East Wing of the National Gallery in Washington, the $22 million, three-story wing complements the Beaux-Arts monument of 1909. It adds 80,000 sq ft (7 432 m^2) to be used not only for more gallery space but also for the educational, commercial, and social activities now considered essential for a museum. The new wing features glass roofing and windows, which bring daylight back to the museum. For the opening, the museum presented the United States' only major international exhibition of works by Camille Pissarro (1830–1903). This French painter had not yet received a comprehensive show that would enable his unique position as an Impressionist and influential Post-Impressionist to be properly evaluated. Organized

"Improvisation No. 33" was a Wassily Kandinsky watercolor seen at the Cleveland Museum of Art.

The Cleveland Museum of Art

for the 150th anniversary of his birth by a committee of French, British, and American scholars, it was previously shown at the Hayward Gallery in London and the Grand Palais in Paris. It included almost 100 paintings, a like number of prints and drawings, and such objects as painted fans and ceramics, photographs, and letters.

In Europe, too, there was the opening of a new museum, the Neue Pinakothek in Munich. In contrast to its counterpart, the Alte Pinakothek, which emphasizes the Old Masters, the new museum is devoted to 19th-century painting. Badly damaged during the war, the building was completely rebuilt at a cost of $44 million. No longer in the same restrained neoclassical style as the facing Alte Pinakothek, it does not have a very attractive exterior. But the interior provides excellent display space, with natural lighting, for the city's great collection of European art from the period when Munich was an important creative center.

Other European exhibitions concentrated on the art of the 20th century. Moscow had its first view in some 50 years of many works by modern Soviet artists that had been banned from public showing. The occasion was the "Paris-Moscow 1900–1930" exhibition organized and shown in 1979 at the Centre Pompidou. If the earlier show—a remarkable assemblage of paintings, sculpture, architectural and industrial designs, cinema, literature, and posters of the modernist period in Russia—excited great interest in Paris, the essentially same show was a revelation in Moscow. Although Soviet museums are rich in works of this era, contemporary audiences are not permitted to see them, as they are considered too revolutionary and bourgeois. While the show had been designed to demonstrate friendly relations between France and the Soviet Union, attempts at censorship and other political intrusions on the part of Soviet officials were deeply resented by the French organizers.

Meanwhile in Paris, Pontus Hulten, the retiring director of the "Beaubourg," staged his last great spectacle. Called "Paris-Paris," the show featured works from the two decades after the Paris fair of 1937. As other Beaubourg shows, the "Paris-Paris" exhibition included not only works of art but also films, photographs, books, and objects from everyday life. It gave a comprehensive picture of tastes and fashions when Paris was truly the center of the art world.

An even bigger exhibition, mounted in Cologne, displayed the panorama of modern European art to the present day; works by American artists also were included. All told, some 860 works by more than 200 artists since 1939 were shown at the Rheinhallen, the city's vast Trade Exhibition Building. Because of the ambitious design, the organizers exhausted all of its municipal funding (more than $1.5 million) before the contemporary section could be installed. They therefore took the unusual and controversial step

Philadelphia Museum of Art

The Philadelphia Museum of Art offered a two-month show of the art of India, including a c.1690 watercolor.

Photos Scala/EPA

Two 5th century B.C. bronze male nudes, found in the Ionian Sea in 1972, were exhibited in 1981.

of asking art dealers to assemble and present those works in private galleries.

Two large overseas shows were arranged by U.S. museums. At the Galerie des Beaux-Arts in Bordeaux, France, 80,000 visitors packed into the small provincial museum to see "Profile of the Metropolitan Museum." A selection of 230 objects—ranging from a Sumerian clay figure to a Tiffany vase, and including European and American paintings—provided a comprehensive view of the Met's riches. Bordeaux was the only city in Europe to benefit from the Met's new policy of sending small traveling shows to audiences too distant to visit New York. The Boston Museum of Fine Arts presented an exhibition of American art in Peking under the sponsorship of the U.S. Government. Included were 13 modern abstract paintings by such artists as Jackson Pollock, Franz Kline, and Helen Frankenthaler. Chinese officials objected. They wanted the abstract works removed but retreated from their position when warned that the entire show might be canceled.

Restorations. From Italy came important news regarding the restoration of two major works of art. The first was the announcement of a 12-year, $3 million project to clean and restore Michelangelo's frescoes in the Sistine Chapel in Vatican City. The work (which includes the famous *Last Judgment*) has undergone many restorations, but previous efforts were not so respectful of the original as current techniques, and often were actually harmful. The paintings have darkened considerably, a fact now very evident by the brightness of the side walls, painted by other Renaissance artists, which were recently cleaned. A small section of the Michelangelo frescoes already cleaned in 1980 shows the startling results possible with modern chemicals, more sophisticated methods, and scrupulous attention. In addition to preserving the paintings for future viewing, the project is expected to reveal much about the working methods of the master.

Another successful restoration was demonstrated in Florence, with the exhibition of two larger-than-life-sized Greek bronzes found in 1972 off the coast of southern Italy. The two nude warriors are among a handful of original Greek bronzes remaining from the golden age of Greek art of the 5th century B.C. Following years of restoration they were exhibited to enormous crowds—half a million during a six-month period at Florence's Archeological Museum and 300,000 at the Quirinal Palace in Rome, where they were shown before going to their permanent installation at the museum of Reggio Calabria.

ISA RAGUSA, *Princeton University*

UPI

Japan's Zenko Suzuki and the Philippines' Ferdinand Marcos participate in a ceremony in Manila.

ASIA

Efforts at greater cooperation dominated the international relations of Asia in 1981—a year in which foreign policy seemed to overshadow internal political developments in the region. Common goals drew governments closer together in an expanding number of areas, but differences also developed among some of the same states that were exploring new avenues of cooperation.

Toward Cooperation. Japan and South Korea—the latter once occupied by the Japanese as a colony—held talks to improve relations between the two northeastern Asian neighbors, linked by their common anti-Communist ideologies but still ill at ease in interaction with one another, a legacy of the imperial period (1910–45). Tokyo refused to link aid to the South Koreans, still fearful of new Communist North Korean military moves, to defense considerations, and no joint communiqué was issued.

The Japanese also sought better relations with other important nations in East Asian international affairs. In a bid to lessen tension with the USSR, Premier Zenko Suzuki announced that his government was willing to resume talks with the Soviets—which had been suspended in late 1979 as a consequence of Moscow's military involvement in Afghanistan. Suzuki, in his first trip abroad since becoming prime minister, opened a year of diplomatic overtures in January with visits to the five Association of Southeast Asian Nations (ASEAN) countries, Indonesia, Malaysia, the Philippines, Singapore, and Thailand. He was given a cordial reception.

In midyear South Korean President Chun Doo Hwan made a comparable swing through the ASEAN capitals—somewhat to Japan's concern. Abandoning his country's prior absorption with the affairs of only northeastern Asia, the Korean leader largely explored economic cooperation—specifically, the sale of heavy industrial equipment and opportunities for South Korean investment—making Seoul a new competitor in Southeast Asia.

China's Premier Zhao Ziyang visited the Philippines, Malaysia, Singapore, and Thailand, but not Indonesia, which does not have diplomatic relations with Peking. He primarily sought to reduce differences between China and the anti-Communist Southeast Asian nations on how to deal with continuing *de facto* Vietnamese occupation of Cambodia (Kampuchea).

The United States, like most of the Asian governments themselves, generally improved relations with states of the vast region. Among other actions, Washington extended $3,200,000,000 worth of military and economic aid to Pakistan (neighbor of war-plagued Afghanistan), significantly increased its assistance to Thailand (adjacent to still-troubled Cambodia), and signaled a continuation of its strategic commitment of troops to South Korea. American aid to Pakistan, however, worsened U.S.-Indian relations, while Taiwan was vocally very critical of Washington's supply of arms to China.

The ASEAN nations continued to cooperate diplomatically in blocking the seating of the Vietnamese-established Cambodian regime in the UN General Assembly and in urging a United Nations peacekeeping presence in Cambodia. In emulation of ASEAN, the foreign ministers of the seven South Asian nations met in Sri Lanka's capital of Colombo in April to discuss regional cooperation.

Developing Differences. Japan and South Korea, pursuing improved relations in northeastern Asia, had clearly become major economic rivals in the southeastern corner of the great continent. On the other hand, the differences between the United States and the anti-Communist countries of the region—the ASEAN nations—were political. The United States was a *de facto* ally of all five of these states, but Washington and the ASEAN governments differed in approaches to restraining Vietnam (which still, in effect, occupied neighboring Cambodia). The Americans agreed with the Chinese policy of bleeding the Vietnamese by aiding Cambodian resistance forces against the 200,000 Vietnamese troops in the country—an extremely heavy drain on Vietnam's economy. Not only did the ASEAN nations seek politically to end the Cambodian civil-foreign war, but some of them also appeared to be apprehensive about the implications of an American policy that encouraged a strong, modernized China.

China provided support to different types of rebels against Vietnamese dominance of the adjacent parts of once-French Indochina. Peking was the chief source of supply of arms and ammunition to the anti-Vietnamese and antigovernment insurgent opposition—both Communist and anti-Communist—to the Hanoi-established Phnom Penh regime in Cambodia. China even permitted right-wing Thai mercenaries to train strongly anti-Communist hill-tribesmen on Chinese soil, with the object of overthrowing the Communist, pro-Vietnamese, and pro-Soviet government of Laos.

Thailand seemed to have no hesitation about siding with China against Vietnam and the USSR, but Malaysia and Singapore in particular were uneasy about the Sino-U.S. alignment, especially U.S. efforts to arm the Chinese with modern weapons. Malaysia's and Singapore's leaders feared that such weapons might find their way into the hands of Communist insurgents in the non-Communist Southeast Asian lands.

India's relations with three of its subcontinent neighbors—Sri Lanka, Bangladesh, and Pakistan—worsened during the year despite the April all-South Asian Colombo conference. Serious communal rioting in August in Sri Lanka, pitting indigenous Sinhalese against Tamil Indians, caused Indian President Sanjiva Reddy to postpone an official visit to Colombo. The border between Bangladesh and India became the site of tension and violence as thousands of illegal Bangladesh refugees flowed across the frontier into Tripura state. The most serious deterioration, however, was in Indo-Pakistani relations—the result of Pakistan's receipt of F-16 fighters under a $3,200,000,000 American aid package.

Even Indo-Soviet relations seemed to have cooled. The tenth anniversary of the 20-year Moscow–New Delhi friendship treaty passed almost unnoticed in India—to visible Soviet disappointment. The USSR, however, did sign a trade agreement with Vietnam in August.

Continuing Conflict. The war in Afghanistan intensified, although there were also signs of a possible early resolution of the conflict. According to the Soviet newspaper *Pravda,* the USSR was prepared to withdraw its forces from the country if Afghanistan's two neighbors, Pakistan and Iran, agreed to peace proposals advanced by the Kabul government's President Babrak Karmal. The Afghan leader also indicated a willingness to accept UN participation in the peace talks. Leaders of various Western governments doubted, however, that an early Soviet disengagement from Afghanistan was likely.

Fighting also continued in Cambodia, where 200,000 Vietnamese troops did limited battle with a multifaction insurgent opposition that was a fraction of the size of Hanoi's forces. The ASEAN nations proposed withdrawal of the Vietnamese forces and a UN peacekeeping presence, but Hanoi and Moscow rejected this.

China's Chairman Hu Yaobang invited Taiwan's President Chiang Ching-kuo to visit the mainland, but Chiang—Generalissimo Chiang Kai-shek's son—proclaimed that his government would never negotiate with Peking.

Domestic Politics. The consolidation of China's unified political leadership continued, as Vice-Chairman Deng Xiaoping and his lieutenants, Chairman Hu Yaobang and Premier Zhao Ziyang, tightened their grip on the reins of government. The post-Mao government's economic policies received a major international boost when the World Bank's long-awaited nine-volume report strongly backed the economic liberalization and trade expansion of the Deng-directed regime. The report warned, however, of a possible energy crisis stemming from China's drive to modernize. According to the World Bank, China's chief problem, the feeding of its 1,000,000,000 people, would remain.

Economic Progress and Difficulty. South Korea's economic development, which has not drawn nearly the attention of the economic advances of nearby Japan, posed foreign market and investment problems for both the Japanese and the United States. Other non-Communist countries exhibited considerable economic progress—not least of all Burma, previously all but stagnant.

Two of Asia's major Communist governments, Vietnam's and North Korea's, experienced serious difficulties, however. North Korea was a badly debt-ridden nation—in stark contrast to adjacent South Korea. Vietnam, plagued by food shortages, clearly displayed the consequences of the economic burden placed upon it by the demands of a "foreign war" in neighboring Cambodia.

RICHARD BUTWELL, *Murray State University*

Economic Growth in the ASEAN Nations

Ted Spiegel/Black Star

Much of Southeast Asia is a "developing region," an area where large-scale poverty remains but where the economic potential is great. It was with this in mind that the governments of Indonesia, Malaysia, the Philippines, Singapore, and Thailand joined together in Bangkok, Thailand, in August 1967 to form the Association of Southeast Asian Nations (ASEAN). The association seeks to promote not only economic growth but also regional cooperation to ensure the stability of the entire area.

Each of the ASEAN members is presently in the midst of a development program. Thailand began its fifth five-year program in 1981. Singapore, the "miniature superstate" of the area, and Malaysia are experiencing real growth in gross national product (GNP) of more than 8 and 7%, respectively. Indonesia hopes to create jobs by promoting small-scale industry through its third five-year plan. Ferdinand E. Marcos, who was again inaugurated as president of the Philippines in 1981, has instituted a program to establish 11 new industrial projects. These two pages offer a photographic glance at the economic status of the ASEAN nations.

Although not new to the Philippines, rice terraces are heavily cultivated to produce the nation's principal agricultural product. With inadequate housing a major problem, projects such as the one, below, in Surabaya, Indonesia, are a prime goal.

Dirck Halstead/Liaison

Founded as a tin-mining camp, Kuala Lumpur, Malaysia, is now a commercial and transportation center.

David Moore/Black Star

T. Schmitt/Sygma

With gasoline very expensive in Thailand, elephants and pedicabs, left, are used for commercial transportation. Below, a welder in Singapore is busy building pipelines. Thanks in large part to petroleum, Singapore's manufacturing boom continues.

Lincoln Potter/Liaison

ASTRONOMY

Two decades of close-up planetary examinations by the United States came virtually to a close on Aug. 25, 1981, when Voyager 2 swept past Saturn. If the spaceprobe can stay alive it may glimpse Uranus in 1986 and Neptune in 1989, but such a lucky happening would be a bonus. Voyager has concluded its primary mission, and no similar spacecraft are being prepared. An era in cosmic exploration has ended; the picture show is over.

Yet, a decade of apathy toward space science may also have ended. In 1981, lobby groups were formed to demonstrate public interest in astronomical space research and to provide financial support for U.S. programs. Such activity is unprecedented in the annals of astronomy.

Instrumentation. After eight years of construction and the expenditure of $80 million, the Very Large Array in New Mexico was completely operational in 1981. Its 27 antennas, each 25 m (82 ft) in diameter, stretch more than 35 km (22 mi) across the Plains of San Augustin. With this instrument, astronomers can now observe at radio wavelengths the tiny details of celestial objects that previously could only be recorded by optical telescopes.

Saturn. The flybys of the ringed planet by Voyagers 1 and 2 in 1980 and 1981, respectively, may have yielded discoveries more bizarre and unexpected than those garnered by any other planetary mission. Saturn's famous ring system was found to be composed not of three broad components, as previously believed, but of hundreds upon hundreds of narrow ringlets. Also totally unimagined before Voyager 1 were radial spokes in the ring system. These seem to rotate as a solid wheel (with the rim moving faster than the hub); this is unlike the planetary motions influenced by gravity. The explanation may involve levitation, whereby particles are lifted out of the ring plane by electrostatic forces that overcome the planet's gravitational pull.

Every image returned by the Voyagers provided surprises for the observers and challenges for the theorists. The gossamer-thin, outermost "F" ring, discovered by the Pioneer 11 spaceprobe in 1979, was revealed at times to be a trio of braided strands unlike anything astronomers had ever before imagined.

As previous flybys of Jupiter's family of moons had shown, the satellites of planets are unique and fascinating worlds. Saturn's retinue is no exception. The Voyager probes confirmed that Saturn's moons are composed mainly of ice, vastly different from those of the giant planets (mainly gas) and the earthlike planets (mainly rock).

Mimas, the innermost of Saturn's classical moons, was found to have a crater 100 km (62 mi) in diameter, a quarter the diameter of the satellite itself. It is the deepest divot known in our solar system; the energy of the impacting body must have been nearly enough to shatter Mimas completely. Saturn's largest moon, Titan, was a pictorial disappointment; its extremely dense atmosphere prohibited views of the surface. However, instruments revealed that Titan's atmosphere consists of 99% nitrogen and 1% methane, in agreement with a theoretical model constructed before the Voyager encounter.

Sun. In 1981, the sun remained near the peak of its current activity cycle. The Solar Maximum Mission (SMM), launched in February 1980, produced a wealth of new insights concerning solar flares—events so powerful that they can release energy equivalent to trillions of hydrogen bombs, enough to interrupt radio communications and perhaps even cause climatic changes on earth. SMM observations seem to confirm a popular theory that flares begin with the colli-

Photos NASA

The Voyager 2 image of Saturn, obtained Aug. 11, 1981, shows two satellites (moons) above the planet, Dion (right) and Enceladus (left and mosaic below). Regions of Enceladus reveal impact craters up to 35 km (22 mi) in diameter.

In 1981 astronomers continued to be fascinated by the findings concerning solar flares revealed by the Solar Maximum Mission satellite, launched in 1980. The mission's coronograph showed coronal spikes shooting more than a million miles west and southwest from the solar limb. Such spikes can extend to one tenth the distance to earth.

NASA

sion of powerful magnetic fields containing hot gas. Ultimately, such knowledge may allow accurate predictions of when a major flare will occur.

Stars. In March 1979, an enormous pulse of gamma rays, the most energetic form of radiation known, was detected by nine spacecraft. The brevity of the pulse, less than 0.001 second, as well as its direction indicated that the emitting source is tiny and probably located in the Large Magellanic Cloud (a companion galaxy to our own). A neutron star, an endpoint of stellar evolution in which neutral atomic particles form an essentially solid body about 20 km (12 mi) in diameter, would correspond in size. Such stars seem to vibrate gravitationally, thus transporting enormous quantities of energy from their interiors to their surfaces at nearly the speed of light. If the pulse were indeed from a neutron star, the March 1979 event would mark the first detection of gravitational radiation and open a new window to the universe.

Curious Object. For several years astronomers have been puzzled by SS 433, a starlike resident of our galaxy that seems to be moving simultaneously toward and away from us at tens of thousands of kilometers per second. According to one recent theory, a highly condensed object, a neutron star or black hole (from which not even light can escape), is surrounded by a disk of gas drawn from an ordinary companion star. When the material in the disk accumulates to a critical density, two jets erupt perpendicularly to the disk. One rushes toward the earth, the other away, thus making SS 433 seem to be going in opposite directions at the same time.

Galaxies. For decades astronomers have observed galaxies with enigmatic twisted shapes and looping appendages that emit huge quantities of radio waves. For at least one such galaxy, called Fornax A, these properties can be explained by the cannibalization of a neighboring system within the last 1,000,000,000 years. In fact, it is being suggested that galactic cannibalism might be a rather common phenomenon. Recent evidence indicates that our own Milky Way may have swallowed a small, nearby companion galaxy as recently as 2,000,000,000 years ago. The evidence stems from the presence of many young stars in the outer halo of our system, where normally they would not be found. The collision of dust carried by the Milky Way and another galaxy could have triggered a secondary burst of star formation some 8,000,000,000 years after our galaxy's initial starburst.

In 1980, two galaxies were photographed at a distance of 10,000,000,000 light-years—the deepest penetration into space yet for imaging such objects. The light from these extremely remote stellar systems is very similar to that from relatively nearby galaxies known to be 6,000,000,000 years old. Thus, 16,000,000,000 years has now been established as the minimum age of the universe.

By definition, primordial galaxies have just begun their initial starburst. An object called IZw 18 seems to be such a system, the youngest known in the universe. Its recency is revealed by its extremely blue color, like that of the hottest and shortest-lived stars known in the Milky Way. Also, the chemical composition of IZw 18 indicates that its luminous material had not been processed in the interiors of an earlier generation of stars. The IZw 18 starburst occurred within the last 20 million years, only a few times longer than man's presence on earth.

Quasi-stellar Objects. For the past two decades, quasi-stellar objects (QSOs) have perplexed the astronomical world. They appear starlike and extremely distant; in order for us to see them, they must have enormous outputs of energy from very small volumes. Evidence is mounting that quasars are not previously unimagined celestial powerhouses, but merely the brilliant nuclei of very distant galaxies whose surrounding disks are masked by the brightness of their starlike cores. The source of the prodigious energy created by these objects remains largely unknown.

See also SPACE EXPLORATION.

LEIF J. ROBINSON
"Sky and Telescope" Magazine

Coretta Scott King joins other blacks in a memorial march for children murdered or missing in Atlanta.

Gubb/Gamma-Liaison

ATLANTA

Atlantans endured the reporting of 11 more child murders and welcomed the arrest of a suspect. They also elected a mayor and watched as the 52-floor Georgia-Pacific building rose.

Crime. The nightmare that began in July 1979 intensified as 11 more murdered children were discovered between January and May 1981, bringing the total to 29. The last victims fit the profile: young, poor, black, street-wise hustlers. The city, state, and federal governments, as well as private citizens, responded to the tragedy with aid. A special police task force was established by the mayor and a city-wide curfew for children was put into effect.

The General Assembly allotted more than $200,000 for expenses associated with the investigation. Gov. George Busbee directed the state bureau of investigation to supplement city enforcement efforts. President Ronald Reagan announced an appropriation of $1.5 million to pay for police overtime. In addition, the federal government gave an estimated $1.7 million in aid for FBI participation in the investigation, and for social programs to alleviate emotional stress imposed upon black families as a result of the slayings. Money poured into the city from private citizens, including a $400,000 donation from Muhammad Ali. Thousands of Atlanta citizens ignored near-freezing temperatures each weekend to search for clues in the wooded areas.

Twenty-three months after the deaths and disappearances began, a suspect was arrested and charged with the murder of Nathaniel Cater. Wayne B. Williams, a 23-year-old free-lance photographer, was stopped on a bridge and questioned by police after they heard a loud splash in the water. Five days later Cater's body surfaced in the Chattahoochee River.

Attempts to monitor Williams' activity covertly were foiled when the local news media began their own surveillance of him. Basing the case on the bridge incident as well as on the discovery that fibers found on the bodies of two victims matched fibers taken from Williams' home and car, authorities charged the suspect with the murders of Nathaniel Cater and Jimmy Payne.

Williams is the only child of an Atlanta couple, both of whom are retired public-school teachers. Friends and former teachers describe Williams as a superior student, energetic, businesslike, but never successful. He worked as a free-lance cameraman, shooting film of fires, wrecks, and murders which he offered to local TV stations. He had tried recently to become a record promoter, auditioning black teenagers.

Following his arrest on June 21, Williams was taken to the Fulton County jail. After an interview with Williams appeared in a national magazine, his visitors were limited.

Mayoral Race. From an initial list of mayoral candidates which included former police commissioner Reginald Eaves and state representative Sidney Marcus, Atlantans chose Andrew Young. Young, 49, has been in the public spotlight as a civil rights activist with Martin Luther King, Jr., a U.S. Congressman, and U.S. ambassador to the UN (1977–79). Young defeated white candidate Sidney Marcus in a run-off election which invoked discussion of racial polarization. White business leaders contributed substantial funds to the Marcus campaign, and Young received endorsements from leading black citizens. Mayor Maynard Jackson intensified the racial debate when he publicly referred to black Marcus supporters as "shuffling, grinning Negroes."

KAY BECK, *Georgia State University*

AUSTRALIA

For Prime Minister Malcolm Fraser it was a year of paradox. In his sixth year leading the Liberal-National Country Party coalition, he was able to restore surplus financing in the federal budget for the first time in ten years, but he found himself the center of heightened political contention when a destabilizing process within the Liberal Party's parliamentary section appeared to lessen his hold. The Australian Labor Party's internal problems, including factionalism and personality clashes, were largely ignored while media attention focused on the prime minister's future. The prolonged speculation about Fraser was seen by some commentators to enhance the possibility of a leadership challenge, but the prime minister weathered opposition parliamentary attacks as well as the resignation from the cabinet of Andrew Peacock, who had been foreign affairs minister and was industrial relations minister when he resigned in April. After suffering illness in August and September, Fraser gained new status as host of the Commonwealth Heads of Government Meeting (CHOGM) in Melbourne.

With inflation running at about 8% in the first half of the year, the economy made a good start in spite of a persistent 6% unemployment. Imports rose strongly, creating a trading shortfall which the strong capital inflow more than corrected. At midyear a big shakeout occurred on stock exchanges in line with world trends, but generally unionists rather than businessmen were complaining about affairs. Most companies, other than mining enterprises, told of profit rises at about double the inflation rate.

From midyear, wage demands were pressed in widespread strikes, leading to a spate of wage increases. These and very high interest rates cast a shadow over profit and employment prospects. At the same time a base for strong future growth was being built through an outpouring of money by business enterprises on plants and equipment, unprecedented in Australia's history. In the second half of the year, inflation neared 10%.

Political Developments. The government made a conscious effort to reduce regulation of business. At the same time the long-awaited National Securities Commission came into operation to monitor stock exchange dealings.

From midyear the L-NCP coalition was a minority in the Senate, where the balance of power was held by five members of the Democratic Party and one Independent. Although government measures were generally passed, the danger of a legislative blockage, leading to a dissolution of parliament, remained.

The coalition faced criticism for its stewardship in overseeing public corporations handling the export of rural commodities. A Senate committee reported unfavorably on dealings by a dairy industry body. The government moved to end substitution of horsemeat and kangaroo meat in ground beef for export to the United States.

Western Mining Corporation Ltd.

A massive new mining operation gets under way in the Roxby Downs area of South Australia. The exploration operations began early in the year.

The ALP was also under some strains. The media speculated on the possibility of Robert Hawke, now a member of Parliament, challenging Bill Hayden as parliamentary leader. However, no overt move was made.

ALP strategy was under review at a major party conference, where gains by the Socialist Left faction colored some policy decisions. The party reaffirmed its 60-year plank supporting the "nationalization" of enterprises where this was held to be socially desirable. The party pronouncements were generally considered the work of moderates. The parliamentary spokesmen were more forthright and took the most clearly anti-U.S. policy line to date. The party also urged an end to ties to the British crown.

For much of the year, Fraser's position as Liberal leader was under question, with Peacock seen as the chief challenger. When Fraser was hosting CHOGM in Melbourne, the barbed attacks became more numerous. The irony was that as Fraser's international stature grew so did the implied leadership crisis. Daily newspaper reports told of Fraser "almost visibly changing from a practical Australian politician to the role of a farsighted statesman," Concurrently, it was being said that "many Australians" felt uncomfortable when observing one of their politicians in such a role. As unfounded rumors of a decline in Fraser's health rippled through the media, a leading political writer noted, "a largely amused and cynical Australian audience" was bound to see the prime minister as "merely playing the role of international statesman."

Seasoned observers considered the Commonwealth meeting a success and said that Fraser could claim considerable credit for it. Fraser encouraged Commonwealth members to study the effect of all trade and tariff barriers on the developing countries. Regarding the North-South dialogue, CHOGM suggested the need for developed countries to bend policies to help the advancement of developing countries. Meanwhile, Hayden had put distance between the ALP and CHOGM with a criticism of the meeting's cost to Australian taxpayers and its unclear value in practical terms.

Fraser visited Washington for discussions with President Ronald Reagan. The two leaders expressed close accord on major issues. However, Fraser was slow to agree to an Australian contingent for the Sinai peacekeeping force. Regarding the Sinai force, Hayden considered it "imperative" for Australia to avoid involvement "in a region beyond Australia's sphere of influence." At CHOGM, Fraser supported an interventionist approach to the South Africa/Namibia issue at variance with U.S. policy.

Economic Developments. The year opened with inflation seemingly under control, but wage policy remained at the center of contention as unions pressed for accelerated rises and the government urged Arbitration Commission restraint in granting the requests. At midyear the Commission abandoned its policy of granting "indexed" wage rises, however, opening the way for rapid wage escalation under pressure of strikes.

The budget, presented in August, was broadly deflationary and set about creating an environment in which it would be difficult for business to accede to union demands for wage rises and work-hours reduction. Union pressure did not abate, and a wave of rises accelerated the price spiral. In the budget, provision was made for personal income tax to increase 19%, and for a 14% rise in indirect taxes, including an across-the-board increase in sales tax. Total revenue was expected to exceed U.S.$45,000,000,000. Social welfare expenditure was to rise 14%, to U.S.$12,700,000,000, and defense outlays were up 16% to U.S.$4,600,000,000. Allocations to assist aborigines rose to U.S.$165 million. Over the year, public borrowings eased 8%.

Meanwhile, state budgets reflected the new emphasis on resources expansion. Mineral- and energy-rich Queensland and Western Australia had "boom" budgets, while other states underwent spending strains.

Mining. The sharp fall in metal prices cut the profitability of nearly all mining companies, which faced higher costs at a time when export earnings were reduced by the strength of the Australian dollar.

Oil and gas finds were made in three regions: Bass Strait off Victoria, where commercial fields have been flowing for a decade; in central Australia; and in the Northwest. Important energy mines were opened, including the Gregory coal mine in Queensland and the Ranger uranium mine in the Northern Territory.

Defense. In October, a four-week military exercise was carried out in the Queensland coastal area and in the Coral Sea with U.S., New Zealand, and British forces. As part of its upgrading of defense equipment, the government decided to order 75 McDonnell-Douglas F-A18 Hornets at a cost of U.S.$2,700,000,000. Ten P-3C Orion tracker aircraft and other Army items, including 105mm artillery and a greater operational reserve of ammunition, also were ordered.

R. M. YOUNGER, *Australian Author*

AUSTRALIA • Information Highlights

Official Name: Commonwealth of Australia.
Location: Southwestern Pacific Ocean.
Area: 2,967,900 sq mi (7 686 861 km^2).
Population (1981 est.): 14,800,000.
Chief Cities (March 1980): Canberra, the capital, 241,300; Sydney, 3,193,300; Melbourne, 2,739,700.
Government: *Head of state,* Elizabeth II, queen; represented by Sir Zelman Cowen, governor-general (took office Dec. 1977). *Head of government,* Malcolm Fraser, prime minister (took office Dec. 1975). *Legislature*—Parliament: Senate and House of Representatives.
Monetary Unit: Australian dollar (0.87 A. dollar equals U.S.$1, Nov. 1, 1981).
Manufactures (major products): Mining and transportation equipment, steel, textiles, chemicals.
Agriculture (major products): Livestock, wheat, wool, fruits, sugar, wine grapes, dairy products.

At a refugee camp in Austria, Polish immigrants check the bulletin board for their names. The list identifies persons allowed to leave the camp and start working. The number of Poles asking for asylum in Austria increased by several hundred percent in 1981.

F. Zeitlhofer, Photoreporters

AUSTRIA

The political and economic affairs of Austria were marked by stability in 1981. Still the major transfer point of Soviet Jews immigrating to Israel, Austria also became the center for rapidly increasing numbers of refugees from Poland.

Politics. On Dec. 11, 1980, Hannes Androsch, who had been serving as finance minister for ten years and as vice-chancellor for four years, resigned in the face of attacks for his links with business. In 1981, Androsch became deputy chairman of the Creditanstalt-Bankverein, Austria's largest commercial bank, in which the state holds 60% of the stock.

In reshuffling his cabinet on Jan. 14, 1981, Chancellor Bruno Kreisky named Herbert Salcher, hitherto minister of health and environment, to be minister of finance, and Dr. Alfred Sinowatz, minister of education, to assume the additional post of vice-chancellor. Dr. Kurt Steyer was appointed minister of health and environment.

Economy. The Austrian economy grew at a rate of 3% in 1980, with a slightly lower rate estimated for 1981. Unemployment averaged 2.7% for the first five months of 1981, compared with 2% for the same period in 1980. The balance of trade deficit rose to 90,000,000,000 schillings (about U.S. $6,000,000,000) in 1980, largely because of rising energy costs, especially for oil. Austria imports about 70% of the energy it consumes. Preliminary figures for the first half of 1981 indicated that efforts to cut the trade deficit had met with some success but that imports were still running well ahead of exports.

Foreign Affairs. Austria's law of permanent neutrality does not forbid the sale of arms to countries which are not at war. Nevertheless, after extended debate, the government in the fall of 1980 forbade the sale of 100 tanks to Chile, largely because of human rights abuses in that country. In June 1981, 57 of those tanks were sold to Argentina by the Steyr-Daimler-Puch Co. Including ammunition, the transaction was worth about $180 million.

On May 1, Heinz Mittel, a leading Social Democrat and president of the Austrian-Israeli Friendship League, was assassinated. On August 29, a bomb explosion in a Vienna synagogue killed two persons and injured about 20 others. Both attacks were attributed to the Black June, a Palestinian terrorist group dissident from Yasir Arafat's Palestine Liberation Organization (PLO). Chancellor Kreisky believed the actions were taken to discredit the PLO and Austria's recognition of it.

In 1980, 21,471 Jewish emigrants arrived in Vienna from the Soviet Union and proceeded to Israel and other countries. Austria is also the main haven for refugees from other Communist states. The minister of interior estimated that Austria would spend about $20 million in 1981 to house and feed these refugees, an increase of 300% over 1979. Between Jan. 1 and June 15, 1981, 6,737 persons asked for asylum in Austria, 4,045 of them coming from Poland; these figures represented a three-fold increase over 1980. The Austrian government appealed to the countries in which these refugees wished to settle (mainly Australia, Canada, and the United States), to speed up the immigration process.

ERNST C. HELMREICH
Department of History
Bowdoin College

AUSTRIA • Information Highlights

Official Name: Republic of Austria.
Location: Central Europe.
Area: 32,376 sq mi (83 853 km^2).
Population: (1981 est.): 7,500,000.
Chief Cities (1978 est.): Vienna, the capital, 1,593,000; Graz, 251,000; Linz, 208,000; Salzburg, 138,000.
Government: *Head of state,* Rudolf Kirchschläger, president (took office July 1974). *Head of government,* Bruno Kreisky, chancellor (took office April 1970). *Legislature*—Federal Assembly: Federal Council and National Council.
Monetary Unit: Schilling (15.29 schillings equal U.S.$1, Oct. 1981).
Manufactures (major products): Iron and steel, chemicals, wool and cotton fabrics, fertilizers.
Agriculture (major products): Livestock, dairy products, grains, barley, oats, corn, sugar beets, potatoes.

General Motors

Ford Motor Co.

The 1982 Cavalier, above, a GM J-car, and the Escort, right, a 1982 Ford EXP four-door hatchback, feature front-wheel drive.

AUTOMOBILES

The U.S. automobile industry entered the 1981-model year with high hopes of rebounding from the 1980 slump that brought each of the five producers severe fiscal losses. But car production remained at the previous year's low levels throughout 1981 despite introduction of new, smaller models by each of the Big Three—General Motors, Ford Motor Co., and Chrysler Corp.

In the minds of the buying public, the luster of the restyled cars was dimmed by unabated rises in list prices and interest rates. This led to a phenomenon called "sticker shock" as even fully-equipped subcompact cars carried suggested retail prices above the $10,000 mark. The prime interest rate exceeded 20% in 1981, resulting in sharply increased consumer loan payment terms and keeping some 3 million potential owners of late-model cars out of the market.

The U.S. auto industry built 6,651,345 cars bearing 1981-model designations, little changed from the 1980-model total of 6,696,170. The United States was displaced by Japan as the world's leading car builder in 1980, when Japan's output surpassed the 7 million mark for the first time, and Japan appeared likely to retain its lead for the second year in a row. U.S. truck production, however, did show a modest recovery in the 1981-model year, rising more than 100,000 units from 1980 to 1,341,893.

Chrysler Corp., operating with federally guaranteed loans after a brush with bankruptcy in 1980, and Ford were the only domestic producers to boost output in 1981. Chrysler's gain of 10.6% to 791,258 cars was due largely to brisk sales of some 317,000 new front-wheel-drive K-cars, the Dodge Aries and Plymouth Reliant compacts. Ford managed to lift its 1981-model output by a slight 1.5%, although its sales declined 4.5% despite arrival of its new subcompacts, the Ford Escort and Mercury Lynx, which were joined in the spring of 1981 by two-seater coupes, the EXP and LN7. Ford's production of 1,395,594 cars reflected sales of more than 375,000 cars in the Escort/Lynx family, but at the expense of larger Ford entries.

General Motors suffered a 20.8% production drop in 1981, finishing with 4,147,793 cars.

Chevrolet's decline of 13.9% from 1980 came despite the fact that its lowest-priced models—the Chevette subcompact and the Citation compact—were the top-selling nameplates in 1981. GM's Oldsmobile and Buick divisions increased their sales 7.3% and 8.5%, respectively, but Pontiac fell 5.6% and Cadillac, 4.9%.

Also on the downside were Volkswagen of America and American Motors. VW's domestic Rabbit fell 19.5%, to production of 179,635 cars, while AMC's loss of 20.8%, to 137,125, was offset by launch of car assemblies in Canada.

In addition to Chrysler's K-cars and Ford's Escort/Lynx, the 1981-model year was highlighted by a third small-car introduction—the J-cars from three GM divisions. But the Chevrolet Cavalier, Pontiac J2000, and Cadillac Cimarron fell below forecasts in the second half of the model year as prospective buyers balked at high sticker prices. Born as 1982 models, the J-car trio accounted for about 86,000 sales, only about 60% of forecasts.

Ford also ran into disappointing response to its early-arriving 1982-model pair—the Escort EXP and Lynx LN7. The company predicted that 90,000 of the two-seaters would be sold from April through September, but sales barely exceeded 55,500.

Chevette ousted Citation from the nameplate championship in 1981-model sales, indicative of the market's emphasis on lowest-priced products. Ford Escort was third, followed by the Olds Cutlass Supreme, Chevrolet Malibu, Buick Regal, Ford Fairmont, Chevrolet Impala/Caprice, Olds Cutlass, Buick Skylark, Plymouth Reliant, and Chevrolet Monte Carlo.

The 1982 Models. Fuel efficiency and "downsizing" remained cardinal aims of the U.S. industry. GM issued revamped and smaller versions of two major body groups—the intermediates and the sporty Camaro/Firebird coupes. The A-body intermediates, now with front-wheel drive, arrived as the Chevrolet Celebrity, replacing the Malibu; the Pontiac 6000, succeeding the LeMans; the Olds Cutlass Ciera; and the Buick Century. A V-6 diesel engine was introduced by GM for its new midsize cars, which joined carryover rear-wheel-drive intermediates relabeled the G-body family. Pontiac abandoned the full-size six-seater market, having joined the Chevrolet Chevette segment with its own T-1000 edition early in 1981.

Ford added a four-door sedan to the Escort/Lynx subcompact lineup and reintroduced the Lincoln Continental with a new V-6 engine on a midsize platform. Chrysler Corp. used the K-car base for larger and dressier models, called the Chrysler LeBaron and Dodge 400. Chrysler also dropped its full-size cars in 1981.

WORLD MOTOR VEHICLE DATA, 1980

Country	Passenger Car Production	Truck and Bus Production	Motor Vehicle Registrations
Argentina	218,640	63,153	3,976,721
Australia	316,149	46,287	7,069,900
Austria	7,528	8,533	2,334,041
Belgium	220,441	39,525	3,345,869
Brazil	600,706	564,501	9,200,000
Canada	846,777	527,522	12,892,290
Czechoslovakia	185,088	53,169	2,486,129
France	2,938,581	439,852	21,049,500
East Germany	176,400	37,200	3,145,000
West Germany	3,520,934*	357,481	24,103,651
Hungary	—	16,315	1,029,000
India	30,538	82,788	1,375,988
Italy	1,445,221	166,635	18,360,000
Japan	7,038,108	4,004,776	36,231,013
Mexico	303,056	186,950	4,734,145
Netherlands	80,779	15,656	4,537,000
Poland	351,400	67,100	2,765,800
Portugal	—	182	1,145,000
Rumania	81,600	49,992	360,000
Spain	1,028,813	152,846	8,361,375
Sweden	235,320	63,080	3,058,825
Switzerland	—	1,250	2,325,816
United Kingdom	923,744	389,170	16,866,958
United States	6,375,506	1,634,335	154,118,099**
USSR	1,330,000	867,000	13,500,000
Yugoslavia	240,762	33,391	2,601,906
Total	28,496,091	9,868,689	396,010,675***

*Includes 281,583 micro-buses. **U.S. total includes 120,247,990 cars and 33,870,109 trucks and buses. ***World total includes 309,667,021 cars and 86,343,654 trucks and buses of which 34,966,649 are from nonproducing countries nor shown above. Source: Motor Vehicle Manufacturers Association of the United States, Inc.

DeLorean Motor Company

The DeLorean sports coupe, which was developed by a former executive of General Motors and built in Northern Ireland, was introduced in the United States in 1981. The car, priced at $25,000, is low and available only in silver.

The Imports. Under U.S. pressure, Japan's authorities arranged voluntary reductions in new-car shipments to the United States for 1981-82 and 1982-83. Japanese producers, who had seen their U.S. sales rise steadily up to 1981, now endured a slowdown. The U.S. imported car sales total, as a result, fell to 1,850,776 units in the first nine months of 1981 from 1,869,801 for the comparable period of 1980.

Toyota and Datsun sales decreased in the 1981 period to 459,787 and 368,110, respectively, but Honda rose to 293,379, Mazda to 131,057, and Subaru to 118,619. Record U.S. sales years were posted in 1981 by higher-priced European makes—Volvo, Mercedes-Benz, BMW, and Peugeot. Two new import entries were Japan's Isuzu and the DeLorean sports coupe.

MAYNARD M. GORDON, *"Motor News Analysis"*

AUTOMOBILES—SPECIAL REPORT:

INTERNATIONALIZATION OF THE INDUSTRY

The world's major auto producers forged multinational links as never before during 1981. The trend was motivated by the impact of home-market sales declines on the cash resources required for future development.

At the center of the growing "world-car company" trend were the five domestic automakers in the United States. The U.S. automakers still held the largest national market but were suffering from the fact that 1980 car production slumped from 1979 by more than 2 million units to 6,416,885, while truck output fell nearly 1.5 million units to 1,593,849 vehicles. The 1980 collapse of the U.S. market for domestic vehicles resulted in substantial monetary losses for each of the five producers—General Motors, Ford Motor Co., Chrysler Corp., American Motors, and Volkswagen of America. This, in turn, prompted a rash of 1981 agreements involving the American manufacturers and auto companies in Japan and Western Europe.

Japan's auto industry, enjoying unabated record new-car sales in the United States throughout 1980 and the first half of 1981, was also a principal factor in the establishment of both production and product-development ties with the Americans and the Europeans. The Japanese industry's fervor to sustain high export volume collided with rising protectionist pressure in its main markets, and Japan's ministry of international trade ordered a reduction of 140,000 cars in 1981–82 shipments to the United States, with a potential second-stage cutback in 1982–83.

Faced with a drop in 1981–82 car exports to the United States, from the 1980 record of 1,820,000 to 1,680,000, Japan's auto producers stepped up their efforts to retain American-market shares through cooperative ventures with receptive U.S. car companies. Such compacts also would head off any enactment of local contents laws by the U.S. Congress, urged in mid-1981 by the United Auto Workers to ensure domestic production of high-volume imports.

Before the imposition of voluntary export restraints by the Japanese government, the Japanese manufacturers Nissan and Honda were already committed to construction of U.S. assembly plants. Honda, third largest seller of imported cars in the United States, planned a 1982 start-up of a car assembly plant at Marysville, OH, where it has been assembling motorcycles. Nissan was building a pickup truck plant at Smyrna, TN, for a 1983 launch.

The first foreign automaker to begin U.S. vehicle production was Volkswagen of West Germany. VW's plant at New Stanton, PA, has assembled Rabbit cars since 1978 and Rabbit pickup trucks since 1980. A second VW plant at Sterling Heights, MI, was scheduled to begin operations in late 1982 as an assembler of Rabbit-derived vehicles.

The year 1982 also was expected to see production at American Motors of a new subcompact car designed by AMC's controlling interest, the French state-owned Régie Renault. The car, called the R-9 in Europe, is to be assembled at the AMC plant in Kenosha, WI, as the first product of a joint-production venture involving American and foreign companies.

Renault became the dominant force at AMC in December 1980, after purchasing 46.4% of AMC stock and seating five persons designated by Renault on AMC's board of directors. The French manufacturer, which also has equity interests in Mack Trucks, Inc. and Sweden's Volvo Cars, exercised options in 1981 that could give it approximately 52% of AMC stock.

Joint-venture agreements, rather than Renault-AMC-type takeover arrangements, were the pattern of negotiations affecting other U.S. car producers in 1981. But whichever the form, the intent was the same: to achieve economies in development and production of future vehicles tailored to popular demand. The following are examples of such joint-venture discussions:

1. General Motors and two Japanese automakers, Suzuki and Isuzu, agreed to cooperate in development of minicompacts for world markets, including the United States. Suzuki, a specialist in building so-called "minis" which sell for less than $2,000 and attain up to 55 miles per gallon (23 km/L) sold at 5.3% stock interest to GM. Suzuki swapped small stock interests with Isuzu, in which GM held a 34.2% equity.

Members of the United Auto Workers, demanding a curb on the number of Japanese cars imported to the United States, destroy a Toyota. Japanese officials later imposed such restrictions.

Wide World Photos

2. Ford and Toyota called off year-long talks on a possible joint-venture vehicle to be built in the United States, though the door was held open for a resumption of negotiations at a future date. The two producers were unable to agree on what kind of vehicle to build, and the recess in the discussions left the number one Japanese auto producer without a commitment for a U.S. vehicle assembly plant. Ford did, however, conclude agreements to buy diesel engines from West Germany's BMW for its larger cars and from its Japanese partner, Toyo Kogyo, for its smaller cars and trucks.

3. Chrysler Corp. renewed agreements to buy engines and import cars from Japan's Mitsubishi Motors Corp., in which it holds a minority equity. Chrysler has purchased cars from Mitsubishi since 1970 and uses Mitsubishi engines in its domestic K-cars. In addition, Chrysler and the French auto manufacturer Peugeot signed a letter of intent to develop and build in the United States a new subcompact car for the 1986-model year. Peugeot also would sell Chrysler 450,000 small diesel engines over a five-year period, beginning in the 1984-model year. Chrysler owns 14% of Peugeot stock, an equity that the American company acquired in exchange for sale to Peugeot of its European vehicle assembly plants.

4. Volkswagen of West Germany and Nissan were also pursuing proposals for a joint-venture car—one which could be built by VW's U.S. subsidiary. Reportedly the car was a minicompact to compete with the potential GM-Suzuki product. But VW also was seeking another precedent-setting development as far as Western automakers were concerned—output in Japan of one of VW's own models.

The 1981-model year also saw the introduction of American-made "world cars" as well as world-car companies. Overseas-based vehicle producers have assembled common cars at world locations for many years, but GM and Ford both reinforced their programs for the international market with the introduction of their new front-wheel drive subcompact models at production sites across both the Atlantic and Pacific.

Ford was first with the world-car concept. Ford's domestic Escort and Lynx cars were launched simultaneously in the fall of 1980 in England and West Germany. The GM J-cars made their debut in the spring of 1981 and were earmarked for assembly in Britain, Japan (at Isuzu), and Australia.

Three of America's heavy-duty truck manufacturers were the objects of takeovers or investments by European producers during 1980 and 1981. Renault's purchase of an equity in Mack Trucks was followed by a Daimler-Benz investment in Freightliner and a Volvo takeover of the bankrupt White Motor Corp.

Closer ties also were established between Japanese and European car manufacturers. England's state-owned BL Ltd., formerly British Leyland, agreed to build a Honda-designed car in 1982. It is to be called the Acclaim.

Sweden's Saab and Italy's Lancia were engaged in a joint marketing arrangement of a Lancia model. Italy's Alfa Romeo was tooling up to build a new Nissan car, starting in 1983. The new DeLorean sports coupe, built in Northern Ireland, was powered by a Renault-Peugeot-Volvo V-6 engine manufactured in France.

"The future," as portrayed by Dale E. Dawkins, vice-president of the AMC product group, "is a group of multinational companies—perhaps as many as a dozen—competing against each other on every continent, with North America, Europe, and Japan simply being parts of the whole. . . . The car business is becoming a world-car business at an accelerating and exciting rate."

MAYNARD M. GORDON

BANGLADESH

The assassination of President Ziaur (Zia) Rahman on May 30 shocked the country and left an immediate leadership void. However, the political system he had headed for nearly six years survived his demise, as did his ruling Bangladesh National Party (BNP) and his economic development programs. Corruption, strikes, demonstrations, and tense relations with India remained major items of public concern.

The Assassination. Conspiracies, coups, and political murders are not unusual in Bangladesh. Ziaur Rahman himself rose to power following a series of coups in 1975 and repeated attempts to seize power by politicized elements within the armed forces have resulted in numerous trials and executions of officers and soldiers.

There remained some degree of skepticism and uncertainty concerning the events surrounding Zia's assassination. The president had gone to the port city of Chittagong to settle some factional disputes within the BNP. Shortly after his arrival, he reportedly had a heated argument with Maj. Gen. Mohammad Abdul Manzur, the military commander in the Chittagong area whom Zia had just ordered transferred to Dacca. Manzur and Zia had been freedom fighters together in the 1971 war but, despite their long-term friendship, had developed policy differences. Manzur had reportedly criticized Zia's government for political corruption and for its favoritism of rightist elements who had not participated in the 1971 independence struggle.

According to an official White Paper, Manzur's ambition and arrogance sparked the coup attempt, which took place early on the morning of May 30. However, his actual role in the event is unclear. He reportedly was sleeping when the attack occurred. Several hours after the fact, however, he was accused of having masterminded the plot. When he was captured a couple of days later, he died under mysterious circumstances, supposedly killed by angry soldiers.

Following an investigation, 12 military officers, who had been convicted in a secret court martial, were executed for complicity in the coup attempt. The secrecy of the trial and executions and the severity of the punishment led to a considerable amount of protest.

Other Domestic Developments. Choosing a new president became the major political task following Zia's death. Vice-President Abdus Sattar, 75, became acting president. Although initially reluctant, because of his age and failing health and a constitutional restriction against the candidacy of government officials, Sattar later agreed to become the BNP's candidate in presidential elections. A controversial constitutional amendment removing the restriction was easily passed by the BNP-dominated National Assembly. Although lacking Zia's dynamism and manipulative skills, Sattar was perceived as the BNP candidate most likely to hold together his badly divided party and to win the presidency. The Awami League, also rent by factional divisions, chose Hasina Wajed, the 33-year-old daughter of Sheikh Mujib, as party president in February. Hasina, who had been out of the country when her father and most of her family were killed in 1975 and who had been living in exile in India, returned to Bangladesh in May. Although she was discussed as a likely candidate for the national presidency, the minimum age requirement of 35 and her need for more experience led her to support Kamal Hossein, who had been foreign minister in her father's cabinet. The Awami League initially planned to boycott the election, but decided to contest after the government acceded to most of its demands, including the postponement of the polling date until mid-November.

Among the total of 83 candidates who registered for the November 15 elections, perhaps the most notable was M.A.G. Osmani, the retired general and 1971 war hero who stood against Zia in the June 1978 presidential elections. Both Osmani and the Awami League favor a return to the type of parliamentary system that existed before January 1974 rather than the present strong presidential form of government. Although the Awami League claimed vote fraud, Sattar won the November 15 election.

Economy. Bangladesh remained one of the poorest countries in the world. Zia's attempts to expand agricultural production through mobilization of local *gram sarkars* (village governments) and expanded irrigation were at least partially successful. President Zia noted in April that canal excavation in the countryside had brought 100,000 acres (40 469 ha) under irrigation and that an anticipated 700 additional canals would irrigate between 1.2 and 1.5 million acres (485 623 and 607 028 ha). However, the 1981 World Bank Development Report noted a slump in the country's financial condition and a sharp rise in its balance of payments deficits because of declining jute prices, higher petroleum prices, and a shortfall in commodity aid. In July, the International Monetary Fund suspended a three-year, $912 million loan, given to Bangladesh in late 1980, because of Bangladesh's inability to reduce government spending and food subsidy programs.

BANGLADESH • Information Highlights

Official Name: People's Republic of Bangladesh.
Location: South Asia.
Area: 55,126 sq mi (142 776 km^2).
Population (1981 est.): 92,800,000.
Chief Cities (1974 census): Dacca, the capital, 1,679,-572; Chittagong 889,760; Khulna, 437,304.
Government: *Head of state,* Abdus Sattar, president (elected Nov. 15, 1981). *Head of government,* Shah Azizur Rahman, prime minister (took office April 1979). *Legislature*—Parliament.
Monetary Unit: Taka (18.29 takas equal U.S.$1, July 1981).
Manufactures (major products): Jute goods, textiles, leather, fertilizer.
Agriculture (major products): Rice, jute, tea.

Political uncertainty during the latter half of the year also had adverse economic consequences. In June, Sattar fired two cabinet ministers, including Nurul Islam, the minister of agriculture whom Zia had appointed to achieve food self-sufficiency by 1985. A strike in the six nationalized banks in September resulted in the dismissal of 4,000 bank employees, banning of union activity in the banks, and legal proceedings against union leaders.

Foreign Affairs. Tense relations with India continued to dominate Bangladesh's foreign policy. One cause of friction was a small island, called South Talpatty by Bangladesh, which was believed to have been formed near the Indo-Bangladesh border after the 1970 cyclone and which is claimed by both countries. Other disagreements occurred over boundary and migration problems, and over India's proposal to link the Brahmaputra and Ganges Rivers by means of a canal through Bangladesh. A rift in relations with the Soviet Union occurred in June when customs officers at Dacca Airport seized a consignment of sensitive electronic equipment which the Soviet Embassy was trying to import without Bangladesh approval. Bangladesh continued to seek a wider role in the United Nations and among the community of Islamic states.

WILLIAM L. RICHTER, *South Asia Center*
Kansas State University

BANKING

The year 1981 was one of turmoil and change for the banking industry, as banks and their competitors reacted to the Depository Institutions Deregulation and Monetary Control Act of 1980. The changes that took place all resulted in more competition for the public's business and thus greater benefits for the individual banking customer.

The greatest change in banking was that for the first time since the beginning of the New Deal in 1934, banks throughout the United States could offer interest on checking accounts, through the NOW (Negotiable Order of Withdrawal) accounts. On top of this, the new act began the slow but inexorable trend toward elimination of interest rate ceilings on what the public could earn on its money. Further facilitating the public's financial transactions was the broadening of the powers of savings banks and savings and loan associations to make consumer loans to the public.

But the public had to pay a price for the deregulation, too. For, as savers slowly got a better return on their funds, the financial institutions of necessity had to earn these higher rates. This meant that borrowing costs also rose substantially. This rise in borrowing costs was catalyzed by two developments. First was a federal preemption of usury ceilings under the 1980 Banking Act, which removed limits on borrowing costs in all states that did not specifically mandate usury ceilings through new legislation. Second was the development of variable rates on mortgages and other loans. This occurred because, with credit becoming extremely tight as the Federal Reserve Board fought inflation, banks and thrift organizations had to make rates flexible, so their interest charges could rise and fall with general market rates. Otherwise, banks and thrift organizations would find themselves again locked in with assets whose yields did not match the cost of funds in a high-interest-rate environment.

But this freedom from usury ceilings and the variable rate loans, while helping lenders meet the higher cost of deposits, still was not able to solve the key problem of banks and thrifts: the staggering rise in the public's use of money market funds. Because banks were not allowed to pay top dollar for the public's savings unless the depositor locked his money up for at least several months, people turned to money market funds, which are not regulated and thus can pay top interest, plus allowing immediate withdrawal of money by check or a phone call.

Money market funds grew to more than $150,000,000,000 in 1981, from practically nothing two years earlier. And most banks and savings institutions found that this drain of deposits into money market funds was the most difficult force facing them in 1981.

The loss of deposits, coupled with the high cost of keeping the retained deposits, made the banks and especially the thrifts turn to Washington for help. The result was the enactment of the all-savers provision of the new tax act of 1981. This made a portion of the public's saving in banks and savings institutions tax exempt for the first time. This development helped out banks and thrifts, but it cost the U.S. Treasury a good deal of revenue and put deposit-type institutions in competition with state and local governments for the money normally put into tax-exempt securities. But to the saver, it meant more options for saving than ever before, and as 1981 ended savers well realized that they had become the kingpins of financial institutions. Consequently, borrowers would be paying more for money—a reverse of the procedure of the preceding two decades, under which borrowing rates were kept low by underpaying the saver.

Finally, 1981 also witnessed the dramatic growth of non-bank competition for business formerly the exclusive province of banks and thrifts. Such brokerage firms as Merrill Lynch, Shearson Loeb Rhoades, and Bache, and even such retailers as Sears Roebuck, broadened their diversification into financial services ranging from money market funds to the financing of real-estate transactions. The public was given the option of deposit accounts that offered banking, brokerage, investment of proceeds from home sale, and borrowing for any purpose combined in one account, with funds automatically transferable on the basis of a phone call.

In sum, financial deregulation has meant greater competition in product line offered the public. Additionally, the automatic movement of funds and the growth of automated access to accounts through machines have expanded the geographical territory of individual institutions. All of this gives the saver and borrower more options than ever before, even though it has made life difficult for the institutions relying on tradition and not willing to compete in the new deregulated environment.

Canada. Canada, too, felt the impact of new banking legislation, the Canadian Banking Act of 1980. This act had the main objective of legitimating the presence of foreign banks in Canada. Foreign banks are now allowed to engage in a full array of banking activities, including taking deposits and making loans. The act, however, placed a strict limit on the percentage of Canadian banking that foreign banks can handle and also placed reserve requirements on these foreign organizations. As a result, many foreign banks feel that the real impact of this legislation is to protect Canadian banks and limit the growth of outside banks—growth that had been taking place through such unregulated sectors as leasing and corporate and real-estate financing.

Both the United States and Canada, however, have seen growing efforts of financial institutions to get out of the straitjacket of regulation and provide a full gamut of public services. In time, the result should be that banking and financial service provisions will become much more automatic. The amount of time that customers must take to handle financial affairs should be reduced substantially as the banks and savings institutions and their non-bank competitors seek out new ways to deliver financial service conveniently and cheaply as part of their fight for a growing share of the banking business.

PAUL S. NADLER
Rutgers University

BELGIUM

Continued political instability and mounting economic problems were very much in evidence in Belgium throughout 1981. In December, the country's ninth government in less than eight years and its 32d coalition since World War II was installed. Economic and financial issues had been largely responsible for the downfall of the Wilfried Martens government in the spring and the Mark Eyskens coalition in the autumn. The center-right coalition formed by Martens on December 14 brought together the Social-Christian and Liberal parties, leaving out the Socialists. Martens announced that the new government would seek emergency powers to address the economic problems and take necessary steps without parliament's approval.

First Martens Government. Prime Minister Martens' package of economic measures failed to gain the approval of the Flemish- and French-speaking Social Christian and Socialist parties. Proposals to slash public spending, limit the government payroll, and combat tax evasion were passed in order to reduce the $50,000,000,000 national debt. The austerity program, including a domestic loan issue aimed at channeling back Belgian capital invested abroad tax free, further split the Martens ministry. Cuts in social benefits contributed to party strife, but the primary issues behind the Martens resignation at the end of March were a wage freeze proposal and general wage index reform. The Socialists refused to suspend or modify the automatic coupling of wage increases to rises in consumer prices. The Social-Christians and opposition Liberals agreed with employer organizations that radical reform was needed. Trade union factions within the Socialist parties continued to resist such change, even under the new Eyskens ministry, which was sworn in April 6.

Eyskens Government. Cutting back the public-sector deficit was the main intent of Prime Minister Eyskens, who, like Martens, was a Flemish Social-Christian. His virtually identical coalition government managed to find cuts without touching the index. Small changes in the value-added tax on luxury goods, a "solidarity" tax of 1% on high-income workers, a raise in the income tax for childless families, and altered family allowances all were passed, but the sensitive wage index issue was evaded completely.

On September 21, the 169-day-old Eyskens ministry fell over coalition differences on aid to the steel industry. The Socialist Party withdrew its participation in the coalition when the Cockerill-Sambre Steel Company's request for $300 million for modernization was not satisfactorily resolved. Clearly reflecting the regional, cultural, and linguistic features of Belgian politics, the Socialists (whose major power base is in the francophone industrialized south) supported the company. Cockerill-Sambre, a major industry in the depressed Borinage region of Wallonia, was losing more than $25 million per month. More than $700 million had been poured into the steel industry, and bankers had requested state guarantees of payment before approving additional loans.

BELGIUM • Information Highlights

Official Name: Kingdom of Belgium.
Location: Northwestern Europe.
Area: 11,781 sq mi (30 513 km^2).
Population (1981 est.): 9,900,000.
Chief Cities (1979 est.): Brussels, the capital, 1,008,715; Liège, 220,183; Antwerp, 194,073.
Government: *Head of state,* Baudouin I, king (acceded 1951). *Head of government,* Wilfried Martens, prime minister (formed new government Dec. 1981). *Legislature*—Parliament: Senate and Chamber of Representatives.
Monetary Unit: Franc (38.10 francs equal U.S.$1, Dec. 21, 1981).
Manufactures (major products): Fabricated metal, iron and steel, coal, textiles, chemicals.
Agriculture (major products): Sugar beets, potatoes, grain, tobacco, vegetables, fruits, livestock.

The dispute over assistance to the sagging steel industry not only toppled the coalition but also led to a national election on November 8. Class and ethnolinguistic concerns were most visible, even though the external debates focused on inflation and related economic woes. In the November balloting, the Socialist and Liberal parties both increased their representation in parliament, apparently necessitating a three- or four-party coalition. Beyond the economy, divisive issues were the deployment of U.S. cruise missiles on Belgian soil and the reorganization of the nation into a loose federal system or separate Walloon and Flemish states. The government crisis lasted nearly three months, until Wilfried Martens was finally able to form his new coalition in mid-December.

Economy. State spending competed with rising unemployment throughout 1981. Joblessness increased from 8.8% in 1979 to 13% by the end of 1981; it was the highest rate among the European Community nations and the highest rate in Belgium's history. Social unrest was probably avoided by the government's many expensive unemployment programs, but most observers saw the near absence of retraining programs as a more worrisome feature of the economy.

PIERRE-HENRI LAURENT
Department of History
Tufts University

UPI

Belize's Prime Minister George Price delivers a few remarks as the new nation's flag is raised outside the United Nations building for the first time.

BELIZE

On Sept. 21, 1981, the Republic of Belize, bordering Guatemala, Mexico, and the Caribbean, became an independent state. It occupies less than 9,000 sq mi (23 310 km^2) and contains about 160,000 people, mostly English-speaking blacks, plus a few thousand whites and some 20,000 descendants of the Mayas. The nation's wealth lies in the forest products of chicle and mahogany, plus citrus, sugar, and bananas. The chief port is Belize City (est. population 35,000), formerly the capital. In the early 1970s the capital was moved to the much smaller inland town of Belmopan to escape the fury of tropical storms.

History. Once part of the Mayan empire, this region was explored and conquered by 16th-century Spaniards, but first effectively settled by British buccaneers and log cutters in the 17th century. Spanish troops unsuccessfully attacked the cutters many times in the next two centuries, but finally accepted the settlement in late-18th-century treaties that continued to affirm Spanish sovereignty. When neighboring Guatemala declared its independence from Spain in 1821, it claimed title to Belice (Spanish spelling) by right of inheritance from Spain.

By an 1859 treaty Guatemala recognized British sovereignty in exchange for British construction of a road from the coast to Guatemala City. The road was never built, and ever since the Guatemalans have considered the treaty nullified. Seeking to strengthen their hold, the British in 1862 declared Belize a colony under the name British Honduras. Throughout the next century the colony remained poor. Tensions were frequently heightened by racial and boundary disputes with neighboring Mexico and Guatemala.

About 1950, new nationalistic groups emerged, seeking complete independence from everyone. Chief among these groups was the leftist People's United Party led by George Price, who became prime minister after the colony achieved self-government status within the empire in 1964. Britain has continued to give financial and military aid to Belize.

Independence. In 1981 agreement was reached that Guatemala would recognize the independence of Belize in exchange for highway and pipeline access to the Caribbean through Belize, plus a number of concessions designed to remove tensions and improve the region's prosperity. Independence was celebrated without incident, but Guatemala suddenly retracted its promise to grant recognition and threatened to bring the matter to the United Nations.

The new nation joined the United Nations in late September.

THOMAS L. KARNES
Department of History
Arizona State University

BIOCHEMISTRY

Genetic manipulation, tumor cells, hormones, contraceptive agents, and caffeine were among the areas of interest to biochemists.

Gene Transfer. Researchers at Ohio University succeeded in transferring a gene from rabbits to mice and thence to their offspring. The transferred gene directs the formation of a component of hemoglobin, the oxygen-carrying protein of red blood cells. The technique involved removing egg cells from oviducts of recently mated female mice, injecting the rabbit hemoglobin gene directly into sperm that had already penetrated the egg cell, and implanting the latter in mouse mothers. Some of the resulting mice produced rabbit hemoglobin. Upon mating these mice together, half of the offspring again produced rabbit hemoglobin, indicating that the rabbit gene had been integrated in the genetic make-up of the mice. This technique, therefore, opens the possibility of transferring specific genes into plants and farm animals, and perhaps of inserting functional genes to correct genetic disorders in humans.

Biochemical Cancer Theory. Certain RNA viruses are known to cause normal cells to become cancerous. But how the transformation occurs has remained a mystery. Research has shown that following viral infection, a protein, called protein kinase, is produced in the cell. This kinase is an enzyme that attaches a phosphate group to a tyrosine amino acid residue of certain cell membrane proteins, thereby modifying them. Such a modification leads to changes in the cell skeleton typical of tumor cells.

Not only do the tumor cells have altered cell skeletons, they also have altered metabolism. Specifically, tumor cells have increased rates of glycolysis, which is a relatively inefficient anaerobic pathway by which cells obtain energy from glucose. This observation, first made by Otto Warburg some 50 years ago, has not been adequately explained. In a series of papers, the last of which appeared in *Science* in July 1981, Professor Efraim Racker and his graduate student Mark Spector at Cornell University proposed a biochemical cancer theory that not only explained the so-called Warburg effect but purportedly tied it in with the cell skeleton changes seen in cancer cells.

However, Racker, in a letter to *Science* published in the September 18 issue, partly retracted the theory because of the possibility that some of the experiments may have been doctored. Essentially, what the group had proposed was that in tumor cells the rate of glycolysis is dependent upon the availability of inorganic phosphate (P_i) and adenosine diphosphate (ADP), both of which are produced from adenosine triphosphate (ATP) by an enzyme called adenosine triphosphatase (ATPase). One of the ATPases is located in the cell membrane, where it serves to pump sodium out of the cell. Racker and his colleagues reported that this ATPase in tumor cells is inefficient—that is, it used ATP but pumped little sodium out of the cell. This generated unusually large amounts of ADP and P_i, which in turn stimulated glycolysis. They then found that a tyrosine amino acid of this ATPase protein was phosphorylated, which made it inefficient. Racker confirmed these findings in his September letter to *Science.* However, his group's earlier claim that phosphorylation of the ATPase was controlled by a cascade of kinases, including the same protein kinase that also controlled phosphorylation of the cell membrane proteins causing cell transformation, is in doubt. Studies were under way to clarify the situation.

Hormones. Corticotropin releasing factor is a substance produced in the brain which stimulates the body's master gland, the pituitary, to release hormones needed to cope with stressful situations. Research, however, has been hampered due to the lack of availability of the releasing factor in adequate amounts. In September 1981, scientists at the Salk Institute announced its production in the laboratory. Their synthetic material was as active as the naturally occurring substance. When injected into the brains of rats, it stimulated movement, increased blood pressure, and produced aggressiveness and other characteristics associated with response to stress. Interestingly, the material showed an opposite effect when injected into veins rather than brain—the animal's blood pressure was lowered. Thus, further research might result in the development of a new class of drugs for the treatment of high blood pressure.

Male Contraceptive Pill. Studies in China in the 1950s suggested that gossypol, a substance found in the cotton plant, might be a contraceptive agent in males. Research now shows that it works by blocking an enzyme called lactate dehydrogenase X found only in sperm and testes cells, but seems not to affect sex-hormone levels or libido. Clinical trials began in 1972 and experience to date with 4,000 men shows that gossypol is 99.89% effective. When its use was discontinued, the sperm levels returned to normal. Because there are serious side effects, much research is needed before it might be used as a contraceptive agent.

Caffeine. John Snyder and his colleagues at Johns Hopkins University explained how caffeine in a cup of coffee delivers the well-known stimulating kick. Caffeine works by countering the effects in the brain of a naturally occurring substance called adenosine. Adenosine is a depressant which binds to specific receptors located in the nerve cell membranes and prevents the release of neurotransmitters, the chemicals that carry nerve impulses. It is proposed that caffeine, which is chemically related to adenosine, binds to the same receptors so that adenosine is blocked from binding. The release of neurotransmitters is, therefore, stimulated.

PREM P. BATRA, *Wright State University*

BIOGRAPHY

A selection of profiles of persons prominent in the news during 1981 appears on pages 121–134. The affiliation of the contributor is listed on pages 589–92. Included are sketches of:

Alda, Alan
Blass, Bill
Calvo Sotelo y Bustelo, Leopoldo
Clausen, A(lden) W(inship)
Crippen, Robert Laurel
Cross, Christopher
De Niro, Robert
Duarte, José Napoleón
FitzGerald, Garret
Gretzky, Wayne
Haig, Alexander Meigs, Jr.
Hawn, Goldie
Kirkpatrick, Jeane
Knight, Bobby
Laingen, L(owell) Bruce
Meese, Edwin, III
Michel, Robert Henry
Mitterrand, François
Mubarak, Hosni
O'Connor, Sandra Day
Percy, Walker
Qaddafi, Muammar el-
Reagan, Nancy
Stockman, David Alan
Viola, Roberto Eduardo
Wales, Princess of
Watson, Tom
Watt, James Gaius
Young, John Watts

ALDA, Alan

Alan Alda's writing, directing, and acting talents came in for high praise with the release, in the spring of 1981, of his film *The Four Seasons,* a warm and sensitive comedy in which he and Carol Burnett portray one of three middle-class couples who spend vacations together. *The Four Seasons* is the first of three films that Alda was scheduled to write, direct, and act in under a $20 million contract with Universal Pictures.

Earlier, Alda had written the screenplay for *The Seduction of Joe Tynan* (1979), in which he starred as a liberal U.S. senator.

Alda, best known as the irreverent, woman-chasing Captain Benjamin Franklin ("Hawkeye") Pierce in the popular comedy series *M*A*S*H* about life in a mobile U.S. Army hospital unit during the Korean War, is, according to polls, America's favorite male television star. His contributions to *M*A*S*H*—which has been consistently among the top ten Nielsen-rated programs since its inception in 1972—have earned him four Emmy awards from the National Academy of Television Arts and Sciences, not only as an actor, but also as a writer and director.

Background. Born Alfonso D'Abruzzo in New York City on Jan. 28, 1936, Alan Alda is the son of actor Robert Alda. He spent much of his childhood at the Catskill resorts and the vaudeville and burlesque houses where his father worked as an entertainer. In 1943 he accompanied his family to Hollywood, where Robert Alda landed the role of George Gershwin in the film *Rhapsody in Blue* and obtained a Warner Brothers contract. Not long afterward Alan Alda was stricken with polio, but although his convalescence was long and painful, he recovered completely. In 1950, Alda returned with his family to New York, where his father appeared in the role of Sky Masterson in the Broadway production of *Guys and Dolls*.

After some experience in summer stock, a year of travel and study in Europe, graduation from Fordham University in 1956, and a stint in the U.S. Army Reserves, Alda studied at the Cleveland Playhouse on a Ford Foundation grant. While working as a cab driver and at other jobs between acting assignments, Alda appeared in Off-Broadway plays and television series and demonstrated his flair for satire at the Second City in Chicago and on TV's *This Was the Week That Was.* On Broadway he appeared in *Only in America* (1959), *Purlie Victorious* (1961), *The Owl and The Pussycat* (1964), *Fair Game for Lovers* (1964), and the revue *The Apple Tree* (1966), which earned him a Tony nomination. His screen credits include *Gone Are The Days* (1963), *Paper Lion* (1968), *Mephisto Waltz* (1971), *Same Time Next Year* (1978), *California Suite* (1978), and the TV movies *The Glass House* (1972), *Playmates* (1972), *6 Rms Riv Vu* (1974), and *Kill Me If You Can* (1977). His family situation comedy *We'll Get By* (1975), which he wrote and coproduced, lasted only a few weeks despite some favorable reviews.

Alan Alda, who is imbued with a strong social conscience, is an ardent champion of feminism. Married since 1957 to former concert clarinetist and photographer Arlene Weiss, he has three college-age daughters. He frequently commutes from coast to coast to be with his family.

HENRY S. SLOAN

Schiffman/Liaison

Alan Alda

UPI

Bill Blass

BLASS, Bill

Bill Blass, one of the first American-born designers to achieve international fame, has become even more of a household fashion word since the return of haute couture to the White House with the presence of Nancy Reagan. His fashions, singularly American and original, are synonymous with glamour, created through a superb blend of luxury, good taste, and sophistication. Blass hallmarks are a highly cultivated sense of color and pattern; exquisite attention to detail; and a knack for creating efficient yet feminine day wear, sensual but ladylike evening clothes, and dramatic but non-theatrical ensembles. His clothes reflect a sense of self-assurance, elegance, and intelligence, qualities found among his socially prominent clientele.

Through numerous licensing arrangements his distinctive design sense has been applied to items as varied as jeans and automobile interiors, and his imprint appears on linens, lounge wear, furs, menswear, leather goods, eyeglasses, and fragrance.

Background. William Blass was born on June 22, 1922, in Fort Wayne, IN, the son of Ralph Aldrich Blass and Ethyl Keyser Blass. His fascination with fashion led him to New York after his graduation from Fort Wayne High School in 1939. After studying fashion drawing at the Parsons School of Design, he became a sketcher for the firm of David Crystal, resigning to join the Army at the onset of World War II.

He returned to Seventh Avenue and fashion in 1947, and in 1951 was hired as designer for the New York firm of Anna Miller and Company. In 1959, when the firm merged with Maurice Rentner, Ltd., he remained as designer, becoming a partner in 1961 and vice-president in 1963. In 1970, in recognition of his eminence as a designer, the name of the company was changed to Bill Blass, Ltd., with the designer as president. In 1978 he became sole owner of the firm.

He has received the Coty American Fashion Critics award three times (1961; 1963; and 1970, which elevated him to the Hall of Fame), and in 1971 he received a special citation of overall excellence. Other awards include the Cotton Council Award (1966), the Neiman Marcus Award (1969), the Print Council Award (1972), and the I. Magnin "Great American Designers" Award (1974). In 1973 he was one of five top American designers invited to Paris to show his collection at a gala held at Versailles, and in May 1977 he received an honorary doctorate from the Rhode Island School of Design.

ANN ELKINS

CALVO SOTELO Y BUSTELO, Leopoldo

The sudden resignation in early 1981 of Adolfo Suárez González, who had headed Spain's government for 4½ years, lofted Leopoldo Calvo Sotelo y Bustelo to the premiership and opened a new, unpredictable phase in the country's experiment in democracy.

Mounting social and economic problems had eroded Suárez' base of support. To address these challenges, Calvo Sotelo urged government incentives to create jobs, wage guidelines to combat inflation, and reduced social security taxes to assist businessmen.

Although known as aloof, Calvo Sotelo displayed oratorical prowess, a literate wit, and coolness under fire during a three-day debate on his program. Yet, on February 20 he fell seven votes short of the absolute parliamentary majority required for confirmation. Five days later, on the heels of an abortive coup attempt by civil guards, he won approval as premier.

Background. In contrast to his predecessor, an outsider to Spain's monied establishment, Calvo Sotelo comes from the country's elite. Born on April 14, 1926, into a Madrid family with deep roots in Galicia, a region of the northwest that also produced Generalissimo Francisco Franco and Suárez, Calvo Sotelo grew up in a political environment. The assassination of his uncle, a well-known monarchist, gave impetus to the conspiracy that Franco and fellow officers launched against the Second Republic in 1936.

Calvo Sotelo earned a doctorate after finishing first in his class in the capital's prestigious engineering school. Following a successful career in banking and industry, he was designated president of the national railway system in 1967. Toward the end of the Franco dictatorship, he dabbled in reformist politics as a deputy in the nation's submissive parliament. His support of Prince Juan Carlos' quest for the throne assured good relations with the king.

After Franco's death in 1975, Calvo Sotelo was appointed, successively, commerce minister and public works and town planning minister. He resigned from the cabinet before the June 1977 parliamentary contests—the first free elections in four decades—to organize the triumphant campaign of the Union of the Democratic Center, the country's largest—but now declining—party, which he currently leads.

He proved himself astute and tough-minded as Spain's negotiator for entry into the European Common Market and, later, as deputy premier for economic affairs.

The premier lives in an exclusive Madrid suburb with his wife, Pilar Ibánez Martín Mellado, the daughter of a former education minister, and their eight children.

GEORGE W. GRAYSON

CLAUSEN, A(lden) W(inship)

A. W. ("Tom") Clausen, president and chief executive officer of the San Francisco-based BankAmerica Corporation and its wholly owned subsidiary, the Bank of America, was nominated by President Jimmy Carter on Oct. 30, 1980, as the sixth president of the International Bank for Reconstruction and Development, or World Bank, which is charged with providing development loans for the world's needy nations. He succeeded Robert S. McNamara, who retired in mid-1981. President Carter, who referred to Clausen as "the individual best qualified to continue the bank's strong leadership in the 1980s," made the nomination shortly before the 1980 elections, with the assent of Republican candidate Ronald Reagan, to head off efforts among member nations to name a non-American to the post, which has traditionally been occupied by Americans.

As president of the Bank of America, Clausen headed one of the world's largest commercial banking institutions, with 1,100 California branches and more than 500 offices in 101 countries. Over the years, he acquired a reputation as a champion of the cause of the developing nations, but his positions have at times clashed with official U.S. government policy. As president of the World Bank, Clausen faces a variety of problems amid the ever-growing needs of the developing nations and indications that the U.S. contribution to the bank's financing would be reduced. In a June 1981 interview, Clausen pointed out that it is in the "vested interest" of the United States to support the bank. According to Clausen, if the United States "can help the Third-World countries expand their economies, ours (the U.S.) will also expand."

Background. Born on Feb. 17, 1923, in Hamilton, IL, where his father published the local newspaper, Alden Winship Clausen, who is of Norwegian ancestry, was graduated from Carthage College with a B.A. in 1944. He obtained his LL.B. degree from the University of Minnesota in 1949 and completed the advanced management program at Harvard University in 1966. After joining the Bank of America as a trainee in 1949, he rose rapidly through the executive ranks, advancing to vice-president by 1961 and becoming president and chief executive officer in 1970. Under his leadership, the bank experienced major reorganization and expansion, quadrupling its assets to $111,000,000,000. In 1976, Clausen, a Republican, was offered the post of secretary of the treasury by Jimmy Carter but turned it down for "personal reasons."

Clausen, who is married and has two sons, has been described as a "workaholic" who gives the job "100% plus." He has served as a director of the U.S.-USSR Trade and Economic Council and of the National Council for U.S.-China Trade.

HENRY S. SLOAN

CRIPPEN, Robert Laurel

"What a way to come to California," said astronaut Robert Crippen as space shuttle Columbia approached the California coast at 140,000 ft (42 672 m) altitude, cruising at seven times the speed of sound. He had waited 15 years as an astronaut to make his first space flight as pilot of Columbia with crew commander John W. Young. As the space shuttle Columbia lifted off on April 12, 1981, Crippen expressed his excitement when he exclaimed, "Man, what a view, what a view." Of the intense effort that he and Young had put into preparing for the flight of Columbia he said, "Work is getting to fly airplanes. [This] is enjoyment itself."

At the White House on May 19, Captain Crippen was presented with NASA's Distinguished Service Medal by President Reagan. His citation read, "For distinguished service as pilot of the first orbital test flight of the reusable space shuttle . . . a new generation of spacecraft whose highly successful first flight promises continued U.S. preeminence in space."

Background. Robert Laurel Crippen was born in Beaumont, TX, on Sept. 11, 1937, and grew up in Porter, TX. He was graduated from New Carey High School in New Carey, TX, and received a bachelor of science degree in aerospace engineering from the University of Texas in 1960. He received his commission as a U.S. Navy pilot and spent 2½ years of duty as an attack pilot aboard the aircraft carrier *USS Independence.* He later attended research pilot school at Edwards Air Force Base in California and remained as an instructor until he entered the USAF Manned Orbiting Laboratory Program in 1966. He became a NASA astronaut in 1969 and was a crew member on the successful 56-day Skylab Medical Experiments Altitude Simulation Test. He was also a member of the astronaut support crew for two Skylab missions and the Apollo-Soyuz test project in 1975.

Robert Crippen, his wife Virginia, and their three children, Ellen, Susan, and Linda, live near Houston, TX.

MICHAEL A. CALABRESE

CROSS, Christopher

Singer, songwriter, guitarist, and bandleader Christopher Cross was the surprise fourfold winner at the 23rd Grammy Awards ceremony at Radio City Music Hall in New York City in February 1981. His hit single "Sailing" earned him awards for record of the year and song of the year; his LP *Christopher Cross* was designated album of the year; and he was named the best new artist of the year.

Cross, whose single "Ride like the Wind" was among the best-selling hits of 1980, is noted for his lively guitar style and the lush, sometimes plaintive, folk-rock sound of his melodies, which owe less to the country idiom of his native Texas than to the influence of classical music, jazz, and Broadway show tunes. Reviewing Cross's New York City debut at the Bottom Line in May 1980, a New York *Times* critic, who was not especially inspired by his lyrics, noted that "as a melodist he shines, and his arrangements betray a pop craftsmanship that's already mature."

Background. Christopher Geppert, who adopted the stage name of Cross in 1974, was born May 3, 1951, in San Antonio, TX, the son of an army physician and a nurse. He spent part of his childhood on military bases in Japan and Washington, DC, before moving back to San Antonio. Inspired by the Beatles, Buddy Holly, and Dave Brubeck, he took up the drums at 12 but soon switched to the guitar and later learned to play the bass. At 13 he formed his first band, the Psychos, and in high school he organized another ensemble, the Flash, which occasionally opened local concerts for such groups as Jefferson Airplane and Led Zeppelin. After a two-year stint as a premedical student at San Antonio College, he dropped out in 1972 to pursue music, with his father's encouragement, and moved to Austin, where he and his band eventually became a "living legend." In 1979, Cross, who has written as many as three tunes a day, signed a recording contract with Warner Brothers.

Cross, who is more than 6 ft (1.8 m) tall and weighs more than 200 lbs (91 kg), calls himself conservative in his tastes and something of a loner. With his wife, RoseAnn, and their son, Justin, he lives in Austin.

HENRY S. SLOAN

DE NIRO, Robert

For his dynamic portrayal of Jake La Motta, who mauled his way to the world middleweight championship, in Martin Scorsese's brutally realistic boxing film *Raging Bull*

Robert De Niro

Liaison

(1980), Robert De Niro received the best actor award of the New York Film Critics Circle on Dec. 30, 1980, and of the Academy of Motion Picture Arts and Sciences on March 31, 1981. Frequently tagged as a successor to Marlon Brando, De Niro—whose typical role is that of a man trapped by his environment and trying in vain to escape—had been awarded an Oscar in 1975 as best supporting actor for his portrayal of the young Vito Corleone in *The Godfather II* (1974) and received an Oscar nomination for his performance as a Vietnam war soldier from a small Midwestern town in *The Deer Hunter* (1978). He also won high praise from the critics for his role in *True Confessions*, which was released in 1981.

Earlier, De Niro had been designated best supporting actor by the National Society of Film Critics for his performance as a happy-go-lucky gambler in *Mean Streets* (1973) and by the New York Film Critics Circle for his portrayal of a terminally ill baseball player in *Bang the Drum Slowly* (1973). His forceful performance as a psychotic New York City cabby in Scorsese's *Taxi Driver* (1976) earned him the New York Film Critics' best actor award and firmly established him as a star of major significance. He also won accolades for his portrayal of the scion of a wealthy Italian land-owning family in Bernardo Bertolucci's epic *1900* (1977).

Background. Robert De Niro, an only child, was born on Aug. 17, 1943, in New York City. He grew up in Greenwich Village and on the Lower East Side. His father is an abstract expressionist painter and sculptor. A high-school dropout, Robert began at the age of 16 to take acting classes with Stella Adler. He also studied with Lee Strasberg. After appearing in various Off-Broadway plays and workshop productions, De Niro made his motion-picture debut in director Brian De Palma's underground film *Greetings* (1968) and also gave creditable performances in *The Wedding Party* (1969) and *Hi, Mom!* (1970). Other films in which he appeared include *Jennifer on My Mind* (1971), *Bloody Mama* (1971), *Born to Win* (1971), *The Gang That Couldn't Shoot Straight* (1971), *The Last Tycoon* (1976), and *New York, New York* (1977).

De Niro takes his acting very seriously and is selective about the roles he accepts. He does not rehearse but prefers to work out his scenes during the filming. Married since 1976 to actress Diahnne Abbot, he jealously guards his privacy.

HENRY S. SLOAN

DUARTE, José Napoleón

UPI

José Napoleón Duarte

Rarely has a Latin American leader faced problems as complex as those of José Napoleón Duarte, president of the junta ruling El Salvador since December 1980. Amid kidnappings, assassinations, and civil war in 1981, Duarte clung to office without ever having the complete support of the military, business, or labor.

Duarte believes that El Salvador wages civil war because a few people are very rich and so many people have nothing, and for 50 years the situation has not improved. Now the poor are demanding change; the rich, aided by the military, fight back, and violence escalates, even to the point of kidnapping and murder.

Duarte's measures for gradual change include an ambitious land-redistribution program and substantial tax reform. He opposes the traditionally heavy reliance upon export crops and seeks as much as $300,000,000 in aid for industrial development and the creation of jobs that for the first time might provide an adequate domestic market. His foreign policy opposes both communism and U.S. military intervention. He considers himself a good friend of the United States.

Background. Duarte was born into a family of moderate means in San Salvador in 1926, was graduated from high school in 1944 and from the University of Notre Dame in South Bend, IN, in 1948. Back home again, he married the daughter of a local businessman and engaged in some teaching and engineering. He took little part in politics until 1960, when he helped form the Christian Democratic Party. Locally very popular, he served as mayor of San Salvador from 1964 until 1970. His achievements in collecting taxes, paying off old debts, remodeling the public markets, and controlling utilities brought him national attention.

In 1972 he was nominated for president by a coalition opposing the governing National Party. In the face of considerable harassment he campaigned ceaselessly and may have won, but the government declared him the loser. Declining supporters' suggestions of a rebellion, he began seven years of voluntary exile, mostly in Venezuela. He returned home in 1979 to be greeted by 100,000 followers just as his nation disintegrated. President Carlos Humberto Romero was forced out of office by the military, which ultimately asked for Duarte's participation in a junta composed of civilians and army officers. By December 1980 he was president of that body. Throughout 1981 he was battered by elements of both political extremes who would like to force him out.

THOMAS L. KARNES

FITZGERALD, Garret

On June 30, 1981, Garret FitzGerald was elected prime minister of Ireland, as a coalition of the Fine Gael and Labour parties won a vote of confidence in the Dail, the lower house of parliament, by the slender margin of 81 to 78 votes. In the general election on June 11, FitzGerald's Fine Gael party had won only 65 seats, compared with 78 for Fianna Fail. FitzGerald negotiated with the Labour Party, led by Michael O'Leary, as well as several independent deputies, and thereby formed the coalition approved by the Dail.

An intellectual with a degree in economics, a pragmatist who talks at times like an idealist, the new prime minister, or Taoiseach, is regarded as having one of the sharpest and most analytical minds in Irish politics. FitzGerald has won wide respect for his honesty and his commitment to improving the condition of his countrymen. Essentially a moderate with both liberal and conservative leanings, he has expressed his determination to restore vitality to the Irish economy and to discourage violence as an instrument of political change. Upon taking office, he announced that his government's two main priorities would be to resolve the crisis over hunger strikes by Irish Republican Army (IRA) prisoners in the north and to repair the damage to the economy from inflation and overspending by the government.

Background. Born in Dublin on Feb. 9, 1926, Garret Michael Desmond FitzGerald is the son of the late Desmond FitzGerald, a prominent member of the Irish Free State government during the 1920s. His mother, Mabel McConnell, came from a northern Presbyterian family with strong sympathy for the republican cause. After schooling at Belvedere College in Dublin, FitzGerald studied history and modern languages at University College, Dublin and then read law at King's Inn. From 1947 to 1958 he worked as research and schedules manager at Aer Lingus and then returned to University College, where he lectured on economics from 1959 to 1973. During the 1960s he wrote a popular column in the *Irish Times* on contemporary issues and events.

FitzGerald's reputation as a pundit helped him gain a seat in the Senate, or upper house, in 1965. Four years later he won election to the Dail, representing southeast Dublin. He soon earned the confidence of the Fine Gael leadership and joined the inner circle of the party. When Liam Cosgrave formed his coalition government in March 1973, FitzGerald became minister of foreign affairs, the very office his father had held almost 50 years before. FitzGerald proved an able and energetic diplomat as well as cabinet member. He worked to ensure Ireland's entry into the Common Market, and was honored for his efforts by serving as president of the council of ministers for the European Economic Community (EEC) from January to June 1975.

After the defeat of Liam Cosgrave's government in June 1977, Garrett FitzGerald took over the leadership of the Fine Gael and set about improving the party's organization.

L. PERRY CURTIS, JR.

GRETZKY, Wayne

Wayne Gretzky, who had earned the nickname "The Great Gretzky" even before his first professional hockey game, had one of the greatest seasons in National Hockey League (NHL) history in 1980–81. The 20-year-old center for the Edmonton Oilers established new records for most points (164) and most assists (109) in a single season, while capturing the league's most valuable player award for the second straight season.

Gretzky's statistics were staggering. His point total of 164 shattered the previous record of 152 set by Phil Esposito in 1970–71; Esposito's record was once thought to be unbeatable. Gretzky became the first NHL player to average two points per game. His closest rival for the league's scoring title, Marcel Dionne of Los Angeles, had 29 fewer points; his closest challenger for team scoring leader had 89 fewer. Gretzky's 109 assists broke the record of 102 set by Boston's Bobby Orr in 1970–71. During the regular season, only five NHL players had as many total points as Gretzky had assists. His 55 goals gave him a total of 106 in only two NHL seasons.

Background. Although Gretzky's success in 1980–81 was stunning, it was nothing new to him. He had begun playing hockey at age two on a rink in his backyard in Brantford, Ont. By his early teens, Gretzky was a childhood star in Canada. In 1978, at age 17, he entered the World Hockey Association (WHA); his 46 goals and 110 points for the Oilers earned him rookie-of-the-year honors. In 1979–80, the WHA folded, Edmonton was absorbed into the NHL, and Gretzky continued to star. In his first NHL season, he led the league with 86 assists, tied Marcel Dionne for the scoring title with 137 points, and was named most valuable player. Despite his size, 5′11″ (1.80 m) and 165 lbs. (75 kg), Gretzky's quickness and intelligence promise to make him one of the NHL's all-time greats.

Not only is Gretzky one of the most highly skilled athletes in the United States and Canada, but he is also one of the highest paid. His lucrative 20-year contract with Edmonton is the longest ever signed by a professional athlete in North America. The number on his jersey—99—indicates the year his contract expires.

PAT CALABRIA

HAIG, Alexander Meigs, Jr.

Alexander Haig, a former career military officer and chief of the White House staff during the final days of the Nixon administration, became U.S. secretary of state early in 1981. President-elect Ronald Reagan had selected the former general for the top Cabinet post "because of the respect he has, and is held in, by foreign leaders, particularly in Europe, his knowledge of world affairs, his integrity." After Haig testified before the Senate Foreign Relations Committee for some 30 hours, his appointment was confirmed, 93-6, by the full Senate on Jan. 21, 1981.

Relevant to his appointment as secretary of state, Haig had served on the inner White House foreign relations team—as military adviser to Henry Kissinger and as deputy assistant to the president for national security affairs. In the latter capacity he briefed President Nixon on security conditions throughout the world, managed National Security Council documents, undertook several missions to Vietnam to provide the president with personal assessments, headed the White House advance party to prepare for the president's visit to Communist China, and assisted Kissinger in Vietnam peace negotiations.

Appearing before the Congressional committees in mid-March 1981, the new U.S. foreign minister said that in the 1980s the United States was confronted with three foreign-policy trends: the additional spread of power among many nations, some of which are against the use of force;

Alexander Meigs Haig, Jr.

UPI

increased international turbulence and violent change; and the Soviet ability to foster "an imperial foreign policy" through its increased military power. During his initial months in office, the secretary toured the Middle East, attended the NATO ministerial meeting, and discussed the export of American technological goods with Chinese leaders in Peking.

Secretary Haig was quoted in the media as having a "lack of enthusiasm" when Vice-President George Bush and not Haig was named director of the administration's "crisis management" team. The former general came under fire immediately following the attempt on the president's life, when the secretary announced at the White House that "As of now, I am in control here . . . pending return of the vice-president." The remark stirred controversy since it represented the immediate though temporary functioning of the National Security Council and did not fully take into account the constitutional order of presidential succession.

Background. Alexander Meigs Haig, Jr., was born in Philadelphia on Dec. 2, 1924. Following a year at Notre Dame University, he was appointed to the U.S. Military Academy, from which he was graduated in 1947. During the following quarter century he advanced rapidly through the military ranks and was promoted to four-star general in 1973. In the meantime, continuing his education, he took advanced courses at Columbia University, was graduated from the Naval War College, and received an M.A. degree in international relations from Georgetown University.

Haig served in combat assignments in Korea and Vietnam, in staff posts in Tokyo and at the Pentagon, and in academic positions at the military and naval academies. Later he held high-level staff and command positions in the Defense Department, and capped his military career as commander-in-chief of U.S. Forces in Europe and as NATO commander (1974–78). After leaving the military, Haig became president of the United Technologies Corporation.

He is married to the former Patricia Fox, the daughter of a former senior Army officer. They are the parents of three grown children. The former general underwent open heart surgery in April 1980.

It is acknowledged that he is hard-working, serious-minded, and demanding of those working with him.

ELMER PLISCHKE

HAWN, Goldie

© 1981 Sipa Press/Black Star

Goldie Hawn

Remembered as the lovable, scatterbrained blonde of Rowan and Martin's popular television series *Laugh-In* and as the star of such Hollywood films as *Cactus Flower*, Goldie Hawn came into her own at the production end of the motion-picture industry as executive producer of the $10-million film *Private Benjamin*, one of the top box-office hits of 1980–81. In that movie she plays a "Jewish-American princess" turned soldier. Miss Hawn, whose combination of humor, sex appeal, intelligence, and an indefinable inner quality ranks her with Judy Holliday and Carole Lombard as one of the great comediennes of the screen, was involved in virtually every aspect of the production of *Private Benjamin*, working as much as 14 hours a day with director Howard Zieff.

Her other hit of the season—in which she starred but had no hand in the production—was Neil Simon's film comedy *Seems Like Old Times* (1980), directed by Jay Sandrich. In it she portrays an idealistic lawyer involved in a love triangle with her present husband and her former spouse, played by Chevy Chase, who had appeared with her in the hit *Foul Play* (1978).

Early in 1981 Miss Hawn shared honors in a television special with her friend Liza Minnelli, with whom she hopes eventually to team up for a film version of the Broadway hit *Chicago*.

Background. Goldie Jeanne Hawn, who was born on Nov. 21, 1945, in Washington, DC, and grew up in the suburb of Takoma Park, MD, is the younger daughter of a Jewish mother and a Presbyterian father, a descendant of one of the signers of the Declaration of Independence who earned his living as a musician. Encouraged by her parents, Goldie studied dancing from the age of three and made her professional acting debut at 17 as Juliet with the Virginia Stage Company. After studying drama for three semesters at American University while operating her own dancing school, she appeared as a can-can dancer at the 1964-65 New York World's Fair, worked as a go-go dancer and chorus girl in New York City and Las Vegas, and performed in summer stock.

She made her television debut in 1967 in the chorus of an Andy Griffith special and appeared in a supporting role in the short-lived situation comedy *Good Morning, World* before auditioning for Dan Rowan and Dick Martin's zany comedy hit show *Laugh-In*. Her wide-eyed, innocent gamine quality impressed producer George Schlatter, who made her inadvertent fluffing of lines a regular feature of her performance; she was one of the most beloved of the *Laugh-In* regulars (1968–70).

After making her film debut in a small role in a Walt Disney production, Goldie Hawn was cast in the film version of the Broadway comedy *Cactus Flower* (1969) as the waif-like paramour of middle-aged dentist Walter Matthau. She won an Academy Award as best supporting actress. Her other films include *There's a Girl in My Soup* (1970), *Dollars* (1971), *Butterflies are Free* (1971), *The Sugarland Express* (1974), *The Girl From Petrovka* (1974), *Shampoo* (1975) and *The Duchess and the Dirtwater Fox* (1976).

Miss Hawn, whose marriages to actor-producer Gus Trikonis and musician Bill Hudson ended in divorce, spends as much time as she can with her children, Oliver and Kate.

HENRY S. SLOAN

KIRKPATRICK, Jeane

In a magazine article entitled "Dictatorships and Double Standards" (*Commentary*, November 1979), Jeane Kirkpatrick, a political science professor and active Democrat, voiced strong opposition to the human-rights campaign of President Jimmy Carter. "The failure of the Carter administration's foreign policy," she began, "is now clear to everyone except its architects." The article contended that American interests were being damaged by the administration's failure to differentiate Communist "totalitarian" dictatorships from the right-wing "authoritarian" regimes that deserve U.S. support. Kirkpatrick's article also served as the stepping stone from which the 54-year-old academic became the highest-ranking woman—and Democrat—in the Reagan administration. Candidate Reagan had read the piece, liked it, and invited Kirkpatrick to join his cabinet as ambassador to the United Nations.

Since taking the job in February 1981, Kirkpatrick has been a force of great influence within the Reagan cabinet and National Security Council, as well as a center of controversy at the UN. Her human rights thesis has been adopted as official U.S. policy, and her views on Latin America—advocating military aid for right-wing governments battling leftist guerrillas—have become the basis of Reagan policy there. Both positions have made her the focus of criticism from human-rights advocates.

Another controversy arose when she met with a group of South African military intelligence officers posing as diplomats, and vetoed three UN resolutions against South Africa. Initial complaints about her inflexibility and inability to deal with Third World diplomats were eased when she worked out a compromise resolution with Iraq that condemned Israel for its June attack on an Iraqi nuclear plant. The final resolution did not impose sanctions, thereby averting a U.S. veto. The triumph won a personal commendation from President Reagan.

Background. Jeane Duane Jordan was born on Nov. 19, 1926, in Duncan, OK, and grew up in Mt. Vernon, IL, two towns in which her father worked as an oil wildcatter. She was graduated from Barnard College and obtained her M.A. (1950) and Ph.D. (1968) degrees in political science from Columbia University. In 1955, she married fellow academic Evron Kirkpatrick, who would become the long-time executive director of the American Political Science Association. After rearing their three sons, Mrs. Kirkpatrick returned to academics and Democratic politics. She taught political science at Georgetown University from 1967 until her UN appointment, served as resident scholar at the American Enterprise Institute, and helped form the neoconservative Coalition for a Democratic Majority in 1972.

MICHAEL J. BERLIN

Jeane Kirkpatrick

UPI

KNIGHT, Bobby

He carries controversy with him like an untreatable case of dandruff, but even the severest critics of Bobby Knight would agree that he is the preeminent coach in college basketball today. He proved it again by guiding his Indiana University Hoosiers to the 1980–81 National Collegiate Athletic Association (NCAA) championship.

Indiana's triumph was a typical Knight production. He took a team that was not expected to be particularly strong—and in fact lost seven of its first 17 games—and drilled and cajoled it to near perfection. If Knight himself did not go through the NCAA tournament without incident—his altercation with a fan in a coffee shop made headlines from the NCAA finals in Philadelphia—his team did. Indiana did not have a close game. Its 63–50 win over North Carolina in the championship game represented its narrowest margin of victory.

Background. Robert Montgomery Knight, an only child, was born on Oct. 5, 1940. The son of a railroad worker, he grew up in Orrville, OH, and played basketball at Ohio State. He was overshadowed there by John Havlicek and Jerry Lucas, among others, but still contributed to Ohio State's three Big Ten titles and its NCAA championship in 1960. He was known as a roll-on-the-floor competitor and a student of the game. After college, Knight became an assistant high school coach at Cuyoga Falls, OH, and a year later an assistant at the U.S. Military Academy. In 1965, at age 24, he was appointed head coach.

Knight coached for six years at West Point, bringing his teams to postseason tournaments four times. His squads were known for their patience and defense tenaciousness. At Indiana, where he took over in 1972, Knight added the defensive toughness of Army to the fast-moving talent of a long-time collegiate power. His teams won the NCAA title in 1976 with a 32–0 record, captured the NIT in 1979, and in ten years won six Big Ten titles.

In 1979, Knight was also the coach of the U.S. team at the Pan-American Games in Puerto Rico. It was another typical performance. He had a highly publicized fight with a local security guard, and his team won the gold medal.

LEIGH MONTVILLE

LAINGEN, L(owell) Bruce

The top-ranking diplomat among the 52 American hostages freed on Jan. 20, 1981, after 444 days in captivity in Iran, L. Bruce Laingen had been serving as chargé d'affaires at the U.S. embassy in Tehran at the time of its takeover by student militants demanding extradition of the deposed shah. A 30-year veteran of the foreign service, Laingen had gone to Tehran in June 1979 to take over the duties of outgoing Ambassador William H. Sullivan and had been slated to become the new U.S. ambassador to Iran. In the months before the crisis, Laingen had tried to restore the sagging morale of the embassy staff and to establish rapport with the revolutionary regime of the Ayatollah Ruhollah Khomeini. His communications with the State Department during that period reflect an understanding of the Iranian mentality and a degree of sympathy for the aims of the Islamic revolution.

At the time of the embassy seizure on Nov. 4, 1979, Laingen and two aides were at the Iranian foreign ministry, where they remained during most of the crisis, out of touch with the other hostages. From his captivity, Laingen managed to send several inspirational and optimistic messages to his family and the State Department.

Freed, along with the other hostages, after the United States agreed to return $8,000,000,000 in frozen assets to Iran, Laingen went home to a tumultuous welcome. In an address at the White House on Jan. 27, 1981, he called the families of the hostages the "real heroes" of the crisis. In the months following his release, he spoke on patriotism to audiences across the nation. He also became vice-president of the National Defense University.

Background. Lowell Bruce Laingen, whose ancestors immigrated to the United States from Norway, was born on Aug. 6, 1922, in Odin Township, MN, and grew up in a rural environment. After World War II service as a naval officer in the Philippines, he was graduated with a B.A. degree, cum laude, from St. Olaf College in 1947. He obtained a masters degree in international relations from the University of Minnesota in 1949. Laingen joined the U.S. foreign service in 1950, specializing in Middle Eastern, Mediterranean, and South Asian affairs, and served in diplomatic posts in West Germany, Iran, Pakistan, and Afghanistan before becoming ambassador to Malta (1976–78). He also served in State Department positions.

Laingen, who has been described as "an idealistic, dedicated career servant," is married and has three sons. He enjoys gardening and skiing.

HENRY S. SLOAN

MEESE, Edwin, III

The key to Ronald Reagan's White House is teamwork, and the captain of the team is an affable former law-school professor with a reputation for never losing his temper. In fact, Edwin Meese III has been called affable so often in print that his colleagues kid him about it. As the chief counsellor to President Reagan, Meese coordinates the development of both domestic and foreign policy, ensuring the collegial approach to decision-making that Reagan favors. Meese is a member of the so-called "Big Three," with Chief of Staff James A. Baker III and Deputy Chief of Staff Michael K. Deaver. Together they form the management nucleus of the Reagan White House. When it comes to policy, however, Meese is preeminent. The only one of the three to hold Cabinet rank, he is known variously as the prime minister, deputy president, and even "Saint Meese," as in "The Gospel According to Saint Meese." He shares Reagan's conservative philosophy and, when shaping policy, is especially mindful of adhering to Reagan's long-held campaign commitments.

Meese takes a special interest in law and order matters, keeping a prized collection of miniature pigs to mock would-be detractors of the nation's police. He stirred controversy with his remark that the American Civil Liberties Union and other similar organizations had come together in "what might be described as a criminals' lobby" because of their zeal in protecting the rights of wrongdoers. Meese was instrumental in Reagan's pardon of two FBI agents convicted of authorizing illegal break-ins during the Nixon administration's crackdown on antiwar activists.

Edwin Meese III

UPI

Background. Edwin Meese III was born in Oakland, CA, on Dec. 2, 1931. He attended Yale on a scholarship, graduating in 1953. He obtained a law degree from the University of California at Berkeley in 1958. After serving as deputy district attorney of Alameda County, CA, he joined Reagan's staff in 1969, having caught the then-governor's eye by his tough approach to campus disorders. Meese soon became chief of staff, his passion for organization very evident. "My wife jokes I need management charts for bedtime reading," he says.

In between his services to Reagan, Meese was a vice-president of Rohr Industries, Inc., an aerospace firm in Chula Vista, CA. He taught law at the University of San Diego, heading the school's Center for Criminal Justice Policy and Management. He was a top adviser in Reagan's 1980 presidential drive. Meese retired in 1980 as a lieutenant colonel in the Army Reserve.

The presidential counsellor is married to his childhood sweetheart, Ursula Herrick, and has three children. The oldest, Michael, is a 1981 graduate of West Point.

ELEANOR CLIFT

MICHEL, Robert Henry

When Ronald Reagan won his first significant budget vote in the House of Representatives, he did it with the help of a number of southern Democrats. But that is not what impressed a top aide of House Speaker Thomas P. "Tip" O'Neill. Congratulating Reagan's men on their victory, the envious Democrat confessed that what amazed him more was that there was not a single Republican defection. Credit for that unity belongs in large part to the careful work of House Minority Leader Robert H. Michel, a veteran of 24 years' experience in the give-and-take bargaining of congressional politics.

"The measure of our success will be how well we harmonize," Michel declared when he beat out Guy Vander Jagt (R-MI) for the prestigious job of Republican leader. The contrast between the two congressmen could not have been more stark. Vander Jagt, a gifted orator with a flair for media politics, had won his colleagues' admiration by his effective stumping on their behalf in the 1980 election. Michel, on the other hand, a keen parliamentarian known for his skill at cutting deals, was seen as the man most able to get Reagan's programs through the House. In the end, Republican congressmen voted 103 to 87 for the "workhorse" over the "showhorse."

Michel's credentials in the House go back even further than his twelve terms as the congressman from the 18th district in Illinois. The son of a French immigrant factory worker, he began his legislative career right out of college in 1949 as the administrative assistant to his predecessor, Rep. Harold Velde. When Velde left office in 1956, Michel successfully jumped into the race to replace him and, with the exception of the 1964 Goldwater debacle, has won reelection by wide margins since.

Michel earned his spurs on the Appropriations Committee, where he gained a reputation for pushing economies regardless of political sensitivities. He once said his goal as a congressman was "saving the taxpayers a few bucks." When the Peoria public schools qualified for federal "impact aid," a program Michel opposed, he wrote a letter to the system's officials to register his opposition.

Background. Robert Henry Michel was born in Peoria on March 2, 1923. He attended Bradley University, graduating in 1948 with a degree in business administration. A combat infantryman in World War II, he was wounded by machine-gun fire and discharged with the Bronze Star, Purple Heart, and four battle stars. He has been elected to the 85th through 97th congresses, serving since 1974 as his party's floor whip before being elected minority leader in December 1980.

Michel is married and has four children. His avocation is singing.

ELEANOR CLIFT

MITTERRAND, François

The new president of France has a quality that even his enemies cannot deny: perseverance. In spite of many setbacks and disappointments during his 37 years in politics, François Mitterrand has shown a remarkable fitness to start again. On May 10, 1981, he reversed a generation-long trend in French politics by being elected the first left-wing president since Charles de Gaulle founded the Fifth Republic in 1958. The victory for the Socialist Party attested to the political skill of its leader. A typical representative of the French bourgeoisie, inclined to a somewhat literary and romantic socialism, Mitterrand managed to establish and maintain an alliance with the Communist Party, even though the rise of his own party came at the Communists' expense.

Background. François Mitterrand was born on Oct. 26, 1916, in Jarnac, a small town in the Cognac country of southwestern France. After studies in law and literature at the University of Paris, he served in the army during World War II. In 1940, he was wounded and captured by the Germans, but he escaped to Vichy, where he eventually joined the French resistance movement. After the war he married another resistance fighter, Danielle Gouze, and today they have two grown sons, Jean-Christophe and Gilbert.

Although General de Gaulle appointed him secretary general for war prisoners, Mitterrand hesitated between careers in journalism and politics. Choosing the latter, he helped found the small Union of Democratic Socialist Republicans in 1946 and was elected to the National Assembly. From 1947 to 1957, he held several government posts in various cabinets of the Fourth Republic. In 1958 he was among the parliamentarians who refused to invest De Gaulle as prime minister, and he lost his seat. His political career seemed over.

Nevertheless, in 1965, he stood as the leftist candidate for the presidency against De Gaulle. He ran well, but lost. He was still a natural leader of the non-Communist left, which he spared no effort to strengthen. He concluded an agreement with the Communists that hurt the Gaullists in 1967 parliamentary elections. However, fresh elections in June 1968, when France was confronted with violent student uprisings, were a tremendous success for the Gaullists, and Mitterrand barely managed to keep his seat.

Apparently not discouraged by the turn of events, he worked to make the Socialist Party, of which he became first secretary in 1971, a more powerful organization, able to counterbalance the Communists. In 1972 he signed an agreement with them called the Common Program of Government, and again in 1974 he was the leftist candidate for the presidency, this time against center-right leader Valéry Giscard d'Estaing. Mitterrand was defeated on the second ballot by only 400,000 votes. Many felt that he had lost his chance to become the president of France, that he would be too old to run again in 1981. Despite the air of confidence with which he announced his candidacy, even Mitterrand must have been surprised by the magnitude of his victory.

See FRANCE.

MONIQUE MADIER

MUBARAK, Hosni

Hosni Mubarak of Egypt, who on Oct. 13, 1981 was elected to succeed slain President Anwar el-Sadat, owed his advancement through the military and political ranks to the favor of his predecessor. Like Sadat to *his* predecessor, Gamal Abdel Nasser, Mubarak was the president's protégé and closest adviser. And like Sadat in 1970, Mubarak at the moment of his accession to power is something of an unknown quantity. But because he was "made" by Sadat, there is reason to presume a substantial identity of views.

Background. Like Sadat, Mohammed Hosni Said Mubarak was born in a village of the Nile Delta province of Minufiya; the year was 1928. He was graduated from the Egyptian military academy in 1949 and from the air academy in 1950. He completed his training as a fighter pilot in the 1950s by taking courses at the Soviet Union's military academy. This was the normal culmination of the education of promising young Egyptian officers in Nasser's days. There is no evidence that Mubarak's three separate stays in the USSR produced in him a liking for the Soviet system—far from it. He has the reputation for being one of the Egyptian leaders most favorably disposed toward the United States.

Gamma-Liaison

Hosni Mubarak

Rapid progress in his career as an air force officer testified to Mubarak's ability. In 1964 he led a military mission to the Soviet Union. He was appointed base commander of the Cairo West airfield in January 1966 and director of the Air Force Academy in 1967. Only two years later, at age 41, he became chief of staff of the Egyptian air force and was advanced to flag rank as air vice-marshal. In April 1972, President Sadat made him commander of the air force. As commander, Mubarak entirely and efficiently reorganized the nation's air force, which had been largely destroyed at the onset of the 1967 Six-Day War with Israel. The result was the good showing of the air force in the Yom Kippur War of 1973, from which Mubarak emerged a national hero. His success earned him a promotion to air marshall in 1974. On April 15, 1975, Sadat named him his vice-president, and from then on no one was closer to the president. The most loyal of subordinates, Mubarak remained in Sadat's shadow.

Appointing him vice-president, Sadat said: "We want a new generation to step forward to the country's leadership." Mubarak was entrusted with innumerable special diplomatic missions to Western Europe, other Arab countries, and the United States. He was in Washington conferring with U.S. Secretary of State Alexander Haig only three days before Sadat's assassination. Although Mubarak had never visited Israel, he participated in the Camp David diplomacy and met Israeli President Menahem Begin more than once.

Hosni Mubarak is married, with two grown sons. His wife Suzy has a degree in anthropology from the American University in Cairo. Less mercurial than Sadat, Mubarak is a quiet and direct man, apparently with a considerable reserve of inner strength. He displays the tranquility of a successful commanding general. These attributes he is likely to need in his new and more demanding post.

See EGYPT.

ARTHUR CAMPBELL TURNER

UPI

Sandra Day O'Connor

O'CONNOR, Sandra Day

On July 7, 1981, President Ronald Reagan announced that he would nominate Sandra Day O'Connor, 51, for the position of associate justice of the United States Supreme Court. A judge of the Arizona Court of Appeals, O'Connor was named to succeed Associate Justice Potter Stewart, who had retired at the end of the 1981 term. After unanimous (99–0) confirmation by the Senate on September 21, she took the oath of office to become the 102nd member of the U.S. Supreme Court. She is also the first woman ever to sit on the nation's highest tribunal.

Justice O'Connor had been active in Arizona Republican politics and the state judiciary. She had held the office of assistant state attorney general and was a member for two terms of the Arizona senate, where she was the first woman to be chosen majority leader. She was elected to the Superior Court of Maricopa County in 1974 and appointed by Gov. Bruce Babbitt, a Democrat, to the state Court of Appeals in 1979.

In submitting her name to the Senate, President Reagan praised O'Connor as "possessing those unique qualities of temperament, fairness, intellectual capacity, and devotion to the public good which have characterized the 101 brethren who have preceded her."

Background. Sandra Day O'Connor was born on March 26, 1930, in Duncan, AZ, where she grew up on a ranch. She was graduated from Stanford University in 1950 and from Stanford Law School two years later. Justice William H. Rehnquist was in the same class; he ranked first and she third. Also in the same class was John Jay O'Connor III, whom she married in 1952. Today they have three sons.

In replacing Justice Stewart on the Supreme Court, O'Connor seemed unlikely to cause any substantial shift in the court's constitutional views. Stewart had generally been near the court's center, tending to reach decisions on the basis of facts and precedents rather than on social or economic philosophy. In the Arizona legislature, O'Connor had compiled a record of mainstream, pragmatic Republicanism. U.S. Attorney General William French Smith, who had recommended her appointment, praised O'Connor's judicial philosophy as one of restraint and deference to the legislative branch in making the law. In a law review article published in January 1981, Justice O'Connor had recommended greater reliance on state courts for the protection of constitutional rights. Her nomination for the Supreme Court had the support of Sen. Barry Goldwater (R-AZ) and other conservatives, but opponents of legalized abortion and the Equal Rights Amendment attacked her legislative record on those issues.

C. HERMAN PRITCHETT

PERCY, Walker

Trained as a physician, Walker Percy did not begin his career as a novelist until a relatively late age. His first published novel, *The Moviegoer* (1961), unexpectedly won the National Book Award and established the reputation of its 45-year-old author. Each of his succeeding works received high praise, and his fifth novel, *The Second Coming* (1980), won the American Book Award. Percy's contribution to American literature also includes his discovery of the late John Kennedy Toole's *A Confederacy of Dunces*, which in 1981 was awarded the Pulitzer Prize for fiction.

The locale for Walker Percy's fiction is not the Old South, haunted by the Civil War, but the New South, dotted with country club golf courses. A master of social satire, he wittily depicts a modern world of shallowness and platitudes through which his usually ironic, alienated heroes must find their way. Though his fiction has a strong sense of place, Percy is not a regionalist. A converted Roman Catholic, he is strongly steeped in the philosophies of Sören Kierkegaard and French existentialism. His novels are fundamentally inquiries into the possibility of faith and meaning among the "noxious particles and sadness of the old dying Western World."

Background. Walker Percy was born on May 28, 1916, in Birmingham, AL. After the suicide of his father in 1929 and the death of his mother in 1931, he was adopted by his father's cousin, William Alexander Percy. Walker's "Uncle Will" was highly cultivated and had a deep influence on the boy. He was the author of a classic work on the South, *Lanterns on the Levee* (1941; reissued in 1974 with an introduction by Walker Percy). Walker earned his B.A. in chemistry from the University of North Carolina in 1937 and his M.D. from Columbia University in 1941. Working at Bellevue Hospital in New York, he contracted tuberculosis

Walker Percy

Wide World Photos

and spent two years in a sanatorium. His readings there turned his interest from science to religion and philosophy. With money left by his uncle he was able to devote his time to reading, thinking, and some writing. He returned to the South and in 1946 married Mary Bernice Townsend. They have two daughters.

Percy's essays on alienation, symbolism, and semiotics started to appear in journals in 1954. His interest in fiction developed out of his readings of Jean-Paul Sartre and Albert Camus, who "see nothing wrong with writing novels that address what they consider the deepest philosophical issues."

The Moviegoer, set mainly in New Orleans, tells of a troubled young man who finds more reality in movies than in the everyday world. Subsequent novels are *The Last Gentleman* (1966), *Love in the Ruins* (1971), *Lancelot* (1977), and *The Second Coming*. His formal essays are collected in *The Message in the Bottle* (1975).

Percy lives in Covington, LA, which he describes affectionately as a pleasant "nonplace."

JEROME H. STERN

QADDAFI, Muammar el-

Since coming to power in late 1969, Col. Muammar el-Qaddafi of Libya has placed himself at the forefront of Arab critics of U.S. policy in the Middle East. American administrations have, in turn, condemned Quaddafi's radicalism and penchant for meddling in his neighbors' affairs. Ironically, Colonel Qaddafi has not curbed the operations of American oil companies in Libya, nor has he ever seriously curtailed oil shipments to the United States. This remained the case even after two incidents in 1981 further strained relations. In May the Libyan embassy in Washington was shut down, and Libyan diplomatic personnel were expelled from the country. In August, U.S. Navy planes downed two Libyan Air Force jets over the Gulf of Sidra in a dispute over territorial rights. (*See* LIBYA.)

Background. Muammar Muhammad Qaddafi, born in the Sirte Desert in 1942, is the son of a nomadic herdsman. Educated in both secular and religious schools, he was graduated from the Libyan Military Academy in 1965. As a junior officer, Qaddafi ardently admired Egyptian President Gamal Abdel Nasser and his efforts to unite the Arab states into a powerful political force. Convinced that the Libyan monarchy was corrupt and unduly influenced by Great Britain, Qaddafi determined to oust King Idris I, taking Nasser's overthrow of Egyptian King Faruk as his model.

On Sept. 1, 1969, Qaddafi led a youthful group of nationalist army officers in a bloodless coup that deposed the king and abolished parliament. Rule passed into the hands of a Revolutionary Command Council. Qaddafi, who had assumed leadership of the armed forces, became prime minister and defense minister in early 1970, but resigned both offices in 1972. He retained the presidency of the Revolutionary Council and the command of the military.

Qaddafi has vigorously advocated Arab unity, but none of his proposals to link Libya with other states has come to fruition. These failures have frustrated the Libyan leader, who regards Arab unity as essential to his primary political goal of defeating Zionism. His espousal of fundamental Islamic views has led him to enforce the laws and proscriptions of the Koran. This fundamentalism has been one of the roadblocks to Libya's unity with its more liberal neighbors. It also accounted for his support of the Iranian revolution in 1978–79.

During the 1970s, most foreign investments in Libya, including those of multinational oil companies, were nationalized. The revenues helped finance a series of development plans to improve the nation's economic infrastructure and to provide more social services for the citizenry. A campaign of Arabization further symbolized Qaddafi's desire to obliterate foreign influence.

Colonel Qaddafi has supported militant Muslim groups throughout the world and has aided a variety of revolutionary movements aimed at regimes in the Middle East and elsewhere. Despite his anti-Westernism, Qaddafi has shown little interest in Communist ideology, arguing that Islam meets the sociopolitical needs of his people. Although there have been occasional indications of internal unrest during Qaddafi's regime, the great wealth generated by Libyan oil, combined with the strength of the government, has kept visible dissent at a minimum.

KENNETH J. PERKINS

UPI

Muammar el-Qaddafi

REAGAN, Nancy

Elegant is the word most frequently used to describe First Lady Nancy Reagan. Those who disapproved of the casual, down-home style of the Carter White House credit Mrs. Reagan with returning elegance and dignity to the presidential home. During 1981 most of Mrs. Reagan's spare time was spent in redecorating the White House.

The role of first lady is defined by the personality of the individual, and Mrs. Reagan has opted for a much more traditional role than that assumed by Rosalynn Carter. Unlike her predecessor, Mrs. Reagan does not have an office in the East Wing of the White House. She prefers to work in the family quarters, and sees her primary role as being one supportive of her husband.

Mrs. Reagan bristles at suggestions that she has undue influence on her husband. She says that after nearly 30 years of marriage they cannot help but influence one another, but she insists that she is not the power behind the throne. Whatever influence Nancy Reagan may have on policy decisions comes from her extraordinarily close relationship with her husband.

After more than a year in Washington, Mrs. Reagan still seems restrained with the press. An intensely private person, she admits to being sensitive to criticism, such as that which followed her disclosure in December 1980 that she kept "a tiny little gun" by her bedside in California. Particularly bothered by charges that the Reagans live extravagantly at a time when her husband is asking Americans to make financial sacrifices, she revealed to the press that she had worn a 17-year-old dress to the state dinner for British Prime Minister Margaret Thatcher.

Still, it is difficult to picture Mrs. Reagan in the proverbial Republican cloth coat. A perfect size six, the first lady is a member of the permanent Hall of Fame of America's best dressed women.

There is more to Mrs. Reagan than clothes, however. She is very active in the Foster Grandparents Program, which brings elderly people together with retarded, handicapped and emotionally disturbed children. She is also very interested in the problems of drug and alcohol abuse by youth.

Background. Nancy Reagan was born Anne Frances Robbins on July 6, 1923. She was adopted by her stepfather, Dr. Loyal Davis, when she was 14. After graduation from Smith College, she moved to Hollywood to pursue an acting career. She made 11 movies between 1949 and 1956, including *Hellcats of the Navy,* in which she appeared with Ronald Reagan, who she had married in 1952. The Reagans together have two children, Patricia Ann and Ronald Prescott.

SANDRA STENCEL

STOCKMAN, David Alan

After staking his presidency on the gamble that cutbacks in federal spending coupled with substantial tax reductions could revive the nation's faltering economy, Ronald Reagan turned to a little-known, two-term Michigan congressman to wield the ax. As director of the Office of Management and Budget (OMB), David Stockman did such a good job that Reagan joked, "We won't leave you out there alone, Dave. We'll all come to the hanging."

With Reagan's support, Stockman chopped more than $40,000,000,000 from previously planned outlays, much of it from "Great Society" social-welfare programs set in place by former President Lyndon Johnson. Denouncing the federal budget as "a coast-to-coast soup-line," Stockman successfully lobbied for cuts in everything from college student loans to aid to cities, preserving only what he called "a safety net for the truly needy."

The OMB director ran into difficulty when in a series of interviews published in the December issue of *Atlantic Monthly* he expressed doubts about the effectiveness of the budget and tax cuts.

David Alan Stockman

UPI

Once a staff aide to former Illinois Congressman John Anderson, Stockman was the logical choice to be Anderson's stand-in, and then Jimmy Carter's, when Reagan practiced for the 1980 presidential debates.

After Reagan won the election, Stockman urged that he declare an economic emergency, circulating his thoughts in a treatise titled, "Avoiding a GOP Economic Dunkirk," which he coauthored with fellow Congressman Jack Kemp (R-NY). Reagan resisted the report's more explosive rhetroic, but in a February 18 speech before the Congress said "If we do not act forcefully, and now, the economy will get worse."

Background. David Alan Stockman was born in Camp Hood, TX, on Nov. 10, 1946. He grew up on his family's 150-acre (60.7-ha) fruit farm outside of St. Joseph, MI, first venturing into politics as a volunteer in Barry Goldwater's 1964 presidential campaign. He attended Michigan State University, graduating in 1968 with a B.A. in history. At MSU, he headed a summer-long protest against the war in Vietnam. Intrigued by the writings of theologian Reinhold Niebuhr, he accepted a scholarship to the Harvard Divinity School, though he had no plans to enter the clergy. At Harvard, he boarded with the family of New York Sen. Daniel Patrick Moynihan, then a Nixon administration aide. Stockman adopted Moynihan's neo-conservative views, leaving behind any liberal leanings he may have had as a campus radical.

Stockman left the divinity school without graduating to join John Anderson's staff in Washington and to head the House Republican Conference, which Anderson then chaired. He was a fellow at the Harvard Institute of Politics (1974–75). Stockman was elected to the 95th Congress by Michigan's 4th district in 1976 and was reelected in 1978 and 1980. He resigned his seat to join the Reagan administration.

ELEANOR CLIFT

VIOLA, Roberto Eduardo

Lt. Gen. Roberto Viola began a three-year term as president of Argentina on March 29, 1981. His cabinet contained more civilian than military ministers. Of the 23 provincial governors appointed, six were civilians. Maintaining that "political parties were irreplaceable elements within the republican system," he set out to reincorporate the many followers of Juan Perón into national life, by first facilitating the release of Perón's widow, Isabel, who had been detained after her administration was overthrown in a March 1976 coup.

At the beginning of Viola's government, the inherited economic crisis deteriorated into the worst in Argentine history, sparking rumors of a possible right-wing coup. The peso was devalued by 64% in the first half of the year. Official reserves fell from $10,000,000,000 to less than $1,000,000,000 during the same period. An inflation rate of up to 175% was forecast for 1981. Unemployment or underemployment skyrocketed to the 40% level as bankruptcies mounted. To surmount the situation, the Viola government announced further devaluations, new credit to be made available to the productive sector by the central bank, and a freeze on government spending.

Viola was confronted with an international conflict at the outset of his administration, when two Argentine army officers were arrested in Chile on espionage charges. The border was closed by Argentina, and troops were mobilized. After six weeks of tension, relations returned to normal through an exchange of the detained officers for five Chileans held in Argentina on spying charges. Pope John Paul II had appealed to Viola, and also to the Chileans, for a relaxation of tensions so that the officers' detention would not prejudice papal mediation of their overlapping claims in the Beagle Channel. On that matter, the Argentine president called for a papal decision that would be satisfactory to both countries. Argentina had been unable to accept a December 1980 mediation decision; deliberations were reopened in June.

Invited to the White House by U.S. President Ronald Reagan, President-designate Viola forged better relations between Washington and Buenos Aires. Although Viola indicated to U.S. congressmen that his administration would identify persons who have "disappeared" in an antiterrorist campaign (1975–present), in order to placate human right activists, his military commanders did not agree.

A three-man military junta forced the president to step down late in the year.

Background. The son of an immigrant Italian tailor, Viola, 56, was chosen for the presidency by the commanders of the army, navy, and air force. As army chief of staff, Viola had been the key planner of the 1976 coup against President Isabel Perón. From 1966 to 1969, he was part of the Argentine delegation to the Inter-American Defense Board in Washington, DC. Viola retired from active duty in 1979. A friend observed that Viola was the most political officer among the current generation of military leaders.

LARRY L. PIPPIN

WALES, PRINCESS of

The Princess of Wales, formerly Lady Diana Spencer, is a beautiful English girl with very little past and an enormous future. At the age of 20 she handled a change of status that few could contemplate. Until her marriage on July 29, 1981, to Prince Charles, heir to the British throne, she knew the relaxed life of the English countryside, where she lived on her father's vast Northamptonshire estate, and the casual whirl of days passed in the smart London flat which she shared with three other girls while working at a kindergarten. With her marriage she joined the world's most formal royal family, who live secluded in palaces, ruled by inflexible schedules. Buckingham Palace announced in November that the couple is expecting their first child in June 1982.

Background. Her lineage makes her a suitable Princess of Wales. Born Diana Frances Spencer on July 1, 1961, the princess is the youngest daughter of the eighth Earl Spencer, a title that goes back to the 18th century. She is related to the British throne through the illicit liaisons of a few of her ancestors with royalty and to notable U.S. presidents through her American great-great-grandfather. Prince Charles is her 16th cousin, once removed. She spent much of her youth on an estate next to the royal home of Sandringham in Norfolk, and as a child knew the children of the royal family. Her parents divorced in 1969, and the princess spent what is for many today a familiar childhood, shuttling back and forth between two households. She was educated until the age of 16 at a girl's boarding school in Kent. A spell at a finishing school in Switzerland saw her return after only six weeks, homesick, to live and work in London.

From all the public attention, she has emerged as a girl with warmth, an unpretentious mind, and with the right youthful flexibility to start training for her future rigorous career. Nor should the princess be dismissed as merely "suitable." A London social magazine, commenting on her first formal appearance alongside Prince Charles after their betrothal, at which she wore a low-cut black taffeta evening dress, decided that she was defiantly signaling to all concerned—"I am not merely suitable, but also gorgeous."

MAUREEN GREEN

WATSON, Tom

UPI

Tom Watson

With his triumph in the 1981 Masters Tournament at the Augusta (GA) National Golf Club—along with his first Masters victory in 1977 and British Open titles in 1975, 1977, and 1980—Tom Watson has established his credentials as one of the finest golfers in the history of the sport.

While victories in prestigious events are important to any golfer, earnings on the professional tour are also a gauge of skill and consistency. In that regard, 1980 was a hallmark season for Watson, who won $530,808 and became the first golfer to earn more than a half-million dollars in one season. In 1980 he played in 22 tournaments, winning six besides the British Open; he finished in the money in all 22 and among the top ten golfers in 16. His career earnings zoomed to $2,202,241. In 1981, Watson won the Masters, the New Orleans Open, and the Atlanta Open and finished second three times through the first week in August. He finished the season third on the money-winners list with $347,660 and had a career total of 25 victories on the Professional Golfers Association (PGA) tour.

Background. Thomas Sturges Watson was born on Sept. 4, 1949, in Kansas City, MO. He was six years old when his father, an insurance executive and scratch golfer (no handicap), introduced him to the sport. Although Watson starred in basketball and football at prep school in Kansas City, he was more fascinated with golf. He spent long hours hitting balls and perfecting his swing. As an amateur, Watson was a four-time winner of the Missouri state championship. He was graduated from Stanford University with a degree in psychology in 1971 and then joined the PGA tour.

Watson's first purse money—$1,065—came in his first tour event, the 1971 Kaiser International Open, in which he finished in a tie for 28th place. Three years later he won his first pro tournament, the Western Open.

For the years 1977 through 1980, Watson was named the PGA's player of the year. Among his tournament victories (besides his two Masters and three British Open titles) were the Tournament of Champions and Memorial Tournament in 1979, the World Series of Golf in 1980, and the Byron Nelson Classic, named after his tutor and friend, four times. He was the winner of the Vardon Trophy, awarded for the lowest average score per round, from 1977 through 1979 and was a member of the U.S. Ryder Cup team in 1977.

The 5′9″ (1.75-m), 160-lb (73-kg) Watson lives with his wife, Linda, and their daughter, Meg, in Mission Hills, KS. His enjoys hunting, fishing, and playing the guitar.

GEORGE DE GREGORIO

WATT, James Gaius

With a reputation for favoring industrial development at the expense of the environment, U.S. Secretary of the Interior James Watt has been likened to the proverbial fox guarding the chicken coop. He is committed to increased offshore drilling for oil and gas, more exploration of wilderness areas by industry, and the easing of regulations that limit such controversial ventures as strip mining. "Conservation is not the blind locking away of huge areas and their resources because of emotional appeals," said Watt, stressing the importance of breaking the nation's dependence on foreign oil.

A fundamentalist Christian who belongs to the Assembly of God faith, Watt stunned environmentalists shortly after taking office in January 1981 by publicly declaring his belief in a Second Coming. "I do not know how many generations we can count on before the Lord returns," he told the House Interior Committee, leaving the impression that natural resources did not have to be protected forever.

Watt insisted he meant nothing of the sort and that he seeks only "to swing the environmental pendulum back to center" after the heightened concern of the 1960s. But such organizations as the National Wildlife Federation and the Sierra Club began calling for his resignation, and even some oil companies protested that his five-year plan to lease 1,000,000,000 offshore tracts for drilling is too much too soon.

A Westerner, Watt was a backer of the "Sagebrush Rebellion," a movement to return publicly-owned land to private interests. He thinks private concessionaires should be given a greater role in managing the country's park system, which he claims has deteriorated to a "sickening" extent. He has urged Congress to stop acquiring new park lands until the government can spruce up what it has. "I wouldn't mind being remembered as the guy who fixed the plumbing," he says with characteristic bluntness.

Despite the controversy he sparked, Watt retained the support of President Reagan, who joked during a 1981 Labor Day appearance in New York that Watt "would have been here but he's working on a lease for strip mining the Rose Garden."

Background. James Gaius Watt was born in Lusk, WY, on Jan. 31, 1938. He is a graduate of the University of Wyoming and its law school. After seven years on Capitol Hill as a Senate aide, he joined the Interior Department in 1969 as director of the Bureau of Outdoor Recreation. In 1975 he was appointed to the Federal Power Commission. In 1977 he left Washington to head the Denver-based Mountain States Legal Foundation, a public-interest group dedicated to challenging government regulations. He resigned that position to join the Reagan administration in 1981. He and his wife of 24 years, Leilani, have two children, who are students at Oral Roberts University.

ELEANOR CLIFT

James Gaius Watt

UPI

YOUNG, John Watts

The crew commander of the first orbital test flight of the U.S. space shuttle, John Young, hailed his aerospace vehicle as the "world's greatest flying machine." The April 12 launch of space shuttle Columbia, the world's first reusable manned space vehicle, marked the beginning of a new era in space transportation and utilization. John Young at 50 feels that "space flight is an old man's business" and indicates he "will keep flying as long as they let me." The 1981 flight made him the first astronaut to make five space flights.

He and Columbia pilot Capt. Robert Crippen received NASA Distinguished Service Medals from President Reagan at the White House on May 19. He also became the seventh astronaut to receive the Congressional Space Medal of Honor. His citation said: "John Young, in a space-flight career spanning two decades, has demonstrated the highest qualities of leadership, courage, and technical skill. The success of each of his five critical space-flight missions has made a major contribution to human progress in the exploration and utilization of space."

Background. John Watts Young was born in San Francisco, CA, on Sept. 24, 1930. He was graduated from Orlando High School in Orlando, FL, and went on to receive a bachelor of science degree in aeronautical engineering from Georgia Institute of Technology, graduating with highest honors in 1952. He then entered the U.S. Navy and received flight- and test-pilot training, after which he flew fighter aircraft and evaluated their weapons systems. He set a world time-to-climb record to altitudes of 3 000 and 25 000 m (9,842 and 82,021 ft) in the Phantom Fighter. He retired from the U.S. Navy in September 1976, completing more than 25 years of active military service, during which he logged approximately 8,000 hours of flying time.

Young was selected as an astronaut by NASA in September 1962. His first of five space flights was as pilot with command pilot Gus Grissom on the first manned Gemini flight on March 23, 1965. On July 18–21, 1966, Young served as command pilot on Gemini 10 with Michael Collins as pilot. On his third space flight Young was command-module pilot on Apollo 10, May 18–26, 1969, with spacecraft commander Thomas P. Stafford and lunar-module pilot Eugene A. Cernan. The fourth space flight for John Young was as spacecraft commander on Apollo 16, April 16–27, 1972, with command-module pilot Thomas K. Mattingly II and lunar-module pilot Charles M. Duke, Jr. Young and Duke spent more than 71 hours on the moon's Cayley Plains at Descartes, where they collected more than 90 kg (200 lbs) of rock and soil samples, operating the lunar rover over the roughest surface encountered on the moon. Young became chief of the astronaut office during his preparation for the flight of Columbia.

John Young, who has two grown children from his first marriage, lives with his second wife, Susy, in the Houston area.

MICHAEL CALABRESE

Gen. Celso Torrelio is sworn in as the president of Bolivia, September 4 in La Paz. He became the country's 37th president in 50 years.

UPI

BOLIVIA

After a year of considerable turmoil, which included the deposition of President Luis García Meza, Bolivia was scarcely nearer resolving the many problems besetting it. The unacceptability of García Meza to the international community, arising out of the regime's close involvement with cocaine smuggling and its bleak human rights record, compounded by the air of perpetual intrigue surrounding the presidency, further prejudiced an already weakened economy. With International Monetary Fund (IMF) backing required for urgently needed loans, the political crisis grew more intense as the economic situation worsened.

The annual growth rate had slipped to less than 1% in 1980, and the gross domestic product (GDP) declined 11% over the last quarter of 1980 and the first quarter of 1981. With oil production at just over 23,000 barrels per day by midyear, and with consumption approaching 26,000 barrels per day, Bolivia's new status as a net importer was confirmed. Renewed negotiations with Brazil for a transcontinental pipeline offered hope for a tripling of natural gas exports by 1985, but in the meantime the only dynamic growth area was the production of cocaine for illicit export, and this hardened U.S. opinion against the regime.

Early in January an extremely unpopular set of economic reforms was imposed. Subsidies on gasoline, wheat, and imported flour were removed, leading to marked price increases in basic commodities, as well as in bus, rail, and air fares. As the domestic situation worsened, García Meza proved unable to make headway either in gaining U.S. recognition of his regime or in renegotiating the large external debt.

In late February the two men most closely identified with the cocaine traffic, Interior Minister Luis Arce Gómez and Education Minister Ariel Coca, were dismissed. García Meza also appointed the first two civilians to his government, Jorge Tamayo Ramos and Mario Rolon Anaya, as ministers of finance and foreign affairs, respectively. Against a background of almost weekly coup attempts from various sectors of the armed forces, talks were pursued for diplomatic recognition and debt rescheduling. In late April agreement was reached on the rescheduling of $460,000,000 of Bolivia's estimated $3,700,000,000 external debt, providing that the IMF granted standby credit.

By May, however, it was clear that García Meza's troubled rule was reaching its end. Following uprisings in Cochabamba, the Army commanders decided jointly to replace him as both commander-in-chief and president. Replaced as commander-in-chief by Gen. Humberto Cayola, García Meza maneuvered to keep the presidency. The IMF refused standby credit in June, and the army commanders again voted for him to step down, but a mishandled coup attempt led by Cayola later that month gave García Meza some breathing space. After an uprising in Santa Cruz led by former President Gen. Natusch Busch and Gen. Lucio Anez, García Meza was finally forced to resign on August 4. He was replaced by a three-man junta led by Air Force Gen. Waldo Bernal; the Army representative was little-known Gen. Celso Torrelio, appointed interior minister after the dismissal of Arce Gómez and commander-in-chief of the army when Cayola was exiled for his coup

BOLIVIA • Information Highlights

Official Name: Republic of Bolivia.
Location: West-central South America.
Area: 424,164 sq mi (1 098 585 km^2).
Population (1981 est.): 5,500,000.
Chief Cities (1976 census): Sucre, the legal capital, 63,625; La Paz, the actual capital, 635,283; Santa Cruz de la Sierra, 254,682; Cochabamba, 204,684.
Government: *Head of state and government,* Gen. Celso Torrelio, president (took power Sept. 1981). *Legislature*—Congress: Senate and Chamber of Deputies.
Monetary Unit: Peso (24.75 pesos equal U.S.$1, Nov. 1981).
Manufactures (major products): Textiles, cottage industry goods, cement, tin, petroleum.
Agriculture (major products): Potatoes, corn, sugarcane, cassava, cotton, barley, rice, wheat, coffee, bananas.

attempt. After protracted negotiations between the junta and a group of military officers that had refused to support it, Torrelio was installed as president September 4. It was Bolivia's third government in little more than a year, but the basic problems remained unresolved.

PAUL CAMMACK
University of Manchester, England

BOSTON

Boston during 1981 seemed almost like two different cities, one booming with new development, the other hard-pressed socially and economically. On the one hand, the city's economy remained strong, with major new construction, including the vast Copley Place development, and high rates of employment. At the same time, many neighborhoods, the school system, and the city government itself faced new and continuing problems.

Schools. The Boston public school system, struggling with court-ordered desegregation since 1974, was further troubled by labor disputes and charges of corruption in the five-member school committee. Committeeman Gerald O'Leary was sentenced early in the year for extortion in connection with a school bus contract. Another committee member, John McDonough, was tried and acquitted in the same case. The scandal further undermined confidence in the city's school system, which has lost some 32,000 students, mostly white, since desegregation began. A new superintendent, Robert Spillane, pledged to take steps to restore the system's reputation.

City Finances. Massachusetts' tax reduction act, "Proposition 2½," went into effect in 1981 and severely strained the finances of the state's largest city and capital. Several hundred city employees, including many police and firefighters, were laid off. An attempt to get the legislature to authorize a special bond issue permitting the city to raise new funds was unfavorably received on Beacon Hill. The consensus among State House knowledgeables was that special tax relief for Boston would come eventually, but not until early 1982 and then only after tight restrictions were placed on the city's use of any new funds. This attitude, in turn, reflected the opposition to Mayor Kevin H. White, who was accused by members of the city council and some state legislators of saving patronage jobs at the expense of public safety and basic service positions.

Elections. Elections for council and school committee in Boston are "at large," and it is often difficult for political newcomers to achieve recognition. Nonetheless, a field of 40 candidates for the council, the largest in memory, vied for two vacancies on that body. Incumbent councillors easily won reelection, and top vote getters among the other candidates included James F. Kelly, a critic of school desegregation.

Cultural Landmarks. Despite the stresses of change, Boston's rich and old cultural institutions continued to flourish. In July, the Museum of Fine Arts opened its new west wing, designed by I. M. Pei. In September, the Boston Symphony Orchestra began its 100th season.

HARVEY BOULAY
Boston University

BOTANY

The eruption of Mount St. Helens in May 1980 captured the attention of scientists as have few events in recent memory. While geologists were busy studying the volcanic activity itself, botanists were afforded a unique opportunity to observe the effects on plant life. In the aftermath of the eruption, they have studied the effects on flora in a variety of aspects, such as plant populations following the reestablishment of flora in devastated areas; the recovery of ecosystems; speciation; gene expression in new populations compared with averages for the species as a whole; and ring patterns in surviving trees. The U.S. Forest Service is observing the effects of the removal of fallen timber from certain areas, as compared with others.

The annual meeting of the Botanical Society of America (BSA) was held Aug. 17–21, 1981, at Indiana University in Bloomington. Titles of symposia and special sessions included Endangered Species vs. Endangered Ecosystems, sponsored by the ecological and physiological sections of the BSA and by the American Institute of Biological Sciences; Germ Plasm Resource Conservation, sponsored by the economic botany section; Plant-Animal Interactions, sponsored by the ecological section; and Secretory Structures and Biology of Pollen, sponsored by the developmental and structural section. Workshops included one entitled The Application of Newer Experimental Techniques and Methods to the Study of Fern Development, Morphogenesis, and Physiology.

A number of plant explorations undertaken in 1980 continued into 1981. Among them were explorations sponsored by the U.S. Department of Agriculture in Australia, China, and Mexico, with special attention to *Gossypium* species, wheat, soybean, forage, vegetables, medicinal plants, and *Phaseolus* species.

Scientists in several states continued to investigate the role of certain bacteria in initiating ice formation on plant leaves, which may lead to frost damage. The phenomenon has been demonstrated in several geographical areas, and attempts are under way to reduce the plant damage by application of bactericides, antagonistic bacteria, or ice nucleation inhibitors. Dr. Steven Lindow reported on the various experimental control methods being studied to resolve the problem (*California Plant Pathology,* No. 48, March 1980).

E. N. O'ROURKE
Department of Horticulture
Louisiana State University

BRAZIL

In 1981, for the first time in more than 17 years, a civilian held the office of president of Brazil. The country's vice-president, Aureliano Chaves, became acting president on September 23 after a heart attack incapacitated Gen. João Baptista Figueiredo, Brazil's president since March 1979. The smooth constitutional transition stood in marked contrast to previous Brazilian experience. By November 12, however, Figueiredo returned to his post.

Liberalization. At the time of his heart attack, President Figueiredo, 63, was vigorously pursuing a policy of liberalization of the nation's political process. Under that policy, known as *abertura,* or opening, elections for the national Congress and state and municipal governments were scheduled to be held Nov. 15, 1982. Figueiredo had committed the military to an eventual withdrawal from the presidency as well.

The policy of *abertura* had come under fire from rightists in the military who opposed a return to civilian rule, and from church and labor leaders who charged that the process was moving too slowly. A wave of terrorist bombings early in the year was blamed on military opponents of *abertura.* In August, the unexpected resignation from Figueiredo's cabinet of Gen. Golbery do Couto e Silva, a strong supporter of *abertura,* set off a wave of speculation that the government was about to turn to a hardline policy. However, Couto e Silva's successor, João Leitão de Abreu, a civilian lawyer, quickly pronounced himself in favor of the liberalization process.

Nuclear Power. Brazil entered the nuclear age in August with the dedication of Angra I, a nuclear-powered electrical generating plant in Angra dos Reis, a town on the outskirts of Rio de Janeiro on the road to São Paulo. The plant, which will have a generating capacity of 626 MW when it goes into operation in March 1982, was built by the American firm Westinghouse at a cost of some $2,000,000,000.

Angra I is the first step in an ambitious nuclear power program involving eight more power plants to be constructed by the year 2000, under a contract with West Germany signed in 1975. Two of the plants, Angra II and Angra III, are already under way. Fulfillment of the rest of the contract is not certain because of the enormous cost—estimated at between $15,000,000,000 and $18,000,000,000. The United States has opposed the Brazilian-West German agreement on the grounds that the new plants will be able to produce material for thermonuclear weapons, which is not the case with Angra I.

Economy. Brazil's chronic economic problems—soaring inflation, a severe payments deficit, and a heavy foreign debt—continued to plague the nation through 1981. Despite a restrictive monetary policy designed, as one observer put it, to "shock" the economy into recession, little headway was made in reducing the inflation rate, which ran as high as 120% during the year.

Signs of the desired recession, however, were visible. Industrial production was off by 3% in the first half of the year; sales of consumer durables were down by 15%; and car sales plummeted by one third. Unemployment rose correspondingly, reaching 800,000.

An aggressive export promotion program, based on subsidies for exporters, helped increase overseas sales of Brazilian products by an estimated 15 to 20%. Imports also rose, but at a somewhat slower pace, narrowing the 1980 trade deficit of $3,000,000,000. Nonetheless, economists predicted that the overall payments gap would actually increase. In August, a leading economic forecaster, Pedro Malan of the Pontifical Catholic University of Rio de Janeiro, said he

UPI

President João Baptista Figueiredo is hugged by schoolchildren during a four-day visit to Portugal in February. Later in the year, Figueiredo suffered a heart attack and was temporarily replaced by his vice-president.

expected the country to run a 1981 current account deficit of $12,000,000,000. Brazil's foreign debt, already the largest in the developing world, would reach $70,000,000,000 in 1981, Malan said.

Exacerbating the problem was the fact that a large part—as much as half—of Brazil's foreign debt had been contracted at floating rates. As a result, in the tight money market of 1981, Brazil paid higher interest rates than many other developing countries.

Despite its enormous debt, or perhaps because of it, Brazil continued to enjoy the confidence of foreign bankers throughout the year. The country was able to roll over some $7,500,-000,000 in repayments and to borrow an additional $6,000,000,000–$7,000,000,000 from foreign sources, not counting $3,000,000,000 in suppliers' credits.

Export Diversification. Two decades ago, a few basic commodities dominated the Brazilian export sector. Coffee was king, accounting for more than 50% of foreign exchange earnings. Since then, however, there has been significant change in the composition of Brazilian exports. Manufactured goods, which amounted to only 2% of total exports in 1961, accounted for more than half in 1980 and reached 60% in 1981.

High technology products figure prominently among Brazil's manufactured exports. In 1981 Brazil sold to the United States such items as a $67 million steel rolling mill, 30 Bandeirante turboprop passenger airplanes, and high performance pistons for light aircraft engines. In other parts of the world, Brazilians sold fighter aircraft, armored vehicles, infantry weapons, and container ships. The total value of manufactured exports was estimated to be $1,600,000,000, while sales of services, mostly engineering projects, reached $2,000,000,000.

Agriculture. Diversification has also taken place within the agricultural sector, with such food crops as soybeans surpassing coffee and sugar in importance. With an annual output of 15 million T (13.6 million t) of soybeans, Brazil is second only to the United States in the international soybean trade.

In July, Brazil and the Soviet Union signed a $5,000,000,000 trade agreement calling for the sale by Brazil of 550,000 T (500 000 t) of soybeans and 440,000 T (400 000 t) of soybean meal each year for the next five years. Other Brazilian agricultural products covered by the agreement are 550,000 T of corn per year, 11,000 T (10 000 t) of cocoa kernels, 11,000 T of cocoa liquor, and an undisclosed amount of methanol. In exchange, Brazil will get 20,000 barrels per day of Soviet oil, hydroelectric equipment, and other machinery.

Production of coffee and sugar was sharply curtailed by a killing frost in July. Forty-five percent of the next year's coffee crop was destroyed; an estimated 2,000,000,000 coffee trees were affected. Prices on world coffee markets jumped 25% as news of the disaster spread, but recovered when it became known that enormous carryover stocks of coffee in both Brazil and Colombia could more than make up for the shortfall.

Sugar exports, on the other hand, were embargoed by the Brazilian Sugar and Alcohol Institute. Sugar is the primary ingredient in Brazil's national alcohol fuel program, designed to ease the country's dependence on imported oil. The sugar institute said its embargo was necessary because 73% of Brazil's sugar plantations were affected by the July freeze. Losses were put at 550,000 T in the 1981–82 crop year and at least 1.2 million T (1.1 million t) the following year.

Foreign Relations. Traditionally isolated in hemispheric affairs, Brazil under President Figueiredo actively sought closer relations with its Spanish-speaking neighbors. Figueiredo visited a number of Latin American capitals in 1980 and 1981, in some cases becoming the first Brazilian president to do so. Before his heart attack, he was scheduled to go to Mexico in October and to Ecuador sometime in 1982.

Argentina has been a particular target of the campaign for closer relations. In July, Argentine President Roberto Viola visited Brasília, where he signed a ratification of agreements on nuclear cooperation and the manufacture and exchange of arms. Later in the year, the two countries agreed to a joint program of offshore oil exploration in the Straits of Magellan.

RICHARD C. SCHROEDER
Syndicated Free-lance Writer

BRAZIL • Information Highlights

Official Name: Federative Republic of Brazil.
Location: Eastern South America.
Area: 3,286,478 sq mi (8 511 965 km^2).
Population (1981 est.): 121,400,000.
Chief Cities (1979 est.): Brasília, the capital, 978,600; São Paulo, 8,407,500; Rio de Janeiro, 5,394,900; Belo Horizonte, 1,856,800.
Government: *Head of state and government,* João Baptista Figueiredo, president (took office March 1979). Legislature—National Congress: Federal Senate and Chamber of Deputies.
Monetary Unit: New Cruzeiro (110.12 n. cruzeiros equal U.S.$1, Oct. 1981).
Manufactures (major products): Steel, chemicals, petrochemicals, machinery, consumer goods.
Agriculture (major products): Coffee, rice, beef, corn, milk, sugarcane, soybeans, cacao.

BRITISH COLUMBIA

Economy and Public Finance. Relatively high levels of capital investment and substantial growth in consumer expenditure were cause for some optimism about the state of the British Columbia economy in 1980–81. Continued adverse conditions in export markets, however, were less encouraging. Also, a record rainfall during a 61-day period in the spring destroyed nearly half of the province's fruit and vegetable crops, threatening substantially higher produce prices. And with a persistent decline in the volume of lumber exports to the United States, the forestry industry produced at only 75% of capacity in the fall despite settlement of the summer's province-wide forestry strike.

Copper displaced natural gas as the most valuable mineral, and oil and gas production continued to decrease. In the wake of an energy-pricing agreement with Alberta on September 1, the federal government signed a similar five-year agreement with British Columbia. The provincial government agreed to share 37% of an estimated (C.) $12,300,000,000 in revenue and agreed to pay the federal domestic natural gas excise tax it had previously withheld. While controversy continued over the financing of the northeast coal development project and its port facilities, construction began on the mining project's $170 million townsite at Tumbler Ridge.

Agreements made in January provided for the annual shipment to Japan of 8.5 million T (7.7 million t) of coal over 15 years, beginning in 1983.

The 1981–82 provincial budget was a balanced one. Operating expenditures were estimated at $6,610,300,000, including a debt reduction of $26.1 million. Expenditures included $48 million in direct aid for the northeast coal project and an allocation of $293.4 million for forestry management. Tax changes included a reduction in the small business corporation income tax, the extension of exemptions from the social service tax, and increases from 4% to 6% in the social service, cigarette, tobacco, and gasoline tax rates.

Politics and Government. The activities of the Ku Klux Klan within the province prompted introduction of the Civil Rights Protection Act. It provides for fines and/or imprisonment for any interference in individual rights on the basis of color, race, religion, ethnic origin, or place of birth. Other major legislation included a new Environmental Management Act and a Financial Administration Act. After protracted negotiations, an agreement was reached with the British Columbia Medical Association for a 40% increase in fees under the medical services plan.

— BRITISH COLUMBIA • Information Highlights —

Area: 366,255 sq mi (948 600 km^2).
Population (April 1981 est.): 2,701,900.
Chief Cities (1976 census): Victoria, the capital, 62,551; Vancouver, 410,188.
Government (1981): *Chief Officers*—lt. gov., Henry Bell-Irving; premier, William R. Bennett (Social Credit party); chief justice, Court of Appeal, Nathaniel T. Nemetz; Supreme Court, Allan McEachern. *Legislature*—Legislative Assembly, 57 members.
Education (1981–82 est.): *Enrollment*—elementary and secondary schools, 537,170 pupils; postsecondary, 50,050 students.
Public Finance (1980–81 est.): $5,800,000,000 balanced budget.
Personal Income (average weekly salary, April 1981): $397.21.
Unemployment Rate (June 1981, seasonally adjusted): 6.1%.
(All monetary figures are in Canadian dollars.)

Attempts by doctors to overbill patients were prohibited by new legislation against balance-billing under medicare. Increased costs of health care resulted in higher medical plan premiums and other service charges for hospital care.

New Ministry of Human Resources regulations tightened eligibility requirements for income assistance available to employable applicants.

Health Minister Rafe Mair resigned early in 1981, and in a May by-election his former seat in Kamloops was retained by the Social Credit Party. Robert Strachan, former provincial leader of the New Democratic Party and British Columbia's agent-general in London, died in July.

NORMAN J. RUFF, *University of Victoria*

BULGARIA

As in recent years, President and First Secretary Todor Zhivkov dominated the national scene, and "eternal friendship" with the Soviet Union dominated foreign policy.

Domestic Affairs and Economy. Government-party controls, censorship, and secrecy regarding the economy, foreign trade, and defense continued throughout the year. Bulgaria's standard of living, the lowest in Eastern Europe, showed some signs of improvement despite January price increases of up to 60% for agricultural products. The government's reports on the national economy were difficult to evaluate, but agricultural production and real income per capita apparently did not reach projected levels.

In March, the 12th congress of the Bulgarian Communist Party, representing 825,000 members, was held in Sofia. The 1,658 delegates called for an improvement in national production and recommended that industrial enterprises and organizations work out their own "supplemental plans." Todor Zhivkov was unanimously reelected head of the party.

On June 7, national and local elections were held, with all candidates for the 400 seats in the National Assembly nominated by the Fatherland Front. Of those citizens entitled to vote, 99.96% reportedly went to the polls. The Fatherland Front nominees reportedly received 99.93% of valid votes. Nine days later, the National Assembly replaced Stanko Todorov as prime min-

BULGARIA • Information Highlights

Official Name: People's Republic of Bulgaria.
Location: Southeastern Europe.
Area: 42,758 sq mi (110 743 km^2).
Population (1981 est.): 8,900,000.
Chief Cities (1979 est.): Sofia, the capital, 1,047,920; Plovdiv, 342,000; Varna, 286,382.
Government: *Head of state,* Todor Zhivkov, president of the State Council and first secretary of the Communist party (took office July 1971). *Head of government,* Grisha Filipov, chairman of the Council of Ministers (took office June 1981).
Monetary Unit: Lev (0.85 lev equals U.S.$1, July 1981).
Manufactures (major products): Processed agricultural products, electric power, crude steel.
Agriculture (major products): Grain, tobacco, fruits, vegetables, livestock.

ister, naming Grisha Filipov, a Politburo member and secretary of the Central Committee, to the post. Todorov was elected chairman of the parliament, but the change was seen as a demotion. The National Assembly also unanimously reelected Zhivkov chairman of the State Council (head of state) for a third five-year term.

In August the 90th anniversary of the Bulgarian Communist Party was nationally celebrated, and on September 7, the first secretary's 70th birthday, Todor Zhivkov was named "The Hero of the People's Republic of Bulgaria." On July 21, Zhivkov's daughter Lyudmila, 38, who had played a prominent political role, died.

Foreign Affairs and Trade. High government-party officials made several visits to COMECON and Third World countries for the purpose of enhancing trade. In December 1980, Politburo member Alexander Lilov visited Belgrade in an attempt to improve Yugoslav-Bulgarian relations. In May 1981, Zhivkov paid a ceremonial visit to Greece and then was host to Austrian Chancellor Bruno Kreisky. Soon after, West Germany's Foreign Minister Hans Dietrich Genscher visited Sofia. In July, representatives of the COMECON nations met in Sofia to thrash out guidelines for coordinating their concurrent five-year plans for 1981–85, and in August Zhivkov conferred with Soviet President Leonid Brezhnev in the Crimea.

According to official statistics, foreign trade increased by 14.1% instead of the expected 7.5%. Imports from and exports to the USSR reached 60% and 55%, respectively.

Bulgaria's reaction to the continuing crisis in Poland faithfully followed the Soviet line.

JAN KARSKI, *Georgetown University*

BURMA

A partial shift in political leadership and accelerating economic growth suggested the possibility of a significantly changed Burma.

Politics. Gen. Ne Win, Burma's leader since the 1962 coup in which he displaced elected Premier U Nu, resigned as president in November and turned over the reigns of government to 63-year-old heir apparent Brigadier San Yu. The 70-year-old nationalist-soldier attributed his decision to advancing age and ill health. But it was also apparent that he was much concerned with a peaceful transition following termination of his own rule and setting a precedent for subsequent switches in leadership. Ne Win, however, accepted the advice of colleagues that he remain as chairman of the ruling single-party. The sudden death, one day before the presidential elections, of Burma's third-ranking leader, Thaung Kyi, secretary-general of Burma's Socialist Program Party, added uncertainty to the succession situation. He was replaced by the former army chief of staff, Aye Ko, number four man in the Burmese political-military hierachy. Maung Maung Kha was reappointed premier.

Some 17 million voters went to the polls in a two-week period in October to "elect" members of state bodies at four levels of Burmese government. The balloting—to select 475 members of the National Congress, 976 holders of seats on people's councils at division and state levels, and additional village and ward officials—was carefully managed, however. The BSPP controlled the resulting deliberative bodies.

Insurgency. Burma's Communist rebels continued to control the northeastern portion of the country. They did not expand the territory under their control, however, partly because they were not given the requisite arms and ammunition by their chief supplier, adjacent China. The Chinese, while continuing to support the Communist insurgents, appeared to aid their Burmese comrades only to the degree necessary to hold territory already under their control.

Economy. The gross national product experienced a post–World War II single-year record growth of 8.3%. Rice production, steadily expanding in recent years, was 45% higher in 1981 than it had been five years earlier. But inflation and scarcities persisted, despite the improvement in the Burmese economic situation. A nationwide gasoline shortage, which spawned an extensive black market, was a factor in a major fire in the former royal capital of Mandalay. The fire left 8 persons dead and 35,000 homeless and destroyed $7 million worth of property. Illegally stored petroleum products caused the fire to spread quickly.

Foreign Relations. Sino-Burmese relations deteriorated in 1981, primarily because of Chinese persistence in aiding Communist insurgents in the country. China's Premier Zhao Ziyang requested an invitation to Rangoon early in the year, but, even though this was tendered, President Ne Win virtually snubbed him. He saw his Chinese visitor only once during a four-day visit.

Foreign Minister Lay Maung visited Vietnam the same month, and Burma hosted the deputy foreign ministers of Thailand and Vietnam in June in an effort to help them resolve the differences between their two countries—principally over de facto Vietnamese occupation of Cambodia. China was clearly displeased at this initiative.

RICHARD BUTWELL, *Murray State University*

BURMA • Information Highlights

Official Name: Socialist Republic of the Union of Burma.
Location: Southeast Asia.
Area: 261,218 sq mi (676 555 km^2).
Population (1981 est.): 35,200,000.
Chief Cities (1975 est.): Rangoon, the capital, 2,100,000; Mandalay, 417,000; Moulmein, 202,000.
Government: *Head of state,* San Yu, president (took office Nov. 1981). *Head of government,* U Maung Maung Kha, prime minister (took office March 1977). Legislature (unicameral)—People's Assembly.
Monetary Unit: Kyat (7.63 kyats equal U.S.$1, July 1981).
Manufactures (major products): Agricultural products, textiles, wood and its products, refined petroleum.
Agriculture (major products): Rice, jute, sesame, groundnuts, tobacco, cotton, pulses, sugarcane, corn.

BUSINESS AND CORPORATE AFFAIRS

U.S. businessmen lived in a difficult economic environment in 1918. Interest rates remained at double-digit levels, peaking with a 20½% prime rate in July. Inflation was a nagging problem, as it, too, held at double-digit levels. Bankruptcies remained high, and several major industries were kept alive only by mergers or government support. Yet American businessmen were buoyed by the new administration, which took a decidedly pro-business approach. Not only did the Reagan administration shepherd through Congress a series of beneficial tax cuts, but it was decidedly less antagonistic in environmental, consumer, and antitrust matters.

Corporate Profits and Spending. In the first quarter of 1981, corporate profits were unchanged from the same quarter a year earlier, despite an 11% growth in sales. Profits margins shrank, and inflation-fed inventory profits accounted for a significant portion of net income. Still, profits in the first quarter were up 11% from the last quarter of 1980. By the second quarter of 1981, profits had rebounded, showing a 20% gain over the same quarter in 1980 and a 5% increase over the first quarter of 1981. Industries that had been badly depressed, such as airlines and automobiles, showed the greatest gains. By the third quarter, earnings had begun to decline, reflecting the recession President Ronald Reagan acknowledged had begun.

Merchants hoped that the tax cuts enacted by Congress would lead to a strong Christmas, as consumers reacted positively to increases in disposable income. In spite of favorable tax legislation, however, the business community was slow in responding. Analysts expected total capital spending to increase by only 2.5%.

The Strong and the Weak. The tire and rubber, oil service, restaurant, steel, and defense and military aerospace industries had the strongest performances of 1981, while airlines, metals and mining, savings and loans, real estate, and housing and building materials had the poorest. International oil companies, after posting sizable gains in 1980, had an off year, as a glut in oil ate into profit margins.

U.S. automobile companies had a second consecutive dismal year. In the 1981-model year, sales were about 6.6 million units, down from 6.8 million in 1980. At the same time, import sales increased from 2.3 million to 2.4 million. The only bright spot in Detroit was some improvement at Chrysler Corp., which reported a sales increase of 18% for the model year.

High interest rates also crippled the U.S. housing industry. Half a million new homes, worth $3,000,000,000, sat unsold. Unemployment in the industry averaged 17%, and the failure rate among contractors was up 40%.

Despite the downturn in autos and housing, American steel manufacturers reported an improvement in earnings. However, by the third quarter, a strong dollar had weakened their competitive position, and imports flooded into the country. The steel companies said they would file anti-dumping suits, which once again raised the specter of a trade war.

Air transportation was one of the hardest hit industries. Deregulation permitted the airlines to lower fares, and transcontinental rate wars continued. Also, a strike by air traffic controllers cut down the number of flights. High fuel costs and a decline in domestic traffic forced Pan American World Airways to sell its most profitable subsidiary, the Intercontinental Hotel chain. William T. Seawell, 64, retired as company chairman, and C. Edward Acker, 52, former chairman of Air Florida, took over.

The savings and loan (S&L) industry continued to be plagued by the ceiling on interest rates they are allowed to pay. Depositors remained aloof for most of the year, preferring to put their money into money market mutual funds, whose assets grew from $19,000,000,000 on January 1 to more than $166,000,000,000 by October 21. At the same time, high mortgage rates kept potential customers away, squeezing profits. With their backs to the wall, three major S&Ls from San Francisco, New York, and Florida were merged into one interstate bank. The new bank was the largest federally chartered S&L, with combined assets of $6,800,000,000.

Mergers. High interest rates did not dampen merger enthusiasm on Wall Street. The nine-month total purchase price in 1,807 mergers came to $60,800,000,000, exceeding the record of $44,300,000,000 for all of 1980.

The largest and most spectacular was between DuPont de Nemours and Conoco, the ninth biggest U.S. oil company, for $7,600,000,000. The bidding began when Seagram Co., the Montreal-based distiller, bid $73 per share for 41% of Conoco's stock. Conoco, however, courted DuPont. Then Mobil Oil jumped in, bidding $90 per share. Seagram countered, only to see the ante raised by DuPont. Mobil ran into antitrust questions, and its highest offer was ignored. Eventually, DuPont prevailed, and Seagram wound up owning 20% of the Wilmington (DE) company's stock.

Other mergers were less contentious. Societé Nationale Elf Aquitaine of France purchased Texasgulf for $4,300,000,000; Fluor bought St. Joe Minerals for $2,700,000,000; Standard Oil of Ohio acquired Kennecott for $2,000,000,000; and Nabisco and Standard Brands joined in a merger valued at $1,800,000,000.

Even Wall Street firms found themselves the subject of takeovers. Sears Roebuck purchased Dean Witter Reynolds for $607,000,000; American Express bought Shearson Loeb Rhoades for $1,000,000,000; Phibro got Salomon Bros. for $483,000,000; and Prudential Insurance paid $385,000,000 for Bache Halsey Stuart Shields.

RON SCHERER
"The Christian Science Monitor"

CALIFORNIA

California in 1981 was spared major earthquake, fire, flood, or other natural disasters, but it did face a major threat to its valuable agricultural crops, severe financial problems, and a political battle over reapportionment.

"Medfly." Early in the summer, the state Department of Agriculture reported a steady, though not yet heavy, infestation of tiny pests known as Mediterranean fruit flies. By laying their eggs under the skin of various fruits and vegetables, the insects can ruin whole crops. The spread of the Medfly posed a serious threat to California agriculture.

Technicians the previous autumn had advised aerial spraying with the chemical pesticide malathion. But Gov. Edmund G. (Jerry) Brown, supported by a vociferous if not large constituency of environmentalists, hesitated. Farmers in the Salinas, Sacramento, and San Joaquin valleys were outraged. The U.S. Department of Agriculture announced a quarantine on California produce, which would have been economically devastating in the long term. Finally the governor ordered malathion aerial spraying, and by autumn the threat of disaster seemed to have passed. Governor Brown's popularity, meanwhile, had fallen to an all-time low.

Redistricting. With the governorship and both houses of the state legislature in Democratic hands, reapportionment of the legislature and U.S. Congressional districts was, as is traditional in such cases, planned to benefit the majority party. Legislative leaders enlisted the aid of Rep. Phillip Burton, a San Francisco liberal, to help draw the lines for the state's 45 Congressional districts. (California's representation in the House was increased by two seats as a result of the 1980 U.S. census.)

Republicans complained that Democratic gerrymandering would cost them two Senate, three Assembly, and six Congressional seats, but by year's end the issue was far from settled. The Republicans planned to seek an initiative proposition for the June 1982 ballot to overrule the legislative action; to have the legislative action overruled in the state courts by invoking a constitutional provision for compactness; and to seek the intercession of the U.S. Department of Justice under the Voting Rights Act.

Financial Problems. Heavy demands by local governments for "bailout" funds in the wake of Proposition 13, together with a faltering national economy, caused the state's budget surplus to evaporate. In fact, the governor and state controller took steps to prevent a deficit in fiscal 1982. In early October, the governor issued an executive order for some $460 million in emergency budget cuts and indicated that additional cuts would come later.

Nuclear Power. A large but peaceful protest against the opening of the Diablo Canyon Nuclear Power Plant near San Luis Obispo resulted in the arrests of more than 1,000 demonstrators on September 21. The demonstrators contended that the facility was unsafe because it is situated near an undersea fault. The Nuclear Regulatory Commission in Washington the same day granted a preliminary license to operate the first of two reactors at the site. In late November, however, it was revoked pending an investigation of design irregularities.

Legislative Session. Republicans, bitter over the apportionment battle, killed scores of bills that required unanimous consent or a two-thirds majority. The most important bill to die was a bispartisan effort to get California to conform to the health and welfare budget changes of the national administration.

Among major pieces of legislation in 1981 were an act lobbied for by organized labor and women's groups to provide comparable pay for jobs of comparable worth; an act supported by developers, passed over the opposition of the state League of Cities, and later vetoed by Governor Brown, to create five new, privately developed cities with planning and regulation controlled by a state agency and with no local government for ten years; acts requiring some persons on welfare to seek job training and accept available employment; and an act barring politicians from using campaign funds for personal purposes. More than 300 "law and order" bills were introduced, and some were passed. Despite spending cutbacks, the state budget again reached an all-time high.

Crime. Crime and criminals continued to make headlines throughout California during 1981. A suspect in the "freeway murders" of 21 young men and boys went on trial in Los Angeles County; an alleged accomplice hanged himself in a county jail. In San Diego, Joseph C. Bonanno, 75, was sentenced to five years in prison and fined $10,000 for taking part in the activities of organized crime. And in San Francisco, a second mistrial was declared in the case of members of the Hell's Angels motorcycle gang charged with racketeering and dealing in narcotics; the case was then dismissed on a motion by the district attorney.

CHARLES R. ADRIAN
University of California, Riverside

CALIFORNIA • Information Highlights

Area: 158,706 sq mi (411 049 km^2).
Population (1980 census): 23,668,562.
Chief Cities (1980 census): Sacramento, the capital, 275,741; Los Angeles, 2,966,763; San Diego, 875,504; San Francisco, 678,974; San Jose, 636,550; Long Beach, 361,334; Oakland, 339,288; Anaheim, 221,847; Fresno, 218,202; Santa Ana, 203,713.
Government (1981): *Chief Officers*—governor, Edmund G. Brown, Jr. (D); lt. gov., Mike Curb (R). *Legislature*—Senate, 40 members; Assembly, 80 members.
State Finances (fiscal year 1980): *Revenues*, $36,087,000,000; *expenditures*, $32,812,000,000.
Personal Income (1980): $259,551,000,000; per capita, $10,938.
Labor Force (July 1981): *Nonagricultural wage and salary earners*, 9,882,400; *unemployed*, 855,000 (7.4% of total force).

CAMBODIA

During 1981, the precarious sense of "normalcy" that had been induced in Cambodia (Kampuchea) by the three-year Vietnamese occupation and by aid from many foreign sources began to be tested. The cooperation between China and ASEAN (Association of Southeast Asian Nations) against Vietnam and the alliance between Vietnam and the USSR also were tested. It was a year in which everyone who had an interest in Cambodia struggled to find some solid ground to stand on.

Politics. In May 1981, carefully controlled elections were held for a 117-member National Assembly. The government made a kind of festival of the assembly elections, and foreign journalists reported that many Cambodians seemed willing to vote for the handpicked candidates. The Assembly then formally approved a new administration and adopted a new constitution. The exercise plainly was designed to invest the Hanoi-supported regime with greater legitimacy in the eyes of the Khmer (Cambodian) people and in the eyes of the world. (Most nations have refused to recognize the Vietnamese-backed regime in Phnom Penh or to allow it to claim the UN seat reserved for Cambodia.)

After the election, the Phnom Penh regime held a congress of the Kampuchea People's Revolutionary Party (KPRP) and chose Penn Sovan, 45, as secretary-general, which seemed to prove that he was the leading personality in the regime. Penn Sovan also tried to adopt a more direct relationship with Moscow, which increased its advisory role in competition with Hanoi. In December, Penn Sovan was suddenly removed from office, apparently at Vietnam's initiation. Also in December, it was announced that the Pol Pot faction, based in China, was disbanding.

Economy. Cambodia's economic life achieved a remarkable but fragile recovery in the three years since Vietnam invaded and expelled the Pol Pot regime. The Pol Pot group had tried to run a primitive form of Communism in the mid-1970s, and they butchered hundreds of thousands of suspected "class enemies." Massive foreign aid was poured into Cambodia during 1979 and 1980, including some $200 million from the Soviet bloc countries, $450 million from Western governments, and $100 million from private Western organizations. Total U.S. government contributions during the 1980 and 1981 fiscal years were $186 million, and American citizens also privately contributed about $70 million.

By their own efforts, backed by the aid, the Khmer people rebuilt many of the homes that were destroyed and replanted many of the rice fields that were abandoned during a decade of war. However, the country still lacked enough seed, tools, and draft animals to produce food to feed the people, much less to export a surplus to pay for vitally needed machinery and raw materials to run existing factories. At the end of 1981, everything in Cambodia was tinged with uncertainty, particularly Vietnam's plans for the country, the value of the currency, and the willingness of foreigners to provide more aid. Even the size of the population was uncertain.

UPI

While Cambodia tries to regain economic order, the black market in Phnom Penh remains active.

Foreign Relations. During 1981, Penn Sovan's regime failed to gain any important new recognition by countries outside the Soviet bloc. In July, a UN conference of 92 nations, which Vietnam and the USSR refused to attend, grappled with the problem of restoring Cambodia's sovereignty. At the conference, the five ASEAN countries took a somewhat more conciliatory posture toward Vietnam than China did. China's hard-line insistence on no Vietnamese political or military role in Cambodia was supported by the conference. Penn Sovan's removal could be a sign that Vietnam wished to open a dialogue with ASEAN on Cambodia's future.

PETER A. POOLE, *Old Dominion University*

CAMBODIA • Information Highlights

Official Name: Democratic Kampuchea.
Location: Southeast Asia.
Area: 69,898 sq mi (181 036 km^2).
Population (1981 est.): 5,500,000.
Chief City (1979 est.): Phnom Penh, the capital, 200,000.
Government: *Head of state and government,* Heng Samrin (took office 1981).
Monetary Unit: Riel.
Manufactures (major products): Textiles, cement, paper products.
Agriculture (major products): Rice, rubber, sugarcane.

CANADA

For Canadians, 1981 was a year of living with decisions made the year before. The federal government's preoccupation with constitutional reform was linked to Quebec voters' rejection of separation in a 1980 referendum. Conflict over domestic energy prices dated from the Liberal victory in the 1980 federal election. Relations with the new Reagan administration in the United States were aggravated by Canada's National Energy Program, announced by Ottawa in November 1980. Inflation, unemployment, and soaring interest rates—the preoccupations of most ordinary Canadians during 1981—were all problems inherited from the past. In a year of unhappy sequels, even Terry Fox, the one-legged runner whose Marathon of Hope had thrilled Canadians in 1980, finally succumbed to lung cancer on June 28, 1981.

The Constitution. For Canada's Prime Minister Pierre Elliott Trudeau, the priority in 1981 was the historic task of ending dependence on Britain for the amendment of the constitution. Simple patriation had scarcely been controversial. What had provoked half a century of debate was an acceptable amending formula. In the long search for a generally agreed solution, provinces had bargained their consent against demands for additional powers in what already was one of the most decentralized of federal systems. In October 1980, an impatient Trudeau had proclaimed his determination to ask Britain for a final amendment of the British North America Act, using an amending formula which had satisfied the provinces in 1971 plus a new Charter of Rights embodying a wide variety of human, economic, and cultural guarantees.

The sharp constitutional debate which Trudeau's announcement provoked continued throughout much of 1981. Of the ten Canadian provinces, only Ontario and New Brunswick supported the Trudeau initiative. The remainder, led by Alberta and Quebec and eventually joined by Saskatchewan, were angrily opposed. In Parliament, Trudeau's Liberal majority was joined by most of Ed Broadbent's New Democratic Party. Joe Clark's Progressive Conservatives, the official opposition, carried all but a few dissenters into opposition. Canadian opinion, reflected by the polls, gave apparently strong support to the prime minister's purpose, opposed his unilateral tactics, and, outside French Canada, indicated that other issues took far higher priority.

While debate in Parliament raged over principles and a special committee considered amendments urged by native groups, feminists, civil libertarians, and other organized pressure groups, three of the dissenting provinces took their case to court. Verdicts in Manitoba and Quebec generally favored the federal government's right to proceed; a Newfoundland decision endorsed that province's objections. Amid rumors that the British parliament might balk at accepting the Trudeau constitutional package if the legal issue was not resolved, the federal government agreed to expedite an appeal to the Supreme Court. It also abandoned its patriation deadline of July 1, Canada's national holiday. Clark agreed to abandon parliamentary delaying tactics, and an agreed Charter of Rights was adopted by the House of Commons.

When, after its lengthy summer recess, the Supreme Court announced its verdict on September 28, the nine justices confirmed that the real issues were political, not legal. By a verdict of 6 to 3, the court ruled that Ottawa's unilateral approach broke past constitutional conventions, though the justices did not define what those conventions were. By a margin of 7 to 2, the justices also ruled that the federal government had a legal right to proceed.

Supporters and critics each took up the part of the verdict that suited their case, but it was soon apparent that the Supreme Court had dealt a serious setback to Trudeau's unilateral approach. Ed Broadbent's NDP withdrew its support unless the prime minister made yet another try at compromise. Fresh from an unexpectedly successful provincial election, Quebec Premier René Lévesque summoned Quebec's National Assembly to denounce any possible invasion of its powers. The Quebec Liberal leader, Claude Ryan, led most of his supporters to back the Lévesque declaration, confessing that he had "suffered enough for federalism."

For a month, British Columbia's premier, William Bennett, new spokesman for the eight dissenting provinces, shuttled between provincial capitals, looking for concessions which might move beyond the bare-bones agreement among the eight provinces in April—simple patriation and an amending formula that allowed provinces to opt out of changes that affected them. On November 2, Trudeau and all ten premiers met in Ottawa for a last bid at a settlement, urged on by rumors that Britain's parliament might balk at a constitutional package backed

CANADA • Information Highlights

Official Name: Canada.
Location: Northern North America.
Area: 3,851,809 sq mi (9 976 185 km^2).
Population (April 1981 est.): 24,150,000.
Chief cities (1980 met. est.): Ottawa, the capital, 726,400; Toronto, 2,856,500; Montreal, 2,823,000.
Government: *Head of state,* Elizabeth II, queen; represented by Edward Schreyer, governor-general (took office Jan. 22, 1979). *Head of government,* Pierre Elliott Trudeau, prime minister (took office March 1980). *Legislature*—Parliament: Senate and House of Commons.
Monetary Unit: Canadian dollar (1.20 dollars equal U.S.$1, Nov. 1981).
Manufactures (major products): Motor vehicles and parts, fish and forest products, petroleum and natural gas, processed and unprocessed minerals.
Agriculture (major products): Wheat, livestock and meat, feed grains, oilseeds, dairy products, tobacco, fruits and vegetables.

P. Breese/Liaison

Pierre Elliott Trudeau was host to the leaders of the six other major industrial democracies. Many Canadians were unhappy with the prime minister for playing a bigger role on the world scene.

only by Ottawa and two provinces. A blizzard of possible changes circulated among the eleven first ministers as successive premiers sought the honorable role of peacemaker. The winner, in the final hours, was Newfoundland's Brian Peckford. In a final, emotional public session, Trudeau and nine of the ten premiers announced an agreement on patriation, an amending formula based on the terms agreed upon in April by eight of the premiers, and a sharply modified charter of rights.

The one province which held out, not altogether reluctantly, was Quebec. Abandonment by seven of its erstwhile allies was fulfillment of separatist arguments. Although other provinces, including Ontario, had at last agreed to guarantee education rights for French-speaking minorities, Quebec refused to allow any such guarantee for its English-speaking minority. Premier Lévesque was angered by a provision which refused financial compensation for any province that opted out of future constitutional changes. He knew that federal financial aid had levered Quebec into health, hospital, and old age security programs.

For the moment, Prime Minister Trudeau and his colleagues could overlook protests from an avowed separatist. Native people and women, whose special clauses had vanished in the November 5th compromise, mobilized successfully to restore most of the earlier language. Despite the Quebec government and other dissenters, Canadians could hope for a new constitution.

Inflation and Interest Rates. Despite the Trudeau government's preoccupation with constitutions, pollsters reported in 1981 that most Canadians were bewildered by the issue and indifferent to its outcome. They wanted politicians to solve economic problems. Forecasts for 1981 had offered mild encouragement in most regions, but Alberta's energy boom went flat. Both American and Canadian exploration companies packed their drill rigs and headed south to the richer incentives promised in Ronald Reagan's America. The two multi-billion-dollar oil sands projects at Alsands and Cold Lake were closed down as an industry counterblow to Ottawa's National Energy Program and to the failure of Ottawa and Alberta to agree on future oil prices.

Canadian inflation in 1981 reached an annual rate of 12.5%, a little higher than in the previous peacetime record year of 1975. Inflation's most public manifestation was unprecedented interest rates. By midsummer, the bank rate hovered above 20%; chartered banks charged favored customers 2–3% more, and Canadian borrowers, from farmers to homebuyers, worried about imminent bankruptcy and foreclosure. Rates eased during the autumn, and financial

UPI

The premiers of the four Western provinces (l-r)—Manitoba's S. Lyon, Saskatchewan's A. Blakeney, Alberta's P. Lougheed, and British Columbia's B. Bennett—discuss such matters of mutual concern as high interest rates, federal-provincial relations, energy prices, and the federal budget deficit. Canada's constitution was also of particular importance for the premiers throughout 1981.

institutions, criticized by Minister of Finance Allan MacEachen, offered mild palliatives to their borrowers. Industries dependent on credit, from home builders to manufacturers of consumer durables, began to feel the pinch of a shrunken market.

National Energy Program (NEP). In November 1980, the Trudeau government had startled the corporate world by carrying through some of the nationalistic energy policies it had promised during the year's political campaign. As advanced by Minister of Energy Marc Lalonde, the NEP promised at least 51% Canadian ownership of its petroleum and gas industry by 1990. To speed the process, old tax incentives would be abolished and a new system of incentive grants for exploration would be available only to Canadian-owned firms. Combined with failure to reach an energy pricing formula with Alberta, the Lalonde program produced confusion in the energy industry and a sharp reduction in exploration activity, as well as angry threats from the new Reagan administration in Washington.

Under pressure, the NEP was softened slightly but multinationals complained that Ottawa, seeking at least 51% Canadian ownership, had devalued their shares by restricting their market. There was little evidence of undervaluation when Petro-Canada, the state-owned oil company, purchased Petrofina's Canadian holdings for C$1,500,000,000 or when Ontario paid half that much for only a quarter of Suncor. The Trudeau government believed that it had strong public support for its policies. Its confidence grew when a report by Robert Bertrand, a respected official, accused major oil companies of price-fixing arrangements that had cost consumers $12,000,000,000 during the 1970s. When hearings into the charges opened in October, the embattled companies mustered some of Canada's ablest corporation lawyers for their counterattack.

For consumers and the economy as a whole, failure to reach an oil pricing agreement was more troubling than the National Energy Program. Meetings between Lalonde and his Alberta counterpart, Mervin Leitch, were punctuated by cutbacks in oil production enforced by the provincial government. By September 1, when the cuts totaled 180,000 barrels a day, an agreement was finally reached. While both sides

THE CANADIAN MINISTRY

Pierre Elliott Trudeau, prime minister
Allan Joseph MacEachen, deputy prime minister and minister of finance
Jean-Luc Pepin, minister of transport
Jean Chrétien, minister of justice, attorney general, and minister of state for social development
John Munro, minister of Indian affairs and northern development
H. A. (Bud) Olson, minister of state for economic development
Herb Gray, minister of industry, trade and commerce
Eugene Whelan, minister of agriculture
André Ouellet, minister of consumer and corporate affairs; postmaster general
Marc Lalonde, minister of energy, mines and resources
Ray Perrault, leader of the government in the Senate
Roméo LeBlanc, minister of fisheries and oceans
John Roberts, minister of state for science and technology; minister of the environment
Monique Bégin, minister of national health and welfare
Jean-Jacques Blais, minister of supply and services
Francis Fox, minister of communications
Gilles Lamontagne, minister of national defence
Pierre De Bane, minister of regional economic development
Hazen Argue, minister of state for the wheat board
Gerald Regan, secretary of state and minister responsible for fitness and amateur sport
Mark MacGuigan, secretary of state for external affairs
Robert Kaplan, solicitor general
James Fleming, minister of state for multiculturalism
William Rompkey, minister of national revenue
Pierre Bussières, minister of state for finance
Charles Lapointe, minister of state for small business
Ed Lumley, minister of state for trade
Yvon Pinard, president of the Privy Council
Donald Johnston, president of the treasury board
Lloyd Axworthy, minister of employment and immigration
Paul Cosgrove, minister of public works and minister responsible for Canada Mortgage and Housing Corp.
Judy Erola, minister of state for mines and minister responsible for the status of women
Charles Caccia, minister of labor
Serge Joyal, minister of state
Bennett Campbell, minister of veterans affairs
Jack Austin, minister of state

made concessions, Alberta forced Ottawa to remove a federal excise tax on natural gas exports to the United States, and the new price formula would double the price of fuel oil and gasoline to Canadian consumers by 1986. Of $212,000,000,000 in new revenues, Ottawa would gain $54,000,000,000, Alberta $64,000,000,000, and the companies, $94,000,000,000.

The settlement delighted the two governments involved, those provinces with *ad valorem* taxes on gasoline, and a bevy of experts who insisted on the economic, ecological, and moral virtues of high energy prices. Consumers were tranquilized by the postponing of big increases until the new year. As for the energy industry, it insisted that its share was still inadequate. By year's end, the two oil sands projects and other major undertakings vital to Canadian self-sufficiency by 1990 remained in limbo.

Making a Living. Faced with big increases in food prices, double-size monthly payments for renegotiated mortgages, and the prospect of $4 for a gallon of gasoline, Canadian consumers lived through the fourth consecutive year in which wage increases lagged behind the cost of living. Only British and Japanese workers, among the advanced industrialized countries, earned lower hourly wages, a dramatic shift from the era when Canadians ranked only behind Americans in wage levels. Although unions mustered more than a third of the work force in their ranks, the strike weapon was blunted by large inventories, high unemployment, and vigorous public hostility. The federal government allowed a strike by 23,000 militant postal workers to tie up the mails for nearly seven weeks. The publicly-owned Canadian Broadcasting Corporation sacrificed its fall season to force striking technicians to settle largely on its terms.

Faced with adversity, Canadian unions appeared to fragment rather than unite. Some 250,000 members of American-based construction unions quit the Canadian Labour Congress to establish their own Canadian Federation of Labour in November 1981.

To improve postal service, Ottawa followed the example of Britain, Australia, and the United States by creating an independent government corporation to handle the mail. Spurred by the biggest wheat harvest in years, the government also moved to improve grain handling and railway facilities while imposing sharp cuts on passenger rail services.

External Affairs. If most Canadians were indifferent to their government's constitutional preoccupation, they sometimes seemed positively annoyed by their prime minister's sudden involvement in international concerns. Trudeau's

Opposition leader Joe Clark makes a point during House of Commons debate. The standing of the Progressive Conservative leader in the polls was low early in the year but later rose.

UPI

travels, notably to prepare for the North-South conference at Cancún in Mexico in October, took him to Latin America, Africa, and the South Pacific. A July 23–24 summit conference of seven national leaders at the Chateau Montebello near Ottawa served to remind Canadians that they still counted, though barely, among the major industrial nations. When North and South did meet at Cancún on October 22–23, Trudeau joined the Mexican president as co-chairman.

Canada's major external concerns, as ever, were with the United States. Although President Reagan's pre-election statements emphasized his eagerness to improve relations with Canada and Mexico, his first year in office only underlined how rapidly Ottawa and the new Washington administration were drifting apart. The Trudeau government's plans to Canadianize a predominantly American-owned oil industry, the pollution of the Niagara River by chemical companies on the U.S. side, and Canadian capital pursuing corporate bargains in the United States all contributed to an unusually acerbic tone in Canadian-American relations in 1981. Ottawa and the province of Ontario campaigned against American sulfur emissions, alleged to cause half the acid rain that destroyed fish and vegetable life in Canadian lakes. Americans asked why Canadians did so little to curb their half of the problem. The possibility that Canada might give teeth to its largely symbolic Foreign Investment Review Agency provoked talk of U.S. retaliation.

With their historic faith in public enterprise and on public-private economic collaboration, Canadians found it hard to adjust to the rhetoric of the Reagan White House, and there was an uncomfortable sense of menace when, in the midst of business and political threats of American retaliation, a senior U.S. State Department official, Myer Rashish, drew a parallel with Soviet-Polish relations. Canadian business interests warned other Canadians of their vulnerability to American economic pressures, reinforcing the Polish analogy.

Canadians went without mail deliveries for 43 days. The summer strike was quite damaging to business.

Brian Willer/"Maclean's"

Politics, Police, and Media. In parts of Canada, President Reagan's economic philosophy gave positive reinforcement to the reiterated beat of Trudeauphobia. The energy battle between a newly wealthy Alberta and Ottawa gave prominence to a variety of western separatist movements in early 1981, although the absence of a credible leader or a persuasive program sent the separatists into eclipse long before the September 1 energy deal. Despite obvious economic difficulties and the constitutional battle, Canadian voters sustained Trudeau and the Liberals in the opinion polls for the first half of 1981. When Progressive Conservatives met in Ottawa at the end of February, a third of the delegates voted no-confidence in Joe Clark by demanding a leadership convention. In July, it was Ed Broadbent's turn to face a party convention in which a third of the delegates repudiated his support for Trudeau's constitutional initiative.

By the summer, however, it was the Liberals whose fortunes were flagging. On August 17, the Conservatives regained their single Quebec seat and in a normally Liberal constituency in Toronto the New Democrats defeated Trudeau's principal aide, Jim Coutts. By the autumn, the governing party trailed the Conservatives in the opinion polls and Cark's leadership looked slightly more secure.

The Liberal government could blame its misfortune on economic difficulties beyond its control. At Montebello, other heads of state had failed to alter President Reagan's commitment to high interest rates and, unless Canada followed NDP advice to cut itself off from the U.S. economy, Canada would win or lose with its American neighbors.

The Liberals were authors of some of their own misfortunes. In January, they enraged their own women supporters by a heavy-handed attempt to stop the federal Advisory Committee on the Status of Women from criticizing the draft Charter of Rights. At the height of the summer postal strike, the postmaster general enraged small businessmen by an ill-judged comment that it was their own fault if they depended on the postal service for their living.

F. C. Elder

According to Canada's Minister of the Environment John Roberts, the effect of acid rain on Canadian lakes, including George Lake in Ontario's Provincial Park (above), "is simply disastrous." The problem caused U.S.-Canadian relations to deteriorate in 1981.

By no means everything went badly for the government or the country. The report of Justice David McDonald on the undercover activities of the Royal Canadian Mounted Police (RCMP) condemned members of the force for clumsy and illegal operations against Quebec separatists and alleged subversives, but it exonerated the politicians responsible for the RCMP. The report recommended a new civilian security agency. Another government report was less welcome, at least to Canada's newspaper publishers. Created in 1980 after long-established newspapers in Ottawa and Winnipeg were simultaneously closed by competing chains, a task force headed by Tom Kent, former journalist and Liberal aide, conducted the second investigation of newspaper management in a decade. Its report, issued in August, claimed that chain ownership had grown from 55 to 77% in the interval. After scathing criticism of editorial and journalistic standards, particularly in the large Thompson chain of newspapers, the task force urged legislation to prevent further concentration, divestiture of media monopolies, and a system of community monitoring of newspaper performance. The Kent proposals drew a torrent of outrage from the newspaper owners. The task force's advice vanished into the care of two committees.

The MacEachen Budget. When Parliament resumed on October 14, the government had much ground to recover. Finance Minister Allan MacEachen had been left with responsibility for remedying a host of contradictory problems—lagging growth, high unemployment, static revenues, rising costs in every public or private activity, and a heavy federal deficit. On November 12, the only certainty about the long-expected budget was that no one would be very pleased. The forecasts were fulfilled.

The Finance Department predicted continuing double-digit inflation, rising unemployment, and the fifth year of falling real incomes for wage-earners. The government had promised help for those in "dire straits" because of high interest rates. However, the aid was meager and patchy. The two main features of MacEachen's budget were halfway fulfillment of his threat to cut federal payments to the provinces for health and higher education and the elimination of a large number of income tax shelters. Plugging loopholes allowed a cut in marginal tax rates from 45 to 34%. Reduced payments to the provinces, still to be negotiated, would cut the federal government deficit.

Canadians were unimpressed. On November 21, 80,000 of them answered a Canadian Labour Congress summons to the largest Parliament Hill demonstration in history. Their fellow citizens shared a gloomy sense of impending economic gloom.

DESMOND MORTON
Erindale College, University of Toronto

THE ECONOMY

For the Canadian economy, 1981 was a year of successive shocks. What had appeared to be a recovery from the 1980 recession slid into a second, W-shaped (down, up, down, up) recession. Beginning with two quarters of relatively strong growth, the economy began to wither by midsummer under the glare of sustained high interest rates imposed in response to the restrictive monetary policies in force in the United States. This brought growth to a virtual standstill during the second half. Indeed, with 1981 marking a deterioration in almost all leading economic indicators—except gross national product (GNP), expected to show a year-to-year real gain of 3.5%, in spite of the weak second half—some economists believe the Canadian economy never recovered from the 1980 recession. The same dim prospects were stretching well into 1982 as well.

What made 1981 a particularly wrenching year was the battering received by the Canadian dollar in international currency trading, especially the sharp decline against the U.S. dollar that took place during the third quarter. In early August, the Canadian dollar declined to a 50-year low of U.S.$0.8043, barely sustained above the psychological breakthrough level of 80 cents by a massive $1,400,000,000 intervention by the Bank of Canada. The dollar's decline reflected the great stress placed on many Western currencies during the height of U.S. monetary restraint. Canada, for example, was forced to raise its central bank rate to a record high of 21.54% during the third quarter simply to maintain a spread over U.S. rates or else risk a massive outflow of short-term capital and an even sharper decline in the currency.

It was capital outflow of a different type—long-term money, associated with government and corporate borrowing—that brought the currency crisis to such a level in the first place. An estimated $10,000,000,000 in Canadian dollars—four times the normal level—were converted into U.S. funds during 1981 to finance takeovers, either "Canadianizing" U.S.-owned subsidiaries operating in Canada or buying up companies outside the country. The takeovers were spurred in part by Canadian incentives offered under the new federal National Energy Program (NEP).

Capital outflows during 1981 were further hastened as a result of continued borrowing by government to finance Canada's growing current account deficit, expected to soar from $1,900,000,000 in 1980 to more than $5,000,000,000 in 1981. Though Canada traditionally records an annual surplus in merchandise trade (chiefly raw materials), the services deficit (interest on foreign loans, foreign dividend payments, travel, and so on) was growing at a dangerous rate annually.

Inflation was up over 1980, with the Consumer Price Index showing a sharp jump from 10.1% in 1980 to an estimated 12.7% by year-end. The increase was caused partially by a considerable rise in Canadian energy prices. This followed a September agreement between the federal government and oil-producing provinces to raise well-head prices nearer to world levels—the end of a long period of uncertainty clouding Canada's energy sector. Nearly every other key indicator was adversely affected by high interest rates: housing starts, expected to increase, remained relatively flat; unemployment, expected to decline, began to creep above the 1980 level of 7.5%; capital spending, expected to grow by about 8% following two years of good profits, began to trail away by year-end.

See also LABOR.

ANTHONY WHITTINGHAM
Senior Writer, "Maclean's"

THE CANADIAN ECONOMY

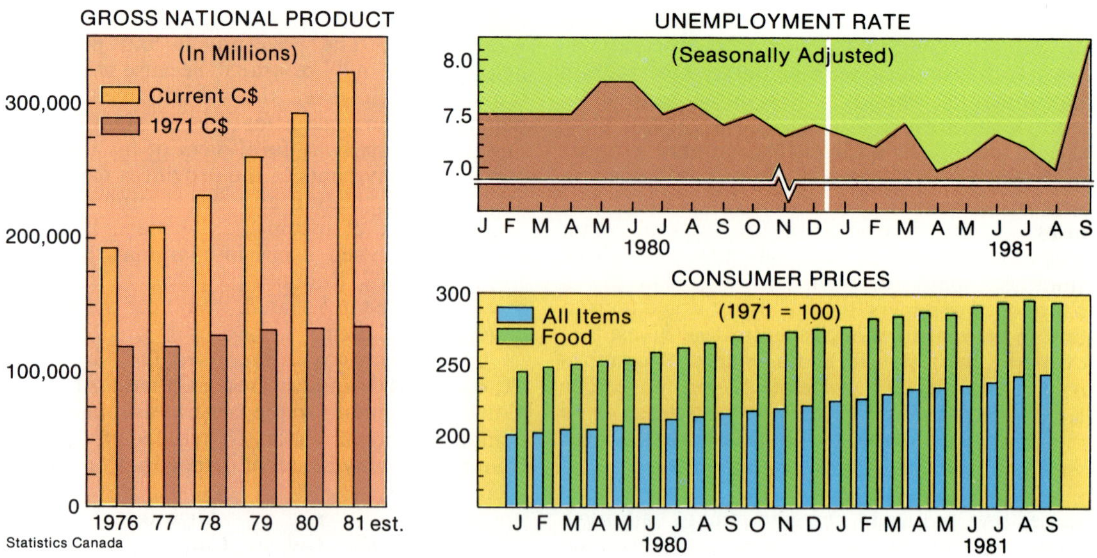

Statistics Canada

Les Grands Ballets Canadiens

Les Grands Ballet Canadiens perform George Balanchine's "Capriccio" during 1981 U.S.-Canadian tour.

THE ARTS

Several years ago, the arts in Canada were set on an unprecedented expansion course. At that time the Canadian economy, according to the federal government's national growth targets for the 1980s, was geared to progress and expectancy. Public funding and spending escalated. The concept of social responsibility toward the cultural sector changed from passive laissez-faire to optimistic, positive activism. The rosy dawn of the 1980s turned gray before the hopeful forecasts for arts, humanities, and social sciences in the new decade could become reality. A freeze on government funding and cutbacks in subsidies became necessary. In retrospect it seems clear that without the Canada Council, the major federal funding agency (established in 1957), and generous provincial, municipal, and corporate support, not only would Canada's evolution from cultural deprivation and colonialism have been seriously delayed, but the threat to the arts would not have aroused so much concern in the more recent times of austerity. According to 1981 statistics, the cultural sector has become the fourth largest employer in Canada. Nearly half the population, 11,200,000 people, visited a public or university-affiliated art gallery or museum in 1980. The government, despite restrictions on funding of the arts, accounts for about 80% of operating revenues. In one generation, "the things we cherish" have become "the things we need" and "the things we are entitled to take for granted" in a modern, civilized society. This attitude was made clear by the thousands of people who spoke up at the public hearings held by the Federal Cultural Policy Review Committee during its three-month, cross-country tour made in 1981. The purpose of the inquiry was to examine the range of current federal policies in culture and the arts and to recommend future directions. A government White Paper was in preparation for presentation to the Ministry of State in 1982.

Visual Arts. Among the hundreds of exhibitions organized by private and public galleries, four were outstanding and of long-term interest. They reflected a growing ambition by Canadian museum directors to compete in the international spectacular-exhibition arena. The 1981 season began on January 24, with "Vincent van Gogh and the Birth of Cloisonism" at the Art Gallery of Ontario (AGO) in Toronto. Guest curator Dr. Bogomila Welsh presented a decisive reassessment of the 1886–91 period in French Post-Impressionist painting. Each of the 147 paintings, drawings, and prints featured stylistic traits of "Cloisonism," a term derived from the French word *cloison,* or partition, originally a generic name associated with stained glass, enamel inlay, and block print. Van Gogh, Paul Gauguin, Louis Anquetin, Emile Bernard, and Henri de Toulouse-Lautrec were major proponents of this style. Also organized by the AGO, "Gauguin to Moore" (November 7–January 3) picked up a fascinating theme—the influence of primitive art on modern sculptors from Gauguin, Auguste Rodin, Pablo Picasso, and Constantin Brancusi to Alberto Giacometti and Henry Moore, a period between 1880 and 1940. At Vancouver's Centennial Museum, the spring exhibition "The Look of Music" (1500 to 1900) brought 328 priceless early instruments from 30 museums and collections in 12 countries together for the first and perhaps only time. The exhibits included a number of instruments from Leningrad, which had been generally inaccessible to musicians and scholars. On September 19, the Museum of Fine Arts in Montreal (MMFA) presented the works of French portraitist Nicolas de Largillière (1656–1746). The 89 paintings, drawings, and prints traced the development of an art that glorifies the 18th-century taste of the rich and powerful Parisian *haute bourgeoisie.*

Performing Arts. Eight major dance companies took part in the "Canadian Dance Spectacular" (May 28–30), a $1 million event staged at the National Arts Centre in Ottawa by the Canadian Association of Professional Dance Organizations (CAPDO, formed 1978). Participants in the gala included Vancouver's Anna Wyman Dance Theatre; Montreal's Les Grands Ballets Canadiens; Ottawa's Le Groupe de la Place Royale; Toronto's National Ballet of Canada, Toronto Dance Theatre, and the Danny Grossman Dance Company; and the Royal Winnipeg Ballet and Contemporary Dancers of Winnipeg. Each company presented chosen highlights from its repertoire. At the prestigious Moscow International ballet competition in June, four young dancers, performing for Canada, reached the finals and won awards. All were trained by Betty Oliphant, director of the National Ballet of Canada School. Canada's newest dance company, the Theatre Ballet of Canada (Artistic Director, Lawrence Gradus), went on its first coast-to-coast tour in 1981.

Theater festivals have developed at an enthusiastic pace. In Ontario highlights included, at Stratford, Friedrich Dürrenmatt's *The Visit,* directed by Jean Gascon, with Alexis Smith in the major role; and at the Shaw Festival, Niagara-on-the-Lake, Robert David MacDonald's *Camille,* which blended the principal versions of the legend—the real life Marie Duplessis and her lover Alexandre Dumas *fils,* Marguerite Gautier in Dumas' novel and play *La Dame aux Camélias,* and Violetta in Giuseppe Verdi's opera *La Traviata.* Toronto's International Theatre Festival, "Onstage '81" (May 11–30), offered in 38 locations 950 performances by 138 companies, including a separate nine-day children's festival and the first conference on theater business, "Stage Directions," for lawyers, producers, directors, and politicians. One of Canada's productions at the festival, David Fennario's *Balconville* (Centaur Theatre Company, Montreal), set in a bilingual Quebec working-class neighborhood, had earlier been the first Canadian play to be performed at London's Old Vic. Theatre Passe Muraille, Toronto, presented *Maggie and Pierre,* with Linda Griffiths in her unique double role. The play was suggested by events in the life of Prime Minister Trudeau and his estranged wife Margaret. It had its New York debut on September 26, at the Marymount Manhattan Theatre, New York City. One of the fastest growing annual events is the Blyth Summer Festival, established in 1975 in a small Ontario community (population 900) 120 mi (193 km) west of Toronto. It features Canadian plays only and encourages a grass-roots approach to theater. At the Charlottetown Festival, Prince Edward Island, the 17th season opened with the sparkling, up-tempo new musical *Aimee!,* written by Patrick Young, with music by Bob Ashley. It is based on the life of Aimee Semple McPherson, the famous evangelist from Ingersoll, Ontario, who attracted publicity, adulation, and a huge radio audience in the 1920s and

Art Gallery of Ontario

Vincent van Gogh's "Vase with Iris Against a Yellow Background" was on display at the "Vincent van Gogh and the Birth of Cloisonism" show at the Art Gallery of Ontario early in the year.

Canadian Opera Company Archives

The Canadian Opera Company's fall season featured Jacques Offenbach's "The Tales of Hoffmann."

1930s in California. The United Nations International Year of the Disabled was marked at Edmonton's Workshop West by a production of Jan Selman's *Creeps.* The play took a deliberately shocking look at the basic problems facing the disabled who suffer from the "protection" of the outside world.

The Canadian Opera Company opened the fall season with Jacques Offenbach's *The Tales of Hoffmann.* The Fritz Oeser edition of the score was first introduced to North America in 1980 by the Greater Miami Opera, which lent the sets for the Toronto production. The Canadian Opera Company also staged Verdi's *A Masked Ball,* with the Metropolitan Opera's Martina Arroyo in the major role.

The Toronto Symphony's 60th anniversary coincided with the National Ballet of Canada's 30th. The Symphony is to move in 1982 from its old home into the New Massey Hall, now under construction. The new Association of Canadian Women Composers plans to establish liaisons with other associations of women composers in the United States and Europe.

Motion Pictures. The celebrated film of 1981 was *Les Plouffe* (The Plouffe Family), an updated and condensed version of Quebec's popular French radio and television serial, based on Roger Lemelin's novel of the same name. It was shown, along with Clay Borris' *Alligator Shoes,* at "Director's Fortnight" (not in competition) at the Cannes Film Festival. *Ticket to Heaven,* based on Josh Freed's book *Moonwebs,* which depicts the dark side of the Rev. Sun Myung Moon's counter-culture utopia, opened 1981's Toronto Festival of Festivals. *Not a Love Story: A Film about Pornography,* the 70-minute National Film Board documentary, was shown, surprisingly uncut by Ontario's strict Board of Censors. It presents a Montreal stripper and the movie director Bonnie Sherr Klein, touring North America and conducting interviews with women, including poet Margaret Atwood and feminist writer Kate Millett. Robin Phillips, former artistic director of the Stratford Festival, directed his first movie in Canada, *The Wars,* based on Timothy Findley's 1977 award-winning novel.

Beginning in 1982, producers must use Canadian stars in one of the two leading roles in their movies and video productions, as well as a Canadian director or screenwriter, in order to qualify for capital cost allowances against taxation.

Television. The Canadian Broadcasting Company's activities in 1981 were seriously restricted by a technicians' strike, which lasted 112 days. Europe continued to be the largest buyer of its productions, with 1980 purchases exceeding $1,500,000.

HELEN DUFFY, *Art Critic, Toronto*

CARIBBEAN

An unusually high number of tropical depressions were spawned in the eastern Atlantic Ocean during the 1981 hurricane season. Fortunately for the Caribbean, however, none of the storms adversely affected any of the land areas of the region. Most of the hurricanes went off to the northwest, and those that did cross into the Caribbean were weak and poorly organized, leaving behind only rain and, in the case of the Dominican Republic in June, some flooding. Temperatures throughout the Caribbean were only two to four degrees higher than average during the summer months, and rainfall also was above normal. There was no dry season in 1981.

In July, speaking in Santo Domingo, Roger Fountaine, a specialist on Caribbean and Latin American affairs and a member of the U.S. National Security Council, stressed the interest and concern for the Caribbean of President Ronald Reagan. At several times during the year, spokesmen for the new administration—including Secretary of State Alexander Haig speaking in Can Cun, Mexico, Special Representative for Trade Bill Brock in Washington in June, and Undersecretary of State for Latin American Affairs Thomas Enders before a congressional committee in Washington—all stressed the interest of the United States in increasing aid to the countries of the Caribbean. In cooperation with Mexico, Venezuela, and Canada, the United States devised an assistance plan for the Caribbean basin, placing emphasis on private investment, relaxed trade restrictions on regional products for U.S. markets, and more flexible conditions for multinational aid programs, either through the World Bank or the Inter-American Development Bank.

Politics. Elections were held in 1981 in Barbados, Trinidad and Tobago, and the French West Indies. In Barbados, Prime Minister J. M. G. (Tom) Adams was returned to power on June 18 by defeating onetime Prime Minister Errol Barrows in a close election. Adams' Barbados Labour Party won a majority of the 27 seats of the island parliament, ensuring a pro-Western government in this densely populated island. The death of one of the great post-World War II political leaders of the Caribbean, Dr. Eric Williams, who had dominated Trinidad's political scene for 25 years, brought an element of uncertainty to the oil-rich island in the southeastern corner of the Caribbean. (*See* TRINIDAD AND TOBAGO.) The voting population of the French West Indies sensed the trend toward the left in France and, after giving Valéry Giscard d'Estaing and his party a 70% majority in the first round of the two-tiered French electoral process, promptly switched to the Socialist Party of the victorious François Mitterrand in the decisive second round. The islanders elected four Socialists and Communists out of seven representatives to the French National Assembly.

On November 1, the Caribbean welcomed another independent ministate. Antigua, with its small satellite island of Barbuda, was granted independence from Great Britain. Princess Margaret, representing her sister, the queen of England, formally handed over the official documents to Prime Minister Vere Bird. The celebration was dampened by the lack of enthusiasm of the 1,500 inhabitants of Barbuda who opposed independence, claiming that Antigua's political leaders neglected the needs of their island.

One of the more bizarre political developments in the Caribbean was the discovery in April of a conspiracy against the democratically elected government of Dominica. In Louisiana, the U.S. Federal Bureau of Investigation (FBI) arrested several members of the Ku Klux Klan who were preparing an invasion of the island to return to power former Prime Minister Patrick John, who was deposed after a general strike in 1979. The Klan mercenaries, who were convicted in U.S. courts, apparently were being paid by interests intending to use the island as a base for international financial schemes. During a U.S. visit in May, Prime Minister Eugenia Mary Charles was briefed on the conspiracy and requested support against future invasions.

THOMAS MATHEWS, *University of Puerto Rico*

CARIBBEAN—SPECIAL REPORT:

JAMAICA

Prime Minister Edward Phillip George Seaga, whose Jamaica Labour Party won a landslide election victory on Oct. 30, 1980, moved rapidly in 1981 to reverse the march toward socialism that had been the objective of former Prime Minister Michael Manley and his People's National Party.

The Jamaica inherited by Seaga had for several years been torn by acts of violence, which at times threatened the island with anarchy. The economy was marked by 30 to 40% unemployment, a heavy balance of payments deficit, and an utterly bankrupt treasury. Seaga promised to restore civil order, making it clear that no reprisals would be taken against the opposition but that any further acts of violence would be met with firm punishment. He announced his government's support of free enterprise capitalism and an economic policy that would encourage business to return to Jamaica. Although the private sector would play the major role in his economic recovery pro-

Once a vital industry, tourism in Jamaica was seriously hurt by the island's economic difficulties and political upheavals. In 1981, the new democratic government began a major ad campaign to bring vacationers back to Jamaica.

Photo by Frank Tedesco, Courtesy of Jamaica Tourist Board

gram, Seaga promised that the government would help create a favorable economic climate by seeking emergency financial assistance from abroad.

While acts of violence did not cease entirely, the incidence of violent crime dropped markedly. The police did not hesitate to take strong action against persons using illegal weapons to carry out crimes. Order returned to the streets of Kingston and, with one or two exceptions, all sections of the capital city were open again to law-abiding citizens. The city carried out a major cleanup campaign, and the island government initiated a program to promote Jamaica as once again a place of peaceful relaxation for tourists.

On Jan. 28, 1981, Prime Minister Seaga became the first foreign head of government to meet with U.S. President Ronald Reagan in Washington. In addition to soliciting emergency financial aid from the United States, Seaga set out to reverse the decision of the International Monetary Fund (IMF) to withdraw its support.

President Reagan quickly promised Seaga the "good will, cooperation, and moral and material assistance" of the United States. In keeping with the desire of both governments to emphasize the role of the private sector in Jamaica's economic recovery, a special investment committee was appointed. David Rockefeller, former chairman of the Chase Manhattan Bank, was named to head the group, which also included such important U.S. industrial leaders as John Blomquist, president of Reynolds Metals, and William Norris of Control Data Corporation. As a result of these and other contacts, some 400 industrial and manufacturing proposals were made to the Jamaican government by foreign investors. By mid-1981, some 311 projects—with a total investment of $730 million and promising employment for 29,000 workers—had been approved.

Seaga was equally successful in his dealings with the IMF. In April 1981, the organization pledged $698 million in aid over a three-year period, of which 40%—more than $300 million—was available in 1981. The terms of the agreement did lead to a series of labor stoppages, as the government had to persuade unions to accept smaller increases in pay. But police, teachers, and nurses finally accepted the conditions. In return, the government agreed to open the island's markets to more foreign products, thus reducing consumer prices but threatening local producers. In addition, Seaga announced a $2,700,000,000 five-year investment program.

THOMAS MATHEWS

CENTRAL AMERICA

History has not often been good to Central America, but future accounts may well contend that 1981 was as turbulent a year as that region has ever experienced. And perhaps never have the republics been more important to the United States as the new Reagan administration, bedeviled by questions of military and economic aid toward the republics, groped throughout the year for a policy.

The forms of disturbance varied from nation to nation, but all of them shared certain problems—political extremes of right and left were nagging at the middle; refugees and exiles were stirring the pot; the public was demanding more services when international credit was drying up; a need for austerity was everywhere; commodity prices were sagging consistently; inflation would not go away; and energy and borrowing costs were increasing.

While various world leaders proposed mini-Marshall Plans—with prospects of aid appearing good from West Germany, Mexico, Venezuela, and Canada, as well as from the United States—the Central American Common Market celebrated its 20th anniversary in June amid signs of disintegration. States were raising tariffs against one another; trade was falling within the market; and breaks were occurring in the common tariff against the outside world. As a whole the region's gross domestic product grew by only 2% during the year, while the foreign debt grew more than one third.

Strife even surrounded the birth of a new nation in the region, as British Honduras became an independent state. (*See also* BELIZE.)

For Central America generally, it was hard to be optimistic.

Costa Rica. As usual the Costa Ricans suffered from little of the violence that beset their neighbors in 1981, but there were spillovers. The government was charged with involvement in questionable arms deals with Cuba and Nicaragua, and the tradition of accepting all refugees was severely tried by the presence of thousands of Central Americans made homeless by wars tearing at other states. Many exiles were economic burdens, but others violated the hospitality and earned deportation for themselves to Guatemala or Nicaragua for their "undesirable" behavior in Costa Rica.

The results of too much government spending, easy credit, falling trade, inflation, and rising costs hit the Costa Rican people hard in 1981. International agencies tightened the purse strings and demanded some semblance of austerity before approving any more loans. The World Bank suggested devaluation of the colón and a program of broad tax reduction. The International Monetary Fund (IMF) delayed for months, then approved a loan of $347 million on

World leaders as well as thousands of Panamanians attend the funeral of Gen. Omar Torrijos Herrera. The Panamanian strongman died in an airplane crash in western Panama, July 31.

Randy Taylor/Sygma

the condition that there would be budget cuts, tariff reductions, suspension of subsidies, and other measures of strict austerity. These stern actions were not popular with much of labor and business, and the national assembly moved slowly to implement the changes. Danger increased that the nearly $3,000,000,000 foreign debt might be defaulted in the face of 63% devaluation and the likelihood that the entire coffee crop would earn only enough for oil purchases. The vice-president resigned in protest against the new measures.

The leading candidates for president in 1982 generally supported President Rodrigo Carazo Odio, but were beginning their campaigns for the February election. No significant political issues surfaced in anticipation of the election; the major parties agreed that the chief enemy was the economy.

Guatemala. Although not drawn into total civil war, the people of Guatemala continued to face unmitigated violence in 1981. The administration of President Romeo Lucas García was blamed for a planned program of murder and torture that had resulted in the death of 3,000 persons during his term of office. Some times the violence was aimed at special groups, such as lawyers or mayors. Increasingly it included the Indians, as they began to play a greater role in opposition to the right-wing government. And one Indian village lacked a mayor simply because so many incumbents had been killed. The Lucas government denied the charges, but they were supported by the recently resigned vice-president. The violence affected enrollment in universities and reduced the production of some crops by frightening workers or killing off managers.

The economy was mixed. Cotton prices were good and the demand very high, but production costs rose even faster. Coffee growers complained of taxes that were eight or nine times the level of a decade ago, and they also suffered from sabotage. Inflation moderated back to about 10%. Oil production accounted for only some 15% of the nation's needs, but some oil was exported, and a new pipeline to Puerto Barrios was planned.

Four leftist groups, even though uniting, found themselves unable to overthrow the government, and elections were held regularly, although often appearing fraudulent. President Lucas talked in terms of economic reform to encourage foreign aid, but nothing resulted. A tiny percentage of landholders still owned two thirds of the land, and wages remained very low. Remnants of President Jimmy Carter's civil rights policies meant that Guatemala could buy little military equipment in the United States, but found Israel a ready supplier. The 14,000-man army could see to it that business continued as usual by day, but nighttime terror remained uncontrolled. In August, the U.S. State Department advised tourists to stay out of Guatemala, a critical blow to the economy.

UPI

Daniel Ortega Saavedra, a Sandinista, serves as a member of Nicaragua's government. The number of junta members was reduced to three in March.

Honduras. Two major themes dominated the Honduran news in 1981—relations with its neighbors and the economy. Historically Honduras has been the focus of Central America's wars, even when Honduras was completely neutral, and the present struggles are no exceptions. Sandinistas from Nicaragua have been reported as both deserting to the Honduran army and trying to spread their revolution; guerrillas in El Salvador complained that Honduras aided the Salvadoran army; yet thousands of Salvadoran

CENTRAL AMERICA • Information Highlights

Nation	Population (in millions)	Area in sq mi (km^2)	Capital	Head of State and Government
Costa Rica	2.3	19,575 (50 700)	San Jose	Rodrigo Carazo Odio, president
El Salvador	4.9	8,260 (21 392)	San Salvador	José Napoleón Duarte, president
Guatemala	7.5	42,042 (108 890)	Guatemala City	Romeo Lucas García, president
Honduras	3.9	43,277 (112 087)	Tegucigalpa	Policarpo Paz García, president
Nicaragua	2.5	50,193 (130 000)	Managua	National Reconstruction Junta
Panama	1.9	29,209 (75 650)	Panama City	Arístides Royo Sanches, president

refugees had found temporary or even permanent homes in Honduras; and arms traffic to the neighbors had become a serious, if profitable business. To express its objectives and its strength, the Honduran navy conducted joint maneuvers with U.S. ships on both coasts.

Amid fears of a 25% deficit, a budget of $675 million was approved for 1981. About one fourth of the budget was expected to come from foreign loans to cope with fleeing capital, increasing imports, rising costs of those imports, and growing military expenditures. Even basics like corn, beans, and clothing rose in price. The government banana monopoly struggled with the transnationals for greater shares of the European market and over the export tax rate. Ceiling prices on many items rose as often as five times during the year. Like Costa Rica, Honduras faced IMF requirements of reduced government expenditures before some loans could be approved and granted, and this added measures of austerity to the regime of President Policarpo Paz Garcia. Not surprisingly, labor unrest was expressed in brief strikes of teachers, doctors and nurses, and farm laborers.

In late November the Hondurans conducted their first presidential election in 18 years. The military government had been reluctant to yield its power to civilians but under pressure from Presidents Jimmy Carter and Ronald Reagan had permitted the election. The chief campaigners, Dr. Roberto Suazo Córdova and Ricardo Zúñiga Augustinus, waged a clean, somewhat issue-less campaign, debating vague promises of reform. Dr. Suazo Córdova, age 54, a small town physician most of his life, won with 54% of the more than one million votes cast. He would take office in January 1982. His Liberal party also won the majority of the Congress.

He was expected to follow the United States in its support of the Duarte junta in El Salvador and keep the Nicaraguan Sandinistas at arms' length. His tasks include finding ways to deal with these neighbors and the refugees from their lands, as well as an economy slowed by high energy and high borrowing costs. As usual, the military would be watching.

Nicaragua. The Sandinista movement faced many crucial moments in 1981. The most important task was the increasing necessity of proving that it could govern. Its followers could claim that in a year unemployment was cut in half, while inflation was reduced from 60 to 35%. They boasted of honesty in government and a broad scale literacy campaign. But their enemies cited their fears of Marxist totalitarianism, weaker unions, growing class hatred, bumbling bureaucracies, and a divided church. Archbishop Miguel Ovando y Bravo, who had once opposed the Somoza government, now ordered priests not to serve in the present cabinet on threat of excommunication.

Government policy favored the consumer over business, and competition declined as the government became the sole buyer and seller of 12 basic items. Probably one half of the economy was in government hands by July when the Sandinistas celebrated the second anniversary of their revolution. Traditionally self-supporting in grains, Nicaragua now found it necessary to import essentials like corn and beans. Food shortages were aggravated by new land-reform programs and the almost complete elimination of loans from the United States. Further strains were caused by the fall of coffee exports and the lack of private investment.

By autumn, the government had decreed a state of economic emergency, banning strikes and salary increases, and placing many new restrictions on the use of private capital. To aid the revolution, the USSR promised $50 million in credits toward the purchase of farm machinery and chemicals. But this was a stopgap. By most estimates, two years of revolution had done little, ironically, for the lower classes who gave the movement its chief support, while the middle groups who had not suffered greatly continued to resist incorporation into the revolution. All that the government could do was ask the people for patience as Nicaragua drifted in unknown directions.

Panama. The most startling 1981 news from Panama was the death in an airplane crash of Gen. Omar Torrijos Herrera, since 1968 Panama's strong man. (*See also* OBITUARIES.) His political successor was not known by late in the year, but to Panamanians his chief legacy was the Panama Canal. With the election of Ronald Reagan, many feared that the treaties matter might be reopened, but Reagan assured the Panamanians that he would abide by those agreements. Already authorities were seeking a loan from Japan to deepen and widen the channel to accommodate supertankers and eliminate long lines of ships waiting to pass through. Now operated by a mixed commission, the canal will be in Panama's control in the year 2000, although U.S. intervention would be permitted.

Canal traffic had risen about 10% since the days of U.S. control. The free trade zone was growing, and tourism and especially banking expanded significantly. U.S. investment in Panama was larger than in all the rest of Central America combined. But unemployment was high, and agriculture remained undeveloped, in part because fuel costs had doubled in 12 months. For much of the year, trade had been hampered by a trucking war with Costa Rica which hauled about 90% of their mutual traffic. Because of its own problems Costa Rica was also reducing commerce with Panama. Panama was engaged in another trade war, this with United Brands over banana shipments to Eastern Europe.

President Arístides Royo Sanches declared that he saw no serious gap without Torrijos. The national guard, the source of Torrijos' power, remained strong, and should continue so.

THOMAS L. KARNES, *Arizona State University*

EL SALVADOR

Tiny tormented El Salvador staggered through another year of cold-blooded murders (reportedly 10,000), kidnappings, and civil war, making it appear to the outside world that the nation was destroying itself. In retrospect, 1981 brought a trifle less death and pillage than the previous two or three years, but that distinction is a fine one and probably not worth much.

Historically this land of mostly mestizo and Indian peoples has existed off the product of its soil, with especial emphasis on coffee and other cash crops. The population totaled less than 1 million in 1900, only 1,443,000 in 1930, but an estimated 4.9 million in 1981. Traditionally the nation has been dominated by a handful of landowners, sometimes inexactly described as "the fourteen." This situation brought stability to politics and society until the collapse of coffee prices toward the end of the Depression.

An unusual Labor Party government was unseated in 1931 as a result of the worsening economic conditions and the government's inability to deal with new forces demanding reform. The military junta accomplishing the overthrow was soon led by Gen. Maximiliano Hernández Martínez. The coup brought reaction from reformers in the land, many of whom were Communists, to attempt a counterrevolt. Although most of the leadership was quickly captured, the peasants and urban poor were now stirred and continued the effort with support from abroad, perhaps the first attempt of the Comintern to revolutionize any nation in Latin America. There followed much looting, raping, and murder, although probably less than the junta reported.

The rebels controlled most of the Western portion of the republic and captured the large town of Sonsonate. Here a pitched battle was waged by the army and police against poorly armed peasants, who were slaughtered as General Martínez retook the entire region. His losses were slight, but the destruction his men meted out amounted to a massacre. It was a class and race war as the ruling groups equated peasant with Communist and resolved to eradicate the threat from Salvadoran soil forever. All over the Western part of the nation men were hunted

El Salvador President José Napoleón Duarte (below) outlined his program during a ten-day, September visit to the United States. Meanwhile fighting between government troops and guerrillas continued in his homeland.

O. Franken/Sygma

Hoagland/Liaison

Hoagland/Liaison

Nurses and troops come to the aid of the wounded. Major guerrilla offensives occurred in El Salvador in May and August, with a high number of casualties.

down, tortured, and put to death. Many were machine-gunned after capture. The number of casualties was never officially revealed, but the leading authorities estimated somewhere between 10,000 and 40,000 deaths. The reprisal appeared deliberately contrived to put the peasants back into their accustomed subservience and even eliminate much of the pure Indian race remaining in the nation.

It is this massacre that the campesinos today solemnize as the *Matanza,* and the young leftist leaders executed back then, such as Agustín Farabundo Martí and Alfonso Luna, are the heroes of today's rebels. But the *Matanza* is also remembered by the oligarchy as the time when their control was most dangerously threatened and when they tightened their resistance to reform. *Matanza* broke the back of the reform movements of the 1930s, and General Martínez ruled with an iron hand until 1944, when he was overthrown and exiled. By then, the social order had returned to its pre-1931 structure, except that the military dominated politics even more completely. The military permitted the planters to serve in minor posts and make money. Occasionally officers fell out with one another, but the system did not change, only the name of the colonels in command.

Often the governments were efficient; all were effective for varying periods; and many paid lip service to reform by passing but not enforcing legislation beneficial to the masses.

The 1960s brought to a head a long, serious trend. Many Salvadorans had found their own release from oppressive government and the heavy population pressure upon the land by migrating into Honduras, which contained hundreds of thousands of acres of underutilized land. Since the migrants could readily pass for Hondurans, and their new employers were pleased to have them, no clear picture of their number can be drawn, but they assuredly were in the scores of thousands. Many were merely the unemployed looking for work or a small piece of land. More evident, though few in number, were small numbers of businessmen who often did well and made themselves objects of jealousy for their industriousness.

Old boundary questions, growing Honduran fear of the sheer number of Salvadoran migrants, economic problems in Honduras, and enforcement of land reform laws selectively against Salvadorans brought great bitterness and tension between the two nations. War was triggered by the unseemly and offensive behavior of both peoples toward the respective visiting soccer teams during the 1969 World Cup preliminaries. El Salvador "won" the brief war, and no great quantities of blood were shed. However, scores of thousands of Salvadorans suddenly found themselves back in their native land, restoring much of the population pressure that had been relieved by the Honduran safety valve.

In 1972 the popular former mayor of San Salvador, José Napoleón Duarte, won the presidency in opposition to the usual ruling groups, but the government declared him the loser, forced him out of office, imprisoned and tortured him, and sent him into exile, making a hero of him.

Force begot force, and by 1973 guerrilla terrorists had stolen the scene. Kidnapping for ransom to support the terrorists became the practice. Banks were robbed, stores were looted, and arms were procured from the military by murder and robbery. Assassination became commonplace, the first targets being leading politicians, later industrialists, often not even of Salvadoran nationality. The underground groups multiplied on the right and on the left. Some probably were dominated by reformers, others by gangs of criminals and hooligans. Attempting to find economic solutions, the government essayed a long overdue land reform program, but by 1976 this had failed.

The poor found themselves an unusual spokesman in 1977 in the person of new Archbishop Oscar Arnulfo Romero, who became very critical of the government's failure to aid the struggles of the peasant and urban poor. But in March 1980 he, too, was assassinated.

Fraud and massacre had marked the election of 1977 when a military junta once again took charge of the nation. The U.S. government, shocked by the increasing horror, aided the government but insisted upon reforms. A massive agrarian reform program was planned and partially implemented in 1980 and 1981, the evident object being not only to aid the peasants but to steal some of the thunder from the Marxists who were so harrying the nation that the economy seemed near failure. Allegedly some 200,000 peasants received grants of land by 1981, totaling about 40% of all croplands. But the results have not been dramatic; crop production is about the same as before, perhaps because of the nation's chaos. The former owners complained of lack of compensation for their losses.

Late in 1979 other officers had overthrown the government and established a reform junta of officers and civilians. They brought some changes, including the land reform mentioned above, but they also increased the repressive tactics of their predecessors. Hoping to improve their image and their support internationally, the military invited José Napoleón Duarte to join the junta in March 1980, and in December he was named to fill the role of president. At once, Duarte began trying to keep his nation together in the face of almost total rebellion on the left and the terror of paramilitary groups on the right, yet maintaining a semblance of the democratic process. (*See also* Biography.)

In 1981 Duarte clung to office, using his once very popular Christian Democratic Party as the nucleus of his support. That support shrank during 1981. But Duarte himself declared that the greatest threat to his government was not the leftist rebellion, but the conservative businessmen who, from exile in Miami or California, supported the extreme right in their opposition to the reform program that now included nationalizing banks as well as cotton, sugar, and coffee exports. It was difficult to judge where the real power lay in the Duarte government. Some observers believed that Duarte was dominated by the military members of the junta, but he continued to plan for the election of a constitutional assembly in 1982 and a president in 1983.

The left-wing opposition consists primarily of Marxist guerrillas who call themselves the Farabundo Martí National Liberation Front (FMLN). They have many allies, some of whom are probably not Marxist in any ideological sense. These would include students, clergy, and politicians who label themselves the Democratic Revolutionary Front (FDR). While they remain tough opposition, there is little evidence that they are winning the military phase of the struggle, and their highly publicized May 1981 offensive made only small inroads. Their August offensive had more success, and often they were able to take and hold towns for days at a time. Government casualties were significant in these campaigns, but the rebels seem more successful in destroying the economy than defeating government forces.

The church opposed the government less vigorously than when Archbishop Romero was alive, but the acting archbishop (the Vatican had not made a permanent appointment to that position) sharply criticized the army for unexplained massacres of civilians. Church-government relations remained badly strained as a result of the December 1980 murder of three nuns and a lay worker from the United States.

Early in 1981 the United States affirmed its support of President Duarte and resumed military aid. Duarte welcomed the help but insisted that he did not want the presence of U.S. troops or any other nation's troops on Salvadoran soil. At first President Ronald Reagan's government spoke of making a determined stand against Communism in the Western Hemisphere by drawing the line in El Salvador. But for many Americans this raised the specter of another Vietnam; the matter was allowed to cool, and the Reagan administration talked less of battle lines and more of reform, financial aid, and political solutions. A 1981 aid bill in July brought to some $200 million the amount of U.S. gifts and loans to El Salvador since October 1979.

In August 1981 the governments of France and Mexico announced that though their relations with Duarte remained unchanged, they would begin to recognize the leftist rebels as a "representative political force" in El Salvador, probably hoping that this small sign of legitimacy might exert pressure upon the government to agree to equal representation in a political solution. Mexico denied subsequently that it was interfering in Salvadoran affairs and claimed that it has not given arms or funds to either side.

In September, President Duarte went to the United States for ten days, defending his program in talks with President Reagan and various groups, including the United Nations, and making a convincing display of confidence. He admitted the continuance of human rights violations in his land but vowed that improvements were taking place. The U.S. Congress seemed determined to promote this development by tying the Salvadoran aid program to requests for proof from Reagan that the junta's human rights record was actually getting better.

Thomas L. Karnes

CHAD

Chad's 15-year-old civil war entered a new phase with the intervention of Libya in the conflict. Muammar el-Qaddafi, responding to pleas for help from Chad's President Goukouni Oueddei, sent troops and tanks into Chad in late December 1980, reconquered Ndjamena, and drove out Hissène Habré's forces. While bringing peace to most areas, the invasion focused international attention upon Chad. The United States, France, and most African states denounced the invasion, believing it a prelude to Libya dominating the savannah regions of West Africa. Qaddafi did little to ease fears by announcing the merger of Libya and Chad on January 6. Pressure from the international community, including the USSR, later caused Oueddei to reconsider the proposed union. Although Qaddafi in March restated his intention to create a federation, he began withdrawing his troops and the bulk of Libyan forces had evacuated Ndjamena by the end of July. Following further pressure from France, the pullout was completed by the end of the year.

The Organization of African Unity (OAU) attempted to mediate between the factions immediately after the Libyan invasion. Its effectiveness was reduced because of deep-seated differences within the organization. Siaka Stevens of Sierra Leone, who met with the leaders of Chad in May and later visited Tripoli, was accused by President Alhaji Shehu Shagari of Nigeria of being pro-Libyan. Shagari, President Anwar el-Sadat of Egypt, and President Jaafar al-Nemery of the Sudan were particularly hostile to Libya's expansion. Sadat admitted that Egypt had sent arms to Habré. Al-Nemery, who had never forgiven Qaddafi for supporting an abortive coup in Sudan in 1976, went even further in stating that Sudan was at war with Libya. He welcomed Habré and continued to support the guerrillas operating near the Sudanese border.

Economy. Rebuilding Chad's economy was complicated by the anti-Western attitudes of Oueddei's government. France, which had supported Chad economically before 1980, was hesitant to repeat that role although direct diplomatic contact was resumed in June. Ndjamena's airport was partially repaired and some businesses, including the Central Bank, were reopened, but the capital remained in ruins, with only a fraction of its original population. Agriculture, the mainstay of 70% of the population, produced less than 50% of its prewar totals. Oueddei's appeal for immediate assistance was ignored. Foreign governments indicated that substantial aid would await the Libyan withdrawal and stabilization of the situation.

HARRY A. GAILEY, *San Jose State University*

CHAD • Information Highlights

Official Name: Republic of Chad.
Location: North-central Africa.
Area: 496,000 sq mi (1 284 640 km^2).
Population (1981 est.): 4,600,000.
Chief Cities (1979 est.): Ndjamena, the capital, 303,000; Moundou, 66,000; Sarh, 65,000.
Government: *Head of state and government,* Gen. Goukouni Oueddei, president of Transitional Government of National Unity (Nov. 1979).
Monetary Unit: CFA franc (285.9 CFA francs equal U.S. $1, June 1981).
Manufactures (major products): Flour, beer, refined sugar, cotton textiles.
Agriculture (major products): Millet and sorghum, cotton, pulses, rice, groundnuts.

CHEMISTRY

Among the year's chemical achievements were successes in synthetic chemistry and new developments in photochemistry.

The Atmosphere. Public attention was directed at the problem of acid rain. (*See* ENVIRONMENT.) Meanwhile, warnings on two other atmospheric problems were sounded. A thin layer of ozone found in the earth's stratosphere protects life on the surface from the sun's harmful short-wavelength ultraviolet rays. In 1974 scientists warned that chlorofluorcarbons (CFCs), chemicals used as propellants in aerosol spray cans and for other purposes, might leak to the stratosphere and cause damage to the ozone layer. In 1978 the government banned use of CFCs in spray cans, but allowed other uses to continue. Still, the charge was controversial, since there was no firm evidence that the ozone layer was being damaged. In August, NASA scientist Donald Heath rekindled the controversy by presenting preliminary evidence from satellite data showing that the ozone concentration at 40 km (25 mi) altitude indeed fell by a small, but significant amount—about 0.5% per year—in the 1970s.

The amount of carbon dioxide in the earth's atmosphere also has been a source of concern. It has been speculated that higher concentrations of this gas might trap heat radiating from the earth's surface and cause the planet's temperature to increase, a phenomenon dubbed the "Greenhouse effect." Higher production of carbon dioxide due to the burning of fossil fuels and lower consumption of the gas because of the destruction of many forest areas may combine to bring this about. The problem was highlighted in August when NASA scientists reported that the earth's mean temperature has increased by 0.4 °C (0.9 °F) in the past century, with half of this increase during the last two decades. They predicted that the effects on climate would continue and become more obvious, possibly leading in the next century to droughts, partial melting of the Antarctic ice sheet, and even "opening of the fabled Northwest Passage."

Synthesis. Leo Paquette and his co-workers at Ohio State University completed the synthesis dodecahedrane, a compound of carbon and hydrogen whose carbon skeleton has the shape of a regular dodecahedron, the Platonic solid with 12 identical, pentagonal faces. Earlier syntheses by others of the polyhedral compounds cubane and tetrahedrane, the latter in substituted form, had left dodecahedrane as an obvious challenge to the skills of synthetic organic chemists. Paquette and his students devised a synthetic route consisting of 20 reactions starting from a pentagonal ion and leading finally to a symmetric dimethyl derivative of dodecahedrane. X-ray analysis confirmed the expected regular geometry and the existence of a small central cavity in the compound. Later, using a modified route, they were able to make the unsubstituted compound.

A team from Harvard University, led by Yoshito Kishi, succeeded in synthesizing the antibiotic erythromycin. Completion of this synthesis marked the culmination of an eight-year effort involving about 50 workers. The Harvard team followed chemical reaction routes originally suggested by the late Nobel laureate R. B. Woodward. One very difficult aspect of the work involved the properly oriented addition of sugar groups at specific locations on the molecule. Kishi's group also reported synthesis of the nonsugar part of aclacinomycin A, a natural compound produced by bacteria that may prove valuable in treating cancer. Two other research groups, at the University of Rochester and Hoffmann-LaRoche laboratories, reported syntheses of this latter compound by different methods.

The rules of electronic orbital symmetry proposed by R. B. Woodward and Roald Hoffmann a decade and a half ago have proven to be a powerful guide to understanding the paths taken in chemical reactions. These rules state that certain pathways are "allowed," that is, favored, and others are "forbidden," or disfavored. The forbidden pathways usually are not followed because they contain a large energy barrier that must be overcome. In 1981 a group of workers in Chicago, led by Robert Gordon, reported a way to get around, or more precisely, over, this problem. Normally *cis*-3,4-dichlorocyclobutene reacts to form a single product with a specific geometry. However, when an intense, infrared laser beam was directed at the reaction vessel two additional symmetry-forbidden isomers were formed, presumably because the laser pulse supplied enough energy to push some molecules over the restricting barrier. The Chicago chemists cited this as the first example of this type of laser-induced reaction.

Photochemistry. More new ways are being found to use light, visible and otherwise, to influence chemical reactions. For example, hydrogen sulfide is a foul-smelling gas that arises as an undesirable by-product in the oil refining business. Workers in Lausanne, Switzerland, and Turin, Italy, revealed that under proper conditions visible light can not only split hydrogen sulfide, but even turn the compound into useful products—gaseous hydrogen, which can be used as a fuel, and sulfur. The key to making the reaction go is the presence in water of colloidal cadmium sulfide particles with ruthenium dioxide on their surfaces. The particles help to transfer electrons and catalyze the conversion.

PAUL G. SEYBOLD, *Wright State University*

CHICAGO

A newspaper series aptly called Chicago the "City on the Brink." The city that for years seemed to work so well appeared to be falling apart in 1981. Daily headlines told of bankruptcy in the city government, public schools, and transit system.

For weeks Chicagoans did not know if the trains and buses would be running the next day, if the schools would open in the fall, or if public employees would be paid. Years of borrowing to pay record high salaries to teachers and transit workers, and thus avoid strikes and public chaos, caught up with Mayor Jane Byrne and the city government.

Chicago banks for the first time said no to easy-money loans to the city to keep the schools going. In Springfield, the state capital, Gov. James R. Thompson and state legislators also said no to state aid for Chicago's ailing financial condition. Behind the long political tug-of-war between Democrat Byrne and Republican Thompson was the constant threat of Chicago breaking down, with no mass transit and no public schools. The threat of a transit shutdown became so real that elaborate plans for alternate transportation were made by individuals and their employers.

In the end the schools and transit system did not shut down, but neither did the financial woes go away. At best the day of reckoning was put off, as it had been in previous years.

Meanwhile, Chicagoans saw their bus and train service cut, fares rise by 50 to 107%, their property taxes soar, a new tax on services, and a hike in their sales tax as Mayor Byrne sought to avoid financial collapse.

Yet the feisty mayor, her political career on the line, seemed to be holding her own through the crises. Moving into Cabrini-Green, a black housing project on the city's North Side, was a political plus for the mayor. Cabrini residents warned her to stay away, telling her that her life would not be worth a dime in the crime-ridden project. She moved in anyway, for five weeks, and when she moved out her popularity had soared in local polls.

And she apparently left behind a better life at Cabrini-Green. City services at the project improved. Crime went down. And the toughs who had terrorized the place for years had moved out.

A scandal struck the Catholic Archdiocese of Chicago. Archbishop John Cardinal Cody was under investigation by a federal grand jury for charges that he had diverted about $1 million in church funds to a Mrs. Helen D. Wilson, a cousin by marriage. Cardinal Cody and church representatives vigorously denied the charge.

ROBERT ENSTAD, *"Chicago Tribune"*

CHILE

Gen. Augusto Pinochet Ugarte formally assumed the presidency of Chile for eight years on March 11, 1981. During the year, there was some economic improvement. Relations with the United States, Great Britain, and Peru improved, while relations with Argentina worsened.

Pinochet Assumes Title. General Pinochet formally assumed the title of president under a new constitution approved in a September 1980 plebiscite. The term lasts until 1989. In that year, the governing military junta will nominate a president whose candidacy will be accepted or rejected in a national referendum. Pinochet reiterated in July that there would be no "political opening" (*apertura politica*) to provide for future participation of traditional political parties, although Gen. Fernando Matthei, commander of the Air Force, expressed support in March for participation of the parties, which have been banned since 1974. He did not mention a date or period when party activity would be permitted legally again.

Terrorism Increases. Leftist terrorists of the outlawed Popular Resistance Militia (MRP) claimed responsibility for attacks on banks, police barracks, and other public buldings several times during the year. Army troops and *Carabineros* (National Police) captured members of the MRP and other guerrilla groups during the year. However, Gen. Humberto Gordon, director of the National Intelligence Center (CNI), announced June 26 that his controversial agency would be reorganized after it was discovered that five CNI officials robbed and murdered two employees of a bank in Calama. Human rights groups inside and outside Chile had also charged other CNI officials with torture and murder of individuals engaged in trade union activity. On August 11, Chilean security forces summarily expelled from the country four prominent opposition politicians, including Jaime Castillo Velasco, president of the Chilean Commission on Human Rights.

Foreign Affairs. On August 9, Jeane Kirkpatrick, U.S. ambassador to the United Nations, completed a visit to Chile. After speaking with Pinochet and other government leaders, Mrs. Kirkpatrick said that the United States intended to "normalize completely its relations with Chile in order to work together in a pleasant way." The ambassador declined to comment on Chile's human rights record. The exile of Castillo Velasco, a former minister of justice, ended the possibility that three Chilean intelligence agents involved in the 1976 assassination of former Ambassador Orlando Letelier in Washington, DC, would be extradited to the United States by Chile.

In June, Foreign Minister René Rojas Galdámes met with U.S. Vice-President George Bush, Secretary of State Alexander Haig, and other U.S. officials in Washington as part of a rapprochement between the two governments, whose relations were strained over human-rights issues during the presidency of Jimmy Carter. Earlier, the U.S. State Department lifted trade sanctions against Chile imposed by the Carter administration. The sanctions banned the U.S. government financing of exports to Chile.

Full diplomatic relations were restored with Peru—severed in 1979 over charges of Chilean spying—and with Great Britain—severed in December 1975 over charges of imprisonment and torture of a British surgeon.

Relations with Argentina remained hostile. Argentina formally rejected on March 17 some of the proposals made on Dec. 12, 1980, by Pope John Paul II as a mediator in the Beagle Channel dispute. Chile accepted the pope's proposals, which included recognition of Chilean sovereignty over the main islands of Nueva, Picton, and Lennox, construction of an airport on Nueva which would permit stopovers of Argentine planes flying to Antarctica, installation by Argentina of navigation buoys on the Chilean islets of Evourt and Bernevelt to the south, and creation of a 200-mi- (370-km-) wide territorial "sea of peace" extending south of Cape Horn to which Argentina would have access. Argentina closed its 2,600-mi (4 160-km) border with Chile on April 29 after Chile imprisoned two Argentine army officers and after Argentina arrested 11 Chileans in Rio Gallegos on charges of spying. (*See also* ARGENTINA.)

Economy. Chile's peso remained stable for the second year in a row. Inflation fell to 7.4% in August, compared with 30% for 1980. Unemployment in Santiago was down to 8.4% in August, compared with 12.5% in August 1980.

Increased imports, especially of automobiles and food, worsened Chile's foreign debt position between January and May 1981, especially since copper prices gradually fell during the year to 83 cents a pound in October. The 1980 average price was $1.10. Since the national budget was based on an average price for copper of 78.36 cents per pound, Chile planned to use the difference to service the foreign debt, which reached $11,240,000,000 in December 1980, compared with $8,460,000,000 in December 1979 and $5,200,000,000 in September 1977.

NEALE J. PEARSON, *Texas Tech University*

CHILE • Information Highlights

Official Name: Republic of Chile.
Location: Southwestern coast of South America.
Area: 292,257 sq mi (756 946 km^2).
Population (1981 est.): 11,200,000.
Chief Cities (June 1980 met. est.): Santiago, the capital, 3,853,275; Viña del Mar, 272,814.
Government: *Head of state and government,* Gen. Augusto Pinochet Ugarte, president (took power Sept. 1973). *Legislature*—Congress (dissolved Sept. 1973).
Monetary Unit: Peso (39.00 pesos equal U.S.$1, Nov. 1981).
Manufactures (major products): Small manufactures, refinery products.
Agriculture (major products): Wheat, corn, rapeseed, pulses, fruit.

CHINA

The year 1981 in China saw formal actions to eradicate the Maoist influence and further efforts by Deputy Chairman Deng Xiaoping to strengthen his leadership. The trial of the Gang of Four and a formal statement criticizing Mao Zedong were meant to bury Maoism forever. The removal of Hua Guofeng from the party leadership in June left Deng Xiaoping at the height of his power. With his own appointees at the helm of the state, China's paramount leader vigorously pursued the goals of the party he controlled.

Stressing the economy as its top priority, the government called for a plan of slow, steady development. Abandoning huge industrial projects, Peking laid emphasis on agriculture and light industry.

In foreign affairs, China gladly agreed to a proposal by U.S. Secretary of State Alexander Haig for strategic cooperation to counter Soviet expansion. But Peking was at the same time perturbed by Washington's friendly relations with Taiwan. In Southeast Asia, China's principal interest was that the various Cambodian opposition groups be united in the struggle against Vietnamese occupation.

UPI

Jiang Qing, wife of the late Chairman Mao, was convicted of counterrevolutionary crimes.

DOMESTIC AFFAIRS

The Great Trial. After a long delay, the trial of ten deposed party radicals and military leaders at last began on Nov. 20, 1980. The chief defendants were the "Gang of Four"—Jiang Qing, widow of Mao Zedong; Zhang Chunqiao, a former member of the Standing Committee of the Politburo; Wang Hongwen, a Shanghai textile mill worker whom Mao made a deputy chairman of the party; and Yao Wenyuan, a polemist whose writings spearheaded the Cultural Revolution. These four were tried along with Chen Boda, Mao's former political secretary, and five military leaders, the associates of the late Defense Minister Lin Biao. Brought before a special court of 35 judges, the party radicals were charged with conducting campaigns against other leaders, persecuting and killing more than 34,000 opponents of the Cultural Revolution, and plotting an armed rebellion in Shanghai. The military leaders were accused of attempting, in conspiracy with Lin Biao, to assassinate Mao Zedong in 1971.

During the trial, Wang Hongwen and Yao Wenyuan tended to cooperate with the prosecution. Chen Boda confessed to persecuting Liu Shaoqi, then China's head of state. Zhang Chunqiao, however, refused to answer any questions, and Jiang Qing raged at the trial judges and prosecutors, calling them "Fascists" and Chinese Nationalist agents. She defended her deeds by arguing that she was acting on behalf of Mao. The five military men admitted to having been involved in a plot to depose Mao.

On Jan. 25, 1981, after more than two months, the court reached its verdict. All ten defendants were found guilty of counterrevolutionary crimes. Jiang Qing received a death sentence, which was suspended for two years. If, after that period, Jiang showed signs of repentance, the sentence would be changed to life imprisonment. If not, the court would then order her execution. Zhang Chunqiao received the same sentence, while Yao Wenyuan was sentenced to 20 years and Wang Hongwen to life imprisonment. The other defendants—Chen Boda and the five military leaders—were given prison sentences ranging from 16 to 18 years.

Jiang's suspended death sentence was a compromise reached in the Politburo to avoid opposition from lurking Maoists. The trial was, in fact, a political struggle in legal disguise, but it was necessary as a final suppression of the Cultural Revolution and a prelude to the formal assessment of Mao's place in history.

Leadership Struggle. After the punishment of the Gang of Four, the political maneuvering was directed against Party Chairman Hua Guofeng, who had been named premier by Mao Zedong in 1976. Although he had played a part in the arrest of the Gang of Four, Hua was admittedly a Maoist. And Deng Xiaoping, now the powerful leader, considered Hua not only a political rival but also an obstructionist to his new line of pragmatism and modernization. In 1980, Deng had begun to place his own men in key party positions. He forced Hua to resign his premiership in favor of Zhao Ziyang and had Hu Yaobang appointed general secretary of the party to circumvent Hua, who was still party chairman. By the end of the year, a high party conference had decided that Hua was to resign that post, but it needed the Central Committee's action to formalize the resignation.

Central Committee Meeting. On June 27, 1981, the sixth plenary session of the Central Committee of the Chinese Communist party was formally convened in Peking. After three days of meetings and maneuvering, the committee on June 29 announced the formal replacement of Hua Guofeng with Hu Yaobang as chairman of the party. It elected Deng Xiaoping as chairman of the party's Military Commission and Zhao Ziyang vice-chairman of the Central Committee. Hua remained a member, though the lowest-ranking one, of the seven-member Standing Committee of the Politburo. With his own men holding the reins of the party, Deng's ascendancy over Hua was complete. A vigorous critic of Mao, Hu Yaobang was expected to be a faithful exponent of Deng's policies.

Assessment of Mao. On June 30, Peking made public a formal evaluation of Mao Zedong—the resolution of "certain questions in the history of our party" that had just been passed by the Central Committee. Surveying the 60-year history of the party, the 35,000-word statement focused its criticism on the Cultural Revolution, which, it said, "was responsible for the most severe setback and the heaviest losses suffered by the party, the state, and the people since the founding of the party." The Cultural Revolution, it went on, "was initiated and led by Comrade Mao Zedong," who acted on the basis of "erroneous left theses." During the period, he "confused right and wrong, and the people with the enemy." He acted "more and more arbitrarily and subjectively, and increasingly put himself above the Central Committee of the party." However, conceded the resolution, Mao in his later years remained alert to safeguarding the country's security, stood up to the pressure of "Social-imperialism," and pursued "a correct foreign policy." For these reasons, and "particularly for his vital contributions to the cause of the revolution over the years," the Chinese people "have always regarded Comrade Mao Zedong as their respected and beloved great leader and teacher." Finally, the resolution stated that "if we judge his activities as a whole, his contributions to the Chinese revolution outweigh his mistakes."

The assessment was plainly a compromise between the Deng group and remnant Maoists, who were looking for a chance to stir up trouble. Moreover, to strike too hard at Mao, a symbol of Chinese Communism for so long, might shake the Communist system too deeply. Nevertheless, Deng achieved his objective of demolishing the image of Mao as an infallible demigod.

Party Platform. The party platform, approved by the Central Committee on June 27, called for orderly economic development and improvement in living standards. While state enterprise and planning would continue to play the dominant role, private enterprises and market forces would complement government efforts to increase production. The platform endorsed a gradual extension of democracy under party control and a legal system that would ensure the rights of the people. It warned, however, that any word or deed that "denies or undermines" the party's leadership would not be tolerated. The platform denounced "fallacious views that denigrate education, science, and culture, and discriminate against intellectuals." It affirmed Deng's program of systematic modernization without resorting to unrealistic plans that would lead to "colossal waste and losses."

Economy. The economic "readjustment" adopted in 1981 was aimed at achieving slow, steady economic growth. It abandoned the huge 1978 ten-year plan which, with its 120 major industrial projects, would have required a capital expenditure of up to $600,000,000,000. The new policy, emphasizing agriculture and light industry, would cut back capital construction and limit outlays for the import of foreign technology.

Inflation was a serious problem. Though officially estimated at 6%, rates three times as high were reported in some cities. To curb the trend, Peking moved to eliminate budget deficits. Gov-

UPI

Senior Deputy Premier Deng Xiaoping consolidated his power by being elected head of the Communist party's Military Commission. That key post had been vacated by Hua Guofeng, who was replaced as chairman of the party by a protégé of Deng.

UPI

During a visit by U.S. Secretary of State Alexander Haig (left) in June, China and the United States agreed that strategic cooperation was necessary to counter Soviet expansionism.

ernment expenditures for 1981 were cut by $9,800,000,000 to $64,600,000,000, with capital construction reduced by 45% and defense and administration costs cut substantially. Priority was given to production of consumer goods so as to stabilize commodity prices, and to development of existing industries to reduce construction expenditures.

During the period of readjustment, which was expected to last a few years, major industrial projects were postponed. In January 1981, the $5,000,000,000 Baoshan Steel Works project was shelved halfway through the first phase of construction. Contracts signed with Japan, West Germany, and the United States for expensive, long-term projects were suspended.

In agriculture, the government decided to relax its control, giving the peasants greater freedom to handle their farming businesses. They were allowed to farm small plots of land and to sell the produce at free markets for their own profit. The government also planned to expand privately cultivated plots until they comprised 15% of the country's arable land.

Despite droughts in northern China, the wheat harvest in 1981 was expected to reach some 62 million t (56 million T), compared with 60 million t (54.2 million T) in 1980. On the other hand, a great flood that swept through the southwestern province of Sichuan in July caused serious damage to area crops.

Society and Culture. Dedicated to modernization, the new leadership in 1981 took a more liberal position regarding social life and cultural trends. American television programs were shown, and Western classical music was played in big cities. While items of beauty were condemned as bourgeois during the Cultural Revolution, they were now displayed without fear of official censure. Flowers, paintings, and vases reappeared in Chinese homes, and women's clothes became colorful again.

Artistic and literary freedom, however, were still remote. Deng Xiaoping personally directed a campaign against "bourgeois liberalism" among Chinese writers and artists whose works, he said, propagated "opposition to the leadership of the party."

Peking's decision to relax religious restrictions stimulated a revival of church activities. In April, thousands of Chinese celebrated Easter in the cathedrals and churches of Peking. But the new freedom was far from total. Much still depended on the sympathy of local officials, and many churches were still not returned to Christian congregations.

On June 6, Pope John Paul II named Monsignor Dominic Tang archbishop of Guangdong province. If the Vatican hoped the move would help improve relations with Peking, it was soon disappointed. China denounced the appointment as an interference in its internal affairs, and the Chinese Patriotic Catholic Association termed it "intolerable." Bishop Tang, 73, had been freed in 1980 after 22 years in prison.

FOREIGN AFFAIRS

United States. Peking was not cheered by the election of Ronald Reagan, who during his campaign had expressed an interest in upgrading relations between the United States and Taiwan. After his inauguration in January 1981, however, President Reagan began to recognize the need for improving relations with China. On June 14, Secretary of State Haig arrived in Peking for a three-day visit. He held talks with the Chinese leadership, including Deng Xiaoping and Zhao Ziyang. In his talks with Foreign Minister Huang Hua, Haig stressed the danger of Soviet expansionism and the "strategic imperative" of the United States and China establishing close ties. Huang agreed, for what Haig proposed was altogether in consonance with China's policy. On June 16, at the end of his visit, Haig announced that the United States had decided in principle to sell arms to China. The move was a significant shift from the policy of previous U.S. administrations, which had refused to sell combat arms to China for fear of provoking the Soviet Union. Haig did not indicate what weapons and equipment would be offered, but it was presumed that they would initially be defensive.

China was not expected to make large purchases, since it had cut its 1981 military budget by 25%.

Both China and the United States expressed gratification with Haig's visit, but the Taiwan issue remained a matter of acute concern to Peking. On June 19, the New China News Agency stated that continued United States arms sales to Taiwan "cannot but cast a shadow on the developing Chinese-American relations."

On October 21, Prime Minister Zhao Ziyang and Foreign Minister Huang Hua called on President Reagan at the North-South summit meeting in Cancún, Mexico, to discuss the Taiwan question. After listening to a Chinese plan for reunification with Taiwan, the U.S. president said he would not interpose in a matter that must be settled by Peking and Taipei, and reaffirmed his intention to continue arms sales to Taiwan.

Western Europe. Peking continued to cultivate friendly relations with Western European countries, with a special interest in arms purchases. In July, Yang Dezhi, China's chief of staff, toured France, Belgium, and England, visiting defense establishments and conferring with military leaders. A negative note, however, was sounded on February 27, when China recalled its ambassador to the Netherlands to protest a Dutch sale of two submarines to Taiwan. Peking demanded that official relations with the Netherlands be downgraded to the chargé d'affaires level.

Soviet Union. Moscow was seriously concerned by the planned Chinese-U.S. strategic cooperation. It charged that Washington's offer to sell weapons to China was a "provocative decision" and accused Secretary of State Haig and the Chinese of joining in a conspiracy of "aggression and imperialism" in Southeast Asia. China, on its side, denounced the Soviets for their expansion into Southeast Asia, their securing of air and naval bases in Vietnam, and their backing of Vietnam's invasion of Cambodia. In June, Peking charged that Moscow reneged on an agreement to negotiate on boundary disputes. Soviet intransigence, said a Chinese official, was "not only malicious but also dangerous, reeking of expansionism and gunpowder."

Japan. Peking's decision to cancel a large number of industrial projects produced considerable disappointment among Japanese businessmen. In 1981, contracts with Japanese companies amounting to more than $1,500,000,000—for ventures in metallurgy, chemicals, steel, and other heavy industries—were postponed or canceled. Japanese officials were gloomy over the chances of restoring the contracts, and the future of economic cooperation looked dim.

In May it was reported that China had requested Japanese credits of more than $3,000,000,000 to restore some key petrochemical and steel projects. But negotiations bogged down over the amount and form of the possible loans. Japan did not want to go beyond the limits of commercial and government credits already pledged, and that was not enough for Peking.

On July 22, China demanded that Japan stop surveying oil resources around the Diaoyutai islands northeast of Taiwan. Peking maintained that the islands had been Chinese territory since ancient times.

Southeast Asia. China's central policy in Southeast Asia was to curb Vietnam, which had occupied Cambodia and set up the puppet government of President Heng Samrin. On July 11, when Vietnam refused to attend a UN conference on Cambodia, China declared that the 200,000 Vietnamese troops in Cambodia must be driven out by force. The Vietnamese regime, said Peking, was a proxy for the USSR and understood only force. Under strong Chinese pressure, a united front of former Cambodian leaders was formed in September to launch a campaign against the Vietnamese occupation of Cambodia. Peking believed the coalition was necessary to improve the image of the former Pol Pot regime, so that it could retain its seat in the UN.

During a visit to Thailand in February 1981, Prime Minister Zhao played down China's support of Asian Communists. China, he said, "has only ideological and moral relations with the Communist parties in Asian countries." And, he went on, China "will take further actions to prevent its relations with these parties from affecting [its] friendly relations" with the non-Communist countries of Southeast Asia. Thailand was pleased, but Malaysia, which wanted Peking to denounce publicly its support for the Malaysian Communist party, was not satisfied.

India. On June 26, Foreign Minister Huang Hua arrived in New Delhi seeking improved Chinese-Indian relations, which had deteriorated since the border war in 1962. The two countries agreed to hold early negotiations on their border disputes, but they differed on the issues of Soviet intervention in Afghanistan and Vietnamese occupation of Cambodia. China did not alter its support of Pakistan in the Indian-Pakistani dispute over Kashmir, nor its opposition to the merger of Sikkim with India in 1974. But China and India declared that differences should not stand in the way of improved relations. Border talks opened December 10.

CHESTER C. TAN, *New York University*

– COMMUNIST CHINA • Information Highlights –

Official Name: People's Republic of China.
Location: Central part of eastern Asia.
Area: 3,705,396 sq mi (9 596 976 km^2).
Population (1981 est.): 985,000,000.
Chief Cities (1980 est.): Peking, the capital, 8,500,000; Shanghai, 12,000,000; Tianjin, 7,200,000.
Government: *Chairman of the Chinese Communist Party,* Hu Yaobang (took office June 1981). *Head of government,* Zhao Ziyang, premier (took office Sept. 1980); Deng Xiaoping, senior deputy premier. *Legislature* (unicameral)—National People's Congress.
Monetary Unit: Yuan (1.61 yuan equal U.S.$1, March 1981—noncommercial rate).
Manufactures (major products): Iron and steel, coal, machinery, cotton textiles, light industrial products.
Agriculture (major products): Rice, wheat, corn, millet, cotton, sweet potatoes.

CITIES AND URBAN AFFAIRS

The "urban renaissance" movement, which had begun to offer new hope for U.S. cities in recent years, experienced serious setbacks in 1981. The major forces influencing the status and direction of cities were 1) the economy, highlighted by "Reaganomic" budget cuts and continued high interest rates; 2) the Reagan administration's "New Federalism," characterized by an historic shift away from Washington's responsibility for urban programs; and 3) fundamental changes in private sector finance mechanisms for both home purchases and urban development processes.

The Economy. The fiscal stress experienced first by New York City in the mid-1970s, followed by Cleveland, Chicago, and Philadelphia, became widespread in 1981. The growing urban fiscal crisis is caused in part by continuing inflation, municipal union demands, mandated pension fund escalations, administration mismanagement, and the growing costs of maintaining a deteriorating urban infrastructure. Simultaneously, economically beleaguered voters in a growing number of local jurisdictions, following the lead of California's Proposition 13 and Massachusett's Proposition 2½, have restricted urban financial flexibility by placing legal limits on spending and taxes.

Further adding to their financial woes, municipalities experienced serious difficulty selling bond issues because of high interest rates and changes in the tax laws which created increased competition for investment dollars.

The most serious blow to the urban economy in 1981 came from Washington, when Congress passed a Reagan budget which drastically reduced or eliminated federal grant programs designed to aid cities and urban residents. In addition to significant reductions in such entitlement programs as Medicare, Medicaid, and Social Security, which provide aid directly to recipients, the categorical grant programs involving mass transit, education, health, housing, economic development, job training, and community services were to suffer severe cuts. Chicago, for example, estimated its loss in federal support for social programs at $250 million.

New Federalism. In addition to deep cuts in urban program budgets, President Reagan quickly moved to implement a campaign promise to reduce the role of the federal government by shifting the responsibility for social programs to states and municipalities. Aided by two high-level committees—The Coordinating Task Force on Federalism and the Presidential Advisory Committee on Federalism—Phase I of the "New Federalism" went into effect on October 1, when 57 categorical grant programs were converted into 9 block grants to the states.

A companion proposal was the transfer of tax resources to the states so that those who spend the tax dollars would be accountable to those who pay them. This so-called "tax-turnback" scheme is ideologically consistent with the intent of Reagan's New Federalism, but it has the potential for protracted political conflict and implementation problems.

Another major concern for cities and urban groups that had benefited from federal programs was the disruption of favorable political relationships with the federal agencies. Under the New Federalism, the focus of lobbying and political maneuvering shifted to the states.

Finance Mechanisms. Despite the gloomy economic outlook for U.S. cities, the imagination and creativity of urban public and private leaders were demonstrated during the year, abetted by the infusion of new sources of investment capital.

With interest rates everywhere remaining too high to sustain the urban housing market, the real estate industry and financial institutions engaged in the "creative financing" of home mortgages through such mechanisms as adjustable rates, shared appreciation, graduated payments, renegotiable rates, variable rates, and wraparounds. The housing market was also enhanced by a continued trend toward condominium and cooperative homeownership, providing for the increased number of single-person and childless-couple households. The adaptive reuse of older buildings for residential use, encouraged by new tax laws, not only helps fill the need for housing but encourages the preservation of sound buildings and sustains the quality of urban life.

During the Carter administration a major incentive was the UDAG (Urban Development Action Grant) program, designed to encourage private-sector investment in urban projects. Intense lobbying by both cities and the private sector in 1981 temporarily saved UDAG, which continued as a major urban development tool.

Perhaps more significant for the development of cities in the long run was the emergence in 1981 of several important trends: large, highly professional, well-financed developers from Canada building major urban projects in a number of U.S. cities; overseas investors, often pension funds, seeking investment opportunities in the U.S. real estate market; and the strong interest of major U.S. insurance companies and pension funds in extending their role in real estate development to equity partner in addition to mortgage lender. Of at least equal consequence was that some large city planning departments moved from simply providing development incentives (land clearance, tax abatement, and service enhancement) to requiring amenities from developers, in exchange for the right to build projects that add to the tax base, the architectural landscape, and the building needs of the city.

(*See* articles on individual cities.)

Louis H. Masotti
Center for Urban Affairs and Policy Research
Northwestern University

COINS AND COIN COLLECTING

The year 1981 was an eventful one for coins and their collectors. The Susan B. Anthony dollar, introduced with much fanfare on July 2, 1979, quickly proved to be a flop. Although production of the Anthony dollar reached nearly 90 million in 1980, few actually circulated. In 1981, it was announced that no additional pieces would be produced in 1982.

The rising price of copper prompted the U.S. Treasury Department to adopt a new format of copper-coated zinc for the cent, with production beginning at the end of 1981.

The Medallic Art Company of Danbury, CT, produced medals in five sizes in honor of the inauguration of Ronald Reagan in January. In the same month, Frank Gasparro, chief engraver of the U.S. Mint for many years, retired. Elizabeth Jones, an accomplished sculptor and medallist, was named as his successor. Later in the year, Donna Pope was selected by President Reagan to replace Stella Hackel Sims as director of the Bureau of the Mint.

The American Arts Gold Medallion Program was launched with a pair of medals, one weighing a half ounce (.014 kg) and the other weighing one ounce (.028 kg), with a market price keyed to the daily bullion price. Sales were less than expected. A John Wayne memorial medal, designed by Frank Gasparro, attracted wide attention.

Two 1787 Brasher doubloons came on the market. An example from the Garrett Collection was sold by Bowers & Ruddy Galleries for $625,000, and another specimen, in better condition, was sold in a private sale for $650,000 by Stack's of New York City. Carlton Numismatics of Michigan paid $325,000 for a 1911 Canadian pattern silver dollar, the highest price ever received for a coin issued by that country.

New releases: Britain's crown-size coin in honor of the royal wedding and Canada's $100 gold coin.

Photos Courtesy, Krause Publications, Inc.

During the year, restrictive legislation affecting coins cropped up in many areas of the United States as a result of silver bullion thefts. Legislation was passed requiring dealers in second-hand goods to hold silver/gold objects for a lengthy period before selling them. In August it was announced that President Reagan's new tax act contained a clause forbidding Keogh Plan participants from investing in such "hard" assets as coins, stamps, and so on. Legislation was later introduced to change this, but as of press time the outlook did not seem hopeful for collectors. Legislation plus a late 1981 recession, coming on the heels of the boom coin market of the preceding two years, caused a reduction in prices for all coins.

The American Numismatic Association (ANA) broke ground for a new addition at its Colorado Springs headquarters. By September, the American Numismatic Association Certification Service announced that more than 11,000 coins were being processed each month. Adna Wilde, Jr., was sworn in as the new ANA president, with Q. David Bowers as vice-president. The organization's 1981 convention was held in New Orleans. The auction, conducted by Bowers & Ruddy Galleries, realized $5.4 million, with $475,000 posted for the 1907 Indian head pattern double eagle struck in gold, the only known example.

Legislation was introduced for a commemorative half dollar to honor the 250th anniversary of George Washington's birth. The coin is to be minted in 1982 to the extent of 10 million pieces. Shortly thereafter, additional legislation was introduced to provide for the minting of 29 special commemorative coins to be issued in conjunction with the 1984 Olympics. President Reagan's proposal that a private firm, Occidental Petroleum, be named to distribute the Olympic coins privately and receive a profit from them caused a tremendous uproar among coin collectors.

An exhibit of papal medals from the Baroque era (1500–1700) was shown at the Mount Holyoke College Art Museum in Massachusetts. Spink & Son, a leading London coin dealer, opened an office in New York City. The British Royal Mint offered crown-size coins observing the July 29 wedding of Prince Charles and Lady Diana Spencer. The pieces were designed by Philip Nathan. The Royal Canadian Mint selected the 100th anniversary of the founding of Saskatoon, Saskatchewan, as a theme for its 1982 commemorative silver dollar.

Q. DAVID BOWERS
Bowers & Ruddy Galleries, Inc.

COLOMBIA

The three major themes in Colombian national life since 1948—guerrilla activity, political maneuvering within the contending elites of the two old-line political parties, and economic difficulties—continued to preoccupy most Colombians during 1981. The major guerrilla organizations—the M-19 and FARC (Colombian Revolutionary Armed Forces)—rejected a government offer of amnesty and proceeded to carry out several violent attacks, one of which cost the life of an American hostage. Both the Liberal and Conservative elites began to gear up for the national presidential election, to be held in 1982, with the Liberal party split along personality lines and the Conservative party united behind one candidate. The Colombian economy performed poorly, with inflation, unemployment, and a large government deficit the biggest problems.

Politics. Both Liberals and Conservatives held their presidential nominating conventions in 1981. The September Liberal convention in Medellín was marked by bitter infighting between former presidents Alfonso Lopez Michelsen and Carlos Lleras Restrepo. Lopez openly campaigned for the nomination while Lleras, perhaps too old to seek another term for himself, worked for the candidacy of Virgilio Barco, the former mayor of Bogotá. After Barco and Lleras boycotted the convention, Lopez was selected as the Liberal standard-bearer. Barco later agreed to support Lopez, but Lleras (who resigned from the National Liberal Directorate) still refused to endorse Lopez. A major factor in the internecine struggle was a contest between Lleras and current President Julio César Turbay Ayala for the mantle of elder statesman within the party. Turbay, who backed Lopez' candidacy, appeared to have won the struggle.

By contrast, the Conservative party, which held its convention in November, unified solidly behind the candidacy of Belisario Betancur. Betancur, who had previously been denied the nomination because he was deemed too liberal by the more conservative wing of the party, is a charismatic campaigner. If the split within the Liberals is not healed by election time, Betancur could well emerge the winner.

Guerrillas. Guerrilla activity increased during the year. A government offer of amnesty made at the end of 1980 expired July 31, with no takers. The M-19, heirs to the failed populist movement of former dictator Gustavo Rojas Pinilla, followed its occupation of the Dominican Republic embassy in 1980 with the kidnapping in 1981 of Chester Alan Bitterman, an American working in Colombia for the Summer Institute of Linguistics (SIL). Bitterman was kidnapped on January 30 and, after demands for ransom and the expulsion of the SIL were not met, was killed on March 7. The M-19 claimed that Bitterman and the SIL had links to the U.S. Central Intelligence Agency (CIA) and that SIL operations were designed to destroy native cultures in the countries in which they operated. The charges had been leveled at the SIL by leftist groups in other Latin American countries as well. The Bitterman episode may have produced a split within the M-19. Moderates within the movement, such as Jaime Bateman Cayon, who had declared his candidacy for the presidency, dissociated themselves from the kidnapping.

The increased activity of both the M-19 and FARC in 1981 evidently inspired a long-dormant guerrilla group, the National Liberation Army (ELN), to re-form.

Guerrilla activities produced reactions in government circles. President Turbay was forced to cancel visits to Moscow and Peking because of army pressure. In April, famed novelist Gabriel Garcia Marquez fled his Bogotá apartment and surfaced in Mexico, claiming that the army wanted to arrest him.

Economy. The Colombian peso deteriorated steadily against the U.S. dollar, reaching 54.2 pesos per $1.00 at midyear. The government deficit for the first five months was between 12,000,000,000 and 15,000,000,000 pesos and was expected to go much higher. Unemployment was at 9.2% in mid-July. Inflation remained a major cause of the nation's economic woes, with the trade deficit increasing dramatically. A loan of $254 million was made by the Bank of America, with a higher interest rate and more rapid repayment schedule than public loans, which all but ceased.

Foreign Affairs. Relations with the United States were quite good, despite the Bitterman incident. On July 31, the U.S. Senate ratified a treaty whereby the United States renounced all claims to three small coastal islands in the Caribbean. Colombia also joined in the condemnation of Mexico and France for their recognition of the guerrillas in El Salvador as a "political force" in that country. The Turbay government sought to mend fences with Venezuela; President Turbay met with Venezuelan President Luis Herrera Campins in September and October.

ERNEST A. DUFF
Randolph-Macon Women's College

COLOMBIA • Information Highlights

Official Name: Republic of Colombia.
Location: Northwest South America.
Area: 439,737 sq mi (1 138 919 km^2).
Population (1981 est.): 27,800,000.
Chief Cities (1979 est.): Bogotá, the capital, 4,055,909; Medellín, 1,506,661; Cali, 1,316,137.
Government: *Head of state and government,* Julio César Turbay Ayala, president (took office Aug. 1978). *Legislature*—Congress: Senate and Chamber of Representatives.
Monetary Unit: Peso (56.49 pesos equal U.S.$1, Oct. 1981).
Manufactures (major products): Textiles, beverages, processed food, clothing and footwear, chemicals, metal products, cement.
Agriculture (major products): Coffee, bananas, rice, cotton, sugarcane, tobacco, corn, plantains, flowers.

Jerry Downs

Roy Romer (left) and Bill Coors serve as cochairmen of Colorado's Blue Ribbon Panel, a committee appointed by Gov. Richard D. Lamm to oversee growth-management efforts in the state.

COLORADO

As Colorado's energy boom continued, political leaders in the state seemingly argued about how much prosperity the state could stand.

Energy. Despite the Reagan administration's emphasis on private energy development, TOSCO Corp. won a $1,100,000,000 federal loan guarantee for development of oil shale production in western Colorado. Union Oil received a $400 million federal purchase guarantee for products from its Colorado oil shale project.

Governor Lamm and the Legislature. As has happened through much of his seven years in office, Democratic Gov. Richard D. Lamm dueled with the Republican-controlled legislature over his growth-management efforts. A Lamm-appointed Blue Ribbon Panel urged a five-year, $500 million program of capital improvements to meet growth needs. The legislature ignored the proposal and killed a Lamm-backed increase in the mineral severance tax that would have helped pay for it. Then, the legislature voted to return a $137 million revenue surplus to taxpayers. Lamm vetoed the tax package but was overridden when many minority Democrats joined majority Republicans on the issue.

In the face of legislative criticism, Lamm scrapped the "Human Settlements Policy," another growth-control effort he had instituted by executive order. Unappeased, legislators passed a bill stripping the governor of the power to set such policies. Lamm vetoed the bill but was again overridden. Part of the governor's problems in sustaining vetoes, ironically, came from his failure to veto a bill repealing Colorado's pioneering bilingual education law. Democratic Hispanic legislators had urged that he veto the bill. When he let it become law, some of the Hispanics voted with Republicans to override the governor on measures he had vetoed.

In October, Lamm promoted the results of yet another growth-management effort, the Front Range Project, which was completing a two-year study at his request.

Urban News. Announcement of three new 50-plus-story office buildings kept downtown Denver's building boom going. But, paradoxically, the city announced cutbacks in key services, including Denver General Hospital. Admission fees were imposed at the once-free Denver Art Museum, and suburban residents were told that they would have to pay $200 a year to use the Denver Public Library.

Part of the financial squeeze stemmed from a Colorado law designed to keep property taxes down. It requires all buildings to be assessed at 1973 values. New construction is computed as if it had been built in 1973, meaning the inflated values of Colorado real estate produce little tax revenue. Many other cities in the state also had to trim their expenses as tax revenues from retail sales grew more slowly than anticipated.

Denver area voters approved $126 million in sewer bonds to help cope with growth. Littleton residents approved a $17.3 million project to ease traffic problems stemming from growing numbers of coal trains running through the city.

The Denver School Board elections in May tipped control to a faction opposed to court-ordered busing. In December, the board sought U.S. District Judge Richard Matsch's approval for a "magnet school" plan which sought to achieve voluntary integration while eliminating forced busing. Matsch was still weighing the proposal at year's end.

Tornado. On June 3, a tornado struck suburban Thornton, killing no one but injuring 60 persons and causing $10 million in damage.

BOB EWEGEN, *"The Denver Post"*

COLORADO • Information Highlights

Area: 104,091 sq mi (269 596 km^2).
Population (1980 census): 2,888,834.
Chief Cities (1980 census): Denver, the capital, 491,396; Colorado Springs, 215,150; Aurora, 158,588; Lakewood, 112,848; Pueblo, 101,686; Arvada, 84,576; Boulder, 76,685; Fort Collins, 64,632; Greeley, 53,006; Westminster, 50,211.
Government (1981): *Chief Officers*—governor, Richard D. Lamm (D); lt. gov., Nancy Dick (D). *General Assembly*—Senate, 35 members; House of Representatives, 65 members.
State Finances (fiscal year 1980): *Revenues*, $3,366,000,000; *expenditures*, $2,805,000,000.
Personal Income (1980): $29,029,000,000; per capita, $10,025.
Labor Force (July 1981): *Nonagricultural wage and salary earners*, 1,273,400; *unemployed*, 78,400 (5.2% of total force).

COMMUNICATION TECHNOLOGY

In 1981, important advances were made in telecommunication systems, in the number and variety of services available, and in techniques for increasing the capabilities and lowering the costs of microelectronics used in computers and microprocessors. The goal of an integrated national network of digital transmission facilities and time-division digital switching centers came noticeably closer to realization.

Transmission and Switching Systems. The Bell System began installing, in New Jersey, the first section of optical fiber cable for its long-distance light-wave communication system connecting Washington, DC, and Boston, MA. Scheduled for completion in 1984, the system will have an initial capacity of 80,000 simultaneous telephone conversations or an equivalent in video pictures and data signals.

In April, the U.S. Federal Communications Commission (FCC) adopted rules clearing the way for the American Telephone & Telegraph's (AT&T's) new Advanced Mobile Phone Service (AMPS). The AMPS will have the capability of serving hundreds of thousands of cars and trucks in major U.S. cities. It is expected to be available in the mid-1980s.

Plans were announced for the installation of digital transmission facilities on a coaxial cable between Plano, IL, and Sacramento, CA, a distance of about 2,300 mi (3 700 km). When completed in 1982, it will be the longest digital high-speed coaxial cable system in the world. It will handle up to 140 million bits of information per second, the equivalent of several hundred newspaper pages.

A new digital microwave radio communication system, designed to link cities up to several hundred miles apart, was put into operation between Eugene and Roseburg, OR. Designated the DR6-30, it carries voice and data in the digital format of coded pulses. It has a capacity of seven working channels, each one capable of carrying 1,344 voice and data circuits.

General Telephone and Electronics (GTE) announced the development of an integrated voice and data switching system for use with existing private branch exchanges. The Bell System's first local digital time-division switching system was put into service in Seneca, IL.

Communication Services. Home antennas and associated electronic equipment for direct pickup of TV broadcasts via satellite became practical in 1981; dishes from 10 to 15 ft (3.0 to 4.6 m) in diameter were available from several manufacturers. An earth station enables the individual to have direct access to satellite transmissions of news, sports, movies, and the full range of TV features already available, with more on the way.

Early in the year, Satellite Business Systems (SBS) began operation of an advanced satellite system for high-speed data transmission to business customers. GTE Satellite Corp. requested permission from the FCC to lease facilities on Canada's Anik B satellite for a similar service in the United States.

Courtesy of The Western Electric

The microwave tower with horn and disk antennas is part of a new communications system in Oregon.

A variety of tests and customer trials were carried out for information systems with visual displays on the home television screen. Knight-Ridder Newspapers, together with AT&T, announced that an expanded Viewtron information test, involving 5,000 participants in southern Florida, would begin in 1983.

Microelectronics. Bell Laboratories announced a major advance in microelectronics with its development of an X-ray technique for producing ultra-miniature integrated circuit patterns on silicon wafers. By using this technique instead of conventional photolithography, line widths of one millionth of a meter (one micron) or less can be obtained. Ten times as many electronic components can be put on a chip of a given size and, compared with conventional step-by-step optical exposure methods, ten times as many wafers can be produced per hour.

IBM developed three new processors to increase the capacity of the IBM 8100 Information System. The new models have up to 60% more computing performance and up to twice the data storage previously available.

Several firms developed 32-bit microprocessors. They can process 32 bits of information simultaneously, twice the capability of previously available devices.

See also SPACE EXPLORATION; TELEVISION AND RADIO

M. D. FAGEN, *Formerly, Bell Laboratories*

Ku Klux Klansmen and police duck to avoid bottles and rocks thrown during a Klan march in Meriden, CT.

UPI

CONNECTICUT

Political, Financial, and Judicial News. State Rep. Thirman L. Milner (47) was elected mayor of Hartford on November 3, the first black ever to be popularly elected a mayor of a New England community. Milner won the Democratic nomination in an October 13 primary (ordered following alleged voting irregularities) after losing a first primary on September 8 by 94 votes.

Two prominent state leaders died during 1981. Former Gov. Ella T. Grasso, 61, who resigned on the last day of 1980 because of illness, died on February 5. U.S. Rep. William R. Cotter, 55, died on September 8. (*See also* OBITUARIES.) William A. O'Neill, who succeeded to the governorship following Mrs. Grasso's resignation, set Jan. 12, 1982, as the date for a special election to choose Cotter's successor.

Governor O'Neill took on the burden of keeping the state treasury solvent in the face of increasing costs and the expected harmful impact of cuts in federal assistance. The state legislature at O'Neill's urging enacted a controversial tax on unincorporated businesses as an alternative to increasing the sales tax.

In other action, consumers were expected to benefit from lower beer and liquor prices resulting from legislative action that repealed a law setting the minimum markup on wholesale and retail prices. The repeal, effective on Jan. 1, 1982, should allow Connecticut liquor merchants to be competitive with merchants in neighboring states. A similar repeal on wine will become effective in January 1983.

The state Supreme Court declared unconstitutional the law that prohibited the sale of alcoholic beverages on Good Friday.

In addition to taking away federal funds from the state, President Reagan also borrowed some talent when he appointed two prominent state residents, Alexander M. Haig, Jr., and Malcolm Baldrige, to his cabinet.

Ku Klux Klan. The Ku Klux Klan, which openly began recruiting members in Connecticut in 1980, stepped up its activities in 1981. It was involved in a March 21 confrontation with anti-Klan protesters in Meriden that resulted in a shakeup in the command of the state police. Meriden police complained that the state police assigned too few troopers to assist them and then failed to respond to a call for more help. A legislative investigation of the incident resulted in Governor O'Neill taking command of the state police from Public Safety Commissioner Donald J. Long and giving it to Deputy Commissioner Lester Forst.

In October, Forst assigned so many troopers to keep the peace at a Klan cross burning in Windham County that troopers outnumbered Klansmen and spectators.

Other News. James F. English, Jr., became the 13th president of Hartford's Trinity College on October 3, succeeding Theodore D. Lockwood. Trinity is the state's second oldest college.

The usually calm waters of Long Island Sound were the scene of a nighttime tragedy on August 9, when a pleasure boat sank and five residents of West Hartford, who were aboard the *Karen E,* perished. The boat's owner was the only survivor and said his craft had been struck by a cement-laden barge being towed by a tugboat. A Coast Guard investigation was pending.

Directors of Bloomfield-based Connecticut General Corp. and of INA Corp. of Philadelphia recommended a merger of the two insurance companies.

The Danbury State Fair, an annual event for 112 years, ended in October. The 150-acre (61-ha) fairground is to become a shopping mall.

ROBERT F. MURPHY, *"The Hartford Courant"*

CONNECTICUT • Information Highlights

Area:
Population (1980 census): 3,107,576.
Chief Cities (1980 census): Hartford, the capital, 136,392; Bridgeport, 142,546; New Haven, 126,109; Waterbury, 103,266; Stamford, 102,453; Norwalk, 77,767; New Britain, 73,840; West Hartford, 61,301; Danbury, 60,470; Greenwich, 59,578.
Government (1981): *Chief Officers*—governor, William A. O'Neill (D); lt. gov., Joseph J. Fauliso (D). *General Assembly*—Senate, 36 members; House of Representatives, 151 members.
State Finances (fiscal year 1980): *Revenues,* $3,472,000,000; *expenditures,* $3,341,000,000.
Personal Income (1980): $36,510,000,000; per capita, $11,720.
Labor Force (July 1981): *Nonagricultural wage and salary earners,* 1,427,900; *unemployed,* 101,600 (6.3% of total force).

CONSUMER AFFAIRS

Inflation continued to be a plague during 1981. There was hope that the double-digit inflation of recent years would slow down to single-digit inflation. Interest rates, housing costs, medical expenses, and energy prices continued to trouble consumers.

Reagan Economics. The Reagan administration made significant changes in the consumer protection area at the federal level. The administration's moves toward less regulation in the marketplace were very apparent in the appointments made to regulatory commissions and agencies, and budget reductions proposed by the president and passed by Congress were having significant impact on consumer protection agencies, including the Federal Trade Commission, the Food and Drug Administration, and the National Highway Traffic Safety Administration. The final budget cuts made by Congress in the summer were not so drastic as the administration's original proposals, and plans for additional reductions were announced.

David Stockman, director of the Office of Management and Budget (OMB), gave an indication of the administration's position regarding consumerism when he stated: "They've (consumer activists) created this whole facade of consumer protection in order to seize power in our society. I think part of the mission of this administration is to unmask and discredit that false ideology."

White House Appointments. Former Federal Trade Commissioner and former deputy director of the White House Office of Consumer Affairs Elizabeth Dole was named to head the White House Office of Public Liaison. Reporting to Elizabeth Dole is Virginia Knauer, former head of the White House Office of Consumer Affairs and special assistant for consumer affairs to Presidents Nixon and Ford, who was named director of the Office of Consumer Affairs and special assistant in the consumer matters as well as matters of the aging and disabled, and of safety, health care, and vocational guidance self-help.

Legislation. In the consumer legislative area, 1981 was a year in which consumer-oriented legislators tried to retain what had been enacted and not push for new legislation. A Cash Discount Act was passed, permitting merchants to offer unlimited discounts to customers paying cash and extending the ban on credit-card surcharges until 1984. Previously the cash discount had been limited to 5%. Merchants who choose to offer discounts for cash will continue to be required to offer the discount to all prospective buyers and conspicuously disclose its availability.

State Legislative Activity. More than a dozen states have enacted legislation that requires child restraint seats in motor vehicles. By a unanimous vote, the Alabama legislature approved a deceptive trade practices act. Alabama had been the

Teresa Zabala/New York Times Pictures

Virginia Knauer, consumer-affairs adviser to Presidents Nixon and Ford, joined the Reagan team.

only state in the nation not to have such a consumer protection statute. During 1981 a number of states boosted or abolished interest-rate ceilings. This was disturbing news to consumer borrowers.

Better Business Bureaus. With the decline in funding for local consumer protection offices in many areas, consumers have been turning more and more to Better Business Bureaus. The Council of Better Business Bureaus reported that in 1980 its bureaus recorded 6,580,847 consumer contacts as follows: inquiries—5,088,421 (77.3%); complaints—1,492,426 (22.7%). Heading the complaint list were general mail-order companies, followed by franchised auto dealers and home-remodeling contractors.

Canada. In the early 1970s, the Consumers Association of Canada's magazine *Canadian Consumer* was a small digest-size publication of 40 pages. Since then it has been through many landmark changes. Its circulation has risen from 85,000 to about 182,000. Effective with the October 1981 issue, the magazine began to be published monthly instead of bimonthly.

Health protection of consumers continued to be a major effort. For example, foam insulation made from urea formaldehyde was banned because of an interim report by the Canadian federal department of health, which found that formaldehyde was cancer causing and had allergenic potential.

STEWART M. LEE
Geneva College

CRIME

Considerable doubt exists as to whether crime rates are rising or declining. But there is no question that, as *The Washington Post* said in an editorial, "the ordinary American now believes a random, vicious criminal incident will disrupt unexpectedly the moral fabric of his or her life." This perception of the ominous threat of crime was what underlay much of the federal decision-making on the subject during 1981.

In addition, the mass murders of children in Atlanta, GA, and the attempted assassinations of President Reagan and Pope John Paul II caused major concern. (*See* Atlanta and special report page 178.)

U.S. Crime Statistics. The Uniform Crime Reports (UCR), published annually by the Federal Bureau of Investigation (FBI), showed a rise of 9.4% in the amount of serious crime between 1979 and 1980. Violent crime was up 11.1%, and within the category of violent crime, the offense of robbery showed a striking 17.5% increase. The FBI statistics are based upon reports forwarded to the bureau from police departments throughout the United States. The departments tabulate what are called "crimes known to the police," matters that involve illegal behaviors that law enforcement officials themselves locate or acts that are reported to them.

The best indication that the FBI figures reflect a true growth in the amount of violent crime is provided by the offense of homicide. Statisticians assume that most murders and manslaughters, the major categories of homicide, are reported accurately. Both the FBI figures and the death certificate totals published by the U.S. Public Health Service indicate a continuously escalating rate of homicide. The figure per 100,000 population in the United States was about 4.5 in 1962. It has inched upward except for a slight decline in the mid-1970s, and now stands at about 10.5 per 100,000 persons.

In White Plains, NY, Jean S. Harris was convicted of the second-degree murder of Dr. Herman Tarnower.

UPI

The foregoing conclusions about rising crime rates are contradicted, however, by a report issued in 1981 by the Bureau of Justice Statistics. The bureau's National Crime Survey (NCS) was based on interviews with a sample of 132,000 persons in 60,000 households across the nation. The NCS secures information on about 3 million violent crimes each year, three times the total reported by the FBI. But in terms of rates, the NCS shows no increase in crime whatsoever. In fact, it reports a decline in violent crime between 1979 and 1980. Rape and robberies showed no change, but there were fewer assaults, burglaries, and larcenies, according to NCS figures. In fact, the NCS materials insist that criminal activity decreased slowly during 1975–80.

The NCS report also found that race had little to do with crime victimization, but that higher-income households were more likely than low-income households, and city and suburban residents more likely than rural residents to become victims of crime.

Trying to reconcile the very different conclusions of the UCR and NCS reports, a *New York Times* editorial writer offered the interpretation that crime has remained steady but that the reporting of crime to the police has increased. The demands of insurance companies for official police reports before they compensate theft losses were said to be one reason for the rise in reporting. Another suggested explanation lay in a growing public confidence in the police, particularly in regard to rape offenses. Women in the past have resisted reporting forcible rape because of fear of hostile police and court response. Today, more sympathetic criminal justice system attitudes may encourage a higher reporting rate.

Public Concern. Notwithstanding the uncertain picture of criminal activity, public concern about crime was dramatically on the increase in 1981. Fifty-eight percent of 1,030 persons contacted by the Gallup organization for *Newsweek* magazine during a national telephone poll said that they believed that there was more crime where they live now than a year earlier. Many reported making changes in their style of life as a precaution against crime. Almost four of five respondents indicated that they do not carry cash because of fear of robbery, while 64% said that they would not go out alone at night if they could avoid it. Other persons reported that they no longer wear expensive jewelry when away from home.

Tough measures were favored by the public to deal with crime. In the *Newsweek* poll, 65% of

The Guardian Angels, New York City youths who try to fight crime by personally patrolling the city's streets and subways, march in honor of Malcolm Brown, a member of the group who was killed while trying to aid two women mugging victims.

UPI

the respondents wanted convicted murderers to be executed, while only 24% opposed the death penalty. Eleven percent did not offer an opinion. A decade ago, Americans were about evenly divided on the issue of capital punishment. About half of the respondents said that they had little or no confidence in the police to guard them against violent crime.

A midyear Associated Press-NBC telephone poll of 1,599 American adults found a similar pattern. Eighty-five percent were more concerned about crime now than they were five years ago. Only 2% said they were less concerned, while 13% said their level of concern had not altered. Women and city residents expressed greater amounts of concern than men or rural dwellers.

Federal Recommendations. The intense public unrest about crime was reflected in the recommendations offered by the Attorney General's Task Force on Violent Crime, which were released in August. The eight-member task force, headed by former Attorney General Griffin Bell and Gov. James B. Thompson of Illinois, proposed that the federal government allocate $2,000,000,000 to help the states construct prisons. It also proposed the abolition of parole for federal prison inmates, tightening of bail laws, and an alteration of evidentiary rules to make convictions easier to obtain. The panel further endorsed pretrial detention of suspects considered dangerous, the limitation of habeas corpus petitions for state prisoners, and the increased uses of computers to facilitate the exchange of criminal records among jurisdictions. Other proposals included mandatory prison terms for persons convicted of using firearms in connection with a federal felony offense and the institution of a verdict of "guilty but mentally ill" for persons pleading insanity.

The need for prison facilities to relieve intense crowding underlay the proposed $2,000,000,000 expenditure. The federal government would pay 75% of the expense of new penal institutions' construction costs. From 1978 to 1980 the number of inmates in state facilities had risen from 60,000 to 329,000. By 1981 at least 39 states were involved in litigation or under court orders regarding inadequate or unsatisfactory prison conditions. The cost of building a maximum-security prison is about $70,000 per bed; minimum-security institutions run about $30,000 to $50,000 a bed.

If the federal task force recommendations are adopted, bail would be denied to "persons who are found by clear and convincing evidence to be dangerous" as well as to persons who in the past had committed serious crimes while on release before trial. The panel also advocated that the current presumption favoring release of persons waiting to be sentenced or appealing convictions should be abandoned.

The task force also supported new methods for dealing with firearms. There would be a ban on the importation of parts for handguns that are illegal in the United States, and gun owners would be required to report to the local police any loss or theft of a firearm.

The task force proposals received general approval from the Department of Justice. But Ira Glasser, executive director of the American Civil Liberties Union, declared that the task force report was "a public relations fraud." He noted that the task force members "want to appear to be doing something about crime, but what they're really doing is fooling with the Constitution."

Prison Statistics. The rapidly rising number of persons held in prisons in the United States is traceable to sentencing legislation passed on a widespread basis in recent years, according to a 1981 Department of Justice study. Between 1976 and 1980, 37 states enacted mandatory sentencing statutes and 15 states passed determinate sentencing laws. While determinate sentencing allows for probation, restitution, or suspended sentences and mandatory sentencing does not, both forms send the offender to prison for a fixed number of years that cannot be shortened by parole. Four states—Illinois, Indiana, Maine, and New Mexico—have completely abolished parole. During 1981 Texas added more than 3,000 inmates to its prison population, and California nearly 2,000.

A 1981 survey by the *National Law Journal* highlighted the extraordinary variations in prison sentences throughout the country. The journal noted that in terms of sentences meted out "it often matters less what crime has been committed than the state in which the felon chose to commit it." It was found that sentences in Massachusetts are the highest in the nation, averaging 53 months for all felony categories, while those in South Dakota, at 13 months, are the lowest. Prisoners sentenced for robbery in South Carolina were found to serve more prison time than those sentenced for murder in six states.

Crime Around the World. The United Nations Crime Prevention and Criminal Justice Branch reported on a worldwide survey of crime trends during the first half of the 1970s. Per 100,000 population, the highest rate of adult criminal behavior—1,683.1 per 100,000 persons—was found in the Caribbean area (Bahamas, Barbados, Jamaica, and Trinidad and Tobago). The lowest rate at 137.6 per 100,000 appeared in Latin American countries (Argentina, Chile, Costa Rica, Ecuador, El Salvador, and Peru). The report noted that the rate of offenses against the person decreases significantly in proportion to offenses against property as a nation develops economically. It also observed "a strong positive correlation . . . between unplanned development and an increase in crime."

Capital Punishment. About 150 persons continue to be sentenced to death each year in the United States, and at the year's end there were more than 800 persons on the death rows of the 35 states that permit capital punishment. More than half were confined in three southern states—Texas, Florida, and Georgia. All told, 78% of the death row inmates are in southern states.

Four states—Idaho, New Mexico, Oklahoma, and Texas—have authorized a new method of capital punishment, the hypodermic needle. Although the safety and effectiveness of the drugs required for such execution have not been tested, proponents believe that the hypodermic needle would be a more humane form of administering the death penalty than the methods used in the past. Convicted murderers Thomas Lee Hays (McAlester, OK, prison) and Charles Milton (Huntsville, TX, prison) were scheduled to be the first persons to be executed by injection. Such executions did not, however, occur in 1981. In March 1981, Steven T. Judy was executed in the electric chair in Indiana.

GILBERT GEIS, *University of California, Irvine*

CRIME—SPECIAL REPORT:

PROTECTING PUBLIC FIGURES

Three attacks on world leaders during 1981 vividly highlighted the vulnerability of public figures to assassination attempts. The dilemma of the situation appears almost insoluble: positions of leadership in the world today demand many occasions of close contact between public figures and their constituents—handshaking, touching, mingling with crowds. Such contact leaves officials open to bullet or knife thrust. The situation bedevils security agencies charged with protecting public officials.

On March 30 in Washington, DC, President Ronald Reagan was struck by two .22 caliber bullets fired from a handgun held by John W. Hinckley, Jr., a 25-year-old drifter from an upper middle-class family. A Secret Service agent and a Washington, DC, policeman also were injured, and James S. Brady, the president's press secretary, received severe head wounds.

What might have been done to forestall the assassination effort? Rerunning the episode in slow motion on television indicated the unfortunate tendency of local security officers to watch the president's progress instead of turning their backs to him and concentrating attention on the crowd. Hinckley had mixed in with television crewmen whose credentials had never been satisfactorily scrutinized. Better security checks and more vigilant protective measures might have thwarted the assassination attempt.

It appears, however, that there is something fundamental in society today that is responsible for the surge of such death-dealing behavior. The past two decades have seen the slayings of President John F. Kennedy (1963), Sen. Robert F. Kennedy (1968), and civil-rights leaders Medgar Evers (1963) and Martin Luther King, Jr. (1968). On Dec. 8, 1980, the onetime Beatles star, John Lennon, was killed in New York City. In addition, injuries have been inflicted on presidential candidate George Wallace (1972) and the black leader Vernon Jordan (1980). Two attempts were made on the life of President Gerald Ford in 1975.

Vigilance probably would not have proven particularly effective in checking the death-dealing attempt by Mehmet Ali Agca, a 23-

year-old Turkish national, against the life of Pope John Paul II on May 13 in Rome's St. Peter's Square. Two American women also were wounded by the assassin's shots. The Pope was greeting more than 10,000 persons.

On October 6 Egypt's President Anwar el-Sadat was murdered while viewing a military parade in Cairo. (*See* EGYPT.)

The Assassins. Individuals who attack prominent public figures show a rather common profile: they tend to be loners, erratic, alienated human beings. Most often they are young men. The use of personality tests to attempt to identify dangerous individuals before they commit violent acts sometimes is suggested as a countermeasure against assassination. But there exist in democracies strict requirements against interfering with citizen freedom on highly speculative grounds, and there are no tests capable of determining potentially assaultive persons with any degree of adequacy. Indeed, it is impossible to predict satisfactorily, even after such behavior, whether the same person will repeat a violent act.

Physical Safeguards. Government agents who seek to protect officials bemoan the tendency of such persons to expose themselves to dangerous conditions. It was asked why President Reagan had not used the more sheltered exit from the Washington hotel, but the answer was self-evident: it is in the nature of a president to be visible, to be capturable by the television cameras. The Pope, of course, as a spiritual leader, must be seen by his flock, to present a living personal inspiration to communicants.

After his recovery, President Reagan at a speech at Notre Dame University in South Bend, IN, stood behind a bullet-proof transparent shield. It seems likely too that vulnerable officials will take to wearing bullet-proof vests, and to riding more often in protected bubble-top cars in which they can clearly be seen but not harmed. A heavily increased cordon of security agents surrounding prominent persons undoubtedly also will be in order in the future.

Gun Control. Bullets are notably suitable for assaults on public figures, since guns overcome the necessity to move into close contact with the intended victim. While Mr. Reagan was recovering from his wounds, Sen. Edward Kennedy (D-MA) urged that the president support national legislation that would restrict the sale of handguns. The president remained adamantly opposed to gun control, maintaining, first, that such laws would not prove effective, and, second, that they would undermine the traditional American right to defend oneself adequately in an emergency.

The Assassination Ethos. The mood of violence said to permeate Western society is believed by some people to be fundamental to assassinations of public figures. Leslie Bennetts has noted that the American mass media may reflect and contribute to such a mood. Writing in 1981 in *The New York Times*, Bennetts pointed out that "in film, as in other media, violence has become commonplace, with people dismembered, impaled, incinerated, blown-up, machine-gunned, or otherwise annihilated with numbing regularity."

Hinckley, the man who shot President Reagan, was said to have been strongly influenced by *Taxi Driver*. The 1976 motion picture portrays the plan of a disturbed young man to murder a political candidate, a plan that ends instead with him slaughtering a group of unsavory characters, an act for which he is proclaimed a hero by the media. Such material, it is claimed, can encourage assaultive behavior, particularly on the part of unsettled young persons. This view finds support in a cross-cultural study comparing Japanese and American television themes in regard to violence. Japan has not suffered an assassination since World War II. Sumiko Iwao, Ithiel de Sola Pool, and Shigeru Hagiwara, writing in the spring 1981 issue of the *Journal of Communication*, noted that television in Japan shows as much violence as is portrayed in the United States, but that Japanese television violence follows a very different pattern than American. On American shows, the authors report, "good" and "bad" characters both are likely to initiate violence, and the villain is most apt to suffer its consequences. Japanese-produced television programs have villains initiating violence and heroes suffering. The authors maintain that this "strikingly different" treatment of violence arouses in Japanese viewers a feeling of distress and sympathy, while in overseas audiences the emotions elicited are those of support and "cheering" for violence.

Public Attention. Some persons insist that assassins are likely to be irrational, and therefore that they are not susceptible to attempts at deterrence. A contrary view is that their acts are logical and reasonable, and that they can best be headed off by undercutting their motivation.

Mark David Chapman, the 26-year-old who killed John Lennon, was portrayed at his sentencing hearing in 1981 by an assistant district attorney as a person who "essentially wanted to draw attention to himself, to make people see how important he was. He was basically looking for fame." Thomas Szasz, an eminent psychiatrist, believes the same motive prompted Sirhan Sirhan, when he fatally wounded Robert Kennedy. Szasz suggests that would-be assassins are well aware that if they carry out their deeds they will become media sensations. He believes that the most effective method to discourage assassination attempts would be to minimize the outpouring of attention focused on perpetrators.

GILBERT GEIS

CUBA

"Production and Defense," a propaganda slogan launched by the Cuban government at the December 1980 Second Communist Party Congress and repeated much thereafter, was the leitmotiv of the country's life during much of 1981. "These are unusual, difficult times," President Fidel Castro told the Congress which set policies and production plans for the 1981–1985 period. "No country is isolated from the rest of the world today," said Castro. He was referring to deleterious effects in Cuba of worldwide inflation and was demanding greater productive effort and urging the strengthening of national defense. "We are facing a really exceptional period. The change in the United States administration unquestionably implied risks for our country," said the president.

Having fared poorly on the production front in the past five years, the Castro government was trying to rebound. The 1981 output of sugar, Cuba's economic mainstay, was about 8 million t (8.7 million T), 1 million t (1.1 million T) more than in 1980. Lower sugar prices on the world market prevented Cuba from benefiting significantly from its good cane harvest. To obtain badly needed dollars and Western goods and technology, Havana, for the first time, sought partnership with foreign corporations, especially tourist industry concerns interested in developing Cuban beach resorts. But at the same time, the country's income from "family visits" by Cuban exiles living in the United States, estimated at more than $120 million in 1980, dwindled to $40 million. For political reasons, Cuba made it harder for the exiles to travel to their native country.

In 1981, Cuba's hard currency debt reached $3,000,000,000, of which $2,000,000,000 was owed to commercial banks in the West. The country continued to be heavily subsidized by the Soviet Union, whose economic aid was estimated at close to $4,000,000,000. Judging by the data of the next five-year plan, Cuba's dependence on Moscow would increase and the country would concentrate on better management of its agricultural resources rather than launching new industrial projects. The projected, much overdue modernization of the sugar industry would accentuate the role of Cuba as the main provider of sugar to the Soviet bloc. Cuba's trade share with the Communist bloc, already close to 80% of the total, would consequently grow even higher.

Military Buildup. Preparing for what Cuban leaders call "the eventuality of a total war" in the face of what they perceived as the Reagan administration's hostility, Havana created a new paramilitary force and began, with Soviet aid, a complete overhaul of its regular military establishment. The new force, the Territorial Militias, comprises hundreds of thousands of men and women who are not part of the regular troops, the reserve, or the civil defense units. According to Castro, the main mission of the Militias, both in peacetime and in wartime, is to replace and complement regular troops in combating paratroop landings, guarding and protecting factories, bridges, and railways, and "carrying out irregular war missions in the case of occupied territories." The Militias are being built up toward a strength of 1 million, about 10% of the country's entire population. In addition in 1981, Cuba had regular forces of some 190,000 and 200,000 reservists. These forces, according to U.S. Secretary of State Alexander M. Haig, Jr., were being reequipped with Soviet weapons whose shipments reached near-record levels in the spring of 1981. In addition to light armament apparently destined for the Militias, Cuba reportedly received a 2,300-ton Koni class frigate, new tanks, artillery, and antiaircraft missiles.

Cuban military involvement abroad did not diminish in 1981. The country maintained some 20,000 troops in Angola, about 16,000 in Ethiopia, and thousands more in other countries, from South Yemen to Nicaragua. Havana officials said that they were no longer sending aid to guerrillas in El Salvador or elsewhere in the Caribbean, although they did admit that arms shipments had been made from Cuba to the Salvadoran rebels before. In all, nearly 50,000 Cuban regular troops and military advisers were supporting various Third World revolutionary forces in 1981.

Foreign Relations. The Cuban government suffered a series of setbacks on the diplomatic front. The turnaround began with the 1980 flight of Cubans through the embassies of Peru and Venezuela, escapes which practically froze relations between Cuba and these two countries. In February 1981, Cuban security forces stormed the Ecuadoran embassy in Havana, against the wishes of the government of Ecuador, to seize a dozen persons who sought refuge there. The break-in, reportedly ordered personally by Castro, resulted in the recall of the Ecuadoran ambassador. In March, Colombia broke off relations with Havana, charging that some 80 guerrillas, captured by government troops after landing in the country, had been trained and armed in Cuba. In May, Costa Rica suspended relations with Cuba. Jamaican ties with Havana,

CUBA • Information Highlights

Official Name: Republic of Cuba.
Location: Caribbean Sea.
Area: 42,823 sq mi (110 912 km^2).
Population (1981 census): 9,796,369.
Chief Cities (Dec. 1978): Havana, the capital, 1,986,500; Santiago de Cuba, 333,600; Camagüey, 236,500.
Government: *Head of state and government,* Fidel Castro Ruz, president (took office under a new constitution, Dec. 1976). *Legislature* (unicameral)—National Assembly of People's Power.
Monetary Unit: Peso (0.78 peso equals U.S.$1, July 1981—noncommercial rate).
Manufactures (major products): Refined sugar, metals.
Agriculture (major products): Sugar, tobacco, rice, coffee beans, meat, vegetables, tropical fruits.

among the closest in the hemisphere until the defeat of former Prime Minister Michael Manley in late 1980, were first downgraded by new Prime Minister Edward Seaga, who asked for the recall of the Cuban ambassador in Kingston, accusing him of interfering in Jamaican internal affairs, and later cut. Cuban-Mexican relations continued as warm as ever. But even that closeness did not prevent Mexican President José López Portillo from disinviting Castro to the October 22–23 North-South meeting in Cancún, Mexico.

Castro was absent from Cancún because Mexico was warned by Washington that should he appear there President Ronald Reagan would not attend. The warning was another sign of a hard-line policy toward Cuba adopted by the United States after Reagan's inauguration. The Reagan administration, in one of its initial statements, accused Havana of arming El Salvador leftist guerrillas and the White House said the United States would take "the necessary steps" to stop such flow of military matériel. Washington was also concerned about a new military and naval facility built at Cienfuegos and the refurbished San Antonio de los Baños air base, home for Soviet TU-95 "Bear" long-range reconnaissance planes. Moscow continued to keep some 5,000 soldiers in Cuba; about 3,000 of them belonged to an armed brigade and the rest were advisers.

On its part, Cuba continued to maintain a taunting posture toward the United States, with Castro declaring that his government would fulfill all its "international obligations." The United States, he suggested publicly, might have been responsible for the introduction of several plagues afflicting Cuba, among them hemorrhagic conjunctivitis and a new strain of dengue-2 fever. Washington called Castro's charge unfounded.

GEORGE VOLSKY, *University of Miami*

CYPRUS

In 1981, almost 40% of Cyprus remained under Turkish control. The Nicosia government, headed by President Spyros Kyprianou, still refused to recognize this "Turkish Federated State of Cyprus" led by its own president, Rauf Denktaş. Intercommunal talks again met with little success.

Elections. On May 24, elections were held for the Cyprus House of Representatives. President Kyprianou's Democratic Party received eight of the 35 seats; 12 went to the right-wing Democratic Rally; 12 went to the Communist AKEL party; and three went to the left-wing EDEK party. The 15 seats reserved for Turkish Cypriots remained empty as they had since 1963, when the outbreak of fighting between Greek and Turkish Cypriots led to the withdrawal of Turkish Cypriots from the central government. When the new legislature convened in June, the eight Democratic and 12 AKEL deputies joined together in electing President Kyprianou's candidate for speaker, George Ladas.

On June 28, elections were also held for the presidency and assembly of the "Turkish Federated State of Cyprus." Rauf Denktaş was reelected president, and though no single party won a majority in the assembly, leftists scored significant gains. Several months later, Turkish Foreign Minister Ilter Turkmen visited the occupied territories to show solidarity with the Turkish Cypriots.

Intercommunal Talks. Under the sponsorship of UN Secretary-General Kurt Waldheim, Greek and Turkish Cypriots continued intercommunal talks, which in past years had been fruitless. In August, proposals for territorial changes were put forth by the Turkish Cypriots, but they proved unacceptable to President Kyprianou, all the Greek Cypriot political parties, and Archbishop Chrysostomos, head of the island's Greek Orthodox Church. The archbishop was especially severe in his condemnation of Turkish Cypriot tactics in the intercommunal talks. Waldheim put forth another plan for continuing the intercommunal discussions, and Kyprianou met with him in New York, but the question of Waldheim's own reelection as secretary-general clouded his role in the Cyprus negotiations.

Greece and Cyprus. Numerous diplomatic initiatives were taken during the year to establish closer ties between Cyprus and Greece. President Kyprianou visited Athens to consult with Prime Minister George J. Rallis. Then, after Rallis' electoral defeat and the installation of Socialist Andreas Papandreou on October 21, Kyprianou traveled to Greece again. Arriving on October 22, he became the first official visitor to be received by the new Greek government. Papandreou voiced strong support for the Greek Cypriots, accusing his predecessor of weakness vis-à-vis the Turks. In a program enunciated on November 22, Papandreou stated that Greece had a specific legal right to protect Cyprus' independence under agreements reached with Great Britain and Turkey before Cyprus became independent in 1960.

GEORGE J. MARCOPOULOS
Tufts University

CYPRUS • Information Highlights

Official Name: Republic of Cyprus.
Location: Eastern Mediterranean.
Area: 3,572 sq mi (9 251 km^2).
Population (1981 est.): 600,000.
Chief Cities (1978 est.): Nicosia, the capital, 121,500; Limassol, 102,400.
Government: *Head of state and government,* Spyros Kyprianou, president (took office Aug. 1977). *Legislature*—House of Representatives.
Monetary Unit: Pound (0.453 pound equals U.S.$1, July 1981).
Manufactures (major products): Processed foods, asbestos, cement.
Agriculture (major products): Potatoes, grapes, citrus fruits, wheat, barley, carobs, livestock.

UPI

Secretary-General Gustav Husák addresses the 16th Congress of the Czechoslovak Communist Party in Prague, April 6. Soviet President Leonid Brezhnev (front row, left) spoke the next day on the crisis in Poland. He predicted that Polish Communists would be able to solve the country's problems without Soviet or other help.

CZECHOSLOVAKIA

In Czechoslovakia, 1981 was a year of elections. The Slovak Communist Party (KSS) Congress was held in March and the 16th Congress of the Communist Party of Czechoslovakia (KSC) was held in April to choose their respective party leaders. Elections were also held in June for representative assemblies on all levels of government. The regime's worries about developments in neighboring Poland were compounded by its concern over the mediocre performance of the Czech economy in the first year of the seventh five-year economic plan.

Party and Government. The 16th congress of the ruling KSC, attended by Soviet President Leonid Brezhnev, was a model of Marxist-Leninist orthodoxy. Gustav Husák was unanimously reelected secretary-general, and all members of the party's Presidium and Secretariat were returned to their respective functions. There was a 30% turnover in the membership of the Central Committee. As of Jan. 1, 1981, the party was said to have 1,538,179 members and candidates, an increase of 157,089 since 1976.

The quinquennial elections for the Federal Assembly, the Czech and Slovak National Councils, and regional, district, and local committees were virtual carbon copies of the 1976 elections. More than 99% of the voters cast their ballots for the official candidates, who had been handpicked by the Communist-controlled National Front. Of some 200,000 candidates, only one failed to be elected.

Economy. In 1981, Czechoslovakia's economy began to operate under a new "Set of Measures to Improve the System of Planned National Economic Management," designed to stimulate productivity, enhance efficiency, and raise the quality of production. Results for the first half of 1981, however, were far from satisfactory. Compared with the first half of 1980, industrial production rose by a modest 1.8%, labor productivity in industry by 2%, and real wages by 1.3%. But the volume of construction fell by 2.3%, and 75% of construction enterprises failed to meet planned targets. A meager 0.2% increase was reported in domestic trade. Prescribed quality standards remained unfulfilled, and 1981 harvests were well below planned goals. Better results were achieved in foreign trade, where exports rose by 7.9% and imports by only 4.6%.

Reaction to Events in Poland. Fearful of a spillover of the Polish quest for more freedom and aware of its similarity to the Czechoslovak reformist movement of 1968, the regime unleashed a harsh campaign of denunciations of what President Husák labeled a counterrevolution instigated and supported by forces of international imperialism. Echoing the notorious "Brezhnev doctrine," he pledged full support for "all true Polish patriots" and cautioned that the defense of the socialist system was "the joint concern of the members of the socialist commonwealth." Anxious to prevent any attempts to emulate the Polish example in Czechoslovakia, the regime stepped up the persecution of dissidents and intensified its struggle against "revisionism."

EWARD TABORSKY
University of Texas at Austin

CZECHOSLOVAKIA • Information Highlights

Official Name: Czechoslovak Socialist Republic.
Location: East-central Europe.
Area: 49,374 sq mi (127 879 km^2).
Chief Cities (Dec. 1979): Prague, the capital, 1,193,345; Bratislava, 374,860; Brno, 372,793.
Government: *Head of state,* Gustav Husák, president (took office 1975). *Head of government,* Lubomir Stougal, premier (took office 1970). *Communist party secretary-general,* Gustav Husák (took office 1969). *Legislature*—Federal Assembly: Chamber of Nations and Chamber of the People.
Monetary Unit: Koruna (11.74 koruny equal U.S.$1, July 1981—noncommercial rate).
Manufactures (major products): Machinery and equipment, iron and steel products, textiles, motor vehicles, footwear.
Agriculture (major products): Sugar beets, potatoes, wheat, corn, barley, livestock, dairy products.

Richard N. Greenhouse/Courtesy of Washington Ballet

In October 1981, Mikhail Baryshnikov (left) and the American Ballet Theatre present "Configurations," a new ballet by Choo San Goh, assistant director of the Washington Ballet.

DANCE

It was a time for reconsideration in the dance world in 1981. The creative upsurge so noticeable the previous year was now replaced by fewer new works of distinction and a tendency to take stock of past achievements. The festival format and the anniversary celebration offered good pretexts for this type of perspective.

The major events included the New York City Ballet's Tchaikovsky Festival and the avant-garde New Dance USA Festival in Minneapolis. The Joffrey Ballet's 25th anniversary season was launched with a gala that summed up the company's history.

While interest continued to center on the major organizations, including American Ballet Theatre's first season under its new director, Mikhail Baryshnikov, there was also greater awareness of the increasing importance of ballet companies in other large American cities. Baryshnikov even took part in a benefit for the Washington (DC) Ballet by dancing with his own company in the gala premiere of a ballet by Washington Ballet's assistant director, Choo San Goh. Seventeen-year-old Amanda McKerrow, the Washington Ballet's leading dancer, made news when she became the first American to win a gold medal, in the junior category, in Moscow's International Ballet Competition.

New York City Ballet. The New York City Ballet's Tchaikovsky Festival was patterned after its 1972 Stravinsky Festival and 1975 Ravel Festival but did not commemorate the birth or death of a composer. George Balanchine, the company's artistic director, explained that he wished to honor one of his favorite composers. At the same time, the 77-year-old Balanchine turned over most of the new choreography to relatively inexperienced choreographers on his staff. With fewer Balanchine premieres than in past festivals, the Tchaikovsky celebration proved uneven in quality.

Jerome Robbins, nonetheless, created two highly successful ballets, "Piano Pieces," which extended the art of partnering, and "Andantino," a pas de deux with ice-skating steps for Darci Kistler and Ib Andersen. "Allegro con Gracia," a waltz led by Helgi Tomasson and Patricia McBride, was Robbins' contribution to the interpretation of the "Symphonie Pathétique" on the festival's closing night. Balanchine himself choreographed a startling and deeply emotional work, "Adagio Lamentoso" to the symphony's last movement. An allegorical view of Tchaikovsky's anticipation of death, the work used few ballet steps. Instead, three female mourners whirled against a sculptural ensemble as others formed a cross and a child blew out a candle.

Other Balanchine ballets for the festival were "Hungarian Gypsy Airs," a new version of his 1933 "Mozartiana" and a version of the "Garland Dance" from "The Sleeping Beauty" for a collection of waltzes called "Tempo di Valse." The other waltzes were Jacques d'Amboise's "Valse Scherzo" and John Taras' "Waltz from Eugene Onegin" and "Trio in A Minor."

Other festival premieres were Taras' "Souvenir de Florence," d'Amboise's "Concert Fantasy" and "Scherzo Opus 42," Peter Martins' "Symphony No. 1" and "Capriccio Italien," and Joseph Duell's "Introduction and Fugue." Earlier, Martins had choreographed "Suite from Histoire du Soldat" to Stravinsky's music.

American Ballet Theatre. American Ballet Theatre's only world premieres were held at year-end: The Choo San Goh–Samuel Barber "Configurations" and Kenneth MacMillan's "The Wild Boy." Most of the novelties were company premieres of ballets from other companies' repertoires such as Paul Taylor's "Airs" and Balanchine's "La Sonnambula." Great interest centered on Baryshnikov's restagings of the 19th-century classics because of the major changes he made in them. Baryshnikov justified them on the grounds that he was drawing upon the versions seen in his former company, the Kirov Ballet in Leningrad. Most of his productions were criticized for looking too abstract. But the successful additions were a pure-dance scene from Petipa's "Le Corsaire," called "Le Jardin Animé" and a pas de deux from "La Fille Mal Gardée." Baryshnikov was highly praised for having raised so quickly the standard of dancing by the corps de ballet.

The Joffrey. President and Mrs. Ronald Reagan attended a special Joffrey Ballet gala at the Metropolitan Opera House, which gave them their first view of their son Ron, a member of the Joffrey II Dancers, in a professional ballet company. Mrs. Reagan also attended the 25th anniversary gala. During the season, the Joffrey offered the premiere of Gerald Arpino's "Light Rain" and the company premiere of Jiri Kylian's "Transfigured Night." The Stuttgart Ballet's Marcia Haydée and Richard Cragun were guest stars in the company premiere of John Cranko's "The Taming of the Shrew." An older revival, Frederic Franklin's staging of Michel Fokine's "Scheherazade" came from the Dance Theater of Harlem, which also presented Taras' "Designs with Strings" and "Belé," by Geoffrey Holder.

Regional Ballet. Greater awareness of regional ballet activity was fostered by the continuation of the Brooklyn Academy of Music's "Ballet America" festival with the Ohio Ballet, the Cleveland Ballet, the Houston Ballet, and the Pennsylvania Ballet. Meanwhile, the Boston Ballet produced an unorthodox "Swan Lake" with British designer Julia Trevelyan Oman's 19th-century Victorian costumes and a "Big Bird" owl outfit for Rothbart, the evil magician.

The Royal Ballet. The most eagerly awaited foreign troupe to visit New York was Britain's Royal Ballet, which was celebrating its 50th anniversary. Although the old star-quality was felt to be missing in the top ranks, the corps was praised for its elegance and style. The highlights included a revival of Frederick Ashton's sophisticated "Scènes de Ballet" and his new virtuosic Sergei Rachmaninoff Ballet, "Rhapsody." Originally created for Baryshnikov in London, it was now danced by Anthony Dowell or Stephen Beagley, with Lesley Collier as the ballerina. Kenneth MacMillan's full-evening "Isadora" was considered either boring or in poor taste in its view of Isadora Duncan, but his "Gloria" and "La Fin du jour" were well received. A revival of

Steven Caras

Heather Watts and Bart Cook demonstrate the art of partnering in "Piano Pieces." The Jerome Robbins ballet was performed during the New York City Ballet's 1981 Tchaikovsky Festival.

The 1981 dance year saw the New Dance USA Festival, sponsored by the Walker Art Center in Minneapolis. Presented during the festival were David Gordon and Valda Setterfield, left, in "Close Up."

Walker Art Center

Robert Helpmann's "Hamlet" allowed Antoinette Sibley to step out of retirement.

Other Companies and Regional Ballet. Other companies to visit the United States included the Netherlands Dance Theater with premieres by Kylian—"Soldiers Mass," "Dream Dances" and "Overgrown Path." Milan's La Scala Ballet made its American debut with guest stars Rudolf Nureyev, Carla Fracci, and—as Lady Capulet in "Romeo and Juliet,"—Margot Fonteyn. Australia's Sydney Dance Theater also made a debut.

In modern dance, the New Dance USA Festival at Minneapolis' Walker Art Center brought together 27 experimental choreographers. Karole Armitage, Trisha Brown, Laura Dean, and Lucinda Childs were among those in this group who presented major premieres elsewhere during 1981. Meanwhile Twyla Tharp presented her company on Broadway in "The Catherine Wheel," to a rock score by David Byrne. "Short Stories" and "Uncle Edgar Dyed His Hair Red" were other Tharp premieres.

Martha Graham received the first $25,000 American Dance Festival–Samuel H. Scripps Award for lifetime achievement in modern dance. Earlier, she created a new piece, "Acts of Light." Paul Taylor's premieres were "Arden Court" and "House of Cards." Premieres by Merce Cunningham were "Channels/Inserts," "Fielding Sixes," and "10's with Shoes." Erick Hawkins did "Agathlon" and "Heyoka." Alwin Nikolais presented "The Mechanical Organ." Alvin Ailey created a pas de deux for Judith Jamison and Alexander Godunov, scheduled for his company's gala.

ANNA KISSELGOFF
"The New York Times"

DELAWARE

In 1981 Delaware enjoyed a respite from the biennial electoral hurly-burly. Gov. Pierre S. duPont, IV (R) was inaugurated for his second term at midnight, January 20. The political scene during the year reflected the usual calm and unpretentiousness of Delaware. The General Assembly began its labors in January with a Democratic Senate and a Republican House. It passed a constitutional amendment, which required a three-fifths vote, to enact an increase in taxes. The state attorney general held that the amendment was not retroactive, but effective upon the adjournment of the General Assembly, which occurred in August.

In October, the legislature agreed to have the state sell its interest in the capital stock of the Farmers Bank of Delaware. Since 1808 the bank had been the state depository, and legislators served on the board of directors until 1976. The state owned 77% of the capital stock. Money received from the sale would be applied to reduction of the state debt.

Toward the end of session the legislature became involved in a reapportionment struggle resulting from shifts in the population noted in the 1980 census. Resolution of the conflict effected changes in several key districts. There was an increase of 8.6% in the state's overall population, but the total number of legislators was retained. Twenty-six of the state's 57 municipalities lost population. Wilmington, the chief city, decreased 14.5%. One new town, Dewey Beach, was incorporated in 1981.

DELAWARE • Information Highlights

Area: 2,044 sq mi (5 294 km^2).
Population (1980 census): 595,225.
Chief Cities (1980 census): Dover, the capital, 23,512: Wilmington, 70,195; Newark, 25,247; Elsmere, 6,493; Milford, 5,356; Seaford, 5,256; New Castle, 4,907; Smyrna, 4,750.
Government (1981): *Chief Officers*—governor, Pierre S. duPont IV (R); lt. gov., Michael N. Castle (R). *General Assembly*—Senate, 21 members; House of Representatives, 41 members.
State Finances (fiscal year 1980): Revenues, $970,000,000; expenditures, $886,000,000.
Personal Income (1980): $6,172,000,000; per capita, $10,339.
Labor Force (July 1981): *Nonagricultural wage and salary earners,* 263,900; *unemployed,* 21,200 (7.3% of total force).

Economy. The economy was slightly improved. Unemployment decreased from 8.8% in July 1980 to 7.3% in July 1981. The automotive assembly plants experienced sustained layoffs. Housing production was up a sharp 79%. A new banking law lifted interest ceilings and provided for a schedule of state taxes on bank earnings that benefited larger banks. This legislation permits out-of-state banks to set up branches in Delaware. The Wilmington marine terminal reported a slight increase in total cargo handled. The death of Edward Ball, 93, chairman of the A.I. du Pont Testamentary Trust, set off speculation as to the future of the trust.

Cash farm income dropped from $360.8 million in 1979 to $332.8 million in 1980. Delaware had approximately 3,600 farms in 1981, a slight increase over the number in 1980.

Schools. The controversial busing issue in northern New Castle County again came to the fore, with the legislature creating four new school districts in place of the single large district set up by the U.S. District Court in 1979. The court acquiesced in the new arrangement, but insisted that busing between Wilmington and the suburban areas be maintained. Controversy continued between the state and local authorities concerning the proper share of state support to public education. A threatened teacher strike over compensation and extracurricular activities failed to materialize. Public school enrollment continued to decrease, with 99,403 attending in 1981, a drop of 4.5%. Private schools showed a slight increase, with more than 23,000 students registered. Parochial school enrollment also increased slightly.

Government. The state budget increased 12.1%, from $634 million in fiscal 1981 to $711 million for fiscal 1982. The state debt as of Sept. 15, 1981, was $527,770,000, a year's decrease of slightly more than 1%.

PAUL DOLAN, *University of Delaware*

DENMARK

Denmark's struggle against inflation and unemployment was not very successful in 1981, and the year ended with an election. Prime Minister Anker Jørgensen called the election on November 12 after Parliament had refused to support his program to divert pension fund money into industrial investment. After Jørgensen's Social Democratic Party suffered heavy losses in the December 8 general elections, the prime minister announced that his government would "only continue as a caretaker until a new government is formed." The various parties then began talks in hopes of forming a coalition.

Oil. The various parts of the North Sea and the shelf that are under Danish sovereignty and have proven to contain oil and gas deposits figured in an agreement between the government and the Danish Underground Consortium, consisting of the giant firm A. P. Møller and other companies. In 1962 the DUC had obtained a fifty-year contract (revised in 1976) regarding exploration for oil, but the government had decided to strive for an early return of the control of these areas. Negotiations were completed on May 10. By January 1986, the government will receive back 99% of the areas involved, while A. P. Møller will retain certain smaller areas in the southwest. Private companies may apply for permission to exploit some of the fields.

Defense. A nuclear weapons-free zone in Scandinavia was discussed by parties and politicians, with the Social Democrats showing sympathy for the idea. However, the refusal of the Soviet Union to place some of its western areas, particularly the Kola peninsula, in the zone, and the wishes of Scandinavian statesmen to make a nuclear weapons-free zone part of a European zone, as well as opposition from NATO, dampened enthusiasm for the plan.

In August, the four nonsocialist parties, the Social Democrats, and the government signed a defense agreement to be in effect for three years. The parties agreed that Denmark should shoulder an annual 1.5% increase in defense outlays instead of the 3% NATO target.

Nordic Council. The 29th annual session of the Nordic Council was held in Copenhagen, March 2–6. No less than 32 economic, social, and judicial recommendations were forwarded to the Nordic Council of Ministers.

Strikes. A strike by the typographers' union lasted from March 27 to June 5. Newspapers, books, and magazines came under the printers' interdict in the longest such strike in Danish history.

Population. Denmark's population fell for the first time in the 20th century. The number of births did not reach the expected total, the death rate rose somewhat, and the number of immigrants was less than estimated.

The Queen. Queen Margrethe II and her husband, Prince Henrik, in February were the hosts to the new president of Iceland, Vigdís Finnbogadóttir. On April 21, the royal couple began a three-week state visit to Japan, Hong Kong, and Thailand to promote Danish products.

ERIK J. FRIIS
The Scandinavian-American Bulletin

DENMARK • Information Highlights

Official Name: Kingdom of Denmark.
Location: Northwest Europe.
Area: 16,631 sq mi (43 074 km^2).
Population (1981 est.): 5,100,000.
Chief Cities (1980 est.): Copenhagen, the capital, 1,214,382; Aarhus, 244,839; Odense, 168,528.
Government: *Head of state,* Margrethe II, queen (acceded Jan. 1972). *Head of government,* Anker Jørgensen, prime minister (took office Feb. 1975). *Legislature* (unicameral)—Folketing.
Monetary Unit: Krone (7.435 kroner equal U.S.$1, Dec. 18, 1981).
Manufactures (major products): Industrial and construction equipment, furniture, textiles, processed foods.
Agriculture (major products): Meat, dairy products, fish, fur.

DISASTERS AND ACCIDENTS

AVIATION

April 17—Near Colorado's Loveland-Fort Collins airport a twin-engine commuter aircraft and a skydiving plane collide in air, killing 15 persons.
May 6—In western Maryland about 45 mi (72 km) west of Baltimore, a U.S. Air Force tracking plane explodes in flight, killing all 21 persons aboard.
May 7—An Argentine jetliner crashes into the Río de la Plata near Buenos Aires, killing all 30 persons on board.
May 26—In an attempted landing, a Marine jet crashes on the flight deck of the carrier *Nimitz* just off the coast of northeastern Florida; 14 men are killed.
July 21 (reported)—A Somali passenger airplane crashes just after takeoff about 22 mi (35 km) north of Mogadishu, the capital, killing 49 persons.
July 28—A Mexican airliner crashes while attempting to land at the Chihuahua, Mex., airport, killing 32.
Aug. 22—A Taiwanese domestic jetliner explodes and crashes near Sanyi, Taiwan, killing 110 persons.
Oct. 6—Near Rotterdam, a Dutch airliner crashes after its wing is torn off in a storm; 17 persons are killed.
Nov. 8—A Mexican jetliner crashes into a mountain slope near Altamirano, Mex., killing 18 persons.
Dec. 1—Near Ajaccio, Corsica, a Yugoslav jetliner crashes into a mountain, killing 178 persons.

EARTHQUAKES

June 11—An earthquake hits the southeastern Iranian province of Kerman, killing 1,027 people.
July 28—An earthquake strikes Kerman in southeastern Iran, killing about 1,500 people.

FIRES AND EXPLOSIONS

Jan. 9—Fire in a Keansburg, NJ, home for the elderly and mentally retarded kills 30 persons.
Jan. 18—Fire in a Toronto hotel kills at least six.
Feb. 7—In Bangalore, India, a circus tent fire kills 66.
Feb. 10—A fire at the Hilton Hotel in Las Vegas claims the lives of eight persons, injures at least 200 others.
Feb. 14—Fire in a Dublin discothèque kills 46 persons.
March 14—Fire in a residential hotel in Chicago kills 19.
April 15—An explosion in a coal mine near Redstone, CO, kills 15 men.
May 10—Fire sweeps through Mandalay, Burma, killing five persons and leaving 35,000 others homeless.
Sept. 3—A coal-mining explosion in Zaluzi, Czechoslovakia, kills 65 miners.
Oct. 16—Explosions in a Japanese coal mine near Sapporo kill 93 workers.
Dec. 7—A coal mine explosion near Topmost, KY, kills eight.
Dec. 8—Near Palmer, TN, an explosion in a coal mine traps at least 12 men.

LAND AND SEA TRANSPORTATION

Jan. 6—An overcrowded river boat sinks in Amazon river currents just off Belém de Cajari, Brazil, killing at least 262 persons; another 49 are missing.
Jan. 27—An Indonesian passenger ship catches fire during a storm and sinks in the Java sea; 380 people are missing and 87 persons are known dead.
Feb. 18—A commuter bus traveling along Virginia's Interstate 95 plunges down a steep embankment at the Stafford-Prince William county line, killing 11 persons.
Feb. 27—In northern Pacific waters, fire severely damages the freighter *Dae Rim;* 23 South Korean seamen are missing, and of three other sailors rescued, one died.
May 7—The collision of a bus and train in central Java kills 31 persons and seriously injures 20 others.
May 12—In New Delhi, India, a bus overturns, killing at least 25 passengers and injuring about 50 others.
June 6—During a storm, a train with several hundred people aboard tumbles off a bridge into the Bagmati River in the Indian state of Bihar, killing 268 people.
June 22—In Pampas Galeras, Peru, a bus plunges into a deep ravine, killing 25 persons.
June 28 (reported)—In the USSR, 70 persons are killed in a collision of express and local trains near the Black Sea coastal district of Gagry.
July 31—Near Bahawalpur, Pakistan, six coaches of a passenger train derail, killing 43 persons.
Sept. 12—A bus blows up after hitting a land mine near Kampala, Uganda; 20 civilians are killed.
Sept. 19—An Amazon riverboat sinks in the northern Brazilian jungle port of Obidos; more than 300 people are missing.
Oct. 21—Near Simla, India, in the Himalayas, a bus plunges off a mountain road, killing 40 persons.
Oct. 26—In the Atlantic just north of Miami, FL, 33 Haitians are drowned when their boat capsizes.
Nov. 27—About 200 mi (322 km) south of Santiago, Chile, a bus and truck collide, killing 32 persons.

STORMS AND FLOODS

Feb. 10—A winter storm stretching from the U.S. Rocky Mountains to the Great Lakes contributes to at least seven deaths; while in the south, tornadoes strike, killing at least one person in Texas and injuring more than 60 people in an Alabama school.
March 18—Rains cause flooding that leaves 100,000 people in Djibouti (one third of the population) homeless.
April 4—Flooding, the result of three weeks of steady rain, isolates the northeastern state of Rio Grande de Norte in Brazil, killing at least seven persons.
April 4—A tornado strikes West Bend, WI; six persons die in storm-related accidents and 100 others are injured.
April 12—A tornado in southern Bangladesh kills 41.
April 17—Near the Bay of Bengal, India, a tornado destroys four villages and causes the deaths of 120.
April 19—In week-long flooding in northern and central Colombia, 21 persons are killed and ten are reported missing.
April 23—Storms and tornadoes in Missouri and Texas contribute to the deaths of five persons.
April 25-26—Floods and mudslides in Venezuela kill 20 persons and leave 4,000 others homeless.
May 6 (reported)—A rainstorm that moved across the Persian Gulf kills 40 persons, 33 from Oman.
May 25—Flash floods sweep through Austin, TX, killing 13 persons; one other is missing.
June 13-14—In the middlewestern states rainstorms and tornadoes kill at least 20 persons, of whom six are killed in tornadoes in Roseville, MN and Cardington, OH.
July 1—Tropical storm *Kelly* hits the central Philippines, killing at least 120 persons.
July 21—In northern India, the states of Assam and Uttar Pradesh are affected by floods; more than 200 people are reported dead.
July 25—In Lahore, Pakistan, five persons are killed under buildings collapsed by monsoon rains; 16 others are killed in flash floods.
August 20 (reported)—Flooding of the upper reaches of China's Yangtze River in Sichuan and Hubei provinces during July and August leaves 768 dead, more than 500 missing, more than 28,000 injured, and 1,500,000 homeless.
Sept. 23—In Bombay, India, torrential rains, causing collapsed houses and landslides, kills at least 15 persons.
Oct. 4 (reported)—Landslides created by storms and flooding in the Sichuan province of China kill 240.
Oct. 9—Tropical storm *Lydia* hits the north Pacific coast of Mexico, killing at least 65 persons.
Nov. 2—A hurricane lashes the Arabian Sea and the western coast of India; at least 470 fishermen are missing.
Nov. 7-8—In central and eastern Yugoslavia, icy roads, dense fog, and snow cause road accidents that kill 17.
Nov. 29—Prior week's typhoon in the Philippines kills 273.
Nov. 29-Dec. 5—A typhoon in southern Thailand causing a week of monsoon rains and flash floods kills 37 persons; six crewmen from a capsized freighter are missing.
Dec. 6—A landslide in Dasun, Java, kills 17.

MISCELLANEOUS

Jan. 25—It is reported that more than 270 people have died in a month-long cold wave in northern India.
Feb. 8—At a soccer match in Athens, Greece, 24 fans are killed in a stampede as crowds leave the match.
March 27—In Cocoa Beach, FL, a condominium collapses, killing at least 11 persons and injuring 14 others.
May 20 (reported)—A landslide on the slopes of Mount Semeru in eastern Java killed at least 184 people; 200 others are missing.
June 21—Eleven mountain climbers are believed dead after being swept off the face of Mount Rainier in Washington and buried in up to 70 ft (21 m) of ice.
July 17—In the Kansas City, MO, Hyatt Regency Hotel two suspended aerial walkways in the lobby collapse, killing 111 persons.
Dec. 3—A coal mine roof collapses near Bergoo, WV, killing three men.
Dec. 4—In New Delhi, 45 persons are killed in a stampede from an Indian monument after a power failure.

Fires and Fire Prevention in the United States

"The majority of people tend to think of a serious fire as they would a serious automobile accident or other tragedy—as something that happens to someone else. This is because the average person suffers a minor burn or experiences a small fire only once or twice in a lifetime, and thus the threat of a truly destructive fire seems improbable and remote. In too many cases, lack of preparation causes panic, death, and destruction that might have been avoided had the victims taken seriously the threat of fire and thus known how to prepare themselves accordingly."

Percy Bugbee, *Principles of Fire Protection*

Fire always has been regarded as mysterious and powerful—a force to be reckoned with. Early myths depicted fire as a "two-sided god"—one side having beneficial qualities, the other side having destructive qualities. Man long ago discovered how to harness fire's benefits but is still struggling to control its destructive nature.

Recent major hotel fires have focused public attention on personal fire safety and the need for adoption and stricter enforcement of fire safety codes in public buildings.

Despite sophisticated technology and increased public awareness, fire remains a major killer. In 1980 alone, fire claimed the lives of 6,505 Americans. In spite of the recent rash of hotel fires, fires in the home, by far, have proven to be the United States' most serious fire problem, accounting for approximately 78% of the total number of fire deaths since 1976.

The problem of fire loss in the United States has been rooted traditionally in public apathy and misunderstanding of fire. During the latter part of 1980 public awareness about fire was certainly increased as a result of major hotel fires in Las Vegas and Harrison, NY. All together, 165 lives were lost in hotel fires during 1980. The fire at the MGM Grand Hotel in Las Vegas, NV, on Nov. 21, 1980, was the second largest loss-of-life hotel fire in U.S. history, with 86 persons killed and more than 600 injured. (The fire at the Winecoff Hotel in Atlanta, GA, in 1946 was the largest, claiming 119 lives.) During November and December 1980, fires in hotels killed 111 guests; 26 persons died in the disaster at the Stouffer Inn in Harrison.

Since 1896, the National Fire Protection Association (NFPA), with 32,000 members, has worked to reduce the nation's fire loss. Today, the NFPA is widely recognized as the leading independent advocate of public fire safety. Its fire protection codes and standards, technical-assistance programs, research, and public-education efforts advance the case for fire safety nationwide.

NFPA has determined that most fatal home fires occur at night, when people are sleeping and are least prepared. Research finds that the leading source of ignition is the cigarette—igniting either upholstered living-room furniture or bedding. In 1980, 4,175 persons were killed by fire in one- and two-family dwellings.

Yet, during the past few years, NFPA has identified a trend toward fewer fire deaths in the home: a decline of 11.2% between 1977 and 1980. NFPA attributes this trend to the considerably increased use of residential smoke detectors and to home fire safety media campaigns, including NFPA's "Learn Not to Burn" television announcements, which feature Dick Van Dyke. This is one reason that the installation of smoke detectors and the creation of home-escape plans are among the key fire-safety cautions advocated by NFPA.

NFPA notes that hotel fires are not a new development, but because today's hotels are much larger, more complex structures, the potential for fire disaster has increased significantly. It is now possible for thousands of people to be exposed to fire and toxic smoke in high-rise hotel superstructures and large assembly areas. In response to this potential danger, NFPA urges strict compliance with fire-safety codes by hotels, frequent inspections by local fire departments and hotel management, and increased cooperation between them. Compliance with these safety codes will help protect life and property from fires in hotels. In addition, NFPA urges hotel guests to familiarize themselves with nearby exits.

The study of human behavior is another way that NFPA addresses the nation's fire problem. By learning more about how people behave in fires, NFPA develops improved fire-safety education programs and fire-fighter techniques, and writes its Life Safety code taking into account the way people generally react in fire emergencies.

Ultimately, no building—even with today's technology and fire-safety features—can be guaranteed as 100% safe. Personal responsibility is the key to reducing the number of people who die in fires. Behaviors such as "crawling in smoke," "finding two ways out," and "feeling the door for heat" are typical actions that must be learned and practiced in order to increase survival chances in a fire.

NATIONAL FIRE PROTECTION ASSOCIATION

ECUADOR

The most important events of 1981 in Ecuador were the accidental death of President Jaime Roldós Aguilera in May and serious border clashes with Peru in January and February.

Government and Politics. In the last weeks of 1980, the political position of the moderate leftist government of President Roldós had been strengthened. Local and provincial elections on Dec. 7, 1980, had provided major gains for the parties supporting the Roldós government. The Frente Radical Alfarista (FRA) received 20% of the total vote, while the Democracia Popular/Unión Democrática Cristiana and Izquierda Democrática together got about 30%. All three supported the government. The Concentracion de Fuerzas Populares (CFP), which had originally selected Roldós but had later broken with him, got only about 8%.

On May 24, 1981, President Roldós, his wife, Defense Minister Marco Subia Martinez, and five other persons were killed in a plane crash in the mountains near the Peruvian border. His funeral two days later was attended by the presidents of Venezuela, Colombia, Costa Rica, and Panama, as well as distinguished figures from other countries.

The death of President Roldós was a severe test of the fragile democracy established by Roldós' decisive election victory in 1979. The democracy did survive, as Vice-President Osvaldo Hurtado Larrea took over the presidency and was not seriously challenged from any quarter.

In a radio address on June 15, Hurtado told the people that he would continue the policies of Roldós and would go through with the economic Five-Year Plan, which he had been largely responsible for drawing up. He also announced, however, that some projects would have to be postponed because of economic circumstances.

The only severe political crisis following Roldós' death was the struggle over who should replace Hurtado as vice-president. Raul Baca Carbo, the president of Congress, temporarily took over the position. But, on June 2, León Roldós, the brother of the late president, was elected vice-president by Congress over Rodolfo Baquerizo of the CFP. The margin of victory was 21-20, with president Hurtado's party, Democracia Popular/Unión Democrática Cristiana, and Izquierda Democrática abstaining. There were two cabinet shakeups, in June and August.

UPI

Osvaldo Hurtado assumed the presidency of Ecuador after a plane crash took the life of Jaime Roldós.

Economy. Ecuador faced difficult economic conditions during the year. The prices of its principal exports—oil, cacao, and coffee—declined. Oil prices fell from $40 a barrel at the beginning of the year to $32.50 by June. However, the government did succeed in raising considerable funds from abroad. In August, the U.S. brokerage house of Shearson Loeb Rhodes undertook to raise $140 million through the sale of Ecuadorean government notes in the New York securities markets.

Foreign Affairs. An armed clash with Peru was the major development in foreign affairs. The incident began with border skirmishes between January 28 and February 1. A cease-fire agreement was reached on February 2, but there were several subsequent incidents. The border of the two countries was sealed by both sides on February 23.

Also on February 23, representatives of the four powers (Argentina, Brazil, Chile, and the United States) that had participated in the Rio agreement after the 1942 Ecuadorean-Peruvian War met in Brasilia. On February 26 they announced that Ecuador and Peru had agreed to pull back their troops 9 mi (14.5 km) behind the border. After further negotiations between the two countries, an agreement was signed March 6 to withdraw troops from the area and to maintain peaceful relations. On April 2 the border was reopened.

ROBERT J. ALEXANDER, *Rutgers University*

ECUADOR • Information Highlights

Official Name: Republic of Ecuador.
Location: Northwest South America.
Area: 104,506 sq mi (270 670 km^2).
Population (1981 est.): 8,200,000.
Chief Cities (1974): Quito, the capital, 635,713; Guayaquil, 941,009.
Government: *Head of state and government,* Osvaldo Hurtado Larrea, president (took office May 1981). *Legislature* (unicameral)—Congress.
Monetary Unit: Sucre (28.42 sucres equal U.S.$1, Oct. 1981).
Manufactures (major products): Food products, textiles, light consumer goods, light industrial goods.
Agriculture (major products): Bananas, coffee, cacao, rice, corn, sugar, livestock.

EDUCATION

In 1981 the Reagan administration's New Federalism affected decades of federal education programs with budget cuts of up to 25%, block grants to restore state and local control, scrutiny of federal affirmative action rules, and proposals to end the U.S. Department of Education. Pressure to desegregate public elementary, secondary, and higher education was eased. The evangelical right in two states gained equal time for teaching creation based on Genesis alongside evolution. Enrollments continued to decline; school costs continued to rise.

Internationally, the new French Socialist government laid plans to decentralize education and to merge private schools with the state system. Mainland China–U.S. cultural and educational accords for 1982–83 were signed.

THE UNITED STATES

New Federal Policy. The Reagan administration put into effect its policy of reducing the federal role in many areas, including education, in order to restore power to the states and to cut federal spending. The intent to reverse the federal government's doctrinal thrust of the last 50 years was expressed in these federal aid to education budget targets for fiscal 1982: elementary and secondary education, $6,000,000,000 (Carter proposal, $7,600,000,000); higher education, $5,000,000,000 (Carter, $6,900,000,000); research, training, vocational education, and other programs, $1,400,000,000 (Carter, $1,600,000,000).

A budget deficit, layoffs, and a canceled pay increase cause Philadelphia teachers to strike.

UPI

The Reagan administration asked Congress to cut all federal aid to education programs by at least 25% and to consolidate almost 50 categorical aid programs into block grants for states and localities to spend as they see fit. Educators reacted with protests and dismay at the dismantling of categorical aid (federal money for specific programs, such as Title I of the Elementary and Secondary Education Act, which provides compensatory education for mainly urban disadvantaged children). While critics said the poor would be irrevocably hurt, the administration responded that block grants shift control from federal to state and local bodies where it belongs and also bypass bureaucrats whose salaries use up much of the money intended for the poor. Opponents such as American Federation of Teachers President Albert Shanker said that, while education funds comprise only 1% of the total federal budget, education is subject to 7% of federal budget cuts. He charged that the billions saved would be used to finance tuition tax credits for private schools.

While further cuts are possible, federal aid to education figures for 1982 were approved in late July by a U.S. House and Senate conference committee. On August 13, President Reagan signed into law the budget, which cut more than 200 domestic programs. Elementary and secondary school aid was held at 25% below current levels; grants to needy college students totaled $2,600,000,000 (cut from $2,900,000,000); block grants to states were $589.4 million (omitted from block grants were categorical aid for the needy and handicapped, vocational education, and bilingual education); college student loans would go to an estimated 10–40% fewer students eligible under stricter rules about family income; school lunches (under the U.S. Department of Agriculture) totaled $2,900,000,000 (cut from $4,400,000,000). In a September 24 speech to the nation, the president announced that additional cuts in the student-loan program would be forthcoming.

Title IX of the 1972 Education Amendments prohibits sex discrimination, and Title VII of the 1964 Civil Rights Act prohibits sexual harassment. Women's rights leaders and others were incensed at announcements on August 12 that Vice-President George Bush's Task Force on Regulatory Relief would reexamine these and other federal regulations considered counterproductive interference. In May, a bill seeking to reduce affirmative action in hiring women and minorities in colleges and industry was introduced in the U.S. House of Representatives. In August, Secretary of Education T. H. Bell asked the U.S. attorney general's approval for narrower interpretation of women's equity measures in order to ease lawsuits involving Titles VII and IX.

On August 4, Secretary of Education Bell urged President Reagan to propose to Congress in January 1982 that the U.S. Department of

Education be reduced to a national foundation (similar to the National Science Foundation) that would disburse funds for education research and provide other educational assistance. In his September 24 speech, the president made plain that he would go forward with plans to dismantle the department. Direction and control of education would be shifted to the states through block grants; the department's civil rights office would be shifted to Justice, and student loans to Treasury. If the appropriate legislation failed, Bell was prepared to achieve dismantling through existing authority by transferring, altering, and discontinuing programs, including bilingual education. Bell, a former U.S. commissioner of education, testified in 1978 in favor of creating the department (inaugurated in May 1980), was the last cabinet member President Reagan appointed, and gained the post after agreeing to find a way to downgrade the department.

On August 26, Bell, formerly Utah's chief higher education officer, named 18 members to a National Commission on Excellence in Education, headed by University of Utah President David P. Gardner. Bell challenged the commission to come up in 18 months with maximum competency recommendations to reverse the long decline in U.S. education quality.

Desegregation. Mandatory busing to integrate white and black schools, key strategy for more than 20 years, was downplayed in 1981, as money problems surpassed racial segregation as the major concern of many U.S. school systems. The political and legal climate has turned against busing for integration as public education costs skyrocketed despite enrollment decline, and voters refused to pay more taxes for public education because of unhappiness over school violence, low test scores, and inflation.

Signs abounded that integration policy was being reversed: Los Angeles dropped mandatory busing in April after the California Supreme Court upheld a constitutional amendment forbidding busing unless segregation by design is proved; Chicago, under Carter administration pressure to desegregate, has delayed mandatory busing until at least 1983 with U.S. Justice Department approval. The antibusing mood was reflected when the House of Representatives on June 9 voted an overwhelming 265–122 to end the Justice Department's role in enforcing busing for integration, a vote the administration wanted. More than two dozen bills were pending in Congress late in 1981 to strip federal agencies of power to require and enforce busing. Conservatives expect to challenge further the courts' powers to order busing. Also, some urban school systems are beginning not to care; their predominantly Hispanic children make busing to hard-to-find white neighborhoods financially burdensome and operationally impossible.

One civil rights leader said: "We are now seeing an even more serious attack on desegregation than under the Nixon administration." Some point out that more than 50% of U.S. schoolchildren are bused to school but only about 4% are bused for desegregation. "Busing is not the real issue," said a former desegregation official, adding, "Busing has become a code word for desegregation."

More subtle signs also indicated less federal action to desegregate higher education. Title VI of the 1964 Civil Rights Act barred discrimination in organizations receiving federal funds. Previous administrations used the threat of withholding federal aid to hasten dismantling of dual white and black college systems in southern and border states. But in North Carolina, Florida, Louisiana, and South Carolina, the Reagan administration's Justice and Education departments backed down, compromising on much less stringent desegregation terms. Removal of a strong federal hand in higher education desegregation fits the administration's desire to restore states' rights. The administration compromise has been characterized as: "Separate and *less* unequal is better than separate and unequal."

Evolution-Creation Controversy. Kelly Segraves brought suit claiming violation of his three children's religious freedom because they were taught evolution dogmatically in California schools without hearing a competing divine-origin view of man and the universe. Segraves heads Creation Science Research Center in San Diego, publisher of fundamentalist creation science books. At issue were the California Education Department's science teaching guidelines which approve teaching evolution but not creation based on Genesis. The media-heralded "Scopes II trial of the century" fizzled when Segraves, early in the five-day nonjury trial, said he would be satisfied if the science guidelines qualified evolution as a theory about which scientists hypothesize. On March 6, State Superior Court Justice Irving H. Perluss rejected Segraves' original request for equal time evolution/creation teaching, but also pleased creationists by ordering wide distribution of a 1973 State School Board rule that evolution be presented in textbooks as theory, not fact.

On March 23, Arkansas Gov. Frank White, a member of a small evangelical sect, signed into law a bill requiring equal time in teaching "evolution theory" and "creation science." The bill passed quickly with little debate during the legislature's last days. Many legislators disliked the bill but voted for it to save their political lives at a time of rising fundamentalist fervor. In May the American Civil Liberties Union and 22 other plaintiffs challenged the constitutionality of the law, first to pass in any state. Critics say that the law was modeled after one drafted by attorney Wendell Bird of the Institute for Creation Research and supplied by South Carolina creationist Paul Ellwanger, who heads Citizens Against Federal Establishment of Evolutionary Dogma. Ellwanger claimed that similar legislation, which contains no references to God or religion in order to avoid constitutional challenge, was being considered in 21 states.

Louisiana became the second state to pass an equal time evolution/creation law when such a bill was signed by Gov. David C. Treen on July 21. Also said to be based on the Institute for Creation Research model, the Louisiana bill was more debated than the one in Arkansas. A state science education official estimated the cost of implementation would be between $1.8 million and $7 million, to pay for books, teacher training, and other expenses. Critics believe the constitutionality of Louisiana's law will also be challenged.

Enrollment Down, Costs Up. Elementary and secondary school enrollment declined for the sixth consecutive year while higher education enrollments reached an all-time high. School statistics for 1981–82 (1980–81 in parentheses) were: Enrollments, kindergarten through grade 8: 31,000,000, −1.2%, decline is expected to reverse in the mid-1980s (31,400,000); high school: 14,400,000, −3.5%, with decline projected through the 1980s (14,900,000); higher: 12,100,000, +3.3%, with decrease projected 1982–90 (11,700,000); total: 57,600,000, −1.4% (58,400,000). The total was 6% below the 1975 record high of 61,300,000.

Education directly involved 61,000,000+ (61,400,000) persons, or 27% of the total population. Expenditures were: public elementary and secondary schools, $112,800,000,000 ($103,500,000,000); nonpublic elementary and secondary, $14,000,000,000 ($12,800,000,000); public higher education, $48,300,000,000 ($43,900,000,000); nonpublic higher education, $23,200,000,000 ($21,100,000,000), a total of $198,300,000,000 ($181,300,000,000). Of this, 10% ($20,000,000,000) would come from the federal government, 39% ($77,000,000,000) would come from state governments, and 25% ($50,000,000,000) would come from local governments; 26% ($51,000,000,000) would come from private sources, including tuition, fees, endowment earnings, and private gifts.

Number of teachers, elementary and secondary, 2,400,000 (2,500,000); higher, 840,000 (830,000); total, 3,270,000 (including 300,000 administrators and other staff).

Graduates, high school, 3,050,000 (3,150,000), with close to 3,000,000 expected in 1982 (high school graduate peak in 1977 was 3,161,000); bachelor's degrees, 945,000 (952,000); first professional degrees, 72,000 (70,000); master's, 300,000 (316,000); doctorates, 33,000 (same).

Fewer Teacher Strikes, More Layoffs. There were 37 teacher strikes in September 1981 (97 strikes in September 1980), mainly in Pennsylvania, New Jersey, Rhode Island, New York, Michigan, and Idaho. In Philadelphia, the site of the largest teachers' strike, the causes were a school-budget deficit, 3,500 teacher and other school employee layoffs, and a canceled 10% pay increase. Some 44,000 teacher layoffs nationally included many teachers with tenure and were caused by enrollment decline, school closings, and cost increases. Massachusetts led with 7,500 teacher layoffs (1,000 in Boston) and some 400 school closings. Most school closings were in the Northeast and Midwest. New schools were opening only in energy-boom western states (Nevada, Wyoming, Idaho, and Montana) and in such sunbelt states as Florida.

INTERNATIONAL

France. Newly elected French President François Mitterrand intends to merge private schools into the state system. Private schools in France are almost all Roman Catholic and enroll about 2 million, one out of every six, schoolchildren. In some areas, such as Brittany, half the schools are church-run and educate two thirds of the children. Parents have increasingly sent their children to Catholic schools and to the few non-Catholic private secondary schools for the same reasons U.S. parents do—better discipline and higher academic standards. Some militant Catholic teachers welcome the state takeover as a way to improve pay and stability. Under the new plan, the state pays all teachers' salaries in private schools, determines much of the curriculum, and also pays textbook and building repair costs.

Education Minister Alain Savary said that incorporating private schools into the state system would take five years. After that, private schools that want to remain private may do so but without receiving government funds. So far, the ruling French Socialists, who also want to decentralize education as well as government administration, have not been opposed by teachers' unions, who in the past complained that the Gaullist elite took money from public schools to help private schools. Nor is the church hierarchy ready for a showdown over private schools. Bishop Pierre Eyt, newly appointed rector of the Catholic Institute of Paris, wants negotiations over private schools to include "a vast debate on the nature and ends of education." The mood to merge is aided by the fact that, for the first time in French history, most of the legislators are former teachers, as are four of Mitterrand's cabinet ministers, including Prime Minister Pierre Mauroy.

People's Republic of China. On September 5, China and the United States signed accords to broaden scholarly and cultural exchanges during 1982–83. The agreement provides for the exchange of cultural and film delegations and dance troupes, direct contacts between Chinese and U.S. universities, sports exchanges, and exchanges of national park experts. Many other private exchanges go on, but the official accords provide a framework under which unofficial arrangements are negotiated. Left unresolved were U.S. complaints about the imbalance of fewer than 300 Americans studying in China compared with some 6,000 Chinese studying in the

United States, charges that in housing and travel Americans are segregated from the Chinese people, and complaints that U.S. scholars are denied access to records and officials needed for research.

Prolonged cultural contacts with foreign scholars pose a problem for Chinese officials trying to prevent their vast population from questioning a lack of freedom in China. In 1981, an incident marred U.S.-Chinese cultural exchanges. When a Chinese dancer married an American in Houston early in the year, Chinese authorities canceled the exchange program, privately arranged for and funded, that would have allowed ten dancers to study with the Houston ballet company during the next five years. One reason advanced by U.S. experts for Chinese restriction of foreign scholars is that China's government is uncomfortable about having outsiders observe closely the pending significant economic and political changes.

FRANKLIN PARKER, *West Virginia University*

EDUCATION—SPECIAL REPORT:

U.S. PRIVATE SCHOOLS

The private schools have always constituted a vital part of the American education system. Their history is checkered: it included the privately-run charity or peer schools provided by many towns and cities in the early part of the 19th century; it included the elite college-preparatory academies; and it included the church-organized schools, often founded in response to the Protestant-dominated public schools which exposed Catholics and members of other minority religions to scorn and ridicule.

The private schools weathered their most serious threat in 1922, when the Oregon legislature passed a law to make public-school attendance compulsory, even though at the time more than 90% of the state's children between the ages of 7 and 13 were enrolled in public schools. A combination of anti-Catholicism and super-patriotism, exploited by the Ku Klux Klan, led to an attempt to outlaw the private schools.

On June 1, 1925, the U.S. Supreme Court held that private schools could not be deprived of their property without due process of law and that, while the state rightfully exercises certain regulatory powers over all schools, public and private, it has no right "to standardize its children." Thus, the ruling in *Pierce v. Society of Sisters* established beyond further question the legitimacy of nonpublic schools.

Although the nonpublic schools are thus protected, the coexistence of the two systems has not been without tensions. Some supporters of the public schools have periodically tried to portray the nonpublic competition as undemocratic and even divisive; supporters of the nonpublic sector, on the other hand, have aggravated the antagonism by seeking public funds for the support of private schools.

Competitive tensions once again became evident in 1981. One factor was the legislative proposal, supported in principle by President Reagan, to provide tuition tax credits for parents whose children are enrolled in private schools; the second factor was the publication of a report, "Public and Private Schools," by University of Chicago sociologist James S. Coleman and a related study by the Rev. Andrew M. Greeley, a Roman Catholic priest and professor of sociology at the University of Arizona.

James S. Coleman

Wide World Photos

The Rev. Andrew M. Greeley

UPI

The Coleman study said, in effect, that private schools show a higher level of academic achievement among their students, maintain better discipline, and are less segregated than public schools. Father Greeley's report called the Roman Catholic parochial schools "impressively superior" in educating members of minority groups. The Coleman study was based on a survey of 58,728 seniors and sophomores in 1,016 public and private high schools.

Other experts challenged the Coleman report's findings. A senior researcher at the Brookings Institution, for example, held that it did not take into account "the behavior of the schools in selecting and excluding students." Others suggested that the reports were intended to provide public and political support for the enactment of tuition tax credits which, public-school supporters fear, could be so costly as severely to undercut federal support for public education. Apart from these controversies, however, the studies underscored the continuing importance of the nonpublic schools as part of the fabric of American education.

While the public schools experienced an enrollment decline of about 5 million in the 1970s, nonpublic schools have shown increases of about 1% annually since 1975. Total nonpublic-school enrollment is estimated at slightly more than 5 million. Eleven percent of the nation's 46 million schoolchildren are in nonpublic schools. The largest nonpublic sector is that of the Roman Catholic parochial schools with an enrollment of 3.1 million, down from 4.3 million in 1970. However, there is evidence that the decline, which forced the closing of 20% of the elementary schools and 25% of the high schools in the 1970s, has ended. In the 1980–81 school year, the loss was less than 1%, and a new upward trend may be indicated by the opening of some new schools in 1981–82. At this time, more than 6 of every 10 nonpublic school students are in Catholic institutions.

However, the largest-growing nonpublic sector is that of the Protestant or Christian schools which are opening, according to the movement's spokesmen, at a rate of three a day. A study by the National Center for Educational Statistics estimated that the number of all non-Catholic private schools increased by 6% a year between 1979 and 1981. This would mean an increase of 1,600 such schools during the two-year period. Since many of these schools are small, it is estimated that the increase represents only about 120,000 pupils. Typically, these small schools enroll 60 students, compared with an average of 350 for Catholic schools.

The most stable nonpublic sector is that of the so-called independent schools, most of them either unaffiliated or only loosely linked through their origins with a religious denomination. They enroll about 320,000 and include some of the most prestigious schools, both day and boarding, such as New York City's Collegiate School, which shares with the public Boston Latin School the claim to be the oldest secondary schools in the United States, and residential institutions such as Groton and Choate. They run the gamut from traditional single-sex schools, such as The Brearley School for girls, to originally progressive and coeducational Dalton, both in New York.

Compared to parochial school, these private or independent schools are costly, with tuition in some exceeding $4,000 annually. However, the National Association of Independent Schools (NAIS) points out that these institutions today are awarding more financial aid to greater numbers of their students. In 1980, scholarship aid went to 51,000, 16.4% of their enrollment, compared with 36,000, 11.7%, ten years earlier. The present total contributed by these schools to student aid is $70 million, 7% of their operating budgets, up from $40 million a decade ago.

A spokesman for the association underscores a growing trend of cooperation between public and private schools, in an effort to improve education. "At a time when events pit public schools against private schools, the emergence of collaborative programs between public and private sectors in education may actually be leading to a new trend in education," William Dandridge, director of academic services at the NAIS, said. He cited the National Network of Complementary Schools, a collaborative of 29 public and independent schools which offer exchange programs for students and teachers. It is because of their long tradition of independence and relative stability that these private schools are less likely to enter into controversies over public support of nonpublic schools.

Finally, the private-school community is pondering the currently discussed possibility of substituting a so-called voucher system for the present method of local, state, or federal school financing. Under such a system, parents would be given vouchers representing a certain number of publicly provided dollars which they could turn over to the school, public or nonpublic, that agrees to educate their children. Since the public schools must accept all comers anyway, the supporters of the voucher plan expect that more parents would take the vouchers to nonpublic institutions. Proponents of the plan say that its main advantage is giving parents greater freedom of choice; opponents charge that it would undercut tax support of public education and endanger the quality of the public schools since the private schools would retain the right to reject less desirable, hard-to-educate youngsters.

FRED M. HECHINGER

Jihan Sadat, wife of slain Egyptian President Anwar el-Sadat, is comforted at the October 10 funeral by his successor, Hosni Mubarak (right), and Prince Reza Pahlavi (center), son of the late shah of Iran.

Gamma-Liaison

EGYPT

The year 1981 in Egypt was one of growing domestic tension, culminating in the assassination of President Anwar el-Sadat on October 6. His murder and the events leading up to it dramatized an increasingly plain fact in Middle Eastern affairs—except in Israel, it is seemingly impossible for a leader to pursue friendly relations with the West, to opt for moderation and realism, and to eschew populism, radicalism, and pan-Arab or pan-Islamic sentiments and at the same time maintain popularity in the home constituency. The shah of Iran found this out in 1978–79, as did President Sadat before his life was cut short.

In the first nine months of the year, Sadat faced increasingly outspoken criticism from left-wing opposition parties, Islamic fundamentalists, members of the intelligentsia, and other groups. While their objectives were not all compatible, the various opposition groups shared the feeling that an egoistic and complacent Sadat was showing too little interest in needed economic and administrative reforms. Sadat and his official spokesmen maintained that the Soviet Union was stimulating, supporting, and financing the dissent. While this was no doubt partly true, there has been more to Egyptian discontent in recent years than mere Soviet fishing in troubled waters.

Dissent and Unrest. Perhaps the most telling indication of the dissatisfaction was a statement issued in February by a self-styled "national coalition" of some 100 Egyptian political figures, including several of Sadat's former cabinet members. The statement indicted Sadat for failing to live up to the promises he had made when he signed the 1979 peace treaty with Israel—the treaty had not brought prosperity to Egypt but had only isolated it in the Arab world.

On January 12, Sadat announced the arrest of a Soviet diplomat and another Soviet citizen on charges of espionage and fomenting sedition. On March 1, he declared that Communists would be barred from working in the communications industries. And on March 29, the government announced the arrest of 70 members of a "secret Communist organization." Even the Socialist Labor Party, launched with official approval in 1978 as a token opponent to Sadat's own National Democratic Party, began to feel the weight of official disapproval. Denunciations by Sadat evoked a libel action against the president, dismissed by a Cairo court in May as "inadmissible." The Egyptian Bar Association, venturing on political criticism, also ran afoul of the government. The People's Assembly on July 22 passed a bill dissolving the association's governing council and empowering the justice minister to appoint a replacement.

A contagion of Islamic fundamentalism, perhaps wafting from Iran, caused more serious upheavals. The southern town of Asyut, a hotbed of Islamic fanaticism and the site of disorders in 1980, flared up again after Sadat's death. And throughout the year there were outbreaks of violence between Muslims and Copts, the ancient Christian sect of Egypt. Clashes in Cairo, June 17–19, left ten persons dead and 55 injured. A bomb explosion at a wedding in a Coptic church in Cairo on August 2 killed three persons and wounded 56.

In an entirely accidental diaster, Egypt lost 14 senior military officers in a helicopter crash on March 2. On the vehicle touring Egypt's western border were Minister of Defense Ahmed Badawi, ten generals, and three colonels.

Favorable Developments. If early 1981 showed signs of tension and repression that in retrospect could be viewed as portentous, not all the news was bad. Egyptian oil production, nearly all from the Sinai fields developed by Israel and later returned, rose to about 700,000 barrels per day by the end of 1980, one half being exported. Oil revenues reached $3,000,000,000 in 1980, up from $1,800,000,000 in 1979. Other factors contributing to Egypt's improved foreign exchange position were a 14% increase in earnings from Suez Canal dues and tourism, and marked increases in expatriate remittances. All statistics for the fiscal year ending June 30, 1981, suggested that Egypt was enjoying an improved—although still not healthy—economy. Per capita income rose 12% above the previous year (to $421), and inflation declined sharply.

On February 16, Egypt ratified the Nuclear Non-Proliferation Treaty, clearing the way for the United States to supply two 900-megawatt reactors (agreement signed June 7), and also for possible nuclear cooperation for peaceful purposes with France and Britain.

On May 13, to mark the tenth anniversary of his undisputed rule, President Sadat released from prison four former associates of the late President Gamel Abdel Nasser, including former Vice-President Ali Sabry, who had attempted a coup against him in 1971.

The September Crackdown. Four months later, however, Sadat began a massive crackdown against his opponents. On September 3–4, more than 1,500 politicians, journalists, religious figures, and academics were arrested. It was the most severe act of political suppression in the 11 years of Sadat's presidency. In a three-hour parliamentary speech on September 5, Sadat accused all the arrested of having exacerbated religious tension. Among them were journalist M. H. Heikal (a former close associate of Nasser), Ibrahim Shukry (leader of the Socialist Labor Party), many former ministers, 16 Coptic priests, and eight Coptic bishops. Sadat in his speech also announced the removal of the Coptic pope, Shenuda III, whose functions would henceforth be discharged by a commission of five bishops. On September 7, the government announced that it would gradually assume direct supervision of Egypt's 40,000 mosques and that political topics would be banned in sermons. On September 15, Sadat expelled the Soviet ambassador and six embassy employees and also terminated a number of Soviet diplomatic activities in Egypt.

Assassination. The assassination of Anwar el-Sadat on October 6 thus occurred in a country in which the atmosphere was already strained and in which the president's prestige had been bruised and damaged by a whole series of demarches. Sadat was gunned down near Cairo while watching the annual military parade commemorating the Egyptian attack on Israel in 1973. One truck in the parade stopped, and four men in Egyptian uniform ran toward the reviewing stand and opened fire with automatic weapons. Sadat died some two hours later in a military hospital. Eight other government officials and foreign dignitaries were killed and dozens wounded. The accused assassins were all Muslim extremists, but whether they were part of a wider conspiracy or acted alone remained uncertain.

Vice-President Hosni Mubarak immediately became the effective ruler of Egypt. He was confirmed as president by a 98% vote in a plebiscite on October 13. In his inaugural speech on October 14, Mubarak pledged a faithful continuation of Sadat's policies. Consistency and continuity were indeed the hallmarks of his government in the last months of the year. (*See* BIOGRAPHY, page 129.)

Sadat was entombed on October 10 near the scene of the fatal attack. The ceremony was attended by three former U.S. presidents—Jimmy Carter, Gerald R. Ford, and Richard Nixon—and by Israeli Prime Minister Menahem Begin and numerous other foreign dignitaries. Security was so tight the Egyptian public was virtually excluded. Mourning among the people was restrained, in sharp contrast to the wild lamentations for Nasser. At the end of November, the chief accused assassin of President Sadat, Lt. Khaled Islambouli, and 23 others were put on trial. Four were accused of assassination and 20 of complicity.

Foreign Affairs. Relations between Egypt and neighboring Libya remained bad throughout the year. In the late summer, the forces of Libya's Col. Muammar al-Qaddafi, already controlling Chad, raided the Sudan. A war between Libya and Sudan would have certainly involved Egypt, and perhaps other countries, but Libyan forces were later withdrawn and the threat receded. President Sadat met with Prime Minister Begin at Sham al-Sheikh on June 4—their first meeting since January 1980—and again at Alexandria, August 25–26. But the follow-up negotiations to the Egyptian-Israeli peace treaty made slow progress, bogging down on the question of Palestinian autonomy. Relations with President Jaafar al-Nemery of the Sudan were increasingly cordial, with the two leaders exchanging official visits. Egypt's isolation in the Arab world was balanced by its more cooperative relations with the United States. Sadat had a splendidly successful state visit to the United States, August 5–10, meeting President Ronald Reagan for the first time and renewing his friendship with Carter. At the end of November, U.S. forces conducted "Operation Bright Star," a large-scale military training exercise in Egypt, Sudan, Oman, and Somalia.

ARTHUR CAMPBELL TURNER
Department of Political Science
University of California, Riverside

EGYPT • Information Highlights

Official Name: Arab Republic of Egypt.
Location: Northeastern Africa.
Area: 386,660 sq mi (1 001 449 km^2).
Population (1981 est.): 43,500,000.
Chief Cities (Nov. 1976 est.): Cairo, the capital, 5,084,463; Alexandria, 2,318,655; El Giza, 1,246,713.
Government: *Head of state and government,* Hosni Mubarak, president and prime minister (took office Oct. 1981). *Legislature* (unicameral)—People's Assembly.
Monetary Unit: Pound (0.69 pound equals U.S.$1, Oct. 1981).
Manufactures (major products): Textiles, processed foods, tobacco, chemicals, fertilizer, petroleum and petroleum products.
Agriculture (major products): Cotton, rice, wheat, corn.

UPI

Offshore exploratory drilling for oil continues. Such drilling aboard the Shell Oil Co. 12-story rig Zapata Saratoga, above, is temporarily halted as a drill becomes stuck.

ENERGY

Two developments dominated the U.S. energy picture during 1981: 1) a world surplus of oil resulting from major conservation achievements and a worldwide movement to alternative fuels and 2) a fundamental change in the approach of the federal government to energy policy.

Oil Surplus. The most striking indication of conservation was the continuing drop in gasoline consumption in the United States. During 1981 the quantity of gasoline consumed in the United States declined by roughly 6% to the lowest level since 1971. Gasoline consumption was down 16.5% or 1.2 million barrels per day from 1978.

The nation's ability to conserve gasoline has been the result of both a reduction in the number of miles driven and replacement of fuel-inefficient automobiles. Federal legislation passed during 1975 required a fleet average of 27.5 miles per gallon (mpg) or 11.6 km/L for new cars sold in 1985. Rapid increases in the price of gasoline have moved public demand for efficient automobiles well ahead of that schedule. General Motors now estimates that its fleet average for 1985 will be 31 mpg (13.1 km/L).

Conservation of gasoline was only the most dramatic case of a broader pattern of energy savings which reduced overall energy consumption in the United States by 3% during the first six months of 1981.

A steady, although gradual, move away from oil to natural gas and coal by many industrial concerns and electric utilities also contributed to oil savings. The passage by Congress in 1978 of the Natural Gas Policy Act put in place a five-year program of incremental increases in natural gas prices leading to total price deregulation. The result of that legislation was clearly evident in 1981 with the existence of a momentary domestic surplus of natural gas which absorbed some of the previous demand taken care of by oil.

The most evident impact of the above developments was a precipitous decline in oil imports to the United States during the year. U.S. imports were about 5.5 million barrels per day, which represents approximately a 40% drop from the nation's peak year of 1978. The import decline between 1980 and 1981 was more than 1.5 million barrels per day. Since domestic oil production has remained relatively constant, the reason for the decline in imports is clearly oil conservation.

What has been occurring in the United States is only one example of a worldwide trend. Conservation combined with slow economic growth contributed to reduced oil consumption in all industrial countries during 1981. Estimates during the last quarter of 1981 indicated that the industrial nations consumed approximately 31.5 million barrels a day in 1981, a big decline from the 1979 peak of 36 million barrels per day.

The world oil surplus also benefited from increased production by non-OPEC (Organization of Petroleum Exporting Countries) oil-producing nations, particularly Mexico. They increased their production by nearly 1 million barrels a day in each of the previous three years.

Energy Policy. The Reagan administration maintained that supply and demand should be managed in the marketplace and energy decisions should be made in the private sector—a 180-degree turn in federal energy policy.

Spokesmen for the Republican administration argued that the striking move toward conservation in the United States was the result of letting the price of oil rise to the world level. It was their contention that higher prices would lead to an increase in production, and they cited the benefits flowing from gradual deregulation of natural gas as an example.

One of the president's first acts in the energy field was to deregulate totally the price of domestically produced oil, thus moving forward eight months the Carter administration deadline of September 1981.

The Reagan administration's approach to energy policy has five characteristics:

1) Both the choice of and the responsibility for funding new sources of energy should rest with the energy industry and not government, the only exception being nuclear power. In the nuclear area, the Reagan administration reversed the policies of the previous administration by lifting the ban on nuclear fuel reprocessing and pushing the development of the fast-breeder reactor.

2) The Department of the Interior, the government's major land-management agency, moved rapidly to make minerals on all public lands, both onshore and offshore, available on an accelerated basis—a pattern previously established by the Carter administration.

The most controversial proposal called for a five-year schedule of leasing on the Outer Continental Shelf (OCS) of the United States, which offered industry a broader selection of leasable areas than was previously the case. The primary emphasis in this new approach to leasing was to accelerate exploration on the very large continental shelf area surrounding Alaska with the hope of finding giant new oil and gas fields.

In December 1981, the Department of the Interior held a lease sale on the National Petroleum Reserve in Alaska. This area, located in northwestern Alaska, was previously withheld from leasing as a part of the Naval Petroleum Reserve System. In January 1981, as part of its new five-year leasing program, the government held the first general coal lease sale on federal lands in more than a decade. Finally, the Department of the Interior moved rapidly in planning a permanent leasing program for the large oil-shale resources existing in northwestern Colorado, southeastern Wyoming, and northeastern Utah.

3) The government acted vigorously to get out of the business of promoting energy conservation either through regulation or by the direct expenditure of federal funds. The new administration's approach to conservation reflected its belief that there should be no governmentally established limits to energy consumption. Many Congressmen and energy researchers questioned the wisdom of this particular policy focus, and some critics argued that establishing uniform federal efficiency standards, promoting better designs, improving building codes, and providing better insulation were the cheapest and most efficient ways to continue the move toward more conservative energy use.

4) The Reagan administration followed a policy of supporting energy research and development under the view that government should support those activities that are sufficiently long-term and where there is little likelihood that the private sector will support them.

5) One powerful and consistent theme of the new administration was the elimination of burdensome regulations that impede the rapid development of energy sources. The rationale behind this approach was that many of the regulations do not provide sufficient benefits to society to justify their costs. Particular concern was focused on regulations that slowed down energy development.

The vast majority of the regulations that were reviewed, modified, or eliminated were put in place during the 1970s to achieve various kinds of human health and environmental protection. The environmental community and certain other interests in society expressed great concern that this process of deregulation would have serious consequences.

There was evidence that membership in many of the environmental interest groups was growing rapidly in response to the Reagan administration's deregulation and public lands initiatives. For example, during 1981 the Sierra Club and the Audubon Society were reported to have gained approximately 20,000 members each, and Friends of the Earth added about 10,000.

During the election campaign, Ronald Reagan indicated a commitment to dissolving the Department of Energy (DOE). The administration's attitude toward the department was reflected in its initial handling of the department's budget, when slightly more than $3,000,000,000 was cut. Nearly everything in the DOE's budget, with the exception of nuclear power, experienced severe cuts. Clearly, however, the department's efforts to promote conservation were a particular focus of attention. The administration requested only $195 million for conservation, as compared with $922 million sought by the Carter administration.

Solar energy research and development were also subjected to major funding reductions. The Reagan budget proposed $172 million, as compared with $516 million in the Carter budget.

Demonstrators in Trenton, NJ, demand an end to nuclear power projects in the state. The energy program of the Reagan administration emphasizes nuclear development.

UPI

Only long-term solar research and development received support. The administration also proposed that government withdraw from all subsidy programs, such as tax credits, aimed at marketing solar space heating and wind power.

In October a Presidential Decision Paper on dismantling the Department of Energy was made public. The paper proposed eliminating all of the department's economic regulatory functions and distributing most remaining functions among other agencies. Under the proposal two new agencies would be created: one to regulate interstate utilities and the other to handle both military and civilian nuclear programs. The administration expected this proposal to save $1,500,000,000 and eliminate 4,400 jobs.

Early evidence indicated that the Reagan administration also desired to eliminate the Synthetic Fuels Corporation, established in 1980, but found such heavy Congressional commitment to that effort that a decision was made not to call for its elimination. Under the Reagan administration, however, the Synthetic Fuels Corporation was primarily in the business of providing loan guarantees and guaranteed prices for the fuels produced by synthetic fuel plants. Clearly the Synfuels Corporation would not provide heavy dollar expenditures to underwrite plant construction, nor would it build its own large facilities as allowed under the legislation.

Reagan administration energy policies, then, reversed a pattern of detailed federal involvement in the nation's energy system that began with the Arab oil boycott of 1973 and continued through both Republican and Democratic administrations.

Saudi Arabia. One thing that did not change during 1981 was the pivotal role of Saudi Arabia in both the world and the U.S. energy systems. Saudi production represented approximately 45% of the production of the OPEC nations and one quarter of the non-Communist world's production. By September 1981 the Saudis were producing 9.2 million barrels per day, and their oil, at $32 a barrel, was the lowest-priced oil in the world. It should be noted that the Saudi need for dollars was substantially less than the quantity of dollars generated by their production. Simply stated, the Saudis could singlehandedly have eliminated the world surplus of oil without doing any damage to their financial needs.

Both the quantity of Saudi production and the relatively low price of Saudi oil resulted from a continuing commitment on their part to a policy which had two objectives: price unification among all OPEC members at roughly the present Saudi price and a long-term freeze of oil prices. The Saudis repeatedly argued that any pattern of continued price escalation similar to that which had been experienced since 1973 would drive consuming nations to alternate sources of energy. The result of that, they maintained, would be a pattern of continuing decline in the available markets for the one commodity they had to sell—oil.

Saudi oil reserves were estimated to be 160,000,000,000 barrels. In comparison, the U.S. oil reserves were estimated to be about 30,000,000,000 barrels. In addition, the Saudis were discovering more oil each year than they were producing. From their vantage point, it was critical that they have a stable market for their oil for the long-term future, if they were to carry out their scheduled economic development programs. It was also doubtless that the Saudis viewed stability to be very important to their transition from an underdeveloped to a developed status.

During 1981, there were continuing struggles among the members of OPEC over both price and production. At the beginning of 1981, prices for OPEC oil ranged from the $32 figure charged by Saudi Arabia to more than $40 a barrel on the part of North African producers. In the last half of 1981, the decline in consumption of oil caused many of the members of OPEC to cut back production and to give special, unannounced discounts to purchasers of their oil.

The proportions of the change being faced by OPEC were illustrated by the fact that OPEC daily production in 1981 averaged about 23 million barrels a day, down from more than 31 million barrels per day in 1977. For a country such as Nigeria, this loss of market was a severe threat to its ambitious economic development program funded by oil revenues.

During an OPEC meeting in August 1981, the Saudis proposed that prices for OPEC oil be set at $34 a barrel, $2 above their present sales price. The Saudi proposal implied that if price unity could be established at that level, they would be willing to cut back their production.

While the OPEC nations rejected the Saudi proposal in August, declining demand for oil led to a special OPEC meeting in October where it was accepted. Under the agreement, prices will vary from $4 a barrel above the $34 Saudi base to $2.50 below depending on oil quality and geographical location of the producer. These prices are to remain frozen through 1982.

It was estimated that the overall effect of the price agreement would be an average increase of 50 cents a barrel in the world cost of oil.

Following the agreement, the Saudis announced they would cut production back to 8.5 million barrels a day. It was expected that the production cut would eliminate some of the world surplus.

Saudi policy resulted in a decline in the actual price of world oil in 1981 for the first time since the Arab oil boycott of 1973. Many Americans, for the first time, experienced an absolute reduction in the price they paid for gasoline. Based on the belief that Saudi policy would be sustained over the next few years, many oil experts projected that the world could, for the first time since 1973, look forward to a number of years of oil price stability.

Soviet Production. One of the continuing uncertainties concerning world oil resulted from conflicting projections of Soviet oil production. In 1977, the Central Intelligence Agency (CIA) indicated that it expected Soviet oil production to peak in the 1970s and drop to 8 to 10 million barrels per day by 1985. Were this to happen, it was expected that the Soviet Union would have to enter the world oil market to make up the difference between its production and demand. During 1981, the CIA revised its estimates upward. The most recent CIA estimates indicated that Soviet production, about 12 million barrels per day, would drop to somewhere between 10 and 11 million barrels by 1985. The CIA estimates, however, were challenged by a report from the Defense Intelligence Agency, which expected production to be above 12 million barrels per day at least through 1985.

The basic difference in these two projections rested on the question of the capability of Soviet oil production technology to produce from more remote and hostile areas in Siberia. The more optimistic estimates of Soviet production capability, tied to the existence of an oil surplus, have resulted in less concern on the part of most analysts about the Soviet need to acquire oil from the Middle East.

Coal Exports. A self-conscious effort by both the European nations and Japan to develop alternatives to oil had one distinctly beneficial effect for the United States—a very rapid increase in the quantity of coal being exported to supply energy to steam-electric power plants.

During 1980, the United States exported 90 million T (81.8 million t) of coal—a 39% leap over 1979 exports. Estimates of the coal export market range from a low of 200 million T (181.8 million t) to as high as 500 million T (454.5 million t) in the year 2000. For comparative purposes, it is useful to note that during 1980 the total production of coal in the United States was 830 million T (754.5 million t). This improved coal export situation was sustained during 1981.

The primary constraint on rapid export increases was the limitation on coal loading in U.S. ports. The coal export market created substantial pressure in the United States for a major program of port expansion and channel deepening over the next several years.

Forecast. Most energy analysts viewed the developments of 1981 as being quite positive. The ability of the United States both to conserve oil and to move to other energy sources occurred at a more rapid rate than most predictions indicated would be possible. For example, the percentage of U.S. energy supplied by imports declined from 24% in 1977 to 13% in 1981. The world oil surplus led to an absolute reduction in the price of oil and contributed significantly to a decline in the U.S. inflation rate—even in the face of very high interest rates. Finally, the commitment of the Saudis to establish a long-term price for oil gave real reasons for optimism.

The dark clouds hanging on the energy horizon came from several sources. First, the inability to resolve the Arab-Israeli conflict left the future stability of the Middle East, including Saudi Arabia, in an uncertain state. Second, even though drilling for oil in the United States was occurring at the highest rate in history, there were no new, large additions to the nation's domestic oil reserves, and additional reserves were only sufficient to maintain the nation's base at about where it had been in 1980. Third, the great potential for additional oil reserves lay mainly on federally controlled lands. Actions by the Reagan administration to accelerate leasing on those lands appeared to be leading to a coalition of states and environmental interests to challenge such moves. And, finally, in spite of administration actions, the nation was no closer in 1981 to resolving what to do about nuclear energy than it had been in 1980. These dark clouds, however, did not negate the fact that the United States was in better shape with regard to energy than it had been since the 1973 Arab oil boycott.

DON E. KASH, *University of Oklahoma*

ENGINEERING, CIVIL

Despite budget and finance problems, the public sector in the United States and other nations continued to design and construct major engineering projects.

BRIDGES

United States. In 1981, Utah completed a pair of high-level twin bridges on a 17-mi (27-km) extension of I-70 through Clear Creek canyon to meet north-south I-15. Replacing a two-lane highway, the new four-lane stretch of I-70 includes a pair of plate-girder twin bridges 1.5 mi (2.4 km) apart. Concrete piers 160 ft (49 m) above the canyon floor support the steel superstructure. One bridge pair crosses Fish Creek on five spans totaling 1,150 ft (351 m). The other pair, crossing Shingle Creek, includes four spans totaling 1,058 ft (322 m). Concrete decks complete the project, which cost $17 million.

Michigan is constructing a 1.5-mi (2.4-km) segmental concrete box bridge over the Saginaw River at Zilwaukee. The twin four-lane crossing on I-75 will replace a bascule lift span that has been a constant traffic bottleneck. With a maximum vertical clearance of 125 ft (38 m), the new bridge has 25 spans, including a 392-ft (119-m) main span flanked by 370-ft (113-m) side spans. Box segments are 8 ft (2.4 m) long, 72 ft (22 m) wide, as deep as 20 ft (6 m), and weigh up to 185 T (168 t). Completion is scheduled for 1984 at a cost of $77 million.

The longest segmental concrete box girder span in the country is under way in Texas, to cross the Houston Ship Channel 170 ft (52 m) above the water. The 750-ft (229-m) main span is flanked by 375-ft (114-m) side spans. The four-lane crossing is 52 ft (16 m) wide, 10,450 ft (3 185 m) long, and will have 2 mi (3.2 km) of approach roadways. The cast-in-place segments are 15 ft (4.6 m) long and 58 ft (18 m) wide, with a maximum depth of 43 ft (13 m). Due to open in 1982, the project will cost $102 million.

Switzerland. In 1981, Switzerland completed a 2,224-ft (678-m) concrete box girder bridge spanning Ganter Valley on concrete piers as high as 394 ft (120 m). The two-lane Highway 9 crossing, near the Simplon Pass leading to Italy, has eight spans. The 571-ft (174-m) center span is flanked by 417-ft (127-m) side spans. The remaining spans vary from 115 ft (35 m) to 262 ft (80 m). The three main spans are stabilized by prestressed concrete cables about 3.5 inches (8.9 cm) in diameter. The four-year project cost more than $14 million.

CANALS

United States. The 1980 eruption of Mount St. Helens in southwest Washington produced a massive debris barrier that plugged the mouth of Cold Water Canyon. Backed-up water behind the dam posed a flood threat that was relieved in 1981 when the U.S. Corps of Engineers dug a canal to drain the water gradually. The canal, 1,600 ft (488 m) long, 30 to 40 ft (9 to 12 m) deep, and 80 ft (24 m) wide, was excavated mostly through mud, but about one quarter of the channel was dug through a rock ridge.

A 6.5-mi (10.5-km) section of the Highline irrigation canal in Mesa County, CO, is being lined with 2.5 inches (6.35 cm) of concrete. The

Swiss National Tourist Office

With seven staunch piers and an elegant S-curve, the Ganter Bridge, near Switzerland's Simplon Pass to Italy, opened during 1981.

canal passes through an area of high salt-content shale and the lining will reduce or prevent seepage. A detention ditch 8 ft (2.4 m) deep is also being dug along portions of the canal to limit runoff. Including road reconstruction and relocation, the U.S. Bureau of Reclamation project is expected to cost $7.5 million.

DAMS

United States. Located 70 mi (113 km) north of San Francisco, the Warm Springs Dam will provide water and flood control for the heart of northern California's vineyard country. Sponsored by the Sonoma County Water Agency and the U.S. Corps of Engineers, the $240-million project was scheduled for completion in 1981. The earth-fill dam measures 3,000 ft (914 m) long, 317 ft (97 m) high, 2,602 ft (793 m) wide at the base, and 30 ft (9 m) wide at the crest. The compacted embankment contains 30 million cu yd (23 million m^3) of fill. During construction, the river at Warm Springs was diverted through a tunnel 3,399 ft (1 036 m) long and from 10 to 14 ft (3 to 4.3 m) in diameter. Lined with concrete, the tunnel will be kept in operation to regulate downstream river flow throughout the year.

Honduras. Construction started in 1981 on the double-curved, concrete-arch El Cajon Dam on the Humaya River. The multipurpose water project will provide flood control, irrigation, and electric energy from an initial 300 Mw power plant. The structure will be 741 ft (226 m) high, 1,246 ft (380 m) long at the crest, 157 ft (48 m) wide at the base, and 23 ft (7 m) wide at the crest. It will contain 2 million cu yd (1.5 million m^3) of concrete. The thin-arch dam will form a 36-sq mi (93-km^2) reservoir. The $550-million project is scheduled for completion in 1985. During construction, the Humaya River is being diverted through a 1,870-ft (570-m) tunnel, 42 ft (13 m) in diameter.

Norway. In 1981, Norway completed Sysen Dam at the head of Hardangerfjord on the Atlantic Coast south of Bergen. The clay-cored earth dam is 230 ft (70 m) high, 3,600 ft (1 097 m) long, and 26 ft (8 m) wide at the crest. It contains 4.7 million cu yd (3.6 million m^3) of fill material. Located at an elevation of 3,281 ft (1 000 m), the catchment area taps rivers on the Hardanger plateau and directs the water down twin 2,822-ft (860-m) penstocks to an underground rock cavern housing four turbine sets. Generating 1,120 Mw, the Sima power station is Norway's largest producer of electric energy.

Great Britain. An unusual type of dam is under construction on the Thames River downstream from London to protect the city from flooding. Located only 40 mi (64 km) from the Thames mouth at the North Sea, London is constantly threatened with life and property loss from severe surging tides. The 1,700-ft (518-m) barrier stretching across the river includes concrete piers and ten sector gates. Six gates are of the rising type; four are 200 ft (61 m) wide and two 103 ft (31 m) wide. The rotating gates rest on concrete pier sills at the river bottom, permitting navigation. At a flood tide surge, they can be hydraulically raised 60 ft (18 m) within 30 minutes. Labor problems have delayed job progress, but London hopes to complete this movable flood defense by 1984. Total cost of the dam and bank raising is expected to reach $1,000,000,000.

TUNNELS

United States. An 8,600-ft (2 621-m) interceptor sewer tunnel through soft ground in the Red Hook section of Brooklyn, NY, was finished in 1981 at a total cost of $62 million. The five-segment, steel liner-plate tube, 10 ft (3 m) in diameter, was constructed under compressed air ranging from 6.5 to 7 psi (.45 to .49 kg/cm^2). Since the top of the sewer had about 15 ft (4.6 m) of cover, open-cut tunneling at first looked feasible. But because of the many utility lines above the interceptor and subway lines running below, it proved impossible. Also, a high water table created dewatering problems for the cut-and-cover approach.

Across the country in San Francisco, another sewer tunnel was finished in 1981 under the Fisherman's Wharf area. This 3,057-ft (932-m) bore, 12 ft (3.7 m) in diameter, was built by a Japanese contractor for $13 million. The bid was almost $5 million below the city's estimate.

Also in California, the U.S. Bureau of Reclamation is building the $50 million Pacheco water tunnel, which is part of the Central Valley Project. The bore under Diablo Mountain, 12 ft (3.7 m) in diameter and 5.3 mi (8.5 km) long, is at a maximum depth of 1,300 ft (396 m). Excavation is handled by the drill-blast-muck method. When lined with concrete, the inside diameter of the tunnel will be 9.5 ft (2.9 m). Completion is scheduled for 1983. The tunnel will carry water from San Luis Reservoir to canals and pumping stations for use in four counties.

Netherlands. A tunnel under the Gouwe Canal near Gouda will remove a traffic bottleneck from a drawbridge carrying Highway E-8, linking The Hague with West Germany. The concrete tunnel is 131 ft (40 m) long, 164 ft (50 m) wide, and 15 ft (5 m) high. The $30-million structure carries eight traffic lanes and four service lanes. The top of its 4-ft- (1.2-m-) thick roof serves as the bed of the canal. Work started in 1975, and the tunnel was scheduled to open in 1981. It was built in sections within sheet-pile cofferdams so as not to interrupt canal navigation.

India. Calcutta hopes to ease traffic congestion in its narrow streets by building a 10.5-mi (17-km) twin-track subway. The cut-and-cover tunnel is 36 ft (11 m) underground and will serve a metropolitan population of 9 million. India's first rapid transit system is due for completion in 1986.

WILLIAM H. QUIRK
Construction Consultant

ENVIRONMENT

In 1981, the United Nations Environmental Program (UNEP) indentified as major world problems the pollution of groundwater, the spread of toxic substances, and misguided environmental economics. New concern about acid rain became a hotly debated political issue between Canada and the United States. And within the United States, thrusts toward greater energy self-sufficiency and less federal environmental regulation brought new unity to conservation groups.

WORLD DEVELOPMENTS

The year brought progress toward stronger regulation of world trade in endangered flora and fauna, and international agreements on restraints of the whaling industry. In his 1981 State of the World Environment message, UNEP Executive Director Mostafa K. Tolba called for new research into the contamination and depletion of groundwater, which collects in subsurface layers and is a main source of fresh water. He also urged tighter international controls over the production and use of such persistent pesticides as DDT, aldrin, and dieldrin and of toxic industrial chemicals. In regard to environmental economics—the cost-benefit ratio of maintaining a healthy ecosystem—Tolba said that improvements in environmental quality can generate health and economic benefits that far outweigh the costs. "Good management of the environment should be based upon avoiding wastage of resources and pollution," he said. "This is more appropriate and certainly more efficient than redressing environmental degradation after it occurs."

Acid Rain. The pollution of land and water by airborn emissions of sulfur dioxide and nitrogen oxide from automobiles, coal plants, and other sources was the subject of a number of international meetings. "Pollutants are not respecters of international boundaries," said Canada's Minister of the Environment John Roberts, speaking before the American Association for the Advancement of Science. "Even if we were able to eliminate our own emissions, we would still be receiving more than six million tons of these chemicals from sources in the United States. . . . I can only hope for the necessary ingredients of political will which can allow an international resolution of this difficulty." In March, U.S. President Ronald Reagan pledged to Canadian Prime Minister Pierre Elliott Trudeau that the United States would fulfill commitments made by the Jimmy Carter administration to curb such emissions. However, the Reagan administration's announced plans to cut back on the activities of the U.S. Environmental Protection Agency (EPA) caused widespread alarm in Canada. In July, Roberts charged that the United States had failed to live up to its commitment.

Meanwhile, the problem of acid rain appeared to be spreading. As many as 50,000 lakes in eastern North America are believed to be affected by acid rain, which kills fishlife by raising the acidity of the water. In August, rain and snow nearly as acid as raw vinegar were reported in a number of lakes in Colorado. In July, at the European Conference on Acid Rain held in Göteborg, Sweden, delegates learned that nearly one third of the spruce forests in northern Germany are suffering needle loss from the effects of acid rain, and that freshwater fish have been extirpated in 5,000 sq mi (13 000 km^2) of lakes in southern Norway since 1950.

Whales. In July, the International Whaling Commission (IWC) met in Brighton, England, and, amid considerable controversy, narrowly rejected a total ban on commercial whaling. Dissenters were led by Japan and the USSR, two of the nine member nations that still engage in whaling. The overall kill quota was set at 13,356, down nearly 500 from the previous year. A "zero quota" was set on the commercial killing of sperm whales after 1981, and the group voted to ban the use of nonexplosive "cold" harpoons beginning in 1983. The IWC now numbers 31 member governments, with the admission in 1981 of China, India, Uruguay, St. Lucia, St. Vincent, Costa Rica, and Jamaica.

Endangered Wildlife. A number of international meetings concerning the world's wildlife populations were held during 1981. In February,

Anne Gorsuch, 38, was appointed administrator of the U.S. Environmental Protection Agency (EPA).

UPI

representatives of the International Convention on International Trade in Endangered Species (CITES) met in New Delhi, India. Delegates voted to restrict trade in parrots and sperm whales. Neither measure was supported by the United States. The U.S. delegation contended that quotas on sperm whales are more properly under the jurisdiction of the IWC and that parrot trade should be curtailed only in those species considered endangered or threatened.

In July, international wildlife specialists met in Zimbabwe to finalize plans to conserve elephants and the black and white species of rhinoceros. The group heard reports that trade in ivory and rhino horns is increasing, while human settlements continue to encroach on the animals' habitats.

U.S. DEVELOPMENTS

With the inauguration of Ronald Reagan, severe budget cuts and pledges of a drive for greater energy self-sufficiency and less government regulation drastically altered such traditional federal programs as pollution control and the management of public lands. At the same time, environmental groups challenged some of those policy directions in the courts and media.

Controversial Appointments. Among the first changes to be challenged were Reagan appointments to key environmental posts. These included John Crowell, former legal counsel of Louisiana-Pacific Corp., a large consumer of timber, who was named assistant secretary of agriculture for environment and natural resources, with direct supervision over the U.S. Forest Service (USFS); Robert Burford, a Colorado rancher and advocate of states' rights to public-domain land, to head the Bureau of Land Management; Anne Gorsuch, a former Colorado legislator who had opposed air-quality and toxic waste regulations, to head the U.S. Environmental Protection Agency (EPA); and James Watt, an attorney who represented the Colorado-based Mountain States Legal Foundation, as secretary of interior. The Watt choice was by far the most hotly contested, with the National Audubon Society, Sierra Club, National Wildlife Federation, and Izaak Walton League of America calling for his removal.

Public Lands. One of the new interior secretary's first moves was to place a freeze on the National Park Service's land-acquisition activities and to direct that agency to concentrate on improving and maintaining existing parks. The action came in the wake of a number of government reports of deteriorating conditions within the park system due to heavy public use. The Interior Department also announced a "good neighbor" policy of less regulation on more than 500 million acres (202 million ha) of public land under its jurisdiction. Under that policy, states would have first rights to water, and more areas would be open to mineral and oil exploration and other "multiple uses."

Offshore Oil. The administration's plans to accelerate oil exploration in nearly 1,000,000,000 acres (404 686 000 ha) of coastal waters hit a major snag in May, when a federal district judge blocked an Interior Department sale of drilling leases on more than 150,000 acres (60 750 ha) along the California coast. The litigation, initiated by the Natural Resources Defense Council on behalf of more than 20 environmental groups, said the planned sale violated state and federal environmental laws.

Water. The quantity as well as the quality of the nation's water resources were major issues in 1981. During the spring months, severe drought hit many states, causing widespread concern about crops and the availability of drinking water. The U.S. Geological Survey reported that 42 states were affected. In Florida, low water tables were blamed for a massive sinkhole in Winter Park, causing multimillion dollar damage.

Some states, including Florida, New Jersey, and New York, initiated stringent water-use controls. In the Midwest, however, late rains were heavy enough to spare wheat, corn, and other crops. The U.S. Soil Conservation Service reported that dry conditions nationwide were partly responsible for a significant increase in soil erosion.

Amid increasing fears about possible future water shortages, hopes dimmed for effective control of pollution. Federal aid for sewage cleanup projects was sharply curtailed, and one government report said that more than half the nation's existing waste treatment plants are inefficient. A federal ban on ocean dumping was scheduled to go into effect at the end of the year, but some municipalities, including New York City, said they would be unable to meet that deadline. There was, however, some progress in the cleanup of industrial pollutants called PCBs (polychlorinated biphenyls) from the Hudson River. New York State's plan to dredge up and bury the substance was approved by the EPA.

The foliage-eating gypsy moth caterpillar wreaked havoc on forestlands from Maine to Maryland.

UPI

The cost of cleaning the contaminants in 40 areas of high concentration was expected to be $26.7 million, with $20 million financed through a Congressional appropriation.

Air. The Clean Air Act was due for Congressional renewal in 1981, but final action was repeatedly delayed as industries pressed for relaxed air standards and environmentalists urged strict enforcement. The EPA, which has primary enforcement responsibilities, found itself with a sharply reduced budget and an insufficient number of field inspectors to do the job.

Insect Pests. In California, following an outbreak of the Mediterranean fruitfly ("Medfly") which threatened the California fruit harvest, the spraying of malathion caused public concern about the insecticide's possible effects on humans. (*See* GARDENING AND HORTICULTURE.) In Montana, 200,000 acres (81 000 ha) of wheat land were sprayed with another, more persistent pesticide, Endrin, to combat army cutworms. Heavy concentrations of the chemical were subsequently found in waterfowl and other game birds in 17 western states, all of which considered closing their fall hunting seasons. In the northeast, a record infestation of gypsy moths defoliated trees on more than 11 million acres (4.5 million ha) of woodlands.

Reptile "Sting." In July, the U.S. Fish and Wildlife Service announced the successful conclusion of an 18-month undercover investigation of illicit traffic in thousands of snakes, turtles, lizards, and migratory birds by more than 175 individuals. Twenty-seven arrest warrants were issued in Georgia, Pennsylvania, and Florida.

Endangered Species. The Interior Department shifted the emphasis of its endangered species program from listing new ones to saving species already on the official roster of threatened plants and animals.

BILL VOGT, *"National Wildlife" and "International Wildlife" Magazines*

ETHIOPIA

In 1981 Ethiopia continued its low-keyed war with Somalia, and strengthened its ties with the Soviet Union as the United States developed a military strategy in the Horn of Africa and the Indian Ocean. Domestically, Col. Mengistu Haile Mariam increased his control over the government and army.

War with Somalia. In January 1981 the United States began delivery to Somalia of $40 million in military aid of a "defensive nature." According to the U.S. State Department the aid is "part of a strategic framework . . . in response to the Soviet threat in the region." At the end of June, just two weeks after Somalia claimed that 30 people were killed during Ethiopian air raids on two border towns, Somalia's President Siad Barre said he was willing to hold peace negotiations with Ethiopia over the disputed territory of the Ogaden. He proclaimed that Somalia had halted its aid to guerrillas who were attempting to wrest the Ogaden from Ethiopia. Ethiopia did not respond to the peace overture. According to the United Nations the world's most intractable refugee problem exists in Somalia, where 1.2 million Ethiopians from the Ogaden have fled.

Foreign Affairs. The United States plans to have a string of military bases in the Red Sea, the Horn of Africa, and the Indian Ocean by 1986, at a cost of more than $2,000,000,000. The U.S. Joint Chiefs of Staff view this plan as a comprehensive strategy for dealing with the growth of Soviet power in the region. Naval bases are planned for development in Egypt, Somalia, Kenya, and Oman, while the U.S. naval position on Diego Garcia is to be strengthened. By 1982, $24 million would be spent in Somalia to repair facilities in the port of Berbera, while $26 million would be spent to dredge the Kenyan port of Mombasa. As part of the U.S. strategy 32 combat and support vessels were deployed in the Indian Ocean during the latter half of 1981.

Ethiopia moved to develop its ties to the USSR. In February 1981 *The New York Times* obtained documents indicating that Ethiopia had provided military arms to leftist guerrillas in El Salvador who were attempting to dislodge the pro-American government there. The equipment was reported to have been transshipped through Cuba. In the first quarter of 1981 the Soviet navy developed its anchorage in the Dahlak Islands of Ethiopia on the Red Sea. It was also reported that the USSR was constructing a naval base in the islands. With the Eritrean war winding down in 1981 due to Eritrean seccessionist losses, the Soviet presence in the Red Sea increased. The Soviets also have naval bases in South Yemen, directly across the Red Sea from Ethiopia.

African Politics. In midyear Ethiopia expelled five senior Secretariat members of the Organization of African Unity. They were accused of being involved in antigovernment activities in Addis Ababa. A Treaty of Friendship and Cooperation was signed by Ethiopia, Libya, and South Yemen on August 19. The three states maintained that they were "a material force taking action on the part of joint struggle against all forms of conspiracy and aggression which threaten the peoples of these countries."

PETER SCHWAB
State University of New York at Purchase

ETHIOPIA • Information Highlights

Official Name: Ethiopia.
Location: Eastern Africa.
Area: 471,777 sq mi (1 221 900 km^2).
Population (1981 est.): 33,500,000.
Chief Cities (1978 est.): Addis Ababa, the capital, 1,125,340; Asmara 373,827; Dire Dawa, 72,202.
Government: *Head of state and government,* Mengistu Haile Mariam, chairman of the Provisional Military Administrative Committee (took office Feb. 1977).
Monetary Unit: Birr (2.07 birrs equal U.S. $1, June 1981).
Manufactures (major products): Cotton yarn, fabrics, cement, sugar, cigarettes, canned food.
Agriculture (major products): sugarcane, roots and tubers.

ETHNIC GROUPS

New policies pursued in 1981 by the administration of Ronald Reagan had special implications for America's minority groups. Reagan's first priority as president was to heal the nation's economy, and his prescription called for painful reductions in the federal budget. The problem for many citizens was that a good deal of the cutting came from programs on which the unemployed and working poor have come to depend. Aid to Families with Dependent Children; medicaid; food stamps; CETA job-training; housing subsidies; and legal, family-planning, and day-care services were all curtailed. Since minority-group members partake of those services in greater proportions than other Americans, their despair was predictable.

Civil Rights. What was worse for minority groups was their lack of clout with the administration. Black voters, for example, cast only 7% of their ballots for Reagan—but he won in a landslide anyway, a situation guaranteed to reduce the political influence of blacks. The conflict of interests was obvious when the president addressed a convention of the National Association for the Advancement of Colored People (NAACP) in Denver. Reagan explained his position: a healthier economy would lead, in the long run, to greater prosperity for all Americans. That rationale was cold comfort to an audience already upset by Reagan's de-emphasis of affirmative-action programs and stunned by the prospect that the hard-won Voting Rights Act of 1965 might be repealed. In November, however, the president called for an extension of the act.

In 1981, Vernon Jordan announced his resignation as president of the National Urban League.

UPI

Civil-rights organizations were stunned in other ways as well. In the same week, Roy Wilkins, longtime chief of the NAACP, died and National Urban League head Vernon Jordan announced his resignation. The loss of Wilkins was largely symbolic; he had retired in poor health four years earlier. (*See also* OBITUARIES.) Jordan's unexpected decision deprived civil-rights forces of one of their most effective and respected spokesmen. Jordan, who said he would sign on with a prestigious Washington law firm, said that his resignation had nothing to do with the sniper attack that nearly killed him in 1980.

At the same time, new voices were being raised. With the coming of the Reagan administration, attention was focused on a small, controversial group of black conservatives whose views ran counter to those espoused by civil-rights groups on a number of issues. Most prominent among the conservatives was Thomas Sowell, an economist who spoke out against affirmative action because, he said, it stigmatizes the beneficiaries; against school busing for racial desegregation because it does not improve education and angers whites; against minimum-wage laws because they hinder the employment of minority youth; against massive federal welfare because it fosters dependency. Sowell and his fellow conservatives could boast no great following—but because they seemed to have the White House ear they could gain in influence.

Desegregation. Several big-city school systems, including Chicago, still struggled to develop an acceptable school-desegregation plan—but the wind seemed to be shifting. In the spring, the California Supreme Court surprised many observers by refusing to review a lower-court ruling that upheld an antibusing referendum. Los Angeles had yielded to a 15-year court case in 1978 and begun a mandatory busing plan, prompting many white families to enroll their children in private schools. In 1979, voters passed a ballot initiative that would put an end to the busing. Since the state supreme court let stand the ruling that the initiative was constitutional, the busing plan was scrapped.

In Washington state, voters approved a similar initiative which would halve a busing program ordered by the Seattle school board. A lower court found the initiative unconstitutional, but the state appealed to the U.S. Supreme Court. In a change of policy, the U.S. Justice Department joined the case on the side of the state—a signal that the administration would oppose busing even when initiated by local authorities, not by federal court order. A final ruling in the case was not made.

The antibusing trend was not limited to ballot proposals or the White House. The House of Representatives voted to bar the Justice Department from pursuing cases that might result in busing, and the Senate took steps in the same direction. The administration, in fact, opposed the Senate bill because it was too restrictive, but

Justice officials did say they would favor racial-balance remedies only in those cases where the imbalance was caused by state action. In other words, discriminatory intent, not simply results, would be the criterion for government action. The NAACP indicated that if Justice held to that view, the association might sue the department for failing to enforce civil-rights law.

There was also a change in school-desegregation policy as it pertained to higher education. Under Jimmy Carter, the U.S. Department of Education issued warnings to officials of several states that their state college systems were illegally segregated. The warnings, which came just before Carter left office, were the result of a ten-year court battle that had seen the federal government threaten to cut off funds to some states. Under President Reagan, though, the government reached accord with several of the affected states, which agreed to provide funds to enhance the facilities and programs at traditionally black state colleges. In return, the government would no longer pressure the states to increase integration. The accord was hailed by many black college administrators, who feared that with integration the schools would lose their black identity. Yet some civil-rights tacticians objected that the tacit approval of separate but equal public colleges would be no bargain for blacks in the long run. (*See also* EDUCATION.)

Hispanics. With the 1980 census, the city of San Antonio, TX, once known mainly for the Alamo, remained the tenth largest city in the United States. It was also the largest city with a Hispanic majority, and in 1981 it became the largest city ever to elect a Hispanic mayor, Henry Cisneros, a popular 33-year-old city councilman.

While the election of Cisneros, a Mexican-American, was a positive sign for Hispanics, there was ground lost in the longstanding controversy over bilingual education. Many Hispanic activists favor strong bilingual programs as a way of assuring that Spanish-speaking children have equal educational opportunity. But one of the first actions taken by Terrel H. Bell, the new secretary of education, was to scrap proposed federal guidelines for bilingual education, an indication that the administration would leave it to the states to decide how much, if any, bilingual instruction to provide. In Colorado, one of the country's most comprehensive programs was repealed. In Texas, a federal judge ruled that the state's program was inadequate.

Immigration. The U.S. Supreme Court agreed to decide whether states must provide free public education for illegal-alien children. A 1975 Texas law barring the use of state funds for that purpose was challenged in 1977 by the Mexican American Legal Defense Fund, and a federal court ruled that the law was unconstitutional. The Justice Department at that time joined the plaintiffs in seeking to strike down the law. In 1981 Justice chose to bow out of the case, in effect supporting the state's decision to deny free access to the schools.

Wide World Photos

Henry Cisneros is the first Hispanic to be elected mayor of a large U.S. city. He won in San Antonio.

A new group of refugees, this time from war-torn El Salvador, captured the attention of beleaguered immigration officials. Since the Salvadorans were fleeing not political oppression but grinding poverty—per capita income was only $639 in 1978—the newcomers were considered illegal aliens. The Border Patrol caught and deported about 12,000 Salvadorans in 1980, but officials believe at least 60,000 others made it safely into the United States.

At the same time, hundreds of Cuban refugees, left over from the 1980 "freedom flotilla" that brought more than 100,000 into the United States unexpectedly, still languished at Fort Chaffee, AR. Also facing an uncertain future were 6,000 Haitians who arrived in the U.S. after October 1980, when those who were already in the country were given leave to stay. Despite threats of deportation, the Haitians, fleeing poverty and an oppressive regime, continued to risk the treacherous journey across 800 mi (1 280 km) of open water in homemade 20-foot (6-m) boats. More than 1,000 of them, having washed up on the Florida shore with nowhere to go, were kept in a makeshift Miami detention center waiting for determination of their fate. The government's efforts to deport them were often frustrated by a group of young lawyers acting on their behalf. In late October, 33 Haitians were drowned when their boat capsized off Florida.

DENNIS A. WILLIAMS, *"Newsweek"*

EUROPE

The year 1981 brought no change in the mood of uneasiness and frustration that had descended on Europe in 1974, when recession, precipitated by rises in the price of imported oil, brought high unemployment and industrial stagnation. In Western Europe, a long-established government was voted out of office in France, and power changed hands in some ten other countries. More violent opposition took the form of terrorist attacks in Northern Ireland and West Germany, street riots in Great Britain, and an attempted military coup against the parliamentary regime in Spain. In Eastern Europe, discontent in Poland led to a serious attempt by the trade union movement to change the very nature of an authoritarian society.

In these volatile circumstances, international negotiation achieved little. Soviet-American relations remained in a deadlock. The summit meeting of the leading non-Communist economic powers in Ottawa in July achieved little more than an agreement to disagree. And even the Soviet Union, still embroiled in Afghanistan, seemed unable to bring either the Polish Communist party or the independent union Solidarity to do more than moderate the pace of change in Poland's institutions.

Continuing Recession. After the average price of crude oil had risen by almost 90% in 1979–80, only small price increases were posted in 1981. A temporary glut in oil supplies, due partly to reduced consumption in such major importing countries as West Germany and the United States, forced prices to drop slightly. But, since oil prices were established in U.S. dollars, the soaring value of the dollar in relation to European currencies then raised the price of oil to Europeans by as much as one third, increasing resentment of high U.S. interest rates which, it was felt, had helped drive European inflation to more than 13%. Most European governments chose to fight inflation by restrictive monetary policies and reduction of government spending, which caused unemployment to rise.

In Great Britain, for example, the austerity policies of Prime Minister Margaret Thatcher brought the number of unemployed to more than three million, or 12% of the labor force. As usual, the countries of southern Europe suffered most. No growth was expected in the Italian economy, in which inflation had exceeded 21%. Greece, which expected to receive not only economic stimulus but also direct financial aid as a result of joining the European Community (EC) in January, expected a growth of no more than 3% in a national product that was already the lowest in the EC. The sagging economies of Spain and Portugal were responsible in part for postponement of their entry into EC, which had been tentatively planned for 1983. Even in northern Europe, difficulties were widespread. West Germany, with Europe's strongest economy, had run a deficit of $15,000,000,000 in 1980 and, by imposing monetary restrictions in 1981, had begun to increase unemployment. In France, where Socialist President François Mitterrand ordered increased government spending to combat unemployment, business confidence slumped in expectation of budget deficits and higher inflation. The most disastrous record, however, occurred in Poland, where the burden of servicing a debt to the West of $23,000,000,000 was combined with problems of inefficient management of state industry and inadequate incentives for private farmers. The Polish national income had declined in 1979 and 1980, and seemed likely to slump precipitously during the labor turmoil of 1981.

Political Repercussions in Western Europe. The most dramatic protest vote occurred in France, where in May Socialist challenger Mitterrand defeated the incumbent president, Valéry Giscard d'Estaing, and led his Socialist Party to victory in parliamentary elections in June. Mitterrand gave notice of his intention to establish a new direction in French politics by appointing four Communists to his government, giving that party a share in power for the first time since 1947. Mitterrand promised more extensive social programs, nationalization of private banks and several leading industrial companies, and a more cooperative attitude toward France's allies. In a similar reversal, Greek voters ended seven years of conservative government by giving the Socialist Party and its leader, Andreas Papandreau, a sweeping victory in October parliamentary elections. Discontent with Ireland's high inflation and unemployment rates led to the narrow defeat of incumbent Prime Minister Charles Haughey (Fianna Fáil party) in June. In Italy, Christian Democratic Prime Minister Arnaldo Forlani was compelled to resign, following disclosures that several members of his cabinet belonged to a secret Masonic organization suspected of plotting against the state. For the first time since 1945, a non-Christian Democrat—Giovanni Spadolini of the Republican Party—became premier.

Rampant Terrorism. Political protest often passed to physical violence. A Turkish gunman wounded Pope John Paul II as he drove through a crowded St. Peter's Square in May. The Italian Red Brigades continued their campaign of kidnapping and assassination, while the Red Army Faction in West Germany engaged in bombing and rocket attacks on American military bases and personnel. Spain was buffeted from both the political right and left. Basque terrorists of the left-wing separatist ETA organization brought to more than 350 the number of political and military officials they had murdered, prompting right-wing military officers to attempt to overthrow the government and restore authoritarian rule. Spanish civil guards seized parliament in February, but the coup was defeated. The beleaguered British government saw the problem of

P. Breese, Gamma-Liaison

UPI

The leaders of the seven major industrialized democracies (above, front row) held a two-day summit in July near Ottawa, Canada. A focus of the discussions was the effect of high U.S. interest rates on European economies. Right, West German Chancellor Helmut Schmidt makes a point with French President François Mitterrand during May talks at the Élysée Palace.

Northern Ireland exacerbated when imprisoned members of the Irish Republican Army (IRA) shocked observers worldwide by starving themselves to death in hunger strikes. The British public, however, was more shaken by summer riots in 30 cities, in which mobs of unemployed youths expressed their frustration in a massive rampage of burning, looting, and violent confrontation with police.

The Polish Cauldron. Annoyance at deteriorating economic conditions and repressive government led Solidarity to demand greater authority and improved living conditions for all. The Communist party leadership was able, however, to maintain a relatively moderate middle course between Soviet demands and Solidarity's pressures. Farmers were permitted their own union. The parliament took a more active role in policy making. The Communist party congress, chosen by secret referendum, purged the party bureaucracy and adopted reforms compelling greater governmental responsiveness to the wishes of the rank-and-file members. And greater freedom was granted to the press, radio, and television. Warnings from the USSR increased throughout the year, especially after Solidarity called for the formation of similar unions in other East European countries, but Soviet options remained limited. With 85,000 troops still tied down in Afghanistan, the Soviet leaders did not wish to provoke a military conflict in Poland. They also feared further disruption of the Polish economy, which they had backed with more than $4,000,000,000 in aid since 1980. Nevertheless, it remained uncertain as to how long the Soviet Union would tolerate the profound process of social and economic change that Poland had undergone since the Gdansk strikes began in mid-1980.

F. Roy Willis
Department of History
University of California, Davis

"Le Figaro" Magazine/Gamma-Liaison

Ballooning harem pants were a glamorous addition to the 1981 fashion scene. With its sensuous billowing lines, bold color, and more formal mien, the outfit (left) exemplified several of the year's notable fashion trends.

FASHION

Opulence, extravagance, and exaggeration were the distinguishing trends in fashion for 1981. After several years of designing sane and sensible clothing, couturiers filled their collections with costumery of the most lavish kind. Infantas and Regency belles shared the runway with tsarinas and medieval troubadors. No period or ethos went unrepresented. Inspired by poets, peasants, pirates, Berbers, Mongols, Incas, Turks, Moors, and others, designers adapted their costumes, creating an unbridled pageantry.

Several factors were responsible for this flood of flamboyance. First, the relative sameness of fashion with its emphasis on classics was becoming boring. Designers felt their creativity stifled, and manufacturers, realizing that customers' closets were stuffed with "preppy" styles, felt the need to excite the consumer and stimulate business. Both encouraged the dramatic change that was a total reversal of past trends.

Another important factor was the presence of the new first lady, Nancy Reagan. Her taste and style as well as her patronage of the couture made her as inspiring a figure as was her predecessor Jacqueline Kennedy. The return to formality and ritual for White House state dinners and receptions set a tone of elegance and taste that stimulated the fashion world and influenced the attitudes and customs of society.

In addition, 1981 was the year of the royal wedding of England's Prince Charles and Lady Diana Spencer. With all the attendant pomp, it further inspired fashion outpourings and gave a boost to the wedding gown business.

The Silhouette. Fashion exaggeration began with a silhouette that was full and generous, moving away from the body. Billowing skirts, flaring smocks, swirling capes, and tent-like coats all bespoke the bravura of a widened shape. Hemlines, which had been slowly inching upward, plummeted to mid-calf to accommodate this silhouette. Clothes ballooned over bodies and made contact only at the neck, waist, wrist, or ankle, where they were secured by ascots, obis, and cuffs. When done in fabrics with bold patterns, such as blanket or block plaids, Berber stripings, massive paisleys, or tapestry florals (which often were mixed in one outfit), the theatrical look of 1981 was achieved.

The Materials. While the silhouette had a certain barbarous panache, the fabrics used were all luxurious and refined. There were soft, drapable cashmeres, woolens, and silks. Jerseys, challis, soft tweeds, brushed blanketing and mohairs, lush velvets, and glittering lamés were the types of fabrics that were combined in layered ensembles, suitable for grand entrances. Designers outdid themselves in the imaginative ways in which they mixed color, pattern, and texture.

Colors were deep, rich, and true earth and desert tones or Renaissance court colors. The patterns represented the ethnic motifs of the culture that was the basis for a particular look or a specific designer's leitmotif. Examples included Ralph Lauren's Navahos, Calvin Klein's Berbers, the Ottoman Empire à la Bill Blass, and de la Renta's gypsies. All were authentic, not derivative. Besides these colors and patterns, there were two promotional colors—Reagan Red, the favorite hue of the first lady, and Winter White, a calm relief from the frenetic designs and bold palette so much in evidence.

By far, however, the most widely used material in 1981 fashion was leather—made pliable and feminine in brilliant colorations of elegantly soft and drapable skins. Kidskin and suede were draped, gathered, tucked, and shaped into the most romantic ruffled blouses and into pantaloons and prairie dresses, as well as such items as camisoles, shorts, T-shirts, and tunics. Leathers—gilded, printed, embossed, perforated, appliquéd, and embroidered—embellished the fashion scene with sophistication and glamour. No collection was complete without a substantial leather grouping.

Accessories. To compete with the strong fashion silhouette, accessories were bold and brazen. Shawls or their counterparts—ponchos, ruanas, and serapes—were the number one item in this category. Touted as the "big wrap-up," these mini-blankets were guaranteed to give this year's look to last year's clothes. In brightly colored mohairs or wool plaids, in challis paisleys or stripes, and in folkloric patterns of silk and wool, they were draped over dresses, suits, coats, and capes for instant achievement of the audacious look of the 1980s.

Next in importance were belts. Wide obis, cummerbunds, and sashes of leather or suede, or bejeweled metallic cinches of American or Middle Eastern design, controlled the flyaway silhouette.

Pierre Vauthey/Sygma

Interest in the look of precious metals carried over into clothing in 1981. The combination of baggy, silver metallic pants, topped by a black box jacket (right), was a guaranteed showstopper. Another color combination featuring the metallic look, black with gold, was nearly obligatory in the fall fashion shows.

Courtesy Saks Fifth Avenue

In fashion's promotion of the ethnic costumed look, traditional gypsy dress was a designer source.

Bertrand Laforet/Gamma-Liaison

Shawls of many sizes, shapes, patterns, and fabrics were a must, adding dash to the feminine wardrobe.

Jewelry was dazzling and distinctive with primitive overtones. Wide cuff-type bracelets, huge chunky necklaces, and oversized dangle earrings provided an ethnic sense. Hammered and textured metals studded with semiprecious or frankly fake "gems," marble-sized wooden or acrylic beads, heavy chains, and rigid sculptured chokers were dramatic complements to costumes.

Quality was epitomized in footwear, which had a refinement and delicacy the other accessories lacked. The boots seen most often in all the major collections were the wafer-heeled crushed boot in rich earth-tone suedes or the highly polished leather riding boot in basic black, brown, or burgundy. The major shoe shape was the classic mid-height pump with a tapered toe and shaped heel. The treatment of the pump was anything but basic, however. Created from rich velvety suedes, high-gloss calfskin, or alligator, snakeskin, or lizard, it was embellished with a bow or cockade, decorated with contrast piping or appliqué, stitched in patterns or trapunto detailing, or highlighted with metallic touches.

Hats were a wide brimmed poet's fedora or its cavalier version with plume, close fitting turbans, helmets, or fur toques à la Russe.

The look of gold in accessories and trims was still important, but its luster took on a more burnished or antique tone. Its competition was other metallics such as copper, bronze, and pewter that likewise became important fashion accents.

Emphasized Apparel. Pants were in. Full and gathered, pleated, or tucked, there were culottes, split skirts, sweat pants, jodhpurs, knickers, harem pants, dhotis, and palazzo pajamas. All were of sensuous and luxurious fabrics and leathers.

Furs made a spectacular comeback this year after a decade of keeping a low profile. The richest and rarest pelts were fashioned into exciting and extravagant coats and jackets. Sable, fitch, fox, beaver, and nutria joined mink, raccoon, and broadtail for an incredible parade of opulence. The coats and jackets, as voluminous as their cloth counterparts, featured furs worked in checkerboard, striped, or herringbone patterns, dyed and patched into mosaics, sheared to velvet

Courtesy Saks Fifth Avenue

Leather, 1981's favorite material, is used here in knee-length pants, tunic, and suede crushed boots.

Marc Bulka/Gamma-Liaison

In a year of opulence and extravagance, rich and rare fur coats and jackets made a comeback.

thinness, or feathered. Many were trimmed in gold braid or appliquéd with leather and fabric.

Menswear. While menswear did not reflect the obvious costumed look of clothes for women, there was a distinct sense of quality, formality, and elegance. There were few casual looks; the emphasis was on refined dressing in the classic mode. The suit had a natural shoulder line and comfortably followed the body's form. Jackets were longer and leaner with side vents, and trousers were less baggy, tapering from the hips to the cuff. Fabrics were traditional, but new colorations included pastel-toned tweeds and unusual English country checks.

Dress shirts were styled with short, narrow collars, French cuffs, and a square body cut in white or soft pastels. Shirt patterns were subtle stripes or plaids, often with contrasting white collars and cuffs. The ties were in paisley, regimental striped patterns, or had club motifs.

Vests reappeared with suits, either in the same fabric or in a knit of Fair Isle or Argyll patterning or in one of the pastels which were the accent colors in menswear this year.

What leisure wear there was had the same elements of quality and style as the more formal dress, and in this category leather and suede were important. Used for jackets, tops, and trousers, they were anything but knockabout.

Accessories for men included cashmere or silk scarves, fine leather wallets and briefcases, the digital watch with gold-link bracelet, dress socks color-matched to the suit, a breast pocket handkerchief, and shoes of suede or polished calf with refined and subtle detailing.

After six, the tuxedo or a dinner suit complete with tucked shirt, cummerbund or vest, and patent leather pumps were *de rigueur* for a night on the town.

It remained to be seen whether the exaggerated looks of 1981, with their correspondingly high prices, would survive. At year's end, there was already a tendency on the part of fashion designers to draw back from this excess. Periodic aberrations in fashion, as in nature, are needed, if only to clear the landscape.

ANN ELKINS
"Good Housekeeping Magazine"

FINLAND

Urho K. Kekkonen resigned as president of Finland on October 27, having completed 25 years in the position. President Kekkonen, 81, had for some time been suffering from a disturbance of the blood supply to the brain. Following a fishing trip to Iceland in August, he went on medical leave on September 11. His contributions to stability in Northern Europe were recognized in June when he was awarded the Peace Prize of the Ralph Bunche Institute in New York City. The award was given for "his historic achievements for democracy, self-determination, and fundamental liberties." Kekkonen had also received the Lenin Prize and the Dimitrov Prize in 1981.

In accordance with the Constitution, Prime Minister Mauno Koivisto took over as acting president and Eino Uusitalo became acting prime minister. A Social Democrat, Koivisto, 57, had managed to keep his cabinet in office for what in Finland is a very long period. Elections were scheduled for Jan. 17–18, 1982, and the new president, who would serve until February 1988, would be sworn in on January 27.

A Gallup Poll taken in February and March showed that the Koivisto government was growing in popularity. No less than 66% of those interviewed said they were satisfied with the government.

In May, 5.1% of the labor force was out of work, a figure that is very high in a Scandinavian country. By midsummer, the unemployment situation had improved somewhat over 1980, and it was expected that the trend would continue. Many industries, however, suffered an acute labor shortage.

Foreign Affairs. A Finnish government early in the year received a request from Egypt for the Finns to participate in a peacekeeping force in the Sinai when Israel withdraws its troops in the spring of 1982. The request, however, was rejected. Foreign Minister Paavo Väyrynen noted that Finland "cannot take part in other peacekeeping actions than those carried out under the direction of the United Nations."

President Leonid Brezhnev of the Soviet Union in June let it be known that he was in favor of a nuclear weapons-free zone to cover the Nordic countries. Foreign Minister Väyrynen responded that such a proposal would be studied with deep interest. At a meeting of foreign ministers from Denmark, Finland, Norway, Iceland, and Sweden, held in Copenhagen in early September, only Finland voiced interest in a convention that would only confirm the status quo. The ministers agreed, however, to study the proposal.

The feeling in Scandinavia was that any such nuclear weapons-free zone (actually, all of Scandinavia, including Finland, is already a nuclear weapons-free zone) should include parts of the Soviet Union, such as the Kola peninsula and the Soviet territorial sea in the Baltic. There was a feeling that such a zone might become viable only in a European setting. A subsequent statement by Soviet leaders to the effect that no parts of their territories would be included in such a zone, combined with opposition from the United States, put the entire project in a political limbo.

ERIK J. FRIIS
The Scandinavian-American Bulletin

FINLAND • Information Highlights

Official Name: Republic of Finland.
Location: Northern Europe.
Area: 130,129 sq mi (337 034 km^2).
Population (1981 est.): 4,800,000
Chief City (1978 est.): Helsinki, the capital, 483,157.
Government: *Head of state,* Mauno Koivisto, acting president. *Head of government,* Eino Uusitalo, acting prime minister. *Legislature* (unicameral)—Eduskunta.
Monetary Unit: Markka or Finnish mark (4.46 markkaa equal U.S.$1, Nov. 1981).
Manufactures (major products): Timber and forest products, machinery, ships, clothing, transportation equipment, appliances.
Agriculture (major products): Dairy products, wheat and other grains, livestock products.

FLORIDA

Issues relating to taxes, growth, and the refugee influx dominated the news in 1981.

Tax Revolt. Although a study of 1978–79 taxes by the U.S. Bureau of the Census revealed that Florida ranked 42d in state and local tax collection per $1,000 personal income, a Proposition 13-type tax revolt appeared in some areas of Florida. Howard Jarvis, who led the 1978 movement in California, was in Florida advising citizen groups. The anti-tax mood convinced legislators to defeat Gov. Bob Graham's request for tax increases to better fund education, highway construction, and law enforcement. Fortunately, higher than expected sales tax collections funded some increases in these programs. Some legislators believe a sales tax increase may become necessary if federal grants substantially decrease.

Local governments took the brunt of the attacks, which were directed against property taxes. Because of the elimination of some state funds which previously went to local government, President Ronald Reagan's deep cuts in CETA and other grant programs, and the higher homestead exemption, local government revenues dropped sharply in some areas, forcing increases in property taxes, one of the few sources of revenue for local government. News of higher property taxes brought thousands of taxpayers to county commission meetings in Broward, Dade, Manatee, and Pinellas counties. Taxpayers were angry because even though the homestead exemption had risen from $5,000 to $20,000 over a two-year period, the assessment rate, previously at 60–70%, was now at 100% of market value. Intimidated officials abandoned most tax increases and cut services.

Growth. The financial problems of local governments were in part the result of rapid growth.

UPI

A large sinkhole, a property-swallowing land subsidence, caved in May in Winter Park, FL.

Of the 25 fastest growing metropolitan areas identified by the 1980 U.S. census, ten were in Florida. By comparison, Texas was second with only five. Providing services for this expanding population, often with money borrowed at the current exorbitant interest rates, contributed to the financial woes. Some local governments planned to seek relief from the state in the form of a local sales tax. The positive news about the growth was that the added population will give Florida four new seats in the U.S. House of Representatives.

Refugees. For Dade County (Miami) the financial problems have been multiplied by the influx of 140,000 or more Cuban and Haitian refugees during the past 18 months. Both the Carter and Reagan administrations refused to fund adequately the public costs resulting from the refugees. For example, Miami's public hospital anticipated a $9 million deficit directly attributable to refugee costs, and the county jail population was 17% above desirable capacity. Constant complaints from Governor Graham and Dade officials brought little response from the Reagan administration, except for a Coast Guard blockade to turn back Haitians.

Crime. The 1980 FBI report evoked increasing concern about crime. Six Florida cities were among the top ten cities with the most serious crime problems in the nation. Not too surprisingly, Miami had the highest crime rate in the nation. Miami officials blamed federal officials who have failed to assist Florida in suppressing drug-smuggling operations centered in south Florida or in handling the refugees who now make up a disproportionate percentage of the jail population. About one third of the homicides are drug-related, including daylight shootings by "cocaine cowboys." Gun sales to frightened citizens were up 46%.

Reagan administration cuts in the Coast Guard budget will reduce the already inadequate efforts to halt drug smuggling into Florida.

Environment. Floridians were reminded by the 1981 drought that water is a vital resource which is less abundant than it might superficially appear. For the first time ever, strict water rationing was imposed over all central and south Florida. Summer rains brought relief, but Lake Okeechobee, crucial to south Florida's water supply, was still dangerously low at year's end.

J. LARRY DURRENCE, *Florida Southern College*

FLORIDA • Information Highlights

Area: 58,664 sq mi (151 940 km^2).
Population (1980 census): 9,739,992.
Chief Cities (1980 census): Tallahassee, the capital, 81,548; Jacksonville, 540,898; Miami, 346,931; Tampa, 271,523; St. Petersburg, 236,893; Fort Lauderdale, 153,256; Hialeah, 145,254; Orlando, 128,394; Hollywood, 117,188; Miami Beach, 96,298.
Government (1981): *Chief Officers*—governor, Bob Graham (D); lt. gov., Wayne Mixson (D). *Legislature*—Senate, 40 members; House of Representatives, 120 members.
State Finances (fiscal year 1980): *Revenues*, $8,223,000,000; *expenditures*, $7,387,000,000.
Personal Income (1980): $88,675,000,000; per capita, $8,996.
Labor Force (July 1981): *Nonagricultural wage and salary earners*, 3,689,100; *unemployed*, 271,700 (6.5% of total force).

A California "swat team" seeks to control the Mediterranean fruit fly, an insect harmful to crops and found in the state in 1981, by the aerial spraying of Malathion.

David Strick/Black Star

FOOD

Throughout 1981 international tensions in different world locations overshadowed two basic needs of the world's people—food and energy. Although the supply of petroleum increased, its cost effect on the production, processing, storage, and transportation of food was little diminished. In developed countries, the food industry continued to initiate programs and research designed to reduce energy or petroleum costs. Several large U.S. food firms reported dramatic savings through the use of recycled waste heat, fluids or waste products, computer controlled lighting and heating systems, and modification of production schedules.

World Food Supply. Feeding the current world's population of some 4,500,000,000 is an enormous task, one that is compounded by weather, politics, distribution systems, and money. Currently, it is estimated that up to one half of the world's population is marginally fed, and about one eighth does not receive an adequate supply of food. World food needs are growing. It is forecast that world food need in 1985 will be 44% greater than that needed in 1970.

Within the Communist bloc, food production and distribution in 1981 made the headlines. In southern Russia and the Ukraine, record high temperatures and heavy rains at harvest time combined to reduce crop yields. Further, the weather vagaries caused unusual maturation of crops, resulting in the need to harvest grain, corn, soybeans, and barley all at once. Lack of machinery and mismanagement resulted in lowered harvests. As a result grain production in the USSR would be some 26% below the target of the 236 million t (260 million T) in the current Soviet Five-Year Plan. The expected grain harvest of less than 175 million t (191 million T) would be the second lowest since 1976.

Soviet planners seemed intent on buying grain to ensure bread for the people and feed for livestock. Evidence of this intent was the October-announced purchase of 23 million t (25.3 million T) of U.S. grains over a 12-month period. U.S. sales to the Soviets had been lower than expected due to the ban resulting from the Soviet invasion of Afghanistan. Offsetting the lowered U.S. sales were Soviet grain contracts with Argentina, Canada, and Australia for more than 50 million t (55 million T) in the next five years. Indicative of livestock production problems in the USSR was a five-year agreement for Argentina to supply 60 000–1 000 000 t (66,-000–1,100,000 T) of meat annually to the Soviet Union.

Food shortages in other Communist bloc nations resulted in strikes by labor unions in Poland and in the replacement of cabinet members in Rumania. Although weather affected other world growing areas, preliminary estimates of food production tonnages seemed to indicate no drastic problems. U.S. farmers, while beset with early drought and late rains, still produced the biggest wheat and corn crops in history. Other areas of the world, with the exception of China where rains and floods may have lowered crop harvests, expected to produce near normal crops.

Future Outlook. Conferences on world hunger and population growth focused on developments in the next 20 years. While birth rates in some countries are dropping, it is forecast that the world's population will increase by 50% to nearly 6,000,000,000 in the year 2000, with the largest increases in developing countries. Although food from grains is expected to rise adequately in the next 20 years, population increases may partially negate this increase. In total food production, forecasts indicate that Asia and Africa will not meet required consumption needs. Of necessity, solutions will be multifaceted.

U.S. Food Supply. While 1981 served up various forms of unwanted weather such as drought and heavy rains, the U.S. crop of essential grains was huge. Of more importance was the partial embargo on grain sales to the USSR (later lifted) which reduced exports. The supply situation was more uncertain than in previous years.

During 1981, a renewed threat to U.S. agriculture appeared in the form of a destructive insect called the "Medfly." The Mediterranean fruit fly, which attacks 253 different species of fruits, nuts, and vegetables, was found in California in early summer. In both a technological and political battle to control the fly, millions of dollars of produce were at stake. Embargoes on California products were threatened by various Southern states and foreign countries. The Medfly threat to California led to widespread aerial spraying with Malathion, a chemical eradicator.

Nutrition. Budget reductions by the Reagan administration have caused and are causing many changes in the social programs of the U.S. Department of Agriculture (USDA). Suggested changes in the school lunch program sparked controversy over a proposal to permit smaller portions and some substitutions—nuts and bean curd for meat, for example—to meet budget cuts. Other proposed changes included lowering of the maximum family income for free-lunch eligibility, ending of school food service equipment reimbursements, and a two-thirds reduction in funding for the Nutrition Education Program. In other actions, wide ranging changes in the Food Stamp program relating to income limits, school lunch duplication, block nutrition grants, and commodity distribution programs were proposed. Expected changes in other programs, including the Aid to Families with Dependent Children, would cut the budget by $1,100,000,000, and directly affect an estimated 680,000 families. The Women, Infants, and Children Program (WIC), which provides supplemental food for 2.2 million mothers and their small children, is similarly affected through maximum income reduction.

The U.S. Food Industry. Inflation, which slowed in 1981, still affected the U.S. food industry. Although consumer buying showed slight changes in food preferences, the industry reacted in new and different ways. The cost of feed grains altered the amount of grain-fed beef coming to market, and, as well, slightly lowered the total number of animals produced for slaughter. In other food groups, prices rose at a slow pace, primarily due to adequate stocks.

Within the food industry itself, it was expected that overseas sales of U.S. agricultural goods should reach about $48,500,000,000 in 1981, an increase of 20% over 1980. While feed grains and wheat sales were expected to rise, soybeans and vegetable oils would be lower. Overall, food exports would be more than double the cost of imports.

In 1981, concern in the food industry was linked to regulatory actions, nutrition, new products, processes, and markets, and application of advanced technology to agriculture. In the regulatory area, artificial sweeteners commanded attention. While the Congress' two-year moratorium applied to a Food and Drug Administration (FDA) ban of saccharin was due to expire on June 30, the Senate passed and sent on to the House a two-year extension. The FDA indicated that it would take no action against saccharin during the legislative period. In another action, the FDA approved aspartame, an artificial sweetener for use as a tabletop sweetener in cereals, chewing gum, dry base beverages, instant coffee and tea, dairy products, puddings, and the like.

Technically speaking, the food industry has introduced or is applying to food many recent scientific advances. New to the American scene is the retort pouch. Initially designed to improve the Army field ration, the pouch is a "flexible can," containing a one serving entree. Easily heated, it provides a nutritious, high-quality, lightweight entree. The pouch is in distribution in Europe, Japan, and Canada. Now, several large companies (Kraft, ITT Continental Kitchens) are test marketing various products. The pouch is flexible and made of three layers of material (polyester, foil, polypropylene). In the United States, the year 1981 saw an estimated 25–35 million pouches go to retail and 80–90 million to the military. In another packaging development, the so-called "two-piece can" was beginning to appear on the market for certain foods. Equal in cost to three-piece cans (top, body, bottom) it reduces inspection costs and aids in the trend toward lower lead content of foods.

KIRBY M. HAYES, *University of Massachusetts*

FORESTRY

The primary challenge for forestry management in the 1980s is to meet the growing demands for forest products, services, and amenities, as the nation's forest base declines. Professional foresters addressed this challenge in 1981 by continuing to explore ways to increase forest productivity by way of modern silvicultural methods and by advancing the public process of long-range forest planning.

Forests provide many essential products and services. The most familiar of these is timber, which is needed for construction, pulp and paper production, and the manufacture of wood products. Increasingly, wood is also in demand as a fuel for industrial as well as home heating uses. Overall, the demand for timber is projected to more than double during the next half century, from 13,300,000,000 cubic feet (376 613 440 m^3) to 28,300,000,000 cubic feet (801 365 440 m^3). Yet timber is not the only important output of forests. They also provide recreation, range, wilderness, wildlife areas, fish, and mineral values, for which demand is also growing. In addition, forests play an integral part in protecting water quality and influencing water runoff. With water consumption demands expected to increase 80% between 1975 and 2000, man will rely more than ever on the watersheds provided by forestlands. Some of these forest uses are mutually compatible, but others conflict. For example, timber production may enhance recreational use of the forest by providing access to recreational sites by way of logging roads, but logging by such methods as clearcutting is quite incompatible with the goal of wilderness preservation. In the face of these growing, sometimes conflicting, demands, the amount of forestland has been steadily declining for more than a decade. From 1970 to 1977, an average of 1.7 million acres (687 966 ha) was lost each year as forests were converted for such uses as agriculture, urban expansion, and energy development. This pattern of decline is expected to continue for the next half century as competing land uses encroach on the forest base. Furthermore, there is now almost no virgin forestland left.

In Colorado (photo), timber harvesting is limited to selected areas so as to conserve the resource.

Tom Stack

Until the 1960s, when the last "old growth" stands in the West began to be depleted, the logging industry had moved from one region of the United States to another. When the virgin timber had been removed from one area, the loggers simply migrated elsewhere. Since this is no longer possible, future demands for timber and for other forest outputs will have to be met by increasing productivity of the shrinking forest base.

Modern forestry has evolved to increase forest production by managing the process of regrowth, rather than leaving the forest to regenerate naturally. Silvicultural methods, such as site preparation and replanting, forest fertilization, genetic improvement of tree species, and crop thinning, contribute to improving the quality and quantity of timber produced. Forest managers also work to protect forest crops from damage during their long growing cycles through systematic programs of fire prevention and control and insect and disease protection.

Even increased forest productivity, however, will not fully resolve the growing conflicts over resource use. The forestry community increasingly recognizes the need for broad-scale planning to allocate the forest resources for multiple use. A major development in this direction was the passage of the Forest and Rangeland Renewable Resources Planning Act (RPA) of 1974. This legislation calls for the U.S. Forest Service to assess every ten years the nation's needs for the products, services, and amenities that could be provided by the nation's forestlands. This assessment would serve as the basis for a program plan, updated every five years, that would focus on that portion of the demand for forest outputs which can be provided by national forests. Although an initial round of the process was completed in 1975, the first full-scale effort under RPA was completed in 1980.

KAREN ELISE PARSONS

FRANCE

While there had been no really major political changes in France since Gen. Charles de Gaulle returned to power in 1958 and founded the Fifth Republic, 1981 marked an entirely new orientation. A left-wing president was elected, and in the National Assembly a Gaullist and center-right majority was replaced by a Socialist one. The new leaders undertook a number of reforms—such as decentralization, nationalization of the leading companies, and abolishment of the death penalty—but they were faced with the continuation, even the aggravation, of the country's economic problems.

DOMESTIC AFFAIRS

Preparations for the spring presidential elections occupied the first months of 1981. Three candidates seemed to have a chance to win—incumbent President Valéry Giscard d'Estaing; Jacques Chirac, the mayor of Paris and the leader of the Gaullist Party; and Socialist François Mitterrand, who was running for the third time and who had chosen as his slogan "the quiet force." (*See* BIOGRAPHY.) Just as Giscard was expected to be hampered by Chirac's candidacy, so many thought that Mitterrand would be handicapped by left-wing rival Georges Marchais, the leader of the Communist Party.

The first round in France's two-part presidential election process was conducted April 26, with no less than ten candidates on the ballot. Giscard obtained 28.3% of the vote, Mitterrand 25.8%, Chirac 18%, and Marchais a mere 15.4%. Before the second round of balloting on May 10, Marchais invited the Communists to support Mitterrand, but Chirac asked his voters not to. The size of Mitterrand's victory—51.75% to 48.25% for Giscard—came as a surprise.

President Mitterrand immediately chose as prime minister a moderate Socialist leader, Pierre Mauroy, 52, who formed a cabinet made up almost entirely of members of his own party. Another one of Mitterrand's first acts was to dissolve the National Assembly, in which center-right forces hostile to his policy held a majority. Legislative elections on June 14 and 21 confirmed the success of the Socialists. The party secured a majority in the Assembly, with 285 deputies out of the total of 491. Mitterrand, himself elected for seven years, thus had a green light to govern on his own terms for at least five years. The defeated parties were, of course, the Gaullist Rassemblement pour la République (RPR), Giscard's Union pour la Démocratie Francaise (UDF), and especially the Communists, whose representation dropped from 86 to 44 seats. Another new cabinet, however, formed by Pierre Mauroy after the parliamentary elections, included four Communists; it was the first time since 1947 that Communists participated in a French government.

Mitterrand seemed in a hurry to put into effect the program of changes he had promised during his campaign. Among the reforms was the important project of government decentralization and regionalization presented by Home Minister Gaston Defferre and passed (329-129) in September by the National Assembly. This program, which dismantled the old Napoleonic system, transferred the powers of Paris-appointed departmental prefects in France to elected regional councils. In overseas departments and territories, the Socialist success had generally been received with hope by supporters of autonomy and independence, but the new Cabinet did not hasten to bring drastic changes. Problems arose in New Caledonia, where Pierre Declercq, secretary-general of the Caledonian Union, the largest pro-independence party, was assassinated on September 19, causing tension between Europeans and Melanesian inhabitants, known as Kanuks.

In metropolitan France, the political life was quieter than usual during the summer. Opinion polls indicated that the "state of grace" had not ended for Mitterrand and that Mauroy was even more popular. Knocked down by their defeat, the former majority parties nursed their wounds and did not say much. But after Mauroy's declaration of policy at the National Assembly on September 15 and Mitterrand's first press conference on September 24, the opposition leaders began to voice severe criticisms, especially of inconsistencies in economic policy.

Economy. As a candidate, Mitterrand had strongly insisted upon the economic reforms proposed by the Socialist Party. The main objectives were to lower unemployment and to redistribute wealth more equitably. As early as June, the new cabinet announced a 10% raise in the minimum wage, a 20% increase in allowances for the aged and handicapped, and a 25% increase in family and housing allowances. All salaried workers would receive a fifth week of paid vacation. A committee composed of employer and trade union leaders would draft a plan for a progressive shortening of the work week to 35 hours by the end of 1985. Some 54,000 new public jobs were to be created, and the state would encourage the hiring of young and unskilled workers by partially exempting employers from social charges. There would be a tax increase on the 108,000 highest incomes and on company expense accounts.

The cabinet had hoped that raising lower incomes would spur economic activity, but results were somewhat disappointing. A high rate of inflation (more than 14%) tended to offset the effects of the raises in income. And lack of confidence in the Socialist government by businessmen inside and outside France had caused the franc to tumble on most exchanges as soon as Mitterrand was elected. The unavoidable devaluation, called a "realignment" to save face,

(continued on page 222)

France Goes to the Polls

In two rounds of balloting, April 26 and May 10, French voters went to the polls to select a president for the next seven years. In the first round, a field of ten candidates was reduced to two—incumbent Valéry Giscard d'Estaing of the Union for French Democracy (UDF) and François Mitterrand of the Socialist Party. This automatically pitted them in the second-round runoff, a repeat of their 1974 confrontation. The balloting was expected to be close, but the approximately 30 million voters gave Mitterrand a 52%–48% victory, solid by French standards.

Gamma/Liaison

Jacques Chirac, leader of the Gaullist party, finished a strong third in the first round of voting.

Laurent Maous, Gamma/Liaison

Gamma/Liaison

The last week of campaigning between Giscard and Mitterrand included a televised debate, above. Neither candidate was seen as gaining an advantage. Right, Giscard waits to cast his ballot at town hall in Chanonat, in central France.

Gamma/Liaison

President Mitterrand takes the traditional inaugural drive up the Champs-Elysées in Paris.

A.F.P. Photo/UPI

occurred on October 4. After discussions with European partners, it was decided that the franc would be devaluated 3% against the European "snake" and 8.5% against the almighty West German mark. Simultaneously, Finance Minister Jacques Delors announced measures designed to hold 1982 inflation to 10%—freezing of food and service prices, a reduction in government spending, and a suggestion to limit wage increases (except for lower wage earners). But just a few days before, on September 30, the 1982 budget had been adopted by the cabinet. It provided for a 27.6% increase in state expenditures and for a record deficit of more than 95,000,000,000 francs.

Nationalization. An important and very controversial part of the Socialist campaign platform had been the program of nationalization. Opponents maintained that a heavily state-controlled economy had failed whenever it had been tried in the past. But President Mitterrand again moved to keep the promises he had made as a candidate. On September 9 the cabinet approved legislation roughly in accordance with the Socialist program. Five leading industrial companies and two major financial groups were to be nationalized, and the state would take over 51% ownership of two other big companies. Also to be taken over were 36 of France's most important banks, which would leave 95% of all deposits under state control. The opposition led a hard battle against the draft.

Nuclear Energy. There were also heated discussions, both before and after the election campaign, about the heavy program of nuclear plant construction developed by the Giscard government. In order to secure the support of ecologists in the June elections, the Socialists had emphasized the need for a great national debate on the issue and had declared themselves in favor of stopping, or at least postponing, the construction of nuclear power plants already under way. Once in power and faced with meeting the nation's energy needs, however, the Socialists had to adopt more realistic views. A highly controversial nuclear facility planned for Plogoff in Britanny was abandoned, but the cabinet decided to go ahead with six out of nine others and to enlarge the La Hague plant for recycling irradiated combustibles. The government's energy plan, adopted by the National Assembly on October 8, ended up being a great source of bitterness for the ecologists.

Justice and Criminality. Before his election, Mitterrand had said that he would abolish the death penalty, which was still in use. One of the first tasks of Justice Minister Robert Badinter, a well-known barrister, was to prepare a bill for the abolishment of the famous guillotine. The bill was approved by a large majority of the National Assembly on October 18. On July 29, the Assembly already had voted to suppress the State Security Court, created in 1963 and considered by the left to be a threat to civil liberties. These measures were accompanied by a sweeping amnesty after Mitterrand's election, which, together with the traditional presidential clemencies granted on Bastille Day, liberated more than one out of seven inmates from France's overpopulated prisons.

Mitterrand's generosity did not, however, result in a decrease in violence, evidenced in particular by a criminal affair which made headlines during the summer. On July 18 police inspector Jacques Massie and five members of his family were killed at Auriol, near Marseille in southern France. It quickly appeared that the mass murder had been executed by a commando of the SAC (Service of Civic Action), a right-wing political protection organization.

Social Rights. The Socialists had placed great emphasis on their plan to change society by giving more rights to certain segments of the population. Under the previous government, loud protests had been made against the expulsion of immigrants. Most often, the immigrants came from North Africa and worked clandestinely for very low wages. At the end of May, the new home minister halted the expulsions of foreigners, and in August invited all illegal immigrants and their employers to regularize their status.

Labor unions, meanwhile, were demanding reinforcement of the rights of workers. At the beginning of October, Labor Minister Jean Auroux presented proposals in this connection but, due to the high unemployment rate and the economic difficulties of a good number of companies, the program was less audacious than some had hoped. Strikes developed late in the year, especially in previously nationalized companies.

Culture and Communication. The literary best-seller of the summer in France was a new "translation" of 16th-century astrologer Nostradamus' prophecies, according to which there are gloomy prospects for the end of the 20th century. The unprecedented success of such a book seemed to indicate that the French were not especially optimistic about their future. However, in the areas of art and literature, they were promised great changes for the better by the new

FRANCE • Information Highlights

Official Name: French Republic.
Location: Western Europe.
Area: 211,207 sq mi (547 026 km^2).
Population (1981 est.): 53,900,000.
Chief Cities (1975 census): Paris, the capital, 2,299,830; Marseille, 908,600; Lyon, 456,716; Toulouse, 373,796.
Government: *Head of state,* François Mitterrand, president (took office May 1981). *Chief minister,* Pierre Mauroy, prime minister (took office May 1981). *Legislature*—Parliament: Senate and National Assembly.
Monetary Unit: Franc (5.67 francs equal U.S.$1, Nov. 1981).
Manufactures (major products): Chemicals, automobiles, processed foods, iron and steel, aircraft, textiles, clothing.
Agriculture (major products): Cereals, feed grains, livestock and dairy products, wine, fruits, vegetables.

The last 50 French nationals to leave Iran arrive in Paris on August 12. The French government, citing the threat of "uncontrollable actions," had urged its citizens to leave that country August 5. The next day, the Iranian government denied a group, including the ambassador, permission to leave.

Jérôme Chatin/Gamma-Liaison

culture minister, Jack Lang, 42, an imaginative and active man, passionately fond of theater. For the average Frenchman, however, the most perceptible changes in connection with culture did not come from Jack Lang's ministry, since they affected television and radio. All the managers and journalists suspected of being favorable to the former government were replaced by people well-disposed toward the new leadership. The reaction of the press was diverse, many saying that the Socialists were doing what they had always criticized. A draft bill designed to legalize private radio stations, which had proliferated during the first months of the year, was less liberal than anticipated—advertising would be forbidden and the broadcasting stations would have only very limited range. The proposal was the subject of harsh discussions in parliament during the month of September.

FOREIGN POLICY

The political changes in France provoked uneasiness in many foreign capitals. As soon as he took charge, Mitterrand reaffirmed that he was an Atlanticist, even if he did not contemplate the return of France to NATO's integrated military command. He also made clear his intention to maintain the independent French nuclear force and said he was opposed to a significant reduction in defense expenditures. He told West German Chancellor Helmut Schmidt in July that close Franco-German relations would go on despite the departure of Giscard.

The new French leadership denounced the Soviet menace in Afghanistan and Poland, and supported NATO's decision to deploy U.S. medium-range nuclear missiles on Western European soil to counteract the buildup of Soviet SS-20 missiles in Eastern Europe. This firm attitude toward the USSR was of course well received in Washington.

Other aspects of the new French policy, however, were less gratifying to the United States. At the beginning of July, Foreign Minister Claude Cheysson visited Central America, where he affirmed that France was in favor of allowing each people in the area to decide freely its own destiny. On August 28, France and Mexico published a joint declaration recognizing as a legitimate political force the guerrilla opposition forces in El Salvador. On a state visit to Mexico, October 20–21, Mitterrand made a clear reference to El Salvador in a solemn speech devoted to the protection of human rights. With regard to Third World economic problems, the French president stressed the need to redress inequities between rich and poor countries. He had an opportunity to express his views to U.S. President Ronald Reagan when they met on October 18–19 to commemorate the Franco-American victory in the 1781 Battle of Yorktown.

In the Middle East, the new French policy was very quickly tested. Mitterrand did not hesitate to assert his deep personal sympathy for Israel, a country with which his predecessor maintained poor relations. But, at the same time, Mitterrand favored the establishment of a Palestinian homeland. On June 7, Israel attacked and destroyed a French-built nuclear reactor near Baghdad, an act vigorously condemned by France. At the end of August, Foreign Minister Cheysson visited Jordan, Lebanon, and Syria, reaffirming France's position on the Palestinian problem. In Beirut he met with the Palestine Liberation Organization (PLO) leader Yasir Arafat, provoking acerbic criticism by Israel. A few days later, on September 4, the French ambassador in Beirut, Louis Delamare, was assassinated. In late September, Mitterrand went to Saudi Arabia on an official state visit, where he expressed interest in Prince Fahd's peace plan.

MONIQUE MADIER, *French Writer and Editor*

GAMBLING

Legalized gambling in the United States has expanded substantially over the past decade. In 1981, some form of gambling was legal in 46 of the 50 states, and 33 allowed some type of gambling other than bingo. The number of states with a lottery or government-run "numbers game" increased from two in 1970 to 16 in 1981; total lottery-ticket sales exeeded $2,000,000,000, with player losses amounting to about half that amount. Pari-mutuel horse racing is presently sanctioned in 30 states, and total wagering now exceeds $9,000,000,000 per year, of which $1,500,000,000 is lost by bettors. Pari-mutuel dog racing expanded its legal presence from seven to 13 states during the 1970s, and total wagering increased from $730 million to $1,900,000,000; player losses were $300 million in 1979. State-sanctioned off-track betting, which did not exist until 1972, now can be found in four states; $1,500,000,000 was wagered in 1979, with player losses of $300 million.

The greatest growth in legal gambling, however, has occurred in the area of casino gambling. In 1970, casinos were legal only in the state of Nevada; that year casinos won $575 million from their patrons. In 1976, the voters of New Jersey approved the legalization of casinos in the declining resort community of Atlantic City. The first casino opened there in 1978, and by the end of 1980 six were in operation. Total casino winnings from Atlantic City patrons were $625 million in 1980, while Nevada casinos won $2,390,000,000. In 1981, three additional casinos opened in Atlantic City, and total winnings were expected to exceed $1,000,000,000. In Nevada, $2,500,000,000 in winnings were anticipated. Thus, as of 1981, casino gambling accounted for about half the total winnings from legalized gambling in the United States.

Construction continues along the Boardwalk in Atlantic City, NJ, now a center for legalized gambling.

Peter Gridley/FPG

The first half of 1981 was marked by considerable debate by a number of states on the advisability of legalizing casinos. In New York, where casino legislation must be passed by two consecutive sessions of the legislature, the 1980 session had passed a number of bills. Only one of them had to be passed in 1981 and then put before the voters for casinos to be legalized. But because of potential political liabilities, support from major public figures waned, and the legislature recessed without passing a casino bill. In Massachusetts, the legislature considered legalizing casinos in two townships, Hull and Adams. Both communities had voted favorably on nonbinding referendums but, mainly because of opposition from neighboring communities, a bill was not forthcoming from the 1981 legislature.

There are a number of arguments both for and against legalized casino gambling. Proponents claim that casinos create jobs and needed tax revenues at the state and local levels. Furthermore, as more states legalize casinos, those tourist and convention centers that do not have them might find themselves at a competitive disadvantage. Opponents of casino gambling, on the other hand, argue that legalization will bring to the community increases in crime, prostitution, loan sharking, and political corruption. The potential problems of compulsive gamblers and of infiltration by organized crime are also cited as significant reasons against widespread legalization of casinos.

The experiences in Nevada and Atlantic City support the arguments of both sides. In mid-1981, the tourist and gaming industry employed about 117,000 in Nevada and 30,000 in Atlantic City. Gross revenue from gaming taxes contributed about $130 million to Nevada's general fund in 1980; Atlantic City's 8% tax on gross winnings generated $50 million. In both places, however, there have also been serious problems. The regularity commissions in Nevada and New Jersey have both been hurt by scandals. In Atlantic City, there have been a number of mob-style killings allegedly linked to union operations in casinos, and the crime rate more than doubled between 1978 and 1980. Finally, increased land values and rapid population growth forced the displacement of many low-income, minority, and elderly residents.

William R. Eadington
University of Nevada, Reno

GARDENING AND HORTICULTURE

The Mediterranean fruit fly, an insect considerably smaller than the common housefly, was at the heart of a major confrontation between political and agricultural interests, and was a focus of the U.S. news media in 1981. Two infestations, the first since 1976, were found about 400 mi (644 km) apart in California in June 1980. Control measures, including stripping trees of fruit, ground-based spraying of the pesticide malathion, and the release of millions of sterile flies, were effected. The southern outbreak was controlled, but the Santa Clara Valley infestation remained active. An article in *California Agriculture* (vol. 35, nos. 3 and 4, March–April 1981) entitled "Mediterranean Fruit Fly: The Worst May Be Yet To Come" warned that its continued presence ten months after detection posed a very real threat to California agriculture. As of early July 1981, however, the state government was still rejecting aerial spraying, and the controversy grew. The U.S. Department of Agriculture (USDA) then announced a quarantine on California produce which, along with the imposition of a quarantine by 11 Southern states, would have been economically devastating. Aerial spraying was begun, but the infestation spread. On August 4, three flies were trapped in Tampa, FL, leading state officials to quarantine an area surrounding the city and to begin control measures. Later in August, the California infestation spread to the rich farmlands of the San Joaquin Valley. Growers began individual control measures, but Japan threatened to stop imports of fleshy fruits from California.

All-America Selections. Gardeners welcomed the announcement of the All-America Rose Selections for 1982: two hybrid teas, Brandy and Mon Chéri; a floribunda, French Lace; and a grandiflora, Shreveport, named after Shreveport, LA, home of The American Rose Center, the headquarters for many affiliated amateur rose societies.

The 1982 All-America Selections for annuals and vegetable plants include a tall double hybrid carnation, Scarlet Luminette; two zinnias, Small World Cherry, a dwarf, and Fantastic Light Pink, a giant-flowered type; Peter Pan hybrid scallop squash; and Jersey Golden Acorn, a squash which can be eaten fresh or stored for winter use.

New Cultivars and Plants. New cultivars of known plants reported in *Hortscience* through June 1981 included 20 vegetables, 25 fruits, and 9 ornamentals. Among breeding lines were 30 vegetables, 4 fruit rootstocks, and 2 hardy roses.

Each year, the Plant Introductions branch of the USDA distributes large numbers of domestic and introduced plant materials, including horticultural plants, to cooperators. In 1980, more than 15,000 plant introductions were distributed by the USDA's Beltsville, MD, office to research workers through appropriate curators.

Production and Sales. Figures from the Crop Reporting Board of the USDA showed that foliage plant sales, which dropped slightly in 1979, rose again in 1980; production was up by about 11%. Moderate increases were noted in production of bedding plants, geraniums, poinsettias, and gladioli, with reduced crops of hydrangeas, lilies, standard and sweetheart roses, standard carnations, and standard chrysanthemums. Prices increased on all crops surveyed but, with the exception of sweetheart roses, the price increases did not equal the inflation rate.

ASHS Meeting. The American Society for Horticultural Science held its annual meeting Aug. 9–14, 1981, in Atlanta, GA.

E. N. O'Rourke
Louisiana State University

GENETICS

The remarkable pace of discoveries and practical applications in the field of genetics continued and even quickened in 1981. Genetics became a household subject with expanded coverage of new research and huge investments in genetic engineering. Celebrated associations between private industry and higher education included a $50-million investment by Hoechst, a German firm, in recombinant DNA (deoxyribonucleic acid) research at Massachusetts General Hospital, affiliated with Harvard University; a $30-million arrangement between Johnson & Johnson and Scripps College in California; and venture-capital firms set up by faculty at several leading institutions. Disputes arose over priority and patents for new discoveries, and a leading researcher was penalized for violating rules of informed consent in his haste to try gene therapy in human subjects.

Cancer Genes. Cancers are triggered by cigarette smoking, chemicals, diet, heredity, viruses, and radiation. All begin with the transformation of a single normal cell into a tumor cell with altered biochemistry and altered surface characteristics. Researchers may have uncovered a final common pathway for tumorigenesis. The early clues came from studies of retroviruses, tiny RNA (ribonucleic acid) viruses that cause cancer in certain animals. When the retrovirus invades a cell, its RNA is converted into DNA, which is integrated into a host-cell chromosome. The malignant sarcoma virus in birds contains only four genes; one of them, *src*, codes for a protein that induces the sarcoma. It is thought that *src* and other virus oncogenes (tumor-causing genes) originate in animal cells. Something must happen to activate these proto-oncogenes for them to become transforming genes.

Robert Weinberg at the Massachusetts Institute of Technology (MIT) has shown that other stimuli can activate a proto-oncogene. Mouse fibroblasts were treated with the chemical carcinogen methylcholanthrene, and the DNA was extracted and introduced into normal mouse

UPI

Quarantines could not keep the Medfly infestation from spreading to rich California farmlands.

fibroblast cells. Some cells were transformed, and their DNA in turn could transform other cells. No virus was involved. Thus, DNA damaged by the chemical agent is itself carcinogenic. Next, the transforming DNA was treated with restriction enzymes, which cut it at specific sites. Analysis of the resulting DNA sequences showed that a single gene accounted for mouse cell transformation. Finally, DNA isolated from several kinds of spontaneous and chemically-induced tumors in mice, rabbits, and humans similarly transformed fibroblasts in the laboratory setting.

Biochemical studies show that *src* and a leukemia virus gene code for certain types of enzymes, which lead to alterations in metabolism, cell structure, and cell membranes.

Gene Structure and Expression. An ever more dynamic and complicated picture of the genetic material emerges from molecular studies of the organization and evolution of DNA in chromosomes. Plant, invertebrate, and vertebrate genes undergo increases in number and transposition in location. For example, genes that govern different portions of antibody molecules must rearrange in response to foreign substances (antigens) in order to make specific antibodies. A primordial globin gene has evolved, over about 500 million years, into two clusters of genes which code for the protein chains of hemoglobin in embryonic, fetal, and adult blood cells. The two clusters have been mapped to different human chromosomes (11 and 16). The five globin genes in the beta cluster are spread over a long stretch of DNA, of which they occupy only 8%.

Creation and Evolution. Arkansas in March and Louisiana in April enacted laws requiring that the Biblical account of creation be taught in public schools whenever a teacher mentions Charles Darwin or the theory of evolution. (*See* special report, page 434.) Meanwhile, public interest was stirred by a dispute in the paleoanthropological community over the fossil remains of *Australopithecus afarensis,* or "Lucy," uncovered by Dr. Donald Johanson in northern Ethiopia. (*See* feature article, page 43.)

Medfly. An infestation of Mediterranean fruit flies in California led to a controversy over the spraying of affected areas with the pesticide malathion. Opponents feared that the pesticide could cause birth defects or cancers. Scientific tests indicated, however, that exposure to the malathion created little or no danger. (*See also* GARDENING AND HORTICULTURE.)

GILBERT S. OMENN
University of Washington

GEOLOGY

During 1981 geologists were deeply involved with the practical problems of mineral shortages, the search for energy sources on continental shelves, shrinking underground water supplies, and the amelioration of earthquake and other hazards. The depletion of geologists through premature hirings of graduate students and the loss of competent teachers from university faculties caused concern. Attention was drawn away from mundane subjects by the astrogeological discoveries concerning faraway Saturn, which was photographed during a successful flyby by Voyager 2 on August 25.

Astrogeology. On Nov. 12, 1980, Voyager 1 passed within 78,100 mi (125 700 km) of the surface of Saturn and on Aug. 25, 1981, Voyager 2 came within 63,000 mi (101 300 km). Information from these missions extends the domain of geology 1,000,000,000 mi (1 600 000 000 km) into space. The United States Geological Survey has an official astrogeology branch, giving status to the study of solid bodies in space where geological processes are evident. At least eight of Saturn's numerous moons qualify as being solid and rocky if ice is admitted as a rock. In order outward, the geologically interesting moons are Mimas, Enceladus, Tethys, Dione, Rhea, Titan, Hyperion, and Phoebe. Voyager 2 got closer to Hyperion, Iapetus, Enceladus and Tethys than did Voyager 1.

Enceladus has been described as being simultaneously cratered, cracked, and smooth. Great faults cut the surface; forces necessary to cause movements may be supplied by gravitational pull of neighboring moons. Photos of Tethys reveal a giant crater 250 mi (400 km) in diameter and a crack-like canyon that extends three quarters of the distance around the satellite. Iapetus is notable in having its forward face about 15 times darker than its opposite hemisphere. Hyperion is being compared in shape to a hamburger patty; evidently internal gravity is not strong enough to force a spherical form. Far out Phoebe, only 130 mi (200 km) across, follows a steeply inclined retrograde orbit and may have been captured by Saturn's gravitational pull. Much of what is observed of Saturn's moons must result from the geological behavior of ice, not only of water but of methane and ammonia, that makes up much of their substance.

Education. Perhaps more than most sciences, geology is suffering from lack of balance in the production and utilization of new recruits. The search for energy sources by ever-increasing, well-financed companies has produced an excessive demand for qualified geologists that cannot be met by the current crop of graduates. New graduates, even those with only bachelor's degrees, are being hired at beginning salaries higher than those of professors who trained them. And professors are being lured away from classrooms and laboratories by salaries that cannot possibly be matched by already hard-pressed universities. Salaries of up to $100,000 are reported in the oil-related fields of stratigraphy, sedimentation, and structure. Continual weakening of university geology departments cannot fail to have serious effects on the profession. One college dean asked: "Who will teach the next generation of students our country [the United States] will desperately need as problems with energy and mineral resources and preservation of a healthy environment become even harder?"

A partial solution to the problem of disseminating new knowledge and technology to industry has been the institution of mini-courses, seminars, and field conferences. Such meetings are directed by qualified persons from industry and academic institutions, last a few days or weeks, and cost less than $1,000. The success of these intensified courses has been phenomenal; most commercial organizations are happy to give leave time and financial contributions to help keep their employees abreast of the times.

Gold. Geological processes govern the formation and distribution of gold deposits and the increasing price of the precious metal has stimulated search at all levels. Amateur prospectors, looking for nuggets and visible grains, are active everywhere and have made newsworthy discoveries. At the opposite extreme are massive mining operations that aim to recover invisible gold from material that has heretofore been valueless. The three major gold-producing states and their 1980 production are: South Dakota (280,000 troy ounces), Nevada (251,000 troy ounces), and Utah (190,000 troy ounces). Practically all of this production came from very low-grade ore taken from deep mines (South Dakota) or large open pits (Utah and Nevada). Nevada is the site of a veritable gold rush with geologists taking credit for the basic discoveries. The potential of a band of low-grade ore 250 mi (400 km) long and 100

Geologist Tony Irving inspects the steam vents (fumaroles) from which heat escaped after the eruption of Mount St. Helens in Washington in 1980.

UPI

mi (160 km) wide was discovered by routine mapping and is paying off in a big way. Mining companies spent $700 million to open 20 new mines during 1980. By 1983 sixteen more mines are expected to open.

Disasters. Geological violence was not so impressive as in 1980. Mount St. Helens quieted down after the eruption of May 18, 1980. Severe earthquakes shook Iran, Pakistan, and Peru.

Disaster in another quarter did not come to pass when predicted major earthquake activity in Peru did not occur. Brian Brady of the U.S. Bureau of Mines, Golden, CO, and William Spence of the Geological Survey, on the basis of elaborate calculations and experiments, had forcast a magnitude 7.5 to 8.0 quake for about June 28, one of 8.8 for August 10, and one of 9.5 for September 16. As these events successively failed to materialize, credence in the Brady-Spence theory lessened. In spite of attempts to reassure the Peruvians, many of those who could afford it arranged to be elsewhere on June 28.

Creeping disasters do not get attention until they are well advanced. A noteworthy example in the geologic domain is the depletion and pollution of groundwater resources. The Ogallala formation and associated sediments, constituting the most important aquifer system in the United States, is slowly being drained. It underlies about 177,000 sq mi (458 430 km^2) of the High Plains and has been pumped for irrigation water since shortly after World War II. There is no way it can be recharged, and once depleted it will be gone forever so far as human use is concerned. Pollution of aquifers by contaminants generated and concentrated by human activities also presents incurable situations. More than 30,000 dangerous waste disposal sites have been catalogued in the United States. Many of these are stagnant canals, landfills, sludge pits, and wells that drain directly into subsurface aquifers. Unlike organic pollutants that are removed by natural processes in soil and rock strata, there are dozens of inorganic substances that stay in solution indefinitely and can emerge to contaminate surface water at distant localities.

Drillings. Ever deeper drilling for scientific and economic purposes is accelerating. The deepest hole in the world, designated primarily for information, is on Kola Peninsula, near the Barents Sea, west of Murmansk, USSR. It was more than 35,371 ft (10 781 m) deep in May. The National Science Foundation combined the eminently successful Deep Sea Drilling Program (DSDP), which has been operating since 1968, with the Ocean Margin Drilling Program (OMDP). Since the ocean margins have great economic potential for oil and gas, it is hoped that the petroleum industry will make substantial financial contributions for experiments and exploration. A new alignment calls for retirement of DSDP's pioneer research vessel, the *Glomar Challenger,* in 1983 and its replacement by the *Glomar Explorer,* former CIA "spy" ship which has five times the carrying capacity of the *Challenger.* Operation costs of the *Challenger* are $25 million (1981 dollars) per year; corresponding costs for the *Explorer* will be $40 million.

Exploration of the Atlantic continental shelf has been very expensive and very disappointing. No commercial discoveries have been announced for the mid-Atlantic area off Atlantic City, NJ, where drilling commenced in March 1978. However, high hopes are held for Georges Bank, a shallow and geologically favorable area offshore of New England. With approval of the U.S. Geological Survey, Shell Oil Company and Exxon Corporation commenced drilling in July 1981. In spite of approval by a Biological Task Force, charged with assessing possible environmental damage to the important fishing grounds, local fishermen demonstrated their objection to the project.

Dinosaurs. More than mere petrified bones have been coming to light from 70-million-year-old Late Cretaceous formations near Choteau, north-central Montana. Paleontologist Donald Baird and colleagues from Princeton University unearthed not only the remains of adult duckbill dinosaurs but clutches of eggs and "nests" of juveniles in associations that reveal for the first time how dinosaurs probably behaved and survived the perils of growing up. Young dinosaurs are virtually absent in previously known major quarries and the question of how they managed to avoid being fossilized has been answered by assuming that they spent their time in upland areas and did not travel with the adults. This has become practically certain with the Montana finds.

From the fact that nestlings of the same size are found concentrated in "nests," it is assumed that they had adult care in the nest and did not leave it until fully able to fend for themselves. From the absence of specimens of intermediate size it is thought that the half-grown, sexually immature individuals left the area in company with adults and did not return until they were ready to produce and care for their own eggs and hatchlings.

The Princeton group also discovered the first carnivorous ornithischian dinosaur. Previously the entire ornithischian order was presumed to be herbivorous.

Celebrations. The period 1980–1990 has been designated officially as The Decade of North American Geology by the Geological Society of America. The aim is to make the "vast fund of information about the North American plate and its surroundings available to the broadest possible audience." Currently, 23 volumes of regional synthesis and probably 3 volumes summarizing the geology of North America are planned for publication by the end of the decade. In addition, many of the eight divisions, six sections, and eight associated societies are planning special volumes.

WILLIAM LEE STOKES, *University of Utah*

GEORGIA

Reapportionment, the state constitution, and crime dominated Georgia news.

Reapportionment. Prompted by population shifts identified in the 1980 census, the General Assembly met to devise a new alignment for congressional districts. Under the adopted plan most counties retain their basic configurations. The controversial portions of the plan concerned the redistricting of metropolitan Atlanta counties, which left Republicans and blacks dissatisfied. Republicans wanted a "suburban horseshoe" district encompassing the GOP strongholds north of the city. The legislature divided that area between the ninth and tenth districts, thereby diluting Republican concentration.

Led by Julian Bond, blacks pushed for a 69% black district in Atlanta. Redistricting left a 59% black area, which significantly lessens the chance for election of a minority congressman. Bond intended to present his alternate plan to the U.S. Justice Department, which has authority to review redistricting proposals.

Constitution. During the special session, legislators also wrote a new constitution which would be submitted to voters for approval in the 1982 general election. Changes include a property tax reduction for farm owners, tougher regulations for repeat crime offenders, and provision for a uniform judicial system. Deleted from the new document were local amendments and a public initiative amendment.

Politics. The Atlanta mayoral race ended in a runoff between former U.S. Ambassador to the UN Andrew Young and state Rep. Sidney Marcus, with Young the winner. Outgoing Mayor Maynard Jackson was mentioned as a successor to Vernon Jordan, who was retiring as Urban League president. A battle over chairmanship of the state Republican Party led to speculation of an ideological split. U.S. Sen. Mack Mattingly's handpicked candidate, Fred Cooper, defeated incumbent Matt Patton, who was more closely allied with Ronald Reagan's presidential campaign in Georgia.

General Assembly. Sponsors of the Equal Rights Amendment chose to wait until 1982 to push for state ratification. Gains were logged, however, when legislators supported women's rights by passing bills that enhance the dignity of homemakers, protect battered wives, and rid the lawbooks of some sexist language.

Environmentalists, too, received legislative support when Gov. George Busbee signed a bill taking control of hazardous waste disposal out of the private sector and making it a government responsibility.

Minorities did not fare so well. The Assembly defeated a bill that would have required one state agency to do 10% of its business with minority-owned firms.

Crime. The nation watched as Atlanta citizens anguished over the disappearance and murder of 28 young blacks. Wayne B. Williams, a free-lance photographer and record promotor, was arrested and charged in the slayings of two of the victims. (*See also* ATLANTA.)

Mike Keza/Gamma-Liaison

Andrew Young, former Congressman and U.S. ambassador to the UN, is elected mayor of Atlanta.

Carter and Associates. Former President Jimmy Carter and his wife, Rosalynn, returned to private life in Plains, GA, where they began writing their memoirs. An Atlanta site for the Carter library was proposed, but no decision regarding the location was announced.

Two former Carter associates appear to have state political ambitions. Max Cleland, former head of the Veterans Administration, expressed an interest in the office of secretary of state. Jack Watson, former Carter adviser, appeared to be preparing for the 1982 gubernatorial race.

Hamilton Jordan, chief of Carter's White House staff, became a visiting fellow in political science at Emory University.

KAY BECK, *Georgia State University*

GEORGIA • Information Highlights

Area: 58,910 sq mi (152 577 km^2).
Population (1980 census): 5,464,265.
Chief Cities (1980 census): Atlanta, the capital, 425,022; Columbus, 169,441; Savannah, 141,634; Macon, 116,860; Albany, 73,934; Augusta, 47,532; Athens, 42,549; Warner Robins, 39,893; Valdosta, 37,596; East Point, 37,486.
Government (1981): *Chief Officers*—governor, George D. Busbee (D); lt. gov., Zell Miller (D). *General Assembly*—Senate, 56 members; House of Representatives, 180 members.
State Finances (fiscal year 1980): *Revenues*, $5,194,-000,000; *expenditures*, $4,901,000,000.
Personal Income (1980): $44,217,000,000; per capita, $8,073.
Labor Force (July 1981): *Nonagricultural wage and salary earners*, 2,151,200; *unemployed*, 151,700 (6.2% of total force).

Regis Bossu, Sygma

On the last leg of a European diplomatic tour, U.S. Secretary of State Alexander Haig (center) met in mid-February with West German Chancellor Helmut Schmidt (right) and Foreign Minister Hans-Dietrich Genscher (left). Throughout the year, the two governments differed on several foreign policy and economic issues.

GERMANY

Relations between the Federal Republic of Germany (West Germany) and the German Democratic Republic (East Germany or DDR) remained stable in 1981. However, due to the tensions between East and West over Afghanistan, Poland, the arms race, and other issues, official contacts between the two states were few.

Occasionally each side signaled to the other its interest in closer relations. The DDR renewed its campaign for recognition as a wholly separate sovereign state and for the acknowledgment of a separate East German citizenship, but it later toned down these demands in the interest of rapprochement. The Federal Republic, in turn, stepped up its coal shipments to East Germany to help make up for Poland's inability to provide sufficient supplies.

In September it was announced that West German Chancellor Helmut Schmidt and Erich Honecker, East German head of state and secretary-general of the DDR's ruling Socialist Unity party, would meet in late 1981 for a discussion of issues of common concern. A few weeks later Günter Guillaume, the East German agent who had managed to become a close aide of former West German Chancellor Willy Brandt and whose arrest led to Brandt's resignation in 1974, was exchanged for a number of West German agents held by the DDR.

FEDERAL REPUBLIC OF GERMANY (West Germany)

Chancellor Schmidt and his Social Democratic-Free Democratic coalition government did not long enjoy the electoral victory they had won in October 1980. Economic problems that had been papered over before the election—rising inflation (6½%) and unemployment (5¼%)—had to be dealt with. Seemingly modest by U.S. standards, the inflation rate was in fact considerably higher if computed by American methods. In addition, high U.S. interest rates forced West German banks to raise their own rates to prevent an excessive outflow of capital, thus further fanning inflation. As a result, the gross national product (GNP) was expected to decrease by 1.3% in 1981.

Budget. The question of how to deal with these difficulties strained the government coalition of the left-of-center Social Democrats (SPD) and the middle-of-the-road Free Democrats (FDP) almost to the breaking point. While the SPD was willing to cut some social programs, it also called for reduced military expenditures and an income surtax to finance a public works program. The FDP, on its part, demanded deeper cuts in social expenditures than the SPD was willing to grant and also proposed tax reductions to aid business.

A compromise reached within the government after lengthy discussions provided for cuts in unemployment benefits and tax allowances for children, as well as for a 1% reduction in the take-home pay of public officials. And although West Germany, like all NATO (North Atlantic Treaty Organization) members, was pledged to increase military outlays by 3%, after inflation, the actual increase in the new budget was to be held to 1%. Subsidies for the modernization of the steel industry, increased tax depreciation rates for the construction industry, and an enlarged public transportation program were to aid the sluggish economy and generate new jobs. It remained to be seen whether the budget would be accepted by Parliament.

Armaments. The government faced also a growing opposition from the left wing of the SPD, as well as from pacifist groups, church circles, and youth movements, over the armaments issue. The opposition focused on a 1979 NATO decision to place U.S. Pershing II and cruise missiles on West German soil, in response to the USSR's SS-20 missile and Backfire Bomber, which presented new threats to Western Europe.

That decision was linked, however, to a commitment from NATO to initiate arms control talks with the Soviet Union in the hope that the deployment could be avoided or limited as part of a mutual reduction of nuclear weapons in Europe. Washington's reluctance to engage in such talks fed the opposition to the deployment of the American missiles. The concern centered on the first-strike capability of the highly accurate Pershing IIs and on the fear that the United States might more readily accept a war with the USSR in the belief that it could be confined to Europe. The U.S. decision to produce neutron bombs, for use in Europe as a counter to Soviet superiority in tanks, added to these misgivings. In October some 250,000 demonstrators staged an antinuclear rally in Bonn.

Chancellor Schmidt, aware of West Germany's dependence on U.S. military support, threatened to resign should his own party, the SPD, reject the installation of the missiles. Yet Schmidt also knew that East-West German relations and the status of West Berlin would be jeopardized by continued U.S.-Soviet tensions, and he continually urged Washington to react more positively to Soviet overtures for arms control talks.

Environment. Environmental problems also caused much concern. In March 70,000 protesters gathered at Brokdorf, south of Hamburg, to block construction of a nuclear reactor. Other protests sought to stop the expansion of the Frankfurt airport because of the anticipated noise pollution. The growing importance of such issues was reflected in the electoral victories of a new environmentalist party, the Greens, which won from four to seven seats in municipal elections in the states of Hesse and Lower Saxony. The Greens were supported also by opponents of nuclear armaments, pacifists, and various social protest groups.

Terrorism. Unlike the nonviolent Greens, a group of militant radicals known as the Red Army Faction sought to stop the deployment of nuclear missiles by physical attacks on U.S. personnel and installations in West Germany. They set off a bomb at the U.S. air base at Ramstein in the Palatinate, injuring 20 persons. They also claimed responsibility for an unsuccessful attempt to assassinate the U.S. army's European commander, Gen. Frederick J. Kroesen. Between February and September there were 14 attacks on American lives and property.

West German authorities also faced increasing terrorist activity on the part of rightist groups. And finally, terrorist groups were active among foreign workers, reflecting conditions in their respective homelands. The problem was especially serious among the large Turkish contingent, which was being harassed by both rightist and leftist extremists.

Economy and Industry. West Germany's economic troubles were caused by rising energy costs, a serious decline in exports, and a tight-money policy designed to contain inflation. The country's wide-ranging social programs weighed as an additional burden on the shrinking econ-

U.S. Army Gen. Frederick Kroesen survived a terrorist attack on his car in Heidelberg, September 15.

Regis Bossu, Sygma

omy. There were, however, structural weaknesses also in West German industry that had to be remedied in the face of stiff competition from such high-quality and/or low-cost producers as Japan, Brazil, and Korea. The proposed 1982 budget focused on these problems.

One serious impediment, however, was the shortage of qualified scientists and engineers. Universities no longer turn them out in sufficient numbers; in 1980 enrollment at technical universities amounted to only two thirds of their capacity. According to the Association of German Engineers, 16,000 engineering jobs were vacant in April 1981.

Absenteeism also remained a major concern. A survey of 265 representative firms revealed an absentee rate of 8.4%. Absenteeism, sickness, vacations, holidays, and time off for personal reasons reduced the average work week to 31.6 hours.

Social Conditions. A growing shortage of low-cost housing led to the occupation of vacant buildings by groups of squatters in Munich, Bremen, and other cities. In some cases the occupiers were forcibly removed, in others they were allowed to stay either because they enjoyed widespread public support or to avoid bloodshed. But there were also some bitter clashes with the police, frequently aggravated by teenage hoodlums and vandals. Where the squatters were allowed to stay, they often repaired and furnished the buildings and sometimes even signed leases. Both federal and state governments sought to encourage construction of new apartment houses and the restoration of old ones through tax relief and other incentives.

Prussia. In their efforts to come to terms with their past, West Germans showed considerable interest in a spate of new books on Prussia, the forerunner and shaper of the defunct German Reich, dissolved by a Big Four decree in 1947. Most of the books tried to present a balanced picture of that state and its rulers and stressed the fact that its history was by now a closed chapter that could be viewed with detachment.

Foreign Policy. West German–U.S. relations suffered not only from disagreements about the attitude to be assumed toward the USSR and the high-interest strategy of American banks, but also from divergent views on the Third World, whose problems Bonn viewed as primarily socioeconomic rather than military. Except for some leftist groups, critics of the United States were not inspired by anti-Americanism but by a genuine concern for world peace and stability.

Vis-à-vis the USSR, the Schmidt government retained its pragmatic, restrained attitude. It continued negotiations with Moscow on a trade agreement by which West German concerns would build a 3,500-mi (5 633-km) pipeline to transport natural gas from Siberia to Western Europe. The pipeline would supply gas to the USSR and Western Europe beginning in the mid-1980s. Some contended that West Germany would become too dependent on the USSR, but the government maintained that the arrangement would preserve the West's own supplies and that West Germany could always revert to its present suppliers—the Netherlands, Britain, and Norway. Soviet President Leonid Brezhnev visited Bonn, November 22-25, for talks with Chancellor Schmidt. Discussions focused on the U.S.–Soviet nuclear buildup in Europe, with Brezhnev rejecting U.S. President Ronald Reagan's call for a bilateral pullout of medium-range missiles.

Throughout the year, West Germany tried hard to help stabilize conditions in Poland, providing credits to Warsaw to buy foodstuffs and other necessities. Bonn feared that a deterioration of the Polish crisis would put new strains on its relations with the DDR.

At a meeting of the finance ministers of the European Monetary Fund in Brussels on October 4, West Germany agreed to revalue its currency to help the ailing French franc and Italian lira. The value of the German mark was raised by 5.5%.

— WEST GERMANY • Information Highlights —

Official Name: Federal Republic of Germany.
Location: North-central Europe.
Area: 97,883 sq mi (253 517 km^2). West Berlin, 186 sq mi (481 km^2).
Population (1981 est.): 61,300,000.
Chief Cities (1980 est.): Bonn, the capital, 286,200; Hamburg, 1,653,000; Munich, 1,299,700.
Government: *Head of state,* Karl Carstens, president (took office July 1979). *Head of government,* Helmut Schmidt, federal chancellor (took office May 1974). **Legislature**—Parliament: Bundesrat and Bundestag.
Monetary Unit: Deutsche mark (2.23 d. marks equal U.S. $1, Oct. 1981).
Manufactures (major products): Iron, steel, coal, cement, chemicals, machinery, ships, vehicles.
Agriculture (major products): Grains, potatoes, sugar beets, meat and dairy products.

GERMAN DEMOCRATIC REPUBLIC (East Germany)

In April the (Communist) Socialist Unity party (SED) held its 10th party congress in East Berlin. Once again, Secretary-General Erich Honecker stressed the sovereignty of the DDR and asked for the establishment of normal diplomatic relations between the DDR and the Federal Republic. He called for an exchange of ambassadors instead of "permanent representatives," on which Bonn still insisted. Honecker noted also that the relationship between the DDR and Federal Republic was directly affected by U.S.–Soviet relations. He described East Germany as the most dependable ally of the Soviet Union, suggesting that such "antisocialist" developments as had taken place in Poland would never be tolerated in the DDR.

A new five-year plan presented to the congress provided for annual production increases of 5 to 6%. Special attention would be paid to consumer goods, in particular housing, refrigerators, washing machines, electric ovens, and sewing machines. As before, rents, food prices, and

UPI

Council Chairman Erich Honecker (left) of East Germany, who in April was elected to a third term as secretary-general of the Communist party, accepts the credentials of a new Canadian ambassador, John Macleod Fraser.

public transportation fares would be kept low by means of state subsidies.

Honecker was elected secretary-general of the party for the third time.

Elections for the People's Chamber were held June 14. There was only one slate of candidates, the National Front, and although it embraced all parties, the nominees of the SED and other Communist organizations were assured a solid majority.

Economy. Rising world prices for raw material continued to exert inflationary pressures on the East German economy. Since the DDR is poorly endowed with mineral resources, it is particularly dependent on the import of raw materials. To redress the adverse balance of payments, plans were being drafted to increase exports. At the same time the country sought greater self-sufficiency through an expansion of the nuclear energy industry, more efficient utilization of available raw materials, and improvements in agricultural production. Whether these changes would be sufficient to meet the twin goals of more consumer goods and increased export production remained to be seen.

Education. School and kindergarten teachers as well as lower-rank university instructors and researchers, whose salaries had long been lagging behind those of skilled workers, were granted raises of up to 25%. Student and apprentice stipends also were raised "in recognition of their contributions to our economic tasks." All post-high school students were to receive a basic stipend of 200 DDR marks (about $88 U.S.) per month; special achievements would be rewarded by additional grants. Apprentice stipends ranged from 105 to 220 marks ($46 to $97), depending on schooling, type of work, and length of service.

Prussia. The DDR, too, began to take a new interest in Prussia. Long condemned as the embodiment of militarism and feudal class interests, the Prussian state was now seen also as the initiator of various progressive economic and judicial reforms. The landowning nobility, the Prussian Junkers, were credited with having introduced capitalism into agriculture. And while the Prussian army was still charged with having fostered a deadening spirit of blind obedience, it was also hailed as a highly effective school of military expertise.

A statue of Prussia's most famous king, Frederick the Great (1712–86), which had been removed from Berlin in 1950, was set up on East Berlin's best known avenue, Unter den Linden. By reclaiming Prussia as part of its heritage, the DDR sought to buttress its own claim to historical legitimacy.

Foreign Policy. East Berlin watched closely the year's developments in Poland. Visas were required for trips to and from that country, and every effort was made to impede contacts between East Germans and Poles in implementation of the "increased vigilance" that the "aggravations of the class struggle" in Poland demanded. To help the Warsaw government sta-

EAST GERMANY • Information Highlights

Official Name: German Democratic Republic.
Location: North-central Europe.
Area: 41,768 sq mi (108 179 km^2).
Population (1981 est.): 16,700,000.
Chief Cities (1979 est.): East Berlin, the capital, 1,133,-854; Leipzig, 563,912; Dresden, 515,387.
Government: *Head of state,* Erich Honecker, Chairman of the Council of State. *Head of government,* Willi Stoph, chairman of the Council of Ministers Presidium. *First secretary of the Socialist Unity (Communist) party,* Erich Honecker (took office 1971). *Legislature* (unicameral)—Volkskammer (People's Chamber).
Monetary Unit: DDR mark (2.44 DDR marks equal U.S.$1, July 1981—noncommercial rate).
Manufactures (major products): Electrical and precision engineering products, fishing vessels, steel, machinery, chemicals.
Agriculture (major products): Grains, fruits and vegetables, meat and dairy products.

bilize conditions and cope with a serious food shortage, the DDR also shipped substantial amounts of meat to Poland—even though it could ill afford to do so. As the Polish Solidarity movement stepped up its demands, however, East Berlin issued veiled threats that further aid might be withheld unless Solidarity showed greater moderation and Poles worked harder for economic recovery.

East German advisers, both military and technical, continued to be active in many Third World countries.

WEST BERLIN

Early in 1981, a serious financial scandal involving loan guarantees carelessly granted by city officials to a near-bankrupt building concern led to the resignation of Mayor Dietrich Stobbe (SPD) and his Social Democratic-Free Democratic coalition government. A new (132-seat) city parliament was elected, with the conservative Christian Democratic Union (CDU) securing 60 seats, the SPD 49, the FDP 7, and the Alternative List—comprising environmentalists, social protesters, and pacifists—9. The FDP, the Social Democrats' long-time partner, switched over to the CDU, and the new coalition elected as mayor the Christian Democrat Richard von Weizsäcker. It was the first time in almost 30 years that the SPD did not participate in West Berlin's government.

West Berlin suffered an even more serious housing shortage than most West German cities. Throughout the year, militant youths and older sympathizers occupied vacant buildings, touching off clashes with the police and some major street battles. While, as elsewhere, the squatters enjoyed considerable popular sympathy, their cause suffered when vandals and looters took advantage of the occupiers' confrontations with the police.

Economy. Economically, West Berlin did a little better than West Germany in 1980, recording an industrial growth of 2% as compared with 1.8% in West Germany. But its population continued to decrease and grow older, and it became increasingly difficult to attract first-rank talent to the city. Tourism, one of the city's major sources of income, also decreased considerably in 1981.

Armaments. Many West Berliners were opposed to the deployment of additional U.S. missiles on German soil. When U.S. Secretary of State Alexander Haig came to the city in September, nuclear protesters staged a large demonstration.

ANDREAS DORPALEN
The Ohio State University

GHANA

The economic situation, although improved, continued to threaten President Hilla Limann's government. Funding the many debts incurred during past regimes placed a continuing strain on the government. The world price for cocoa, Ghana's major export, fell from a high of $5,100 to below $2,150 per ton, cutting government revenues sharply and creating a large budget deficit and a need for increased taxes.

Economy. A loan of $750 million was floated in April to cover the deficit and the government borrowed further to finance agricultural and industrial development. The proposed new taxes created a budget crisis in August and Limann was forced to compromise. The government established a minimum wage of $4.25 per day. However, inflation remained at more than 50%, gasoline and kerosene sold as high as $18 per gallon, and a loaf of bread in Kumasi brought the illegal price of $7. In some parts of the Volta region, severe water shortages allowed water sellers to charge 75 cents a barrel.

There were threats, but no major strikes, partially because the government specified 15 staple foods as having priority and was obviously trying to get these items to the areas of greatest need. Distribution was difficult because of the poor condition of the roads and railroad, the cost of gasoline, and the shortage of spare truck parts. Direct aid from Britain, Germany, the United States, and South Korea allowed Ghana to plan to improve its communication, agricultural, and industrial sectors, but the gradual upturn in the price of cocoa was the most helpful sign.

Politics and Foreign Affairs. The five opposition parties united in a compact in May but posed little immediate threat to the People's National Party. Flight Lt. Jerry Rawlings remained a spokesman for the military, warned the government about the economic situation, and finally staged a coup against Limann at year-end.

Students ransacked the Ivory Coast embassy in March to protest the death of 46 Ghanaian prisoners in an Abidjan jail. Normal relations were restored after a meeting at Lomé between the two presidents, Limann and Félix Houphouët-Boigny. The most serious internal problem was the resurgence of tribalism in the north, where clashes between the Nanumba and Konkomba tribes in June left an estimated 1,500 dead before peace was restored.

HARRY A. GAILEY
San Jose State University

GHANA • Information Highlights

Official Name: Republic of Ghana.
Location: West Africa.
Area: 92,100 sq mi (238 539 km^2).
Population (1981 est.): 12,000,000.
Chief Cities (1977 est.): Accra, the capital, 840,000; Kumasi, 353,000; Tema, 169,500.
Government: *Head of state and government,* Jerry Rawlings (assumed power Dec. 1981). *Legislature*—Constituent Assembly.
Monetary Unit: New cedi (2.75 new cedis equal U.S.$1, July 1981).
Manufactures (major products): Minerals, lumber, cement, aluminum.
Agriculture (major products): Cocoa, timber, coconuts, coffee, subsistence crops, rubber.

GREAT BRITAIN

In 1981, Britain endured another exceedingly difficult and demanding year. The worldwide recession continued to affect the country far more than other Western industrialized nations; Britain's cities experienced the worse street violence of the century; and the country's time-hallowed two-party political system showed clear signs of breaking up. Amid the gloom, the only cheer was the wedding of the heir to the throne, Prince Charles, to Lady Diana Spencer. This, at least, was an unambiguous success.

The Thatcher Government. The worst problems were faced by the Conservative government headed by Margaret Thatcher. Mrs. Thatcher, having committed herself to a policy of tight money and lowered public expenditure, refused to be shifted from the path even when it led to an unemployment figure of almost three million people (about 12% of the working population), a pound sterling that dropped as low as $1.75, and interest rates that touched 15.5%. Arguing, against mounting unpopularity in the country and a crescendo of criticism within her own party and government, that there was no alternative to her policies, she made it clear time and time again that she would refuse to switch.

Critics said that her attempts to control the country's money supply had inevitably contributed to the high interest rates that were in turn starving industry of necessary investment funds. Thus, people who were unemployed as a result of the cuts in public spending were finding it almost impossible to find alternative work. As their numbers mounted, extra public money had to be diverted for their welfare payments, and the Treasury lost the money they would have paid in tax. The subsequent drain on the public purse necessitated more spending cuts and higher tax and interest rates, three more twists to the vicious spiral the government found itself lost in.

Mrs. Thatcher, for her part, argued that any relaxation of her policies would simply lead to more inflation and hence prevent any real, lasting solution to Britain's economic woes. Her problems were exacerbated by President Ronald Reagan's similar economic policies. While Mrs. Thatcher praised the president's strategy, she was obliged to recognize that high U.S. interest rates were a principal cause of her own difficulties.

The traditionally docile and subservient Conservative Party began to indicate toward the end of the year that it would not continue to accept unchanged "Thatcherism" for very much longer. In January, she was able to dismiss one or two dissenting ministers from her government without incurring too much wrath. When in September, however, she sacked three prominent Cabinet ministers, all of them highly critical of her activities, the opposition within her own party became far more critical.

Former Conservative Prime Minister Edward Heath began a series of speeches which accused her in the most outspoken terms of being a disaster for the country. Heath, who had never masked his scant regard for his successor, has little following in his own Conservative Party, but his powerful words made it necessary for other Thatcher critics to be equally vehement if they wished to be heard. At the annual Conservative Party conference, normally a love-in for the party leader accompanied only by heartfelt expressions of loyalty, a number of senior party figures made forthright attacks on government policy. Increasingly, the prime minister looked like a lonely and beleaguered figure, surrounded only by those who agreed with her and determined to ignore those who did not.

Labour. Britain's other great political party, Labour, faced a similar threat. For many years, the party's activists, its keenest supporters and those who do the work at the grass-roots level, had been trying to push the party in a leftward direction. In the previous two or three years they had scored several successes, chiefly gaining greater control over Members of Parliament (MPs) who might be tempted to move away from a leftish, socialist position. They had also found a figurehead in a controversial former aristocrat, Anthony (Tony) Benn.

The activist left, or the "Bennites" as they were sometimes known, scored a remarkable

Riviere/Gamma-Liaison

Great Britain's Prime Minister Margaret Thatcher addresses the Commonwealth Heads of Government Meeting, held in Melbourne, Australia, September 30–October 7, 1981.

victory at a special party conference in January, when they arranged for the leader and deputy leader to be chosen by the whole party rather than merely by its MPs. Benn himself, in spite of pleadings from the present leader, Michael Foot, determined to stand as Foot's deputy against the rightist Denis Healey. When the vote took place in September, Healey scraped home by less than 1% of the ballot, leading many to believe that Benn was on the brink of a lasting success.

All this was against a background of a party which had swung sharply to the left already. It is, among other things, against Britain's membership in the European Common Market and in favor of the country's unilateral renunciation of nuclear weapons. The net effect was to prove more than a number of senior Labour politicians could bear. In March, 14 MPs set themselves up as a new party, the Social Democratic Party, and with a briskness and efficiency not common in British politics, set about getting a national membership. They had four former Cabinet ministers at their head, and within a few months had a membership of more than 50,000 persons and an alliance with the old, middle-of-the-road Liberal Party.

Faced with an unpopular and unsuccessful Conservative government, and a Labour opposition heading leftward at a reckless pace, the British electorate at first gave a warm welcome to the new SDP/Liberal alliance. SDP member Roy Jenkins, a former Labour chancellor of the exchequer, came close to winning an almost rock-solid Labour seat in northern England. Then a Liberal candidate with a poor electoral record easily won a middle-class seat in a London suburb, and in late November Shirley Williams became the first SDP member to be elected to Parliament. The new SDP seemed to appeal to all classes, and while its opponents at first tried to pretend it did not exist, and then scoffed at its lack of coherent policies, its supporters argued that any policies would be preferable to the alternatives offered.

Police, equipped with protective shields, prepare to confront rioters in London's Brixton area.

UPI

Opinion polls and these by-elections appeared to indicate that, as the SDP put it, the old "two-party mould" of British politics was about to be broken. Since the 1920s, apart from wartime, the Labour and Conservative parties have shared power between them. Both appeared to have great reserves of loyal supporters who would vote for them under all circumstances, with each election being determined by the handful of people who floated between the two. In the period between 1950 and 1979, both parties tended to follow broadly similar policies, and it was the failure of these policies in the period from 1964 into the late 1970s which helped to push the parties to the political extremes. The early success of the new third party, steering a course between these new extremes, appeared to indicate that the natural moderation and conservatism of the British remained intact.

Riots. Undoubtedly one of the greatest shocks to the nation occurred in July, when for the first time in most people's memory, rioting gangs took to the streets of many British cities. The first serious street riots had occurred in April in Brixton, a largely but not exclusively black area of London. The origin was undoubtedly racial and reflected the deep suspicion that existed between the black residents, especially young men, and the police. Another vicious circle had been established: young blacks found it difficult to get work, and thus were more likely to be involved in casual street crime. The police subsequently paid them more attention, so creating greater antagonism. It proved to be a constantly recurring pattern.

Curiously, however, the British riots also turned out to be multiracial. They reached their apogee in July in Toxteth, an area of decayed, downtown Liverpool, where hundreds of young men hurled bricks, paving stones, and Molotov cocktails at police, with black and white rioters standing together. Britain could claim, with some justice, to have the only multiracial riots in the world.

The Toxteth riots were swiftly copied in other big cities: Manchester, Birmingham, Leeds, Leicester, and London. In the course of one week, thousands of shops and public buildings were boarded up, and for a few days at least there was a sense of siege throughout many of the country's biggest towns.

The riots ended partly because they ran out of steam, as most riotous behavior in Britain generally has, and partly because the police began arresting people in large numbers. Early fears that swift action by the authorities might

Left to right, Roy Jenkins, David Owen, William Rodgers, and Shirley Williams join together to form Britain's Social Democratic Party.

UPI

create a situation similar to that which has occurred in Northern Ireland, with the local population resenting a crackdown, proved ungrounded. The rioting ended, if only temporarily, as quickly as it had begun.

The inquest into what had caused it went on for much longer. No definite conclusions could be reached, but it was generally agreed that the extraordinarily high incidence of unemployment, combined with boredom and a dislike of the police had all contributed. Some rioters had perhaps been copying the scenes from Northern Ireland, which they had seen frequently on television. It was a significant week, however, since it ended once and for all the complacent British assumption that such scenes could not take place at home.

One contributory factor had been a terrible fire in Deptford, a south London suburb, where 13 young black people died. Officials and ministers were notable by their absence after this disaster, and that fact, combined with black suspicions that the police were covering up a murder, stirred black resentment. A horrifying incident, which in the white community would have passed with no more than deep regret, caused a lasting resentment among the blacks.

Disarmament. Britain moved nearer to a policy of unilateral nuclear disarmament. As had been expected for some time, the opposition Labour Party and the influential Trades Union Congress voted for this action, and in October, a crowd estimated at between 100,000 and 250,000 gathered in Hyde Park to protest nuclear weapons. The Campaign for Nuclear Disarmament, moribund since the 1960s, began to recruit new members at the rate of more than 500 a week.

More significantly, the main political parties showed marked shifts toward the antinuclear position. The SDP was opposed to the British purchase of the Trident missile program from the United States. Others were angry about the decision to accept U.S. cruise missiles on British soil. President Reagan's implication that a nuclear war could be fought entirely on European land, while the United States remained unscathed, was a powerful boost to the antinuclear campaign. The suggestion that Europe might suffer obliteration in order to keep the United States free was, not surprisingly, greeted with great resentment.

Bombers came nearer to home for Londoners when the Irish Republican Army resumed its campaign on the British mainland (*see* accompanying special report).

Crime and the Law. More happily, the year brought the capture and conviction of the so-called "Yorkshire Ripper," a man who had murdered 13 women in the north of England. Like the victims of Jack the Ripper, the 19th century sex maniac, most of the dead women were prostitutes. The man convicted was a truck driver, named Peter Sutcliffe, who had confessed to all the crimes. He was sentenced to life in prison. There were urgent demands for an inquiry into the competence of the police when it emerged that Sutcliffe had been interviewed by investigating officers several times during the murders, but had been released because of the officers' belief that the murderer had a northeastern accent. This mistake undoubtedly cost the lives of several women.

Other legal cases involved a mongol or Down's syndrome baby whose life was saved in August, after the Appeal Court ruled that her parents did not have the right to refuse her an operation that would keep her alive. The parents

GREAT BRITAIN • Information Highlights

Official Name: United Kingdom of Great Britain and Northern Ireland.
Location: Island, western Europe.
Area: 94,250 sq mi (244 108 km^2).
Population (1981 est.): 55,900,000.
Chief Cities (June 1979 est.): London, the capital, 6,877,100; Birmingham, 1,033,900; Glasgow, 794,316; Leeds, 724,300; Sheffield, 544,200; Liverpool, 520,200.
Government: *Head of state,* Elizabeth II, queen (acceded Feb. 1952). *Head of government,* Margaret Thatcher, prime minister (took office May 1979). *Legislature*—Parliament: House of Lords and House of Commons.
Monetary Unit: Pound (0.5329 pound equals U.S.$1, Dec. 18, 1981).
Manufactures (major products): Steel, metal products, textiles, motor vehicles, aircraft.
Agriculture (major products): Cereals, livestock, livestock products, fish.

Sygma

The bride and bridegroom—the new Princess of Wales and Prince Charles—members of their families, pages, and flower girls greet the crowd from a Buckingham Palace balcony following the July 29 royal wedding.

had wished to allow their 12-day-old child, hopelessly handicapped, to die quietly, but were prevented by an appeal from a doctor.

Royal Wedding. One—perhaps the only—source of good cheer for British people was the royal wedding. Even here, many felt that it was an attempt to provide a diversion from the genuine problems that the country faced. It was certainly attended by difficulties. In June, a young unemployed man fired six blank shots at Queen Elizabeth as she rode in a procession. This event, combined with the recent rioting, created some fears that the wedding might not proceed as peacefully as hoped. Tourists from abroad failed to arrive in the expected numbers, largely because at that time the pound sterling was overpriced. King Juan Carlos of Spain decided not to come because the royal couple were to begin their honeymoon from Gibraltar, a speck of land that is still a source of British-Spanish friction.

But in the end, all went smoothly and in a spirit of genuine pleasure, peace, and harmony. The prince, who will succeed to the throne on the death of his mother, had chosen a ceremony in St. Paul's Cathedral, the vast domed church designed by Sir Christopher Wren, Britain's greatest architect, rather than in the more traditional Westminster Abbey. He had also asked for a musical wedding, and for the first time this century, Britain's royal family, not usually noted for their artistic tastes, brought some superlative works of art into the nation's homes. The undoubted popularity of the couple, the splendor of the wedding, the peaceful contrast with the riots, as well as the November announcement that the couple is expecting a child in June 1982, did more than anything else could have done to restore the battered and bruised national morale.

SIMON HOGGART
"The Observer," London

GREAT BRITAIN—SPECIAL REPORT:

NORTHERN IRELAND

In 1981, Northern Ireland, the six northeasternmost counties of Ireland, entered the 14th year of civil war. Although there were fewer deaths than in many previous years, the political situation grew, if possible, even worse. The end of the year saw a solution to the problem as distant as ever.

Among those who were murdered in the course of the year were Sir Norman Stronge, an 86-year-old former politician, and his son James, who were shot at home by the Irish Republican Army (IRA). The IRA is the guerrilla organization that represents the population, largely Roman Catholic, who believe that the whole of Ireland should be united. They were also responsible for the death of five British soldiers who were killed in a landmine explosion in the south of the province in May, and for the murder of a Northern Ireland member of the British Parliament, the Rev. Robert Bradford, shot dead while advising his constituents on a Saturday morning in November.

However, the IRA's most effective weapon in 1981 turned out not to be random murders but the deaths of several of their own members in a hunger strike. The hunger strike has a long tradition in Irish politics. Because of the immense sacrifice made by those taking part, the effort of will required by them, and the fact that innocent people do not suffer, a hunger strike can attract powerful waves of sympathy. This effort lasted for just more than seven months and attracted support for the IRA from all over the world.

The success of the IRA tactic inevitably produced a reaction from the Protestant majority in Northern Ireland. These people, numbering about one million, compared with the province's 500,000 Catholics, describe themselves as "Loyalists," meaning that they remain loyal to union with Great Britain. However, they showed through the year that they were quite prepared to defy the government of Britain in order to avoid their ultimate fear: union with the largely Catholic Irish Republic to the south.

Early in the year, the Rev. Ian Paisley, the most aggressive of all Protestant spokesmen, announced the readiness of a third force, outside the British Army and the police, that would be prepared to defend Protestant people against IRA attack and against forcible union with the south. Paisley held a dramatic press conference in the middle of the night on a windswept hill at which hundreds of masked men waved pieces of paper which they claimed to be firearm licenses. The event was greeted with some derision in Britain, but it was quite clear that many armed men would be available to Paisley if he decided to mobilize.

The IRA hunger strike began in March. It was confined to prisoners in the so-called "H-blocks," cell blocks in the shape of the letter 'H' in the Maze Prison, near Belfast. These prisoners had been engaged in a "dirty protest," which involved refusing to wear prison clothes or to clean excrement from their cells, in the hopes of winning political prisoner status.

The British authorities had always maintained that the prisoners, since they were guilty of such offenses as murder and bombings, should be treated in the same manner as ordinary criminals. The IRA claimed that the prisoners, because they had been politically motivated, should have a separate and superior status. They were demanding the right to civilian clothes, less prison work, more frequent visitors, and various other privileges. However, the principal reason for the hunger strike was a desire to attract worldwide sympathy and publicity, and in this the IRA succeeded.

The first man to go on strike was Bobby Sands. He died blind, painfully thin, and unconscious in the tenth week of his fast. In April, after 40 days, he had been the surprise winner of a British parliamentary by-election in the constituency of Fermanagh and South Tyrone. He was, of course, both unwilling and unfit to take up his seat at Westminster.

As each hunger striker died, he was replaced by another, so that at any one time four or five IRA men would be fasting. Numerous attempts to break the deadlock were tried, but for months all negotiations failed, largely because of the obduracy of the IRA and the British government. Margaret Thatcher, the British prime minister, refused all appeals to seek a compromise, including those from statesmen in other countries. Finally, after ten men had died in considerable pain, the strike collapsed, largely because of increasing pressure from the families of the men who were perishing. It ended in October, after which the British government, freed from duress, granted some of the concessions that the strikers had been demanding.

Meanwhile, in June, there had been a general election in the Irish Republic. Two of the seats in the sensitive border areas were won by Maze hunger strikers, but the net effect of the poll was to replace a hard-line Republican, pro-Irish-unity prime minister, Charles Haughey, with the far more moderate and pragmatic Garret FitzGerald. FitzGerald immediately showed himself willing to make numerous concessions in the hopes of attracting support from the Protestant population of Northern Ireland. Ironically, this alarmed the Protestants even more, because they feared the effect of this reasonableness on the British government. A summit meeting between FitzGerald and Mrs. Thatcher in November fueled their fears, especially because the willingness of Britain and Ireland to consider joint institutions for the whole of Ireland struck them as the first step toward the hated Irish unity.

Mrs. Thatcher had appointed as her new secretary of state for Northern Ireland—in effect, the governor of the province—James Prior, one of the most moderate of her ministers. Prior had been appointed as a punishment for his opposition to her economic policies, and this fact, coupled with his unwillingness to strike aggressive poses, led to further resentment by the Protestants. Inflamed by the Bradford murder, the Thatcher-FitzGerald summit, and what they saw as a dangerously conciliatory attitude to the IRA, the Protestants began a series of protests.

The IRA, having lost the hunger strike, began a new tactic of attacking targets in Britain. In a few weeks in October and November, two civilians were killed in London in a botched attempt to destroy a bus carrying British soldiers; Sir Steuart Pringle, commandant-general of the Royal Marines, was maimed when a bomb blew up his car; and a police bomb disposal officer was killed trying to defuse a bomb in a busy central London hamburger bar.

The British government found itself, once more, at an impasse. It continued to insist that no form of government could be established in the province without the support of both main religious groups. Equally, the two groups showed no willingness to compromise. Various vague plans for constitutional assemblies and elections were floated, but these tactics had been tried before without success. The British public showed itself increasingly angered by the expense of maintaining a vast garrison of soldiers in Northern Ireland, the cost in human life, and the extension of the war to the mainland. But so far there was no indication that the British public would cease to tolerate these drawbacks altogether.

SIMON HOGGART

THE ECONOMY

The economic policies of the Thatcher government in Great Britain faced a severe test in 1981, but it became apparent during the course of the year that the widely predicted abandonment of strict monetary control for a less demanding regime was not going to take place. British industry and financial markets began to accept that, in contrast with most other post-World War II governments, Mrs. Thatcher intends to fight the next election campaign (due at the latest in May 1984) on the basis of the policies on which she was elected.

The steep fall in output, which was sharper in Britain than in most other countries in the wake of the second jump in oil prices, leveled off by the middle of the year. But there was little sign of any significant recovery by the final quarter. Cutthroat competition on prices, especially by retailers, produced a boom in consumer spending at the beginning of the year, but this faded later as pay increases fell below the rate of inflation. Companies continued to run down their inventories in response to high interest rates, though investment remained relatively buoyant. Export industries were hampered by a very high exchange rate for sterling which at the beginning of the year traded at more than $2.40. By late 1981 it had fallen 25% against the dollar and by a lesser amount against the deutsche mark, holding out some hope of an export revival.

With output stagnant, unemployment continued to rise, nearing the emotive 3 million mark, equivalent to about 12.5% of the work force. The high birthrate of the 1960s is helping to swell the number of new entrants to the labor force, increasing the pressure on available jobs and postponing, possibly for some years, any significant reduction in the numbers out of work.

The government's strategy for countering the recession—a sharp fall in interest rates—was undermined by the persistently high rates in the United States. The March budget contained unpopular increases in taxes in order to maintain a conservative fiscal balance and enable a rapid fall in interest rates. Monetary data were obscured for several months by a civil service strike, but in the event bank lending and the money supply grew faster than intended. High interest rates in the United States helped put pressure on sterling, and eventually rates in Britain, far from falling, had to be raised twice within two weeks to 16%.

Inflation, as measured by the rise in retail prices during the past twelve months, continued to fall until midyear. Thereafter it leveled off at about 11%. Pay settlements in the private sector continued to decelerate and competition kept margins low. But local government and the nationalized industries, especially in the energy sector, put up their charges very rapidly.

Perhaps the major achievement of the Thatcher strategy has been that the underlying level of productivity appears to be rising significantly as commercial pressures force managers to be tougher and trade unions to abandon a variety of restrictive practices. This could lead to a rapid increase in output on any revival in world demand. Meanwhile the unemployment cost of years of uncompetitive practices is proving painful.

RODNEY LORD
"The Daily Telegraph," London

Britain's Trade Union Congress holds a "People's March for Jobs" as unemployment exceeds 12%.

UPI

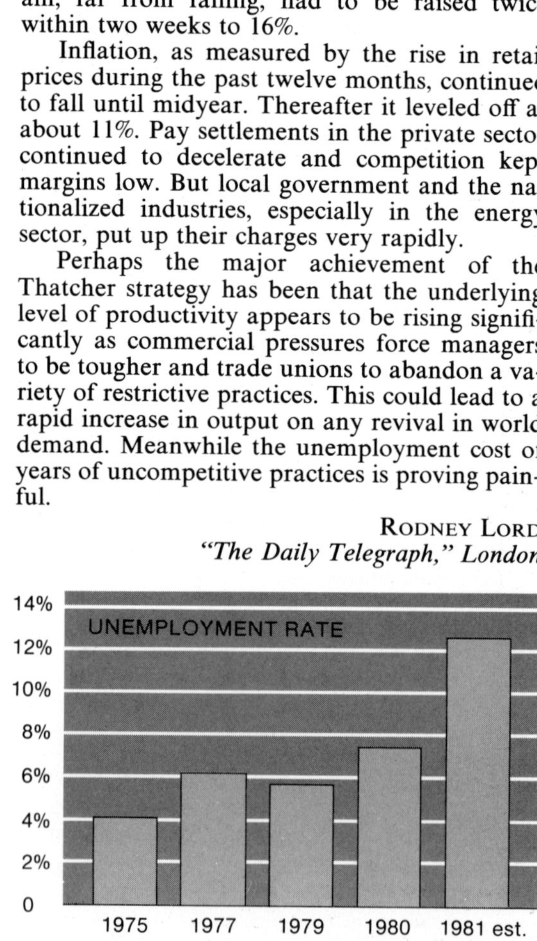

THE ARTS

The state of the arts in Britain was decidedly gloomy in 1981. Government inability to increase the arts budgets to keep pace with inflation led to some tough decisions. The Arts Council of Great Britain announced as 1981 began that it would withdraw its financial support from 41 organizations, among them the well-known Old Vic Company, and the amateur seedbeds of the National Youth Orchestra and National Youth Theatre. The outcry had reached fever pitch when, in January, the staunchly supportive arts minister, Norman St. John-Stevas, was sacked from the cabinet. The gloom dissipated somewhat when the Arts Council's pruning of funds from less successful companies was matched by financial rewards to thriving institutions.

Theater. No year that sees the Old Vic Theatre steadily dark can be counted a good year for British drama. Nor can one that sees the English Stage Company at the Royal Court theater trembling in the face of an uncertain future. However, the year's compensations included new plays by Tom Stoppard, Peter Nichols, Howard Brenton, Colin Welland, and Simon Gray, as well as glittering classical productions from the leading companies and lively experiments from the fringe theaters.

In the competition that keeps the two big subsidized theater companies on their toes, the National Theatre marginally drew ahead of the Royal Shakespeare Company in 1981, partly through a fascinating choice of unfamiliar foreign plays. *The Mayor of Zalamea,* a dazzling Spanish play by Pedro Calderón hitherto unknown to British audiences, was dubbed by one critic "the most important classical revival" of 1981. The production followed an elegant version of *A Month in the Country* by Ivan Turgenev, directed by Peter Gill. A new play about Ireland, *Translations,* by Brian Finch, plus verbal fireworks from Tom Stoppard's *On the Razzle,* brought 1981 to a fittingly brilliant close at the National.

At the Royal Shakespeare Company, the 1981 season opened with Peter Nichols' new *Passion Play,* which contrasted to a rollicking revival of *The Knight of the Burning Pestle,* by Francis Beaumont and John Fletcher, contemporaries of Shakespeare. At the year's end Alan Howard brought his award-winning roles in *Richard II* and *Richard III* from their Stratford run to London.

In London's commercial theater, Simon Gray's *Quartermaine's Terms,* directed by Harold Pinter, was welcomed as Gray's best in years. Other big hits were the lampoon *Anyone for Denis?,* a farce about the home life of Prime Minister Margaret Thatcher and her husband, and *Cats,* the Andrew Lloyd Webber musical.

Music. Cutbacks in Arts Council support sounded the death knell for eight local music festivals in 1981. Only the British Broadcasting Corporation (BBC), able to count on the radio and television audiences, could afford to be adventurous as usual.

As the year began the Royal Opera launched *The Tales of Hoffmann,* directed by John Schlesinger, with Placido Domingo, which, while widely appreciated, created controversy because of the use of three sopranos to sing the three roles usually all done by one. A month later the first London performance of Alban Berg's *Lulu* was presented. The Welsh Opera in Cardiff gave the first performance of *The Greek Passion* by Bohuslav Martinu, and the Scottish Opera mounted a successful *Beggar's Opera.* Private festivals at Buxton and Glyndebourne mounted superb productions of Domenico Cimarosa's *The Secret Marriage* and Benjamin Britten's *A Midsummer Night's Dream.* The latter was accounted the most magical of the year.

Dance. Amid the general cutbacks, dance fared better than most other artistic endeavors in Britain. In October, "Dance Umbrella '81" saw 70 performances by 35 different dance groups from three continents fill small London art theaters. New works emerged at the Royal Ballet, celebrating its 50th anniversary in 1981. Most notable was Kenneth MacMillan's full-length ballet *Isadora,* which was considered an exciting failure despite the brave efforts of Merle Park in the title role. A new generation of British dancers was evident, especially at the Royal Ballet, Sadler's Wells, and the Festival Ballet. A deliberate policy of the Royal Ballet is the limiting of the number of guest stars in order to spotlight the talents of the company's own younger dancers. Bryony Brind and Fiona Chadwick, two promising young ballerinas, survived with honor the testing roles of leading dancer in *Swan Lake* and *The Firebird.*

Visual Arts. The vast spaces of the Hayward Gallery were never so well filled as in the summer of 1981 when "Picasso's Picassos" from the Musée Picasso in Paris were exhibited.

At the National Gallery "El Greco to Goya" brought together, from British and Irish museums, several centuries of Spanish masterpieces, charting a long history of Anglo-Spanish involvement. The Royal Academy presented "The Great Japan Exhibition," which introduced a more distant and less well-known culture.

Among contemporary British artists, Bridget Riley's two London shows provoked renewed appreciation of one of Britain's finest abstract painters, while David Hockney used his reputation and flair to contrast his own works with major masterpieces in the National Gallery exhibit "The Painter's Eye."

Cinema. The British film industry, so often declared dead, brought out a rash of vital, low-budget movies, notably Ken Loach's *Looks and Smiles* and Bill Forsyth's *Gregory's Girl.*

MAUREEN GREEN
Author and Journalist, London

Actress Melina Mercouri was named minister of culture and science in the new socialist government of Greece.

Argyropoulos/Sipa-Black Star

GREECE

A Socialist victory in October parliamentary elections brought a radical change in Greece's political outlook.

Rallis Government. For most of 1981, Greece was under the government of Prime Minister George J. Rallis of the New Democracy party. Rallis had become prime minister in the spring of 1980, when Constantine Caramanlis relinquished that position to become president.

On Jan, 5, 1981, Greece formally entered the European Community (EC), an occasion for which President Caramanlis had worked for years. Ominously, the head of the Panhellenic Socialist Movement (PASOK), Andreas Papandreou, refused to attend the accession ceremony. In the months that followed, Papandreou showed the political skill that had enabled him and his party to become the major opposition to New Democracy. Prime Minister Rallis, meanwhile, grappled with problems of unemployment; an inflation rate that stood at more than 20% for the third straight year; and international complications, including the still-unresolved Cyprus question and a dispute with Turkey over air and sea rights in the Aegean Sea.

With parliament's term scheduled to end no later than November 1981, Papandreou stepped up his criticisms of Rallis' pro-NATO stand. He called for a revision of Greece's role in NATO, citing Turkey as a greater threat than the Soviet Union. Though Papandreou had lived in the United States for 20 years, had once been a U.S. citizen, and was married to an American, he was considered by many to be anti-American, especially for urging that Greece end American control of four major military bases in the country. In addition, Papandreou affirmed that, if in power, he would reconsider Greece's ties to the Common Market. All the while, he criticized Rallis' general economic policies.

Elections and Post-Election Politics. In parliamentary elections October 18, Papandreou and PASOK won a smashing victory. PASOK won 170 of 300 seats, with 112 going to New Democracy, 13 to the Communists, and 5 to independents. On October 21, Papandreou and his cabinet were sworn in.

In outlining his programs before parliament on November 22, Prime Minister Papandreou established as major goals the gradual transfer of American bases on Greek territory to Greek control, an eventual withdrawal of Greece from NATO's military wing, and a referendum in which the Greeks could vote on EC membership. He also indicated a desire for socialization in such areas of the economy as banking, transportation, and industries related to defense needs. Papandreou won a vote of confidence for his program a few days later. In late November he attended a conference of EC heads of governments in London, and at a December meeting of NATO in Brussels spoke vaguely about a partial withdrawal from the military wing and demanded a guarantee of protection against Turkey.

Death of Queen Frederika. Queen Frederika of the Hellenes, 63, widow of King Paul I (reigned 1947–1964) and mother of deposed King Constantine II, died suddenly in Madrid, on Feb. 6, 1981, while visiting her daughter, Queen Sofia of Spain. Her burial in Greece raised such a furor among the political opposition that King Constantine and his family spent only a few hours in the country. It was his first visit to Greece since December 1967, when he fled in the wake of an unsuccessful attempt to topple the military regime that had taken power in April of that year.

GEORGE J. MARCOPOULOS, *Tufts University*

GREECE • Information Highlights

Official Name: Hellenic Republic.
Location: Southwestern Europe.
Area: 50,961 sq mi (131 990 km^2).
Population (1981 est.): 9,600,000.
Chief Cities (1971 census): Athens, the capital, 867,023; Salonika, 345,799; Piraeus, 187,458.
Government: *Head of state,* Constantine Caramanlis, president (took office May 1980). *Head of government,* Andreas Papandreou, prime minister (took office Oct. 1981). *Legislature*—Parliament.
Monetary Unit: Drachma (56.30 drachmas equal U.S.$1, Oct. 1981).
Manufactures (major products): Food products, textiles, metals, chemicals, electrical goods, cement, glass.
Agriculture (major products): Grains, citrus fruits, grapes, vegetables, olives and olive oil, tobacco, cotton.

GUYANA

Continued political tension between the government of President Lynden Forbes Burnham and the opposition, a severe economic crisis, and unsettled relations with neighboring Venezuela marked 1981 in Guyana.

Politics. On January 10, Burnham, who had been acting president since October 1980, was inaugurated as president under a new constitution. In the December 1980 election, his People's National Congress was credited with winning 53 of 65 seats in parliament, with the opposition People's Progressive Party and United Force taking 10 and 2, respectively. Two other opposition groups, the Working People's Alliance (WPA) and Vanguard for Liberty and Democracy, had boycotted the election.

In 1981, the results of the balloting were denounced by various foreign groups. An international team of observers headed by Lord Avebury of the British parliamentary human rights group said in a report on February 15 that the election had been rigged. In March, the U.S. State Department annual human rights report said that the election had been "fraudulently conducted and cannot be considered a free and fair test of public opinion."

On June 13, the first anniversary of the murder of WPA leader Walter Rodney, some 5,000 people held an antigovernment demonstration in Georgetown, and a bomb exploded at the central post office.

Economy. Guyana's economic situation remained critical. The WPA charged that unemployment was running at 42%. In February, the World Bank provided a loan of U.S. $14 million; its affiliate, the International Development Association (IDA), granted a loan of 6.3 million SDR (Special Drawing Rights) units. Later, the World Bank provided an additional $1.5 million in loans for technical development.

In June the government announced a revised budget, providing for various austerity measures but increased military expenditures. At the same time, Guyana devalued its dollar (from U.S. 39 cents to 33 cents) and broke its link with the U.S. dollar, substituting a basket of currencies. As a result of these measures, the International Monetary Fund (IMF) raised the funds available to Guyana from SDR 100 million to 150 million.

GUYANA • Information Highlights

Official Name: Cooperative Republic of Guyana.
Location: Northeast coast of South America.
Area: 83,000 sq mi (214 970 km^2).
Population (1981 est.): 800,000.
Chief City (1976 est.): Georgetown, the capital, 205,000 (met. area).
Government: *Head of state,* Lynden Forbes Burnham, president (took office Jan. 1981). *Head of government,* Ptolemy Reid, prime minister (took office Oct. 1980). *Legislature* (unicameral)—National Assembly.
Monetary Unit: Guyana dollar (3.00 G. dollars equal U.S.$1, July 1981).
Manufactures (major products): Bauxite, wood products.
Agriculture (major products): Sugar, rice, coconuts.

Foreign Affairs. President Burnham visited Venezuela April 2–3 but did not succeed in mitigating that nation's claim to more than half of Guyana's territory. Shortly after, Venezuela announced that it would not renew a 1970 agreement to suspend the border controversy and that it refused to extend to Guyana the preferential terms for purchases of oil that it had granted other Caribbean countries.

ROBERT J. ALEXANDER, *Rutgers University*

HAWAII

For Hawaii, 1981 appeared to be a year of adjustment and caution. The economy slowed down, and the state and local governments assessed the effects on social services of President Ronald Reagan's budget cutbacks and considered ways to adapt to these changes.

Economy. Hawaii's economy, after adjusting for inflation, continued to show signs of a slight decline. The major industry, tourism, after years of rapid growth, entered its second year of a slowdown, due in large part to the continuing national recession and higher air fares. Hotels were offering special rates to entice local residents to have stay-at-home vacations, made doubly attractive by lower air fares for interisland travel. A third major carrier, Mid-Pacific, entered the local market and aggressively challenged the two established airlines, Hawaiian and Aloha.

Hawaii's garment industry, the third largest export industry after sugar and pineapple, had a slow but steady growth. The state's efforts in diversified agriculture showed little progress. Modest beginnings were made in aquaculture, particularly prawn farming, but developments did not match some early optimism. The state continued its pursuit of high technology industries but again met with very limited success. The same could be said for its efforts to become the business and communications hub of the Pacific. Hawaii's unemployment rate, however, remained below the national average, and state tax revenues did not decline.

Energy. Permission was granted by federal authorities for Hawaii's major electricity com-

HAWAII • Information Highlights

Area: 6,471 sq mi (16 760 km^2).
Population (1980 census): 965,000.
Chief Cities (1980 census): Honolulu, the capital, 365,048; Pearl City, 42,575; Kailua, 35,812; Hilo, 35,269; Aiea, 32,879; Kaneohe, 29,919; Waipahu, 29,139; Mililani, 20,351; Schofield Barracks, 18,851; Wahiawa, 16,911.
Government (1981): *Chief Officers*—governor, George R. Ariyoshi (D); lt. gov., Jean Sadako King (D). *Legislature*—Senate, 25 members; House of Representatives, 51 members.
State Finances (fiscal year 1980): *Revenues,* $1,895,000,000; *expenditures,* $1,660,000,000.
Personal Income (1980): $9,775,000,000; per capita, $10,101.
Labor Force (July 1981): *Nonagricultural wage and salary earners,* 407,600; *unemployed,* 22,600 (5.5% of total force).

Marine police in Hong Kong patrol a fleet of junks during an influx of Chinese refugees in April. The Chinese said they had fled because authorities had warned them of an impending earthquake.

UPI

pany to use oil with a higher sulfur content, and therefore cheaper, in energy production. Consumers could look forward to a halt in the steady rise of electricity costs. The state's much heralded efforts to develop alternative energy resources—geothermal, solar, wind, and ocean thermal energy conversion—continued in 1981 despite technical and equipment problems and a cutback in financial support from federal and private sources.

Politics. While the Democrats continued their political dominance through the 1980 elections, intraparty conflicts became so serious that they were not able to organize the state senate. Consequently, a coalition of 10 Democrats and 8 Republicans assumed the leadership of that body, with the remaining 7 Democrats playing the role of minority party. The coalition held firm through the session, but the lasting effects and long-term consequences of the arrangement were difficult to determine. For the first time in years, Republicans did enjoy the spoils of leadership and were more determined than ever to unseat the Democrats. The Republicans also took full advantage of their ties with the party's national administration and were expected to mount a serious challenge to Hawaiian Democrats in the 1982 elections. Among their successes in 1981 was convincing President Reagan to reconstitute and appoint Republicans to a federal commission to investigate the conditions under which Hawaii was annexed at the turn of the century, with an eye to possible reparation for native Hawaiians.

RICHARD H. KOSAKI
University of Hawaii

HONG KONG

Sir Murray MacLehose, Hong Kong's longest-serving governor, announced in March 1981 that he would not be staying on after the expiration of his fourth term in April 1982.

Economy. In the first half of 1981, Hong Kong's exports increased by 14%, imports by 26%, and reexports by 48%, compared with the same period in 1980. The textile and garment industries accounted for 41% of the territory's exports.

Heavy trading on July 17 pushed the local stock market barometer, the Hang Seng Index, to a record high of 1,810.20, surpassing the previous record, set March 9, 1973, by 35.24 points. Amid fears of increased bank interest rates, however, the index plunged to 1,688.56 by July 24.

A diamond exchange, the first in Asia, was opened in Hong Kong in August.

Construction and Transportation. The first Y-shaped Trident blocks, newly-designed public residential buildings, were under construction in Fan Ling. Under the government's Home Ownership Scheme, nine housing projects had been completed and 11 others were under way.

A 1.4-mile (2.3-km), two-track railway tunnel through Beacon Hill was opened April 27. The 7.8-mi (12.5-km) Mass Transit Railway Island Line, along the northern shore of Hong Kong Island, was expected to be completed in 1986. In July 1981, Laker Airways was granted a license to fly from Hong Kong and Tokyo to Honolulu, San Francisco, and Los Angeles.

Population. Preliminary results of the 1981 census indicated a population of 5,022,000. To facilitate the arrest of illegal aliens, the government passed a law in October 1980 compelling Hong Kong residents to carry proof of identity at all times. On July 15, 1981, the government began sending back to China the 2,500 Vietnamese refugees who had arrived from there.

Links with China. China provides about 50% of Hong Kong's food and 30% of its oil, and is cooperating with Hong Kong to develop its offshore oil industry. In 1980, China earned $7,000,000,000 from trade with Hong Kong.

Regular air service from Hong Kong to Peking, operated by the Civil Aviation Administration of China, began in November 1980. A bus service between Hong Kong and Canton began in July 1981.

Guangdong Enterprise Ltd., representing the province of Guangdong in its dealings with local and foreign investors, was established in Hong Kong in June 1981. The company will spend $80 million to build a wharf in Kowloon Bay for Chinese cargo vessels. Another wharf for Chinese vessels was being built in Tai Tam-dui.

CHUEN-YAN DAVID LAI
University of Victoria, British Columbia

HOUSING

The U.S. housing market continued in the worst slump since the 1974–75 recession. Interest rates soared to record levels, and the real estate industry labeled the situation a crisis. Worldwide, the slow economy was felt in all countries, and the undeveloped countries were becoming more outspoken about their housing needs.

THE UNITED STATES

The production of new homes was down severely from 1980's level of 1.29 million units. In January, housing starts were at the seasonably adjusted rate of 1.6 million units. However, the rate declined throughout the year. By June, housing starts were down to 1.0 million units and the November rate was .871 million units. The production levels for the last months of the year were the lowest since 1966. U.S. society requires approximately 2.0 million new housing units each year to meet the demands of new household formation and to compensate for the demolition of the unusable portion of the current housing stock. The housing industry produced 2.0 million units per year during 1977 and 1978 but production has been well below that mark during the last three years. The unmet demand creates the potential for a significant and dramatic rebound in housing production. The sale of existing single family homes was also down dramatically during 1981. The decline was significant in all areas of the country, including the "Sun Belt" that had been immune to the housing slump. The number of homes for sale increased and was the highest on record. Prices for existing homes stopped increasing in almost all areas and started to decline slightly in many areas. Real estate sales people were labeling this the greatest buyers' market ever.

The incredibly bad market for new homes and for existing homes can be directly attributed to the highest mortgage loan rates ever. During the last half of 1981, mortgage loan rates were between 17% and 18.5%. These rates forced the vast majority of buyers to the sidelines. Home buyers have viewed 10% as a very high interest rate and 7% to 9% as normal rates. It was surprising that anyone was borrowing money at 18%. Most potential buyers do not qualify for a home at such interest rates, or, if they do qualify, they feel the home they can afford is not up to their expectations. The median price for new homes sold in 1981 was approximately $72,000. The lender determines if a potential buyer qualifies for a loan by adding together certain costs of home ownership (mortgage payments, property taxes, and property insurance). Using the current national average rates and a 30-year mortgage at 18%, for 80% of the home's value, the monthly costs of ownership for the $72,000 home would be $991. The buyer would need an annual income of $47,500 to qualify for the loan. The same $47,500 income would qualify the buyer for a home costing $123,500, if the mortgage rate were 10%.

The builders of new homes and the sellers of existing homes both realize the importance of financing and are using "creative financing" to improve the terms. Builders are offering mortgage "buy-downs." The builder will arrange for financing at a market interest rate but will agree to "buy down" the interest rate to a tolerable level, such as 12%, for a limited period of time, usually one to three years. Using the buy-down scheme, the buyer can afford the home he or she wants and may expect to refinance the property at more favorable rates during the buy-down period. Subsidizing the mortgage is expensive for the builders, but many builders feel that reducing the interest rate to the buyer makes the home more affordable than reducing the price of the home. Of course, part of the builder's profit will go toward reducing the interest rate. The sellers of existing homes are using "purchase money mortgages" to make the homes more attractive to buyers. A seller may supply a second mortgage or purchase money mortgage to a buyer at a reduced rate. The rate is typically in the 10%-to-12% range for a term of three to five years. The buyer can combine the low interest debt from the seller with the high interest debt from the institutional lender to obtain an acceptable overall rate. The buy-downs and the purchase money mortgages may have profound effects on the housing market in the coming years. These creative financing arrangements will force many thousands of home buyers to refinance their homes in the coming years. If interest rates are down to normal levels, the refinancing will not be a problem. However, if interest rates remain high, then the home-owner may not be able to afford the high payments and may be forced to default on the loan. This high-risk interest rate speculation engaged in by current home buyers reveals a very different attitude toward home ownership from that of the home buyer of the 1950s, who sought safety of investment and had the goal of owning his home free and clear of all debt.

Merrill Lynch led a parade of corporate giants into various areas of the real estate field. The volatile market created exceptional opportunities for Merrill Lynch, which was actively purchasing residential real estate brokerage firms. Sears was also actively entering the personal finance and real estate market. The new "corporate look" to the market, and the current poor market that is forcing many small operations out of business, will dramatically alter the way people buy and finance their homes.

Outlook. Many economists expect interest rates to remain high in 1982. They see high federal deficits and low corporate cash reserves as placing a burden on the financial markets. If rates do remain high, above 15%, then the housing industry will remain in the worst slump since the depression. If interest rates decrease signifi-

Ryan Homes, Inc.

Home buyers are forced to look for ways to overcome high prices. The "closed wall" system of home building (above), featuring manufactured wall assemblies, can offer savings for the buyer.

cantly to the 12–15% range, then home sales may rebound dramatically. President Ronald Reagan has supported altering regulations to allow pension funds to invest more of their money in home mortgages, and the all-saver certificate was enacted to attract more funds to savings and loan associations. Both of these moves were designed to bring funds into the housing market. Another hopeful sign for 1982 was the lower rate of inflation. Generally, the long-term interest rate is 2% to 3% above the rate of inflation. By the end of 1981, the inflation rate had declined to less than 10% per year. Based on the rate of inflation, the mortgage interest rate should be between 12% and 13% and not 18%. Taking all of these factors into account, there should be a low level of housing production for the first six months of 1982 and a rapidly expanding rate in the last half. Interest rates should fall during 1982 and should be at 15% by midyear and 13% by year-end. The production of new homes should be at a rate of .85 million units per year during the first half of 1982 and 1.25 million units per year during the second half, for a total of just more than 1.0 million units for the year. If the housing industry does not recover substantially in 1982, then as many as 40% of the nation's home builders may be out of work by the end of the year.

INTERNATIONAL

Canada. The Canadian housing market remained slow and did not have bright prospects for improvements until interest rates decline. Many large Canadian developers were pursuing very large projects in the United States and forcing U.S. developers to do business on a larger and more corporate scale.

Arab Countries. The Arab countries were still experiencing a construction boom. Many of the housing units were factory manufactured units and much of the construction was assisted by European and American architectural and engineering expertise.

South America. The population growth of South America continues to exert a demand on the housing market. Most of the South American urban areas are unable to build water supply systems and sewerage treatment systems fast enough to keep pace with the market. The resultant crowding tends to cause faster deterioration of the existing housing stock. New projects were being constructed in the luxury housing market.

Europe. Many European investors see the United States as a relatively safe and viable economy. Condominiums are a favored mode for investment in the United States. Dutch and German investors have been especially active but foreign investments may be discouraged by rising exchange rates.

See also BANKING; UNITED STATES—*The Economy;* and articles on individual countries throughout the volume.

EDGAR J. MCDOUGALL
Stadler Development Corp.

HUMAN RIGHTS

The changeover from the Carter administration to the Reagan administration resulted in a different set of U.S. policies and principles regarding international human rights. UN Ambassador Jeane Kirkpatrick distinguished between authoritarian dictatorships which are mildly repressive, and totalitarian regimes which are systematically ruthless. Michael Novak, U.S. delegate to the UN Human Rights Commission, stated: "We tend to spend more time criticizing countries that are partly free and making progress toward freedom than those where little freedom exists." He believed that the greatest violation of human rights is the "new international terrorism, supported by various international networks." This was an echo of the view of Secretary of State Alexander M. Haig, Jr., announced in his first news conference.

Ernest W. Lefever, assistant secretary of state-designate for human rights and humanitarian affairs, shared this world view, which he described as "compassionate realism." At his confirmation hearings, Lefever attacked the Soviet Union for human rights violations but said he would use "quiet diplomacy" to correct abuses by regimes friendly to the United States. Earlier he had written that American foreign policy should be exclusively concerned with the "external policies" of other countries, "but not [devised] to reform domestic institutions or practices, however obnoxious." Attending his hearings was Jacobo Timerman, a publisher who was jailed and tortured in Argentina without being charged with a crime and who was set free after intervention by Lefever's predecessor in the Carter administration. Timerman told the press: "Silent diplomacy is silence. Quiet diplomacy is surrender." The U.S. Senate Foreign Relations Committee, including a majority of its Republican members, rejected Lefever's nomination, feeling he would be an unlikely promoter of human rights. The Reagan administeration withdrew his name and chose a new nominee, 33-year-old Elliott Abrams, who had no problems in his confirmation hearings.

One region where the Reagan administration sought to take a more pragmatic position on violations of human rights was Latin America, where in 1981 there were murders, disappearances, and other violations of human rights and fundamental freedoms wrought by paramilitary and guerrilla groups, as well as officially sanctioned imprisonments for exercising rights of conscience, arrests without warrants, torture, and detentions and executions without trials. Arguing that there had been significant improvements in the human rights situation in these countries, the Reagan administration instructed its delegates to the international development banks to support loans to Argentina, Chile, Paraguay, and Uruguay. The United States sided with the junta in El Salvador's civil war and considered resuming arms sales to the government of Guatemala, where government-allied death squads had killed several thousand opponents. At international meetings, the United States abstained on or opposed resolutions that were allegedly selective and discriminatory. At the UN Commission on Human Rights, the United States and the USSR both sided with Argentina in opposing further investigations of the 6,000–15,000 citizens who had disappeared in that country.

Elsewhere, the Reagan administration accorded a measure of legitimacy to the regimes of the Philippines (where U.S. Vice-President George Bush attended the inauguration of President Ferdinand Marcos) and South Korea (whose President Chun Doo Hwan was one of the first chiefs of state to visit Washington after Reagan took office). In continuing to play a "China card," the United States at the July UN conference on Cambodia refused to side fully with the five ASEAN countries when China disapproved of parts of their resolution designed to preclude a return to power of former Prime Minister Pol Pot.

The 1975 Helsinki agreement had committed the USSR to respect fundamental freedoms and assure freer movement of people and information. A 1980–81 conference to review compliance with the Helsinki accords was held in Madrid. The USSR was taken to task for harassment of Helsinki Watch Groups who monitored Soviet compliance. These dissidents were arrested for subversion or slander or on trumped-up criminal charges. They were subjected to psychiatric terrorism, bureaucratic intimidation, and officially-inspired hooliganism.

The United Kingdom and the Commonwealth also had their share of human rights controversies in 1981. In Northern Ireland, IRA hunger strikers demanded political prisoner status and refused to wear prison clothes or do regular prison work. The British, who until 1976 treated terrorists as "special category prisoners" with a status similar to prisoners of war, did not wish to reestablish this political status, under which prisoners organize their own command structure and guards rarely enter their compounds. In New Zealand and Australia there were protests when South Africa's national rugby team was allowed to play. The Commonwealth retaliated by shifting a meeting of its finance ministers from New Zealand to the Bahamas.

Amnesty International, the London-based human rights organization, marked its 20th year in 1981. During that time it has succeeded in ameliorating the conditions of at least half the political victims—approximately 13,000—whose causes it took up. The organization has pushed to increase its membership in the Third World to dispel any image of "do-gooders" forcing Western morality on developing nations.

MARTIN GRUBERG
University of Wisconsin-Oshkosh

UPI

First Secretary János Kádár (left) welcomed Libya's Muammar el-Qaddafi in Budapest, September 22.

HUNGARY

A blending of the Communist system and Western free enterprise continued to give Hungary a generally higher standard of living than that of the other COMECON (Council for Mutual Economic Assistance) countries.

Domestic Affairs. In December 1980, First Secretary János Kádár urged delegates to the Congress of Trade Unions to be more sensitive to workers' grievances and to assume more responsibility. In March 1981, the Seventh Congress of the Patriotic People's Front was held in Budapest. First Secretary Kádár and László Cardinal Lekai addressed the delegates. As evidenced at both congresses, the government was promoting more private ownership to boost the economy. Despite bad weather in 1980, the gross value of agricultural production rose by 4%, and personal savings climbed to $5,000,000,000. More than 50% of the housing stock had been built by private groups relatively free from government interference. In January 1981, the government began to auction off formerly government-managed restaurants. Would-be entrepreneurs were promised guaranteed minimum taxes and allowed to employ up to 12 laborers. In April, all industrial workers were granted five-day, 40-42-hour workweeks at no reduction in wages. In June, all adults were allowed to participate in sharecropping, as the government sought to increase the country's acreage of arable land. And in October legislation was passed that would permit Hungarian citizens, beginning in 1982, to form companies with up to 30 employees.

In January 1981, broad price increases of 6 to 30% were instituted, with foods, services, gasoline, fertilizers, telephones, and construction materials most seriously affected. Acute shortages in construction materials, exchange parts, coal, and coke were caused in part by the work stoppages in Poland.

Foreign Trade. In 1980, Hungarian foreign trade amounted to $20,000,000,000, 55% with the COMECON countries and 28% with the Soviet Union alone. All imported oil, more than 57 million barrels, came from the USSR at half the going world price. Exports to the West represented some 50% of the country's total export income and for the first time in many years exceeded imports, by $150 million. Hungary's 1981–1985 Five-Year Plan calls for an increase in exports of 39%, about twice the planned increase in imports. To enhance the balance of trade further and to attract more tourists, the forint was devalued against Western currencies.

JAN KARSKI
Professor of Government
Georgetown University

HUNGARY • Information Highlights

Official Name: Hungarian People's Republic.
Location: East-central Europe.
Area: 35,920 sq mi (93 033 km^2).
Population (1981 est.): 10,700,000.
Chief Cities (1979 est.): Budapest, the capital, 2,060,000; Miskolc, 207,436; Debrecen, 193,122.
Government: *Head of state,* Pál Losonczi, chairman of the presidential council (took office April 1967). *Head of government,* György Lázár, premier (took office 1975). First secretary of the Hungarian Socialist Workers' party, János Kádár (took office 1956). *Legislature* (unicameral)—National Assembly.
Monetary Unit: Forint (29.54 forints equal U.S.$1, July 1981, noncommercial rate).
Manufactures (major products): Iron and steel, pharmaceuticals, textiles, transportation equipment.
Agriculture (major products): Corn, wheat, potatoes, sugar beets, fruits.

ICELAND

Public opinion polls in 1981 showed a strong and somewhat surprising popular backing for the coalition government of Prime Minister Gunnar Thoroddsen, deputy chairman of the conservative Independence Party (IP). Very few IP legislators, however, supported it in Althing (parliament). Bitterness over Thoroddsen's early-1980 desertion of the IP caucus to form the cabinet was evidenced at the party's caucus in late autumn. The government commanded only a tiny majority in the 60-seat Althing, as most IP delegates and the Social Democrats were in the opposition. The main parliamentary support for the strange coalition came from the centrist Progressives and the leftist People's Alliance. Cabinet infighting over the U.S. military presence and related issues was in some evidence, but it did not affect Iceland's longstanding dependence on the United States for national security.

Economy. A currency reform, price freeze, and other economic measures were put into effect Jan. 1, 1981, in an effort to control runaway inflation. The currency law provided for a new króna equivalent to 100 old krónur. The economic package was intended to bring the annual inflation rate down to 40% by the end of 1981, but by midyear a 50% level was forecast. The government's policies were aided by a rise in the U.S. dollar, falling oil prices, and a continuing truce with organized labor. By autumn, however, both blue- and white-collar unions seemed to be girding for a showdown. While there was a marked improvement in the terms of trade, export industries suffered from a cost squeeze due to high inflation and the fairly steady value of the króna. Icelandair tried to cope with losses by seeking further state aid. Foreign borrowing remained heavy, contributing to monetary expansion, and farm subsidies remained an economic burden.

Fisheries. Although catches were generally good, inflation and government policies strained the fishing industry. The 1980 take of cod, the most valuable species, was about 471,000 T (428,000 t), with a prospect for at least that much in 1981. Capelin landings in 1980 reached just 836,000 T (760 000 t), and the condition of the stock dictated a further cutback in 1981. There were mounting worries over foreign fishing off Greenland and excessive growth of the domestic fleet.

Energy. High priority was again given to harnessing domestic energy sources, both geothermal and hydro, which account for more than 50% of the energy used by Iceland.

HAUKUR BODVARSSON
"News From Iceland"

ICELAND • Information Highlights

Official Name: Republic of Iceland.
Location: North Atlantic Ocean.
Area: 39,709 sq mi (102 846 km^2).
Population (1981 est.): 200,000.
Chief Cities (Dec. 1978): Reykjavik, the capital, 83,376; Kópavogur, 13,269; Akureyri, 12,889.
Government: *Head of state,* Vigdís Finnbogadóttir, president (took office Aug. 1980). *Head of government,* Gunnar Thoroddsen, prime minister (took office Feb. 1980). *Legislature*—Althing: Upper House and Lower House.
Monetary Unit: Króna (7.499 krónur equal U.S.$1, July 1981).
Manufactures (major products): Fish products, aluminum.
Agriculture (major products): Hay, potatoes, turnips, meat and dairy products.

IDAHO

A depressed economy was the major news in Idaho in 1981.

In agriculture, all groups suffered from escalating prices for their needs but stable or lower prices for what they had to sell. Beef raisers were hurt hardest. Potatoes and spring wheat sustained damage from May and June frosts. Spring wheat production was off 22% and potatoes were down 10%. Fall wheat in northern Idaho, aided by heavy June rains, held up well, but prices were lower.

Tourism, affected by high gasoline prices and slumping economies, was reduced.

The timber industry was in a shambles because high interest rates reduced housing starts nationwide. Idaho depends on national sales. Of the 74 sawmills in the state, 28 curtailed production and 15 closed. Idaho has 9,400 sawmill workers; 5,050 were laid off or put on reduced working hours. The state delayed collecting $1.4 million on timber sale money to help the industry.

In mining, Bunker Hill and Sullivan was closing its smelter in Kellogg, which employs 2,100 persons. The loss of 2,100 primary jobs in a community of 30,000 will be a devastating blow.

On the bright side, Cyprus-Amoco Minerals was developing an open pit molybdenum mine in the mountains near Challis in central Idaho.

The Legislature. The legislature appropriated $420.6 million, about 3.4% more than 1980. Public education received $185.9 million, 3.2% more, and higher education $67 million, up 1.8%. Health and welfare appropriations did not fare so well. With inflation at 12%, these appropriations amounted to serious cuts.

IDAHO • Information Highlights

Area: 83,564 sq mi (216 431 km^2).
Population (1980 census): 943,935.
Chief Cities (1980 census): Boise, the capital, 102,160; Pocatello, 46,340; Idaho Falls, 39,590; Lewiston, 27,986; Twin Falls, 26,209; Nampa, 25,112; Coeur d'Alene, 20,054; Caldwell, 17,699; Moscow, 16,513.
Government (1981): *Chief Officers*—governor, John V. Evans (D); lt. gov., Philip E. Batt (R). *Legislature*—Senate, 35 members; House of Representatives, 70 members.
Senate Finances (fiscal year 1980): *Revenues,* $1,108,000,000; *expenditures,* $1,041,000,000.
Personal Income (1980): $7,626,000,000; per capita, $8,056.
Labor Force (July 1981): *Nonagricultural wage and salary earners,* 326,700; *unemployed,* 29,000 (6.7% of total force).

The session, which lasted 75 days, failed to pass a right to work bill and a Sagebrush Rebellion bill calling for the state to take over 12 million acres (4 860 000 ha) of federal land. It also beat back attempts to repeal the Land Use Planning Act of 1975, wipe out public kindergartens, eliminate an educational program for the gifted and talented, close Lewis-Clark State College in Lewiston, impose tuition on residents attending state universities, and raise the state speed limit above 55.

It passed bills allowing tax deductions for families supporting relatives above age 65 at home, raising gasoline taxes two cents per gallon to increase highway repairs, allowing Idaho to join the Pacific Northwest Electric Power Planning and Conservation Council, imposing a 2% severance tax on any gas and oil found in Idaho, reducing inheritance taxes, and requiring adult recipients of Aid to Dependent Children to take jobs "where feasible."

A 16-day special session in July redistricted the state for the U.S. Congress and the state legislature. The bill districting the legislature was vetoed by the governor because of too large a population disparity between districts.

Other. A dry August caused a rash of range fires. The Idaho Public Utilities Commission imposed a fee of $50 per kilowatt hour of capacity on newly constructed, electrically heated houses. The U.S. Army Corps of Engineers was accused of paying $2.3 million to acquire a fish hatchery at Buhl alleged to be worth only $300,000.

CLIFFORD DOBLER, *University of Idaho*

ILLINOIS

Political bickering, labor strife, and a sluggish economy made 1981 a year many Illinoisans would like soon to forget.

Labor. A costly strike by operating engineers shut down about $2,000,000,000 in building and road work during two months of the summer. About 50,000 tradesmen were idled by the walkout, called "one of Illinois' more costly work stoppages" by Gov. James R. Thompson. The governor intervened as a mediator before both sides agreed to a $6.55 an hour increase in wages and benefits over three years—an agreement that building industry spokesmen said had "no winners."

In downstate Galatia, violence by union miners temporarily stopped construction of a new nonunion coal mine in August. State police were sent to Galatia to quell the disturbance.

The Economy. Illinois' economy, which is heavily pegged to agriculture and heavy industry, was mixed. The state's jobless rate stood at more than 8% at year's end. The economic outlook also appeared bleak. An economic prospectus by a Washington, DC, consulting firm said Illinois and four other Midwest states (Ohio, Indiana, Michigan, and Missouri) face grim times in the 1980s. The study blamed the bleak outlook on rising energy costs and the decline of the region's largest industries—steel, cars, farm and industrial machinery, and metals.

There was a brighter picture for Illinois farmers, who are first in soybean production and second in corn and the nation's leading agricultural exporter. The state's 1981 corn harvest was projected at 1,435,000,000 bushels, 127 bushels per acre. Soybean yields were projected at 356 million bushels, 38 bushels an acre—well above the 1980 harvest of 309 million bushels.

Redistricting and Transportation. In Springfield, the state's capital, legislators spent much of their time in partisan bickering over transportation funding and a new legislative redistricting map.

The state lost two Congressional seats following the 1980 census. After the legislature was unable to agree on a redistricting plan, a three-judge federal panel approved the Democratic-sponsored Congressional proposal. Although the population shifts of the 1970s occurred in Democratic districts, the accepted plan eliminates two Republican-held seats. A new plan for state legislative districts also favored the Democrats. Republicans predicted that the new map would give Democrats control of the Illinois General Assembly for the next decade. "It's not a Republican map," said a disappointed Governor Thompson, a Republican.

The legislators quibbled over a much-needed transportation package to fund the state's deteriorating roads and the transit system in metropolitan Chicago. Politics, the old regional rivalry between Chicago and downstate legislators, as well as the fear of raising taxes combined to produce a stalemate. No new funding program was approved, and the roads and transit system got worse.

Politics. Governor Thompson's leadership in the protracted transportation debate helped heat up the 1982 gubernatorial race, which got off to an early start. Former Sen. Adlai E. Stevenson, son of a former governor and two-time presidential candidate, received the endorsement of the Democratic Party slatemakers in November. A Thompson-Stevenson match was seen as a classic battle.

See also CHICAGO.

ROBERT ENSTAD, *"Chicago Tribune"*

ILLINOIS • Information Highlights

Area: 56,345 sq mi (145 934 km^2).
Population (1980 census): 11,418,461.
Chief Cities (1980 census): Springfield, the capital, 99,637; Chicago, 3,005,072; Rockford, 139,712; Peoria, 124,160; Decatur, 94,081; Aurora, 81,293; Joliet, 77,956; Evanston, 73,706; Waukegan, 67,653.
Government (1981): *Chief Officers*—governor, James R. Thompson (R). *General Assembly*—Senate, 59 members; House of Representatives, 177 members.
State Finances (fiscal year 1980): *Revenues*, $12,730,000,000; *expenditures*, $12,429,000,000.
Personal Income (1980): $120,434,000,000; per capita, $10,521.
Labor Force (July 1981): *Nonagricultural wage and salary earners*, 4,864,400; *unemployed*, 430,000 (7.7% of total force).

INDIA

During the second year of her latest tenure as prime minister, Indira Gandhi seemed to retain her personal popularity in spite of internal tensions and the lackluster performance of her government. Her only surviving son, Rajiv, was elected to parliament, increasing speculation that he is being groomed as his mother's successor. The economy showed signs of rebounding from two years of stagnation, but there were many adverse trends as well. In foreign affairs the year was an unusually busy one, with an important conference of foreign ministers of nonaligned states in New Delhi in February, a large number of official visits to India, and several trips abroad by Prime Minister Gandhi. Relations with Pakistan and the United States, already under strain, deteriorated further.

Politics. On August 14, in a radio-TV message on the eve of the 34th anniversary of India's independence, President Neelam Sanjiva Reddy told the nation, "We cannot but view with concern the frequent and violent manifestation of divisive forces in the country which brought about the loss of several lives and caused avoidable suffering in diverse ways to a large number of innocent persons. Regional and linguistic differences, religious, caste, and communal differences were allowed to gain the upper hand and to spread disorder and violence." Acts of violence were particularly numerous and serious in Gujarat, Uttar Pradesh, Bihar, West Bengal, and the entire northeastern part of the country. Because of continuing unrest and the collapse of local Congress (I) governments, "president's rule" (direct rule by the central government) was proclaimed in Assam and Manipur. On October 21, president's rule was also proclaimed in Kerala after the government coalition, headed by the Communist Party-Marxist (CPI-M), had been weakened by the defection of the Congress (S), an opposition Congress party.

In July, President Reddy promulgated an ordinance called the "Essential Services Maintenance Ordinance," which prohibited strikes in essential services, initially for a period of six months. The action was criticized by opposition parties and trade union spokesmen as unwarranted and arbitrary.

On June 14, in by-elections for seven seats in the Lok Sabha (lower house of the Parliament) and for 23 State Assembly seats in Bihar, Uttar Pradesh, Karnataka, and West Bengal, Prime Minister Gandhi's Congress (I) party won five of the Lok Sabha seats and more than two thirds of the State Assembly seats. But in West Bengal, the CPI-M, which controlled the state government, won four of the six contested State Assembly seats. The most publicized by-election was in the Amethi parliamentary constituency in eastern Uttar Pradesh. Rajiv Gandhi, the prime minister's older son, was the candidate of the Congress (I) to succeed his brother, Sanjay, who held the seat from January 1980 until his death in a plane crash in June of that year. Rajiv Gandhi, 36, won an overwhelming victory, and thereafter he was a marked figure in Indian politics, regarded by many as Prime Minister Gandhi's "heir apparent."

Economy. Between Feb. 9 and March 5, 1981, a decennial census, involving 1.2 million enumerators and supervisors, was conducted throughout the country. The Census Commission reported in July that the population of India as of March 1 was 683,810,051, at least 12 million more than had been projected. This represented an increase of 24.75% over the previous decade; the lack of any decline in the rate of population growth had serious implications for the society and the economy.

A major goal of the delayed, draft Sixth Five-Year Plan (1980–85), approved by the National Development Council in mid-February, was to reduce the percentage of Indians below the poverty line from an estimated 48.4% to 30% by 1985. The draft plan envisaged a public sector outlay over the five-year period of Rs. 97,500 crores (1 crore equals 10 million; 1 crore of rupees equals about U.S.$1.1 million), and an annual growth rate of 5.2%, considerably higher than in earlier plans. The plan assumed that about 5% of the necessary funds would be obtained from foreign aid and that increased deficit-financing would be covered by higher taxes, import and export duties, postponement of debt repayment, and foreign loans, especially from the International Development Association (IDA) and the International Monetary Fund (IMF).

A UN-subsidized dairy development project pays for milk deliveries from rural collectives to cities.

UPI

UPI

Indian men working on an irrigation project in West Bengal are paid in food donated by CARE (Cooperative for American Relief Everywhere).

In early summer, India entered into negotiations with the IMF for a loan of $5,800,000,000 which, if granted, would be the largest loan ever extended by the fund. Negotiations were bogged down by India's reluctance to accept some of the conditions imposed by the IMF, but the loan was granted in early November.

In February, the ministry of finance reported that the economy was rebounding after two bad years. It predicted that for the fiscal year ending March 31 the gross national product (GNP) would rise by 6.5% (compared with a 4.5% decline in fiscal 1980), that agricultural production would rise by 19% (after a 16% decline), and that industrial production would increase by 4% (after a 1.4% drop). But the ministry also predicted a huge trade deficit of $5,000,000,000, with a 50% rise in the value of imports and only a 4% increase in exports.

In its annual report, released in September, the World Bank stated that the Indian economy was "substantially stronger" than at any time in the previous five years. In support of its evaluation, the bank cited gradual elimination of food imports, "substantial" food-grain reserves, a low external debt, and comfortable foreign exchange reserves. But in fact, in spite of a good harvest in 1981, India had to import substantial amounts of food grains, including 1.65 million T (1.50 million t) of wheat from the United States. Its foreign exchange reserves declined to a near-critical level of Rs. 3,600 crores. The negative aspects of the Indian economy mentioned in the World Bank report, including "persisting structural deficiencies"—such as power shortages and transportation bottlenecks—became more serious by the end of the year.

The rate of inflation, which reached 21% in 1979–80, was expected to be reduced substantially—to about 13%—but the continuing rise in prices for essential commodities, including basic foodstuffs, imposed added burdens on the poor. In his address to the nation on August 14, President Reddy declared that "the rising prices of foodstuffs and consumer goods, and hardship which the poor and the fixed income groups are being put to, have been a cause of concern to all of us."

In 1981, largely as a result of a new trade agreement, the Soviet Union became India's principal trading partner. Total Indo-Soviet trade, much of it on a barter basis, was estimated at more than $3,000,000,000, compared with about $2,000,000,000 in trade between India and the United States.

Foreign Policy. A major Nonaligned Nations Foreign Ministers' Conference was held in New Delhi, February 9–13. Representatives of 91 countries and two liberation movements participated, together with 15 observer and 22 guest delegates. A special session on February 11 commemorated the 20th anniversary of the first nonaligned summit conference in Belgrade. Although the delegates disagreed on many issues, a joint declaration was adopted "by consensus" on February 13. It called for a political settlement of the Afghanistan problem and strict observance of the principle of nonintervention; affirmed the right of the people of Kampuchea (Cambodia) to determine their own destiny; expressed serious concern over growing military activity in the Indian Ocean and urged all states in the region to treat the waterway as a zone of peace; declared the Camp David agreements and the Egypt-Israel Treaty invalid; called for a complete withdrawal by Israel from all Arab territories, including Jerusalem; and gave full support to "the inalienable rights" of the Palestinian people.

An usually large number of distinguished official visitors went to India in 1981. Among them were the presidents of Botswana, Ghana, Guinea, Kenya, Madagascar, Mexico, Tanzania, Venezuela, and West Germany; the king of Bhutan; the emir of Bahrain; and the prime ministers of Australia, Great Britain, South Yemen, and Zimbabwe. Of special interest were official visits in June by Chinese Foreign Minister Huang Hua, the first by a senior official of the People's Republic since 1960; and in August by Jeane Kirkpatrick, U.S. ambassador to the UN, the first member of President Ronald Reagan's cabinet to visit India.

President Reddy made state visits to Kenya and Zambia in late May and early June; to Great Britain in late July for the wedding of Prince Charles and Lady Diana Spencer, and to Sri Lanka in December. Prime Minister Gandhi visited a number of countries and participated in four important international conferences. In May she went to Switzerland on an official visit and addressed the 34th World Health Assembly in Geneva. On her return trip she stopped briefly in Kuwait and the United Arab Emirates. In August she went to Kenya to give the keynote address at the United Nations Conference on New and Renewable Sources of Energy. On her return trip she made a brief official visit to the Seychelles. From September 23 to October 9 she visited Indonesia, Fiji, Tonga, Australia (where she participated in a Commonwealth summit meeting), and the Philippines. In late October she went to Mexico to participate in the important North-South summit meeting in Cancún, having made brief stops in Rumania, Canada, and Great Britain. From November 6 to 15 she visited Bulgaria, Italy (with an audience with Pope John Paul II), and France.

India's relations with Pakistan seemed on the verge of significant improvement in 1981. This was symbolized by a visit to Pakistan by India's Foreign Minister P. V. Narasimha Rao, June 9–13. The goodwill generated by that visit, however, was soon eroded by a series of developments. India repeatedly objected to Pakistan's military buildup, especially its agreement with the United States for $3,200,000,000 worth of economic and military assistance—including sophisticated F-16 fighter planes—over the next six years. India was troubled by continuing rumors that Pakistan was developing nuclear weapons capability. And India strongly objected to alleged anti-Indian propaganda in Pakistan, a charge denied by the latter country. Pakistan, in turn, was annoyed by India's opposition to its application to rejoin the Commonwealth, from which it had withdrawn in 1972.

The long-professed desire of both India and China to improve their relations seemed closer to realization as a result of the visit of Chinese Foreign Minister Huang in late June. According to an official Indian spokesman, "the two sides . . . agreed that their differences need not stand in the way of improving Sino-Indian relations" and that on the major issues in dispute, including the border question, "purposeful discussions to arrive at settlement should be undertaken at appropriate levels between the two governments." It was also agreed that "a program should be drawn up for annual cultural, scientific, technological, and economic exchanges." Prime Minister Gandhi accepted an invitation from Huang to visit China at some future date. On December 10 in Peking, the two countries opened talks on their longstanding border dispute.

The same assessment could be made of official Indo-U.S. relations. The political philosophies, world outlook, and economic and social views of Prime Minister Gandhi and President Reagan were obviously far apart. Whether the United States would comply with a 1963 agreement to supply enriched uranium for the nuclear power plant at Tarapur, near Bombay, remained a bone of contention. Abrogation of the treaty, either unilaterally by the United States or by mutual consent, remained a real possibility. An added irritation was the adoption by the U.S. Senate of an amendment to the Foreign Assistance Act of 1982 requiring a cutoff of foreign aid to India or Pakistan if either country detonates a nuclear device. Other major foreign policy differences concerned Soviet activities in Afghanistan; Pakistan (with India strongly objecting to the U.S. military aid package); Kampuchea (with India recognizing the Heng Samrin regime and the United States recognizing the Pol Pot regime); the U.S. naval buildup in the Indian Ocean area; and a variety of Middle East issues. The long-delayed appointment of career foreign service officer Harry Barnes as U.S. ambassador to India was regarded in some quarters as a further indication of India's low-priority status in the eyes of the Reagan administration. Almost all previous U.S. ambassadors had been distinguished citizens and noncareer diplomats.

APPLE. On June 19, India's first geostationary experimental communication satellite, christened APPLE (Ariane Passenger Pay Load Experiment), was launched by the European Space Agency's Ariane rocket from French Guiana.

NORMAN D. PALMER
University of Pennsylvania

INDIA • Information Highlights

Official Name: Republic of India.
Location: South Asia.
Area: 1,269,346 sq mi (3 287 606 km^2).
Population (1981 census.): 683,810,051.
Chief Cities (1971 est.): New Delhi, the capital, 3,600,-000; Bombay, 6,000,000; Calcutta, 3,200,000.
Government: *Head of state,* Neelam Sanjiva Reddy, president (took office July 1977). *Head of government,* Indira Gandhi, prime minister (took office January 1980). *Legislature*—Parliament: Rajya Sabha (Council of States) and Lok Sabha (House of the People).
Monetary Unit: Rupee (9.09 rupees equal U.S.$1, Nov. 1981).
Manufactures (major products): Textiles, processed food, steel, machinery, transport equipment, cement.
Agriculture (major products): rice, pulses, oilseeds, cotton, jute, tea, wheat.

INDIANA

A "lean" budget, lobby reform, and redistricting highlighted the regular 61-day legislative session, and disagreement on school funding necessitated a later three-day special session for the 1981 Indiana General Assembly. Various sports activities, including Indiana University's NCAA basketball win and a disputed Indianapolis 500, and the conviction of Marine Pfc. Robert R. Garwood for collaboration with the Vietnamese were other headline events during the year.

Legislature. Amid charges of gerrymandering, the Republican-controlled legislature redrew the state's Congressional districts in response to a 1980 census mandate reducing the number of districts from 11 to 10. The reapportionment jeopardizes the political futures of three of six incumbent Democratic Congressmen and moves two others outside the districts they now represent. New state legislative boundaries also favor the Republicans.

Reacting to recent scandals involving prominent state legislators, the General Assembly established more stringent requirements for registering lobbyists and reporting lobbying expenditures. Other legislative measures included a package of four "home rule" bills aimed at lessening state control of local government; a two-cent-a-gallon increase in the gasoline tax, with further increases mandated for January 1982; a hazardous waste bill giving the state authority to preempt local zoning boards in approving dump sites; and a $10 million package of seven bills to spur economic development.

Ronald Reagan addresses Notre Dame University graduates. It was the president's first public trip outside of Washington after an attempt on his life.

UPI

Failing to pass were bills that would have reformed nursing home laws, increased the 55 mph (89 km/hr), speed limit on interstate highways to 65 (105 km/hr), and limited the power of judges to close court hearings to the public. Despite a federal investigation into alleged illegalities, a measure abolishing the state Alcoholic Beverage Commission also failed to pass. Gov. Robert D. Orr vetoed a "Liberty Amendment" bill that would have voided any actions by federal agencies in Indiana and allowed any state resident to go to court against cooperation between those agencies and state or local government.

The legislature adjourned without establishing a plan for the distribution of $960 million in state funds to public school districts. In a special three-day session in June, legislators provided new funding of some $80 million per year for teachers' salary increases, allowed schools to shift $40 million annually from cumulative building funds to other areas, froze school tax rates but not levies, and withdrew $19 million from state property tax replacement funds during the biennium.

Budget. Lawmakers approved three budget bills totaling $11,600,000,000 for the biennium—about $2,000,000,000 higher than for the preceding two-year period. Proposed raises for teachers and for state and university employees ranged from 4 to 6%, and the operating budget assumed that universities would raise fees for both in-state and out-of-state students. The spending program would leave an extremely low $5 million balance in the General Fund surplus by mid-1982 and $15 to $16 million by the end of the biennium.

Other. Hoosier Marine Pfc. Robert R. Garwood was convicted by court martial of collaborating with the enemy during the Vietnam War and of assaulting an American POW. He was sentenced to a reduction in rank to the lowest pay grade and a dishonorable discharge, but no prison term. Litigation continued.

Heavy rains throughout the spring and early summer delayed corn and soybean planting. The resulting late harvest affected farm yields and contributed to farmers' further economic distress.

LORNA L. SYLVESTER, *Indiana University*

INDIANA • Information Highlights

Area: 36,185 sq mi (93 719 km²).
Population (1980 census): 5,490,179.
Chief Cities (1980 census): Indianapolis, the capital, 700,807; Fort Wayne, 172,196; Gary, 151,953; Evansville 130,496; South Bend, 109,727; Hammond, 93,714; Muncie, 77,216; Anderson, 64,695; Terre Haute, 61,125.
Government (1981): *Chief Officers*—governor, Robert D. Orr (R); lt. gov., John Mutz (R). *General Assembly*—Senate, 50 members; House of Representatives, 100 members.
State Finances (fiscal year 1980): *Revenues,* $4,794,000,000; *expenditures,* $4,867,000,000.
Personal Income (1980): $49,177,000,000; per capita, $8,936.
Labor Force (July 1981): *Nonagricultural wage and salary earners,* 2,108,500; *unemployed,* 235,900 (9.1% of total force).

Indonesia's Foreign Minister Mochtar Kusumaatmadja confers privately with UN Secretary-General Kurt Waldheim.

UPI

INDONESIA

For many years the trend in Indonesian politics has been toward concentration of power in the hands of the bureaucracy, the armed forces, and President Suharto. The trend continued in 1981, with a number of signs that the president was establishing himself more firmly than ever as the center of the political system.

Politics. Perhaps the single most important political event was the appointment in April of Judo Sumbono as president-director of the state oil company, Pertamina, replacing Maj. Gen. Piet Haryono. Haryono had disapproved of Suharto's attempts to bypass Pertamina in petroleum projects in which the president's personal business interests were involved. Sumbono was expected to return Pertamina to its pre-1976 role as principal financier of presidential economic and political activities. The president also did nothing to discourage a campaign begun by Minister of Information Ali Moertopo to have Suharto awarded the title "Father of Development" by the People's Consultative Assembly at its next session in March 1983. "Spontaneous" appeals by many groups for the reelection of Suharto as president at the same assembly session were reminiscent of the political style of the late President Sukarno.

Preparations for the May 1982 parliamentary elections also occupied the government. Its annual budget statement promised a massive subsidy for fuel oil prices, of greatest benefit to the urban middle class, and continued large fertilizer subsidies for rice farmers. Devout Muslims were deprived of an election issue by the government's closing of gambling casinos on April 1. At the same time, dissenting voices in the universities were suppressed by Minister of Education and Culture Daoed Joesoef. In June, citing security considerations, the government banned the first two volumes of a tetralogy of novels on the early nationalist movement by noted writer Pramoedya Ananta Toer.

There were few signs of active political opposition. In November 1980, a quarrel between an Indonesian Chinese and an indigenous youth sparked anti-Chinese rioting in towns across Java. In late March 1981, a small group of radical Muslims hijacked a Garuda Indonesian Airways jet to Bangkok before being overpowered by Indonesian military commandos. Neither of these events was connected to recognized nationalist or Islamic political organizations.

Economy. In his Independence Day speech in August, President Suharto claimed that the government's third five-year plan goals of equality, growth, and stability were all being met or exceeded. Indicators of growth in petroleum exports and exploration, manufacturing, and agriculture (especially rice) were indeed all positive, as were the high foreign currency reserves (more than $7,000,000,000 in March) and continued low inflation rate (about 17%). Evidence of growing equality was more difficult to find, and an early report of the 1980 census indicated a substantial increase in landless agricultural laborers in Java.

In a confidential document leaked to the press early in the year, the World Bank took a more negative view of Indonesian development. It deplored increasing regulation of the economy, arguing that the government's own goals of equalization and preference for indigenous entrepreneurs would be better served by more reliance on market forces.

R. WILLIAM LIDDLE, *The Ohio State University*

INDONESIA • Information Highlights

Official Name: Republic of Indonesia.
Location: Southeast Asia.
Area: 735,432 sq mi (1 904 769 km^2).
Population (1981 est.): 148,800,000.
Chief Cities (1979 est.): Jakarta, the capital, 5,690,000; (1974 est.): Surbaya, 2,000,000; Bandung, 2,000,000; Medan, 1,000,000.
Government: *Head of state and government,* Suharto, president (took office for third five-year term March 1978). *Legislature* (unicameral)—People's Consultative Assembly.
Monetary Unit: Rupiah (630 rupiahs equal U.S.$1, Oct. 1981).
Manufactures (major products): Textiles, food and beverages, light manufactures, cement, fertilizer.
Agriculture (major products): Rice, rubber, cassava, copra, coffee, soybeans, palm oil, tea.

INDUSTRIAL PRODUCTION

Industrial production staged a feeble recovery in the United States in the first half of 1981, only to falter toward year-end. Production also declined in Europe, and Japan saw its brisk rate of gain of previous years cut to less than half. As major industrial countries registered output declines, industrial activity turned sluggish in the rest of the world as well. Unemployment rose sharply in the European Community and in the United States.

United States. Industrial production in the United States increased less than 3% in 1981, according to preliminary estimates by the Federal Reserve Board of Governors (FRB). The gain did not make up for the 3.6% production loss recorded for 1980. The rate of capacity utilization for manufacturing remained practically unchanged from the 79% recorded for 1980.

While manufacturing industries increased production by about 2.5%, following a 4.5% drop in 1980, utilities increased at the same rate as in the preceding year—1%. The best production record was in mining, where output rose more than 7%, after rising 5.8% in 1980. Oil and gas extraction and exploration activity increased 10% in 1981, while other mining edged ahead 1%.

Production of consumer goods increased 2% after a 3.5% drop in 1980. Business equipment output advanced about 4% after a 1% gain in 1980. Production of defense equipment also gained 4% after a 5% gain in 1980.

Gains well above the average were posted by those manufacturers who had suffered the steepest cuts in 1980. Thus, tire producers bounced back with a 16% gain following a 23.5% drop in 1980. Primary metals production increased about 7% after a nearly 16% drop. Production of mobile homes increased 6% following a 17% drop. Furniture production increased 4% after dropping nearly 11%, and fixtures and office furniture also advanced 4%. Household appliances advanced about 5% following a 9% drop. Production of construction equipment overcame the depressed state of residential construction in 1981 as brisk demand from the mining sector helped boost production by 4%.

Production of chemicals increased about 5% after declining 2%. Synthetic materials advanced 9% after an 8% drop. Drugs and medicines also increased 9% following a 3% gain in 1980. Production of agricultural chemicals grew 5% following a 4% increase. Output of soaps and toiletries gained nearly 5% after a 0.5% decline. Reflecting the depressed residential construction industry, the production of paints was practically unchanged, after dropping 5% in 1980.

Registering average increases of about 3% were ordnance, paper and paper products, printing and publishing, fabricated metal products, electrical machinery, television and radio sets, ships and boats, and concrete. Production increases in the 1–2% range were posted by food, tobacco, basic chemicals, stone-clay-glass, hardware, industrial machinery, electronic components, and equipment instruments manufacturers.

Output declines were shown for textile mill products, down 1%; apparel, down more than 4%; plastic products, down 1%; cement, down 5%; petroleum products, down 3%; farm equipment, down 8%; aircraft and parts, down 1%; railroad equipment, down 50%; and consumer instrument products, down 3%.

Steel production increased 14% in 1981 to about 127 million T (115 million t). The increase did not make up for the 18% drop in 1980, but helped boost the industry's rate of capacity utilization to about 80%. That was a sharp improvement from the 71% rate of 1980. Steel shipments recovered nearly 9% after plummeting 16% in 1980. The industry grew increasingly unhappy with foreign competition as it watched imports capture 14% of the domestic market in the first quarter of 1981, 18% in the second, and 22% in the third. Steel production in major industrial countries lagged behind 1980. The Organization for Economic Cooperation and Development reported production in its member countries was 1% lower than in 1980.

The American auto industry sold 6.4 million cars in 1981, fewer than the 6.6 million domestic units sold in 1980. Production declined sharply in the closing months of 1981, dropping the unit output by 100,000 under the 6.4 million level of 1980, which was the lowest since 1961. With the economy in recession again in the second half of 1981, consumers had little incentive to buy, given the rising unemployment and high prices, including interest rates. U.S. truck production increased slightly in 1981, but the number of units was just about half the record 3,489,000 trucks produced in 1978.

Auto-industry employment has declined sharply from the peak 1,033,000 that the five domestic automakers employed in 1978. Jobs totaled 750,000 at year-end 1981, representing a 27% drop over the four-year period. Industries supplying the auto manufacturers lost almost 400,000 workers in the same period, dropping to an employment level of 1 million.

While high prices were cited as a deterrent to domestic car sales, they apparently did not discourage import sales. Imports claimed 26.5% of the U.S. market in 1981, just about the same as the record share of 26.7% in 1980. Import sales were 2.3 million in 1981, down slightly from the 2.4 million units sold in 1980. Import sales would have been higher than in 1980, but Japan imposed export restrictions on its auto manufacturers. Since Japanese cars account for 80% of all import sales in the United States, the export restraint program helped reduce total import sales 4%. The automobile industry worldwide is capable of producing some 48 million cars and trucks a year. About 80% of that capacity was utilized in both 1980 and 1981. The industry produced at 100% of capacity in Japan and at 95% in South America. In Western Europe, the industry's production claimed 75% of capacity, and in North America the industry produced at a 70% rate of capacity. Of the worldwide excess capacity of about 10 million units, half is located in North America.

The prototype of a new generation of quiet, fuel-efficient passenger aircraft was rolled out in 1981. The Boeing 767 is the first completely new passenger plane to go into production since 1969 when the 747 was introduced. The 767 has a range of 3,000 nautical miles (nmi) and can carry up to 290 passengers. American manufacturers of large transports shipped 402 units in 1981. That includes 35 Boeing 747s, all but one for export.

Production of bituminous coal was stunted by a 72-day strike in 1981. Despite the strike and the recession, mine output amounted to 805 million T (730 million t), only 2% less than in 1980. The strike, along with slowing economic activity abroad, also held the increase in bituminous coal exports to 5.6% in 1981. That was sharply less than the 39% increase in 1980. Even so, exports reached a record 95 million T (86 million t) in 1981.

Crude oil production in the United States in 1981 lagged only 0.2% behind the daily output rate of 8,595,000 barrels of 1980. The rate of capacity utilization in petroleum refineries dropped to less than 69% compared with the almost 76% rate in 1980. Since petroleum prices were decontrolled in early 1981 and a worldwide oil glut developed, small "teapot" refiners were especially hard hit. "Teapots" represented about 25% of the U.S. refining capacity in early 1981. As decontrol ended their price advantage over foreign refiners, many "teapots" were forced out of business.

Capital spending by U.S. business amounted to $322,000,000,000 in 1981, 8.8% more than in 1980. But after adjusting for inflation, there was little increase in volume, just 0.8%. Manufacturers increased dollar expenditures 9.5%, sharply less than the 17.5% increase in 1980. The highest increase was 27% by the petroleum industry. Sizable increases were recorded also for the food and beverage industry. Spending for new plant and equipment was reduced slightly for paper and textile industries.

Among durables manufacturers, producers of instruments and other durables hiked spending 16.5%. Machinery producers raised investment by 15%, and increases of 11–13.5% were recorded for motor vehicles, nonferrous metals, and electrical machinery producers.

Capital investment was reduced sharply by the stone-clay-glass industry, which reported a 15% drop. Declines on a smaller scale were reported for aircraft, fabricated metals, and iron and steel industries.

World Trend. After a minuscule drop of 0.1% in 1980, industrial production declined 1.5% in West Germany. Output losses were especially

Oriental-design rugs, which are made of wool, cotton, or a synthetic material and are less expensive than genuine Orientals, were heavily advertised and a big favorite among 1981 carpet buyers.

Karastan

Minnetonka Inc.

Liquid hand soap, in pump-dispenser plastic bottles, was a major new product of 1981. The year's sales of the item were expected to total $100 million.

large in glass manufacturing, almost 10%; primary metals, about 7%; rubber, about 6%; and motor vehicles, nearly 5%. Among major industries, gains were posted for chemicals and machinery.

In France, industrial production dropped almost 6% in 1981, after a slight 0.1% decrease in 1980. The largest cutback was in motor vehicle production, which dropped about 45% in 1981, after a 6.3% decline in 1980.

Production dropped about 6% in the United Kingdom, after dropping 6.6% in 1980. Ireland posted an increase of 6%. Italy experienced a decrease of about 4%, following a 5% gain in 1980. The Netherlands recorded a 2% decline, after a 0.1% slide in 1980. Following no change in 1980, Belgium saw its industrial output decline more than 3% in 1981. Production stagnated in Sweden and Norway.

Industrial output plummeted in Poland by 13% in the first eight months of 1981. Polish industry is estimated to be functioning at less than 70% of capacity. Especially damaging was the collapse of coal production, down more than 20% in the same time span. Coal exports provided much of the foreign exchange needed to buy parts and materials for heavy industrial projects. An example of the difficulty is a television factory that was programmed to produce 600,000 sets in 1981 but turned out only 50,000. With much of the industrial base lacking crucial imports of Western technology and materials, the country's industrial output headed for the worst disaster to hit any European country since World War II.

Among countries that registered production gains in 1981 was Australia, with an increase of 6%, thanks to its rapid development of mineral resources. Canada increased output by 5%. Japan saw a 2.5% increase, compared with a 6.8% gain in 1980.

Having gained world leadership in automobile production, Japan is forging ahead in the production and development of semiconductors and electronic equipment. Long a leader in the production and development of cameras, Japan's camera industry announced a new camera that uses advanced electronic and video technology to take still pictures without the use of traditional photographic film. The new camera records images on a small magnetic videodisc, and images can be viewed instantly on a home television screen.

As for developing countries, the information available is sketchy at best. Industrial production declined about 1% in India in 1980, and industrial sluggishness was evident in 1981. Afghanistan reported a 13% production drop for 1980, and events pointed to a severe decline in 1981 as well. While 1980 gains were reported in Taiwan (7%), Pakistan (8%), Thailand (6%), Singapore (12%), and the Philippines (5%), indications were that production gains were much slower in 1981. South Korea registered a 4% drop in 1980, and growth prospects were dim in 1981.

Crude oil production declined worldwide by 5% in 1980 to a production rate of 59.4 million barrels a day. As energy conservation efforts increased and economic activity slowed, crude production dropped in 1981 by nearly 5%. Adding to the downward pressure on crude petroleum production was the growing shift to bituminous coal by industrialized countries.

Members of the Organization of Petroleum Exporting Countries (OPEC) cut their production 13% in 1980 to a daily rate of 26.7 million barrels. A reduction of the same magnitude occurred in 1981 as production dropped sharply in Libya, Nigeria, the United Arab Emirates, Saudi Arabia, and Iran. Non-OPEC, less-developed countries increased production moderately.

The Soviet Union increased crude oil production by 1% in 1981, as new oil fields were developed in western Siberia. The production goal for 1981 was a record 12.2 million barrels a day.

China reduced its production target for 1981 to a level 6% below 1980, as production at existing fields continued to decline.

AGO AMBRE
U.S. Department of Commerce

Photo by Paul G. Beswick, Courtesy of Southern Accents

Harmony is the key to arranging antique furniture, as seen in the Memphis home of the George Treadwells.

INTERIOR DESIGN

The reasons people collect things range from a basic squirrel instinct to, as *The Wall Street Journal* sees it, a more complex desire to convert paper money and weak investments into durable goods, such as antiques and works of art. Prices paid at auctions in 1981 proved that the appreciation in value of antiques and art objects far outstrips inflation, and that more and more people are investing in them.

Whether collecting for investment or pleasure, living with an accumulation of collectibles becomes a home decorating problem. The major challenges are how to organize them, how to group them, and how to light them.

Having many of the same or similar types of objects creates the unique problem of organization without boredom, a problem adroitly solved by the Ivan Karps in SoHo, New York City. She, an art historian, and he, a gallery owner, lined their pristine white kitchen with ceiling-high shelves for the display of their extensive collection (more than 200 pieces) of salt-glaze stoneware.

The placement of large antique furniture becomes a problem of spatial logistics. The walls of most homes are punctuated with windows, doors, and fireplaces, often leaving oddly placed, uninterrupted flat areas for furniture. Antiques generally have to be juggled with more ordinary functional pieces, such as sofas and chairs. The organizational problem is to keep them all related in terms of scale and function, with an overall sense of harmony and in an esthetically pleasing relationship. The living room of the George Treadwells in Memphis, TN, designed by Kenneth Kimbrough, is a serene example of well-organized space.

The grouping of similar or diverse small objects may end up in confusion, or worse, clutter. Los Angeles designer Walter Boxer arranged Jody Powell's collection of dissimilar Oriental ceramic objects on a cloth draped around a table set into the recesses of a bay window. Important to the display is a vase of brilliantly colored flowers, which acts both as a visual focus and as a diversion from the otherwise monotonous blue and white of the objects. Boxer also created an asymmetrical composition with a collection of cut crystal and crystal decanters. Another approach to the grouping of similar small objects is simply to lay them in rows on an unused table or desk. Such was the solution of Lisa Taylor, director of The Cooper Hewitt Museum in New York.

Where art objects—paintings, sculpture, or ceramics—are large and individually exhibited, lighting is the important ingredient. The ceiling-recessed spotlights used by New York designer Angelo Dinghia cast a concentrated beam, dramatizing the color and colossal scale of paintings by Colombian artist Fernando Botero.

JEANNE G. WEEKS

Photos Chris Callis Studio

Organizing a collection of similar objects is a special challenge for the home decorator. With an extensive collection of early American stoneware and an extremely high-ceilinged kitchen, Marilyn and Ivan Karp of New York solved two problems at once by displaying the pottery on shelves. Lisa Taylor avoided the cluttered look by grouping her pen collection on an antique writing desk.

INTERNATIONAL TRADE AND FINANCE

One development overshadowed all others in the area of international trade and finance in 1981—record high interest rates. This was a reflection of the determination by several industrial nations, especially the United States, to tackle their severe inflation problems with stern monetary policies. As noted in the 1981 annual report of the Bank for International Settlements, "sustained growth in output, and hence in employment, will take place only if the process of inflation is brought under control. The fight against inflation has therefore tended to become a declared policy target of first priority; and anti-inflationary policies have in fact been adopted in many countries with the main burden falling on monetary policy."

Monetary Policy and Interest Rates. This tough economic stand began to have modest positive results as the year wore on. Inflation among the 24 non-Communist industrial nations belonging to the Organization for Economic Cooperation and Development (OECD) averaged 5% in the six months through August 1981, compared with 12.9% for all of 1980.

But the stringent monetary policy also had its price. High interest rates throughout the world also slowed down business activity. By summer, the United States had slipped into a mild recession, as acknowledged in October by President Ronald Reagan. Western Europe, too, was suffering from economic stagnation. The strict monetarist policy of Britain's Prime Minister Margaret Thatcher succeeded in bringing retail inflation down from some 18% in 1980 to about 11% in 1981, but unemployment soared to 12.5%, causing a political storm. In West Germany, growth also petered out as the year progressed, and unemployment had risen to more than 5% of the work force by October, highly uncomfortable by German standards. For the first time in the history of the postwar Federal Republic, German workers experienced no real growth in wages, though they did benefit from an income tax cut. In France, the slowdown was partially responsible for the spring election victory of the Socialist party. The administration of former President Valéry Giscard d'Estaing launched a massive pre-electoral fiscal expansion—with little benefit politically. The new government followed suit with a traditional Keynesian-style expansion, sharply stepping up government lending programs, hiring more civil servants, and continuing rapid expansion of the money supply to finance a huge budget deficit.

In fact, unemployment rose in most of the non-Communist industrial world and was expected to reach 25 million, or 7.5% of the labor force, by late 1981.

In the United States the year began with the prime interest rate reaching 21.5%. By March it had dropped to 17% but, to the surprise and dismay of most investors in the bond market, it bounced back to 20.5% in May. The prime slid below 19% in June and then rose to 20.5% in early July, before gradually falling off as the year went on.

Effects of High Interest Rates. The long-term bond market was devastated by the climb in U.S. interest rates. The traditional institutional buyers of such investments saw the value of their portfolios clobbered repeatedly by climbing interest rates. Few were willing to commit themselves to buying 10- or 20-year obligations. Capital markets concentrated in the medium and short-term maturities. With mortgage interest rates in the 17–19% range, the housing industry suffered severely. Auto sales also plummeted as financing costs soared. Economists were puzzled by the stubbornness of the high interest rates, as the U.S. economy moved along at a lackadaisical pace. Washington politicians complained about Wall Street's reluctance to lower interest rates.

Abroad, many developing countries suffered what they termed "an interest rate shock." Some leaders of countries with large external debts said it was worse than the "oil shocks" of 1973–74 or 1979. One estimate was that each rise of 1% in the average interest rate in the industrial world cost the Third World an extra $2,000,000,000 in interest payments on their variable-interest-rate foreign obligations. These debts amounted to some $415,000,000,000 at the end of 1980, up about 13% from the previous year. Payments of principal and debt ran some $75,000,000,000 in 1980 and undoubtedly even higher in 1981.

The Philippines, for instance, had to pay an extra $490 million in interest payments on its

Foreign visitors got more French francs for their money. European currencies were unstable.

Alain Keler/Sygma

Laffont/Sygma

Japan's heavy volume of exports caused friction with its major trading partners.

debt. According to Prime Minister Cesar Virata, who also held the portfolio of finance minister, that amount was about equal to the nation's total annual earnings from its burgeoning exports of electronic goods. In 1981, Virata chaired the so-called "Group of 24," a committee of finance and economic ministers from poor countries that convenes regularly at the annual meeting of the World Bank and the International Monetary Fund (IMF). In a communiqué September 25, the group noted that the current account deficits of non-oil producing, developing countries were rising rapidly from \$84,000,000,000 in 1980 to \$97,000,000,000 in 1981 and a projected \$100,000,000,000 in 1982.

The ministers complained that their difficulties "have been further compounded by the worsening in their terms of trade which, in effect, has resulted in a transfer of resources from developing to developed countries." They also expressed grave concern over protectionist measures by industrial countries, stressing that they seriously impair adjustment by non-oil developing countries by placing limitations on markets for their exports.

Nor were leaders of the industrial nations happy about the high interest rates that prevailed in 1981. When the seven major industrial nations held their seventh annual heads of state summit meeting in July at the Chateau Montebello, a secluded resort some 40 mi (64 km) downriver from Ottawa, Ontario, West German Chancellor Helmut Schmidt described American bank interest rates as "the highest since the birth of Christ." These high rates were drawing capital out of European money markets and into New York, pushing up the price of the dollar, and shoving down the price of the West German mark, French franc, British pound, and other currencies. The Europeans generally tried to stem the outflow by jacking up their own interest rates. But with their economies already performing sluggishly, the Europeans worried that these high interest rates would worsen their economic prospects even further. And the drop in the value of their currencies made it more difficult to stem inflation as imports became more expensive. Indeed, some Germans spoke of a third "oil shock" because of the higher price they had to pay for petroleum, which is usually priced in U.S. dollars.

Currencies. The worst period on the foreign exchange markets came after the victory of the Socialists in France, when panicky traders paid 2.31 West German marks per U.S.\$1, up 18% from the 1980 year-end level. Nor did the continuing Polish labor crisis and food shortage help the status of the mark, since Germany has lent huge sums to its troubled eastern neighbor. On a weighted basis against the United States' major trading partners, the dollar appreciated 13.5% in the first four-and-a-half months of 1981. Later in the year, the dollar lost some of its strength against the mark.

The Europeans had some difficulty getting their own currency relationships straightened out. In October, when the dollar was a bit weaker, the European Monetary System underwent a realignment of parities. The West German mark was revalued upward by 8.5% against the French franc and the Italian lira, and by 5.5% against the other currencies of the bloc except the Dutch guilder, which is closely tied to the German economy.

Oil Prices. Another significant development during the year was the considerable success of the industrial nations in containing the repercussions of the 1978–79 upsurge in energy costs. Commented the IMF in its annual report, "... adjustment to the latest round of oil price increases has been much better managed than was the adjustment of the mid-1970s. In particular, the rise in wages has been distinctly more moderate in relation to current increases in consumer prices during the period 1978–81 than it was following the oil price increases of 1973–74." If wages rise too fast, this sustains high inflation rates.

Further, oil consumption grew more slowly in relation to economic growth than it had in the past. During 1980 total energy consumption in the industrial countries was about the same as in 1973 despite a 19% growth in real gross national product (GNP) since then. Moreover, business and consumers have been rapidly substituting such non-oil energy sources as natural gas and coal. Those trends continued in 1981.

One help to oil-importing nations was a large surplus of petroleum on world markets. At an August meeting in Geneva, the members of the Organization of Petroleum Exporting Countries (OPEC) were unable to agree on a unified price structure. Saudi Arabia announced that it would maintain its price at $32 per barrel until the end of the year and reduce production by 1 million barrels per day. Because the world surplus was estimated at 2 million barrels per day, however, the Saudi action was not enough to ease pressure to lower prices. Subsequently, several other OPEC members did trim their oil prices and cut back production because of poor sales. An emergency meeting of OPEC in Geneva October 29 produced an agreement to fix a new unified base price of $34 per barrel and to freeze it through the end of 1982. That meant Saudi Arabia would boost its price by $2 and other OPEC members would lower theirs.

The recycling of "petrodollars"—the surplus oil earnings of such petroleum-rich countries as Kuwait, Saudi Arabia, and the Persian Gulf sheikhdoms—was carried out with ease, primarily by commercial banks and other private channels. Noted the Bank for International Settlements (BIS): "As in 1974–75, financing the payments imbalances has so far proved less difficult than had been feared. . . ."

Gold and Silver. After its spectacular increases in 1980, the price of gold tended to fluctuate slowly during much of 1981. In London, gold's price had risen from $236.40 an ounce on April 20, 1979, to $850 on Jan. 21, 1980. But by October 1981 it was floating around $430–$440 an ounce and showing somewhat less inclination to bounce upward dramatically with each international political disturbance. Silver prices were similarly depressed. The start of an autumn sale from strategic U.S. stocks attracted such weak bids that only some were accepted. In October 1981, the price of silver was running somewhat above $9 an ounce.

Trade Patterns. International trade, hit by the slowdown in the economies of the industrial nations, was expected to decline in volume for the year ending Dec. 31, 1981. That accentuated the trend of 1980, when trade grew by only 1.5% in terms of volume but rose 20% in terms of current U.S. dollars. Equally significant in 1981 were sharp changes in the terms of trade for various groups of nations. The oil-exporting countries saw their trade terms improve 28% in 1979 and 42% in 1980, but lower oil prices were expected to cause a decline in 1981. The terms of trade for the industrial countries fell 3% in 1979 and 6.5% in 1980, but were expected to improve in 1981 as the price of commodities, including oil, dropped. The oil-importing developing countries saw their

Photo News/Gamma

Gaston Thorn (right) of Luxembourg, the new president of the European Community (EC) Commission, is welcomed by his predecessor, Roy Jenkins, at the January 1981 meeting in Brussels. Interest rates, monetary policy, and price supports were among the controversial issues faced by the EC during the year.

terms of trade deteriorate by 8.5% over 1979 and 1980, but the decline was offset somewhat in 1981 by lower oil import costs.

Trade between East and West climbed from $15,000,000,000 in 1970 to more than $106,000,000,000 in 1980, but the growth appeared to slow in 1981. The United States accounted for only 9.5% ($10,000,000,000) of total 1980 East-West trade. But it ran a $5,100,000,000 overall trade surplus with the East and led all Western countries in agricultural exports to the Communist countries. President Reagan's decision in early 1981 to permit more grain exports to the Soviet Union and a subsequent poor harvest in that country indicated that U.S. farm exports would continue at a healthy pace.

Third World. Despite the economic turbulence, the developing countries showed what the World Bank termed "remarkable" resilience. Their economies grew an average 4.6% in 1980, substantially higher than the 1.3% average growth of the industrial countries. Moreover, many developing nations increased their penetration of markets in industrial countries as well as their trade with each other. In 1981, however, the poor countries had trouble overcoming the various economic obstacles to growth, such as high interest rates.

In addresses to the IMF-World Bank meeting on September 29, the World Affairs Council of Philadelphia on October 15, and the North-South conference in Cancún on October 22, President Reagan sounded the same theme regarding the world's developing nations—there should be greater reliance on the free-enterprise system.

DAVID R. FRANCIS
"The Christian Science Monitor"

IOWA

In 1981 the first session of Iowa's 69th General Assembly met in regular session for a period of 131 days. Two additional six-day special sessions were held in July and in August. The Republicans held a 29 to 21 edge in the Senate and a 59 to 42 majority in the House.

Legislation. Gov. Robert D. Ray, a Republican, listed at the beginning of the session 32 priority items. Of these, 25 were enacted into law. The governor's budget recommendations were followed with very few exceptions. The total appropriations for fiscal year 1982 equaled $1,770,000,000 and the amount appropriated for fiscal 1983 totaled $1,870,000,000.

The state gasoline tax was increased three cents per gallon, effective Sept. 1, 1981. One cent per gallon was added to the tax on gasohol and two cents were added to the diesel fuel tax, also effective on the same date. Another two cents will be added to the diesel fuel tax in 1982. The increases would add about $34.5 million to the state road use fund. The state cigarette tax was increased five cents per pack; the increased annual revenue is expected to be about $17.5 million, which will be placed in the state's general fund. The second special session saw passage of a bill allowing the state to sell up to $200 million worth of bonds to finance loans for railroad rehabilitation.

For the first time in the state's history a nonpartisan reapportionment plan was approved by the Iowa legislature. The congressional and state legislative district plan for reapportionment approved in the second special session was drafted by the nonpartisan Legislative Research Bureau and was enacted without amendment. The new congressional district map will place two incumbent Democrats, Neal Smith and Tom Harkin, in the same district.

Other major legislation enacted in the regular session included the permanent indexing of the state income tax law; salary increases of 8% for fiscal year 1982 and an additional 8% for fiscal 1983 for nearly all state employees; and a change in the state's inheritance tax law, which will generate an additional $10 million in the first year but will lower the inheritance tax due on most estates in succeeding years.

Economy. The state's corn and soybean crops were both reported to be at record levels, and the state was expected to rank number one in total bushels harvested.

Education and City Government. It was estimated that more than 1,000 public-school teachers in Iowa lost their positions in the 1981–82 academic year because of budget reductions. The University of Iowa reported an all-time record high enrollment of more than 26,000 for the 1981–82 academic year. Willard Boyd, president of the University of Iowa since 1969, resigned to become president of the Field Museum of Natural Science in Chicago. James Freedman, dean of the Pennsylvania School of Law, was named to the position. The appointment is effective April 1, 1982.

Ottumwa, Burlington, and Fort Dodge voted to abandon the commission form of city government. Only Cedar Rapids of Iowa's 955 cities now uses the commission government.

RUSSELL M. ROSS
University of Iowa

IOWA • Information Highlights

Area: 56,275 sq mi (145 752 km^2).
Population (1980 census): 2,913,387.
Chief Cities (1980 census): Des Moines, the capital, 191,003; Cedar Rapids, 110,243; Davenport, 103,264; Sioux City, 82,003; Waterloo, 75,985; Dubuque, 62,321; Council Bluffs, 56,449; Iowa City, 50,508; Ames, 45,775; Cedar Falls, 36,322.
Government: *Chief Officers*—governor, Robert D. Ray (R); lt. gov., Terry E. Branstad (R). *General Assembly*—Senate, 50 members; House of Representatives, 100 members.
State Finances (fiscal year 1980): *Revenues,* $3,479,000,000; *expenditures,* $3,412,000,000.
Personal Income (1980): $27,328,000,000; per capita, $9,358.
Labor Force (July 1981): *Nonagricultural wage and salary earners,* 1,063,600; *unemployed* 89,200 (6.1% of total force).

Kalari/Sygma

National funeral services were held June 30 for 72 persons, including numerous government officials, killed in a bomb blast at the Islamic Republican Party offices in Tehran.

IRAN

It was the year Iran had three presidents. It was also a year when leftists challenged the clergy-run regime with a bloody guerrilla war that resulted in the deaths of many government leaders and regime supporters. The government responded by intensifying executions of political opponents, even ones who had not resorted to violence. The country's economy and social structure were further weakened. But for the supreme religious leader, the Ayatollah Ruhollah Khomeini, no price was too high if hardline Islamic rule could be maintained and if Western values could be eliminated from Iranian culture and daily life.

Political Struggle. The first part of the year was marked by political infighting between President Abolhassan Bani-Sadr and the clergy-run government and parliament (*Majlis*). Bani-Sadr used his presidential veto whenever possible to thwart Islamic fundamentalist Prime Minister Mohammed Ali Rajai. Bani-Sadr also challenged the parliament, which was controlled by the Islamic Republican Party (IRP), the extremist faction among Khomeini's supporters. The Ayatollah Mohammed Beheshti, leader of the IRP and head of the country's supreme court, was a key figure in the campaign that was to force Bani-Sadr into exile.

Hostages. No punches were pulled in the political struggle over what to do with the remaining 52 hostages taken at the U.S. embassy in Tehran in November 1979. Although Bani-Sadr had been against the taking of the American hostages from the outset, he questioned whether Rajai got the best possible deal from the Americans when the hostages were finally released in January 1981.

The agreement for the release was signed January 19 in Algiers, with Algerian officials acting as mediators between U.S. and Iranian negotiators. Originally Iran had claimed $14,000,000,000 in assets frozen in American accounts by President Jimmy Carter after the seizure of the embassy. Iran also demanded $10,000,000,000 that it said represented the wealth of the former shah and his family in the United States. The final agreement provided for the repayment of only $8,000,000,000 in frozen assets and, because of claims by U.S. companies against Iran, the Tehran government was to get even less than that figure.

The fact that the agreement was signed one day before President Ronald Reagan took office was dramatic proof that the Rajai government feared that Reagan would exact swift and severe retribution if the hostages were not released.

Turning Point. Until May, Khomeini seemed to take a mediatory role in the feud between Bani-Sadr and the fundamentalists. But then Khomeini's tone changed, much to Bani-Sadr's disadvantage. Finally, on June 10, Khomeini dismissed Bani-Sadr as commander-in-chief of the armed forces, a post the president had used to strengthen his political position by taking an active role in leading the war effort against Iraq. Bani-Sadr found himself living under virtual house arrest, menaced by hostile mobs and Khomeini's revolutionary guards. Bani-Sadr issued a statement saying his life was in danger, and then he disappeared. The fundamentalist regime staged a massive but fruitless manhunt. On June 21 parliament impeached Bani-Sadr, and Khomeini followed through by formally removing him from the presidency.

Until the ouster of President Bani-Sadr, leftist violence had been minimal. Most of the killing had been done by the regime's firing squads carrying out the orders of ad hoc Islamic courts. But now the left, led by the Islamic Marxist Mujahedeen-e-Khalq (People's Freedom Fighters or Holy Warriors) stepped up its activities from demonstrations to large-scale street battles, which resulted in heavy losses by both the leftists and the government forces. Lacking mass support, the Mujahedeen had to go underground, from which it gained its biggest victories.

On June 28, the leftists pulled off a major coup by bombing the IRP headquarters in Tehran, killing 72 IRP leaders and officials. Among the dead was the Ayatollah Beheshti.

In July, rigged presidential elections resulted in Rajai assuming Bani-Sadr's post as president. Hojatolislam Jad Bahonar, a clergyman and IRP official, was named prime minister. On August 30, however, both were killed when a bomb went off in the prime minister's office. An official on Bahonar's staff was suspected of planting the bomb.

The next president was Hojatolislam Mohammed Ali Khamenei, who was elected in October. An IRP stalwart, Khamenei had been wounded in an assassination attempt earlier in the year, and had been noted for waving a rifle while conducting prayer services in Tehran. The new premier was Mir Hussein Moussavi, once editor of the IRP newspaper.

By using hit-and-run tactics, the Mujahedeen managed to kill hundreds of IRP and government officials, sometimes using bombs but more frequently gunning them down from speeding motorcycles.

The government's answer to the leftist terror was simple. The new chief justice, the Ayatollah Moussavi Adebeli, announced that executions would be stepped up. He proclaimed that dissidents, whether armed or unarmed, would be put to death immediately if two people testified against them. There was no way to keep track of

Muslim fundamentalists rallied in opposition to President Bani-Sadr, who was forced to flee the country.

Ledru/Sygma

A nine-member peace mission of the Islamic Conference visited Tehran February 28, seeking a resolution to the Iran-Iraq war. The Ayatollah Khomeini (center) rebuffed it and other mediation efforts during the year. To his left are then President Bani-Sadr and the ayatollah's son, Ahmad Khomeini.

Francolon/Gamma-Liaison

all the people killed as a result of this ad hoc justice, but the leftist terror continued.

Protests. The indiscriminate nature of the executions brought protests from many international agencies, including the London-based human rights organization Amnesty International. In October, former prime minister Mehdi Bazargan told parliament that many of those executed were guiltless and many of them young people. He was shouted down by the IRP clergy in parliament.

Opposition. The mass executions cut the strength of the leftists, but the Mujahedeen was still potent as an underground force. Abroad, Bani-Sadr and Mujahedeen leader Massoud Rajavi proclaimed a government in exile on October 1. The two men had surfaced in France, where they were granted political asylum. Relations between Paris and Tehran deteriorated, and the French ambassador was expelled in April. France moved to withdraw its embassy personnel to avoid a repetition of what happened to the U.S. embassy personnel, but more than 100 of its nationals were detained for five days before being allowed to leave. Ironically, France had provided asylum to both Khomeini and Bani-Sadr when they were opposing the shah's regime.

Minorities. Full-scale battles between Kurds and government troops broke out several times during the year. The general political and social chaos gave the Kurds an opportunity to reassert their demands for independence, or at least a form of autonomy very near to independence. Other ethnic groups, including the Azerbaijanis, were also restive.

War with Iraq. The fact that Iraq was unable to defeat Iran militarily boosted Khomeini's prestige. Toward the end of the year, Iranian forces lifted the siege of the oil refinery port of Abadan, but Iraq still held much of the border area it seized in 1980. Meanwhile, there were reports that the Soviet Union was supplying arms to Iran through Libya. Although technically allied to Iraq through a treaty, Moscow also wanted to play the Iranian card wherever possible. The Iranian Communist Party, the Tudeh, remained a force to be reckoned with. The Moscow-controlled Tudeh was better organized than the much larger IRP and was allowed to operate as a legal party.

There were also reports, including one from the exiled Bani-Sadr, that Israel had provided spare parts to Iran for its American-made weapons. Jerusalem and Tehran denied these reports, but it was clear that while Israel does not support the Khomeini regime, it has an even greater dislike for Iraq.

Peace Efforts. Iran took a hard line toward various efforts to mediate the conflict with Iraq, demanding that all Iraqi forces leave Iranian territory before peace talks begin. Tehran turned a cold shoulder to mediation efforts by the UN, the Nonaligned Movement, the Conference of Islamic Nations, and the Socialist International. For Khomeini, the Iraqis were not only invaders but also infidels. Khomeini is a Shiite Muslim, while the Iraqi government is dominated by Sunni Muslims.

IRAN • Information Highlights

Official Name: Islamic Republic of Iran.
Location: Southwest Asia.
Area: 636,300 sq mi (1 648 017 km^2).
Population (1981 est.): 39,800,000.
Chief Cities (1976 census): Tehran, the capital, 4,496,159 (met. area): Isfahan, 671,825; Meshed, 670,180.
Government: *Head of state,* Mohammed Ali Khamenei, president (took office Oct. 1981). *Head of government,* Mir Hussein Moussavi, premier (took office Oct. 1981). *Legislature* (unicameral)—Parliament.
Monetary Unit: Rial (80.95 rials equal U.S.$1, Oct. 1981).
Manufactures (major products): Petrochemicals, textiles, cement, processed foods, steel, aluminum.
Agriculture (major products): Wheat, rice, barley.

Economy. OPEC officials estimated that Iran was exporting only about half a million barrels of oil per day, compared with more than six million barrels per day during the final years of the shah's reign. Tehran claimed that production was about one million barrels. The lifting of the U.S. trade embargo helped the financial situation, as did the return of assets from American banks. But the Khomeini regime was printing great quantities of money and inflation was running rampant. Shortages were reported for virtually everything. Even European and Japanese firms that had resisted the U.S. embargo were not eager to resume many of their operations in Iran because of the nation's economic instability.

Support. In spite of the agony the country was going through, Khomeini still had the support of a large segment of Iran's population, particularly among the illiterate majority. The Mujahedeen's base was small, many guerrillas coming from a middle-class background. In some ways, the killings of Beheshti, Rajai, and others mobilized many devout Muslims to support the regime. But the key to the regime's survival was Khomeini's charisma, and one day he must leave the scene. Even in 1981 he began to surrender powers to his likely successor, Ayatollah Hussein Ali Montazari.

AARON R. EINFRANK
Free-lance writer

IRAQ

The prestige and ambitions of Iraqi President Saddam Hussein suffered two major blows in 1981. One was his inability to defeat Iran or to bring the war with that country to an honorable end. The other was the humiliating Israeli attack that destroyed the French-built Osirak nuclear reactor near Baghdad.

War with Iran. Hussein had counted on a quick victory over Iran when he ordered the Iraqi invasion in September 1980. His goal was modest—to gain control of the Shatt-al-Arab waterway, the lifeline through which most of Iraq's oil exports flowed to the Persian Gulf and the outside world.

But Iranian forces proved too tough for the Iraqis even though Iran remained in a chaotic state. In the first part of 1981, the fighting was stalemated; it was a war of attrition. In the latter part of the year, however, Iranian forces launched major offensives, even lifting the Iraqi siege of the oil refinery port of Abadan. Iraqi troops held on to most of the border territory taken in 1980, but they were largely on the defensive and in no position to strike a knockout blow.

It was estimated that Iraq was losing 700 men per month. Hussein had put a quarter of a million men under arms, an enormous economic and social strain on a country with a population of less than 14 million.

The Iranian navy controlled the Persian Gulf, posing military as well as economic problems for Iraq. Arms and other supplies had to come overland from friendly Jordan and Saudi Arabia. Israeli Defense Minister Ariel Sharon in October charged that the United States was supplying Iraq with military equipment, a charge that was denied by the U.S. State Department. But it was highly likely that Jordan and Saudi Arabia were sending American-made equipment from their own arsenals and that the United States was turning a blind eye to the situation.

The Soviet Union, which is allied to Iraq through a treaty, had been Baghdad's biggest arms supplier. But once the war broke out, Moscow cut off arms sales in an obvious attempt to curry favor with Iran, which—like Afghanistan—has always been one of the major targets of Soviet expansionism. After the Israeli attack on the nuclear reactor, Iraq announced that the USSR was resuming arms shipments. But it was questionable just how generous Moscow would be. The Kremlin was not happy with Hussein's independent-mindedness. Moscow also did not want to offend Syria, which was supporting Iran and engaged in a bitter feud with President Hussein.

Peace Bids. Throughout the year Hussein made peace offers to Iran, offering a cease-fire without preconditions. While maintaining that Iraq must have control of the Shatt-al-Arab waterway, Hussein indicated that he would be flexible on other territorial questions. The Iraqi president proved most cooperative with mediation efforts by the United Nations, the Nonaligned Movement, and the Conference of Islamic Nations. But it was all to no avail. Iran would not cooperate, demanding that all Iraqi troops leave Iranian soil before any peace talks were held. This would have meant outright capitulation by Hussein, a gift he would not give his domestic enemies.

Economic Consequences. President Hussein did his best to mitigate the formidable economic consequences of the war. In 1981, Iraq exported about 1 million barrels of oil per day, compared with some 3.5 million per day before the war. With the gulf closed and pipelines through Syria and Syrian-controlled Lebanon insecure, most Iraqi oil was piped through Turkey. To make matters worse, a glut in world oil supplies made high-priced Iraqi oil hard to sell on the international market.

To pay the country's bills, Hussein had to dig deep into Iraq's foreign currency and gold reserves. He also raised large loans from Saudi Arabia, Kuwait, and other friendly Gulf States. Thanks to these financial manipulations, consumer goods were plentiful in Iraqi stores, giving at least the impression of economic normalcy. Industrial and agricultural projects continued to be built under Hussein's ambitious development program. Foreign workers had to be brought in to take the place of Iraqi men serving in the

Iraq's President Saddam Hussein (near right) sought an end to the conflict with Iran, welcoming the efforts of various international organizations. On March 2, the peace mission of the Islamic Conference arrived in Baghdad. Among the nine members were President Ahmed Sekou Toure of Guinea (far right) and Pakistani President Zia ul-Hag (center, back).

Francolon/Gamma-Liaison

armed forces. Hussein was most generous in granting pensions to families who had lost men at the front, but there were reports of discontent about the unsuccessful war. International bankers wondered just how long President Hussein could continue to provide Iraq with both guns and butter.

Attack. The June 7 Israeli air attack that destroyed the Osirak reactor outside Baghdad was a great psychological defeat for Hussein. Iraq denied Israeli charges that the reactor would be used to produce nuclear weapons. But whatever the truth in the Israeli charges, Iraq's possession of such a nuclear reactor would have bolstered Hussein's campaign to make Iraq the most influential country in the Persian Gulf region and the entire Arab world. His anti-Israeli rhetoric was aimed at undermining Egypt's rapprochement policy with Israel and at the same time asserting Iraq's leadership role among Arab states. The Osirak reactor was a symbol of power and influence, and the dream of Iraqi supremacy went up in the smoke.

Although the Arab world as well as other countries condemned the Israeli attack, underlying the protests of Arab leaders was a feeling of satisfaction that the ambitious Hussein had been put in his place. The prospect of a nuclear-armed Iraq was almost as much a cause of concern to Hussein's Arab neighbors as it was to Israel. Iraq even had to mute its anger over the fact that Israel had used U.S.-built planes in the devastatingly accurate attack. At the UN, Iraqi and American diplomats worked out a compromise Security Council resolution that condemned Israel but took no punitive action against the Jewish state. Iraq failed to get Israel expelled from the UN's International Atomic Energy Agency.

Nonaligned. In 1982, Iraq takes over from Cuba the chairmanship of the Nonaligned Movement. During 1981, work continued on the huge conference center in Baghdad that will be the site of the meeting of nonaligned leaders. But Iran and such countries as Syria and Libya are not expected to show up for the conference unless the war takes a dramatic turn. If anything, Iraq's chairmanship merely underlines the disunity that exists within the ranks of the nonaligned nations.

Politics. From all appearances, Hussein maintained his control over the ruling Baath (Arab Socialist) Party and the country's military establishment. However, Iraq remains a one-party police state, and its failure to win the war with Iran, plus the humiliation of the Israeli air attack, were definite blows to Hussein's prestige. As the year 1981 drew to a close, President Hussein's position still seemed relatively secure, but a serious domestic challenge to his rule was not so remote a possibility as it had been in the past.

AARON R. EINFRANK
Free-lance writer

IRAQ • Information Highlights

Official Name: Republic of Iraq.
Location: Southwest Asia.
Area: 169,284 sq mi (438 446 km^2).
Population (1981 est.): 13,600,000.
Chief Cities (1970 est.) Baghdad, the capital, 2,183,800 (met. area); Basra, 370,900; Mosul, 293,100.
Government: *Head of state and government,* Saddam Hussein Takriti, president (took office July 1979).
Monetary Unit: Dinar (0.29532 dinar equals U.S.$1, July 1981).
Manufactures (major products): Leather, consumer goods.
Agriculture (major products): Barley, wheat, dates, vegetables, cotton.

Brian Farrell, Photoreporters, Inc.

Although Ireland's Fine Gael won only 65 of 166 parliamentary seats in the June 11 general election, party leader Garret FitzGerald (center) was able to form a coalition government.

IRELAND

A change of government dominated the Irish political scene in 1981.

Elections. On May 21, Prime Minister (Taoiseach) Charles J. Haughey dissolved the Dail (lower house of parliament) and called for a general election on June 11. Troubled by the high cost of living and mounting unemployment, the electorate did not give the Fianna Fail party the endorsement sought by Haughey. The government's supporters in the Dail fell from 84 (elected in 1977) to 78, and Fine Gael won 65 seats, compared with 43 in 1977. (The overall number of seats in the Dail had been increased from 148 to 166.) Two successful independent candidates were members of the Irish Republican Army (IRA) imprisoned in Northern Ireland.

Garret FitzGerald, the Fine Gael leader, negotiated an alliance with the 15-member Labour party, led by Michael O'Leary. With the support of several independents, FitzGerald formed a coalition government, and on June 30 he won a vote of confidence by the slender margin of 81 to 78 votes. Among those named to ministries with cabinet rank were Michael O'Leary (deputy premier and energy minister), John Bruton (finance), James Dooge (foreign affairs), John Kelly (industry and commerce), James Tully (defense), Liam Kavanagh (labor), and Eileen Desmond (health and social welfare.)

FitzGerald's Tasks. An astute politician who had served as foreign minister in Liam Cosgrave's coalition government from 1973 to 1977, FitzGerald is an expert in economic theory and practice. (*See* BIOGRAPHY.) Aware of the country's serious financial problems, he introduced in July an interim budget designed to reduce the national debt and to restore confidence in the Irish pound. His austerity measures included raising the minimum rate of the value-added tax (VAT) on consumer goods. By August the price of a pint of beer or stout had reached one pound, and gasoline cost more than two pounds (about U.S. $3) per imperial gallon. The new government also strove to end the hunger strike of IRA prisoners in the Maze prison in Northern Ireland, a strike that cost ten lives between May and September. FitzGerald's diplomatic skills and his support of such groups as the Irish Commission for Justice and Peace helped persuade the families of the starving prisoners to call off the strike on October 3. (*See* special report, page 238.) Handicapped by its precarious majority, the coalition government faced an uphill battle against the relentless forces of inflation and political violence.

Protest. The prolonged struggle of IRA prisoners in Northern Irish jails for political prisoner status prompted their sympathizers to organize numerous protest rallies. On July 18 thousands of protesters, carrying the banners of the National H-Block Committee and other allied groups, converged on Dublin from all over the country. The extremists among them hurled stones at the cordons of police who were protecting the British Embassy in Ballsbridge. In the

IRELAND • Information Highlights

Official Name: Republic of Ireland.
Location: Island in the eastern North Atlantic Ocean.
Area: 27,136 sq mi (70 282 km^2).
Population (1981 est.): 3,400,000.
Chief Cities (1979 est.): Dublin, the capital, 544,586; Cork, 138,267; Limerick, 60,665.
Government: *Head of state*, Patrick J. Hillery, president (took office Nov 1976). *Head of government*, Garret FitzGerald, prime minister (took office June 1981). *Legislature*—Parliament: House of Representatives (Dail Eireann) and Senate (Seanad Eireann).
Monetary Unit: Pound (0.63 pound equals U.S.$1, Oct. 1981).
Manufactures (major products): Processed foods, textiles, construction materials, machinery, chemicals.
Agriculture (major products): Cattle, dairy products, wheat, potatoes, barley, sugar beets, turnips, hay.

ensuing riot, police batons and demonstrators' bricks inflicted scores of injuries. Protesters marching through Dublin a week later managed to avoid confrontation with the police.

Early in July, a work stoppage by maintenance men in several CIE bus depots resulted in a three-week bus strike in the Dublin area.

Disco Fire. On February 14, a fire broke out in a disco club in north Dublin, where more than 700 young people had gathered for a St. Valentine's Day dance. After flames had engulfed the main ballroom of the Star Dust Club, panic-stricken youths rushed to escape and found some of the exit doors locked. Fire and smoke killed 44 persons and injured 130 others. The official investigation lasted through the summer and proved to be the longest and costliest court inquiry in modern Irish history.

Economy. Rising unemployment and declining productivity continued to depress the Irish economy. As a result of a 30% increase in unemployment in 1980 (affecting a record 12% of the labor force by December), the government promised in January 1981 to invest $3,200,000,000 in the industrial and commercial sectors in order to create 10,000 new jobs. But it would take more than this subsidy to stimulate an economy already weakened by excessive government spending and high interest rates.

L. PERRY CURTIS, JR., *Brown University*

ISRAEL

The year 1981 was one of dramatic developments for the State of Israel. It saw an increase in violence and turmoil in neighboring states, as well as socioethnic division at home. In 1981, Israel faced a Syrian missile crisis in Lebanon, Palestinian attacks on northern Galilee, world condemnation for the bombing of an Iraqi nuclear reactor, the AWACS issue, a critical election campaign, a bitter archaeological controversy, unabated Arab terrorism, and uncertainty caused by the assassination of Egyptian President Anwar el-Sadat.

Regional Turmoil. A flare-up of hostilities in Lebanon among Syrian forces, Lebanese Christians, Palestinian terrorists, and local militiamen; the reign of Islamic terror in Iran and assassinations in other Arab countries; and the escalation of the Iran-Iraq war posed a constant threat to Israel's security.

A crisis between Syria and Israel developed in May, when the Syrians deployed in southern Lebanon three batteries of Soviet-made surface-to-air missiles, which Israel vowed to destroy. The situation was ultimately defused through American mediation.

Early in the year, Palestinian terrorists fired Katyusha rockets from southern Lebanon into Israel, causing numerous injuries and considerable damage. Israeli retaliatory raids on Palestinian positions in southern Lebanon escalated the hostilities, and by May northern Israel had turned into a war zone. Continuous Palestinian shelling and rocket attacks during June and July on such population centers as Nahariya, Kiryat Shmona, and Metulla claimed many civilian lives and devastated the countryside. Israel retaliated by bombing Palestine Liberation Organization (PLO) offices in Beirut in mid-July. The heavy death toll elicited worldwide condemnation. The United States postponed delivery of ten advanced F-16 jet fighter planes to Israel.

A shipment of U.S. fighter planes had been put off the previous month in response to Israel's destruction of Iraq's Osirak nuclear reactor near Baghdad, June 7. Although Iraq claimed the facility was used exclusively for research, the French-built 70-MW Tammuz 1 reactor was 14 times more powerful than most research reactors and had the potential for manufacturing nuclear

F. Lochon, Gamma-Liaison

Shimon Peres of the opposition Labor Party casts his ballot in Israel's general election June 30. No party was given a clear parliamentary majority, and the Likud bloc of Prime Minister Menahem Begin remained in power by winning the support of the country's religious parties.

Ira Wyman, Sygma

The delivery of U.S. F-16 (above) and F-15 fighter planes to Israel was resumed in August after a ten-week suspension. The Reagan administration had delayed shipments after Israeli raids on an Iraqi nuclear power plant and on Palestinian strongholds in Lebanon. Right, Prime Minister Begin arrives in Cairo for the funeral of Egyptian President Anwar el-Sadat in October.

Gamma-Liaison

weapons. Israel's rationale for the raid was a statement by Iraq in September 1980, after an unsuccessful Iranian attack on the reactor, that "the Iraqi nuclear reactor . . . is not intended to be used against Iran but against the Zionist enemy." Israel's Prime Minister Menaham Begin called the attack "an act of national self-defense." However, the UN Security Council and the International Atomic Energy Commission both censured Israel for the bombing.

In Israel, national pride in the mission was tempered by partisan criticism of the government. The election campaign for the Tenth Knesset (parliament) was at its peak, and the opposition intimated that there were political motives behind the operation.

Election and the National Mood. More than a political contest between ideologically conflicting parties, the election campaign became a catalyst for latent socioethnic problems. As June 30—election day—approached, deep-seated resentments surfaced. Polarization became manifest between Sephardim, Jews of Middle Eastern descent, and Ashkenazim, Jews of European background; between orthodox and secular Jews; and between nationalists and socialists. The right-wing nationalist Likud bloc, headed by Menahem Begin, drew its main support from Sephardic Jews, predominantly unskilled laborers and small entrepreneurs; the socialist Labor Party, headed by Shimon Peres, was backed by "kibbutzniks," unionists, and professionals mostly of Ashkenazic parentage.

The election results dramatized two features of the national mood. The virtual elimination of small parties, hitherto a major force, made the religious parties a decisive factor in the formation of a government. Although the contest was close (Likud, 48 seats, Labor, 47) and both parties made attempts to form a coalition that would control at least 61 seats in the 120-member parliament, Labor had to concede to Likud because its antireligious stance precluded an agreement with the religious bloc. Likud's sympathies with traditional values facilitated such a coalition, which increased the political power of the orthodox and deepened the antireligious sentiment among secular groups.

In July, ultra-orthodox Jerusalemites clashed with archaeologists excavating a site believed to be an ancient Jewish cemetery. The incident touched off mass protests. An injunction against the dig by the chief rabbinate was challenged by a High Court decision according to which "the Supreme Rabbinical Council is not by law empowered to determine facts necessary for the implementation of the law."

Nationalist sentiment was given added impetus during the second half of the year by an increase in Palestinian terrorist violence. Attacks on Israeli public offices abroad and on civilian targets at home rose sharply. Hand grenades thrown at public and private vehicles and bombs planted in populous areas killed or injured countless civilians. In August, a Palestinian grenade hurled at a group of Italian pilgrims near the Church of the Holy Sepulcher in Jerusalem killed one and seriously wounded 28 others.

On October 16, Israel mourned the passing of Moshe Dayan, a former chief of staff of the Israeli army, former minister of defense, and national hero of the 1967 Six-Day War. His death of a heart attack marked the end of an era in Israel's history. (*See* OBITUARIES.)

Diplomacy and the Peace Process. In August, Saudi Arabia announced its version of a peace plan with Israel. Although the plan, which called for Israeli withdrawal behind pre-1967 borders, was unacceptable to Israel, the move indicated a dramatic departure from the earlier Saudi approach, which had called for "jihad," a holy war against the Jewish state.

The changed Saudi attitude toward Israel was apparently a gesture of accommodation to the United States, which proposed to sell five E-3A sentry planes with AWACS (Airborne Warning and Control Systems) and other advanced air weaponry to Saudi Arabia. The news alarmed Israel, whose military leaders believed that AWACS in Saudi possession could expose the country's military secrets. The U.S. Congress at first appeared to oppose the sale, but in a late October vote it narrowly (52–48) allowed the sale to go through.

During a visit to Washington in September, Prime Minister Begin failed to dissuade President Ronald Reagan from making the AWACS deal. Instead, the talks concentrated on a proposed strategic alliance between the United States and Israel against possible Soviet military moves in the Middle East. Immediately after the summit, top advisers to the two leaders began working out the details. The final agreement was announced November 30 in Washington.

Other unprecedented developments in foreign diplomacy took place during the year. Among them were meetings in New York between Israel's Foreign Minister Yitzhak Shamir and the foreign ministers of the Soviet Union and Poland; it was Israel's first such contact with both countries since 1967, when they broke diplomatic relations. Visits to several Latin American countries by the Israeli foreign minister resulted in improved bilateral contacts. And a high-level dialogue between Israel and the government of newly-elected French President François Mitterrand opened a new era of friendly relations between the two countries.

A September summit meeting in Alexandria between Prime Minister Begin and Egyptian President Sadat resulted in a projected revitalization of the normalization process and the resumption of the autonomy talks broken off by Egypt in May 1980.

However, on October 6, the eighth anniversary of the Yom Kippur War, President Sadat was assassinated by gunmen believed to be Muslim fanatics. Despite assurances from Hosni Mubarak, the new Egyptian president, that his government would continue Sadat's peace initiatives, the sudden violence created a sense of uncertainty in Israel about the future of the Camp David accords.

Under the terms of the 1979 peace treaty, Israel is scheduled in April 1982 to turn over to Egypt the last segment of the Sinai peninsula. Nationalist opposition to the withdrawal process was bolstered by Sadat's death. Members of the "Stop the Withdrawal Movement" joined in a mass demonstration with residents of Yamit, the largest Israeli town to be handed over to Egypt. A great number of nationalists, some of them members of the Knesset, began settling in the region to exert pressure on the government to change its policy.

Jewish settlements also proliferated in Judea and Samaria during the year, bringing the total to 82, with a Jewish population of 24,000. In October, the cabinet approved Defense Minister Ariel Sharon's plan to transfer administrative functions from the military to civilian officials in the territories of Judea, Samaria, and Gaza to prepare for autonomy.

On December 14, the cabinet and parliament abruptly passed a measure formally annexing the strategically sensitive Golan Heights along the Syrian border. Days later, the United States suspended the November 30 pact.

LIVIA E. BITTON JACKSON
Herbert H. Lehman College, CUNY

ISRAEL • Information Highlights

Official Name: State of Israel.
Location: Southwest Asia.
Area: 7,848 sq mi (20 326 km^2).
Population (1981 est.): 3,900,000.
Chief Cities (1979 est.): Jerusalem, the capital, 386,600; Tel Aviv-Jaffa, 339,800; Haifa, 229,000.
Government: *Head of state,* Yitzhak Navon, president (took office May 1978). *Head of government,* Menahem Begin, premier (took office June 1977). *Legislature* (unicameral)—Knesset.
Monetary Unit: Shekel (13.55 shekels equal U.S.$1, Oct. 1981).
Manufactures (major products): Processed foods, textiles, metal products.
Agriculture (major products): Wheat, hay, citrus fruits, dairy products, cotton.

ITALY

A major shift in Italy's political pattern occurred in June 1981, when the Christian Democrats were forced to relinquish the premiership, which they had controlled since 1945, to Giovanni Spadolini of the secular Republican Party.

POLITICS

The year began with much of the nation still reeling from the devastating earthquake that struck southern provinces on Nov. 23, 1980, taking at least 2,600 lives and leaving thousands of others homeless. The Communist Party and others bitterly criticized the four-party government headed by Christian Democrat Arnaldo Forlani for alleged inadequacies in its response to the needs of the afflicted population. Adding to the woes of the ruling Christian Democratic Party was a huge oil scandal, involving $2,000,000,000 in tax evasions, bribery, and corruption.

Terrorism. In January 1981, a group calling itself the Communist Fighting Unit claimed responsibility for the murder in Rome of Enrico Galvaligi, deputy commander of Carabinieri (national police) antiterrorist forces in northern Italy. Galvaligi had worked with a Rome magistrate, Giovanni D'Urso, who had been kidnapped by leftist Red Brigades a few weeks earlier in what many feared might be a replay of the Aldo Moro tragedy of 1978. But on January 15 the Red Brigades released D'Urso unharmed after certain newspapers agreed to publish statements by the terrorists. When coalition partners decided not to press criticisms of Forlani's handling of the case, the government won (353 to 243, with 7 abstentions) a vote of confidence in the Chamber of Deputies on January 16.

Giovanni Spadolini formed Italy's first non-Christian Democrat government since 1945.

UPI

In Naples, Ciro Cirillo, a prominent Christian Democratic leader, was kidnapped by the Red Brigades on April 27 and held prisoner for 90 days. His two-man escort was killed.

On December 17, U.S. Brig. Gen. James L. Dozier was kidnaped from his Verona apartment by members of the Red Brigades. The group made no formal demands but did issue a statement that Dozier would be put on "trial." By year's end, a massive police manhunt had still turned up nothing.

Despite these incidents, Italian law enforcement efforts did show signs of success. In February, the head of the Carabinieri declared that his police had crushed the Prima Linea terrorist group. And in April, police in Milan arrested Mario Moretti, the most senior known leader of the Red Brigades. By midyear, police officials believed that terrorism was on the wane. In 1976 there were 1,198 cases; in 1977, 2,128; in 1978, 2,395; in 1979, 2,366; in 1980, 1,264; and in 1981 the figure was expected to drop below 1,000. The situation in Turin and Genoa appeared to have been brought under control, but Rome and Milan remained trouble spots.

Referendum on Abortion. On May 18 a national referendum was held on the question of whether to uphold the liberal abortion law that parliament had enacted in 1978. The law permitted women over the age of 18 to have free abortions in state hospitals during the first 90 days of pregnancy.

When Pope John Paul II strongly urged Roman Catholics to join a "holy cause" against the law, much resentment was aroused over Vatican "interference" in Italian politics. But some observers expected a large sympathy vote for the pope's position after he was the victim of an attempted assassination a few days before the referendum. This was not to be the case. Italian voters rejected by a 2-to-1 margin the proposal to repeal the abortion law. Even the staunchly religious South voted to uphold the law. By an even larger margin, however, voters also rejected another proposal that would have further liberalized the abortion law.

Masonic Lodge Scandal. In May, a major political scandal exploded as a result of the activities of one Licio Gelli, grand master of a secret (and therefore illegal) Masonic Lodge known as "Propaganda-Due," or P-2. Gelli, a self-made industrialist with a Fascist background, escaped to South America, but police found in his Tuscan villa a suitcase containing the names of 953 dues-paying lodge brothers. Among them were 3 cabinet ministers, 30 generals, 8 admirals, 43 members of parliament, hundreds of other prominent citizens, and some persons suspected of illicit activities.

Most important was the revelation that the P-2 Lodge was planning to exercise political power upon any indication of a Communist takeover of the government. The three cabinet members implicated were Justice Minister Adolfo Sarti and Labor Minister Franco Foschi, both Christian Democrats, and Foreign Trade Minister Enrico Manca, a Socialist. Sarti resigned on May 23. The rapidly escalating affair led to the resignation of the entire government on May 26, after the Socialists, key partners in the coalition, refused to go along with Prime Minister Forlani's plans for a small reshuffling of the cabinet.

Caretaker Government. Invited to stay on as caretaker, Forlani had the defense ministry ask for the voluntary suspension of all active-duty military personnel whose names were on the list of lodge members.

Forlani tried for two weeks to form a new coalition government but gave up the task when he was unable to persuade the Socialists and Republicans to join. Both parties had made as a condition for any coalition Forlani's dissolution of the Masonic P-2 lodge. But Forlani's efforts in that regard were complicated by the fact that Pietro Longo, secretary of the Social Democratic Party, was one of the most prominent names on the list of alleged lodge members.

Bettino Craxi, secretary of the Socialist Party, also aspired to form a government, but in mid-June agreed to let Giovanni Spadolini, secretary of the small, moderate leftist Republican Party, have a try. Spadolini, a professional historian and journalist, was able to gain the support of the Socialist, Liberal, and Social Democratic parties, as well as the Christian Democrats.

Final action on the coalition was postponed, however, until the results of local elections in Rome, Genoa, Bari, and Sicily on June 21 could be studied. The Socialists nearly doubled their vote to 23% in the Rome elections and posted moderate gains elsewhere. The Communists held their own in Rome and Genoa. And the ruling Christian Democrats lost ground everywhere except in Sicily.

Spadolini Government. Finally, on June 28, Spadolini was sworn in to head the new five-party coalition government. In the 27-member cabinet, the Christian Democrats held 15 seats, the Socialists 7, the Social Democrats 3, and Liberals and Republicans 1 each. It was, in Spadolini's words, "the first secular government in the history of the Republic." Christian Democrats had held the premiership in every previous government since Alcide de Gasperi was appointed in 1945. Many observers felt that Spadolini would be able to hold office only for a brief time before Socialist Party leader Craxi would claim the post.

Prime Minister Spadolini quickly won Senate approval of a decree dissolving the P-2 lodge. Outlining his new government's program, Spadolini promised to fight terrorism by increasing appropriations for modernizing law enforcement technology, to strengthen Italy's role in NATO (North Atlantic Treaty Organization) and the EC (European Community), and to try to curb indexing of wages. The government imposed a rent freeze for two months, modified some tax policies, and increased the share paid by patients for some public health care. On July 11, the new government won (369 to 247) a vote of confidence in the Chamber of Deputies.

On July 16, Walter Pelosi, head of the Office of Intelligence Coordination, resigned after prosecutors implicated him in the P-2 scandal. Two days later, the government appointed Gen. Vittorio Santini to be chief of the defense staff, replacing Adm. Giovanni Torrisi, who also resigned after being implicated in the scandal. New appointments were also announced for the chiefs of staff of the army, navy, paramilitary police, and customs police.

ECONOMY

Italy's economy, often labeled a hopeless problem, actually recorded the fastest growth in the EC in 1979 (5% real growth in gross domestic product) and again in 1980 (3.8%). But in 1981 the worldwide economic recession definitely arrived. Many forecasters believed the most that could be hoped for would be zero growth.

In 1980, the trade deficit had quadrupled to $19,000,000,000, primarily because of huge outlays for imports of energy. In 1981, the trade deficit was expected to total $25,000,000,000. Italy has to import 70% of its energy, compared with about 44% imported by its neighbors.

Inflation climbed to a rate of more than 20% early in 1981, some 9% higher than the rate of Italy's competitors. Because of this, the government imposed a tight monetary squeeze on February 1, limiting domestic credit expansion to 13%. On March 22, the lira had to be devalued by 6% against other EC units, while the discount rate was raised from 16½% to 19%, an Italian record. On October 8 the lira was devalued by another 3-8.5% against other EC units.

Italy's budget deficit in 1981 was about $45,000,000,000, partly because of a reluctance to raise taxes. Viewed as a proportion of production, the deficit was 8.4%—much higher than that of Italy's major competitors (United States, 0.8%; France, 0.8%; Great Britain, 2.3%; Japan,

ITALY • Information Highlights

Official Name: Italian Republic.
Location: Southern Europe.
Area: 116,318 sq mi (301 264 km^2).
Population (1981 est.): 57,200,000.
Chief Cities (Dec. 1978): Rome, the capital, 2,914,640; Milan, 1,693,351; Naples, 1,255,377; Turin, 1,172,-482.
Government: *Head of state,* Sandro Pertini, president (took office July 1978). *Head of government,* Giovanni Spadolini, prime minister (took office June 1981). *Legislature*—Parliament: Senate and Chamber of Deputies.
Monetary Unit: Lira (1,188 lire equal U.S.$1, Nov. 1981).
Manufactures (major products): Automobiles, machinery, chemicals, textiles, shoes.
Agriculture (major products): Wheat, rice, corn, fruits, vegetables.

UPI

Officials check referendum ballots in May. A move to overturn the law allowing abortion was defeated.

3%; and West Germany, 4.5%). Despite massive expenditures on job preservation in both the public and private sectors, unemployment reached 7.7% and was very serious in the automobile, steel, chemical, and office machinery industries.

Milan Stock Market Collapse. The P-2 Masonic Lodge scandal involved a number of financiers, including Roberto Calvi, president of the Banco Ambrosiano in Milan and of La Centrale Finanziaria. Calvi was arrested in June and convicted the next month on charges of illegally exporting large amounts of capital. He was also alleged to have helped arrange the 1979 fake kidnapping in New York of Michele Sindona, an Italian financier now serving a 25-year sentence in the United States for bank fraud and conspiracy.

All of these developments, along with a flood of selling by speculators, contributed to the collapse of share prices on Milan's stock market early in July. The treasury minister had to intervene and close down the bourse for four days—its first closing since 1917.

FOREIGN AFFAIRS

Attempted Papal Assassination. Italians of all religious and political persuasions were shocked by the attempted assassination of Pope John Paul II in St. Peter's Square on May 13. The would-be assassin was arrested moments after the shooting. He was Mehmet Ali Agca, a fugitive Turkish right-wing fanatic.

Under provisions of the Lateran Treaty of 1929, Italian courts have jurisdiction over crimes committed in the enclave of Vatican City. Italian police, therefore, assisted by Turkish law enforcement officials, conducted the interrogation of Agca, and his trial took place in Rome July 20–22. Agca admitted shooting the pope but refused to accept the Italian court's jurisdiction. When his plea to be tried in Vatican City was rejected, he boycotted the proceedings. Agca was found guilty and sentenced to life imprisonment.

NATO and the United States. At a meeting of NATO foreign ministers in Rome in May, Italy pledged to stand behind its promises to the United States and West Germany to allow American Pershing II and Cruise missiles to be based on Sicily to help counter the Warsaw Pact's deployment of SS-20 missiles. For its part, the United States agreed to an early resumption of talks with the Soviet Union on reducing European-based nuclear weapons. By autumn, however, there was growing opposition in Italy to further deployment of nuclear weapons in Western Europe. On October 24, a crowd of about 200,000 marched through Rome, denouncing the nuclear arms race.

Italian units took part in NATO naval maneuvers in the Mediterranean Sea during the summer. After American planes shot down two Libyan planes over the disputed Gulf of Sidra in August, Libyan terrorist activities in Italy accelerated. When Italian authorities discovered an alleged Libyan plot to assassinate U.S. Ambassador to Italy Maxwell M. Rabb, he was quickly flown to safety in Washington on October 14.

Malta. Early in 1981, Italy entered an accord to guarantee Malta's neutrality and thereby foreclose Soviet naval use of that strategic island.

Egypt. President Sandro Pertini represented Italy at the funeral of Egypt's slain President Anwar el-Sadat in October.

Industrialized "Big Seven." In midsummer, Prime Minister Spadolini represented Italy at the annual conference of the "Big Seven" industrialized countries, held in Ottawa. A major topic of discussion was the effect of high interest rates in the United States on European economies.

Italy was not invited to the North-South economic conference at Cancún, Mexico, in October but President Pertini had made a state visit to that country in March, where he enjoyed a warm reception.

Gas from the USSR. In autumn Italy, along with several other European countries, agreed to buy large amounts of natural gas from the USSR in future years. Italy also expressed support for European financing of a new pipeline to Siberian gas fields, despite U.S. concern that Western Europe may become too dependent on the Soviet Union for energy.

CHARLES F. DELZELL
Vanderbilt University

JAPAN

Once again in 1981, Japan was proud of its standing among the world's advanced industrialized democracies, delegates of which gathered at a summit meeting held near Ottawa in July. After his return to Tokyo, Prime Minister Zenko Suzuki expressed relief that the conference had sent "a message to the world" calling for liberal trade policies. Prior to the summit, Japan had felt great pressure to reduce exports, particularly of automobiles and electronic goods, to the United States and the European Community (EC). Delegates at the summit had expressed a common concern over the Soviet Union's military buildup but did not publicly press Japan for an increased defense effort. Suzuki had promoted Japan's policy of "comprehensive security," which would focus on North-South relations, the problems of global development, and cooperative revitalization of the world economy.

At home, the Liberal-Democratic Party (LDP), which had emerged from the unprecedented dual election of June 1980 with comfortable majorities in both houses of the Diet (parliament), staked the future of the Suzuki cabinet on administrative reform. In order to reduce a huge budget deficit, the finance ministry announced plans to hold the budget for fiscal 1982 to zero growth. The plan was also designed to cut the number of central government employees by 5% (almost 45,000 employees) over the five-year period beginning April 1982.

FOREIGN AFFAIRS

On several occasions during the year, Japanese officials announced that the nation would make greater efforts to assume a more significant economic and political role in the international community. Although Japan's security continued to rest on the foundation of the U.S.-Japanese alliance, severe strains were felt in the structure. One source of tension was the huge Japanese trade surplus, which approached $14,000,000,000 in 1981 (compared with $9,900,000,000 in 1980). Another was the steadily increasing pressure from Washington for Japan to increase its defense expenditures.

During Prime Minister Suzuki's ten-day, six-nation tour of Western Europe in June, he stated that Japan sought to develop closer, more active relations with European democracies. Because of its vast automobile exports, however, Japan faced rising protectionist sentiment among the EC nations as well.

Closer to home, Tokyo agreed with Seoul that the Republic of Korea (ROK—South Korea), aided by a renewed U.S. defense commitment, had contributed to stability in East Asia by its efforts to keep up with the military expansion taking place in North Korea. Japan balked, however, at linking aid to the ROK with a promise of security. Severe problems in the "four modernizations" undertaken by China sharply reduced the expectations of Japanese industry, which since the signing of a friendship treaty in 1978 had hoped to profit from plant exports to the mainland. (*See also* CHINA.)

In January 1981, Prime Minister Suzuki completed a tour of the member states of the Association of Southeast Asian Nations (ASEAN). The prime minister promised cooperation with ASEAN in economic development and supported members' demands for a conference to study the issue of whether Vietnam was interfering in the domestic affairs of Cambodia.

United States. Even before the administration of President Ronald Reagan took office in January, Tokyo officials and the Japanese media sensed a new outlook in Washington. President Reagan, Secretary of State Alexander Haig, and National Security Adviser Richard Allen referred to "the decade of crisis," a "diplomacy of strength," and restoration of the "traditional balance of power." The implications were clear—the United States expected Japan to adhere to a "sharing-of-roles" doctrine and take more responsibility for guarding its own territory and the Western Pacific in general, as American attention shifted to the Middle East and the Indian Ocean. Moreover, U.S. congressmen objected to Japan's "free ride" in the area of national security while its trade policies—specifically, the heavy export of automobiles—were having a

Prime Minister Suzuki visited six European capitals, including Rome (below), seeking closer ties.

Edoardo Fornaciari/Gamma-Liaison

damaging effect on American industry and defense capability.

It was reported that Japanese exports of four-wheel vehicles reached a record 5,967,000 units in 1980 (54% of total output), with 2,407,000 going to the United States (up 16% over 1979). In January 1981, a report of the Japan-U.S. Economic Relations Group (the "Wise Men") recommended regular, ministerial-level monitoring of bilateral trade. In his meeting with the new U.S. president in Washington on March 24, Japanese Foreign Minister Masayoshi Ito agreed that an early solution to the automobile issue was essential and that one should be reached before the planned summit meeting of President Reagan and Prime Minister Suzuki in May.

The summit was threatened by the attempted assassination of President Reagan on March 30, but former President Gerald Ford, in Tokyo at the time, reassured the Japanese that Reagan's condition remained stable.

Meanwhile, Tokyo had observed with great interest the Reagan administration's first international contact. In January, President Reagan welcomed President Chun Doo Hwan of South Korea and reaffirmed the U.S. commitment to the defense of the ROK. Foreign Minister Ito, in Washington in March, welcomed the renewed pledge but disturbed both the United States and the ROK by remarking that Japan did not foresee any attack being launched from North Korea. Secretary Haig insisted that stability was being maintained by South Korea's defense capability and the U.S. presence.

Tokyo approached the Washington summit, scheduled for May 7–8, with two advantages, at least according to Japanese media. First, the United States was placed in an embarrassing position by a collision between one of its nuclear-powered submarines and a Japanese freighter in the East China Sea. The sub hastily left the scene, where two Japanese crew members were lost, and Washington neglected to notify Tokyo for more than 24 hours. Although U.S. Ambassador Mike Mansfield delivered a report dated May 6 accepting U.S. "liability" for the collision, Japanese maritime officials involved in rescue operations found the account "not very convincing."

The second advantage, or so the Japanese believed, lay in an agreement reached on the very eve of the summit, whereby Japan promised to limit auto exports to the United States. In the fiscal year beginning April 1981, exports would be limited to 1,680,000 units, a reduction of 7.7%.

Despite these apparent advantages, the final joint communiqué summarizing the Suzuki-Reagan meeting appeared to the Japanese media and political opposition to be highly favorable to the United States. The tone of the final report suggested Tokyo's indebtedness to the United States for defense of sea lanes approaching Japan and hinted at the need for Japan to increase its defense efforts. Moreover, Prime Minister Suzuki criticized the foreign ministry for issuing the communiqué before he had a chance to brief the press. A passage referring to an American-Japanese "alliance," used for the first time and taken to have a military meaning, was emphasized in the press reports. Suzuki himself was criticized for a lack of leadership. On May 16, Foreign Minister Ito resigned "to take responsibility for . . . the confusion."

The defense issue was exacerbated by continuing differences over the interpretation of the U.S.-Japan security treaty, first signed in 1953, renewed after an internal struggle in 1960, and automatically continued in 1970. Upon the reversion of Okinawa to Japanese control in 1972, Tokyo had attempted to calm Japanese fears by adopting the so-called "three non-nuclear principles." Successive governments had promised not to produce, possess, or allow the introduction of nuclear weapons on Japanese territory. In May 1981, former U.S. Ambassador Edwin Reischauer stated flatly that, under a "verbal agreement" between Tokyo and Washington, U.S. ships carrying nuclear arms could enter Japanese waters and call at Japanese ports. The situation was complicated further when retired U.S. Adm. Gene LaRocque, director of a Washington defense institute, was widely quoted as saying that all U.S. aircraft carriers and 70% of other naval ships making port calls in Japan had nuclear arms aboard.

After the Reischauer statement, the Japanese government took the somewhat unrealistic position that the United States had never made any "prior consultation" on the bringing in of nuclear weapons and that Tokyo could only "trust" its ally to respect Japan's nuclear policies. On June 5, the aircraft carrier *Midway* of the U.S. Seventh Fleet returned to base at Yokosuka and received a mixed welcome. About 2,500 demonstrators protested the ship's presence.

USSR. Tokyo was somewhat puzzled by remarks from Gen. William H. Ginn, commander of U.S. Forces in Japan, who was scheduled to retire October 1. Ginn urged Japan to increase defense efforts in the face of the Soviet military buildup in the north but admitted that he did not expect an immediate attack. Japan repeatedly protested continued Soviet occupation of the "Northern Territories," islands northeast of Hokkaido. Soviet Gen. Michael Kiriyan, director of a military research institute in Moscow, in an interview with Japan's Kyodo News Service warned, "We have to respond if Japan tries to settle [the issue] by force." Moscow denounced as "an anti-Soviet campaign" various "Northern Territories Day" rallies held throughout Japan in February.

Western Europe. On June 10, Prime Minister Suzuki arrived in West Germany for meetings with Chancellor Helmut Schmidt in Hamburg. To head off protectionist moves by EC nations, Suzuki publicly promised to restrict surging Japanese automobile exports. Suzuki made a similar pledge to Britain's Prime Minister Margaret Thatcher in London and promised Foreign Secretary Lord Carrington to open up the Japanese market. On the last leg of his tour, in Paris on June 19, Suzuki agreed with French President François Mitterrand to establish a "Wise Men's" group similar to the Japan-U.S. economic committee.

Third World. In the course of its European diplomacy and at the Ottawa summit in July, Japan stressed the importance of coming to some understanding regarding the distribution of wealth and resources between the developed North and the developing South, or Third World. Tokyo remained particularly sensitive to events in the Middle East, from which Japan received most of its oil supplies. In October, Prime Minister Suzuki articulated Japan's shock over the assassination of President Anwar el-Sadat, particularly in light of the planned state visit of the Egyptian leader to Tokyo. The carefully arranged, "officially-unofficial" visit to Tokyo October 12–14, by Yasir Arafat of the Palestine Liberation Organization (PLO) underscored Suzuki's belief that a solution to the Palestinian problem was a key to peace in the Middle East.

Prime Minister Suzuki represented Japan at the North-South summit at Cancún, Mexico, October 22–23. He agreed with the other delegates on the need for global negotiations to resolve issues between the industrialized North and the developing South.

UPI

PLO representative F. Abdel Hamid (second from right) in March hoists a Palestinian flag at the PLO office in Tokyo for the first time.

DOMESTIC AFFAIRS

The Suzuki-led LDP continued to enjoy the support of a relatively high plurality of voters, according to Kyodo News Service polls. In surveys conducted September 26–27, almost 47% of respondents backed the LDP, while the support rate for opposition parties dropped to only 26.3%. Of equal significance, the percentage of voters who consistently withheld support from any party increased to 23.3%, a trend that reflected subtle social changes in Japan.

Society. That Japan had reached mature, post-industrial status was clearly revealed in three demographic trends. First, in fiscal 1980 (April 1980 through March 1981) the population increased by only 814,104, to a total of 117,009,000. Thus, the year-to-year growth rate continued to fall—to 0.7% from 0.8% in 1979—approaching zero population growth.

Second, populations of the older industrial cities—such densely inhabited districts (DIDS) as Tokyo and Osaka—remained nearly static because of a continued outflow to service-centered, suburban prefectures. The population of Tokyo (metropolitan area), for example, declined for the first time in postwar history to 11,615,000 (1980 census). Meanwhile, the populations of Saitama, Chiba, and Kanagawa prefectures, which border on Tokyo, rose rapidly. The average size of the Japanese family unit continued to decline, to 3.22 members nationally and 2.7 in Tokyo.

Third, Japan's population began to grow older. The birth rate declined sharply from a high during the postwar "baby boom" of 1947–1949, falling to 13.7 per thousand persons in 1980. Meanwhile, life expectancy showed a dramatic increase—in 1980 rising to 73.46 for males (the highest in the world) and 78.89 for females. The net result was widely referred to as "the graying of Japan," with profound implications for such public policy issues as retirement age, social security, and transfer payments.

Economy. Like most advanced industrial democracies, Japan in 1981 felt the simultaneous impact of worldwide recession and inflation. In April, the government announced a package of stimulative measures, including reduction in the official discount rate, to reinvigorate the economy. In June 1981, the jobless rate of 2.39% represented a sharp (20%) increase over the June 1980 figure. In September, the consumer price index showed an abrupt (2%) increase over the previous month, reaching 106.0 (1980=100). Part of the increase was attributable to vegetable prices, which had risen significantly after extensive typhoon damage.

Late in December 1980, the LDP government adopted an austere budget for fiscal year 1981, balanced at 46,790,000,000,000 yen. It incor-

Kyodo News Service

An explosion of methane gas in a coal mine at Yubari, Hokkaido, in mid-October killed 93 workers and slowed Japan's conversion to coal as a major source of energy.

porated the lowest expansion of government expenditures and the largest tax increases in two decades. But because of social trends and the recession, outlays for social welfare were up 7.6% over the previous year. Although defense spending went up much less than the pace suggested by the United States, the increase of 7.61% was for the first time, as opposition parties pointed out, larger than the increase for welfare.

Despite stagflation, Japan's economic growth rate was impressive. According to the Economic Planning Agency (EPA), the April-June quarter showed a 5.1% increase (seasonally adjusted annual rate) in gross national product (GNP). Nominal GNP totaled 250,085,200,000,000 yen (about U.S. $1,087,000,000). According to one projection, the per capita GNP of Japan in 1990 ($29,100) would exceed that of the United States ($27,730). The value of the yen against the U.S. dollar was predicted to rise to 130 yen to the dollar by the end of the decade.

Party Politics and Elections. There were no national elections in Japan during 1981, but on June 23 some 230 candidates took to the streets to open a 12-day campaign for the 127 seats in Tokyo's Metropolitan Assembly. The election, held on July 5, was viewed as a midterm referendum on the conservative-coalition regime of Gov. Shunichi Suzuki. Two years before, Suzuki had taken over from Ryokichi Minobe and his leftist coalition administration. Despite a poor performance by the LDP, the governor's coalition won a two-thirds majority in the assembly.

At the national level, the LDP held strong majorities in both houses of the Diet—287 of 511 seats in the House of Representatives, and 135 of 252 seats in the House of Councillors.

Major cabinet changes were made in mid-May and late November. On May 17, Sunao Sonoda replaced Foreign Minister Ito, who had resigned over the U.S. communiqué incident. On November 29, Prime Minister Suzuki thoroughly reorganized his cabinet, with only five ministers retaining their posts. Yoshio Sakurauchi replaced Sonoda as foreign minister, and Shintaro Abe was named minister of international trade and industry.

Disasters. On August 25, the National Police Agency (NPA) announced that the number of persons killed by floods and landslides caused by Typhoon No. 15 totaled 31, with 12 missing and 113 injured. The typhoon struck the Boso Peninsula, Chiba prefecture, on August 23 and then slashed through northern Honshu and Hokkaido, bringing damage to 21 prefectures.

On October 16, Japan suffered one of the worst coal mining accidents in its history, at Yubari in Hokkaido. An explosion of methane gas in a mine owned by the Kokutan Yubari Mining Company killed 93 workers. Beyond the personal tragedy, the accident dealt a blow to Japan's efforts to shift its reliance from imported oil to coal to meet its energy needs. The mine was heavily subsidized by the government and produced about 1 million T (900 000 t) of Japan's total annual output of 18 million T (16.4 million t) of coal. The total domestic output represented only about one fifth of total consumption; the remaining four fifths had to be imported, mainly from Australia, the United States, and Canada.

ARDATH W. BURKS, *Rutgers University*

JAPAN • Information Highlights

Official Name: Japan.
Location: East Asia.
Area: 147,470 sq mi (381 947 km^2).
Population (1981 est.): 117,800,000.
Chief Cities (1979 est.): Tokyo, the capital, 8,448,382; Yokohama, 2,763,270; Osaka, 2,682,221; Nagoya, 2,089,332.
Government: *Head of state,* Hirohito, emperor (acceded Dec. 1926). *Head of government,* Zenko Suzuki, prime minister (took office July 1980). *Legislature*—Diet: House of Councillors and House of Representatives.
Monetary Unit: Yen (232.50 yen equal U.S.$1, Nov. 1981).
Manufactures (major products): Machinery and equipment, metals and metal products, textiles, automobiles, chemicals, electrical and electronic equipment.
Agriculture (major products): Rice, vegetables, fruits, milk, meat, natural silk.

JORDAN

In 1981, Jordan's King Hussein made no new efforts to lead the Arab world toward a unified position on how to solve the Arab-Israeli problem. Instead, he sought to retain his political options in the involuted environment of Middle Eastern affairs.

Israel and the United States. Hussein's challenge in dealing with what he regarded as Israel's intransigence was to balance his solidarity with other Arab leaders and his traditionally friendly ties with the United States, Israel's major ally. Although Hussein had high hopes for a more evenhanded U.S. policy and was encouraged by talks with President Ronald Reagan in early November, events early in the year severely strained relations.

On January 27, at the Islamic summit in Taif, Saudi Arabia, Hussein again rejected the so-called "Jordanian option," whereby Jordan would join the Camp David peace negotiations. During a stop in Amman by U.S. Secretary of State Alexander Haig, April 6–7, Hussein not only repeated his position but insisted that the only acceptable settlement must include complete Israeli withdrawal to its 1967 borders and self-determination for the Palestinians.

Given no U.S. support, Hussein made a May 26–28 visit to Moscow, his first since 1976, and expressed support for a Soviet proposal to convene an international peace conference. Hussein's displeasure with U.S. policy was increased by tacit U.S. acceptance of Israel's June 7 air attack on an Iraqi nuclear installation. On July 8, Hussein declared that the reality in the Middle East was that "the United States is Israel and Israel is the United States."

Shortly after the late summer announcement of a U.S.-Israeli agreement to allow the stockpiling of strategic U.S. supplies in Israel, Hussein remarked that it was characteristic of the United States' "rather simplistic attitude" toward the region. Relations deteriorated to the point that, on September 23, the United States rushed to assure Jordan that rumors of U.S. support for an Israeli plan to dismember the Jordanian state were false. Hussein said that his November 2–3 meetings in Washington "left me more reassured than any in the past," but he also announced plans to purchase additional arms from the Soviet Union.

Tension with Syria. Differences between Jordan and Syria continued in 1981. Hussein was openly critical of both Syria's role in Lebanon and its refusal to join an anti-Soviet resolution on Afghanistan at the Islamic summit in January. Syrian President Hafez al-Assad held Hussein responsible for aiding the antigovernment activities of Syria's fundamentalist Muslim Brotherhood. Tensions were exacerbated when Syrian gunmen kidnapped a Jordanian diplomat in Beirut on February 6. On March 24, Assad denounced Hussein as the man who lost the West Bank to Israel. The tension eased when the kidnapped official was released on April 14, but relations never really improved. During the prolonged regional crisis over the installation of Syrian surface-to-air missiles in Lebanon, Hussein announced on June 2 that Jordan would provide no military aid if Syria were attacked by Israel. Hussein was the only major Arab leader to refuse assistance to Syria.

Wide World Photos

King Hussein of Jordan was left "reassured" by talks with President Reagan in November.

Economy. On March 16, Jordan announced a new five-year plan designed to attract foreign investment and develop export industries. The 1981 trade deficit was expected to surpass the $1,808,000,000 level of 1980, but subsidies from oil-rich neighbors helped ease the financial difficulties. Between July 6 and August 14, Jordan received $250 million of the annual Arab grant of $1,250,000,000 pledged in 1978.

F. NICHOLAS WILLARD
Georgetown University

JORDAN • Information Highlights

Official Name: Hashemite Kingdom of Jordan.
Location: Southwest Asia.
Area: 37,738 sq mi (97 740 km^2).
Population (1981 est.): 3,300,000.
Chief Cities (Nov. 1979): Amman, the capital, 648,587; Zarqa, 215,687; Irbid, 112,954.
Government: *Head of state,* Hussein ibn Talal, king (acceded Aug. 1952). *Head of government,* Mudar Badran, prime minister (took office Aug. 1980). *Legislature*—National Consultative Assembly
Monetary Unit: Dinar (0.3310 dinar equals U.S.$1, Nov. 1981).
Manufactures (major products): Cement, phosphate, petroleum products.
Agriculture (major products): Wheat, fruits, olive oil, vegetables.

KANSAS

The Kansas economy remained relatively stable in 1981. The state ranked among the leaders in aircraft production and in agricultural exports. The unemployment rate remained low.

In spite of a mild winter, a late frost on May 10 severely damaged the wheat crop. Great Bend and other towns in central Kansas were flooded in June after heavy rains. A tornado struck Lawrence in June, causing numerous injuries, at least one death, and extensive damage.

Agriculture. The drought of the previous fall, insects, the late frost, rains, and flooding combined to reduce significantly the 1981 wheat harvest. The frost was particularly damaging because mild spring weather had caused the crop to be two to three weeks ahead of schedule. The freeze caught the wheat in the critical bloom period. The total 1981 wheat crop was 305 million bushels, 27% below the yield of the previous year. The average yield per acre was 25 bushels, a significant decrease from the 35-bushel average of 1980 and well below the 32-bushels-per-acre average of the last ten years. Acreage left uncut either due to low yield or overripeness was nearly double the total for 1980.

Legislation. Dissension in the 1981 Kansas legislature centered on money matters. In his budget message, Gov. John Carlin (D) called for increased state aid for schools and highways and proposed to provide increased funding through a severance tax on oil, natural gas, and coal. The Republican leadership in the legislature generally opposed the tax and it was never debated by the full Senate.

The legislature balanced the budget for the first time since 1972. The omnibus appropriation bill, passed in the closing days of the session, however, was the subject of controversy after adjournment. Governor Carlin used his line-term appropriation veto power to delete a section that set limits on the percentage increase allowed school districts, arguing that the section was an appropriation because it determined the amount of money available to school districts. Attorney General Robert Stephan, at the urging of the Republican leadership, filed a suit against Carlin that charged the veto was unconstitutional because the section in question was substantive law. The Kansas Supreme Court heard the case and ruled that the governor's veto was illegal because the section was substantive law but also that the legislature had exceeded its constitutional power by including a substantive issue in an appropriation bill.

Prisons. On September 6, seven inmates at the state penitentiary in Lansing, including five convicted murderers, assaulted a guard and escaped. It took Kansas and Missouri law officers a week to capture two escapees. An investigation of prison security followed. Later in September one inmate stabbed another to death and in October a guard was killed by an inmate. A shake-up in prison administration followed with the dismissal of the prison director and a deputy director. The directions for the state corrections program have been under discussion for several years.

PATRICIA A. MICHAELIS
Kansas State Historical Society

KANSAS • Information Highlights

Area: 82,277 sq mi (213 097 km²).
Population (1980 census): 2,363,208.
Chief Cities (1980 census): Topeka, the capital, 115,266; Wichita, 279,272; Kansas City, 161,087; Overland Park, 81,784; Lawrence, 52,738; Salina, 41,843; Hutchinson, 40,284; Olathe, 37,258; Leavenworth, 33,656; Manhattan, 32,644.
Government (1981): *Chief Officers*—governor, John Carlin (D); lt. gov., Paul V. Dugan (D). *Legislature*—Senate, 40 members; House of Representatives, 125 members.
State Finances (fiscal year 1980): *Revenues,* $2,419,000,000; *expenditures,* $2,254,000,000.
Personal Income (1980): $23,648,000,000; per capita, $9,983.
Labor Force (July 1981): *Nonagricultural wage and salary earners,* 943,400; *unemployed,* 49,800 (4.0% of total force).

KENTUCKY

The most important development in the state was the continuation of the economic downturn. High interest rates had a serious impact on the building industry and on the automotive and appliance industries that are heavily concentrated in Louisville. The number and length of layoffs increased during the year. Another serious blow to the state was the 72-day coal strike early in the year. It affected other business in the counties producing coal and reduced state revenue from the severance tax. The coal strike was also marked at times by violence around the mines and on the highways where trucks, hauling nonunion coal, were fired on.

In the spring heavy rains and flooding damaged crops, but excellent weather later in the year contributed to a record corn crop and higher than usual tobacco and soybean crops. Because the national corn crop was high, however, Kentucky farmers faced a drop in prices.

In late October the state agreed to new boundary lines, ending 15 years of litigation between Ohio and Kentucky.

KENTUCKY • Information Highlights

Area: 40,409 sq mi (104 659 km²).
Population (1980 census): 3,661,433.
Chief Cities (1980 census): Frankfort, the capital, 25,973; Louisville, 298,451; Lexington-Fayette, 204,165; Owensboro, 54,450; Covington, 49,013; Bowling Green, 40,450; Paducah, 29,315; Hopkinsville, 27,318; Ashland, 27,064; Henderson, 24,834.
Government (1981): *Chief Officers*—governor, John Y. Brown, Jr. (D); lt. gov., Martha Layne Collins (D). *General Assembly*—Senate, 38 members; House of Representatives, 100 members.
State Finances (fiscal year 1980): *Revenues,* $4,168,000,000; *expenditures,* $4,569,000,000.
Personal Income (1980): $27,939,000,000; per capita, $7,613.
Labor Force (July 1981): *Nonagricultural wage and salary earners,* 1,187,400; *unemployed,* 117,100 (7.1% of total force).

Retrenchment in Government. Because of the economic slump and the coal strike, tax revenues for the 1980–82 fiscal years fell far below estimates, and there was no budget surplus to accommodate the shortfall. As a result, it became necessary to make further reductions in state spending in 1981. The reductions, effective over a two-year period and announced by Gov. John Y. Brown, added up to a reduction of about $500 million or about 11% of the biennial budget.

As a result, sharp cuts were made in spending for welfare programs and for elementary, secondary, and higher education. On the college campuses, building projects were postponed, tuition was increased, and vacancies were left unfilled, but the universities were able to avoid firing faculty. A state study commission urged both more funding for higher education and the elimination of duplication of programs.

Governor Brown made the decisions on cutting expenditures himself, without calling a special session of the legislature, as some had urged. Most legislators seemed to agree with the governor that the state should avoid raising taxes.

The reduction in federal funding for programs that took effect late in 1981 added to the problems of state government; the effects on welfare programs were particularly severe.

Elections. Kentucky was one of the few states electing state legislators in 1981. Representatives were to serve terms of three years and senators were elected for five years, as a transition to legislative elections in even-numbered years. Democrats retained legislative control.

The most controversial issue in the November elections was a constitutional amendment to allow the governor and other statewide officials to serve a second consecutive term. Governor Brown endorsed the amendment, and the vote was widely perceived in advance as a referendum on Brown and his administration. The elections returns produced a substantial majority against the amendment.

MALCOLM E. JEWELL, *University of Kentucky*

KENYA

A surface stability hid some deep-seated social and economic problems in Kenya in 1981.

Economics. A shortage of basic foodstuffs caused widespread unrest in Kenya. Due to drought and to misguided government policies regarding farm supports, the nation was faced with the need to import 320,000 tons of grain at a cost of $70 million, and to subsidize the retail sale of the grain to keep the price at about $1.00 per bag. This not only cost Kenya needed foreign exchange, but also led to smuggling and hoarding as profiteers took advantage of the situation.

Kenya also saw its hope for a revival of the East African Community vanish in disagreements with Uganda and Tanzania. As a result, Kenya lost about $125 million in trade and was forced to continue operating the money-losing national airline alone. The Kenyan economy also suffered from the New Year's Eve bombing of the famed Norfolk Hotel in Nairobi, which killed at least 15 persons and injured dozens more. Though terrorism is rare in Kenya, and the bombers were soon identified, it was feared the incident would seriously hurt Kenya's $500 million tourist industry.

Overall, the economy stagnated, as 35% of the nation's foreign earnings went to pay for oil imports and the average world price for Kenyan agricultural products (especially coffee) fell by some 30%.

Military Affairs. Kenya had to face continued unrest in the Northeast Frontier Province, where ethnic Somalis have been agitating for autonomy or even secession and union with the Somali Republic. "Bandit" attacks and random violence led to the death of dozens, including a priest, and the government was worried by the presence of sophisticated weapons in the hands of the bandits. Cattle raids from Uganda and Ethiopia are the usual cause of violence in the region, but the unrest there has taken on political overtones. One result was a series of meetings between President Moi and Ethiopian leader Mengistu Haile Mariam. Though the two countries are radically different in foreign and domestic policies, both fear the threat of Somali expansionism and recognize the need to coordinate border security.

Foreign Affairs. Kenya continued its close cooperation with the United States. The latter agreed to dredge Mombasa harbor for large ships, while Kenya accepted U.S. Navy personnel for R and R and allowed U.S. Marines of the Rapid Deployment Force to conduct training exercises in the Northeast. An agreement exists between the two countries on joint base use for Indian Ocean regional security. President Moi met with President Reagan and other U.S. officials in Washington in September.

Kenya and India signed agreements covering technical and economic cooperation and cultural exchanges. President Moi visited Nigeria and Ghana during 1981. Kenya played host to the 18th annual summit of the Organization of African Unity (OAU). President Moi served as chairman.

ROBERT GARFIELD, *DePaul University*

KENYA • Information Highlights

Official Name: Republic of Kenya.
Location: East Coast of Africa.
Area: 224,961 sq mi (582 649 km^2).
Population: 16,500,000.
Chief Cities: Nairobi, the capital, 959,000; Mombasa, 401,000.
Government: *Head of state and government,* Daniel arap Moi, president (took office Oct. 1978). *Legislature* (unicameral)—National Assembly, 170 members.
Monetary Unit: Kenya shilling (8.45 shillings equal U.S. $1, April 1981).
Manufactures (major products): Petroleum products, cement, beer.
Agriculture (major products): Corn, wheat, rice, sugarcane, coffee, tea, meat, hides.

KOREA

In 1981 untested new leaders in both South and North Korea consolidated their positions in the midst of sharp domestic and international tensions. Chun Doo Hwan, who had brutally crushed mass opposition and silenced the major opposition political parties in the South in 1980, strengthened the sinews of the dictatorship and its ties with the United States and Japan. The regime continued, however, to face acute economic problems and periodic outbursts of protest by students, Christian groups, and workers. In the North, Kim Chong Il, son and designated successor to Kim Il Sung, strengthened his political and military position. North-South and international tensions were at high levels as both sides traded recriminations.

SOUTH KOREA

Politics. Elections for a new parliament in February-March paved the way for the inauguration of the 50-year-old Gen. Chun Doo Hwan as president of South Korea, formally ending the 16-month interregnum following the assassination of military dictator Park Chung Hee. Park had ruled South Korea with an iron hand during 18 years of tumultuous social change and high speed export-led economic growth. Chun's personal military dictatorship, beneath a transparent parliamentary facade, continues important traditions characteristic of South Korean politics since 1961. It also retains the loyalty of Western-trained technocrats, including Premier Nam Duck Woo, a key planning figure under the previous regime.

President and Mrs. Chun Doo Hwan join 16 million S. Koreans in voting in parliamentary elections.

UPI

The extraordinary measures taken to assure Chun's election for a seven-year term as president testify to the insecurity of the regime. They included the purge of 800 politicians active under the former regime. Deposed New Democratic party opposition leader Kim Young Sam remained under house arrest and popular dissident leader Kim Dae Jung was serving a life term on charges of sedition. Under conditions combining direct repression and division of the opposition, Chun's Democratic Justice Party won 90 out of 92 district seats in the 1981 election and claimed a total of 151 out of 276 seats in parliament despite collecting only 35% of the 16 million votes cast. "They've changed the rusty old Park barbed wire for shiny new barbed wire," one diplomat commented, "but it is still barbed wire." In September, reacting to international charges that as many as 15,000 dissidents were being detained without trial, a South Korean embassy spokesman in Tokyo said that 3,000 people were being held without trial.

The most dangerous opposition to the Chun regime in 1981 stemmed not from political dissidents and human-rights advocates, however. It sprang rather from acute economic problems.

Economics. Following the worst economic performance in 20 years in 1980—including a 5.7% decline in gross national product (GNP), a 28% rate of inflation, a 36% drop in the value of the won, and an agricultural disaster—the regime promulgated new economic guidelines. Even official figures recognized a 6% unemployment rate by the end of 1980, the highest in many years. A new course was spelled out in the five-year economic and social development plan unfurled in September for the years 1982–87. The plan projects continued export-led growth. Despite the more than $19,000,000,000 medium- and long-term debt burden, South Korea looked to an estimated $8,400,000,000 in international financing in 1981. For the second year in a row, South Korea obtained emergency loans from the International Monetary Fund ($706 million). The current plan, nonetheless, signals the end of the era of galloping growth.

The new plan projects annual GNP growth rates of 7.6% and export growth of 11.4%, both well below the performance of the preceding decade. The focus of the plan, however, is a restructuring, backing away from the costly and grandiose heavy industrial projects of the former plan and attempting to bring the nation's rampant inflation under control. Electronics, auto, and textile industries are slated for rapid expansion, but no new heavy industrial complexes are projected. Meanwhile skyrocketing oil prices, chronic trade deficits ($3,200,000,000 in 1980), and heavy debt continued to threaten efforts to turn the economy around.

Typhoon Agnes dumped heavy rains on the extreme southern section of Korea in 1981, killing several persons.

UPI

Restructuring can also be observed in the changing relationship between labor and capital charted by the present South Korean administration. If the initial impulse of the Park regime in the early phases of rapid industrialization was to outlaw labor organization, the labor law which went into effect in January 1981 provides the clearest indication of changing winds. The new law requires each enterprise to establish an employee-management council, a vehicle both for worker indoctrination and the mediation of disputes. This corporatist approach seeks to undercut further the role of unions which represent 1.7 million workers, approximately one fourth of the seven-million-member industrial labor force. These moves followed the 1980 "purification" of the leadership of the Korean Federation of Trade Unions. The new policies explicitly bar industrial unions from negotiating directly with companies. At the same time, the government has effectively attacked the church-supported Urban Industrial Mission that supported several of the most militant strikes during the late 1970s. The regime has succeeded in lowering real wages in an effort to regain its comparative advantage in international markets.

The five-year economic plan projects increased social spending, but it ignores the polarization of Korean society, including growing divisions between rich and poor and between city and countryside. For example, official figures revealed that the top 20% of income earners increased their share of national income from 42 to 47% between 1970 and 1975 while the share of the bottom 40% dropped from 20 to 17% in the same years. By 1980 the latter had fallen to just 15%. At the same time Korea's headlong industrialization rush has produced an urban blight of mammoth proportions, with more than eight million people crowding into Seoul alone.

Foreign Relations. The year brought about the strengthening of a de facto U.S.–Japan–South Korea military alliance. The very first state visitor welcomed to the United States by the Reagan administration was Chun Doo Hwan, symbolizing the end of the Carter human-rights diplomacy and the importance which the new U.S. administration accorded the South Korean leader. The visit was smoothed by the commutation of Kim Dae Jung's death sentence to life imprisonment, and President Chun's promise to build a "democratic welfare state" in Korea. The White House welcome was nothing less than effusive. "In the short time you've had, Mr. President," President Reagan commented, "you've done much to strengthen the tradition of 5,000 years' commitment to freedom." The Carter plan for phased withdrawal of U.S. ground forces from South Korea, suspended in 1979, was now formally buried beneath U.S. assurances of continued military presence for the indefinite future.

SOUTH KOREA • Information Highlights

Official Name: Republic of Korea.
Location: Northeastern Asia.
Area: 38,022 sq mi (98 477 km^2).
Population (July 1981): 38,900,000.
Chief Cities (July 1980): Seoul, the capital, 8,450,000; Pusan, 3,100,000.
Government: *Head of state,* Chun Doo Hwan, president (formally inaugurated March 1981). *Head of government,* Nam Duck Woo, prime minister (took office Sept. 1980). *Legislature*—National Assembly.
Monetary Unit: Won (689.9 won equal U.S.$1, July 1981).
Manufactures (major products): Textiles, clothing, electronic equipment, petrochemicals, plywood, processed foods, metal products.
Agriculture (major products): Rice, barley, wheat, soybeans, sweet potatoes, fish, livestock.

The most concrete expression of the new U.S.–South Korean relationship was Team Spirit '81, joint military exercises conducted in South Korea on an unprecedented scale with 180,000 troops. The United States later opened negotiations with South Korea for the sale of 36 advanced F-16 fighter bombers.

Though Japanese-Korean relations remained somewhat strained throughout 1980, the first year of the Chun administration, Japan's 19,000,000,000 yen (about $90 million) loan, formalized in January 1981, symbolized the strengthening of their relationship. Nevertheless, Japanese-Korean frictions remained evident, notably in Korean bitterness over the large trade deficit ($15,000,000,000 in 16 years) with Japan. The September Japan-Korea ministerial meeting did not produce agreement on South Korea's demand for $6,000,000,000 in loans during its forthcoming five-year plan.

With the Reagan administration's strengthening of U.S.–South Korea and U.S.–Japan military relations, and its encouragement to tighten Japan-Korea security ties, pressure was growing for a three-way military alliance as the pivot of U.S. strategy in North Asia and the Pacific.

The relationship between external and internal security was, moreover, invariably close. Not all U.S. weapons support is directed toward strengthening the South against the North. In October 1981, for example, the State Department proposed the sale to South Korea of $1.4 million worth of crowd control weapons and police equipment.

NORTH KOREA

Politics. Political attention centered on consolidating the October 1980 decisions of the Sixth Congress of the Korean Workers' Party (KWP), the first held in ten years. Most important was the elevation of Kim Chong Il, son of President Kim Il Sung, as designated successor. As a February 1981 radio broadcast observed, "Comrade Kim Chong Il, who is unanimously admired by all compatriots, is the dear leader who is inheriting the *juche* (self-reliance) revolutionary cause holding aloft the great banner of Kimilsongism." This "unanimity" permitted Kim Chong Il to attain membership in the select new five-member Politburo Presidium, the supreme policymaking organ of the party, the secretariat (the party's executive organ), and the Military Commission. He thus moved to positions of power within all three key organs of the party-state-military apparatus. The rise in the number of military men in the politburo (now 11 of 34 members) suggests strong military as well as party backing for the new leader, at least as long as Kim Il Sung remains at the helm.

Economy. Critical economic questions centered on the ability of the North to accumulate or borrow in international markets sufficient capital to approach the ambitious targets outlined in the economic program put forward at the 1980 party congress. Nevertheless there is no evidence that the high industrial growth rates, officially estimated at 15.9% per year in the 1970s, have slowed significantly. Recent U.S. visitors to the North have attested to the high levels of education, social welfare, security, and income equality.

North-South Relations. North-South relations were bitter and volatile in 1981. The modified plan for reunification put forward in October 1980 by Kim Il Sung was soon set aside as the North bitterly denounced the Chun regime. "We will never sit at the same table with the butcher of the nation," the *Nodong Sinmun* editorialized in January 1981, attacking the Southern leadership and looking forward to negotiations after Chun's overthrow.

North-South and international tensions were inflamed in March with large-scale U.S.–South Korean joint military exercises, in Team Spirit '81. One result, according to a Korean news agency dispatch, was the "most strained relations since the *Pueblo* incident in 1968."

Both North and South actively pursued diplomatic routes to win international support and isolate rival regimes. In June, Chun Doo Hwan toured the states within the Association of Southeast Asian Nations (ASEAN), and South Korea bid successfully to host the 1988 Summer Olympics. In September, North Korea hosted a conference of developing and nonaligned nations on world food problems as a means of emphasizing its position of nonalignment and proclaiming achievements in the area of food self-sufficiency. In 1981 at least ten American and Korean scholars from the United States.

North Korea reiterated its close ties with China. In July, on the 20th anniversary of the Treaty of Friendship, Cooperation, and Mutual Assistance, Kim Il Sung reaffirmed the treaty and the "blood-sealed relation of fraternal friendship and cooperation between Korean and Chinese peoples." The Chinese message noted the role of the treaty not only in "strengthening and developing ... friendship" but also in "maintaining peace in Asia and the world."

MARK SELDEN
State University of New York at Binghamton

NORTH KOREA • Information Highlights

Official Name: Democratic People's Republic of Korea.
Location: Northeastern Asia.
Area: 46,540 sq mi (120 539 km^2).
Population (July 1981 est.): 18,300,000.
Chief Cities (July 1980 est.): Pyongyang, the capital, 1,445,000; Hamhung, 780,000.
Government: *Head of state,* Kim Il Sung, president (nominally since Dec. 1972; actually in power since May 1948). *Head of government,* Li Jong Ok, premier (took office Dec. 1977). *Legislature* (unicameral)—Supreme People's Assembly. The Korean Workers (Communist) Party: General Secretary, Kim Il Sung.
Manufactures (major products): Cement, coke, pig iron, ferroalloys, textiles, fertilizers.
Agriculture (major products): Rice, corn, potatoes, barley, millet, soybeans, livestock, fish.

LABOR

For American labor, the year of its centennial celebration, 1981, brought frustrations, disappointments, and disasters.

Employment. Widespread layoffs hit major industries and their suppliers. They included the construction industry, handicapped by high interest rates; the automobile industry, challenged by popular imports and high interest rates; the air transport industry, crippled by an air traffic controllers strike; and federal, state, and local government agencies, where cuts in federal expenditures curtailed operations and reduced grants.

As the recession deepened, layoffs spread. The number of unemployed grew by nearly 800,000 in the first ten months. By November, more than 8 million (8.4% of the workforce) were job hunting and another estimated 1.1 million "discouraged" workers were no longer seeking jobs. This meant that sometime during the year an estimated 25 million in the United States suffered the indignities of joblessness. Those gainfully employed totaled a record 98,025,000. On the recommendation of the President's Office of Management and Budget, Congress curtailed unemployment benefits and reduced funds for retraining and relocating jobless workers.

Air Traffic Controllers. Labor's biggest disaster was an illegal strike by 85% of the nation's air traffic controllers, employees of the Federal Aviation Administration (FAA). The strike grounded much of the air traffic at major airports, delayed commercial flights, and forced the layoff of airline personnel.

The union, the Professional Air Traffic Controllers Organization (PATCO), had backed Ronald Reagan in his presidential campaign and had received from him a letter indicating sympathy for the air traffic controllers' complaints.

Nonetheless, when the strikers ignored the president's 48-hour back-to-work ultimatum, he blacklisted them from all government jobs, including military service, and the FAA began the long, expensive task of recruiting and training replacements.

The AFL-CIO disbursed nearly $1 million in financial aid to strikers' families. After 86 days, PATCO offered to call off the strike but by then the Federal Labor Relations Authority had revoked the union's right to represent air traffic controllers. The union was bankrupt and faced heavy damage suits from the airlines.

Efforts to persuade the FAA to rehire the strikers—on any terms—was rebuffed. Most of the 11,500 strikers and their families were reduced to poverty. PATCO's defeat was one of the worst suffered by a labor organization since 1936, when the government began to encourage collective bargaining.

Strikes. In all, 3,519 strikes were reported to the Bureau of Labor Statistics (BLS) in the first ten months. They involved 1,120,000 workers and resulted in 23,985,000 days of idleness. This number was less than a year earlier when, in the same period, 3,590 strikes were reported, involving 1,295,000 workers and resulting in 30,621,000 days of idleness. The year's lost time due to strikes amounted to less than .0001% of the time worked.

BLS reported that 288 strikes involved public employees, the most recently unionized workers. Most public employee strikes involved schoolteachers. The largest was a 50-day walkout by 23,000 teachers and other employees of the Philadelphia school system protesting a 10% salary cut and the layoff of 3,500 teachers, in violation of the American Federation of Teachers' agree-

U.S. PUBLIC EMPLOYEE UNIONS

The fastest growing U.S. labor organizations are the public employee unions. The ten largest are:

Union	Membership
National Education Association (NEA)	1,684,000
American Federation of State, County and Municipal Employees (AFSCME)*	1,098,000
American Federation of Teachers (AFT)*	551,000
American Federation of Government Employees (AFGE)*	255,000
American Postal Workers Union (APWU)*	251,000
National Association of Letter Carriers (NALC)*	230,000
National Association of Government Employees (NAGE)	200,000
American Nurses Association (ANA)	180,000
International Association of Firefighters (IAFF)*	178,000
Fraternal Association of Police (FAP)	150,000
National Association of Postal and Federal Employees (NAPFE)	125,000
California State Employees Association (CSEA)	105,000

*AFL-CIO Affiliate

Source: U.S. Bureau of Labor Statistics

Addressing the AFL-CIO convention, union President Lane Kirkland criticizes Reagan budget cuts.

UPI

ment. The strike ended after a court ordered the laid-off teachers reinstated and the strikers back to the classrooms.

The biggest strike in the private sector was a 72-day stoppage by 160,000 bituminous coal miners. They settled for wage and benefit improvements amounting to 37.5% over 40 months. The settlement restored union rules that management had demanded governing the processing of nonunion coal and the use of nonunion labor.

Settlements. Major labor-management agreements reached in the first nine months provided wage increases averaging 9.3% a year over the three-year life of most contracts, plus cost-of-living adjustments. "Give-backs" of union-negotiated raises and benefits became more frequent. At Chrysler Corp. workers accepted a give-back package amounting to $822 million or 13% of potential earnings for each worker. In turn the troubled automaker agreed to a profit sharing plan that may allow workers to recoup some of the concessions. Employees of Conrail gave up $200 million to save their jobs.

In November, railroad unions concluded a 39-month agreement with the nation's class one carriers providing for wage increases totaling 32.5% over three years, including cost of living allowances. Health plans, pensions, and vacations were improved.

In July the U.S. Postal Service concluded negotiations with four unions representing its 600,000 employees. The pact called for salary increases of $2,100 spread over three years, some of it based on reaching productivity quotas, plus a cost-of-living escalator.

Earnings. Weekly earnings for nonsupervisory employees averaged $259.35 in October, up from $240.77 a year earlier. Real, spendable earnings continued to decline. A drop of 1.9% in September was the largest in one month since April 1979. In that month consumer prices were advancing at an annual rate of 14.8%, a figure that abated in November.

On January 1, the federal minimum wage for anyone working in interstate commerce rose to $3.35 an hour.

AFL-CIO. Seldom has anyone been more frustrated than union leaders who were powerless to stop the budget cuts pushed through Congress by the Reagan administration. Union officers saw their most prized programs cut, everything from food stamps to the Comprehensive Employment and Training Act (CETA). To protest the Reagan policies, the AFL-CIO with other civic organizations sponsored Solidarity Day on September 19. More than 250,000 showed up in Washington, DC.

The protest was echoed at the AFL-CIO's biennial convention two months later in New York. AFL-CIO President Lane Kirkland lamented in his keynote: "He promised us a boom but brought us a bust." The delegates set Nov. 2, 1982, election day, as "Solidarity Day II" to continue the protest. Voting in the convention were 835 delegates. They represented 91 national and international unions, including the newly reaffiliated United Auto Workers (UAW); 43 state federations; and 178 local central bodies. Together the affiliates claim more than 15 million members. Affiliates will support the national labor federation with monthly per capita payments of 24 cents in 1982 and 27 cents during 1983.

Union Organizing. Management efforts to establish a "union-free" environment continued in some industries. A House Labor Committee reported in March that outside management consultants grossed more than $500 million a year helping management resist employee unionization—legally and illegally. Anti-union specialists were partly responsible for the fact that unions won only 45% of plant elections in 1981.

Discrimination. The U.S. Supreme Court ruled that women may sue their employers for sex discrimination, even if the jobs performed by women are not the same as those of male employees.

UPI

Smoke rises from an abandoned building as striking firemen in Yonkers, NY, refuse to leave the picket line. Overall, the number of strikes throughout the United States decreased during the first ten months of the year.

Unemployed blacks tell New York City construction workers that they want jobs. "We don't work, you don't work," they yelled. U.S. unemployment among blacks and other nonwhites registered 15.5% in October 1981.

UPI

Sears, Roebuck reached an agreement with the Equal Employment Opportunity Commission to modify personnel policies at all its facilities and to promote the hiring of black and Hispanic workers. Sears employs more than 400,000 in 855 stores.

INTERNATIONAL

ILO. U.S. delegates to the June Conference of the International Labor Organization (ILO) returned from Geneva, Switzerland, reporting that the tripartite (labor, management, government) ILO had come closer than usual to fulfilling its mission. The political rhetoric of Communist bloc delegates cooled after they sat in silence during a standing ovation given Lech Walesa, Poland's worker delegate. Walesa credited the ILO's standard on freedom of association and trade union rights for the Polish government's acceptance of Solidarity, an independent, self-managed trade union, the first ever in a Communist nation.

Later, over bitter Soviet objections, the conference adopted a report criticizing the USSR's violation of that same standard by failing to allow freedom of association. The ILO urged the USSR to take "concrete measures" to guarantee Soviet workers the right to form free trade unions. Irving Brown, U.S. worker delegate and AFL-CIO representative, was elected to the workers' governing body.

Poland. Solidarity, Poland's free trade union movement, observed its first birthday in August. In one year it had achieved a shorter workweek, the right to strike, worker self-management in some industries, and the right to publish its own material. In May, a delegation from the Polish labor organization attended a conference in Washington, DC, of the International Metalworkers Federation, trade secretariat of metalworking unions in 70 non-Communist countries.

In September, Solidarity convened its first national congress in Gdansk. AFL-CIO President Lane Kirkland was invited to speak. After the Polish government refused him a visa, the convention heard Kirkland on videotape.

Shortages of food and fuel increased and desperate Polish workers took to wildcat strikes. On October 18, the Polish Armed Forces Commander, Wojciech Jaruzelski, was installed as secretary of Poland's Communist Party. Jaruzelski's immediate goals were a return to the six-day week and reversal of labor's other achievements.

Tension between the government and Poland's workers continued to mount as winter came on. A one-hour nationwide general strike on October 28 failed to calm the frustrated workers. By November, unauthorized strikes were reported in two thirds of Poland's 49 provinces. In December, martial law was decreed, the operations of Solidarity were suspended, and its leaders were interned.

France. In May, France elected a labor-supported Socialist government, its first in 23 years. The new government moved to deal with inflation of some 14% and unemployment of 8%.

The legal minimum wage was increased 10%, family allowances 25%. The legal workweek was trimmed to 39 hours with a further cut to 35 hours promised by the end of 1985. Rent subsidies and minimum social security benefits for the aged and the disabled were increased. To create job opportunities, small enterprises were given financial aid, as were housing and other construction projects. Prices for most services were frozen for six months. Manufacturers were urged to hold price increases to 8%. Unions were asked to show wage restraint.

To pay for social programs and for an 18% increase in military expenditures, the government boosted prices for heating gas, electricity, railroad and bus fares, and automobile, gasoline, and cigarette taxes. It also introduced a special tax on higher incomes.

Great Britain. With Britain's recession more than two years old, nearly 3 million workers were unemployed in 1981.

UPI

Poles in February support Solidarity, a union movement seriously threatened as the year ended.

Increases in the Consumer Price Index slowed from an annual rate of 22% in early 1980 to 11.5% in September 1981. In August, average earnings had increased 13% over a year earlier. As in the United States, some unions have been forced to "give back" some negotiated raises and benefits to save their jobs. The number of strikes declined. In 1980, 1,250 strikes were reported, the fewest since 1941. For the first half of 1981, only 666 strikes were reported.

Relations between the Trade Union Congress (TUC) and the Tory government were distant. TUC ties with the Labour Party were strengthened. Both the Labour Party and the TUC adopted policies favoring withdrawal from the Common Market, unilateral nuclear disarmament, and—less clearly—withdrawal from the North Atlantic Treaty Organization. All three positions are opposed by the newly founded Social Democratic Party.

Japan. The annual nationwide negotiations between the unions and management, the "Spring Offensive," produced wage increases ranging from 7 to 8%. For the first time in 17 years, the agreement was reached with few strikes. The increases correspond to expected increases in prices and productivity. Unemployment amounted to about 2% of the labor force.

Federal Republic of Germany. High interest rates plagued the German economy. By August, unemployment had reached 5.5%. In September, consumer prices were advancing at an annual rate of 6.5%. Real average earnings increased 10% in 1980 and were expected to show a similar rise in 1981. Unions lost an important decision when the federal court held that employers can lock out employees in industrial disputes, but only in response to a strike.

Canada. Canada continued to suffer from inflation and unemployment. In September, consumer prices were rising at an annual rate of 12.5%, the unemployment rate reached 8.2%. In the third quarter, wages were up 12.2% but purchasing power, which dropped 0.5% in 1980, continued to decline. The federal minimum wage rose to $3.50 an hour.

Strikes continued at a rate of more than 1,000 annually. A strike by hospital employees in Ontario led to the jailing of the union president and 17 others. Major strikes included a 43-day postal stoppage, a 54-day strike by Halifax police, and a month-long walkout by 60,000 woodworkers in British Columbia. Alberta adopted legislation banning strikes by provincial employees.

The Canadian Labour Congress suspended for nonpayment of dues 12 U.S.-based building trades unions. They represent 20% of CLC membership. The dispute is over the Quebec Federation's accepting affiliation of an independent union of 12,000 electrical workers. Also in dispute were jurisdictional lines in British Columbia between the building trades and the industrial unions, especially the Woodworkers and Steelworkers, and CLC's convention rules giving disproportionate representation to unions with many small locals. Negotiations for a solution to this dispute continued.

See also articles on the various individual countries.

GORDON H. COLE and JOSEPH MIRE

LAOS

Vietnam's virtual occupation of Laos stabilized the country in 1981, at least for the short run, but foreign powers both intervened in Laotian internal affairs and considered how to do so without provoking a crisis.

Political. Premier Kaysone Phomvihane and longtime Communist Pathet Lao leader Prince Souphanouvong, president of the National Assembly, played essentially figurehead roles, as 40,000 Vietnamese soldiers controlled almost all aspects of Laotian public life. Many of the Laotian soldiers and officials who had served in the pre-Communist regime and subsequently become de facto prisoners in remotely located "political re-education" camps returned to Vientiane and their families. But they played no role in the governing of their country.

The Lao People's National United Liberation Front (LPNULF), established in May 1980, was the main antigovernment force within the country. Led by onetime anti-Communist Defense Minister Phoumi Nosavan and former Gen. Khambou Bourrasath, the LPNULF had an estimated 3,000 partisans under arms in southern Laos. The LPNULF posed no immediate threat to the survival of the Communist regime, largely because its leadership had been discredited previously. In alliance with anti-Communist forces in adjacent countries, however, it represented a potential rallying point for opposition to de facto Vietnamese occupation of Laos.

Insurgencies. Harassment activity by the LPNULF in southern Laos, which was aided by anti-Vietnamese insurgents in adjacent and also occupied Cambodia (Kampuchea) and probably by both China and Thailand, stepped up by the year's end.

Opposition to both the indigenous Pathet Lao leadership and the Vietnamese military also continued in the mountainous highlands, where Hmong tribesmen, once heavily financed by the United States, persisted in their armed activity. Estimates of Hmong military strength ranged from 2,000 to 10,000 partisans. The Hmong were much weaker than they had been in the days when their CIA-funded "secret army," led then and in the early 1980s by the durable Vang Pao, was the most effective fighting force against the Communist Pathet Lao. During the decade of the 1970s, however, the ethnic minority Hmong suffered extraordinary casualties in their seemingly perpetual war with the Communists.

A third group in armed uprising against the government were the Yao and related ethnic minorities, along the northern border with China. Yao guerrillas numbered 5,000 fighting men.

Yao chieftain Chou La, Hmong leader Vang Pao, and the LPNULF's Phoumi Nosavan met in northeastern Thailand in June and formed a united front.

Economy. Persisting economic difficulties, reflected in widespread scarcity of goods and high prices, resulted in major relaxation of state control of the economy. "All existing regulations" limiting "free" circulation of goods were "abrogated." "Free markets" were specifically endorsed,. except for certain commodities under state monopoly.

The country's economic problems rather than political persecution led to a continued outflow of refugees. An official U.S. government panel on refugee policy recommended the voluntary repatriation of Laotian refugees in Thailand.

Foreign Relations. China was the major power most actively involved in opposing continued Vietnamese control of Laotian politics and foreign policy. The Chinese not only directly provided arms assistance to Yao rebels but also allowed anti-Pathet Lao groups, including some 2,000-3,000 followers of onetime Laotian neutralist leader Kong Le, to train on their soil.

The USSR, China's chief rival in Indochina, entertained Laotian Premier Kaysone Phomvihane, his Cambodian counterpart, and the secretary-general of the Vietnamese Communist party in September. Although there are official U.S.–Laotian diplomatic relations, Sisouk Na Champassak, a pre-Communist Laotian defense minister, met with U.S. officials in Washington.

RICHARD BUTWELL, *Murray State University*

LAOS • Information Highlights

Official Name: Lao People's Democratic Republic.
Location: Southeast Asia.
Area: 91,429 sq mi (236 800 km^2).
Population (1981 est.): 3,600,000.
Chief Cities (1973 census): Vientiane, the capital, 176,637; Savannakhet, 50,690.
Government: *Head of state,* Prince Souphanouvong, president. *Head of government,* Kaysone Phomvihane, prime minister. *Legislature* (unicameral)—National Congress of People's Representatives.
Monetary Unit: Liberation kip (400 liberation kips equal U.S.$1, 1980).
Manufactures (major products): Tin, lumber.
Agriculture (major products): Rice, corn, tobacco, coffee, cotton.

LATIN AMERICA

Arguably, the most important event of 1981 in Latin American affairs occurred not in Latin America itself, but in Washington, DC. The inauguration of Ronald Reagan as president of the United States led to major changes in the political and economic relations between Latin America and the United States.

During 1981, President Reagan reversed many of the policy directions of the Jimmy Carter administration. In keeping with his campaign platform, the new president de-emphasized public expressions of concern for human rights violations by Latin American governments, and substituted more subtle behind-the-scenes pressures under the banner of "quiet diplomacy." One result of this policy change was an almost immediate improvement in relations with such military governments as those of Argentina, Brazil, and Chile.

President Reagan, to a greater extent than his predecessors, tended to view hemispheric terrorism and insurrection as the product of Soviet and Cuban meddling. While acknowledging that a large part of the hemisphere's unrest stems from economic and social inequities, the president stressed the need to strengthen security mechanisms in countries friendly to the United States in order to cope with rising violence. During the year, arms aid was restored to Argentina and Chile. Military equipment worth $20 million was sent to El Salvador, along with U.S. technical advisers. And arrangements were made to sell 24 F-16 fighter planes to Venezuela.

In the area of economic development, the Reagan administration's austere domestic economic programs found an echo in its plans for aid to Latin America. Governments of the region were cautioned to rely less on official development assistance and to look more to the private sector—especially private trade and investment—as the most viable route to economic growth.

Throughout 1981, Latin America was the object of heightened awareness and intense scrutiny by Washington, a development that was received with mixed feelings in many Latin capitals. Not only were there disagreements over U.S. policies in such areas as Central America and the Caribbean, but there was also a perception that Latin America was drawing unaccustomed attention from the United States at a time when governments of the region were increasingly steering an independent course.

The oil wealth of such countries as Mexico and Venezuela, and the relatively sophisticated industrial technologies of such others as Argentina, permit these countries to challenge the United States not only on the economic front, but on the political as well. As a result, the 1980s promise to be, if not precisely a "post-American decade," then at least a period of increasing competition between the United States and its hemispheric neighbors.

Central America. There was widespread concern in both the United States and Latin America during 1981 over the continuing internecine violence in El Salvador and Guatemala. (*See* CENTRAL AMERICA and special report, page 158.) The two conflicts drew in, to one degree or another, most of the other nations of the hemisphere. The United States supplied the Salvadoran military junta and condemned Cuba for aiding the guerrilla rebels. Both Mexico and Venezuela condemned outside intervention, but Mexico sided with the opposition, while Venezuela supported the government junta. Mexico and France issued a joint statement recognizing the political legitimacy of the Salvadoran guerrillas, and nine Latin countries immediately published a declaration condemning the Mexican-French initiative.

Caribbean Basin Development. Talks began at midyear among the United States, Canada, Mexico, and Venezuela on a proposed long-term development plan for Central America and the Caribbean. From the beginning, it was clear that the plan faced formidable obstacles.

The potential beneficiary countries saw in the proposal the promise of massive inputs of external capital to solve their pressing economic problems. At one point, there was a Central American consensus on an infusion of $20,000,000,000 over the next nine years. The United States, however, argued that it could offer only limited official capital, along with increased trade concessions and incentives to promote private-sector financing and investment. The United States and Mexico also split on the question of Cuban involvement in the plan. By year's end, the plan seemed in serious trouble.

Latin American Economies. Latin America's economic performance in recent years has been somewhat better than that of the average developing nations, but the region shares with the rest of the Third World a number of troublesome problems—a slowdown in economic growth, unemployment, inflation, and large balance of payments deficits.

In the decade 1961–70, the majority of Latin countries had annual inflation rates of less than 5%, with only four experiencing rates greater than 15%. By 1980, according to estimates of the Inter-American Development Bank (IDB), no Latin country had single-digit inflation, and 19 countries were over 15%. Preliminary IDB calculations showed the trend continuing in 1981.

The region's trade performance showed similar signs of stress. According to data released by the Organization of American States (OAS), Latin America had a $4,500,000,000 trade deficit with the United States in 1980, the highest level in recent years. The biggest deficits were shown by Argentina, Brazil, Chile, Colombia, and Mexico. The deficit would have been $2,000,000,000 more were it not for the surpluses registered by oil exporters Venezuela and Trinidad and Tobago.

Border Disputes. Long-standing arguments over national boundaries continued to plague relations among the Latin American countries in 1981. The independence of Belize (formerly British Honduras) in September was bitterly protested by Guatemala, which has claimed the entire territory for more than a century.

Guyana and Venezuela wrestled over Venezuela's claim to almost two thirds of Guyana's territory of 83,000 sq mi (215 000 km^2). At the same time, Surinam claims 6,000 sq mi (15 540 km^2) of Guyanese land. Papal mediation continued in the dispute between Argentina and Chile over ownership of three small islands in the Beagle Channel. Nicaragua and Colombia contested rights to several small Caribbean islets and cays.

RICHARD C. SCHROEDER
Syndicated free-lance writer

LAW

The highlight of 1981 for the U.S. Supreme Court was the appointment of Sandra Day O'Connor to replace Associate Justice Potter Stewart, who retired at the end of the 1980–81 term. O'Connor, a 51-year-old appellate court judge and former state legislator from Arizona, became the first woman to sit on the nation's highest court. (*See also* BIOGRAPHY.) In international law, the UN Law of the Seas Conference again was a major focus of attention.

U.S. SUPREME COURT

Justice Stewart, appointed to the court by President Dwight Eisenhower in 1958, was one of that body's most influential members. He was second to Justice William Brennan in seniority but, at age 66, only the sixth oldest justice. His announcement on June 18 that he would retire from the court as of July 3 came as a surprise to his colleagues and clerks. Generally near the court's center and one of five "swing" justices, Stewart tended to support First Amendment rights but frequently dissented in liberal criminal law rulings.

With a reputation as a moderate conservative, O'Connor did not appear likely to cause any great change in the court's basic constitutional philosophy. Even before President Reagan announced her appointment, the court seemed to be limiting its intervention in public policy controversies and deferring to the political branches. During the 1980–81 term, the justices upheld statutes controlling strip mining and protecting workers from cotton dust and lead poisoning. They affirmed the right of the State Department to suspend the passport of an American citizen on grounds of national security. They permitted state courts to televise criminal trials (*see* special report, page 296). They erected no barriers to affirmative action programs for minorities, and they upheld state limits on abortion.

The court handed down 123 signed opinions, of which only 39 were unanimous. The two liberals, Marshall and Brennan, were the most frequent dissenters (49 and 43). Rehnquist, the previous term's most active dissenter, found the more conservative climate more agreeable and dissented only 26 times.

Separation of Powers. Deferring to the executive, the court unanimously upheld President Carter's agreement with Iran for freeing the 52 American hostages (*Dames & Moore v. Regan*). The agreement had canceled all attachments against Iranian assets in the United States and transferred from U.S. courts to an international tribunal all legal claims by American firms against Iran. The court ruled that the agreement was supported by statute and by longstanding congressional acquiescence in presidential settlements of foreign claims disputes. The court also upheld (7–2) the State Department's revocation of the passport of a former Central Intelligence Agency (CIA) member who had publicized the names of CIA operatives (*Haig v. Agee*).

Deferring to Congress, the court rejected (6–3) contentions that the military draft law denied equal protection because it applied only to men (*Rostker v. Goldberg*). As a coequal branch of government, Congress was held to be entitled to utmost support on military matters.

First Amendment. The two religion clauses of the First Amendment were interpreted in an unusual number of decisions. North Carolina's practice of printing a "motorists' prayer" on official highway maps was held to be in violation of the prohibition against establishment of religion, and a Kentucky law requiring public schools to post copies of the Ten Commandments in their classrooms also was deemed unconstitutional (*Bradshaw v. Hill, Stone v. Graham*). Expenditures of public funds by the city of Philadelphia to build a platform for a mass to be conducted by Pope John Paul II were held in violation of the establishment ban (*Philadelphia v. Gilfillan*).

On the other hand, the court refused to hear a challenge to the observance of Christmas and other religious holidays in public schools, and dismissed a suit to stop references to God in the daily opening ceremonies of a federal court (*Florey v. Sioux Falls, O'Hair v. Cooke*).

Denial of unemployment benefits to a member of the Jehovah's Witnesses who, because of

After 23 years on the U.S. Supreme Court, Associate Justice Potter Stewart, 66, retired July 3.

UPI

On September 25, Sandra Day O'Connor took two oaths of office to become the 102d justice—and first woman—to sit on the Supreme Court. The first oath was that given to all new federal judges. The second, left, for the Supreme Court, was administered by Chief Justice Warren Burger, with O'Connor's husband John looking on.

Michael Evans/The White House

his religious beliefs, quit his job with a machine company when he was transferred to a division that manufactured turrets for military tanks was held to be a violation of his right to free exercise of religion (*Thomas v. Review Board*).

The court unanimously upheld restrictions on the right of Hare Krishna members to solicit money in such crowded public places as state fair grounds. Selling of literature or other money-making activities could be limited to booths or other fixed locations (*Heffron v. ISKCON*). In a decision that could handicap the operation of civic groups and nonprofit organizations, the court voted (7–2) to uphold a federal law prohibiting the placement of any unstamped material in postal boxes (*U.S. Postal Service v. Council of Greenburgh*).

The court struck down (6–3) a San Diego ordinance banning all billboards, even those carrying noncommercial messages (*Metromedia v. San Diego*). By refusing to review a number of lower court libel decisions limiting the category of "public figures," the court made libel awards easier to secure. For example, the founders of California's Rancho La Costa health resort, alleged by a magazine to be mobsters, were held not to be "public figures" and allowed to proceed with a $630 million libel suit (*Penthouse v. Rancho La Costa*).

Equal Protection. The term's decisions on sex discrimination tended to make distinctions based on sex easier to justify and more likely to survive legal challenge. In addition to upholding the male-only draft law, the court ruled (6–3) that divorced spouses of military personnel have no legal claim to a share of military retirement benefits (*McCarty v. McCarty*). The court likewise rejected (5–4) equal protection arguments against the California statutory rape law that makes it criminal for a male to have sexual relations with a female under 18 to whom he is not married, but that exempts females from criminal liability in the reverse situation (*Michael M. v. Superior Court*).

In employment discrimination cases brought by women, the court ruled that an employer is not required to prove that a male appointee is better qualified than a female applicant, but only that there is some legitimate, nondiscriminatory reason for the decision (*Texas Dept. of Community Affairs v. Burdine*).

A decision favorable to women was *County of Washington v. Gunther*, which held that women can bring suits for sex discrimination in pay even if they work in jobs that men have never performed. A Louisiana law giving husbands the unilateral right to dispose of jointly-owned property was invalidated, and the court let stand a ruling that an economic boycott organized by women against states that had failed to ratify the Equal Rights Amendment (ERA) was not a violation of the Sherman Antitrust Act (*Kirchberg v. Feenstra, Missouri v. NOW*).

Affirmative action plans to increase minority representation in the uniformed services of three cities, approved by lower courts, were not disturbed; in three other cities, the court declined to review lower court rulings ordering school busing or pupil assignment.

Criminal Prosecutions. Police searches of homes and automobiles created constitutional problems for the court. In *Steagald v. U.S.* it held (7–2) that police armed with a single arrest warrant have no right to enter the home of someone other than the person they seek to arrest. However, officers with a valid search warrant may detain for the duration of the search any persons found on the premises (*Michigan v. Summers*).

In two confusing opinions, the court held that police need a warrant to search a closed container found in an automobile, but not if they already have enough evidence to arrest the owner of the item (*Robbins v. California, New York v. Belton*). The special training and experience of border patrol officers were held to justify them in stopping suspicious vehicles and questioning the occupants (*U.S. v. Cortez*).

Broadening the *Miranda* right to counsel, the court held unanimously in *Estelle v. Smith* that the defendant in a capital case should have been warned in advance that the results of a psychiatric interview might be used against him in fixing sentence, and that he had a right to consult an attorney before agreeing to the interview. This ruling voided the death sentences of 30 Texas prisoners, most of whom had been interviewed by the same "hanging" psychiatrist.

Lassiter v. Department of Social Services held (5–4) that failure to appoint counsel for indigent parents in a proceeding for termination of parental rights did not violate due process, since the case presented no troublesome points of law.

Upon a defendant's request, the judge must instruct the jury that the defendant's failure to testify cannot be considered evidence of guilt (*Carter v. Kentucky*). But the court upheld the conviction of a Mexican-American even though the lower court judge had refused to question prospective jurors about their possible prejudice toward Mexicans (*Rosales-Lopez v. U.S.*).

Lower federal courts have held that prison conditions in 24 states violate the Eighth Amendment against cruel and unusual punishment. But the Supreme Court in *Rhodes v. Chapman* held (8–1) that it is not unconstitutional for two prisoners to be confined for long periods in a cell designed for a single inmate. Writing the controlling opinion, Justice Powell contended: "The Constitution does not mandate comfortable prisons."

A statute giving federal prosecutors the right to appeal sentences they regard as too lenient does not amount to double jeopardy (*U.S. v. DeFrancesco*). *Bullington v. Missouri* held that a defendant sentenced to life imprisonment who was granted a new trial could not be sentenced to death on the second conviction. Both were 5–4 decisions. The court refused to hear a challenge to the California capital punishment law, thereby permitting resumption of death sentencing in that state.

Privacy. Two state laws limiting abortion were upheld by the Supreme Court. One was a Utah law requiring a doctor to notify the parents of a minor upon whom an abortion is to be performed (*H.L. v. Matheson*). The second was an Indiana law requiring all abortions after the first three months of pregnancy to be performed in a hospital (*Gary-Northwest Indiana Women's Services v. Orr*). Both were 6–3 rulings.

The court let stand lower court decisions on two other controversial privacy issues. In *Rutherford v. U.S.* the federal ban on interstate shipment of laetrile had been upheld, and in *New York v. Onofre* a state law prohibiting sodomy between consenting adults had been declared unconstitutional.

Voting and Elections. *Ball v. James* upheld (5–4) an Arizona law restricting to landowners the right to vote for directors of a large water district. Even though the district exercised a number of general governmental powers, it was held to be exempt from the one-person, one-vote rule.

In *Democratic Party v. LaFollette,* the court ruled (6–3) that political parties have the right to determine their own process for choosing delegates to their national conventions. In *California Medical Assn. v. FEC* it upheld (5–4) the federal election law limiting to $5,000 a year the amount of money individuals or unincorporated groups may contribute to a political action committee.

The court ruled against television stations that had refused to make time available for a campaign speech by President Carter in December 1979. The networks contended that it was too early for the presidential campaign of 1980 to begin (*CBS et al. v. FCC*).

Business and Commerce. The court upheld (5–3) an Occupational Safety and Health Administration (OSHA) regulation limiting the exposure of textile workers to cotton dust, rejecting the Reagan administration contention that such regulations must be subjected to cost-benefit analysis (*American Textile Manufacturers v. Donovan*). The federal strip-mining law was upheld against claims by the coal industry and 22 states that the law infringed state sovereignty (*Hodel v. Virginia*). The court let stand strict federal controls on exposure to lead in the workplace (*Lead Industries Assn. v. Donovan*).

In two cases, the court struck down state interference with interstate commerce—an Iowa law banning from the state's highways trucks exceeding 60 ft (18 m) in length, and a Louisiana tax on gas from offshore wells passing through the state to out-of-state customers (*Kassel v. Consolidated Freightways, Maryland v. Louisiana*). But, the court also ruled, Montana's 30% tax on coal production does not unconstitutionally burden interstate commerce (*Commonwealth Edison Co. v. Montana*).

Other Rulings. Dividing 4 to 4, the justices left in effect a lower court ruling that Richard Nixon and three former White House officials could be sued for damages for violating the constitutional rights of a former national security aide by tapping his private phone (*Kissinger v. Halperin*).

Legislation rescinding federal salary increases was held to have reduced the salaries of federal judges unconstitutionally (*U.S. v. Will*). A law exempting members of Congress from paying income taxes to their states of residence while attending sessions of Congress was upheld (*Maryland v. U.S.*). The appeal of former U.S. Rep. Michael Myers (D-PA) of his conviction on Abscam bribery charges was rejected.

C. HERMAN PRITCHETT
University of California, Santa Barbara

INTERNATIONAL LAW

It had been hoped in 1980 that the International Law of the Seas Conference, after seven years' effort by more than 150 countries on 440 draft articles, was on the verge of completion and that a convention could be signed in Caracas, Venezuela, before the end of 1981. However, some U.S. mining companies opposed measures requiring them to divide up revenues from international waters with other countries and to share technology with Third World nations. Other Americans feared that future supplies of such strategic minerals as cobalt, nickel, copper, and manganese would fall under Third World control and that there would be production limits. These concerns led to a Republican Party platform plank contending that the conference had slighted "United States long-term security requirements." When the Reagan administration took office in January 1981, it announced its intention to hold up further negotiations pending a policy review.

Less than 24 hours before the conference resumed in March, President Reagan removed the acting director of the U.S. delegation and six of his top aides, replacing some of them with avowed enemies of the treaty. The purpose of the New York session had been merely to "polish the language" of the draft treaty. Instead, the seven-week session mostly marked time. Until the U.S. position was clarified, the Group of 77 developing countries decided not to undertake negotiations on the issue of a "grandfather clause" protecting deep seabed investments during the preparatory period before the convention went into effect.

The impasse continued in August, when the conference resumed. The United States had said that it would not complete its review by August and had made an effort to persuade the Group of 77 to postpone the next session until 1982. However, neither this bloc nor the Soviet bloc was agreeable.

Some feared that U.S. footdragging would tempt Third World countries to reopen issues on which they had made concessions. Elliot Richardson, the Carter administration's chief delegate and still a member of the 1981 delegation, argued that the text was a compromise based on a sound balance which should not be upset by reopening issues. He said that all but 14 of the 130 changes made in the seabed mining provision since mid-1977 were favorable to the United States. Without the treaty, a mining company would lack the legal right to mine any part of the sea bottom. Any company that began mining could be challenged in international court.

U.S. oil, shipping, and fishing companies, unlike the mining companies, favored the treaty. The Pentagon had been among the treaty's staunchest supporters because it would guarantee passage for ships and submarines through the world's oceans and strategically important straits. However, the new secretary of the interior, James Watt, and the CIA director, William Casey, both opposed the treaty.

As if to underscore what could happen in the absence of an accord, in August two Libyan planes were shot down by U.S. Navy jets during Sixth Fleet maneuvers in the Gulf of Sidra, 60 mi (97 km) off Libya, which claimed 200 mi (370 km) as territorial waters. In the absence of a convention, there had been creeping jurisdiction by the coastal states. The Law of the Seas draft agreement was highly protective of the strategic, navigational, and other military-related concerns of the major maritime powers.

The United States was having coastal difficulties with its neighbors, Canada and Mexico. The three countries had a dispute in the Pacific over the harvesting of albacore tuna. The United States does not recognize the right of a country to include "migratory species" within its claim to resources extending 200 mi out to sea. However, when American boats followed the tuna into Mexican and Canadian waters, they were seized and fines were levied. In retaliation, under U.S. law, imports of Canadian and Mexican albacore tuna were embargoed. The government of Mexico notified the United States that it was terminating the U.S.–Mexican bilateral fisheries agreement as of December 1981. Most of the vessels affected would be U.S. One of the major reasons for the termination was that Mexican citizens had failed to receive allocations to harvest New England squid. New England fishing interests also tied up in the Senate a treaty with Canada providing for sharing of fish resources in the Georges Bank. To the frustration of the Canadians, the Reagan administration recalled the treaty from the Senate.

Controversial international law issues continued to be generated in the Middle East powder keg. In June, Israel attacked and destroyed a nuclear installation in Iraq, claiming that the facility would produce fuel for nuclear weapons and that it was normal international practice for a nation to take preemptive armed action in the face of clear, imminent, and provoked danger of enemy attack. Nevertheless, Israel was condemned for the attack by the United Nations.

In September, arbitration began in The Hague on claims by U.S. corporations that did business with Iran before the revolution in 1979.

The continuing tension over possible Soviet military moves into Poland caused the governments of Sweden and Denmark to prepare contingency plans to rescue Poles fleeing ships of the Soviet Baltic fleet. Under international law, Danish and Swedish ships would be entitled to open fire against Soviet pursuers in their coastal waters.

Work also began in 1981 on an international convention for the protection of the rights of migrant workers and their families.

MARTIN GRUBERG
University of Wisconsin-Oshkosh

LAW—SPECIAL REPORT:

TELEVISION IN THE COURTROOM

On Jan. 26, 1981, Chief Justice Warren Burger delivered the opinion of the U.S. Supreme Court in the case of *Chandler et al v. Florida*. The court held, 8-0, that televising trials is not necessarily and inherently unconstitutional. It pointedly rejected any constitutional right of camera access to courts but declined to assert, as it had in 1964 in *Estes v. Texas*, that televising criminal trials is *per se* a violation of "due process." The court thus allowed states to experiment with television in the courts despite the admitted risk of prejudice. Further research, it added, might reveal that broadcasting criminal trials jeopardizes due process.

At the time of the *Chandler* ruling, more than half the states had already proposed, or were conducting, experiments with cameras in courtrooms. (No such experiments were allowed in federal courts.) Nevertheless, with several studies challenging the validity of the experiments, with some state legislatures moving to block the trend, with the continued opposition of the American Bar Association (ABA), and despite strong media pressure on state courts, it remained to be seen whether the bandwagon would continue to roll or would stall.

History. The issue dates back to 1937, when the ABA House of Delegates banned all recording devices in courtrooms. A series of sensational trials—especially that of Bruno Hauptmann in 1935 for the Lindbergh kidnapping-murder—had been disrupted by media coverage. Although ABA canons are only advisory, all state courts except those of Colorado and Texas followed the ban. In 1965, the U.S. Supreme Court overturned Texas' conviction of financier Billie Sol Estes for swindling, on the grounds that the psychological effects and potential political abuses make television trials inherently prejudicial. The *Estes* case appeared to settle the issue. However, the lure of sensational trials, lobbying by the media, changes on the courts, and a shift toward states' rights slowly turned the tide.

Proponents of cameras in court noted that the *Estes* decision may have been limited to circumstances prevailing at the time and that the opinion lacked empirical verification—claims that the Burger court was to revive. By 1977 several states, including Florida, began widely publicized experiments. In 1978, a conference of state chief justices approved a resolution to allow the highest court in each state to decide if, when, and how cameras should be allowed. Prompted by that decision and armed with available reports from early television trials, a dozen states opened their courtrooms, 17 continued with experiments, and another 15 began to examine the issue.

Pros and Cons. Proponents argue that improvements in technology have made TV coverage unobtrusive. The principles of public trial and public interest make coverage desirable. Witnessing trials on television improves public understanding of the judicial process, generates support for court reform, and instills public confidence in the courts.

Opponents insist that the main issues are the effects on participants and on the public of televising selected and edited scenes from sensationalized trials. Notoriety from television coverage would hurt some defendants and help ambitious judges and attorneys. Competition for high ratings rather than the need for public information would determine what is televised. Picked and edited to grab audiences raised on fictional courtroom drama, real trial scenes would fortify rather than rectify the myths.

The legal profession is split on the issue. In a survey of ABA members published in September 1979, 75% of respondents agreed that "television cameras in the courtroom would tend to distract witnesses"; 70% thought that television would broadcast only the sensational; 64% believed that lawyers and judges "grandstand for the television audience"; and 37% responded that "televised courtroom proceedings would enhance the public conception of our system of justice."

The media generally welcomed the *Chandler* decision, but there were dissenting voices. "The courts are playing with social dynamite," wrote syndicated columnist Richard Reeves. A *Washington Star* editorial warned that "only the very naive will suppose that television, once admitted to trials, may not change the texture and even the substance of justice, as it has changed the texture and substance of politics." And James Reston of *The New York Times* pointed out that although the chief purpose of a trial is to ensure fairness, "it's hard to argue that the cameras would increase the rights of the defendant by increasing the size of the audience."

Jury Still Out. Despite, or perhaps because of, the *Chandler* decision, the issue of cameras in the courtroom remains one of the most crucial and troublesome in the history of judicial administration. It involves questions of public information and enlightenment, risk of prejudice and further distortion, and the integrity and independence of the judicial process itself. The many dangers that the court said lurk in its decision are still not completely clear.

GEORGE GERBNER

UPI

The foreign ministers of Kuwait, Syria, Lebanon, and Saudi Arabia (left to right) arrive at Beit Eddine Palace in Lebanon, June 7, seeking a solution to the continuing Lebanese crisis.

LEBANON

In 1981, Lebanon again failed to escape the cycle of sectarian violence and foreign interference that has devastated the mountainous republic since the 1975–76 civil war. The government of President Elias Sarkis exercised only nominal sovereignty, with Israel and Syria orchestrating Lebanon's seemingly endless tragedy.

Israel continued to provide military and financial support to Christian forces—both those of Maj. Saad Haddad in the south and those of Phalangist Party militia leader Bashir Gemayel in the north—and to mount air and sea operations against guerrilla positions of the Palestine Liberation Organization (PLO).

Syria, with 22,000 troops dominating the Arab League's peacekeeping Arab Deterrent Force (ADF), contributed to the instability by its support of the PLO and its determination to thwart the Phalangists' avowed goal of expelling both the Syrians and the guerrillas from Lebanon. Hostilities between the Syrians and the Phalangists in April turned Lebanon into the scene of yet another Arab-Israeli crisis.

Government Impotence. President Sarkis and his government were ineffectual in several attempts to stabilize the forces responsible for 60,000 Lebanese deaths in seven years. Speaking before the Islamic Summit Conference in late January at Taif, Saudi Arabia, Sarkis demanded without result that the PLO cease using Lebanon as a base against Israel. On February 14, Prime Minister Chafiq al-Wazan called for the establishment of an international court to prosecute Israel for its aggression against Lebanon—again without result.

To emphasize Sarkis' impotence, Haddad threatened to shell the port of Sidon unless Sarkis met his demand for $5 million. Following the attempted extortion and an Israeli air strike, Sarkis met with Syrian President Hafez al-Assad on March 10 to discuss how to establish internal security. The talks achieved little, as major fighting broke out April 1 at Zahle, 25 mi (40 km) east of Beirut.

Zahle Struggle. Commanding the strategic Beirut-Damascus highway, Zahle had been occupied by Phalangists since December 1980. When militia units began building a road that threatened a linkup with Haddad in the south, ADF forces besieged the city. On April 7, Sarkis met with Syrian Foreign Minister Abdul Halim Khaddam in an attempt to end the siege and the sectarian violence it had sparked in Beirut and between PLO units and Haddad's forces in the south.

After 18 cease-fires in eight days, Wazan and Khaddam began talks with the political factions in Beirut on April 15. By April 24, a tentative settlement on Zahle was reached but, while Sarkis and Khaddam were meeting with Beirut factions on April 28, Israeli warplanes destroyed two Syrian helicopters over Zahle.

Arab-Israeli Crisis. The Syrian decision on April 29 to deploy surface-to-air missiles in the Bekaa Valley near Zahle and Israel's subsequent threat of military action led to a major international effort to avoid another Arab-Israeli war.

While U.S. Special Envoy Philip Habib shuttled between Israel and Damascus to defuse

LEBANON • Information Highlights

Official Name: Republic of Lebanon.
Location: Southwest Asia.
Area: 4,000 sq mi (10 360 km^2).
Population (1981 est.): 3,200,000.
Chief Cities (1974 est.): Beirut, the capital, 1,000,000; Tripoli, 128,000.
Government: *Head of state,* Elias Sarkis, president (took office Sept. 1976). *Head of government,* Chafiq al-Wazan, prime minister (took office Oct. 1980). *Legislature* (unicameral)—National Assembly.
Monetary Unit: Lebanese pound (4.71 pounds equal U.S.$1, Oct. 1981).
Manufactures (major products): Petroleum products, lumber, cement.
Agriculture (major products): Fruits, wheat, corn, barley, potatoes, olives, onions, tobacco.

the Syrian-Israeli dispute, an Arab League committee of the foreign ministers of Syria, Saudi Arabia, and Kuwait worked with Sarkis and Lebanese Foreign Minister Fuad Butros to negotiate a settlement acceptable to both the Syrians and the Phalangists. The Arab League committee met in Lebanon, June 7–8, to discuss the situation with Gemayel and leaders of the other factions. Progress was disrupted by Israel's June 7 raid on the Osirak nuclear reactor near Baghdad but, following the committee's June 23–24 meeting in Saudi Arabia, an agreement was achieved.

On June 30, the Phalangist militia evacuated Zahle and the 91-day siege was ended. In return for Syria's acquiescence to the deployment of regular Lebanese army troops in Zahle, Gemayel announced on July 7 that he would not seek future ties with Israel.

July Crisis. Two days after U.S. envoy Habib returned to Lebanon on his third attempt to resolve the Syrian-Israeli crisis, Israel responded to reports that Palestinian guerrillas had been receiving heavy weapons from Libya by intensifying its air attacks on southern Lebanon to a level unmatched since the Israeli invasion of March 1978. Israeli planes struck four times between July 10 and 17.

On July 17, in a raid coordinated with widespread attacks that destroyed three bridges in the south, Israeli planes bombed a densely populated area in west Beirut where a PLO headquarters was located. The bombing, which failed to destroy the guerrilla offices, killed an estimated 300 civilians and wounded more than 800 others.

Despite international criticism, Israel stepped up its attacks the following week while diplomats tried to arrange a cease-fire. On July 22, two more Litani River bridges were destroyed, 50 persons were killed, and Lebanon's main source of petroleum, the Saudi TAPLINE terminus at the Zahrani refinery, was set on fire.

To the relief of President Sarkis and the Lebanese people, American and UN representatives on July 24 arranged for an Israeli-PLO cease-fire, which held through the end of the year. However, the lull in the fighting in the south yielded to an outbreak of sectarian violence during August and September in Beirut. The militant Front for the Liberation of Lebanon from Foreigners claimed credit for a series of car bombings in September and October.

Economic Dislocation. The fierce fighting of the spring and summer had severe economic repercussions. Power and fuel rationing were put into effect after the Israeli attack on the Zahrani refinery complex. Customs revenues, normally 47% of the government's receipts, fell to 14% by early September. More importantly, critical Arab aid was slow to arrive. On September 21, Lebanon announced that it had received only $236 million of the $400 million annually pledged since the Tunis Summit of 1979. Finally, on September 21, the government apparently accepted its inability to control economic affairs by announcing a $1,266,000,000 budget that included no development funds.

F. NICHOLAS WILLARD
Georgetown University

LIBRARIES

On May 17, 1981, the Office for Intellectual Freedom of the American Library Association (ALA) reported that between November 1980 and May 1981 there had been attempts to remove, restrict, or deny access to 148 different books in 34 states. Compared with the same period in 1979–80, efforts to censor books in school and public libraries had tripled. Joining Kurt Vonnegut's *Slaughterhouse-Five* and J. D. Salinger's *The Catcher in the Rye* as censorship targets were such works as *Our Bodies, Ourselves* by the Boston Women's Health Collective and the young people's stories of Judy Blume. Conservative organizations, most prominently the Moral Majority, insisted on their particular conceptions of morality. Librarians, on the other hand, renewed their dedication to the intellectual pluralism embodied in the First Amendment to the U.S. Constitution and in the *Library Bill of Rights.*

Budgets. Inflation and tightened purse strings deprived libraries of much financial support. The Reagan administration's budget for the 1982 fiscal year called for substantial cuts in the appropriations for the Library Services and Construction Act and for library funding in the Elementary and Secondary Education Act and the Higher Education Act. The economic position of elementary and secondary school libraries was rendered especially precarious with the advent of the Elementary and Secondary Education Program Consolidation and Improvement Act. This legislation requires school libraries to compete for funds with other programs from a single block grant. The block-grant concept offers no guarantee that federal moneys will not be substituted for the state and local funding of education or that state education agencies, as opposed to state legislatures, will make allocation decisions.

In San Francisco and Boston, open hours and branch library services were reduced in response to Propositions 13 and 2½, respectively. In California, a state budget surplus has been exhausted and by mid-1981 could no longer compensate for the decrease in local governmental revenues brought on by Proposition 13. Massachusetts' Proposition 2½, approved in 1980, had a more immediate effect since there was no state surplus.

American Library Association. At a meeting in Chicago on April 9 and 10, the power of the centrifugal forces within the ALA became more visible than ever before. Many of ALA's constituent units desire their autonomy, the freedom to control their own financial, personnel, programmatic, and publications operations. Their disenchantment with a unified association has both political and economic roots. Politically, unit leaders believe that they are in much closer touch with the interests and opinions of the members of their units than are the association's general officers or the members of ALA's permanent secretariat. Economically, the units are increasingly unhappy with the way association headquarters allocates the dollars derived from general membership fees. While unit autonomy might ensure a greater responsiveness to the needs of those who share a common interest in a type of library service or a type of library operation, it would most certainly reduce the ALA's capacity to offer more general services and programming and its ability to address national funding and intellectual freedom issues in the name of an integrated American library community.

The ALA's 100th annual conference was held in San Francisco, June 26–July 2, 1981. Presiding over the meeting was Elizabeth W. Stone, administrative head of the School of Library and Information Science, Catholic University of America. Carol A. Nemeyer, associate librarian for national programs, Library of Congress, became vice-president and president-elect. The association sponsored National Library Week, April 5–11, 1981, employing as its theme, "America, The Library Has Your Number."

Other Developments. The U.S. House of Representatives' Subcommittee on Science, Research, and Technology held hearings in Washington on May 20 and 21 and on June 9 on the Information Science and Technology Act of 1981. Introduced by Rep. George Brown (D-CA), the legislation would create an Institute for Information Policy and Research. In late 1980, the National Commission on Libraries and Information Science appointed Toni Carbo Bearman as its executive director, replacing Alphonse Trezza. The Reagan budget for the 1982 fiscal year included a slight increase in funds for the commission.

Major Library Awards of 1981

Beta Phi Mu Award for distinguished service to education for librarianship: Haynes McMullen, professor, School of Library Science, The University of North Carolina at Chapel Hill

Randolph J. Caldecott Medal for the most distinguished picture book for children: Arnold Lobel, *Fables*

Melvil Dewey Award for creative professional achievement of a high order: Henriette Avram, director, Processing Systems, Networks, and Automation Planning, Library of Congress

Grolier Foundation Award for unusual contribution to the stimulation and guidance of reading by children and young people: Jane McGregor, former children's services specialist, Ohio Valley Area Libraries

Joseph W. Lippincott Award for distinguished service to the library profession: Eric Moon, former president, American Library Association

John Newbery Medal for the most distinguished contribution to literature for children: Katherine Paterson, *Jacob Have I Loved*

Ralph R. Shaw Award for outstanding contribution to library literature: Ruth A. Velleman, librarian, Human Resources Center, Albertson, NY, *Serving Physically Disabled People*

Linking the Bibliographic Utilities: Benefits, and Costs, an important report from Battelle-Columbus Laboratories, recommended the establishment of on-line links among the Library of Congress, the Online Computer Library Center, the Research Libraries Information Network, and the Washington Library Network. The Electronic Library Association (ELA), formed in Columbus in March, seeks "to ensure that information delivered electronically remains accessible to the general public." ELA expects to become an ALA unit.

The Copyright Office awarded a contract to King Research, Incorporated, for an investigation of whether the copyright law "has achieved a fair balance between the rights of copyright owners and the needs of the users of libraries and archives in respect to photocopying." This study will be used in the preparation of the Register of Copyrights' 1983 report to Congress on the workings of existing copyright legislation. At a meeting in Minneapolis late in 1980, the Committee of 118, consisting of librarians and interested lay people in equal numbers, laid plans for the implementation of the resolutions of the 1979 White House Conference on Library and Information Services.

Vartan Gregorian, provost of the University of Pennsylvania, became president and chief executive officer of the New York Public Library. The John Crerar Library at the Illinois Institute of Technology announced that it would move to a new facility on the campus of The University of Chicago in 1984. Its collections will be merged with the science collections of the university.

The 47th council meeting of the International Federation of Library Associations and Institutions convened in Leipzig, East Germany, Aug. 17–23, 1981. National institutions, professional organizations in librarianship, and national library planning were discussed.

DAN BERGEN
Graduate Library School
University of Rhode Island, Kingston

LIBYA

Libya's foreign policy, particularly its aggressive behavior in Africa and its strong support for the Palestine Liberation Organization (PLO) and other terrorist organizations, strained the country's relations with the West in 1981. But despite the expulsion of Libyan officials from Washington, an armed confrontation between Libyan Air Force and American Navy planes, and disclosures that Libyan "hitmen" had been sent on a mission to kill U.S. President Ronald Reagan, the United States continued to purchase 40% of the 1.6 million barrels of oil Libya produced daily.

Chad and the Sudan. Col. Muammar el-Qaddafi, Libya's leader, announced in January that his country would merge with Chad, its southern neighbor. Libya had previously supported one faction in Chad's civil war, occasionally hinting at the possibility of a future union. Nevertheless, many African leaders denounced the plan as a violation of an agreement not to interfere with Chad's interim government, established to supervise elections scheduled for 1982. A few African states broke off diplomatic relations with Libya over the issue.

The growth of Libyan influence in Chad brought accusations by Sudan's President Jaafar al-Nemery that Libyan troops were using bases there as launching points for forays into Sudanese territory. Nemery also charged that Qaddafi intended to overthrow his government because of its pro-Western policies. Tensions between Libya and Sudan increased after the assassination of Egyptian President Anwar el-Sadat in October. Sadat had been Qaddafi's most outspoken critic, frequently asserting that Libya, with a Soviet-supplied arsenal worth some $15,000,000,000, served as a proxy for Moscow in the region. Sudan's close ties to the Sadat regime raised questions about the stability of the Nemery government after the assassination. There was a renewed spurt of Libyan activity along the Chadian-Sudanese frontier, but no serious attacks were reported. On October 29, President Goukoni Oueddei of Chad requested the immediate withdrawal of Libyan troops from the capital Ndjamena and other regions. By November 5, reports were confirmed that the Libyan forces had indeed been flown out.

Middle East. Elsewhere, Libyan troops and surface-to-air missiles were deployed in southern Lebanon to support PLO forces. Guerrillas opposing the governments of Oman and Somalia also received financial and technical assistance from Libya, and a loan estimated at $100 million was granted to the leftist government of Nicaragua. Many of these ventures were financed by Libyan oil revenues, estimated to exceed $10,000,000,000. For much of 1981, Libyan oil was the most expensive in the Organization of Petroleum Exporting Countries (OPEC), selling for as much as $41 per barrel.

In a series of diplomatic maneuvers to offset Western condemnations of the regime, Libya strengthened its links with other states in the region that advocated policies similar to its own. In August, Libya, South Yemen, and Ethiopia signed a treaty of friendship and cooperation. In September, in response to American pledges to Israel, Libya convened a summit conference attended by Syria, Algeria, South Yemen, and the PLO to explore the prospects for establishing closer and more formal ties with the Soviet Union.

United States. The U.S. reaction to Libya's activities was highly critical. In addition to attacking Libya's foreign adventures, the Reagan administration charged Libya with conducting assassination campaigns against Libyan dissidents abroad. In May, the United States expelled Libyan representatives from Washington, reducing diplomatic contacts between the countries to a minimum. Relations deteriorated further in August, when Libyan planes fired on American naval aircraft over the Gulf of Sidra. The incident occurred over waters claimed by Libya but which the United States maintained were international. Two Libyan aircraft were shot down and a wave of anti-American demonstrations followed. Despite denials from Washington, Libya and other Arab governments insisted that the United States had provoked the encounter to demonstrate its military strength in the area.

Even with all these problems, there were still no efforts by either Libya or the United States to limit commercial exchanges. Almost 2,000 American citizens, most of them employees of oil companies, were assured of their safety by Libyan officials and remained in the country until late in the year.

On December 10 President Reagan appealed to Americans living and working in Libya to leave immediately. The official administration statement cited a worsening "security climate" and "increased risk" for U.S. citizens there; American passports were invalidated for travel to Libya. U.S. oil companies complied immediately, evacuating their employees.

The U.S. move came in the wake of intelligence reports that Libyan "hitmen" had been dispatched by Colonel Qaddafi on a mission to assassinate President Reagan. Verbal attacks by the Libyan leader further heightened the tension.

Still, Washington stopped short of embargoing Libyan oil. Libya supplied some 10% of U.S. imported oil during the year, and the value of American exports to that country in the first half of 1981 rose significantly.

To help African and Middle Eastern states defend themselves against possible threats from Libya, U.S. military aid to several countries in the region, most notably Tunisia, was increased dramatically. After the Sadat assassination, the United States sent two Airborne Warning and Control System (AWACS) planes to Egypt for monitoring activities in the troubled areas where Egypt and Sudan border Libya and Chad.

KENNETH J. PERKINS, *University of South Carolina*

LIBYA • Information Highlights

Official Name: Socialist People's Libyan Arab *Jamahiriya* ("state of the masses").
Location: North Africa.
Area: 679,360 sq mi (1 759 542 km^2).
Population (1981 est.): Tripoli, the capital, 295,000; Benghazi, 190,000.
Government: *Head of state,* Muammar el-Qaddafi, secretary-general of the General People's Congress (took office 1969). *Head of government,* Abdullah Obeidi, chairman of the General Popular Committee. *Legislature*—General People's Congress (met initially Nov. 1976).
Monetary Unit: Dinar (0.29605 dinar equals U.S.$1, July 1981).
Manufactures (major products): Crude petroleum, processed foods, textiles, paper products.
Agriculture (major products): Wheat, barley, dates, olives, peanuts, citrus fruits, livestock.

LITERATURE

American Literature

The disparity between "have" and "have not" American authors seemed to grow even more pronounced in 1981. A handful of writers remained or became national figures whose books commanded huge advances and were aggressively promoted. They appeared on television talk shows and were mentioned in gossip magazines. Publishers devoted less time and money to other fine writers, who thus remained in relative obscurity.

Novels. John Irving's appearance on the cover of a national news magazine made clear that he had become a literary celebrity. His new novel, *The Hotel New Hampshire,* tells of a talented family that undergoes odd, sometimes frightening adventures while owning a succession of hotels. The book's clever mixture of joy and sorrow, sex and death made it a great popular success. Irving keeps reassuring his readers that "Art is fun" and contrives satisfying endings for all his characters. Although several critics were displeased at what they regarded as a squandering of Irving's talent, he deserves recognition for an intelligent, contemporary fairytale that understands its own limitations. Irving's previous bestseller, *The World According to Garp,* was being made into a movie.

Toni Morrison also received major media attention, but her *Tar Baby* is a more challenging work. A black man is, by chance, on a tiny Caribbean island, where he enters the lives of a rich, retired American white couple, their black servants, and the servants' beautiful, cultivated niece. His love affair with the niece and their attempt to live in the United States precipitate a series of realizations about the lives of each of the characters. The reader sees how both whites and blacks have trapped themselves psychologically and politically. The idea of the tar baby, an attractive but inescapable snare, develops through the novel. Morrison verges on the supernatural and allegorical as she describes Caribbean legends and the white couple's spiritual self-destruction, but her command of the language holds together her fictional world.

By contrast, Mary Gordon's *The Company of Women* is most successful when it is most narrowly focused. The author traces the lives of a group of Roman Catholic women who devote themselves to an austere priest. When Gordon leaves this world to depict a liberal professor and his confused followers she becomes condescending, but her understanding of the spiritual and emotional intensity of the priest and his devout circle successfully renders the richness of their constricted lives.

John Updike continues his portrait of middle-class American life—begun in *Rabbit Run* (1960) and *Rabbit Redux* (1971)—with *Rabbit is Rich.* In the new work, Harry Angstrom has in-

Novels by John Irving and Toni Morrison were among the most popular—and heavily promoted—of 1981.

Courtesy E. P. Dutton

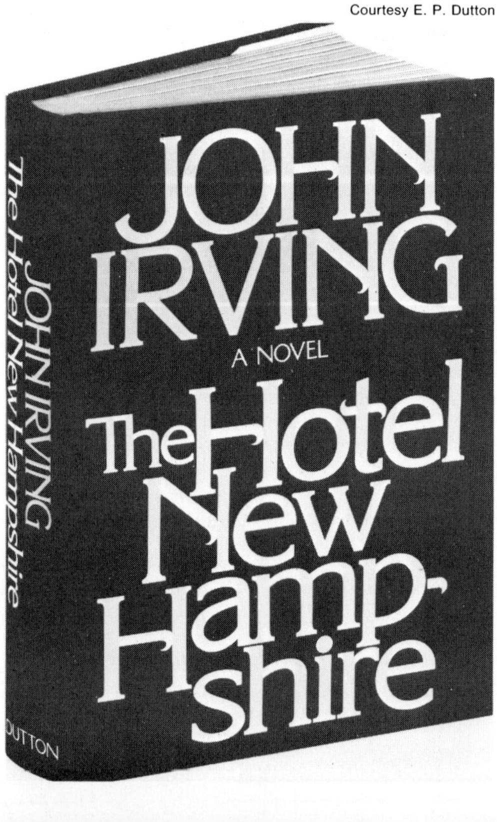

Courtesy Knopf

herited an interest in his father-in-law's successful Toyota car dealership. Somewhat more complacent now, Harry still suffers from a sense that the world is changing too fast, that he is trapped by his family, and that his attempts to get more out of life have been futile. Updike impressively renders what America felt like in 1979, but the book lacks the concentrated brilliance he showed in *The Coup* (1978).

Writers themselves are the subject of two new sequels. Philip Roth's *Zuckerman Unbound* has the hero of *The Ghost Writer* (1979) no longer learning about the problems of art, but finding out how to cope with wealth and notoriety. Roth seems to be trying to deal satirically with the difficulties he suffered after the success of *Portnoy's Complaint* (1969), but there is a certain self-indulgence that dulls the book's edge. Reynolds Price's ambitious *The Source of Light* is about an aspiring poet who was born toward the end of *The Surface of Earth* (1975). Price's rich prose creates an intense world where a sense of the past weighs heavily on the present as the poet tries to understand himself.

Although domestic problems, psychological relationships, and the psyche of the artist are still important concerns, new American fiction cannot fairly be accused of being parochial. David Bradley utilizes Pennsylvania history in *The Chaneysville Incident,* a tale of 13 escaped slaves who choose to die rather than return to the South. The legend, which is being explored by a black historian trying to understand his own past, becomes a complex meditation on religion and culture. Robert Stone's *A Flag for Sunrise* invents a Latin American country struggling with revolution. It is a tale of violence, moral squalor, and convoluted motives, which led critics to compare Stone to Joseph Conrad and Graham Greene.

But perhaps the most remarkable novel of the year was *Riddley Walker,* by the American expatriate Russell Hoban. Taking place about 2,000 years after civilization has been destroyed by atomic holocaust, the story is told in a highly imaginative, acutely fractured English which signifies the loss of cultural continuity yet manifests a yearning to create meaning and poetry.

Short Stories. The last few years have seen a resurgence of interest in American short fiction, and there are fresh new voices daringly redefining the art. Raymond Carver's *What We Talk About When We Talk About Love* employs severely stripped-down, minimalist narrative; Mark Helprin's *Ellis Island* is exuberantly, surrealistically textured; and Guy Davenport's *Eclogues* are highly allusive intellectual exercises. Other collections—such as Richard Yates' *Liars in Love,* Alice Walker's *You Can't Keep a Good Woman Down,* and Barry Holstun Lopez' *Winter Count*—are more traditional in form but no less fresh in their language and perception.

Publishers, apparently heartened by the response to recent retrospective collections, produced *The Stories of Elizabeth Spencer* and *The Collected Stories of Caroline Gordon.* Both Spencer and Gordon are Southern writers with long, distinguished careers whose achievements can now be more fully appreciated. In lively contrast is Donald Barthelme's *Sixty Stories,* a sustained attack on narrative convention, but still often witty and poignant.

Poetry. Despite the accomplished and provocative work being done by contemporary poets, their work seems destined to be read by an extremely small audience unless they capture the public's interest by some other means. Sylvia Plath's *The Collected Poems* makes clear her power, and Anne Sexton's *The Complete Poems* demonstrates that her better works are still moving, but it was not until their tragic suicides that these poets became newsworthy and received widespread attention. Similarly, Adrienne Rich's *A Wild Patience Has Taken Me Thus Far* shows her continued commitment as a poet, but her feminist writings and lectures have given her greater visibility. Robert Penn Warren's *Have You Ever Eaten Stars?* is a remarkable collection of his latest verse, but he is still better known as a novelist and critic. And Lawrence Ferlinghetti's *Endless Life,* a selection of work going back to the 1960s, shows his lyric and satiric gifts, but his fame came more from his association with the City Lights Book Store and the Beat movement than from his poetry.

The lack of any strong movement or charismatic eminence in American poetry today may be due more to public inattention than to poetic failure. A. R. Ammons' *A Coast of Trees* makes immediate the sensations of geological time as indelibly as Robert Bly's *The Man in the Black Coat Turns* makes eternal the most ephemeral of moments. John Ashbery's enigmatic *Shadow Train* contrasts with David Ignatow's appealing *Whisper to the Earth.* John Logan's *Only the Dreamer Can Change the Dream* is as oblique as Roger Peterson's *Leaving Taos* is direct. But perhaps the work that will gain the widest circulation is William Zaranka's *Brand-X Anthology of Poetry,* "Burnt Norton Edition," a parody of the widely used college text, *The Norton Anthology of Poetry.*

Nonfiction. As evidenced by new works in 1981, nonfiction can also challenge the imagination. George W. S. Trow's *Within the Context of No Context* comments on contemporary American culture through a collage of aphorisms, inquiries, and striking observations. Peter Matthiessen's *Sand Rivers* is not merely a travel book about a game preserve in southeastern Tanzania, but also a poetic evocation of an awesome and fragile part of the earth. Impeccable prose helps make John McPhee's description of U.S. geology, *Basin and Range,* an inquiry into the culture itself.

Interesting criticism came from writers not known primarily as critics. Joyce Carol Oates' *Contraries* and Guy Davenport's *The Geography*

American Literature: Major Works, 1981

NOVELS

Alther, Lisa, *Original Sins*
Auchincloss, Louis, *The Cat and the King*
Berger, Thomas, *Reinhart's Women*
Bradley, David, *The Chaneysville Incident*
Burroughs, William, *Cities of the Red Night*
Busch, Frederick, *Take This Man*
DeVries, Peter, *Sauce For the Goose*
Friedman, B. H., *The Polygamist*
Gordon, Mary, *The Company of Women*
Gould, Lois, *La Presidenta*
Grumbach, Doris, *The Missing Person*
Higgins, George V., *The Rat on Fire*
Hoban, Russell, *Riddley Walker*
Irving, John, *The Hotel New Hampshire*
Knowles, John, *Peace Breaks Out*
Michaels, Leonard, *The Men's Club*
Morrison, Toni, *Tar Baby*
Neugeboren, Jay, *The Stolen Jew*
Oates, Joyce Carol, *Angel of Light*
Potok, Chaim, *The Book of Lights*
Price, Reynolds, *The Source of Light*
Purdy, James, *Mourners Below*
Roth, Philip, *Zuckerman Unbound*
Smith, Martin Cruz, *Gorky Park*
Stone, Robert, *A Flag for Sunrise*
Updike, John, *Rabbit is Rich*
Vidal, Gore, *Creation*
Wambaugh, Joseph, *The Glitter Dome*
Wharton, William, *Dad*
Woiwode, Larry, *Poppa John*

SHORT STORY

Banks, Russell, *Trailerpark*
Barthelme, Donald, *Sixty Stories*
Carver, Raymond, *What We Talk About When We Talk About Love*
Davenport, Guy, *Eclogues*
Gardner, John, *The Art of Living*
Hall, James B., *The Short Hall*
Helprin, Mark, *Ellis Island*
Kornblatt, Joyce Reiser, *Nothing to do with Love*
L'Heureux, John, *Desires*
Lopez, Barry Holstun, *Winter Count*
Silko, Leslie Marmon, *Storyteller*
Sommer, Scott, *Lifetime*
Walker, Alice, *You Can't Keep a Good Woman Down*
Wolff, Tobias, *In the Garden of the North American Martyrs*
Yates, Richard, *Liars in Love*

POETRY

Ammons, A. R., *A Coast of Trees*
Ashbery, John, *Shadow Train*
Bensko, John, *Green Soldiers*
Bly, Robert, *The Man in the Black Coat Turns*
Carter, Jared, *Work, For the Night is Coming*
Ferlinghetti, Lawrence, *Endless Life*
Ignatow, David, *Whisper to the Earth*
Logan, John, *Only the Dreamer Can Change the Dream*
Meinke, Peter, *Trying to Surprise God*
Meredith, William, *The Cheer*
Pastan, Linda, *Waiting for my Life*
Peterson, Roger, *Leaving Taos*
Plath, Sylvia, *The Collected Poems*
Ramke, Bin, *White Monkeys*
Rich, Adrienne, *A Wild Patience Has Taken Me Thus Far*
Rosenthal, M. L., *Poems 1964–1980.*
Ryan, Michael, *In Winter*
Saner, Reg, *So This Is the Map*
Sexton, Anne, *The Complete Poems*
Smith, Dave, *Homage to Edgar Allen Poe*
Sorrentino, Gilbert, *Selected Poems 1958–1980*
Soto, Gary, *Father is a Pillow Tied to a Broom*
Squires, Radcliff, *Gardens of the World*
Stern, Gerald, *The Red Coal*
Warren, Robert Penn, *Have You Ever Eaten Stars?*
Zaranka, William, *Brand-X Anthology of Poetry*

CRITICISM AND AMERICAN CULTURE

Arlen, Michael J., *The Camera Eye: Essays on Television*
Balliett, Whitney, *Night Creatures: A Journal of Jazz 1975–1980*
Brooks, John, *Showing Off in America*
Davenport, Guy, *The Geography of the Imagination*
Flippo, Chet, *Your Cheatin' Heart: A Biography of Hank Williams*
French, Marilyn, *Shakespeare's Division of Experience*
Friedan, Betty, *The Second Stage*
Giddins, Gary, *Riding on a Blue Note: A Jazz Chronicle*
Goldman, Albert, *Elvis*
McGuane, Thomas, *An Outside Chance: Essays in Sport*
McPhee, John, *Basin and Range*
Oates, Joyce Carol, *Contraries*
Sowell, Thomas, *Ethnic America*
Trow, George W. S., *Within the Context of No Context*
Wolfe, Tom, *From Bauhaus to Our House*
Ziff, Larzer, *Literary Democracy*

HISTORY AND BIOGRAPHY

Allen, Gay Wilson, *Waldo Emerson*
Baker, Carlos, *Ernest Hemingway: Selected Letters 1917–1961*
Bridenbaugh, Carl, *Early Americans: Collected Essays 1933–1980*
Bruccoli, Matthew J., *Some Sort of Epic Grandeur*
Dillon, Millicent, *A Little Original Sin*
Epstein, Barbara Leslie, *The Politics of Domesticity: Women, Evangelism, and Temperance in Nineteenth-Century America*
Frederickson, George M., *White Supremacy: A Comparative Study in American and South African History*
Jones, James H., *Bad Blood: The Tuskegee Syphilis Experiment*
Lears, T. J. Jackson, *No Place of Grace: Antimodernism and the Transformation of American Culture*
Levy, Leonard W., *Treason Against God: A History of the Offense of Blasphemy*
Lewis, David Levering, *When Harlem Was in Vogue*
Malone, Dumas, *The Sage of Monticello*
Mariani, Paul, *William Carlos Williams*
McCullough, David, *Mornings on Horseback*
McFeely, William S., *Grant*
Mee, Charles L., *The Ohio Gang: The World of Warren G. Harding*
Mendelson, Edward, *Early Auden*
Rawley, James A., *The Transatlantic Slave Trade: A History*
Rugoff, Milton, *The Beechers*
Shi, David, *Matthew Josephson: Bourgeois Bohemian*
Tuchman, Barbara, *Practicing History*
Wills, Garry, *Explaining America: The Federalist*

AUTOBIOGRAPHY

Angelou, Maya, *The Heart of a Woman*
Galbraith, John Kenneth, *A Life in Our Times*
Mebane, Mary E., *Mary*
Morris, Wright, *Will's Boy*
Perelman, S. J., *El Sid*
Toback, David, *The Journeys of David Toback*
Vonnegut, Kurt, *Palm Sunday: An Autobiographical Collage*

SCIENCE AND PHILOSOPHY

Fuller, R. Buckminster, *Critical Path*
Gould, Stephen Jay, *The Mismeasure of Man*
Hook, Sidney, *Philosophy and Public Policy*
Kidder, Tracy, *The Soul of a New Machine*
Kohlberg, Lawrence, *The Philosophy of Moral Development*
May, Rollo, *Freedom and Destiny*
Nozick, Robert, *Philosophical Explanations*

Passmore/Sygma

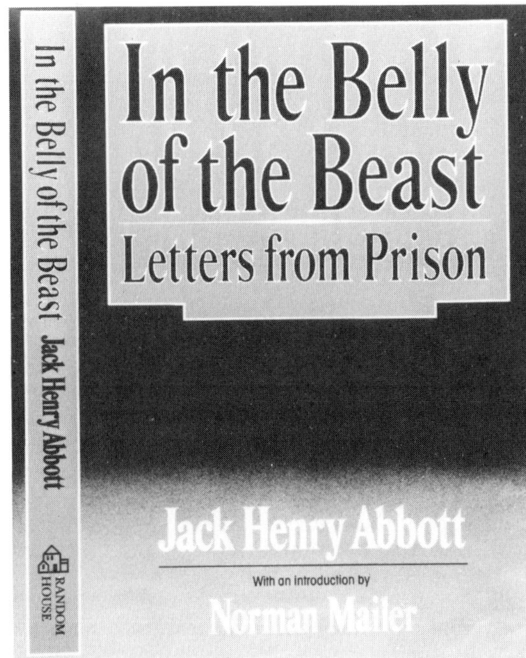

Courtesy Random House

Jack Henry Abbott's account of life in prison, in the form of letters to friend Norman Mailer, won high praise. Then in September, after a month-long search by police, Abbott was arrested for murder.

of the Imagination are energetic, personal reactions to a wide range of works. Marilyn French's feminist analysis, *Shakespeare's Division of Experience,* is provocative though partial.

But perhaps the year's most significant contribution to the understanding of literature is Larzer Ziff's *Literary Democracy,* a study of 19th-century American writers who declared and established the nation's cultural independence. Ziff centers on great literary figures from Edgar Allan Poe to Walt Whitman, his sensitivity to social context providing a new understanding of their achievements and their times. Gay Wilson Allen's excellent *Waldo Emerson* describes the tensions of Ralph Waldo Emerson's struggle for independence from cultural orthodoxy. Milton Rugoff traces an awesomely energetic family in *The Beechers.*

Good biographies not only record lives, they also add new perspectives to history and the individual's role in it. Paul Mariani's *William Carlos Williams* argues that Williams' discovery of the poetry in American vernacular made him far more influential than has generally been recognized. Edward Mendelson's *Early Auden* asks the reader to reevaluate the poet's achievement. Matthew J. Bruccoli is scrupulously careful in sorting fact from fiction in his life of F. Scott Fitzgerald, *Some Sort of Epic Grandeur.* There are figures who might be lost to us were it not for the careful work of their biographers. Millicent Dillon's life of Jane Bowles, *A Little Original Sin,* tells of a unique talent lost to disease. David Shi's *Matthew Josephson: Bourgeois Bohemian* recalls a man who was associated with the exciting avant-garde artists of the 1920s before becoming a biographer himself.

Donald Hall's *The Oxford Book of American Literary Anecdotes* is a rich and often revealing collection of stories.

Literary documents can also provide new understandings of history and culture. Carlos Baker's collection *Ernest Hemingway: Selected Letters 1917-1961* reveals a paradoxical man, heedless in some ways and haunted in others, whose self-image seemed to be at war with his artistic goals. *Robert Frost and Sidney Cox: Forty Years of Friendship,* and *The Republic of Letters in America: The Correspondence of John Peale Bishop and Allen Tate* quietly illuminate aspects of American Modernism, as well as the personalities of the correspondents. Scholars welcomed the complete, unedited version of Theodore Dreiser's *Sister Carrie* (1900); the original text of William Faulkner's *Sanctuary* (1931); and the long-suppressed autobiographical novel of the Imagist poet Hilda Doolittle (H.D.), *HERmione,* telling of her tangled relationship to Bryher and Ezra Pound.

In the Belly of the Beast, a searing revelation of prison life by Jack Henry Abbott, won wide acclaim. In September, a month after disappearing from a federal halfway house where he was finishing a 14-year sentence for killing a prison inmate, Abbott was arrested for the murder of a waiter in New York City.

JEROME H. STERN
Florida State University

Children's Literature

Publishers of children's books placed increased emphasis on mass-market merchandise during 1981, following a trend that began several years earlier with the slackening of library sales. Individual title production in the United States increased by some 300 over the previous year, to approximately 2,000. Nearly a quarter of the total output was devoted to calendars, diaries, address books, collections of jokes and riddles, pop-ups (the best being Eric Carle's *The Honeybee and the Robber*), movie and television tie-ins, and construction and coloring books.

With 1981 being the International Year of Disabled Persons, there were numerous books featuring young people with physical afflictions. There were many newly illustrated editions of the classics, particularly works by the Grimms, Hans Christian Andersen, and Aesop. Cookbooks remained strong, as did books on dinosaurs, trucks, and ballet. Noteworthy was the appearance in paperback of Random House's "Landmark Books," volumes of history and biography originally published in the late 1940s and early 1950s.

The year also marked the 100th anniversary of the creation of Pinocchio and the 50th of Babar. Both were honored in new books, but only *Babar's Anniversary Album,* by Jean and Laurent de Brunhoff, was a critical success.

The American Library Association's (ALA's) John Newbery Medal for most distinguished contribution to American children's literature went to Katherine Paterson for *Jacob Have I Loved,* a first-person narrative about the rivalry between twin sisters living on a Chesapeake Bay island in the 1940s. Paterson had won the Newbery in 1978 for *Bridge to Terabithia.* The ALA's Randolph Caldecott Medal for most distinguished picture book was awarded to Arnold Lobel for *Fables,* containing 20 original tales about eccentric animal characters. The American Book Award (ABA) for children's fiction went to Betsy Byars for *The Night Swimmers,* about the daughter of a country and western singer who takes care of her two younger brothers; and in nonfiction to Alison Herzig and Jane Mali for *Oh, Boy! Babies!,* a photodocumentary of a boys' class in baby care. The ABA for children's paperback fiction went to Beverly Cleary for *Ramona and Her Mother.* Maureen Crane Wartski won the Child Study Children's Book Committee Award for *A Boat to Nowhere,* about the escape of a Vietnamese family.

Perhaps the outstanding book of the year—and the most controversial—was Maurice Sendak's *Outside Over There,* carried on both the adult and juvenile lists of its publisher, Harper & Row. Ostensibly the story of a baby's kidnapping by goblins and rescue by her nine-year-old sister, the tale conveys Freudian hints of fear, hostility, and rivalry. The book's art derives from the German Romantic tradition.

For the picture book audience (ages 3 to 7), the most noteworthy books were *Jumanji,* by Chris Van Allsburg, in which two children play a bizarre magic board game; *On Market Street,* by Anita Lobel, a decorative alphabet book adapting the style of 17th-century French trade engravings; *Light,* by Donald Crews, a spectacular display of nighttime lights in the country and city; Hans Christian Andersen's *The Wild Swans,* elegantly illustrated by Susan Jeffers; James Stevenson's *The Night After Christmas,* about a discarded doll and teddy bear rescued by a dog; and *The Maid and the Mouse and the Odd-Shaped House,* a cleverly designed picture-puzzle story by Paul O. Zelinsky.

For children between 7 and 10, the best books were Nancy Willard's *The Marzipan Moon,* illustrated by Marcia Sewall, a wry tale about a poor priest and a magic crock; Dick Gackenbach's *McGoogan Moves the Mighty Rock,* a tale of generosity and friendship between a traveling man and a rock; and Olaf Baker's *Where the Buffaloes Begin,* an Indian legend illustrated by Stephen Gammell.

In the 9–12 category, the most outstanding books were Lynne Reid Banks' *The Indian in the Cupboard,* in which a three-inch- (7.6-cm-) high plastic Indian comes to life; *Let the Circle Be Unbroken,* by Mildred D. Taylor, a powerful novel of black family life in 1934 rural Mississippi; Beverly Cleary's *Ramona Quimby, Age 8,* episodes in the life of a third-grader; Vera and Bill Cleaver's *The Kissimmee Kid,* in which a 12-year-old girl discovers that her idolized brother-in-law is a cattle rustler; Lloyd Alexander's *Westmark,* a tale of adventure in an imaginary kingdom; and *Lester's Turn,* by Jan Slepian, a touching story of a young cerebral palsy victim and his friends.

Among the year's best novels for teenagers were M. E. Kerr's *Little Little,* a contemporary satiric romance involving three dwarfs; *Rainbow Jordan,* by Alice Childress, about a tough, proud black girl trying to make her way despite an often-absent mother; Cynthia Voigt's *Homecoming,* about the long journey of a family of four abandoned children; and Lois Duncan's *Stranger with My Face,* a spine-chilling tale of a girl with an evil twin sister.

Among many volumes of poetry published in 1981, two stood out—Nancy Willard's *A Visit to William Blake's Inn,* illustrated by Alice and Martin Provensen; and Shel Silverstein's *A Light in the Attic,* a companion volume to his best-selling *Where the Sidewalk Ends.* The most impressive new biography was Jean Fritz's *Traitor,* the life of Benedict Arnold. Another outstanding volume of nonfiction was Melvin Zisfein's *Flight,* a panoramic history of aviation, handsomely illustrated in watercolors by Robert Andrew Parker.

George A. Woods
Children's Book Editor
"The New York Times"

Canadian Literature: English

The year 1981 was another outstanding one for Canadian fiction in English. In nonfiction, a great many books appeared about Canada's history, economics, and people; native Indians claimed particular attention.

Nonfiction. In *Flames Across the Border 1813–1814,* the second of two volumes on the War of 1812, Pierre Berton once again brings history to vivid life, making the complicated campaigns both understandable and exciting. Peter C. Newman's *The Acquisitors* in his second volume on financial leaders, the first being his popular *The Canadian Establishment.*

A Pour of Rain: Stories from a West Coast Fort is Helen Meilleur's well-informed history of the first few decades of the Hudson's Bay Company's Fort Simpson, now Port Simpson, B.C., where she was born and grew up among the Indians she writes about so engagingly. Sylvia Van Kirk's *"Many Tender Ties": Women in Fur-Trade Society* describes the problems of intermarriage between white fur traders and Indian women in the 19th century. Marjorie Halpin's *Totem Poles: An Illustrated Guide* authoritatively explains these art works of the Pacific Northwest's coastal Indians. In *Human Rights and Dissent in Canada,* Justice Thomas R. Berger tells of Canada's dissenters and minorities and their causes through the years, including today's Indian land claims. Hugh Brody depicts the life of the Beaver Indians of the subarctic in *Maps and Dreams.*

Elspeth Cameron's *Hugh MacLennan: A Writer's Life* is a meticulously researched biography of the man many consider Canada's leading writer. Christopher Ondaatje's *The Prime Ministers of Canada: Macdonald to Trudeau, 1867 to 1982* describes 16 widely different men. Betty Keller's *Pauline* is a biography of poetess Pauline Johnson. Edith Iglauer's *Seven Stones* is a well-illustrated study of famed architect Arthur Erickson.

Ginette Bureau's *Mona* is a mother's touching account of her four-year-old daughter's fight against leukemia. Peter Nichols traveled the world for a year to research his study of the Roman Catholic Church today, *The Pope's Divisions.* In *The Canadian Caper,* Jean Pelletier and Claude Adams describe how the Canadian embassy in Tehran helped six U.S. diplomats escape from Iran during the hostage crisis. In *By Reason of Doubt,* Ellen Godfrey reports the murder trial of Prof. Cyril Belshaw.

Richard Rohmer's *Patton's Gap: An Account of the Battle of Normandy 1944* blames Gen. B. L. Montgomery for the escape of German troops through the Falaise Gap but praises Gen. George S. Patton. Tom Naylor's *Canada in the European Age 1453–1919,* Volume I, is the first of two volumes on Canada from the time of the early Spanish and Portuguese explorers. In *The Politics of Water Power,* Harold Foster and Derrick Sewell argue that Canada's water supply is not endless and that governments must act to preserve it. David Godfrey's *The Telidon Book* describes the techniques and impact of electronic information. Peter Lyman's *Canadian Culture and the New Technology* also deals with advances in communications systems.

Poetry. A new collector's item in Canadian poetry is *The Lines of the Poet,* edited by D. G. Jones. This richly produced book was limited to 100 copies, selling for $2,500 each. It contains short works by 14 poets, including F. R. Scott, A. J. M. Smith, and Leonard Cohen.

Margaret Atwood's new collection, *True Stories,* contains poems of painful truth and remarkable beauty. In *Europe and Other Bad News,* Irving Layton again eschews the quiet and conventional. Louis Dudek's two volumes, *Cross-Section: Poems 1940–1980* and *Poems from Atlantis,* show his awareness of both language and technique. Andrew Suknaski's *In the Name of Narid* celebrates the author's Ukrainian ancestors and their building of a new life on the prairies. *Field Notes: The Collected Poems of Robert Kroetsch* arranges fragments from conversations, letters, seed catalogues, and other unlikely sources into convincing verse. George

Courtesy, Macmillan of Canada

W. O. Mitchell's first novel in ten years helped make the fall 1981 season an especially bright one for Canadian publishing.

Bowering's *Particular Accidents* enhances his reputation. And at age 72, Dorothy Livesay added to her long list of poetry collections with *The Raw Edge, voices from our time.*

Fiction. The spring and fall seasons brought several important works by major Canadian novelists. *How I Spent My Summer Holidays,* W.O. Mitchell's first novel in 10 years, is a story of childhood on the prairies. Brian Moore's *The Temptation of Eileen Hughes* concerns an Irish girl who becomes part of a complex triangle. *The Marriage Bed,* by Constance Beresford-Howe, is an extraordinary work about an ordinary Ottawa couple. Timothy Findley's new novel, *Famous Last Words,* has Hugh Selwyn Mauberley, a friend of Ezra Pound, in hiding near the end of World War II and writing the controversial story of his life and times. One of Canada's great journalists, Bruce Hutchison, turned to fiction in *Uncle Percy's Wonderful Town,* a look at a small western town 70 years ago. Robertson Davies' *The Rebel Angels* is about academic life, and Margaret Atwood's *Bodily Harm* concerns a troubled woman journalist.

In *Doomsday Minus Four,* Larry Clark presents an exciting tale of electronic war between East and West. Marian Engels' *Lunatic Villas* describes a woman writer's unusual life among unusual Toronto neighbors. Matt Cohen's *Flowers of Darkness,* set in the fictional Ontario town of Salem, is a powerful tragedy.

DAVID SAVAGE
Simon Fraser University

Canadian Literature: Quebec

The 1981 literary scene in Quebec was a stimulating one, with a wealth of new works in all genres.

Novels. The prestigious Governor General's Award for French fiction went to Pierre Turgeon for *La Première Personne,* a detective story blending exciting suspense with beautiful prose to convey a sense of contemporary alienation. Quebec's Prix David was awarded to Gilles Archambault for *Le Voyageur distrait.* In *La Dame qui avait des chaînes aux chevilles,* the prolific Roch Carrier explores the themes of love, death, and solitude in a 19th-century rural Quebec setting. Humor, a relatively rare phenomenon in Quebec writing, characterizes Yves Beauchemin's *Le Matou,* in which a young Montrealer attempts to rid himself of his paternalistic past. Louis Caron, carefully documenting the social conditions at the time of the 1837 rebellion, describes the plight of a French Canadian farmer in *Le Canard de bois.*

Women writers reflect the rapidly expanding feminist movement in Quebec. Using the popular language of Montreal's colorful Saint-Denis quarter, the young poet and novelist Yolande Villemaire offers a multidimensional view of the female writer and her "doubles" in *La Vie en prose.* Carol Dunlop's *Mélanie dans le miroir* shows maturity of expression, while Gabrielle Poulin offers differing feminine perspectives in *Un Cri trop grand.*

Short Stories. Several prominent novelists published short story collections in 1981. *La Femme Anna et autres contes* contains 30 previously unpublished selections by Yves Thériault. After several years of silence, Jacques Ferron came out with two new works, *Gaspé Mattempa* and *L'Exécution de Maski.* His sister, Madeleine Ferron, describes the real and imaginary Maskinongé county in *Histoires édifiantes.* Louis Maheu-Forcier's volume, *En toutes lettres,* contains 25 well-crafted stories; Jean-Yves Soucy's *L'Etranger au ballon rouge* uses irony, humor, and the fantastic to buttress political reflections; and Marilú Mallet offers a recent immigrant's view of Montreal's alienating landscape in *Les Compagnons de l'horloge-pointeuse.*

Poetry. Michel van Schendel's *De l'oeil et de l'ecoute* received the 1981 Governor General's Award for poetry in French. *En la nuit, la mer* is a retrospective of Fernand Ouellette's poetry from 1972 to 1980. Robert Mélançon's *Territoire,* Jacques Brault's *Trois fois passera,* Madeleine Ouellette-Michalska's *Entre le souffle et l'aine* were well-received, as were Rina Lasnier's *Entendre l'ombre* and Paul Chamberland's *L'Enfant doré* and *Le Courage de la poésie.*

Theater. Jovette Marchessault's *La Saga des poules mouillées,* one of the year's most interesting plays, presents four sketches about female Quebec writers concerned with the problems of a "feminine mode of expression." *Sur le matelas* is Michel Garneau's latest play. Louisette Dussault's *Moman* and Marie Laberge's *C'était avant la guerre à l'Anse-à-Gilles* provide feminine perspectives; and Antonine Maillet's humorous *La Contrebandière* portrays forceful and heroic women.

Essays and Criticism. Paul Chamberland's mix of poems and essays, *Emergence de l'adultenfant,* synthesizes the major currents of his intellectual development in the past decade. Madeleine Ouellette-Michalska's extraordinary essay *L'Echappée des discours de l'oeil* explores male-dominated visions of the world in an "archaeology of the written word." In the realm of criticism, Annette Saint-Pierre's *Le Rideau se lève au Manitoba* graphically illustrates a century of French theater in her province, and Pascal Normand sketches a brief history of song in Quebec with a discography in *La Chanson québécoise.*

Children's Literature. An Acadian Paddington is delightfully presented in *Christophe Cartier de la Noisette dit Nonours,* by Antonine Maillet. *La Vengeance de l'original* by Doric Germain, a Franco-Ontarian, takes place in the woods of northern Ontario. *Le Visiteur du soir,* a detective story by Robert Soulières, is about a theft from a Montreal museum and the sabotaging of the James Bay hydro project.

RAMON HATHORN
University of Guelph

English Literature

Publishing in Great Britain during 1981 gave the impression of a pause, perhaps of a change. In fiction and poetry, there were fewer books by famous writers than in recent years. The void was filled, however, with books by lesser-known and new writers. In nonfiction, significant new studies and memoirs were published steadily throughout the year.

Nonfiction. Two novelists, Daphne du Maurier and Muriel Spark, and a playwright, John Osborne, published memoirs that cast new light on their work. Du Maurier's *The Rebecca Notebook and Other Memories* contains several personal essays and the notebook in which she planned her most famous novel. In *Loitering with Intent,* Muriel Spark uses the disguise of a narrator to reflect on her own life and work. In his first autobiographical work, *A Better Class of Person,* Osborne reveals a personality as abrasive as that of Jimmy Porter, the hero of his play *Look Back in Anger.*

Several less famous Britons also published autobiographies. In *Memories,* Frances Partridge, the wife of a friend of Lytton Strachey, looks back on her life and relationships with members of the Bloomsbury Group. Geoffrey Keynes, a surgeon, bibliographer, and brother of the economist John Maynard Keynes, also looks back, in *The Gates of Memory.* Sarah Churchill, the actress and daughter of Winston Churchill, considers the vicissitudes of her life in *Keep on Dancing.* In *How to Become a Virgin,* Quentin Crisp describes with happy astonishment how the abuse he received for his unusual dress and manners changed to adulation with the help of television. On his return to England after an absence of 45 years, William Campbell wrote, in *Villi the Clown,* about his experiences in the Soviet Union as factory worker, singer, actor, journalist, and clown.

Important editions of letters and diaries also appeared during the year. *Like It Was,* edited by John Bright-Holmes, presents selections from the diaries of Malcolm Muggeridge, journalist and television host, for the years 1932 to 1962.

Vera Brittain's diary for the period 1913 to 1917, *Chronicle of Youth,* edited by Alan Bishop, was published posthumously. The book reveals the personal consequences of World War I, including the deaths of her brother and his two closest friends, one of whom was her fiancé. Many of the experiences recorded in the diary were used in Brittain's novel, *Testament of Youth.*

Other posthumous collections were the letters of J. R. R. Tolkien, edited by Humphrey Carpenter; *Siegfried Sassoon Diaries, 1920–1922,* edited by Rupert Hart-Davis, which takes up Sassoon's life where his autobiography, *Siegfried's Journey,* left off; *A Lonely Business: A Self Portrait of James Pope-Hennessy,* selected by Peter Quennell from Pope-Hennessy's letters and diary; and *The Diaries of Sir Robert Bruce Lockhart, 1939–1965.* Lockhart, author of *Memoirs of a British Agent,* about his experiences in Russia during World War I, was also head of the British Political Warfare Executive during World War II.

Important new biographies were David Carlton's *Anthony Eden;* Nigel Hamilton's *Monty: The Making of a General;* Silvia L. Horwitz's *The Find of a Lifetime: Sir Arthur Evans and the Discovery of Knossos;* Henrietta Sharpe's *A Solitary Woman: A Life of Violet Trefusis;* Carolyn Scott's *The Heavenly Witch,* a life of the evangelist Kate Booth, daughter of the founder of the Salvation Army; T. A. J. Burnett's *The Rise and Fall of a Regency Dandy,* the life and times of Scrope Davies, a friend of Byron; Winifred Gérin's *Anne Thackeray Ritchie;* Georgina Battiscombe's *Christina Rossetti;* June Badeni's *The Slender Tree: A Life of Alice Meynell;* John Conrad's *Joseph Conrad: Times Remembered;* Brian Taylor's *The Green Avenue: The Life and Writings of Forrest Reid;* James Brabazon's *Dorothy L. Sayers;* Victoria Glendinning's *Edith Sitwell;* and Humphrey Carpenter's *W. H. Auden.*

Works of literary history and criticism included Roger Knight's *Edwin Muir: An Introduction to His Work;* G. S. Fraser's *A Short History of English Poetry;* and Walter Allen's *The Short Story in English.*

Humphrey Carpenter's new biography of W. H. Auden, emphasizing his career as a teacher as well as a poet, was greeted as an enlightening study.

Courtesy Houghton Mifflin

A number of books were published in celebration of the centennial of the birth of P. G. Wodehouse. Perhaps the most significant was Iain Sproat's *Wodehouse at War.* Sproat extracted from the British government a report on Wodehouse's broadcasts from Berlin, where he and his wife were held prisoner during World War II. The report cleared Wodehouse of accusations of disloyalty.

Fiction. Several writers whose names have become familiar over the last decade published new novels in 1981. Keith Waterhouse's *Maggie Muggins* recounts a day in the life of a drifter. In *Who Was Oswald Fish?,* A. N. Wilson wittily explores the manners and sexual activities of a Victorian architect and his 20th-century descendants. In *Feelings Have Changed,* P. H. Newby combines fantasy and comedy with a realistic account of life in a radio department of the British Broadcasting Corporation (BBC). Piers Paul Read's *The Villa Golitsyn* is set near Nice, France, where a couple near death are investigated by a friend from the Foreign Office who has ostensibly come to help them. Venice becomes a place of horror for a middle-aged couple on vacation in Ian McEwan's *The Comfort of Strangers.* In Jennifer Johnston's *The Christmas Tree,* a dying woman tries to relive the past by accepting a lover she had rejected years before. Martin Amis' *Other People* is about the uneasy experiences of a young woman who has lost her memory.

Two older novelists also published new books. John Braine's *One and Last Love* is about the love affair of a middle-aged writer. And Pamela Hansford Johnson's posthumous *A Bonfire* describes the girlhood and three marriages of its central character.

Five of the year's most interesting novels have a regional flavor. Alasdair Gray's *Lanark* is partly a psychological allegory and partly a developmental novel about a young artist in Glasgow. Anne Smith's *The Magic Glass* is about the growth of its energetic heroine in a working-class district of a Scottish city; and Michael Bassi's *The Kilted Parrot* describes the middle-class career of a flamboyant Edinburgh man. In G. B. Edwards' posthumous novel *The Book of Ebenezer Le Page,* a Guernsey man observes with disdain the changes that the 20th century has brought to his island. *Silver's City,* by Maurice Leitch, is about the effects of terrorism on Belfast.

With *The Sirian Experiments,* Doris Lessing continues her series of novels about the history of the earth and other empires in the galaxy. Bruce Arnold published the second and third novels, *The Song of the Nightingale* and *The Muted Swan,* in his series, in which a narrator looks back on his youth. *The Dew* concludes John Tofts' series of novels about families in the Potteries district of England. Michael Moorcock published the first volume, *Byzantium Endures,* of the fictional life of a Ukrainian engineer who survived the Russian Revolution and fled to England.

Other notable novels were Anita Mason's *Bethany,* Nicholas Salaman's *The Frights,* Janice Elliott's *Secret Places,* Nina Bawden's *Walking Naked,* Lynn Reid Banks' *Defy the Wilderness,* Caroline Blackwood's *The Fate of Mary Rose,* Mary Hobson's *Oh Lily,* Anita Brookner's *A Start in Life,* Mary Hocking's *March House,* Ann Schlee's *Rhine Journey,* and George Steiner's *The Portage to San Cristobel of A.H.*

Among collections of short stories were William Trevor's *Beyond the Pale,* Gillian Tindall's *The China Egg,* Desmond Hogan's *Children of Lir,* Alan Sillitoe's *The Second Chance,* Helen Lucy Burke's *A Season for Mothers,* Patricia Zelver's *A Man of Middle Age,* and Fay Weldon's *Watching Me, Watching You.*

Poetry. Britain's best-known poets published little in 1981. Ted Hughes spoke of his volume *Under the North Star,* illustrated by Leonard Baskin, as "a simple picture book," but its concrete images are intended for adults as well as children. John Heath-Stubbs' *Birds Reconvened* is a series of carefully crafted poems on various birds. John Betjeman's *Church Poems* contains 30 poems on churches, illustrated by John Piper.

Peter Porter, an Australian who settled in England and contributed much to its poetry in recent years, must perhaps by now be considered an English poet. Porter's new work, *English Subtitles,* is typical of his eloquence and style.

The poems in several new collections are rooted in particular regions. Jeremy Hooker, a Hampshireman, has lived in Wales for ten years. Not quite at home there, he writes of Wales with the sharp eye of a stranger in *Englishman's Road.* The Sussex coast is the locale for several of the poems in Ian Caws' *Boy With a Kite.* The epigrams and poems in Robert Shaw's *The Wrath Valley Anthology* are set in Yorkshire; and Norman Nicholson's *Sea to the West* examines in free verse his native town and its Cumberland environs. Douglas Dunn, having lived for some time in England, returns in imagination and memory to his native Scotland in *St. Kilda's Parliament.*

Among other collections were John Fuller's *The Illusionists,* Thomas Blackburn's *Bread for the Winter Birds,* Anthony Thwaite's *Victorian Voices,* Joan Barton's *A House Under Old Sarum,* Dannie Abse's *Way Out in Centre,* Gerda Mayer's *Monkey on the Analyst's Couch,* Richard Burns' *Learning to Talk,* Penelope Shuttle's *The Orchard Upstairs,* Medbh McGluckian's *Portrait of Joanna,* Francis Horovitz's *Water Over Stone,* Louis Gluck's *Descending Figure,* and David Constantine's *A Brightness to Cast Shadows.*

Among the year's poetry anthologies were John Wain's *Poems 1949–1979,* David Holbrook's *Selected Poems 1961–1978,* Roy Fisher's *Poems 1955–1980,* and D. J. Enright's *Collected Poems.*

J. K. JOHNSTONE, *University of Saskatchewan*

Non-English Literature

In European literature generally and in French belles lettres specifically, the year 1981 brought the expected sizable selection of esoteric, hybrid, often unclassifiable texts that have followed in the wake of the *nouveau roman* and the era of *écriture.* Michel Butor, one of the prime practitioners of the New Novel in the 1950s and 1960s, issued the fourth part of his *Matière de rêves* (Stuff of Dreams) series, *Quadruple fond* (Fourfold Foundation), like its predecessors a free-form blend of fiction, verse, philosophy, fantasy, and satire presented as a successive and self-referential set of dream states. Claude Simon, another of the New Novelists and France's likeliest current candidate for the Nobel Prize, published perhaps his richest and most ambitious novel ever: *Les Géorgiques* (The Georgics, in imitation of Vergil) is a long, multilevel work involving several "readers" and "writers" and incorporating the Spanish Civil War, the French Revolution, and the Roman conquests in a virtuoso effort of modernistic prose. And from Samuel Beckett came another in a series of stark, brief, cryptic fictional exercises, *Mal vu mal dit* (Ill Seen Ill Said).

During the same year, however, there appeared several works of genuine nostalgia, books of a traditional nature either in style or substance or both. Previously unseen correspondence from Albert Camus and Jean Cocteau added little to their high reputations, but François Mauriac's posthumous reminiscences, *Souvenirs retrouvés* (Rediscovered Memories), illumine both an earlier age and one of its finest authors. Daniel Gillès's *Laurence de la nuit* (Laurence of the Night), the fifth in a projected seven-volume *roman fleuve* tracing the fortunes of two noble families in Austria and Belgium during World War II, evokes memories of Tolstoy and Romain Rolland in technique and sweep. François Clément's *Les procédures champêtres* (Rustic Red Tape), in which a middle-aged businessman exchanges his daily routine for a new life in the country, brought favorable comparisons with Flaubert in its clean, concise style and sharp, full characterizations.

The year also witnessed two stunning public "events" in French letters: the induction of Marguerite Yourcenar (a resident of Maine for more than 30 years) as the first female Immortal in the long history of the Académie Française; and the revelation of the much-celebrated but reclusive novelist "Emile Ajar" as none other than the late Romain Gary, a literary hoax unequaled in postwar France either in success or duration.

In Spanish and Spanish American letters, 1981 was not a strong year, although four major novelists did bring out important works. In Spain, Juan Goytisolo published the first Peninsular edition of his 1962 exile novel *La chanca* (a kind of old shoe), the work in which the author began his evolution into a social novelist and realist with a genuine understanding of historical forces and movements. Colombia's celebrated Gabriel García Márquez followed his phenomenal earlier successes with *Una muerte anunciada*

Elias Canetti, a 76-year-old Bulgarian-born Jew who lives in England and writes in German, was awarded the 1981 Nobel Prize in Literature. In its citation, the Swedish Academy said his writings are "marked by a broad outlook, a wealth of ideas, and artistic power."

Educated in Switzerland, Germany, and Austria, Canetti received a doctorate in chemistry in 1929 and then turned to writing. His best-known work is his only novel, *Die Blendung* (1935), published in England under the title *Auto-da-Fé* (1946) and in the United States as *Tower of Babel* (1947). His major nonfiction work, *Masse und Macht* (*Crowds and Power,* 1960), is a long study of the origins, structures, and effects of mass movements. Canetti's oeuvre also includes several plays, memoirs, notes and aphorisms, a travel book, and literary portraits. Considered in the tradition of Goethe, Canetti was described in the academy's citation as having "one native land, and that is the German language. He has never abandoned it, and he has often avowed his love of the highest manifestation of classical German culture."

Gamma

(A Foretold Death). By labeling this retrospective tale of avenged dishonor a "chronicle," or fact-based novella, the author remained faithful to his vow not to write fiction so long as Augusto Pinochet rules Chile. Peruvian novelist Mario Vargas Llosa explored the history of the Amazon's colonization and early development in another of his multiple-strand Faulknerian narratives, *La señorita de Tacna.* And returned Chilean exile José Donoso's *El jardín de al lado* (The Side Garden) continued to plumb the world of grotesqueness and corruption that the author has virtually made his own through several novels over the past 15 years.

From the other Romance-language areas came several works on and of bygone days. The late Portuguese author José Rodrigues Miguéis' old-fashioned novel of the tribulations of farm laborers versus big landowners and big government, *O pão não cai do céu* (Bread Doesn't Fall from the Sky), appeared in book form for the first time. Brazilian writer Sergio Sant'Anna offered in *Um romance de geração* (A Generational Novel) a brilliant satire on stagnating intellectual life during the early 20th-century turmoil in Brazil. Catalan author Manuel de Pedrolo's *Anònim II* (Anonymous II), written in 1970 but only now released after six years of Spanish democracy, viciously indicted a "fictitious" totalitarian regime and accurately predicted the emergence of a moderate government which would subsequently collapse under attack from both the Left and Right. Leading Catalan poets Salvador Espriu and Pere Gimferrer continued the post-Franco boom of publications in Spain's minority languages with their respective new verse collections *Aspectes* and *Mirall, espai, aparicions* (Mirror, Space, Apparitions). The novels and stories of Rumanian sage and fiction-writer Mircea Eliade have been steadily appearing in French and German translations for more than a decade, and 1981 saw the publication of his *Uniformes de général,* a collection of fantastic tales. Eliade's work has slowly begun to appear in English as well, and the year also saw the English-language publication of the first volume of his *Autobiography,* covering the period 1907–37, which included his long stays in Calcutta and the Himalayas and his first years as a professor of philosophy at the University of Bucharest.

West German Siegfried Lenz published a new novel, "Der Verlust" (The Loss), about muteness.

German Information Center

German-language writing arguably outdistanced much that was produced elsewhere in Europe during 1981, with East Germany—perhaps surprisingly—leading the way. East German Stefan Heym brought forth what may well be his masterpiece in *Ahasver* (Ahasueris, or the Wandering Jew), a superbly crafted novel which recounts both the story of a North German cleric's spiritual rise and fall through contact with the title figure, and a fictional exchange of letters between scholars in Berlin and Jerusalem on the nature and supposed continued existence of Ahasueris. The combination makes for a resonant study of myth and an enthralling evocation of that myth's import for the betterment of mankind, not merely its salvation or damnation. The foremost representative of East German literary life, novelist-playwright Hermann Kant, gathered 23 years' worth of criticism and commentary in *Zu den Unterlagen* (Concerning the Enclosed Information), which reads like a cultural history of the young nation since 1957. Volker Braun, termed by many the most exciting and inventive playwright currently active in East or West Germany, issued the second volume of his collected plays and continues to produce and direct his work at the famous Berliner Ensemble. Expatriate Peter Weiss, long a resident of Sweden but an East German sympathizer, completed his huge trilogy *Ästhetik des Widerstands* (Esthetics of Resistance), a novelistic investigation of the role of art in European political life using the example of Brecht and others. And recently exiled poet Günter Kunert published *Verspätete Monologe* (Belated Monologues), 152 often aphoristic utterances comprising a movingly candid and highly intelligent reckoning with the author's past and present life.

From West Germany came Siegfried Lenz's newest novel *Der Verlust* (The Loss), which explores the consequences of muteness through the story of a travel guide who loses the faculty of speech and must painstakingly reestablish connections to words, language, concepts, and meaning as well as to himself and to his friends. The short stories collected in Gabriele Wohmann's *Stolze Zeiten* (Proud Times) affirm her mastery of this genre but offer an unrelievedly bleak vision of human weakness, stupidity, selfishness, narrow-mindedness, and cruelty in even the subtlest of gestures and most trivial of events. The equally misanthropic Austrian novelist-playwright Thomas Bernhard presented the fourth installment of his reminiscences, *Die Kälte* (The Cold), dealing with the period of his confinement for a near-fatal lung disease at age 18 and his later "escape" and private convalescence, viewing the entire experience as a metaphor for hopelessness. Swiss-born Urs Jaeggi's prizewinning novel *Grundrisse* (Fundamentals) depicts a German executive's change from a wholly structured existence to a wholly aimless one as an inner journey of existential self-discovery.

In the other Germanic languages, 1981 was a stronger year for poetry than for fiction. The Netherlands' two principal contemporary poets, Hans ten Berge and Lucebert, brought out the collections *Nieuwe gedichten* (New Poems) and *Oogsten in de dwaaltuin* (Harvest in the False Garden), respectively. Swedish poet and Nobel Committee member Östen Sjöstrand's *Dikter* (Poems) offered a selection of his lyric output from the last two decades, an unusual poetry which draws on the disparate sources of ancient religions, modern physics, and music. His countryman Tobias Berggren probed the problematic relationships among language, sociopolitical forces, and abstract reality in *Threnos* (Threnody). Leading Norwegian poet Paal Brekke collected his essays and critical writings since 1970 as *Farvelets rester* (Parting Remnants), while prominent Danish poet Thorkild Bjørnvig continued his recent fascination with ecological matters in the new verse collection *Abeguder* (Ape Gods). Klaus Rifbjerg, "the Danish Updike," kept up his incredibly prolific production with the short novel *De hellige aber* (The Holy Apes).

Soviet Russian literature continues to be a creatively rich but humanly tragic field, as more and more writers are muzzled, forced into exile, imprisoned—or silenced forever. Out of the past in 1981 came the voice of the late Eugenia Ginzburg in *Within the Whirlwind,* the translation of the second part of her posthumous 1977 "autobiographical novel," recounting her grim years at hard labor in a desolate Siberian prison camp. Ginzburg's son Vasily Aksyonov, a recent émigré and one of the leading contemporary Russian prose writers, brought out a disappointingly weak satirical novel, *Ostrov Krym* (The Crimean Island), clumsily transposing the mores and practices of the West during the 1960s onto present-day Soviet types. Better efforts came from Vladimir Maramzin in the story collection *Tyanitolkai* (Push-Pull) and from the "regional" writers Chingiz Aitmatov of Kirgizia with the novel *I dolshe veka dlitsya den* (And a Day Lasts for Ages) and Fazil Iskander of Abkhazia with

German Information Center

Gabrielle Wohmann of West Germany displays her mastery of the short story in a new collection.

an expanded version of his highly original 1979 comic novel *Sandro iz Chegema* (Sandro from Chegema).

The transforming power of the Nobel Prize continued to work its magic, this time in the case of Polish poet-novelist-essayist Czesław Miłosz. The 1980 laureate's triumphant three-week return to his native country in the spring of 1981, after three decades of exile in France and the United States, was accompanied by huge printings of his complete works for the first time ever in Warsaw and Cracow. In Toronto, meanwhile, there appeared the first original-language edition of the superb novel of memory and hope, *Kniha smíchu a zapomnění* (*The Book of Laughter and Forgetting*), by Czech émigré Milan Kundera; translations had created a literary sensation in Paris, New York, and Frankfurt during the preceding year.

Among the smaller European literatures, such as Greek and Hungarian, Greek poet Nikifóros Vrettákos' exuberant nine-part hymn to Hellenism *Litouryia káto apó tin Akrópoli* (Liturgy Beneath the Acropolis) deserves special mention. Two significant translations into English also appeared: 1979 Nobel laureate Odysseus Elytis' *Maria Nephele,* a complex antiphonal poetic dialogue between an older Greek writer and a liberated but blasé young woman of the 1970s; and *Ocean at the Window,* a flawed but nonetheless useful anthology of postwar Hungarian poetry containing the work of 24 established and new poets.

Much African literature is composed in English, but Kenyan novelist Ngugi wa Thiong'o (formerly James Ngugi, author of *A Grain of Wheat*) pulled a startling reversal in 1980 by publishing the first novel ever written in his native Gikuyu tongue—*Caitaani Mutharaba-ini,* dealing principally with the conflict between native tradition and outside forces; in 1981 there followed Ngugi's own English version, entitled *Devil on the Cross.* Francophone Africa produces frequently fine writing as well, with the most unusual work in 1981 being Tunisian author Mahmoud Messadi's heavily symbolic play *Le Barrage* (The Dam), a set of eight tableaux depicting in mythical, archetypal fashion the conflicts engendered among Man, Woman, Tribe, earth spirits, and the Divinity by a massive dam project on a vital river. South African émigré author-scholar Daniel Kunene brought out a new English translation of the story of Shaka, the great Zulu king who unified his people in what is now Natal; and prominent Afrikaans poet N. P. van Wyk Louw issued *Versamelde gedigte,* his collected poems of several decades.

The literatures of Asia and the Near East make their way westward largely through translation into English and French, and 1981 saw a continued flood of first-rate works. Renowned Turkish novelist Yashar Kemal's *Seagull* presented the fascinating and absorbing story of a child's developing perceptions of an exotic world mixed with fantasies, myths, fabrications, and misapprehended facts. The respected Egyptian authors Taha Hussein and Nagib Mahfuz were represented by the autobiographical work *An Egyptian Childhood* and the short-story collection *Children of Gebelawi,* respectively. From Israel came not only the English editions of new verse collections by the two finest active Hebrew poets, T. Carmi (*At the Stone of Losses*) and Yehuda Amichai (*Love Poems*), but also the translation of an important volume of essays by novelist-playwright A. B. Yehoshua, *Between Right and Right,* and the magnificent *Penguin Book of Hebrew Verse,* edited by Carmi and covering 3,000 years of uninterrupted literary creativity in a beautifully arranged bilingual presentation.

Chingiz Aitmatov, board secretary of the Soviet Writers' Union, published a new "regional" novel.

Tass from Sovfoto

From the Country of Eight Islands was a similar effort on behalf of Japanese poetry, offering samples of the finest work from 1,300 years of lyric tradition, with more than one third of the selections coming from the modern period. From the Malay came translations of both Ishak Haji Muhammad's excellent 1937 novel of British colonialism, *The Prince of Mount Tahan,* and Ahmad Shahnon's collection *The Third Notch and Other Stories,* tales notable for their linguistic resourcefulness and their adept psychological insights. Umar Kayam's Baha Indonesian tales translated as *Sri Sumarah and Other Stories* reveal a thematic range far wider than the provincial limitations or stereotyped prose which might be expected by Western readers.

Among many fine translations from the Chinese were two new examples of contemporary writing and new renditions of two superb classics: mainland-born author Hualing Nieh's novel *Two Women of China,* loosely based on her own immigration experiences in Taiwan and the United States, quickly sold out in a first printing of 130,000 in Peking, went into a large second printing, and was available in her own English version published simultaneously in Peking and New York; *Literature of the Hundred Flowers,* a two-volume anthology produced under Hualing Nieh's editorial supervision, collects the best poetry, prose, and polemical writings produced during China's brief period of liberalization in 1956 and 1957; *The Warning Voice* represents the third of five installments comprising Cao Xueqin's great 18th-century novel of manners *The Story of the Stone;* and a new, two-volume edition of *Outlaws of the Marsh,* as translated by Sidney Shapiro, far outstrips Pearl Buck's 1931 version (*Dream of the Red Chamber*) of this celebrated novelistic amalgam of Chinese martial tales long popular in song and film as well as in literature and myth.

WILLIAM RIGGAN
Associate Editor, "World Literature Today"

LONDON

On television around the world, Londoners were seen at their best and worst during 1981.

After an incident in which a stabbed black youth was picked up by the police on April 10, the streets of Brixton in South London erupted into riots, and for two successive nights battles raged between the local, mostly black, inhabitants and the police. The official inquiry into the riots, headed by Lord Scarman, heard evidence throughout the summer from community leaders, local police, and residents. Indications were that after many months of widening hostility between police and the community in Brixton (an area with a high immigrant population, high unemployment, and a growing crime rate) such tension existed as to culminate in April's explosion. Lord Scarman's report was given to the Home Office at the year's end. Major rioting also broke out in London and various other cities in Britain and Scotland in July. (*See also* Great Britain.)

On July 29, Londoners ignored their worries and reached a fever of celebration when they lined the streets to watch the wedding procession of Prince Charles, the heir to the throne, and Lady Diana Spencer. After the grandeur of the marriage ceremony in St. Paul's cathedral, the royal couple, in an open carriage festooned with balloons, set off on their honeymoon, across Westminster Bridge and past County Hall.

In County Hall, the leader of London's government, 32-year-old Ken Livingstone, sat working, having pointedly refused his invitation to the royal wedding. The elections of May 7 overthrew the Conservative majority in favor of a new chamber made up of 50 Labour councillors, 41 Conservatives, and 1 Liberal. However, the day after the election results were announced the moderate Labour leader Andrew Mackintosh was replaced by left-winger Ken Livingstone, whose opinions, notably on the wedding, Northern Ireland, and the riots made him a household name nationally.

MAUREEN GREEN

LOS ANGELES

On Sept. 4, 1981, Los Angeles commemorated the 200th anniversary of its founding. In 1781, 44 Mexican peasants founded *El Pueblo de Nuestra Señora la Reina de los Angeles de Porciuncula* (the Village of Our Lady, Queen of the Angels of Porciuncula). Celebrations of the event actually took place throughout the year. And, as if nature wished to be included in the activities, the city was struck on the morning of September 4 by an earthquake measuring Richter 5.1, the strongest temblor in more than ten years. Skyscrapers swayed and pedestrians braced themselves against buildings, but there were no injuries and virtually no property damage, a tribute to a strict city building code.

Ron Butcher

Los Angeles is rendered on a bicentennial cake. Real buildings were shaken by an earthquake.

Politics. In April, Mayor Thomas Bradley, 63, was elected to a third term, winning by more than two-to-one over former mayor Samuel Yorty. In June, voters rejected a plan to raise the property tax so as to increase the size of the police force by 20%. The proposal needed a two-thirds majority but received only 42%.

The county board of supervisors, now with a conservative majority and facing the effects of Proposition 13, drastically cut back the budget and eliminated about 4,400 jobs, one third of them in social services. The city made an across-the-board budget cut of 3%, and the police chief agreed to cuts in management positions so as to increase the number of patrolmen.

Schools. School board politics saw the end of mandatory busing on April 20, after an 18-year battle in the nation's second largest school district. The California Supreme Court let stand a lower-court decision upholding the constitutionality of a voter-approved referendum banning all compulsory busing except to end deliberately planned segregation. But the board encountered a new problem, as protests grew against the implementation of year-round schooling in overcrowded, mostly poor areas of the city.

Sports. Al Davis, managing general partner of the Oakland Raiders football team, sought to move the franchise to Los Angeles, but the move was opposed by the rest of the league owners. The case came to trial, which ended in an inconclusive hung jury. The city celebrated the Dodgers' win in the 1981 World Series.

CHARLES R. ADRIAN
University of California, Riverside

LOUISIANA

The state legislature passed a controversial bill requiring equal time for the teaching of the theories of scientific creationism and evolution in public school science classes. Other notable new legislation included an anticrime package, a bill to reform the racing commission, and a $5,100,000,000 operating budget. For the first time ever, the legislature ejected one of its own members, Sen. Gaston Gerald of Greenwell Springs. Gerald had been convicted of attempted extortion from a Baton Rouge contractor.

Crime. Carlos Marcello, reputed New Orleans rackets figure, and Charles E. Roemer II, former state commissioner of administration, were convicted in federal court of conspiring to use bribes and kickbacks to obtain a state insurance contract. Two defendants, Washington lobbyist I. Irving Davidson and New Orleans lawyer Vincent A. Marinello, were acquitted. Charges had been dropped against Aubrey Young, a longtime state office holder. The Brilab (bribery-labor) case had been cracked by undercover FBI agents.

Civil Rights. Another Louisiana court case drew national attention when a federal judge ordered the busing of three junior high school girls 15 mi (24 km) from the village of Buckeye to a mostly black school in the city of Alexandria. A state court judge tried to remove the girls from the busing plan. According to a compromise agreement, the girls, known as the "Buckeye 3," were forced to go to school in Alexandria, and possible contempt charges against the state judge were dropped. In yet another important federal court case, the state reached a settlement to upgrade two predominantly black universities, Grambling and Southern, by sharing programs and teachers among those schools and mostly white universities. And more blacks are to be recruited in the white schools. The NAACP claimed the settlement did not go far enough.

Oil Port. The Louisiana Offshore Oil Port (LOOP) became the nation's first deepwater oil port when it opened in May. The offshore platform, 18 mi (29 km) off the town of Grand Isle, will allow the offloading of imported oil from supertankers that could not be handled by U.S. inland ports.

The drinking water in New Orleans and smaller Mississippi River communities was fouled in February when the Georgia Pacific Co. illegally discharged phenol into the river. The company at first denied dumping huge amounts of the chemical, which is said to be harmless but ruins the taste of water. Georgia Pacific was fined $308,000 by the state Environmental Control Commission and was sued by several towns for the cost of purifying their drinking water.

New Orleans. New Orleans proceeded with plans for its 1984 World's Fair. Mayor Ernest N. Morial questioned whether the expense of the fair would balance benefits to the city. But after meeting with Gov. David C. Treen and fair officials, he said an agreement had been reached to help the city cope financially with the fair.

New Orleans suffered racial tensions but no violence through much of 1981. Six active policemen and a former officer were charged with brutality against blacks in an investigation that followed the unsolved shooting death of another officer. A state grand jury refused to indict the policemen. Although a federal grand jury did later indict them, a federal judge threw the charges out because he said the U.S. prosecutor pressured the grand jury into the indictment.

JOSEPH W. DARBY III
"The Times-Picayune," New Orleans

LOUISIANA • Information Highlights

Area: 47,752 sq mi (123 678 km^2).
Population (1980 census): 4,203,972.
Chief Cities (1980 census): Baton Rouge, the capital, 219,486; New Orleans, 557,482; Shreveport, 205,815; Lafayette, 81,961; Lake Charles, 75,051; Kenner, 66,382; Monroe, 57,597; Alexandria, 51,565; Bossier City, 49,969; New Iberia, 32,766.
Government (1981): *Chief officers*—governor, David C. Treen (R); lt. gov., Robert L. Freeman (D). *Legislature*—Senate, 39 members; House of Representatives, 105 members.
State Finances (fiscal year 1980): *Revenues,* $5,412,000,000; *expenditures,* $4,887,000,000.
Personal Income (1980): $35,645,000,000; per capita, $8,458.
Labor Force (July 1981): *Nonagricultural wage and salary earners,* 1,638,400; *unemployed,* 147,200 (8.2% of total force).

LUXEMBOURG

The European economic recession of 1981 was deeply felt in Luxembourg, where more than 80% of the gross national product (GNP) is related to foreign trade. Estimated real growth in the duchy's GNP fell to less than 1% in 1981.

Despite completing a long-range employee reduction program, which mainly affected migrant workers from Italy and Portugal, the ARBED steel combine announced plans for a cold steel strip mill with a capacity of 1.2 million t (1.32 million T). Belgian, French, and German competitors complained, and after government negotiations with the Belgians the mill's capacity was halved. The incident stimulated conjecture of further cooperation among Benelux steel in-

LUXEMBOURG • Information Highlights

Official Name: Grand Duchy of Luxembourg.
Location: Western Europe.
Area: 999 sq mi (2 587 km^2).
Population (1981 est.): 400,000.
Chief Cities (1978 est.): Luxembourg, the capital, 79,600; Esch-sur-Alzette, 26,500; Differdange, 17,100.
Government: *Head of state,* Jean, grand duke (acceded 1964). *Head of government,* Pierre Werner, prime minister (took office July 1979). *Legislature* (unicameral)—Chamber of Deputies.
Monetary Unit: Franc (39.26 francs equal U.S.$1, June 1981).
Manufactures (major products): Steel, rubber products, synthetic fibers.
Agriculture (major products): Grains, livestock, dairy products.

Two reigning families pose for an informal portrait at the Luxembourg palace in March. They are (left to right), Prince Henri and the Grand Duchess of Luxembourg, Queen Beatrix of the Netherlands, the Grand Duke of Luxembourg, Prince Claus of the Netherlands, and Princess María Teresa of Luxembourg. Prince Henri and Maria Teresa were wed one month earlier.

UPI

dustries. It also underlined the need for agreement within the European Community (EC) on production quotas and the elimination of government subsidies for steel industries if protectionist tariff hikes are to be avoided.

Such agreement was reached on June 25, 1981. The duchy was represented in the negotiations by a new foreign minister, Colette Flesch. Flesch succeeded Gaston Thorn, who commenced official duties as president of the EC Commission in January. Flesch, a ranking member of the Liberal party and the mayor of the city of Luxembourg, also assumed the post of deputy prime minister and the portfolios of foreign trade, economic affairs, middle classes, and justice.

Hopes that the duchy would become the permanent seat of the European Parliament faded, as the monthly plenary sessions stayed in Strasbourg. Luxembourg is left with the embarrassment of a $100 million assembly hall, but the duchy does remain administrative headquarters for the secretariat's staff of about 2,000.

In March, the Belgium-Luxembourg Monetary Union was renewed for ten years, with the duchy gaining greater economic autonomy so as to avoid being pulled further into the Belgian economic crisis. The duchy will be represented in the International Monetary Fund by a purely Luxembourg Monetary Institute.

Luxembourg's large international banking complex continued to thrive. Inflation for 1981 was estimated at 6–8%, a low figure compared with that of nearby countries and especially so considering the fact that about 90% of Luxembourg consumer goods are imported. Unemployment also remained low.

J. E. HELMREICH, *Allegheny College*

MAINE

The economy was the central focus in Maine in 1981.

Troubled Industries, Transportation, Energy. Potato farmers in Aroostook County continued to worry about the shipment and sale of Canadian potatoes. The poultry industry faced financial troubles caused by the high cost of the shipment of grains into Maine. The shoe industry confronted problems caused by foreign competition.

Also at issue was the continued operation of the Maine Milk Commission, which has the power to set minimum milk prices in retail stores.

Still another problem was the funding of the state Department of Transportation (DOT). The DOT was financially hampered by a decline in revenue due to inflation and the drop in sales of gasoline. This loss of revenue led the DOT to trim its maintenance and road-building activities. A new tax on interstate trucking resulted in the initiation of litigation to prevent its continuation.

Gordon Weil, state energy director, and his staff began establishing a statewide energy plan. The cost of heating oil in the northeast is a major concern.

Environment. The safety of Maine Yankee Atomic Power Plant, run by Central Maine Power Company, was a matter at issue. A request to enlarge the storage capacity for spent fuel rods at Wiscasset aroused severe opposition.

Acid rain, which reaches Maine from the Midwest, received more attention than in the past. Water and air pollution also remained in the public consciousness.

MAINE • Information Highlights

Area: 33,265 sq mi (86 156 km^2).
Population (1980 census): 1,124,660.
Chief Cities (1980 census): Augusta, the capital, 21,819; Portland, 61,572; Lewiston, 40,481; Bangor, 31,643; Auburn, 23,128; South Portland, 22,712; Biddeford, 19,638; Sanford, 18,020; Waterville, 17,779; Brunswick, 17,366.
Government (1981): *Chief Officer*—governor, Joseph E. Brennan (D). *Legislature*—Senate, 33 members; House of Representatives, 151 members.
State Finances (fiscal year 1980): *Revenues*, $1,369,000,000; *expenditures*, $1,326,000,000.
Personal Income (1980): $8,940,000,000; per capita, $7,925.
Labor Force (July 1981): Nonagricultural wage and salary earners, 428,000; unemployed, 45,900 (8.6% of total force.)

In the emotional debate over whether or not to allow hunting of the state animal, the moose, proponents prevailed. Opponents pointed to the moose's status as the state animal, the fact that the animal has not been hunted regularly for years, and that many moose are too tame to be hunted.

Legislation. The Public Utilities Commission, an appointed body, was challenged by a referendum which, if enacted into law, would transform the commission into an elected body. Those who favored an elected commission felt that it would be more responsive to the needs of the public. However, the referendum was defeated by voters in November.

A new law dealing with the apprehension and punishment of motor vehicle operators driving under the influence of alcohol (OUI) took effect in September. Under the law, penalties for conviction include severe fines and the possibility of a jail term.

Other Problems. Smuggling of illegal drugs along the Maine coast continued in 1981. This problem is one which is hard to deal with since Maine has such a long and indented coastline.

Heavy rains during the summer caused difficulties for the state. Rains washed out roads and threatened homes in Aroostook County, especially in the vicinity of Caribou.

Teachers faced problems in obtaining contracts before the school year opened in September. The Maine Teacher's Association and its college affiliate, the Associated Faculties of the University of Maine, and the state did not reach any agreement until year's end. Also unable to come to terms with the state were the Maine state employees, numbering about 10,000.

EDWARD SCHRIVER
University of Maine, Orono

MALAYSIA

Mahathir Mohamad, a 56-year-old physician, became Malaysia's fourth prime minister on July 16, 1981, following the resignation of Hussein Onn for health reasons.

Politics. Dr. Mahathir advanced from the post of deputy prime minister following his unopposed June bid for the presidency of the United Malays National Organization (UMNO), the dominant party of the ruling National Front coalition. The previous prime minister decided to relinquish his political and governmental posts while convalescing from a February heart operation. Mahathir's ascendancy followed the tradition of the deputy moving to the prime ministership.

The major political battle focused on choosing a successor to Mahathir as deputy president of UMNO. Finance Minister Tunku Razaleigh Hamzah and Education Minister Musa Hitam were the prime contenders in an occasionally bitter campaign. Musa's substantial victory at the June party conference made him deputy prime minister and heir-apparent to Dr. Mahathir.

One of the early acts of the new government was the release of a number of political detainees for the main Islamic holiday in August. Included was Harun Idris, who had served 3½ years for corruption and forgery and, although in jail, had been elected one of three vice-presidents at the June party conference.

In the East Malaysian state of Sarawak the chief minister, Abdul Rahman Yaakub, relinquished his post to become the titular head of the state. In the neighboring state of Sabah, the Berjaya Party overwhelmingly defeated its fellow National Front party, the United Sabah National Organization, to continue control of the state government. Other, primarily Chinese, parties in the National Front escalated their competition for members. Defections between the Malaysian Chinese Association (MCA) and the Gerakan Rakyat Malaysia continued through the year, with the most notable being the departure of MCA deputy president Michael Chen to become vice-president of Gerakan. Even the largely Chinese opposition Democratic Action Party suffered from defections and expulsions.

The Economy. Despite a stock market plunge in July and August which led the Mahathir government to announce new restrictions on trading, the economy remained strong with a real growth rate of more than 7%. The Fourth Malaysia Plan, which charts development efforts until 1986, was announced.

The key economic issue remains increasing Malay ownership in the economy to 30% by 1985. To achieve this, a new national investment company was formed to hold shares in trust on behalf of the Malays, who were urged to buy mutual shares in the company. This new capital enabled the company to buy control of the Guthrie Corp. on the London stock market and the Malaysian assets of other plantation companies. The London market restricted future takeovers, which prompted anti-British reaction from the Malaysian government and press.

Foreign Affairs. Malaysia resurrected its call to make Southeast Asia a zone of neutrality, but dramatically increased its defense budget.

K. MULLINER, *Ohio University*

MALAYSIA • Information Highlights

Official Name: Malaysia.
Location: Southeast Asia.
Area: 127,315 sq mi (329 746 km²).
Population (1981 est.): 14,300,000.
Chief Cities (1975 est.): Kuala Lumpur, the capital, 500,000; George Town, 280,000; Ipoh, 255,000.
Government: *Head of state,* Sultan Ahmad Shah (took office April 1979). *Head of government,* Mahathir Mohamad, prime minister (took office July 1981). *Legislature*—Parliament: Dewan Negara (Senate) and Dewan Ra'ayat (House of Representatives).
Monetary Unit: Ringgit (Malaysian dollar) (2.36 ringgits equal U.S.$1, July 1981).
Manufactures (major products): Steel, tin, automobiles, electronic equipment, rubber products.
Agriculture (major products): Rubber, palm oil, timber, cocoa, rice, pepper.

MANITOBA

Economic uncertainty and an upset election victory by the socialist New Democratic Party (NDP) marked 1981 in Manitoba.

Economy. Economically, the year began with optimism in several sectors, including real estate, where a short-lived boom petered out in the face of rising interest rates. Manitoba Hydro reported a $16.3 million loss for the year ending March 31, while the 25th anniversary of the northern mining town of Thompson was marred by a United Steelworkers' strike at Inco Metals Ltd.

Politics and the Election. Speculation over when a provincial election would be held ended October 13, when Conservative Premier Sterling Lyon named November 17 as the polling day. The government campaigned on its past achievements, including restraint in public spending, cutting back of the bureaucracy, and encouragement of private enterprise. It also proposed three "mega-projects" to fuel the stagnating economy—a $2,000,000,000 hydroelectric development project, if other western provinces would agree to build a power grid; a $600 million potash mine, to be developed by the government and International Minerals and Chemical Corporation; and a $500 million aluminum smelter, to be built by Alcan if feasibility and market studies warranted it. NDP opposition leader Howard Pawley attacked Lyon for resource giveaways and the province's generally poor economic performance, while other critics added that there was no guarantee that any of the "mega-projects" would come to fruition.

The NDP opposition had its own problems earlier in the year, when former cabinet minister Sidney Green and two other members broke away to form the Progressive Party, charging that Pawley was a tool of organized labor.

In the election, however, four years of Conservative government ended when the leftist NDP was returned to power with a solid majority in the legislative assembly. It won 34 of the 57 seats, an increase of 14; the Conservatives took the remaining 23, a loss of 9. Howard Pawley, 47, was sworn in as Manitoba's 19th premier on November 30. The election result was seen as a reflection of discontent with provincial and national economic policies of fiscal restraint, like those of the United States and Great Britain.

In other political events, Conservative MLA (member of legislative assembly) Bob Wilson lost legal appeals and was sent to jail for seven years for his part in a drug importing conspiracy. And on October 23, Pearl McGonigal became the first woman lieutenant governor of the province, replacing Francis (Bud) Jobin.

Agriculture. Following news of a bumper 1981 wheat harvest—estimated by Statistics Canada at 45 million T (41 million t)—the Canadian Wheat Board announced a record grain-export target of 29 million T (26 million t), worth $6,000,000,000. In July, Health Minister Bud Sherman declared a state of emergency after an outbreak of western equine encephalitis, caused by diseased mosquitoes. Major rural centers and Winnipeg were aerially sprayed with the chemical Baygon, and the state of emergency lasted 57 days.

Winnipeg. The federal, provincial, and city governments announced a $96 million downtown renewal program for Winnipeg, with demolition and construction expected to begin in 1982. *Winnipeg Magazine,* on the verge of closing, was taken over by the *Winnipeg Sun* and revamped for free distribution to the newspaper's subscribers. The *Sun* also switched to morning delivery but made little dent in the massive circulation of the rival *Winnipeg Free Press.*

PETER CARLYLE-GORDGE
Manitoba Correspondent, "Macleans" Magazine

MANITOBA • Information Highlights

Area: 251,000 sq mi (650 090 km²).
Population (April 1981 est.): 1,028,800.
Chief City (1976 census): Winnipeg, the capital, 560,874.
Government (1981): *Chief Officers*—lt. gov, Pearl McGonigal; premier, Howard Pawley (New Democratic Party); chief justice, Court of Appeal, Samuel Freedman; Court of Queen's Bench, A. S. Dewar. *Legislature*—Legislative Assembly, 57 members.
Education (1981–82 est.): *Enrollment*—elementary and secondary schools, 217,560; postsecondary, 20,220 students.
Public Finance (1980–81 est.): *Revenues,* $1,900,000,000; *expenditures,* $2,000,000,000.
Personal Income (average weekly salary, April 1981): $305.90.
Unemployment Rate (June 1981, seasonally adjusted): 5.9%.
(All monetary figures are in Canadian dollars.)

MARYLAND

Maryland's economy remained in the spotlight during 1981.

Economy. Statewide unemployment was about 7%, slightly below the national average, and some 86,000 persons were out of work in the Baltimore metropolitan area.

General Motors postponed indefinitely its plans for a $220 million expansion and renovation of its Baltimore midsize-car plant, blaming the delay on sluggish auto sales. About 3,500 auto workers remained on furlough: GM officials talked of recalling some of them early in 1982. About 5,000 workers in the construction industry were without jobs in the Baltimore area because of a slump in building.

The Food Fair supermarket chain, involved in a Chapter 11 bankruptcy after losing $6 million in less than a year in the Maryland-Delaware region, closed its 54 Pantry Pride stores in the two states. It laid off 4,300 employees, of whom 2,600 were in the metropolitan area. The closings were attributed to a prolonged price war among major food chains in the area, which sharply reduced profits for all involved. After the Pantry Pride closings were announced, five other major chains asked their employees to forgo pay raises provided in their union contracts. Two local meat processors and a steel company approached workers about accepting pay reductions to help the companies weather financial difficulties.

The Legislature. The state legislature prohibited banks from requiring membership fees from holders of their credit cards, including VISA and MasterCard, causing some banks to threaten to move out of the state. A judge ruled that the bank credit card operations fall under the state laws that regulate small loan companies—freeing banks to charge as much as 33% interest on the first $500 of the bill and to begin charging interest from the day of the purchase, rather than giving the consumer 25 days to pay without interest.

The legislature adopted tougher drunk-driving laws, including the reduction of the blood-alcohol level defined as intoxicated, but Motor Vehicle Administration (MVA) officials said they were having trouble keeping dangerous drivers off the roads. Of about 16,000 motorists who annually have their licenses suspended or revoked, MVA officials estimated that 12,000 continue to drive illegally. A list of the 29,000 worst offenders was distributed to police agencies.

Agnew, Mandel, and Politics. A Maryland judge ruled that Spiro Agnew took thousands of dollars in kickbacks from contacts during the years that he was state governor and national vice-president. The judge ordered Agnew to repay the state $248,735 ($147,500 in bribes plus $101,235 in interest). Agnew's lawyer announced that the decision would be appealed.

In December, President Ronald Reagan commuted the prison sentence of former Gov. Marvin Mandel.

Shortly after being elected to the U.S. House of Representatives in November 1980, Gladys Spellman (D) suffered a heart attack. The House seat was declared vacant in April and was won by Steny Hoyer in a special election in May. Sen. Paul Sarbanes, a Democrat who is up for reelection in 1982, was selected as one of the primary targets for defeat by the National Conservative Political Action Committee.

Other. The $21 million National Aquarium in Baltimore opened in August. More than 300,000 persons toured the modernistic, multilevel aquarium in its first two months.

The Guardian Angels, a volunteer brigade organized in New York City to oppose street crime, formed a chapter in Baltimore, with a cautious welcome from police.

A plaque commemorating the 1767 arrival from Africa of Kunta Kinte, the slave memorialized in the book and television drama *Roots,* was placed at the waterfront in Annapolis and dedicated by the book's author, Alex Haley. Two days later, it was stolen and a calling card of the Ku Klux Klan was left in its place. Private organizations joined to raise the $2,000 needed to replace it with a more secure plaque.

PEGGY CUNNINGHAM
"The News American," Baltimore

MARYLAND • Information Highlights

Area: 10,460 sq mi (27 091 km^2).
Population (1980 census): 4,216,446.
Chief Cities (1980 census): Annapolis, the capital, 31,740; Baltimore, 786,775; Rockville, 43,811; Hagerstown, 34,132; Bowie, 33,695; Frederick, 27,557; Gaithersburg, 26,424; Cumberland, 25,933; College Park, 23,614; Salisbury, 16,429.
Government (1981): *Chief Officers*—governor, Harry R. Hughes (D); lt. gov., Samuel W. Bogley III (D). *General Assembly*—Senate, 47 members; House of Delegates, 141 members.
State Finances (fiscal year 1980): *Revenues,* $5,564,000,000; *expenditures,* $5,435,000,000.
Personal Income (1980): $44,210,000,000; per capita, $10,460.
Labor Force (July 1981): *Nonagricultural wage and salary earners,* 1,690,100; *unemployed,* 157,800 (7.3% of total force).

MASSACHUSETTS

The year 1981 was a turbulent one for public affairs in Massachusetts. Attempts to cope with a new tax reduction law, a lengthy budget battle, and deepening problems with public transportation were among the major issues.

New Tax Measure. On Jan. 1, 1981, Massachusetts became one of the few states to follow

The new $21 million National Aquarium in Baltimore is owned by the city and operated by a private, nonprofit institution. It holds more than 5,000 specimens of fish, mammals, birds, reptiles, and amphibians.

Residents of Massachusetts, including senior citizens, marched to the statehouse in May to protest cuts in the fuel assistance program and the legislature's failure to revise electric rates.

UPI

the lead of California's "Proposition 13" in enacting a property tax reduction law. Dubbed "Proposition 2½," the measure was overwhelmingly approved by voters in November 1980. It required communities to set property taxes at no more than 2½% of the "average fair market value" of all real estate. The law also reduced the excise tax on automobiles, long one of the most unpopular taxes in the state. For older cities, where the average value of property has declined in recent years, Proposition 2½ meant a large reduction in tax income. For many of the state's 340 cities and towns, substantial reductions in public employment—including police, fire, school, and service personnel—were necessary. Groups representing municipal employees, along with many affected citizens, angrily demonstrated against the cuts.

Budget Battle. Although technically unrelated to the issues of Proposition 2½, a protracted struggle over the state budget kept fiscal issues before the public through the middle of the year. As fiscal 1981 came to an end on June 30, the two houses of the legislature were unable to agree on a budget. A $6,350,000,000 budget was finally passed in the second week of July, after state employees, working without pay for two weeks, threatened job actions. The conflict within the legislature was complicated by a dispute between the legislative branch and Gov. Edward King (D) over so-called "riders" to the budget act. King claimed selective veto power over such riders, some of which would have made sweeping changes in state administration. The matter was settled by the state supreme court, which ruled in favor of the governor.

For Governor King, the budget clash was only one in a series of difficult problems during the year. King, who would be up for reelection in 1982, suffered a dramatic loss in voter popularity. A statewide poll in October, for example, showed only 10% of registered Democrats preferring King to potential opponents.

Public Transportation. The Massachusetts Bay Transportation Authority (MBTA), which serves 79 communities in the populous eastern third of the state, has been in trouble since 1980. Operating problems and growing criticism of the management and staffing of the system were evident throughout 1981. On May 3, State Transportation Secretary Barry Locke, who had also served as the MBTA's general manager for several months, was suspended by Governor King following allegations that he had received payoffs to influence the awarding of contracts. Locke's removal marked the system's second major change in leadership in less than a year. In August, the MBTA raised basic subway fares from 50 to 75 cents and doubled bus fares. The immediate result was a sharp drop in ridership, which led the beleaguered MBTA to request still more operating funds.

Nuclear Plant Stopped. In September, Boston Edison Company stopped construction on a second nuclear generating plant at Plymouth. In a controversial move, the utility announced that it intended to bill customers for the $291 million already spent on the plant. This would have the effect of raising average residential electric bills by 6.5% per year for ten years. Immediate protests were lodged.

Winter Storm. On December 6, an early winter storm dumped up to 2 ft (.6 m) of snow on parts of the state, including Boston.

(*See also* BOSTON.)

HARVEY BOULAY, *Boston University*

— MASSACHUSETTS • Information Highlights —

Area: 8,284 sq mi (21 456 km^2).
Population (1980 census): 5,737,037.
Chief Cities (1980 census): Boston, the capital, 562,994; Worcester, 161,799; Springfield, 152,319; New Bedford, 98,478; Cambridge, 95,322; Brockton, 95,172; Fall River, 92,574; Lowell, 92,418; Quincy, 84,743; Newton, 83,622.
Government (1981): *Chief Officers*—governor, Edward J. King (D); lt. gov., Thomas P. O'Neill III (D). *General Court*—Senate, 40 members; House of Representatives, 160 members.
State Finances (fiscal year 1980): *Revenues,* $7,457,-000,000; *expenditures,* $7,336,000,000.
Personal Income (1980): $58,232,000,000; per capita, $10,125.
Labor Force (July 1981): *Nonagricultural wage and salary earners,* 2,632,100; *unemployed,* 200,700 (6.7% of total force).

MEDICINE AND HEALTH

The year in medicine and health saw increasing evidence to support contentions that nutrition and environmental factors play major roles in determining the state of a person's health. What a person eats and breathes is being clearly linked to that person's chances of contracting such illnesses as heart disease and cancer.

Among the most exciting medical news of 1981 were developments in surgery. Advances were made in transplanting organs and in the use of artificial organs. And in California, surgeons performed a successful operation on an unborn child.

Improved methods of treatment are resulting in longer life spans for people suffering from a variety of illnesses. But the development of drug-resistant microbial strains necessitates the search for new drugs and new treatment modes.

Heart Disease. Evidence linking dietary habits and heart disease continued to mount. Dr. Robert W. Mahley of the University of California at San Francisco discovered a specific mechanism by which dietary fats and cholesterol can produce atherosclerosis. The Seven Countries Study, led by Dr. Ancel Keys of the University of Minnesota, compared over a period of ten years the diets of 12,763 men who ate the foods typical of their lands: Crete, Finland, Italy, Japan, Yugoslavia, the Netherlands, and the United States. The major difference in the diets occurred in the percentage of calories that came from fats. Figures ranged from 9% in Japan to 39–40% in Crete, Finland, the Netherlands, and the United States. The researchers found that the death rate from heart disease is closely related to the ratio of saturated fats to unsaturated fats. In Crete, where the ratio is low, there was 1 coronary death among 686 men. In Finland, where the ratio is high, there were 78 deaths among 817 men.

Scientists at Boston University Medical Center reported that hardening of the arteries in monkeys can be prevented by including anticalcium drugs in the animals' diet. Diets high in butter and cholesterol caused the deposit of fat in the blood vessels of untreated monkeys. Monkeys that received the same diet but with the addition of anticalcifying agents had substantially less buildup of fat and less hardening of arteries.

A Norwegian study indicated that timolol, a drug developed by Merck Sharp & Dohme Research Laboratories, reduces the death rate of heart attack victims by almost 40%. The reduction in mortality is especially great in high-risk patients—those who are most susceptible to subsequent heart attacks. Timolol acts by blocking the action of hormones that affect heart action, blood pressure, and other body functions.

Cancer. A study prepared by the American College of Surgeons showed that there has been a marked improvement in the five-year survival rate for cancer patients. Improvement was particularly striking in the survival rates of patients with such less common cancers as leukemia and Hodgkin's disease. Among the types of cancer shown to have higher survival rates were breast cancer, 73% survival in 1979, up from 65% in 1969; prostate cancer, 68% in 1979, up from 57% in 1969; and Hodgkin's disease, 72%, up from 54%.

A study at the National Cancer Institute in Milan, Italy, compared the survival rates of two groups of women with early breast cancer. One group of women were treated by conventional radical surgery, in which the entire breast, the

Drs. Torsten Wiesel (far left) and David Hubel of Harvard University toast each other after being named co-winners of the 1981 Nobel Prize for Medicine. They shared the award with Dr. Roger Sperry (far right) of Caltech. The three researchers were cited for their studies of the human brain.

Photos UPI

Rosa Skinner cuddles her two-month-old twins, Michael (left) and Mary, who had become part of medical history. In April, Michael underwent the first successful surgical treatment of an unborn child.

UPI

underlying chest muscle, and the lymph nodes in the armpit are all removed. The second group had partial mastectomies, in which only about one quarter of the breast is removed. There was no significant difference between the survival rates of the two groups. The findings provided further evidence to support the trend toward more conservative surgery for breast cancer. The researchers emphasized, however, that the findings apply only to women whose cancers are very small at the time of diagnosis.

Postmenopausal breast cancer patients whose disease has spread to other parts of the body have usually had their adrenal glands removed. This is done to stop the production of estrogen, which is used by the cancer cells. A study headed by Dr. Richard J. Santen of the Milton S. Hershey Medical Center of the Pennsylvania State University indicated that the drug aminoglutethimide decreases estrogen production as effectively as does removal of the adrenal gland, and with fewer side effects than other drugs currently used against estrogen-dependent breast cancer.

Improved treatment methods may double the survival rates for people with soft tissue sarcoma, a form of cancer that develops in tissues around bones. Most commonly, the cancer affects an arm or leg. Heretofore, the standard treatment was to amputate the affected limb. But two studies done at the U.S. National Cancer Institute indicated that limiting surgery to removal of the tumor and using an aggressive drug and radiation treatment program is much more effective—and spares many patients the loss of a limb. The five-year survival rate for the traditional treatment is about 40%. Dr. Steven A. Rosenberg, head of the institute's surgery branch, believes that the survival rate of patients receiving the new treatment may "level off substantially in excess of 80%."

Another study sponsored by the National Cancer Institute found that laetrile is not an effective treatment for cancer. According to an institute report, the study showed that "no substantive benefit from laetrile has been observed in terms of cure, improvement or slowing the advance of the cancer, improvement of symptoms related to cancer, or extension of life span." Laetrile, a chemical obtained from apricot pits, has long been controversial. Despite a lack of supporting medical evidence, many people believe it is effective, and 22 states have legalized its use.

Evidence gathered by several research groups indicated that certain genes can cause a normal, healthy cell to become cancerous. Such genes have been found in leukemia cells, as well as in lung, breast, colon, and bladder cancer cells. Dr. Frank J. Rauscher, Jr., director of research of the American Cancer Society, pointed out: "If we learn what switches these things on, we ought to be able to intervene in the process. That would be a whole new way of getting at control or prevention of cancer." However, Dr. Rauscher and other cancer researchers emphasize that learning how to control or inactivate the genes is probably many years away.

Surgery. Surgeons at the University of California at San Francisco performed the world's first known successful operation on a fetus. The unborn child, a male, had a urinary blockage that would have seriously damaged his kidneys and lungs and might have caused his death. To drain urinary wastes, the doctors inserted a catheter, a very thin plastic tube, through the mother's abdominal wall and uterus and into the fetus' bladder. The catheter was removed after the baby—and his healthy twin sister—were born, at which time additional surgery was performed.

Microsurgeons continued to perform feats unimaginable only a short time ago. In September, a 21-year-old man lost eight fingers in an accident. In a 46½-hour operation, a medical team at Massachusetts General Hospital successfully reattached seven of the fingers. (The eighth finger was also replanted, but it began to lose circulation and had to be partially amputated.)

Organ Transplants. An experimental new drug, cyclosporin A, dramatically improves short-term survival of persons receiving liver transplants. The drug suppresses the body's immune system so that it will not attack the new organ. However, unlike azathioprine, the drug usually used to suppress the immune system, cyclosporin A does not interfere with the patient's ability to fight bacterial infections.

Cyclosporin A has also been used in other transplant operations, including three heart-lung transplants conducted at Stanford University in 1981. One patient died of complications, including kidney and liver failure. The other two became the longest surviving heart-lung transplant patients in medical history.

The University of Texas Health Science Center opened a coordinated program for "bankable" organs for transplantation. "Bringing bankable organs together in one facility is definitely the wave of the future," said Dr. Charles R. Baxter, director of the facility. "For the first time transplant services [are] located in one central area, leading to greater cooperation between medical areas, a higher rate of efficiency in operation, and an opportunity for all areas of transplantation to expand this valuable work." Organs handled by the program include skin for transplantation in major burn injuries, corneas and other eye tissues, joints for patients with certain bone and cartilage problems, and the iliac crest, a portion of the upper pelvic bone that is often used for fusions.

Dr. Robert Jarvik holds the heart he designed for permanent implantation in human patients.

UPI

Artificial Organs. Dr. Denton Cooley of the Texas Heart Institute implanted an artificial heart in a 36-year-old man. After 54 hours the mechanical device was replaced by a donated human heart. The man lived for a total of ten days before succumbing to kidney failure, lung problems, and infections. It was only the second time that an artificial heart had been implanted in a human being. The first operation, also performed by Dr. Cooley, was in 1969.

An artificial heart under development for more than 20 years was approved for use by the University of Utah. This device would be a permanent replacement of the patient's heart, unlike those used by Dr. Cooley, which were used to keep the patients alive until human heart donors could be found. The Utah heart was successfully implanted in calves and sheep. It is pneumatically driven and uses an external power source.

A new demineralized bone powder is being used by Harvard researchers to assist bone formation in patients with certain birth defects. When implanted in patients with cleft palates, missing noses, or other facial deformities, the powder stimulates certain body cells to make cartilage and then bone. For example, using demineralized bone, the researchers were able to construct a nose in a person born without a nose bone. Demineralized bone can also be used to help mend broken bones that fail to heal in a normal length of time.

An artificial skin developed by I. V. Yannas of the Massachusetts Institute of Technology and John F. Burke of Harvard University was successfully used to replace skin destroyed by burns. The artificial skin has two layers. The inner layer is made of connective tissue from cattle, and is meant to be permanent. The outer layer is made of silicon. It is removed about a month after implantation and replaced with epidermal cells taken from healthy skin on the patient's body. Because supplies are limited, the artificial skin has been used only on patients with extensive burns. At least some of the patients "probably would have died" without it, acccording to Burke.

Environmental Health. A report prepared for the U.S. Environmental Protection Agency by the National Academy of Sciences called indoor air pollution a serious and growing problem. Such pollution can cause discomfort, illness, and even death. Pollutants found in homes, offices, and public buildings include microorganisms, tobacco smoke, cooking fumes, formaldehyde and asbestos from insulating and decorating materials, and radon from construction materials. Energy conservation measures are aggravating the problem. Such measures make buildings more airtight, thereby reducing ventilation and increasing the concentrations of contaminants.

It has long been known that smokers exposed to asbestos are 92 times more likely to die from lung cancer than nonsmokers. Scientists at the Puerto Rico Cancer Center have discovered the mechanism behind the cancer-causing ability of asbestos. They showed that when white blood cells are exposed to asbestos, the cells release hydrogen peroxide. This chemical reacts with potential cancer-causing substances, such as those found in cigarette smoke, and changes them into powerful carcinogens.

The Puerto Rico Cancer Center also studied the effects of coating rice with talc. This has been a common practice in Puerto Rico for many years. Processors say the coating is added to preserve the rice and to enhance its appearance. Experiments conducted at the center by Dr. Angel Román-Franco suggest that when stomach lining cells ingest the talc, compounds are released that can change potential cancer-causing substances into carcinogens.

Radiologists at the Royal Victoria Hospital in Montreal reported a relationship between hairspray use and lung disease. Two patients who used aerosolized hairspray twice daily for a number of years developed small nodules in their lungs. They also developed persistent coughs and suffered weight loss. The symptoms disappeared following steroid treatments and discontinuation of the use of hairspray.

Smoking. Do spouses of smokers run a greater risk of contracting lung cancer than spouses of nonsmokers? Two studies reported in 1981 gave conflicting answers to this question.

A 14-year study conducted by Dr. Takeshi Hirayama of Japan's National Cancer Center Research Institute indicated that nonsmoking wives of smokers are much more likely to develop lung cancer than nonsmoking wives of nonsmoking husbands. According to Dr. Hirayama, the more the men smoked, the greater the risk to their wives. The U.S. Tobacco Institute reported that the Japanese study contained mathematical errors that invalidated the conclusions. Dr. Hirayama disagreed.

Another study, prepared by the American Cancer Society, found no evidence that nonsmoking women whose husbands smoke have a greater chance of contracting lung cancer than wives of non-smoking husbands.

New findings from the Framingham (MA) Heart Study indicated that switching from nonfiltered to filtered cigarettes does not decrease a smoker's chances of developing heart disease. Filters reduce tar and nicotine but do not necessarily reduce the amount of carbon monoxide that a smoker inhales. This suggests that carbon monoxide may be more important than nicotine as a promoter of heart disease. Carbon monoxide competes with oxygen in red blood cells, thereby decreasing the amount of oxygen that reaches the heart muscles. It may also facilitate the formation of fatty deposits in arteries.

UPI

Dr. Robert Fischell helped develop a unique electronic painkiller. It is implanted beneath the skin and can be adjusted by radio command.

Harvard researchers reported that smokers are at least 2½ times more likely to get acute respiratory illness (ARI) than nonsmokers. And among patients with ARI, those who smoked were more apt to have phlegm and abnormal chest sounds. Their coughs lasted an average of 9 days, compared with 7 days for nonsmokers.

Venereal Disease. *Chlamydia trachomatis* appears to have become the leading venereal pathogen in the United States. Early-stage symptoms usually are minimal or nonexistent, making detection difficult. Dr. Paul J. Wiesner of the Centers for Disease Control in Atlanta estimated that there are 2.5 to 3 million cases and that about half of the approximately 200,000 babies born each year to infected women develop eye infections or chlamydial pneumonia.

The Centers for Disease Control reported a sharp rise in the number of penicillin-resistant gonorrhea infections and recommended routine resistance tests for all gonorrhea patients. Penicillin-resistant cases are currently treated with spectinomycin. In 1981, however, the world's first known case of gonorrhea resistant to both penicillin and spectinomycin was detected in California. (The infection was successfully treated with tetracycline.)

JENNY TESAR
Science and Medical Writer

Dentistry

The dental profession in the United States during 1981 continued its concerted drive to expand access to dental care for underserved population groups, especially the elderly. Noting that the Medicare program ignores the dental needs of the nation's 24 million senior citizens, the American Dental Association (ADA) intensified its efforts to include dental-care benefits under Medicare. The ADA worked with major senior-citizen organizations to convince Congress that providing preventive dental care for the elderly under Medicare would help them solve many of their oral health needs.

Meanwhile, more Americans received regular dental care through the burgeoning of dental insurance. In 1981, more than 75 million persons were covered; the number was expected to rise to 100 million by 1985. Since virtually all major industries now have group dental coverage, the focus of expansion efforts has begun to shift to smaller companies.

Although the bulk of dental treatment in the United States continues to be furnished by private practitioners in solo or group practices, other care systems are being explored. One type of facility is the dental center or clinic, many of which are being established in shopping centers and department stores. Because there have been no formal studies published as to how these facilities compare with more traditional dental practices, the American Dental Association has taken a wait-and-see attitude. The ADA maintains that these centers should be evaluated the same way as other dental practices. There should be sufficient emphasis on prevention, continuing and regular care, and the doctor-patient relationship.

Broadening access to dental care also depends on sufficient manpower. To overcome the problem of uneven distribution of dentists, organized dentistry has had success with a relatively new system. Called the National Health Professions Placement Network (NHPPN), this ADA-sponsored computer matching service was established by a $1.17-million grant from the ADA and the W. K. Kellogg Foundation, of Battle Creek, MI.

Tooth Decay Research. Dental researchers looking for new methods to fight tooth decay have defined a triple approach: increasing resistance, reducing or modifying cariogenic (decay-producing) potential of substances, and developing mechanical, chemical, and immunochemical techniques. Dr. Irwin Mandel of the Columbia University dental school maintains that the multiple use of fluoride—water and dietary supplements; topical application; and self-application with dentifrices, rinses, and gels—remains the most effective method of reducing the incidence of caries (decay). Researchers are now studying an intra-oral device which would be attached to a molar to control the release of fluoride. Other studies are focusing on plastic sealants for the biting surfaces of teeth, which have been used successfully in protecting children's back teeth against cavities.

Antibacterial strategies for controlling dental plaque also are being investigated. (Dental plaque is a colorless film forming constantly on the teeth; it is considered a major factor in the development of tooth decay.) Such approaches are "a classic case of good/bad news," according to Dr. Mandel. A Scandinavian study showed that thorough plaque removal can prevent virtually all dental caries in persons over age 20. "The bad news," Mandel added, "is the exquisite . . . oral hygiene required and the continuing need for reinforcement and professional intervention." Chemical methods for retarding plaque formation have proved disappointing, said Mandel. However, low concentrations of chlorhexidine in combination with sodium fluoride as a bactericidal agent "look promising." The most dramatic research in the antibacterial area is immunochemical—attempts to modify the inherent antibody response in saliva. Although there has been steady progress in the development of an anticaries vaccine, such a vaccine, in Mandel's words, "must be examined not only from the biological point of view but from the regulatory and pharmaceutical points of view as well." Animal experiments have indicated that effective vaccination against caries is "certainly possible," but the choice of antigen or antibody, the method of immunization, and the role of supplemental agents "still need considerable exploration," Mandel concluded.

Replacing a Missing Tooth. Dr. Dan Nathanson of Tufts University dental school developed a new, inexpensive, and simple technique for replacing a single front tooth. The method offers a one-appointment approach to a dental emergency common among children and adolescents. A plastic tooth crown is bonded directly to abutment teeth on either side of the vacant space. The plastic crown is contoured on the bottom to fit tightly over the vacant space on the ridge of the underlying bone. Conventional techniques utilize either a fixed bridge, which is more costly and time-consuming to construct, or a removable bridge, which frequently causes interference with proper oral hygiene.

Relaxation in the Dental Chair. A dental researcher at the State University of New York at Buffalo has found that relaxation instructions are better than soft music for putting patients at ease in the dentist's chair. Dr. Norman L. Corah reported that studies of both techniques showed that music provides, at best, a placebo effect, while relaxation induced by instructions from a recorded voice seems to be a surer way of reducing stress. The research also showed that although the relaxation technique is preferred more by women than by men, it is effective with both male and female patients.

LOU JOSEPH

Mental Health

Rapidly accumulating information about brain chemistry and function, and novel applications of computer technology to psychiatric research highlighted advances in mental health. The 1981 Nobel Prize for medicine was shared by three scientists—Roger W. Perry of the California Institute of Technology, and David H. Hubel and Torsten N. Wiesel of Harvard University for their work in brain research.

Basic Research. During the year, scientists at the National Institutes of Health and at The Johns Hopkins University in Baltimore successfully developed an analogue of adenosine—a naturally occurring neuromodulator, or substance found in the brain that appears to have a sedative effect. Scientists at the National Institute of Mental Health (NIMH) subsequently used analogues to map, by means of autoradiography and computerized image processing techniques, adenosine receptor sites—areas in the brain to which the analogues bind to exert their calming effect. The scientists discovered also that the analogues are 10 to 100 times more powerful than existing sedatives. The discovery may lead to a new class of psychotropic drugs which would be administered in amounts only a fraction of the therapeutic dosages now necessary, offering more effective treatment with fewer risks of adverse side effects.

To make sense of the staggering amount of data generated by brain studies, mental health researchers are exploiting the computer's ability to store, analyze, and display vast quantities of information. Image processing techniques entail, first, converting qualitative measures of brain function—such as electrical and chemical activity levels—into numbers and then displaying the numerical values in a meaningful visual pattern.

NIMH's Louis Sokoloff had previously developed the deoxyglucose method of mapping brain metabolism. That technique, which involves injecting minute amounts of radioactively labeled substances into the brain, made possible the development of the PETT (positron emission transaxial tomography) scan, which, incorporating computer image processing, has proven useful in diagnosing serious mental illness.

Behavioral Research. A comprehensive review of research on the relationship between television and social behavior upheld the U.S. surgeon general's 1972 determination that there is a causal relationship between televised violence and later aggression. Moreover, "the newer research shows influences of television on the viewer much beyond the issue of violence," said behavioral scientist Eli Rubenstein, noting that much of television programming offers a discrepant view of the world through reliance on sex, age, and occupational stereotypes. Though the research suggests that TV may take up time that youngsters might otherwise devote to development of cognitive skills needed in school, studies also found that parental involvement in children's viewing can boost the positive effects and buffer the negative effects of a program.

Scientists at NIMH and Harvard University reported new findings to the effect that mild caloric deficiencies in the diet of an infant or a pregnant woman can disrupt a child's emotional stability by school age. (Physical and mental effects of malnutrition are well documented.) The conclusions were based on a five-year study of 6- to 8-year-old Guatemalan village children and a survey of children of low-income families in San Diego. It was the first research to link poor nutrition with social and emotional development in children more than three years old.

Mental Health Services. The introduction of federal block grants will give states and local governments responsibility for the development and operation of local mental health service programs. Since the enactment of community mental health center (CMHC) legislation in 1963, nearly 800 federally funded CMHCs have been established in the United States, contributing to a dramatic turnaround in the ratio of inpatient to outpatient mental health care episodes.

This shift toward locally accessible mental health care encourages increased interaction between the mental health and general health fields, a trend supported by research evidence of the contribution of psychological factors to many forms of physical illness. Studies indicate that the incorporation of mental health services in general health settings tends to reduce both the inappropriate use and unnecessary cost of medical services. University of Colorado researchers identified a variety of chronic medical illnesses for which the "offset" effect of psychiatric treatment is most apparent. The illnesses include airway limitation diseases, such as asthma and emphysema, ischemic heart disease, and hypertension. In a separate study, clinicians at New York's Columbia University demonstrated the benefits of a psychiatric liaison service to elderly patients hospitalized for orthopedic surgery. Patients who received psychiatric support services were hospitalized for a shorter period and were discharged more frequently to their own homes, rather than to nursing homes, than were patients who did not receive such service. Of note to the health system broadly are the medical savings realized over the cost of psychiatric service.

Stigma. The National Restaurant Association collaborated with NIMH in a survey of its membership to determine the extent to which food service industries provide employment opportunities to mentally restored workers. Twenty-nine percent of respondents had employed former mental patients and commented favorably on the workers' reliability and productivity. The survey was part of a larger federal initiative to combat discriminatory attitudes toward people with a history of mental illness.

HERBERT PARDES
National Institute of Mental Health

THE U.S. NURSING PROFESSION

Because it is a profession in transition, nursing in the 1980s is in turmoil, with factions both within nursing itself and within the traditionally bureaucratic structure of hospitals pressuring to keep nurses in submissive roles. Perhaps the strongest ally modern nurses have in their efforts to enhance their influence and strengthen their contribution to patient care is a vocal public that is increasingly demanding more of them.

Overall View. There are today in the United States more nurses than ever before. The latest official count by the *American Journal of Nursing* shows more than 1.4 million registered nurses (RNs) holding active licenses. Approximately 975,000, almost 70%, are employed in nursing positions. In the 1970s, the ratio of RNs to the population grew from 313 to 487 per 100,000 persons.

Yet, nationwide, dramatic headlines proclaim a critical shortage. Throughout the United States, the demand for nursing services is outstripping the supply. With the publicity, however, many of the problems that have plagued the nursing profession for years are surfacing and receiving long-warranted attention.

Nursing, as a predominantly women's profession (about 2% of the nurses are men and although the number of male nurses has increased, the proportion has not), suffered for many years the problems of all women's occupations—low salaries and status, exclusion from top-level decision making, responsibility without authority, and the expectation that nurses would behave in the presence of physicians in the traditional wife-to-husband role.

Although there had been early seeds of discontent with that status, they burgeoned slowly, but by the mid-1960s, societal, scientific, and professional trends converged, compelling new attitudes in nurses themselves and in other health professionals with whom they work.

The 1960s and 1970s. In the late 1960s, the women's movement, which had submerged its own goals to march in the mainstream of the peace movement, became much more vocal and more militant. During that same period, Lyndon Johnson's visions of a "Great Society" were emphasizing health care for all as a right, rather than a privilege. Comprehensive national health insurance was discussed regularly in the halls of Congress. Although such a bill was never legislated, other pieces of legislation, including Medicare with supporting care for those over 65 and for many of the disabled, were enacted. Federal funds supported research into the causes and treatment of diseases, scientific and technological advances multiplied, and the demands for nurses exploded.

In 1963, the U.S. surgeon general appointed a Consultant Group on Nursing, whose report called for 130,000 more nurses by 1970. As a result, an intense program of federal funding of nursing education began with the Nurse Training Act of 1964; it continues, although currently at much lower levels.

To prepare for licensure as a registered nurse, an applicant can take one of four routes. He or she can enroll in a baccalaureate program in a university or college; in an associate degree program in a community or junior college; in a diploma program in a hospital school; or in a graduate program offering either a master's degree or a professional doctorate as the basic nursing degree.

In 1965, the American Nurses' Association, nursing's professional organization, issued a position paper that stated that the education of all those who are licensed to practice nursing should take place in institutions of higher learn-

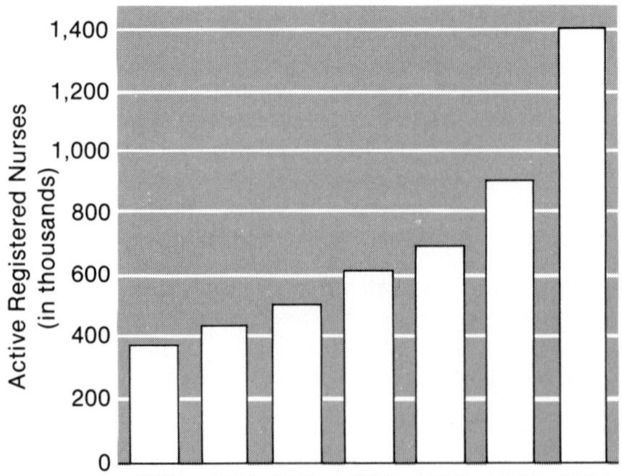

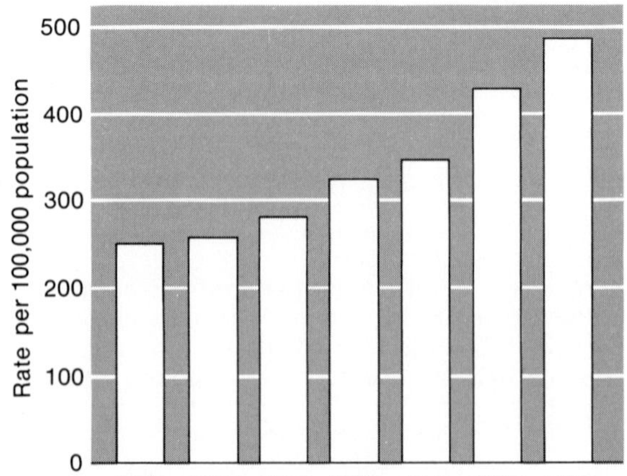

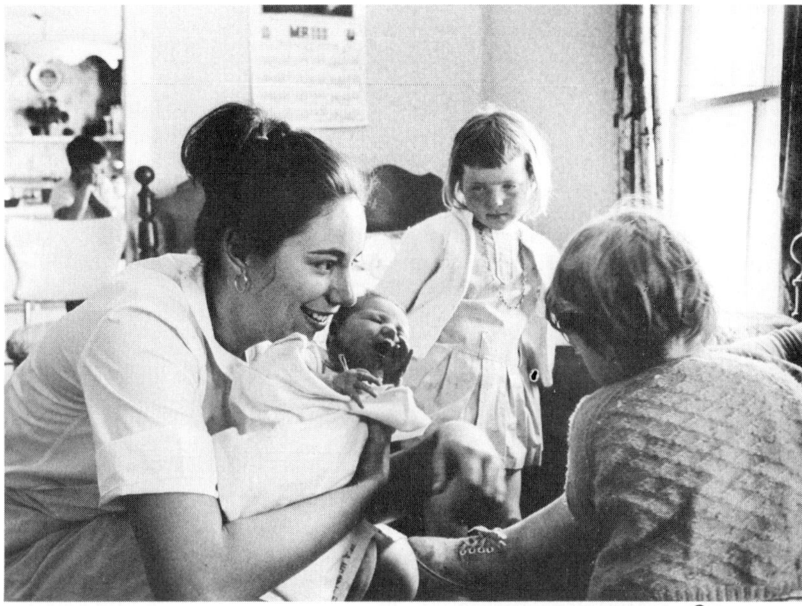

Nurse practitioners, nurses who take care of well children in ambulatory settings, now play a large role in U.S. health care, particularly in the nation's rural areas.

Michael Mauney/"Life" Magazine © Time Inc.

ing. It differentiated between two levels of nursing practice: professional nursing practice, requiring a bachelor's degree, and technical practice, requiring an associate degree. Although the term "technical nursing practice" never took hold in the minds of either the public or of the nurses themselves, the 1970s saw an enormous growth of associate degree nursing programs. In 1965 there were 174; in 1980, 707. During that same period, the number of baccalaureate programs rose from 198 to 385, and the number of diploma schools dropped from 821 to 311.

In addition to the emphasis on basic collegiate education, the 1970s brought a strong emphasis on master's and doctoral preparation both for administrative and teaching positions and for the increasing number of nurses who found themselves specializing in particular clinical fields. The findings from nursing research have provided the knowledge base for such programs, and both federal and private sector funding have supported the research as well as fellowships for graduate studies.

The 1980s. As a result, there are today increasing numbers of nurses with more advanced academic backgrounds, with higher career expectations, and with greater professional commitment than their forebears might have expected. They no longer are willing to accept a handmaiden role; they want autonomy in nursing care decisions and full participation in the decisions of the health care team. They are fighting to achieve legislation that will legitimize functions they have been carrying out for years but that are suddenly being viewed as impingements on medical practice.

One impetus to expansion of nurses' roles was the advent of nurse practitioners. This title was first used in a special demonstration program at the University of Colorado in the mid-1960s. The program showed that nurses could handle the primary care of well children in ambulatory settings. The concept soon spread, and nurses, particularly in rural areas, began to assume responsibility for routine monitoring of selected adult patients and families, for care during normal pregnancies, for screening programs, and for collaboration with physicians and other health professionals in planning a community's health services.

Health Maintenance Organizations are another setting in which nurse practitioners are being used increasingly. Nurse practitioners also direct ambulatory clinics where chronically ill persons and those needing health counseling are assisted routinely.

While nurse practitioners were proving their mettle in out-of-hospital situations, clinical nurse specialists—generally with master's degrees—were offering advanced skills in acute hospitals. By the 1970s, hospitals were increasingly providing special care units in which highly technological, expensive equipment could be concentrated. Intensive care units, coronary care units, renal units, pulmonary units, dialysis units, and special care situations in a variety of other specialties began to appear. The breadth and depth of information and experience needed by nurses who staff these critical care units have led to specialization in nursing just as they have in medicine.

With nurse practitioners and clinical nurse specialists setting the example, nurses throughout the United States have begun agitating for greater autonomy, greater participation in decision making, and better salaries to recognize the increase in their preparation and in their responsibilities.

THELMA M. SCHORR, R.N.

METEOROLOGY

Technology continues to play a major role in meteorological studies. A new weather satellite was launched in May 1981. Doppler radar provides forecasters with better information about severe storms. And a whole arsenal of sophisticated new observing aids has come into use.

Satellites. On May 22, 1981, an improved geostationary environment satellite (GOES) was launched by the United States to hover at 85° W longitude. In addition to providing cloud pictures and surface temperatures, the satellite scans for vertical temperature and moisture distribution. With a companion satellite at 135° W longitude, it provides stereoscopic pictures by which the intensities of storms and hurricanes can be scaled. For thunderstorms breaking through the tropopause into the stratosphere with cloud top temperatures below −63° C (−81.4° F), rainfall rates of 1 000 m^3/sec (264,000 gals/sec) occur. By counting the number of highly reflecting clouds on satellite pictures, therefore, scientists can estimate monthly rainfall. Calibrated over a dense network of rain gauges in the Midwest, this method is used to estimate rainfall in areas where gauges are sparse. GOES observations over the Indian Ocean indicate the arrival of the Indian monsoon one month before it occurs.

Satellites help meteorologists in other ways. Microwave observations provide sea surface temperatures, estimates of sea surface wind, the boundaries of sea ice, and the thickness of dry snow. In cloudy regions, microwave scanning in the oxygen bands gives estimates of vertical temperature distribution. A trace molecule spectrometer on Nimbus 7 has mapped ozone concentration at jet flight levels; the data are transmitted to commercial airlines so that planes can avoid areas with high values.

Severe Storms. Doppler radar reveals to forecasters three-dimensional flow patterns inside tornadoes. It identifies tornado vortices earlier than conventional radar and permits warnings 20 to 30 minutes in advance, compared with only 2 minutes' warning from funnel sightings. The method covers a larger area, and there are fewer false alarms.

Tornadoes have been more precisely measured and severe hailstorms better understood. Tornadoes are between 30 and 130 m (98 and 427 ft), in diameter, with maximum wind speeds from 22 to 92 m/sec (49 to 206 mph). In severe hailstorms there are updrafts of 51 m/sec (167 ft/sec) and downdrafts of 25 m/sec (82 ft/sec). Hail particles occur in many parts of the storm, explaining why hail suppression experiments have been unsuccessful: targeting of seeding agents has been inadequate. Extensive convective circular cloud shields with top temperatures below −32° C (−26° F), covering several hundred thousand square kilometers, and lasting more than 12 hours, are indicative of severe storm outbreaks. Such storm systems are seen by satellites but are often missed by present computer weather models. In the midwestern United States, 60 to 100 occur annually.

Winter tornadoes, often ignored because of the popular belief that tornadoes occur only in spring, hit the same regions as spring tornadoes and are usually accompanied by severe blizzards. Tracks run from northern Texas to the Great Lakes and from Oklahoma to Georgia. Even though notice can be given several hours in advance, popular disbelief results in a substantial number of casualties.

Weather Modification. Weather modification activities have shifted from haphazard cloud seeding to development of rationales for specific technologies. Observations of natural precipitation in Utah have shown that orographic (associated with mountains) winter precipitation occurs when five criteria are fulfilled: cloud top temperatures must be below −22° C (−8° F); clouds must be at least 1 km (0.6 mi) thick; the cloud base must be at or below the mountain peak; normal mountain wind speeds must exceed 8 m/sec (18 mph); and vertical updrafts must exceed 1 m/sec (2.2 mph), with maximal yields of more than 2 m/sec (4.5 mph).

In a seeding experiment in Alberta, Canada, three different agents were tested on convective clouds extending above a stratocumulus cloud deck—silver iodide, solid carbon dioxide pellets, and neutral particles. The neutral pellets had no effect. The carbon dioxide pellets produced rain which reached the ground 20 minutes after seeding and lasted 10 minutes. Rainfall induced by the silver iodide also began within 20 minutes but lasted one hour.

Inadvertent Weather Modification. Acid rain remained a focus of attention, both in industrial and remote areas. High levels were recorded in Colorado and Hawaii. In northern Illinois, where there is heavy air traffic, condensation trails from jets have increased cloudiness, reducing sunshine and the number of clear days. Studies of atmospheric transparency at Davos, Switzerland, have indicated that changes do take place after volcanic eruptions.

New Observational Equipment. Sophisticated new technology is being used for atmospheric sounding. LIDAR (light detection and ranging) measures temperature, humidity, and wind speed by use of lasers. DIAL (a differential absorption Lidar) can map when plant plumes hit the ground by using two ultraviolet laser beams. Sonar (sound navigation and ranging) using Doppler acoustics to detect temperature inversions, tops of ground fogs, and low-level winds, has become a powerful tool in boundary layer meteorology. WOTAN (weather observations through ambient noise) has been tested in 1 800 m (5,900 ft) of water. From the noise produced by waves, it gives reliable estimates of surface winds.

H. E. LANDSBERG, *University of Maryland*

METEOROLOGY—SPECIAL REPORT:

THE WEATHER YEAR

December 1980–February 1981. The outstanding feature of the winter season in the United States was a widespread drought that affected most of the nation. Satellite imagery revealed that the snow cover over North America was the least since measurements began in 1966. West of the Mississippi River, average temperatures were from 2 to 8° F (1 to 4° C) warmer than expected values, while the eastern third of the country was slightly cooler than average.

December 1980 was warm and dry over the Great Plains, the Ohio Valley, and the southern mid-Atlantic region. The Great Lakes and New England recorded below-average temperatures. Frigid Arctic air swept across the eastern half of the country on Christmas Eve, plunging temperatures to record or near-record lows in many areas. Winds of 40 mph (64 km/h) combined with the low temperatures to produce a wind-chill equivalent of −50° F (−45° C) on Christmas Day. Records showed that New England experienced its coldest Christmas Day of the century. Heavy rain and melting snow caused severe flooding in western Oregon and Washington.

Warm weather in January continued to deplete the snowpack in the Rockies to below its average June value in some locations. Daily high temperatures during the second week of the month were as much as 15 to 20° F (8 to 11° C) above average in the northern Plains and the prairie provinces of Canada. East of the Mississippi River, temperatures were from 4 to 10° F (2 to 5° C) cooler than normal. The Ohio and Mississippi Valleys and the Atlantic Coastal States received less than one quarter their average January precipitation. Severe to extreme drought was persistent in New York and northern New Jersey, with mandatory water rationing measures in effect. Hard freezes on January 13 and 14 in Florida caused an estimated $232 million damage to the state's crops.

Heavy and regular rainfall in February eased drought conditions in parts of the South and Northeast. Almost all of the United States recorded above-average temperatures in February. Positive departures of 6 to 14° F (3 to 7° C) were recorded in northern New England. A major winter storm swept across the Great Plains in mid-February, causing 38 deaths. Spring-like temperatures enveloped the country during the latter part of the month.

Much of Europe and the western Soviet Union recorded above-average temperatures for the winter. Rainfall was only 25% of the average winter value for the Iberian peninsula, while parts of the Ukraine received more than 200% of the normal winter snowfall. Elsewhere in Europe, precipitation was near the average seasonal values. In the first week of January, an intense storm in the Mediterranean brought 2 inches (5 cm) of snow to Tunisia, its first snow since 1955. Freezing temperatures were recorded deep in the Sahara desert. A severe snowstorm in Japan in early January killed 33 persons and destroyed scores of homes. Heavy rain the same month left 71 dead and more than 300,000 homeless in the Philippines. Food supplies were threatened by lack of winter rainfall in the African countries of Kenya, Mozambique, and Tanzania. In the Southern Hemisphere, heavy summer rainfall produced flooding in parts of Argentina, Brazil, and Uruguay.

March–May. Temperatures for the spring season were generally well above average in the northern and central Plains and the West, while the middle and southern Atlantic Coast were slightly cooler than normal. Precipitation was well above average in the Rocky Mountains. Along the Eastern Seaboard, spring rain was from one half to three quarters its average value.

March was wet in the West, but the Northeast experienced near-record dryness. The northern Plains averaged 10 to 14° F (5 to 7° C) warmer than normal. During the latter part of the month, a cold spell pushed freezing temperatures as far south as central Florida.

April was an active month for severe weather. Hail, high winds, and tornadoes plagued many areas east of the Rockies. In the second week of the month, heavy rain produced flooding in Texas and southern Ohio.

May was cooler than average throughout much of the United States. Warmer than normal temperatures prevailed in the Southwest, the northern Plains, and the New England states. The month was unusually wet, but the excess precipitation helped compensate for the lack of moisture over the previous winter and summer. Corn planting was delayed in many areas because of waterlogged fields. As the water table in Florida continued to lower, huge sinkholes developed in the limy soil, swallowing up automobiles and even houses. In the Everglades, thousands of acres of grassland burned.

Much of Europe experienced a cloudy, mild, and wet spring. In the second week of April, however, a severe snowstorm dropped 8 to 10 inches (20 to 25 cm) of wet snow throughout Scotland and southwest England. Heavy April rain caused flooding in parts of East Africa, Iran, and Afghanistan. A two-week heat wave in India and Pakistan sent temperatures soaring to 120° F (49° C). Northwest China experienced its worst drought in a century, while heavy rain in the Yangtze River (Chang Jiang) Valley killed

UPI

Los Angeles firefighters battle a blaze in the Mt. Washington area, as three-digit mercury readings in mid-June caused fires throughout southern California. The Northern Hemisphere recorded its warmest winter and spring in 100 years.

38 persons and left thousands homeless. Dry weather posed problems in the grain-growing areas of Australia, Argentina, and Brazil.

June–August. Summer temperatures were near average values throughout the United States, except for the Desert Southwest and the Plateau region, where seasonal temperatures averaged 6° F (3° C) above normal. Rainfall was unusually heavy from the southern Plains to the middle Mississippi Valley. Parts of Texas and Illinois received more than twice the normal seasonal precipitation. Pockets of dryness remained in sections of the Southeast and along the Appalachian Mountains.

In June, all of the continental United States except the Pacific Northwest and southwest Texas experienced above-average temperatures. An inflow of tropical air over eastern Texas and Oklahoma produced heavy rains and flooding during the first two weeks of the month.

July was a wet month in the middle Mississippi Valley. Temperatures were 2 to 4° F (1 to 2° C) above average in the Southeast and the northern Plains, while the Pacific Northwest was cooler than average by the same amount.

A heat wave persisted throughout the West during the month of August. The Great Plains and the southern Atlantic Coast recorded slightly below-average temperatures. Rainfall was heavy in eastern New Mexico, western Texas, and the central Rockies. Tropical storm Dennis produced heavy rain in central and southern Florida in the third week of the month.

Europe had unusually wet weather during the first two months of summer, with widespread flooding occurring in parts of Italy, West Germany, and Poland. Drier weather prevailed on the continent in August. A heat wave in the western USSR sent temperatures soaring to 97° F (36° C) in Moscow on July 20, one of the highest temperatures ever recorded in that city. Central China continued to experience heavy rain, which caused extensive flooding and agricultural damage. Seasonal temperatures were as much as 6° F (3° C) above average in the interior of the Australian continent. Torrential rains from Typhoon Thad flooded 7,400 acres (3 000 ha) of farmland and 3,000 homes as the storm moved through northern Japan in late August.

September–November. Several invasions of cold polar air into the eastern United States proved September to be the first autumn month. Monthly average temperatures were 2 to 4° F (1 to 2° C) below normal in the Southeast, while the Rockies and Great Plains registered positive departures from normal by a similar amount. Precipitation was heavy along the Appalachians, from southwest Texas to the high plains of Nebraska, and along the West Coast from northern California to the Canadian border.

A series of storm systems moved through the Pacific Northwest in October, dumping heavy snow in the Cascades and northern Rockies. Remnants of two tropical storms moved across northern Mexico and into western Texas and Oklahoma during two successive weeks at the beginning of the month, triggering strong thunderstorms and several tornadoes throughout the region. Floodwaters as high as 15 ft (4.6 m) were reported in Texas, with crop and property damage exceeding $25 million. Rainfall remained below average in the Southeast.

The third week in November brought heavy snow to the Midwest. One storm dumped 11 inches (28 cm) on Minneapolis and St. Paul, with another 14 inches (36 cm) in some places only days later. Twelve persons were killed, and property damage was extensive.

Flooding was a problem in parts of Europe, Nepal, and China during autumn. As of the first week in September, the death toll from flooding in the Shaanxi province of China stood at 764, with 260,000 acres (105 000 ha) of farmland under water and 200,000 persons homeless. In Nepal, the worst flooding in 30 years left a reported 1,500 persons dead and thousands more homeless. The East Asian monsoon retreated two to four weeks ahead of schedule in northwest India, causing reduced rice crop yields.

IDA HAKKARINEN

MEXICO

The naming of the next president of Mexico was the political highlight of 1981, followed by continued national opposition to the policies of the United States in Central America and the Caribbean. Mexico also announced increases in its oil reserves.

Politics. The September announcement that Minister of Budget and Planning Miguel de la Madrid Hurtado had been chosen by President José López Portillo to be his successor in 1982 ended months of political jockeying and speculation. The election of the 47-year-old de la Madrid was a foregone conclusion even though he was not officially nominated by the government's Institutional Revolutionary Party until November and elections would not be held until July 1982. No government-backed presidential candidate has lost an election in this century. De la Madrid, the author of Mexico's economic development plan, is expected to continue the conservative policies of López Portillo. His selection was widely seen as a signal to the world business community that Mexico is a safe place for investment.

De la Madrid is well-qualified to guide the nation's economy for the 1982–88 presidential term. He holds a law degree from the national university (his thesis was on economics) and a master's degree in public administration from Harvard University. He has served as subdirector general of credit in the finance ministry and as subdirector of finances in the state petroleum monopoly, Petróleos Mexicanos (PEMEX). That he has never held an elective political office is not expected to be a handicap, for recent Mexican presidents have been bureaucrats, not politicians.

The political scene was relatively quiet during the year, but discontent with the government's authoritarian policies flared on several occasions. In the spring, in a private document obtained by the press, Mexican bishops criticized governmental power abuses, corruption, institutional violence, and the presidential selection process. Such criticism is rare in this anticlerical nation. When the leader of the Chamber of Deputies reminded the nation that the church was forbidden to speak on politics, the bishops fell silent. In January, peasants in Chiapas blockaded roads to oil and gas fields in protest of environmental pollution. Former President Luis Echeverría criticized the conservative agrarian policies of the government, in particular the "Mexican Food System," a plan that creates a partnership between communal landholders and private enterprise in an effort to increase production. Echeverría saw the plan as a retreat from the goals of the Mexican Revolution. His comments drew considerable attention, since former presidents are expected to stay out of politics. Some observers wondered if Echeverría was trying to establish himself as the leader of the Mexican left.

Economic Policy. The government concentrated its efforts on promoting economic growth to provide food and jobs for the nation's burgeoning population. Industrial development and expansion of energy production received the major attention. To combat the effects of inflation, more credit was extended to food-processing plants, small- and medium-sized industries, and transportation, while import duties were suspended on essential goods. Minimum wages were raised an average of 31%.

The 1981 federal expenditure budget of 2.3 trillion pesos (up 31% over 1980) shifted more fiscal power to the central government and away from the public sector agencies, thus giving the president more direct control over economic policy. Federal government expenditures were programmed to rise 42.7%, whereas the public sector agencies would increase expenditures by only 17.5%. Similarly, administrative costs were increased 55%. Debt service for the federal government went up 36%, while that of the agencies went down 31%. The federal government began

UPI

John Gavin (center), a former actor and the new U.S. ambassador to Mexico, shares a laugh with President Ronald Reagan (left) and Mexican President José López Portillo (right) at Camp David, MD.

to take more direct action in fostering economic development, formerly a major role of agencies.

Mexico continued to program deficit spending, although at a reduced rate. Total national government income was expected to be only 1.6 trillion pesos, with the deficit to be met by borrowing 298 million pesos. The public debt, however, decreased in proportion to the gross domestic product. When oil revenues continued to fall in the first half of 1981, López Portillo reduced expenditures by 4%.

Economic Performance. The economy performed well in spite of high inflation and sluggishness in some sectors. The gross domestic product increased 8%, a rate higher than that of other industrial nations. A 197% increase in seed production during the first eight months of the year promised reductions in future food imports. Increases in corn production made Mexico the world's fifth largest producer of that basic food. Steel production rose 7%, and cement production was programmed to increase 8.4%. The inflation rate, however, surpassed 28% and caused dislocations. Tourism and border transactions, important for foreign exchange, dropped. The commercial balance of trade for the manufacturing industry deteriorated, largely as a result of production problems. Petroleum exports fueled the economy even though the nation derived only 38% of its export income from that mineral.

Energy. President López Portillo announced on September 1 that Mexican oil reserves, at 72,000,000,000 barrels, are the fourth largest in the world and are expected to increase. Mexico exports 1.25 million barrels per day, earning an annual revenue of $15,000,000,000. Nevertheless, oil revenues constituted only about 7% of the gross domestic product. López Portillo again used Mexico's oil strength to call for a world energy plan. It was announced that henceforth no country would receive more than 50% of Mexico's oil exports, to keep Mexico from becoming too dependent upon a single market. Concerted efforts were made during 1981 to diversify oil export markets. In the face of falling world oil prices, Mexico lowered its prices an average of $4 per barrel in June. Strong nationalistic opposition, however, forced the government to raise them by $2 in August. In spite of buyer protest of the latter move, Mexico held firm to the new price even though revenues dropped as contracts were canceled. The director of Petróleos Mexicanos, Jorge Diaz Serrano, was replaced by Julio Moctezuma in response to nationalists' complaints and to reduce Diaz Serrano's growing domestic political power.

Foreign Policy. Mexico actively pursued its policy of encouraging stability in Central America and the Caribbean, recognizing the inevitability of change and advocating the self-determination of peoples. In May, Mexico welcomed as a hero the leader of the Nicaraguan junta. In cooperation with Venezuela, Mexico continued to subsidize oil exports to Central America. Throughout the year, López Portillo's government criticized U.S. policy in strife-torn El Salvador, warning against making a great power confrontation out of what Mexico considers to be a domestic conflict. In August, France joined Mexico in recognizing El Salvador's guerrilla-led opposition as a representative political force with the right to participate in negotiations to settle that country's civil war. López Portillo called Cuba Mexico's "dearest" friend in Latin America and admonished the United States for continued opposition to Castro's government. Cuba and Mexico signed trade and petroleum agreements, thus strengthening their ties and diversifying the Mexican market.

In spite of three cordial meetings between presidents López Portillo and Ronald Reagan of the United States, relations between the two nations were often labored. The appointment of former actor John Gavin as ambassador to Mexico caused considerable dismay even though Gavin has an Hispanic ancestry and a graduate degree in Latin American studies. Some Mexicans took the appointment as a signal that their country was less important to Washington than it had been previously. Mexico joined the United States and Canada in discussing a joint assistance plan for Central America but protested Washington's assertions that definite agreements had been reached.

Overall, however, relations between Mexico and the United States remained close. The United States continues to be Mexico's largest trading partner, while Mexico is the third largest trading partner of the United States. Washington welcomes Mexico's interest in promoting stability among its southern neighbors and demonstrated the fact by selling Mexico 12 F5E fighter planes. The planes are expected to be used to protect southern oil and gas fields from possible turmoil spilling over from Central America.

In October, the 22-nation North-South summit conference met in Cancún, Mexico. The developing nations demanded that the rich industrial nations redistribute international wealth more in their favor. In order to get President Reagan to attend, Mexico persuaded the Cubans to stay home.

DONALD J. MABRY
Mississippi State University

MEXICO • Information Highlights

Official Name: The United Mexican States.
Location: Southern North America.
Area: 761,602 sq mi (1 972 549 km^2).
Population (1981 est.): 69,300,000.
Chief Cities (1979 est.): Mexico City, the capital, 9,191,295; Guadalajara, 1,906,145; Monterrey, 1,064,629.
Government: *Head of state and government,* José López Portillo, president (took office Dec. 1976). *Legislature*—Congress: Senate and Chamber of Deputies.
Monetary Unit: Peso (25.34 pesos equal U.S.$1, Oct. 1981).
Manufactures (major products): Processed foods, chemicals, basic metals and metal products, petroleum products.
Agriculture (major products): Corn, cotton, sugarcane, wheat, coffee.

Family members join Mark Siljander (second, left) in celebrating his special election to the U.S. House of Representatives. The 29-year-old Republican won the seat vacated by Budget Director David Stockman.

UPI

MICHIGAN

Economic problems dominated in Michigan for the third consecutive year. The auto industry fought to resume profitable operations (*see also* AUTOMOBILES), unemployment remained high, and all levels of government reduced services in the face of declining revenues and public outcries for tax relief.

Auto Industry. The major automakers reported modest profits in the spring but the industry continued to stagnate. The most optimistic forecasters predicted a combined total loss of more than $600 million for the year despite cost-cutting efforts and rebate and discount sales schemes.

The failure of the auto industry to recover was blamed for continued high unemployment, which stood near double digit levels much of the year.

State Finances. The depressed economy and demands for tax relief prompted Gov. William G. Milliken to ask state legislators on September 17 to approve a complex development program, including a 20% cut in property taxes over three years. But four weeks later, the governor withdrew his call for a tax cut, citing the continuing recession and a swelling state budget deficit.

Detroit Survival Plan. Detroit, the state's largest city, faced a deficit of $119 million for fiscal year 1981, which was expected to rise during 1982. Mayor Coleman A. Young launched a "Detroit survival plan." The three-point program called for an increase in the city income tax, which was approved by the voters June 23; wage concessions from city employees totaling $51 million, which were ultimately ratified by all city unions; and the borrowing of $125 million to finance the 1981 deficit, which was completed November 2.

Schools. Detroit voted overwhelmingly on September 15 to end an 11-year experiment with decentralized control of its public schools. The district is to return to the one central board of education in 1983.

Poletown Controversy. Detroit's condemnation of land in an older portion of the city, known as Poletown, for a General Motors Corp. assembly plant aroused bitter opposition. The final battle took place July 16 when police evicted protesters from historic Immaculate Conception Church and stood guard while wreckers razed the structure, which had become a symbol of the opposition.

Election. Detroit Mayor Young was reelected easily to a third term. His opponent was Perry Koslowski, a city accountant. Detroit residents were asked in the city election if they favored casino gambling. The vote, which favored the measure, was advisory only, but the question had prompted vigorous campaigning.

Wayne County. On November 3, voters in Wayne County, the state's most populous county, approved a new charter designed to streamline county government. Detroit's black leaders, including Mayor Young, opposed reorganization as an effort to dilute the power of Detroit's black majority in favor of white suburbanites.

Bishop Edmund Szoka of Gaylord, a northern Michigan diocese, was installed May 17 as Roman Catholic archbishop of Detroit. He succeeded John Cardinal Dearden, who resigned.

CHARLES THEISEN, *"The Detroit News"*

MICHIGAN • Information Highlights

Area: 58,527 sq mi (151 585 km^2).
Population (1980 census): 9,258, 344.
Chief Cities (1980 census): Lansing, the capital, 130,414; Detroit, 1,203,339; Grand Rapids, 181,843; Warren, 161,134; Flint, 159,611; Sterling Heights, 108,999; Ann Arbor, 107,316; Livonia, 104,814; Dearborn, 99,-660; Westland, 84,603.
Government (1981): *Chief Officers*—governor, William G. Milliken (R); lt. gov., James H. Brickley (R). *Legislature*—Senate, 38 members; House of Representatives, 110 members.
State Finances (fiscal year 1980): *Revenues,* $12,357,-000,000; *expenditures,* $12,634,000,000.
Personal Income (1980): $92,339,000,000; per capita, $9,950.
Labor Force (July 1981): *Nonagricultural wage and salary earners,* 3,458,500; *unemployed,* 529,800 (11.8% of total force).

MICROBIOLOGY

In 1981, recombinant-DNA research involving microbes continued to offer promise of solutions to some serious problems. Microbes were also being used to produce fuel-grade alcohol and to combat pollution. There was an increased understanding of magnetic bacteria and of the role bacteria play in a deep-sea community.

Recombinant-DNA Research. Scientists at the U.S. Department of Agriculture and at Genentech Inc. used the bacterium *Escherichia coli* (*E. coli*) to develop a vaccine against foot-and-mouth disease. The vaccine consists of a surface protein of the virus that causes the disease, one of the world's most serious agricultural problems. Tests indicate that the vaccine is safe and effective against one common type of the virus; efforts were under way to develop a more general vaccine.

Scientists at the University of California at San Francisco incorporated the gene for a hepatitis-B surface protein into yeast. Instead of synthesizing the surface protein, the yeast produced a complex chemical resembling the immunizing particles formed by the blood of hepatitis-B patients. (A clinical trial has indicated that immunizing particles are an effective vaccine against hepatitis-B.)

The hepatitis-B gene had previously been spliced into bacteria, but yeast offers certain advantages over bacteria for commercial production of biochemicals. The techniques for growing large quantities of yeast have already been developed by bread, beer, and wine makers. Also, yeast does not produce endotoxins, poisonous substances manufactured by bacteria.

In 1980, *E. coli* was genetically engineered to produce human interferon. In 1981, the human interferon gene was spliced into two additional organisms: the soil bacterium *Bacillus subtilis* and yeast. Both offer safety and other advantages over *E. coli.*

Researchers at the Imperial Cancer Research Fund in London used gene-splicing techniques to develop a vaccine for one type of influenza. They inserted the viral gene that controls the production of hemagglutinin (HA) into the DNA of bacteria. The bacteria then produced HA, which can be injected into human beings to make them resistant to the flu virus.

Fuel Production. Henry Schneider of Canada's National Research Council discovered a yeast, *Pachysolen tannophilus,* that eats both 5- and 6-carbon sugars. This promises to make the production of fuel-grade ethanol from agricultural and wood industry wastes economically attractive. Standard fermentation yeasts metabolize 6-carbon sugars but not 5-carbon sugars. The latter comprise a significant portion of the waste materials. Metabolism of both types of sugars could increase yields by 50 to 80%.

Another source of ethanol was reported by scientists at the University of Oklahoma. They treated whey with lactose-fermenting yeast, which turned lactose in the whey into ethanol. Whey is a by-product of cheese production and a serious pollution problem in some places.

Chemical Cleanup. Two Cornell University engineers have developed a bacterium that thrives on a diet of pentachlorophenol (PCP). This widely-used wood preservative is biodegradable in most circumstances. However, accidental spills or steady buildups of the material, particularly in wastewater discharges of plants that use the chemical, can cause fish kills and other problems. The laboratory-grown bacterium can clean up soil or water contaminated with PCP about 50 times faster than current methods.

Virus in Milk. Bovine leukemia virus (BLV) is widespread in commercial dairy herds. Researchers at the University of Pennsylvania inoculated lambs with milk collected from 24 dairy cows naturally infected with BLV. The lambs were later examined for the development of BLV antibodies. Using this technique, it was shown that 17 of the cows released the infectious virus into their milk. It has not been proven that BLV does—or does not—infect human beings. The infectivity of BLV is apparently destroyed by the pasteurization process, but people in many parts of the world continue to consume unpasteurized milk.

Magnetic Bacteria. Research has provided insights into the behavior of bacteria that contain magnetite crystals. Bacteria found in the Northern Hemisphere always swim north. Those found in the Southern Hemisphere always swim south. Among those collected from waters directly on the magnetic equator, about half swim north and half swim south. The magnetite crystals are aligned in the direction of movement. Researchers can realign the crystals and thereby reverse the bacteria's direction by using hand-held magnets. It is believed that the magnetite's function is to make the bacteria swim toward bottom sediments, their preferred habitat. The magnetite could also aid in escaping from enemies and harmful chemicals.

Bacteria and Giant Worms. A unique biological community was discovered several years ago living around hot springs on the floor of the Pacific Ocean off the coast of Latin America. A major element of the community is giant tube worms, since named *Riftia pachyptila* Jones. The worm lacks a mouth and digestive system. Meredith L. Jones of the Smithsonian Institution and his colleagues believe that the worm obtains nourishment with the aid of symbiotic bacteria. In the rear section of the worm's body is a structure that contains billions of sulfur-oxidizing bacteria. These bacteria oxidize hydrogen sulfide emitted from the hot springs. They use the resulting energy, as well as special enzymes, to change the carbon dioxide from the water into carbohydrates.

JENNY TESAR
Science and Medical Writer

MIDDLE EAST

The Middle East in 1981, as always, witnessed a plethora of seemingly important events—most of them violent or merely ominous, a few encouraging and positive. Among them all, two stood out as being genuinely significant. One was the release of the Americans held hostage in Iran since 1979. The other was the assassination of President Anwar el-Sadat of Egypt. These two events, each in its own way, marked a definite end to a historic phase. But, however many striking events occurred, it was not a year in which things really changed very much. Any evaluation of general trends would have to conclude that, if anything, they changed for the worse.

Things were not helped by the fact that U.S. policy was in the hands of a new administration and an inexperienced president. There were the usual signs of fumbling, no novelty in such a situation. The Reagan administration early on developed a fairly clear idea of the two objectives it would pursue in the Middle East—regional security, primarily for the purpose of safeguarding oil supplies, to be attained by stepping up actual U.S. military presence in the region; and the pursuit of intraregional harmony by the muting and diminishing of area conflicts, whether between Israel and the Arabs or among the Arab states themselves. While these objectives were entirely worthy, their attainment was far from realized. Within the calendar year, some degree of success was achieved on the first point. The U.S. presence was increased, and the utilization of bases and working arrangements with area governments progressed. But this did not necessarily contribute toward attainment of the second objective—which, if anything, receded. Partly as a result of American policy, polarization seemed to increase rather than grow less. The prospects of a general Arab-Israeli peace, or even of a wholly successful Egyptian-Israeli peace, grew dimmer.

Iran. For the families of the 52 U.S. hostages held in Tehran since Nov. 4, 1979, as well as for the hostages themselves, January 1981 was a happy month. Their departure from durance in Iran took place on the day of Ronald Reagan's inauguration, January 20, exactly 444 days since the storming of the embassy. But, except for the fate of the hostages themselves, there was little to cheer about. The popular perception that ransom had been paid was not altogether mistaken. A revolutionary government that had defied all canons of international behavior, however long-established, had essentially won out. Several billion dollars of Iranian assets in the United States were unblocked and returned. U.S. assets of every kind in Iran—buildings, installations, machinery, and contract claims—were to be disposed of by the decisions of a mixed international tribunal, which by year's end had not even begun proceedings.

Conditions within Iran continued to deteriorate. Oil production did not cease completely but was down to about one quarter of the prerevolutionary capacity. The standard of living continued to decline. Assassinations and random violence were the order of the day. Executions of all those supposed to be in any way against the regime of the Ayatollah Khomeini continued at a heavy rate. Meanwhile, disillusioned revolutionaries, many of them now in exile, exhibited their naiveté by complaining that conditions were now far worse than they had been under the shah. It was highly significant that three dissident groups, all fairly well organized, were emerging as potential challengers to the Khomeini regime of religious zealotry. The *mujahadeen,* generally described as "Islamic Socialists," were perhaps the most important of these. The *Tudeh* party, or pro-Moscow Left, was experiencing a revival. And the *fadayan,* Marxist-Leninist but anti-Soviet, appeared also to be growing in strength. The monarchists, supporters of the former regime, seemed to be a negligible quantity inside Iran; numerous outside Iran, they were seriously weakened by factionalism.

In terms of regional trends, the most momentous fact about Iran in 1981 was that it was drifting more and more into the Soviet orbit. Nothing so crude as an Afghanistan-style takeover seemed to be immediately in prospect, but Iran remained cut off from all U.S. contact and aid, and the trend of its economic orientation was clearly toward the Soviet Union. Economic agreements for practical cooperation on a number of matters were concluded or in process.

Iran-Iraq War. The war between Iran and Iraq, the only actual international war in progress in the region, continued to drag on. More than a year after it had begun in September 1980, the fighting was still totally inconclusive. Although reliable information was lacking, the course of military events in the fall of 1981 seemed to favor Iran, which, with a population three times that of Iraq, has an enormous advantage in manpower resources. It was, however, a war of limited commitment by both countries; the total number of killed on each side seemed to be about 10,000 by year's end. In economic terms, however, the loss of oil revenues made it perhaps the most costly two-power conflict ever waged. Researchers calculated the cost of the war to Iran as being at least $100,000,000,000 by the end of 1981, and $50,000,000,000 to Iraq, whose oil output and sales were better maintained. Politics and the standard of living in Iran were far more adversely affected than in Iraq. Several mediation efforts were made during the year, all in vain.

Threats to Kuwait. Early fears that the Iraq-Iran war would spread to other states fortunately proved groundless. The only hint of an expansion occurred when tiny but oil-rich Kuwait provided Iraq, whose Persian Gulf outlet is unusable, with facilities for overland transportation

UPI

An Israeli armored personnel carrier patrols the Golan Heights during the May crisis over Syria's deployment of missiles in southern Lebanon. In December, Israel annexed the Golan.

of supplies. Minor attacks on Kuwait were made by Iran on Nov. 12 and 16, 1980, and on June 13, 1981, with a more serious air attack on the Ommul-Aish oil facility on October 2 (for which Iran denied responsibility).

A New Configuration? A novel configuration in Middle East politics appeared to be emerging, whereby Iraq was linking up with certain conservative states which would not, prior to the war with Iran, have been considered suitable ideological bedfellows for the Baghdad regime. The government of President Saddam Hussein, always notably pragmatic, seemed to be cooperating well with Jordan and Saudi Arabia, both monarchies. On May 16, King Hussein of Jordan was in Baghdad, and on July 19 the president of Iraq publicly thanked Saudi Arabia for offering to pay the cost of rebuilding the Iraqi nuclear reactor that had been destroyed in the notorious Israeli air raid of June 7.

Trends and Alignments. It was still too early to assess the long-term effects on Middle East politics of the assassination of President Sadat of Egypt on October 6 and the succession of his vice-president, Hosni Mubarak. In all his early speeches and actions, Mubarak stressed continuity, but the skepticism would persist at least until continuity has been demonstrated after April 25, 1982—when Israel is obliged, under the peace treaty of 1979, to hand over to Egypt the third and final installment of the occupied Sinai, which happens to contain two major Israeli airfields. After April, to put it crudely, Egypt will have nothing further to gain by remaining on good terms with Israel. Normal relations—to say nothing of improved relations—will rest on good faith alone. But the price, if that honorable course is chosen, will no doubt be continuing, or even deepening, Egyptian isolation in the Arab world.

Egypt's relations with the United States appeared to be on a firm footing. Sadat had made a very successful official visit to the United States (August 5–10), his funeral was attended by three former U.S. presidents, and Egypt received assurances of U.S. support during the mini-crisis with Libya in late summer. Later, almost two months after Sadat's death, "Operation Bright Star" brought U.S. forces to Egypt to conduct large-scale military maneuvers. In late November, Mubarak announced his intention of visiting both the United States and Israel in February 1982.

It appeared for a time that there might be some hitch in the arrangements, signed August 3, for an international peacekeeping force in the Sinai. Israel in November objected to the proposed participation of Great Britain, France, Italy, and the Netherlands because these countries had said publicly that they favored an eventual negotiating role for the Palestine Liberation Organization (PLO). A compromise was worked out by December 4, whereby these countries agreed to base the peacekeeping force on the Camp David accords and the Egyptian-Israeli peace treaty, thus isolating the matter from broader considerations. On the question of the PLO, as on many others, a growing divergence existed between U.S. policy and the policies of Western European governments; Western Europe found it easier than Washington to overlook the PLO's terrorist role.

Saudi Arabia. While maintaining close relations with Egypt, the Reagan administration moved increasingly to buttress the government of Saudi Arabia, the Middle East's largest exporter of oil. In a move that generated sustained and bitter controversy, the Reagan administration decided to sell to Saudi Arabia a number of sophisticated AWACS (Airborne Warning and Control System) surveillance planes. The political struggle lasted the whole summer and part of the fall, until the U.S. Senate finally gave its consent in October. The debate centered chiefly on the question of the stability of the Saudi regime. Its supporters saw it as the one genuinely stable and important conservative regime in the Middle East; its opponents tended to draw analogies, perhaps of questionable applicability, with Iran. Inevitably, the government of Israel and its supporters in the United States were bitterly opposed to the sale, which they regarded as a betrayal.

There was evidence, both in the AWACS issue and others, of some long-term "tilt" on the part of the United States away from unconditional support of Israel and in the direction of pro-Arab policies. Political reality in the region, however, made it unlikely that this would go very far.

The Quest for Stability. Things were certainly easier for the United States when the Pahlavis were still in power in Tehran, because Iran is non-Arab and the shah sold oil to Israel in peace and war. It was tempting, but not altogether accurate, to see U.S. policy in the Middle East since the fall of the shah as the search for another friendly pillar of stability in the region. No thoroughly satisfactory substitute was available, and the former role of Iran seemed now to be shared by Egypt and Saudi Arabia; there were also prospects of closer military cooperation with Israel.

If the United States was pursuing friendly policies in various Middle East quarters, there was no doubt as to which state was regarded in Washington as the villain of the region—Libya. Denunciations of Col. Muammar el-Qaddafi's terrorist activities, of his temporary takeover of Chad, and of his threat to the Sudan, were underscored on August 19 when, over the Gulf of Sidra 60 mi (97 km) off the Libyan coast, two F-14 fighters from the U.S. aircraft carrier *Nimitz* responded to an airborne missile attack and shot down two Libyan fighter planes. In the fall, Exxon Corporation voluntarily decided to close down all its Libyan oil operations, and at the beginning of December all U.S. companies operating in Libya were requested to do the same.

The "Peace Process." Meanwhile, the crucial issue in the Middle East peace process—namely, the "autonomy" provisions of the Camp David accords and the 1979 peace treaty agreements relating to the West Bank and Gaza, as well as the procedures for carrying them out—remained unresolved. Egyptian-Israeli negotiations on the question, suspended for more than a year, got going again only very tentatively in late 1981. The basic documents speak of some vaguely defined "autonomy," totally inadequate in Palestinian eyes; Egypt feels obliged to push, beyond the terms of the treaty, for "independence" for Palestinians. Israel, however, considers independence for the Palestinians to be incompatible with its very existence.

A possibly significant novelty of 1981 was the marginal involvement, for the first time and briefly, of Saudi Arabia in the stalled peace process. This took the form of a diplomatic trial balloon launched by Prince Fahd on August 8. His eight-item peace plan called for Israeli withdrawal from all occupied territories and the removal of all Israeli West Bank settlements; the creation of a Palestinian state with East Jerusalem as its capital; and the recognition of the right of all states in the area "to live in peace." The final vague phrase was interpreted as a cautious acceptance of Israel's legitimacy, and for this reason the proposals were rejected out of hand by the PLO. Prince Fahd's plan was accorded respectful attention in the gulf emirates and in Western Europe, and was even given favorable mention by President Reagan. Yet no conceivable Israeli government could agree to the Palestinian state, still less to the yielding up of East Jerusalem. The main interest in the Fahd proposals lay in the fact that they did constitute the first real Saudi contribution to the peace process. However, since the proposals were summarily rejected by the radical Arab states at the Arab summit at Fez, Morocco, November 25, and turned that meeting into a short-lived fiasco, the Fahd proposals may prove the last, as well as the first, Saudi initiative of this kind.

Golan Heights. On December 14, Prime Minister Menahem Begin of Israel pushed rapidly through the Knesset (parliament) a measure to annex the Golan Heights, formally extending Israeli law and civil administration. The Golan had been conquered from Syria in 1967 and occupied by Israel ever since. Explanations for this unanimously condemned demarche lay chiefly in Israel's internal politics. Begin's Likud party had won the election of June 30, but by a narrow margin that left the premier's political base more precarious. The AWACS sale, the assassination of Sadat, the fact that the United States restrained Israel in early summer from extirpating the new Syrian missiles in Lebanon, and similarly ominous events made many Israelis question the reliability of U.S. support, as well as the wisdom of carrying out the April 1982 evacuation of the Sinai. The U.S. response, intended to reassure, was a short-lived "strategic accord," signed in Washington on November 30 by Israeli Defense Minister Ariel Sharon and U.S. Secretary of Defense Caspar Weinberger. The accord looked to Israeli-U.S. military cooperation and, rather indiscreetly, mentioned the Soviet Union as a potential enemy. This unusual document did not placate Israeli critics of Begin's government, and the annexation of the Golan Heights was intended to strengthen Begin's position internally. It did, being approved in the Knesset by 63 votes to 21. But the move not only roused the fury of the Arab world, especially of Syria, but was formally condemned by the UN Security Council, the United States concurring.

There has never been the slightest prospect that Israel could be persuaded to hand back the Golan Heights to Syria, which for many years prior to 1967 had used the commanding high ground to harass settlements in the lower lands of northern Israel. Egypt's President Mubarak denounced Israel's move as a "violation" of the peace treaty, but this would be hard to prove. The Golan Heights are nowhere mentioned in the peace treaty. Secretary Weinberger, more justifiably, spoke of the Golan move as a breach of the spirit of Camp David. As a reprimand to Israel, the United States "suspended" the November 30 agreement, which Israel then canceled.

ARTHUR CAMPBELL TURNER
Department of Political Science
University of California, Riverside

MILITARY AFFAIRS

In 1981 military affairs were dominated by allegations from the Reagan administration that massive increases in Soviet military capability, plus an expansion in Soviet influence about the world, justified what could become the largest peacetime military buildup in U.S. history. True to his word that he would rearm America against the Communist threat, President Ronald Reagan made a series of decisions in late summer and early fall which, if Congress appropriates the funding, will affect the military capacity of the United States into the beginnings of the 21st century. Associated with the rearming programs was a willingness by the Reagan administration to use military force also in situations where it was thought that American rights were in jeopardy. The most dramatic example of this philosophy occurred when two Navy F-14 fighters shot down two Soviet-built Libyan SU-22 jets over Mediterranean waters claimed by Libya. Previous to the August air encounter, the State Department had disputed the Libyan government's claim of sovereignty extending 200 nautical miles (nmi) or 370 km out from the coastline.

The Neutron Bomb. In August the Reagan administration announced that the United States would move beyond President Jimmy Carter's decision to stockpile the components of the so-called neutron bomb and commence building the new weapons, which will be stored in the United States until needed. More accurately described as an enhanced radiation weapon, the device employs advanced technology to increase the amount of energy released in the form of radiation while decreasing the energy released as blast and heat. The consequence, claim proponents, is a weapon that is more effective against troops in the field while being less destructive of the nearby countryside and its inhabitants and structures. The specific threat against which the enhanced radiation weapons are being readied is the tank forces possessed by the Soviet Union and its Warsaw Pact allies. The president put the need for the neutron weapons this way: "This weapon was particularly designed to offset the great superiority that the Soviet Union has on the Western Front."

Domestic and foreign objections to the enhanced radiation weapon decision were quick to develop. The Soviets charged that Reagan was taking a step toward war in Europe and hinted that they, too, might develop such weapons. In Western Europe the president's action was described by growing numbers of peace movement supporters as further evidence that the United States intended to make their homelands into nuclear battlegrounds while America itself might be spared. U.S. opposition reflected the fear that because the new weapons were less destructive they might be more easily used, thus opening the door for expanded nuclear weapon employment. The administration responded that the rationale for the weapons was not to make war easier or more attractive, but to deter Soviet attack by making an effective U.S. response more certain.

Strategic Nuclear Weapons. After years of discussion over what has become known as the "window of vulnerability" problem, President Reagan announced a number of decisions designed to assure the survivability of American strategic nuclear forces in the event of a Soviet first strike. The concern over vulnerability arose in the 1970s as defense planners watched the Soviet Union replace relatively inaccurate and unreliable intercontinental ballistic missiles (ICBMs), which carried one modest-sized warhead, with more accurate and reliable missiles equipped with three or more warheads of substantially larger yield. U.S. Department of Defense officials worried that the more effective Soviet missiles could be used in a sneak attack which might destroy up to 90% of the U.S. land-based ICBM force. Compounding Washington's fears was the possibility that Soviet air defenses would be capable of destroying substantial numbers of the aging B-52 bomber force before the aircraft could reach their targets.

To negate the possibility of a successful Soviet attack, and thus to deter such an attack, President Reagan announced in October a plan to deploy a scaled down version of the MX ICBM program, to build 100 B-1 bombers, and to conduct additional research intended to lead to the production of a Stealth aircraft by the 1990s.

In deciding to deploy some MX missiles in existing silos now housing Titan ICBMs, President Reagan dramatically altered the MX deployment mode favored by the Carter administration. That administration had developed plans to shuttle 200 MXs between 4,600 shelters to be constructed in desolate areas of such Western states as Utah and Nevada. The rationale for the "shell game" deployment mode was that the Soviets would not know in which of the 4,600 shelters the MXs would be housed. Thus, to guarantee a successful strike the Soviet planners would have to target all 4,600 shelters, 4,400 of which would be empty. Carter advisers thought the cost and difficulty of targeting 4,600 shelters would make such a strike unlikely. In a reversal of the Carter perspective, Reagan officials stated their belief that the Soviets could build sufficient warheads to destroy all the shelters.

Although rejecting the multiple shelter basing mode, President Reagan did not fully commit himself to any single alternative basing plan. For now the United States will build 100 of the MX missiles. The first 36 will be installed in silos now containing the older Titan missiles. These silos will be reinforced with steel and concrete in the expectation that they then will be able to withstand anything less than a direct hit by a one megaton or larger warhead. Fifty-two Titan silos are available for MX deployment in Arkansas, Kansas, and Arizona. Where and how the re-

Gen. David Jones, who was retained as chairman of the Joint Chiefs of Staff by the Reagan administration, and Secretary of Defense Caspar Weinberger (right) testify on the 1982 fiscal year defense budget.

UPI

mainder of the initial 100 MXs will be deployed, and how additional missiles will be based if they are built, had not been indicated by the Pentagon by mid-November.

In comparison with the most advanced of the currently deployed American ICBMs, the Minuteman III, the MX missile represents a substantial increase in capability and firepower. For example, the Minuteman III is capable of carrying three 170-kiloton warheads for a distance of approximately 7,000 mi (11 265 km). The MX carries ten 350-kiloton warheads to a distance of up to 8,000 mi (12 874 km). The MX is far larger, with a weight of 190,000 lbs (86 070 kg), as compared with a weight of 78,000 lbs (35 334 kg) for the Minuteman III. Because of its impressive potential some feared that the deployment of the MX would appear to Moscow to suggest the United States was seeking a weapon that could be used in a first strike, thus adding a destabilizing factor to the strategic nuclear relationship between the two nations.

Part of the solution to the vulnerability of the B-52s is President Reagan's decision to ask Congress for funding to construct 100 B-1 strategic jet bombers. In making this request the president significantly altered President Carter's plan to halt production of the aircraft and only to permit further research on the plane. Over the years critics have noted that the B-52s, because they are large, slow, and old, were losing their capability to penetrate the extensive and modernized Soviet air defenses. The B-1, of which three prototypes have been built, is designed to overcome the limitations of the B-52. A swept-wing intercontinental jet, the B-1 will carry 32 air-to-ground missiles and sophisticated electronic jamming equipment.

Anticipating the decade of the 1990s, when the B-1s could be vulnerable, President Reagan ordered accelerated research upon a new aircraft concept termed Stealth. The Stealth bomber would incorporate new technology into an aircraft that its supporters believe will be extremely difficult to track by radar.

There are other components of the president's strategic military package. In regard to the submarine-launched ballistic missile (SLBM) force, Reagan announced his intention to place the larger D-5 missile on the new Trident submarines. The D-5 SLBM can carry 14 warheads with a longer range and greater accuracy than the currently deployed missiles. The sea-based nuclear deterrent force will also be bolstered by the addition of several hundred cruise missiles to be carried aboard general purpose submarines.

Further, President Reagan stated his desire to improve radar capabilities against enemy bombers by augmenting continental air defenses with AWACS (airborne warning and control system) planes and up to five more squadrons of F-15 jet interceptors. He also ordered steps to be taken to increase the protection of the nation's command and control system against the effects of a nuclear attack.

The president's new strategic proposals were met with a mixed response. Tass, the official Soviet news agency, stated that the new U.S. military building program "signals a new stage in the nuclear arms race and increases the danger of war." The Soviet government indicated Moscow's intention to balance whatever new or additional weapons the United States deployed. In America a number of observers wondered whether the president could dramatically increase expenditures for the military and still be able to cut taxes and balance the budget. Others criticized the president for increasing military expenditures while cutting back social services.

In an unprecedented move to support the administration's request for higher levels of military spending and preparedness, Secretary of

Defense Caspar Weinberger ordered the publication of a 99-page booklet detailing the parameters of the Soviet military capacity. The defense secretary described the booklet, *Soviet Military Power,* as providing information concerning the "total dimension" of Soviet armed might. Weinberger added, "This is a very real and growing threat. It is not scare talk. . . . It requires actions on the part of all of us to meet this kind of threat." Critics of the document noted that the Soviet forces were not analyzed in terms of offsetting U.S. military forces. For example, the booklet does not inform the reader that the three small Soviet aircraft carriers are pitted against 13 heavy U.S. carriers. Further, no mention is made of threats perceived by Moscow, such as China, which could account for a portion of the Soviet military establishment's size.

Military Assistance to the Middle East. In addition to the customary sales of military equipment to Israel, such as the F-15s and F-16s which bombed the Iraqi nuclear reactor (*see* special report, below), the Reagan administration sought to increase the sale of military equipment and the provision of military assistance to Egypt and Saudi Arabia. Shortly after the assassination of Egyptian President Anwar el-Sadat the Pentagon stepped up joint U.S. and Egyptian military exercises. Military assistance was offered to the Sudan, Egypt's southern neighbor, when Sudanese officials expressed fear that the weakening of Egypt might tempt Libya to invade.

More controversial was an $8,500,000,000 arms package to Saudi Arabia that included AWACS radar warning planes, air-to-air missiles, and extra fuel tanks to extend the range of previously purchased F-15s. Proponents of the sale argued that peace and the maintenance of oil sales required the United States to assist friendly governments. Opponents stated it was dangerous to introduce advanced equipment into unstable areas where political upheavals could result in the equipment falling into radical hands. Others argued that further arming of the Saudis constituted a threat to Israel. With a two-vote margin, President Reagan won acceptance for the Saudi arms deal in the Senate in October.

World Wide Arming. Dwarfed by the allegations of Soviet military building, and the compensatory responses ordered by President Reagan, were widespread increases in the military capability of many lesser nations, subnational entities, terrorist groups, and revolutionary organizations. The United States and the Soviet Union directly supplied much advanced weaponry to their client states. Old American and Soviet equipment indirectly passed through the hands of shadowy arms dealers to those who could pay. Many European states on both sides of the East-West dividing line supplied automatic weapons, light missiles, armored cars, and ammunition to eager buyers in the Third and Fourth Worlds. Because of the political and religious turbulence in the Middle East, and the abundance of petro-dollars with which to purchase weapons, that region ranked highest in the acquisition of weapons except nuclear.

Standing in direct contrast to much of the world were antimilitary demonstrations that attracted thousands in some of the NATO nations, particularly West Germany. There protesters demonstrated against the projected deployment of American Pershing II missiles and cruise missiles, both of which carry nuclear warheads. Washington claimed the deployments were necessary in order to balance the installation of SS-20 missiles by the Soviets in their eastern European satellites. In November, President Reagan offered an arms control deal to the Soviets. It was that the United States would refrain from deploying Pershing II and cruise missiles to NATO if the Russians would withdraw missiles such as the SS-20 from Eastern Europe. Moscow rejected the proposal since it did not include other U.S. forces nor British and French nuclear forces.

ROBERT M. LAWRENCE
Colorado State University

MILITARY AFFAIRS—SPECIAL REPORT:

NUCLEAR PROLIFERATION

Since shortly after the dawn of the nuclear age the world has been haunted by the fear that an expanding number of nations will develop the capability for launching nuclear war. Gradually that fear has materialized to the point where currently six nations—the United States, the Soviet Union, Great Britain, France, China, and India—have developed nuclear explosives. All but India have moved beyond research to deploy a wide range of nuclear weapons. One additional nation, Israel, is thought either to possess untested nuclear weapons or to have built the components for such weapons but not yet assembled them. The source of the fissionable material for the Israeli nuclear weapons program is believed to be the secret nuclear reactor located in the desert at Dimona.

Until 1981 a variety of peaceful and diplomatic means were used to prevent the proliferation of nuclear weapons among a larger number of nations. The foci of such activity are the treaty on the nonproliferation of nuclear weapons (NPT) and the International Atomic Energy Agency (IAEA), an inspection organization located in Vienna, Austria. If a nonnuclear weapons state accepts the NPT it agrees to refrain from acquiring nuclear weapons and to permit IAEA inspection of civil nuclear facilities to verify compliance. States possessing nuclear weapons that adhere to the NPT, such as the United States, the USSR, and Great Britain, agree not to assist others to obtain nuclear weapons.

Several problems exist regarding the NPT. While most nations have ratified the treaty, a few have not. Even those nations that are signatories may legally withdraw from the treaty by citing a threat to their national security. Ninety days later they are free of NPT constraints. Further, the NPT provides no punishment for a nation that violates its provisions.

In addition to the NPT, a number of agreements have been made among advanced nations to restrict and control trade in fissionable materials and equipment needed for a nuclear program. To some extent the Reagan administration has relaxed restrictions in favor of expanded trade. The basic argument for the change is that the United States can be more influential regarding a nation's nuclear activities if Washington is more a partner than a watchdog.

A New Initiative. In 1981, the Israeli government, led by Prime Minister Menahem Begin, used a new antiproliferation policy that had been analyzed years before by the United States as a possible response to the Chinese nuclear program, but never implemented. The policy is called assertive disarmament. Its objective is to destroy physically the components of a nation's nuclear research and development capability in order to prevent the use of such facilities for nuclear weapons development. Assertive disarmament is also designed to discourage others from even considering a nuclear weapons option.

Because the Begin government employed assertive disarmament and hinted it would do so again, it must be inferred that the Israelis are not sanguine that the peaceful antiproliferation efforts will be effective, at least in the Middle East.

The Raid on the Osirak Reactor. Late in the afternoon of June 7, Israeli planes bombed and destroyed a nuclear reactor, patterned after the French Osirak model, that was nearly completed a few miles outside the Iraqi capital of Baghdad. The raid was carried out by eight U.S.-built F-16 fighter-bombers using conventional bombs. Six U.S.-built F-15 fighters escorted the bombers along the 600-mile (960-km) flight path to and from the target area. No Israeli pilots were injured, but one French technician was killed. Engineers stated that it could take three to four years to rebuild the reactor.

Despite almost universal criticism of the raid by both Arab and non-Arab nations, there was no direct punishment of or retaliation against Israel. There was some "wrist slapping," however. Three days after the raid the Reagan administration announced that four F-16s scheduled for delivery to Israel would not be shipped until it was determined whether the Israelis had violated a 1952 arms sale agreement that limits Israeli use of American arms to "legitimate self-defense." The next month, as the State Department officials wrestled with that problem, the Israeli air force bombed Beirut, Lebanon, with an estimated loss of some 300 lives. This act led to the embargo of more U.S. jets, so that by August, 14 F-16s and 2 F-15s were being held from delivery. Finally, in mid-August, the Reagan administration released all the planes to Israel. According to Secretary of State Alexander Haig, an investigation had failed to determine whether the bombing raids were in fact offensive or defensive in character. In September the IAEA voted 51–8, with 27 abstentions, to suspend Israel from future participation in the organization unless Israeli nuclear facilities are opened up to international inspection. The United States joined in opposing the proposition. Many Western European nations abstained.

Israeli Justification for Assertive Disarmament. For several years the Israeli government has contended that the real objective of the Iraqi government in building the Osirak reactor was neither to engage in civil nuclear research nor to produce electricity, but to obtain fissionable materials for nuclear weapons fabrication. Iraq, a signatory of the NPT, disclaims such charges.

If one assumes the Israeli contention is correct, two possibilities exist whereby the Osirak reactor could have led to an Iraqi bomb. One is that the few pounds of highly enriched U-235 reactor fuel could have been diverted to make an atomic bomb. The other possibility is that neutrons produced in the reactor core could have been used to bombard natural uranium and so produced an artificial element, plutonium, that is fissionable and can be used to manufacture nuclear weapons.

The Future. A number of technically advanced nations, including Australia, Canada, Italy, Japan, Sweden, and West Germany, clearly possess the scientific capability to develop nuclear weapons, but at this time seemingly have little incentive to do so. In addition to Iraq, there is another group of nations which may have both the technical capability and the incentive to develop nuclear weapons. Among these are Argentina, Brazil, Pakistan, South Africa, South Korea, and Taiwan. Will these, and possibly other nations, voluntarily eschew nuclear weapons; can they be persuaded from nuclear weapons development by peaceful diplomacy; or will they be subjected to assertive disarmament by a single nation or a group of nations acting collectively?

ROBERT M. LAWRENCE

MINING

The year 1981 could not be regarded as a good year for the world's mining industry as a whole. Among market economy nations, the effects of inflation, due significantly to energy costs, were felt both in the industry's investment in facility expansion and improvement and in exploration and development of new mines. Inflation was also tied to reduced demand for consumer goods, which tended to curtail plant output of mineral commodities. Other factors contributing to cutbacks in development/actual production increases included the major workers' strikes in Poland, a second year of drought conditions in the northern areas of China, war conditions in the Middle East and Afghanistan, recurrent civil disorder in Central America, and a variety of political and economic problems in a number of African states.

Firms with a traditional involvement in fuel mineral supplies made substantial efforts to acquire interest in nonfuel mineral properties. This placed the fuel mineral firms in direct competition with major nonmineral industry conglomerates that have been acquiring mining firms for several years.

Value of World Output. The value of world crude mineral output (including fuels) in 1981 was estimated at $610,000,000,000 in terms of constant 1978 dollars, less than 10% above the $560,000,000,000 for 1980. Comparable recent figures (also in constant 1978 dollars) were, in billion dollars: 1976—$515; 1977—$538; 1978—$536. The USSR accounted for nearly 20% of the 1978 total (exact figures for 1979 and 1980 not available), with the United States ranking second at about 15.4%, followed by Saudi Arabia (8.2%), China (6.6%), Iran (5.2%), and Canada (3.7%). Other countries accounting for more than 1% of the 1978 total, listed in order from the largest to the smallest, were: United Kingdom, Iraq, Libya, Venezuela, West Germany, Nigeria, Kuwait, United Arab Emirates, Indonesia, Poland, South Africa, Mexico, Australia, Algeria, and the Netherlands. On a commodity basis, petroleum accounted for 49.6% of the 1978 total, coal (all types) for 15.7%, natural gas for 10.2%, iron ore for 2.2%, natural gas liquids for 1.7%, copper for 1.6%, gold for 1.4%, and all other mineral commodities for less than 1% each and for only 17.6% in total.

Ferrous Ores and Metals. Final results for 1980 showed a significant reduction in world iron ore output relative to that of 1979, and preliminary results for 1981 suggested only a very modest increase, with a total in the 890-to-900-million-t (979-to-990-million-T) range. Similarly, for crude steel, little increase over the 708-million-t (779-million-T) level of 1980 was expected.

Curtailment of steel industry activity was expected to have a stagnating effect on output of manganese ore, of which major producers, such as Brazil, already held substantial unsold inventories. Prospects were slightly brighter for producers of chromite, molybdenum, tungsten, and other steel alloying components. Production of alloy steels seemed to be accounting for a somewhat higher proportion of world steel output.

Nonferrous Ores and Metals. Incomplete returns indicated that 1981 total world output of copper, lead, zinc, and nickel, both in terms of mines and smelter/refined output, probably would prove to be marginally below the levels shown for 1980. The labor situation in Poland was expected to have a damaging effect on that nation's copper output. Generally poor worldwide market conditions were regarded as influential in retarding growth of lead and zinc, and of nickel to an even greater extent. Production of tin and titanium materials at or near 1980 levels was expected. In contrast, a higher level of output was suggested by partial returns for bauxite and its metallic product, aluminum. Likewise, a marginal increase was anticipated for magnesium. Mercury production, down for several years as producers reduced unmarketed inventories, was expected to be but little above the 1980 level. There were prospects of increase for 1982 or 1983, with Spanish producers contemplating an increase in mine output and Italian and Yugoslav producers considering mine reopenings.

Uranium. Indications were that world output of uranium advanced in 1981. Although figures for the USSR and China are not known, these nations undoubtedly increased production. Among market economy countries, the return of Australia to the ranks of producers in the mid-1970s and the development of a substantial production in South-West Africa (Namibia) in recent years were particularly notable.

Precious Metals. Although precious metal prices remained far higher in 1981 than the levels of a few years ago, the all-time record highs of 1980 were not matched. Higher prices led to the reopening of some gold properties and to a "gold rush" into placer mining areas in Brazil, but increases in reported world output were not evident. In the case of silver, where a substantial share of total world production is as a by-product of copper, lead, and zinc mining, output growth was held back by reductions in output of the principal mine products. World platinum production apparently was somewhat higher in 1981.

Fertilizer Materials and Asbestos. Preliminary and partial data from major producing countries indicated that output of all three major fertilizer commodities (nitrogen, phosphate, and potash) exceeded 1980 levels. The hopes of asbestos producers that demand for their insulation product would grow as a result of the even higher cost of fuel materials proved overly optimistic. World output declined in 1980, and there seemed to be little to suggest a 1981 upturn.

See also Production Tables pages 578–79.

CHARLES L. KIMBELL, *U.S. Bureau of Mines*

The new 62,000-seat Hubert H. Humphrey Metrodome in downtown Minneapolis was expected to be completed in time for the 1982 baseball and football seasons. Builders expected the final cost to be below the $55 million budget. Part of the inflatable dome collapsed in a mid-November snowstorm, but it was quickly repaired.

UPI

MINNESOTA

A weakening economy, spending cutbacks, revenue shortfalls, and striking public employees were constant concerns in Minnesota in 1981.

Economy. The economy was generally sluggish, with agriculture and iron mining especially hard-pinched. Yields were at or near record levels for the state's seven leading crops—corn, soybeans, wheat, hay, oats, barley, and sunflowers—but prices were off sharply. Corn production, for example, hit an all-time high of 737 million bushels but in September was selling at $2.25 a bushel 50 cents under 1980.

Mining. Reflecting the national drop in demand for steel, Minnesota's iron mines faced sharp cutbacks. In 1979 taconite production reached an all-time high when 16,000 workers produced 56.2 million T (51 million t). In 1980 it dropped 20%, made a brief comeback in early 1981, but dropped sharply in the last half of the year.

Unemployment. The state's overall unemployment rate held at 5.6%, which was still below the national average of 7.2%. But the spread between the state and national averages had dropped from 2% to 1.6%, giving cause for concern that the state's economy was becoming more sensitive to national fluctuations.

Personal Income. A sharp reversal in personal income added to the state's concern over the economy. For the year ending March 31, 1981, personal income grew only 8.1%, compared with 11.1% nationally. Wages and salaries grew 5.9%, compared with 9.7% for the nation.

Cutbacks. County government and welfare agencies, both public and nonprofit, scurried to deal with a drop of $200 million in federal funds for medicaid, food stamps, and Aid to Families with Dependent Children. State appropriations were substantially under requests, forcing widespread spending cuts.

Revenue Shortfalls. State tax revenues were off sharply, reflecting the economic downturn. The escalating money problem led to a continuing confrontation between Independent-Republican Gov. Albert H. Quie and the Democratic-Farmer-Labor-controlled legislature. In early November, Quie was preparing to convene the year's third special session of the legislature to find ways to make up an estimated $600 million revenue deficiency.

Sales Tax Increase. In May, the money problem appeared settled when the second special legislative session modified income tax indexing and increased the state sales tax from 4% to 5%. But the economic downturn sent revenues off during the summer and fall.

Strikes. In the face of the revenue shortage, public school teachers in more than a score of districts went on strike in October. Making widespread use of a new law permitting teachers to strike, the Minnesota Education Association orchestrated a statewide pattern of walkouts aimed at boosting salaries.

A 22-day strike by 14,000 state employees was settled in August with wage increases ranging from $100 to $184 per month, representing increases of 8.9% to 13.3%.

Refugees. Minneapolis and St. Paul became a major center for Southeast Asian refugees. New residents included 10,000 Hmong, 8,500 Vietnamese, 3,500 Cambodians, and 3,000 Laotians.

ARTHUR NAFTALIN
University of Minnesota

MINNESOTA • Information Highlights

Area: 84,402 sq mi (218 601 km^2).
Population (1980 census): 4,077,148.
Chief Cities (1980 census): St. Paul, the capital, 270,230; Minneapolis, 370,951; Duluth, 92,811; Bloomington, 81,831; Rochester, 57,855; Edina, 46,073; Brooklyn Park, 43,332; St. Louis Park, 42,931; St. Cloud, 42,-566; Minnetonka, 38,683.
Government (1981): *Chief Officers*—governor, Albert Quie (I-R); lt. gov. Lou Wangberg (I-R). *Legislature*—Senate, 67 members; House of Representatives, 134 members.
State Finances (fiscal year 1980): *Revenues,* $5,700,-000,000; *expenditures,* $5,418,000,000.
Personal Income (1980): $39,744,000,000; per capita, $9,724.
Labor Force (July 1981): *Nonagricultural wage and salary earners,* 1,753,700.

MISSISSIPPI

The 90-day regular session of the legislature ended April 4 with relatively few major enactments. Among them were an increase in maximum truck weight limits, an extension and expansion of the program diverting motor fuel sales tax revenues from the general fund to the state highway program, a three-year extension of the Department of Corrections, and a revamping of the state's justice courts in the wake of a Fifth U.S. Circuit Court of Appeals ruling that the system for handling civilian cases was unconstitutional.

Public kindergarten and compulsory education bills were defeated easily, despite their backing by Gov. William Winter. Also defeated was a "variable" gasoline tax measure.

Municipal Elections. Almost all of Mississippi's 293 municipalities held elections in June. While Democrats continued to dominate municipal offices across the state, 20 Republican mayors and more than 70 aldermen/councilmen/commissioners were elected or reelected. This represented a doubling of the number of municipal offices held by the GOP. In Jackson, Republicans did not recapture the mayor's position that they lost four years ago; but for the first time in more than 100 years, they won control of the city council. Black mayors were elected or reelected in 20 municipalities.

Congressional Election. In the July 7 runoff election to fill the Fourth Congressional District seat made vacant by Republican Jon Hinson's April resignation, Wayne Dowdy, the Democratic mayor of McComb, pulled votes from labor, blacks, and rural whites to win a narrow upset victory (50.4%) over Republican Liles Williams, Clinton businessman and front-runner in the first-round balloting two weeks earlier. The 12-county district, which contains the city of Jackson, had been represented by a Republican since 1973.

Budgetary Cutbacks. In the face of bleak revenue projections that pointed to a potential $78 million shortfall in state receipts by June 1982, Governor Winter acted on July 2 to impose tight budget controls on state agencies rather than to recommend a tax increase. Chief among his expenditure containment actions were a 50% cutback in the budget increases given to state agencies during the 1981 legislative session and a freeze until January 1982 on all capital improvements.

Congressional Redistricting. A special legislative session was called in August to redraw the lines of the state's five Congressional districts so as to reflect the almost 14% increase in Mississippi's population between 1970 and 1980. Despite considerable pressure to create a black-majority Delta district, lawmakers approved a redistricting plan that provided as little change as possible in existing jurisdictions.

Miscellaneous. State and local officials continued to oppose the possible storage of high-level nuclear waste within Mississippi salt domes. Construction of the Tennessee-Tombigbee Waterway continued to spark controversy and litigation.

The state of the economy, including the effect of federal expenditure cuts, continued to cause widespread concern.

DANA B. BRAMMER
Bureau of Governmental Research
University of Mississippi

MISSISSIPPI • Information Highlights

Area: 47,689 sq mi (123 515 km^2).
Population (1980 census): 2,520,638.
Chief Cities (1980 census): Jackson, the capital, 202,895; Biloxi, 49,311; Meridian, 46,577; Hattiesburg, 40,829; Greenville, 40,613; Gulfport, 39,676; Pascagoula, 29,318; Columbus, 27,383; Vicksburg, 25,434.
Government (1981): *Chief Officers*—governor, William F. Winter (D); lt. gov., Brad Dye (D). *Legislature*—Senate, 52 members; House of Representatives, 122 members.
State Finances (fiscal year 1980): *Revenues*, $2,885,000,000; *expenditures*, $2,691,000,000.
Personal Income (1980): $16,626,000,000; per capita, $6,580.
Labor Force (July 1981): *Nonagricultural wage and salary earners*, 817,100; *unemployed*, 83,700 (8.2% of total force).

U.S. Army Corps of Engineers

Construction of the Tennessee-Tombigbee Waterway, left, with the relocated Illinois Central Railroad in the background, is a concern to many Mississippians.

Hotel investigators survey the damage after two aerial walkways collapsed and fell into the lobby of the Hyatt Regency Hotel in Kansas City, MO, July 17. One hundred and thirteen persons were killed in the disaster.

UPI

MISSOURI

Finances. Declining tax revenues forced Republican Governor Christopher S. Bond to veto $20.6 million in appropriations and withhold $75 million in allocations to state agencies. Salaries of state employees were frozen and capital expenditures were deferred. Bond refused to talk about a tax increase, but other leaders argued that something had to be done if Missouri was to catch up with national norms. The state already ranked 50th among the states in spending and 47th in taxation. The only solution seemed to lie in an overhaul of the tax structure rather than in a simple sales or income tax hike.

The state was already committed to statewide reassessment, itself a thorny matter. All real estate is required by law to be assessed at one third its value; in practice residential property has been assessed in terms of market value, commercial property on the basis of acquisition minus depreciation, and farm property on productivity. Since the average home assessment has been less than 10% of market value, it is generally conceded that reassessment would sharply increase the total tax base. It is less clear that the process would significantly raise revenue because of a provision to reduce tax rates to a level that would produce no more return than before reassessment. Many observers feared the result would be a massive shift of the property tax burden from industry to homeowners. For owners of older homes this might constitute a tax increase of 30–40%.

Federal budget cuts, which resulted in a loss of money for jointly funded programs mostly in the area of welfare, added to the gloomy financial picture. The state eliminated free day-care centers for children of working mothers, free lunches for the aged, free legal advice for the elderly, and aid to dependent children for about one seventh of the recipients.

Redistricting. Following publication of the 1980 census report, Missouri politicians began the ordeal of redistricting. With the loss of 1 of the state's 10 seats in the U.S. House of Representatives, congressional districts had to be realigned. The question of who lives where and how the people of a given area normally vote made the matter a partisan battle in which the fate of individual officeholders hung in the balance. A plan to merge the first and third Congressional districts, which would pit two incumbent Democrats—William L. Clay, Missouri's only black congressman, and Richard A. Gephardt—against each other in 1982, brought sharp protests from blacks and from St. Louisans who argued that the greater metropolitan area deserved to retain its three representatives. The General Assembly adjourned without taking action on the matter.

Schools. St. Louis public schools survived the first year of court-ordered desegregation with no major violence, with improved scores on standardized tests, and with scattered signs of better racial attitudes. Faculty attendance improved and pupil attendance was no worse than in recent years. These encouraging indications came despite dislocations occasioned not only by busing students but also by massive transfers of teachers to comply with the order that each school's faculty conform to the racial balance of the district as a whole, and by the creation of 23 middle schools for grades six through eight.

Disasters. One of the worst disasters in recent Missouri history occurred on July 17 when two steel and concrete aerial walkways crashed into the lobby of the Hyatt Regency Hotel in Kansas City, killing 113 and injuring 186 persons. The hotel reopened in the autumn.

RUTH W. TOWNE
Northeast Missouri State University

MISSOURI • Information Highlights

Area: 69,697 sq mi (180 515 km^2)
Population (1980 census): 4,917,444.
Chief Cities (1980 census): Jefferson City, the capital, 33,619; St. Louis, 453,085; Kansas City, 448,159; Springfield, 133,116; Independence, 111,806; St. Joseph, 76,691; Columbia, 62,061; Florissant, 55,372; University City, 42,738; Joplin, 38,893.
Government (1981): *Chief Officers*—governor, Christopher S. Bond (R); lt. gov., Kenneth J. Rothman (D). *General Assembly*—Senate, 34 members; House of Representatives, 163 members.
State Finances (fiscal year 1980): *Revenues,* $4,258,000,000; *expenditures,* $3,996,000,000.
Personal Income (1980): $44,273,000,000; per capita, $8,982.
Labor Force (July 1981): *Nonagricultural wage and salary earners,* 1,964,000; *unemployed,* 163,000 (6.8% of total force).

UPI

A small dam collapsed near Helena, MT, in late May, causing heavy flooding and severe property damage.

MONTANA

The legislature cut income and auto taxes while imposing a new severance tax on oil production. It created a new Department of Commerce and committed the state to financing water use projects. Bills to override some voter initiatives and to amend the initiative process failed. A voter-initiated ban on nuclear wastes and a constitutional amendment to return to annual legislative sessions will be on the 1982 ballot. The legislature rejected proposals for optional taxes and revenue sharing as means of aiding local governments.

Two U.S. Supreme Court decisions bore special significance for the state. One ruling gave the state the right to regulate hunting and fishing on that part of the Big Horn River that flows within the Crow Indian reservation. The other upheld Montana's coal severance tax. Following the decision, opponents of the tax asked Congress to limit such taxes to 12.5%. The state legislature responded by hiring a Washington lobbyist to oppose this latest effort to alter the coal tax.

The Burlington Northern will eliminate about 500 mi (800 km) of branch lines and haul grain in large unit trains that can be loaded only by huge regional grain terminals. This will close most of the state's small grain handling facilities.

Oil, Gas, Mining. The state witnessed a boom in oil and gas exploration. By midyear completed wells were up 64% over 1980. Some of this was the result of Canadian firms bringing in capital and equipment. The two most active areas were the Williston Basin in the northeast portion of the state and the Cut Bank and Sweetgrass Arch east of Glacier Park. But drilling occurred in most other parts of the state as well. Environmental groups were concerned about permits for exploration in roadless wilderness and wildlife management areas.

After shocking the state by eliminating 1,500 jobs in 1980, the Anaconda Copper Company responded to sagging copper prices by eliminating 400 more jobs in Butte. In other parts of the state, new metal mines were in various stages of development. The extreme northwest corner of the state saw much exploration work, while in the area just north of Yellowstone Park, Anaconda and others were about to open new mines.

The Environment. Pesticides were in the news. Officials used compound 1080 in western Montana to kill ground squirrels. Although nontargeted species also died, the state Department of Agriculture will ask the federal Environmental Protection Agency for permission to conduct a similar program in 1982. Use of endrin, a chlorinated hydrocarbon, to kill army worms in eastern Montana resulted in high levels of residue in upland game birds and waterfowl. Because of the threat to human health, state game officials considered closing hunting in some areas and eliminating the waterfowl season. Officials invoked an emergency rule to ban the sale and use of endrin and began formation of a state advisory council on pesticides.

A wet spring ended the 1980 drought, but a hot dry summer reduced an expected bumper year for grains down to yields slightly above average.

Federal Cuts. As the year drew to a close, the legislature met in special session to assess and find ways to adjust to President Ronald Reagan's changes in federal aid programs.

RICHARD B. ROEDER
Montana State University

MONTANA • Information Highlights

Area: 147,046 sq mi (380 849 km^2).
Population (1980 census): 786,690.
Chief Cities (1980 census): Helena, the capital, 23,938; Billings, 66,798; Great Falls, 56,725; Butte-Silver Bow, 37,205; Missoula, 33,388; Bozeman, 21,645.
Government (1981): *Chief Officers*—governor, Ted Schwinden (D); lt. gov., George Turman (D). *Legislature*—Senate, 50 members; House of Representatives, 100 members.
State Finances (fiscal year 1980): *Revenues*, $1,153,-000,000; *expenditures*, $1,005,000,000.
Personal Income (1980): $6,732,000,000; per capita, $8,536.
Labor Force (July 1981): *Nonagricultural wage and salary earners*, 284,200; *unemployed*, 24,800 (6.1% of total force).

MOROCCO

The government of King Hassan II was shaken by the worst rioting in its 20-year history in June 1981 when, under pressure from the International Monetary Fund (IMF), price subsidies on basic foodstuffs were cut.

Hassan agreed to an Organization of African Unity (OAU) plan for a cease-fire and referendum to end the war in the Western Sahara, and after an implementation meeting in August, Morocco and the Polisario Front were scheduled to negotiate conditions for the cease-fire. Acceptance of the OAU peace plan provoked criticism from the opposition party, the Socialist Union of Popular Forces (USFP).

Sahara War. While the war between Morocco and the Algerian-backed Polisario Front continued on the ground, King Hassan accepted the OAU's proposals for a cease-fire and referendum for the disputed territory during the organization's June summit in Nairobi, Kenya. A meeting of the OAU committee on the Sahara in August, attended by Hassan, Algerian President Benjedid Chadli, and Polisario secretary-general Mohamed Abdelaziz, worked out a compromise plan to narrow the differences between the adversaries' positions on implementation of the cease-fire and referendum. Polisario and Moroccan officials were to hold direct negotiations through the OAU committee on the proposed cease-fire.

Following the June OAU summit, Hassan met with Mauritanian President Mohammed Khouna Ould Haidala and agreed to restore diplomatic relations, broken in March when Mauritania accused the Rabat leadership of masterminding an abortive coup. Relations between the two countries, once allies in the Sahara war, had deteriorated when Mauritania withdrew from the conflict in 1979 and signed a peace agreement with Polisario.

The United States agreed to sell Morocco M-60 tanks and reconnaissance planes early in the year, dropping the Carter administration's attempt to link the arms sales to Rabat's efforts toward negotiating a settlement to the war. In October, Rabat accused Libya and Algeria of backing a major Polisario attack on the key Moroccan garrison of Guelta Zemmur, in which two planes were shot down.

And in September, five leaders of the opposition USFP were arrested and sentenced to one-year prison terms for issuing a statement critical of Hassan's acceptance of a referendum to decide the Sahara's future. They had said the Moroccan populace should be consulted as well regarding any vote on the Sahara issue.

Economy. Morocco was granted a $1,000,000,000 credit from the IMF in 1981. The assistance was intended to ease Morocco's severe balance of payments difficulties resulting from the cost of the Sahara war, estimated at $1.5 million per day; a collapse in the price of phosphates, the country's leading currency earner; and a spiraling oil bill.

UPI

Moroccan youths display a photo of the crown prince, backing the king's Western Sahara policy.

In return for the credit, the IMF set conditions to be met by the government, including a cut in budget expenditures, particularly subsidies on basic foods. In May, the government announced that the price of five basic foods would be increased by an average of 30%, later halving the increase. But the two leading labor unions, the socialist Democratic Confederation of Labor (CDT) and the Moroccan Union of Labor (UMT), called a general strike and unrest turned to violence in Casablanca in June. Police were called in to quell the disturbances. According to government figures, more than 60 were killed and 100 injured in the rioting, looting, and burning touched off by the strike. But the leaders of the USFP and CDT said that more than 600 died in the violence. Some 2,000 people were arrested, including the top leadership of the USFP and CDT, and were standing trial late in 1981.

MARGARET A. NOVICKI, *"Africa Report"*

MOROCCO • Information Highlights

Official Name: Kingdom of Morocco.
Location: Northwest Africa.
Area: 180,602 sq mi (467 759 km^2).
Population (1981 est.): 21,800,000.
Chief Cities (1973 est.): Rabat, the capital, 385,000; Casablanca, 2,000,000; Marrakesh, 330,000; Fez, 322,000.
Government: *Head of state,* Hassan II, king (acceded 1961). *Head of government,* Maati Bouabid, prime minister (took office March 1979).
Monetary Unit: Dirham (5.58 dirhams equal U.S.$1, July 1981).
Manufactures (major products): Coal, electric power, phosphates, iron ore, lead, zinc.
Agriculture (major products): Barley, wheat, citrus fruit, sugar beets, grapes.

MOTION PICTURES

Despite the inroads made by the burgeoning home entertainment market, Americans flocked to the movies in large enough numbers during 1981 to send box-office receipts soaring and to temporarily ease the minds of industry leaders who had feared the worst. By October the Motion Picture Association of America was able to announce the most lucrative first eight months in movie history. Nearly $2,000,000,000 in tickets were sold, representing a 5.3% increase from 1980. A record-breaking summer was largely responsible; business from June through August leaped by 15.6%. The ever-mounting cost per ticket also played a role, but that figure increased by only 3.2%. A fall slump, however, stirred new anxieties.

A problem still confronting the industry was the concentration by viewers on a few select films. The blockbuster phenomenon continued. Released in the summer, *Raiders of the Lost Ark* and *Superman II* quickly grossed more than $100 million, which meant that the major companies, increasingly attuned to economic factors, could be expected to seek similar blockbusters. Filmmakers wanting to make special films for more limited audiences would have an ever more difficult time financing their projects, especially in light of current high interest rates.

Another development that eased concern about the overall well-being of the movie business was the settling of the 13-week screenwriters' strike and the heading off of a threatened directors' strike. The disputes did take some toll, particularly through delaying television production, but the disastrous results that had been anticipated did not materialize. The agreements constituted a further step toward meeting demands of creative artists for a share in the profits expected from the broadening market of pay television, cable, cassettes, and discs.

Reissues. By the end of the year there had been a virtual turnaround of the gloomy New Year's outlook fueled by the shattering *Heaven's Gate* fiasco. The abrupt failure of the multi-million-dollar film and its speedy withdrawal for reediting, brought resolve on the part of producers that henceforth they would clamp down on directors, often hitherto allowed carte blanche after initial successes, and keep a tighter rein on budgets. At United Artists, the distributor of *Heaven's Gate,* there not only were personnel changes, but the company was sold by Transamerica to Metro-Goldwyn-Mayer.

As for *Heaven's Gate,* the rerelease of a shortened version also failed, but refusing to give up, United Artists Classics, the subdivision which had taken over the distribution, announced plans to edit the film further and release a third version under another title, *The Johnson County Wars.* Director Michael Cimino would have no involvement in the patchwork, which was to end with the "good guys" winning. If it was any consolation, when the film was shown in France, it won admirers who argued that Americans had turned their backs on a minor masterpiece.

The French were in the position of having an undisputed major masterpiece of their own rediscovered after it had been abandoned for more than half a century. When Abel Gance's silent epic *Napoléon* opened in 1927, it was judged too unwieldy to be shown extensively. Gance, using an array of techniques far ahead of his time, predated Cinerama with his wide screen and triptych sequences. Film historian Kevin Brownlow dedicatedly restored the original, and producer Francis Ford Coppola was so impressed that he presented the film in a four-hour version at Radio City Music Hall. A new score was composed by Francis Coppola's father, Carmine, and played under the elder Coppola's baton by the American Symphony Orchestra. The extraordinary event had to be rescheduled to accommodate the crowds, and it was duplicated in London and Rome, as well as in numerous American cities. The end was nowhere in sight for the spectacular revival. Gance, 92, was too ill to attend any of the showings. He was reported in newspaper interviews to be gratified, but also embittered that the accolades had come too late in his life to affect his career. (Gance died on November 10.)

Eastern Europe. The rumblings in Poland and their implications for the rest of Eastern Europe had their counterpart in the cinema of that region. At both the Cannes International Film Festival and at the New York Film Festival the most astonishing piece of work was *Man of Iron* by Polish director Andrzej Wajda. Its predecessor, *Man of Marble,* was boldly political in its examination of past injustices under Polish communism, but *Man of Iron* was far more outspoken than any film in memory that had been made in a Communist country. It gave voice to the depth of dissatisfaction of shipyard workers and others, shedding light on the intensity of the labor upheaval. The fact that the film could be completed under government funding and then, apparently after considerable deliberation, be exported, raised expectations that Wajda's work could to some extent mark a turning point for free expression in his country.

From Hungary came *The Witness,* an attention-getting broad satire of the faking of trials in 1948 Hungary, as well as a collection of barbs at life under Communism. The film had been banned for ten years, but so many people had seen it in private viewings that it finally was permitted to surface. The film's discovery by critics from the West led to its being shown first at

(*continued on page 353*)

Seymour Krawitz & Co.

MOTION PICTURES—SPECIAL REPORT:

KATHARINE HEPBURN

As 1981 drew to a close, the drama and cinema sections of U.S. newspapers and magazines were dominated by a single name, Katharine Hepburn. Not only was Miss Hepburn appearing on Broadway in *The West Side Waltz,* but the film *On Golden Pond,* in which she stars with Henry and Jane Fonda, was being released nationally. In addition, the 50th anniversary of her debut in films was about to occur. Since, as *Time* magazine noted in its November 1981 cover story, "Hepburn triumphantly skirts sentimentality," it seems appropriate to ask why she has remained such a favorite. For in a moment of self-evaluation, Katharine Hepburn once said, "I'm a personality as well as an actress. Show me an actress who isn't a personality, and you'll show me a woman who isn't a star."

Certainly it is her individuality which initially catapulted Hepburn to stardom. Blessed with a singular beauty—superb cheekbones, a fine, athletic body, and a crown of auburn hair—and a metallic voice that was like no one else's on earth, she cut a striking and original figure in her early stage and screen appearances. From her very first performances, she had an aura of intelligence and aristocratic breeding, an independence of spirit that set her apart from her contemporaries. Forthright, often intimidatingly so, she was often abrasive, but beneath the brash exterior lurked a vulnerability that was as unexpected as it was appealing. For her admirers, Hepburn came to represent the modern American woman, determined to find her place in a man's world and yet struggling with private insecurities and deep personal needs.

It was a very definite personality, but one that was nonetheless flexible enough for Hepburn to play a wide variety of heroines, including a society playgirl (*The Philadelphia Story,* 1940, perhaps her most famous role); a Chinese peasant (*Dragon Seed,* 1944); queens (*Mary of Scotland,* 1936; *The Lion in Winter,* 1968); a hillbilly (*Spitfire,* 1934); and love-starved spinsters (*The African Queen,* 1951; *Summertime,* 1955). And she proved versatile in a wide range of performing styles, everything from giddy farce (*Bringing Up Baby,* 1938) to stark tragedy (*Long Day's Journey Into Night,* 1962). On stage she has run the gamut from musical comedy to Shaw, from Philip Barry to Shakespeare, and nearly always with successful results. Her awards have been many, including a trio of Academy "Oscars" as best actress (*Morning Glory, Guess Who's Coming to Dinner,* and *The Lion in Winter*), a record that is yet to be equaled.

Born in Hartford, CT, on Nov. 8, 1907, Hepburn's interest in acting awakened while she was a student at Bryn Mawr, where she participated in amateur theatricals. She made her professional debut in 1928, and after being hired for and fired from a number of important plays, she scored a personal triumph in an indifferent Broadway comedy, *The Warrior's Husband* (1932). Hollywood beckoned immediately, and that same year Hepburn made her film debut opposite John Barrymore in *A Bill of Divorcement.* Her performance brought her enormous acclaim, and during the next five years, she appeared in many widely admired movies, notably *Little Women* (1933) and *Alice Adams* (1935). Then in swift succession, she was cast in a series of dismal vehicles that caused critics to complain

"Woman of the Year" was the first of nine movies to feature Katharine Hepburn and Spencer Tracy.

The Museum of Modern Art Film Stills Archive

Miss Hepburn won her third Oscar for "The Lion in Winter," which also starred Peter O'Toole.

of her mannerisms and affectations, and that eventually earned her the label of "box-office poison."

In 1939 she returned in glory to the stage in *The Philadelphia Story,* and a year later reestablished herself as a major film star through her appearance in the film adaptation of Philip Barry's comedy. She was to have another smash hit with *Woman of the Year* (1942), the first of nine films she was to make with Spencer Tracy, who would become her close companion for the next 25 years. (Hepburn had married Ludlow Ogden Smith, a Philadelphia socialite, in 1928; they divorced in 1934.) The Tracy-Hepburn pictures, especially *Adam's Rib* (1949) and *Pat and Mike* (1952), were admired for the intimacy and polished interplay that the co-stars brought to their Punch and Judy romantic interludes.

After *Long Day's Journey Into Night,* in which Hepburn gives what is widely acknowledged as her most accomplished and moving screen performance, she was professionally inactive for several years, a period when Spencer Tracy was seriously ill. Following his death in 1967, just after the completion of *Guess Who's Coming to Dinner,* Hepburn picked up her professional pace drastically. The third phase of her career was opening, during which she would rise from star to the status of legend.

In the years since Tracy's death, Hepburn has appeared in six films of varying quality, but in each she has been very much the star attraction. She has not been nudged into character roles or reduced to cameo appearances in disaster movies, like so many actresses of her age. She branched out into television, giving critically praised performances in three productions, *The Glass Menagerie* (1973), *Love Among the Ruins* (1975), and *The Corn Is Green* (1979). Interspersed were stage engagements in *Coco* (1969) and *A Matter of Gravity* (1976), both of which did sell-out business on Broadway and on their cross-country tours, thanks to the powerful allure of the Hepburn magic.

Now as she is nearing her 50th anniversary as a film actress, Hepburn is as vital as ever, despite a series of illnesses incurred during the past few years. She has changed amazingly little—she is nearly as outspoken and astringent as ever, though today she seems more agreeable to talking to the press than she was during the earlier phases of her career when she was publicity shy and fiercely protective of her privacy.

In typical fashion, she accepts her enduring popularity with a touch of Yankee common sense. "I'm a legend because I've survived over a long period of time," she said recently. "I think people are beginning to think I'm not going to be around much longer, and what do you know—they think they'll miss me like an old monument, like the Flatiron Building."

GARY CAREY

Cannes and then in the United States. *The Witness* also had been financed by the state.

New Stars. Meryl Streep had already made her mark with *Kramer vs. Kramer,* but her popularity soared in 1981. By the time she appeared in *The French Lieutenant's Woman,* the adaptation of John Fowles' novel, she had been crowned in the media as the brightest woman star of her generation. Both her beauty and her talent were celebrated, and the promise of a glowing future was solidified when she was given one of the most coveted parts in recent movie history, the title role in the pending adaptation of the William Styron best-seller *Sophie's Choice.* Among other women given special attention were Jessica Lang, whose steamy performance in the remake of *The Postman Always Rings Twice* rescued her from the ignominy of the *King Kong* remake; Sissy Spacek and Mary Steenburgen, who won best-actress and best-supporting-actress Oscars, respectively, for their performances in *Coal Miner's Daughter* and *Melvin and Howard;* and Bo Derek, who suffered derision, but nevertheless enjoyed media coverage for her remake of *Tarzan, the Ape Man.*

William Hurt was a strong contender for the position of frontrunner among new male actors. In *Body Heat* and *Eyewitness,* he showed a strength and charisma that no newcomer had displayed in some time. His reputation as a first-rate stage actor also stood him in good stead. Robin Williams, until now known as Mork of television's *Mork and Mindy* series and for his stand-up comedy routines, took the plunge into serious acting, playing the lead in the film version of *The World According to Garp,* due for release in 1982. Timothy Hutton was awarded an Oscar for his supporting performance in *Ordinary People.*

Several established actors enhanced their reputations. Robert De Niro, who won an Oscar for *Raging Bull,* gave a restrained, exquisitely subtle performance as a priest in *True Confessions.* Robert Duvall, long recognized among his peers as one of America's finest film and stage actors, received plaudits for playing De Niro's brother, the cop in *True Confessions.* The extremely funny Dudley Moore attained new popularity through the success of *Arthur.*

Directors. Ingmar Bergman, regarded as one of the world's greatest filmmakers, announced in Stockholm that he would retire from filmmaking after completing two pending projects. He indicated that he would continue to direct plays. On the other hand, another international master, Japan's Akira Kurosawa, said he had many more films he wished to make. He visited the United States in October to open a complete retrospective of his work at Japan House in New York. Robert Altman, who has been lauded as

Alan Alda wrote, directed, and starred in "The Four Seasons," a summer hit.

Warner Brothers

United Artists

"Superman II," with a notable director, writer, and cast—headed by Margot Kidder and Christopher Reeve (above)—was a summer blockbuster.

English cinema, often considered in decline, scored royally with "The French Lieutenant's Woman." Screenwriter Harold Pinter triumphed in the task of adapting John Fowles' unique novel for the screen. The novel imposes the insights of a modern narrator on a story of Victorian life, and its adaptation had been considered for some years a cinematic problem. A solution was found through use of the technique of a film-within-a-film. In their duel roles, Meryl Streep and Jeremy Irons (left) turned in top-notch performances.

French director François Truffaut's "Le Dernier Metro" (The Last Metro) is set in Paris during the Nazi occupation of France. Ostensibly about a Parisian theater company's production of a play, it actually deals with a specific time in history and how the actors relate to each other and respond to the condition of being occupied. The film's stars, Catherine Deneuve and Gerard Depardieu, give splendid performances.

French Film Office

one of America's most original contemporary directors, found it necessary to sell his Lion's Gate production company, following the failure of his last three films. He announced that he was taking temporary leave from the cinema in order to work in the theater. Alan Alda achieved new stature directing his comedy *The Four Seasons.* Andrew Bergman, a comedy writer, used his own script as a springboard to direct his first film, *So Fine,* starring Ryan O'Neal. Mel Brooks ran into a hail of criticism regarding his bad taste in his *History of the World, Part I,* which, among other things, featured a musical number spoofing torture during the Spanish Inquisition and including a bevy of swimming nuns. Veteran Sidney Lumet's work gained new respect as a result of his impressive *Prince of the City,* about police corruption and informing; the Museum of Modern Art honored him with a retrospective. (The museum also scheduled retrospectives of works by Indian filmmaker Satyajit Ray, a survey of India's historical films as well as featured works by many contemporary Indian directors, and the largest reprise of French films ever held in the United States.)

Topicality. Hollywood usually lags behind major events, as it takes time to catch up with the headlines, and in some cases, to get nerve enough to deal with controversy. One past exception was *The China Syndrome,* released prophetically just before the Three Mile Island nuclear accident that thrust the film into the headlines. A less ominous 1981 exception was *The First Monday in October.* Based on a Broadway play, the film starred Jill Clayburgh as the first woman justice of the United States Supreme Court, with Walter Matthau as her antagonistic colleague. History had not yet been made at the time of the film's completion, but when President Ronald Reagan did in fact appoint the first woman justice, Paramount rushed the film into distribution. Unfortunately, the diversion was a weak affair that made events within the Court resemble an ordinary situation comedy.

Pressure Groups. Uneasiness overtook the film industry, although to a lesser extent than it did television, over the rise of pressure groups demanding purification of the arts. The vocal Moral Majority and their threat of a boycott against entertainment that stresses sex and violence evoked fears that a new era of blacklisting might be on the horizon. During the years of blacklisting, countless performers, writers, directors, and others were prevented from working because of their political views, real or imagined. The boycott did not materialize, but there were indications that television executives were trying to forestall it by self-censorship. Movies remained unfettered, but it was too early to tell what effects, if any, the pressures might have on them. Those adamant against any repetition of the sort of damage done to individuals and to the arts in general by the blacklisting of the late 1940s and the 1950s were committed to vigilance against and to organized opposition to threats of censorship and retaliatory measures. However, there were also those who felt that some voluntary restraint was wise. Both television and films have in many instances gone to excesses that have put off audiences, neither fanatical nor narrow-minded, but merely deeply concerned about the trend toward exploitation and the escalation of bad taste. In the final analysis, there is the public marketplace and the need to be responsive to consensus.

WILLIAM WOLF, *"New York Magazine"*

Harrison Ford plays a daring archaeologist, Indiana Jones, in the adventure "Raiders of the Lost Ark."

MOTION PICTURES | 1981

ABSENCE OF MALICE. Director, Sydney Pollack; screenplay by Kurt Luedtke. With Paul Newman, Sally Field.

. . . ALL THE MARBLES. Director, Robert Aldrich; screenplay by Mel Frohman. With Peter Falk, Burt Young.

AMERICAN POP. Director, Ralph Bakshi; screenplay by Ronni Kern. (animated)

ARTHUR. Written and directed by Steve Gordon. With Dudley Moore, Liza Minnelli, John Gielgud.

ATLANTIC CITY. Director, Louis Malle; screenplay by John Guare. With Burt Lancaster, Susan Sarandon.

BLOW OUT. Written and directed by Brian De Palma. With John Travolta, Nancy Allen.

BODY HEAT. Written and directed by Lawrence Kasdan. With William Hurt, Kathleen Turner, Richard Crenna.

CATTLE ANNIE AND LITTLE BRITCHES. Director, Lamont Johnson; screenplay by Davie Eyre and Robert Ward. With Burt Lancaster, Rod Steiger, Amanda Plummer.

CHARIOTS OF FIRE. Director, Hugh Hudson; screenplay by Colin Welland. With Ben Cross, Ian Charleson, John Gielgud.

CITY OF WOMEN. Director, Federico Fellini; screenplay by Mr. Fellini and Bernardino Zapponi with collaboration by Brunello Rondi. With Marcello Mastroianni.

CONTINENTAL DIVIDE. Director, Michael Apted; screenplay by Lawrence Kasdan. With John Belushi, Blair Brown.

CUTTER AND BONE. Director, Ivan Passer; screenplay by Jeffrey Alan Fiskin. With Jeff Bridges, John Heard.

ENDLESS LOVE. Director, Franco Zeffirelli; screenplay by Judith Rascoe. With Brooke Shields.

ESCAPE FROM NEW YORK. Director, John Carpenter; screenplay by Mr. Carpenter, Nick Castle. With Kurt Russell, Lee Van Cleef, Ernest Borgnine, Donald Pleasence, Isaac Hayes, Adrienne Barbeau.

EXCALIBUR. Director, John Boorman; screenplay by Mr. Boorman, Rospo Pallenberg. With Nigel Terry, Helen Mirren, Nicol Williamson, Cherie Lunghi.

EYEWITNESS. Director, Peter Yates; screenplay by Steve Tesich. With William Hurt, Sigourney Weaver, James Woods, Irene Worth, Christopher Plummer.

FIRST MONDAY IN OCTOBER. Director, Ronald Neame; screenplay by Jerome Lawrence and Robert E. Lee, from their play. With Walter Matthau, Jill Clayburgh.

FORT APACHE, THE BRONX. Director, Daniel Petrie; screenplay by Heywood Gould. With Paul Newman.

FOR YOUR EYES ONLY. Director, John Glen; screenplay by Richard Maibaum and Michael Wilson. With Roger Moore.

FOUR FRIENDS. Director, Arthur Penn; screenplay by Steve Tesich. With Craig Wasson, Jodi Thelen, Michael Huddleston, James Metzler.

THE FOUR SEASONS. Written and directed by Alan Alda. With Alan Alda, Carol Burnett, Len Cariou, Sandy Dennis, Rita Moreno, Jack Weston.

THE FRENCH LIEUTENANT'S WOMAN. Director, Karel Reisz; screenplay by Harold Pinter, based on the book by John Fowles. With Meryl Streep, Jeremy Irons.

GALLIPOLI. Director, Peter Weir; screenplay by David Williamson, from a story by Mr. Weir. With Mel Gibson, Mark Lee.

GHOST STORY. Director, John Irvin; screenplay by Lawrence D. Cohen from the novel by Peter Straub. With Fred Astaire, Melvyn Douglas, Douglas Fairbanks, Jr., John Houseman.

THE GREAT MUPPET CAPER. Director, Jim Henson; screenplay by Tom Patchett, Jay Tarses, Jerry Juhl, Jack Rose. With The Muppets, Diana Rigg, Charles Grodin.

HEAVEN'S GATE. Written and directed by Michael Cimino. With Kris Kristofferson, Isabelle Huppert.

HEAVY METAL. Director, Gerald Potterton; screenplay by Dan Goldbert and Len Blum, based on original art and stories by Richard Corben, Angus McKle, Dan O'Bannon, Thomas Warkentin, and Berni Wrightson.

HISTORY OF THE WORLD—PART I. Written and directed by Mel Brooks. With Mel Brooks, Dom DeLuise, Madeline Kahn, Harvey Korman, Cloris Leachman, Sid Caesar, Orson Welles, Bea Arthur, Henny Youngman.

LA CAGE AUX FOLLES II. Director, Edouard Molinaro; screenplay by Francis Veber, story by Mr. Veber, Jean Poiret, Marcello Danon. With Ugo Tognazzi, Michel Serrault.

LE DERNIER METRO (The Last Metro). Director, François Truffaut; screenplay by Mr. Truffaut and Suzanne Schiffman. With Catherine Deneuve, Gérard Depardieu.

MAN OF IRON. Director, Andrzej Wajda; screenplay by Aleksandr Scibor-Rylski. With Jerzy Radziwilowicz.

Dirck Halstead/Liaison

Burt Lancaster (right) stars in Louis Malle's romantic ghost story, "Atlantic City."

MOMMIE DEAREST. Director, Frank Perry; screenplay by Mr. Perry, Frank Yablans, Tracy Hotchner, Robert Getchell, based on the book by Christina Crawford. With Faye Dunaway, Diana Scarwid.

MODERN ROMANCE. Director, Albert Brooks; screenplay by Mr. Brooks and Monica Johnson. With Albert Brooks, Kathryn Harrold.

MOSCOW DOES NOT BELIEVE IN TEARS. Director, Vladimir Menshov; screenplay by Valentin Chiornykh. With Vera Alentova, Irina Muravyova.

MY DINNER WITH ANDRE. Director, Louis Malle; screenplay by Andre Gregory, Wally Shawn. With Andre Gregory, Wally Shawn.

ON GOLDEN POND. Director, Mark Rydell; screenplay by Ernest Thompson, based on his play. With Henry Fonda, Katharine Hepburn, Jane Fonda.

ONLY WHEN I LAUGH. Director, Glenn Jordan; screenplay by Neil Simon. With Marsha Mason, Kristy McNichol, James Coco, Joan Hackett.

OUTLAND. Written and directed by Peter Hyams. With Sean Connery, Peter Boyle, Frances Sternhagen.

PENNIES FROM HEAVEN. Director, Herbert Ross; screenplay by Dennis Potter. With Steve Martin, Bernadette Peters.

PIXOTE. Director, Hector Babenco; screenplay by Mr. Babenco and Jorge Duran. With Fernando Ramos da Silva.

THE POSTMAN ALWAYS RINGS TWICE. Director, Bob Rafelson; screenplay by David Mamet, based on the novel by James M. Cain. With Jack Nicholson, Jessica Lange.

PRIEST OF LOVE. Director, Christopher Miles; screenplay by Alan Plater. With Ian McKellen, Janet Suzman.

PRINCE OF THE CITY. Director, Sidney Lumet; screenplay by Mr. Lumet, Jay Presson Allen. With Treat Williams.

RAGGEDY MAN. Director, Jack Fisk; screenplay by William D. Wittliff. With Sissy Spacek, Sam Shepard.

RAGTIME. Director, Milos Forman; screenplay by Michael Weller. With James Cagney, Mary Steenburgen, Howard E. Rollins, Jr., Brad Dourif.

RAIDERS OF THE LOST ARK. Director, Steven Spielberg; screenplay by Lawrence Kasdan, story by George Lucas, Philip Kaufman. With Harrison Ford, Karen Allen.

REDS. Director, Warren Beatty; screenplay by Mr. Beatty, Trevor Griffiths. With Diane Keaton, Warren Beatty, Jack Nicholson.

RICH AND FAMOUS. Director, George Cukor; screenplay by Gerald Ayres. With Jacqueline Bisset, Candice Bergen.

S.O.B. Written and directed by Blake Edwards. With Julie Andrews, William Holden, Shelley Winters, Marisa Berenson, Larry Hagman, Loretta Swit, Robert Vaughn.

SO FINE. Written and directed by Andrew Bergman. With Ryan O'Neal, Jack Warden, Mariangela Melato.

STEVIE. Director, Robert Enders; screenplay by Hugh Whitemore, based on his play and the works of Stevie Smith. With Glenda Jackson.

STRIPES. Director, Ivan Reitman; screenplay by Len Blum, Dan Goldberg, Harold Ramis. With Bill Murray.

SUPERMAN II. Director, Richard Lester; screenplay by Mario Puzo, David Newman, Leslie Newman. With Christopher Reeve, Gene Hackman, Margot Kidder.

TALES FROM THE VIENNA WOODS. Director, Maximilian Schell; screenplay by Mr. Schell, Christopher Hampton, from a play by Odon von Horvath. With Birgit Doll.

TAPS. Director, Harold Becker; screenplay by Darryl Poniscan, Robert Mark Kamen. With George C. Scott, Timothy Hutton.

TARZAN, THE APE MAN. Director, John Derek; screenplay by Tom Rowe, Gary Goddard, based upon the characters created by Edgar Rice Burroughs. With Bo Derek, Richard Harris, Miles O'Keeffe, John Phillip Law.

THEY ALL LAUGHED. Written and directed by Peter Bogdanovich. With Ben Gazzara, John Ritter, Audrey Hepburn.

TRUE CONFESSIONS. Director, Ulu Grosbard; screenplay by John Gregory Dunne, Joan Didion, based on a novel by Mr. Dunne. With Robert De Niro, Robert Duvall.

VICTORY. Director, John Huston; screenplay by Evan Jones, Yabo Yablonsky. With Sylvester Stallone, Michael Caine, Pelé, Max von Sydow.

WHOSE LIFE IS IT ANYWAY? Director, John Badham; screenplay by Brian Clark, Reginald Rose, based on the play by Mr. Clark. With Richard Dreyfuss, John Cassavetes.

WOLFEN. Director, Michael Wadleigh; screenplay and screen story by Mr. Wadleigh, David Eyre, based on the novel by Whitley Strieber. With Albert Finney.

THE WOMEN NEXT DOOR (La Femme d'à Côté). Director, François Truffaut; screenplay by Mr. Truffaut, Suzanne Schiffman, Jean Aurel. With Gérard Depardieu, Fanny Ardant.

Michael Grecco/Picture Group

A free concert on the Boston Common in October was one of several programs celebrating the 100th birthday of the Boston Symphony Orchestra.

MUSIC

Classical

An outward sense of prosperity and calm belied the actual effect of the sluggish U.S. economy on the music world. In reality, the posture of the nation's performing institutions was more one of holding the line in the face of both the recession and President Ronald Reagan's reduction of federal funds for the National Endowment for the Arts. The mood was conservative, with performers and audiences in a period of assimilation rather than innovation. The search in music was for reassurance and confirmation rather than for change.

Symphony Orchestras. Symphony orchestras sustained the trend toward a more regular presentation of contemporary and American music, though the increase was slight. If there was no clear identification of the outstanding newer composers or new landmark works, institutional approaches, which might better assure such discovery and selection, became more obviously defined.

The Boston Symphony Orchestra reaffirmed its historic role as pioneer by awarding 12 commissions for new works to major composers in celebration of its 100th anniversary. One of these works was Peter Maxwell Davies' Symphony No. 2, which Seiji Ozawa introduced with conspicuous success in Boston concerts during February and on the orchestra's March tour in New York, San Francisco, and Los Angeles. The Boston Symphony's centennial celebration was observed with a tour to Japan and Europe (October 26–November 28) and by two gala birthday concerts (October 18 and 22). In addition, the commemoration included programming of famous American and world premieres which the orchestra had given in its illustrious past.

In September, the San Francisco Symphony tried the saturation or festival approach, featuring one composer, Sir Michael Tippett, with seven performances of three different programs of his works. (One was given by the Oakland Symphony.) The Los Angeles Philharmonic initiated a comprehensive new music project, first appointing William Kraft composer-in-residence. Kraft conducted two "Showcase of American Music" concerts. He formed and, in November, directed the 30-member Philharmonic New Music Group in its first concert. Michael Tilson Thomas conducted the Philharmonic in three programs of music by resident composers of Los Angeles. Music by Arnold

Schoenberg and Igor Stravinsky was performed on November 28 and December 13, and works by Ernst Křenek, Hanns Eisler, Lukas Foss, Ingolf Dahl, Morton Subotnick, and others were performed on December 5.

Most American orchestras brought out new pieces singly on regular concert programs. The major premieres included Roger Sessions' *Concerto for Orchestra* (Boston Symphony, October 23), Rhian Samuel's *Elegy Symphony* (St. Louis Symphony, October 1), Robert Starer's *Violin Concerto* (Boston Symphony, October 4), Peter Mennin's *Capricciosa: Sinfonia* (National Symphony, March 10), Morton Gould's *Burchfield Gallery* (Cleveland Orchestra, April 9), Ezra Laderman's Symphony No. 4 (Los Angeles Philharmonic, October 23), and Ned Rorem's *Double Concerto in 10 Movements for Cello and Orchestra* (Cincinnati Symphony, November 13).

The Chicago Symphony opened its 91st season in its newly renovated and acoustically improved Orchestra Hall; a new pipe organ was installed as well.

Almost without exception, American orchestras celebrated the centennial of Béla Bartók's birth (March 25, 1881), each playing at least two of his larger compositions. The Detroit Symphony, whose music director, Antal Dorati, turned 75 in April and was named Conductor Laureate in June, held a nine-day Bartók Festival (March 12–21).

Samuel Barber, whose 70th birthday was honored in 1980 by extensive performances of his compositions, died on January 23. (*See also* OBITUARIES.) Performance tributes in memorial were widespread.

New Music. The slender modern violin concerto repertory received a noteworthy addition in Boston at a concert of the Emmanuel Chamber Orchestra with the premiere on January 24 of the *Violin Concerto* by John Harbison (the 1980 Kennedy Center Friedheim Award winner and also recipient of a Boston Symphony centennial commission).

An ambitious week-long festival of contemporary music, which began on January 30th, was held by the Juilliard School of Music. The six concerts presented works by 22 composers, including Francis Thorne's *The Eternal Light.*

The freer styles in music of the avant-garde tended to decrease in influence and incidence. Popular offshoots of the movement, such as the works of Steve Reich and Philip Glass, continued to hold favor with younger audiences. The West Coast was the most active region in avant-garde activity, beginning in February with the New Sounds San Jose (CA) Festival and the festival jointly produced by the University of California, San Diego, and the California Institute for the Arts. The New Music America '81 festival held in San Francisco (June 7–13) made shallow waves, introducing no essentially new kinds of

The University of Michigan's May Festival included a tribute to Béla Bartók; the pianist is Gyorgy Sandor.

Bob Kalmbach

Joan Marcus/The National Symphony

Maksim Shostakovich, son of the renowned Russian composer Dmitri Shostakovich, conducts the National Symphony. Maksim and his son Dmitri defected from the USSR in April while on tour in Bavaria. They later were admitted to the United States as refugees.

music or procedures. As part of a John Cage Festival (September 1–October 3) held by Real Art Ways in Hartford, CT, there was an American premiere of Cage's 12-hour marathon work, *Empty Words.*

American interest in advanced European composers decreased, but the New York Philharmonic's U.S. premiere of Karlheinz Stockhausen's *Jubilee* on September 10, with Zubin Mehta conducting, was an exception.

Operas. There were fewer premieres than usual, and those given were generally traditional in approach and conservative in style. They included the double bill by Dominick Argento, *A Water Bird Talk* and *Miss Havisham's Wedding Night* (Minnesota Opera, May 1) and Carlisle Floyd's *Willie Stark,* based on Robert Penn Warren's novel, *All the King's Men* (Houston Grand Opera, April 24).

More venturesome operas performed were Conrad Susa's *Black River,* greatly expanded and rewritten from its 1975 version (Minnesota Opera, February 21), Philip Glass' *Satyagraha* (text in Sanskrit) given its American premiere in July at Artpark theater in Lewiston, NY, and the American premiere of Minoru Miki's *An Actor's Revenge,* about a kabuki actor in 18th century Edo (Tokyo) (Opera Theater of St. Louis, June 11).

The San Francisco Opera attracted national attention as it opened its new summer season with the American premiere of Aribert Reimann's *King Lear.* Highly theatrical and melodramatic effects in an unrelievedly dissonant score supported a production of forceful impact. In Kurt Herbert Adler's 28th and final season as general director, the San Francisco Opera presented the first American performance in 45 years of Dmitri Shostakovich's *Lady Macbeth of Mtsensk* in its original (1932) version, and in Russian. It made a stirring impression and revealed that its social protest and satire were directed at ongoing conditions in the Soviet Union, not simply at Tsarist Russia. This revelation clarified the political basis for the Stalin regime's historic denunciation of the work and its composer in 1936.

Observing the centenary of Modeste Mussorgsky's death, his *Khovanshchina* in Dmitri Shostakovich's orchestration was given its first American performance on March 1 by the Opera Orchestra of New York, with Eve Queler conducting. Gian Carlo Menotti's 70th birthday was honored by a new production of his opera *The Last Savage* at the fifth annual Spoleto Festival U.S.A. in Charleston, SC.

Bohuslav Martinu's opera *The Greek Passion,* given its American premiere by the Indiana University Opera Theater in April, was repeated later in the Metropolitan Opera House and became the first opera to be taped and used for cable television.

Ardis Krainik became the new general manager of the Chicago Lyric Opera, after the retirement on January 8 of Carol Fox, co-founder of the company in 1952. On July 21, Miss Fox died of a heart attack. (*See also* OBITUARIES.)

News Events: To honor the 90th anniversary of New York's Carnegie Hall, a special series of concerts were held there, including a Great American Orchestras series, with the Boston Symphony and Cleveland and Philadelphia orchestras performing their original Carnegie Hall debut programs, and the New York Philharmonic recreating the hall's opening program.

The convocation of the First National Congress on Women in Music, at New York University (March 26–29), demonstrated the heightened status of a new field already under study in regional conferences around the country.

Mozart's Symphony in F, K. 19a, composed in 1765 when he was nine years old and discovered in 1980, received its world premiere on May 17 in the Castle Herrenchiemsee, Bavaria. Its American premiere was given on July 8 by the Mostly Mozart Festival orchestra, Leonard Slatkin conducting, at the Kennedy Center, Washington, DC.

On April 12, the son and grandson of the late Dmitri Shostakovich, the Soviet Union's most celebrated composer, defected in Bavaria after performing there with the Soviet Radio Symphony. Admitted to the United States as refugees, Maksim, 42, conductor, and Dmitri, 19, pianist, announced their intention to seek U.S. citizenship. On May 30, Maksim Shostakovich conducted the National Symphony in its Memorial Day concert on the White House grounds. The 75th anniversary of Dmitri Shostakovich's birth, September 25, was observed with concerts that week by the National Symphony, with Mstislav Rostropovich, its music director and a Shostakovich family friend, as cello soloist, son Maksim as conductor, and grandson Dmitri as pianist.

The most extensive musical event in Europe, and perhaps in the world, took place in Leipzig, East Germany, in connection with the October 8 opening of the new Leipzig Gewandhaus (concert hall) and the 200th anniversary of that institution. On 20 programs between October 8 and December 4, the premieres of ten large-scale compositions were given, along with works by Mendelssohn, Schumann, Brahms, and others associated historically with the Gewandhaus.

Awards. Gregory Fulkerson, concertmaster of the Honolulu Symphony, won the Kennedy Center Rockefeller Competition for American music performance. His prize included $10,000, a $25,000 recording contract, and $35,000 for concert promotion. Nadja Salerno-Sonnenberg, 20, an American violinist of Italian birth, won the Walter W. Naumburg International Violin Competition.

André-Michel Schub, 28, of New York City, won the sixth Van Cliburn International Piano Competition, receiving a $12,000 prize, a recording contract, and two years of concert engagements. The Leventritt Foundation Gold Medal was awarded to pianist Cecile Licad, 19, of the Philippines.

ROBERT COMMANDAY
Music Critic, "San Francisco Chronicle"

Courtesy Education Department, Metropolitan Opera Guild/Curt Kaufman

One of the Metropolitan Opera season highlights was the production of "L'Enfant et les Sortilèges." The Maurice Ravel opera was part of a triple-bill production that included "Parade" and "Les Mamelles de Tirésias." It was designed by David Hockney, staged by John Dexter, and conducted by Manuel Rosenthal.

Dizzy Gillespie and his band entertain as the Newport Jazz Festival returns to Rhode Island for the first time since 1971. The festival attracted many jazz celebrities and a big crowd.

Daniel G. Dunn/Picture Group

Jazz

The jazz scene of 1981 produced no new trends or substantial changes that would seem likely to influence the music of the 1980s. The financial climate, the uncertainty of government grants and support for the arts, and unemployment all contributed to the lessening of live jazz-club activity, new record releases, and festival and jazz-clinic growth.

Festivals. Despite the rather bleak economic picture, the two most important 1981 festivals, the Newport Jazz Festival and the Kool Jazz Festival—New York, were very successful. The year saw a Newport Jazz Festival again held in Newport, RI. George Wein, the festival's impresario, had moved the original Newport festival from Newport to New York City in 1972, following the 1971 storming of the stage by a mob of gate-crashers. A changing economic and social climate contributed to the return of the festival to Newport. Established jazz names at the festival, including Dizzy Gillespie, Lionel Hampton, Art Blakey, Buddy Rich, Nancy Wilson, and Dexter Gordon, dominated the festival program.

The musical content of the ten-day Kool Jazz Festival—New York appealed to the varied jazz tastes of American audiences. The festival's broad musical spectrum included salutes to the Blakey legacy, Chicago-style jazz ("Goin' to Chicago"), jazz singing ("The Art of Jazz Singing"), women in jazz ("Wild Women Don't Have the Blues," "Women Blow Their Own Horns"); and programs featuring the Crusaders, Spyro Gyra, and Miles Davis, whose return to the stage was much heralded.

Jazz Recordings. For several years the decision by recording companies to record jazz has often been the result of the efforts of a few committed company executives, willing to record on the basis of a return of profits via slow and steady sales. In such a situation the departure of even a single individual from a company can critically influence that label's decision to record jazz. At present there are not a great number of jazz recordings being made. The economic slump experienced by recording companies in the late 1970s adversely affected jazz-recording operations.

Awards. Winners in the 29th International Jazz Critics Poll included: record of the year—Art Ensemble of Chicago, *Full Force;* reissue of the year—Lennie Tristano, *Requiem;* big band—Toshiko Akiyoshi/Lew Tabackin; jazz group—Art Ensemble of Chicago; alto sax—Phil Woods; tenor sax—Dexter Gordon; baritone sax—Pepper Adams; trumpet—Dizzy Gillespie; trombone—Jimmy Knepper; drums—Max Roach; electric bass—Jaco Pastorius; and the 53d person inducted into the *Down Beat* Hall of Fame, the late Bill Evans.

Other News. The year found the Mel Lewis Orchestra without Thad Jones and the Ornette Coleman jazz-rock group, Prime Time, performing in New York. Prime Time, which had not played in New York since 1978, was considered by some to be potentially the most influential jazz voice of the 1980s. Jazz great Lionel Hampton was honored by President Ronald Reagan with a formal dinner at the White House. Woody Herman and His Thundering Herd became the permanent house band of "Woody Herman's" club after its November opening on the plaza level of the New Orleans Hyatt Regency hotel.

Milestones in jazz education during 1981 included the establishment of a jazz master's degree program at Indiana University and the retirement of Leon Breedon as director of jazz activities at North Texas State University.

People who will be missed include William Alonzo "Cat" Anderson, Eddie Sauter, Mary Lou Williams, George "Pee Wee" Erwin, Shep Fields, and Dr. Herb Patnoe.

DOMINIC SPERA, *Indiana University*

Michael Putland/Retna

The Rolling Stones begin a 25-city American tour before a Philadelphia crowd of 90,000.

Popular

With minor variations, the pop music trends established in 1980 held steady in 1981. As the U.S. population grew older (the 1980 census revealed a median age of 30), maturing tastes became apparent. Rock remained the preferred music of the majority, but soft rock became dominant. Country music, largely MOR (middle of the road), followed rock in popularity, while a broad variety of pop music genres maintained devoted, if smaller, followings.

This new maturity was evident not only in the softening of rock, but also in a renaissance of such long-established performers as Frank Sinatra, Tony Bennett, Lena Horne, and Mel Tormé. The Big Band sound appealed to nostalgia, but was new to young listeners. Some rock stars experimented with unusual material, and their explorations exposed to other sounds a generation raised solely on rock. Carly Simon made an album of torch songs, containing Rodgers and Hart selections. Joe Jackson unearthed gems of Forties jazz for his New Wave fans, and Willie Nelson, the country outlaw, once put out a disc of pop standards.

Although heavy metal was still favored by the segment of the population aged 12–20, and although New Wave retained an active following, the hegemony of blander rock was symbolized by balladeer Christopher Cross' unprecedented five-award sweep of the 1980 Grammy awards, presented in February 1981.

Ascertaining the listening climate, radio stations abandoned the teen audience and sought to capture the prime 25–54 age group by adopting A/C (Adult Contemporary) or country formats. Even a revival of *Your Hit Parade,* a program of the 1940s, gained a new audience.

As rock artists lost the radio exposure once essential to sell their records and faced an economy that made concert tours unprofitable, especially for new acts, they turned to the video media. MTV, a pioneering 24-hour, nationally broadcast stereo music cable-TV channel, became the visual equivalent of AOR (Album Oriented Radio), playing videocassettes instead of records. Many local cable channels featured musical acts that fell outside mass commercial taste.

Established commercial rock acts continued to sell, but a new trend developed; it became common for a supergroup member to take a solo flight without departing from the group, as seen in albums released by Stevie Nicks of Fleetwood Mac, Pete Townshend of the Who, Deborah Harry of Blondie, and Michael Jackson of the Jacksons. Pop artists became more commercially

Gary Gershoff/Retna

Kim Carnes, a new star at the age of 34, had the summer's top hit, "Bette Davis Eyes."

Sorce/Retna

REO Speedwagon dominated the charts with the album "Hi Infidelity" and the single "Keep on Loving You."

active and were highly visible in ads for products.

It was also the year of the "slugger." Many artists who had hovered in the shadows broke through to stardom. After six albums, husky-voiced Kim Carnes topped the charts with *Bette Davis Eyes* and joined Pat Benatar as one of the hot new female rock singers. REO Speedwagon's success after years of obscurity was aided by the new visual media. MTV presented REO in concert, an event that attracted 25 million viewers.

However, the largest single-act live concert in U.S. history occurred when 500,000 people saw Simon and Garfunkel reunited in New York after an 11-year separation. Other long-lost pop performers returned to the music scene with great success, among them the Moody Blues, Gary U.S. Bonds, and Don McLean. Bill Haley, who helped start it all, passed away quietly.

In jazz, Miles Davis broke a seven-year silence with an appearance at the Kool (formerly Newport) Jazz Festival. Jazz vocalist Al Jarreau managed to win a substantial pop audience. A new hybrid, punk jazz, attracted critical notice.

Several types of music had substantial audiences but could not "cross over"—gain the cachet of mass commercial appeal. Rhythm and Blues (R&B) expanded into the vacuum left by disco's demise, but it failed to gain the same wide acceptance. Kurtis Blow popularized an offshoot called rapping, a kind of jive-talking to music, but it took Blondie's song *Rapture* to put the form on the charts.

A further indication of maturing tastes was a boom in Broadway musicals. Of the 26 shows on the Great White Way, 16 were musicals. Despite exorbitant ticket prices, attendance was up 15% over record-breaking 1980. As many as 28 new musicals were projected for the 1981–82 season, including two from the modern majordomos of the musical, Stephen Sondheim (*Merrily We Roll Along*) and Weber and Rice (*Cats,* already a hit in London). John Williams remained the accepted master of the film score, but the title duet of the film *Endless Love* by Diana Ross and Lionel Richie was the year's chart topper.

The international scope of the pop music community was enlarged by worldwide satellite broadcasts. The World Music Awards at MUSEXPO, a music business trade fair, were broadcast live to 40 countries. The influx of foreign performers to the United States continued to grow. U.S. exchange with England was, as always, the heaviest, although such Australian groups as AC/DC and Air Supply made inroads in the American pop market. From Britain came the New Romanticism, a flamboyant pop style that involved more costume than innovative sound. Adam and the Ants became an enormous cult favorite, although their pirate garb, 19th-century costumes, and garish makeup was a style created by Steve Strange. The Village People adopted the New Romantic look in an abortive effort to save a career that had died with disco.

The year 1981 also marked the 150th anniversary of the federal copyright covering music. Disputes over copyright protection for the new video media, which had caused massive strikes by musicians and writers, were being gradually settled with the aid of the performance protection agencies ASCAP, BMI, and SESAC.

PAULETTE WEISS, *"Stereo Review"*

COUNTRY MUSIC

Country music, a genre of American popular music that developed in the rural southeastern United States in the late 19th and early 20th centuries, has achieved unprecedented popularity in the 1970s and early 1980s.

In 1961 there were 81 radio stations programming country music full time in the United States; by 1980 that number had grown to 1,534. Country music was featured on television throughout the 1960s and 1970s. Such films as the Loretta Lynn biography *Coal Miner's Daughter,* Willie Nelson's *Honeysuckle Rose,* and *Urban Cowboy* introduced American audiences to large doses of country music. In addition, the 1970s witnessed the emergence of major new country entertainers who gave definition to contemporary country music. Ronnie Milsap, Crystal Gayle, and Kenny Rogers emerged from the Nashville sound tradition developed during the 1960s. Their performances contain many musical elements drawn from popular music, and their recordings are played on both country- and pop-music radio stations. These performers, who combine pop and country elements in their recordings, are an important reason for the contemporary acceptance of country music.

Of equal importance are the singers who perform in a pure country style based on the honky-tonk or bluegrass music of an earlier era. Emmylou Harris arrived in the 1970s and has achieved success performing songs in styles drawn from the early days of country music. Willie Nelson's work evokes the honky-tonk singing of the early 1950s. Waylon Jennings and Merle Haggard also sing in styles little influenced by pop music.

History. Country music has had an important impact on popular music throughout its history. Though previously associated with rural white culture, country music combines elements of several musical traditions, including Anglo-American folk music, 19th-century popular music, and the blues of rural blacks. These elements were found in combination by the record-company pioneers who first discovered the commercial value of Southern white music. The fiddle solo "Sallie Goodin'" by "Eck" Robertson, recorded in July 1922, is considered to be the first country recording.

From the 1920s forward, country music has evolved as a commercial-music form. Regional and cultural performing styles have influenced one another, and each distinct sub-style has itself changed through time. Change in the technology of recording, the development of radio and television, and innovations in the business of selling records also have altered the sound of country music. These forces of change produced distinctive sub-styles of country music.

Photos David Redfern/Retna

Loretta Lynn and Merle Haggard are major stars on the 1980s country-music scene.

Shelly Katz/Black Star

A ride on a mechanical bull is a side-attraction at many country and western nightclubs.

Western swing developed in the Southwest in the mid-1930s. It combined the repertory and instrumentation of country music with those of big-band jazz. Western-swing bands (for example, Bob Wills and his Texas Playboys) featured fiddle and guitars, but also included brass sections, reed sections, and drums.

Bluegrass music is a sophisticated form of string-band music that developed just after World War II. Instruments are generally not electronically amplified, and include fiddle, five-string banjo, mandolin, guitar, and string bass. Bluegrass vocals are high-pitched, and instrumental selections are fast-paced. Bill Monroe and Earl Scruggs are major artists associated with the development of bluegrass.

Honky-tonk music is named for the working-class nightclubs in which the style developed in the late 1940s and early 1950s. Honky-tonk music emphasized singing and deemphasized instrumental selections. Songs were frequently about real-life situations of love and work, and sometimes told about the suffering that followed immoral behavior.

Rockabilly, which emerged in the mid-1950s, is a combination of country music and the blues of rural blacks. Rockabilly carried the repertory and style of the blues to a large white audience, and paved the way for the commercial success enjoyed by rock 'n roll. Elvis Presley, Carl Perkins, and Jerry Lee Lewis were important rockabilly performers.

The *Nashville-sound* recording style was developed in Nashville in the late 1950s and lasted through the 1960s. The style combined country songs with violin sections, background vocal groups, and other pop-music conventions. Such singers as Jim Reeves, Eddy Arnold, and Patsy Cline performed in this pop/country style, and their recordings frequently "crossed over" from a country to a pop music market.

Country songs use realistic language and present real-life situations in a direct manner. Early country songs frequently told stories of events. Many country performances were of religious songs or hymns, and even secular selections frequently presented a moral or lesson based on the strict Protestant doctrine of Southern mountain people. Since World War II country songs have come to narrate situations of concern to urban adults, and fewer religious songs are performed. However, the view that evil is real and that sin will be punished remains an important moral basis for country songs.

Country music's recent success has been achieved both by accommodation with popular music and through the preservation of historical country styles. The median age of the U.S. population is increasing, and many adult listeners have come to prefer the mature themes, simple language, and uncluttered instrumentation of country music.

WILLIAM IVEY

NEBRASKA

Excellent crops, the legislature, and controversies gained attention in 1981.

Agriculture. Drought plagued Nebraska farmers from the fall of 1980 to midsummer 1981 when bountiful rains came and continued into the fall. Wheat production was 103.7 million bushels, somewhat less than in 1980 but more than in 1979. Corn production (772.8 million bushels) was the second largest on record and both grain sorghum (166.1 million bushels) and soybeans (81.9 million bushels) posted record yields. Production costs and land prices for both farmers and stockmen continued to rise as prices of grain and livestock declined.

Legislature and State Government. The legislature completed congressional and legislative redistricting, gave greater protection to farmers with grain in commercial storage, and made judges responsible for releasing those acquitted of violent crimes by reason of insanity. Likewise, it enacted certain government reorganization suggestions of Gov. Charles Thone, including extending the governor's responsibility over the Department of Health. The legislature also made permanent Omaha's controversial special half-cent sales tax, increased liquor and tobacco taxes (part of the proceeds are to be used to combat diseases caused by smoking and drinking), approved initial funds for a veterinary college, and passed a controversial banking act. Tax lids on the Omaha and Nebraska City school districts were removed and a new formula was provided to make possible distribution of $70 million in school funds. The formula replaced one included in the 1980 state aid to schools act, later declared unconstitutional. Further litigation was expected. Most notably, three laws on the vital subject of water policy were passed. One sets the policy for transferring underground water for industrial purposes; another provides for control of water pollution from nitrates and other chemicals; and a third deals with transfer of surface water from one river basin to another.

Governor Thone called a surprise special session of the legislature which, in early November, voted to cut the approved state budget by $24 million to prevent increased taxes.

NEBRASKA • Information Highlights

Area: 77,355 sq mi (200 349 km²).
Population (1980 census): 1,570,006.
Chief Cities (1980 census): Lincoln, the capital, 171,932; Omaha, 311,681; Grand Island, 33,180; North Platte, 24,479; Fremont, 23,979; Hastings, 23,045; Bellevue, 21,813; Kearney, 21,158; Norfolk, 19,449; Columbus, 17,328.
Government (1981): *Chief Officers*—governor, Charles Thone (R); lt. gov., Roland A. Luedtke (R). *Legislature* (unicameral)—49 members (nonpartisan).
State Finances (fiscal year 1980): *Revenues,* $1,506,000,000; *expenditures,* $1,392,000,000.
Personal Income (1980): $14,738,000,000; per capita, $9,365.
Labor Force (July 1981): *Nonagricultural wage and salary earners,* 629,300; *unemployed,* 30,600 (3.8% of total force).

Miscellaneous. Various issues aroused considerable interest in the state in 1981. In a very close election, Mike Boyle defeated incubment Al Veys for mayor of Omaha. Issues concerning the separation of church and state appeared when a federal judge held that the legislature may not pay a chaplain and when a Baptist minister, who operated a private "Christian" school in his church building, challenged state education laws. The former matter was resolved by the chaplain's offer to serve as an unpaid coordinator who would arrange with various clergymen to lead daily prayer in the legislature. In the school controversy a state court ordered the school to remain closed because its teachers were uncertified. It opened and after considerable maneuvering and publicity the issue remained unresolved.

Concern about water resources was not limited to the state legislature. Rapid expansion of center-pivot irrigation into the Sand Hills disturbed many. Likewise, the possibility that South Dakota might sell large amounts of Missouri River water for use in a coal slurry line concerned Nebraskans.

ORVILLE H. ZABEL, *Creighton University*

NETHERLANDS

Worsening economic difficulties and uncertainty about foreign and defense policies dominated public life in the Netherlands during 1981, giving rise to a tense and confused political situation.

Economy. A small country extremely dependent on exports of industrial and agricultural products, the Netherlands in 1981 found its foreign sales impeded by the high value of the guilder. This was caused in part by the expanding sale abroad of natural gas from the great field in the northern province of Groningen, and in part by the linkage of the guilder to the West German mark. The linkage of the Dutch monetary system to that of West Germany, the country's largest trading partner, was vividly illustrated in October, when the two currencies were simultaneously revalued upward by 8½% and others in Europe were revalued downward.

The competitive position of Dutch industry was also made more difficult by a high wage scale and the high cost of the welfare system, among the most generous in the world. Furthermore, a steady increase in unemployment—reaching 423,000 in September, the highest level since the depression of the 1930s—was a drain on the treasury at the very time that the business downturn sharply reduced tax revenues.

The nation was deeply divided on national economic policy. Economic conservatives, represented politically by the Liberal party (VVD), favored reduction of both wages and welfare benefits in the hope of spurring industrial investment. The Labor party (PvdA) favored the maintaining of income levels for the lowest-paid

UPI

Dutch Prime Minister Andreas van Agt (right) conferred with U.S. Vice-President George Bush at the White House, March 31. Bush was standing in for President Ronald Reagan, who was hospitalized after an assassination attempt the day before.

workers and welfare recipients; it also looked to the state rather than to private capital to revitalize industry and provide new jobs. The two principal center parties, the Christian Democrats (CDA) and the progressive Democrats-1966 (D'66—named for the year the party was founded), adopted intermediate positions in the spring election campaign for the Second (lower) Chamber of parliament.

Politics. The political situation was further complicated by a bitter dispute over the role of the Netherlands in the North Atlantic Treaty Organization (NATO). A vigorous antinuclear movement opposed the government's agreement to deploy U.S. cruise missiles in the country, favoring unilateral nuclear disarmament. Influential in both Catholic and Protestant church groups, the movement gained broad support in the Labor party for limitation of the Dutch commitment to NATO.

The government of Prime Minister Andreas van Agt, resting on a coalition of his CDA, the Liberals, and the D'66, followed a moderately conservative course. This was reflected in the budget submitted to the States General (parliament) in mid-September. At that time, the new coalition government had only just been formed, some three and a half months after the national election of May 26. The election had increased the strength of the political center at the expense of both the right and left. The Liberals lost two seats in the 150-member Second Chamber, dropping to 26. The Labor party fell from 53 to 44. Prime Minister van Agt's CDA, an alliance of Catholics and Protestants, held its own, losing only a single seat (from 49 to 48). The D'66 showed the greatest gain, increasing from 8 to 17 seats.

The van Agt ministry resigned after the election but remained in office until the conclusion of lengthy and mistrustful negotiations for the center-left coalition. Not until the issue of nuclear arms was set aside for later decision was it possible for van Agt to form a ministry, with Labor party leader Joop den Uyl as vice-premier and minister of social affairs, and D'66 leader Jan Terlouw as vice-premier and minister of economic affairs.

The new government had been in office only four weeks when it submitted its resignation to Queen Beatrix on October 16. The immediate issue was den Uyl's demand for a more extensive job program than van Agt was willing to concede. Rather than attempt to form a coalition with the Liberals and right splinter parties, van Agt accepted a compromise, and the resignation of the government was withdrawn on November 5. With the question of armament policy still unresolved, the government faced uncertainty as to how long it could stay in office, even though there was no obvious coalition ready to take over and no indication that a new election would yield any different distribution of seats in the Second Chamber.

HERBERT H. ROWEN
Department of History, Rutgers University

NETHERLANDS • Information Highlights

Official Name: Kingdom of the Netherlands.
Location: Northwestern Europe.
Area: 13,054 sq mi (33 810 km^2).
Population (1981 est.): 14,200,000.
Chief Cities (Jan. 1980 est.): Amsterdam, the capital, 716,919; Rotterdam, 579,194; The Hague, the seat of government, 456,886.
Government: *Head of state,* Beatrix, queen (acceded May 1980). *Head of government,* Andreas van Agt, prime minister (took office Dec. 1977). *Legislature*—States General: First Chamber and Second Chamber.
Monetary Unit: Guilder (2.44 guilders equal U.S.$1, Dec. 1981).
Manufactures (major products): Metals, textiles, chemicals, electronic equipment.
Agriculture (major products): Sugar beets, wheat, barley, fruits, potatoes, oats, flax, bulbs, flowers, meat and dairy products.

NEVADA

Property tax relief and plans for the MX missile were dominant news items in Nevada in 1981. The gambling industry continued to sputter following sensational growth in the 1970s.

Legislative Session. Although the 1979 legislature enacted a large tax-cut package, including reduction of the property tax and the removal of the sales tax from food, skyrocketing housing valuations, especially in the Reno area, brought pressure for more relief. Gov. Robert List proposed a massive tax shift from the property tax to the sales tax. Despite resistance from some Clark County (including Las Vegas) legislators, a bill was passed reducing the property tax an average of 50% and increasing the total sales tax from 3.5 to 5.75%. A two-stage six-cents-per-gallon increase in the motor vehicle fuel tax also was approved for road repair.

The 1980 U.S. census disclosed that the state's population increased by 63.5% in the 1970s. Consequently, the state legislature increased the size of its two houses, with the addition of two Assembly seats and one Senate seat going to Clark County, which continued to grow at a faster rate than the remainder of the state. After more than 100 years with one U.S. congressman, the state received a second House seat. The threat of a veto by Governor List prevented the passage of a redistricting bill that would have placed half the population of Clark and Washoe counties in each of the two districts. The List-approved plan places most of Clark County in one district, with the remainder of the state and 60,000 persons from Clark County making up the other district.

The legislature passed a stringent state fire code for high-rise buildings in the wake of the disastrous fire at the MGM Grand Hotel in Las Vegas in November 1980. In other legislative action, the state's drunken driving law was strengthened, a six-member watchdog agency was created to defend the public against unfair utility rate increases, and state employees received an average 14% salary increase.

MX Missile. At the start of the year, most political leaders were resigned to the plan backed by the Carter administration for the placement of a configuration of MX missile sites in the desert of eastern and southern Nevada. However, Governor List, who had originally supported the plan, joined with Sen. Paul Laxalt and Rep. Jim Santini in a strong effort against the proposal. Most Nevadans indicated opposition to the plan. The general feeling was that the close friendship between Laxalt and President Ronald Reagan paid a dividend to the state when the latter announced the decision in early October not to base the missiles in Nevada.

Economy. Gambling and sales taxes, which account for the bulk of the state's general fund revenues, increased by 9 and 10%, respectively, for the 1980–81 fiscal year. Although the increases were disappointing and below inflation levels, less-than-expected gambling revenues could be partially explained by the closings for most of the year of the MGM Grand Hotel in Las Vegas and of Harvey's at Lake Tahoe, scene of a bombing. Spurred by the increase in value of precious metals, mining production in the rural counties continued to rise. The unemployment rate for the state reached a high of 7% in February and a low of 6.5% in May.

DON W. DRIGGS
University of Nevada, Reno

NEVADA • Information Highlights

Area: 110,561 sq mi (286 353 km^2).
Population (1980 census): 799,184.
Chief Cities (1980 census): Carson City, the capital, 32,022; Las Vegas, 164,674; Reno, 100,756; North Las Vegas, 42,739; Sparks, 40,780; Henderson, 24,363; Boulder City, 9,590; Elko, 8,758.
Government (1981): *Chief Officers*—governor, Robert List (R); lt. gov., Myron E. Leavitt (D). *Legislature*—Senate, 20 members; Assembly, 40 members.
State Finances (fiscal year 1980): *Revenues,* $1,221,000,000; *expenditures,* $1,098,000,000.
Personal Income (1980): $8,597,000,000; per capita, $10,727.
Labor Force (July 1981): *Nonagricultural wage and salary earners,* 418,300; *unemployed,* 26,800 (6.7% of total force).

NEW BRUNSWICK

A federal royal commission urged the breakup of the Irving newspaper empire. A partial collapse of law and order accompanied police strikes in two provincial centers.

New Brunswick, like the other provinces and territories of Canada, was concerned with developments regarding a new national constitution. (*See also* CANADA.)

Newspapers. A federal commission of inquiry recommended in August that the Irving interests, which control New Brunswick's daily press, divest themselves of either their two Moncton newspapers or their two Saint John papers. The commission, headed by Tom Kent of Dalhousie University, said that if the Irving family chose to keep the Saint John papers they should sell their television and radio stations in that city, New Brunswick's largest.

John Irving owns the Moncton *Times,* Monc-

NEW BRUNSWICK • Information Highlights

Area: 28,354 sq mi (73 437 km^2).
Population (April 1981 est.): 709,600.
Chief Cities (1976 census): Fredericton, the capital, 45,248; St. John, 85,956; Moncton, 55,934.
Government (1981): *Chief Officers*—lt. gov., Hedard Robichaud; premier, Richard B. Hatfield (Progressive Conservative). *Legislature*—Legislative Assembly, 58 members.
Education (1981–82 est.): *Enrollment*—elementary and secondary, 151,700 pupils; postsecondary, 13,520 students.
Public Finances (1980–81 est.): *Revenues,* $1,561,024,000; *expenditures,* $1,506,700,000.
Personal Income (average weekly salary, April 1981): $307.81.
Unemployment Rate (June 1981, seasonally adjusted): 11.4%.
(All monetary figures are in Canadian dollars.)

ton *Transcript,* and Fredericton *Gleaner.* His brothers James and Arthur own the *Telegraph Journal* and *Times-Globe* in Saint John. (*See also* PUBLISHING.)

Strikes. A police strike in late May brought turmoil to Saint John. An evening riot broke out within hours after the city's 190 policemen quit their jobs in a contract dispute. Store windows were smashed, shops looted, and park benches overturned. The strike was settled 27 hours after it began. A similar walkout by police at Sackville resulted in three nights of public rowdyism in August.

Case Dropped. The case of Francis Atkinson, a Fredericton lawyer whose trial broke open a long-simmering scandal in New Brunswick politics, was officially closed by Justice Minister Rodman Logan. The minister announced in March that outstanding charges would be dropped. Atkinson had been fined $10,000 for corruption in the payment of money to a civil servant for inside information on government business, and faced nine counts of influence peddling as well. Logan said, however, that the "principles of justice" had been served and there would be no point in proceeding with the influence charges.

CBC Under Attack. Dissatisfaction with the CBC's television service in New Brunswick surfaced in the provincial legislature in July. Premier Richard Hatfield led a vigorous attack against the "negligent attitude" of CBC management. Supported by the Liberal opposition, he declared the legislature "unanimous in its condemnation" of the network's performance in New Brunswick.

Industrial. Mitel Corp., a high-technology firm based in Kanata, Ont., was building two plants in Buctouche at a cost of $48 million. The project, announced in midsummer, would provide residents of southeastern New Brunswick with 1,000 new jobs.

JOHN BEST
Canada World News

NEWFOUNDLAND

The issue of the federal constitution and provincial jurisdiction continued to dominate public life in Newfoundland during 1981. From the beginning, the Progressive Conservative government of Premier Brian Peckford had sought three major provisions for Newfoundland—the acknowledgement of provincial jurisdiction over offshore oil and gas; an ending of Canada's exclusive jurisdiction over commercial fisheries; and changes that would permit the export of Newfoundland hydroelectric power through the province of Quebec to markets in the United States. In October 1980, however, federal Prime Minister Pierre Elliott Trudeau announced that the various efforts at compromise had failed and that he was prepared to present a constitution to Great Britain without the unanimous consent of the provinces. Newfoundland, together with Manitoba and Quebec and backed by four other provinces, took the matter to court. On March 31, 1981, the Newfoundland Court of Appeal ruled unanimously that the federal government was acting unconstitutionally. The matter was then placed before the Supreme Court of Canada, which held in late September that the government's patriation plan was constitutional but that it "offends the federal principle" because of the lack of overall provincial consent. Throughout the year, Premier Peckford and the Newfoundland legislature debated the various jurisdictional issues among themselves, with leaders of other provinces, and with the federal government. Finally in November, with Peckford playing the role of peacemaker, Ottawa and the provinces agreed on a new constitution. (SEE CANADA.)

Politics and the Legislature. On April 10 a by-election was held to fill the assembly seat vacated by former Liberal Party leader Don Jamieson, who resigned in October 1980. Liberal Wilson Callan won the Bellevue riding, leaving the 52-seat provincial legislature with 33 Conservatives and 19 Liberals.

The throne speech opening the third session of the province's 38th legislature on February 25 had dealt heavily with the question of patriation. The constitution and related issues—such as offshore fishing and mining rights and hydroelectric exports—took up much of the assembly's time throughout the session.

Budget and the Economy. The fiscal 1982 budget tabled by the provincial government called for a total expenditure of $1,700,000,000, an increase of $200,000,000 over the previous year. Taxes would be raised for tobacco, alcohol, and gasoline and diesel fuel.

In late April, the Conference Board of Canada forecast improved economic growth throughout the country and especially "noteworthy accelerations" in Newfoundland. It predicted that the province's overall production would increase by 5% for 1981, after a decline of 3.8% the previous year.

SUSAN MCCORQUODALE
Memorial University, Newfoundland

NEWFOUNDLAND • Information Highlights

Area: 156,185 sq mi (404 520 km^2).
Population (April 1981 est.): 584,500.
Chief Cities (1976 census): St. John's, the capital, 86,576; Corner Brook, 25,198.
Government (1981): *Chief Officers*—lt. gov., Anthony J. Paddon; premier, A. Brian Peckford (Progressive Conservative). *Legislature*—Legislative Assembly, 51 members.
Education (1981–82 est.): *Enrollment*—elementary and secondary schools, 146,110 pupils; postsecondary, 9,750 students.
Public Finance (1980–81 est.): $2,000,000,000 balanced budget.
Personal Income (average weekly salary, April 1981): $317.27.
Unemployment Rate (June 1981, seasonally adjusted): 13.5%.
(All monetary figures are in Canadian dollars.)

NEW HAMPSHIRE

Throughout 1981 fiscal and economic issues dominated the public consciousness, reflecting changes in Washington and the economy of the state. The principal concern of the regular biennial session of the General Court was balancing the budget while meeting basic needs. The reduction of federal funding, which had supported many state programs, added to the dilemma. For New Hampshire, the avoidance of any general sales or income tax was crucial, forcing any increases in revenue to be done in a piecemeal fashion. However, more and more influential persons and organizations in the state are supporting an income or general sales tax.

Budget and Economy. The fiscal problems resulted in a heated political battle between Gov. Hugh Gallen (D) and the Republican-controlled legislature. The governor vetoed the state budget in late June, causing a flurry of activity before a compromise was reached. Principal stumbling blocks included the funding of a pay raise for state employees and the level of state aid for social services. Gallen signed a compromise budget one-half hour before the new fiscal year began on July 1. The budget mandated 10% reductions in spending by state agencies. With uncertainties about the amount of federal monies available to New Hampshire, the many fiscal problems remain unresolved.

The revenue issues facing state government arose in part from a sluggish economy in 1981. The unemployment rate of approximately 5% was well below the national average, but slowdowns in such areas as housing construction and auto sales hurt the state as they did the nation. One bright spot was tourism. Despite a second straight winter of poor snow conditions, the summer season ensured a good, if not outstanding, tourist year. Most indications were that the summer of 1981 approached the record level achieved in 1978.

Railroad and Redevelopment. After years of public indifference, the Boston & Maine Railroad gained a lot of attention because of Timothy Mellon's effort to purchase control of the principal railroads in northern New England so that he might put together a regional system. Key to this is control of the Boston & Maine, which Mellon seemed on the verge of achieving. His success would fulfill a dream shared by many during the last 80 years.

The redevelopment of Rockingham Park, a Salem racetrack, made slight progress in 1981, despite periodic speculation about several schemes. A reported move by the Boston Bruins hockey team to Salem did not materialize. By late in the year, the burned out track remained unused.

Loeb. The death of William Loeb, conservative publisher of the *Manchester Union Leader,* marked the passing of an era. Always a controversial figure, his editorials and comments vilified or praised people and issues in a way seldom found in modern journalism. How his death would affect the *Union Leader* was debatable.

Environment. Severe defoliation by gypsy moths and the increasing evidence of the harmful effects of acid rain made media headlines. In August, the state gained its own public radio station.

The immediate future of the state's overall economy seemed uncertain. Unless the state can find additional revenue through a revised tax structure, residents can expect diminished support from the public sector.

WILLIAM L. TAYLOR, *Plymouth State College*

— NEW HAMPSHIRE • Information Highlights —

Area: 9,279 sq mi (24 033 km²).
Population (1980 census): 920,610.
Chief Cities (1980 census): Concord, the capital, 30,400; Manchester, 90,936; Nashua, 67,865; Portsmouth, 26,254; Salem, 24,124; Dover, 22,377; Rochester, 21,560; Keene, 21,449; Derry, 18,875; Laconia, 15,575.
Government (1981): *Chief Officer*—governor, Hugh J. Gallen (D). *General Court*—Senate, 24 members; House of Representatives, 400 members.
State Finances (fiscal year 1980): *Revenues,* $894,000,000; *expenditures,* $889,000,000.
Personal Income (1980): $8,429,000,000; per capita, $9,131.
Labor Force (June 1981): *Nonagricultural wage and salary earners,* 389,800; *unemployed* (July 1981), 24,900 (5.2% of total force).

NEW JERSEY

Gubernatorial politics dominated events in New Jersey in 1981.

Election. Gov. Brendan Byrne was constitutionally ineligible to run for a third term and any candidate in the primaries who could raise at least $50,000 through private sources could receive matching funds from the State Election Law Enforcement Commission. The combination of these two factors caused an unusually large number of persons from both parties to run for the governorship. Many people were fearful that the election finance law was too liberal, and Governor Byrne sponsored a move to increase the amount a person must raise to $150,000, but it was defeated in the legislature. All told, 13 Democrats and 8 Republicans filed nominating petitions for the June 2 primary. Among the Democrats, the most prominent were congressmen James J. Florio and Robert Roe, mayors Kenneth Gibson of Newark and Thomas F. X. Smith of Jersey City, and state Sen. Joseph P. Merlino, while the Republican aspirants were headed by former assembly speaker Thomas H. Kean and Paterson Mayor Lawrence F. Kramer. As the primary campaign neared completion, more than $4.5 million had been allocated from public funds. The winners were Florio and Kean.

With the primaries ended, the campaign developed national importance as the first major test of support for President Ronald Reagan's social and economic policies at the state level.

Wide World Photos

Republican Thomas Kean (left) and Rep. James Florio (D), the candidates for the governorship of New Jersey, exchange greetings following a debate. Assembly Speaker Kean was elected in one of the closest races in the history of New Jersey.

Kean ran on a supply-side platform calling for reduced taxes on business corporations and a possible 1% reduction in the sales tax. The president himself, Vice-President George Bush, Secretary of Labor Raymond Donovan, and other administration members made several visits to the state. Kean, 46-year-old scion of a wealthy and socially prominent family, made efforts to court the working class ethnic voters in the northern cities, and mounted an extensive program of television commercials. Florio's strategy, on the other hand, played down substantive issues and stressed personal ability and independence from Governor Byrne, although he frequently expressed skepticism over Kean's tax program. The 44-year-old congressman also emphasized his Italo-American background and lower-middle-class origins. In spite of energetic campaigning by both candidates, a poll taken by the Eagleton Institute of Politics at Rutgers University in October revealed general public apathy. Less than half those polled could name who was running, and the expectation was that the election would be decided by a voter's traditional ethnic and party affiliation, which gave the edge to Florio. He was strongest in the southern counties near his Camden base, while Kean had a slight lead in the central part of the state.

The election turned out to be about the closest in state history. In fact, the winner was not known until Representative Florio conceded defeat on November 30. A recount of the ballots had revealed that Kean won by some 1,700 votes. New Jersey voters also elected a new legislature and approved bond issues to improve water-supply systems, to clean up hazardous waste, and to preserve farmland.

Abscam. The Abscam scandal of 1980 was still an important problem because of the bribery conviction of Sen. Harrison Williams. Pressure for Williams to resign his Senate seat was brought from many sources, but Williams refused to do so. The Senate was scheduled to consider expulsion proceedings against Williams in December but such hearings were postponed.

1980 Census and Federal Aid. The 1980 census revealed a steady decline in the rate of population increase in New Jersey. In the 1970s the population grew 2.7% to 7,364,158, whereas in the 1950s and 1960s the rates of increase were 25.5% and 18.2%, respectively. The census showed a movement away from the cities and suburban areas into counties that had been rural. Also as a result of the census, the state lost one seat in Congress. Overall reapportionment was scheduled for early 1982.

An additional sign of future problems lay in the Reagan administration's proposed reductions in federal aid, which were estimated for New Jersey at $265 million for fiscal 1981 and $1,000,000,000 for fiscal 1982.

Miscellaneous. The naming of the new Meadowlands sports arena in East Rutherford, home of the New Jersey Nets basketball team, in honor of Governor Byrne aroused much controversy. The state adopted the tomato as its emblem.

HERMANN K. PLATT, *Saint Peter's College*

NEW JERSEY • Information Highlights

Area: 7,787 sq mi (20 168 km^2).
Population (1980 census): 7,364,158.
Chief Cities (1980 census): Trenton, the capital, 92,124; Newark, 329,248; Jersey City, 223,532; Paterson, 137,970; Elizabeth, 106,201; Camden, 84,910; East Orange, 77,025; Clifton, 74,388; Bayonne, 65,047; Irvington, 61,493.
Government (1981): *Chief Officer*—governor, Brendan T. Byrne (D). *Legislature*—Senate, 40 members; General Assembly, 80 members.
State Finances (fiscal year 1980): *Revenues*, $8,822,000,000; *expenditures*, $8,537,000,000.
Personal Income (1980): $80,724,000,000; per capita, $10,924.
Labor Force (July 1981): *Nonagricultural wage and salary earners*, 3,133,100; *unemployed*, 246,100 (6.8% of total force).

NEW MEXICO

New Mexicans in 1981 remained preoccupied with continuing problems at the state penitentiary near Santa Fe, which in 1980 witnessed one of the worst prison riots in U.S. history. They were also warned by officials that the state would lose approximately $200 million in federal funds as a result of the Reagan administration's budget cuts.

During June, ceremonies were held in Grants inaugurating the new county of Cibola, created out of the western portion of Valencia County by the 1981 legislature. Cibola is New Mexico's 33rd county and the first addition since establishment of Los Alamos County in 1949.

Politics. In regular session, the legislature passed an omnibus liquor control code and a bill permitting use of DMSO, a controversial drug used to combat the pain of arthritis.

Substantial increase in the 1980 census figures indicated the need to reapportion the state's 112 House and Senate districts. New Mexico gained a seat in the U.S. House of Representatives. A special legislative redistricting session was scheduled for January 1982. Local Democrats and Republicans sought to influence redistricting plans.

Crime. At least seven different state and federal agencies initiated investigations into charges of prison corruption, mismanagement, and brutality, and theft of prison supplies. A report published on September 2 after a five-month probe alleged that 20 inmates from the 1980 riot were still unaccounted for. Violence in the penitentiary continued with deaths of several prisoners and two guards. Also, court action was begun against riot participants. In October, 300 inmates filed a petition with the U.S. attorney seeking to have the federal government take control of the penitentiary. They charged criminal negligence on the part of state officials and violation of their civil rights.

Environment. Test drilling got under way near Carlsbad for the Waste Isolation Pilot Plant (WIPP) designed for disposal of low-level nuclear waste. A series of court actions intended to halt the project were unsuccessful. Environmentalists and some geologists charged that the WIPP site is unsafe for such waste disposal. A protest rally on Labor Day resulted in the arrest of 28 persons.

Energy. More than 3,000 jobs were reported lost in the state's distressed uranium mining industry during 1980–81. New legislation provided for the practical application of solar devices produced by the energy research program at New Mexico State University. Scientists there contributed to the installation of the world's largest flat-plate photovoltaic system in a shopping center at Lovington. Utilizing the sun's energy, the system provides partial power for the center.

Indian Affairs. Pueblo Indian leaders, concerned over federal funding cutbacks, met with Congressional representatives to search for alternatives to programs scheduled to be dismantled. New census figures showed Albuquerque to rank fifth in the nation for its Indian population. The figures were up 257% from the 1970 count for a total of 20,780 in 1980.

MARC SIMMONS
Author, "New Mexico, A History"

NEW MEXICO • Information Highlights

Area: 121,592 sq mi (314 923 km²).
Population (1980 census): 1,299,968.
Chief Cities (1980 census): Santa Fe, the capital, 48,899; Albuquerque, 331,767; Las Cruces, 45,086; Roswell, 39,676; Clovis, 31,194; Farmington, 30,729; Hobbs, 28,794; Carlsbad, 25,496; Gallup, 18,161; Las Vegas, 14,322.
Government (1981): *Chief Officers*—governor, Bruce King (D); lt. gov., Roberto A. Mondragon (D). *Legislature*—Senate, 42 members; House of Representatives, 70 members.
State Finances (fiscal year 1980): *Revenues*, $2,183,000,000; *expenditures*, $1,744,000,000.
Personal Income (1980): $10,219,000,000; per capita, $7,841.
Labor Force (July 1981): *Nonagricultural wage and salary earners*, 466,300; *unemployed*, 40,000 (7.1% of total force).

NEW YORK

The results of the 1980 U.S. Census confirmed what many experts had predicted for New York State—the population dropped somewhat from 1970, down 3.8% from 18,241,391 to 17,557,288. The decline was most severe in large urban areas, but there were considerable population gains in seven of eight counties in the mid-Hudson Valley.

As record interest rates kept money tight, and with federal budget cuts estimated to cost the state $900 million in funding, New York became the first state to invest public retirement funds in residential mortgages. During the spring, more than $85 million of a planned $300 million was so invested.

Business and Finance. The U.S. Treasury Department released figures showing that New York State continued to rank first among the 50 states in federal aid received, with $9,470,000,000 in 1980.

Noting the prohibitive cost of borrowing money, Comptroller Edward V. Regan planned to delay construction projects throughout the state. Regan noted that the newly introduced all-savers certificates were luring many potential investors away from New York State's tax-free municipal bonds.

Politics and the Legislature. A bitter 42-day impasse ended on April 29, when the legislature finally enacted a budget for fiscal 1982, which had begun April 1. The agreement reached between Gov. Hugh L. Carey (D) and Senate Majority Leader Warren M. Anderson (R) called for $16,600,000,000 in outlays, but it did not include funding for the state takeover of local medicaid costs, which Carey had made a top priority. Projected total income was $16,323,000,000, including $16,053,000,000 in current revenues and $270 million in bond funds.

During its 204th session, the legislature did go along with the governor on several proposals. It enacted a broad program of tax cuts for individuals and businesses, allowed a 15% increase in state welfare grants, and approved Carey's five-year, $5,850,000,000 physical improvement plan for the Metropolitan Transit Authority (MTA). The body also passed a plan of its own to hold MTA fares at current levels for at least two years.

After a fierce struggle with the state's labor movement, and in the face of certain opposition by the Republican majority in the State Senate, Meyer S. Frucher withdrew his name as Governor Carey's nominee for State Labor Commissioner. The move came as a major political defeat for the governor, who faced a reelection campaign in 1982.

Crime. Jean S. Harris, 57, was sentenced to 15 years to life in prison for the 1980 murder of Dr. Herman Tarnower, author of the best-selling *The Complete Scarsdale Medical Diet.* Craig S. Crimmins, 22, was sentenced to serve 20 years to life for the 1980 murder of violinist Helen Hagnes at the Metropolitan Opera House in New York City. Mark David Chapman received 20 years to life for the December 1980 murder of former Beatle John Lennon.

Jack Henry Abbott, author of the acclaimed *In the Belly of the Beast,* based on his letters to friend Norman Mailer from prison, where Abbott has spent most of his adult life, was the alleged murderer of waiter Richard Adan on July 18 outside an all-night restaurant on New York City's Lower East Side. The 37-year-old Abbott had just received parole with the help of Mailer and others. He was captured two months after the murder outside Morgan City, LA.

On October 20, three members of the Weather Underground—a radical protest group spawned during the Vietnam War era—and a fourth suspect were arrested after an attempted $1.6 million armored truck robbery in Nyack, Westchester County. Two police officers and a Brink's guard were killed in a shootout after the bungled robbery attempt.

Environment. The explosion of an electric generator in a large state office building in upstate Binghamton left every floor contaminated with dust found to contain polychlorinated biphenyls (PCBs). The building was closed down, but to prove that it was safe Governor Carey said he would drink a glass of PCBs.

A new leak discovered at the Indian Point 3 nuclear facility delayed plans by The Power Authority of New York State to put the plant back into service after routine maintenance work in early October.

People. On April 11, Governor Carey wed Evangeline Gouletas, a principal owner of American Invisco, one of the largest real estate companies in the United States. The two had met at Ronald Reagan's inauguration in January.

New York's master builder Robert Moses, who did more to shape the physical environment of the city and state than anyone else in the 20th century, died July 29 at the age of 92. (*See* OBITUARIES.)

MICHAEL SPECTER
"The New York Times"

NEW YORK • Information Highlights

Area: 49,108 sq mi (127 190 km²).
Population (1980 census): 17,557,288.
Chief Cities (1980 census): Albany, the capital, 101,727; New York, 7,071,030; Buffalo, 357,870; Rochester, 241,741; Yonkers, 195,351; Syracuse, 170,105; Utica, 75,632; Niagara Falls, 71,384; New Rochelle, 70,794; Schenectady, 67,972.
Government (1981): *Chief Officers*—governor, Hugh L. Carey (D); lt. gov., Mario M. Cuomo (D). *Legislature*—Senate, 60 members; Assembly, 150 members.
State Finances (fiscal year 1980): *Revenues,* $27,199,-000,000; *expenditures,* $24,978,000,000.
Personal Income (1980): $180,646,000,000; per capita, $10,260.
Labor Force (July 1981): *Nonagricultural wage and salary earners,* 7,264,400; *unemployed,* 630,500 (7.7% of total force).

UPI

New York's Gov. Hugh Carey and his bride, Evangeline Gouletas of Chicago, cut the cake at their wedding reception in Manhattan's St. Regis-Sheraton Hotel.

New Yorkers jam the Brooklyn Bridge on their way home from work September 9, after an electric generator explosion left much of Manhattan without power and subway service.

UPI

NEW YORK CITY

Mayor Edward I. Koch, the first politician in the history of New York City to carry both the Democratic and Republican mayoral endorsements, was elected to a second term in a landslide victory on Nov. 3, 1981. Mayor Koch garnered more than 75% of the votes cast and captured every assembly district in the city. In addition to the mayoral contest, Democrats swept the citywide and boroughwide races. City Council President Carol Bellamy and Comptroller Harrison J. Goldin overwhelmed their opposition to win reelection, and Manhattan Borough President Andrew J. Stein succeeded with a narrow victory over David Dinkins to win a second term in office.

Census. Final population figures from the 1980 U.S. Census indicated a sharp drop in New York City's white population, a moderate rise in its black population, and a substantial increase in Hispanic residents over the previous decade. The total number of city residents was declared to be 7,071,030, representing a 10.4% decline from 1970.

In a 7–0 vote on September 9, the U.S. Supreme Court refused to overturn a lower court ruling that had banned primary voting throughout New York City. The lower court had ruled that newly-drawn city council lines discriminated against blacks and Hispanics by diluting their voting strength. The council was ordered to redraw its lines.

Business and Finance. According to a U.S. Bureau of Labor Statistics survey, New York City has lost more than 50% of 1,073,000 manufacturing jobs since 1947, about 40,000 of them since 1978.

City Budget Director James R. Brigham, Jr., predicted that New York would end 1981 with a $243 million surplus, its first surplus since the early 1960s and almost twice the originally projected figure. In February, the New York State Financial Control Board, which oversees the finances of New York City, pronounced the city financially healthy for the first time in years. On March 23, New York reentered the long-term lending market by offering the sale of $75 million in municipal bonds. It was the first such sale by the city since early 1975.

Development. On July 31, after ten years of wrangling between the city and state governments, Mayor Koch and Gov. Hugh Carey agreed on a plan to build Westway, a 4.2-mi (6.8-km) stretch of highway on Manhattan's West Side. The $2,300,000,000 project, expected to be begun in 1982, is to be financed 90% by the federal government and 10% by the state.

New York City and New York State also released a proposal, formulated by several city and state agencies together, to develop the Times Square area in mid-Manhattan. The proposal calls for a major rehabilitation of one of the city's most famous but most crime-ridden areas.

The Landmark Preservation Committee approved the creation of a Historic District on Manhattan's Upper East Side, conferring landmark status on 1,044 buildings on almost every block between 61st and 79th streets from 5th to Lexington avenues.

Power Failure. On September 9, an explosion in a Consolidated Edison electric generator on 14th Street left most of lower and mid-Manhattan without power for four hours in the late afternoon. The approximately 3.5 million persons who normally use the subway to get home from work were forced to find other means of transportation.

MICHAEL SPECTER
"The New York Times"

UPI

Police in Auckland, New Zealand, arrest two youths during a protest in mid-July against a tour by South Africa's national rugby team, the Springboks. Opponents of the tour maintained that taking part in matches against the team amounted to acceptance of South Africa's apartheid policy.

NEW ZEALAND

Although public opinion polls consistently rated unemployment and the economy as the two matters of most concern, New Zealand's biggest news in 1981 were a general election and the tour of a South African rugby team.

Election. With polls showing his National Party holding an average 10% lead over the opposition Labor Party, Prime Minister Robert D. Muldoon confidently expected to be returned for a third successive term. But continued high support (27% in the polls) for the Social Credit Party made the result the most unpredictable in decades. The campaign was a bruising affair, centering on the issue of a shaky economy.

The preliminary result on November 28 was a hung parliament, with the National Party apparently losing its majority in the 92-seat House of Representatives but retaining the largest representation, 46 seats. The Labor Party was credited with 44 seats, and the Social Credit Party with two. By December 9, however, nearly 250,000 absentee ballots had been counted, and the final result left Prime Minister Muldoon's National Party with a thin majority—47 seats, to Labor's 44 seats and Social Credit's two.

Economy. Inflation (about 17%), external borrowing, climbing interest rates, devaluing of the dollar, and a steady rise in unemployment engendered serious doubts about the soundness of the economy. The budget tabled in July was aptly described as "an election year budget without the usual largesse." With an anticipated 19.5% jump in government spending, an unprecedented deficit of $2,090,000,000 was to be covered by loans. Additional taxes on alcohol and tobacco were not offset by any cut in income tax rates. Credit cards were made subject to a five-cent duty per transaction. And first-home buyers were afforded tax relief on mortgages, but overall the budget lacked any real substance or definite theme.

Foreign Affairs. Prime Minister Muldoon made five major overseas visits during 1981. A visit to Japan concentrated on trade issues, as did one to European Community (EC) capitals in June. In July, he met U.S. President Ronald Reagan in Washington, where they discussed freight and trade policies, and then he traveled to London for the royal wedding. At the Commonwealth Prime Ministers' Conference in Melbourne in October, Muldoon caused a stir by raising the issue of the implementation of the Gleneagle Agreement on sporting contacts with South Africa. In June, New Zealand hosted a conference of the ANZUS (Australia, New Zealand, and United States) Treaty Council, with Secretary of State Alexander Haig leading the U.S. delegation.

Springbok Tour. The arrival of the South African Springboks rugby team for a tour in July bitterly polarized the nation. Street demonstrations started in May, but the government clung

NEW ZEALAND • Information Highlights

Official Name: New Zealand.
Location: Southwest Pacific Ocean.
Area: 103,736 sq mi (268 676 km^2).
Population (1981 est.): 3,100,000.
Chief Cities (March 1980): Wellington, the capital, 349,000; Auckland, 808,800; Christchurch, 326,200.
Government: *Head of state*, Elizabeth II, queen, represented by David Beattie, governor general (took office Nov. 1980). *Head of government*, Robert Muldoon, prime minister (took office Dec. 1975). *Legislature* (unicameral)—House of Representatives.
Monetary Unit: New Zealand dollar (1.2121 N.Z. dollars equal U.S.$1, Oct. 1981).
Manufactures (major products): Processed foods, wood products, cement, fertilizer, beverages, domestic appliances.
Agriculture (major products): Wheat, corn, barley, potatoes, dairy products, wool.

to its stated policy that while it disapproved of the tour it would not force a cancellation. As a consequence, a meeting of Commonwealth finance ministers planned for Auckland was moved to the Bahamas. Demonstrations grew larger and more violent as the tour proceeded, finally forcing the cancellation of two matches. The largest police operation ever organized in New Zealand led to the arrest of nearly 2,000 protesters, and the day of the final contest witnessed probably the most severe street violence in the history of the nation.

GRAHAM BUSH
Political Studies Department
University of Auckland, New Zealand

NIGERIA

The second year of civilian government was disturbed by riots, criticism of President Alhaji Shehu Shagari's leadership, factionalism, and a serious decline in oil revenues.

Politics. In January dissatisfaction within the coalition central government, dominated by Shagari's National Party of Nigeria (NPN), focused upon revenue allocation. President Shagari wanted the federal government to retain more revenues than did the House of Representatives. The House sought to give more funds to the states. Members of the National People's Party (NPP) threatened to resign from the government. A compromise confirmed most of Shagari's proposals and the NPP did not then withdraw from the government. However, in April the governors of nine states, whose parties were in opposition to the NPN, issued a manifesto charging the central government with a number of provocations. Finally, in July, the NPP voided its accord with the NPN and four NPP ministers resigned from Shagari's government preliminary to the formation of a united opposition to the NPN.

Political differences within the states were even more serious. A split developed within the People's Redemption Party (PRP). Those elements loyal to Alhaji Aminu Kano engineered the expulsion of governors of Kaduna and Kano states. In a highly publicized case, Gov. Alhaji Balarbe Musa of Kaduna state was later impeached and was succeeded by his lieutenant governor. There was violence in many states. The most serious began in Kano in late December 1980 when members of a fanatical Muslim sect began indiscriminate attacks on people and property. The government sent troops which brought order, but only after an estimated 1,000 persons died and extensive damage was done to property. In July, crowds in Kano reacting to a supposed insult to the Emir Ado Bayero from Gov. Alhaji Abubakar Rimi ranged through the streets, destroying government property and causing a number of deaths. Violence also occurred in June at Ijebu-Ode between supporters of the United Party of Nigeria (UPN) and NPN; at Ife, where police clashed with students; and at Owerri, where politically motivated students destroyed government buildings. One reaction of the central government to such disorders was the arrest of editors of four main opposition newspapers, who were charged with libel and sedition.

Economics. Nigeria's petroleum revenue decreased by about one third because of the world's oversupply. Production fell from 2 million barrels per day in January to only 500,000 in September. After the Geneva OPEC meeting in August, Nigeria lowered its crude price from $40 to $36 per barrel. Despite loss of revenue, the government continued to support the development of five new steel plants, the improvement of three refineries, the Kiri Dam project, and the plans for the world's largest liquefied gas plant. Foreign loans and private investment allowed the continued development of sugar refineries, plastic plants, cement factories, flour mills, and hotels. The fourth development plan (1981–85) appropriated $5,700,000,000 for agriculture to counter Nigeria's dependence upon imported food, which increased twenty-fold from $122 million in 1975 to $2,500,000,000 in 1980.

Foreign Policy. During the year, President Shagari visited a number of African and European states and entertained representatives from the United States, Benin, and Angola. Shagari's moderate position remained unchanged, and he reiterated to U.S. Assistant Secretary of State for African Affairs Chester Crocker Nigeria's opposition to South African apartheid and his fears of a change in U.S. policy. The president also visited a number of African and European nations in 1981.

Libyan diplomats were sent home in protest of the invasion of Chad, and Shagari openly criticized the peace efforts by the Organization of African Unity (OAU). In May, a major crisis developed over the killing of five Nigerian soldiers by Cameroon troops near the eastern border. The Cameroon embassy was stoned, but the issue was eventually settled by an apology from Cameroon. The failure of OAU to act caused Shagari to boycott the heads of state meeting in Nairobi, Kenya, in June.

HARRY A. GAILEY
San Jose State University

NIGERIA • Information Highlights

Official Name: Federal Republic of Nigeria.
Location: West Africa.
Area: 356,669 sq mi (923 773 km^2).
Population (1981 est.): 79,700,000.
Chief Cities (1976 est.): Lagos, the capital, 1,100,000; Ibadan, 850,000; Ogbomosho, 435,000; Kano, 400,-000.
Government: *Head of state and government,* Alhaji Shehu Shagari, president (took office Oct. 1979). *Legislature*—Senate and House of Representatives.
Monetary Unit: Naira (0.64616 naira equals U.S.$1, June 1981).
Manufactures (major products): Petroleum, textiles, cement, food products, footwear, metal products, lumber.
Agriculture (major products): Cocoa, rubber, palm oil, yams, cassava, sorghum, millet, corn, rice, cotton.

NORTH CAROLINA

Adjustment to the new mood expressed by the citizenry in the 1980 elections provided the chief topic of conversation in 1981.

Government and Politics. James B. Hunt, Jr., the first governor to begin a second full four-year term, was confronted by public demands for stricter controls over state spending, and the General Assembly responded by cutting expenditures of some state programs in proportion to reductions in federal assistance. Passage of a three-cents-per-gallon increase in the gasoline tax came only after spirited Republican opposition. For the first time, the legislature adjourned without passage of a full biennial budget, and a second session was required in October for adoption of the remaining money bills. A bill to ratify the Equal Rights Amendment never came out of committee.

Precedent was broken in the traumatic decennial task of redrawing lines for congressional and legislative districts. For the first time, a county (Moore) was split between two congressional districts. The plan for legislative redistricting was so deficient that the state attorney general recommended a third session of the Assembly to draw new lines.

Revelation of a bid-rigging scandal in the awarding of road construction contracts led to conviction of several corporation executives. William R. Robertson, Jr., was appointed to head the state's troubled Department of Transportation. Howard Lee, the state's top black officeholder, resigned as secretary of the Department of Natural Resources and Community Development and was succeeded by Joseph W. Grimsley, Jr., who in turn was replaced as secretary of the Department of Administration by Jane Patterson.

The Economy. The microelectronics industry was boosted by a $25 million legislative appropriation; the number of motion picture and television productions increased in the state. Farmers began adjusting to the prospective end to federal price supports for peanuts and tobacco. Unemployment dropped to 5.6% in October. After years of objections by environmentalists, water began filling the B. Everett Jordan Lake.

— NORTH CAROLINA • Information Highlights —

Area: 52,669 sq mi (136 413 km²).
Population (1980 census): 5,874,429.
Chief Cities (1980 census): Raleigh, the capital, 149,771; Charlotte, 314,447; Greensboro, 155,642; Winston-Salem, 131,885; Durham, 100,831; High Point, 64,107; Fayetteville, 59,507; Asheville, 53,281.
Government (1981): *Chief Officers*—governor, James B. Hunt, Jr. (D); lt. gov., James C. Green (D). *General Assembly*—Senate, 50 members; House of Representatives, 120 members.
State Finances (fiscal year 1980): *Revenues*, $6,202,000,000; *expenditures*, $5,733,000,000.
Personal Income (1980): $46,043,000,000; per capita, $7,819.
Labor Force (July 1981): *Nonagricultural wage and salary earners*, 2,357,200; *unemployed*, 173,900 (6.1% of total force).

Education. Under a consent decree signed in federal court ending a U.S. Department of Education suit, the University of North Carolina system agreed to continue efforts to increase minority representation on the various campuses and to improve facilities and programs at predominantly black institutions. In return, the government accepted "goals" in place of "quotas," and university officials viewed the decision as evidence that educational policies should be made by educators, not politicians.

Population. The 1980 census indicated that North Carolina had displaced Massachusetts as the tenth most populous state. The state's population grew by 15.5% during the decade. The number of Indians showed a decennial increase of 45%, while blacks increased almost 17% and whites 14%. Nearly half of the citizens lived in urban areas, a sharp increase in recent years.

Names in the News. Sen. Jesse Helms commanded wide media coverage from both supporters and opponents. Shake-ups in cultural programs brought new directors: William S. Price in archives and history; Edgar P. Bowron in art, and Patrick Flynn in music (symphony).

H. G. JONES
University of North Carolina

NORTH DAKOTA

Agriculture and the energy industry in North Dakota each attained "first in the nation" status in 1981. The state harvested more wheat than any other and the nation's first commercial-scale coal gasification plant obtained government backing for completion.

Agriculture. North Dakota raised a record 338 million bu (9.2 million t) of wheat, dethroning Kansas as national champion. But when harvested, it was a crop no one wanted, so most of the bumper production, plus the state's other grains, stayed in storage. Falling commodity prices and rising production costs left farmers only slightly better off financially than in dry 1980 when losses were $650 million.

Energy. Reagan administration approval of a $2,000,000,000 loan guarantee ensured continued construction of a North Dakota energy complex that will produce synthetic natural gas from lignite coal for Midwest cities by 1984.

In other energy industry developments, construction started on the state's 273-mi (437-km) segment of a natural gas pipeline linking Alaska and the lower 48 states; North Dakota approved a 17-mi- (27-km-) wide corridor for a controversial 500-kilovolt electrical transmission line; six proposed energy plants applied for various state permits; oil lease auctions of state mineral rights set sales and average price records; ten strip mining companies produced nearly 20 million T (18 million t) on which they paid the state 96 cents per ton severance tax; and the double-taxed oil industry contributed 17% of the state's 1981 revenue.

NORTH DAKOTA • Information Highlights

Area: 70,702 sq mi (183 118 km²).
Population (1980 census): 652,695.
Chief Cities (1980 census): Bismarck, the capital, 44,485; Fargo, 61,308; Grand Forks, 43,765; Minot, 32,843; Jamestown, 16,280; Dickinson, 15,924; Mandan, 15,513; Williston, 13,336; West Fargo, 10,099.
Government (1981): *Chief Officers*—governor, Allen I. Olson (R); lt. gov., Ernest Sands (R). *Legislative Assembly*—Senate, 50 members; House of Representatives, 100 members.
State Finances (fiscal year 1980): *Revenues,* $1,013,000,000; *expenditures,* $910,000,000.
Personal Income (1980): $5,723,000,000; per capita, $8,747.
Labor Force (July 1981): *Nonagricultural wage and salary earners,* 248,300; *unemployed,* 16,440 (4.8% of total force).

The oil industry challenged the 6.5% extraction tax and lost in the courts. North Dakota fought in courts and Congress against federal tampering with state-imposed severance taxes. Citizen groups prodded state government to order a utility to equalize gas rates in a regional system, while state agencies, grain dealers, and labor opposed Burlington Northern Railroad's plan to abandon more than 1,000 mi (1 600 km) of branch lines. Railroads sued North Dakota for equality of taxation with other industrial property and won. The beleaguered Garrison Diversion water project was again in court and a federal judge ruled work could not proceed without reauthorization by Congress.

Legislature. The legislature implemented the oil extraction tax mandated by an initiative but substituted a water pipeline project for a voter-approved energy research trust fund provision. Then it used the new revenue source to enact tax relief measures. It federalized income tax rates, cut property and sales taxes by $92 million, raised personal and capital gains exemptions, and adopted simplified income tax return forms.

The 1981 session increased aid to schools as provided by the oil tax measure; created a Human Services agency; approved the addition of blackjack in the gambling-for-charity law; adopted a uniform county court system; enacted a corporate farming law; and reapportioned legislative districts and added three.

Free Land. Harley Kissner, a 72-year-old bachelor, objected when the Antler, ND, school closed because of lack of pupils. He offered to give 9-acre (3.6-ha) plots of land to families who would come to the small town, population 150, establish residency, and remain at least five years. Hundreds answered his advertisements; he selected six families with 21 children. Antler school reopened with 34 enrolled.

STAN CANN
"The Forum," Fargo

NORTHWEST TERRITORIES

As in other parts of Canada, constitutional reform was a major issue in the Northwest Territories during 1981. Because the majority of people living in the Northwest Territories are of native origin, the protection of aboriginal rights was of primary concern in the constitutional debates.

Constitution. The November 5 agreement between Prime Minister Pierre Elliott Trudeau and nine of Canada's ten provincial premiers (René Lévesque of Quebec being the lone opponent) on patriation of the federal constitution removed aboriginal rights from the Charter of Rights and Freedoms, part of the legislative resolution for patriation from Great Britain. In a dramatic move, the entire 22-member legislative assembly of the Northwest Territories traveled to Ottawa, where they engaged in extensive lobbying to have the protection reinstated. Their efforts, combined with those of native organizations, achieved the desired result, and a compromise provision for aboriginal rights was included in the final resolution passed by the Canadian Parliament on December 2. The Territorial Council members were not successful, however, in changing the provisions that would allow provincial governments to be involved in the establishment of new provinces and in extending the boundaries of existing provinces into the Northwest Territories.

Economy. Although the economy of the Northwest Territories continued to be adversely affected by inflation and high energy costs in 1981, exploration of oil and natural gas remained at high levels, easing pressure. There was also a significant growth in the tourist industry.

In April, the National Energy Board (NEB) announced its approval for construction of a $400 million buried pipeline to transport crude oil from Imperial Oil's field at Norman Wells in the Mackenzie Valley to existing pipelines in northern Alberta. The Dene Nation, representing about 20,000 Indians of the Mackenzie Valley, appealed to Ottawa officials to delay construction of the pipeline for two years, pending settlement of all land claims by the natives. The federal government accepted the NEB approval for construction but recommended the two-year delay to give the land-claim negotiations a fair chance.

ROSS M. HARVEY
Assistant Director of Information
Government of the Northwest Territories

NORTHWEST TERRITORIES • Information Highlights

Area: 1,304,903 sq mi (3 379 700 km²).
Population (April 1981 est.): 43,100.
Chief City (1980 est.): Yellowknife, the capital, 9,550.
Government (1981): *Chief Officers*—commissioner, John H. Parker; chief justice, Court of Appeal, William A. McGillivray; judge of the Supreme Court, C. F. Tallis. *Legislature*—Legislative Assembly, 22 elected members.
Education (1981–82 est.): *Enrollment*—public and secondary schools, 12,567 pupils. *Public school expenditures* (1980–81), $52,211,000.
Public Finance (fiscal year 1980–81): *Revenues,* $335,027,000; *expenditures,* $327,129,000.
Mining (1981 est.): Production value, $540,866,400.
(All monetary figures are in Canadian dollars.)

NORWAY

The Norwegian Labor Party, which had governed Norway since 1973, was defeated in parliamentary elections Sept. 13–14, 1981, to be replaced by the country's first purely Conservative administration in about half a century.

The new makeup of the 155-member Storting (parliament) was as follows: Labor, 65 seats (76 previously), Conservatives, 54 (41), Christian Peoples' Party (CPP), 15 (22), Center (Farmers') Party, 11 (12), Liberals, 2 (2), and Socialist Left, 4 (2). The Progressives, a rightist, anti-tax, and anti-immigration party, which won no seats in the previous (1977) election, did better than expected and got four.

The main issue in the campaign was the Labor government's handling of the economy, particularly its use of revenues from Norwegian offshore oil and gas. The Labor and Conservative parties agreed on many other key issues, such as the pace of petroleum exploration and development and Norway's commitment to NATO, and so the Conservatives concentrated their criticism on such economic issues as the high rate of inflation (nearly 14% in the first nine months of 1981), high taxes, and what they called excessive government spending.

Government and Politics. On February 4, Norway had got its first woman prime minister when Gro Harlem Brundtland, 41, succeeded Odvar Nordli as head of the minority Labor government. Under Nordli, who had been ailing for some time, the party had steadily lost support in public opinion polls. It was split on a number of questions, notably foreign policy, with a vocal pacifist minority that advocated a nuclear weapon "free zone" in the Nordic countries and opposed the stockpiling of U.S. weapons on Norwegian soil. Brundtland proved adept at reconciling the party's various factions and fought an aggressive, confident election campaign. Although the party was defeated, it did better than expected.

The Conservatives, CPP, and Center Party campaigned on a promise to form a coalition if together they could win a parliamentary majority. Soon after the election, however, attempts to form such a coalition failed. The main stumbling block was the CPP's demand for a change in the law allowing abortion on demand.

Abortion was one of several special interests espoused by smaller parties—ecology, decentralization of employment, and more cautious exploitation of offshore resources were others—that failed to catch the voters' attention. The exceptions to the trend were at the extremes of the political spectrum, where the Socialist Party won some votes with its campaign against U.S. nuclear arms policies, and the Progressives gained support with their promises to slash taxes, enforce law and order, and take a tough line on Third World immigration.

It was the Conservatives, however, who emerged as the big winners. Party leader Kare Willoch, the new prime minister, formed an all-Conservative cabinet, which took office on October 14. There was an understanding that the CPP and Center Party would support the new government on most questions in parliament, with the Labor Party providing the necessary votes on such disputed issues as offshore oil strategy.

Gro Harlem Brundtland (left) became Norway's premier in February; Kare Willoch replaced her in October.

UPI

Norwegian Information Service

NORWAY • Information Highlights

Official Name: Kingdom of Norway.
Location: Northern Europe.
Area: 125,181 sq mi (324 219 km^2).
Population (1981 est.): 4,100,000.
Chief Cities (Jan. 1980): Oslo, the capital, 454,872; Bergen, 208,910; Trondheim, 134,726.
Government: *Head of state,* Olav V, king (acceded Sept. 1957). *Head of government,* Kare Willoch, prime minister (took office October 1981). *Legislature*—Storting: Lagting and Odelsting.
Monetary Unit: Krone (5.77 kroner equal U.S.$1, Oct. 1981).
Manufactures (major products): Pulp and paper, ships, oil and gas, food products, aluminum, ferroalloys.
Agriculture (major products): Potatoes, barley, wheat, apples, pears, dairy products, livestock.

Economy. The election result looked like a vote of no confidence in the way Labor had managed the economy. There was widespread resentment at high tax levels and rising prices, and many workers were annoyed about the government's efforts to hold down wage increases.

In fact, Norwegians were generally better off than their European neighbors. Unemployment was less than 2%, reflecting high government spending, financed by oil and gas revenues, and the economic stimulus of offshore activities. Businesses and industries sheltered from foreign competition generally prospered. The rate of inflation was, however, above the European average, and rising costs affected the competitiveness of some industrial sectors. In addition, the world recession hit several important export industries.

The budget tabled by the outgoing Labor government was moderately expansionist, providing for a slight increase in personal income taxes, which the Conservatives were expected to change.

All in all, Prime Minister Willoch's new government appeared to be facing a difficult four years. Oil and gas earnings had been leveling off, and no new large fields were due to start production in the first half of the 1980s. Politically, the support of his two parliamentary allies seemed half-hearted at best.

THØR GJESTER, *"Økonomisk Revy," Oslo*

NOVA SCOTIA

Nova Scotians during 1981 voted in provincial elections, suffered rising interest rates, and expected discovery of gas and oil reserves on Sable Island. The economic well-being of the average Nova Scotian declined, as average real income dropped and unemployment rose.

Legislature and Government. Just after three years in office, the Tories, led by John Buchanan, declared a general election and won a sweeping majority. Liberal A.M. (Sandy) Cameron remained the leader of the legislative opposition, and Alexa McDonough became the sole representative of the National Democratic Party, whose stronghold on Cape Breton was shattered by the Tories. The government had started the year with a record operating deficit of $150 million. This enabled it to increase funding for education, health, and social welfare, establish a Small Business Corporation, and subsidize electric power use.

Though the legislature, before its dissolution, was largely preoccupied with Liberal accusations of government scandals—such as the Portland Estate land expropriation deal—it did consider some 155 bills, of which 121 became law. Areas covered included financial aid to senior citizens, freedom of information, redistribution of the electoral boundaries for Yarmouth and Inverness, workmen's compensation, and tidal power.

Economy. Despite a buoyant provincial economy, Nova Scotians suffered high unemployment and a decline in real income. Trade unions sought to protect the well-being of their members by declaring strikes. A strike by 4,000 Cape Breton coal miners lasted more than two months, and police struck for eight weeks. A strike by nonmedical hospital workers paralyzed provincial hospitals late in the year.

Despite labor unrest, double-digit real growth was recorded by the mining, fishing, and construction sectors. Coal mining had a second year of substantial growth, and fishing recovered the output lost in 1980. Construction activity, which increased by 12.5% in the first three quarters of the year, gave additional impetus to economic growth. Above all, the expected discovery of gas and oil reserves on Sable Island created optimism among investors.

Energy. Coal mining took its place at the center of provincial energy planning for the 1980s. By 1988, coal-burning thermal generators are expected to eliminate the province's dependence on oil. Efforts are under way to find new oil and gas reserves on the Scotian Shelf. Gulf Canada Resources announced an expenditure of $674 million for an exploration project on Beaufort Sea holdings, and the National Energy Boards sanctioned the construction of a gas pipeline from Montreal to Halifax. These efforts appear to put Nova Scotia on the threshold of a new era of economic prosperity.

R.P. SETH
Department of Economics
Mount Saint Vincent University, Halifax

NOVA SCOTIA • Information Highlights

Area: 21,425 sq mi (55 490 km^2).
Population (April 1981 est.): 856,600.
Chief Cities (1976 census): Halifax, the capital, 117,882; Dartmouth, 65,341; Sydney, 30,645.
Government (1981): *Chief Officers*—lt. gov., John E. Shaffner; premier, John Buchanan (Progressive Conservative). *Legislature*—Legislative Assembly, 52 members.
Education (1981–82 est.): *Enrollment*—elementary and secondary schools, 184,790 pupils; postsecondary, 21,570 students.
Public Finance (1981–82 est.): *Revenues,* $1,704,580,-200; *expenditures,* $1,844,466,100.
Personal Income (average weekly salary, Aug. 1981): $300.00.
Unemployment Rate (Sept. 1981, seasonally adjusted): 11.1%.
(All monetary figures are in Canadian dollars.)

Obituaries[1]

Wide World Photos

GRASSO, Ella Tambussi

U.S. politician: b. Windsor Locks, CT, May 10, 1919; d. Hartford, CT, Feb. 5, 1981.

Ella Grasso made history when she was elected Connecticut's 83d governor in 1974, the first woman ever elected a U.S. state governor without having her husband precede her in the office. Despite her achievement, she never made much of it. She did not want it thought that in a period when feminism was on the rise, her sex had played a role in her election. She preferred to credit her successes to political instincts honed during her years in public service.

On the other hand, feminists were not willing to call Ella Grasso one of their own. She supported some of their causes (appointing the first woman to the Connecticut Supreme Court), but opposed the public funding of abortions.

BRADLEY, Omar Nelson

U.S. army officer: b. Clark, MO, Feb. 12, 1893; d. New York, NY, April 8, 1981.

General of the Army Omar N. Bradley, the last of the American five-star generals, played a key role in the victories of Allied forces in North Africa and Europe during World War II. Although he had not had any battlefield experience when he was assigned to the Tunisian front in early 1943 to act as field adviser to Gen. Dwight D. Eisenhower, he served with distinction as commander of the 2nd Corps in the Northern Tunisian and Sicilian campaigns and of the First Army during the June 6, 1944, assault landing in Normandy. As commander of the 12th Army group he led some 1,300,000 troops of four armies—the largest U.S. force ever commanded by one man—through the remainder of the fighting in France and Germany and established the first linkage with Soviet forces in 1945.

A brilliant tactician, Bradley preferred to rely on meticulous calculation rather than intuition when preparing for battle. His concern for the welfare of the common soldier earned him a reputation as the "G.I.'s general."

Background. The son of a seamstress and a schoolteacher of modest means who died when his son was 13, Omar Nelson Bradley developed a love for hunting and fishing in the rural Missouri environment in which he grew up. On advice of his Sunday school superintendent he applied to and was accepted at the U.S. Military Academy, where his graduating class of 1915 eventually provided more than 30 World War II generals, including Dwight D. Eisenhower. In the years that followed, Bradley rose through the

Photoworld

LOUIS, Joe

American boxer: b. Lafayette, AL, May 13, 1914; d. Las Vegas, NV, April 12, 1981.

For 11 years, 8 months, and 8 days between 1937 and 1949, Joe Louis reigned as the heavyweight boxing champion of the world. The "Brown Bomber" successfully defended his crown 25 times and held the title longer than any other boxer. Beyond that, his simple dignity won him a respect that far transcended sport.

Background. Born Joseph Louis Barrow, he was the eighth child of an Alabama sharecropper. Joe began boxing as an amateur in Detroit, where his family moved when he was a teenager. Assuming the name Louis after a ring announcer forgot his last name, Joe turned pro in 1934 and within two years was touted as the next heavyweight champion. He won that title on June 22,

[1] Arranged chronologically by death date

Background. The daughter of an Italian-immigrant baker, she was, despite humble origins, educated with the daughters of the wealthy. She attended exclusive Chaffee School in Windsor, CT, on a scholarship and was graduated *magna cum laude* from Mount Holyoke College in 1940. She later earned a master's degree there.

Mrs. Grasso's early political career transpired during a time when male camaraderie excluded most women from an election ticket. The experience shaped her personality. She was tough in public debate, and in private, when provoked, she was as salty in her speech as any ward heeler.

A Democrat, she was elected a state representative in 1952 and again in 1954. Elected Connecticut's secretary of the state in 1958, she spent 12 years seeing that election laws were implemented and that town clerks correctly recorded documents. She also made the office accessible to ordinary citizens. Her service as secretary of the state made her an advocate of open government, and later, in her first term as governor, she helped enact a strong freedom of information law.

In 1970 she was elected to the first of two terms in the U.S. House of Representatives but found living in Washington disruptive to her home life. She asked her mentor, Democratic state chairman John M. Bailey, to get her the Democratic party's nomination for governor. Elected governor in 1974, she proved to be conservative on fiscal matters and was often at odds with free spenders in the state legislature. She was able to block enactment of a state income tax by threatening the use of a veto. She was halfway through her second four-year term when she resigned on Dec. 31, 1980, because she was ill with cancer.

She is survived by her husband and two children.

ROBERT F. MURPHY

---

ranks in a variety of training, teaching, and administrative assignments, including a stint at Schofield Barracks, Hawaii. As commandant of the Infantry School at Fort Benning, GA, February 1941-February 1942, he converted it into a massive officer training center.

Bradley served as the first post-World War II head of the Veterans Administration (1945–47). Then, under the newly established U.S. Department of Defense, he was the first chairman of the Joint Chiefs of Staff (1949–53). From 1958 to 1973 he was chairman of the Bulova Watch Co.

Bradley spent his last years at Fort Bliss, TX, occasionally lecturing on military leadership. His death came shortly after a dinner given in his honor by the New York chapter of the Association of the U.S. Army. His 69 years' military service was the longest of any U.S. soldier.

HENRY S. SLOAN

UPI

1937, in Chicago, by knocking out James J. Braddock in the eighth round. Louis went on to defend his crown more times than any other heavyweight champion. His many quick knockout victories earned his victims the collective nickname "Bums of the Month."

The most famous of Louis' fights was a return match with Max Schmeling on June 22, 1938. Two years earlier, Louis was knocked out by the German in the 12th round. Now with Hitler expounding his Nazi propaganda, German leaders made disparaging remarks about black Americans and the bout was regarded as a test of Aryan supremacy. In just two minutes and four seconds of the first round, Louis destroyed the man and the myth.

Joe Louis was to fight for another 11 years before announcing his retirement as undefeated champion on March 1, 1949. A year-and-a-half later, he tried to regain the crown but lost to Ezzard Charles on a decision. After an 8th round knockout at the hands of Rocky Marciano, Louis retired with a professional record of 68 wins (54 by knockout) and 3 losses.

Louis is perhaps as well-remembered for his simple articulation outside the ring as for the eloquence of his fists inside. When asked about the "running" tactics that Billy Conn was expected to use in their second meeting, Louis said simply, "He can run but he can't hide." Speaking at a bond rally, Louis also put into succinct language the U.S. rallying cry for World War II. We would win, he said, "because we are on God's side."

Despite earning nearly $4.5 million in purses, Louis, in his own words, "wound up broke" and finally owed nearly $1 million in back taxes. He spent the last years of his life as a public relations representative at Caesars Palace in Las Vegas.

BERT RANDOLPH SUGAR

WYSZYNSKI, Stefan Cardinal

Churchman, Roman Catholic Primate of Poland; b. Bialystok Province, Russia (now Poland), Aug. 3, 1901; d. Warsaw, May 28, 1981.

The most influential leader of the Roman Catholic Church in Poland in the 20th century, Stefan Cardinal Wyszynski achieved notable success in his lifelong struggle for the preservation of religious values, Catholic institutions, and Polish nationalism. From the late 1940s until his death, Wyszynski led the major unofficial opposition to the Polish Communist regime. Through confrontation and compromise he strengthened the position of the church, and in his last years was a moderating force in the struggle between the government and disenchanted labor forces. Wyszynski was also the mentor and friend of Karol Cardinal Wojtyla, who in 1978 became Pope John Paul II. In his eulogy, the pope praised his countryman as "the keystone of the unity of the church in Poland."

Background. Born in rural surroundings and modest circumstances, Wyszynski was the son of a village teacher and church organist. He was ordained as a priest in 1924, and in 1929 received a doctorate in sociology and canon law from the Catholic University of Lublin. Interested in the problems of working people and the poor, Wyszynski in 1935 founded the Catholic Workers University and throughout the 1930s helped resolve industrial and labor disputes. During World War II he was a leader of the resistance against Nazi occupation. In 1946 Wyszynski was consecrated Bishop of Lublin, and in 1948 Pope Pius XII named him Archbishop of Gniezno and Warsaw and the Primate of Poland.

The major challenge of his career came in the early 1950s, when the church faced official per-

Wide World Photos

MOSES, Robert

New York State official: b. New Haven, CT, Dec. 18, 1888; d. West Islip, NY, July 29, 1981.

Known as New York's "master builder," Robert Moses, who took pride in his ability to "get things done," did more to change the physical appearance of the state and city of New York than any other person of his generation. Through his various appointive public posts, he was instrumental in the building of such New York landmarks as the Triborough Bridge, the Brooklyn-Battery Tunnel, the Verrazano-Narrows Bridge, the Long Island parkway system, the Cross Bronx Expressway, the Niagara and St. Lawrence power projects, Jones Beach State Park, Lincoln Center, the New York Coliseum, the UN headquarters, Co-op City in the Bronx, and Shea Stadium in Queens. He helped create

TORRIJOS HERRERA, Omar

Panamanian military and government leader: b. Santiago, Panama, Feb. 13, 1929; d. in a plane crash in western Panama, July 31, 1981.

Gen. Omar Torrijos Herrera, 52, commander-in-chief of the National Guard and former chief of government of Panama, was killed in an airplane accident July 31. The crash, which occurred about 60 mi (97 km) west of Panama City, took the lives of all on board. Torrijos will be remembered by Americans as the tough negotiator of the Panama Canal treaties, concluded with President Jimmy Carter in 1978. Difficult to assess, Torrijos probably best represented a new breed of Latin American leader, possessing old-fashioned *machismo,* a Marxist vocabulary, and a pragmatism that permits close cooperation with Western capitalists when it is useful.

No intellectual, Torrijos was nevertheless a stirring orator. Representing no special ideology, he used his native rural wit to charm private listeners or exhort vast mobs. To the United States he had been an enigma; he fought tenaciously for the canal, supported Sandinistas in Nicaragua and guerrillas in El Salvador, and was a friend of Fidel Castro. Yet he condemned the Soviets over Afghanistan, boycotted the 1980 Olympics, and befriended the Shah of Iran when no one else would.

Background. Torrijos attended military schools in El Salvador, Venezuela, and the United States. In 1952 he was commissioned a second lieutenant in the National Guard. Very popular with troops, he rose through the ranks to become the commander-in-chief of that 4,500-man organization. In 1968 he led the coup that overthrew President Arnulfo Arias Madrid, and after months of intrigue, Torrijos emerged as secution by the Communist authorities. Wyszynski was successful in rallying the clergy and the faithful, and in 1952 he was elevated to the rank of cardinal. In 1953 Wyszynski was arrested and was confined for the next three years.

The struggle between church and state continued, but the late 1950s and the 1960s saw a remarkable upsurge in Polish Catholic life. The cardinal marked the millennium of Polish Christianity in 1966.

In 1970, when Wladislaw Gomulka was replaced by Edward Gierek as Communist Party leader, government pressure on the church was eased. Cardinal Wyszynski, however, maintained his role as critic, especially of government violence during the labor riots of 1976. In 1980, his encouragement of Lech Walesa's "Solidarity" movement was tempered with concern for the economy and fear of Soviet intervention.

ALEXANDER J. GROTH

UPI

parks, bridges, roadways, and housing throughout the state. The work implemented in New York proved a model in shaping the physical environment of urban areas throughout the world.

Background. Born of prosperous Jewish parents, Robert Moses studied at Yale (B.A., 1909), Oxford (B.A., 1911; M.A., 1913), and Columbia (Ph.D, 1914).

After working with the New York City Bureau of Municipal Research (1913–18), he was appointed by Gov. Alfred E. Smith to head a commission established to study means of streamlining state government. Most of the proposals made by the commission became law in 1924. In that same year, Moses became chairman of the New York Council of Parks and president of the Long Island State Park Commission, positions that gave him a power base from which to impose his vision of New York. He held several other state and city offices (many of them simultaneously), including secretary of state of New York (1927–28); city park commissioner (1934–60); chairman of the Consolidated Triborough Bridge and City Tunnel Authority (1946–68); member of the New York City Planning Commission (1942–60); and chairman of the state Power Authority (1954–63). He was also president of the New York World's Fair of 1964–65. He sought elective office only once, an unsuccessful attempt at the New York governorship in 1934.

Long a controversial figure and sometimes accused of running roughshod over the concerns and sensibilities of individual citizens and political figures, Moses resigned his state posts, effective Jan. 1, 1963, after Gov. Nelson Rockefeller accepted his resignation bluff. His legacy includes 12 bridges, 35 highways, 658 playgrounds, and some 2 million acres (810 000 ha) of parks.

SAUNDRA FRANCE

dictator, governing without parties or congress under the strictest censorship. From 1972 until 1978, he served as chief of government, behind puppet presidents.

His pose was strongly anti-United States, but he wooed foreign investment and brought considerable growth to Panama, especially in manufacturing and banking. Much of his success resulted from Torrijos' promise to acquire the Panama Canal from the United States. Talks had begun in the 1960s, but it was not until President Carter came into office that treaties were completed. They were very popular with most Panamanians, and Torrijos became a hero.

He left a Panama which is prouder if still hungry, better off than most of Latin America, with credit good and canal traffic up about 10% over the last year under U.S. jurisdiction.

THOMAS L. KARNES

UPI

WILKINS, Roy

U.S. civil-rights leader: b. St. Louis, Mo, Aug. 30, 1901; d. New York City, Sept. 8, 1981.

By the time he died, Roy Wilkins' name had become synonymous with the National Association for the Advancement of Colored People, the oldest and largest civil rights organization in the United States, which he served for nearly half a century. His name was also closely tied to the cause of racial equality, to which he dedicated his life.

Background. Wilkins' father was a college-educated Methodist minister who had to tend a brick kiln for a living. His mother died when Roy was four years old, and he, his brother, and his sister went to live with an aunt and uncle in St. Paul, MN. There he attended an integrated high school and was editor of the school paper. He went on to study sociology and journalism at the University of Minnesota, supporting himself with jobs as a redcap, Pullman car waiter, and slaughterhouse worker and still finding time to edit a local black weekly, the St. Paul *Appeal.* After graduation in 1923, Wilkins got his first taste of widespread racial segregation, and he used his editorial position to argue against such injustices. At one point, he even led a successful campaign to prevent the reelection of a U.S. senator from Missouri whom many blacks considered a racist.

That triumph brought Wilkins to the attention of NAACP chief Walter White, who invited the young journalist to work for the organization in New York City in 1931. One of his first projects was to investigate the working conditions of blacks laboring on Mississippi River levees. Wilkins went undercover and lived in the work camps, where men were paid only ten cents an hour, and produced a report entitled "Mississippi Slave Labor" that helped prompt Congressional action to improve the situation. That mission, Wilkins said later, "took all the theory out of the race relations business for me and put it on a realistic basis." Later, Wilkins succeeded W.E.B DuBois, one of the NAACP's founders, as editor of *The Crisis,* the association's official publication.

UPI

In 1934, Wilkins suffered the first of several arrests while picketing the office of the U.S. attorney general to protest the fact that lynching was not a high law-enforcement priority. Lynching was one of Wilkins' own preoccupations during the early days of his NAACP career. He never got the national legislation against it that he wanted, but his efforts added enough public pressure and awareness to help ease the situation. But his attentions were not limited; he was also passionately concerned about voting rights, fair housing, and educational equality. In fact, what Wilkins considered to be the greatest success of his career was in the field of education. He was the NAACP's point man for the school-desegregation case that resulted in the landmark 1954 U.S. Supreme Court ruling that outlawed "separate but equal" public schools.

Upon the death of Walter White in 1955, Wilkins was named the association's executive secretary, a post that was later changed to executive director. In that job, Wilkins continued the approach that had become the NAACP's trademark: legal and political action, working within the system to secure and enforce constitutional rights for black Americans. As other leaders, including the Rev. Martin Luther King, Jr., led the black rights struggle into the streets and before television cameras, Wilkins' NAACP did the homework, providing funds, legal expertise, and persuasive counsel in places as high as the White House.

As the movement grew more militant in the late 1960s, however, that role was increasingly misunderstood or unappreciated by younger activists who derided Wilkins as an "Uncle Tom." He was not deterred, and when the riots and demonstrations had ended, Wilkins was still on the scene. In the 1970s he took the Nixon and Ford administrations to task for what he perceived as footdragging in the national commitment to civil rights, and the NAACP continued to press legal cases across the country. But by the mid-1970s, Wilkins was in failing health and under challenge by those within his own organization who wanted him to step aside for younger leadership. He did so at the NAACP's 68th annual convention in his native St. Louis in 1977.

Wilkins was hospitalized on the eve of his 80th birthday, and he died days later of kidney failure. He was survived by his wife, the former Aminda Badeau. More than 900 persons, including U.S. Vice-President George Bush, attended his funeral service in New York City.

DENNIS A. WILLIAMS

SADAT, Anwar el-

President of Egypt: b. Mit Abul Kom, Egypt, Dec. 25, 1918; d. Cairo, Oct. 6, 1981.

The prospects for peace and stability in the Middle East were perceptibly dimmed on Oct. 6, 1981, when Anwar el-Sadat, the president of Egypt, was gunned down by assassins as he reviewed a parade of his troops in a suburb of Cairo. During his 11 years as president, Sadat established himself as a courageous and original leader, both in domestic affairs and regional diplomacy. He never eschewed violence as a means to political or diplomatic ends, and not all of his actions were free of a touch of the Machiavellian, but he will be remembered best for the bold initiative of his approach to Israel in November 1977, which he hoped would break the weary round of Arab-Israeli hostilities and inaugurate a new era of peace.

Though a devout Muslim, Sadat was entirely without the hegemonial and messianic ambitions of his predecessor, Gamal Abdel Nasser, or certain present-day Middle East leaders. Above all an Egyptian nationalist, he was profoundly suspicious of the Soviet Union and friendly to the United States. In domestic policy, he encouraged private enterprise and foreign investment. He tried gallantly, and the tragedy of his death was that he left much unfinished business.

Mohammed Anwar el-Sadat was born in a small village in the Nile Delta, into a family whose circumstances were modest but not poverty-stricken; his father was a clerk in a military hospital. Little is known of Sadat's boyhood, though contemporaries tell of his energy, originality, eccentricity, and penchant for solitary brooding.

Sadat attended the Royal Military Academy, graduating in 1938. Like many other young Egyptian officers, he developed strongly revolutionary and anti-British views. During World War II, he did whatever lay in his power to bring about a German victory. He engaged in several ineffectual conspiracies and was arrested and stripped of his rank for an unsuccessful attempt to convey military information to German Gen. Erwin Rommel.

Freed from jail but unemployed, Sadat in the postwar years engaged in various kinds of legal and illegal political activity. He apparently belonged briefly to both the Young Egypt party and the fundamentalist Muslim Brotherhood. Much more important to Sadat's career, however, was his role as a founding member of the secret Free Officers group, which had as its aims to end both the monarchy and the remaining aspects of British control over Egypt.

Restored to the rank of army captain in 1950, Sadat was one of the inner group of the Free Officers who overthrew King Farouk on July 23, 1952. During the Nasser era, Sadat held several high-level jobs but never a ministerial post. He was chairman of the National Assembly from 1959 to 1969, when Nasser appointed him vice-president.

UPI

When Nasser died in September 1970 and Sadat took over the presidency, it was widely assumed that he would be a weak figurehead and that he would soon lose his power to some rival. Such suppositions proved mistaken. In May 1971, a plot by Vice-President Ali Sabry was uncovered and punished. From then on, Sadat was indubitably in command. He first caught world attention in 1972 with the overnight expulsion of 20,000 Soviet military advisers who had been invited by Nasser in the wake of the Egyptian military debacle in the 1967 war with Israel. In 1973 Sadat went to war again with Israel to restore the nation's self-respect. Despite Israel's eventual victory, Egypt put up a strong showing and purged the earlier humiliation.

Sadat's visit to Jerusalem in November 1977 was an extraordinary and unique gesture. A magnificent gamble, it led successively to the Camp David draft agreement in September 1978; the awarding of the 1978 Nobel Peace Prize to Sadat and Israeli Prime Minister Menahem Begin; the signing of the Egyptian-Israeli Peace Treaty on March 26, 1979; and the normalization of relations between the two states. But the peace effort did not improve the economic lot of the ordinary Egyptian, and Sadat was almost totally isolated from the rest of the Arab world.

The year 1981 witnessed an increasing edginess and ruthlessness in Sadat's domestic policies. In September, some 1,500 political opponents, most of them Islamic fundamentalists, were rounded up and arrested. The same month, Sadat expelled the Soviet ambassador and 20 other Soviet officials.

ARTHUR CAMPBELL TURNER

DAYAN, Moshe

Israeli military leader and government official: b. Kibbutz Degania, Palestine, May 20, 1915; d. Tel Aviv, Israel, Oct. 16, 1981.

One of the most vivid and versatile of contemporary statesmen was lost to the world scene when Moshe Dayan succumbed to a heart attack on Oct. 16, 1981. A former Israeli chief of staff, defense minister, and foreign minister, Dayan was a hero in war and a pursuer of peace. A *sabra* (native Israeli) and passionate nationalist, he was a resilient but controversial figure in the domestic political arena. Also an archaeologist of note, Dayan owned one of the world's largest collections of Middle Eastern relics.

Background. Moshe Dayan was born at Degania, the first kibbutz in what is now Israel, on the southern shore of the Sea of Galilee. He was the son of Russian immigrants who helped found the kibbutz. Later the family moved to Nahalal in the Jezreel Valley, where Moshe went to an agricultural high school. He began to serve his apprenticeship as a soldier in his teens, guarding the settlement at night from Arab attacks. He enrolled in *Haganah,* the Jewish self-defense force, and in 1936–39 served in an auxiliary force used by the British to combat Arab terrorism. In 1939, however, Haganah was declared illegal, and Dayan was given a ten-year jail sentence. But two years later he was released. Trained by the British, he served in a force that advanced into Syria to oppose the Vichy French. It was in combat there that he lost his left eye and began wearing his familiar eye-patch.

When Israel became independent in 1948, Dayan was made a regularly commissioned officer. He distinguished himself in the Arab war that year. A rapid rise made him a major general in 1950 and chief of the general staff, 1953–58. He emerged as a hero in the 1956 war with Egypt. Leaving the military, he took a law degree in 1959 and entered parliament as a Labor Party member. He was minister of agriculture, 1959–64 and in 1967 became minister of defense in time to head the Israeli forces in the Six-Day War. The lightning victory made him the most popular man in Israel. As administrator of occupied territories, he unified Jerusalem and permitted free movement for all its inhabitants.

If he was too highly praised in 1967, Dayan suffered too much opprobrium for Israel's initial poor performance in the 1973 Yom Kippur War. Out of government for three years, he was the surprise choice for foreign minister in Menahem Begin's 1977 Likud Party cabinet. As ardent in peace as he had been in war, he played a leading part in bringing Egyptian President Anwar el-Sadat to Jerusalem in 1977, the Camp David negotiations of 1978, and the Israeli-Egyptian Peace Treaty in 1979. Dayan resigned from the cabinet in October 1979, favoring more leniency for Palestinian Arabs in occupied territories than did Prime Minister Begin. He returned to politics in June 1981 as leader of the small, new Telem party.

ARTHUR CAMPBELL TURNER

The following is a selected list of prominent persons who died during 1981. Articles on major figures appear in the preceding pages.

Algren, Nelson (né Nelson Algren Abraham) (72), writer; his works include the novels *A Walk on the Wild Side* and *The Man with the Golden Arm:* d. Sag Harbor, NY, May 9.

Princess Alice (97), Countess of Athlone; last surviving grandchild of Queen Victoria: d. London, Jan. 3.

Altschul, Frank (94), financier and philanthropist, an investment banker and senior partner in the firm of Lazard Freres & Company (1943–45) and chairman of General Investors Corporation until his retirement in 1961. In 1934 he established the Overbrook Press, which specialized in exquisitely printed and illustrated limited edition books: d. Stamford, CT, May 29.

Anders, Glenn (92), actor; appeared in numerous stage roles in the 1920s and 1930s, including the Pulitzer Prize-winning *Hell Bent for Heaven* (1924), *They Knew What They Wanted* (1924), and *Strange Interlude* (1928). He occasionally appeared in films: d. Englewood, NJ, Oct. 26.

Anderson, Jack Z. (76), California member of U.S. House of Representatives (1939–53) and an administrative assistant of Dwight Eisenhower's White House Staff (1956–61): d. Hollister, CA, Feb. 9.

Prince Andrew of Russia (84), member of the Romanov Dynasty that ruled Russia from 1613 until 1917 and the oldest surviving relative of Czar Nicholas II: d. Teynham, England, May 8.

Arieti, Silvano (67) psychoanalyst; wrote extensively on schizophrenia and creativity. His books include *Interpretation of Schizophrenia,* which won him a National Book Award in 1975 and *Creativity: The Magic Synthesis.* He was editor in chief of the *American Handbook of Psychiatry:* d. New York City, Aug. 7.

Astaire, Adele (née Adele Marie Austerlitz) (83), dancer-comedian; performed in many musical comedies of the 1920s with her brother and dance partner Fred: d. Phoenix, AZ, Jan. 25.

Auchinleck, Sir Claude (96), British field marshal. A decorated hero of World War I, he served during World War II in India and the Middle East. Auchinleck was dismissed by Winston Churchill in August 1942 for refusing to launch an immediate counterattack when Rommel halted outside Cairo: d. Marrakesh, Morocco, March 23.

Bagnold, Enid (91), British playwright and novelist. Her six novels include *National Velvet* (1935), later made into a film, and her ten plays include *The Chalk Garden* and *A Matter of Gravity:* d. London, March 31.

Baldwin, Roger (97), freedom crusader; founded the American Civil Liberties Union in 1920, retiring as its head in 1950. Baldwin and the ACLU defended people of all political persuasions. Educated at Harvard, Baldwin became a sociology instructor at Washington University in St. Louis in 1906. In 1909 he met anarchist Emma Goldman, after which he "never departed far from the general philosophy represented in libertarian literature." In his later years, Mr. Baldwin taught civil liberties law at the University of Puerto Rico: d. Ridgewood, NJ, Aug. 26.

Ball, Edward (93), financier; chief trustee of the billion-dollar Alfred I. du Pont Testamentary Trust. The brother-in-law of Alfred du Pont, he began working for Du Pont interests after World War I, and following the death of his brother-in-law in 1935 he became one of Florida's most influential and controversial citizens through control of the huge estate. He was said to have led the "red scare" campaign that forced Florida's Claude Pepper from the Senate in 1950. Mr. Ball built the Alfred du Pont estate, originally estimated at about $33 million, to a value of about $2,000,000,000: d. New Orleans, June 24.

Barber, Samuel (70), composer; he won Pulitzer Prizes in 1958 and 1963 and his piece *Adagio for Strings* is one of the most popular orchestral works. He began studying piano at age 6, wrote his first piece at age 7. In 1938 conductor Arturo Toscanini gave world premieres of two Barber works in a single year. His opera *Vanessa,* for which his longtime friend, composer Gian Carlo Menotti, supplied the libretto, won the Pulitzer Prize of 1958. He experienced two major disappointments—his opera *Antony and Cleopatra,* which opened the Metropolitan Opera's new home at Lincoln Center, was a fiasco; and Mr. Barber considered his

Wide World Photos
ROGER BALDWIN

Wide World Photos
SAMUEL BARBER

Wide World Photos
ALFRED H. BARR

UPI
MARCEL BREUER

Second Symphony an inferior work and tore up all available scores of the symphony. His music was conservative and neo-Romantic: d. New York City, Jan. 23.

Barr, Alfred Hamilton, Jr. (79), art scholar, developer of New York's Museum of Modern Art; he was instrumental in acquiring much important 20th-century art for the museum—acquisitions that built the museum into the world's most significant collection of modern art. He brought to the museum innovative multidepartmental plans in architecture, film, photography, industrial and theater design, and commercial art. He wrote major works on modern art: d. Salisbury, CT, Aug. 15.

Beard, Matthew (Stymie) (57), actor; he was one of the "Our Gang" comedy actors, known on television as "The Little Rascals": d. Los Angeles, Jan. 8.

Becker, Frank J. (82), U.S. representative from New York (1953–65): d. Lynbrook, NY, Sept. 4.

Beheshti, Ayatollah Mohammed (52), political leader of Iran. As head of revolutionary Iran's Islamic Republican Party and the Iranian Supreme Court, he had steadfastly whittled away at President Bani-Sadr's power until Bani-Sadr was removed from office. He died in a bomb explosion: d. Tehran, June 28.

Benchley, Nathaniel (66), novelist, humorist, and journalist; wrote 15 novels of which the most celebrated was *The Off-Islanders,* which became the film *The Russians Are Coming, the Russians Are Coming.* He also worked as a journalist for *The New York Herald Tribune* and *Newsweek,* wrote for *The New Yorker, Harper's Bazaar,* and *Playboy,* did children's books, and occasionally wrote for motion pictures: d. Boston, Dec. 14.

Bennett, Robert Russell (87), musical composer and conductor. He was famed for his orchestrations of such Broadway hits as *Show Boat, Oklahoma, My Fair Lady, Rose Marie, Of Thee I Sing, Anything Goes, Carmen Jones, Annie Get Your Gun, Kiss Me Kate, South Pacific, The King and I, The Sound of Music,* and *Camelot.* Mr. Bennett also did guest conducting with symphony orchestras; had the radio program *Russell Bennett's Notebook* on which he arranged, conducted, and composed music; was musical director of the National Broadcasting Company; and spent four years in Hollywood contributing original music and orchestrations to films: d. New York City, Aug. 18.

Betancourt, Rómulo (73), president of Venezuela (1959–64); he earlier had been leader of the country (1945–48) as head of the junta that overthrew Gen. Isaías Medina Angarita: d. New York City, Sept. 28.

Blackwell, Randolph T. (53), civil-rights activist; joined Martin Luther King, Jr.'s Southern Christian Leadership Conference in 1963 and in 1966 became director of Southern Rural Action, a nonprofit corporation specializing in economic development in the South: d. Atlanta, GA, May 21.

Bliss, Ray (73), national chairman of the Republican Party (1965–69); held a seat on the Republican National Committee (1952–80). In 1949 he took over as the Republican Party's state chairman in Ohio. Over the next 16 years, he turned that state's party unit from one of disarray into one of the smoothest running in the country. Upon taking over the national chairmanship he rebuilt the party after the Goldwater debacle in 1964 and was helpful in getting Richard Nixon elected in 1968. He quit the chairmanship in 1969 in a power struggle with Richard Nixon: d. Akron, OH, Aug. 6.

Böhm, Karl (86), Austrian musical conductor; his specialties were Mozart, Wagner, and Richard Strauss. Educated in the law as well as in music, his conducting debut was at the Graz Opera in 1917. He was conductor in various provincial European opera houses before becoming in 1934 general director of the Dresden Staatsoper. In the years from 1934–43 Böhm produced a golden age in music for the city of Dresden. He became friends with composer Richard Strauss and led the world premieres of the composer's *Die schweigsame Frau* (1935) and *Daphne* (1938). He also built an enviable ensemble of opera singers. After leaving Dresden he served two terms as general director of the Vienna State Opera (1943–45 and 1954–56). After 1956 he gave up his administrative duties to conduct on a free-lance basis throughout the world. He debuted with the New York Metropolitan Opera in 1957 and with the New York Philharmonic in 1973: d. Salzburg, Austria, Aug. 14.

Bolotowsky, Ilya (74), painter; embraced the approach to art known as Neo-Plasticism, a style in which color and line were harmonized in simple right-angle forms. He was given his first museum show, a retrospective at the Guggenheim, in 1974: d. New York City, Nov. 22.

Bondi, Beulah (92), actress; most famous for her performances in the motion pictures *Make Way for Tomorrow* (1937) and *On Borrowed Time* (1939): d. Hollywood, CA, Jan. 12.

Boni, Albert (88), publisher; in the post–World War I period, he brought out the works of Thornton Wilder, Ford Madox Ford, Theodore Dreiser, and Leon Trotsky and was one of the pioneers of the paperback and book-club fields. Along with Horace Liveright he founded Modern Library and selected the first 100 titles before selling out to Liveright. In 1929 he attempted to combine soft-cover and book-club publishing with the creation of the Paper Books program. This company faded during the Depression. Boni began Readex Microprint Corporation, a publisher of reference materials on microfilm, in 1950. He retired in 1974: d. Ormond Beach, FL, July 31.

Boone, Richard (63), actor; most famous for his appearances in the television series *Have Gun, Will Travel.* He appeared in 65 movies and 11 plays: d. St. Augustine, FL, Jan. 10.

Bordes François (61), French archeologist; authority on the culture of Neanderthal man and on the study of the making and use of ancient tools. Dr. Bordes, author of *The Old Stone Age,* was director of the Laboratory of Quaternary Geology and History at the University of Bordeaux and had made more than 100,000 stone tools, most resembling ancient tools so closely that they had to be labeled to avoid confusion: d. Tucson, AZ, April 30.

Breit, Gregory (82), physicist; active in the development of atomic weapons. In 1942 he was chosen to start designing a bomb, but resigned from the project to go into ballistics research at the Aberdeen Proving Ground in Maryland. J. Robert Oppenheimer was his successor. Dr. Breit, along with Nobel Prize physicist Eugene Wigner, is credited with the resonance theory of nuclear reactions—that every object has characteristic frequencies at which it vibrates: d. Salem, OR, Sept. 13.

Breuer, Marcel (79), architect; famed as the designer of the Cesca and Wassily chairs and as the architect responsible for such structures as the Whitney Museum in New York, the Parisian headquarters of UNESCO, the IBM Research Center in La Gaude, France, and St. John's Abbey in Collegeville, MN. Born in Hungary, Breuer began the study of art in Vienna in 1920, leaving after just five weeks upon hearing of the new Bauhaus school in Weimar, Germany. He enrolled during the same year and by 1924 was a Bauhaus Master in charge of the carpentry and furniture department. In his furniture designs he was interested in exploring the potential of modern technology. In 1928 he left the Bauhaus for Berlin and set up his own architectural practice. Two major commissions in Germany—the Harnischmacher House in Wiesbaden and the Doldertal Apartment in Zurich—were designed before Breuer departed for England in 1936. He left England after just one year to join Walter Gropius, an old Bauhaus associate, in the United States at Harvard University. In 1946 Breuer moved his practice to New York City, and in 1964 added a branch office in Paris: d. New York City, July 1.

Brown, Christy (49), Irish author; handicapped with cerebral palsy, he wrote by typing with his left foot. His works include *My Left Foot* (1954) and his autobiographical novel *Down All the Days* (1970): d. Parbrook, Somerset, England, Sept. 6.

Burke, James (58), musician; principal cornet soloist with the Goldman Band for more than 30 years: d. June 26.

Wide World Photos

EMANUEL CELLER

UPI

PADDY CHAYEFSKY

Butler, Paul (89), aviation executive; founder of Butler Aviation: d. near Oak Brook, IL, June 24.

Cabot, John Moors (79), U.S. career diplomat; joined the Foreign Service in 1927 and in his 41-year career served as U.S. ambassador to Brazil, Colombia, Finland, Poland, and Sweden. During the Eisenhower administration, Cabot was the assistant secretary of state for Latin American affairs. He also served as the last U.S. Consul General in Shanghai before the 1949 Communist victory in China: d. Washington, DC, Feb. 23.

Carmichael, Hoagy (82), composer; wrote such standards as *Stardust, Georgia on My Mind, Lazy Bones,* and *The Nearness of You.* He acted in some movies, including *To Have and Have Not* and *The Best Years of Our Lives,* and occasionally appeared on radio and television: d. Rancho Mirage, CA, Dec. 27.

Celler, Emanuel (92), served 50 years (1923–73) in the U.S. House of Representatives from New York's Tenth District. A liberal, he supported major New Deal and Fair Deal programs. In 1949 he became chairman of the Judiciary Committee and as such handled civil-rights legislation: d. Brooklyn, NY, Jan. 15.

Chase, Mary Coyle (74), playwright; author of the Pulitzer Prize-winning *Harvey:* d. Denver, Oct. 20.

Chayefsky, Paddy (né Sidney) (58), playwright; winner of three (1955, 1971, 1976) Oscars for screenwriting for *Marty, The Hospital,* and *Network.* His early television dramas were a part of what was later referred to as television's golden age. Other stories and screenplays that he wrote included *The Bachelor Party* (1957); *Middle of the Night* (1959); *The Americanization of Emily* (1964); and *Altered States* (1979), based on his novel. His stage plays include *The Tenth Man, Gideon,* and *The Passion of Josef D:* d. New York City, Aug. 1.

Clair, René (82), French film director-writer; he was the first person elected to the French Academy solely for film work. A master of comedy of a satiric or philosophic nature, his most famous films include *Un Chapeau de Paille d'Italie, A Nous la Liberté, Paris Qui Dort, Le Million, It Happened Tomorrow.* In all, he made 28 films between 1923 and 1965: d. Neuilly, France, March 15.

Cole, Cozy (né William R.) (71), jazz drummer. In 1953, along with drummer Gene Krupa, he formed the Krupa and Cole Drum School; the school closed after Krupa's death in 1973: d. Columbus, OH, Jan. 29.

Conley, Eugene (73), tenor; sang with the Metropolitan and New York City opera companies and was the first American tenor to open the season at Milan's La Scala Opera Company: d. Denton, TX, Dec. 18.

Connelly, Philip M. (77), labor militant; convicted of trying to overthrow the U.S. government after a six-month trial in 1952 in which he and other Communist Party members were found guilty under the Smith Act of 1940. He was sentenced to a five-year prison term. In 1955 an appeal to the U.S. Supreme Court resulted in the overturning of the sentence. A newspaperman, Connelly became a professional labor organizer in 1938. He was a full-time Council of Industrial Organizations executive until 1949 and thereafter edited a West Coast Communist newspaper: d. Torrance, CA, May 20.

Coolidge, Peggy Stuart (67), composer, pianist, and conductor; she was a soloist with the Boston Symphony Orchestra: d. Cushing, ME, May 7.

Coon, Carleton S. (76), anthropologist; he made contributions to the study of transitional human development from the hunter-gatherer culture to the early agricultural communities. In 1948 he became curator of ethnology at the University Museum in Philadelphia and professor of anthropology at the University of Pennsylvania. He wrote a basic textbook, *A Reader in General Anthropology* (1948), and is perhaps best known for *The Story of Man* (1954) and *The Seven Caves* (1957): d. Gloucester, MA, June 3.

Corner, George (91), professor of medicine; his research in human reproduction and sexuality led to the development of the birth control pill. Along with Dr. Willard M. Allen, he is credited with the identification of the hormone progesterone, key to the development of the birth control pill: d. Huntsville, AL, Sept. 28.

Cotter, William Ross (55), Democratic congressman from Connecticut's First District (1971–81): d. East Lyme, CT, Sept. 8.

Cronin, A(rchibald) J(oseph) (84), Scottish author; he had earlier been a physician, serving as a medical inspector of mines in South Wales and later building a practice in Glasgow and London. In 1931 he wrote *Hatter's Castle.* It became a best-seller in England, and thereafter Dr. Cronin wrote full time. Other novels are *The Stars Look Down, The Citadel,* and *The Keys of the Kingdom:* d. Glion, Switzerland, Jan. 6.

Crowther, Bosley (75), film critic for *The New York Times* (1940–67). He authored five books and two plays: d. Mount Kisco, NY, March 7.

Curran, Joseph (75), founder of the National Maritime Union of America. Mr. Curran organized the union in May 1937 and was elected its first president. Despite accusations that he was a Communist, he continued to be elected until 1973: d. Boca Raton, FL, Aug. 14.

Daniel, Dan (91), sportswriter; expert on baseball: d. Pompano Beach, FL, July 1.

Daniels, Jonathan (79), editor and aide to presidents Franklin Roosevelt and Harry Truman. Daniels trained for the law, but never practiced. He began working for his father on *The Raleigh* (NC) *News and Observer* as the paper's Washington correspondent in 1925, leaving in 1928 to write a novel. He returned to the paper in 1932, became editor in 1933 and remained until 1942 when President Roosevelt persuaded him to become assistant director of the Office of Civil Defense. He later became Roosevelt's press secretary and was an adviser to President Truman: d. Hilton Head, SC, Nov. 6.

Davis, James Curran (86), publisher and Georgia Democratic congressman; served in the U.S. House of Representatives from 1947 until 1963. A champion of segregation, in 1964 he began publication of *The Atlanta Times,* a conservative newspaper which closed after 14 months because of financial problems: d. Atlanta, Dec. 28.

Davis, Jim (65), actor; best known as the patriarch Jock Ewing on the highly successful *Dallas* television series: d. Northridge, CA, April 26.

Dean, Paul (Daffy) (67), baseball pitcher; along with his older brother Dizzy, he helped win the 1934 World Series for the St. Louis Cardinals. In his first two major league seasons he won 19 games each and pitched a no-hitter, but developed arm trouble in 1936: d. Springdale, AR, March 17.

Dean, William F. (82), major general of the U.S. Army. He received the Medal of Honor for attacking an enemy tank armed only with a hand grenade during the Korean War. For 20 days following, he wandered in the hills below Taejon, South Korea, before being betrayed by two South Korean civilians. He was a prisoner of war for the remainder of the conflict and withstood all efforts to extract military information from him: d. Berkeley, CA, Aug. 24.

Delbrück, Max (74), biologist; a major pioneer of modern molecular genetics. Born in Berlin and trained as a theoretical physicist, his greatest contributions to science were his studies of groups of viruses called bacteriophages. In 1969 he shared the Nobel Prize for physiology or medicine with Salvador Luria and Alfred Hershey: d. Pasadena, CA, March 9.

Dinkeloo, John (63), architect and engineer; joined the firm of Eero Saarinen in 1950, becoming a partner in 1956. After Saarinen's death in 1961, he continued the firm with Joseph Lacy and Kevin Roche. The firm became Kevin Roche, John Dinkeloo Associates in 1966. Its widely acclaimed buildings include the Oakland (CA) Museum and the Ford Foundation headquarters in New York: d. Fredericksburg, VA, June 15.

DiSalle, Michael V. (73), Democratic governor of Ohio (1959–63) and formerly a member of the Ohio House of Representatives, a mayor of Toledo, and director of Price Stabilization under President Harry Truman. He championed the Kennedy election causes: d. Pescara, Italy, Sept. 15.

Dixon, Jean (85), stage and motion picture actress; she appeared in the stage hits *June Moon* (1929) and *Once in a Lifetime* (1930) and in the films *My Man Godfrey* (1936) and *Holiday* (1938): d. Feb. 12.

Dominick, Peter H. (65), U. S. representative (R-CO, 1961–63) and U.S. senator (1963–75): d. Hobe Sound, FL, March 18.

Douglas, Donald W., Sr. (88), airline industrialist; he produced in 1936 the DC-3 airliner (military version—the C-47) which brought mass airline travel to the world. In 1967 his company was absorbed by the McDonnell Aircraft Corporation, and Douglas retired: d. Palm Springs, CA, Feb. 1.

Douglas, Melvyn (né Melvyn Edouard Hesselberg) (80), actor; well known for his Academy Award-winning performances in the movies *Hud* and *Being There.* He had begun his film career as a debonair actor of Hollywood romantic comedies, and between 1931 and 1942 made 45 motion pictures. After World War II he abandoned Hollywood for ten years and made numerous appearances on the Broadway stage (where he had performed prior to his movie success). His Broadway successes included

Time Out for Ginger (1952) and *Inherit the Wind* (1955), in which he portrayed Clarence Darrow: d. New York City, Aug. 4.

Durant, Ariel (née Ida) (83), historian; she collaborated with her husband Will on the 11-volume series *The Story of Civilization:* d. Hollywood Hills, CA, Oct. 25.

Durant, Will (96), historian and philosopher; wrote *The Story of Civilization,* an 11-volume history of more than 110 centuries begun in 1927 and completed in 1975. All 11 volumes were best-sellers and one of the volumes, *Rousseau and Revolution,* won a Pulitzer Prize. Dr. Durant's parents had intended that he study for the Roman Catholic priesthood, but after some study in a seminary he withdrew and shortly thereafter was excommunicated. As a young man, he was part of New York's radical circles, teaching at the anarchist-sponsored Francisco Ferrer School. It was there he met his wife, Ariel, a 14-year-old pupil whom he married in 1913 when she was 15. Together they collaborated on several volumes. Durant also wrote *Adventures in Genius, Program for Americans,* and *Tragedy of Russia.* He and his wife wrote their biography, *A Dual Biography* (1977): d. Los Angeles, Nov. 7.

Dwan, Allen (96), motion picture director of an estimated 1,850 films, many of them very early one-reelers. His major films include *Zaza, The Iron Mask, Heidi, Rebecca of Sunnybrook Farm, Suez,* and *Sands of Iwo Jima*: d. Woodland Hills, CA, Dec. 21.

Eberly, Bob (65), singer; performed with the Dorsey brothers and was a popular singer of the "Swing" era: d. Glen Burnie, MD, Nov. 17.

Edwards, Joan (61), singer; was the star of the 1940s radio show *Your Hit Parade.* In later years she wrote scores for nightclub revues and did successful advertising jingles: d. New York City, Aug. 27.

Ernster, Dezsö (82), Hungarian bass singer; debuted with the Metropolitan Opera in 1946 as King Marke in *Tristan.* His final appearance there was in the role of the Grand Inquisitor in *Don Carlo:* d. Zurich, Feb. 15.

Evans, Madge (71), actress; she appeared in such films as *Dinner at Eight* (1933) and *David Copperfield* (1935) and on Broadway in *Daisy Mayme* (1926), *Here Come the Clowns* (1938), and *The Patriots* (1943): d. Oakland, NJ, April 26.

Fisk, James B. (70), executive of Bell Laboratories. He was president of the company from 1959–73, becoming chairman in 1973, a year before his retirement. He was a key figure in the development of radar, and on several occasions left Bell to work for the government: d. Elizabethtown, NY, Aug. 10.

Fitzsimmons, Frank Edward (73), president of the International Brotherhood of Teamsters. Starting as a bus driver for the Detroit Motor Company, he worked briefly in New York City before returning to Detroit as a truck driver. In 1934 he joined the teamsters' Local 299 in Detroit. The newly-elected president of that Local was Jimmy Hoffa. Fitzsimmons worked through the union ranks and in 1961 as a protégé of Hoffa was elected a union international vice-president. When Hoffa was sent to prison in 1967, Fitzsimmons, with the newly created title of general vice-president, assumed the day-to-day running of the union. In 1971, after Hoffa gave up the union presidency in exchange for freedom from prison, Fitzsimmons became president: d. La Jolla, CA, May 6.

Fox, Carol (55), co-founder and former general manager of the Lyric Opera of Chicago: d. Chicago, July 21.

Fox, Terry (22), Canadian hero. As a college student he was stricken with bone cancer, resulting in an amputated right leg. He began a marathon run across Canada to raise money for cancer research. He was unable to complete his cross-country run, but through his efforts $20 million had been raised for research. He was awarded the Order of Canada: d. New Westminster, B.C., June 28.

Queen Frederika (63), Queen of Greece from 1947 until the death of her husband, King Paul I, in 1964: d. Madrid, Feb. 6.

Frings, Katherine Hartley (Ketti) (61), screenwriter and playwright; she dramatized Thomas Wolfe's *Look Homeward Angel* for the Broadway stage, winning the Pulitzer Prize in 1958: d. Los Angeles, Feb. 11.

ARIEL DURANT

UPI

FRANK FITZSIMMONS

UPI

Gance, Abel (92), French cinematic pioneer; he was the first filmmaker to use three screens simultaneously (a forerunner of wide-screen cinematography) and a camera on a moving track. He is also credited with introducing stereophonic sound to the motion picture industry. His 1927 masterpiece *Napoléon* enjoyed renewed acclaim in 1981 when it was shown in several cities throughout the world: d. Paris, Nov. 10.

Garnett, David (88), British novelist; one of the last members of the Bloomsbury group. His best known novel was *Lady into Fox* (1922): d. Le Verger de Charry, Montcuq, France, Feb. 17.

George, Chief Dan (82), motion picture actor and chief of the Burrard Indian tribe from 1951 to 1963; best known for his role in *Little Big Man,* which earned him an Academy Award nomination: d. Vancouver, British Columbia, Sept. 23.

Gimbel, Sophie (83), fashion designer; credited with introducing the culotte or divided skirt. Mrs. Gimbel headed the Saks Fifth Avenue custom-order department from 1931 until her retirement in 1969: d. New York City, Nov. 28.

Golden, Harry (né Harry L. Goldhurst) (79), editor, author, and publisher. Born in New York City, he moved to the South, first working as a salesman and then as a reporter for *The Charlotte (NC) Observer.* He founded *The Carolina Israelite* in 1941; it folded in 1968. His books include *Only in America, For 2 Cents Plain, Enjoy! Enjoy!,* and a biography of Carl Sandburg: d. Charlotte, NC, Oct. 2.

Gordon, Caroline (86), writer and critic; in her career of more than 50 years nine of her novels were published. Her short stories were published in 1981 as *The Collected Stories of Caroline Gordon:* d. San Cristobal de las Casas, Chiapas, Mexico, April 11.

Grahame, Gloria (née Gloria Hallward) (55), actress; she appeared in more than 30 films and won an Academy Award in 1952 for her supporting role in *The Bad and the Beautiful:* d. New York City, Oct. 5.

Green, Paul (87), playwright; winner of the Pulitzer Prize in 1927 for *In Abraham's Bosom.* He also wrote *Johnny Johnson* (1936) and with Richard Wright adapted *Native Son* (1941) for the theater. His screenplays include *State Fair* (1945): d. Chapel Hill, NC, May 4.

Guyer, Tennyson (67), Republican U.S. representative from Ohio (1973–81): d. Alexandria, VA, April 12.

Hagerty, James (71), White House press secretary under Dwight Eisenhower (1953–61): d. Bronxville, NY, April 11.

Haley, Bill (né William John, Jr.) (55), singer–band leader; he was one of the pioneers of rock 'n' roll. Haley's most famous recording is *Rock Around the Clock:* d. Harlingen, Texas, Feb. 9.

Handler, Philip (64), biochemist; served as the president of the National Academy of Sciences for 12 years, retiring in June 1981, and was a member of the Duke University faculty. At Duke, Handler made a key discovery regarding pellagra, tracing the disease's cause to a corn-rich diet. He was also credited with the discovery of at least 15 enzymes, chemicals that promote various biological processes. In 1962 Dr. Handler was appointed to the National Science Board and in 1966 he was elected its chairman. He was reelected chairman in 1968 and a few months later was elected president of the National Academy of Sciences: d. Boston, Dec. 29.

Hanson, Howard (84), composer, conductor, and educator; he directed the Eastman School of Music in Rochester, NY, from 1924 until his retirement in 1964. He was a guest conductor of many orchestras. In 1944 he received a Pulitzer Prize for his Fourth Symphony: d. Rochester, NY, Feb. 26.

Harburg, E. Y. (Yip) (84), lyricist; he wrote the lyrics to *Over the Rainbow, April in Paris, Brother, Can You Spare a Dime,* and the musical *Finian's Rainbow* (1947), for which, along with Fred Saidy, he also wrote the libretto. Because of his political views he was black-listed after World War II: d. Los Angeles, March 5.

Harding, Ann (née Anna Gately) (79), actress: made numerous stage and film appearances in the 1920s and '30s. She had important stage successes in such plays as *Tarnish* (1923) and *The Trial of Mary Dugan* (1927): d. Sherman Oaks, CA, Sept. 1.

Harrison, Wallace (86), architect; played an important role in the planning of Rockefeller Center, the United Nations, Lincoln Center, the 1939 World's Fair, and the Empire State Plaza in Albany, NY, and was also the architect of the Metropolitan Opera House at Lincoln Center: d. New York City, Dec. 2.

Hays, Lawrence Brooks (83), U.S. Representative from Arkansas (1943–59), a moderate Democrat, he helped with explosive civil rights issues during the Eisenhower administration. Later he was a special assistant to presidents Kennedy and Johnson: d. Bethesda, MD, Oct. 11.

Head, Edith (80s?), motion picture costume designer. In a career spanning more than 50 years she received a record eight Academy Awards. She worked on 1,000 films and was nominated for 35 Oscars: d. Hollywood, CA, Oct. 24.

Hirsch, Joseph (71), painter; well known for his realistic art; also described as an allegorical, figurative, still-life, and portrait painter: d. New York City, Sept. 21.

Hirshhorn, Joseph (82), financier and art patron. As his art collection grew, an institution to house it became necessary, and Mr. Hirshhorn, taken with Lyndon Johnson, selected Washington as the city in which to place his collection. The Joseph Hirshhorn Museum and Sculpture Garden was opened in 1974, a miscellaneous museum of American and European art: d. Washington, DC, Aug. 31.

Holden, William (né William Franklin Beedle, Jr.) (63), motion picture actor; won the Academy Award for his performance in *Stalag 17*. In a career of more than 40 years he appeared in several important films, including *The Country Girl, Sunset Boulevard, Born Yesterday, Picnic,* and *the Bridges of Toko-Ri*. He also appeared in the television series *The Blue Knight*. Respected by directors and critics, he was a particularly popular film star. The actor also was a devoted animal conservationist: d. Santa Monica, CA, Nov. 16.

Hollowood, Bernard (70), editor of the British humor magazine *Punch* (1957–68); during his 11-year tenure with the magazine he expanded its format to include political and social commentary: d. England, March 28.

Holm, John Cecil (76), actor and playwright; coauthored, with George Abbott, the Broadway comedy *Three Men on a Horse:* d. Rhode Island, Oct. 24.

Horan, James D. (67), historian, novelist, and newsman; he was the author of 40 books, including *Matthew Brady: Historian with a Camera* (1955) and *The Authentic Wild West* (1977): d. New York City, Oct. 13.

Humes, Helen (68), singer; known as both a ballad and blues singer. A recording artist at age 14, she was a vocalist with Count Basie's band (1938–42). Thereafter she made recordings and toured Australia and Europe, but gave up singing professionally in the 1960s after the death of her mother. In 1973 she went to New York to take part in a tribute to Count Basie, and subsequently took up her career again: d. Santa Monica, CA, Sept. 13.

Ilg, Frances L. (78), pediatrician, authority, and writer on child behavior. In the 1930s and 1940s she was an associate at Yale University of Dr. Arnold Gesell, founder of the Yale Clinic of Child Development and a pioneer in the study of infant and child behavior. After Dr. Gesell's retirement from Yale in 1950, Dr. Ilg, along with two collaborators, established the Gesell Institute of Child Development, later changed to the Gesell Institute of Human Development. Dr. Ilg was coauthor of more than 20 books tracing children's behavior patterns from infancy through their teens: d. Manitowish Waters,WI, July 26.

Jaffee, Irving (74), speed skater; won the 10,000-meter race in the 1928 Olympic Games at St. Moritz, Switzerland, and four years later at Lake Placid, NY, he won gold medals in the 5,000- and 10,000-meter events. In 1940 he was elected to the U.S. Skating Hall of Fame: d. San Diego, CA, March 20.

Jessel, George (83), comedian; began as a performer on the vaudeville circuit, later performed on Broadway and in films, and in recent decades was known as a "toastmaster general." His most famous Broadway appearance was in the title role of *The Jazz Singer* (1925). He appeared in and produced several other stage shows. In Hollywood he appeared in some films and produced others, often Hollywood musicals. As a toastmaster who appeared all over the world, he raised millions of dollars for charities and social and political causes: d. Los Angeles, May 24.

Johnson, Pamela Hansford (69), British novelist; also wrote plays, biographies, and criticism. Her novels include *An Impossible Marriage, The Sea and the Wedding, The Good Husband,* and *Night and Silence, Who Is Here?* Her plays include *Corinth House* and *The Rehearsal,* and her literary studies include *Thomas Wolfe* (published in the United States as *Hungry Gulliver* and later *The Art of Thomas Wolfe*). She was the widow of C. P. Snow: d. London, June 18.

Kaiser, Edgar Fosburgh (73), industrialist; the son of Henry J. Kaiser, founder of the Kaiser industrial empire. Mr Kaiser worked with the Kaiser company's World War II shipbuilding program; as general manager of the Kaiser–Frazer Corporation, which put out post World War II automobiles; as president of the Kaiser Industries Corporation; and as chairman of the board of the Kaiser Steel Corporation: d. California, Dec. 11.

Kanner, Leo (86), child psychologist; Dr. Kanner, known in psychiatric circles as the father of child psychology, founded the Johns Hopkins Children's Psychiatric Clinic in 1930: d. Sykesville, MD, April 3.

Kelly, Patsy (née Bridget Veronica) (71), actress; she played in vaudeville, later made several motion pictures in which she played amusing sidekicks to Hollywood leading ladies. She won a Tony Award for her appearance in the Broadway revival of *No, No, Nanette* (1971): d. Woodland Hills, CA, Sept. 24.

Knight, John S. (86), founder of the Knight publishing empire and editor emeritus of Knight-Ridder Newspapers Inc.; he had retired as editorial chairman of the Knight-Ridder chain in 1976. By 1981 the organization included 32 daily papers in 17 states and four television stations: d. Akron, OH, June 16.

Knott, Walter (91), founder of Knott's Berry Farm, a 150-acre (61-ha) amusement complex in California with major pavilions featuring the Old West, early Spanish California, and 1920s flapper era themes. The third largest such park in the United States, it attracts more than 4,000,000 people each year: d. Buena Park, CA, Dec. 3.

Kondrashin, Kiril (67), Soviet symphony conductor; he reportedly revitalized the Moscow Philharmonic after taking over its direction in 1960. He became known in the Western musical world for two recordings in which he conducted Van Cliburn, after the latter had won the Tchaikovsky Competition in Moscow. He defected to the Netherlands in 1978 and became conductor of Amsterdam's Concertgebouw Orchestra in 1979: d. Amsterdam, March 8.

Krebs, Sir Hans (81), German-born biochemist; awarded the 1953 Nobel Prize in physiology or medicine for his discovery of the means by which food is converted to energy in the body. His major discoveries were of two basic biochemical chain reactions—the urea cycle and the citric acid cycle (now called the Krebs cycle): d. Oxford, England, Nov. 22.

La Barba, Fidel (76), flyweight boxing champion, he fought as a professional, 1925–27 and 1928–33. He was a 1924 Olympic gold medalist: d. California, Oct. 2.

Lacan, Jacques (80), psychoanalyst; considered the most influential figure in French psychiatry; he set up and later abolished the Freudian School of Paris, replacing it with the Freudian Cause. His major work is *Ecrits* (1966): c. Paris, Sept. 9.

Lane, Frank (85), baseball executive; he was general manager of the Cincinnati Reds, Chicago White Sox, St. Louis Cardinals, and Kansas City Athletics and executive vice-president of the Cleveland Indians: d. Richardson, TX, March 19.

Lane, Lola (née Dorothy Mulligan) (75), actress; she was a Hollywood leading lady of the 1930s and 1940s, and appeared in 38 movies before her retirement in 1946. She often appeared with two of her sisters: d. Santa Barbara, CA, June 22.

Lenya, Lotte (née Karoline Blamauer) (83), actress; appeared on the German and American stage and in films. She attracted great attention in the 1928 Berlin production of *The Threepenny Opera,* written by Bertolt Brecht and Miss Lenya's husband, Kurt Weill. She also appeared in the film version of 1931. After Weill's death in 1950 she became more active in stage work and in 1954 appeared in the Off-Broadway revival of *The Threepenny Opera*. Thereafter she appeared in other works of Weill and Brecht and also supervised and sang in a series of Weill recordings. She won a theater Tony Award for *Cabaret* and a motion picture Oscar for *The Roman Spring of Mrs. Stone:* d. New York City, Nov. 27.

Leontovich, Mikhail A. (78), Soviet nuclear physicist. He worked during World War II on defense-related radio research, becoming a full member of the Soviet Academy of Sciences in 1946. From 1951 he headed theoretical research on controlled nuclear fusion and plasma physics at the academy's Institute of Atomic Energy and was said to have made important contributions to the development of the experimental Tokamak fusion reactor: d. Moscow, reported April 1.

Levin, Meyer (75), writer; works include novels, plays, documentary films, and scenarios. His highly successful novel *Compulsion* (1956), about the 1920s' Leopold-Loeb murder case, was made into a play and a film: d. Jerusalem, July 9.

Lewis, David (71), member of Canadian parliament; founder of Canada's New Democratic Party. First elected to the House of Commons in 1962, he became leader of his party in 1971: d. Ottawa, May 23.

Liebman, Max (78), television producer; most famous for the television series *Your Show of Shows* (1950–54), the highly successful Sid Caesar–Imogene Coca variety show: d. New York City, July 21.

Lilienthal, David Eli (81), atomic energy developer; former chairman of the Tennessee Valley Authority (TVA) and the first chair-

WILLIAM HOLDEN

UPI

DAVID LILIENTHAL

UPI

man of the Atomic Energy Commission. President Franklin Roosevelt appointed him one of the triumvirate to head TVA. He left the chairmanship of TVA when he accepted the apointment to the Atomic Energy Commission in 1946. As chairman of the Atomic Energy Commission he sought to build up a stockpile of atomic bombs and worked for atomic weapons development. He wrote several books: d. New York City, Jan. 15.

Lindsay, Margaret (70), actress; she made 88 movies in her 30-year career in motion pictures: d. Los Angeles, May 8.

Lindstrom, Fred (75), baseball player; for nine seasons he was a New York Giants third baseman and outfielder. In all he played professional baseball for 13 seasons. Elected to the baseball Hall of Fame in 1976, his lifetime batting average was .311: d. Chicago, Oct. 4.

Loeb, William (75), conservative U.S. newspaper publisher; owner of *The Manchester Union Leader* and *The New Hampshire Sunday News:* d. Burlington, MA, Sept. 13.

Loos, Anita (88), screenwriter, playwright, and novelist. She wrote *Gentlemen Prefer Blondes,* a book published in 1925 that went through 85 editions, was translated into 14 languages, and became a play and the basis of two movies and two musical comedies. Miss Loos was an innovator in the use of screen captions, which she first wrote for *Macbeth* in 1916. Her subtitles for *Intolerance* (1916) are considered classics: d. New York City, Aug. 18.

Ludden, Allen (62–63?), television personality; hosted the television game show *Password* (1961–67); and appeared on the *G.E. College Bowl* (1959–63): d. Los Angeles, June 9.

McCain, John S., Jr. (70), admiral and commander in chief of Pacific forces in the Vietnam War, and a World War II hero. Following his promotion to the rank of rear admiral (1959) he became chief of information for the Navy. He also was an amphibious specialist, a military representative to the United Nations, and commander of Naval forces in Europe: d. aboard a military aircraft returning from Europe, March 22.

McHugh, Frank (82), stage and film actor; probably best known for his sidekick roles. He made his Broadway debut in *The Fall Guy* (1925): d. Greenwich, CT, Sept. 11.

McNamara, Margaret Craig (65), founder of Reading Is Fundamental, a nationwide program to encourage poor children to read. She was married to former Secretary of Defense Robert S. McNamara in 1940 and was always active in community affairs: d. Washington, DC, Feb. 3.

Markey, Enid (91), actress; played in a number of silent films, including the first Tarzan film in 1918. In 1920 she embarked on a stage career and for the next 25 years appeared in numerous productions. She returned to films in 1945 and later appeared on television: d. Bay Shore, L.I., NY, Nov. 15.

Marley, Bob (36), singer, composer, and arranger of reggae music. His concerts were considered mystical and often mesmerizing experiences: d. Miami, FL, May 11.

Martin, Ross (reared as Martin Rosenblatt) (61), actor; probably best known for his role in the television series *The Wild, Wild West:* d. Ramona, CA, July 3.

Matthews, Jessie (74), British musical-comedy actress. Well known to American audiences for such 1930s British film musicals as *Evergreen, First a Girl,* and *It's Love Again.* On the London stage she introduced Cole Porter's *Let's Do It,* Noël Coward's *A Room with a View,* and Richard Rodgers' *My Heart Stood Still* and *Dancing on the Ceiling.* She made her Broadway debut in 1924: d. England, Aug. 20.

Maugham, Robin (né Robert Cecil Romer) (64), British author, Viscount Maugham of Hartfield, he was the nephew of Somerset Maugham. He wrote about his famous uncle and about his father, a former Lord High Chancellor, in *Somerset and All the Maughams* (1966) and *Conversations with Willie* (1978): d. Brighton, England, March 13.

Mecom, John W. (70), one of the world's largest independent oil operators: d. Houston, TX, Oct. 12.

Montale, Eugenio (84), Italian poet; recipient of the 1975 Nobel Prize for Literature: d. Milan, Italy, Sept. 12.

Montgomery, Robert (né Henry Montgomery, Jr.) (77), stage and film actor; well known for his screen portrayals of sophisticated men-about-town. He appeared on television during the 1950s and did stage and film directing as well: d. New York City, Sept. 27.

Muhlen, Norbert (72), writer; best-known work is probably *The Incredible Krupps: The Rise, Fall, and Comeback of Germany's Industrial Family* (1959): d. New York City, Aug. 20.

Myers, C. Kilmer (65), theologian; Episcopal bishop of California (1966–79). He held radical social and political views—criticizing the Vietnam War, attacking racism and official corruption—and conservative theological positions—opposing the ordination of women to the priesthood: d. San Francisco, June 27.

Northrop, John Knudsen (85), aviation design pioneer and founder of the Northrop Corporation; his contributions to aviation development included the original Lockheed Vega, the A-17 attack plane, early Navy dive bombers and the World War II P-61 night fighter known as the Black Widow. After World War II he was associated with the design and production of the F-89 jet interceptor and the intercontinental winged Snark missile. He was most closely associated with the highly innovative Flying Wing: d. Glendale, CA, Feb. 18.

O'Connell, Arthur (73), film and stage actor; famed for his role in *Picnic;* twice a nominee for an Oscar: d. Los Angeles, May 18.

Oldfield, Sir Maurice (65), former chief of intelligence of Great Britain; spent 40 years in intelligence service. He is believed to be the inspiration for the fictional character George Smiley in John Le Carré's spy novels and the character "M" in Ian Fleming's James Bond books: d. Northern Ireland, March 10.

Osborne, John (74), columnist; for 13 years he wrote a column for *The New Republic* magazine: d. Washington, May 2.

Patrick, Nigel (68), British stage and screen actor; well known as a featured player who presented portrayals of sophisticated English gentlemen. He appeared in nearly 24 plays and in nearly 30 films: d. London, Sept. 21.

Peabody, Mary Parkman (89), prominent civil-rights and antiwar activist of the 1960s. Married to the Rev. Malcolm E. Peabody and the mother of former Massachusetts governor Endicott Peabody, Mrs. Peabody served on a variety of community and social organizations prior to the 1960s: d. Cambridge, MA, Feb. 6.

Pella, Giuseppe (79), Italian economist; served briefly as Italy's prime minister (1953–54) and foreign minister (1957–58, 1959–60). In addition he held Italy's top economic post (1947–52), served 22 years in the Chamber of Deputies and two terms in the Senate, and was Budget Minister (1960–62): d. Rome, May 31.

Piccard, Jeannette (86), high-altitude balloonist and Episcopal priest. In 1934 she piloted a balloon above Lake Erie, the first U.S. flight in which the balloon remained under control for the entire flight and the first successful stratospheric flight made through a layer of clouds. She worked for the U.S. space program from 1964 to 1970 and then began theological studies. She was ordained an Episcopal priest in 1974: d. Minneapolis, MN, May 17.

Ponselle, Rosa (née Ponzillo) (84), operatic soprano; debuted with the Metropolitan Opera in 1918 having had little, if any, formal voice or opera training. She appeared with Enrico Caruso. During her 19 seasons at the Met, she sang 22 dramatic and dramatic-coloratura roles. She was for many years artistic director of the Baltimore Opera: d. Stevenson, MD, May 25.

Powell, Wesley (65), governor of New Hampshire (1958–62): d. Hampton Falls, New Hampshire, Jan. 6.

Price, Winston Harvey (58), epidemiologist; internationally known in the fields of rickettsia and virus diseases. He developed the first successful vaccine against the JH virus (a major cause of the common cold) and the vaccine for encephalitis: d. Baltimore, MD, April 30.

Rajai, Mohammed Ali (47), president of Iran July 24–Aug. 30, 1981. He had earlier served as prime minister of Iran's revolutionary government, having been appointed by President Bani-Sadr to that post in Aug. 1980, despite Bani-Sadr's strong objections to him: d. Tehran, Aug. 30.

Raymond, James C. (64), artist; had worked on the "Blondie" comic strip for more than 40 years. He had collaborated with Chic Young, the strip's creator, until Mr. Young's death in 1973, and thereafter had worked with Mr. Young's son until 1980: d. Boynton Beach, FL, Oct. 14.

Reiser, Pete (62), baseball outfielder; played for the Brooklyn Dodgers (1939–42; 1946–52); won the 1941 National League batting title: d. Palm Springs, CA, Oct. 25.

Richter, Karl (54), conductor and organist; leader of the Munich Bach Choir and Orchestra which he developed in the 1950s. Mr. Richter during the 1950s and 1960s presented a de-Romanticized approach to Baroque music considered quite revolutionary at the time, but one that later passed out of fashion: d. Munich, Feb. 16.

Roldós Aguilera, Jaime (40), president of Ecuador (1979–81). In 1979, in the first elections held since 1968, he was elected to office by the greatest majority in Ecuadoran history. A lawyer, his only other government service was as a national legislator (1968–70): d. near Guachala, Ecuador, May 24.

Roosevelt, John A. (65), New York investment banker; youngest son of President Franklin D. Roosevelt: d. New York City, April 27.

Roszak, Theodore (74), sculptor; known for his work in welded steel: d. New York City, Sept. 3.

Ryden, Ernest Edwin (94), Lutheran minister, journalist, and hymnologist; wrote and translated more than 40 hymns. An ecumenicist, he helped unify four denominations to form the Lutheran Church in America in 1962: d. Providence, RI, Jan. 1.

Saroyan, William (72), writer. His first real success as a writer came in 1934 with the magazine publication of *The Daring Young Man on the Flying Trapeze.* Within months his first book of short stories was collected, and between 1936 and 1938 five more collections appeared. He achieved fame as a playwright when *The Time of Your Life* was performed on Broadway in 1939. He won the Pulitzer Prize for that play, but refused the award because he felt that businessmen were not qualified to judge art. He also worked, although not very successfully, as a salaried Hollywood writer. In 1941 he wrote *The Human Comedy* for M-G-M, and later tried to buy back the script. He fashioned the

Wide World Photos
SOONG CHING-LING

UPI
LOWELL THOMAS

UPI
BARBARA WARD

Wide World Photos
NATALIE WOOD

novel of the same name from the scenario. He later wrote television plays and his memoirs: d. Fresno, CA, May 18.

Sharp, Zerna (91), originator of the "Dick and Jane" reading textbooks for the elementary school which were widely used in the classroom for 40 years: d. Frankfurt, IN, June 17.

Sheares, Benjamin Henry (73), president of Singapore (1971–81). Dr. Sheares was a well-known gynecologist before his unanimous election by Parliament in 1971; d. Singapore, May 12.

Siegel, Carl L. (84), German mathematician; made fundamental discoveries in the theories of numbers, of analytic functions, and celestial mechanics: d. Göttingen, West Germany, April 5.

Smith, Joe (né Joe Sultzer) (97), vaudeville star; he was a partner for 73 years in the vaudeville team of Smith and [Charles] Dale: d. Englewood, NJ, Feb. 22.

Soong Ching-ling (90), political activist and widow of Sun Yat-sen, founder of the Chinese Republic. Educated in Shanghai and in the United States, over the objections of her father she became Dr. Sun's secretary and in 1914 his second wife. In 1927, two years after her husband's death, she broke with the Nationalists of her brother-in-law Chiang Kai-shek (a sister was married to him) because of their killing of Chinese Communists and trade-unionist supporters. Elected to the Nationalists' Standing Committee in 1946, she was the only woman on the State Council of the Nationalist government. She was elected honorary chairman of the Nationalists' Revolutionary Council (an anti-Chiang group) in 1948. After the Communist takeover in 1949 she was made deputy chairman of the government and in 1951 was awarded a Stalin Peace Prize. In 1959 Miss Soong was appointed one of two deputy chairmen of the republic. On her deathbed she was made honorary chairman of the nation: d. Peking, May 29.

Speer, Albert (76) associate in the German Third Reich; he was Hitler's architect and, during World War II, Minister of Armaments and War Production. At the Nuremberg trials he was the only war criminal who admitted guilt for his actions. Books in which he expressed his views include *Inside the Third Reich, Spandau: The Secret Diaries,* and *Infiltration: The SS and German Armament:* d. London, Sept. 1.

Stein, Julian Caesar (Jules) (85), founder of the Music Corporation of America: d. Los Angeles, April 29.

Teague, Olin E. (70), member of the U.S. House of Representatives (D-TX, 1946–79): d. Bethesda, MD, Jan. 23.

Thomas, Lowell (89), broadcaster and author; he broadcast a weekday radio news program for nearly 46 years until it was discontinued in 1976. In addition, for 17 years he was the voice of Movietone News. Besides his career as a radio broadcaster, he was a war propagandist, lecturer, author, world traveler, and skier, who played an important role in developing ski resorts: d. Pawling, NY, Aug. 29

Trippe, Juan (81), founder of Pan American World Airways; was the company's operating head for 41 years: d. New York City, April 3.

Urey, Harold C. (87), chemist; discoverer of heavy (isotope) hydrogen, which made possible thermonuclear devices. He won the Nobel Prize in chemistry in 1934. Other important contributions were to space exploration and to scientific explanations for the evolution of the universe and the origin of life: d. La Jolla, CA, Jan. 5.

Urrutia Lleo, Manuel (79), president of Cuba; he took office in January 1959, the first president of revolutionary Cuba, and served for six months until his dismissal by Fidel Castro. He went to the United States in 1963. Urrutia's book *Fidel Castro Company, Inc.: Communist Tyranny in Cuba* was published in 1964: d. New York City, July 6.

Vaughan, Harry H. (87), U.S. Army Major General. During the Truman administration, he was a military aide to President Truman: d. Fort Belvoir,VA, May 20.

Vera-Ellen (née Vera-Ellen Rohe) (55), actress-dancer; appeared in several stage and film musicals of the 1930s and 1940s: d. Los Angeles, Aug. 30.

Vinson, Carl (97), U.S. representative (D-GA 1914–65): d. Milledgeville, GA, June 1.

Von Zell, Harry (75), radio announcer and actor; best known for his appearance on the George Burns and Gracie Allen radio and television shows: d. Calabasas, CA, Nov. 21.

Voskovec, George (76), actor; known for his character roles on the New York stage. He made his first appearance in New York in 1945 in *The Tempest* and went on to act in numerous Off-Broadway and Broadway productions during the next 25 years: d. Pearblossom, CA, July 1.

Wallace, (William Roy) DeWitt (91), founder of *Reader's Digest.* With the help of his wife, Lila Bell Acheson, whom he had married in 1921, the magazine was published in 1922. It proved an immediate success, and at the time of Mr. Wallace's death was published in 16 languages and reached readers in 163 countries: d. Mount Kisco, NY, March 30.

Ward, Barbara (67), British economist and author; she stressed the necessity of helping the world's poor and underprivileged, the fundamental unity of the West, and the need for accommodation with the Communist powers of the East, and worked closely with the United Nations throughout her life. Her first book, *The International Share-Out,* was published in 1938 and in 1939 she began working for *The Economist* in London. Highly respected in the United States, she was a visiting scholar at Harvard (1958–68) and held the Schweitzer Chair of International Economic Development at Columbia (1968–73). She was created a life peeress in 1976 with the title Baroness Jackson of Lodsworth: d. Lodsworth, England, May 31.

Warren, Harry (né Salvatore Guaragna) (87), songwriter; his career spanned 59 years during which he composed more than 300 songs for some 50 motion pictures: d. Los Angeles, Sept. 22.

Waugh, Alec (83), British author; his first novel created a stir as it was the first book to refer to homosexual relations in English public schools. He is best known for the novel *Island in the Sun* (1956): d. Tampa, FL, Sept. 3.

Wechsler, David (85), psychologist and author of widely used intelligence tests: d. New York City, May 2.

Lord Widgery (70), former British Lord Chief Justice; John Passmore Widgery was knighted in 1961 and made a life peer in 1971. He became Queen's Counsel in 1958; a judge in 1959; a High Court judge in 1961; and a Lord Justice of Appeal in 1968, serving until 1971: d. London, July 25.

Williams, Eric E. (69), prime minister of Trinidad and Tobago (1962–81): d. St. Anne, March 29.

Williams, Mary Lou (né Mary Elfrieda Scruggs) (71), jazz musician: d. Durham, NC, May 28.

Wood, Natalie (née Natasha Gurdin) (43), motion picture actress; she began her career at the age of four. She was nominated three times for an Academy Award—for *Rebel Without a Cause* (1955), *Splendor in the Grass* (1961), and *Love with the Proper Stranger* (1963): d. near Santa Catalina Island, CA, Nov. 29.

Wortman, Sterling (58), plant geneticist; he worked during most of his career for the Rockefeller Foundation. He was involved with the development of high-yielding "miracle grains": d. Greenwich, CT, May 26.

Wyler, William (79), motion-picture director; his career began in 1929. He was nominated 13 times for the Academy Award for directing and won the award three times, a record surpassed only by John Ford: d. Beverly Hills, CA, July 28.

Yost, Charles Woodruff (73), U.S. Foreign Service officer and U.S. delegate to the United Nations (1969–71); served as ambassador to Laos, Syria, and Morocco: d. Washington, DC, May 21.

Yukawa, Hideki (74), Japanese physicist; the 1949 winner of the Nobel Prize in physics and Japan's first Nobel Prize laureate. Dr. Yukawa had predicted the existence of a new type of subatomic particle which came to be known as the meson. In 1949 such particles were confirmed: d. Kyoto, Japan, Sept. 8.

Ziaur Rahman (45), president of Bangladesh (1975–81): d. Chittagong, Bangladesh, May 30.

OCEANOGRAPHY

Recent oceanographic projects have measured energy exchanges between the sea and the atmosphere which control weather processes and are critical in the growth and development of storms. A U.S.-Canadian project, known as STREX (Storm Transfer and Response Experiment), examined the area of winter storm formation in the Gulf of Alaska and observed the development of nine storms, using aircraft, ships, dozens of buoys, and various satellites. STREX focused on measurements of critical boundary layers in the atmosphere and the surface waters of the sea, where energy exchange occurs. Heat exchange processes were found to be radically altered as atmospheric cold fronts swept across the sea. Analysis of the data was under way late in 1981 and it was hoped that the results would lead to improved weather forecasts and better long-range predictions of climate trends.

Shuttle Experiment. A shuttle experiment was conducted in the Pacific Ocean from Hawaii to Tahiti by research vessels and aircraft making cruises for 16 months over three meridional sections across the equator. Earlier studies, off the coast of Peru as a part of the Coastal Upwellings Ecosystems Analysis Program (CUEA), had led to a theory that the occurrence of El Niño, a warm equatorial current inshore near South America that displaces the usual cold, nutrient-rich upwellings in the Peru Current, was related to a reduction of the Southeast trade winds and the alteration of major currents across the Pacific. Preliminary results of the shuttle experiment indicate that monitoring of such changes in the mid-ocean region is feasible and could in time be covered by island stations, earth satellites, and passing ship traffic. Such a network would provide early warning of the changes that disrupt the highly productive inshore fisheries.

Gulf Stream Rings. In the Atlantic Ocean, the effect of Gulf Stream rings is a major study. Cyclonic (counterclockwise) eddies 100 to 300 km (62.5 to 187.5 mi) in diameter in the warm Sargasso sea are composed of a ring of Gulf Stream water surrounding a core of cold water from the inshore side of the Gulf Stream which is rich in plants, animals, and nutrients. As a ring decays the inshore properties of its core are gradually replaced by those of the Sargasso sea, where standing crops of plants, animals, and nutrients generally are low. The rate of decay suggests a lifetime of 2 to 4 years, but a cold-core eddy usually rejoins the main Gulf Stream after 6 to 12 months. Such rings are a major means of transfer and mixing between the distinct warm and cold currents of the North Atlantic. These eddies have been observed by United States scientists in project MODE (Mid-Ocean Dynamics Experiment) and in a joint U.S.–USSR program called POLYMODE. A 200-km (125-mi) square area southwest of Bermuda, known as the LDE (Local Dynamics Experiment), with a grid of observation sites spaced only 25 km (15.6 mi) apart, has given evidence of small eddies (20 km or 12.5 mi in diameter) both at depth and near the surface, which may carry water hundreds and perhaps thousands of kilometers across the ocean.

"Glomar Challenger." Since 1968 the Deep Sea Drilling Program (DSDP) drillship *Glomar Challenger* has obtained deep water seafloor samples worldwide during more than 70 cruises. In 1981, the vessel was used to sample the oldest rocks ever recovered from the deep ocean, estimated to be 145 to 155 million years old, thus dating from mid-Jurassic time. The rocks were found at a depth of 1 647 m (5,404 ft) beneath the seafloor at a drill site located some 500 km (300 mi) east of Florida in nearly 5 km (3 mi) of water depth. The core sample obtained also gave much information of the early Atlantic Ocean basin at about this time in the past. Scientists from the USSR, Germany, Japan, France, and the United Kingdom were involved in the drilling program, which was part of the International Phase of Ocean Drilling (IPOD). Planning is under way for an Ocean Margin Drilling Program (OMDP) to start in 1984 and to make use of the *Glomar Explorer,* with expanded capabilities to operate in deeper waters, in rougher weather, and in colder, more ice-strewn seas.

Hot Springs. A French expedition in the tropical section of the East Pacific Rise has found more areas of hydrothermal activity on the seafloor. One area near 13° N was producing new ocean crust from volcanic activity at a rate of 10 cm (3.9 inches) per year (fast) and another area between 20° and 21° S had a rate of spreading of 16 cm (6.3 inches) per year (superfast). Near 21° N, where American researchers first discovered hot springs on the Rise, the rate of spreading is only 6 cm (2.4 inches) per year. The zones of volcanism and hot springs are quite narrow—only 0.5 to 1 km (0.3 to 0.6 mi) in spite of their high spreading rates—and they lack the large, rapid outpourings of fluid lava associated with mid-Atlantic rift sites. Instead, a heavy deposit of metal-bearing sediments is found.

Rift Organisms. Organisms first seen along the spreading center of the mid-Pacific rift near the Galapagos Islands have now been identified and described. They represent a major new subdivision of the phylum Pogonophora, a group of deep-sea bottom-dwelling worms unknown until the 20th century. The whole group is unique among animals as the only collection of free-living animals that has no digestive system. The newly-named rift organisms operate in a unique food chain associated with the spreading centers in which the gaseous venting from deep in the earth includes nutrients to support sulfur-eating bacteria, which in turn are used by the pogonophorans. Analysis of 63 specimens recovered from the hot spring sites showed that the bacteria are kept in colonies in special portions of the worm's body, where they convert hydrogen sulfide and form carbohydrates that in turn are utilized by the worm.

Biological Research Cruise. In surface waters, the world's largest biological research cruise, comprising some 20 ships from about a dozen countries, began in February 1981 in waters near Antarctica. The cruise, known as the First International Biomass Experiment (FIBEX), is the first part of Project Biomass, a ten-year program for study of the area. The FIBEX cruise found a huge swarm of krill, thought to be perhaps the largest aggregation of sea creatures ever encountered. The small shrimp-like creatures covered several square miles and ranged in depth from 20 to 200 m (60 to 600 ft) with the total weight of the swarm estimated at about 10 million t (11 million T). The swarm was measured by sonar and by netting techniques. These krill are an important link in the Antarctic food chain and a potentially important, but still largely untapped, source of protein for human consumption.

DAVID A. MCGILL
U.S. Coast Guard Academy

OHIO

Budget and tax problems, plus worries about business growth concerned Ohio in 1981.

A six-month, 1% "bite" added to the regular 4% sales tax helped raise extra millions, but it expired June 30. The principal goal of the legislature's early autumn deliberations was to try to find acceptable taxation for education and other services.

Four persons were killed and 200 homes were destroyed by a June tornado that hit Cardington, OH.

UPI

OHIO • Information Highlights

Area: 41,330 sq mi (107 045 km^2).
Population (1980 census): 10,797,419.
Chief Cities (1980 census): Columbus, the capital, 564,871; Cleveland, 573,822; Cincinnati, 385,457; Toledo, 354,635; Akron, 237,177; Dayton, 203,588; Youngstown, 115,436; Canton, 94,730; Parma, 92,548.
Government (1981): *Chief Officer*—governor, James A. Rhodes (R). *General Assembly*—Senate, 33 members; House of Representatives, 99 members.
State Finances (fiscal year 1980): *Revenues,* $12,180,000,000; *expenditures,* $11,397,000,000.
Personal Income (1980): $102,410,000,000; per capita, $9,462.
Labor Force (July 1981): *Nonagricultural wage and salary earners,* 4,364,900; *unemployed,* 495,300 (9.4% of total force).

A report to the Northeast-Midwest Congressional Coalition, a meeting of 200 congressmen from 28 states, showed that of Midwest states, Ohio had the greatest "outmigration" in the 1970s—565,000 persons; that the state can expect only a 2.9% population growth in the next 20 years, a sixth of the national rate; and that Ohio suffered a loss of 154,000 manufacturing jobs in the 1970s, an 11% decline.

A demographic report publicized in October stated that in 50 years, Ohio, with a renascent industry based on available raw materials, markets, and water transportation, could become the nation's second most populous state (behind California), with about 17 million persons.

An embarrassment involving state finances arose in August when an audit revealed that the Ohio treasurer's cashier department had received $1.3 million more than was deposited in banks. A former employee was questioned and an official probe begun.

Two constitutional amendments were decided November 3. Voters refused to open workers' compensation coverage to private insurance companies. The creation of a reapportionment and redistricting commission for defining new borders for Ohio legislative and congressional districts was rejected.

Effective October 19, Ohio reinstated capital punishment for murderers who kill while involved in rape, robbery, or burglary. Killing a high official, murder for hire, or murder to escape detection of a crime also may lead to the penalty. The state's previous death penalty was overturned by the U.S. Supreme Court July 3, 1978.

Schools. Teachers in about 20 Ohio systems struck during 1981. On April 13 Ravenna, in north-central Ohio, settled what then was the longest public school teachers' strike in U.S. history—85 days.

A bizarre interlude came August 31 when U.S. District Judge Frank J. Battisti briefly jailed the president and treasurer of Cleveland's Board of Education for contempt of court. The issue was Cleveland's temporary failure to approve the school's desegregation office. A strike by the board's bus drivers, who were needed to implement Battisti's desegregation orders, narrowly was averted in mid-October.

The U.S. Court of Appeals in Cincinnati (6th District) October 21 upheld a 1980 finding by Battisti that the state's school officials had failed to prevent "intentional school segregative practices," and Ohio should share desegregation costs. Cleveland public school officials said that they believed Ohio owed between $30 and $40 million for 1980 and the first half of 1981.

Cleveland. A second attempt in four months to increase Cleveland's revenues by raising the municipal income tax to 2% from 1.5%, effective March 1, won in a February 17 election. The issue, supported by Mayor George V. Voinovich and opposed by his predecessor Dennis J. Kucinich, got 62% of votes. With this added taxation (expected to total $24.5 million in 1981 and nearly $40 million in 1982) and with the benefits of a 1980 balanced budget, Cleveland emerged from its 1978 default. Rating agencies raised judgments of the city's general obligation.

By nearly 2 to 1, voters on June 30 ordered the City Council reduced from 33 to 21 members. This came after the Ohio Supreme Court overturned a Cleveland official's refusal, on a technicality, to verify petitions for the balloting. Two earlier reduction attempts in the prior eight years had failed. Mayor Voinovich was reelected November 3 for four years.

The Cleveland *Press,* first paper founded by E. W. Scripps, started a Sunday edition August 2. Control of the afternoon daily passed from Scripps-Howard Broadcasting Co. to Joseph E. Cole, Cleveland businessman-millionaire.

JOHN F. HUTH, JR.
Reporter
"The Plain Dealer," Cleveland

OKLAHOMA

The state legislature met from Jan. 6 to June 26, 1981, and reconvened on July 20 to pass a congressional redistricting bill that had been opposed as a gerrymander by Republican legislators. The plan stretches the 5th District, held by Republican Mickey Edwards, from Oklahoma City to Bartlesville and retains five Democratic incumbents in safer districts.

During its regular session, the legislature appropriated a record $1,688,000,000. A record $624.4 million common school bill was passed to raise teachers' pay by an average of $1,600 per year. A $327.4 million appropriation for higher education represented 98% of the state regents' request. A $23 million welfare "bailout" bill was passed, as was a bill revising the state school aid financing formula. State employees received salary increases averaging 15% to 18%, and their classification system was revised; the legislation included a checkoff provision for employee union dues. The state gift tax was abolished and the inheritance tax reduced. A proposal to remove the sales tax on prescription drugs was passed. A bitter controversy over reapportionment was resolved near the session's end.

County Commissioners Scandal. FBI and Internal Revenue Service investigations led 75 present or past county commissioners, as well as 35 equipment salesmen and suppliers, to be indicted or to sign agreements to plead guilty to criminal charges. Prosecutors alleged that the commissioners took kickbacks on delivery of materials, especially road construction equipment, and split payments with suppliers for phony orders. It was predicted that more than 250 persons might be charged before the investigation ends. The scandal is seen as the largest in state history.

Gov. George Nigh (D) called a special session of the legislature in August to consider the county commissioner scandal. Counties were authorized to seek reimbursement from the state for the cost of holding special elections to replace commissioners who resigned. The special elections were expected to cost up to $1 million. Commissioners who pleaded guilty to felonies were to be ousted from office, and in the future commissioners must obtain competitive bids on purchase contracts of $1,500 or more. The governor appointed a special "blue ribbon" committee to recommend corrective legislation.

Business. Oklahoma is in the midst of an oil boom, ranking high among the states in new oil and gas wells. The number of oil and gas exploration companies also continued to increase. These trends reverse a ten-year decline in oil production.

Conoco, Inc., with major facilities in Ponca City, the nation's ninth largest oil company, was the object of a bidding war among Dupont, Seagrams & Sons, and Mobil. Dupont received tenders for a majority of the Conoco stock. Fear was expressed that other natural resource firms might face similar takeovers.

The Oklahoma Supreme Court upheld Att. Gen. Jan Eric Cartwright's opinion that corporations are included in the state constitution's ban on alien ownership of property, but that if foreign-based corporations have domesticated and paid a filing fee they are considered legal residents and can own property.

JOHN W. WOOD
University of Oklahoma

OKLAHOMA • Information Highlights

Area: 69,956 sq mi (181 186 km²).
Population (1980 census): 3,025,266.
Chief Cities (1980 census): Oklahoma City, the capital, 403,213; Tulsa, 360,919; Lawton, 80,054; Norman, 68,020; Enid, 50,363; Midwest City, 49,559; Muskogee, 40,011; Stillwater, 38,268; Broken Arrow, 35,761; Moore, 35,063.
Government (1981): *Chief Officers*—governor, George Nigh (D); lt. gov., Spencer Bernard (D). *Legislature*—Senate, 48 members; House of Representatives, 101 members.
State Finances (fiscal year 1980): *Revenues,* $3,433,000,000; *expenditures,* $3,249,000,000.
Personal Income (1980): $27,645,000,000; per capita, $9,116.
Labor Force (July 1981): *Nonagricultural wage and salary earners,* 1,176,200; *unemployed,* 42,400 (3.0% of total force).

CP Picture Service

Ontario Premier William Davis, a Conservative, campaigned successfully for reelection in March.

ONTARIO

For Canada's most populous province, 1981 was a year of hard economic realities. Squeezed by rising fuel prices and a manufacturing sector in recession, Ontario technically became a "have not" province, eligible for federal equalization payments even if it was too proud to ask for them.

Thirty-three years of uninterrupted Tory rule were extended on March 19, when Premier William Davis' Progressive Conservatives (PCs) were not only reelected but given the outright majority denied them in two previous elections. Premier Davis had called the unusual winter election after public opinion polls showed strong favor for his government. After a rather dull campaign, in which few real issues caught fire, the PCs won 70 seats, a gain of 12; the Liberals won 34 seats, no change; and the New Democratic Party (NDP) took 21, a loss of 12. The Liberals, attacking the government for the province's poor economic performance, had expected major gains. Although they held on to their 34 seats, they garnered only 33.6% of the popular vote, compared with 39.7% in 1977. Some speculated that either the electorate simply did not wish to hear bad economic news or that it preferred to stick out the hard times with the government it knew. Both opposition party leaders, Stuart Smith of the Liberals and Michael Cassidy of the NDP, announced their resignations. Cassidy received particularly heavy criticism for his party's poor showing.

The major initiative to stimulate the Ontario economy and create new jobs was the formation in January 1981 of BILD (Board of Industrial Leadership and Development), a $1,500,000,000 program that formed the main plank of the PC election platform.

Backed by a majority in the legislature, Treasurer Frank Miller tabled a tough, $19,400,000,000 budget in May. To offset a mounting deficit, personal income taxes were raised by 4%, the first rate increase since World War II; medicare premiums were increased 15%; and taxes on alcohol and gasoline were substantially increased, with the assessment changed from a flat rate to an ad valorem basis. To stimulate investment and provincial manufacturing, corporate taxes were left unchanged, and sales taxes on major household appliances and furniture were suspended temporarily. Hopes for a balanced budget by 1984 were abandoned, however, as a $17,400,000,000 deficit was forecast for 1981.

In October, Transportation Minister James Snow and his deputy minister were convicted and fined for violating the provincial Environmental Protection Act. The two officials had permitted construction to begin on a superhighway extension before the end of the period in which an environmental hearing could be requested.

Concerned by the threat of acid rain to the province's lakes and rivers, Ontario stepped up its publicity campaign in the United States and began to intervene more forcefully in U.S. legislative hearings and court proceedings.

With their new majority—dubbed the "Reality of March 19th" by Premier Davis—PC legislators were able to block further investigation by the Judiciary Committee of the alleged failure of the Ontario Securities and Exchange Commission to protect small investors after the bankruptcy of two Niagara Falls financial companies. Equally controversial was the province's purchase in October of 25% of the Suncor oil company for $650 million. The stated purposes were to give Ontario a "window" on the oil industry and to support the federal program of increased Canadian ownership in the oil industry.

PETER J. KING, *Carleton University*

ONTARIO • Information Highlights

Area: 412,582 sq mi (1 068 587 km^2).
Population (April 1981 est.): 8,614,200.
Chief Cities (1976 census): Toronto, the provincial capital, 633,318; Ottawa, the federal capital, 304,462.
Government (1981): *Chief Officers*—lt. gov., John Black-ard; premier, William G. Davis (Progressive Conservative); chief justice, Supreme Court, High Court of Justice, Gregory T. Evans. *Legislature*—Legislative Assembly, 125 members.
Education (1981–82 est.): *Enrollment*—elementary and secondary schools, 1,883,760 pupils; postsecondary, 243,200 students.
Public Finance (1980–81 est.): *Revenues*, $16,160,000,000; *expenditures*, $17,121,000,000.
Personal Income (average weekly salary, April 1981): $340.69.
Unemployment Rate (June 1981, seasonally adjusted): 6.3%.
(All monetary figures are in Canadian dollars.)

OREGON

High interest rates and low building starts devastated Oregon's economy during 1981.

Economy. The closure of lumber and plywood mills across the state was accelerated during the year. Unemployment stood at an October figure of 10% of the state's labor force. This figure excluded some 74,000 unemployed who had exhausted their unemployment benefits. Cost of unemployment compensation was $4.1 million per week at the beginning of the fourth quarter, double the figure of 1979. Paper mills escaped closure because of a favorable paper market, but Oregon paper mills rely, to some extent, upon timber by-product for raw material. Some mills were experiencing difficulty maintaining stable pulp supplies.

The aluminum industry located in the Columbia Basin during World War II to take advantage of long-term contracts for low-cost Bonneville power. Contracts are now maturing and energy rates to large users are escalating. This, together with lessened demand for aluminum products, has forced several major producers to cut production, idle a share of their capacity, and lay off workers.

Faltering state revenues necessitated cuts in most areas of the state budget. Close examination of welfare rolls resulted in a reduction, by some 6,000, in the number of benefit recipients. Projections of state revenues portend further far-reaching cuts. Higher education was targeted for severe cutbacks.

In order to prevent widespread default of logging contracts in federal forests, the U.S. Forest Service was permitting the postponement for up to two years of the harvest of timber sold at regular government auctions.

Court decisions favorable to Indian fishing rights caused the closing of the Columbia River to commercial non-Indian Chinook salmon fishermen. The commercial catch of ocean salmon was so poor that many fishermen earned less than their fuel costs.

Population. Oregon's population increased by 25.9% in the 1970s—from 2,091,533 in 1970 to 2,632,663 in 1980. The added 541,130 was sufficient to warrant a fifth U.S. congressional district. The new district was drawn to encompass the Mid-Willamette Valley, where population growth was the greatest.

The Democratic state legislature redrew state legislative districts but the plan failed an Oregon Supreme Court test. Secretary of State Norma Paulus, a Republican, drew up a redistricting plan incorporating the court's prescription.

Other. In January, the Oregon Supreme Court declared the state's capital punishment law unconstitutional. In July, Oregon became the tenth state to ratify the U.S. Constitutional amendment granting the District of Columbia voting representation in Congress.

Governors Victor G. Atiyeh of Oregon and John Spellman of Washington ageed to appoint a committee, made up of members from both states, to study hazards to the scenic quality of the Columbia River Gorge. The committee is to suggest means by which the gorge, shared by Oregon and Washington, may be protected from commercial and industrial despoliation.

L. CARL BRANDHORST
Department of Geography
Western Oregon State College, Monmouth

OREGON • Information Highlights

Area: 97,073 sq mi (251 419 km^2).
Population (1980 census): 2,632,663.
Chief Cities (1980 census): Salem, the capital, 89,233; Portland, 366,383; Eugene, 105,624; Springfield, 41,621; Corvallis, 40,960; Medford, 39,603; Gresham, 33,005; Beaverton, 30,582; Hillsboro, 27,664; Albany, 26,546.
Government (1981): *Chief Officers*—governor, Victor Atiyeh (R); secy. of state, Norma Paulus (R). *Legislative Assembly*—Senate, 30 members; House of Representatives, 60 members.
State Finances (fiscal year 1980): *Revenues*, $4,041,000,000; *expenditures*, $3,456,000,000.
Personal Income (1980): $24,587,000,000; per capita, $9,317.
Labor Force (July 1981): *Nonagricultural wage and salary earners*, 1,010,700; *unemployed*, 117,200 (8.8% of total force).

OTTAWA

Ottawa was in the international spotlight in 1981. In July, amid unprecedented security, it was the site of the International Economic Summit Conference attended by the leaders of the world's seven major industrial nations. The conference marked U.S. President Ronald Reagan's second visit of the year to the Canadian capital. In March, on his first official visit outside the United States as president, he was met by noisy demonstrations on Parliament Hill. The protesters objected to U.S. policy in Latin America and to acid rain from across the border.

Downtown Ottawa began to undergo a drastic change in appearance with the start of construction on the $250 million Rideau Centre. The complex, with more than 200 stores and services, a major hotel, and a 4,000-delegate convention center about .5 km (.3 mi) from Parliament Hill, has stimulated other hotel and commercial developments and given the region's sluggish construction industry a much needed boost. The city and regional municipalities were, nevertheless, at odds over their respective contributions to the convention center's expected deficit.

The continued expansion of the high technology and electronics industry has caused the Ottawa area to be dubbed "Silicon Valley North." Led by Mitel Corp., whose expansion alone will create more than 1,000 new jobs, the industry is providing a vital economic stimulus and a welcome lessening of dependence on federal civil service. The continuing effort to develop Ottawa as an industrial center produced intense and successful lobbying by civic and business leaders for a direct link with New York City. Transportation facilities are to be further improved by a $43 million expansion of the terminal facilities at Ottawa airport.

PETER J. KING
Carleton University

PAKISTAN

During 1981, Gen. Zia ul-Haq further consolidated his control over Pakistan. He thwarted some serious challenges to military rule by widespread arrests and political manipulation.

Domestic Politics. Opposition to the perpetuation of military rule mounted during the first quarter of the year. Students, university teachers, journalists, and lawyers defied bans on political activity and protested against government repression. Representatives of nine political parties met in Lahore to launch a Movement for the Restoration of Democracy (MRD). Court cases questioned the action of martial law authorities and noted the tenuous legitimacy of the regime. More violent protests also erupted, with several deaths on university campuses, the burning of a Pakistan International Airways DC-10 at Karachi Airport, and, on March 2, the dramatic hijacking of a PIA Boeing jet. The hijackers turned out to be members of the al-Zulfikar, a clandestine group led by Murtaza Bhutto, son of Zulfikar Ali Bhutto, the former prime minister whom Zia had executed in 1979.

The hijacking alienated the late prime minister's Pakistan People's Party (PPP), presently led by his widow Begum Nusrat Bhutto and his daughter Benazir, from other components of the MRD. Moreover, it also occasioned widespread arrests which successfully squelched the incipient protest movement. Then, on March 24, Zia promulgated a new Provisional Constitutional Order which gave the government added powers and banned judicial questioning of martial law actions. At least 19 Supreme Court and Provincial High Court judges refused to sign the new oath of office and were dismissed. These developments effectively eliminated the judiciary as an impediment to the government's increased use of military courts, preventive detention, torture, and execution to control dissent. In September, Amnesty International submitted written testimony to the U.S. House Foreign Affairs Committee which "noted a steady deterioration in the human rights situation in Pakistan."

As 1981 ended, Zia announced that at the present time parliamentary elections were not possible despite our "best efforts." Instead the president formed a 350-member consultative council to help him govern. The council would consider legislative and budgetary issues but its decisions would be nonbinding.

The Economy. A major factor which has prevented discontent from igniting a mass protest movement, as occurred in Pakistan in 1968–69 and 1977, is the relative well-being of the economy. Agricultural production, industrial production, and exports were all significantly higher in 1981. Although energy imports and heavy foreign debt continued to burden the economy, Finance Minister Ghulam Ishaq Khan declared that stagnation had "given way to a resurgent vitality, sound fiscal management has replaced budgetary indiscipline, and the growing balance of payments disequilibrium has been arrested." In June, the World Bank's Aid Pakistan Consortium pledged a record $1,170,000,000 in economic aid. The continued migration of Pakistani workers to other Persian Gulf nations benefited the economy.

The government established new interest-free banking arrangements on January 1. By the end of June, 3,000,000,000 rupees (Rs) (about $300 million) had been deposited in the profit-and-loss sharing accounts, and estimated profits were approximately 9% for the six-month period. Other interest-free investment programs, established earlier, appeared to be enjoying similar success. The collection and distribution of *zakat,* a charitable wealth tax, and *ushr,* an agricultural tax, was having mixed results. Zakat collections, which began in June 1980, totaled more than Rs 800 million ($80 million) by the end of April 1981. The government claimed that more than two million orphans, widows, handicapped, and other deserving people had been assisted by the program. Ushr, on the other hand, encountered problems in implementation, and remained on the drawing board.

Foreign Affairs. The war in Afghanistan dominated Pakistan's foreign policy concerns. Already affected by the pressures of more than two million Afghan refugees, Pakistan has suffered border incursions and overflights by Soviet-supported Afghan forces. Pakistan has resisted Soviet pressures to recognize the Babrak Karmal regime in Kabul and has continued to urge the withdrawal of Soviet troops. A UN special representative appeared unable to negotiate an end to the impasse.

The United States and Pakistan arrived at a mutually acceptable package of military and economic assistance. The Reagan administration package promised $3,200,000,000, half of it in military sales credits, over a five-year period. In addition, the United States pledged to sell Pakistan, on a cash basis, up to 40 F-16 fighter aircraft. Although various issues and objections were raised in the American press and in Congress, including Pakistan's nuclear program and human-rights violations, the package appeared likely to get Congressional approval with only minor modifications.

PAKISTAN • Information Highlights

Official Name: Islamic Republic of Pakistan.
Location: South Asia.
Area: 310,403 sq mi (803 944 km^2).
Population (1981 est.): 88,900,000.
Chief Cities (1974): Islamabad, the capital, 250,000; Karachi, 3,500,000; Lahore, 2,100,000.
Government: *Head of state and government,* Mohammed Zia ul-Haq, president (took power July 5, 1977). *Legislature*—Parliament: Senate and National Assembly (dissolved July 1977); consultative council (formed Dec. 1981).
Monetary Unit: Rupee (9.90 rupees equal U.S.$1, July 1981).
Manufactures (major products): Textiles, processed foods, tobacco, chemicals, natural gas.
Agriculture (major products): Wheat, cotton, rice.

A hijacked Pakistani airliner sits on an airfield runway in Damascus, Syria, in March. To obtain the release of more than 100 persons held on the plane, the Pakistan government agreed to free 55 political prisoners.

Claude Salhani/Gamma-Liaison

Pakistan continued to view India as a greater threat to its security than Afghanistan. India objected to the U.S.-Pakistan assistance package, particularly the F-16 sales, and warned of a new arms race in the subcontinent. Both countries attempted to alleviate tensions through bilateral discussions.

Relations with other Islamic countries and with China flourished. Chinese Premier Zhao Ziyang visited Pakistan in June.

WILLIAM L. RICHTER, *Director*
South Asia Center, Kansas State University

PARAGUAY

Uncertainty over the availability of Gen. Alfredo Stroessner, 69, for a seventh consecutive presidential term beginning in 1983, was causing political realignments among opposition forces. Factions of the Liberal Party were rejoined in August. Earlier, the Christian Democrats, the Revolutionary Febrerista Party, dissident members of the official Colorado Party, and the Authentic Liberal Radical Party formed a coalition.

Civil-rights violations continued under the 27-year-old Stroessner dictatorship. Luis Alfonso Resk, founder and former president of the fledgling Christian Democrats, was arrested in June and later exiled to Venezuela. The Christian Democrats had publicly supported an attack on the Stroessner regime by the Venezuelan senate. Adolfo Pérez Esquivel, 1980 Nobel Peace Prize winner for his civil-rights work in Argentina, was denied entry into Paraguay on August 6. He was to speak before the Paraguayan human-rights commission.

Pressure on the government by local and foreign Indian rights groups resulted in an accord on August 14, under which the Institute of Rural Welfare and the church obtained 19,000 acres (7 689 ha) of grazing land in the Chaco, from an agribusiness firm, for the resettlement of 700 Toba Indians. The Indians had been forcibly removed from their ancestral lands in January.

Economics. Soybean production for 1981 was forecast at 1.1 million t (1.2 million T), after having risen to more than 800 000 t (887,360 T) in 1980. Most of that harvest was exported, accounting for 13.6% of Paraguay's foreign exchange earnings in 1980.

A U.S. $27.5 million loan was obtained in August from the Inter-American Development Bank for rural development in central Paraguay. The World Bank extended a $12 million loan for water and sanitation services among poorer communities in the southeast. The Paraguayan government awarded a contract for $160 million to a French group for the construction of a cement factory, about 300 mi (480 km) north of Asunción.

Foreign Relations. Paraguayan Foreign Minister Alberto Nogués and his Argentine counterpart, Oscar Camilión, discussed in Ayolas in July a Paraguayan complaint concerning the diversion by Argentina of waters from the Pilcomayo River. Another priority item considered was a $2,000,000,000 civil engineering contract for the stalled binational Yacyretá hydroelectric project. In April, a $66 million contract for supplying 20 turbines for Yacyretá was awarded to an Argentine-Paraguayan consortium.

LARRY L. PIPPIN, *Elbert Covell College*
University of the Pacific

PARAGUAY • Information Highlights

Official Name: Republic of Paraguay.
Location: Central South America.
Area: 157,047 sq mi (406 752 km^2).
Population (1981 est.): 3,300,000.
Chief Cities (June 1979 est.): Asunción, the capital, 481,706; Caaguazú, 74,337; Coronel Oviedo, 67,956.
Government: *Head of state and government,* Gen. Alfredo Stroessner, president (took office Aug. 1954). *Legislature*—Congress: Senate and Chamber of Deputies.
Monetary Unit: Guarani (126 guaranies equal U.S.$1, July 1981).
Manufactures (major products): Processed foods, wood products, consumer goods, cement, hydroelectric power.
Agriculture (major products): Wheat, corn, manioc, sweet potatoes, beans, rice, sugarcane, fruits.

PENNSYLVANIA

Pennsylvanians wrestled with a number of problems, including Three Mile Island, reapportionment, a sluggish economy, the abortion issue, funding of education, teacher strikes, and a steep cut in federally funded programs.

Three Mile Island. Many proposals were offered for funding the remaining $760 million of the more than $1,000,000,000 needed to clean up radioactive wastes from the March 1979 nuclear power accident, the nation's worst. But a solution remained elusive until October, when President Ronald Reagan countered previous congressional and administration opposition to federal support by backing a plan offered by Gov. Dick Thornburgh. The governor's formula called for shared funding over a six-year period by the plant's owners, the nuclear industry, insurance, the federal government, and the states of Pennsylvania and New Jersey. With Reagan's support, a settlement seemed near. Firm commitments were needed, however, from each of the parties involved.

Meanwhile, the federal Atomic Safety and Licensing Board concluded eight months of testimony, which filled 95 volumes, on a request by the plant's owners to restart the undamaged companion reactor. The reactor was shut down for refueling at the time of the accident and has been idle since. It was expected that permission would be granted to restart the generator in early 1982.

In other developments, the courts approved a $25 million settlement of a class action suit filed in behalf of area residents and businesses against the owners, operators, and builders of the damaged reactor. And the owner, General Public Utilities, readied a $4,000,000,000 suit against the federal government, charging that negligence on the part of the Nuclear Regulatory Commission contributed to the accident.

Reapportionment. Political leaders debated the relative merits of the state congressional delegation's redistricting plan—favoring the incumbents of both parties—and one offered by the Republican-dominated legislature, which targeted four seats held by Democrats for extinction. As a result of the 1980 census, the legislature was required to trim the number of congressional districts by two.

Education. On September 8, the 22,000-member Philadelphia Federation of Teachers went on strike, disrupting for the second consecutive year the opening of school for the city's 223,000 public school pupils. The union charged that the school board reneged on the contract settlement of the 1980 strike by ordering large-scale layoffs and cancellation of a 10% salary increase in attempting to deal with the district's $223 million deficit. The strikers returned to work October 28 in compliance with a court order.

New Laws. A 3.5% tax on motor fuels at the refinery level was adopted to fund road repairs. The state Supreme Court stayed an August 16 deadline for ending medicare-funded abortions as provided under a legislative statute.

Abscam and Other Crimes. Former Congressmen Michael Myers and Raymond Lederer were sentenced to three-year prison terms and fined $20,000 following their convictions in Abscam trials. Nine members of the radical group MOVE were sentenced to 30- to 100-year terms each, stemming from the cult's 1978 shootout with Philadelphia police, in which an officer was slain. The Rev. Daniel Berrigan, his brother, Philip, and six others received prison terms for breaking into the GE plant near Philadelphia and damaging two missile nose cones.

RICHARD ELGIN, *"The Patriot-News" Harrisburg*

The tall ships came and the fifers and drummers marched as Pennsylvania marked the 300th anniversary of Wm. Penn's receiving title to the region.

Philadelphia Visitor & Convention Bureau

PENNSYLVANIA • Information Highlights

Area: 45,308 sq mi (117 348 km²)
Population (1980 census): 11,866,728.
Chief Cities (1980 census): Harrisburg, the capital, 53,264; Philadelphia, 1,688,210; Pittsburgh, 423,938; Erie, 119,123; Allentown, 103,758; Scranton, 88,117; Reading, 78,686; Bethlehem, 70,419.
Government (1981): *Chief Officers*—governor, Dick Thornburgh (R); lt. gov., William W. Scranton, III (R). *General Assembly*—Senate, 50 members; House of Representatives, 203 members.
State Finances (fiscal year 1980): *Revenues*, $14,004,000,000; *expenditures*, $12,644,000,000.
Personal Income (1980): $112,220,000,000; per capita, $9,434.
Labor Force (July 1981): *Nonagricultural wage and salary earners*, 4,686,200; *unemployed*, 448,300 (8.1% of total force).

PEOPLE, PLACES, and THINGS

The Empire State Building, once the world's tallest edifice and always a must with the tourist to New York City, turned 50 years old in 1981. Red and turquoise laser lights, which were widely visible, were beamed from the building to mark the occasion.

Andy Levin/Black Star

With the cost of living increasing, more and more Americans turned to flea markets and garage sales to increase their incomes and add to their purchasing power.

O. Schatz/FPG

F. Lochon, Gamma/Liaison

The "Solar Challenger," the first sun-powered airplane, crossed the English Channel in July 1981. The plane was powered by 16,000 photovoltaic cells, which converted the solar energy to electricity.

Attempting to solve Rubik's Cube was a major 1981 pastime. More than 10 million cubes were sold worldwide between mid-1980 and mid-1981. Even books on the puzzle were published and became big sellers.

Ideal

Martha Swope

Joe Namath, known as Broadway Joe during his years as quarterback of the New York Jets, tried summer theater in 1981. He teamed with Susan Elizabeth Scott and Eddie Bracken in the Jones Beach Theater (Wantagh, NY) production of "Damn Yankees."

John Benson
Jelly Belly is the registered trademark of Herman Goelitz, Inc.

Once the public learned that jelly beans are a Ronald Reagan favorite, sale of the candy rose sharply. The presidential brand is Jelly Belly, available in 36 flavors.

An expedition led by Peter Gimbel succeeded in finding a safe from the Italian liner Andrea Doria, *which sank off Massachusetts in 1956. The safe was to be opened during a live television documentary.*

Yvonne Hemsey, Gamma/Liaison

The Gerald R. Ford Museum (below), with exhibits of the former president's life, was dedicated in Grand Rapids, MI, in September. The Ford presidential library had opened in Ann Arbor in April.

The Gerald R. Ford Museum

U.S. State Department

The U.S. embassy in Lima, Peru, was among buildings struck by predawn, terrorist bombings in late August.

PERU

Peru's major events in 1981 were a short-lived war with Ecuador in January, increased political terrorism, and economic problems marked by a continuing decline in the value of the Peruvian sol.

Border Disputes. A 165-year-old border dispute between Peru and Ecuador erupted into fighting between troops January 28 in the remote Cordillera del Condor north of the Marañon River and lasted until a February 2 truce was declared. On January 22, a Peruvian army helicopter was hit by ground fire while over the Peruvian base of Paquisha on the Camaina River, on the western slopes of the mountain range. The cease-fire was broken February 20 in several disputed mountain passes. After another cease-fire was declared March 6, Ecuador's foreign minister stated that his country was not interested in regaining all the territory lost to Peru after a brief 1941 flare-up was ended by the January 1942 Protocol of Rio de Janeiro. Ecuador said it would accept access to the Amazon River so that it could ship goods to Brazil and the Atlantic Ocean.

Political Terrorism. Dynamite bombs thrown August 31 at the U.S. Embassy and several U.S. business subsidiaries by members of the ultra-left *Sendero Luminoso* (The Shining Path) highlighted outbreaks of terrorism that disrupted the return to civilian rule under Fernando Belaúnde Terry.

While few people were killed or wounded, a year-long campaign by Peruvian supporters of Jiang Qing, the widow of Mao Zedong, against banks, electric power lines, government buildings, and a Roman Catholic Maryknoll office caused millions of dollars worth of damage, and uneasiness throughout the country. The government issued a decree law in March providing harsh penalties and permitting the police to arrest anyone suspected of supporting terrorists. Several church and human rights groups said at least 1,000 persons were imprisoned in September, not for links with the terrorists but for organizing or defending peasants in disputes over wages and access to land.

Economic Slowdown. The Peruvian sol declined in value from 317.12 to the dollar in November 1980 to 467 in mid-November 1981 as inflation approached 80% in 1981, compared with 50% in 1980 and 66.7% in 1979. The Belaúnde regime continued its policy of transferring ownership of various government-owned industries to private hands, reducing business and consumer subsidies, and encouraging savings and investment through high interest rates. Strikes were expected to increase to more than the 739 counted in 1980 which resulted in nearly 18 million man-hours being lost in the country. Unemployment reached 15% in June, and many workers did not receive the official monthly minimum wage of $82.00.

Peru's Minister of Mining and Energy Pedro Pablo Kuczynski launched a campaign in July

PERU • Information Highlights

Official Name: Republic of Peru.
Location: West Coast of South America.
Area: 496,223 sq mi (1 285 218 km^2).
Population (1981 est.): 18,100,000.
Chief Cities (1972 census): Lima, the capital, 3,158,417 (met. area); Arequipa, 304,653; Callao, 296,220.
Government: *Head of state,* Fernando Belaúnde Terry, president (took office July 1980). *Head of government,* Manuel Ulloa Elías, prime minister (took office July 1980). *Legislature*—Congress: Senate and Chamber of Deputies.
Monetary Unit: Sol (467 soles equal U.S.$1, Nov. 12, 1981).
Manufactures (major products): Mineral and petroleum products, fish meal, textiles.
Agriculture (major products): Cotton, sugar, coffee.

with Canada and Mexico to oppose a proposed U.S. government sale of one million ounces of silver from excess government reserves as world silver prices fell to $9.53 an ounce in October from a 1980 high of more than $50.

Up to 23 exploratory and 220 secondary recovery wells were to be drilled in 1981 by Petro-Peru, the state oil firm, and by two American firms under a new petroleum law signed on Dec. 26, 1980.

Foreign Relations. Full diplomatic relations with Chile were restored July 14 after two years of conflict over charges of Chilean spying. Brazil's President João Baptista Figueiredo and President Belaúnde signed ten agreements June 24–26 involving joint highway construction, technology, trade, and development of portions of the Amazon Basin.

NEALE J. PEARSON
Texas Tech University

PHILIPPINES

President Ferdinand E. Marcos had his 16-year rule extended for an additional six years by election, but the managed balloting did not reflect national consensus in support of the Filipino leader.

Politics. President Marcos, 63, who established martial law in the Philippines in September 1972, formally terminated such rule in January. But the government retained authority to arrest persons without formal charges, and both lay and church critics claimed that no real change had taken place. The army, which increased in size from 46,000 in 1972 to 150,000 in 1981, remained the prime prop for perpetuation of Marcos' rule.

Filipinos went to the polls in June in a presidential election in which Marcos had no opposition. Voters were told that they faced arrest if they failed to cast ballots, and 88% of them obeyed by supporting extension of Marcos' 16-year rule, which began with a free election in 1965, for another six years.

Voters also approved a new French-style presidential system in carefully manipulated balloting in April. The new arrangement provides for a strong president, who appoints the prime minister. Marcos named to the new post one of the most respected and honest figures in Filipino political life, Finance Minister Cesar Virata. Virata, also much respected in international monetary circles, was the leading member of the technocrat bloc in the government. His designation as premier did not mean the abandonment of the so-called "old guard" in the Marcos regime, however.

One of Marcos' most outspoken critics was Jaime Cardinal Sin, who accused the president of a "deliberate" effort to stifle religious freedom—comparing his tactics with those of the Nazis in Germany in the 1930s. Marcos hoped that the February visit of Pope John Paul II could be interpreted as a kind of approval of his authoritarian regime, but the pontiff spoke out strongly against "any violation of the fundamental dignity of the human person."

Not all opposition to the Marcos regime, however, was peaceful. The biggest demonstration ever against the president's rule took place in Manila in mid-September, when upward of 10,000 workers, students and other protesters attacked the "United States–Marcos dictatorship." This was followed in early October by the worst rioting in Manila under Marcos' rule. Some 1,500 demonstrators, most of them rock-throwing students, participated.

Rebellion and Subversion. A chief problem of the Philippine political process was the absence of legal opportunity for protest. The United Democratic Opposition campaigned for boycott of the June presidential election, while both moderate as well as leftist clergy—in a country with 40 million Roman Catholics—became increasingly alienated from the regime.

UPI

Flanked by President and Mrs. Ferdinand Marcos, Pope John Paul II blesses the crowd during his February visit to the Philippines.

In Manila on June 30, Ferdinand Marcos is sworn in for another six-year term as president of the Philippines.

UPI

A major Muslim secessionist rebellion persisted on Mindanao and adjacent southern islands with no early ending seemingly in sight. The Community New People's Army (NPA), with an estimated 5,000 insurgents in the field, continued to grow in strength in the countryside in its 12th year of existence. The NPA fought government troops on both the northern island of Luzon and Mindanao in the south. Affiliated with the pro-Chinese Communist Party of the Philippines (CPP), the NPA followed a different strategy than the pro-Moscow PKP (*Partido Komunista ng Pilipinas*), whose activities were limited to Luzon and largely included infiltration of the government and unions.

Economy. Rising unemployment and high inflation contributed to the mounting dissatisfaction with the Marcos government. An external debt of $13,800,000,000—owed mainly to American banks, the World Bank, and the International Monetary Fund—indicated the heavy dependence of the Philippine economy on borrowed funds from abroad. The United States, Japan, and major European nations pledged $1,200,000,000 in aid to the Philippines.

U.S. investment in the Philippines, according to the U.S. Department of Commerce, was somewhat greater than $1,000,000,000, but other sources suggested that it might be significantly higher. Major Philippine corporations, owned by relatives and friends of President Marcos and his wife, were reported in serious economic difficulty in several instances. Their potential collapse threatened to add to the financial troubles of the nation.

Bad weather contributed to a reduced rice crop, causing the government to halt exports of the cereal. A major increase in the cost of imported fertilizer lowered yields of the grain. Rising oil-product prices at retail outlets not only reflected international cost increases but also Filipino foreign exchange problems.

Foreign Relations. U.S. Vice-President George Bush represented President Ronald Reagan at Marcos' June 30 "inauguration." Regime critics were outraged, however, when Bush toasted Marcos' "adherence to the democratic principles." The U.S. vice-president promised full U.S. commitment and support to the Philippines and its non-Communist neighbors. The U.S. stake in the island nation was also evident in the continued importance of Clark Airfield, headquarters for 30,000 service and civilian personnel, and Subic Bay Naval Base. President Reagan did not invite Marcos to Washington in 1981—clearly annoying the Filipino leader.

The Philippines served as host in June to the second foreign ministers' meeting of the Association of Southeast Asian Nations (ASEAN). Earlier, Filipino Foreign Minister Carlos P. Romulo, claiming to speak for ASEAN, endorsed a "united front" against the Vietnam-established Phnom Penh government. But the ASEAN lands, he said, would not give aid to the Kampuchean rebels.

China's Premier Zhao Ziyang, Japan's Prime Minister Zenko Suzuki, and South Korean President Chun Doo Hwan were state guests of the Marcos government. The Philippines also signed an agreement with Canada establishing the framework for possible future transfer of Canadian nuclear technology to Manila.

RICHARD BUTWELL, *Murray State University*

PHILIPPINES • Information Highlights

Official Name: Republic of the Philippines.
Area: 115,830 sq mi (300 000 km^2).
Population (1981 est.): 48,900,000.
Chief Cities (May 1975): Manila, the capital, 1,479,116; Quezon City, 956,864; Davao, 484,678; Cebu, 413,025.
Government: *Head of state,* Ferdinand E. Marcos, president (took office Dec. 30, 1965). *Head of government,* Cesar Virata, premier (appointed April 8, 1981). *Legislature* (unicameral)—National Assembly.
Monetary Unit: Peso (8.083 pesos equal U.S.$1, November 1981).
Manufactures (major products): Processed foods, tobacco, beverages, rubber products, cement, glass, textiles.
Agriculture (major products): Rice, corn, sugar, copra, coconut oil.

PHOTOGRAPHY

The year 1981 in photography was highlighted by clarifying and mystifying pictures of Saturn via the Voyager 2 satellite, incredible views of the inside of the human brain, and, according to Eastman Kodak, more than 10,000,000,000 images snapped by amateurs.

Though each year of the 1970s was marked by a major photo event—from the electronics takeover and reduction-in-size revolution in equipment to the acceptance of the medium as a first-rate art form—the early 1980s have been experiencing a more subtle coming of age, especially in regard to color. Two major technological breakthroughs were announced in 1981: the first video single-lens reflex camera that takes color pictures without film, and a new one-step color printmaking system. In the world's museums and galleries alike, manipulated and multimedia images as well as photographs in the classic documentary tradition made frequent appearances.

Hardware. Refinements, rather than major new equipment, told the story of the single-lens reflex (SLR) camera. From Canon came the AE-1 Program model, an updated version of the bestselling multi-mode, compact, automatic-exposure SLR, with programmed exposure. Canon also brought out a new version of its professional quality F-1 as an answer to Nikon's flagship F-3. The Japanese Nippon Kogoku of Tokyo purchased Nikon's longtime U.S. marketing subsidiary, Ehrenreich Photo-Optical Industries. While the photographic world awaited the first auto-focusing SLR, expected by year's end, Canon's AF35ML Super Sure Shot, a rangefinder compact, sported the fastest-yet auto-focusing lens (by a full f-stop), a 40mm f/1.9.

The first fundamental change in concept and technology since Louis Daguerre announced the invention of the silvered copper plate in 1839 was introduced by Sony in Japan. The Mavica, a video camera resembling a conventional 35mm, does not require the chemical processing of film. The SLR (expected to be priced at $650) uses an easy-to-load magnetic disc called a Mavipak ($2.65 and reusable), measures ⅛ inch (.3 cm) thick by 2 inches (5 cm) wide, and takes 50 images, which are viewable on a television screen via a disc player ($220). The camera was not expected to be available in U.S. retail stores until at least 1983.

Home moviemakers continued to scrap their Super-8 equipment in favor of video cameras and recorders. Kodak eliminated its XL movie camera and projector lines.

In the instant camera/film arena, Polaroid introduced its new 600 System. The 660 Sun camera, its Sonar auto-focusing model, costs $95 and the 640, with a fixed-focus lens, is priced at $70. At the system's heart is the new ASA 600 High Speed Color Film, costing $9.95 for a ten-exposure pack. The film ejects automatically, develops in 90 seconds, and can only be used with the two new cameras.

New compact zoom lenses, introduced at the annual Photographic Manufacturers Association trade show, stretched focal-length ranges even farther. Close focusing ("macro") became more common. And a tidal wave of new "dedicated" (electronically synchronized with camera exposure) flash units rolled in from independent manufacturers.

In Color. Technologically, 3M introduced the fastest-ever color emulsion, its ASA 640-T slide film, balanced by tungsten lighting. Manufactured in Italy, it is available under private labels in 20- and 36-exposure cartridges. And Kodak announced the Ektaflex one-step color printmaking system—a film, paper, activator solution, and printmaker (costing about $135) that makes possible printmaking from negatives or transparencies in as little as six minutes. Based on the same image-transfer technology that Kodak uses in its instant color print films, the system is expected to revolutionize the darkroom

An autographed photo of Charles Dickens was on display at the "This Is My Favorite Photograph of Myself" show at the Boston Athenaeum Gallery.

Courtesy of M. Wesley Marans

Courtesy of International Center of Photography (ICP)

The above David Hockney photograph was one of 200 "New Color" photos shown at New York City's International Center of Photography late in the year.

market because it requires only a single solution, has a wide usable temperature range, and eliminates the need for precise timing, mixing chemicals, and washing finished prints.

Aesthetically, color works were exhibited or published for the first time by heretofore master black-and-white photographers: Harold Feinstein's flowers and Mary Ellen Marks' prostitutes of Bombay. Ruffin Cooper hired a helicopter to produce striking color abstractions of the Statue of Liberty, while William Wegman posed his weimaraner, named Man Ray, in visual puns on 20-24-inch (51-61-cm) color Polaroid. And at the International Center of Photography (ICP) in New York City, "The New Color: A Decade of Color Photography" included 200 works by 47 photographers in the first comprehensive critical perspective on color in the 1970s.

Exhibitions. A two-part retrospective of the master works of photojournalist W. Eugene Smith comprised the opening shows for Photograph gallery in New York City. The gallery's owners had bought Smith's works (he died in 1978) for slightly more than $1 million, the largest amount ever paid for the work of a single photographer. Other unique aspects of the gallery include a Daguerrian Room, a first of its kind, and a policy whereby substantial profits will be turned into grants for photographers. And at the Philadelphia Museum of Art, a major retrospective included the landscapes and Western expeditionary views of 19th-century photographer Timothy O'Sullivan. The antithesis of the classic documentary style was dramatically evident in 1981, as in "The Markers" at the San Francisco Museum of Art, in which 11 contemporary Americans scrawled and scribbled, tore and colored their images.

While proposed funding cuts in the arts raised concern about a comparable decrease in corporate spending, Springs Mills expanded its support of photography, begun in 1978, at New York's Museum of Modern Art (MoMA), with three major shows and the publishing of accompanying books: "American Children," "American Landscape," and "Old France." The latter consists of Eugène Atget's views of the French countryside and is the first of four annual exhibits of the 19th-century documentarian's images, each with a companion volume encompassing *The Work of Atget.* Two other Atget exhibits opened concurrently in New York.

MoMA's most controversial show was "Before Photography: Painting and the Invention of Photography." The show's curator and catalogue-essay writer Peter Galassi proposed the theory that the direct result of the new pictorial vision—Realism—that was being pioneered in painting was the invention of photography, which in turn played a primary role in determining the entire subsequent course of modern painting. And in New York City, a number of undervalued 20th-century photographers received the attention they deserve: "Frederick Sommer at 75: A Retrospective" at ICP, Bill Brandt's "Nudes 1945–1980" at Marlborough, and Louis Faurer's 1950s street photography at the Light Gallery.

BARBARA LOBRON
Copy Editor, "Camera Arts"

PHYSICS

During 1981 excited states of the upsilon meson were found, the direction of controlled fusion research was decided, and the properties of neutrinos were debated.

Neutrinos. Questions about the fundamental properties of neutrinos remained unanswered. Neutrinos interact extremely weakly with matter, are assumed to have zero rest mass, and always travel at the speed of light. There are three varieties—the electron, muon, and tau neutrinos. In 1980 the co-discoverer of the neutrino, Frederick Reines, presented results which suggested that neutrinos do not have fixed identities, but instead oscillate between electron and muon neutrinos. This would imply a neutrino rest mass. A Soviet group reported a precise measurement of the maximum energy of the electrons emitted in radioactive decay. The latter findings also implied a non-zero neutrino rest mass. Other experiments were in progress at the Laue-Langevin Institute in Grenoble, France; at Savannah River, SC; and at Brookhaven National Laboratory, NY. If neutrinos have a rest mass, then a significant fraction of the mass of the universe—possibly enough to overcome expansion and close the universe—could be undetected. A neutrino rest mass might also resolve a variety of astrophysical problems, including the solar neutrino question (the fact that the measured solar neutrino flux is below expectations).

Controlled Thermonuclear Fusion. Fusion remains an appealing long term solution to the energy problem—unlimited fuel, few radioactive wastes, no nuclear proliferation. The problem is how to sustain the temperature required to initiate fusion (10 to 100 million degrees Kelvin). Majority opinion seems to favor magnetic confinement. Since charged particles leak from the hot plasma, the shape of the magnetic field is crucial. A doughnut shape (torus) is the most common, but particles drift away from the center of its curved system and are lost. Another system has a cylindrically shaped magnetic field with magnetic mirrors at the ends. Results at Lawrence Livermore (CA) encouraged the U.S. Department of Energy to accelerate the mirror approach in the planned Mirror Fusion Test Facility. Another solution combines the toroidal shape with periodic constrictions (mirrors). The combination, called a "bumpy" torus, has no ends to leak particles, and the bumps correct for radial drift.

Implosion by lasers or charged particles provides an alternate method to attain fusion. The implosion methods seem to have lost ground to the magnetic approach. However, the Nova laser, planned for completion in 1985 at Lawrence Livermore, will be the world's most powerful laser (200–300 terawatts) and may even reach breakeven. The Magnetic Fusion Engineering Act, federal legislation enacted in 1980, calls for the development of a fusion engineering device by 1990. For such demonstration systems, the doughnut-shaped magnetic confinement method seems to be the clear first choice.

Particle Physics. Elementary particles, such as protons, are thought to consist of subparticles called quarks. The discovery of the psi particle in 1974 required a fourth type, or flavor, of quark—the charm quark. The psi particle consists of a charm quark and antiquark and itself has total charm zero. A family of mesons has been observed that are excited states of the psi meson. The combination of a charm quark with other quarks is said to possess naked charm.

Since quarks are expected to come in threes, the next step was the search for the fifth or bottom quark. The upsilon meson was first observed at Fermilab, IL, in 1978. This massive (10 GeV) particle consists of a bottom (beauty) quark and antiquark and does not display the bottom flavor directly. The search began for the excited states of the upsilon meson. "Bare bottom" states have been observed at the Cornell electron-positron storage ring. There is now no evidence for the expected sixth (top) quark.

These results provide more evidence for the theory of quantum chromodynamics (QCD). Just as there is a quantum of electromagnetism (the photon), there should be a quantum of the strong interaction (the gluon). Although gluons cannot be directly observed, their existence has been implied by experiments at DESY (Hamburg, West Germany). Evidence has now been obtained at DESY that the gluon has spin one, in agreement with theory. Although the quark model is highly successful, some physicists are beginning to consider the next question—are quarks really fundamental particles, or are they, too, composite particles with substructures?

Science Policy, Manpower, and Education. The future of science research and development (R&D) funding and of science education seemed at a crossroads in 1981. Sharp increases in R&D funding for the Department of Defense were expected, while National Science Foundation funding may be reduced. With increased emphasis on development, both the magnetic fusion and laser applications should have increased support, but the future of high-energy accelerators seemed in doubt. A consensus supports more R&D to increase productivity and to maintain U.S. parity in such areas as microelectronics.

Unfortunately, surveys of U.S. science and engineering education and manpower reveal gloomy findings. The results of standardized tests on science and mathematics have been declining for more than 15 years. Only a sixth of the nation's high-school students take 11th grade science and mathematics; many fewer take physics. The percentage of physicists earning doctorates is half that of ten years ago. The demand for physicists is expected to exceed the supply for some time.

GARY MITCHELL
North Carolina State University

Laski/Black Star

Gen. Wojciech Jaruzelski (left) was named Poland's premier in February. Eight months later he replaced Stanislaw Kania (right) as first secretary of the Communist party.

POLAND

The year 1981 in Poland was marked by unprecedented economic and political turbulence. Strikes, strike threats, hunger marches, and demonstrations continued throughout the year, while economic conditions declined to levels unseen since the end of World War II. Political tension between the Communist Polish United Workers Party (PZPR) and the independent trade unions culminated in the imposition of martial law on December 13.

Government and Labor. In early January, amid continuing labor unrest in Rzeszów and Ustrzyki Dolne, the leader of the Solidarity trade union movement, Lech Walesa, negotiated with Deputy Premier Mieczyslaw Jagielski over the union's demand for a national five-day workweek. No agreement was reached. On January 8, the Solidarity leadership declared that workers would not work on Saturdays and would not accept cuts in pay or additional weekday hours. In response, the government threatened to withhold pay of workers absent from their jobs. Solidarity countered with a nationwide strike on January 10. According to union estimates, some 80% of the work force joined in the one-day walkout.

Locally, strikes were taking place in western and southeastern parts of Poland. In early January, a local union chapter in Zielona Gora resorted to strike action to force the government to dismiss its minister-without-portfolio in charge of unions, Stanislaw Ciosek. On January 13, demonstrators in Nowy Sacz, demanding an investigation into Communist Party misuse of funds and sanatorium privileges, were forcibly cleared out of the town hall. Demands for the recognition of an independent farmer's union led to a two-hour warning strike by Solidarity in Rzeszow on January 14. Two days later, bus and streetcar workers in Warsaw staged a four-hour strike in support of the demand for a five-day workweek. In the same cause, Solidarity's national leadership called for a series of warning strikes in Gdańsk, Bydgoszcz, Konin, and Grudziadz. Hundreds of thousands of workers responded with brief work stoppages. In late January, strikes and sit-ins by workers and farmers were augmented by student protests. Some 2,000 Łódź University students staged demonstrations. In early February, Solidarity called for a nationwide strike to back up the demand of farmers for an independent trade union of their own.

On February 9, Prime Minister Jozef Pinkowski was replaced by Defense Minister Gen. Wojciech Jaruzelski. The new premier called for a three-month moratorium on strikes.

In early March, the government announced a 50% cut in sugar rations and scheduled meat rationing for April. It also began arrests and prosecutions of political activists, including Jacek Kuron and Leszek Moczulski. Moczulski, leader of the Confederation for Independent Poland, was accused of trying to overthrow the regime.

On March 8 a rally was held in Warsaw to commemorate the suppression of student demonstrations in 1968, and on March 10 Jaruzelski's moratorium was shattered by a one-hour warning strike in Łódź, as well as strike threats affecting 300 plants in Radom within the next 48 hours. The most serious incident of early 1981 occurred March 19 in Bydgoszcz, where police used violence against Solidarity demonstrators. This triggered local sympathy strikes in Szczecin and Toruń and a nationwide warning strike, called for by Solidarity, on March 27.

On April 10, after Premier Jaruzelski threatened to resign, the parliament (Sejm) approved a resolution calling for a two-month suspension of strikes and strike threats. On April 13, the government announced plans to ration butter, wheat, flour, rice, and cereals for the first time since World War II. On April 17, the regime reversed its previous position and recognized an independent union of farmers.

A major government reorganization took place in early July, when Premier Jaruzelski streamlined the cabinet by firing eight ministers and consolidating 11 economy-related ministries into just six. The months of April through June were relatively strike-free, and on June 25 Lech Walesa actually announced that the period of union-government confrontation was over.

Party Congress. A special national congress of the PZPR in Warsaw on July 14 proved to be a milestone in Eastern European political history. The 1,964 delegates to the congress were elected competitively by secret ballot; about 20% of them were members of Lech Walesa's Solidarity. A 200-member Central Committee and an expanded 15-member Politburo were also elected competitively and by secret ballot. As expected, Stanislaw Kania was reelected first secretary. Kania pledged before the congress to follow a policy of "renewal"—a democratization of party and political life in Poland. He balanced that commitment with a pledge to keep Poland's place in the Warsaw Pact, a reaffirmation of the strong alliance with the Soviet Union, and a condemnation of "anti-Soviet and anti-Socialist excesses" among some Solidarity elements.

Resumption of Strikes. On July 9, on the eve of the party congress, employees of LOT, the Polish national airline, resorted to a strike over the issue of the workers' right to choose the airline's director. Strike activity was also undertaken by some 40,000 dockworkers and other transportation employees. In late July, Solidarity began a series of demonstrations in various cities to protest food shortages. On August 1, monthly meat rations were cut by the government from 8.1 lbs (3.7 kg) per person to 6.6 lbs (3.0 kg). Simultaneously, new price increases on food, ranging in some cases from 100 to 400%, were being considered by the regime. In August, hundreds of thousands of persons participated in food protests in such cities as Łódź, Lublin, and Gdańsk. On August 3, the city of Warsaw was brought to a standstill for several hours by a transport workers' protest strike. On August 7, more than half a million coal miners and steel workers in Silesia struck for four hours in protest of the critical food situation. Most party and government newspapers were forced to close because of

The continuing food shortage forced smaller rations. A family of four displays one week's allowance.

Laffont/Sygma

UPI

At the University of Łódź, left, students held a 26-day sit-in to protest Communist party control of the institution, its curriculum, and student associations. Demonstrations of support spread to other educational institutions throughout the country before an agreement was reached on February 18.

strikes, and even private fruit and vegetable vendors went on strike in the latter part of August. On August 20, Lech Walesa announced that Solidarity was headed for a "total confrontation" with the government because of its failure to improve the economic situation. He also indicated that political reforms were needed before genuine economic improvement could be achieved. One of these political reforms was union access to the media. Negotiations with the government in late August, designed to increase Solidarity's access, proved fruitless. In September, the government tripled the price of bread and doubled the price of flour.

Solidarity Congress. On September 5, Solidarity began its first national congress in Gdańsk with nearly 900 delegates in attendance. Among the resolutions adopted by the congress was one expressing support for free unionism throughout the Soviet bloc. The delegates declared that Solidarity was "not a trade union anymore but a social movement," and that Poland was to be a country of self-management. There were also demands for free elections and a national referendum on self-management; freedom for political prisoners; price rollbacks; and union control over the mass media. One resolution called for tribunals to punish party and government officials for past wrongs. If the regime failed in this, Solidarity declared, it would constitute its own tribunals.

The congress also saw some dissension over the Solidarity leadership and an unsuccessful challenge to the role of Lech Walesa. During the second part of the congress in early October, Walesa was reelected chairman.

Change in Government Leadership. On October 18, Stanislaw Kania—long believed in disfavor with the Soviets for his inability to curb Solidarity—was ousted as party leader. General Jaruzelski was named first secretary by the Central Committee, thus combining the portfolios of party chief, premier, and minister of defense. In replacing Kania, the Central Committee adopted a resolution calling for a "temporary" ban on strikes; a return to the six-day work week; and a renegotiation of the agreement that had sanctioned Solidarity's activities in August 1980.

Continuing Unrest. In late October, police battled demonstrators in Katowice in the worst outbreak of violence since 1980. Hundreds of thousands of people across the country participated in wildcat strikes. In the face of mounting unrest, Premier Jaruzelski issued crisis orders to the armed forces on October 19, deploying military detachments at various localities throughout the country. On October 27, Solidarity called for a one-hour nationwide strike to protest widespread food shortages. On October 28, life in Poland came to a virtual halt, just as it had during the general strike in March. Jaruzelski appealed to parliament for new legislation curbing walkouts and fired six cabinet ministers. In early November, the parliament enacted a resolution calling for workers to halt strikes but failed to pass the kind of legal strike ban that Jaruzelski

POLAND • Information Highlights

Official Name: Polish People's Republic.
Location: Eastern Europe.
Area: 120,727 sq mi (312 683 km^2).
Population (1981 est.): 36,000,000.
Chief Cities (Dec. 1980): Warsaw, the capital, 1,552,300; Łódź, 825,200; Cracow, 693,200.
Government: *Head of state,* Henryk Jablonski, president of the Council of State (took office 1972). *Head of government,* Gen. Wojciech Jaruzelski, chairman of the Council of Ministers (Feb. 1981) and first secretary of the United Polish Workers' Party (Oct. 1981). *Legislature* (unicameral)—Sejm.
Monetary Unit: Zloty (33.20 zlotys equal U.S.$1, July 1981).
Manufactures (major products): Iron and steel, chemicals, textiles, processed foods, ships, transport equipment.
Agriculture (major products): Grains, sugar beets, potatoes, hogs, livestock.

had sought. Lech Walesa's appeals in November against wildcat strikes proved ineffective. Warning that he might resign if workers did not respond, Walesa on November 4 took part in an unprecedented but futile summit meeting of labor, government, and church leaders.

In late November and early December, food shortages and strikes by factory workers, farmers, and students increased. At the same time, however, government denunciations of Solidarity, calls for an anti-strike law, and police repression also were stepped up. Talks among church, party, and union leaders in early December broke down once again. On December 12, Solidarity's national committee adopted a resolution urging a national referendum on Communist party rule and Poland's role in the Warsaw Pact. On December 13, Premier Jaruzelski declared martial law, subjecting strikers to possible death penalty, cutting communications, imposing a strict curfew, and placing limitations on travel and public assembly. Lech Walesa and other Solidarity leaders were arrested, along with some 5,000 persons throughout the country, according to official figures, and perhaps as many as 50,000, according to unofficial estimates. Army units were used to break up strikes and worker occupation of mines, factories, shipyards, and port facilities. A number of detention camps were set up, and strict censorship made it difficult to assess the death toll or to know the real fate of those arrested. The government acknowledged eight fatalities, but some estimates put the number in the hundreds. Varying reports of passive resistance and industrial sabotage continued to reach the West throughout December. Food shipments from the Soviet bloc and Western countries did arrive, but on December 28 the government announced severe cuts in meat and butter rations, as well as huge price increases, especially of coal.

Church-State Relations. The political and social significance of church involvement in Poland greatly increased during the year. As evidenced by the November 4 "tripartite crisis summit" in Warsaw, the Roman Catholic church came to be viewed as one of the principal political forces in the country. Church officials participated in the settlement of several disputes and strike actions throughout the country during 1981. Pope John Paul II and the Polish hierarchy were generally supportive of Solidarity and of the so-called "renewal" process. They defended the right of Poles to determine their own fate, free of foreign (Soviet) intervention. Nevertheless, they urged caution and social self-discipline as advocated by the late Cardinal Stefan Wyszynski, who had died in Warsaw on May 28. (*See* OBITUARIES, page 384.) On July 6, Bishop Jozef Glemp of Warmia, 52, was named by Pope John Paul II to succeed Cardinal Wyszynski as the primate of Poland.

Both Archbishop Glemp and the pope repeatedly expressed church opposition to the martial law, although urging the Polish people to refrain from fratricidal bloodshed. A Vatican mission to Warsaw in late December apparently failed to bring about an easing of the government repression.

Foreign Affairs. External economic assistance—in the form of deferred loan repayments, new credits, and shipments of food and raw materials—was vital to Poland, especially in view of its huge foreign debt, estimated at about $27,000,000,000. In January, West Germany agreed to extend a new $153 million loan. The United States agreed in February to defer loan payments. The U.S. labor federation AFL-CIO assisted Solidarity with some $160,000. And in July, the U.S. Food for Peace Program made $55 million available to Poland. At the same time, Poland's relationship with the USSR and the rest of the Warsaw Pact bloc was perilous. Between January and August, Marshal Kulikov, commander of the Warsaw Pact forces, conferred four times with Polish leaders in Warsaw amid charges in the official Soviet and Polish press that subversive and anti-Soviet activities were occurring in Poland.

On February 6, Chancellor Helmut Schmidt of West Germany and then President Valéry

Lech Walesa (front, left) was reelected Solidarity chairman at the federation congress in October.

Czarnecki/Liaison

Photoreporters

Soviet military maneuvers along the Polish frontier were a tacit threat against further upheaval.

Giscard d'Estaing of France warned against any foreign intervention in Poland. Within a week, the Soviet Union and East Germany began large-scale military maneuvers near Polish frontiers, even though Soviet President Leonid Brezhnev expressed confidence that the PZPR would be able to overcome the crisis.

Among Poland's more important contacts with the West in 1981 were the visit of Foreign Minister Jozef Czyrek to Washington in late September and several visits by Lech Walesa to France, Italy, and Japan. The U.S. government made numerous warning statements about impending Soviet military intervention, and Western bankers held several conferences on the handling of Poland's multibillion-dollar debt. In the second half of the year, however, it appeared that new Western loans would be extremely difficult to obtain. Polish coal production was officially estimated to have fallen more than 19% in the first nine months of 1981, and some food and resource stocks declined by as much as 30%.

On June 22, Marshal Kulikov declared that "counterrevolutionary forces were trying to tear the country out of the socialist community." Early in July, Soviet Foreign Minister Andrei Gromyko conferred with Polish leaders in Warsaw. In mid-August, the USSR conducted large-scale naval and amphibious maneuvers in the Baltic Sea close to Polish frontiers. Simultaneously, Secretary Kania and Premier Jaruzelski held talks with Soviet President Leonid Brezhnev in the Crimea. The ensuing communiqué promised Poland a five-year moratorium on the repayment of loans but declared that strikes and demonstrations created "serious perils to the security and independence" of Poland. A letter from the Soviet party's Central Committee published in Poland September 17 declared: "Further leniency shown to any manifestation of anti-Sovietism does immense harm to Polish-Soviet relations and is in direct contradiction to Poland's obligation to its alliances. . . ." In late October, President Brezhnev publicly called on the Jaruzelski government to "stifle the encroachments of counterrevolution."

The imposition of martial law was strongly criticized by the United States and Western Europe. Within one week, it also led to the resignations of two Polish ambassadors—Romuald Spasowski in the United States and Zdzislaw Rorarsz in Japan. Both were granted political asylum in the United States. On December 29, President Reagan announced U.S. economic sanctions against Poland and the USSR, charging that the Polish government, with Soviet support, had violated the 1975 Helsinki Accords by its mistreatment of the Polish people. During 1981, thousands of Poles sought asylum in Austria and other non-Communist countries.

ALEXANDER J. GROTH
University of California, Davis

POLAR RESEARCH

Antarctic. During the 1980–81 field season, more than 270 researchers conducted 74 scientific projects as part of the U.S. Antarctic Research Program. At Siple Station in the continent's interior, a major upper-atmosphere research project included approximately 40 scientists from ten U.S., Norwegian, and United Kingdom research groups. Three Nike-Tomahawk and four Super Arcas rockets provided by the U.S. National Aeronautic and Space Administration (NASA), along with 12 instrumented balloons, were used for detailed investigations of the magnetosphere and ionosphere. The data from these experiments were expected to improve understanding of the earth's radiation belts and of the composition and processes of the magnetosphere.

On Ross Island, about 50 mi (80 km) off the coast of southern Victoria Land, U.S., New Zealand, and Japanese scientists installed on Mt. Erebus, an active volcano, a series of seismic stations, which telemeter data to New Zealand's antarctic station. The surveillance revealed microearthquakes not associated with the volcano. The findings are significant because Antarctica is considered to be nearly aseismic.

In 1980 and 1981, the research vessel *Melville* spent 100 days in the eastern Scotia Sea (between Antarctica and South America). Scientists conducted geophysical investigations of the boundary of the antarctic tectonic plate as well as a multidisciplinary investigation of the life cycle and abundance of krill and their relationship to the circulation patterns and other physical and chemical characteristics of the Scotia Sea. Krill, shrimp-like crustaceans, are a major component of the antarctic food web. In March 1981, marine biologists discovered a krill swarm covering several square miles and containing an estimated 10 million t (11 million T) of the animals, probably the largest school of marine animals ever recorded.

Astronomers at the South Pole continued to study the sun. Preliminary data analysis affirmed that the sun's chemical composition is much the same as that of other stars.

Biologists in the ice-free valleys of southern Victoria Land studied stromatolites (composed of blue-green algae, microorganisms, and sediments), found in the region's cold, glacier-fed lakes. Antarctic stromatolites, the first to be discovered in freshwater lakes, are similar to stromatolites of the Precambrian Age.

Marine geologists recovered a core containing sediments deposited 100–120 million years ago, before Australia and Antarctica rifted apart. Because the core contains well-preserved fossils of pollen from temperate vegetation, more data were expected to be generated on the ecology and climate of East Antarctica before and during the breakup of Australia and Antarctica 40 million years ago.

Arctic. In the final year of the Greenland Ice Sheet Project, a joint U.S., Swiss, and Danish study, glaciologists reached the bottom of the ice sheet at 2 037 m (6,683 ft). The ice core was expected to provide climatic and atmospheric data for the past 130,000 years. Other investigations associated with the project include a study of the ice-flow dynamics of the Greenland ice sheet, as well as stable isotope analysis, particulate analysis, and electrical conductivity measurements of the ice core.

Marine scientists completed their fourth year of ecological investigations in the Processes and Resources of the Bering Sea Shelf project, which focuses on the relationship between biological processes and oceanographic structures.

WINIFRED REUNING
National Science Foundation

PORTUGAL

The resignation and subsequent return to power of Premier Francisco Pinto Balsemão had an unsettling effect on Portugal as it continued to cling precariously to democracy in the face of severe political and economic problems.

Government and Politics. President António Ramalho Eanes named Balsemão head of government following Premier Francisco Sá Carneiro's death in a Dec. 4, 1980, air crash. Balsemão, a 44-year-old journalist and lawyer and cofounder with Sá Carneiro of the Social Democratic Party, proved less combative than his predecessor, especially in dealings with the nation's left-leaning chief executive. The premier's preference for conciliation over confrontation drew mordant criticism from leaders within the moderate-to-conservative Democratic Alliance (AD), the governing coalition composed of Social Democrats, Center Democrats, and the tiny monarchist party. The carping continued despite Balsemão's readiness to make concessions to different groups in the coalition and to invite well-known politicians into the cabinet. These overtures were spurned.

After his own party's executive committee offered a less-than-unanimous vote of confidence, Balsemão stepped down on August 10. Within a month, the Social Democrats, the AD's largest number, implored him to retake the reins of power as they failed to find a credible alternative.

In forming the eighth government since Portugal shed dictatorship for democracy in 1974, Balsemão extracted broader commitments of support than he had previously enjoyed. For example, he persuaded one of his most strident detractors, Diogo Freitas do Amaral, head of the Democratic Center, to join the new cabinet as deputy premier and defense minister.

Yet, the AD may be in for rough times before the next general elections are held in 1984. It proposes to delete from the "revolutionary" Constitution specific references to socialism,

UPI

Portugal's new Premier Balsemão (right) is congratulated by President Eanes (left) and Freitas do Amaral, the outgoing caretaker premier. Balsemão resigned August 10 but was later persuaded to form a new government.

Marxism, and collectivism, and to modify clauses that restrict certain industrial activities to the public sector. Such changes would require two-thirds approval in the 250-member parliament, where the alliance boasts only an 18-seat majority. Moreover, the tensions between Premier Balsemão and Freitas do Amaral may explode the fragile coalition.

Economy. The most important new face in Balsemão's second cabinet is Finance and Planning Minister João Salgueiro. He has the thankless task of broadening an austerity program emphasizing wage controls and decreased public spending. Such bitter medicine was prescribed for Western Europe's poorest country because inflation, which fell from 24.2% in 1979 to 16.4% in 1980, was on the upswing. Even worse, the balance of payments deficit, which soared from $34 million in 1979 to $1,200,000,000 in 1980, approached $1,800,000,000 in 1981.

In May the government reduced personal and sales taxes as part of its effort to cut inflation and stimulate investment. Meanwhile, levies on earnings of long-term bank deposits were raised from 15 to 18%.

Balsemão must be prepared for opposition from the armed forces to efforts to trim the role of the public sector as he liberalizes the nation's economy. On July 18, the military Council of the Revolution (CR), headed by President Eanes, exercised its right of veto over a parliamentary bill to return nationalized banks and insurance companies to private hands. Even though civilians stressed the importance of the measure to economic recovery, the CR labeled the proposal unconstitutional and insisted that it would permit businessmen to recreate the kind of economic system that had bolstered the dictatorial regime overthrown by military officers seven years before. Communist and socialist legislators applauded the military's bold action.

Foreign Affairs. The government hopes that new investments will help reform productive structures, thereby facilitating full membership in the European Community (EC), possibly as early as 1984. Despite a government monopoly on banking, representatives of international financial institutions have flocked to Lisbon in hopes of helping to finance the wave of industrial development anticipated when Portugal joins the EC, and multinational corporations take advantage of its low-cost but skilled work force to make it an export base.

Some air flights had to be rerouted in mid-August as Portuguese air traffic controllers launched a two-day work stoppage to show sympathy for their striking American colleagues.

GEORGE W. GRAYSON
College of William and Mary

PORTUGAL • Information Highlights

Official Name: Republic of Portugal.
Location: Southwestern Europe.
Area: 34,553 sq mi (92 082 km²).
Population (1981 est.): 10,000,000.
Chief Cities (1979 est.): Lisbon, the capital, 1,100,000; Oporto, 350,000.
Government: *Head of state,* António Ramalho Eanes, president (took office July 1976). *Head of government,* Francisco Pinto Balsemão, prime minister (took office Jan. 1981). *Legislature* (unicameral)—Assembly of the Republic.
Monetary Unit: Escudo (63.65 escudos equal U.S.$1, Oct. 15, 1981).
Manufactures (major products): Textiles, footwear, wood and pulp, paper, cork, metalworking.
Agriculture (major products): Grains, potatoes, olives, wine grapes, rice, almonds.

POSTAL SERVICE

The U.S. Postal Service (USPS), the government corporation established July 1, 1971, by the Postal Reform Act of 1970, ended its first decade of operations in 1981. During this period, total mail volume rose by more than 20%, nearing 110,000,000,000 pieces in 1981. Delivery was aided by a new marketing approach of discounts for presorting by big volume mailers. Productivity was up 34% and personnel down some 75,000 from an all-time high of 741,000 in 1970 under the former Post Office Department. The level of subsidy to the USPS dropped from 25% of total revenues to about 4%.

First-class letter rates have been almost the lowest in the world, second only to Canada in 1981. The system services an average of 1.5 million new households each year. Underlying these developments was the growth of a new nonpolitical, professional career management system. Except for military service, Postmaster General William F. Bolger has been with the USPS and its predecessor for his entire career.

While productivity is up, per unit costs have risen. Behind this is a combination of inflation, increased fuel costs for heating nearly 40,000 offices and operating some 205,000 vehicles, plus greatly increased personnel costs. As a percentage of the whole, personnel's level has risen slightly, to about 86% of annual expenditures. Postal pay scales exceed those for most comparable employment, except in the competitive United Parcel Service (UPS).

The five-digit ZIP coding permitted mechanization of the sorting system, but approximately $1,000,000,000 of capital expenditure in the early 1970s for the machine handling of bulk package mail in 21 centers has resulted in only modest improvements in service. Competitors, such as UPS, have made inroads into the USPS package volume which, unlike first-class mail, is not protected by any monopoly statutes. Moreover, the new electronic message capabilities of competitors threaten the entire postal system. A 1981 report by the U.S. General Accounting Office concluded that, without much greater participation in electronic message transmission, the USPS could lose 200,000 workers and 25% of its mail volume by the year 2000.

During the fiscal year (FY) ending Sept. 30, 1981, several important events suggested a partial resolution of these problems. In February 1981, Postmaster General Bolger predicted that, given approval of a rate increase, requested in April 1980 from the Postal Rate Commission (PRC), and a reasonable pay agreement with the postal unions, the service could limit rate increases to at least three-year intervals. This would greatly aid planning by both bulk mailers, who originate the majority of postal volume, and the USPS.

The labor agreement reached in late July could be termed close to reasonable. But the PRC was uncooperative and allowed only a raise from 15 to 18 cents instead of to 20 cents for first-class postage, effective March 22. Turned down twice more, the USPS Board of Governors, in an unprecedented use of a clause in the 1970 act, unanimously (a requirement) overruled the PRC on September 29 and approved most of the rates sought. First-class mail rose to 20 cents and postcards to 13 cents on November 1.

In February, Bolger also predicted that use of the proposed voluntary nine-digit ZIP code would allow the USPS to move from mechanization toward the maximum potential of automation. Scheduled for introduction in 1981, "ZIP + 4" was delayed until Oct. 1, 1983, by the Omnibus Budget Reconciliation Act of 1981. However, the act authorized full implementation of the new code, including purchase of needed equipment. By December 1981, business mailers and boxholders were to be notified of their expanded numbers. Residential notification was delayed. The new system is designed to pinpoint sorting to city blocks or apartment buildings.

On May 29 the PRC's claim of broad authority to regulate postal policy as well as rates was rejected by a decision of the U.S. Court of Appeals for the District of Columbia. Although subject to other regulatory agencies, principally the Federal Communications Commission, the USPS is now much freer to chart its own future. Its two electronic mail systems, INTELPOST for international and E-COM for domestic use, have been allowed to proceed. The former was to expand and E-COM was to commence on Jan. 4, 1982. Main barriers to bringing the USPS fully into the automated and electronic age have been breached.

The postmaster general expects the service to break even for FY 1982, and the Reagan administration has plans to reduce the postal subsidy to zero by 1984.

Canada. A six-week postal strike ended in the middle of August. On October 16, in accordance with a parliamentary act approved April 23, 1981, the Canada Post Office became the Canada Post Corporation (CPC). As is now U.S. and British policy, the agency is expected to become self-sustaining.

This will be difficult. The postal deficit for the year ending March 1981 was unofficially estimated at $500 million. The deficit is as much as, or more than, that predicted for the far larger USPS.

As a beginning attack on its deficit, the CPC proposed in October to raise rates effective Jan. 1, 1982. First-class mail would jump 13 cents to 30 cents Canadian. Third and fourth classes, mainly for use by publishers, were to be increased in April. The Cabinet had 60 days to accept (no action is also acceptance), amend, or return with recommendations the proposal. Meanwhile, in Canada as in the United States, electronic mail systems were expanding.

PAUL P. VAN RIPER, *Texas A&M University*

PRINCE EDWARD ISLAND

The constitutional debate which dominated the Canadian political scene in 1981 had echoes in Prince Edward Island (P.E.I.).

Constitution. The Throne Speech opening the provincial legislature in February said that unilateral action by the federal government on constitutional reform was "contrary to Canadian convention, custom, and practice." Premier J. Angus MacLean was one of eight provincial leaders who lined up against the federal plan to bring home the Canadian Constitution from Britain, complete with an entrenched bill of rights and a constitutional amending formula.

Politics. The voters of the federal constituency of Cardigan, in a by-election on April 13, chose a Liberal to represent them in Ottawa. Bennett Campbell, a former provincial premier, narrowly defeated Conservative candidate Wilbur MacDonald, who held the seat during the short-lived Tory government of 1979–80. The result left the island's four seats in Parliament split evenly between the Liberals and Conservatives. Campbell later was named veterans affairs minister.

Provincially, a by-election held July 6 resulted in A. A. (Joey) Fraser winning the Kings 3rd legislature seat. He defeated Liberal Paul DesRoches, giving the Tories 22 seats in the provincial House compared with the Liberals' 10.

Soon after, the Conservatives found themselves faced with choosing a new leader when MacLean decided to step down as premier. A Tory member of Parliament for 25 years, he entered provincial politics in 1976 and less than three years later led the Conservatives to power in Charlottetown. Health and Social Services Minister James Lee, 44, was selected for the party post and took over as premier in November.

Federal-Provincial. Federal government plans to cut financial help to the provinces, while reducing its control over health care and postsecondary education, caused concern in P.E.I. Finance Minister Lloyd MacPhail told a parliamentary committee in Charlottetown May 5 that his government was "apprehensive" about the plan. Federal money accounts for 55% of the island government's revenue.

PRINCE EDWARD ISLAND • Information Highlights

Area: 2,184 sq mi (5 657 km^2).
Population (April 1981 est.): 124,200.
Chief Cities (1976 census): Charlottetown, the capital, 17,063; Summerside, 8,592.
Government (1981): *Chief Officers*—lt. gov., Gorden L. Bennett; premier, James Lee (Progressive Conservative); chief justice, Supreme Court, John Paton Nicholson. *Legislature*—Legislative Assembly, 32 members.
Education (1981–82 est.): *Enrollment*—elementary and secondary schools, 26,420 pupils; postsecondary, 2,080.
Personal Income (average weekly salary, April 1981): $244.41.
Unemployment Rate (June 1981, seasonally adjusted): 10.5%.
(All monetary figures given in Canadian dollars.)

Ferry Service. The federal government agreed to provide 60% of the funding needed for a feasibility study of a proposed ferry between Souris, P.E.I., and Port Hood, N.S.

Seal-Hunt Aftermath. A Royal Canadian Mounted Police (RCMP) constable was convicted in Charlottetown in March on an assault charge arising from the land-based seal hunt off P.E.I.'s coast. Narca Moore-Craig, a California woman filming the controversial hunt for the Animal Protection Institute of America, laid the charge. She claimed that Constable Lloyd Vassallo assaulted her while seizing film of the event. Vassallo was given an absolute discharge after conviction, while a Canadian fisheries officer, also charged with assaulting Moore-Craig, was acquitted. Officials stopped the hunt.

JOHN BEST, *Canada World News*

PRISONS

In 1981, the population of American prisons continued to grow, and the problem of overcrowding reached new levels of severity. Violent eruptions seldom reached headline proportions, but there were major and costly riots in a number of large prisons, including ones in Hawaii, Illinois, Indiana, Louisiana, Michigan, New Mexico, New York, Pennsylvania, and Washington. Violence among inmates and between inmates and guards is not subject to accurate measurement, but the number of incidents and their severity is almost certainly increasing. In 1981, the number of prisoners rose by 5%, bringing the total to more than 329,000. The increase continued a decade-long trend, during which the number of incarcerated rose by 61%. Budget constraints have added to the burden of confining larger numbers of inmates, and most agree that the entire U.S. prison system is in deep trouble.

Riots. A New Year's Eve (1980) rampage among inmates at the Washington State Corrections Center was quickly quelled, but not before close to $1 million of destruction was inflicted on the facility's school, library, prison store, and a guard lookout post. Only about 100 of the more than 600 prisoners were directly involved in the eruption, but the aftermath saw a radical change in what had been considered a model for progressive prison policies.

The pattern implicit in the Washington State riot was repeated, with minor variations, throughout the year. On May 22, at the Southern Michigan Prison in Jackson, more than 800 of the 5,000 inmates took control of the largest walled prison in the world and set fires that caused extensive damage. The riot apparently triggered three others in the state within the same week. Although there were no deaths, property damage, due largely to fires, was estimated at $5 million. A preliminary report, ordered by Gov. William G. Milliken, identified overcrowding and an unauthorized search by prison guards as the basic causes.

In July, at the Westchester County Jail in Valhalla, NY, prisoners took over the facility in protest against what they called injustices in the criminal justice system, specifically overcrowding. Property damage and the cost of overtime and outside assistance for retaking the institution totaled more than a half million dollars. Thirty-five police departments, 13 fire departments, and two Civil Defense units were called in before order was restored.

Legal Guidelines. Litigation concerning prison conditions, which began to grow precipitously following the Attica uprising and its bloody suppression in 1971, continued to occupy a considerable portion of the agendas of U.S. courts. More than half the states were under court orders to relieve overcrowding and improve living conditions, with additional court challenges under consideration in at least 12 other states. In a number of instances, judges ordered the early release of prisoners to keep down the prison population. In June, the U.S. Supreme Court ruled on the *Rhodes v. Chapman* case, which initially had been filed by inmates at the Southern Ohio Correctional Facility in Lucasville. This maximum security prison, one of the state's newest, contained about 1,400 prisoners doubled up in cells originally designed for a single inmate. Lower courts had ruled that the double-celling violated the Eighth Amendment restriction on cruel and unusual punishment. The Supreme Court reversed those decisions and ruled that the overall conditions at Lucasville had not led to violence or particular unrest among the prisoners and that double-celling in itself did not exceed "contemporary standards of decency."

Violence Among Inmates. As prison conditions have become more highly charged, a gradual shift to an often brutal and swift jail-house justice, in which formal means of settling disputes are bypassed and the inmates themselves rule on what is permissible and what is to be punished, appears to be taking place. Homosexual rape, the possession of contraband, the stealing of personal possessions, and murder are increasingly a part of the reality of prison life. Fistfights, stabbings, and other forms of violence take their daily toll.

In January 1981, Vernon Robert Butts, awaiting trial for a series of brutal murders, was found dead in his Los Angeles cell. Officials ruled the incident a suicide, but there were suggestions that his death was a case of fellow inmates not waiting for formal procedures to exact retribution. In June, James Earl Ray, imprisoned for the assassination of the Rev. Dr. Martin Luther King, was attacked and stabbed repeatedly by four fellow prisoners at Brusky Mountain State Prison in Petros, TN.

Economic Pressures. The costs of incarceration continue to mount. A single cell can cost from $50,000 to $100,000, and the annual costs of keeping a single prisoner behind bars, including guards and support services, ranges from $10,000 to $30,000. The voting public has generally rejected bond issue referendums designed to raise money for state prison systems, leaving them overcrowded and understaffed. Guards, locked in with the prisoners on a day-to-day basis, are finding the situation increasingly intolerable. The number who are leaving to seek other employment is increasing dramatically, with the turnover rate in some institutions doubling or tripling over recent years.

UPI

A special police team stands guard after a series of uprisings at the Westchester County (NY) Jail.

Alternatives. While the public seems to want more systematic and severe use of incarceration, and even though the construction of facilities continues to increase, the present state of U.S. prisons will not permit that desire to be implemented as policy.

Alternatives to imprisonment are increasingly coming up for discussion and are being put into practice in some localities, though not in any systematic way. Programs are emerging in which prison cells are reserved for violent offenders. Some localities are looking at programs of restitution, in which the offender pays back the injured party in the form of money or community work. Other jurisdictions are experimenting with programs in which the offender, under close supervision, performs public-service tasks or takes part in programs not located within prison walls.

DONALD GOODMAN
John Jay College of Criminal Justice
City University of New York

PRIZES AND AWARDS

NOBEL PRIZES

Chemistry ($180,000 shared): Kenichi Fukui, professor of physical chemistry, Kyoto University, Japan; Roald Hoffmann, chairman of chemistry department, Cornell University; cited for work involving the application of "the theories of quantum mechanics, a highly mathematical theory of the behavior of atoms and molecules, to predict the course of chemical reactions."

Economics ($180,000): James Tobin, Yale University; his work, considered a breakthrough in the relationship between financial markets and "real" markets, was cited as having dealt with a "classic problem in economic research."

Literature ($180,000): Elias Canetti, Bulgarian-born writer; cited for "writings marked by a broad outlook, a wealth of ideas and artistic power, . . . held together by a most original and vigorously profiled personality."

Peace Prize ($180,000): Office of the United Nations High Commissioner for Refugees for dealing effectively with "a veritable flood of human catastrophe and suffering, both physical and psychological."

Physics ($180,000 shared): Nicolaas Bloembergen, Harvard University ($45,000) and Arthur Schawlow, Stanford University ($45,000); cited "for their contribution to the development of laser spectroscopy"; Kai M. Siegbahn, Uppsala University, Sweden ($90,000); cited for "his contribution to the development of high-resolution electron spectroscopy."

Physiology or Medicine ($180,000 shared): David H. Hubel, Harvard University ($45,000) and Torsten N. Wiesel, Harvard University ($45,000); cited for work primarily concerned with the manner in which the brain processes visual information; Roger W. Sperry, California Institute of Technology ($90,000); cited for succeeding "brilliantly" in "extracting the secrets from both hemispheres of the brain and demonstrating that they are highly specialized and also that many higher functions are centered in the right hemisphere."

ART

American Academy and Institute of Arts and Letters Awards
- Academy-Institute Awards ($5,000 ea.): art—John Duff, Friedel Dzubas, Mimi Gross, Leo Manso, Jane Wilson; music—Edwin Dugger, Robert Erickson, Meyer Kupferman, Ursula Mamlok
- Arnold W. Brunner Memorial Prize in Architecture: Gunnar Birkerts
- Charles Ives Award ($11,000): Charles Ives Society
- Charles Ives Scholarship ($4,000 ea.): Tamar Diesendruck, Allan Gimbel, Thomas Allen LeVines, William Neil, Russell F. Pinkston, Daniel C. Warner
- Distinguished Service to the Arts: Joseph Papp
- Goddard Lieberson Fellowship ($10,000): Chinary Ung
- Gold Medal for Painting: Raphael Soyer
- Marjorie Peabody Waite Award ($1,500): Normand Lockwood (in music)
- Richard and Hinda Rosenthal Foundation Award ($3,000): Alan Magee (in art)

American Institute of Architects Gold Medal Award: Josep Lluis Sert

Dance Magazine Awards: Selma Jeanne Cohen, Anton Dolin, Twyla Tharp, Stanley Williams

Ernst von Siemens Music Prize ($78,500): Elliott Carter

International American Music Competition ($75,000): Randall Hodgkinson

John F. Kennedy Center for the Performing Arts Awards for career achievement in the performing arts: Count Basie, Cary Grant, Helen Hayes, Jerome Robbins, Rudolf Serkin

National Academy of Recording Arts and Sciences Grammy Awards for excellence in phonograph records
- Album of the year: *Christopher Cross,* Christopher Cross
- Classical album: *Berg: Lulu (Complete Version),* Pierre Boulez, conductor, Orchestre de l'Opéra de Paris
- Country music song: *On the Road Again,* Willie Nelson, songwriter
- Jazz vocal performance, female: *A Perfect Match/Ella & Basie,* Ella Fitzgerald
- Jazz vocal performance, male: *Moody's Mood,* George Benson
- New artist: Christopher Cross
- Record of the year: *Sailing,* Christopher Cross
- Song of the Year: *Sailing,* Christopher Cross

Moscow International Ballet Competition (16-to-19-year-old section): Amanda McKerrow

Pritzker Architecture Prize ($100,000): James Stirling

Pulitzer Prize for Music: no prize awarded

Samuel H. Scripps Award ($25,000): Martha Graham

Van Cliburn International Piano Competition ($12,000): André-Michel Schub

W. Eugene Smith grant for humanistic photography ($10,000): Eugene Richards

JOURNALISM

George Polk Memorial Awards
- Commentary: Roger Angell, *The New Yorker*
- Cultural reporting: *Art News*
- Editorial: *The New York Times*
- Foreign reporting: Shirley Christian, *The Miami Herald*
- Local radio reporting: KMOX, CBS, St. Louis
- Local reporting: *The Miami Herald* for "Police Brutality—the Violent Few"
- Local television reporting: Stephen Talbot and Jonathan Dann, KQED, San Francisco
- National radio reporting: National Public Radio
- National reporting: Jonathan Neumann and Ted Gup, *The Washington Post*
- National television reporting: Charles Kuralt, CBS
- News photography: Oscar Sabetta, United Press International
- Political reporting: Bill Moyers, *Bill Moyers' Journal,* Public Broadcasting System
- Regional reporting: *The Charlotte* (NC) *Observer* for "Brown Lung"
- Satiric drawing: Edward Sorel

Maria Moors Cabot Prizes ($1,000 ea.): Karen DeYoung, Marlise Simons, Jacobo Timerman; special citations to Elizabeth Cabot and Stanley M. Swinton

National Magazine Awards
- Design: *Attenzione*
- Essays and criticism: *Time*
- Fiction: *North American Review*
- General excellence awards: *Glamour, Business Week, Audubon, ARTnews*
- Public service: *Reader's Digest*
- Reporting excellence: *National Journal*
- Single topic issue: *Business Week*

Overseas Press Club Awards
- Book on foreign affairs: Dan Kurzman, *Miracle of November: Madrid's Epic Stand—1936*
- Business news reporting from abroad: Thomas L. Friedman, United Press International
- Cartoon on foreign affairs: Paul Conrad, *Los Angeles Times*
- Daily newspaper or wire service reporting from abroad: Richard Ben Cramer, *The Philadelphia Inquirer*
- Magazine interpretation of foreign affairs: *Time,* "Inside the U.S.S.R."
- Magazine reporting from abroad: Joseph Kraft, *The New Yorker*
- Photographic coverage from abroad: Gilles Peress, *The New York Times Magazine*
- Photographic reporting from abroad: Abbas, *American Photographer*
- Radio interpretation of foreign news: Robert Trout, ABC News Radio
- Radio spot news from abroad: Frank Sesno, Associated Press Radio
- Television interpretation of foreign affairs: Bill Moyers, David Grubin; WNET-TV
- Television spot news reporting from abroad: Richard Threlkeld, CBS-TV
- Bob Considine Memorial Award: Guy Gugliotta, *The Miami Herald*
- Robert Capa Gold Medal: Steve McCurry, *Time*
- Madeline Dane Ross Award: Bill Kurtis, WBBM-TV
- Reporting which describes human rights abuses and supports the principles of human rights: Chris Wallace, Morton Silverstein, NBC-TV

Pulitzer Prizes
- Commentary: David Anderson, *The New York Times*
- Criticism: Jonathan Yardley, *The Washington Star*
- Editorial cartooning: Mike Peters, *The Dayton* (OH) *Daily News*
- Feature photography: Taro M. Yamasaki, *The Detroit Free Press*
- Feature writing: Teresa Carpenter, *The Village Voice*
- General local reporting: *The Longview* (WA) *Daily News*
- International reporting: Shirley Christian, *The Miami Herald*
- National reporting: John M. Crewdson, *The New York Times*
- Public service: *The Charlotte* (NC) *Observer*
- Special local reporting: Clark Hallas, Robert B. Lowe, *The Arizona Daily Star*

Spot news photography: Larry C. Price, *The Fort Worth Star-Telegram*

LITERATURE

American Academy and Institute of Arts and Letters Awards
- Academy-Institute Awards ($5,000 ea.): Louise Gluck, Gail Godwin, Howard Frank Moser, James Salter, Elizabeth Sewell, William Stafford, Hilma Wolitzer, Jay Wright
- American Academy in Rome Fellowship in Creative Writing ($2,000): Edwin Field
- Award of Merit Medal ($1,000): John Guare (for drama)
- Gold Medal for Belles Lettres and Criticism: Malcolm Cowley
- Harold D. Vursell Memorial Award ($5,000): Edward Hoagland
- Loines Award for Poetry ($1,000): Ben Belitt
- Medal for Spoken Language: James Earl Jones
- Morton Dauwen Zabel Award ($2,500): Guy Davenport
- Richard and Hinda Rosenthal Foundation Award ($3,000): Jerome Charyn (in writing)
- Sue Kaufman Prize for First Fiction ($1,000): Tom Lorenz
- Witter Bynner Prize for Poetry ($1,350): Allen Grossman

The American Book Awards ($1,000)
- Autobiography/Biography (hardcover): *Walt Whitman*, Justin Kaplan
- Autobiography/Biography (paperback): *Samuel Beckett*, Deirdre Bair
- Book design, pictorial: *In China*, photographed by Eve Arnold; designed by R. D. Scudellari
- Book design, typographical: *Saul Bellow, Drumlin Woodchuck*, designed by Richard Hendel
- Book illustration, collected or adapted: *The Lost Museum*, by Robert M. Adams, designed by Michael Shroyer
- Children's Books, fiction (hardcover): *The Night Swimmers*, Betsy Byars
- Children's Books, fiction (paperback): *Ramona and Her Mother*, Beverly Cleary
- Cover design (paperback): *Fiorucci: the Book*, designed by Quist-Couratin
- First novel: *Sister Wolf*, Ann Arensberg
- General fiction (hardcover): *Plains Song*, Wright Morris
- General fiction (paperback): *The Stories of John Cheever*, John Cheever
- General nonfiction (hardcover): *China Men*, Maxine Hong Kingston
- General nonfiction (paperback): *The Last Cowboy*, Jane Kramer
- History (hardcover): *Christianity, Social Tolerance, and Homosexuality*, John Boswell
- History (paperback): *Been in the Storm So Long: Aftermath of Slavery*, Leon F. Litwack
- Jacket design (hardcover): *In China*, R. D. Scudellari, designer
- Poetry: *The Need to Hold Still*, Lisel Mueller
- Science (hardcover): *The Panda's Thumb*, Stephen Jay Gould
- Science (paperback): *The Medusa and the Snail*, Lewis Thomas
- Translation: *The Letters of Gustave Flaubert 1830–1857*, translated by Francis Steegmuller; Arno Schmidt's *Evening Edged in Gold*, translated by John E. Woods

Bancroft Prizes ($4,000 ea.): Ronald Steel, *Walter Lippmann and the American Century;* Jean Strouse, *Alice James: A Biography*

Canada's Governor General's Literary Awards
- English fiction: George Bowering, *Burning Water*
- French fiction: Pierre Turgeon, *La Premier Personne*
- English nonfiction: Jeffrey Simpson, *Discipline of Power*
- French nonfiction: Maurice Champagne-Gilbert, *La famille et l'homme a delivrer du pouvoir*
- English poetry and drama: Stephen Scobie, *McAlmon's Chinese Opera*
- French poetry and drama: Michel Van Schendel, *De l'oeil et de l'écoute*

Edward MacDowell Medal: John Updike

National Medal for Literature ($15,000): Kenneth Burke

PEN/Faulkner Award ($2,000): Walter Abish, *How German Is It*

Pulitzer Prizes
- Biography: Robert K. Massie, *Peter the Great: His Life and World*
- Fiction: John Kennedy Toole, *A Confederacy of Dunces*
- General nonfiction: Carl E. Schorske, *Fin-de-Siècle Vienna: Politics and Culture*
- History: Lawrence A. Cremin, *American Education: The National Experience, 1783–1876*
- Poetry: James Schuyler, *The Morning of the Poem*

UPI

Actor Robert Redford wins an Oscar for his first attempt at film directing, "Ordinary People."

MOTION PICTURES

Academy of Motion Picture Arts and Sciences ("Oscar") Awards
- Actor: Robert De Niro, *Raging Bull*
- Actress: Sissy Spacek, *Coal Miner's Daughter*
- Cinematography: Geoffrey Unsworth and Ghislain Cloquet, *Tess*
- Costume design: Anthony Powell, *Tess*
- Director: Robert Redford, *Ordinary People*
- Film: *Ordinary People*
- Foreign language film: *Moscow Does Not Believe in Tears*
- Music—original score: Michael Gore, *Fame*
- Music—original song: *Fame*, music by Michael Gore, lyric by Dean Pitchford
- Original screenplay: Bo Goldman, *Melvin and Howard*
- Screenplay based on material from another medium: Alvin Sargent, *Ordinary People*
- Supporting actor: Timothy Hutton, *Ordinary People*
- Supporting actress: Mary Steenburgen, *Melvin and Howard*
- Academy Award of Merit: Linwood G. Dunn, Cecil D. Love, and Acme Tool and Manufacturing Company for concept engineering and development of the Acme-Dunn optical printer
- Honorary Award: Henry Fonda
- Special Achievement Award: (for visual effects)—Brian Johnson, Richard Edlund, Dennis Muren, Bruce Nicholson, *The Empire Strikes Back*

American Film Institute's Life Achievement Award: Fred Astaire

Cannes Film Festival Awards
- Actor: Ugo Tognazzi, *The Tragedy of a Ridiculous Man*
- Actress: Isabelle Adjani, *Quartet* and *Possession*
- Director: no award given
- Film: *Man of Iron* (Poland)
- Special jury prize: Alain Tanner, *The Years of Light*

PUBLIC SERVICE

Albert Einstein Peace Prize ($50,000): George F. Kennan

American Institute for Public Service Jefferson Awards
- $1,000 awards: Hank Williams, Irene Auberlin, David Crockett, Homer Fahmer, Noey Somchay
- $5,000 awards: Warren Christopher, Marva Collins, Walter Cronkite, David A. Stockman
- Outstanding public service award: Justice Potter Stewart

Congressional Gold Medal (presented by President Ronald Reagan on June 16): Kenneth Taylor, Canadian diplomat
Congressional Robert Kennedy Gold Medal (presented by President Ronald Reagan on June 5): to Ethel Kennedy in memory of Sen. Robert Kennedy
Freedom Award of the International Rescue Committee: Lane Kirkland and Irena Kirkland
Hans J. Morgenthau Memorial Award: Angier Biddle Duke
Harry S Truman Public Service Award: Jimmy Carter
Presidential Citizen's Medal (presented by President Ronald Reagan on March 23): Elmer Staats
Ralph Bunche Institute Peace Award: Dr. Urho Kekkonen, president of Finland (1956–81)
Rockefeller Public Service Awards ($10,000 each): Marian Wright Edelman, for her leadership in advocating the rights of children; Robert A. Hatcher, for promoting the well-being of families; Herbert Scoville, Jr., for his work in promoting world peace; Betty Jean Hall and Charles Prejean (shared), for broadening employment opportunities; Ruth Watson Lubic, Phyllis R. Farley, and Richard Smith (shared), for developing new methods of health care
Templeton Prize for "progress in religion" ($220,000): Dr. Cicely Saunders
U.S. Presidential Medal of Freedom (presented by President Jimmy Carter on January 16): Roger Baldwin, Harold Brown, Zbigniew Brzezinski, Warren Christopher, Walter Cronkite, Kirk Douglas, Margaret Craig McNamara, Karl Menninger, Edmund S. Muskie, Esther Peterson, Gerard C. Smith, Robert Strauss, Elbert Parr Tuttle, Andrew Young, and Earl Warren (posthumously)
U.S. Presidential Medal of Freedom (presented by President Ronald Reagan on October 9): Eubie Blake, Ella Grasso (posthumously), Bryce N. Harlow, Walter H. Judd, Morris I. Liebman, Charles B. Thornton
William J. Donovan Award for distinguished service in the interest of the democratic process and the cause of freedom: Margaret Thatcher, prime minister of Great Britain

SCIENCE

Albert Lasker Awards ($15,000): Barbara McClintock, Cold Spring Harbor (L.I., NY) Laboratory for the Carnegie Institution, Washington, DC, cited "for discovering that certain genetic elements are not stationary as in a string of pearls but can move from one location to another on DNA, the genetic material of heredity"; Louis Sokoloff, National Institute of Mental Health, Bethesda, MD, cited for developing a pioneering method for measuring the function of the brain as well as its specialized sections.
General Motors Cancer Research Foundation Awards ($100,000 ea.): E. Donnall Thomas, Wallace P. Rowe, Cesar Milstein, Takashi Sugimura
International Space Hall of Fame: Charles Yeager
Louisa Gross Horwitz Prize for research in biology or biochemistry ($22,000): Aaron Klug, Cambridge University
MacArthur Foundation Prize Fellow Laureate ($60,000 per year tax free for life): Barbara McClintock
National Medal of Science: Philip Handler

TELEVISION AND RADIO

Academy of Television Arts and Sciences ("Emmy") Awards
- Actor—comedy series: Judd Hirsch, *Taxi* (ABC)
- Actor—drama series: Daniel J. Travanti, *Hill Street Blues* (NBC)
- Actor—limited series: Anthony Hopkins, *The Bunker* (CBS)
- Actress—comedy series: Isabel Sanford, *The Jeffersons* (CBS)
- Actress—drama series: Barbara Babcock, *Hill Street Blues* (NBC)
- Actress—limited series: Vanessa Redgrave, *Playing for Time* (CBS)
- Children's program: "Donahue and Kids," *Project Peacock* (NBC)
- Classical program in the performing arts: "An Evening of Jerome Robbins' Ballets with Members of the New York City Ballet," *Live from Studio 8H* (NBC)
- Comedy series: *Taxi* (ABC)
- Drama series: *Hill Street Blues* (NBC)
- Individual achievement—special class: Sarah Vaughan, *Rhapsody and Song—A Tribute to George Gershwin* (PBS)
- Informational series: *Steve Allen's Meeting of Minds*
- Informational special: "The Bionic Breakthrough," *The Body Human* (CBS)
- Limited series: *Shōgun*, (NBC)
- Special—comedy: *Lily: Sold Out* (CBS)
- Special—drama: *Playing for Time* (CBS)
- Supporting actor—comedy series: Danny De Vito, *Taxi* (ABC)
- Supporting actor—drama series: Michael Conrad, *Hill Street Blues* (NBC)
- Supporting actress—comedy series: Eileen Brennan, *Private Benjamin* (CBS)
- Supporting actress—drama series: Nancy Marchand, *Lou Grant* (CBS)
- Governors Award: Elton H. Rule, president of the American Broadcasting Company

George Foster Peabody Awards
- Radio: Canadian Broadcasting Corporation, Toronto, for "Peniel" from the *Hornby Collection* series and for *The Wonderful World of Science;* Minnesota Public Radio, St. Paul, for *A Prairie Home Companion;* NBC Radio, NY, for *The Hallelujah Caucas;* National Public Radio, Washington, DC, for *Jazz Alive!;* San Francisco Opera, San Francisco, for the San Francisco Opera radio broadcasts; Studs Terkel, WFMT Radio, Chicago; WNCN Radio, NY, for overall station performance
- Television: ABC, NY, for *Amber Waves* and for *IBM Presents Baryshnikov on Broadway;* British Broadcasting Corporation, London, for *All Creatures Great and Small;* Carroll O'Connor, CBS, for "Edith's Death," an episode of *Archie Bunker's Place;* CBS Entertainment, NY, for *Gideon's Trumpet* and for *Playing for Time;* CBS News, NY, for *Universe;* Elaine Green, WCPO-TV, Cincinnati, for the *Hoskins Interview;* KCET, Adrian Malone, and Carl Sagan, for *Cosmos;* KQED-TV, San Francisco, for *Broken Arrow: Can a Nuclear Weapons Accident Happen Here?;* KTEH, Carol Mon Pere and Sandra Nichols, for *The Battle of Westlands;* KUED-TV, Salt Lake City, and WNET/13, NY, for "The MX Debate," special edition of *Bill Moyers' Journal;* Maryland Instructional Television, Owings Mills, for *Terra: Our World;* Mary Nissenson, WTVJ, Miami, for *Poland: Changing Nation;* NBC and Paramount Television, for *Shōgun;* Phil Donahue, for *The Phil Donahue Show;* PBS and Robert Geller, for *The American Short Story* series; Sol Taishoff, *Broadcasting* magazine; Walter Cronkite, CBS News; WQED and National Geographic Society, for National Geographic Specials

Humanitas Awards
- Two-hour category ($25,000): television version of Michael Cristofer's *The Shadow Box*
- One-hour category ($15,000): Michael Kozoll, Steven Bochco, for an episode of *Hill Street Blues*
- One-half-hour category ($10,000): Hugh Wilson, for a segment of *WKRP in Cincinnati*

THEATER

Antoinette Perry ("Tony") Awards
- Actor—drama: Ian McKellen, *Amadeus*
- Actor—musical: Kevin Kline, *The Pirates of Penzance*
- Actress—drama: Jane Lapotaire, *Piaf*
- Actress—musical: Lauren Bacall, *Woman of the Year*
- Choreography: Gower Champion (posthumously), *42nd Street*
- Costume design: Willa Kim, *Sophisticated Ladies*
- Director—drama: Peter Hall, *Amadeus*
- Director—musical: Wilford Leach, *The Pirates of Penzance*
- Featured actor—drama: Brian Backer, *The Floating Light Bulb*
- Featured actor—musical: Hinton Battle, *Sophisticated Ladies*
- Featured actress—drama: Swoosie Kurtz, *The Fifth of July*
- Featured actress—musical: Marilyn Cooper, *Woman of the Year*
- Musical: *42nd Street*
- Musical—book: Peter Stone, *Woman of the Year*
- Musical—score: John Kander, Fred Ebb, *Woman of the Year*
- Play: *Amadeus*
- Special awards: Lena Horne; Trinity Square Repertory Company, Providence, RI

New York Drama Critics Circle Theater Awards
- Best new play: *A Lesson from Aloes*, Athol Fugard
- Best new American play: *Crimes of the Heart*, Beth Henley
- Special citations: *Lena Horne: The Lady and Her Music;* New York Shakespeare Festival production of *The Pirates of Penzance*

Pulitzer Prize for Drama: Beth Henley, *Crimes of the Heart*
Richard Rodgers Production Award ($60,000): *Child of the Sun*, by Damien Leake
Susan Smith Blackburn Prize ($2,000): Wendy Kesselman, *My Sister in This House*

PUBLISHING

The media world became more complex in 1981. Publishers acquired electronic holdings; networks bought publications; and large publishing corporations became larger. Everyone in the industry was affected by rapidly changing technological developments. Revenues climbed, often due more to inflation than to increased sales. The industry's future will be influenced by the U.S. economy, interest rates, growth in education, and additional leisure time.

Books. Book sales increased, as did schoolbook censorship. The American Library Association feared more complaints, with nothing safe from censors. (*See* LIBRARIES.)

Publishers Weekly, however, said prospects for the industry were the brightest in 15 years. According to the Association of American Publishers, 1980 sales topped $7,000,000,000, up 11.2% from 1979. R. R. Bowker's *Weekly Record* reported 42,377 titles for 1980, including 34,030 new books and 8,347 new editions, down 6% from 1979. Average prices continued upward.

Publishers feared federal budget cuts. In a move to curb increasing costs, electronic publishing expanded through computers, word processors, videocassettes, text-fiche, data banks, and other operations.

James A. Michener had 1980–81 leaders: *The Covenant* and *USA The People and the Land. Publishers Weekly*'s tabulation of 1980 best-sellers noted Judith Krantz's *Princess Daisy;* Milton and Rose Friedman's *Free to Choose: A Personal Statement;* Herman Tarnower's *The Complete Scarsdale Medical Diet; Mary Ellen's Best of Helpful Hints* by Mary Ellen Pinkham and Pearl Higginbotham; and Alex Comfort's *The Joy of Sex.*

Money topics sold well too, such as Douglas R. Casey's *Crisis Investing: Opportunities and Profits in the Coming Great Depression;* Jerome F. Smith's *The Coming Currency Collapse and What to Do about It;* Howard J. Ruff's *How to Prosper During the Coming Bad Years and Survive and Win in the Inflationary Eighties;* Adam Smith's *Paper Money;* and George Gilder's *Wealth and Poverty.*

Other leaders included such diet books as Richard Simmons' *Never-Say-Diet Book* and Judy Mazel's *The Beverly Hills Diet. Miss Piggy's Guide to Life,* as told to Henry Beard, poked fun at diets.

Carl Sagan's *Cosmos* and Stephen King's books, *Firestarter* and *Cujo,* enjoyed wide readership. Sagan received $2 million for *Contact,* based on his outline and plot synopsis.

"The V. C. Andrews Phenomenon," as *Publishers Weekly* termed it, called attention to a previously unknown writer, V. C. Andrews. Led by *If There Be Thorns,* her earlier books included *Flowers in the Attic* and *Petals on the Wind.* These paperback originals sold nearly 10 million copies in 18 months.

James Herriot's *The Lord God Made Them All* was sold for $3,520,000 for paperback, book club, and condensed book rights.

Cats had their day. Top sellers were Skip Morrow's *The Official I Hate Cats Book* and Simon Bond's *101 Uses for a Dead Cat.*

Editor Lisa Birnbach's *The Official Preppy Handbook* appealed to many, as did Joe Graedon's *People's Pharmacy 2.* James Clavell's *Noble House* sold well, and so did Lawrence Sanders' *The Third Deadly Sin. The Living Bible* passed the 25 million milestone.

John Lennon's death revitalized the market for publications about the Beatles. Louis L'Amour had another success, *Comstock Lode.* Other paperback leaders in 1981 included Jeffrey Archer's *Kane & Abel;* Robert Ludlum's *The Bourne Identity;* John le Carré's *Smiley's People;* John Kennedy Toole's *A Confederacy of Dunces;* Jim Davis' *Garfield Gains Weight* and *Garfield at Large;* Ken Follett's *The Key to Rebecca;* and James G. Nourse's *The Simple Solution to Rubik's Cube.*

Sidney Sheldon's *Rage of Angels* approached 3 million sales. Harlequin Books, the "most profitable romances in the world," sold millions.

Some 18,000 American books were exhibited uncensored in six cities of China.

Magazines. The Magazine Publishers Association adopted a new slogan, "Nothing opens your eyes like a magazine." Industry leaders, discouraged as 1981 opened, became more optimistic later. Advertising income, flat at midyear, was expected to be up 9% over 1980. Robert J. Koen predicted that 1981 revenues would total $3,430,000,000.

Specialization remained the keynote, with newcomers seeking a part of an already fragmented audience. *Folio,* the industry publication, created a new measuring system, determining the value of each reader in relationship to that publication's advertising and circulation revenues.

Gentlemen's Quarterly went monthly; *US* planned to go weekly. Some, including *Black Stars, Panorama,* and *Quest,* faded. *Texas Monthly* earned ADWEEK's title of hottest 1980 publication, based on ad gains. *Texas* owner Mike Levy bought *New West* and renamed it *California.*

Circulation leaders, according to Audit Bureau of Circulation, were *TV Guide,* 18,084,966; *Reader's Digest,* 17,876,545; *National Geographic,* 10,732,973; *Better Homes & Gardens,* 8,034,009; *Family Circle,* 7,437,863; *Woman's Day,* 6,896,819; *McCall's,* 6,206,424; *Ladies' Home Journal,* 5,516,511; *Good Housekeeping,* 5,305,545; and *Playboy,* 5,200,936.

Advertising leaders for mid-1981, according to the Gallagher Report, were *TV Guide,* $120,841,000; *Time,* $119,807,944; *Newsweek,* $98,173,708; *Sports Illustrated,* $75,060,449; *Business Week,* $65,629,190; *People,* $61,920,072; *Reader's Digest,* $54,231,140; *Good Housekeeping,* $49,-

248,245; *Better Homes & Gardens,* $47,158,464; *Family Circle,* $40,106,029; and *Woman's Day,* $39,616,965.

Advertising page leaders at mid-1981 were *BYTE, Business Week, The New Yorker, TV Guide, People, Newsweek, Sports Illustrated, Time, Forbes,* and *Fortune.*

The increased interest in science was reflected in circulation growth for *Science 81, Discover, Science Digest, Omni, Scientific American, GEO,* and others. More computer/technical orientated magazines appeared.

Canadian magazines increased their advertising and circulation revenues.

Newspapers. Publishers planned to spend more than $750 million for plant expansion, modernization, and equipment in 1981. With forecasts of limited growth in a sluggish economy, several newspapers bought cable operations to offset loss of readers.

The Washington *Star,* the U.S. capital's 128-year-old afternoon newspaper, ceased publication on August 7. Time Inc., which had purchased the paper in 1978 and had spent a reported $85 million to keep it competitive, claimed to have lost more than $35 million on the paper. *The Washington Post* took over the *Star*'s plant. The New York *Daily News* closed its *Tonight* edition for lack of readers. The *Philadelphia Bulletin* reported a loss of $23.7 million in 18 months but was saved when unions agreed to new contract concessions.

American Newspaper Publishers Association (ANPA) President Katharine Graham called for "ways to better meet the needs of our readers," asking if people still need newspapers. "The new technologies will give us an opportunity to meet the increased challenge of competition for advertising dollars by introducing a greater variety of printed products for a greater variety of markets." ANPA officials cited the following problems: the cable television boom, the shrinking number of good independently-owned newspapers, and soaring interest rates. Two thirds of all dailies are now owned by groups, with Gannett having 83.

American Society of Newspaper Editors President Thomas Winship said newspapers "will be covering the kind of stories on which newspapers do best . . . big change . . . economics . . . energy . . . plight of poor." Yankelovich, Skelly and White researchers noted that newspaper readers complain about lack of local coverage, over-emphasis on bad news, political bias, factual errors, and printing mishaps.

Predictions that Americans may soon read newspapers from a television screen focused attention on technological growth, especially satellite delivery, information retrieval, and portable picture transmitters.

The Denver Post was acquired by the Times Mirror Company for $95 million. New York *Post* owner Rupert Murdoch paid $27 million for the *Times* of London, while the Chicago Tribune surprised the industry by buying baseball's Cubs.

The Detroit *Free Press* observed its 150th anniversary, and the Cleveland *Press* started a Sunday edition, the first in its 103-year history. Gannett experimented with a national paper, *USA Today.* Dow Jones & Co. and Knight-Ridder agreed to spend $250 million for a cable television operation with 420,000 subscribers. The Chicago Tribune, Times Mirror, and other companies bought cable.

Newsprint consumption was down slightly to 10 088 000 metric tons (11,116,976 tons) for 1980, while the price edged toward $500 per ton. A record 432,000 persons were employed in the newspaper industry.

Circulation figures reported by *Editor & Publisher Yearbook* showed a slight decline to 62,201,840 for dailies and slight gain to 54,671,755 for Sunday editions. There were 1,745 dailies, down from 1,763; there were 753 Sunday editions, up from 720. In Canada, there were 105 dailies, down from 121, while circulation lagged, from 5,159,841 to 5,081,567. Sunday sales improved, with 14 newspapers selling 1,700,000 copies weekly.

Circulation leaders in mid-1981 were *The Wall Street Journal,* 1,948,121; New York *Daily News,* 1,491,556; *Los Angeles Times,* 1,026,092; *The New York Times,* 930,546, *Chicago Tribune,* 790,475; New York *Post,* 732,158; Chicago *Sun-Times,* 661,531; *The Washington Post,* 618,111; *The Detroit News,* 617,879; Detroit *Free Press,* 613,311; and *San Francisco Chronicle,* 515,453.

The National Newspaper Publishers Association called for a single editorial policy for its 115 member newspapers catering to blacks.

Big companies became bigger. Time Inc. reported 1980 revenues of $2,800,000,000; Times Mirror, $1,800,000,000; Gannett, $1,200,000,000; and Knight-Ridder, $1,100,000,000. Time Inc. became the first $3,000,000,000 publishing firm.

In Canada, a three-member commission, appointed by Prime Minister Pierre Elliott Trudeau in 1980 after the Southam Inc. and Thomson Newspapers Ltd groups announced a consolidation of their operations and following the closing of *The Ottawa Journal* and *The* (Winnipeg) *Tribune* on the same day, issued its report "for freeing the press in Canada" in August. The report said: "The public has been, and is now, shortchanged. Legislation is needed to protect this freedom of the press from ownership to whom a particular newspaper is merely one business among other businesses." The commission also pointed out that newspaper competition "is virtually dead in Canada" since to advertisers "one newspaper for a community is much more efficient than two." The Southam and Thomson groups, who were under federal indictment for conspiracy to reduce newspaper competition, severely criticized the report.

WILLIAM H. TAFT, *University of Missouri*

PUBLISHING—SPECIAL REPORT:

INVESTIGATIVE REPORTING

In April 1981, the annual announcement of journalism's most prestigious awards, the Pulitzer Prizes, included one for a frequent winner, *The Washington Post.* In 1973, the paper won the Pulitzer gold medal for "meritorious public service," as well as international fame, for its investigation of the Watergate scandal. Now, eight years later, the award for "feature writing" went to a newcomer to the *Post,* Janet Cooke, 26, whose vivid description of an eight-year-old drug addict shocked the city of Washington, DC, and was reprinted around the country. The Pulitzer was a sensational honor for so young a reporter. Two days later there was an even more sensational event: the *Post* returned the prize; Cooke had confessed that the story was a complete fabrication.

This shock came less than three weeks after a jury in Los Angeles had ruled in favor of actress Carol Burnett in her suit for libel against *The National Enquirer.* The publication was ordered to pay a startling $1,600,000 to Burnett for printing a damaging gossip item despite knowledge that it was untrue.

April was the cruelest month for American journalism. Two stories that were themselves headline news carried the same message: the news media had lied. A reporter on a respected newspaper had invented a story that had upset an entire city. In the aftermath, prominent stories in other papers were criticized for such questionable practices as fictionalizing characters and inventing quotations. The *Enquirer* case said something more. By voting for so large an award (which was later reduced), the jury apparently was seeking to teach a lesson to *The National Enquirer* and, perhaps, to the entire fourth estate. A succession of large punitive judgments against the press in libel suits, as well as declining percentages in public opinion surveys on the standing of the press, suggested that the news media were losing the confidence of the public.

The stories in the *Post* and *Enquirer* both relied on unnamed sources. And since this is a common practice for investigative journalists, it focused attention on the issue of investigative journalism as a whole and on the use of unidentified sources in particular.

"Investigative reporting" as a term and as a specialty is relatively new. Some editors feel the term is redundant, that all reporting should involve investigation, exploring below the surface of events. But most accept the idea that some projects require such prolonged effort and sophisticated data collection that they constitute a distinct category in journalism. A specialized professional organization, Investigative Reporters and Editors (IRE), has existed for several years.

Investigative reporting won worldwide status most dramatically through the Watergate

Scrawls/"Atlanta Journal"

stories of *Washington Post* reporter Bob Woodward and Carl Bernstein. "Deep Throat," the nickname for a crucial figure in their investigation, subsequently became a nationally-used term for any secret source. (Ironically, it was Woodward who supervised Janet Cooke at the *Post*.)

In the first half of this century, by contrast, news coverage was devoted almost exclusively to reporting the public actions and words of authorities. Every act and statement had to be attributed to someone with a title or other relevant credentials. This practice was encouraged by the growth of newspaper monopolies and wire services, both of which provided the same material to readers of widely differing tastes and opinions. Attributing almost everything to a named authority reduced suspicion that the reporter was inaccurate or biased. This method was incorrectly termed "objective reporting." It was not objective in the scientific sense of natural phenomena unaffected by personal judgment, such as the law of gravity or the addition of numbers. So-called "objective reporting" did not remove the burden of judgment from the reporter, since the reporter and editor still had to select which authorities to quote and with how much emphasis.

Even in its most dispassionate form, the old "objective" style failed a serious test: what if the authorities were wrong? Or lied? Or if no authority would take personal responsibility for announcing something true and significant?

As society became more complex, the problem became more pressing. As society was being shaped increasingly by remote forces, the press became more important as a monitor of the public and private powers that the public itself could not observe. It was a slow change and was accompanied by a gradual professionalization of journalists. Especially after World War II, reporters were required to have higher education degrees and to understand the basic forces in local, national, and international affairs. And since the 1960s, they have been expected to investigate and report on events when formal appearances seem misleading.

Most news—estimated by some to be about 85%—is still largely the words and acts of public figures. This is inevitable because of leadership's impact on society. But if these words and acts are unclear in meaning or seem to be misleading, it is considered legitimate for the reporter to take the initiative to pursue the truth.

This new standard gives reporters greater discretion and greater responsibility. Investigative journalism should, therefore, be applied only to subjects with a potentially serious impact on the public. The *Enquirer's* item about Carol Burnett did not meet this test; even if it had been true, it would not have been one of the urgent issues of our time.

Good investigative journalism requires competence and discipline in judging the validity of information. It calls for sufficient documentation or description by credible witnesses. It cannot depend on speculation or suspicion. The reporter unearthing previously concealed or neglected material is expected to disclose to the reader not only the evidence that points to corruption or negligence, but also to give the target of the investigation a chance to respond to the evidence.

Ordinarily, serious investigations depend on such documents as memoranda, court records, official reports, affidavits, or credible eyewitnesses. Exceptions, however, do occasionally arise. For example, what if a crucial source in the investigation will speak to a reporter only on the condition that his or her identity will remain secret? What about a government employee disturbed by grave corruption but afraid of losing his or her job if identified? A criminal willing to confess to a reporter but fearful of being killed in retaliation? Or an ordinary citizen who can describe a serious neighborhood problem but fears harassment? Or a diplomat or head of state who wishes to have the press present an idea but for some reason does not, at the moment, wish to be identified as the source? In cases such as these, the reporter may promise to keep the source's identity a secret. The result is stories with such phrases as "One source said . . ." or "An official who will be called Mr. X said. . . ."

The unnamed source is a useful and sometimes necessary mechanism, but it is obviously open to abuse. The reporter in the 1981 Pulitzer Prize-winning feature story used this excuse to invent a story in which there was no real source. The mechanism permits distortion of real information given by a source who, being anonymous, cannot be checked. Or it permits the source, taking advantage of anonymity, to give misleading information without taking public responsibility, a course periodically taken by high-ranking diplomats and even heads of state.

Periodic attempts have been made by news organizations to refuse all unattributed information. But they have never succeeded. Too many possessors of important data have demanded anonymity.

The dilemma of journalism after the unhappy events of April 1981 was not that reporters and editors need more stringent standards on the use of unnamed sources. Almost all agree on that. The dilemma is that if public pressure forces the elimination of articles that rely on unnamed sources, the public may regain confidence in the press, but at the same time the press will fail to present important stories, such as Watergate, whose evidence would be withheld by fearful sources.

BEN H. BAGDIKIAN

PUERTO RICO

Political uncertainty and tensions, coupled with budget cutbacks and economic reverses, marked the year 1981 in Puerto Rico.

One year after the November 1980 elections, the Puerto Rican people still did not have the final results. Carlos Romero Barceló was elected governor by a margin of 3,007 votes out of more than 1.6 million. Control of the Senate was taken by the opposition Popular Democratic Party (PPD), but the situation in the House of Representatives was still very much in doubt. Both the PPD and the New Progressive Party (PNP) claimed an equal number of seats, with the one remaining seat so hotly contested that the courts were asked to decide on the validity of disputed ballots. The unofficial vote count was so close that judicial decisions concerning one or two ballots could change the result. For the time being, the House organized itself by electing a speaker belonging to the PNP, but both parties recognized that this agreement was only temporary. Only the most noncontroversial legislation could be approved under these conditions.

Economy. The year started with a two percentage point rise in unemployment over December 1980. In the next six months two more percentage points were added, bringing the rate to 21%; more than 213,000 workers were looking for jobs. By the end of the year, some 250,000 workers would be out of work, with the unemployment rate at about 25%. The governor announced a downward revision in income from local taxes. A $100 million shortfall was anticipated for fiscal 1982, with declines in excise and property taxes. All agencies of the local government were ordered to cut back their operations. The most devastating reduction in government operations, however, would come as a result of the expected $450 million cutback in federal funds for the island. The food stamp program, education, and the Comprehensive Employment and Training Act (CETA) program would be most affected by the cuts. In September, a special White House task force went to Puerto Rico to meet with local officials to prepare them for the substantial cutbacks in programs previously federally supported.

In an effort to cultivate the good will of the White House, the local government, led by the governor, reversed its position on accepting Haitian refugees. Previously, the government had gone to the courts to prevent Haitians from being sent to Fort Allen, an inactive military camp on Puerto Rico's southern coast. Now the government agreed to the transfer of some 800 refugees under rigidly supervised conditions. In mid-August the Haitians were flown in and established at the camp, which was being run by the U.S. Immigration and Naturalization Service.

Two prolonged strikes affected the island during the last half of 1981. The workers of the government-run electric agency struck for higher wages. The strike began in August and lasted for approximately three months. The students at the main campus of the University of Puerto Rico, a state institution with a student body of more than 40,000, went on strike over a tuition increase shortly after the beginning of the fall semester in September. The nominal fee of $5.00 per credit had been raised to $15.00. In spite of this being the lowest fee of any state university, the students refused to attend classes, paralyzing the institution.

THOMAS MATHEWS, *University of Puerto Rico*

PUERTO RICO • Information Highlights

Area: 3,421 sq mi (8 860 km²).
Population (1980 preliminary census): 3,186,076.
Chief Cities (1980 preliminary census): San Juan, the capital, 432,973; Bayamon, 195,965; Ponce, 188,219.
Government (1981): *Chief Officers*—governor, Carlos Romero Barceló (New Progressive Party); secretary of state, Samuel R. Quiros. *Legislative*—Senate, 27 members; House of Representatives, 51 members.
Manufactures (major products): Rum, distilled spirits, beer, cement, electricity.
Agriculture (major products): Sugarcane, coffee, tobacco, pineapples, molasses.

QUEBEC

Provincial elections and the debate over the federal constitution highlighted political affairs in Quebec during 1981.

Elections. On April 13, the Parti Québécois (PQ), under the leadership of Premier René Lévesque, was reelected to a five-year term as the province's governing party. The PQ won 49% of the popular vote and 80 of 122 seats in the legislative assembly. Claude Ryan's Parti Libéral du Québec (PLQ) captured 46% of the popular vote and the remaining 42 seats. After the public's resounding "no" in the May 1980 referendum on the PQ's quest for a mandate to negotiate independence, the 1981 election results suggested that Quebec's voters favored the PQ purely on the basis of "good government." Thus, the party was forced to defend traditional autonomist positions as opposed to its ultimate goal of sovereignty.

The Union Nationale, which obtained only 4% of the vote and lost the five seats it had in the previous assembly, and the Crédit Social party were practically eliminated from the political scene. Former Union Nationale leader Rodrigue Biron was elected as a PQ candidate and named minister of trade and commerce. His successor, Roch La Salle, was not successful in the provincial balloting but was reelected as a federal representative from Joliette.

Almost two thirds of the successful Liberal candidates represented constituencies in the heavily Anglophone, western districts of Montréal Island and its surroundings. All in all, the PLQ gained eight seats in the expanded assembly (from 110 to 122 seats), while the majority PQ increased its representation by 13. The latter party won most of its new seats from the

UPI

Quebec's Premier René Lévesque holds up the agreement reached in November between the federal government and the provinces on patriation of the Canadian constitution. Lévesque was the only provincial premier who refused to sign.

Union Nationale and the newly-created constituencies. The election apparently represented a return to the traditional two-party system.

Constitutional Issues. Following the September 28 ruling by the Supreme Court of Canada that Prime Minister Pierre Elliott Trudeau's move to patriate the federal constitution was legal (*see* CANADA), the Quebec assembly on October 2 passed a resolution condemning any such unilateral action by the federal government. Premier Lévesque had called the body into emergency session, and even the Liberal party joined in the vote. The resolution specifically opposed any unilateral action to diminish the powers of the provincial assembly and urged a new round of federal-provincial negotiations.

When Ottawa and the provinces finally reached a compromise agreement on November 5, Quebec dissented. It was the only province to oppose the plan, as Canada's nine English-speaking provinces all accepted the proposed new constitution. Resisting the compromise on the grounds that it would restrict the province's legislative powers, Premier Lévesque denounced what he called the construction of "a Canada without Quebec."

Social and Economic Indicators. In October, the Quebec Bureau of Statistics published figures that again revealed the province's demographic problems. In 1980, there were 44,849 registered births and 43,515 registered deaths. The population that year showed a net increase of 25,000, the result of a slightly positive migratory balance. The population as a whole continued to grow older, while unemployment, at more than 10%, has been especially heavy among the young and educated. A new law, if adopted, would abolish compulsory retirement at age 65. High inflation and interest rates were a threat to home ownership and to the province's many small and medium-sized business enterprises. There were indications that Quebec would soon suffer from a lack of consumption and would continue to export its labor forces, the training of which represents a considerable public expense to the province.

Territorial Changes. The administrative map of the province was in the process of being reshaped in 1981. In addition to the increase in electoral districts, the regional regrouping of local municipalities involves the creation of more than 100 MRCs (Municipalités régionales de comté) invested with new jurisdictions and powers. Each MRC has to select a new name, which must then be accepted by the provincial commission on toponymy; each must have an exclusive French designation.

The traditional system of superimposed Catholic-Protestant school board districts also faced reform. Religion-based geographical distinctions will be eliminated, and citizens of all creeds and idioms will join within the territorial limits of new school corporations. It was widely felt that the old system encouraged linguistic shelters under religious covers.

In October, the largest lake in the province was born. The completion of the Caniapiscau was a major step toward the completion of the James Bay hydroelectric project.

FERNAND GRENIER, *Inter-American Organization for Higher Education, Quebec*

QUEBEC • Information Highlights

Area: 594, 860 sq mi (1 540 687 km^2).
Population (April 1981 est.): 6,334,700.
Chief Cities (1976 census): Quebec, the capital, 177,082; Montreal, 1,080,546; Laval, 246,243.
Government (1981): *Chief Officers*—lt. gov., Jean-Pierre Coté; premier, René Lévesque (Parti Québécois). *Legislature*—Legislative Assembly, 122 members.
Education (1981–82 est.): *Enrollment*—elementary and secondary schools, 1,189,990 pupils; postsecondary, 225,300 students.
Public Finance (1980–81 est.): *Revenues*, $14,850,000,000; *expenditures*, $17,150,000,000.
Personal Income (average weekly salary, April 1981): $343.11.
Unemployment Rate (September 1981, seasonally adjusted): 11.2%.
(All monetary figures are in Canadian dollars.)

RECORDINGS

The year 1981 found the recording industry still feverishly adjusting to changing demographics, new technology, and stiff competition for the entertainment dollar. A CBS Records report estimated the Amerian record-buying public at 90 million. A survey by the National Association of Recording Merchandisers (N.A.R.M.) revealed that rock/pop still outsold all musical forms combined. Country showed the greatest growth over the previous year, with black music close behind and disco the biggest loser. The breakdown of purchases was: rock/pop, 51.2%; country, 14.3%; soul, 10.5%; easy listening, 6.2%; children's, 5.7%; jazz, 4.2%; classical, 4.0%; comedy, 1.3%; disco, 1.0%; miscellaneous, 1.6%.

Classical. The new classical label Musicmasters was launched in the United States by the Musical Heritage Society, but Europe continued to be the source of many new classical releases. Arista entered the classical market with albums produced in Germany by Ariola-Eurodisc. RCA resumed importing records made in France by Erato, and CBS Masterworks began U.S. distribution of recordings produced in Italy by Fonit-Cetra.

Angel's digital recordings by such American artists as flutist Ransom Wilson sold well, and the word "digital" on a recording of any standard work doubled its sales. Eurodisc announced the first digital recording of Wagner's four-opera cycle *Der Ring des Nibelungen* and issued the first installment in September, but Philips snatched away the claim with a complete 16-disc digital recording of it in October. Such major labels as RCA and Columbia finally moved into the classical audiophile recordings race.

Popular. The major recording labels—CBS, the WEA group, Capitol/EMI, PolyGram, RCA, and MCA—were still recovering from the economic slump of 1979, establishing strict merchandising policies, and trimming their artist rosters to regain fiscal stability. Sales of 100,000 units, once the industry standard for an album to be profitable to a big label, climbed to 200,000 in 1981. In response, these labels concentrated on artists with the broadest commercial appeal.

Album prices increased to an \$8.98–\$9.98 average. CBS took the unprecedented step of eliminating list pricing. The 45-single and the EP (extended play) formats were used as tools to promote more profitable album sales.

Hundreds of small independent labels, able to prosper with sales of a few thousand records, took on artists neglected by the majors and flourished. The National Association of Independent Record Distributors & Manufacturers reported 145 active members, specializing in jazz, blues, folk, and new music. Successful independents, such as Stiff, continued to release controversial or esoteric New Wave discs. Solar became the Motown of the 1980s. Traditional and progressive jazz found fortune on such labels as Concord and Pablo. The new Applause label tapped a wealth of older Broadway material.

Technology. Audiophile recordings, an active specialty market, became a mass consumer possibility with the introduction of CBS's CX noise-reduction encoding. The standard-price CX disc, even without its inexpensive decoder, gave improved audio quality on ordinary equipment.

New technology threatened to alter drastically the character of the recording industry. Although music videocassettes and discs were not yet commercially popular, they became an important tool in selling the original audio formats. MTV, a 24-hour music channel, debuted on 252 U.S. cable TV systems and directly increased album sales of the artists who appeared on it. The elimination of the record album entirely became feasible with the introduction of the Home Music Store. This service, employing digital encoding, satellites, computers, and cable, made it possible for the consumer to tape a selected album automatically through his home stereo system. Another threat to the standard album was the Sonadisc. Digitally encoded, nonspinning, and theoretically impossible to wear out, this disc, the size of a 50-cent piece, had the potential to contain multiple-disc opera.

Prerecorded tapes approached the disc in popularity, tied to a boom in car stereo systems and in portable tape equipment, such as the featherweight "Walkman" type players first developed by Sony. Another N.A.R.M. study showed that prerecorded tapes accounted for 39% of total recording sales in the United States and the percentage was swiftly increasing.

Taxing of blank tape to discourage home taping was still a controversial issue. Piracy remained a major problem, costing the recording industry \$1,500,000,000 globally each year, \$600 million in the United States.

PAULETTE WEISS, *"Stereo Review"*

Edith Mathis recorded Joseph Haydn arias to mark the 250th anniversary of the composer's birth.

Photo Courtesy Polygram

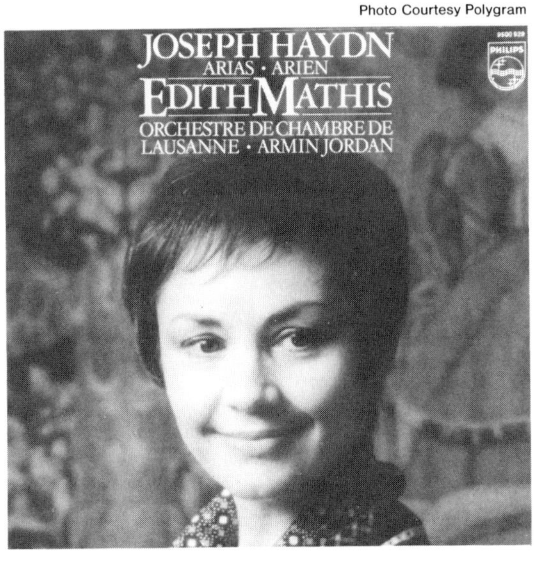

CLASSICAL

BRAHMS: *Symphony No. 4*, Vienna Philharmonic, Carlos Kleiber (Deutsche Grammophon).
DEL TREDICI: *Final Alice*, Barbara Hendricks, Chicago Symphony Orchestra, Sir Georg Solti (London).
LISZT: *Piano Concertos Nos. 1 & 2*, Jorge Bolet, Rochester Philharmonic, David Zinman (Vox Cum Laude).
MOZART: *Symphonies* (*Volume 5*), Academy of Ancient Music, Christopher Hogwood and Jaap Schroeder (L'Oiseau Lyre).
PUCCINI: *Tosca*, Renata Scotto, Placido Domingo, Renato Bruson, Philharmonia Orchestra, James Levine (Angel).
ROSSINI: *L'Italiana in Algeri*, Marilyn Horne, Samuel Ramey, Kathleen Battle, Solisti Veneti, Claudio Scimone (RCA).
SUTHERLAND/HORNE/PAVAROTTI: *Live at Lincoln Center* (works by Bellini, Ponchielli, Puccini, Rossini, and Verdi), New York City Opera Orchestra, Richard Bonynge (London).
VERDI: *Falstaff*, Giuseppe Taddei, Rolando Panerai, Raina Kavaivanska, Christa Ludwig, Vienna Philharmonic, Herbert von Karajan (Philips).
WEILL: *The Unknown Kurt Weill*, Teresa Stratas, Richard Woitach (Nonesuch).
WILSON: *Pleasure Songs for Flute*, Ransom Wilson (Angel).

JAZZ

COUNT BASIE: Kansas City Five (Pablo Today).
RAN BLAKE: Film Noir (Novus/Arista).
CARLA BLEY: Social Studies (ECM).
RON CARTER: Patrão (Milestone).
ROSEMARY CLOONEY: With Love (Concord Jazz).
CHICK COREA: Three Quartets (Warner Bros.).
MILES DAVIS: The Man with the Horn (Columbia).
PETER DEAN: Where Did the Magic Go (Monmouth/Evergreen).
JACK DeJOHNETTE'S SPECIAL EDITION: Tin Can Alley (ECM).
BILL EVANS: Re: Person I Knew (Fantasy).
DAVID FRISHBERG: The David Frishberg Songbook, Vol. I (Omnisound).
HELEN HUMES: Helen (Muse).
AL JARREAU: Breakin' Away (Warner Bros.).
KEITH JARRETT: Invocations to the Moth & the Flame (ECM).
SUSANNAH McCORKLE: Over the Rainbow (Inner City).
SPYRO GYRA: Free Time (MCA).
MEL TORME: And Friends (Finesse).
GROVER WASHINGTON, JR.: Winelight (Elektra).

MUSICALS, MOVIES

ARTHUR: soundtrack (Warner Bros.).
ENDLESS LOVE: soundtrack (Mercury).
HEAVY METAL: soundtrack (Full Moon).
LENA HORNE: THE LADY & HER MUSIC: original cast (Qwest).
MARCH OF THE FALSETTOS: original cast (DRG).
THE PIRATES OF PENZANCE: original cast (Elektra).
SOPHISTICATED LADIES: original cast (RCA).
WOMAN OF THE YEAR: original cast (Arista).

POPULAR

ABBA: Super Trouper (Atlantic).
AC/DC: Dirty Deeds Done Dirt Cheap (Atlantic).
ADAM & THE ANTS: Kings of the Wild Frontier (Epic).
AIR SUPPLY: The One That You Love (Arista).
MARTY BALIN: Balin (EMI/America).
BEE GEES: Living Eyes (RSO).
PAT BENATAR: Precious Time (Chrysalis).
GARY U.S. BONDS: Dedication (EMI/America).
KIM CARNES: Mistaken Identity (EMI/America).
ROSANNE CASH: Seven Year Ache (Columbia).
PHIL COLLINS: Face Value (Atlantic).
THE COMMODORES: In the Pocket (Motown).
ELVIS COSTELLO: Almost Blue (Columbia).
JOHN DENVER: Some Days Are Like Diamonds (RCA).
DEVO: New Traditionalists (Warner Bros.).
BOB DYLAN: Shot of Love (Columbia).
EARTH, WIND & FIRE: Raise (Arc).
SHEENA EASTON: Sheena Easton (EMI/America).
ELECTRIC LIGHT ORCHESTRA: Time (Jet).
JOHN ENTWISTLE: Too Late the Hero (Atco).
FLEETWOOD MAC: Live (Warner Bros.).
DAN FOGELBERG: Innocent Age (Full Moon).
FOREIGNER: 4 (Atlantic).
FOUR TOPS: Tonight (Casablanca).
ARETHA FRANKLIN: Love All the Hurt Away (Arista).
ART GARFUNKEL: Scissors Cut (Columbia).
CRYSTAL GAYLE: Hollywood Tennessee (Columbia).
GENESIS: ABACAB (Atlantic).
TERRI GIBBS: I'm a Lady (MCA).
GRATEFUL DEAD: Dead Set and Reckoning (Arista).
HALL & OATES: Private Eyes (RCA).
TIM HARDIN: Memorial Album (PolyGram).
EMMYLOU HARRIS: Cimarron (Warner Bros.).
DEBORAH HARRY: Koo Koo (Chrysalis).
J. GEILS BAND: Freeze Frame (EMI/America).
JERMAINE JACKSON: I Like Your Style (Motown).
JOE JACKSON: Jumpin' Jive (A&M).
RICK JAMES: Street Songs (Gordy).
JEFFERSON STARSHIP: Modern Times (Grunt).
BILLY JOEL: Songs in the Attic (Columbia).
ELTON JOHN: The Fox (Geffen).
GEORGE JONES: I Am What I Am (Epic).
QUINCY JONES: The Dude (A&M).
RICKIE LEE JONES: Pirates (Warner Bros.).
JOURNEY: Captured (Columbia).
KID CREOLE & THE COCONUTS: Fresh Fruit in Foreign Places (Ze/Sire).
THE KINKS: Give the People What They Want (Arista).
KRAFTWERK: Computer World (Warner Bros.).
LITTLE RIVER BAND: Time Exposure (Capitol).
BARBARA MANDRELL: Live (MCA).
BARRY MANILOW: If I Should Love Again (Arista).
BOB MARLEY: Chances Are (Cotillion).
DON McLEAN: Chain Lightning (Millennium).
MEATLOAF: Dead Ringer (Cleveland Intl.).
STEVE MILLER BAND: Circle of Love (Capitol).
STEPHANIE MILLS: Stephanie (20th Century).
RONNIE MILSAP: There's No Gettin' Over Me (RCA).
MINK DeVILLE: Coup de Gras (Atlantic).
MOODY BLUES: Long Distance Voyager (Threshold).
ANNE MURRAY: Where Do You Go When You Dream (Capitol).
WILLIE NELSON: Somewhere Over the Rainbow (Columbia).
JUICE NEWTON: Juice (Capitol).
STEVIE NICKS: Bella Donna (Modern).
YOKO ONO: Season of Glass (Geffen).
RAY PARKER JR. & RAYDIO: A Woman Needs Love (Arista).
DOLLY PARTON: 9 to 5 and Odd Jobs (RCA).
TEDDY PENDERGRASS: It's Time for Love (Philadelphia Intl.).
TOM PETTY & THE HEARTBREAKERS: Hard Promises (Backstreet).
POINTER SISTERS: Black & White (Planet).
THE POLICE: Ghost in the Machine (A&M).
THE PRETENDERS: Pretenders II (Sire).
EDDIE RABBIT: Step By Step (Elektra).
REO SPEEDWAGON: Hi Infidelity (Epic).
SMOKEY ROBINSON: Being With You (Tamla).
KENNY ROGERS: Share Your Love (Liberty).
ROLLING STONES: Tattoo You (Rolling Stones).
DIANA ROSS: Why Do Fools Fall in Love (RCA).
RUSH: Moving Pictures (Mercury).
SANTANA: Zebop! (Columbia).
BOB SEGER & THE SILVER BULLET BAND: Nine Tonight (Capitol).
CARLY SIMON: Torch (Warner Bros.).
FRANK SINATRA: She Shot Me Down (Reprise).
RICK SPRINGFIELD: Working Class Dog (RCA).
SQUEEZE: Eastside Story (A&M).
BILLY SQUIER: Don't Say No (Capitol).
RINGO STARR: Stop and Smell the Roses (Boardwalk).
STARS ON: Stars on Long Play (Radio).
STEELY DAN: Gaucho (MCA).
ROD STEWART: Tonight I'm Yours (Warner Bros.).
STYX: Paradise Theatre (A&M).
JAMES TAYLOR: Dad Loves His Work (Columbia).
THE TUBES: The Completion Backward Principle (Capitol).
TOM VERLAINE: Dreamtime (Warner Bros.).
THE WHISPERS: This Kind of Lovin' (Solar).
THE WHO: Face Dances (Warner Bros.).
HANK WILLIAMS JR.: Rowdy (Elektra).
DON WILLIAMS: Especially for You (MCA).
STEVE WINWOOD: Arc of a Diver (Island).

REFUGEES AND IMMIGRATION

American attitudes toward immigration are undergoing noticeable change. Where they once held to an "open door" policy, and made the Statue of Liberty a symbol of welcome to immigrants, Americans have come increasingly to look on large-scale immigration—especially illegal immigration—as a threat rather than a boon. The recent influx of millions of Mexicans, Indochinese, Cubans, and Haitians, together with a high rate of U.S. unemployment, have strained the traditional sympathy for newcomers.

Policy Studies. Recent administrations, both Democratic and Republican, have created high-level groups to study immigration and refugee problems. Two such groups released their reports in 1981. The first was the Select Commission on Immigration and Refugee Policy, set up by Congress in 1978 to conduct a comprehensive review of U.S. immigration laws. Composed of eight members of Congress, four public members, and four from the president's cabinet, the commission worked 19 months and issued its recommendations in February. In general, the commission called for tightening safeguards against illegal immigration, slight liberalization of legal immigration, and no change in the current policy on refugees.

The commission's recommendations included (1) an increase in immigration quotas from 270,000 to 350,000 a year, (2) a temporary additional quota of 100,000 a year for five years to clear up current backlogs, (3) an amnesty to legalize the status of illegal aliens already in the United States, (4) increased funding for the Immigration and Naturalization Service (INS), (5) civil and criminal penalties for employers who knowingly hire illegal aliens, and (6) the use of a more secure (but unspecified) method of worker identification. The commission recommended against any massive guest worker program, a campaign proposal made by Ronald Reagan.

The second study group was an interagency task force created by the Reagan administration to review the select commission's report and to recommend legislation. The task force released its report late in July. It accepted, in modified form, many of the commission's recommendations. Among its proposals were 1) a quota increase of 40,000 a year, to be assigned to Canada and Mexico, 2) amnesty for illegal aliens in the United States before Jan. 1, 1980, and permanent resident status for them after a ten-year wait, 3) increased funding for the INS, and 4) fines of up to $1,000 for employers who knowingly hire illegals. The task force turned down the recommendation for an improved identification card, and endorsed a two-year experimental guest worker program that would permit 50,000 Mexicans to enter the country each year on temporary work permits.

Dealing with Refugees. Throughout 1981, the United States continued to feel the impact of the massive flow of Cubans and Haitians the year before. In June the government announced that a total of 130,080 Cubans and Haitians had entered the country between April 1 and Sept. 30, 1980. It was revealed in July that 1,815 Cubans were still being held in federal prisons, either as undesirables or for commiting federal crimes after arriving in the United States.

The government began deportation proceedings against nearly 5,000 Haitians in March. All had come to the United States after Oct. 10, 1980, when a temporary amnesty giving Cubans and Haitian "boat people" a special entrant status expired. Many of the Haitians were held in detention facilities in Florida, New York, West Virginia, and Kentucky. In July agreement was reached with Puerto Rican authorities for still another facility on that island.

President Reagan signed an Executive Order on September 30 ordering the Coast Guard to intercept ships in international waters if they were suspected of carrying illegal Haitian immigrants to the United States. Previously the Coast Guard could intercept ships only when they entered U.S. waters. The president's action was facilitated by agreement of the Haitian government that refugees returned to Haiti would not be prosecuted. The U.S. Coast Guard cutter *Hamilton* arrived in Port-au-Prince in October to begin enforcing the order.

Also in October, the U.S. government reduced the yearly quota for admission of Indochinese refugees from 168,000 to 125,000 for fiscal year 1982. The quota for refugees from all parts of the world was set at 173,000.

International Migration. The U.S. refugee quota was large in comparison with other countries' quotas, but miniscule in terms of world refugee needs. The international refugee situation showed little improvement throughout 1981. Millions in Asia, Africa, and Latin America were pushed out of their homes by civil wars, guerrilla activity, tribal strife, natural disasters, and hunger.

In Africa, an estimated 500,000 refugees from Chad, Uganda, and Ethiopia were living in Sudan in 1981. In Latin America, Costa Rican officials said their tiny country was host to nearly 100,000 refugees from other Central American countries. Venezuelan newspapers reported that more than 1 million "undocumented" persons entered that country in less than a year. And, ironically, Mexico—the source of much of the illegal immigration into the United States—found itself struggling with a large and growing refugee problem of its own, as thousands of Guatemalans and Salvadorans streamed into the Mexican state of Chiapas, fleeing violence and poverty in their homelands.

The United Nations High Commissioner for Refugees was awarded its second Nobel Peace Prize for its work with the "tremendous and increasing number of refugees."

RICHARD C. SCHROEDER

RELIGION

Survey

The support of Pope John Paul II for Solidarity, the independent trade union of his native Poland, was offered as a possible explanation for the attempt on his life. Authorities investigated the possible involvement of secret agencies of the Soviet Union in the May 1981 assassination attempt. Earlier, the pope had continued his practice of pastoral visits abroad, with a February tour of Asia that included several days in the Philippines and Japan and stopovers in Pakistan, Guam, and Anchorage (AK).

The renewal of Christianity in China continues to be a matter for observation and study. Numerous additional churches have opened after years of forced neglect. In Nanjing a Protestant theological school began operating early in 1981. A class of 47 was chosen by written examination from more than 400 applicants. A Roman Catholic school was expected to open in Peking, where currently ten priests serve a constituency of about 10,000.

The emergence of reactionary Islam, which has accounted for much of the trouble in Iran, found its way into Egypt, where it stirred up enmity between Muslims and the Coptic Christian minority. President Anwar el-Sadat, who took militant action against the insurgents just prior to his assassination, claimed that Communist subversion was behind the unrest.

The Reorganized Church of Jesus Christ of Latter-day Saints, with headquarters in Missouri, has always understood itself to be in a familial line of descent from Joseph Smith, founding prophet. The Utah-based Mormons, on the other hand, have claimed the descent of the prophet through a selection process that began with Brigham Young. In 1981 a document came to light that is purported to contain Joseph Smith's blessing and choice of his son, Joseph 3d, as his successor.

Kelly Segraves, who challenged California's policy regarding the teaching of evolution in the public schools, glances over his son's science textbook.

UPI

The Creationists. One of the most curious and interesting subjects to claim recent interest in the field of religion is "creationism." Followers of creationism believe that the direct fashioning of all that exists is the work of a God-Creator, as described in the Genesis accounts of the Jewish-Christian scriptures. Creationists believe that scientific evidence can be used to substantiate this position and they wish to have their own "scientific" thesis presented in any educational situation where evolutionism is taught.

The controversy is not so simple as the creationists, the evolutionists, the courts, and many intellectuals wish to make it. At stake is the freedom of science and education to pursue the truth. Involved also is the freedom of the individual and the family to promote their own values, without having values forced upon them by an established authority. There is little doubt that a form of authoritarianism has gradually emerged in science classrooms and among the lower echelons of the scientific community. In many such quarters it is simply assumed that evolutionary theory is singular, final, incontestable, and that it is obviously in opposition to any understanding of creation. Missing from the minds and methods of many has been a kind of humility before the awesomeness of truth that acknowledges the tentative character of much evolutionary investigation. Many people have become "true believers" in something called Evolution or Science. And so there emerge evolution*ism* and scient*ism.*

On the other side of the controversy are the "true believers" for whom the Bible is a scientific document that explains the process of creation. Many creationists are slaves to reactionary modes of explanation rather than explorers on behalf of a Creator for whom the truth is one. Suffice it to say, if all people were educated to a proper understanding of the realms of science and religion, there would be no need for creationists who expound the matters of creation as if they were science, nor for evolutionists who present the struggles of explanation as if they were religion.

It must be remembered, of course, that varieties of fundamentalism that belong to the creationist connection have been with us for about a century. They surface from time to time, as they did in the Scopes trial of 1925. The 20th century has been a century of cultural schism in which an elite has failed to take full measure of the beliefs of a great part of the populace. The fundamentalism behind creationism has been present all along and among great numbers.

It should have come as no surprise when in March 1981 Kelly Segraves, director of the Creation Science Research Center in San Diego, challenged in court the right of the California Education Department to require the teaching of evolution in the public schools. Segraves and others were concerned that children were being taught ideas in school that conflicted with the teachings of home and church. Sacramento Superior Court Judge Irving H. Perluss ruled that science teachers were to avoid dogmatism in the interpretation of Darwinism. Both sides of the controversy were satisfied with the ruling.

A further manifestation of the controversy occurred when the Arkansas legislature passed a bill requiring creationist theories to be present in courses where evolutionary theory is taught. However, the law prohibits the teaching of religion or references to religion in presenting the creationist theory. Later in the year, Louisiana became the second state to enact an equal time evolution/creation law. (*See also* EDUCATION.)

RICHARD E. WENTZ, *Arizona State University*

Far Eastern

There appears to be a revitalization of Buddhism in Cambodia. When the Communist regime replaced the former pro-Western government in 1975, it sought to eradicate all popular manifestations of religion. Temples were destroyed, monastaries looted, thousands of monks were murdered, and statues of the Buddha were burned or desecrated. Today the task of rebuilding the religion and the culture has begun with impressive results.

Jainism. One of the world's lesser known religions is Jainism. It is a very ancient tradition, dating back to the 6th century B.C., and today numbers 3 million members in India. Its principle founder was Vardhamāna Mahāvīra, a contemporary of Gautama Buddha. Jainism holds that there is no supreme spiritual being or God; the process of time and space functions in accordance with its own inner laws. Full enlightenment is called kervala and serves as the model of attainment for all followers. In eras of time such as the present, such enlightenment is impossible and one seeks to prevent further accumulation of karma (action). Jainism is strongly ascetic, and in its most strenuous form, practices ahimsa, the principle of noninjury to all forms of life. There are two sects, the Digambaras ("sky-clad" or nude) and the Svetambaras ("white-clad"). Nudity is the ideal practice among the former. Digambara idols are nude.

The largest sculpture in India is a 58 ft., 8 in. (17.9-m) gray granite image of Lord Bahubali, the first mortal to reach kervala, located in Shravana Belgola in Mysore, south India. More than 600 steps lead up to the sky-clad statue. In March 1981 pilgrims from all over India visited the open-air temple to participate in the Digambara ritual bathing of the image, which is held every 12–14 years. Ghee (clarified butter) is the basic element of the ritual cleansing. No absolution, propitiation, or removal of karma results from this participation.

RICHARD E. WENTZ

Islam

The dramatic and violent events in Iran, pitting fundamentalist Muslim leaders associated with the Islamic Republican Party against secularists opposed to the mullah-dominated government, kept that country's revolution in the foreground of news about Islam in 1981. Elsewhere, Muslims found other ways to express their hope that Islamic values and traditions might come to play a major role in their societies.

A series of rallies staged by conservative Muslims in northern Nigeria precipitated riots which claimed thousands of lives in the course of the year. In both Syria and Egypt, the Muslim Brotherhood, an organization dedicated to the revival of pristine Islamic principles, was blamed by governmental authorities for inciting sectarian strife. Minority Muslim groups, particularly the Alawis, bore the brunt of the Brotherhood's attack in Syria, while in Egypt secular politicians and Coptic Christians were singled out. Serious disorders in June and again in September prompted Egyptian President Anwar el-Sadat to order the arrest of several Muslim and Christian leaders for fomenting unrest. In the Philippines, the regime of President Ferdinand Marcos, long harassed by guerrillas who claimed it was anti-Islamic, arrested scores of Muslims who were alleged to be plotting a campaign to disrupt the country's elections.

In some areas, the year 1981 saw a backlash against fundamentalism. Increased disenchantment with Pakistan's President Zia ul-Haq derived, at least in part, from his insistence on literal enforcement of the Islamic legal code (*sharia*). In Turkey, the military government, which assumed power late in 1980 with a pledge to end terrorism, jailed some prominent right wing politicians whom it accused of attempting to establish an Islamic state. This was a strong reassertion of the principle of secularism, one of the pillars of Turkish political life since the founding of the state in the 1920s.

But not all calls for the institution of Islamic ideals were so fraught with turbulence. In Kuwait's spring parliamentary elections, fundamentalist influence came peacefully through the electoral process. Conservative candidates swept aside the secular nationalists who had previously controlled the sheikdom's legislature. Another example of the peaceful implementation of Muslim concepts came in June, when businessmen and political leaders from ten Muslim states led by Saudi Arabia established an international banking and investment group, the Dar al-Maal al-Islami (House of Islamic Funds). The agency will operate in accordance with Islamic law, charging no interest on loans but instead taking a share in the profits of ventures it helps to finance. The organization aimed to accumulate a total capital of $1,000,000,000, the bulk of it to be raised by public subscription.

In the political sphere, the Islamic Conference Organization took initiatives to resolve disputes between Muslim states as well as to address some major international problems of specific concern to Muslims. Representatives from 37 states and the Palestine Liberation Organization (PLO) met in Taif, near Mecca, in January. The theme of the conference, voiced by Saudi King Khalid, was the desirability of the Muslim world's nonalignment with the East and West. The Mecca Declaration, issued at the close of the sessions, called for the return of territories seized by Israel during the 1967 war; the creation of a Palestinian state with Jerusalem as its capital; and the withdrawal of Soviet forces from Afghanistan. The delegates also made overtures to both Iran and Iraq to accept a commission to arbitrate the differences which had led them to war in 1980; Iran's (and Libya's) refusal to attend the Taif meeting, however, hampered these efforts. Also missing from the gathering was Egypt, which had not been invited as a sign of dissatisfaction over its inability to gain significant concessions from Israel on the Palestinian issue.

Although the conference did later establish a delegation to try to arrange a cease-fire between Iran and Iraq, neither nation cooperated with it. Efforts persisted through the spring, with the mediators suggesting a variety of proposals and agendas, but finding each rejected by one or both sides. Eventually, Habib Chatti, the conference's secretary general, acknowledged the failure of the peace effort.

KENNETH J. PERKINS
University of South Carolina

Judaism

Religious controversy in Israel threatened a deep rift between "religious" and "secular" Jews in 1981. The conflict was precipitated by the election campaign for the Knesset (Israeli parliament) in June and escalated during the archaeological excavations in Jerusalem's City of David in September. Although both events seemed remote from religion, the unique nature of Judaism—a blend of ethical, legal, nationalistic, theological, and cultural traditions—gave them religious significance.

The election campaign provoked a confrontation between the religious parties potentially aligned with the traditionalist Likud coalition and the Labor Alignment, which took an antireligious stand. Deep-seated resentment surfaced over debates on marriage and divorce laws, religious conversion, autopsies, army service for women, and religious educational institutions, all of which were retained under rabbinic authority when the Likud coalition won reelection.

The religious-secular controversy came into sharper focus with a clash between ultra-orthodox opponents of the Jerusalem excavation, who were supported by an injunction of the chief rabbinate, and the archaeologists, who were backed by the academic community. The rabbinical ban was based on the contention that the site is an ancient Jewish cemetery and that the dig desecrated human remains. The dispute led to a High Court decision with far-reaching implications: the authority of the rabbinate was subordinated to that of the state.

Responding to an alarming rise in anti-Semitism, the World Jewish Congress established, in close cooperation with Jewish communities throughout the world, an International Commission on Anti-Semitism. Manifestations of anti-Semitism in 1981 included the dissemination of virulent hate literature by Saudi Arabia in collusion with new-Nazi groups and vandalism of synagogues, Jewish homes, and Jewish cemeteries in England, France, West Germany, and the United States. In September, worshipers leaving a Vienna synagogue were attacked by Arab terrorists. A middle-aged holocaust survivor and a young woman shielding the small child of a friend were killed. Arab terrorists also attacked the Israeli embassy in Vienna, the Israeli diplomatic mission in Athens, the El-Al Airlines office in Rome, pilgrims and shoppers in Jerusalem's Old City, worshipers at the Western Wall, and vacationers en route to southern shores.

Reports from Ethiopia disclosed the persecution of Falasha Jews, and from Iran news came of arrests and executions of Jewish leaders. In Poland, the specter of political anti-Semitism was raised by the government's use of anti-Semitic propaganda as a weapon against the independent union Solidarity.

In the Soviet Union, conditions of Jews worsened. The number of exit permits was the lowest in ten years, and harassment of "refusniks," those who had been denied visas, increased. They were dismissed from jobs, expelled from organizations, and their children denied higher education. Harsh prison sentences were meted out on trumped-up charges of "parasitism," "defamation of the state," or "illegal possession of firearms." The campaign of persecution was concentrated against scientists and intellectuals. All Jewish cultural expression was stifled. In April, the KGB prevented a holocaust commemoration in the woods near Moscow, and in May it raided a seminar on Judaism, arresting all 80 participants.

Demonstration of support for Soviet Jewry came from prominent scientists, among them nine Nobel laureates and members of the Academy of Science in the United States, Sweden, Norway, and Denmark. Efforts were made to free certain Jewish prisoners, such as the ailing Ida Nudel in Siberian exile, Anatoly Shcharansky in a maximum security cell, and Victor Brailovsky in "internal exile."

During the visit of Israel's Prime Minister Menahem Begin to New York City, Hasidic Jews protest the archaeological excavations in Jerusalem's City of David.

UPI

Against this disheartening backdrop of events, the first World Gathering of Jewish Holocaust Survivors took place in Jerusalem in June 1981. Some 6,000 survivors from 23 countries met to commemorate the holocaust and warn against any recurrence.

The Christian-Jewish dialogue was one area that offered promise for the future. Protestant, Catholic, and Jewish scholars participated in an International Bible Contest in Jerusalem. In West Germany, a church-sponsored organization established at Auschwitz an International Youth Center to foster international cooperation. The German Evangelical Congress warned against a lapse into anti-Semitism and appealed to the West German government to support Israel.

LIVIA E. BITTON JACKSON
Herbert H. Lehman College, CUNY

Orthodox Eastern

Plans for a Great Council of the world's Eastern Orthodox Churches continued, while hopes faded that such a gathering would take place in the near future due to the political conditions in which the majority of the Orthodox find themselves. The administrative divisions among the Orthodox Churches in Western Europe, Australia, Africa, and the Americas continued to disrupt plans for the council, as well as to cause dissension among the Orthodox generally.

In 1981 the Church of Constantinople reasserted its right to administer all Orthodox churches in the so-called "diaspora." The newly elected Exarch of the Ecumenical Patriarchate in Great Britain, Methodios of Thyatira, reaffirmed this position in an encyclical letter. An official statement by Archbishop Paul of Kuopio, primate of the Orthodox Church in Finland, asked that the ecumenical patriarchate either care for the diaspora churches as a whole or relinquish its administration of the diaspora Greeks to the Church of Greece, where it belongs if the Orthodox outside their homelands are to be organized and administered according to ethnic lines. Archbishop Paul, with Archbishop Theodosius of the Orthodox Church in America, leads the movement for regional, self-governing church administrations for the Orthodox in "diaspora" areas.

At a Pan-Orthodox Consultation, held in Sophia, Bulgaria, in May, the Orthodox reaffirmed their conviction that ecumenism, particularly involving the World Council of Churches (WCC), has as its only goal the unity of all Christians in doctrine and worship. The Orthdox also reiterated criticism of the WCC's political policies and programs and demanded greater participation in WCC planning and activity. This view was repeated at the WCC Central Committee meeting in Dresden, East Germany, in August.

At a WCC-sponsored consultation on The Community of Women and Men in the Church, held in Sheffield, England, in July, the Orthodox rejected the views of the majority of participants and of the WCC itself regarding the role of women in church and society. Orthodox in America, because of their disagreements with the WCC tendencies, published their own study guides on the subject. While Orthodox churches in America and Europe include women in all church assemblies, councils, and departments, the world Orthodox remain united in their opposition to the ordination of women to the ministerial priesthood and episcopate.

The movement for the administrative unity of all Orthodox in North America appeared to be gaining support among the members, while the hierarchs generally continued to defend the status quo. Official negotiations toward greater cooperation and eventual unification were established between the Orthodox Church in America (made up of the former Russian, Albanian, Rumanian, and Bulgarian groups) and the Antiochian Orthodox Christian Archdiocese in America, which belongs to the patriarchate of Antioch in Syria. Schisms persist among the Orthodox in East Africa.

Archbishop Diodoros was elected to succeed the late Benedictos I as Greek Orthodox patriarch of Jerusalem.

THE REV. THOMAS HOPKO
St. Vladimir's Orthodox Seminary

Protestantism

In a year when fundamentalist Protestant evangelists and church members exercised considerable political power regarding local and national issues, there was an irony to be found in the fact that at the same time churches of all theological positions were beginning to worry about government intrusion into their freedom.

After playing a role in the election of new members to Congress and contributing to the presidential victory of Ronald Reagan in 1980, fundamentalist leaders, including the Rev. Jerry Falwell, set their sights on political change in the legislative process. At the urging of conservative political leaders, the "social agenda" of the religious right—constitutional amendments on abortion, prayer in the public schools, and changes in federal laws affecting families—was deferred for most of the year. Sen. Jesse Helms (R-NC) appeared to emerge as a congressional spokesman for the fundamentalists and conservatives, and he promised that the agenda would be pursued in 1982. The appointment of Arizona Judge Sandra Day O'Connor to the U.S. Supreme Court angered many fundamentalist leaders because they felt she had not been specific enough in opposing abortion in her earlier career and in her testimony before the Senate judiciary committee.

But these developments took place at the same time that certain trends emerged in which the federal government appeared willing to redefine religious eligibility for tax exemption. A group of 300 church leaders representing 90% of organized religion in the country met in Washington in February to develop a coalition that would seek to protect them from government encroachment. The diversity of the group, which included Episcopalians, Southern Baptists, and the Unification Church of the Rev. Sun Myung Moon, indicated that there is agreement that defining "religion" should not be left to random members of government.

Specific cases were examined. One of considerable interest involved the Worldwide Church of God in California. That state's attorney general moved to take over the church after receiving reports of financial irregularities. He argued that the public is finally the owner of churches. The case, however, was dropped without any legal determination. In a related case, the federal government removed Bob Jones University, of Greenville SC, from its tax-exempt status because it does not comply with federal racial equality standards. The university forbids interracial dating and marriage. As a fundamentalist Christian institution, Bob Jones has argued that it has a right to set social standards contrary to public law. Earlier, the school had forbidden black students to enroll, but changed this policy with the understanding that the students would comply with the dating regulations. Declaring that this was not enough, the Internal Revenue Service (IRS) withdrew the school's tax-exempt status.

Many liberal religious leaders, strongly opposed to the fundamentalist position and the racial bias of Bob Jones, nonetheless argued that the IRS is intruding on religious freedom when it "defines" what standards the college must adopt.

And, of course, Protestant leaders were looking with considerable alarm at the developing case of Chicago's Roman Catholic Archbishop, John Cardinal Cody. Late in the year, a federal grand jury was investigating charges that the cardinal had used church (tax-exempt) funds to benefit a personal friend. Again, if this case proceeds, it will raise serious church-state issues as to the right of a church to spend its funds as it sees fit.

Liberal Protestants, who had never been very fond of former President Jimmy Carter (they felt he was not aggressive enough in pursuing traditional liberal goals), nonetheless recalled his administration fondly when discussing his emphasis on human rights. And during 1981 they joined secular groups in successfully blocking the Senate confirmation of Ernest W. Lefever as assistant secretary of state for human rights and humanitarian affairs in the Reagan administration. An ad hoc committee of the Human Rights Community testified before Senate Foreign Relations Committee hearings, calling Lefever "the antithesis of the congressionally mandated concern for human rights that has been a component of U.S. foreign policy since 1973."

Although social issues, including the ordination of women, were not priority items for denominational meetings in 1981, a new problem emerged for the United Presbyterian Church. Heresy, normally associated with the Middle Ages, suddenly became an issue in that denomination when Mansfield Kaseman, a United Church of Christ clergyman, asked to be admitted to the National Capital Union Presbytery in March 1979. In answer to a question put to him prior to his admission, Kaseman could not state without qualification "that Jesus Christ is God." Conservatives in the presbytery tried to reject his request for admission. Failing in this effort, they appealed to the church's highest judicial body, which ruled that the decision to admit Kaseman was a local decision, and they turned down the conservatives' complaint. Nonetheless, the definition of orthodoxy in Protestant churches appeared to haunt organized religion after several decades of preoccupation with social issues.

In developments affecting individual denominations, Dr. Ralph A. Bohlmann was elected president of the Lutheran Church Missouri Synod and the Rev. Bailey Smith was reelected president of the Southern Baptist Convention.

Bishop James Armstrong, 57-year-old United Methodist Bishop, was elected president of the National Council of Churches.

JAMES M. WALL
Editor, "The Christian Century"

Roman Catholicism

The attempted assassination of Pope John Paul II was easily the most dramatic event in a year which ironically saw a definite shift by Roman Catholic leaders toward strong, almost uncompromising opposition to violence, particularly the growing nuclear arms race.

The year was marked by the pope's 12-day trip to Asia, including Japan and the Philippines; by a new social encyclical, *Laborem Exercens* (On Human Work), which focused on the dignity of the worker and called for new socio-economic systems; by a strong Catholic presence in efforts by the Polish labor movement to gain more freedom; and by widespread calls for the protection of human rights in developing regions, particularly Latin America.

The probe of the slaying in 1980 of four U.S. missioners in El Salvador, as well as constant protests over the torture and killing of clergy and lay catechists in Honduras and Guatemala, continued with little result.

Beginning with his January 1 "state of the world" message, Pope John Paul II became the leader of an emerging movement by Catholic leaders toward stronger initiatives for disarmament. At Hiroshima, the site of the first atomic attack, the pope echoed his United Nations call for an end to the nuclear arms buildup.

A leading U.S. prelate, Archbishop Raymond Hunthausen of Seattle, suggested that taxpayers withhold revenue used for military purposes, and Bishop L.T. Matthiesen of Amarillo, TX, and Archbishop John R. Quinn, former president of the National Conference of Catholic Bishops, condemned the U.S. intent to produce a neutron bomb and urged workers in the nuclear arms industry to seek other employment.

Peace activists' acts were challenged by some Church leaders, and members of a U.S. antiwar group called "Plowshares 8," which included Daniel Berrigan, a Jesuit priest, were sentenced to jail for damaging a missile warhead.

Besides his calls for peace, the pope used his Asian journey to appeal, particularly in the Philippines, for greater efforts by governments to assure the human and religious rights of their people.

Though controversy over Church matters was dampened somewhat by the attempted assassination of the pope by the 23-year-old Turkish militant, Mehmet Ali Agca, it was acknowledged by the Vatican that the pope was concerned over "hasty" annulments of marriages, and that the Church's administration was looking at a $25 million deficit.

Michele Cardinal Pellegrino, retired archbishop of Turin, challenged the Church's position on priestly celibacy in light of the Church's need for priests. In the United Nations, the Vatican altered its traditional neutrality on the death penalty to take a stand opposing capital punishment.

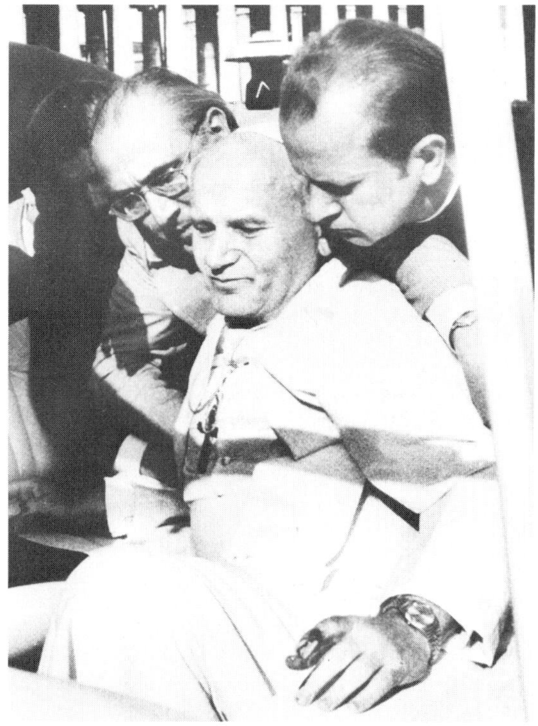

UPI

Pope John Paul II is assisted by aides moments after he was shot in St. Peter's Square, May 13.

In May, a papal envoy visited IRA hunger strikers in Ulster's Maze prison but his pleas went unheeded as Bobby Sands, the first of many, fasted to death to protest British prison conditions. Later, joining the Irish hierarchy, U.S. bishops urged British authorities to be more flexible in dealing with IRA prisoners. The pope also called for peace and negotiations in the strife-torn Middle East, in Central America, and in his native Poland.

Following the death of Stefan Cardinal Wyszynski, primate of Poland, who had served as mediator between the labor union Solidarity and the Communist regime, the pope named Bishop Jozef Glemp to succeed the late primate. (*See also* OBITUARIES.)

An American, the Rev. Vincent O'Keefe, S.J., was made temporary head of the Jesuits after the superior general, the Rev. Pedro Arrupe, S.J., suffered a stroke. Later the pope named the Rev. Paolo Dezza, S.J., as his personal "delegate" to the Jesuits until the order elects a new leader.

The would-be assassin of the pope, Mehmet Ali Agca, was sentenced to life in prison by a court that ordered a conspiracy investigation.

In the United States, a food-lift to Poland was undertaken by Catholic Relief Services; the bishops attacked Reagan administration cuts in social programs and called for increased voluntarism; and John Cardinal Cody of Chicago was accused of misusing Church funds to aid a lifelong friend.

ROBERT L. JOHNSTON, *"The Catholic Review"*

RHODE ISLAND

As the year opened, the state, which had given its 1980 electoral vote to President Jimmy Carter, awaited with mixed hope and apprehension the party change in Washington. Gov. J. Joseph Garrahy (D) and the legislative leaders were braced for budget cuts that could hit Rhode Island hard.

Legislature. The 1981 General Assembly session was billed as dull, with austerity rather than new programs the keynote. A budget was adopted, calling for only limited expenditure increases and no tax rise, against a background of impending proposed federal budget reductions. Estimates of federal money that might be lost to the state exceeded $20 million.

A restructuring of the educational system was enacted. The single Board of Regents responsible for all public education was eliminated and separate ones, each with its own commissioner, were established for higher and for elementary-secondary education. Comprehensive plans for dealing with hazardous waste disposal failed to pass.

Redistricting plans were being prepared for the January 1982 legislative session. Some adjustment would be needed in the two Congressional districts, and much redrawing of state legislative district lines was foreseen.

The Economy. February saw employment in the state at its lowest level in five years, due largely to a sharp decline in the jewelry industry, one of Rhode Island's largest employers. Total employment continued to decline, with fluctuations, into the summer, but rose encouragingly in September. Unemployment was 8.7% in February, but fell to 7.4% in August.

Electric Boat caused much concern. The submarine manufacturer based in Groton, CT, has a major facility at Quonset, RI, which employs many Rhode Islanders. The Navy, highly critical of completion delays and large cost overruns, threatened to withhold new contracts. Layoffs of 1,700 workers resulted, with threats of more dismissals, though the tension later eased.

Providence. The financial woes of the capital city mounted. A huge deficit loomed, its bond rating dropped, and banks were reluctant to provide loans. A supplementary property tax increase of more than $11 per thousand-dollar valuation was adopted to ease the crisis.

To trim expenses, the city laid off workers. In the summer a move to fire garbage collectors and use a private contractor precipitated a strike that crippled the city. Strife between the city and its unions continued into the fall.

Politics. Republican Sen. John Chafee, a popular former governor, would be up for reelection in 1982, and by late 1981 two Democrats, former Attorney General Julius Michaelson and Marvin Holland, had announced that they would seek their party's nomination for the post.

Providence Mayor Vincent Cianci, Jr., showed signs that he would seek a third term, despite his crushing 1980 defeat in the race for governor. Several Democrats indicated active interest in running. The 1982 election would be the first under the new home rule charter.

ELMER E. CORNWELL, JR., *Brown University*

RHODE ISLAND • Information Highlights

Area: 1,212 sq mi (3 139 km^2).
Population (1980 census): 947,154.
Chief Cities (1980 census): Providence, the capital, 156,-805; Warwick, 87,123; Cranston, 71,992; Pawtucket, 71,204; East Providence, 50,980; Woonsocket, 45,-914; Newport, 29,259; North Providence, 29,188; Cumberland, 27,069; Coventry, 27,065.
Government (1981): *Chief Officers*—governor, J. Joseph Garrahy (D); lt. gov., Thomas R. DiLuglio (D). *Assembly*—Senate, 50 members; House of Representatives, 100 members.
State Finances (fiscal year 1980): *Revenues,* $1,393,-000,000; *expenditures,* $1,361,000,000.
Personal Income (1980): $8,975,000,000; per capita, $9,444.
Labor Force (July 1981): *Nonagricultural wage and salary earners,* 391,000; *unemployed,* 37,800 (8.2% of total force).

RUMANIA

The year 1981 in Rumania was marked by a growing foreign debt burden and a decline in the national product.

Domestic Affairs. The government's rigid control over the economy was relaxed somewhat, although repression of any political opposition was not. In July, the World Confederation of Labor protested against political persecution and violations of human rights in Rumania, but the personal rule of President and Secretary-General Nicolae Ceauşescu continued in full force.

The economic situation worsened. Agricultural production fell below expected levels. Oil production dropped to 11.5 million t (12.6 million T), and 15 million t (16.5 million T) had to be imported, at a cost of more than $4,000,000,-000. To alleviate the crisis, the 1981–85 plan provided for a 20% increase in arable land and an increase in coal, hydroelectric, and nuclear-generated power from 27 to 47%. To help meet the latter goal the government signed a $1,000,-000,000 contract with Canada for four Candu reactors and a $250 million contract with General Electric for steam turbines.

RUMANIA • Information Highlights

Official Name: Socialist Republic of Rumania.
Location: Southeastern Europe.
Area: 91,700 sq mi (237 503 km^2).
Population (1981 est.): 22,400,000.
Chief Cities: (July 1979 est.): Bucharest, the capital, 1,-960,097; Braşov, 229,172; Iaşi, 282,493.
Government: *Head of state,* Nicolae Ceauşescu, president and secretary-general of the Communist Party (took office 1965). *Head of government,* Ilie Verdet, premier (took office March 1979). *Legislature* (unicameral)—Grand National Assembly.
Monetary Unit: Leu (4.47 leu equal U.S.$1, May 1981).
Manufactures (major products): Power; mining, forestry and construction materials; metal products; chemicals; machines; processed foods; textiles.
Agriculture (major products): Corn, potatoes, wheat, oilseeds.

There were some signs of a more liberal economic policy. Labor unions were promised a greater voice in government. Shorter work weeks were phased in, with workers getting two free Saturdays every month. A broader base of decision making was announced. And in July, several individuals with independent views were allowed to be elected to the Council of the Writers' Union.

Foreign Affairs and Trade. In June, Finance Minister Stefan Andrei paid an "official friendship visit" to China. Several exchange visits followed. Trade with the West grew to 55%, while trade with the Communist-bloc countries, including the Soviet Union, fell to 34%. The trade deficit, mostly due to technological imports from the West and to oil from the OPEC countries, rose to $1,500,000,000 in 1980, up from $1,200,000,000 in 1979. It continued to rise in 1981.

Hard currency debts rose to more than $9,500,000,000, including $5,000,000,000 owed to Western commercial banks and $1,300,000,000 to the International Monetary Fund (IMF) and the World Bank. Unable to make installment payments of some $2,500,000,000 and to meet interest charges of $800 million, the government applied for and received a $205 million loan, at 9.6% interest, from Western private banks and $1,475,000,000 in new credit from the IMF. The foreign debt was expected to reach $12,000,000,000 by the end of 1981.

On March 26, at a meeting of the Communist Party Central Committee, Secretary-General Ceauşescu criticized administrative deficiencies and made several personnel changes in an effort to resolve the economic situation. Later, he ordered all industries not to accept Western imports unless equivalent purchases of Rumanian goods were guaranteed.

In May, Foreign Minister Andrei conferred in Washington with President Ronald Reagan and Secretary of State Alexander Haig. About the same time, a delegation of the House of Representatives Armed Services Committee visited Bucharest. Soon after, President Reagan approved an emergency loan of $120 million, and in August, the United States agreed to increase exports of surplus butter, wheat, and soybeans.

JAN KARSKI, *Georgetown University*

SASKATCHEWAN

Government. The provincial legislature was dominated in 1981 by the New Democratic Party, which maintained 44 of 61 seats in the House; the Conservative Party held 15 seats and the Unionest Party 2. The provincial by-election, involving three constituencies, did not change the number of seats held by the incumbent and opposition parties.

Government initiatives during the year included passing amendments to the Continuing Education and Farm Security acts, as well as strengthening the regulatory powers of the Department of the Environment and responding to recommendations of the Law Reform Commission.

Premier Alan Blakeney responded to the federal government's proposals for repatriation of the Canadian constitution with a request for an amending formula rather than a referendum procedure in the event of constitutional conflict. The New Democratic Party also favored entrenchment of English and French language rights, guarantees of provincial equalization payments, safeguards for native Indian treaty rights, and confirmation of provincial ownership and control of resources. Dissatisfied with Ottawa's response, Premier Blakeney actively opposed the constitutional reforms. On March 2, he introduced a motion in the legislature saying the changes "would upset the balance of the Canadian federal system." The next day, the legislature unanimously (43–0) passed a resolution condemning the government's proposals.

Agriculture and Resource Development. Half the normal level of rainfall and snowfall created drought conditions in the province in early spring. A succession of windstorms reduced topsoil levels and damaged rangelands. However, expectations of low crop and livestock yields were averted in the summer with a return to average rainfall levels. A drought assistance program involving a 50–50 cost sharing formula between the provincial and federal governments was implemented to respond to the precarious weather conditions. Final crop yields for the province as a whole in 1981 reached an unprecedented high of 19 million t (17.3 million T). In resource development, the Saskatchewan government moved to acquire 100% of shares in the Prince Albert Pulp Company and began negotiations for the operation of the first heavy oil processing and gold mining facilities in the province.

Economy. Economic forecasts for the province were positive, with the 1981 gross domestic product reflecting real growth of 6.7%. On March 5, Finance Minister Ed Tchorzewski submitted to the legislature a balanced provincial budget for 1981–82. It called for revenues of $2,287,000,000 and expenditures of $2,285,000,000.

JENNIFER JOHNSON
Regina Public Library

SASKATCHEWAN • Information Highlights

Area: 251,700 sq mi (651 900 km^2).
Population (April 1981 est.): 977,400.
Chief Cities (1976 census): Regina, the capital, 149,593; Saskatoon, 133,750; Moose Jaw, 32,581.
Government (1981): *Chief Officers*—lt. gov., C. Irwin McIntosh; premier, Allan Blakeney; chief justice, Queen's Bench, F. W. Johnson. *Legislature*—Legislative Assembly, 61 members.
Education (1981–82 est.): *Enrollment*—elementary and secondary schools, 210,710 pupils; post-secondary, 17,180 students.
Personal Income (average weekly salary, April 1981): $327.63.
Unemployment Rate (June 1981, seasonally adjusted): 4.4%.
(All monetary figures are in Canadian dollars.)

UPI

The new King Abdulaziz International Airport in Jidda, opened in the spring, has a special pavilion for King Khalid and leading government officials. The building is a self-contained terminal, where visiting dignitaries are greeted.

SAUDI ARABIA

Foreign wars and revolutions and the resulting need for armaments disturbed oil-rich Saudi Arabia during 1980–81.

Foreign Affairs. Saudi Arabia felt itself threatened by Israeli military superiority, Libyan criticism, Soviet expansionism, and the Iran-Iraq war. When Libya urged Muslims to avoid the 1980 pilgrimage to Mecca because Saudi Arabia was allegedly a puppet of the United States, the Saudis broke diplomatic ties with Libya. A cooperative council established by Saudi Arabia and the smaller Gulf States on March 10, 1981, declared that regional security was a local responsibility. While nominally neutral in the Iraq-Iran war, the Saudis lent money to Iraq and allowed foreign arms shipments to Iraq to be landed in Saudi ports. Prince Saud al-Faisal, the foreign minister, and Ahmed Zaki Yamani, the oil minister, condemned Israel in April as the chief cause of instability in the Middle East and said Israel was a greater danger to Saudi Arabia than was Soviet expansionism in Afghanistan.

U.S. Airborne Warning and Control System (AWACS) airplanes under American control were sent to Saudi Arabia on Oct. 1, 1980, to monitor the Iran-Iraq fighting and to help protect Saudi oil fields. The Saudi purchase of five AWACS, advanced missiles, and flight-extending fuel tanks for already-purchased F-15 fighter planes, at a cost of $8,500,000,000, was delayed by U.S. Secretary of State Alexander Haig after a visit to Riyadh in April 1981. On October 28, however, the U.S. Senate voted (52-48) to permit the controversial sale, dispelling Saudi fears that Israel was a more important and influential American ally than Saudi Arabia.

Earlier in October, U.S. Secretary of Defense Caspar Weinberger and President Ronald Reagan pledged American intervention, if requested by the Saudis, to stop the establishment of an unfriendly new government in that country.

A summit conference of 37 Islamic countries at Taif in late January, the successful Saudi mediation of Syrian-Jordanian border tension, and larger loans by Saudi Arabia to the International Monetary Fund (IMF) demonstrated the increasing international role of Saudi Arabia. However, Crown Prince Fahd's August 8 Middle East peace plan, which called for Israeli withdrawal from occupied territories and settlements, a Palestinian state with East Jerusalem as its capital, and mutual recognition of all states was rejected by Israel, Syria, and others.

Military and Government. Despite a growing arsenal of increasingly sophisticated arms, Saudi Arabia continued to purchase great quantities of new weapons. More than one fourth of all U.S. arms sales in the world went to Saudi Arabia. In 1981, Saudi military salaries were increased 100%. But despite the new weapons and training programs, Israeli warplanes were able to fly undetected over northern Saudi Arabia on June 7 on their way to bomb an Iraqi nuclear reactor near Baghdad. Saudi Arabia offered to pay Iraq to help rebuild the reactor.

According to Defense Minister Prince Sultan, military conscription would be adopted in 1982. A shortage of manpower and a strong demand for labor in the civilian sector have made recruitment and retention of soldiers difficult.

SAUDI ARABIA • Information Highlights

Official Name: Kingdom of Saudi Arabia.
Location: Arabian peninsula in southwest Asia.
Area: 830,000 sq mi (2 149 690 km^2).
Population (1981 est.): 10,400,000.
Chief Cities (1976 est.): Riyadh, the capital, 667,000; Jidda, 561,000; Mecca, 367,000.
Government: *Head of state and government,* Khalid ibn Abd al-Aziz al-Saud, king (acceded March 1975).
Monetary Unit: Riyal (3.41 riyals equal U.S.$1, Oct. 1981).
Manufactures (major products): Petroleum products, cement, fertilizers.
Agriculture (major products): Dates, vegetables, grains.

Since military forces suppressed the group that seized the Meccan Haram in 1979, no substantial changes have been made in the Saudi government. An elected consultative council has not been established, and there have been no steps toward the granting of civil liberties or the adoption of a constitution. All power has remained in the hands of the royal family and a few technocrats. Crown Prince Fahd remains the most powerful leader in the government because of the continued illnesses of King Khalid.

Oil and Finance. In 1981, Saudi Arabia continued to pump more oil than it needed for current expenditures so as to maintain pressure on the Organization of Petroleum Exporting Countries (OPEC) to unify prices and production along lines suggested by the Saudis. The cost of Saudi light crude oil was raised Nov. 1, 1980, to $32 per barrel and kept at that price until OPEC agreed on a uniform $34 in late October 1981. Oil production, which had been increased to 10.3 million barrels per day because of the Iraq-Iran war, was reduced to 9.8 million barrels in June 1981 and 9.2 million in September.

A new pipeline linking Gulf oil fields and Red Sea ports opened in July 1981, and a $12,000,000,000 natural gas separation and storage system neared completion. A 40-sq mi (100-km^2) airport was opened in Jidda, with the construction work done largely by foreigners. By 1981 foreigners represented more than 40% of the Saudi labor force and numbered at least 1.5 million, including 45,000 Americans.

William Ochsenwald
Department of History
Virginia Polytechnic Institute

SINGAPORE

The new cabinet, announced by Prime Minister Lee Kuan Yew in January following the December 1980 electoral sweep, featured the exit of old leaders and the rise of the designated heirs.

Politics. Gone from the cabinet were Health Minister Dr. Toh Chin Chye, past chairman of the ruling People's Action Party (PAP) and former deputy prime minister, and Environment Minister Lim Kim San. Both had been outspoken by Singapore standards in objecting to the government's policy to compel the use of Mandarin by the nation's Chinese majority.

Lee's two deputies and confidants since the founding of the party, Goh Keng Swee and Sinnathamby Rajaratnam, retained their posts. A cadre of young leaders, who have been identified as the successors of the current leadership (who are nearing or past 60), were elevated to key cabinet responsibilities. Foreign Minister Suppiah Dhanabalan further stepped into Rajaratnam's shoes as he also gained responsibility for culture, while Goh Chok Tong took over health as well as assuming responsibility for trade and industry.

In October, C. V. Devan Nair was named president of the republic, the titular head of state, to succeed Benjamin Sheares, who died in May. Nair had served as president of the National Trade Union Congress and in the parliaments of both Singapore and Malaysia.

The Economy. Although affected by the lagging world economy, the nation's gross domestic economy grew by more than 8% in real terms, down from 10% in 1980. Spiraling wages as a result of the government's policy of discouraging labor-intensive industries through economic pressures sparked consumer price rises, particularly for housing.

Goh Keng Swee, first deputy prime minister, demonstrated his unchallenged control of the economy by taking over the monetary authority of Singapore and dismissing the senior staff for what he felt were too conservative investment policies. He also was instrumental in the formation of the government of the Singapore Investment Corporation, which will seek to increase returns on the nation's assets through foreign investments. To provide for future growth, the government sought to encourage research and development (R & D) efforts.

Yet amid the evident prosperity, the island was shaken in midyear by the bankruptcy of the German Rollei Company, followed by a July plunge of the Singapore stock market which continued into the last quarter of the year. Also, the wage policy seemed to discourage more than just labor-intensive industries as three moderately technological Japanese companies announced that they would build new plants in Malaysia rather than in Singapore and other international companies closed tire and automobile assembly factories.

Foreign Affairs. Singapore continued as the most vocal of the Association of Southeast Asian Nations (ASEAN) members in attacking the Vietnamese presence in Cambodia (Kampuchea). It succeeded in getting feuding, anti-Vietnam Cambodian leaders to unite to preserve the UN seat of Democratic Kampuchea from the challenge of the Vietnamese-backed government. With Singapore spearheading the defense, the Vietnamese challenge on credentials was defeated.

K. Mulliner, *Ohio University*

SINGAPORE • Information Highlights

Official Name: Republic of Singapore.
Location: Southeast Asia.
Area: 224 sq mi (580 km^2).
Population (1981 est.): 2,400,000.
Chief City (1974 est.): Singapore, the capital, 1,327,500.
Government: *Head of state,* C. V. Devan Nair, president (took office October 1981). *Head of government,* Lee Kuan Yew, prime minister (took office 1959). *Legislature* (unicameral)—Parliament.
Monetary Unit: Singapore dollar (2.09 S. dollars equal U.S.$1, Oct. 1981).
Manufactures (major products): Refined petroleum, processed rubber.
Agriculture (major products): Tobacco, vegetables, fruits, rubber and coconut palms.

SOCIAL WELFARE

Widespread hunger once again was the most serious welfare problem on a global scale. Record grain harvests, especially in the United States, barely matched the demand of importing nations, and could not meet the desperate shortages in the Third World. By most estimates, more than 500 million people (roughly 12% of world population) suffer from serious, persistent malnutrition. Most victims live in Africa, Asia, and Latin America. Often, as in Somalia, El Salvador, and Cambodia, they also are refugees from political upheaval. The awarding of the Nobel Peace Price to an organization aiding such refugees symbolized the problem's urgency. A World Bank report projected that $600,000,000,000 in investments would be needed over the next decade for irrigation systems and other improvements merely to maintain the current levels of food supplies on a per capita basis. That agency was the chief source of loans for such projects, while further aid, as to the tune of $1,000,000,000, was supplied by the new International Fund for Agricultural Development, based in Rome and financed mainly by Arab oil-producing nations. The same problem dominated the meeting of the Commonwealth nations in September-October and, later in October, the more publicized meeting in Cancún, Mexico, of the leaders of eight industrialized nations of the North and of fourteen developing nations of the South. The Cancún meeting resulted in few concessions or commitments. U.S. President Ronald Reagan, who earlier in the year had called upon United Nations members to rely more on free markets and private investment to achieve economic growth, had also sought reforms in the World Bank under its new president, A. W. Clausen, that would make it less of a welfare agency. (World Bank loans have grown from $1,000,000,000 in 1968 to more than $12,000,000,000 in 1981.) Although Third World hopes that plans for a new international economic order might emerge in some form from the Cancún meeting were dashed, there was agreement that bilateral, private talks toward that goal would continue.

Meanwhile, the return of economic recession to the industrialized nations led to rising unemployment, wage scales lagging behind an inflation more endemic than ever, and associated social disorder. In the spring, youth movements in several Western European nations continued their violent protests of the previous year against the lack of housing and jobs, and often against foreigners. The worst of these demonstrations took place in London's working class district of Brixton in April, when attacks on black and brown residents accompanied a three-day riot, the worst in post–World War II England. Yet they were but a prelude to the "days of rage" in July, when protests against rising unemployment and when racism, often directed at police, among young dark-skinned slum dwellers in several British cities brought a series of shocks to a nation with a tradition of calm civility. More than 800 police were injured by the end of July in cities from Dundee, Scotland, to London. The Thatcher government, increasingly besieged, altered its austere course a bit to authorize an increase in emergency welfare spending. In France, the new Socialist government of President François Mitterrand moved slowly, but firmly, toward implementing its election mandate to improve unemployment benefits and social security payments (extending them to overseas departments), while calling for a "decentralized" socialism and for a Common Market effort to create more jobs through financing research in science and technology. In Eastern Europe, most nations faced a grim time as farm production fell farther behind demand and the Polish workers' challenge to bureaucracy sparked further protests in neighboring countries. By the late fall, Solidarity leader Lech Walesa was appealing for aid from Western nations to help Poles meet anticipated food shortages. In the Soviet Union itself, in spite of announcements at year's beginning that wages would rise and the minimum old-age and disability pensions would improve, there were serious shortfalls in farm output. In the provinces, especially, shortages of meat and dairy products were the rule, and for the third straight year the national grain harvest was critically short, requiring large-scale importations. Moreover, several studies indicated that the quality of Soviet health care, after vast improvement from 1917 to 1967, had deteriorated during the last 15 years, with infant mortality probably 13% higher than in 1960 and the life span of the average Soviet male dropping by as much as four years since 1965.

Responding to this spectrum of problems, Pope John Paul II issued his third encyclical in September, entitled *Laborem Exercens* (On Human Work). It called for "radical and urgent changes" in the Third World to improve life for the masses there, expressed broad support for labor unions, and asserted that workers everywhere should receive a "just" wage, defined as enough for a father to support a family adequately. Partially responding to this call, some 10,000 persons in Buenos Aires, Argentina, attended a mass on November 7 to protest rising unemployment and continued military rule. On the other hand, in South Africa, police evicted by force hundreds of black squatters from a large shantytown near Cape Town, while the United Nations Human Rights Commission reported that there were at least 100,000 slaves and 300,000 serfs and slaves in Mauritania, subject to harsh discrimination.

The United States. The Reagan administration's retrenchment program in welfare spending came into conflict with a new, sharp recession that sent unemployment above the 8% level by late fall. Reflecting the "new federalism" out-

U.S. Health and Human Services Secretary Richard Schweiker comments on the recent history of welfare spending before the House budget committee in March.

UPI

look, the budget called for sharp reductions in medicaid and food stamps, hoping to shift more of the welfare burden to state governments. But losses of jobs put further strains on the federal and state systems by making more workers and their families eligible for food stamps and other aids. The administration's commitment to maintain a "safety net" for the truly needy seemed to be weakening by year's end as various welfare problems mounted, and state governments increasingly found themselves unable to assume a larger share of the costs as the recession cut their revenues. A study, sponsored by the National Governors Association and issued in October, depicted the fiscal condition of state governments as critically bad, with their capacity for meeting welfare needs reduced by as much as 25% because of cuts in federal funds for health and social service programs. One symbol of the change in Washington was the closing at midyear of the Community Services Administration, which once conducted much of the War on Poverty in the Johnson years, and had run 878 community action agencies. The Comprehensive Employment and Training Act (CETA), which had provided more than $3,500,000,000 annually for about 300,000 public-service jobs, also was scrapped. Benefits (under tighter eligibility requirements) for Aid to Families with Dependent Children were reduced, and more than 50 smaller health and social service programs, such as that under the Runaway Youths Act, were shifted to the states with the support of block grants. By December, the details of such cuts were still unclear.

In spite of great efforts by federal agencies, including the Drug Enforcement Administration, to catch major dealers, chemical abuse continued to grow among all strata of American society, with several raids taking place in the ultra-respectable Wall Street district. For the first time in several years, heroin addiction reportedly rose sharply, while use of cocaine and marijuana spread further. Chemicals in various forms that serve as substitutes for more common drugs, including quaaludes, were beginning to rival heroin as a threat. Studies showed that more teenagers than ever were immersed in a "drug culture."

Reductions in federal spending for abortions did not cause a significant decline in their number among poor women, according to an American Medical Association (AMA) report issued in September. State money continued to fund them. The number of teenage pregnancies and illegitimate births among minority groups still skyrocketed. More than 50% of births among blacks, for example, were illegitimate. According to a poll, many Catholic women did not regard abortion as sinful. Catholic bishops, however, reiterated in their annual meeting a denunciation of abortion and gave near-unanimous endorsement to the so-called Hatch amendment, which would give states the right to outlaw abortions, switching, in company of most other abortion foes, from the previous strategy of pushing an amendment that would have banned them at the federal level. A sign of the administration's stand and of the strength of anti-abortion forces associated with the Moral Majority and right-to-life groups, was the appointment of Dr. C. Everett Koop, an avowed opponent of abortion, as U.S. surgeon general. Another symbol of the changed attitude was the sole vote by the United States in the UN World Health Organization against an otherwise unanimous resolution condemning the promotion of bottle-feeding of babies under primitive conditions in developing countries. Such bottle-feeding is linked to much infant disease and mortality.

Criticisms of the welfare retreat came from many quarters, but the administration sought to explain some of its positions during two White House conferences addressing such issues, one in October on children and youth and the other in December on aging.

MORTON ROTHSTEIN
University of Wisconsin-Madison

SOCIAL WELFARE—SPECIAL REPORT:

SOCIAL SECURITY AND RETIREMENT INCOME

Basic economic security for individuals has become the foundation of stability within modern industrial society. Confidence in the social insurance systems has remained high in Europe and Japan, though the cost for workers is generally two or three times greater, as a percentage of salaries, than in the United States, and the benefits are lower. Moreover, the savings rate is considerably higher in these countries. Behind the iron curtain, several nations were extending benefits slightly during 1981, even as budgetary problems worsened.

The persistence of inflation and rising unemployment has weakened the pillars of income security in the United States, making retirement and its future a hot political issue. An inflation rate of 10% can erode away two thirds of the value of a pension in ten years; growing awareness of that harsh reality shook confidence in the Social Security system. Public controversy swirled mostly around efforts to make basic changes in the system, but the issues were related to the whole pattern of demographic and employment pattern changes since World War II. Polls in mid-1981 showed that most Americans were growing fearful about their retirement, particularly the ability of the Social Security Administration to continue providing benefits. Inevitably, too, the system has come in for reexamination since it was made part of the unified national budget in the mid-1960s, representing now about 23% of federal expenditures and providing some form of income to 36 million retired or disabled Americans and their survivors, at a level of about $11,000,000,000 per month.

Pension. The Reagan administration's tax program was justified in part as an encouragement to individual savings and to the spread of small pension plans through Individual Retirement Accounts, Keogh plans, and lower inheritance taxes. At the same time, there has been concern over the power of larger funds, whether administered by professional investers, the employing firms, or by unions. Pensions, as long-term commitments to providing retirement incomes, came into widespread use for the first time in the United States during World War II, as a device for recruiting high-level workers and executives without breaching the wage freeze then in effect.

Pension funds now control literally hundreds of millions of dollars and are the largest components of many insurance company, bank trust, and investment counseling businesses, as well as an apparent major source of corruption in some unions. Still, less than half the work force is covered by pension plans. They pay on the average significantly less than average Social Security benefits and provide little or nothing in most cases for survivors (spouses or minor children). Also, many are in apparently precarious financial condition. One of the first responses of pension fund managers to the sharp rise in inflation during the early 1970s was to shift the investment of those funds from bonds and other stable securities to stocks, real estate, etc., in an effort to keep returns even with inflation, but there were few gains and many losses from that strategy. Concerns about the financial strength or weakness of pension plans and about the perceived inequities in their coverage led to the first federal regulation of such plans, the Employee Retirement Income Security Act (ERISA) of 1974. The act is designed to increase the likelihood that covered workers would actually receive a benefit.

McColough Report. The President's Commission on Pension Policy, headed by C. Peter McColough, issued its final report, *Coming of Age: Toward a National Retirement Policy,* in February 1981 after two years of study. The report called for strengthening pensions with a Minimum Universal Pension System (MUPS) for all workers, to be funded by employer contributions, with 3% of payroll as a minimum standard. Employees more than 25 years of age, with at least one year of service and 1,000 hours on the job (thus covering seasonal and part-time workers) would participate, and would have portable, vested rights to benefits. A separate, nonintegrated supplement to Social Security, MUPS could use that agency's administrative resources to keep the records of workers. The report also proposed that pensions protect survivors of retirees and the divisibility of pension entitlements after divorce. The report further proposed laws making it easier for private pension plans to raise the normal retirement age in tandem with similar raises in the Social Security system, and for uniform retirement age for federal employees. At the same time, the report recommended that the protections of ERISA be extended to state and local employees with a Public Employee Retirement Security Act (PERISA). It also expressed concerns about the ownership and control of pension fund assets. Finally, the commission addressed some of the short-term problems of funding the Social Security system, calling for authority for inter-fund borrowing and the acceleration of payroll tax increases as stopgap measures.

The main parts of the report were attacked by conservatives as advocating too centralized a governmental scheme, as being especially costly for small businesses, and as potentially

The future solvency of the U.S. Social Security system is a worry for the American public and a major concern of the U.S. government.

© Tim Menees/"The Pittsburgh Post Gazette"

undermining the insurance and thrift industries. Organizations representing the elderly, including the Citizens' Commission on Pension Policy, denounced the report for not going far enough in its list of reforms. By May, one aspect of the problem received special attention when the caucus of Congresswomen introduced a 100-page "economic equity" bill in the hope that it would eliminate some of the discriminations against women in the current pension systems. They pointed out that 9 of 10 women become widows at some time, and that more than 1 in 3 over age 65 has an annual income of less than $3,000 and lives alone. Women are still heavily concentrated in work that is not covered by pensions, earn 60% less than men on average, and interrupt their work careers for child-rearing and other reasons, all of which means a far more meager retirement.

Social Security. The pension policy report was soon overshadowed, with little action, when the National Commission on Social Security, chaired by Milton Gwirtzman, issued its final report and recommendations in March. It reaffirmed that the system is sound in principle and the best structure of basic income support for the nation. It concluded that the current financial difficulties of the system arose in part because of economic conditions outside the system's control; inflation that is not offset by increased wages eats into the trust funds because benefit payments are indexed (automatically increase with rising prices), while unemployment reduces the flow of taxes into the trust funds. The commission's major recommendations would shift Medicare funding so that one half its costs would be met from general revenues, would adjust the index used to match price increases, and would put a ceiling on payroll taxes beyond which the general revenue funds would be used to keep the system solvent. There were more than 80 other recommendations about benefits, taxes, trust funds, and the administration of the system, but the main thrust of the report was to uphold the basic program. The report called for a full recommitment to the original aims, as well as the long-run reform, of Social Security. It stressed the need to raise the eligibility age, to adjust the method of indexing, and to shift the disability, Supplemental Security Income (SSI), and/or Medicare to other funding sources.

President Reagan discovered how emotional and pervasive the sense of entitlement has become under the system when he recommended to Congress reductions in benefits.

Two key elements of his proposals, a gradual 23% reduction in benefits for all future retirees and an immediate 40% cut for those who choose to retire at age 62, created an uproar in Congress. The Senate not only defeated the proposals by a 96–0 vote, but came within one vote of passing a resolution censuring the president for a "breach of faith" with the millions of workers approaching retirement.

Less controversial and on a smaller scale were the changes in benefits which Congress approved as part of the complex Omnibus Budget Reconciliation Act of 1981, such as the elimination of the automatic lump sum death benefit of $225 (payable in the future only if there is a surviving spouse or child) the gradual reduction and phasing out of benefits for college students who are surviving children of a retiree (they can still get into this program if they start school full time before May 1982), postponement of the drop in age from 72 to 70 for exemption from income restrictions, and the stopping at 16 years of age rather than 18 of benefits for a child being raised by a surviving low-income parent whose spouse is retired, disabled, or dead. The provision that stirred controversy was the elimination of the minimum benefit of $122 (later rescinded by the Senate).

In his September appeal for more budget cuts, President Reagan refrained from any further suggestions that would affect the Social Security system, except for inter-fund borrowing authority and shifting of some Medicare costs.

MORTON ROTHSTEIN

SOUTH AFRICA

Prime Minister P. W. Botha's unexpected decision to call an election on April 29, 1981, two years before it was due, was in direct response to an increasing backlash by the Right against his proposed limited reforms of some of South Africa's discriminatory legislation. He was particularly concerned about the growing strength of the conservative Herstigte Nasionale Party (HNP) and of right-wing or *verkrampte* discontent within his own National Party.

By calling the election in 1981, instead of at the end of 1982, the prime minister hoped to stem the growing move to the right, and to reunite his party with a win. In the context of South African internal politics it was necessary for him to mount a campaign in which he appeared as the decisive and tough leader of the party who would have no hesitation in using South Africa's military and police strength, and who would not deviate too far from basic principles of racial separation.

Even though the National Party's parliamentary strength was only marginally diminished (it won 131 seats out of a total of 165 seats, a loss of 7 seats from 1977), the election was perceived as falling far short of providing the prime minister with a full mandate for the next five years. For Botha, the liberal Progressive Federal Party's (PFP) winning nine new seats and thus increasing its parliamentary representation from 17 seats to 26 seats was not significant. Nor was the appeal of the charismatic PFP leader, Dr. F. van Zyl Slabbert. What really counted was that the HNP demonstrated that it had the support of an increasing number of right-wing Afrikaners. The HNP received 189,654 votes, or 15% of the total cast. However, because of the scattered nature of its support, HNP did not win a single seat in Parliament. The National Party won 57% of the votes cast, dropping from 65% in the 1977 election. The exuberant HNP leader, Jaap Marais, saw the election as marking a fundamental shift in white South African politics. The HNP was no longer a party that could be ignored. The HNP, formed in 1971 by a splinter group from the National Party under the leadership of Dr. Albert Hertzog, has advocated unadulterated white supremacy. It has appealed to ultra conservatives and blue collar workers and is strongest in the Orange Free State and the Transvaal. The HNP stands to the right of the *verkramptes* or conservatives within the ruling National Party who gravitate to Dr. Andries Treurnicht. The significance of the HNP's election showing is not that it can challenge the National Party, but rather that it poses a threat to Afrikaner unity and in order to avoid widening differences, Botha will have to cut back on his proposed limited reforms.

The President's Council. In February 1981, a new policy advisory and consultative body, the President's Council, began deliberations. The President's Council replaced the South African Senate, which had been abolished. The council included nominated whites, a few Coloured and Asian members, as well as one Chinese, but excluded Africans, who comprise over 70% of South Africa's population. Prime Minister Botha was adamant in his exclusion of Africans because of the existence of the "homelands" where he maintained they had their own representation. This diminished the importance of the council. Because of the exclusion of Africans, the PFP boycotted the Council.

Economics. In 1980 gold brought in half of South Africa's export earnings and as a consequence of its high price, South Africa's gross national product (GNP) increased 7.9%, one of the highest GNP increases in the world. With the fall in the price of gold to about $400 an ounce in 1981, the August budget of Minister of Finance Owen Horwood was a conservative one. The drop in the price of gold plus inflationary military spending (15.5% of total government spending and up 30% from 1980) necessitated what has been referred to as a tough wartime budget.

Afrikaner Student Opposition. An important development on the Afrikaner left is POLSTU (Politieke Studente or Political Student Society), which was formed in July 1980 at the University of Potchefstroom, as a break away from the conservative ASB (Afrikaanse Student Bond). The movement has spread to other universities, including Stellenbosch and the Rand Afrikaans University. It rejects *apartheid* and one of its declared principles is citizenship and full participation for all South Africans. POLSTU points to the concern of young Afrikaners with the current political dispensation. Its importance lies in the fact that these young students, from the strongholds of Afrikaner culture and education, are calling for a just and free South Africa with equal citizenship for all.

POLSTU is not a political movement, but the NP, the HNP, and POLSTU are indicative of the fragmentation of Afrikaner solidarity and the inability of the ruling white group, which consists of 60% of the white population, to deal with the nation's racial problems.

Angolan Invasion. Two South African armored columns invaded Angola from Namibia (South-West Africa) in August 1981 and mounted ground attacks with air support. Prime Minister Botha acknowledged that South Afri-

SOUTH AFRICA • Information Highlights

Official Name: Republic of South Africa.
Location: Southern tip of Africa.
Area: 471,445 sq mi (1 221 043 km^2).
Population (1981 est.): 29,000,000.
Chief Cities (1970 census): Pretoria, the administrative capital, 543,950; Cape Town, the legislative capital, 691,296; Durban, 729,857; Johannesburg, 654,682.
Government: *Head of state,* Marais Viljoen, president (took office June 1979). *Head of government,* P. W. Botha, prime minister (took office Sept. 1978). *Legislature*—Parliament: President Council and House of Assembly.
Monetary Unit: Rand (0.9574 rand equals U.S.$1, Nov. 9, 1981).

South African troops are jubilant following their August incursion into nearby Angola in search of South West Africa People's Organization (SWAPO) guerrillas.

Abbas/Gamma-Liaison

can forces were pursuing South West Africa People's Organization (SWAPO) guerrillas based in Angola. Some fighting, however, also took place between South African forces and the Angolan military. South Africa's invasion appears to have been based on the concern that an early warning radio system and land-to-air missiles were being installed in southern Angola by the Cubans and East Germans. The military action by South Africa led to considerable international condemnation. The Reagan administration stood alone, however, in vetoing a UN Security Council resolution condemning South Africa. Unlike the Carter administration, the Reagan administration favors a less hostile position toward South Africa.

Squatters. In August, more than 1,500 black squatters at a campsite near Nyanga, Cape Town, were expelled from the squatter settlement and deported to the Transkei as illegal aliens. Most of those deported were wives and children of men who were prepared to undergo any hardships to remain with their families. Many of the squatters were arrested and imprisoned, but most returned and stayed on in defiance of the government and in spite of the inadequacy of their temporary plastic huts against the cold winter.

The Nyanga squatters are only one example of a major problem that exists in many other parts of South Africa. Clearly the homeland policy of the government has failed in its objective of developing self-sufficient entities. The homelands are underdeveloped rural slums. Migratory labor continues.

The African National Congress. The African National Congress (ANC) has operated from other African countries and from London since it was banned in 1960. The ANC engaged in several urban guerrilla acts during 1981. On January 30, South African military forces raided ANC buildings in Maputo, Mozambique. At least 13 people died in the raid.

Sporadic guerrilla attacks subsequently occurred in Durban, Port Elizabeth, Pretoria, and East London. They indicate the improved capability of the ANC and of its military wing, *Umkhonto We Sizwe* (the Spear of the Nation), and the beginning of elusive urban guerrilla activities inside South Africa.

Black Labor. Black trade unions continued to play an important political role in South Africa. Black unions can now essentially operate on the same footing as white unions and have begun to move forcefully and to express black political grievances. These unions are, however, hampered by existing apartheid legislation, such as influx control, and by police harassment. Numerous strikes by black workers occurred in major industrial areas throughout South Africa, but particularly among motor industry workers in Port Elizabeth. It is of particular importance that in 1981 black workers began to stage strikes in support of fellow workers in other parts of the labor force.

There are now more than six million black workers in South Africa. Those who are members of unions are now aware of their increasing power and many see their efforts as a part of a total struggle involving both political and labor considerations.

Namibia. The year saw a greater incentive toward the resolution of the Namibian (South-West African) question. After the failure of the Geneva Conference, the "contact group"—Britain, France, West Germany, Canada, and the United States—agreed in September on an independence plan that it hoped would lead to independence by 1983. South Africa now appeared willing to accept UN Security Council Resolution 435 of 1978, which authorized the UN to take the lead in bringing independence to Namibia, as the basis for a settlement, as well as the presence of an international force to ensure free elections. African nations were concerned about the "contact group's" effectiveness because of the Reagan administration's tilt toward South Africa. Sam Nujoma, president of SWAPO, said that he would be willing to attend an all-parties conference on Namibia, based on UN Resolution 435. He also said that while SWAPO would prefer to participate in an open and free election under UN supervision, it was prepared to continue the guerrilla war until this could be guaranteed. From the U.S. viewpoint, the resolution of the Namibia question must be seen in the context of the presence of Cuban troops in Angola.

Rugby. The year also saw a major international controversy surrounding the visit of the South African national rugby team to New Zealand and the United States. The outcry in the two nations against the team (which is integrated) highlights the continuing concern abroad about South Africa's discriminatory policies.

PATRICK O'MEARA
Africa Studies Program, Indiana University

SOUTH CAROLINA

Redistricting the state House of Representatives and the Congressional districts caused conflict within the General Assembly. Blacks contended that the Congressional redistricting plans offered were unfair, and the issue was put off until 1982. The state Senate would be reapportioned later, in time for the 1984 election.

Government. The General Assembly had an unusually long session. Debates on reapportionment, appropriations, and tax increases were extensive. A small state deficit was eliminated by using moneys in the reserve fund. Overcrowding in the state correctional system was partly resolved by permitting prisoners to be paroled after serving one fourth of their terms, by the opening of a major new facility, and by the approval of funds for further construction. The administration of juvenile correctional services was consolidated. Two cents per gallon were added to the gasoline tax. Funds for a number of capital improvements were vetoed. The legislature strengthened the laws on drug smuggling, purchasing precious metals, and child custody. A purchasing code was adopted, fees for hunting and fishing licenses were increased, and milk prices for the dairyman were raised.

Economy and Agriculture. Inflation and high interest rates affected the economy. Unemployment exceeded 7% and construction decreased. State tax revenue did not meet expectations. Significant new industries were added, including a $600 million paper mill. Yet, industries continue to be needed in undeveloped counties. Being capital intensive, the new industries, however, added only about one half of the desired jobs. Several old textile mills closed, severely injuring the economy of some towns. Numerous environmental questions were raised over the storage of toxic and nuclear waste, the operation of nuclear electric plants, and the possible pollution of major river systems.

SOUTH CAROLINA • Information Highlights

Area: 31,113 sq mi (80 583 km^2).
Population (1980 census): 3,119,208.
Chief Cities (1980 census): Columbia, the capital, 99,296; Charleston, 69,510; Greenville, 58,242; Spartanburg, 43,968; Rock Hill, 35,344; Florence, 30,062; Anderson, 27,313; Sumter, 24,890; Greenwood, 21,613; Myrtle Beach, 18,758.
Government (1981): *Chief Officers*—governor, Richard W. Riley (D); lt. gov., Nancy Stevenson (D). *General Assembly*—Senate, 46 members; House of Representatives, 124 members.
State Finances (fiscal year 1980): *Revenues*, $3,484,000,000; *expenditures*, $3,325,000,000.
Personal Income (1980): $22,726,000,000; per capita, $7,266.
Labor Force (July 1981): *Nonagricultural wage and salary earners*, 1,184,600; *unemployed*, 102,800 (7.5% of total force).

Zimberoff/Sygma

Following a meeting at the White House, Sen. Strom Thurmond (R) is interviewed by the press. With the Republicans taking control of the Senate in January 1981, South Carolina's senior senator became president pro tempore and chairman of the judiciary committee.

Although dry weather seriously curtailed yields of soybeans and corn in some areas, agricultural production improved. Tobacco and fresh peach yields and prices were good. Tobacco was still the chief money crop. In acreage, soybeans were the major crop.

Education. Reductions in federal funds seriously affected educational programs, especially for the many children from families of low income. Basic skill assessment tests were given in grades 3, 6, and 8. The results showed major weaknesses in reading, math, and composition. Special programs for gifted and talented students were provided in 88 of the 92 districts. Per student expenditure increased in the economically deprived districts. The pay for public school teachers was increased but remained below the Southeastern average. A leadership academy was established to train public school administrators. Although the number of graduate students increased, lack of funds caused the two major universities to reduce freshman enrollments.

Social and Cultural. The restored Exchange Building in Charleston, famous during the Revolutionary War period, was opened in October. Restoration projects in Columbia and other areas progressed significantly. The first village-type facility for the mentally ill opened.

ROBERT H. STOUDEMIRE
University of South Carolina, Columbia

SOUTH DAKOTA

Early in the 1981 legislative session, the majority Republicans worked amid sharp criticism to fund a $275.4 million state budget for fiscal year 1982 with a new tax program that would increase revenues by $30 million. Rejecting the Democrats' call for a corporate income tax, as well as Gov. William Janklow's plan for a high severance tax on gold produced by the Homestake Mining Company, the legislature voted to establish a moderate 6% levy on gold production, to add 1¢ per gallon to the fuel tax, to extend for six months the term of the 1¢ sales tax created in the previous year to fund a core railway system, and to raise additional funds with assessments on cigarette and liquor sales.

SOUTH DAKOTA • Information Highlights

Area: 77,116 sq mi (199 730 km²).
Population (1980 census): 690,178.
Chief Cities (1980 census): Pierre, the capital, 11,973; Sioux Falls, 81,343; Rapid City, 46,492; Aberdeen, 25,956; Watertown, 15,649; Brookings, 14,951; Mitchell, 13,916; Huron, 13,000; Yankton, 12,011.
Government (1981): *Chief Officers*—governor, William J. Janklow (R); lt. gov., Lowell C. Hansen II (R). *Legislature*—Senate, 35 members; House of Representatives, 70 members.
State Finances (fiscal year 1980): *Revenues,* $762,000,000; *expenditures* $740,000,000.
Personal Income (1980): $5,408,000,000; per capita, $7,806.
Labor Force (July 1981): *Nonagricultural wage and salary earners,* 235,000; *unemployed,* 16,800 (4.8% of total force).

Legislators later approved a redistricting plan. It establishes 28 multiple-member districts in which the voters of each will elect one state senator and two state representatives. Constituents of the district containing Aberdeen will elect two senators and four representatives; those of the district containing Rapid City will choose three senators and six representatives; those of the district containing Sioux Falls will elect five senators and ten representatives. Critics of the plan hoped for revision in the next session.

Economy. The economic indicators of 1981 brought renewed optimism. Ample rainfall produced bumper crops in most areas. Prices were nearly equal to those of the previous year for all principal products except cattle. Reverses in construction industries, caused by high interest rates, brought a slight increase in nonagricultural unemployment. Average personal income increased more than 2%. Farmers reaped the greatest harvests they have had in several years.

Citibank, a subsidiary of Citicorp, chartered in Sioux Falls on February 19. Its managers worked on construction plans for new buildings, hired 250 persons, and promised to employ others. Transferring 5.8 million credit accounts, Citibank leaders also increased capitalization and loan capacity of the state's banking system.

Indian Affairs. Two small groups of Sioux assembled in the Black Hills to express rejection of $105 million offered by the federal government in 1979 as compensation for the loss in the 19th century of the 60-million-acre (24.3-million-ha) Black Hills Region. A group of approximately 40, headed by American Indian Movement leaders, established "Yellow Thunder Camp" on federal land 12 mi (19.2 km) from Rapid City and ignored removal orders, demanding the restoration of 800 acres (323.7 ha). A contingent of Oglalas held temporary encampments at Wind Cave National Park and Sheridan Lake, demanding the return of 7 million acres (5.8 million ha) plus financial damages. Federal officers spurned the demands; the U.S. Supreme Court had already upheld the Black Hills award.

The United Sioux Tribes Executive Director was alarmed by the loss of some 500 reservation jobs after curtailment of Comprehensive Education and Training Act (CETA) funds, and by the threat of drastic reductions in federal supports.

Along with financial cuts, tribal leaders faced adjustment to new procedures, including the replacement of federal contracts by grants for goods and services on reservations, the prospect of block grant instead of line item allocations by Congress, and the transfer of responsibility for socioeconomic services from federal to state and local governments.

State-owned Railroads. The governor's work to create a state-owned railroad system to transport farm products continued in the face of opposition, especially from people west of the Missouri River where no rails had been purchased.

HERBERT T. HOOVER, *University of South Dakota*

NASA

Cape Canaveral, 7 AM (EST), April 12, 1981, the space shuttle Columbia lifts off.

SPACE EXPLORATION

The world's first reusable space shuttle was flown in 1981. The flight was a milestone in manned space flight, culminating a decade of work and ushering in a new era of space transportation. The USSR continued its manned utilization of the Salyut 6 Space Station, accumulating 1,900 man-days in space since Yuri Gagarin was orbited in Vostok 1 in 1961. This record was double the U.S. astronaut time in orbit. Voyager 2 encountered Saturn with its many moons and rings and provided more than 18,000 images, which were more detailed than those obtained from Voyager 1 in 1980.

Manned Space Flight. The successful test flights of the U.S. Space Transportation System, designated STS 1 and STS 2, were the highlights of 1981. The USSR, meanwhile, continued its active use of the Salyut 6 while testing out a newer and larger version of the space station to replace it.

Space shuttle Columbia's first of a series of four orbital test flights (STS 1) took place with a launch at Kennedy Space Center (KSC) on April 12 to a 172-mile or 277-km altitude, circular orbit at 40 degrees inclination. The flight lasted 54½ hours before landing at Dryden Flight Research Center (DFRC) in California on April 14, meeting all primary objectives. The astronauts who commanded this first flight were crew commander John W. Young and Robert L. Crippen. (*See also* BIOGRAPHY.)

After launch and ascent, Columbia's solid rocket boosters were jettisoned and parachuted for recovery from the Atlantic Ocean and eventual reuse. Following cutoff of the space shuttle's main engines and disposal of the external tank, which reentered and impacted in the Indian Ocean close to the predicted impact point, the orbital maneuvering system (OMS) engines were ignited twice to complete insertion into circular orbit. The OMS engines were also used in a retrograde firing to slow the vehicle for return to earth. Although several noncritical thermal protection tiles were lost during the flight, the overall performance of the thermal protection system was very encouraging.

The landing of Columbia marked the first time that a manned nonballistic reentry had ever been performed. It involved flying a space vehicle/glider from near-earth orbit by deorbiting over the Indian Ocean, enduring temperatures of 2700 °F (1482 °C) upon reentry into the atmosphere, approaching the California coast at 120,000 ft (36 585 m) at ten times the speed of sound, and landing on a 3-mi- (5-km-) long runway in the Mojave Desert at 196 knots. This first orbital flight test on STS 1 carried two engineering experiments in the payload bay. These experiments served to increase the technology reservoir for development of future space transportation systems. They included an Aerodynamic Coefficient Identification Package (ACIP) and Infrared Imagery of Shuttle (IRIS).

The second orbital flight test, on STS 2, commanded by Joe H. Engle and Richard H. Truly, was launched on November 12 from KSC and landed at DFRC on November 14. Malfunction of the auxiliary power units that operate the oil hydraulic system caused the mission to be postponed. The launch of OFT 2 had already been delayed approximately one month as a result of an accidental nitrogen tetroxide spill during fueling of the orbiter. Approximately 370 thermal tiles were removed and replaced because of adhesive bond deterioration resulting from the spill. The flight was shortened from 124 hours to 54 hours because of a failure of one of the three fuel cells which supplies Columbia's electrical power. However, in spite of the shortened mission, the major scientific and engineering objectives were accomplished. The largest experiment was the shuttle imaging radar (SIR-A) which successfully acquired eight hours of data over a wide variety of geological terrain. The SIR-A data recorded differences in surface roughness and delineated such geological features as faults and will be combined with landsat data to provide more detailed mapping of earth's resources. The Shuttle Multispectral Infrared Radiometer (SMIRR), which was designed to identify rocks and soil types, acquired about 108 cloud-free minutes of earth observations. The ocean color experiment (OCE), designed to map chlorophyll in the world's oceans, acquired 78 minutes of cloud-free data. Columbia also flew an aggressive reentry maneuvering profile which demonstrated wing performance.

The USSR prepared the Salyut 6 Space Station for reuse by launching an unmanned supply satellite, Progress 12, on January 24 and linking it with Salyut 6. The Soyuz T-4 spacecraft was launched on March 12 with cosmonauts Vladimir Kovalenok and Viktor Savinykh aboard. They remained in orbit aboard Salyut 6 for 75 days, returning on May 26. They were joined by Vladimir Dzhanibekov of the USSR and Jugderdemidiyn Gurragcha of Mongolia, who were launched in Soyuz 39 on March 22 and returned on March 30. The Soyuz T-4 crew were also joined by a second group of cosmonauts, Leonid Popov and Dumitru Prunariu of Rumania in Soyuz 40 on May 14. Popov and Prunariu also remained aboard Salyut 6 for one week and returned on May 22. Experiments conducted aboard Salyut 6 included photosurveys of the earth, material processing of semiconductor materials, gamma-ray measurements with a telescope, and sub-millimeter wave radiation measurements of the earth's atmosphere.

Salyut 6 accumulated an in-orbit time of 43 months in May, which was double its original design life. Twenty Soyuz spacecraft and 12 Progress spacecraft were launched over the four-year period in support of five extended missions by cosmonauts—in Soyuz 26 for 96 days, Soyuz 29 for 140 days, Soyuz 32 for 175 days, Soyuz 35 for 185 days, and Soyuz T-4 for 75 days. Cosmos 1267 was launched on April 25 to serve as a test for Salyut 7. This new space station will weigh twice as much as Salyut 6, be modular in construction, and carry science laboratories, telescopes, and living quarters. The new space station will employ in-orbit assembly of modular station components to a central core with multiple docking ports. The station may be designed to handle as many as 12 cosmonauts simultaneously. The flight of the new station is expected to be in 1982. It is being designed with a four-to-five-year life and is aimed at accommodating long duration missions. Research is continuing

Joe H. Engle (front) and Richard H. Truly prepare for the second launch of the space shuttle.

UPI

on understanding the limitations of long duration flights and providing countermeasures to offset the ill effects, such as bone losses of calcium and other minerals. Regular exercise has been shown to be important in combating these effects, along with regular rest and good nutrition and water supply.

Fourteen U.S. life-science experiments were conducted jointly with the USSR aboard Cosmos 1129, an unmanned Soviet satellite. These experiments yielded valuable information on the effects of weightlessness on animals and plant growth. Bone mineral content in rats used in the experiment decreased 20% as a result of the flight. This supports the theory that new bone production slows down during spaceflight while resorption continues, resulting in net loss of bone and decreased strength. A Vostak satellite was used for the 18-day flight, which was orbited and recovered in the USSR.

Planetary Probes. Voyager, Pioneer Venus, and Viking Lander continued to gather new data on Saturn, Venus, and Mars. The Voyager 2 spacecraft passed through the magnetic tail of Jupiter and made its closest approach to Saturn on August 25, passing 16,500 mi (26 500 km) closer than Voyager 1 on Nov. 12, 1980. The Jovian wake is caused by the solar wind stretching Jupiter's magnetic field at least 252 million mi (406 million km) beyond the planet. These magnetic tails are similar to those encountered by Jupiter, the earth, and the comets.

Voyager 2 passed within 72,500 mi (116 800 km) of Saturn and took more than 18,000 images before continuing on to an encounter with Uranus in 1986 and Neptune in 1989. The mission's major objectives were accomplished in spite of experiencing a jammed azimuth drive in the pointing mechanism of the sensor platform. A manual drive was used to rotate the platform about 50° to acquire images of Saturn as Voyager 2 sped outbound toward Uranus. The platform response improved with use and is expected to function normally for the Uranus encounter.

Voyager 2 traveled more than 1,428,000,000 mi (2 300 000 000 km) before its encounter with Saturn and its photographing of five of the planet's satellites—Enceladus, Tethys, Hyperion, Iapetus, and Phoebe. Voyager 2 showed greater detail than Voyager 1 because of the performance of the camera system coupled with a different angle of approach and higher sun angle.

Voyager 2 provided a closer look at Enceladus, which showed varied topography in lieu of the smooth surfaces indicated by the Voyager 1 photos. This indicates a different geological thermal history, with expansion and contraction of the planet's crust as a possible explanation of the varied relief exhibited by the surface.

The largest crater in the Saturnian system was seen on Voyager images of Tethys at a distance of 715,000 mi (1.15 million km). The crater is approximately 287 mi (463 km) in diameter or one third the diameter of Tethys.

Hyperion was found to be irregularly shaped at 214 mi (345 km) by 143 mi (230 km) with its axis at an angle to the orbital plane. Images of the Saturnian moon, Iapetus, show one side to be very dark with a surface reflectivity of only 4–5%. Radio science data from Voyager 2 indicate a composition of 35% rock, 55% water, and 10% solid methane.

Voyager 2 passed within about 1.5 million mi (2.4 million km) of Phoebe on September 4. Voyager 1 did not attempt to acquire imagery of Phoebe because its approach was not close enough. Voyager 2 also studied Saturn's ring system in detail with emphasis on the B-Ring and its spokes, the braided F-ring and its satellites, and the eccentric rings in the C-Ring, Cassini Division and Encke Division. A new "Kinked Ring" was discovered inside the Encke Division.

Voyager 2's infrared spectrometer showed that Saturn's temperature ranges from 80 °K (−193 °C) to 92 °K (−181 °C) and is correlated as a function of latitude or height. Saturn's jet streams were also seen in more detail from Voyager 2, with easterly flows occurring in the northern latitudes and extending to higher latitudes than do those on Jupiter. High resolution photos of seven newly discovered Saturnian satellites were also taken. They appear to be irregularly shaped and heavily cratered by impacts, with cosmic debris ranging in size from 7 to 230 mi (11 to 370 km) across.

Pioneer Venus orbiter, launched in May 1978, continued to provide important scientific data on the atmosphere and space environment of Venus. The radar altimeter has provided first order characterization of the surface of Venus in preparation for a detailed study proposed by the Venus Orbiting Imagery Radar.

Analysis of Pioneer Venus Orbiter data indicates that Venus' predominant weather pattern is east to west at velocities up to 189 mi/hour (304 km/hr). Two kinds of circulation have been seen, both around the planet and from the equator to the poles, causing the atmosphere to mix thoroughly. This results in identical pressures and temperatures at the equator and polar regions and on the day and night sides. This understanding can be translated to the earth's atmosphere by providing insight into the "greenhouse effect," transport of heat to the polar regions, and interactions between the lower atmosphere and the stratosphere.

Analysis from the Pioneer Venus probe mass spectrometer also yielded insights regarding the concentration of noble gases, including argon, neon, and krypton, in the atmosphere of Venus. Venus' atmosphere has a much higher concentration of these gases than is contained in the earth's atmosphere. The concentration is more like that of the sun, possibly an indication that the gases came from the sun. The information provides real evidence about the formation of the solar system.

The Pioneer Venus orbiter is expected to return pictures and other data until 1985. These data will be supplemented by a Venus Probe that was launched by the USSR on October 30. Venera 13 and 14 are scheduled to arrive at Venus in March 1982. Pioneer 10 and 11 spacecraft continued to operate, providing interplanetary fields and particles measurements on their way out of the solar system. Pioneer 6, which was launched in December 1965, began its 15th year of operation.

Meanwhile, the Viking Lander 1, which arrived at Mars in 1976, continued to operate on the planet. The lander was redesignated the Thomas Mutch Memorial Station in honor of Dr. Mutch, the leader of the Viking imaging team, who was killed in a climbing accident in the Himalayas. The station operates in automatic mode, collecting and storing selected seasonal images of the Martian surface, and transmitting these to earth on command.

Scientific Satellites. Two scientific satellites were launched by the United States in 1981. A pair of Dynamics Explorer (DE) satellites was launched on August 3 and a Solar Mesosphere Explorer (SME) on October 10 by Delta vehicles from Western Space and Missile Center (WSMC) in California. The DE satellites would study the coupling between the ionosphere and magnetosphere at high latitudes. Simultaneous measurements would be made by the two coplanar polar orbiting satellites in the two coupled regions. DE 1 is in a 411 mi (661 km) by 16,000 mi (25 760 km) orbit while DE 2 has an orbit of 435 mi (700 km) by 724 mi (1 166 km). These satellites are designed to provide a better understanding of the processes by which solar radiation and the solar wind enter the earth's magnetosphere and deposit in the upper atmosphere to produce the aurora or northern lights, affect radio signals, and possibly influence weather patterns.

The SME is an atmospheric research satellite, designed to measure the density and altitude distribution of ozone and to measure the solar input, water vapor, and nitrogen dioxide which react with ozone. These data will test models for ozone production and depletion worldwide.

The High Energy Astrophysical Observatories (HEAO 2 & 3) completed their scientific missions on April 26 and May 30 when altitude control gas was expended and all systems were powered down. Three HEAO satellites performed at least twice as long as their design life. HEAO 2 provided X-ray images of astronomical objects such as galaxies and nebulae following a mapping of these X-ray sources by HEAO 1. HEAO 3 conducted an all-sky survey of gamma and cosmic rays. These data suggested that cosmic rays derive their enormous energies from forces acting on the interstellar medium and not from supernova explosions as originally believed. New theories are being developed to determine the nature of these forces.

Sovfoto

Vladimir Dzhanibekov and Mongolia's Jugderdemidiyn Gurragcha rode in the flight of Soyuz 39.

Other scientific satellites launched in the USSR included Intercosmos 21 on February 6 and Intercosmos Bulgaria 1300 on August 7, and a French-Soviet joint mission, OREAL 3, launched on September 21. OREAL 3 was launched by the European Space Agency (ESA) from French Guiana. The satellite would study physical processes in the earth's magnetosphere and ionosphere, including the nature of the aurora.

Earth Observation Satellites. The United States launched two Environmental Observation Satellites in 1981 to continue monitoring of severe storms and global weather. The National Oceanic and Atmospheric Administration (NOAA) maintains four operational civilian weather satellites, two at geostationary orbit and two in near-earth orbit. These new satellites were the Geostationary Operational Environmental Satellites (GOES-E), launched from Eastern Space and Missile Center (ESMC) by a Delta vehicle on May 22, and NOAA-C, which was launched from WSMC by an Atlas F vehicle on June 22. These satellites were later designated GOES 5 and NOAA 7, respectively, when their operations were initiated. GOES 5 carried the second

NASA

The 1981 Voyager II view of Saturn (right) and the Voyager I view of the planet are compared.

Visible Infrared Spin-Scan Radiometer Atmospheric Sounder (VISSR/VAS), which continues sounding of the atmosphere from geostationary orbit initiated by GOES 4 in its position at 135° West longitude. This sensor provides frequent soundings over large areas and is being used in a research mode by NASA and NOAA to track the development of severe storms, including hurricanes. These soundings provide vertical profiles of atmospheric temperatures and the amount, distribution, and movement of water vapor. The sensor also provides sea surface temperature data which are useful for monitoring ocean currents. GOES 5 replaced an older GOES satellite at 75° West longitude.

The TIROS-N weather observation satellite, which was launched in 1978, failed in late February after exceeding its expected lifetime. A significant result obtained from this new series with improved capability was that temperature soundings were significantly better than any previously obtained. These sounding data are important for global weather analysis and forecasts. NOAA 7 replaced TIROS-N and complemented NOAA 6 in providing atmospheric profiles.

In Earth Resources Surveys, Land Satellite (LANDSAT) 2 and 3 continued to provide synoptic, repetitive coverage of the earth's land cover from which information can be derived for management of renewable and nonrenewable resources. Aircraft research flights were conducted to obtain simulated Thematic Mapper data in preparation for the launch of Landsat D in 1982. The Thematic Mapper on Landsat D will have higher spectral, spatial, and radiometric resolution than the Multispectral Scanner presently carried aboard Landsat 2 and 3. This capability should improve the ability to identify crops and monitor their condition, to map vegetated and nonvegetated land cover, and to identify and map geologic features.

The USSR also continued space observations of weather and earth resources with the launching of two Meteor Series Satellites on May 14 and July 10 and five Cosmos Series satellites. Cosmos 1273 was launched on May 22 and Cosmos 1284 on July 30 for earth resources monitoring. Three Nuclear Power Radar Ocean Surveillance Satellites, Cosmos 1249, Cosmos 1266, and Cosmos 1299 were launched on March 5, April 21, and August 25, respectively. The USSR also launched an earth observation satellite for India.

Communication Satellites. Eighteen communication and navigation satellites were launched in 1981, serving both private and military communication needs. Seven U.S. communication satellites—Comstar D, Navy 20 (NOVA 1), Intelsat V-B and C, FLTSATCOM-E, SBS-B, and RCA-D—were sent off in 1981. The USSR launched ten satellites, including five in the Molniya series, one each in the Ekran and Cosmos series, and three in the Raduga series. The last is to support amateur radio use. The Indian Space Research Organization launched an Apple Communication Satellite on June 19 using the ESA Ariane Launcher.

MICHAEL A. CALABRESE

SPAIN

An attempted coup d'etat on Feb. 23, 1981, illuminated the fragility of Spain's short-lived experiment in democracy and dramatized the need for effective solutions to the economic and social problems that afflict the country.

Politics and Government. In the face of mordant criticism from the press, opposition parties, and elements of his own Union of the Democratic Center (UDC), Adolfo Súarez, who had served as premier for 4½ years, abruptly resigned in January. This move plunged Spain into a severe political crisis and indirectly set the stage for a brief takeover of the parliament building by a contingent of dissident civil guards. On the heels of this attempted coup, the national parliament (Cortés) confirmed Leopoldo Calvo Sotelo y Bustelo (*See* Biography) as successor to Suarez, with whom he had closely worked, most recently serving as deputy premier for economic affairs.

Initially, seven members of the UDC's 35-person executive committee opposed Calvo Sotelo's selection. These politicians belonged to the party's "critical sector," composed of right-wing Christian Democrats and Liberals, who believe that Suárez led the party too far away from its conservative roots.

Gaining control of a military in which many officers prefer the discipline and authority imposed by the late Generalissimo Francisco Franco to the fluidity and uncertainty of present-day Spain poses a major challenge to the new government. Although the office of the chiefs of staff was reorganized and at least two generals dismissed following the abortive putsch, elements of the army, national guard, and police have yet to commit themselves to democracy.

Calvo Sotelo's determination both to launch an investigation of the approximately 300 men who participated in the conspiracy and to impose severe sentences on the wrongdoers, including prison terms of up to 30 years for the ringleaders, will test the principle of civilian control over the military.

In June, the government arrested three army officers and five civilians in an effort to quash another possible insurrection.

Economy. Adverse economic conditions, exacerbated by the annual expenditure of $12,000,000,000 on oil imports, have produced headaches for the new premier. Although the gross national product (GNP) grew slightly in 1981, both inflation (14.5%) and unemployment (12%) remained disturbingly high.

In a speech to parliament, Calvo Sotelo supported government incentives to put more people to work, the establishment of guidelines to limit wage increases, and a reduction in business contributions to social security. He also backed the continuation of his country's nuclear power program and endorsed the creation of a state-managed holding company to coordinate a national energy policy.

The escalation of terrorist attacks intensified the discontent caused by economic stagnation. The violence was centered in the Basque region, where 27 political killings reportedly occurred between January and August. Demonstrations and protests by advocates of separatism marred the visit of King Juan Carlos and Queen Sophia to the Basque provinces in early February.

A scandal erupted in late summer over the inadequacy of food and sanitation inspections. Adulterated cooking oil is believed to have killed at least 120 persons and harmed 11,000 others. Thousands of tons of pork sold in northeast Spain came from pigs infected with African swine fever and other diseases. While refusing to dismiss his health minister, the premier ordered the appointment of new health inspectors and offered compensation to the victims.

Foreign Relations. Calvo Sotelo announced his support for legislation for Spain's entry into the North Atlantic Treaty Organization (NATO). Although this proposal is opposed by both Communists and Socialists, who want a referendum on membership, it appears certain to win parliamentary approval. The issue has accentuated political divisions; however, many moderates believe that affiliation with NATO will broaden the outlook of Spanish officers.

The Soviet embassy inadvertently aided the pro-NATO cause when it objected to Spain's probable application for membership. Even the Spanish Communist party applauded the foreign minister's rejection of Moscow's "interference in Spanish affairs."

Despite friction with France over agricultural exports, Spain tenaciously held to its commitment to join the European Community, with full integration scheduled for 1983.

A perceived diplomatic insult—following their marriage, Prince Charles and Princess Diana boarded a yacht at Gibraltar, whose retention by Great Britain infuriates the Madrid regime—prevented Spanish representation at the wedding.

See also EUROPE.

GEORGE W. GRAYSON
College of William and Mary

SPAIN • Information Highlights

Official Name: Spanish State.
Location: Iberian Peninsula in southwestern Europe.
Area: 195,270 sq mi (505 750 km^2).
Population (1981 est.): 37,800,000.
Chief Cities (Dec. 31, 1978 est.): Madrid, the capital, 3,467,438; Barcelona, 1,902,713; Valencia, 750,994.
Government: *Head of state,* Juan Carlos I, king (took office Nov. 1975). *Head of government,* Leopoldo Calvo Sotelo y Bustelo, prime minister (took office February 1981). *Legislature*—Cortés: Senate and Chamber of Deputies.
Monetary Unit: Peseta (94.13 pesetas equal U.S.$1, Oct. 15, 1981).
Manufactures (major products): Processed food, textiles, footwear, petrochemicals, steel, automobiles, ships, cement.
Agriculture (major products): Cereals and feed grains, vegetables, citrus fruits, wine, olives and olive oil, livestock.

Kevin Horan/Picture Group

SPORTS
THE YEAR IN REVIEW

It was like an all-out attack. In 1981, the oldest institutions and most powerful authorities in sport came under siege. League officials, team owners, organizing bodies, and referees faced a steady barrage of challenge and abuse. For fans, the 1981 sports year was a test of patience.

Baseball went on strike. For more than seven weeks in the heart of summer, America did without its national pastime. Since the organization of the professional game in 1876, baseball faced no greater crisis. The issue was free agency, but few could explain the details. The season was split in half and a special play-off round was added, but the team with the best overall record in the National League (Cincinnati Reds) didn't qualify. Every record would have an asterisk.

At Wimbledon, the world's oldest (104) and most prestigious tennis tournament, men's champion John McEnroe berated the judges and linesmen, snubbed the traditional banquet, and otherwise thumbed his nose at what he considered a stuffed-shirt affair.

For the first time in the 70-year history of the Indianapolis 500, the apparent winner was stripped of his title. The United States Auto Club, which makes and enforces the rules for the most venerated U.S. automobile race, responded to a protest and named a new victor. The arguing went on for months, and the body reversed itself. The winner was the winner after all.

A new organization, the College Football Association (CFA) challenged the powerful NCAA. The Canadian Football League (CFL) lured some name players away from the NFL with big salaries. And a new free-agency mechanism in the NBA sent players' salaries—and team owners—through the roof.

Not all, however, was upheaval. Sugar Ray Leonard unified the world welterweight boxing title in a showdown with the touted Thomas Hearns. The Boston Celtics extended their dynasty in basketball. The World Series was a renewal of the longstanding Dodger-Yankee rivalry (though this time the Dodgers won). And the New York Islanders seemed on the verge of their own dynasty after winning hockey's Stanley Cup for the second straight year.

Finally, as a reminder that change can be refreshing, there were new champions, new records, and new faces on the scene. The New York Cosmos *lost* Soccer Bowl, to the Chicago Sting. Wayne Gretzky rewrote the NHL record book. And Marcus Allen emerged as the next great running back at the University of Southern California.

JEFF HACKER

Mark Richards/Picture Group

Major league baseball stadiums sat empty for many a midsummer afternoon during the 712-game players' strike. Die-hard fans survived, but attendance dropped when play resumed.

Bobby Unser (3) crossed the finish line first in the Indy 500, but Mario Andretti (40) was ruled the winner. The decision was later reversed.

Indianapolis Motor Speedway Corp.

Fred Mullane/Sports Photo File

At Wimbledon, John McEnroe upset Björn Borg in the finals and tournament officials throughout the two weeks of competition. The 22-year-old American was fined for "bad language and verbal abuse" and "conduct bringing the game of tennis into disrepute."

Richard Mackson/"Sports Illustrated"

Following in the footsteps of many great USC tailbacks, Marcus Allen set a new collegiate record for most yards rushed in a single season. His dazzling performance won him the Heisman Trophy.

Sugar Ray Leonard sent Thomas Hearns through the ropes on the way to a late-round, come-from-behind victory in their welterweight championship bout.

Dirck Halstead/Liaison

UPI

The New York Islanders hoisted the Stanley Cup for the second straight year after beating the Minnesota North Stars in five games in the NHL play-off finals.

AUTO RACING

The Indianapolis 500-mile race, which has been the scene of disaster and tragedy in the past, was the subject of a 137-day dispute in 1981.

Bobby Unser won by a comfortable margin. But the following morning, when the official results were posted, chief steward Tom Binford took down Unser's name and declared Mario Andretti the winner. Unser was penalized one lap for passing too many cars when he exited the pits during a yellow light situation.

Unser and car owner Roger Penske protested the decision. The United States Auto Club (USAC) conducted a hearing and named a three-man panel to review the race. After 137 days, the panel gave the race back to Unser but fined him $40,000 for rules infractions.

Rick Mears, who was burned seriously at Indianapolis, came back one month later and made a tremendous late charge to take the Championship Auto Racing Teams (CART) national driving title.

CART demonstrated clear superiority over USAC in 1981, with nearly all of the top drivers and teams racing under its banner.

Nelson Piquet of Brazil won the 1981 Formula One World Championship. He edged Carlos Reutemann of Argentina by one point.

Defending champion Alan Jones of Australia announced he would retire at the conclusion of the 1981 season and finished in style with a victory at Las Vegas.

Richard Petty won the Daytona 500-mile race for the seventh time. It was the 193d victory for Petty, the all-time leader in the National Association for Stock Car Racing (NASCAR).

BOB COLLINS
"The Indianapolis Star"

AUTO RACING
1981 CHAMPIONS

World Champion: Nelson Piquet, Brazil
CART: Rick Mears, U.S.
NASCAR: Darrell Waltrip, U.S.
Can-Am: Geoff Brabham, Australia

Major Race Winners

Indianapolis 500: Bobby Unser, U.S.
Michigan 500: Pancho Carter, U.S.
Daytona 500: Richard Petty, U.S.
Pocono 500: A. J. Foyt, U.S.

Grand Prix for Formula One Cars, 1981

Long Beach: Alan Jones, Australia
Brazil: Carlos Reutemann, Argentina
South Africa: Carlos Reutemann
Argentina: Nelson Piquet, Brazil
San Marino: Nelson Piquet
Belgium: Carlos Reutemann
Monaco: Gilles Villeneuve, Canada
Spain: Gilles Villeneuve
France: Alain Prost, France
Britain: John Watson, Ireland
Germany: Nelson Piquet
Austria: Jacques Laffite, France
Netherlands: Alain Prost
Italy: Alain Prost
Canada: Jacques Laffite
Las Vegas: Alan Jones

BASEBALL

The glittering promise of the 1981 baseball season was shattered June 12 when major league players went on strike to protest the owners' free-agent compensation plan. By the time play resumed with the All-Star Game on August 9, the labor impasse had become the longest and costliest in the history of American sports.

Estimated daily loss to the 26 clubs from ticket revenue alone was $1.25 million, while the 650 players lost a combined average of $600,000 per day. The owners did receive some relief from a strike fund that paid each club $50,000 per game from June 24 through August 8.

Under terms reached July 31, the "Basic Agreement" between players and owners was extended through 1984; players received full service credit for strike time, and a limited compensation plan provided clubs that lose "ranking" free agents with professional players from a pool to which all teams contribute.

Split Season. In an effort to rekindle fan interest after the strike, the owners adopted a "split season" format that matched pre-strike and post-strike winners in four intra-divisional "mini-series." By this format, the teams with the best overall records could be excluded from post-season play if they did not finish first in either half. In the National League (NL), the Cincinnati Reds had the best record in the Western Division, and the St. Louis Cardinals had the best combined mark in the Eastern Division, but neither qualified for play-off berths.

The New York Yankees won the American League (AL) East title by defeating the Milwaukee Brewers, three games to two, in the division "mini-series." The Oakland A's advanced to the pennant play-offs by holding the Kansas City Royals to two runs in a three-game sweep of the AL Western Division series. In National League play, the Montreal Expos defeated the Philadelphia Phillies, three games to two, when Steve Rogers twice outpitched Steve Carlton. In the West, the Los Angeles Dodgers rebounded from a two-game deficit to win three straight over the Houston Astros at Dodger Stadium.

Play-offs and World Series. Oakland, with the best overall record in the AL West, was unable to make its aggressive style of play—dubbed "Billy Ball," after manager Billy Martin—pay off against the Yankees in the AL championship series. New York won three straight.

Montreal failed to become the first foreign entry in the World Series when it was unable to win either of two final home games after taking a 2–1 lead in the best-of-five series against Los Angeles. In Game 5, Rick Monday slammed a two-out home run in the ninth inning to give the Dodgers a 2–1 victory.

In the World Series, Los Angeles lost the first two games in Yankee Stadium, but then unveiled its patented capacity for comebacks. The Dodgers swept three games in California and concluded a stunning upset with a resounding 9–2 victory at Yankee Stadium in Game 6.

Bob Watson's three-run homer in the first inning of the opener helped starting pitcher Ron Guidry prevail, 5–3, with an assist from the bullpen. Then former Dodger Tommy John combined with reliever Goose Gossage for a 3–0 shutout. But Ron Cey's three-run homer in the first inning of Game 3 gave Fernando Valenzuela a fast advantage, and the 20-year-old Dodger rookie, though far off his usual form, went the route in a 5–4 victory. The Dodgers also won the next day, 8–7, when the New York bullpen failed to protect a 6–3 lead in the sixth inning. Los Angeles recorded its third straight one-run victory with a 2–1 triumph behind Jerry Reuss in Game 5. The big hits were consecutive homers by Pedro Guerrero and Steve Yeager off Ron Guidry in the seventh inning. Guerrero homered again, and knocked in five runs, as the Dodgers won the October 28 finale. He later shared World Series Most Valuable Player (MVP) honors with Yeager and Cey.

The 1981 World Series will be most remembered by Yankee George Frazier, the first rookie pitcher to lose three games in the same series; by Dodger second baseman Dave Lopes, who made six errors; by Yankee owner George Steinbrenner, who suffered a fractured hand in a Los Angeles elevator brawl with two hostile Dodger fans; and by Yankee manager Bob Lemon, who watched his hitters set a mark for futility in a six-game World Series—55 runners left on base. Dave Winfield, after a fine first season under a ten-year Yankee contract worth more than $13 million, had one single in 22 at-bats.

Regular Season. Had the strike not intervened, 1981 might have been a year of records. Montreal rookie Tim Raines, with 50 stolen bases in 55 games, was ahead of Lou Brock's record pace. Fernando Valenzuela became the first rookie pitcher since 1945 to win his first eight starts but missed a chance to exceed the rookie record for shutouts; he tied the 1913 mark of eight, held by Ewell Russell. Valenzuela became the first rookie ever to win the Cy Young Award for pitching excellence. American League MVP and Cy Young Award-winner Rollie Fingers of Milwaukee seemed certain to exceed John Hiller's record of 38 saves, but was limited to 28 because of the strike. No starter won more than 14 games, no hitter reached 100 runs batted in, and only one player—Philadelphia's Mike Schmidt—hit as many as 30 home runs. Schmidt led the majors with 31 homers and 91 runs batted in (RBI) in 102 games, winning the league MVP award for the second straight year.

Four players tied for the AL lead with 22 homers. One of them, Baltimore's Eddie Murray, led the league with 78 RBI. Batting champions were third basemen Bill Madlock of Pittsburgh (.341) and Carney Lansford of Boston (.336).

On June 10, Philadelphia star Pete Rose tied Stan Musial's National League record of 3,630

Rookie lefthander Fernando Valenzuela led L.A. to the World Series and won the Cy Young Award.

Focus on Sports

Houston fireballer Nolan Ryan pitched a record fifth no-hitter and had the league's lowest ERA.

Focus on Sports

hits. But the Phils were off June 11, so Rose had to wait until August 10 to break it. Rose's teammate, Steve Carlton, became the National League's career strikeout king September 21, when he exceeded Bob Gibson's total of 3,117. Carlton and Cincinnati's Tom Seaver became the fifth and sixth pitchers to reach 3,000 career strikeouts, while Boston's Carl Yastrzemski became the fourth man to play in 3,000 games.

National League earned run average (ERA) king Nolan Ryan (1.69) tossed a record fifth career no-hitter, a 5–0 win over the Dodgers in Houston on September 26, while Cleveland's Len Barker hurled the first perfect game since 1968, a 3–0 whitewash of Toronto in Cleveland on May 15. Montreal's Charlie Lea no-hit San Francisco, 4–0, in Olympic Stadium on May 10.

There were four ownership changes in 1981. On January 29, the American League approved George L. Argyros as principal owner of the Seattle Mariners and okayed the purchase of the Chicago White Sox by Jerry M. Reinsdorf and Eddie Einhorn. On June 16, the Wrigley family ended its record 66-year ownership of the Cubs by selling the team to the Chicago Tribune Co. A group headed by Bill Giles purchased the Philadelphia Phillies from the Carpenter family for a record $30 million on October 29.

Three men were elected to the Baseball Hall of Fame: former Cardinal pitcher Bob Gibson, slugging first baseman Johnny Mize, and the late Andrew (Rube) Foster, reputed to be "the Father of Black Baseball."

DAN SCHLOSSBERG
Baseball Writer

Mickey Palmer/Focus on Sports

George Steinbrenner, controversial owner of the Yankees, made as many headlines as his team.

BASEBALL

Professional—Major Leagues

AMERICAN LEAGUE
(First-Half Standings, 1981)

Eastern Division	W	L	Pct.	Western Division	W	L	Pct.
New York	34	22	.607	Oakland	37	23	.617
Baltimore	31	23	.574	Texas	33	22	.600
Milwaukee	31	25	.554	Chicago	31	22	.585
Detroit	31	26	.544	California	31	29	.517
Boston	30	26	.536	Kansas City	20	30	.400
Cleveland	26	24	.520	Seattle	21	36	.368
Toronto	16	42	.276	Minnesota	17	39	.304

(Second-Half Standings, 1981)

Milwaukee	31	22	.585	Kansas City	30	23	.566
Boston	29	23	.558	Oakland	27	22	.551
Detroit	29	23	.558	Texas	24	26	.480
Baltimore	28	23	.549	Minnesota	24	29	.453
Cleveland	26	27	.491	Seattle	23	29	.442
New York	25	26	.490	Chicago	23	30	.434
Toronto	21	27	.438	California	20	30	.400

NATIONAL LEAGUE
(First-Half Standings, 1981)

Philadelphia	34	21	.618	Los Angeles	36	21	.632
St. Louis	30	20	.600	Cincinnati	35	21	.625
Montreal	30	25	.545	Houston	28	29	.491
Pittsburgh	25	23	.521	Atlanta	25	29	.463
New York	17	34	.333	San Fran	27	32	.458
Chicago	15	37	.288	San Diego	23	33	.411

(Second-Half Standings, 1981)

Montreal	30	23	.566	Houston	33	20	.623
St. Louis	29	23	.558	Cincinnati	31	21	.596
Philadelphia	25	27	.481	San Fran	29	23	.558
New York	24	28	.462	Los Angeles	27	26	.509
Chicago	23	28	.451	Atlanta	25	27	.481
Pittsburgh	21	33	.389	San Diego	18	36	.333

"Mini" Play-offs—American League: New York defeated Milwaukee, 3 games to 2; Oakland defeated Kansas City, 3 games to 0; National League: Montreal defeated Philadelphia, 3 games to 2; Los Angeles defeated Houston, 3 games to 2.

Play-offs—American League: New York defeated Oakland, 3 games to 0; National League: Los Angeles defeated Montreal, 3 games to 2.

World Series—Los Angeles defeated New York, 4 games to 2.

All-Star Game (Municipal Stadium, Cleveland, Aug. 9): National League 5, American League 4.

Most Valuable Players—American League: Rollie Fingers, Milwaukee; National League: Mike Schmidt, Philadelphia.

Cy Young Memorial Awards (outstanding pitchers)—American League: Rollie Fingers; National League: Fernando Valenzuela, Los Angeles.

Managers of the Year—American League: Billy Martin, Oakland; National League: Whitey Herzog, St. Louis.

Rookies of the Year—American League: Dave Righetti, New York; National League: Fernando Valenzuela.

Leading Hitters—(Percentage) American League: Carney Lansford, Boston (.336); National League: Bill Madlock, Pittsburgh (.341). (Runs Batted In) American League: Eddie Murray, Baltimore (78); National League: Mike Schmidt, Philadelphia (91). (Home Runs) American League: tie, Tony Armas, Oakland; Dwight Evans, Boston; Bobby Grich, California; and Eddie Murray, Baltimore (22); National League: Mike Schmidt (31). (Hits) American League: Rickey Henderson, Oakland (135); National League: Pete Rose, Philadelphia (140).

Leading Pitchers—(Earned Run Average) American League: Steve McCatty, Oakland (2.32); National League: Nolan Ryan, Houston (1.69). (Victories) American League: tie, Dennis Martinez, Baltimore; Steve McCatty; Jack Morris, Detroit; and Pete Vuckovich, Milwaukee (14); National League: Tom Seaver, Cincinnati (14). (Strikeouts) American League: Len Barker, Cleveland (127); National League: Fernando Valenzuela, Los Angeles (180).

Professional—Minor Leagues, Class AAA

American Association (play-offs): Denver
International League (Governor's Cup): Columbus
Pacific Coast League (play-offs): Albuquerque

Amateur

NCAA Division I: Arizona State
NAIA: Grand Canyon (Arizona)
Little League World Series: Taiwan

Focus on Sports

With second-year forward Larry Bird setting the pace, the 1980–81 Celtics hung another championship banner in Boston Garden. Left, Bird fakes a Houston defender in the play-off finals.

BASKETBALL

Every time the Boston Celtics win a professional basketball championship, they add a new chapter to one of the shiniest success stories in all of sport. They added another one in 1980–81, when a new cast of characters, headed by second-year pro Larry Bird, carried them past the Houston Rockets, four games to two, in the championship series of the National Basketball Association (NBA) play-offs; it was the Celtics' 14th title in the 35-year history of the league. Indiana University, a perennial power in college basketball, rolled to its fourth NCAA men's championship. Louisiana Tech captured the women's collegiate crown.

THE PROFESSIONAL SEASON

In their march to the title, the Celtics fought through adversity as even the earlier Celtic teams of Bob Cousy and Bill Russell had never done. The story was not so much what they did in the finals against the Rockets as what they did in the semifinals against the Philadelphia '76ers.

Trailing three games to one in the best-of-seven series, the Celtics proceeded to win three unusually close games to eliminate the '76ers. The margins of victory were two points, two points, and one point. A swing of one basket in any of the games would have sent Philadelphia to the finals. The finish of each contest was a study in sustained excitement.

The '76ers apparently had the series won with 1:51 remaining in the fifth game in Boston. They had a 109–103 lead and possession of the basketball. Rookie guard Andrew Toney missed a jump shot, however, and the Celtics' Nate Archibald came back with a three-point play at the other end of the court. The Sixers became flustered and never scored again. Bird, who scored 32 points in the game, hit a jump shot, and forward M.L. Carr hit three free throws, to give Boston a 111–109 victory.

The next problem for the Celtics was to win in Philadelphia, something they had not done in 11 games over a two-year period. Again the '76ers took an early lead. Again the Celtics came back. With 2:16 left in the game, Boston took the lead, 96–95, but still needed two free throws by forward Cedric Maxwell, with only two seconds on the clock, to close out a 100–98 win.

The Boston Garden was packed and crazy for the final game of the series. By now the plot was familiar. The '76ers, led by forward Julius "Dr. J" Erving, took an 89–82 lead with 5:23 remaining. But then they fell apart, not scoring another basket in the game, and the Celtics climbed back again. The winning basket was another jumper by Bird. As a last-gasp in-bounds pass by the Sixers went awry, the scoreboard showed 91–90 in favor of Boston, and its fans poured onto the Garden floor.

After all this, the final series with Houston was a relatively quiet affair. The Rockets were a surprise finalist, becoming the first team with a losing record (40–42) in the regular season ever to reach the championship play-off series. Their major accomplishment was the elimination of the defending champion Los Angeles Lakers, two games to one, in the first round of post-season play.

The only spice in the final series was added by Rockets center Moses Malone, who continually criticized the Celtics. "I could find four other guys in my hometown in Petersburg, VA, and we could beat this team," he said. The two teams split the first four games, but then the Celtics won games 5 and 6 to take the crown. Maxwell was named most valuable player (MVP) of the play-offs after Boston's final win, 102–91, at The Summit in Houston.

The MVP for the regular season was Erving of the '76ers. Darrell Griffith of the Utah Jazz won rookie of the year honors, and Jack McKinney of the Indiana Pacers was named coach of the year. Adrian Dantley of the Jazz won the scoring championship with an average of 30.7 points per game, ending a three-year reign by San Antonio's George Gervin. Malone of Houston was the rebounding leader, averaging 14.8 per game. Calvin Murphy of Houston set a record for free-throw percentage with .947; in doing so he also topped Rick Barry's mark of 60 consecutive foul shots by hitting 78 in a row. Kevin Porter of the Washington Bullets led the NBA in assists, with a 9.1 per game average.

PROFESSIONAL BASKETBALL

National Basketball Association
(Final Standings, 1980–81)

Eastern Conference

Atlantic Division	W	L	Pct.
*Boston Celtics	62	20	.756
*Philadelphia '76ers	62	20	.756
*New York Knickerbockers	50	32	.610
Washington Bullets	39	43	.476
New Jersey Nets	24	58	.293
Central Division			
*Milwaukee Bucks	60	22	.732
*Chicago Bulls	45	37	.549
*Indiana Pacers	44	38	.537
Atlanta Hawks	31	51	.378
Cleveland Cavaliers	28	54	.341
Detroit Pistons	21	61	.256

Western Conference

Midwest Division	W	L	Pct.
*San Antonio Spurs	52	30	.634
*Houston Rockets	40	42	.488
*Kansas City Kings	40	42	.488
Denver Rockets	37	45	.451
Utah Jazz	28	54	.341
Dallas Mavericks	15	67	.183
Pacific Division			
*Phoenix Suns	57	25	.695
*Los Angeles Lakers	54	28	.659
*Portland Trail Blazers	45	37	.549
Golden State Warriors	39	43	.476
San Diego Clippers	36	46	.439
Seattle SuperSonics	34	48	.415

*Qualified for play-offs

Play-offs

Eastern Conference

First Round	Philadelphia	2 games	Indiana	0
	Chicago	2 games	New York	0
Semifinals	Boston	4 games	Chicago	0
	Philadelphia	4 games	Milwaukee	3
Finals	Boston	4 games	Philadelphia	3

Western Conference

First Round	Houston	2 games	Los Angeles	1
	Kansas City	2 games	Portland	1
Semifinals	Houston	4 games	San Antonio	3
	Kansas City	4 games	Phoenix	3
Finals	Houston	4 games	Kansas City	1
Championship	Boston	4 games	Houston	2
All-Star Game:	East 123, West 120			

Individual Honors

Most Valuable Player: Julius Erving, Philadelphia
Most Valuable Player (play-offs): Cedric Maxwell, Boston
Most Valuable Player (all-star game): Nate Archibald, Boston
Rookie of the Year: Darrell Griffith, Utah
Coach of the Year: Jack McKinney, Indiana
Leading Scorer: Adrian Dantley, Utah; 2,452 points, 30.7 per game
Leading Rebounder: Moses Malone, Houston; 14.8 per game

In the college game, Ralph Sampson stood head and shoulders above the crowd. The sophomore center won the Adolph Rupp Trophy as men's player of the year.

UPI

Harley Soltes/"Eugene Register-Guard"

Lori Scott of Louisiana Tech drives to the hoop in the AIAW championship game against Tennessee. Tech won the game, ending the season undefeated.

COLLEGE BASKETBALL

Conference Champions*

Atlantic Coast: North Carolina
Big East: Syracuse
Big Eight: Kansas
Big Sky: Idaho
Big Ten: Indiana
East Coast: St. Joseph's
Eastern Athletic: Pittsburgh
Ivy League: Princeton
Metro: Louisville
Mid-American: Ball State
Missouri Valley: Creighton
Ohio Valley: Western Kentucky
Pacific-10: Oregon State
Pacific Coast Athletic: Fresno State
Southeastern: Mississippi
Southern: Tennessee-Chattanooga
Southland: Lamar
Southwest: Houston
Southwestern Athletic: Southern
Sun Belt: Virginia Commonwealth
West Coast Athletic: San Francisco
Western Athletic: Utah, Wyoming (co-champions)

*Based on post-season conference tournaments, where applicable

Tournaments

NCAA: Indiana
NIT: Tulsa
NCAA Div. II: Florida Southern
NCAA Div. III: Potsdam State
NAIA: Bethany Nazarene College
AIAW (Women): Louisiana Tech

THE COLLEGE SEASON

The major question before the NCAA final game at the Spectrum in Philadelphia was not whether Indiana would beat North Carolina or North Carolina would beat Indiana, but whether the game would be played at all. Earlier in the day, President Ronald Reagan had been wounded by an assassin's bullet, and many urged that the game be postponed.

NCAA authorities stalled until they received word that Reagan was out of danger. They decided at last to have the game played and, after a moment of silence in the filled arena, Indiana went onto the court and completed an impressive glide to the title with a 63–50 win.

Indiana, a team which at the beginning of the season coach Bobby Knight (*see* BIOGRAPHY) hoped "could be competitive," was clearly the best in the country by the end. Its 13-point win in the final was its narrowest margin of victory in five NCAA tournament games. The Big Ten champs rocked Louisiana State, 67–49, in the semifinals, while North Carolina defeated Atlantic Coast Conference rival Virginia, 78–65.

The biggest news of the 48-team tournament came on the first day of competition. Favorites fell everywhere. DePaul, which for the second straight year came into the tournament as the top-ranked team in the nation, exited early for the second straight year. This time the Blue Demons lost, 49–48, on a game-ending shot by John Smith of St. Joseph's College. Second-ranked Oregon State lost to Kansas State, 50–48, and third-ranked Arizona State lost to Kansas, 88–71. The most dramatic loss of all was sustained by defending champion Louisville, which was ousted, 74–73, on a desperation midcourt shot by U.S. Reed of Arkansas.

The tournament MVP was Indiana guard Isiah Thomas, a sophomore. Sophomore center Ralph Sampson (7′4″, or 2.24 m) of Virginia won the Adolph Rupp Trophy as the outstanding men's player of the year. Danny Ainge of Brigham Young, whose full-court drive to beat the clock eliminated Notre Dame 51–50, was voted player of the year by several organizations.

Tulsa outlasted Syracuse, 86–84, in overtime to win the National Invitational Tournament (NIT) in New York City.

Louisiana Tech easily defeated Tennessee, 79–59, to win the AIAW (women's) championship. In doing so, the Lady Techsters completed an undefeated (34–0) season. Angela Turner, who scored 16 points for Tech in the final, was the tournament MVP. Lynette Woodard of Kansas received the Margaret Wade Trophy as the nation's top women's college basketball player.

LEIGH MONTVILLE, *"The Boston Globe"*

BOXING

In 1981, World Boxing Council (WBC) welterweight champion Sugar Ray Leonard emerged as the most celebrated figure in boxing by virtue of two classic performances.

In his fight with World Boxing Association (WBA) junior welterweight champion Ayub Kalule on June 25, Leonard's speed and right-hand leads dominated the action against the southpaw from Uganda. Toward the end of the ninth round, Leonard connected with a combination that sent Kalule to the canvas. Sugar Ray had a new title, but he still faced one major problem—Thomas Hearns, the WBA welterweight title holder.

"The Showdown" between Leonard and Hearns to unify the welterweight title was held at Caesars Palace Sports Pavilion in Las Vegas on September 16, in front of 24,000 screaming fans, joined by millions more via worldwide closed-circuit television. Leonard, the 6-5 betting underdog, faced an opponent 4 inches (10 cm) taller, with a reach 4 inches longer and a devastating right hand that had stopped 30 of 32 opponents and earned Hearns the nickname "Hitman."

Hearns dominated the early rounds, unleashing his long jab while stalking Leonard. Sugar Ray first circled his angular opponent, then stood his ground waiting for his chance. In the sixth round, a sudden Leonard flurry hurt Hearns and turned the tide in Ray's favor, but Leonard was too arm-weary to finish his man. Hearns, using his reach to full advantage, moved backward and kept Leonard off while piling up points. In the 13th, Leonard finally caught up with the retreating Hearns and punished him with combinations to the head. Hearns fell, but it was ruled a slip. Leonard again volleyed and Hearns again fell, but this time there was no question as to the cause. The next round produced more of the same, and it was clear to referee Davey Pearl that Hearns could no longer defend himself. Sugar Ray was pronounced the undisputed welterweight champion of the world at 1:45 of the 14th round.

Although Ray Leonard was the brightest star in boxing's firmament, there were other shining lights. Two men became three-time world champions, the fifth and sixth fighters ever to do so. Wilfred Benitez used a merciless right hand to end the WBC junior middleweight reign of Maurice Hope and claim his own third world crown. Alexis Arguello easily gained a 15-round decision over WBC lightweight champ Jim Watt on June 20, also winning a third world title.

In what had to be the shortest important fight of the year, heralded heavyweight Gerrie Cooney needed just four seconds to knock out an aging Ken Norton. Michael Spinks followed his brother Leon's championship lead by defeating Eddie Mustafa Muhammad for the WBA light heavyweight title. Sammy Serrano regained the WBA junior lightweight crown he had lost to Yasutsune Uehara in 1980. Cornelius Boza-Edwards became the WBC junior lightweight champ with a unanimous decision over Rafael "Bazooka" Limon, but he lost it just months later to Rolando Navarette. Antonio Avelar knocked out Soji Oguma in the seventh round to become the WBC flyweight champ, while Santos Laciar lost his WBA flyweight crown to Luis Ibarra by decision. Laciar had won the crown from Peter Mathebula only months before.

Many of the events affecting boxing in 1981 took place in the courtroom. Sean O'Grady, who had soundly beaten Hilmer Kenty by unanimous decision, was stripped of his WBA lightweight title by U.S. District Court Judge Stanley Brotman, who had ordered the winner to fight Trinidadian Claude Noel within 90 days. O'Grady refused, and Noel was declared champion.

Promoter Don King and the WBC were codefendants in a suit brought by another promoter, Teddy Brenner, who charged that they conspired to monopolize the ratings and championships. The jury ruled in favor of King and the WBC.

In the most bizarre incident of the year, the "This is It" four-bout championship card scheduled for February 23 at New York's Madison Square Garden was canceled amid a scandal involving the alleged embezzlement of $21.3 million from the Wells Fargo Bank by promoter Ross Fields (alias Howard J. Smith).

The year saw the passing of former champs Joe Louis, Mickey Walker, Lew Jenkins, and Fidel LaBarbra.

BERT RANDOLPH SUGAR, *"The Ring" Magazine*

World Boxing Champions
(Year of achieving title in parentheses)

Junior Flyweight—Katsuo Tokashiki, Japan (1981), World Boxing Association (WBA); Hilario Zapata, Panama (1980), World Boxing Council (WBC).
Flyweight—Luis Ibarra, Panama (1981), WBA; Antonio Avelar, Mexico (1981), WBC.
Bantamweight—Jeff Chandler, Philadelphia (1980), WBA; Lupe Pintor, Mexico (1979), WBC.
Junior Featherweight—Sergio Palma, Argentina (1980), WBA; Wilfredo Gomez, Puerto Rico (1977), WBC.
Featherweight—Eusebio Pedroza, Panama (1978), WBA; Salvador Sanchez, Mexico (1980), WBC.
Junior Lightweight—Sammy Serrano, Puerto Rico (1981), WBA; Rolando Navarette, the Philippines (1981), WBC.
Lightweight—Arturo Frias (1981), WBA; Alexis Arguello, Nicaragua (1981), WBC.
Junior Welterweight—Aaron Pryor, Cincinnati (1980), WBA; Saoul Mamby, New York City (1980), WBC.
Welterweight—Ray Leonard, Palmer Park, MD (1980), WBA and WBC.
Junior Middleweight—Tadashi Mihara, Japan (1981), WBA; Wilfred Benitez, Bronx, NY (1981), WBC.
Middleweight—Marvin Hagler, Brockton, MA (1980), WBA and WBC.
Light Heavyweight—Michael Spinks, St. Louis, MO (1981), WBA; Dwight Braxton, Camden, NJ (1981), WBC.
Heavyweight—Mike Weaver, Gatesville, TX (1980), WBA; Larry Holmes, Easton, PA (1978), WBC.

FOOTBALL

With a victory in the 1981 Orange Bowl, Clemson emerged as the No. 1 collegiate football team in the United States. Following an unusually exciting series of play-off games, the San Francisco 49ers and the Cincinnati Bengals went to the Super Bowl, both for the first time. Led by quarterback Joe Montana, the 49ers won Super Bowl XVI, 26-21. The 49ers scored two touchdowns in the first half after turnovers by the Bengals and four field goals.

THE PROFESSIONAL SEASON

At least the Super Bowl combatants did not have to be concerned about the weather in the roof-protected Silverdome in Pontiac, MI. That was a far cry from the American Football Conference (AFC) championship game, hereafter to be known as the second "Ice Bowl," in which the Bengals managed to dispatch the San Diego Chargers, 27-7. For the record, the first "Ice Bowl" was the National Football Conference's title contest at Green Bay in 1967.

AFC. At Cincinnati's Riverfront Stadium for the AFC showdown on Jan. 10, 1982, the Bengals and the Chargers had to cope with −9° F (−23° C) weather and a wind-chill factor of −54° F (−48° C) with gusts that reached 35 mi per hour (56 km/h). The brunt of the climatic conditions fell on the Chargers. San Diego had not played in freezing weather since a victory over the Vikings in Bloomington, MN, in 1978. To add to their discomfort, the Chargers only eight days before had endured 80° F (27° C) in Miami to beat the Dolphins in an overtime battle, 41-38, for the right to play the Bengals.

The AFC title finale had been expected to be a high-scoring, explosive affair. The Chargers' offense, nicknamed Air Coryell after its pass-minded coach, Don Coryell, had racked up the third most touchdowns (61) and the second highest total of points (478) in a National Football League season. And Cincinnati's point-making machine had not been far behind (421).

At the crucial position, quarterback, the elements hampered San Diego's Dan Fouts more than they did Ken Anderson. The cold passing hand went to Fouts, who admitted afterward that he could not grip the frozen ball properly. The winds also virtually nullified San Diego's long-ball aerial attack. Coming off a season in which he bettered his own NFL record by throwing for 4,802 yards, Fouts found his passes fluttering and sailing short of their mark. An important play that typified Fouts' plight occurred late in the second period with the Chargers, trailing by 17-7, driving to the Cincinnati 21. He tried to connect with his all-pro tight end, Kellen Winslow, in the end zone. But the wind held up the ball and Bobby Kemp, the Bengal safety, intercepted in front of Winslow.

Anderson, who was named AFC quarterback of the year, was more successful with a short passing game and threw for two TDs.

The Bengals never trailed. They went ahead in the seventh minute of action on Jim Breech's 31-yard field goal. Then the first of four turnovers proved damaging to the Chargers. James Brooks fumbled away the kickoff return on the San Diego 18. A minute later Cincinnati tallied on an 8-yard pass to M. L. Harris.

In its one scoring sally San Diego capped a 55-yard advance as Winslow, taking a screen

PROFESSIONAL FOOTBALL

National Football League
Final Standings

AMERICAN CONFERENCE

Eastern Division

	W	L	T	Pct.	Points For	Points Agst.
Miami	11	4	1	.719	345	275
Jets	10	5	1	.656	355	287
Buffalo	10	6	0	.625	311	276
Baltimore	2	14	0	.125	259	533
New England	2	14	0	.125	322	370

Central Division

	W	L	T	Pct.	Points For	Points Agst.
Cincinnati	12	4	0	.750	421	304
Pittsburgh	8	8	0	.500	356	297
Houston	7	9	0	.438	281	355
Cleveland	5	11	0	.313	276	375

Western Division

	W	L	T	Pct.	Points For	Points Agst.
San Diego	10	6	0	.625	478	390
Denver	10	6	0	.625	321	289
Kansas City	9	7	0	.563	343	290
Oakland	7	9	0	.438	273	343
Seattle	6	10	0	.375	322	388

Play-offs

Buffalo 31, Jets 27
Cincinnati 28, Buffalo 21
San Diego 41, Miami 38
Cincinnati 27, San Diego 7

NATIONAL CONFERENCE

Eastern Division

	W	L	T	Pct.	Points For	Points Agst.
Dallas	12	4	0	.750	367	277
Philadelphia	10	6	0	.625	368	221
Giants	9	7	0	.563	295	257
Washington	8	8	0	.500	347	349
St. Louis	7	9	0	.438	315	408

Central Division

	W	L	T	Pct.	Points For	Points Agst.
Tampa Bay	9	7	0	.563	315	268
Detroit	8	8	0	.500	397	322
Green Bay	8	8	0	.500	324	361
Minnesota	7	9	0	.438	325	369
Chicago	6	10	0	.375	253	324

Western Division

	W	L	T	Pct.	Points For	Points Agst.
S. Francisco	13	3	0	.813	357	250
Atlanta	7	9	0	.438	426	355
Los Angeles	6	10	0	.375	303	351
New Orleans	4	12	0	.250	207	378

Play-offs

Giants 27, Philadelphia 21
San Francisco 38, Giants 24
Dallas 38, Tampa Bay 0
San Francisco 28, Dallas 27

Super Bowl: San Francisco 26, Cincinnati 21

UPI

With seconds remaining, San Francisco's Dwight Clark (87) grabs the winning TD pass as the 49ers defeat the Dallas Cowboys, 28–27.

pass, ran 33 yards into the end zone early in the second quarter. Pete Johnson's 1-yard plunge made it 17-7 for the Bengals before the half.

Breech's second field goal, a 38-yarder midway in the third period, increased the margin to 20-7, and Cincinnati locked up the decision with a time-consuming, 68-yard drive in the last quarter, capped by Anderson's 3-yard toss to Don Bass.

The irony of the finest season of Anderson's 11-year pro career was that he almost lost his job in the opening game. Not up to par in recent years because of injuries, he had become a target for the Cincinnati boo-birds. After three early interceptions in the opener, Anderson was benched and Turk Schonert rallied the Bengals to a 27-21 victory over the Seattle Seahawks.

Coach Forrest Gregg nearly relegated Anderson to the sidelines for the second game but decided to stick with him. From there on Anderson, who started every game, compiled his glittering statistics: 300 completions in 479 attempts for a 62.6% completion ratio and 29 touchdowns. As befits the owner of the lowest interception percentage in the league record book, he was intercepted only ten times. Anderson also had the benefit of a protective line, headed by Tony Munoz, an all-pro 278-lb (126-kg) tackle. A vital first-time contributor to the Bengals' success was Cris Collinsworth, a fast and sure-handed rookie wide receiver from Florida, who caught 67 passes. The major factor in the Cincinnati ground attack was 250-lb (113-kg) Johnson, who stayed healthy and rushed for 1,077 yards on 274 carries. The result of all this was that the Bengals, who finished in last place in the AFC Central with a 6-10 mark in 1980, rebounded to the top of the conference with the best record (12-4), which gave them the homefield advantage for the play-offs.

The NFC. In marked contrast to the arctic conditions in Cincinnati, the NFC championship was decided in a mild (58° F; 14° C) and sunny climate in San Francisco's Candlestick Park. In a melodramatic finish, the 49ers prevailed over the Cowboys, 28-27, in the last 58 seconds. Joe Montana's 6-yard toss to Dwight Clark, who leaped high for the ball in the end zone, tied the score and Ray Wersching's conversion provided the difference.

On the winning 89-yard drive, Coach Bill Walsh fooled Dallas, which was using its nickel defense (six backs and one linebacker), anticipating an aerial barrage. Walsh mixed up his signal-calling so well (six of the 13 plays were rushes) that the Cowboys acknowledged later that on the scoring play they could not guess pass or run. Lenvil Elliott, a late pickup and playing only because Ricky Patton was injured, made the limelight with several key rushes.

The Cowboys put on a last-minute threat, reaching the San Francisco 44 and needing only one or two gains to be in the field-goal range of their all-pro kicker, Rafael Septien. But Danny White was sacked for the fourth time and fumbled, the 49ers recovering the ball.

Early in the fourth period the Cowboys had gone ahead, 27-21, for the third time in the close contest. White tossed 21 yards to Doug Cosbie, ending a 50-yard march, which was set up by Everson Walls, Dallas' rookie star at cornerback, when he pounced on Walt Easley's fumble. That was the sixth turnover for the 49ers, a high number that usually leads to defeat. They also had to surmount a controversial pass-interference call that prevented a 49er TD.

Montana, as he did all season, sparked the 49ers with three scoring passes. The former Notre Damer, who was in his first full campaign at the San Francisco helm and his third year as a pro, became the highest-rated passer in the NFC by completing 311 of 488 attempts for 3,565 yards and 19 touchdowns. Montana is the third current top quarterback to be developed by Walsh. The San Francisco head man, in prior stints as an assistant coach, molded Anderson from his rookie days and later helped Fouts to join the elite.

Like the Bengals, the 49ers rebounded from a 6-10 record and third place in the NFC West in 1980. Already noted for his offensive wizardry, Walsh concentrated on upgrading his porous defensive unit in 1981. In a rare move, he made three defensive backs high draft choices: Ronnie Lott of USC, Eric Wright of Missouri, and Carlton Williamson of Pittsburgh. They became instant starters, with Dwight Hicks the only holdover from the 1980 secondary. Lott, who was the No. 1 pick, received all-pro accolades.

Walsh also was fortunate to obtain Fred Dean midway in the season when the pass-rush specialist was traded by the Chargers after a salary dispute. The 49er coach solidified his linebacking corps by dealing for Jack Reynolds, a steady veteran, who was disenchanted with the Los Angeles Rams.

Regular Season. A distinction for the 49ers and the Bengals was that they were the first teams to reach the Super Bowl after posting losing records in 1980. Other teams that shot up spectacularly to attain play-off berths were the Tampa Bay Buccaneers, who went from 5-10-1 to 9-7; the Giants, from 4-12 to 9-7, and the Jets, from 4-12 to 10-5-1. After a long play-off drought, the Giants, with a valuable contribution from defensive rookie-of-the-year linebacker Lawrence Taylor, and the Jets, with two specialists in sacks—Joe Klecko and Mark Gastineau—brought on delirium in their fans when they gained wild-card places. The Giants had been out of post-season competition since 1963 and the Jets since 1970 following the Joe Namath-inspired upset of the Baltimore Colts in Super Bowl III.

Showing an equally sharp reversal of fortune—but downward—were the Oakland Raiders, the Atlanta Falcons, the Cleveland Browns, and the Rams. The Raiders' fall was the most noteworthy. After being the first wild-card team to win the Super Bowl in January 1981, Oakland stumbled badly early in the season. Jim Plunkett, the most valuable player in the Super Bowl, performed so poorly that he was benched after the sixth game.

Two other players deserve mention for their regular-season performances—George Rogers of the New Orleans Saints, who led the NFL in rushing (1,674 yards), and Tony Dorsett of the Cowboys, who was second in rushing (1,646 yards).

THE COLLEGE SEASON

It could well be said of the 1981 college football season, "Uneasy lies the head that wears a crown." Never before were so many teams accorded the honor of being ranked No. 1 in the country so quickly deposed. Here is the upset-strewn tale:

No. 1. Michigan was rated the king of the hill before the blocking and tackling began in earnest, and the Wolverines promptly tumbled in their opener, a 21–14 loss to Wisconsin. Notre Dame moved up and was immediately dethroned by a rebounding Michigan, 25–7. The Irish, under their new head coach, Gerry Faust, were to falter to a 5–6 record for their first losing season since 1963.

Southern California was the next No. 1, for two weeks, before Arizona humbled the Trojans, 13–10. Then it was the turn of Texas, and the Longhorns stepped down after losing to Arkansas, 42–11. Penn State followed in the top spot for a week before succumbing to Miami, 17–14. Pittsburgh then managed the longest reign of the year, four weeks, until Penn State administered a 48–14 walloping in the regular-session finale. Whom did that leave before the bowl games for the wire-service polls to select for what had proved to be a jinxed distinction?

It left Clemson. Unheralded and unranked before the season, the Tigers were the only major

On November 28, Bear Bryant won his 315th game—the most ever by a college football coach.

UPI

COLLEGE FOOTBALL

Conference Champions

Atlantic Coast—Clemson
Big Eight—Nebraska
Big Sky—Idaho State
Big Ten—Iowa, Ohio State (tied)
Ivy League—Yale, Dartmouth (tied)
Mid-American—Toledo
Missouri Valley—Tulsa
Pacific Coast Athletic—San Jose State
Pacific Ten—Washington
Southeastern—Georgia, Alabama (tied)
Southern—Furman
Southwest—Southern Methodist
Western Athletic—Brigham Young

Heisman Trophy—Marcus Allen, USC
Lombardi Trophy—Kenneth Sims, University of Texas

NCAA Champions

Division I-AA—Idaho State
Division II—Southwest Texas State
Division III—Widener

NAIA Champions

Division I—Elon
Divison II—Austin and Concordia

Major Bowl Games

Holiday Bowl (San Diego, CA, Dec. 18)—Brigham Young 38, Washington State 36
California Bowl (Fresno, CA, Dec. 19)—Toledo 27, San Jose State 25
Tangerine Bowl (Orlando, FL, Dec. 19)—Missouri 19, Southern Mississippi 17
Sun Bowl (El Paso, TX, Dec. 26)—Oklahoma 40, Houston 14
Gator Bowl (Jacksonville, FL, Dec. 28)—North Carolina 31, Arkansas 27
Liberty Bowl (Memphis, TN, Dec. 30)—Ohio State 31, Navy 28
Bluebonnet Bowl (Houston, TX, Dec. 31)—Michigan 33, UCLA 14
Hall of Fame Bowl (Birmingham, AL, Dec. 31)—Mississippi State 10, Kansas 0
Peach Bowl (Atlanta, GA, Dec. 31)—West Virginia 26, Florida 6
Cotton Bowl (Dallas, TX, Jan. 1)—Texas 14, Alabama 12
Fiesta Bowl (Tempe, AZ, Jan. 1)—Penn State 26, Southern Cal 10
Orange Bowl (Miami, FL, Jan. 1)—Clemson 22, Nebraska 15
Rose Bowl (Pasadena, CA, Jan. 1)—Washington 28, Iowa 0
Sugar Bowl (New Orleans, LA, Jan. 1)—Pittsburgh 24, Georgia 20

Final College Rankings

	AP Writers	UPI Coaches		AP Writers	UPI Coaches
1	Clemson	Clemson	6	Georgia	Alabama
2	Texas	Pittsburgh	7	Alabama	Washington
3	Penn State	Penn State	8	Miami (FL)	North Carolina
4	Pittsburgh	Texas	9	North Carolina	Nebraska
5	Southern Methodist	Georgia	10	Washington	Michigan

eleven to survive the regular season undefeated and untied. And yet Clemson had not convinced all observers of its right to the No. 1 ranking and even was deemed to be an underdog in its Orange Bowl confrontation with No. 4 Nebraska. Coach Danny Ford and the Tigers' fans were particularly resentful of talk of Clemson's having a weak schedule and of the Atlantic Coast Conference being more noteworthy for basketball than for football.

But Clemson finally ended the 1981 hoodoo over the holder of the top spot by defeating Nebraska, 22–15, in the Orange Bowl and clinching the title of national champion. The Tigers silenced the disbelievers with an opportunistic offense that produced a 22–7 lead and a stubborn defense that thwarted Nebraska's fourth-quarter rally. Heroes for Clemson were Homer Jordan, the junior quarterback who passed for 134 yards, including a 13-yard scoring strike to Perry Tuttle, and Jeff Davis, a senior line-backer, who made seven tackles and recovered a Cornhusker fumble that set up a major second-period touchdown.

Bowl Games. The bowl games provided Georgia, ranked No. 2, and Alabama, No. 3, with a last opportunity to claim the title in case Clemson was beaten by Nebraska. But both challengers lost.

Georgia, the undefeated national champion of 1980 thanks to the extraordinary talents of freshman Herschel Walker, was upended by Pitt, 24–20, in the Sugar Bowl. Dan Marino, the Panthers' star quarterback, threw for three touchdowns, the last one with 35 seconds left, to beat the Bulldogs and outshine Walker. The latter scored twice but was held to 84 yards, his lowest one-game rushing total of the season. Alabama lost to Texas, 14–12, in the Cotton Bowl when the Longhorns fashioned two scoring drives in the last period.

Honors. But the season was still a memorable one for coach Paul (Bear) Bryant of Alabama. At the age of 68, he achieved a long-sought goal by posting his 315th victory as the Crimson Tide downed Auburn, 28–17. It had taken Amos Alonzo Stagg 57 years of coaching to establish the previous record of 314, which he set in 1946. Bryant, who received his nickname after he wrestled a bear in his youth, compiled his total in 37 seasons as head coach at Maryland (1945), Kentucky (1946–53), Texas A & M (1954–57), and Alabama (1958–).

The 47th Heisman Memorial Trophy went to Marcus Allen, the latest in a lengthening line of all-America tailbacks at USC. The 6′2″ (1.9 m) 202-lb (92-kg) workhorse earned the cherished trophy by becoming the first collegian to rush for more than 2,000 yards in a season. He gained 2,342 yards, an average of 5.8 yards a carry, and set or tied 12 National Collegiate Athletic Association (NCAA) records. The previous mark of 1,948 yards was made in 1976 by Tony Dorsett of Pittsburgh. In being voted the nation's outstanding player, Allen followed in the steps of three other USC backs—Mike Garrett (1965), O. J. Simpson (1968), and Charles White (1979). Walker of Georgia was second in the balloting.

LUD DUROSKA
"The New York Times"

GOLF

Texans Bill Rogers and Tom Kite produced the fireworks in the 1981 Tournament Professionals Association Tour, the new name for the Professional Golfers Association (PGA) Tour.

Rogers, who had won only one tournament in the United States in six previous seasons on tour, overcame an early-season slump to win the Heritage Classic, the British Open, the World Series of Golf, and the Texas Open. The 30-year-old Texarkana resident was named Player of the Year by the PGA, ending Tom Watson's four-year domination of that honor.

Kite, a 32-year-old from Austin in his ninth full season on tour, won only once, at the Inverrary Classic in March, but he was the talk of the golf world the last half of the season. He finished eighth or better in 17 of his last 18 tournaments, won the Vardon Trophy with a scoring average of 69.8, and finished as the No. 1 money-winner with $375,699. Kite topped the *Golf Digest* Performance Averages with an .815 percentage that has been bettered by only three other players and was named the magazine's Most Improved Male Professional.

Raymond Floyd, winner of the Tournament Players Championship, finished second in the money race with $359,360. Watson, who won the Masters in April and two other tournaments before slumping in the second half of the year, was third with $347,660, and Bruce Lietzke finished fourth with $343,446. Rogers was fifth with $315,411. It was the first time that many players earned more than $300,000 in one season.

David Graham shot an impeccable final-round 67 at Merion to win the U.S. Open with a seven-under-par 273, and Larry Nelson outsteadied the field to win the PGA championship.

Honors on the Ladies Professional Golfers Association (LPGA) tour were as fragmented as on the men's circuit. Donna Caponi won five tournaments, including her second LPGA crown, for the second straight year, but money-winning honors went to Beth Daniel. Miss Daniel tied for second in the year's final tournament, the Mazda Classic in Japan, to win $19,600 and edge JoAnne Carner by $329 with a total of $206,978. It was the second straight money title for Miss Daniel, who also topped the *Golf Digest* Performance Averages with a .681 mark. Mrs. Carner, a four-time money-winner, won the Vare Trophy with a scoring average of 71.75. Jan Stephenson was the recipient of *Golf Digest*'s Most Improved Female Professional award.

Veteran Kathy Whitworth became the first woman to go over the million-dollar mark in earnings, an exploit which earned her *Golf Digest*'s Comeback of the Year award. Mrs. Carner and Miss Caponi also surpassed the million-dollar barrier, and by the end of the year Mrs. Carner had become the all-time leading money-winner in women's golf with $1,042,545.

LARRY DENNIS, *Senior Editor, "Golf Digest"*

GOLF

TPA (PGA) 1981 Tournament Winners

Joe Garagiola-Tucson Open: Johnny Miller (265)
Bob Hope Desert Classic: Bruce Lietzke (335)
Phoenix Open: David Graham (268)
Bing Crosby National Pro-Am: John Cook (209)
Andy Williams-San Diego Open: Bruce Lietzke (278)
Hawaiian Open: Hale Irwin (265)
Glen Campbell-Los Angeles Open: Johnny Miller (270)
Bay Hill Classic: Andy Bean (266)
American Motors-Inverrary Classic: Tom Kite (274)
Doral-Eastern Open: Raymond Floyd (273)
Tournament Players Championship: Raymond Floyd (285)
Sea Pines-Heritage Classic: Bill Rogers (278)
Greater Greensboro Open: Larry Nelson (281)
Masters Tournament: Tom Watson (280)
MONY-Tournament of Champions: Lee Trevino (273)
Tallahassee Open: Dave Eichelberger (271)
USF&G New Orleans Open: Tom Watson (270)
Michelob-Houston Open: Ron Streck (198)
Byron Nelson Classic: Bruce Lietzke (281)
Colonial National Invitation: Fuzzy Zoeller (274)
Memorial Tournament: Keith Fergus (284)
Kemper Open: Craig Stadler (270)
Atlanta Classic: Tom Watson (277)
Manufacturers Hanover-Westchester Classic: Raymond Floyd (275)
U.S. Open: David Graham (273)
Danny Thomas-Memphis Classic: Jerry Pate (274)
Western Open: Ed Fiori (277)
Greater Milwaukee Open: Jay Haas (274)
Quad Cities Open: Dave Barr (270)
Anheuser-Busch Classic: John Mahaffey (276)
Canadian Open: Peter Oosterhuis (280)
PGA Championship: Larry Nelson (273)
Sammy Davis, Jr.-Greater Hartford Open: Hubert Green (264)
Buick Open: Hale Irwin (277)
World Series of Golf: Bill Rogers (275)
B.C. Open: Jay Haas (270)
Pleasant Valley Classic: Jack Renner (273)
LaJet Classic: Tom Weiskopf (278)
Hall of Fame: Morris Hatalsky (275)
Texas Open: Bill Rogers (266)
Southern Open: J.C. Snead (271)
Pensacola Open: Jerry Pate (271)
National Team Championship: Vance Heafner and Mike Holland (246)

LPGA 1981 Tournament Winners

Whirlpool Championship of Deer Creek: Sandra Palmer (284)
Elizabeth Arden Classic: Sally Little (283)
S & H Golf Classic: JoAnne Carner (215)
Bent Tree Ladies Classic: Amy Alcott (276)
Arizona Copper Classic: Nancy Lopez-Melton (278)
Sun City Classic: Patty Hayes (277)
Desert Inn Pro-Am: Donna Caponi (286)
Women's Kemper Open: Pat Bradley (284)
Colgate-Dinah Shore: Nancy Lopez-Melton (277)
American Defender/WRAL Golf Classic: Donna Caponi (208)
Florida Lady Citrus: Beth Daniel (281)
Birmingham Classic: Beth Solomon (206)
CPC Women's International: Sally Little (287)
Lady Michelob: Amy Alcott (209)
Coca-Cola Classic: Kathy Whitworth (211)
Corning Classic: Kathy Hite (282)
Golden Lights Championship: Cathy Reynolds (285)
McDonald's Classic: Sandra Post (282)
LPGA Championship: Donna Caponi (280)
Lady Keystone Open: JoAnne Carner (203)
Sarah Coventry: Nancy Lopez-Melton (285)
Peter Jackson Classic: Jan Stephenson (278)
Mayflower Classic: Debbie Austin (279)
WUI Classic: Donna Caponi (282)
U.S. Women's Open: Pat Bradley (279)
Boston Five Classic: Donna Caponi (276)
Mary Kay Classic: Jan Stephenson (198)
World Championship of Women's Golf: Beth Daniel (284)
Columbia Savings LPGA Classic: JoAnne Carner (278)
Rail Charity Golf Classic: JoAnne Carner (205)
United Virginia Bank Golf Classic: Jan Stephenson (205)
Henredon Classic: Sandra Haynie (281)
Inamori Classic: Hollis Stacy (286)
Mazda Japan Classic: Patty Sheehan (213)

Other Tournaments

British Open: Bill Rogers (276)
U.S. Men's Amateur: Nathaniel Crosby
U.S. Women's Amateur: Julie Inkster
U.S. Men's Public Links: Jodie Mudd
U.S. Women's Public Links: Mary Enright
USGA Senior Men's Amateur: Dr. Ed Updegraff
USGA Senior Women's Amateur: Dorothy Porter
USGA Senior Open: Arnold Palmer
USGA Men's Mid-Amateur: Jim Holtgrieve
Ryder Cup: U.S., 18½; Europe, 9½
Walker Cup: U.S., 15; Great Britain-Ireland, 9

UPI

Pleasant Colony, trained by John Campo, won the Kentucky Derby and the Preakness.

HORSE RACING

Veteran campaigner John Henry was named Horse of the Year and became thoroughbred racing's all-time leading money winner in 1981. The 6-year-old gelding earned $1,798,030 during the year, to raise his career total to $3,022,810, breaking Spectacular Bid's record of $2,781,607.

John Henry, owned by the Dotsam Stable, won eight of ten starts in 1981, including a come-from-behind victory by a nose over The Bart in the Arlington Million, an international race with the richest purse in thoroughbred racing history. John Henry's other triumphs came in the San Luis Obispo Handicap, Santa Anita Handicap, San Luis Rey, Hollywood Invitational Turf Handicap, Sword Dancer Stakes, Jockey Club Gold Cup, and Oak Tree Invitational.

Pleasant Colony, owned by Buckland Farm, triumphed in the Kentucky Derby and Preakness but finished third in the Belmont, the third leg in the Triple Crown series. His victory in the Derby represented the first success for both his jockey, Jorge Velasquez, and trainer, John Campo, in a Triple Crown race. Velasquez had been winless in 18 previous Triple Crown rides, while Campo had failed 20 times.

In the two-year-old division, Timely Writer captured the prestigious Champagne Stakes by 4 3/4 lengths, and Deputy Minister reigned as champion colt. Before Dawn, a two-year-old filly representing Calumet Farm and trained by John Veitch, won five of six races and placed second in the Champagne.

Providential II, a four-year-old son of Run the Gantlet, won the Washington D.C. International and the Hollywood Turf Cup, two important grass races.

Harness Racing. Three-year-old Fan Hanover became the first filly to win the Little Brown Jug, the most famous event in pacing. Fan Hanover, the daughter of Albatross, won $497,717 in 1981, a record for a filly.

Quarter Horse Racing. Special Effort scored a four-length victory in the $1.53 million All American Futurity at Ruidoso Downs in New Mexico. He also finished first in the Kansas and Rainbow futurities, becoming the first winner of quarter horse racing's Triple Crown.

Horse Sales. A colt sired by Northern Dancer sold for a world-record $3.5 million at Keeneland's July Selected Yearling Sale.

JIM BOLUS, *Sports Department*
"The Louisville Times," Louisville, KY

HORSE RACING

Major U.S. Thoroughbred Races

Arlington Million: John Henry, $1,000,000 (value of race)
Beldame: Love Sign, $218,500
Belmont Stakes: Summing, $284,300
Brooklyn Handicap: Hechizado, $230,500
Californian: Eleven Stitches, $342,600
Champagne Stakes: Timely Writer, $150,250
Charles H. Strub Stakes: Super Moment, $235,000
Coaching Club American Oaks: Wayward Lass, $136,250
Hollywood Futurity: Stalwart, $715,100
Hollywood Invitational: John Henry, $200,000
Hollywood Turf Cup: Providential II, $550,500
Jockey Club Gold Cup: John Henry, $568,000
Kentucky Derby: Pleasant Colony, $413,450
Man o' War Stakes: Galaxy Libra, $165,300
Marlboro Cup: Noble Nashua, $400,000
Matron: Before Dawn, $135,350
Oak Tree Invitational: John Henry, $300,000
Preakness: Pleasant Colony, $270,800
Santa Anita Handicap: John Henry, $418,150
Spinster: Glorious Song, $164,700
Washington D.C. International: Providential II, $250,000
Wood Memorial: Pleasant Colony, $163,800
Woodward: Pleasant Colony, $229,000

Major U.S. Harness Races

Cane Pace: Wildwood Jeb, $373,850
Hambletonian: Shiaway St. Pat, $838,000
John Chapman Memorial: Three Diamonds, $284,200
Lawrence B. Sheppard: Icarus Lobell, $463,000
Meadowlands Pace: Conquered, $1,000,000
Mistletoe Shalee Pace: JEF's Eternity, $330,750
Peter Haughton Memorial: Soky's Atom, $512,800
Sweetheart Pace: Savilla Lobell, $700,000
Woodrow Wilson Memorial: McKenzie Almahurst, $1,760,000
World Trotting Derby: Panty Raid, $540,870

ICE HOCKEY

The 1980–81 National Hockey League (NHL) season was marked by glorious triumphs and surprising failures, by spectacular goal-scoring and frustrated defenses, and by the entrance of long-forgotten teams into the corps of hockey's elite. The New York Islanders became only the sixth franchise in the 64-year history of the league to win a second straight Stanley Cup. After finishing first in the regular-season standings, the Islanders were one of the few quality teams to perform well in a play-off that was full of upsets. There was no upset in the world amateur championship, won by the Soviet Union for the 14th time in 19 tournaments. The Soviets later won the Canada Cup series by beating the host team, made up of NHL stars, in the championship game, 8–1.

NHL. Of all the remarkable players in the league, there were two who dominated competition as few others ever have. Wayne Gretzky (*see also* Biography), Edmonton's 20-year-old center, scored a record 164 points on 55 goals and a record 109 assists. While leading his Oiler team to a play-off berth, Gretzky became the first player in NHL history to average at least two points per game over the 80-game regular season. Only New York Islander right wing Mike Bossy challenged Gretzky for new entries in the record book. Bossy, 24, became only the second player in history—and the first since Maurice Richard in 1944–45—to score 50 goals in the first 50 games of the regular season; Bossy finished with a league-leading 68 goals, the third-highest total ever, and had a record 85 goals including the play-offs.

The Islanders' march to the championship was ruthless and methodical. In the semifinal round they disposed of their rival New York Rangers in four games, and in the finals beat the Minnesota North Stars in five. Meanwhile, the other high-place finishers and perennial powers were felled in early rounds. Montreal, with a record 22 Stanley Cups, was defeated by upstart Edmonton in the first round; it was the Canadiens' worst showing in 11 years. The Philadelphia Flyers, Stanley Cup finalists the year before, were beaten by the Calgary Flames in the quarterfinals. The St. Louis Blues, who finished a surprising second during the regular season, were ousted by the Rangers in the quarterfinals.

If the biggest surprise of the play-offs was not the ease with which the Islanders repeated as champions, then it was Minnesota's ability to reach the final round. The North Stars had finished ninth during the regular season and drew the Boston Bruins as their first-round opponents. Having never beaten the Bruins at the Boston Garden in their 14 years in the league, the North Stars swept the first two games of the best-of-five series in Boston and clinched the series back in Minnesota. The North Stars went on to defeat Buffalo in five games and Calgary in six games to earn their first-ever berth in the finals. The Islanders, meanwhile, beat Toronto and Edmonton before facing the Rangers, who had upset the Isles in the 1979 semifinals. This time, however, the Islanders crushed the Rangers in the first two games at Nassau (Long Island) Coliseum, 5–2 and 7–3, and completed a stunning four-game sweep with 5–1 and 5–2 victories at Madison Square Garden.

By winning their first three games against Minnesota in the finals, the Islanders threatened to become the first team since the Bruins in 1970 to sweep the last two rounds of the play-offs. The Islanders took Games 1 and 2 by identical 6–3 scores at Nassau and then won 7–5 in Minnesota, as Butch Goring scored three goals. But the North Stars rallied for a 4–2 victory in Game 4, ending the Isles' streak. It was only their third loss in the play-offs, and it would be their last. The Islanders clinched the series back on Long

ICE HOCKEY

National Hockey League
(Final Standings, 1980–81)

Campbell Conference

					Goals	
Patrick Division	W	L	T	Pts	For	Against
*N.Y. Islanders	48	18	14	110	355	260
*Philadelphia	41	24	15	97	313	249
*Calgary	39	27	14	92	329	298
*N.Y. Rangers	30	36	14	74	312	317
Washington	26	36	18	70	286	317
Smythe Division						
*St. Louis	45	18	17	107	352	281
*Chicago	31	33	16	78	304	315
*Vancouver	28	32	20	76	289	301
*Edmonton	29	35	16	74	328	327
Colorado	22	45	13	57	258	344
Winnipeg	9	57	14	32	246	400

Wales Conference

Adams Division						
*Buffalo	39	20	21	99	327	250
*Boston	37	30	13	87	316	272
*Minnesota	35	28	17	87	292	263
*Quebec	30	32	18	78	314	318
*Toronto	28	37	15	71	322	367
Norris Division						
*Montreal	45	22	13	103	332	232
*Los Angeles	43	24	13	99	337	290
*Pittsburgh	30	37	13	73	302	345
Hartford	21	41	18	60	292	372
Detroit	19	43	18	56	252	339

*Made play-offs

Stanley Cup: New York Islanders

INDIVIDUAL HONORS

Hart Trophy (most valuable player): Wayne Gretzky, Edmonton Oilers
Ross Trophy (leading scorer): Wayne Gretzky
Vezina Trophy (top goaltender, shared): Richard Sevigny, Denis Herron, and Michel Larocque, Montreal Canadiens
Norris Trophy (best defenseman): Randy Carlyle, Pittsburgh Penguins
Selke Trophy (best defensive forward): Bob Gainey, Montreal Canadiens
Calder Trophy (rookie of the year): Peter Stastny, Quebec Nordiques
Lady Byng Trophy (sportsmanship): Rick Kehoe, Pittsburgh Penguins
Conn Smythe Trophy (most valuable in play-offs): Butch Goring, New York Islanders
Coach of the Year: Gordon "Red" Berenson, St. Louis Blues

Island with a 5–1 win; Butch Goring added two more goals. Goring won the Conn Smythe Trophy as the most valuable player in the play-offs, outpolling Bossy, who set a play-off record with 35 points, and Bryan Trottier, who set a record by scoring at least one point in all 18 of the Islanders' play-off games. En route to their second straight Stanley Cup, the Islanders set play-off records for most goals (97), most power-play goals (31), and most shorthanded goals (9). Their performance off the ice was nearly as impressive; just three years after plunging $22 million in debt, the club reported its largest profit ever—more than $1 million.

While the Islanders were the league's biggest winners, the biggest losers were the lowly Winnipeg Jets, who finished dead last and out of the play-offs for the second straight year. The Jets won only nine games and in one stretch went 30 games without a victory (0–23–7), the longest winless streak in NHL history. Winnipeg's first move after the season was to hire a new coach, Tom Watt. Among other coaching changes, Claude Ruel resigned from the Canadiens and Bob Berry resigned from the Los Angeles Kings; Berry then took over for Ruel, while Parker MacDonald was named to replace Berry in Los Angeles. But probably the most publicized switch came in New York: 1980 U.S. Olympic coach Herb Brooks was hired to succeed Craig Patrick at the helm of the Rangers; Patrick, Brooks' assistant at Lake Placid, was moved up to general manager.

World Cup. The national team of the Soviet Union won its third consecutive world championship in Goteborg, Sweden with a 13–1 rout of the host country. The Soviets, held scoreless in the first period, scored six times in the second period to clinch the title. Sweden, Czechoslovakia, and Canada rounded out the "A" pool of the tournament. The United States won the "B" pool.

PAT CALABRIA, *"Newsday"*

ICE SKATING

In a post-Olympic year when most winners have turned professional or retired, 1981 provided a crop of new amateur champions in figure skating. Americans did well. Scott Hamilton, a 22-year-old from Haverford, PA, won the world and United States senior men's singles titles and 15-year-old Elaine Zayak, a high school sophomore from Paramus, NJ, took the United States senior women's championship and finished second in the world tournament.

Hamilton, who is 5′3″ (1.6 m) tall and weighs 110 lbs (50 kg), went into the finals of the world competition trailing David Santee of Park Ridge, IL, but his performance in the five-minute free-skating segment gave him the crown, and Santee finished as runner-up.

Denise Biellmann of Switzerland, the new women's champion, brought a distinctive artistic style to her performance at Hartford, CT, in March. Although there were no perfect scores of 6.0, Miss Biellmann had ten 5.9s and five 5.8s in her 18 marks. Miss Zayak, who stressed an athletic style, compiled three 5.9s and nine 5.8s.

The world pairs championship was taken by the husband-and-wife team of Irina Vorobieva and Igor Lisovski of the Soviet Union. It was the 16th time in 17 years that a Soviet pair had captured the title. A British team of Jayne Torvill and Christopher Dean won the world dance gold medal.

In the United States championships in February at San Diego, CA, ten new champions were crowned. Hamilton, who had used skating as a means of combating a childhood illness that stunted his growth, received two perfect scores of 6.0 for composition and style in his freestyle segment. His lowest score was 5.8. Hamilton replaced Charles Tickner, a four-time champion from 1977–1980. Miss Zayak, whose early training on trampoline enabled her to execute seven triple-revolution jumps on her way to the title, replaced Linda Fratianne as champion. The brother-and-sister team of Caitlin and Peter Carruthers of Wilmington, DE, took the gold medal in senior pairs. Judy Blumberg of Tarzana, CA, and Michael Seibert of Washington, PA, won the dance.

Elaine Zayak, 15, of Paramus, NJ, took a silver medal in the world figure skating championships (below) and a gold in the U.S. tournament.

UPI

UPI

Phil Mahre slaloms to victory en route to an overall World Cup title, the first ever for an American.

Speed Skating. Amund Sjobrend of Norway and Natalya Petruseva of the Soviet Union won the world championships, and the world sprint titles went to Frode Roenning of Norway and Karin Enke of East Germany.

GEORGE DE GREGORIO
"The New York Times"

SKIING

Phil Mahre of Yakima, WA, became the first American ever to win the overall World Cup skiing championship in 1981, when he finished second in the giant slalom, the final event of the season, at Laax, Switzerland. The nine points he earned enabled him to beat Ingemar Stenmark of Sweden for the trophy by a score of 266–260 in the final standing.

Since the World Cup competition began in 1966–67, the men's overall title had never been won by a non-European. Nancy Greene of Canada won the women's crown twice (1967 and 1968).

Stenmark, who had taken the cup in 1976, 1977, and 1978, already had earned the maximum points in the giant slalom and his third-place finish did not reward him with a point. The victory in the final race went to Aleksandr Zhirov of the Soviet Union, who won for the fourth time in a row and served notice that the Soviets were ready to become formidable World Cup skiers.

Mahre's achievement was notable because in 1979 he had suffered a broken ankle at Lake Placid, NY, and it almost ended his career. He had thought of quitting the sport, but made a comeback and captured a silver medal in the slalom at the 1980 Winter Olympics. The broken ankle had required seven screws and a metal plate to set, and for three months Mahre hobbled on crutches.

In the three individual disciplines that make up the cup competition—slalom, giant slalom, and downhill—Stenmark emerged as the winner in the slalom (120 points) and giant slalom (125). Mahre finished third in the slalom and second in the giant slalom for an outstanding all-around performance that enabled him to pile up points and overtake Stenmark, who did not enter the downhill, his weakest discipline. The downhill title was won by Harti Weirather of Austria.

The women's overall title, after 28 events, went to Marie-Thérès Nadig of Switzerland, who beat out a countrywoman, Erika Hess, 289–251. Hanni Wenzel, the 1980 cup champion from Liechtenstein, finished third, with 241 points. Miss Nadig took the downhill title with 120 points, and Miss Hess captured the slalom with 125. The giant slalom was won by Tamara McKinney of Olympic Valley, CA, at 18 the youngest member of the U.S. team.

Utah took the NCAA crown by defeating Vermont 183–172 in Park City, UT.

GEORGE DE GREGORIO

SOCCER

For U.S. soccer, the year 1981 was one of flux, as professional franchises came and went and new champions were crowned in two of the country's three major leagues.

NASL. In the North American Soccer League (NASL), two new champions were crowned and neither of them was the New York Cosmos.

In the league's first full indoor program, the Edmonton Drillers came through to win the title, disposing of the Chicago Sting in the finals. It was the first title of any kind for the two-year-old Edmonton franchise, coached by Timo Liekoski, an indoor genius who previously had outstanding teams at Houston in the Major Indoor Soccer League (MISL).

In the outdoor season, the Sting won its first title ever and the first for a professional Chicago sports team in 18 years by edging the defending champion New York Cosmos, 1–0, in a shootout before 36,971 in Soccer Bowl-81 at Toronto's Exhibition Stadium. American Rudy Glenn scored the winning shootout goal for Chicago after the two teams had battled through 90 minutes of regulation time and two 7½-minute sudden-death overtimes without a goal.

New York and Chicago dominated the NASL during the regular season, finishing first and second in points among the league's 21 teams. Both clubs won 23 games, also tops in the league. In the play-offs, New York received a first-round bye, then eliminated Tampa Bay in three games and Fort Lauderdale in two. Chicago had a harder road. The Sting needed three games each to take care of Seattle, Montreal, and San Diego. It had to win the final two games at home in both the Montreal and San Diego series in order to advance. The latter series went to a third-game shootout, played in front of 40,000 fans at Comiskey Park in Chicago, a record soccer crowd for the Windy City. Chicago (Central), New York (Eastern), San Diego (Western), Vancouver (Northwest), and Atlanta (Southern) were the five division champions for the regular season.

Shortly after the play-offs, the Atlanta franchise suspended operations, citing $6 million in losses over three years. California, Washington, and Calgary also folded, and Dallas merged with Tampa Bay.

Among individual award winners, Cosmos striker Giorgio Chinaglia won the scoring championship and the most valuable player award (MVP) for the regular season. Chicago's Willy Roy was honored by his peers as the league's best coach, and midfielder Joe Morrone, Jr., of Tulsa won rookie of the year honors.

Rudy Glenn of the Chicago Sting celebrates his winning shootout goal in Soccer Bowl-81.

UPI

SOCCER

North American Soccer League
(Final Standings, 1981)

	W	L	G.F.	G.A.	Pts.
Eastern Division					
*New York	23	9	80	49	200
*Montreal	15	17	63	57	141
Washington	15	17	59	58	135
Toronto	7	25	39	82	77
Central Division					
*Chicago	23	9	84	50	195
*Minnesota	19	13	63	57	163
*Tulsa	17	15	60	49	154
Dallas	5	27	27	71	54
Southern Division					
*Atlanta	17	15	62	60	151
*Ft. Lau'dale	18	14	54	46	144
*Jacksonville	18	14	51	46	141
Tampa Bay	15	17	63	64	139
Western Division					
*San Diego	21	11	68	49	173
*Los Angeles	19	13	53	55	160
California	11	21	60	77	117
San Jose	11	21	44	78	108
Northwest Division					
*Vancouver	21	11	74	43	186
*Calgary	17	15	59	54	151
*Portland	17	15	52	49	141
*Seattle	15	17	60	62	137
Edmonton	12	20	60	79	123

*Made play-offs

NASL Champion: Chicago Sting
NASL MVP: Giorgio Chinaglia, New York Cosmos
NASL Indoor Champion: Edmonton Drillers

ASL Champion: Carolina Lightnin'
MISL Champion: New York Arrows
European Cup: Liverpool
NCAA Champion: University of Connecticut

ASL. The Carolina Lightnin', an expansion team, won the American Soccer League (ASL) championship by defeating New York United, 2–1, before a league record crowd of 20,103, in Charlotte, NC. Carolina trailed 1–0 before scoring two late goals to give Rodney Marsh, a former English international and standout player for the NASL's Tampa Bay Rowdies, his first title as a coach. In a major off-season move, first-year commissioner Mario Machado was fired.

MISL. It was the same old story in the Major Indoor Soccer League. Steve Zungul led the New York Arrows to the league championship, winning both the scoring title and MVP award in the process.

International. It was a year of both disappointment and achievement for the U.S. national soccer program.

The disappointment came when the U.S. National Team was eliminated from 1982 World Cup competition in a three-team round robin with Canada and Mexico. The U.S. team won only one game—the last—in the four-game series, but its 2–1 defeat of Mexico was its first victory over that country in 34 years.

The achievement came when the U.S. National Youth Team qualified for the Youth World Cup in Australia. The U.S. squad earned its berth with a win over Honduras in a dramatic penalty kick contest. In the October world tournament, however, the U.S. squad was eliminated in the first round, losing to Uruguay and Poland and tying Qatar. West Germany won the championship match against Qatar, 4–0.

JIM HENDERSON, *"Tampa Tribune"*

SWIMMING

Ten individual world records were set on the international swimming scene during 1981. In the men's division, four records fell, three to Americans, one to a Canadian. Four women's records tumbled and were accounted for by an American and an East German, both previous record-holders.

The most consistent performers were Mary T. Meagher, the 16-year-old butterfly sensation from Louisville, KY, who burst on the international scene in 1979, and Ute Geweniger of East Germany, the durable breaststroke champion.

Miss Meagher, 5′7″ (1.7 m), 128 lbs (58 kg), has been one of the most dominant swimmers in her discipline, having registered 10 of the 11 fastest times in the 200-meter butterfly and four of the five fastest at 100 meters, since she first shattered the marks at the age of 14 in 1979. She excelled at the 1981 United States Long Course Championships at Brown Deer, WI, in mid-August by breaking her world marks for both distances. Her time of 2 minutes, 5.96 seconds in the 200 bettered her previous mark by .41 of a second and her 57.93 effort for 100 clipped 1.33 seconds from her previous standard.

The long course event, held indoors for only the third time in 80 years, did not produce an expected assault on the record book. Except for Robin Leamy's 22.54-second clocking for the 50-meter freestyle, the world's best time for a distance that is not counted as a world record, no men swimmers broke a world record.

Tracy Caulkins of Nashville, TN, was unable to break a world mark although she won four events, the two breaststrokes and the two individual medleys, and lifted her total of national titles to 35, only one short of the record held by Johnny Weissmuller.

The women's 'A' team from Mission Viejo, CA, set the 800-meter freestyle relay world mark with a time of 8:07.44.

The week following the long course championships, the American team competed in a dual meet at Kiev in the Soviet Union against a Russian team. That meet also held great expectations, but only one world record was broken—by Craig Beardsley of the United States, whose 1:58.01 lowerd his mark for the 200 butterfly. Americans clearly outclassed the Soviets, however, in a meet that was supposed to be close, winning 20 of the 29 men's and women's events and outscoring their opponent, 203–141.

Miss Geweniger improved her world standard in the 100-meter breaststroke three times during the year. On July 2, she clocked 1:09.39 at East Berlin to clip .13 of a second from the mark she had lowered on April 21. In September, she brought the record down to 1:08.60 in a meet at Split, Yugoslavia. On July 4 she swam the 200-meter breaststroke in 2:11.73, breaking by 1.27 seconds the mark set in 1980 by Petra Schneider of East Germany.

On April 3, in time trials sanctioned by the International Swimming Federation at Austin, TX, two Americans broke world records. Rowdy Gaines swam the 100-meter freestyle in 49.36 seconds, breaking the 49.44 clocking set by Jonty Skinner of South Africa in 1976, and William Paulus's 53.81 in the 100-meter butterfly lowered the 54.15 set by Sweden's Par Arvidsson, in 1980.

Alex Baumann of Canada did 2:02.78 for the 200-meter individual medley at Heidelberg, West Germany, on July 29 to better the 2:03.24 done by Bill Barrett of the United States in 1980.

In December, Vladimir Salnikov set two world records—14:44.09 in the 1,500 meters and 3:45.10 in the 400-meter freestyle—to lead the Soviet team to victory in the European Cup.

In the National Collegiate Athletic Association championships in March at Austin, TX, ten American records were set, with Gaines leading the way with 42.38 for the 100-yard freestyle.

Jill Sterkel of Texas set an Association for Intercollegiate Athletics for Women (AIAW) record with five firsts in the AIAW meet in March at Columbia, SC. Among her victories were American records in the 50-yard freestyle (22.41) and 100-yard freestyle (53.10).

GEORGE DE GREGORIO

UPI

Chris Evert Lloyd has reason to smile: she has just won Wimbledon and is again ranked No. 1.

TENNIS

Professional tennis consolidated further in 1981 after years of growing pains. The game has now surpassed golf as both a participant and spectator sport and boasts gross revenues in excess of $1,000,000,000 annually.

Youth and Women's Tour. Even the support systems of tennis—television, journalism, and sponsorship—have steadily become more professional and capable of withstanding the devastations of those awkward doubles partners—inflation and recession. Youth continued to be served in the ranks of touring pros with John McEnroe (age 22) replacing Björn Borg (25) as the world's number one player. Chris Evert Lloyd (27) reemerged as the ladies premier pro by winning Wimbledon and the Italian Open. She received some help from Tracy Austin (19), who was forced out of the game for four months because of a back injury. Martina Navratilova (25) continued to perplex her followers with an emotional inconsistency that saw her defeat Andrea Jaeger at the Avon Championships and Evert Lloyd in the semifinals at the U.S. Open, and yet lose to Austin in the final.

Hana Mandlikova (19), the Czech blessed with an unusual combination of stroking power and grace, demonstrated that she is not just a pretty face by winning the French Open and reaching the finals of Wimbledon. And Andrea Jaeger (15) firmly entrenched herself fourth in the world rankings, the youngest player to be so highly placed. The youth movement did not end

TENNIS

Major Team Competitions

Davis Cup: United States
Federation Cup: United States
Wightman Cup: United States

Major Tournaments

U.S. Open—Men's Singles: John McEnroe; women's singles: Tracy Austin; men's doubles: John McEnroe and Peter Fleming; women's doubles: Kathy Jordan and Anne Smith; mixed doubles: Anne Smith and Kevin Smith; men's 35 singles: Jaime Fillol (Chile); junior men's singles: Thomas Hoegstedt (Sweden); junior women's singles: Zina Garrison.

U.S. Clay Court Championships—Men's Singles: José-Luis Clerc (Argentina); women's singles: Andrea Jaeger; men's doubles: Kevin Curren (South Africa) and Steven Denton; women's doubles: Joanne Russell and Virginia Ruzici (Rumania).

U.S. National Indoor—Men's Singles: Gene Mayer; men's doubles: Gene Mayer and Sandy Mayer.

National Men's 35 Clay Court Championship—Men's Singles: Jim Parker; men's doubles: Jim Parker and Butch Seewagen.

U.S.T.A. Women's Clay Court Championship—Women's Senior Singles: Judy Alvarez; 35 doubles: Judy Alvarez and Charleen Hillebrand; 45 singles: Jane Crofford; 45 doubles: Sally Bondurant and Carol Wood; 55 singles: Bunny Vosters; 55 doubles: Doris Hart and Bunny Vosters.

National Junior—Singles: Jimmy Brown; doubles: John Ross and Bill Baxter.

National Girls' 18's Singles—Singles: Lisa Bonder; doubles: Linda Gates and Gretchen Rush.

Volvo Grand Prix Masters—Men's Singles: Björn Borg (Sweden); men's doubles: John McEnroe and Peter Fleming.

Other U.S. Championships

NCAA (Division 1)—Singles: Tim Mayotte; doubles: David Pate and Carl Richter; team: Stanford.

NAIA—Men's Singles: Brian Lusson; doubles: Brian Lusson and Bart Bernstein; team: Southwest Texas State; women's singles: Pat Smith; doubles: Pat Smith and Karen Regman; team: Grand Canyon College and Guilford College.

AIAW—Singles: Anna Maria Fernandez; doubles: Alycia Moulton and Caryn Copeland; team: UCLA.

Professional Championships

U.S. Pro Indoor Championships—Men's Singles: Roscoe Tanner; men's doubles: Marty Riessen and Sherwood Stewart.

World Championship Tennis Tour—Men's Singles: John McEnroe.

Avon Championships Tour—Women's Singles: Martina Navratilova; women's doubles: Martina Navratilova and Pam Shriver.

Toyota Championships Tour—Women's Singles: Tracy Austin.

Other Countries

Wimbledon—Men's Singles: John McEnroe; women's singles: Chris Evert Lloyd; men's doubles: John McEnroe and Peter Fleming; women's doubles: Martina Navratilova and Pam Shriver.

Australian (1981-82)—Men's Singles: Johan Kriek (South Africa); men's doubles: Mark Edmondson (Australia) and Kim Warwick (Australia); women's singles: Martina Navratilova; women's doubles: Kathy Jordan and Anne Smith.

French Open—Men's Singles: Björn Borg, Sweden; women's singles: Hana Mandlikova (Czechoslovakia); men's doubles: Heinz Gunthardt (Switzerland) and Balazs Taroczy (Hungary); women's doubles: Tanya Harford (South Africa) and Rosalyn Fairbank (South Africa).

Italian Open—Men's Singles: José-Luis Clerc (Argentina); men's doubles: Hans Gildemeister (Chile) and Andres Gomez (Ecuador); women's singles: Chris Evert Lloyd; women's doubles: Candy Reynolds and Paula Smith.

Canadian Open—Men's Singles: Ivan Lendl (Czechoslovakia); men's doubles: Raul Ramirez (Mexico) and Ferdi Taygan; women's singles: Tracy Austin; women's doubles: Martina Navratilova and Pam Shriver.

N.B. All players are from the United States, unless otherwise noted.

Leading Money Winners

John McEnroe	$991,000	Martina Navratilova	$865,437
Ivan Lendl	846,037	Chris Evert Lloyd	572,162
Guillermo Vilas	405,872	Tracy Austin	453,404
Jimmy Connors	402,267	Andrea Jaeger	392,115
Peter McNamara	218,291	Pam Shriver	366,530
Jose-Luis Clerc	217,375	Hana Mandlikova	339,602
Tomas Smid	198,175	Wendy Turnbull	225,161
Vitas Gerulaitas	193,475	Anne Smith	192,311
Björn Borg	189,075	Sylvia Hanika	190,898
Brian Gottfried	188,340	Virginia Ruzuci	179,115

UPI

Björn Borg (left) extends congratulations to John McEnroe, winner of the U.S. Open.

with Austin, Mandlikova, and Jaeger. Immediately below this trio was Pam Shriver (19), who apparently reharnessed the angular power of her six-foot (1.8-m) frame that took her to the U.S. Open final in 1978. And Kathy Rinaldi (15), Kathy Horvath (16), and Pam Casale (18)—two of whom were not old enough to drive in many states—made enough money on the tour to buy any model Mercedes with all the extras.

Overall, women's tennis continued to flourish despite the sensation stirred by Billie Jean King admitting her lesbian relationship with her former secretary Marilyn Barnett and enough other insinuations to conclude that King's case is not an isolated one in women's tennis. But tennis has always turned its thick hide against scandal. From force of habit it has had to. Since Open tennis premiered in 1968, the game has been rocked by lawsuits, strikes, bankruptcy, and unconscionable on-court behavior.

The Men. If Evert Lloyd marginally resisted assaults to her queen's throne, Björn Borg was not so successful. After winning a record five consecutive Wimbledon titles and six French Opens in all, Borg was defeated by McEnroe at Wimbledon in four sets, suggesting that the Swede's day as the world's unofficial champion was done. To further this view, McEnroe defeated Borg in the Flushing Meadow finals by an even wider margin. McEnroe became the first champion to win three consecutive Open titles since the legendary Bill Tilden took the crown (1920–25). McEnroe clearly outclassed his foe in all the requisite departments to excel on grass—at serve, volley, and half volley.

McEnroe was fined more than $2,000 for his poor conduct at Wimbledon and afterward suspended for 21 days for further transgressions later in the season. Vitas Gerulaitis, who gave McEnroe his stiffest test in a five-set semifinal at the U.S. Open, was also suspended for 21 days for ill temper, marking the first time in almost 20 years that two American stars have been disciplined in the same year. The suspensions pointed up a weakness in the Code of Conduct, which permits Davis Cup and exhibition playing, enabling pros to earn more money during their purgatory than on the Grand Prix tour. Nonetheless there are specific rules and fines for misconduct, an improvement over the "bad old days" when officials could whimsically single out and make an example of any nonconforming player.

EUGENE L. SCOTT
Publisher, "Tennis Week"

TRACK AND FIELD

In the span of 10 days in August of 1981, Sebastian Coe and Steve Ovett of Britain, the world's two fastest milers, made an assault on the world mile record unequaled in history.

The Mile. The two had been playing cat-and-mouse with the record since 1979, when Coe registered a 3-minute, 49-second clocking on July 17 at Oslo to break the four-year-old mark of 3:49.04 set by John Walker of New Zealand at Göteborg, Sweden, on Aug. 12, 1975. Ovett, who holds 5 of the 10 fastest times ever run in the mile, had shattered Coe's record on July 1, 1980, with 3:48.80 at Oslo. Then on Aug. 19, 1981, Coe lowered the standard to 3:48.53 in Zurich, Switzerland, in a meet in which Renaldo Nehemiah, of Scotch Plains, NJ, became the first hurdler to break the 13-second barrier at 110 meters, lowering the mark to 12.93.

Ovett's rivalry with Coe continued on August 26 in Koblenz, West Germany. Before the race, Ovett predicted that he would regain the world record from Coe. He did just that, clocking 3:48.40. It was the third time the record had changed hands between the two runners and it was believed to be only the fifth time that the mile record had been broken at least twice in the same year.

All that became academic two days later. Coe, who was born on Sept. 29, 1956, and is trained by his father, regained the record on August 28 with a time of 3:47.33 in Brussels, Belgium, before a crowd of 50,000 at Heizel Stadium. Ovett had originally been entered in the race, but withdrew several weeks before the event, saying that when he raced Coe for the first time in the mile he wanted to be on English soil. The two have never run the mile head-to-head. The 1.07 seconds Coe clipped from the mark was the largest drop in the mile record since Walker reduced Bayi's 3:51.0 to 3:49.4 in 1975.

The women's mile record was also under assault. Ludmilla Veselkova of the Soviet Union became the new record-holder with 4:20.89, set in September in Bologna, Italy. She lowered the 4:21.68 mark registered by Mary Decker of the United States on Jan. 26, 1980.

Other Records. In July, Coe shattered his world mark for 1,000 meters with 2:12.18. Henry Rono of Kenya, the holder of four world long-distance marks, bettered his mark at 5,000 by 2.2 seconds with a 13:06.20 clocking. He had set the record of 13:08.4 in Berkeley, CA, on April 8, 1978. The women's 5,000-meter mark also fell—to Paula Fudge of Britain, whose 15:14.51 in September clipped almost 14 seconds from the 15:28.43 set by Ingrid Kristiansen of Norway in July.

In the field events, Ben Plucknett of Beatrice, NE, became the center of controversy in his attempts to claim the discus world record. In May, at Modesto, CA, he broke Wolfgang Schmidt's 1978 record with a throw of 233′ 7″. Then in Stockholm in July he bettered that with 237′ 4″. The 6′ 7″ (2.01 m), 287-lb (130-kg) Plucknett, however, became the subject of an inquiry by the International Amateur Athletic Federation and six days later the I.A.A.F. announced it was banning him for life and discounting his record-breaking performances. A urine sample, taken at the meet in January in New Zealand, had shown that illegal anabolic steroids were present. The 27-year-old Plucknett would have to wait 18 months to appeal.

In the pole vault, the 19-foot barrier fell. Thierry Vigneron of France bettered the world mark of 18′ 11½″ set by Wladyslaw Kozakiewicz of Poland in 1980. Then Vladimir Polyakov of the Soviet Union exceeded that, with 19′ ¾″ before Konstantin Volkov, also a Soviet, turned in the best vault so far—19′ 2″. Among the women, Antoaneta Todorova of Bulgaria set a world mark in the javelin throw (235′ 10″) and Ramona Neubert of East Germany set a heptathlon mark (6,716 points).

Carl Lewis of Houston became the first athlete since Jesse Owens in 1936 to capture separate titles in track and field events in the National Collegiate Athletic Association outdoor championships, taking the 100 meters (9.99) and the long jump (27′ ¾″).

The World Cup. The World Cup competition in Rome did not produce any startling times, but Europe won the men's division by outscoring East Germany, 147–130. The United States was third with 127 points. East Germany won among the women, beating Europe, 120½–110.

Marathons. Alberto Salazar of Eugene, OR, and New Zealand's Alison Roe set world records in the 12th New York City Marathon—2:08:13 and 2:25:28, respectively. Mrs. Roe had earlier won the Boston Marathon, which was taken by Japan's Toshihko Seko among the men.

GEORGE DE GREGORIO

UPI

Alberto Salazar and Alison Roe are crowned with victory wreaths after their record-setting wins in the New York City Marathon.

SPORTS SUMMARIES[1]

ARCHERY—U.S. Champions: men: Rich McKinney, Glendale, AZ; women: Debra Metzger, Lancaster, PA.
BADMINTON—U.S. Champions: men's singles: Chris Kinard, Pasadena, CA; women's singles: Utami Kinard, Pasadena.
BIATHLON—World Champions: men's 20 km: Heikki Ikola, Finland; men's 10 km: Frank Ullrich, E. Germany.
BILLIARDS—World Champions: men's pocket: Mick Sigel, Towson, MD; women's pocket: Loree-Jon Ogonowski, Garwood, NJ.
BOBSLEDDING—World Champions: two-man: B. Germeshausen and H. J. Gerhardt, E. Germany; four-man: B. Germeshausen, H. Gerlach, H. J. Gerhardt, and M. Truebner, E. Germany.
BOWLING—Professional Bowling Association: leading money winner: Earl Anthony, Dublin, CA; national champion: Earl Anthony. **American Bowling Congress:** regular division: singles: Rob Vital, Lancaster, PA (780); doubles: Jim Kontos, Munster, IN, and Al Bruder, Chicago (1,362); all-events: Rod Toft, St. Paul, MN (2,107); team: Strachota's Milshore Bowl, Milwaukee (3,188); master's division: Randy Lightfoot, St. Charles, MO (2,107). **Women's International Bowling Congress:** open division: singles: Virginia Norton, South Gate, CA (672); doubles: Donna Adamek, Duarte, CA, and Nikki Gianulias, Vallejo, CA (1,305); all-events: Virginia Norton (1,905); team: Earl Anthony's Dublin Bowl, Dublin, CA (2,963).
CANOEING—U.S. Champions (flatwater): men's kayak: 500 m: Terry White, VT; 1,000 m: Matt Streib, Bristol, IN; 10,000 m: Bruce Barton, Homer, MI; women's kayak: 500 m: Theresa DiMarino, WA; men's canoe: 500 m: Roland Muhland, Cincinnati; 1,000 m: Rod McLain, New York City; 10,000 m: Bruce Merrit, WA.
CHESS—World Champion: Anatoly Karpov, USSR, defeated Viktor Korchnoi, Switzerland, 6 games to 2, to retain title at Merano, Italy.
CRICKET—World Series Cup: Australia.
CROSS-COUNTRY—World Champions: men: Craig Virgin, United States; women: Grete Waitz, Norway. **NCAA:** Mathew Motshwarateu, Texas-El Paso; **AIAW (women):** Dorothy Rasmussen, Iowa State.
CURLING—World Champions: men: Switzerland; women: Sweden; **U.S. Champions:** men: Superior, WI; women: Seattle Rink.
CYCLING—Tour de France: Bernard Hinault, France. **World Pro Champions:** sprint: Koichi Nakano, Japan; pursuit: Alain Bondue, France; road: Freddy Maertens, Belgium; women's road: Ute Enzenhauer, W. Germany. **U.S. Road Racing Champions:** men: Tom Broznowski, Seattle; women: Connie Carpenter, Boulder, CO.
DOG SHOWS—Westminster (New York): best: Ch. Dhandy's Favorite Woodchuck, pug owned by Robert Hauslohner, Philadelphia. **International** (Chicago): best: Ch. Dhandy's Favorite Woodchuck.
FENCING—World Champions: men: foil: Vladimir Smironov, USSR; épée: Z. Szekely, Hungary; saber: W. Wodke, Poland; women: foil: Cornelia Haenisch, W. Germany. **U.S. Champions:** men: foil: Mark Smith, Atlanta; épée: Lee Shelley, Rutherford, NJ; saber: Peter Westwood, New York City; women: foil: Jana Angelakis, Peabody, MA; épée: Susan Badders, Portland, OR.
GYMNASTICS—World Champions: men: all-around: Yuri Korolev, USSR; floor exercises: tie, Li Yue Jiu, China, and Yuri Korolev; pommel horse: tie, Michael Nikolay, E. Germany, and Li Xiaoping, China; rings: Aleksandr Dityatin, USSR; vault: Peter Ralf Herman, E. Germany; parallel bars, tie, Dityatin and Koji Gushiken, Japan; horizontal bar: Aleksandr Tkachev, USSR; team: USSR. Women: all-around: Olga Bicherova, USSR; floor exercise, Natalia Illenko, USSR; balance beam: Maxi Gnauck, E. Germany; uneven parallel bars: Maxi Gnauck; vault: Maxi Gnauck; team: USSR. **U.S. Gymnastics Federation Champions:** men's all-around: Jim Hartung, Omaha; women's all-around: Tracee Talavera, Eugene, OR. **NCAA:** all-around: Jim Hartung, Nebraska; team: Nebraska. **AIAW (women):** Sharon Shapiro, UCLA; team: Utah.
HANDBALL—U.S. Handball Association Champions (4-wall): men: singles: Fred Lewis, Tucson, AZ; doubles: Tom Kopatich and Jack Roberts, Chicago; women: singles: Rosemary Bellini, New York City; doubles: R. Bellini and Sue Oakleaf, Texas.
HORSE SHOWS—World Cup: Michael Matz riding Jet Run.
ICE SKATING, FIGURE—World Champions: men: Scott Hamilton, United States; women: Denise Biellman, Switzerland; pairs: Irina Vorobieva and Igor Lisovsky, USSR; dance: Jayne Torvill and Christopher Dean, Great Britain. **U.S. Champions:** men: Scott Hamilton; women: Elaine Zayak, Paramus, NJ; pairs: Caitlin and Peter Carruthers, Wilmington, DE; dance: Judy Blumberg and Michael Seibert, Colorado Springs, CO.
ICE SKATING, SPEED—World Champions: men: Amund Sjobrend, Norway; women: Natalia Petruseva, USSR. **World Sprint Champions:** men: Frode Roenning, Norway; women: Karin Enke, E. Germany. **U.S. Outdoor Champions:** men: Tom Grannes, Minneapolis, MN; women: Lisa Merrifield, Butte, MT. **U.S. Indoor Champions:** men: Scott Drebes, Champaign, IL; women: Mary Polaski, Colorado Springs.
JUDO—U.S. Champions: men: 132-lb class: Rod Condurages, Wantagh, NY; 143: James Martin, Alhambra, CA; 156: Mike Swain, Bridgewater, NJ; 172: Nicky Yonezuka, Watchung, NJ; 189: Robert Berland, Chicago; under 209: Leo White, U.S. Army; over 209: Douglas Nelson, Englewood, NJ; open: Mitch Santa Maria, Rochelle Park, NJ. Women: 106: Darlene Anaya, Albuquerque, NM; 114: Robin Takemori, Alexandria, VA; 123: Darlene Hill, Memphis, TN; 134: Robin Chapman, Cranford, NJ; 145: Chris Penick, San Jose, CA; 158: Heidi Baversachs, New York City; over 158: Juanita Cardwell, Tallahassee, FL; open: Karen Mackey, Sioux City, IA.

KARATE—U.S. Champions: men's form: Domingo Llanos, Haverstraw, NY; women's form: Pam Glaser, Hartford, CT.
LACROSSE—NCAA: Div. I: North Carolina; Div. II: Adelphi; Div. III: Hobart. **AIAW (women):** Maryland.
LUGE—World Champions: men: Sergei Demilin, USSR; women: Melitta Sollman, E. Germany.
PLATFORM TENNIS—U.S. Champions: men: singles: Doug Russell, New York City; doubles: Steve Baird, Port Chester, NY, and Rich Maier, Allendale, NJ; women: singles: Robin Fulton, Norwalk, CT; doubles: Yvonne Hackenburg, Kalamazoo, MI, and Hilary Hilton, Glen Ellyn, IL.
POLO—Gold Cup: Boca Raton, FL; **World Cup:** Boehm Palm Beach; **America Cup:** Boca Raton; **U.S. Open:** Rolex A and K.
RACQUETBALL—U.S. Champions: men's amateur open: John Prenn, San Diego, CA; women's open: Cindy Baxter, Lewiston, PA; men's pro: Marty Hogan; women's pro: Heather McKay, Toronto.
RODEO—Professional Rodeo Cowboy Association: all-around: Jimmie Cooper, Monument, NM.
ROLLER SKATING—U.S. Champions: figure: men's singles: Tony St. Jacques, Virginia Beach; women's singles: Rita Drago, Landisville, NJ; pairs: Tina Kneisley and Paul Price, Brighton, MI; dance: Holly Valente and Bill Richards, Walthum, ME. Speed: men: Robb Dunn, Farmington Hills, MI; women: Linda Swain, High Point, NC.
ROWING—U.S. Collegiate Champions: men: pair with coxswain: Pennsylvania; pair without coxswain: Wisconsin; four with coxswain: Syracuse; four without coxswain: Cornell; eight: Cornell. Women's Nationals: single: Dartmouth; quad: Dartmouth, Lake Washington Rowing Club, and Pennsylvania; pair without coxswain: Lake Merritt Rowing Club and 1980 Rowing Club; four with coxswain: 1980 Rowing Club and Lake Washington Rowing Club; double: Dartmouth; eight: University of Washington and Lake Washington Rowing Club.
RUGBY—U.S. Champion: Old Blues, Berkeley, CA; **Test Matches:** Canada 6, United States 3; South Africa 38, United States 7.
SKIING—Alpine World Cup Champions: men: overall: Phil Mahre, United States; downhill: Harti Weirataher, Austria; slalom: Ingemar Stenmark, Sweden; giant slalom: Ingemar Stenmark. Women: overall: Marie-Theres Nadig, Switzerland; downhill: Marie-Theres Nadig; slalom: Erika Hess, Switzerland; giant slalom: Tamara McKinney, United States. **NCAA:** Utah. **AIAW (women):** 4-event: Vermont; Alpine: Wyoming; Nordic: Middlebury.
SOFTBALL—U.S. Amateur Softball Association: men: major fast pitch: Decatur, IL; class-A fast pitch: S.H. Good, Narvon, PA; major slow pitch: Elite Coating, Gordon, GA; class-A slow pitch: Ray Sears & Son, Gambrills, MD; modified pitch: Clinica Asociacion, Miami; 16-inch: Budweiser, Harvey, IL. Women: major fast pitch: Orlando (FL) Rebels; class-A fast pitch: Montclair (NJ) 81's; major slow pitch: Tomboys, Tifton, GA; class-A slow pitch: Orlando (FL) stars.
SQUASH RACQUETS—World Champion: pro: Sharif Khan, Toronto. **U.S. Squash Racquets Association:** singles: Mark Alger, Toronto. North American Open: Sharif Khan; College Team: Harvard. **U.S. Women's Squash Racquets Association:** singles: Barbara Maltby, Philadelphia; doubles: Joyce Davenport, King of Prussia, PA, and Carol Thesieres, Broomall, PA.
SQUASH TENNIS—U.S. Open Champion: Dave Stafford, Bronxville, NY.
TABLE TENNIS—World Cup Champion: men: Guo Yuehua, China; women: Tong Ling, China. **U.S. Open Champions:** men: singles: Xie Saike, China; doubles: Li Zhenshi and Cai Zhenhua, China; team: China. Women: singles: Tong Ling; doubles: Zhang Deying and Cao Yanhua, China; team: China.
VOLLEYBALL—U.S. Champions: USVBA Open: Nautilus/Nike, Long Beach, CA; USVBA Women's Open: Utah State. **NCAA:** UCLA. **AIAW (women):** Southern California.
WEIGHTLIFTING—U.S. Weightlifting Association Champions (men): 114-lb class: Wrenn Norvell, Chicago; 123: Albert Hood, Chicago; 132: Phil Sanderson, Billings, MT; 148: Cal Schake, Butler, PA; 165: Fred Lowe, E. Lansing, MI; 181: Val Balison, Superior, MT; 198: Kevin Winter, San Jose, CA; 220: Ken Clark, Pacifica, CA; 242: Guy Carlton, Decatur, IL; over 242: Jerome Hannan, Colorado Springs; team: York (PA) Barbell Club.
WRESTLING—AAU Freestyle: 105.5-lb class: Bill Rosado, Las Vegas, NV; 114.5: Joe Gonzales, Bakersfield, CA; 125.5: John Azevedo, Mesa, AZ; 136.5: Lee Roy Smith, Stillwater, OK; 149.5: Andy Rein, Madison, WI; 163: David Schultz, Norman, OK; 180.5: Dan Zilverberg, St. Louis Park, MN; 198: Eric Wais, Norman, OK; 220: Greg Gibson, Redding, CA; heavyweight: Jimmy Jackson, Grand Rapids, MI; team: Sunkist Kids. **AAU Greco-Roman:** 105.5: T. J. Jones, Little Creek, VA; 114.5: Wilfredo Leiva, Quantico, VA; 125.5: Dan Mello, Triangle, VA; 136.5: Abdurrahim Kazu, Omaha, NE; 149.5: Doug Yeats, Montreal; 163: David Schultz, Norman, OK; 180.5: Dan Chandler, Minneapolis, MN; 198: Mike Houck, Watertown, WI; 220: Jeff Blatnick, New York; heavyweight: Ron Carlisle, Riviera Beach, FL; team: U.S. Marines. **NCAA:** 118: Gene Mills, Syracuse; 126: Dan Cuestas, Cal State-Bakersfield; 134: Jim Gibbons, Iowa State; 142: Andre Metzger, Oklahoma; 150: Nate Carr, Oklahoma; 158: Rick Stewart, Oklahoma State; 167: Mark Schultze, Oklahoma; 177: Ed Banach, Iowa; 190: Tom Martucci, Trenton (NJ) State; heavyweight: Lou Banach, Iowa; team: Iowa.
YACHTING—U.S. Yacht Racing Union: champion of champions: John Kolius, Seabrook, TX; world women's champion: Marit Soderstrom, Sweden; Mallory Cup (men): Mark Foster, Corpus Christi, TX; Adams Trophy (women): Ann Boyd Sloger, Charleston, SC; Prince of Wales: Marvin Beekman, Houston; half-ton North American: Toy Boat, R. Lester and T. Boehlke, Indiana; three quarter-ton North American: Mandala, John Zerenacher, Annapolis, MD; U.S. women's double: Martha Starkweather, Newport, RI; U.S. women's single-handed: Betsy Gelenitis, Brick Town, NJ.

[1] Sports not covered in pages 458–481.

SRI LANKA

In April 1981, Sri Lanka began a year-long celebration of the 50th anniversary of the adoption of universal franchise. This reminder of the country's impressive democratic record was marred, however, by an increase in social tension and violence, whose main victims were of the minority Tamil community. The economic situation remained somber, with some increases in employment and foreign investment. In foreign affairs, the highlight was a conference of foreign ministers of the South Asian states.

District Council Elections. Elections to the National Development Council on June 4 marked the inauguration of a new system of decentralized authority. The ruling United National Party (UNP), led by President Junius R. Jayewardene, won a majority of seats in 11 of the 17 councils for which elections were held. The Tamil United Liberation Front (TULF) won majorities in six northern districts, and UNP candidates were returned unopposed in seven others.

Violence. Communal violence in the northern districts prompted the government to proclaim a state of emergency 48 hours before the June 4 elections. The emergency was soon lifted, but it was reimposed August 17 after an extended period of attacks on police stations and other targets by terrorist groups in Jaffna District, Colombo, and other parts of the country. Alarmed by the deteriorating situation, the government entered talks with the TULF, which led to the formation of a committee, chaired by President Jayewardene, charged with devising steps to restore law and order and national unity.

Economy. The nation was plagued by budget deficits, high inflation, an unemployment rate of about 13%, and recurrent power shortages. Encouraging trends were an increase in the gross domestic product of about 6%, and substantial increases in foreign investment and tourism. In June, at a meeting in Tokyo, the Sri Lanka Aid Consortium pledged $834 million in economic assistance. Sri Lanka was dependent on foreign aid for about 60% of its development budget.

Foreign Affairs. In late April, Sri Lanka hosted the first conference of foreign ministers of the seven nations of South Asia. A suggestion by Sri Lanka's foreign minister for more formalized regional cooperation was endorsed "in principle." In July, President Jayewardene attended the wedding of Prince Charles and Lady Diana Spencer in London; in late September and early October he participated in the Commonwealth summit conference in Australia. Queen Elizabeth II of Great Britain visited in October for celebrations commemorating universal franchise. On May 30, Sri Lanka formally applied for membership in the Association of Southeast Asian Nations (ASEAN).

NORMAN D. PALMER
University of Pennsylvania

SRI LANKA • Information Highlights

Official Name: Democratic Socialist Republic of Sri Lanka.
Location: Island off the southeastern coast of India.
Area: 25,332 sq mi (65 610 km^2).
Population (1981 est.): 14,900,000.
Chief City (1978 est.): Colombo, the capital, 624,000.
Government: *Head of state,* Junius R. Jayewardene, president (took office Feb. 1978). *Head of government,* Ranasinghe Premadasa, prime minister (took office Feb. 1978). *Legislature* (unicameral)—National State Assembly.
Monetary Unit: Rupee (19.135 rupees equal U.S.$1, July 1981).
Manufactures (major products): Consumer goods, textiles, chemicals and chemical products.
Agriculture (major products): Tea, rubber, rice, coconuts, spices.

STAMPS AND STAMP COLLECTING

Only days after the February announcement from Buckingham Palace of the engagement of Prince Charles to Lady Diana Spencer, postal administrations and their merchandisers rushed to print stamps to mark the wedding. Most issues were handled by two major agencies, and a complete collection cost about $750. It was the most lucrative philatelic event in decades.

On Jan. 30, 1981, on orders from the secretary general, the United Nations issued three stamps publicizing the "Rights of Palestinians." Equating this with sympathy for the Palestine Liberation Organization (PLO), some collectors and dealers boycotted the set as being anti-Israel. The UN also drew criticism from the American Philatelic Society for the second set of stamps in a "flags" series begun in 1980, which the society considered "exploitative."

International Exhibitions and Organizations. There were two major international exhibitions in 1981, one in Switzerland for aero- and astrophilately, the other in Vienna for traditional competition. Unlike previous Austrian shows (1933 and 1965), private dealers and government

SELECTED U.S. COMMEMORATIVE STAMPS 1981

Subject	Denomination	Date
Trans-Pacific Flight	28¢ postal card	Jan. 2
Everett Dirksen	15¢	Jan. 4
Battle of Cowpens	10¢ postal card	Jan. 17
Whitney Young	15¢	Jan. 30
Americana series	12¢	April 8
Native flowers	4x18¢	April 23
Flag definitives	18¢	April 24
Red Cross	18¢	May 1
Isaiah Thomas	12¢ postal card	May 5
George Mason	18¢	May 7
Savings & Loan	18¢	May 8
Space Achievements	8x18¢	May 21
Rachel Carson	17¢	May 28
Charles Drew	35¢	June 3
Professional Management	18¢	June 18
Wildlife Habitats	4x18¢	June 26
Disabled Persons	18¢	June 29
Edna Millay	18¢	July 10
Blinded Veterans	18¢ envelope	Aug. 13
Alcoholism	18¢	Aug. 19
Architecture	4x18¢	Aug. 28
Eutaw Springs	12¢ postal card	Sept. 8
Babe Zaharias	18¢	Sept. 22
Bobby Jones	18¢	Sept. 22
Lewis & Clark	12¢ postal card	Sept. 23
Frederic Remington	18¢	Oct. 9
Yorktown-Virginia	2x18¢	Oct. 16
Desert plants		Oct. 23
Christmas mail		Oct. 28

stamp sellers did not do enough business to justify expensive booth rentals. Less important shows were held in Tokyo and Buenos Aires.

Since its establishment in 1926, the International Philatelic Federation has had Western leadership. At its 1981 convention in Germany, however, the outgoing Belgian president was replaced by Ladislav Dvoracek, an active philatelist and Czech diplomat.

United States and Canada. Demands for increased postal rates caused several problems with regard to new issues. Early in the year, not knowing how much the Postal Rate Commission would allow, U.S. Postmaster General William F. Bolger ordered the printing and distribution of stamps and envelopes inscribed simply with a letter "B." They would be used for whatever rate the commission allowed (18 cents instead of the requested 20 cents). Also, some commemoratives had to wait for release until they could be given 18-cent inscriptions. When the basic rate was increased again, to 20 cents on November 1, stamps and envelopes inscribed with the letter "C" had to be printed and distributed. New commemoratives were once more delayed, and most of the year's previous issues were already obsolete.

After the announcement of two new stamps promoting "Consumer Education," Washington received so many protests against the Spanish inscription on one stamp that the release was pigeonholed.

In Canada, a prolonged postal strike forced Ottawa to postpone the release of stamps originally scheduled for July, August, and September.

The Market. A conspicuous withdrawal of speculative money in stamps brought down the value of formerly "hot" items. A dealer in Switzerland, however, reported that he had sold, for $1,000,000, a five-cent stamp issued by the postmaster of Annapolis, MD, before U.S. federal stamps were introduced in 1847. It was the highest price ever paid for a philatelic gem.

ERNEST A. KEHR
Director, Stamp News Bureau

STOCKS AND BONDS

While the administration of President Ronald Reagan tried to steer the U.S. economy on a radically new course, the U.S. stock and bond markets had a rocky year in 1981.

When Reagan won a landslide election victory in late 1980, the stock market responded with a vigorous rally. But as the new government began to put its "supply-side" program of tax and budget cuts into place, investors began to display more and more misgivings.

Wall Street executives and other business leaders repeatedly stated their faith in, and support of, the Reagan program as the best hope for solving the country's chronic inflation problem. Yet the bond market, which is especially sensitive to changes in inflationary expectations, fell to new low after new low through much of the year. The stock market, which reached an eight-year high in late April, lapsed into a steep decline through the summer and early fall.

Wall Street's doubts focused on the prospective size of the federal budget deficit. With sky-high interest rates swelling the Treasury's borrowing costs and depressing the economy at the same time, Reagan's stated aim of a balanced federal budget within the next few years was met with widespread skepticism.

By autumn, most economists agreed that the United States had entered its second recession in two years. Late in the year, forecasters were warning of a long, cold winter for the economy.

At the close on New Year's Eve, the Dow Jones average of 30 industrial stocks stood at 875.00, down 88.99, or 9.2%, for the year. The New York Stock Exchange (NYSE) composite index dropped 8.7%, and the American Stock Exchange market value index fell 8.1%.

Though the bull market of the past few years seemed to be over, trading volume at the NYSE set a record for the fourth straight year. The 1981 total of 11,850,000,000 shares topped the 1980 figure of 11,350,000,000.

The markets' woes were a particular problem for Reagan, since his program depended so heavily on increased confidence among the nation's investors and business planners. The situation was made particularly ironic by the fact that Reagan's landmark Economic Recovery Tax Act of 1981, which Congress approved in early August, contained many provisions specifically intended to stimulate investment in stocks and bonds. Among other things, it lowered the maximum tax on investment income from 70 to 50%, and the top rate on long-term (one year or more) capital gains from 28 to 20%.

Thus, it was not surprising that relations grew chilly between the political capital in Washington and the financial capital on Wall Street. Asked about the markets at one point, Reagan remarked, "I have never found Wall Street a source of good economic advice." Economists in the financial world, he said, see things "through a very narrow glass."

While it fell far short of 1980, when the Dow Jones industrial average gained 125.25 points, the year had its share of dramatic developments. The first came January 7, when an overnight "sell everything" recommendation by controversial advisor Joseph Granville helped touch off a frenzy of activity. The Dow Jones industrials fell almost 24 points that day, with a single-day record of 92.89 million shares changing hands on the New York exchange.

With summer came the biggest takeover battle in Wall Street history, a three-way struggle among DuPont Co., Mobil Corp., and Seagram Co. for control of Conoco, a large oil concern. DuPont eventually prevailed, completing a deal with a $7,300,000,000 price tag. Mobil went ac-

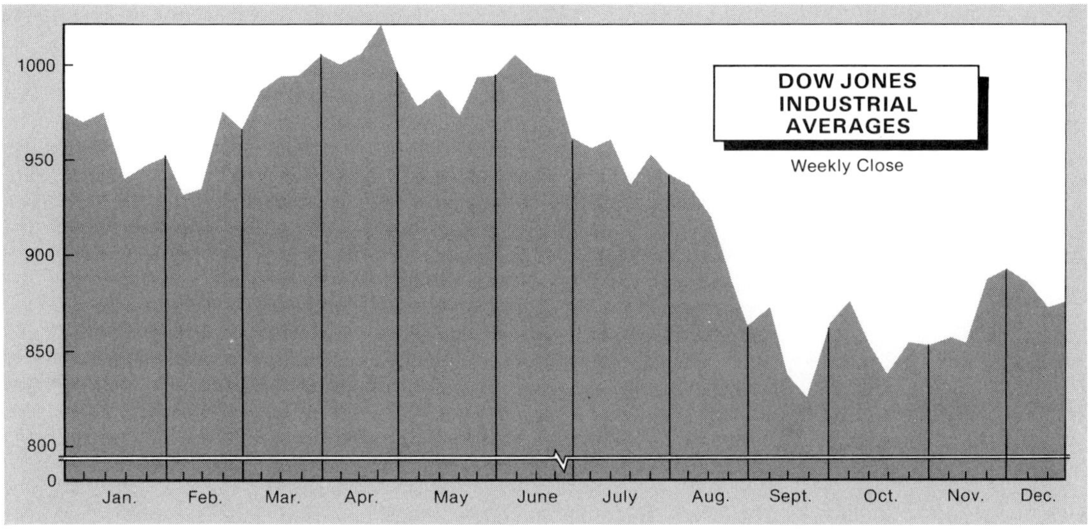

quisition hunting again a few months later, with a bid for Marathon Oil Co. Its offer was countered soon afterward by U.S. Steel Corp., which proposed to spend about $6,300,000,000 for Marathon.

While many Wall Street firms were busy advising major corporations in such battles, several of their own number became merger targets. Prudential Insurance paid $385 million for Bache Group; American Express about $1,000,000,000 for Shearson Loeb Rhoades; and Phibro Corp., a large but little-known commodities company, about $500 million for Salomon Brothers. In October, Sears, Roebuck & Co., struck a $607 million deal for Dean Witter Reynolds, only three days after Sears had agreed to acquire a large real estate and mortgage broker, Coldwell, Banker & Company.

Mergers involving four of the securities industry's ten largest firms within a matter of months clearly amounted to more than a coincidence. Acquirers, such as Sears, openly stated their belief that rapid change, and potentially rapid growth, lay in store for the financial services industry. And indeed, evidence abounded that the old traditional structure of the financial world—with clearly defined distinctions between the roles of bankers, brokers, insurance companies, and other institutions—was undergoing a major shakeup.

The upstart money-market mutual funds, which had grown rapidly in 1979 and 1980, picked up even more steam in 1981. After starting the year with total assets of about $75,000,000,000 they reached the $180,000,000,000 mark by late December. Meanwhile, some other "futuristic" investment products were also establishing themselves as successes.

By late 1981, Merrill Lynch & Co.'s Cash Management Account, a hybrid plan combining such features as checks, a credit card, and money-market investing with a traditional brokerage account, had attracted 500,000 customers in just four years of existence.

At year-end, financial institutions were poised to scramble after still another new market, individual retirement accounts (IRAs). Previously, personal retirement plans of this type had been available only to the self-employed and workers not covered by group plans. The Reagan tax bill, however, opened them up to anyone bringing home a paycheck, starting in 1982. The Investment Company Institute, a mutual-fund trade group, projected growth of IRAs at $20,000,000,000 annually over the next several years.

International Markets. As the world of investing has grown more complex, it has also grown more international. That was evidenced by the fact that most overseas stock markets closely matched the course of prices on Wall Street during 1981.

As of late November, an index of nine world markets published by *The Wall Street Journal* showed a 10.1% decline from the start of the year. The biggest losers included Australia, down 27.3%; Canada, down 17.1%; Hong Kong, down 9.8%; and Switzerland, down 13.9%. In France, a 21.3% drop was attributed in large part to the Socialist party's victory in elections in May. The sole exceptions were Britain, up a modest 0.9%, and Japan, whose industrial prowess has become a subject of world study and recognition. The Japanese market was up 21.3%.

Amid the generally gloomy atmosphere on Wall Street as 1981 grew to a close, there were a few encouraging developments. The depressed bond market staged its best rally of the year in November as interest rates fell. The bank prime lending rate, stuck at 20.5% for months, was down to the 15.75% range by year-end. But it seemed certain that "Reaganomics," if it was to work its promised magic, would need much more good news than that in 1982.

CHET CURRIER, *The Associated Press*

UPI

President Jaafar al-Nemery of Sudan casts his ballot for Hosni Mubarak in an October 13 referendum in Egypt to determine the successor to slain President Sadat. Nemery insisted on voting because he considers Egypt and Sudan to be one country.

SUDAN

Sudan turned increasingly to the United States in 1981 in hopes of gaining military support to counter alleged Libyan destabilization activities, particularly after the death of Egyptian President Anwar el-Sadat in October. Relations with Egypt were normalized earlier in the year after several years of distance-keeping, and Sudan's security was guaranteed by a defense pact with Cairo. A troubled economy acted as an additional threat to the stability of President Jaafar al-Nemery's 12-year-old regime.

Politics and Foreign Relations. In October, Nemery dissolved Sudan's two parliaments in order to decentralize power further. Elections for the National People's Assembly in the north and the Southern Region People's Assembly, governing the autonomous, predominantly Christian south, were planned. Abel Alier, the senior southern official, was replaced by a southern Muslim, Gen. Gasmallah Rassas, as president of a transitional government in the region.

The National People's Assembly would be cut in size from 366 to 151 members, reducing its responsibilities in the areas of health, education, and welfare, and transferring them to the five regional assemblies set up in 1980.

The decentralization moves were believed linked to Sudan's concerns over internal security due to troubles in 1981 with Libya. The Khartoum government maintained that Libyan air forces have been attacking Sudanese towns from the western border with Chad and intend to destabilize the Nemery government. Col. Muammar el-Qaddafi's troops were in the area to combat the Chadian rebel forces of Hissène Habré. Habré's Armed Forces of the North took refuge along the Chad-Sudan border after having been defeated in Ndjamena by government forces with Libyan military assistance.

Just prior to the assassination of President Sadat, Egypt's then Vice-President Hosni Mubarak visited the United States to urge Reagan administration assistance for Sudan's armed forces in the face of the Libyan threat. Following President Sadat's death, the U.S. government decided to speed up deliveries of arms to Sudan, under a $100 million military sales credit package which would include the provision of F-5 jets, M-60 tanks, and other air-defense equipment.

Although the Sudanese government was warning of an incipient Libyan invasion after Sadat's death, analysts believed internal destabilization of Nemery's regime was more likely. In September, more than 10,000 persons were arrested in a security sweep in Sudan for alleged involvement in a Libyan-backed coup attempt, the latest of a series that have been targeted against Nemery during his tenure. Nemery also claimed that Libya was setting up an underground army, the Libyan Salvation Army for the Liberation of Sudan, with revolutionary committees in Khartoum, to work for his overthrow. In addition, thousands of Sudanese workers have reportedly been expelled from Libya for not joining the liberation army. Under a defense

SUDAN • Information Highlights

Official Name: Democratic Republic of Sudan.
Location: Northeast Africa.
Area: 967,500 sq mi (2 505 825 km^2).
Population (1981 est.): 19,600,000.
Chief Cities (April 1973): Khartoum, the capital, 333,906; Omdurman, 299,399; Khartoum North, 150,989.
Government: *Head of state,* Gen. Jaafar Mohammed al-Nemery, president (took office following election, Oct. 1971). *Legislature* (unicameral)—National People's Assembly.
Monetary Unit: Pound (0.50 pound equals U.S.$1, July 1981).
Manufactures (major products): Cement, textiles, pharmaceuticals, shoes, processed foods.
Agriculture (major products): Cotton, peanuts, sesame seeds, gum arabic, sorghum, wheat, sugarcane.

pact, Cairo has guaranteed Sudan's security against a Libyan invasion.

Economy. Compounding the alleged Libyan threat is the continued desperate state of the Sudanese economy. With a foreign debt of $3,000,000,000, a 50% inflation rate, and a severe shortage of foreign exchange, Sudan requested $250 million from the International Monetary Fund to cover balance of payments problems. Discussions with the fund were continuing in October.

Production of and earnings from cotton, the leading cash crop, continued to decline in 1981, complicated by a brain drain of skilled workers from the country. A transport workers' strike during the summer crippled the country, and an influx of Chad refugees, added to those already in Sudan from Ethiopia, Uganda, and Zaire, increased strains on the deteriorating economy. Hopes were still being pinned on petroleum as a potential foreign exchange earner, but imports of crude oil still absorb more than 85% of Sudan's earnings.

MARGARET A. NOVICKI, *"Africa Report"*

SWEDEN

A dispute over tax policy led to the fall of Prime Minister Thorbjörn Fälldin's three-party, non-Socialist coalition in May 1981, but two weeks later Fälldin was reappointed as the leader of a new, two-party minority government. In the second half of the year, steps were taken to improve the nation's lagging economy.

Government. On May 4, the Conservative party withdrew from the governing coalition in a disagreement over how much to lower marginal taxes. The Conservatives refused to go along with a preliminary agreement that the Center Party (led by Prime Minister Fälldin), together with the People's Party (Liberals), had made with the Social Democrats, Sweden's largest political party. The Conservatives insisted on a 50% cap on marginal taxes, while the other party leaders were close to the Social Democrats' compromise of between 75 and 80%. Faced with a certain no-confidence vote, Fälldin handed in his resignation on May 8. On May 22, however, Fälldin announced the formation of a two-party, non-Socialist minority government made up of Liberals and the Central Party. Parliament approved the new 18-minister cabinet by a vote of 174 against and 102 for, with 62 abstentions and 11 absences. This was enough to confirm Fälldin's reappointment, because under the Swedish constitution a prospective prime minister need not be supported by a parliamentary majority. The 174 votes against Fälldin were all by the Social Democratic and Communist members, while the Conservatives abstained.

Although the crisis was clearly set in motion by the nation's economic situation, the crucial factor was ultimately the tax question. The new arrangement left Conservatives in a position to make their promises without having to take the government into consideration. The split also robbed the Social Democrats of a clear-cut opposition. The Center and Liberal parties appeared likely to join with the Social Democrats on a number of issues in parliament, making it more difficult to mount an attack against the government in the 1982 election campaign.

Economy. According to the annual report of the Organization for Economic Cooperation and Development (OECD), made public in mid-1981, Swedish industrial production in the 1970s increased by only 11%, while Denmark and The Netherlands reached 25–30%, and Austria and Finland 40%. Productivity, exports, and the gross national product (GNP) were similarly low, while inflation was 13.5–15% in early 1981. Expansion of the public sector, now absorbing some 65% of total production, and wage policy and extreme tax pressure were considered the main reasons for Sweden's loss of competitiveness in international markets. The July unemployment figure of 104,000 was expected to double during the winter months.

A strike by white-collar workers in May caused the affected companies to call for a lockout of 250,000 employees. Just before the lockout was to take effect, however, a two-year agreement, affecting some 500,000 workers, was reached. It called for an 8.8% increase in wages.

On September 14, Sweden devalued the krona by 10%. The government also announced an immediate price freeze to help slow inflation; a proposal to reduce the value-added sales tax from 23.46 to 20%, pending parliamentary approval; and a $120 million employment program for housing and road construction projects.

Soviet Submarine. On October 27 an old, diesel-powered Soviet submarine ran aground in restricted waters near a Swedish naval base. Sweden refused to assist the sub or allow any Soviet ships to come to its assistance until the sub's captain submitted to questioning. The captain insisted that foul weather was to blame, an explanation dismissed by the Swedes. Radiation was detected in the forward part of the vessel, suggesting that it carried nuclear warheads. The submarine was finally released on November 6, after strong protests had been lodged against Moscow.

MAC LINDAHL, *Harvard University*

SWEDEN • Information Highlights

Official Name: Kingdom of Sweden.
Location: Northern Europe.
Area: 173,000 sq mi (448 070 km^2).
Population (1981 est.): 8,300,000.
Chief Cities (1979 est.): Stockholm, the capital, 649,384; Göteborg, 434,699; Malmö, 235,111.
Government: *Head of state,* Carl XVI Gustaf, king (acceded Sept. 1973). *Head of government,* Thorbjörn Fälldin, prime minister (took office Oct. 1979). *Legislature* (unicameral)—Riksdag.
Monetary Unit: Krona (5.68 kronor equal U.S. $1, Sept. 1981).
Manufactures (major products): Machinery, electronics, metal products, automobiles, aircraft.
Agriculture (major products): Dairy, grains, sugar beets, potatoes, wood.

UPI

Youth protests in Zurich erupted in violence and spread to other Swiss cities.

SWITZERLAND

Youth unrest, civil-rights issues, and mounting trade deficits caused major concern in Switzerland during 1981.

Youth Riots. The discontent of many young Swiss, evidenced by demonstrations and riots during much of 1980, continued into 1981. The focal point was a Zurich youth center that had been closed by police in September 1980. On March 21, 1981, a demonstration in Zurich by 4,000 youths demanding the reopening of the center escalated rapidly into a violent confrontation with police. An attempt by 200 persons to seize the center the next day was repulsed.

Sympathy shown by youth in other cities indicated a widespread malaise among Switzerland's young people. The discontent manifested itself also in expressions of concern over a lack of women's rights, inadequate and expensive housing, crowded universities, a view of Switzerland as an armed camp, and what was regarded as a conservative, ultra-traditional, elitist governing establishment.

Civil Rights. The issue of women's rights appeared to be defused on June 6, when voters approved a national referendum calling for a constitutional amendment stating, "Men and women have equal rights. The law provides for equality, particularly within the family, in education, and in work. Men and women have the right to equal pay for equal work." The last provision was the major source of opposition, as some business interests claimed that an equal pay requirement could lead to bankruptcies.

Passage of the amendment constituted the nation's first major advance in women's rights since 1971, when women were granted the right to hold federal office and vote on federal issues. It was hoped that the amendment would encourage the three cantons that still denied women the right to vote in cantonal affairs to alter their policy.

Swiss voters took a much more conservative line in dealing with civil rights for the 110,000 foreign workers employed each year in Switzerland on a seasonal basis. As the law stands, these persons must work nine months each year for four consecutive years before being allowed to bring their families into the country, to receive full Social Security coverage, to change jobs, or to live outside specially designated residence halls. A referendum to remove these provisions and grant seasonal workers essentially the same rights as the 893,000 registered foreigners who

SWITZERLAND • Information Highlights

Official Name: Swiss Confederation.
Location: Central Europe.
Area: 15,943.4 sq mi (41 293.4 km^2).
Population (1981 est.): 6,300,000.
Chief Cities (1980 est.): Bern, the capital, 141,300; Zurich, 374,200; Basel, 180,900.
Government: *Head of state*, Kurt Furgler, president, (took office Jan. 1981). *Legislature*—Federal Assembly: Council of States and National Council.
Monetary Unit: Franc (1.82 francs equal U.S.$1, Nov. 1981).
Manufactures (major products): Watches, clocks, precision instruments, machinery, chemicals, pharmaceuticals, textiles, generators, turbines.
Agriculture (major products): High-quality cheese and other dairy products, livestock, fruits, grains, wine.

reside in Switzerland year-round was solidly defeated on April 5.

Trade Deficits. Economically, 1981 began with great concern over rapidly rising trade deficits, evidenced by an increase in the surplus value of imports over exports from $2,818,000,000 in 1979 to $6,713,000,000 in 1980. The first half of 1981 saw a sharp reversal of this trend. Imports declined 17.5% to $15,084,000,000, while exports fell 11.4% to $13,108,000,000. The projected gap was less than half of what it had been in 1980, but this did little to dissipate concern over the general decline in international trade.

PAUL C. HELMREICH, *Wheaton College*

SYRIA

In 1981, Syria strengthened its ties to the Soviet Union and maintained its leadership of the radical Arab bloc against Israel. Economic reforms were instituted to build Syria's meager foreign currency reserves, and strict guidelines were imposed to cut government spending. In addition, new funds were allocated for the nation's programs for housing and rural electrification. However, the government of President Hafez al-Assad labored under the strain of its involvement in Lebanon, an international crisis, and continued domestic strife.

Lebanon. On Jan. 22, 1981, the Arab League extended for six months the mandate of Syria's 22,000-member Arab Deterrent Force to maintain a balance of power in Lebanon.

On March 10, Assad met with Lebanese President Elias Sarkis to discuss security problems, the first such face-to-face meeting in more than two years. The consultation was without effect, as heavy fighting erupted between Christian Phalangist militiamen and Syrian troops March 24. On April 2, the Israeli-supported Phalangists began shelling Syrian positions around Zahle, a Greek Christian center east of Beirut. The fighting led to the year's major crisis.

Syrian-Israeli Face-off. On April 28, while Foreign Minister Abdel Halim Khaddam met in Beirut with Lebanese leaders, Israeli warplanes shot down two Syrian helicopters over Zahle, prompting Assad to deploy SAM-6 surface-to-air missiles near the city by April 30.

Assad insisted he was just protecting his troops against Israeli air attacks. Israel's charge that the deployment violated its security and its threat to remove them militarily led both countries to place their forces on alert.

While Syria had no viable military option against Israel, Assad was able to bend the crisis to his political advantage by gaining support throughout the Arab world. The crisis was at its height for two months, with neither side backing down. U.S. Special Envoy Philip Habib shuttled between Damascus, Beirut, and Jerusalem in an effort to buy time and ease tension, while Syria cooperated with other Arab states to resolve the original problem in Lebanon.

In May and again in June, Foreign Minister Khaddam met with representatives of Lebanon, Saudi Arabia, and Kuwait; by June 30 he achieved a settlement satisfactory to the Christian faction besieged in Zahle. To cement the agreement, Syria accepted $1,000,000,000 in Saudi aid, the resumption of Kuwait's $48 million ADF subsidy, and additional Arab peacekeeping troops in Lebanon. The missiles were never removed, but the crisis ebbed as world attention turned to Israel's June 7 raid on an Iraqi nuclear facility and on extremely heavy fighting in southern Lebanon in July.

Foreign Affairs. In the wake of Syria's 1980 Friendship and Cooperation Treaty with the USSR, Assad moved quickly to obtain advanced military equipment. On January 13, Army Chief of Staff Hikmat Shihabi met with Soviet military planners in Moscow and, by early February, some 200 advanced T-72 tanks were delivered.

In June, Assad announced a new Syrian-Soviet agreement to increase trade 150% by 1985. In mid-July, the Soviet Union staged major naval maneuvers off the Syrian coast.

On September 19, following the announcement of a proposed U.S.-Israeli strategic agreement, Syria led the Steadfastness Front (Algeria, Libya, South Yemen, and the PLO) to declare that it would seek closer ties with the Soviet Union.

Domestic. On January 5, Economics Minister Muhammad Atrash cited tax reform, revamping the price subsidy system, and spurring private investment as cornerstones of the effort to curb government spending. Although revenues were 81% higher in the first half of 1981 than in the same 1980 period, government agencies were ordered in July to slash spending by 10%.

On February 3, the second stage of Syria's rural electrification project, to bring power to 3,400 remaining villages, was announced. In July, a housing project to build 60,000 units annually was initiated.

Assad was forced to continue his two-year crackdown on antigovernment fanatics. Syrian troops reportedly gunned down hundreds of Muslim Brotherhood agitators in Hama province in April.

F. NICHOLAS WILLARD
Georgetown University

SYRIA • Information Highlights

Official Name: Syrian Arab Republic.
Location: Southwest Asia.
Area: 71,500 sq mi (185 185 km^2).
Population (1981 est.): 9,300,000.
Chief Cities (1975 est.): Damascus, the capital, 1,042,245; Aleppo, 778,523; Homs, 267,132.
Government: *Head of state,* Lt. Gen. Hafez al-Assad, president (took office March 1971). *Head of government,* Abdel Raouf al-Kasm, prime minister (took office Jan. 1980). *Legislature* (unicameral)—People's Council.
Monetary Unit: Pound (3.95 pounds equal U.S.$1, July 1981).
Manufactures (major products): Petroleum, textiles, cement, glass, soap, processed foods, phosphates.
Agriculture (major products): Wheat, barley, sugar beets, tobacco, sheep, goats, grapes, tomatoes.

TAIWAN (Republic of China)

In 1981, Taiwan remained firm in its anti-Communism, refusing to consider national reunification talks unless Peking renounced Communism. Despite assurances, Taiwan was worried by U.S. moves to strengthen ties with Peking. Taipei was particularly upset by the U.S. State Department's unwillingness to supply it with advanced fighter planes.

The economy was mixed, as the inflation rate moderated, but economic growth had trouble reaching the projected rate of 7.5%.

Party Congress. The 12th National Congress of the Kuomintang, the ruling party of Taiwan, was held in Taipei from March 29 to April 5. The Congress reelected President Chiang Ching-kuo as chairman of the party. In a manifesto issued at the conclusion of the Congress, the party called for unification of China under the Three Principles of the People, the Kuomintang doctrine. With regard to internal policy, the party stressed the common good of the people, with special attention to "equitable distribution of wealth" and raising the standard of living. "We will seek," said the manifesto, "what is good for the people and eliminate anything that is harmful to them."

Anti-Communism. On September 30, Peking proposed to hold reunification talks with Taiwan and offered the Nationalists "posts of leadership" in the government of a reunited China. Taiwan, said Peking, could also retain its armed forces, preserve its socioeconomic system, and maintain its economic and cultural relations with foreign countries. The Nationalists immediately rejected the overture as a propaganda ploy to damage Taiwan's international position and undermine its morale. Denouncing the Communist regime as tyrannical, Taiwan held firmly to its position that the only way to solve the China problem was to eliminate Communism. Said President Chiang Ching-kuo, "We shall never negotiate with the Chinese Communists."

President Chiang Ching-kuo was reelected chairman of the Kuomintang at the party congress.

Wide World Photos

Taiwan refused any contact, including commercial exchanges, with the People's Republic. As for indirect trade, the government maintained that it was beyond Taiwan's power to prevent shipments of its products to Communist China by a third country.

Policy Priorities. In 1981, Taiwan assigned top priority to national defense, internal government, and higher education. In national defense, efforts focused on modernizing the military forces. The government aimed at equipping the air force with high-performance jet fighters and increasing its arsenal of advanced missiles. Taiwan was to accelerate development of its own defense industry and move toward the manufacture of sophisticated weapons. In internal politics, the government sought to gear the democratic process to the rule of the law and to promote self-government in villages and townships. In education, its aim was to raise the academic standard of colleges and universities, stressing applied science and technology.

Economy. Taiwan's economic efforts were directed toward sustained growth and stability. Emphasis was laid on the development of machinery and electronics industries. In the face of soaring prices for imported oil, conservation of energy was considered imperative. Construction of power plants that use oil for fuel was suspended, and heavy and chemical industries that consume large amounts of energy were ordered to limit their production to items badly needed in domestic markets.

In June 1981, Taiwan launched the "second phase of land reform" to combat difficulties caused by industrialization. As more and more people went to work in factories, only 21% of the country's labor force worked on the land. To cope with that situation, the government en-

TAIWAN (Republic of China) • Information Highlights

Official Name: Republic of China.
Location: Island off the southeastern coast of mainland China.
Area: 13,885 sq mi (35 962 km^2).
Population (1981 est.): 18,200,000.
Chief Cities (Dec. 1979): Taipei, the capital, 2,196,237; Kaohsiung, 1,172,977; Taichung, 585,205.
Government: *Head of state,* Chiang Ching-kuo, president (installed May 1978). *Head of government,* Sun Yun-suan, premier (took office May 1978). *Legislature* (unicameral)—Legislative Yüan.
Monetary Unit: New Taiwan dollar (36 NT dollars equal U.S.$1, Oct. 1981).
Manufactures (major products): Textiles, electronic equipment, light manufactures, cement.
Agriculture (major products): Sugarcane, sweet potatoes, rice, vegetables.

couraged extensive use of farm machinery to reduce labor. Mechanical farming, however, requires larger tracts of land than most existing farms. Under the reform, the government would lend money to farmers to enlarge their farms.

For the first eight months of 1981, Taiwan's foreign trade totaled $29,956,800,000, an increase of 15.45% over the corresponding period the previous year. Exports amounted to $15,109,100,000 and imports $14,847,700,000, yielding a surplus of $261,400,000.

Foreign Affairs. Taiwan's chief foreign policy objective was to strengthen its ties with the United States, with which it had only "unofficial" relations. Taipei was dependent on Washington's support to ensure its defenses against Peking, as well as on American trade to sustain its economy. It had entertained high hopes for the China policy of U.S. President Ronald Reagan, who during his 1980 election campaign had shown much interest in elevating Taiwan's status. The Nationalists were greatly upset when in June U.S. Secretary of State Alexander Haig visited China to align Peking in a global strategy against the Soviet Union. They believed that the U.S. plan to sell weapons to Peking could only cause harm to the free world. Still, Taiwan found some relief in Reagan's statement on June 16 that he had not changed his "feelings about Taiwan" and that he intended to "live up to" the Taiwan Relations Act of 1979, which provided for the sale of defensive weapons to the island.

Good progress was made in Taiwan's trade and financial relations with Western European countries, including Great Britain, France, West Germany, Austria, The Netherlands, Belgium, Spain, and Greece. And to diversify Taiwanese markets, the government approved direct trade with Eastern European countries, though it did not allow contact with the Soviet Union.

CHESTER C. TAN
New York University

TANZANIA

The beginning of political change and the continuing economic difficulties marked the year in Tanzania.

Politics. Elections held on Oct. 26, 1980, resulted in the defeat of half the members of Parliament. Even though all candidates belonged to the ruling Chama Cha Mapinduzi Party, the defeat of so many incumbents was seen as a strong protest against the poor economy and as a growing restlessness. President Julius K. Nyerere himself was reelected with a 93% "yes" vote, his lowest percentage total in four elections, and he announced that his new five-year term would be his last. Already, in 1981, the new prime minister, Cleopa Msuya, and the foreign minister, Salim Salim, were lining up support to succeed Nyerere in 1985. Meanwhile, Aboud Jumbe was chosen president of the autonomous region of Zanzibar in a separate election on Oct. 26, 1980. He had held the office for many years, but this represented the first attempt to legitimize his rule by a popular election.

The elections were followed by a massive crackdown on corruption early in 1981. Dozens of government officials were suspended, and the transport minister, who was also the head of the state airline and the head of the State Investment Bank, was fired for misuse of government funds.

Economics. Despite severe economic problems, Tanzania refused to reverse its socialist and self-sufficient course. Drought caused widespread hunger, and the nation had to borrow up to $200 million from the International Monetary Fund (IMF) to meet the cost of imported food. However, Tanzania got the IMF to forego the tight economic and budgetary controls usually imposed for such a loan, and insisted on continuing its program of exchange control, government regulation of the economy, and large public-sector spending. Even with the loan, the economy suffered, as 50% of Tanzania's foreign exchange went to pay for imported petroleum, and the decline in usage of the Tan-Zam Railway caused the line to be closed to passenger traffic to save costs.

Tanzania finally withdrew its troops from Uganda, thus saving $5 million a month; nevertheless, the war and occupation had cost the country $500 million. Uganda's pledge to repay the costs of the war remained unfilled.

Foreign Affairs. Tanzania completed removal of its 10,000 troops from Uganda in June 1981, despite Ugandan pleas for its continuance as the one reliable law-enforcement organization in that nation. Tanzania also became involved with Kenya when late in 1980 Kenyan police killed armed Tanzanians far inside Kenya and recovered 400 stolen cattle. Kenya refused to allow Tanzanian participation in the investigation of the incident, and said that some of the raiders wore Tanzanian militia uniforms. In February 1981 both sides agreed to tighten border security. Nevertheless the incident and the failure to revive the East African Community or reopen the common border further strained relations between the two East African neighbors.

ROBERT GARFIELD, *DePaul University*

TANZANIA • Information Highlights

Official Name: United Republic of Tanzania.
Location: East Coast of Africa.
Area: 364,900 sq mi (945 091 km^2).
Population (1981 est.): 19,200,000.
Chief Cities (1978 est.): Dar es-Salaam, the capital, 870,020; Mwanza, 170,823; Tanga, 143,878.
Government: *Head of state,* Julius K. Nyerere, president (took office Jan. 1964). *Head of government,* Cleopa Msuya, prime minister (took office Nov. 1980). Aboud Jumbe, vice-president and president of Zanzibar (elected Nov. 1980). *Legislature* (unicameral)—National Assembly, 230 members.
Monetary Unit: Tanzanian shilling (8.27 shillings equal U.S.$1, May 1981).
Manufactures (major products): Textiles, cement, fertilizer, petroleum products.
Agriculture (major products): Sugar, maize, wheat, sisal, rice, cotton, coffee, tea.

TAXATION

Tax policy changes in 1981 reflected a diversity of fiscal attitudes among major industrial nations, most of whom were concerned with bringing inflation under better control and limiting government deficits.

THE UNITED STATES

Congressional Action. Congress approved the Economic Recovery Tax Bill of 1981, which was signed by President Ronald Reagan on Aug. 13, 1981. The law provides the largest tax reductions in U.S. history and will affect virtually every U.S. taxpayer. Over the period from 1981 through 1986, the new law will cut taxes by $749,000,000,000. The reduction will be $37,656,000,000 in fiscal year 1982, and the amount will rise in succeeding years to $267,626,000,000 in 1986, when the provisions are fully effective.

Individual taxpayers will benefit from many provisions of the new law, including reduced income tax rates, new tax incentives to encourage savings, easing of the so-called "marriage penalty" for two-earner married couples, more liberal tax provisions for U.S. citizens working abroad, and lower estate and gift taxes. The rate reductions apply across the board to all brackets and were to be phased in over 33 months beginning Oct. 1, 1981. In 1981, the reduction for the year would be 1.25%; in 1982, 11%; in 1983, 19%; and in 1984 and thereafter, 23%. The top marginal rate on investment income was cut from 70% to 50% ("earned" income had previously been taxed at the 50% maximum rate); and the top rate on long-term capital gains was lowered to 20%, retroactive to June 9, 1981. Beginning in 1985, the income tax brackets, zero bracket amount, and the personal exemption are to be adjusted for inflation, as measured by the consumer price index. In 1982, two-earner married couples filing a joint return will be able to deduct 5% of the first $30,000 of income of the lower-earning spouse (a maximum of $1,500), and in 1983 and thereafter, the deduction will be 10% (a $3,000 maximum).

The savings incentive provisions of the new law include exclusion from tax of up to $1,000 ($2,000 for joint returns) of interest on qualified one-year savings certificates issued between Sept. 30, 1981, and Jan. 1, 1983—the so-called "all-savers" certificates; increases in the allowable deductions for contributions to an individual retirement account (IRA) from up to 15% of compensation or $1,500 ($1,750 for a spousal IRA) to up to 100% of compensation or $2,000 ($2,250 for a spousal IRA); eligibility, for the first time, of active participants in tax-qualified pension plans for IRA deductions; increases in the maximum annual deduction for a contribution to a self-employed retirement plan (Keogh or H.R. 10 plan) from $7,500 to $15,000; liberalization of the maximum allowable deduction for employer contributions to employee stock option plans; and exclusion from tax of income up to $750 ($1,500 for joint returns) of dividends from public utilities which are reinvested in the stock of the company under a dividend reinvestment plan, effective for the years 1982 through 1985. Starting in 1985, taxpayers will be able to exclude 15% of net interest income (net of interest expense on consumer borrowing) up to a maximum of $450 ($900 for a joint return). The new law, however, repealed the partial exclusion of dividend and interest income for 1982 (formerly up to $200 for a separate return and $400 for joint returns), and reinstated the lower dividend-only exclusion applicable before 1981 ($100 on separate returns and $200 on joint returns).

For qualified U.S. citizens and residents working abroad, the maximum income exclusion for tax purposes will be $75,000 in 1982. It will rise in $5,000 annual increments to a permanent level of $95,000 in 1986. There is also an exclusion for excess housing costs above a base amount, currently $6,059.

Other provisions of the new law reducing individual income taxes for some taxpayers include liberalization of child and dependent care allowances; limited adoption expense deductions; limited charitable contributions deductions for nonitemizers; extension from 18 months to 2 years of the reinvestment period on tax-free gains on sales of residences; and an increase in the one-time exclusion of capital gains on home sales for persons 55 or older, from $100,000 to $125,000.

Estate and gift taxes will be reduced sharply by several provisions of the new law. The 1981 maximum rate of 70% on taxable transfers will drop five percentage points a year starting in 1982, to 50% for taxable transfers exceeding $2 million in 1985 and thereafter. Through increases in the unified credit against estate and gift taxes, the cumulative transfers exempt from tax will rise from $175,625 under previous law to $225,000 in 1982, and by additional amounts reaching $600,000 in 1987 and thereafter. The new law also removed the limits on both lifetime and death transfers between spouses made after 1981, and increased the annual limit on the gift tax exclusion from $3,000 to $10,000 to any single donee.

The business tax provisions of the 1981 law include new capital cost recovery provisions, liberalized investment tax credits, rate reductions for smaller corporations, and new tax incentives for research and experimentation. More than 95% of the business tax reductions will result from the new Accelerated Cost Recovery System (ACRS), which replaces the previous system of depreciation allowances, under which there were hundreds of asset classifications for tax purposes. The ACRS depreciation deductions are specified for predetermined recovery periods, which generally are shorter than the useful life as determined under previous law. For tangible personal property (machinery and equipment) assets are grouped into four classes with recovery periods of 3, 5, 10, and 15 years. Real property will also be written off over a 15-year period. ACRS applies to property placed in service after Dec. 31, 1980. The cost recovery amount will be accelerated in several stages and will become fully effective in 1986 and thereafter.

Many firms will also benefit from the more liberal leasing provisions of the 1981 law, which in effect allow firms to sell unusable depreciation deductions and investment tax credits. Also included in 1981 were provisions easing the windfall profits tax for royalty owners, independent producers, newly discovered oil, and certain charities, and tightening the tax treatment of "commodity straddles."

Supreme Court. The two major tax cases before the court in 1981 dealt with state powers to tax natural resources.

In *Maryland et al. v. Louisiana*, nine states challenged the validity of Louisiana's "first-use" tax on natural gas. Enacted in 1978, the tax was imposed at the rate of 7 cents per 1,000 cubic feet of gas not previously taxed, and produced mainly in the federally controlled outer continental shelf (OCS). The gas was piped to processing plants in Louisiana and, for the most part, eventually sold to out-of-state consumers. The OCS gas used in the state was excluded from taxation through a system of exemptions and credits. The "first-use" tax law also prohibited any attempt to allocate the tax to any party except the ultimate consumer. The Supreme Court ruled that the tax violated the commerce clause of the Constitution because it discriminated against interstate commerce in favor of local interests. The tax also violated the supremacy clause, the court said, because the provision prohibiting pipeline companies, which pay the tax, from passing it back to gas producers conflicted with the authority of the Federal Energy Regulatory Commission to regulate gas pricing.

Following its decision, the court ordered the state of Louisiana to stop collecting the tax and to refund to consumers the amounts it had collected, including interest. Revenue from the tax, totaling $548 million, had been held in escrow since 1979, when the suit was filed in the Supreme Court.

In *Commonwealth Edison Co. et al. v. Montana,* the court considered the right of the state to impose a high severance tax on coal. Montana has levied a severance tax on coal since 1921; the tax schedule at issue in the case was enacted in 1975. The tax is levied at varying rates, depending on the value, energy content, etc., of the coal, and may equal at a maximum 30% of the contract sales price. Four Montana coal producers and 11 of their out-of-state utility company customers filed suit in Montana state court in 1978, asking for more than $5.4 million in refunds and arguing that the tax was in violation of the commerce and supremacy clauses of the U.S. Constitution. The Montana Supreme Court had ruled that the facts alleged by the plaintiffs were insufficient in law to justify proceeding to trial.

The appellants did not challenge the state's right to levy a severance tax on coal, but argued that the high rate enacted in 1975 imposed an unconstitutional burden on interstate commerce. The Supreme Court did not agree. The court said there is no real discrimination since the tax is computed at the same rate, regardless of the final destination of the coal, and the tax burden is borne according to the amount of coal consumed, not according to any distinction between in-state and out-of-state consumers. Because the tax is measured as a percentage of the value of the coal taken, and is a general revenue levy, the court held that it is in proper proportion to the appellants' activities within the state. The court also struck down claims that the tax violated the supremacy clause by frustrating national energy policies, saying that the tax is not preempted by, or inconsistent with, any federal law. The court noted that the question of the tax rate was properly a matter for legislative, not judicial, resolution. Several bills to limit state taxation of natural resources have been introduced in Congress.

In *Western and Southern Life Insurance Co. v. California State Board of Equalization,* the court

U.S. Treasury Secretary Donald Regan was a major spokesman on taxes for the new administration.

UPI

considered the validity of California's retaliatory tax on foreign insurance companies. California first imposes a uniform tax on all insurance companies. For out-of-state companies doing business in California, it levies an additional tax to equal the tax that would be levied on a California company doing business in the company's home state. The insurance company, headquartered in Ohio, challenged the tax, claiming that it was in violation of the commerce and equal protection clauses of the Constitution.

The court held that the tax did not violate the commerce clause because Congress had passed legislation (the McCarran-Ferguson Act) that leaves the regulation and taxation of insurance companies to the states. As to the "equal protection" argument, the justices said that the tax should be sustained if the distinction it makes between domestic and out-of-state insurers is rationally related to the achievement of a legitimate state purpose. The case was of interest in the insurance industry, since 46 other states have laws based on the same theory.

State and Local Taxes. State and local governments collected $241,925,000,000 in tax revenues in fiscal year 1981, an increase of $20,529,000,000 or 9% over fiscal 1980. The percentage rise was just slightly above the 8.7% experienced in the previous year.

Mainly as a result of sluggishness in the economy, which threatened revenue shortfalls, many state legislatures in 1981 sought new taxes to balance budgets in forthcoming fiscal periods. The 1981 legislative sessions resulted in tax increases in 30 states, netting $2,500,000,000 a year, the highest annual statutory increase in ten years. The 1981 increment compares with a net increase of $420 million enacted in 1980, and with substantial reductions in the two preceding years. Higher general sales taxes, approved in four states in 1981, will account for a sizable portion ($860 million) of the total increase. Reacting to shortages of highway funds brought on by rising costs and declining gasoline sales, 24 states and the District of Columbia approved increases in gasoline tax rates.

INTERNATIONAL

Canada. The 1982 budget plan of the Canadian government, presented in November, calls for a "major overhaul" of the personal tax system. The budget's cutback of tax preferences includes removal of various provisions allowing tax deferrals, ending the tax-free status of a number of employee benefits (e.g., employer contributions to private health and dental plans, free travel passes, low-interest or interest-free employee loans for buying houses or company shares); and others. The combined federal-provincial individual income tax rate would be reduced from an average of 64% to 50%, thus cutting tax rates for some 5.8 million taxpayers with taxable income of more than $11,120. The federal tax reduction, previously 9% of tax with a minimum of $200 and a maximum of $500, would be set at a flat $200 for all taxpayers, with married taxpayers allowed to claim an additional $200 for their dependent spouses. Full indexation of the personal income tax is to be retained, providing a 12.2% increase in exemptions and tax brackets for 1982. The corporate surtax would be extended for two years, for large corporations, at rates of 5% in 1982 and 2.5% in 1983; and corporate depreciation allowances for tax purposes would be restricted.

Europe. Britain's Chancellor of the Exchequer Geoffrey Howe in March announced tax increases which would have major effects on individual taxpayers and banks. The 1981 finance bill sharply raised excise duties on alcohol, cigarettes, and petrol; extended the car tax to motorcycles, mopeds, and scooters; and imposed a one-time tax on banks, designed to recapture an estimated $886 million from record profits resulting from high interest rates. Individuals will also be subject to higher income taxes because the government did not follow its customary practice of adjusting the tax brackets and exemptions for inflation. Other tax increases cover a variety of gambling levies. There was some easing of gift taxation by reductions in the capital transfer tax rates and an increase in the annual exemption for tax-free transfers.

The West German government's budget proposal for 1982, announced in July, was aimed at limiting government expenses and reducing or abolishing certain tax incentives. The proposal included a special tax surcharge on individual income taxes, a rise in tobacco taxes, and reductions in some tax benefits.

In August the French government approved an amendment to the 1981 finance law, which included a 25% one-time surcharge on 1981 income for approximately 108,000 taxpayers in the highest income bracket; a rise from 7% to 17.6% in the value-added tax rate on services rendered by four-star and luxury hotels; and a 10% one-time tax on "lavish" expenditures of businesses which use a substantial part of their income for expenses such as gifts, entertainment, and free motor cars for staff members. Special one-time taxes were imposed on banks and credit institutions and on oil companies. The 1982 French budget included a new wealth tax at the rate of .5%, affecting about 2% of the taxpayers.

Italy increased the standard value-added tax rate from 14% to 15%, and simplified the structure of the tax by reducing the number of different rates applicable to various types of transactions.

Japan. The 1981 budget in Japan proposed an increase in the corporate income tax rate of two percentage points; higher commodity taxes on passenger cars, videotape recorders, and sporting goods; and increases in liquor taxes, stamp duties, and security transactions taxes.

ELSIE M. WATTERS
Tax Foundation, Inc.

TELEVISION AND RADIO

In 1981, the three office towers on New York City's Avenue of the Americas that house the headquarters of the three major television networks were like fortresses under siege. The far-flung conservative and religious groups that had been denouncing commercial programming for decades—without effect—suddenly presented a powerful united front called the Coalition for Better Television, led by a Mississippi clergyman, the Rev. Donald B. Wildmon.

Although the coalition and its high-profile spokespersons, the Rev. Jerry Falwell of the Moral Majority and antiabortion activist Phyllis Schlafly, canceled at the eleventh hour their threatened boycott of companies that advertised on what the coalition considered prurient or immoral programs, they made their point. Procter & Gamble, one of the nation's largest television advertisers, announced that it would voluntarily refrain from sponsoring certain programs. Even those who condemned the proposed July boycott as censorship stressed that they were defending only the principle of free speech, not the content of such racy programs as *Flamingo Road* or *Knots Landing.*

And the attack came from other quarters. By late 1981, cable television had reached into one fourth of all American households, and as it developed more and more of its own programming sources it began to gnaw away at network audience shares. The baseball strike sent TV executives scrambling for alternative—and much less popular—programming, such as minor league baseball and reruns of past World Series. And a three-month strike by the Writers Guild of America over profits from the sale of videocassettes and videodiscs made the opening of the fall season a halting, drawn-out affair.

But the American Broadcasting Company (ABC), the Columbia Broadcasting System (CBS), and the National Broadcasting Company (NBC) did not respond to the siege by throwing hot pitch over the ramparts; on the contrary, they appeared to yield a little. The new fall lineup, which featured the return of such TV warhorses as James Arness and Robert Stack, seemed to most columnists to be literally the grayest, and least risky, in many years. Titillating entertainment was slowly receding, and the only concessions to the womens' movement or alternative lifestyles appeared to be *Jessica Novack,* a new drama about a TV newswoman, and a Tony Randall vehicle about a discreetly homosexual businessman in search of a family.

But the networks threw themselves into the cable industry with more gusto than anyone had expected, announcing the establishment of new cable networks devoted to culture and the performing arts. Cynics—and there are always cynics when the networks make what appear to be enlightened gestures—said the Big Three were backing quality programming on cable so as not to create any overlap with what they were already offering on the airwaves.

Programs. With its second straight ratings victory in 1981, CBS appeared to be rebuilding the empire that programming whiz Michael Dann had fashioned in the 1960s. For not only did the network place four of its well-established shows—*Dallas, 60 Minutes, Dukes of Hazzard,* and *M*A*S*H*—at the top of the ratings chart, but it introduced a pair of innovative comedies late in the season that could be the core of a new generation of CBS hits. They were *Private Benjamin,* starring Eileen Brennan, and *The Two of Us,* with British actor Peter Cook.

NBC's *Hill Street Blues* was a textbook case in how far apart the critics and the general public can be. Though its ratings were low enough to spell death for any ordinary program, the critics raved about it and Fred Silverman, before stepping down as NBC president in July, granted the sophisticated police drama some extra time to establish itself. The ratings improved modestly and *Blues* dominated the Emmy Awards, receiving a record 21 nominations and winning 8.

ABC distinguished itself with the season's blockbuster—the critically acclaimed miniseries *Masada,* starring Peter O'Toole and Peter Strauss as a Roman general and a Jewish rebel leader locked in combat—but otherwise the net-

Picketers at a Philadelphia TV station protest the airing of a movie they consider too violent.

UPI

NBC Photo

NBC's weekly police drama "Hill Street Blues" won a record 8 Emmys, including best drama series.

work continued to lose ground to CBS. Critics found the new action/comedy *The Greatest American Hero,* about a bumbling, would-be superman, to be one of the few bright spots in an ABC schedule that was beginning to run out of gas.

After another miserable, third-place finish in the ratings in the spring, NBC introduced ten new series in the fall, but critics were baffled by how little new blood had actually been injected. Mickey Rooney, Rock Hudson, James Garner, and other middle-aged actors were showcased in what appeared to be an effort at retrenchment, as Grant Tinker took over the reins from Fred Silverman.

News. With the retirement of Walter Cronkite and the defection of David Brinkley from NBC to ABC after a very brief retirement, 1981 marked the end of an era in broadcast journalism. Ironically, the most beloved and credible figures in network news were leaving just when the public's interest in serious TV news was peaking.

To capitalize on this growing interest, CBS began to phase in five additional hours of news each week, expanding *Morning* by a half-hour and introducing a daytime spinoff of *60 Minutes* called *Up to the Minute.* But CBS' traditional superiority in news was facing a strong challenge. ABC's *World News Tonight* passed *The CBS Evening News* in the ratings at midyear. Polls indicated that the new CBS anchor, Dan Rather, was perceived as "too harsh" compared with the grandfatherly Cronkite. Another reason was that ABC, led by their intelligent and unflappable late-night anchor, Ted Koppel, had visibly upgraded its news operations. NBC sought to do the same, naming Tom Brokaw and Roger Mudd to co-anchor the evening news in the spring of 1982, replacing John Chancellor.

Overall, it was a year of uncertainty and introspection in TV news, an extension of the controversies that had been plaguing print journalism since Janet Cooke of *The Washington Post* had been stripped of her Pulitzer Prize for a fabricated article. (*See* special report, page 427.) Questions were being raised about the propriety of the "ambush interview" technique used on network newsmagazines. *60 Minutes,* in fact, invited some of its critics to a televised round-table discussion of the pros and cons of this type of investigative journalism. On ABC, a *20/20* report called "Arson and Profit" was attacked as "erroneous" by *Watching the Watchdog,* a news-critique program on WBBM-TV, the CBS affiliate in Chicago, setting off a series of televised rebuttals and counter-rebuttals. Columnists saw the Chicago battle as a symptom of the public's growing resentment of the power of television news.

Public Affairs and Regulation. In what many observers believed to be a landmark case (*Chandler v. Florida*), the U.S. Supreme Court ruled in January to admit television cameras into courtroom proceedings or, at least, to allow state supreme courts to decide whether to permit TV coverage. (*See* special report, page 297.)

Television and the courts were brought together in other ways in 1981. The prosecution of U.S. congressmen in the Abscam case hinged largely on videotaped evidence of the suspects receiving cash bribes; and the adaptation of the Jean Harris trial into a "docu-drama," aired just eight weeks after her conviction for the 1980 murder of diet doctor Herman Tarnower, was widely attacked as "exploitative."

The antiregulatory climate of the Reagan administration brought forth a proposal that the "Fairness Doctrine," which requires TV stations to allow time for opposing viewpoints on any editorial or paid political announcement, be abolished. Since the rule has always been vague and easy to evade—and is constantly being invoked by politicians who feel that their opponents have so staged a news conference as to be, in effect, a campaign speech—many, including liberals, thought the rule useless in its present form. But the proposal was given little chance of passage if congressmen perceived it as a threat to their reelection.

Public Television. Facing cuts of 35% in federal aid and sudden competition for foreign programming from the new cable networks, the Public Broadcasting System (PBS) got a glimpse of the abyss in 1981. Even its tax-exempt status was challenged over the use of advertising in its monthly guide, "The Dial," but PBS was upheld in court on that issue. A gift of $150 million from the Annenberg School of Communications of the University of Pennsylvania to help set up a

THE 1981 TELEVISION SEASON—Some Sample Programs

The American Family—Documentary on the changing family; with Robert MacNeil. Independent, May 28.
Angel Dusted—A 1981 TV-movie about a family whose son is a user of the drug PCP; with Jean Stapleton, John Putch, Arthur Hill. NBC, Feb. 16.
Barbara Walters Special—1) interviews with Nancy Reagan, Katharine Hepburn, and Lauren Bacall; and 2) with President Reagan. ABC, June 2, Nov. 26.
A Behind-the-Scenes Transition Diary—A documentary chronicling the transfer of presidential power from Jimmy Carter to Ronald Reagan. PBS, Jan. 21.
Berlin Tunnel 21—A 1981 TV-movie involving an escape attempt from East Berlin; with Richard Thomas, Horst Bucholz. CBS, March 25.
Beverly! Her Farewell Performance—In a benefit performance for New York's City Opera, Beverly Sills ended her opera-singing career. PBS, Jan. 5.
Bitter Harvest—A 1981 TV-movie about a chemical disaster; with Ron Howard. NBC, May 18.
Boston Symphony Celebration—Leontyne Price, Rudolf Serkin, Isaac Stern, Itzhak Perlman, and Mstislav Rostropovich appeared with the symphony in concert, celebrating its 100th anniversary. PBS, Nov. 4.
The Bunker—A 1981 TV-movie about Adolf Hitler's final days; with Anthony Hopkins. CBS, Jan. 27.
The Changing West: Reflections on the Stillwater—An *NBC Reports* telecast examining the problems of the small family-owned ranch; with Tom Brokaw. NBC, June 19.
The Christians—Thirteen-part British documentary series chronicling the impact of Christianity on world history and culture. Independent, June 29.
Cinderella—Frederick Ashton ballet performed at London's Royal Opera House. Independent. June 28.
Crisis at Central High—A 1981 TV-movie about the 1957 school desegregation showdown in Little Rock, AR; with Joanne Woodward. CBS, Feb. 4.
Danger UXB—Thirteen-part *Masterpiece Theatre* series set in World War II London. PBS, Jan. 4.
The Day after Trinity—A documentary on the life of J. Robert Oppenheimer. PBS, April 29.
Dear Liar—A comedy based on the 40-year correspondence between George Bernard Shaw and Mrs. Patrick Campbell; with Jane Alexander, Edward Herrmann. PBS, April 15.
The Defense of the United States—A five-part telecast examining U.S. defense policy; with Dan Rather. CBS, June 14.
Don't Look Back—A 1981 *ABC Theatre* film biography of Leroy "Satchel" Paige. ABC, May 31.
Dr. Jekyll and Mr. Hyde—A dramatization of the Stevenson tale; with David Hemmings. PBS, Jan. 6.
East of Eden—Three-part miniseries based on Steinbeck's 1952 novel; with Timothy Bottoms, Jane Seymour, Warren Oates. ABC, Feb. 8.
Elektra—Richard Strauss' opera; with Birgit Nilsson, and conductor James Levine. PBS, Jan. 28.
Escape from Iran: The Canadian Caper—A true-life dramatization of the escape of six Americans from Iran with the help of the Canadian Embassy personnel. CBS, May 17.
Evita Peron—A dramatization of the life of Argentina's Eva Peron; with Faye Dunaway. NBC, Feb. 23.
Family Reunion—Two-part 1981 TV-movie about a retired schoolteacher who visits her relatives and plans a reunion; with Bette Davis. NBC. Oct. 11.
Frederic Chopin: A Voyage with Byron Janis—Pianist Byron Janis surveyed Chopin's life and work. PBS, May 4.
Giulini Concerts: Los Angeles Philharmonic—A series of four concerts in celebration of the Los Angeles bicentennial. PBS, Nov. 25.
Good Evening, Captain—A television special commemorating Captain Kangaroo's 25th year on television. CBS, Aug. 21.
Hard Times—Charles Dickens' novel dramatized in a four-part presentation. Independent, Nov. 16.
Jacqueline Bouvier Kennedy—A drama based on the former first lady's early life; with Jaclyn Smith, Rod Taylor, James Franciscus. PBS, Oct. 14.
Kennedy Center Tonight—A birthday tribute to composer Aaron Copland aired from the Kennedy Center. PBS, April 1.
Kent State—1981 TV-movie about the shooting of student protesters by National Guardsmen at Kent State University in Ohio in 1970. NBC, Feb. 8.
La Traviata—Verdi's opera performed from the Metropolitan Opera House; with Ileana Cotrubas, Placido Domingo, PBS, Sept. 30.
L'Elisir D'Amore—A *Live from the Met* telecast of Gaetano Donizetti's comic opera; with Luciano Pavarotti, Judith Blegen. PBS, March 2.
Lily: Sold Out—A variety special starring Lily Tomlin, who in the storyline for the show prepares for a Las Vegas opening. CBS, Feb. 2.
Live from Lincoln Center—The American Ballet Theatre restaged a trio of works from the repertoire of Marius Petipa. PBS, May 20.
Lost to the Revolution—Documentary on the craftsmanship found in imperial Russia. PBS, May 11.
Manions of America—A three-part drama which opens in Ireland in 1845 and chronicles an Irish family's move to America. ABC, Sept. 30.
Masada—Four-part miniseries about a first-century Jewish insurrection against Rome, with Peter O'Toole, Peter Strauss. ABC, April 5.
The Monastery—An *ABC News Closeup* telecast of life inside the St. Joseph's Trappist monastery in Spencer, MA. ABC, Aug. 20.
Of Mice and Men—1981 TV-movie dramatizing Steinbeck's novella; with Robert Blake, Randy Quaid. NBC, Nov. 29.
The People vs. Jean Harris—A 1981 TV-movie based on the real-life court trial of school headmistress Jean Harris; with Ellen Burstyn. NBC, May 7.
Peter and Paul—Two-part biblical drama; with Anthony Hopkins, Robert Foxworth. CBS, April 12.
Shakespeare Plays—In the third of six seasons, the plays presented were *The Taming of the Shrew, The Merchant of Venice, Antony and Cleopatra, All's Well That Ends Well,* and *Othello*. PBS, Jan. 26, Feb. 23, April 20, May 18, Oct. 12.
Shock of the New—An eight-part series on modern art; with host Robert Hughes. PBS, Jan. 11.
Sinatra: The Man and His Music—Frank Sinatra in concert; with Count Basie. NBC, Nov. 22.
Skokie—A drama based on the true-life incident in Skokie, a predominantly Jewish suburb of Chicago, where a small group of neo-Nazis sought to stage a demonstration; with Danny Kaye. CBS, Nov. 17.
Staying On—A *Great Performances* drama, adapted from a novel by Paul Scott; with Trevor Howard, Celia Johnson. PBS, May 11.
Tales of Hoffmann—Jacques Offenbach's opera presented from London's Covent Garden Opera House; with Placido Domingo. Independent, Jan. 4.
The Tempest—A *Great Performances* telecast of the San Francisco Ballet company's performance of Michael Smuin's adaptation of Shakespeare's play. PBS, March 30.
Thérèse Raquin—A three-part dramatic adaptation of Emile Zola's novel; with Kate Nelligan. PBS, April 12.
Three Stories by Irwin Shaw—Dramatizations of *The Girls in Their Summer Dresses, The Monument,* and *The Man Who Married a French Wife*. PBS, June 1.
A Touch of Churchill, A Touch of Hitler—Special biography of Cecil John Rhodes, the man who acquired vast sections of Africa for the British crown. PBS, July 15.
Vietnam Veterans—Special report included two documentaries on the Vietnam veteran, *Frank: A Vietnam Veteran* and *The Warriors' Women*. PBS, Nov. 11.
Vladimir Ashkenazy in Concert—A *Live from Lincoln Center* telecast; with pianist Vladimir Ashkenazy, conductor Zubin Mehta, and the New York Philharmonic. PBS, Feb. 18.
Why Didn't They Ask Evans?—The dramatization of an Agatha Christie mystery; with Francesca Annis, James Warwick, Eric Porter. Independent, May 21.
Willie Stark—1981 musical drama by Carlisle Floyd, based on Robert Penn Warren's novel *All the King's Men;* with Timothy Nolen, Alan Kays. PBS, Sept. 28.

UPI

Tom Brokaw (left) and Roger Mudd (right) were named co-anchors of the "NBC Nightly News," to replace veteran John Chancellor (center) in 1982.

"college-of-the-airwaves" could not have been more timely.

Before austerity set in, PBS was able to present *Shock of the New,* an absorbing survey of modern art, with *Time* magazine art critic Robert Hughes, and to introduce one of the best examples of the growing Australian school of television drama, *A Town Like Alice.*

Cable TV and the New Technologies. ABC, CBS, and NBC managed to steal some of the thunder from their cable competitors when they announced their own cultural cable networks. ABC's "ARTS" was the first off the mark in the spring, competing directly with PBS to purchase European programming; "CBS Cable" bowed in the fall; and RCTV, a network owned jointly by Rockefeller Center Inc. and RCA, the parent company of NBC, will air in 1982 with exclusive access to programs produced by the British Broadcasting Corporation. RCTV will be a subscription service, like the other major cable programmers, while "ARTS" and "CBS Cable" are forging into the relatively untested waters of advertising on cable.

Meanwhile, the other cable programmers continued to develop software to fill the 120 channels that state-of-the-art hardware would allow, especially programs targeted to special interests. Getty Oil and ABC announced a joint sports channel that would offer one "blockbuster" event every week or month. ABC also joined with the Hearst newspaper empire to set up a network devoted to women's interests.

Newspapers were among the most conspicuous investors in cable during 1981, partly because they wished to avoid being pushed out of business by "videotext," or electronic newspaper technology. The Times-Mirror Company in Los Angeles set up a subscription channel able to buy movies directly from studios, possibly undercutting "Home Box Office" (HBO). Another proposed movie channel, "Premiere," founded by Getty and four of the major studios, would have obtained films free, in effect, but remained stalled all year in antitrust litigation. "Showtime," meanwhile, tried to distinguish itself from the larger HBO by presenting tapes of legitimate stage productions.

In the other technologies, the law opened and closed doors. The Federal Communications Commission (FCC) gave Comsat, the satellite operator, permission to begin direct satellite-to-home TV transmissions in 1985, opening the way for a revolution in technology that could make all other delivery systems, including broadcast stations and cable systems, obsolete. But for videocassettes, an October ruling by a federal appeals court in California that taping programs in the home violates copyright law, could be devastating. The case was passed to the Supreme Court and was not expected to be resolved for up to three years.

Radio. The deregulation of radio, agonized over for years, finally became a reality in 1981, though with an anticlimactic absence of any profound effects. The act lifted limits on the number of commercial-minutes per hour and eliminated the requirement to devote a certain number of hours to public affairs. But since many of the public affairs programs had already been relegated to early Sunday mornings (when few people listen), and since the natural trend of the marketplace has been to reduce the number of commercials, particularly on music stations, the transition to unregulated radio appeared relatively smooth.

Another sign of the antiregulatory mood in Washington was the Supreme Court decision in March that the FCC need not consider music format when licensing a radio station. A group called the WNCN Listener's Guild—named after the New York station that was challenged by angry listeners when it attempted to change its format from classical music to rock—had filed suit against the FCC, arguing that a station's public responsibility included catering to the musical taste of its constituents.

DAN HULBERT, *"Dallas Times Herald"*

TELEVISION AND RADIO—

SPECIAL REPORT:

VIDEODISCS

RCA

Though videodiscs were available in a limited way a few years earlier, 1981 marked the first year of nationwide distribution. With special playback equipment, these high-quality video recordings can be viewed on the home television screen. Major American and Japanese electronics corporations have invested hundreds of millions of dollars for development of this latest form of video technology.

What They Are. Videodiscs look like long-playing (LP) phonograph records but, unlike the familiar sound-reproducing record, they contain video (as well as audio) information. A special videodisc player converts the recorded material, which is in a TV-compatible FM format, so that it can be viewed on an ordinary TV set. A single disc can provide programs up to two hours long (one hour on each side), and both the picture and the audio quality are even better than that provided by over-the-air TV.

For home entertainment use, as well as potential educational, industrial, and commercial applications, the new videodisc technology is in competition with the already established video cassette recorder (VCR) which, while more expensive than the disc system, does have the ability to record TV programs. The videodisc is bought as a prerecorded item; it can not be recorded on home equipment. In 1981, a videodisc player cost between $500 and $750, compared with about $1,000 for a VCR. A full-length movie disc cost about $25, a cassette about $60.

How They Work and Who Makes Them. Because the potential market is so great, competing videodisc systems are being introduced by the largest U.S. and Japanese electronics manufacturers, combined in three joint ventures: RCA and Zenith Radio; North American Philips, Magnavox, and Pioneer Electronics; and Victor Co. of Japan (JVC), Matsushita Electric, and General Electric. In addition, a number of record makers and music companies have helped meet the public demand for discs.

The three different videodisc technologies are not compatible; discs from one system cannot be played on equipment made by either of the others. The RCA SelectaVision system was introduced in early 1981. The picture and sound information is stored in very fine grooves on a 12-inch (30-cm) record, which rotates at a speed of 450 rpm. Minute depressions within the groove are tracked by an electrode or "capacitance probe," which responds to changes in the electric capacitance (ability to store electric charge) between the stylus and the bottom of the groove.

The Philips/Magnavox (MagnaVision) system uses a laser beam for recording and playback. The video information is stored in tiny pits burned into the disc by the recording laser. Another laser in the player "looks" at the microscopic pits and opto-electronically converts the FM-encoded record into pictures and sound.

The third system—that developed and marketed by JVC/Matsushita/GE—uses a capacitance pickup, but there is no groove. A tiny, flat metal shoe rests on the surface of the disc; its position is controlled electronically as the disc spins at a rate of 900 rpm.

The three systems have different capabilities in terms of search-time for particular frames or sequences, displaying pictures as stills, and exhibiting portions of the record in slow motion. The laser system appears to be the most flexible, but the technology is developing so rapidly that another year might bring a better system.

Growth and the Future. The demand for videodisc systems is expected to be very large in coming years—as many as 500,000 players by the end of 1982, a 50% increase for each subsequent year, and an annual rate of 5,000,000 players sold by 1990. The number of videodiscs would, of course, be many times greater; annual sales of 200,000,000 records by the end of the decade have been predicted. The business could be worth as much as $7,000,000,000.

Such estimates, however, are highly conjectural. In this age of microelectronics and microprocessors, a decade is a long time indeed.

M. D. FAGEN

Ray Blanton and Mrs. Blanton are the center of attention by the media after the former Tennessee governor was found guilty of extortion, conspiracy, and mail fraud.

UPI

TENNESSEE

In legislative action, lawmakers approved an unprecedented $4,000,000,000 appropriation measure for the 1981–82 fiscal year. The sales tax was continued at 4.5%, but the gasoline and diesel fuel taxes were increased 2 and 4 cents per gallon, respectively. Lack of adequate funding for schools and other programs continued to generate discussion of an income tax, but political leaders predicted that such a tax, declared unconstitutional decades ago, may not be forthcoming for some time. While state employees received very little by way of pay increases, the state did agree to assume full costs of their retirement system.

The crime rate continued to soar—in the rural counties as well as in the cities. Memphis, Nashville, Chattanooga, and Knoxville each experienced an increase of about 20% above that of 1980, but a half dozen cities in the 10,000 population bracket had increases of 30–50% over that of a year ago. For the first time in the state's history, a former governor was convicted of a felony and sentenced to prison. Ray Blanton, governor from 1975 to 1979, was convicted of extortion, conspiracy, and mail fraud in the issuance of liquor licenses and sentenced to three years in prison. Two aides, James Allen and Clyde Edd Hood, Jr., tried with Blanton, were sentenced to lesser terms for the same offenses. Two other Blanton associates had been sentenced a few months earlier after conviction for bribery. In separate trials, the governor's brother, Gene Blanton, and uncle, Jake Blanton, were sentenced and fined for rigging bids on road construction projects.

The largest tobacco crop since 1946 was expected to exceed 140 million lbs (63.5 million kg)—up 46% from 1980. Soybean production was up 31%, cotton 24%, and corn 95%. The potato and sweet potato crops were up about 50%. For the first time, the value of farm land exceeded an estimated value of $1,000 per acre.

While enrollments in grades K-12 remained steady, institutions of higher learning experienced small enrollment declines. Higher admission and retention standards, increased tuition, and cuts in federal student aid were blamed. Tennessee State University, a predominantly black institution, had a decline in freshman enrollment of more than 25%.

In September, 70,000 Metro Nashville students experienced a three-week delay in school opening when the U.S. Court of Appeals issued a last-minute stay of the Board of Education's new desegregation plan. Among other things, the plan had abolished busing and emphasized the neighborhood school concept. Civil-rights attorneys successfully argued before the court that the plan as proposed by the board would accentuate segregation, especially in the suburbs.

The unemployment rate for the major cities increased slightly. Nevertheless, tax collections were up across the state, due in large measure to a brisk tourism business during the summer and fall months and to the increase in the gasoline and diesel fuel tax receipts.

TENNESSEE • Information Highlights

Area: 42,144 sq mi (109 153 km^2).
Population (1980 census): 4,590,750.
Chief Cities (1980 census): Nashville, the capital, 455,651; Memphis, 646,356; Knoxville, 183,139; Chattanooga, 169,565; Clarksville, 54,777; Jackson, 49,131; Johnson City, 39,753; Murfreesboro, 32,845; Kingsport, 32,027; Oak Ridge, 27,662.
Government (1981): *Chief Officer*—governor, Lamar Alexander (R). *General Assembly*—Senate, 33 members; House of Representatives, 99 members.
State Finances (fiscal year 1980): *Revenues*, $4,028,000,000; *expenditures*, $3,874,000,000.
Personal Income (1980): $35,525,000,000; per capita, $7,720.
Labor Force (July 1981): *Nonagricultural wage and salary earners*, 1,705,300; *unemployed*, 176,400 (8.6% of total force).

Tennesseans who died in 1981 included Joe Carr, Democratic leader and for 30 years the state's secretary of state, and Alexander Marchant, distinguished Vanderbilt University professor and former head of the Brazilian Institute.

ROBERT E. CORLEW
Middle Tennessee State University

TEXAS

The prospects for continued growth and development in Texas remained highly favorable. According to the 1980 U.S. census, the state had 6.3% of the nation's population and accounted for 13% of its growth in the 1970s. During that decade, Texas expanded at a rate more than double the national average, second only to Florida among the 50 states.

Economy. In 1981, the Lone Star State continued to benefit from the nation's preoccupation with finding new sources of oil and gas. Spurred by favorable legislation from Washington, exploratory drilling has increased markedly. Geologists estimate that Texas leads the nation in proven reserves of both natural gas and oil with 25% of the former and 28% of the latter. As a result, the state ranks first in crude oil refineries, crude oil production, and exploratory drilling. While predominance in the energy field comes as no surprise, growth in the agrarian phase of the economy is a new and welcome development. Texas ranks first in all forms of livestock and produces one third of the nation's cotton. Yet another healthy sign is the fact that the jobless rate in Texas is far below the national average despite heavy migration to the Sunbelt.

Politics. The regular session of the state legislature convened Jan. 31, 1981, and considered a number of controversial issues, including legislative redistricting, bilingual education, prison reform, and educational funding.

As a result of the 1980 census, Texas was one of 12 states to increase its representation—from 24 to 27—in the U.S. House of Representatives. Reapportionment mandated by the census was not completed in the regular session of the state legislature that ended in June, and a special session had to be called. Before the body's redistricting plan could be implemented, however, it was struck down in a federal lawsuit.

Bilingual education has become an increasingly important issue in Texas politics. After much debate, the legislature acted to grant $50.00 per pupil toward the cost of a bilingual program through the primary grades. The issue of illegal Mexican aliens remained divisive as well, with the controversy focusing on a state law denying free public education to illegal alien children.

Along with several other states, Texas was the object of a suit to improve conditions in its prison system. A ruling in an Ohio case of the same nature indicated that Texas was in general compliance with national constitutionally mandated standards.

Speaker of the Texas House of Representatives Billy Clayton was acquitted in Houston after a lengthy and complex trial on misconduct charges. Exonerated and with a successful legislative session behind him, Clayton indicated that he was considering running for governor in 1982. The announcement did not seem to faze the incumbent, Gov. William Clements, who stated that he would probably run for reelection.

On May 4, Henry Gabriel Cisneros, 33, was elected mayor of San Antonio, becoming the first Mexican-American mayor of a major U.S. city. On November 17, Houston elected its first woman mayor, Kathryn Jean Whitmire, 35.

Education and the Arts. Long thought to be inadequate, funding for higher education was increased somewhat by the state legislature. By statute, the Permanent University Fund, a bonanza to the state in the form of oil royalties, can be shared only by the University of Texas and Texas A&M University. The desire of other state-supported institutions to share in that fund gave rise to an intense political struggle. The question was left unsettled. Meanwhile, college enrollments showed a substantial increase despite decline in other parts of the country.

The Houston and Dallas symphonies continued to attract artists of national repute. The Houston Grand Opera Company revived Scott Joplin's *Treemonisha* for local audiences and then presented the work on Broadway to critical acclaim. The Kimball Art Museum in Fort Worth attracted thousands of visitors when it hosted the popular exhibit from China, "The Age of Bronze."

STANLEY E. SIEGEL, *University of Houston*

TEXAS • Information Highlights

Area: 226,807 sq mi (691 030 km^2).
Population (1980 census): 14,228,383.
Chief Cities (1980 census): Austin, the capital, 345,496; Houston, 1,594,086; Dallas, 904,078; San Antonio, 785,410; El Paso, 425,259; Fort Worth, 385,141; Corpus Christi, 231,999; Lubbock, 173,979; Arlington, 160,123; Garland, 138,857.
Government (1981): *Chief Officers*—governor, William P. Clements, Jr. (R); lt. gov., William P. Hobby (D). *Legislature*—Senate, 31 members; House of Representatives, 150 members.
State Finances (fiscal year 1980): *Revenues*, $12,924,-000,000; *expenditures*, $11,487,000,000.
Personal Income (1980): $136,146,000,000; per capita, $9,545.
Labor Force (July 1981): Nonagricultural wage and salary earners, 6,150,300; unemployed, 369,800 (5.5% of total force).

THAILAND

The collapse of the government and the appointment of a new government, a failed coup attempt in April, and a new development plan highlighted an eventful year in Thailand.

Politics. Oil split the two main parties of the civilian government, headed by Gen. Prem Tinsulanonda. At issue were negotiations with Saudi Arabia and termination of a commercial refining

UPI

Soldiers loyal to the government assume guard positions during a successful countercoup against military officers who tried to take over the Thai government in April.

lease. The coalition collapsed on March 3, and on March 10 a new government was formed minus the largest parliamentary party. Controversy erupted over the ministerial appointment of Sudsai Hasdin, a rightist whose organizations were blamed for killing students and leftists in the mid-1970s.

These events, plus the perennial jostling for power among military leaders, prompted a coup on April 1. Led by Gen. Sant Chipatima and a number of colonels known as the "Young Turks," military units seized Bangkok and surrounding areas. But Prem escaped to Nakhon Ratchasima, a military base, where he was soon joined by the royal family and loyal military and civilian leaders. This was the first time that the king and queen had publicly intervened in the country's coup-ridden politics. By April 3, the coup collapsed, with only two persons killed. The plotters were later given amnesty.

In July, Prem announced his retirement as army commander in chief. His reluctance to retire in 1980, when General Sant was in line to replace him, may have led to Sant's coup leadership. Prem protégé Lt. Gen. Arthit Kamlang-ek was placed in line to become commander in 1982.

The Economy. In a move with greater psychological than economic impact, the baht was devalued against the U.S. dollar from 21 to 1 to 23 to 1 as the dollar's strength reduced the competitiveness of Thai exports in European and Japanese markets.

On October 1, the fifth five-year development plan began. The new plan seeks economic stability by reducing deficits and limiting government spending, while attempting to redress imbalances in wealth by taxing the wealthy more and focusing on increasing productivity in the agricultural and industrial sectors. Per capita income is projected to double under the plan, as are gross domestic product and imports.

Refugees. Thailand is a first haven for emigrés from Laos, Cambodia, and Vietnam, and more than 250,000 refugees remained at midyear. Although the government canceled its threatened forced repatriation, by July it began moving new arrivals to detention rather than refugee camps. The hardening of Thai policy paralleled the announced one-third reduction in U.S. refugee admissions.

Security. Despite continuing attacks by Communist groups and Muslim separatists in the South, the most dramatic event was a raid by Indonesian commandos on a hijacked Indonesian airliner at the Bangkok airport on March 31. Domestically, student and labor leaders, who fled or joined forces with the Communists following the 1976 coup, increasingly sought to return to civilian life.

Foreign Affairs. Thailand looked to the Association of Southeast Asian Nations (ASEAN) in formulating its policies. It remained friendly toward China, which it sees as countering Vietnamese forces in Laos and Cambodia.

K. MULLINER, *Ohio University*

THAILAND • Information Highlights

Official Name: Kingdom of Thailand.
Location: Southeast Asia.
Area: 198,000 sq mi (512 820 km^2).
Population (1981 est.): 48,600,000.
Chief Cities (1980 est.): Bangkok, the capital, 4,870,509; Chiang Mai, 105,230.
Government: *Head of state,* Bhumibol Adulyadej, king (acceded June 1946). *Head of government,* Gen. Prem Tinsulanonda, prime minister (took office March 1980).
Monetary Unit: Baht (23.00 baht equal U.S.$1, July 1981).
Manufactures (major products): Processed foods, textiles, wood, cement.
Agriculture (major products): Rice, rubber, tapioca, corn, sugar, pineapples.

THEATER

In 1981 the public image of Broadway was one dominated by the star. Celebrated performers known either entirely or mostly for their film careers—Elizabeth Taylor, Lauren Bacall, and Lena Horne—appeared. However, the most notable, publicized, meritorious, extensive, and expensive show of the year had no stars at all in its cast. Featuring a gifted multitude of total strangers, it was *Nicholas Nickleby,* an importation from a British repertory theater, the Royal Shakespeare Company.

Nicholas Nickleby. *The Life and Adventures of Nicholas Nickleby,* adapted by David Edgar and directed by Trevor Nunn and John Caird, crammed an astonishing amount of Charles Dickens' novel into its two segments of four and four-and-a-half hours. In London it was possible to buy an individual ticket for either half, but in New York purchasers were required to buy tickets for both halves at a cost of $50 each. Even $50 (the price of any seat in the house) would have been a record high for a single Broadway ticket; $100 set a mark that it is hoped will not be surpassed for many years. In this episodic chronicle of a decent young country gentlemen's alternating encounters with virtue and vice in Victorian England, Dickens' promise to his readers to make them laugh, cry, and wait is fulfilled. The play's length and the number and variety of its characters had the special virtue of creating the impression that the audience was confronting an entire world. An additional virtue was the in-depth display of the human resources of this extraordinary acting company. The skill of the performers—Roger Rees (in the title role), Emily Richard, David Threlfall, and their colleagues—served as a reminder of what is missed by not encouraging the development of permanent acting companies trained in the classics and by permitting older permanent theaters to die and new ones like the Vivian Beaumont (built to house a permanent company) to fall into disuse.

Repertory Theater. At a time when the British system was giving such striking evidence of glowing good health, some of New York's closest equivalents were in trouble. The BAM Theater Company (of the Brooklyn Academy of Music) and the Chelsea Theater Center went out of business. The prestigious Vivian Beaumont Theater of Lincoln Center, having originated two unremarkable productions in 1981, closed for more than a year so that extensive changes could be made in its auditorium. On the other hand, the New York Shakespeare Festival (the umbrella term for Joseph Papp's producing empire, which includes free shows in Central Park, the off-Broadway Public Theater, and occasional Broadway productions) continued to flourish, not especially for any personal quality that Papp gave to it, but because of the distinctive talents that he attracted and encouraged. Probably its most important achievement of 1981 was getting a new money-making hit established on Broadway, Gilbert and Sullivan's *The Pirates of Penzance* (in an inventive production first seen in Central Park in 1980), to help pay for the festival's more adventurous and less profitable projects in the park and at the Public.

"Nicholas Nickleby," a "great theatrical experience of our time," set a ticket-price record.

UPI

BROADWAY OPENINGS OF 1981

MUSICALS

Bring Back Birdie, book by Michael Stewart, music by Charles Strouse, lyrics by Lee Adams; conceived and directed by Joe Layton; with Donald O'Connor, Chita Rivera; March 5–8.

Camelot, book and lyrics by Alan Jay Lerner, music by Frederick Loewe; directed by Frank Dunlop; with Richard Harris, Meg Bussert; Nov. 15–.

Can-Can, book by Abe Burrows, music and lyrics by Cole Porter; directed by Mr. Burrows; with Zizi Jeanmaire; April 30–May 3.

Copperfield, book, music, and lyrics by Al Kasha and Joel Hirschhorn, based on Charles Dickens' *David Copperfield;* directed by Rob Iscove; with Brian Matthews; April 16–26.

Dreamgirls, book and lyrics by Tom Eyen, music by Henry Krieger; directed by Michael Bennett; with Obba Babatunde, Cleavant Derricks, Loretta Devine, Ben Harney, Jennifer Holliday, Sheryl Lee Ralph; Dec. 20–.

Fiddler on the Roof, book by Joseph Stein, music by Jerry Bock, lyrics by Sheldon Harnick; directed by Jerome Robbins; with Herschel Bernardi; July 9–Aug. 23.

The First, book by Joel Siegel, with Martin Charnin, music by Bob Brush, lyrics by Mr. Charnin; directed by Mr. Charnin; with David Alan Grier; Nov. 17–Dec. 12.

The Five O'Clock Girl, book by Guy Bolton and Fred Thompson, music and lyrics by Bert Kalmar and Harry Ruby; with Lisby Larson; Jan. 28–Feb. 8.

Marlowe, book by Leo Rost, music by Jimmy Horowitz, lyrics by Mr. Rost and Mr. Horowitz; directed by Don Price; with Patrick Jude, Margaret Warncke, Lennie Del Duca, Jr.; Oct. 12–Nov. 22.

Merrily We Roll Along, book by George Furth, music and lyrics by Stephen Sondheim, from the play by George S. Kaufman and Moss Hart; directed by Harold Prince; with Ann Morrison, Lonny Price, Jim Walton; Nov. 16–28.

The Moony Shapiro Songbook, book by Monty Norman and Julian More, music by Mr. Norman, lyrics by Mr. More; directed by Jonathan Lynn; with Jeff Goldblum, Judy Kaye; May 3.

My Fair Lady, book and lyrics by Alan Jay Lerner, music by Frederick Loewe; directed by Patrick Garland; with Rex Harrison, Nancy Ringham, Jack Gwillim, Cathleen Nesbitt, Milo O'Shea; Aug. 18–Nov. 29.

Oh, Brother!, book, lyrics, and direction by Donald Driver, music by Michael Valenti; with Harry Groener, Alan Weeks, Larry Marshall, Judy Kaye; Nov. 10–12.

The Pirates of Penzance, by W. S. Gilbert and Arthur Sullivan; directed by Wilford Leach; music adapted by William Elliott; with Rex Smith, Linda Ronstadt, Estelle Parsons, George Rose; Jan. 8–.

Song of Norway, book by Milton Lazarus, lyrics and musical adaptation by Robert Wright and George Forrest, based on the life and music of Edvard Grieg; with Stephen Dickson, Sheryl Woods; Sept. 3–13.

Woman of the Year, book by Peter Stone, music by John Kander, lyrics by Fred Ebb, based on the film; directed by Robert Moore; with Lauren Bacall, Harry Guardino; March 29–.

PLAYS

Candida, by George Bernard Shaw; directed by Michael Cristofer; with Joanne Woodward, Jane Curtin, Ron Parady, Tait Ruppert; Oct. 15–.

Crimes of the Heart, by Beth Henley; directed by Melvin Bernhardt; with Lizbeth Mackay, Mary Beth Hurt, Mia Dillon, Peter MacNicol; Nov. 4–.

The Dresser, by Ronald Harwood; directed by Michael Elliott; with Tom Courtenay, Paul Rogers; Nov. 9–.

Duet for One, by Tom Kempinski; directed by William Friedkin; with Anne Bancroft, Max Von Sydow; Dec. 17–.

Einstein and the Polar Bear, by Tom Griffin; directed by J. Ranelli; with Peter Strauss, Maureen Anderman; Oct. 29–31.

The Father, by August Strindberg; translated by Harry G. Carlson; directed by Goran Graffman; with Ralph Waite, Frances Sternhagen; April 2–26.

The Floating Light Bulb, by Woody Allen; directed by Ulu Grosbard; with Beatrice Arthur, Jack Weston, Brian Backer, Danny Aiello; April 27–June 21.

Fools, by Neil Simon; directed by Mike Nichols; with John Rubinstein, Pamela Reed; April 6–May 9.

Frankenstein, by Victor Gialanella; directed by Tom Moore; with David Dukes, Keith Jochim; Jan 4.

Grown Ups, by Jules Feiffer; directed by John Madden; with Bob Dishy, Frances Sternhagen, Harold Gould; Dec. 10–.

Heartland, by Kevin Heelan; directed by Art Wolff; with Larry Nicks, J. C. Quinn, Sean Penn, Martyn St. David; Feb. 23–March 15.

Inacent Black, by A. Marcus Hemphill; music and lyrics by Gene McFadden, John Whitehead, and Melba Moore; directed by Mikell Pinkney; with M. Moore; May 6–17.

It Had to Be You, by and with Renée Taylor and Joseph Bologna; directed by Robert Drivas; May 10–June 21.

I Won't Dance, by Oliver Hailey; directed by Tom O'Horgan; with David Selby, Gail Strickland; May 10.

Kingdoms, by Edward Sheehan; directed by Paul Giovanni; with Armand Assante, Roy Dotrice, Maria Tucci; Dec. 13–27.

The Life and Adventures of Nicholas Nickleby, by Charles Dickens, adapted by David Edgar, music and lyrics by Stephen Oliver; co-directed by Trevor Nunn and John Caird; with Roger Rees, Emily Richard, John Woodvine, Priscilla Morgan, Oct. 4–.

The Little Foxes, by Lillian Hellman; directed by Austin Pendleton; with Elizabeth Taylor, Maureen Stapleton, Tom Aldredge; May 7–Sept. 5.

Lolita, by Edward Albee, adapted from the novel by Vladimir Nabokov; with Ian Richardson, Donald Sutherland, Blanche Baker; March 19–24.

Macbeth, directed by Sarah Caldwell; with Philip Anglim, Maureen Anderman; Jan. 22–March 8.

Mass Appeal, by Bill C. Davis; directed by Geraldine Fitzgerald, with Milo O'Shea, Michael O'Keefe; Nov. 12–.

Ned and Jack, by Sheldon Rosen; directed by Colleen Dewhurst; with John Vickery, Peter Goetz; Nov. 8.

Passionate Ladies, by Barbara Perry; directed by Edmund Balin; with Barbara Perry; May 5–10.

Piaf, by Pam Gems; directed by Howard Davies; musical direction and arrangements by Michael Dansicker; with Jane Lapotaire, Zoë Wanamaker; Feb. 5–June 28.

Rose, by Andrew Davies; directed by Alan Dossor; with Glenda Jackson, Jessica Tandy; March 26–May 23.

Scenes and Revelations, by Elan Garonzik; directed by Sheldon Epps; June 25–July 19.

The Supporting Cast, by George Furth; directed by Gene Saks; with Hope Lange, Betty Garrett, Sandy Dennis, Jack Gilford, Joyce Van Patten; Aug. 6–Sept. 6.

The Survivor, by Susan Nanus; directed by Craig Anderson; with David Marshall Grant; March 3–8.

A Talent for Murder, by Jerome Chodorov and Norman Panama; directed by Paul Aaron; with Jean-Pierre Aumont, Claudette Colbert; Oct. 1–Dec. 6.

A Taste of Honey, by Shelagh Delaney; directed by Tony Tanner; with Valerie French, Amanda Plummer, Keith Reddin; June 19–Nov. 8.

To Grandmother's House We Go, by Joanna M. Glass, directed by Clifford Williams; with Eva Le Gallienne, Kim Hunter, Ruth Nelson; Jan. 15–March 8.

Wally's Cafe, by Sam Bobrick and Ron Clark; directed by Fritz Holt; with Rita Moreno, James Coco, Sally Struthers; June 12–23.

The West Side Waltz, by Ernest Thompson; directed by Noel Willman; with Katharine Hepburn, Dorothy Loudon; Nov. 19–.

REVUES

Broadway Follies, music and lyrics by Walter Marks; concept and direction by Donald Driver; with Robert Shields, Lorene Yarnell; March 15.

Emlyn Williams as Charles Dickens; Jan. 14–Feb. 1.

Lena Horne: The Lady and Her Music; May 12–.

Shakespeare's Cabaret, concept and music by Lance Mulcahy; directed by John Driver; with Larry Riley, Catherine Cox, Patti Perkins, Pauletta Pearson; Jan. 21–March 8.

Sophisticated Ladies, concept by Donald McKayle, based on the music of Duke Ellington; directed by Michael Smuin; with Gregory Hines; March 1–.

This Was Burlesque, musical satire based on Ann Corio's recollections; with Ann Corio; June 23–28.

Meanwhile, other permanent theaters in North America and elsewhere were undergoing serious changes. The recently revived American Shakespeare Theatre of Stratford, CT, acquired a new director, Peter Coe, who is British, like the departing head of BAM. The Stratford Festival of Stratford, Ontario, acquired a new director, John Hirsch, who is, for a change, not British but Canadian. The Guthrie Theater of Minneapolis began a new life under Rumanian director Liviu Ciulei. But in London one of the spiritual ancestors of all English-speaking permanent theaters, the Old Vic, closed its doors.

The Stars. Earlier in the year, the *grandes dames* arrived in force. Elizabeth Taylor, who had no previous professional experience on the stage, played the leading role of the malevolent Regina Giddens in *The Little Foxes,* Lillian Hellman's 1939 drama of iniquitous business practices in the American South of the Reconstruction period. Maureen Stapleton appeared as her virtuous but ineffective sister-in-law. The news media were ecstatic. Experience will tell, however, and in the view of some, Miss Taylor's lack of stage experience told against her. Even so, playgoers flocked to see her, and no doubt the whole enterprise did some good, if only to proclaim that the theater's magnetism is so great as to compel even a famous film actress to respond to it.

Lauren Bacall starred in *Woman of the Year,* a moderately pleasant musical based on an old Spencer Tracy–Katharine Hepburn film of the same name. Playing a television news interviewer who encounters a cartoonist (Harry Guardino) unawed by her fame, Miss Bacall again showed that she has a vivid stage presence and that the qualities of her personality more than outweigh the relative lack of professional polish in her singing and dancing. She now has a second Tony award to prove it.

In *Lena Horne: The Lady and Her Music,* Miss Horne simply came on stage to sing and occasionally to reminisce—and to bewitch her audience thoroughly. Her recital was somewhat in the increasingly popular new vogue of bookless musical performances drawing upon the rich tradition of black American song. In Miss Horne's evening, while the gifted singer was black, the selection of music was color-blind. (*Sophisticated Ladies,* interpreting the music of Duke Ellington mainly through choreography and most emphatically in the tap-dancing fireworks of Gregory Hines, was a more representative example of this new and exceptionally attractive Broadway fashion.)

Other Musicals. The primacy of plot in musicals was asserted aggressively late in the year by *Merrily We Roll Along,* directed by Harold Prince, with a score by Stephen Sondheim and a book adapted by George Furth from the 1934 play of the same name by George S. Kaufman and Moss Hart. Like the earlier play, the new musical runs backward in time to show the buoyant hopes that preceded the ultimate selling out, but in this updated version the time span was moved into the relative present.

UPI

"Lena Horne: The Lady and Her Music" was such a hit that its limited Broadway run was extended.

Most of the rest of the year's musicals fed off the successes of past seasons. Revivals included *My Fair Lady,* with Rex Harrison repeating his original role; *Camelot,* with Richard Harris (who replaced the stricken Richard Burton on the road) repeating his role of the film version; *Fiddler on the Roof,* with Herschel Bernardi; and—notably less successful—Cole Porter's *Can-Can* and a relic of 1927, *The Five O'Clock Girl. Bring Back Birdie,* a sequel to *Bye Bye Birdie,* a popular 1960 musical about a rock singer, had none of the charm of the original. *This Was Burlesque* tried but failed to capitalize on the success of the previous season's *Sugar Babies.* Other failed musicals had literary origins—*Copperfield,* a cheerless interpretation of Charles Dickens' novel, and *Marlowe,* a rock musical about the Elizabethan dramatist.

Plays. Among Broadway's straight plays of American origin, high acclaim went to Beth Henley's comedy of small town life in Mississippi, *Crimes of the Heart.* The play began a brief limited engagement at the off-off-Broadway Manhattan Theater club late in 1980, won the Pulitzer Prize in the spring of 1981, and opened on Broadway in the fall. It is probable that no earlier play ever has won the Pulitzer Prize after being seen by so few people in New York, but *Crimes of the Heart* had previously been acted in four regional theaters. Its amazing success conferred glory on both off-off-Broadway and on a burgeoning regional network. Miss Henley's chief characters are three sisters, flightier than Chekhov's, who make grounds for farce out of the legion of disasters and disgraces that beset them. The ensemble performances of Mary Beth Hurt, Mia Dillon, and Lizabeth Mackay, ably directed by Melvin Bernhardt, lost none of their glitter during the long hiatus between off-off-Broadway and Broadway. A few days before this play reached New York another comedy by Miss Henley, *The Miss Firecracker Contest,* opened in Buffalo and gave new evidence of Miss Henley's talent for dramatizing the comic possibilities of misfortune.

Another of the Manhattan Theater Club's 1980 plays made its mark on Broadway, Bill C. Davis' *Mass Appeal,* about the confrontation between a cynical older priest (played by Milo O'Shea) and a disillusioned seminarian. After a long tour, Katharine Hepburn came to town, playing an aging pianist in Ernest Thompson's *The West Side Waltz.* Another film queen arrived in a less fortunate vehicle, Claudette Colbert playing a mystery novelist in a mystery play, *A Talent for Murder,* by Jerome Chodorov and Norman Panama. A stage queen, Eva Le Gallienne, returned at 82 for a brief run as a firm but genial matriarch in Joanna M. Glass' *To Grandmother's House We Go.*

Leading U.S. dramatists had scant success in 1981. Edward Albee's *Lolita,* a dramatization of Vladimir Nabokov's novel about a mature man's infatuation with a pre-teen girl, betrayed little true sympathy for the original. Neil Simon's *Fools,* directed by Mike Nichols, revealed that a single comic idea, a Russian village inhabited entirely by imbeciles, is not enough to hold an audience for an evening. At the Whitney Museum, Arthur Miller narrated a new concert version of his *The Creation of the World and Other Business* titled *Up From Paradise,* set to music by Stanley Silverman. Tennessee Williams' frank autobiographical play, *Something Cloudy, Something Clear,* was staged off-off-Broadway.

Among the many American plays that came and went quickly, Victor Gialanella's *Frankenstein* had the twin distinctions of lasting only one night and losing a large amount of money.

Some British importations generated interest. They were Pam Gems' *Piaf* (from the Royal Shakespeare Company), with Jane Lapotaire as Edith Piaf; *Rose,* by Andrew Davies, with Glenda Jackson as a rebellious feminist wife and schoolteacher, impressively supported by Jessica Tandy as her mother; and Ronald Harwood's *The Dresser,* with Paul Rogers as a veteran Shakespearean actor and Tom Courtenay as his dresser.

Two permanent theaters belong to the category of Broadway. One is the Vivian Beaumont, which offered two productions—*Macbeth,* in which Philip Anglim in the lead made little impression, and Woody Allen's *The Floating Light Bulb,* a gentle, apparently autobiographical comedy of Jewish family life during World War II. The other is the Circle in the Square, which presented August Strindberg's *The Father,* George Bernard Shaw's *Candida,* with Joanne Woodward in the lead (overshadowed for many by Shaw's *Misalliance* at the Roundabout Theater), and a new American play with Chekhovian echoes, Elan Garonzik's *Scenes and Revelations.*

Off Broadway. For new plays, it was arguable that the real action was off Broadway—even for the less recent new plays, like David Mamet's *American Buffalo,* revived effectively with Al Pacino as a violent lowbrow. Off-Broadway musicals were few; the most notable were William Finn's *March of the Falsettos,* a highly original treatment of a homosexual's family life, and *I Can't Keep Running in Place,* Barbara Schottenfeld's exploration of feminist issues. Kevin Wade's first play, *Key Exchange,* amusingly examined the problems of young people who are wary of entanglements, Christopher Durang wittily lampooned therapy in *Beyond Therapy* and later satirized religion in *Sister Mary Ignatius Explains It All for You.* At the Circle Repertory Theater, Lanford Wilson added a new chapter to his chronicle of the Talleys, showing the rest of the family in a less favorable light in *A Tale Told.* For a week at La Mama it was possible to see more than 70 performers in Wallace Shawn's *Hotel Play,* a mordantly bitter portrait of an extremely unpleasant hotel. Charles Fuller's *Zooman and the Sign,* graphically recording a black family's response to the loss of a child, began with presentation by the Negro Ensemble Company but moved on from there to performances in another theater.

Samuel Beckett's *Rockaby,* the monologue of a woman facing death, opened on the dramatist's 75th birthday. Other foreign plays included Irish Brian Friel's *Translations,* which showed the establishment of English education in Ireland, English Caryl Churchill's *Cloud Nine,* and several German dramas, among which Franz Xavier Kroetz's *Request Concert* won the most attention for Joan McIntosh's performance.

The New York Shakespeare Festival presented a disastrous version of *The Tempest* and a commendable *Henry IV: Part One* in Central Park during the summer. The regular season at the Public Theater offered some extremely mixed fare, including two promising plays of Chinese-American life, David Henry Hwang's *The Dance and the Railroad* and *Family Devotions;* Meryl Streep in Elizabeth Swados' musical adaptation of Lewis Carroll, *Alice in Concert;* Richard Foreman's experimental *Penguin Touquet;* JoAnne Akalaitis' arresting documentary on nuclear power, *Dead End Kids;* and, from the German, Wolfgang Hildesheimer's *Mary Stuart,* a cynical new view of the Scottish queen's death.

HENRY POPKIN
State University of New York at Buffalo

THIRD WORLD

The Third World and the Reagan administration were on a collision course, and there was more than one unpleasant confrontation during 1981.

Economics. In September, U.S. President Ronald Reagan addressed the annual meeting of the World Bank and the International Monetary Fund (IMF) in Washington. Reagan's message was in many ways an extension of his domestic economic policies—the countries of the Third World had to make greater efforts to help themselves or foreign aid would be meaningless. Reagan also preached free enterprise economics as opposed to socialist planning. A similar message was delivered to the UN General Assembly by U.S. Secretary of State Alexander Haig.

In late October, President Reagan attended the summit meeting in Cancún, Mexico, which brought together 23 leaders from industrialized and developing countries and the UN to discuss Third World problems. Reagan was conciliatory in his attitude, but the basic lines of U.S. policy remained unchanged.

Neither Reagan nor Haig was threatening to end American assistance to the poor countries of the Third World. The United States is the biggest single contributor to international aid programs (although other countries give more per capita), and it is a foregone conclusion that Washington will remain the largest source of economic aid to the Third World. But the conditions of American cooperation with the Third World had become more stringent—"soft" loans were not going to be quite so soft, and more performance and efficiency would be demanded from the poor countries.

It was also clear that with tensions between Washington and Moscow increasing, the United States was going to be looking very closely at the behavior of Third World states in East-West issues. No longer could a Third World state expect American-financed aid while at the same time taking an anti-American position on East-West issues.

Washington was not only willing to throw its economic weight around in bilateral dealings with Third World states, but it was also quite prepared to use its predominant influence in such international agencies as the World Bank, IMF, and various UN aid organs.

Plight. Although World Bank statistics showed that the Third World countries had not done so badly as many had thought during the decade of the 1970s (often having had higher growth rates than developed countries), the confrontation between the United States and the Third World came at a particularly bad time. The world economy was in a recession in 1981. Some Third World states had trouble finding markets and adequate prices for their exports. The rise in the value of the U.S. dollar on international currency exchanges meant the poor countries had to pay more for the dollars they needed in order to purchase oil. Again, OPEC (the Organization of Petroleum Exporting Countries) was not very generous to the poor.

The private banking system of the capitalist countries was already over-extended. These banks had already given large loans to Third World countries, and in some cases there was the possibility of default. A lot of international money had gone to Communist countries, particularly bankrupt Poland and nearly-bankrupt Rumania. The Soviet Union was shopping around for loans to develop its oil and mineral resources in Siberia. All this diverted aid from the Third World, and high interest rates in the United States meant high interest rates for other countries.

Although the countries of the Communist bloc preached brotherhood to the Third World, little aid was forthcoming, except to those places where Soviet military expansionism could be served.

Meetings. Little was achieved at such meetings as the UN conference on energy in Nairobi in August or the UN conference on the world's poorest countries in Paris in September. The best that could be achieved was a papering over of differences between the United States and the Third World.

Sea Law Conference. Perhaps the biggest shock for the Third World came at the UN Law of the Sea Conference in Geneva, where the Reagan administration rejected the sea law treaty worked out by the Carter administration. The new government in Washington feared that the treaty provisions on international control of the seabed would discriminate against U.S. mining companies (*see* LAW—International).

UNESCO. The effort to create a "new world information order" caused more friction between the West and the Third World at UNESCO (UN Educational, Scientific, and Cultural Organization). The United States and its allies considered this effort nothing more than an attempt by Third World states (with the support of Moscow) to muzzle the free press, particularly the work of foreign correspondents.

Nuclear Proliferation. The Israeli air strike on the Osirak nuclear reactor in Iraq in June highlighted the danger of the spread of nuclear weapons to the Third World. India already has nuclear-weapons capability, and Pakistan is moving in the same direction. (*See* special report, page 342.)

Nonaligned Movement. With Cuba heading the Nonaligned Movement, the moral and political prestige of the movement reached a new low. Nonaligned states were concerned about Communist expansionism in Cambodia and Afghanistan, but with Cuban President Fidel Castro as chairman, the Nonaligned Movement seemed to find it easier to criticize the United States than the Soviet Union and its allies.

AARON R. EINFRANK, *Free-lance writer*

Leslie Lowman

Small commuter airlines, operating from medium-sized U.S. communities, such as Danbury, CT, above, have recently increased across the United States, a result of deregulation of the airlines.

TRANSPORTATION

The year was a difficult one for all types of commercial carriers. Significant gross national product (GNP) growth in the first quarter was followed by weakened economic conditions, continued high interest rates, and inflation only somewhat abated. The significant strengthening of the dollar against European currencies and economic recession in Europe adversely affected both tourist and goods traffic on the North Atlantic, though the Pacific trade continued to flourish. A prolonged coal strike and the continued prostration of the U.S. automotive industry bit heavily into rail traffic. Yet rail traffic measured in ton miles held up well against 1980 traffic, while motor carrier, air, and Great Lakes water volumes recorded declines.

Economic Regulation. While 1980 produced major legislation to reform regulation of domestic motor carrier, railroad, and freight forwarder transportation, 1981 was a year of interpretation, adaptation, and controversy as industry attempted to adjust to changed circumstances, and the Interstate Commerce Commission (ICC) sought to put flesh on the bones of the new statutes. Complaint was loud from the American Trucking Associations and its member conferences and from shipper organizations that the commission, in its efforts to implement the Motor Carrier Act of 1980 and the Staggers Rail Act, was denying due process, proceeding with undue haste, and exceeding the discretion conferred on it by Congress. The Reagan administration professed the intention to continue the movement toward deregulation, but no significant legislation affecting transportation was put forward. The appointment of Reese H. Taylor, Jr., to the commission and his designation as chairman, together with the departure of the two commissioners most devoted to administrative deregulation, strongly suggested a slower pace and more care to adhere to the principles laid down in the 1980 statutes.

Major changes in the application of regulation occurred in 1981. Perhaps the most important was exemption from regulation on March 23 of railroad piggyback traffic (trailer on freight car/container on freight car), which represents some 7.5% of all railroad carloadings. The exemption applies to intermodal rail-ocean traffic in international trade as well as to domestic rail-truck movements. It was strongly protested by ocean carriers, ports, and the Federal Maritime Commission. Late in the year, the Association of American Railroads was attempting to exclude from the exemption intercarrier agreements for the interchange of trailers and containers which, otherwise, may violate the antitrust laws. The exemption means, among other things, that railroads may quote piggyback rates from day to day without notice of change, alter their limits of liability for loss and damage, close existing joint routes, and otherwise alter the conditions under which piggyback transportation will be performed. Whether the railroads would benefit remained to be seen. Competitive pressures and the burden of fuel costs, however, were causing some motor carriers to look more favorably on surrendering long hauls to the railroads for movement in piggyback service.

Since the rail act of 1976, the commission has been barred from prescribing maximum rail rates unless it is shown that the railroads possess "market dominance," essentially a monopoly of the traffic in issue. The Staggers Act of 1980 prescribed a floor for market dominance by an escalating percentage of rail variable costs commencing with 160%. Above that the commission has discretion to consider other factors that may indicate that it has or has not jurisdiction to prescribe a maximum reasonable rate at or above the statutory floor. The commission abandoned its presumptions, which had been laboriously developed following the 1976 statute, and laid down new principles. Substantial investment in rail-related facilities by shippers no longer counts—the availability of alternative materials or geographic origins does. Many shippers contend that the new standards render proof of market dominance well-nigh impossible and the standards were under challenge in the courts. Coal, which represents 30% of originated rail tonnage, and other bulk commodities are those principally affected. Hence the issue is of great significance to the public.

The motor carrier industry was greatly disturbed by the cavalier fashion in which the commission granted new operating rights. Dissenting commissioners pointed out the failure of the majority even to test the fitness of applicant carriers, a standard prescribed by law. Broad territorial rights were frequently granted even though it was plain that applicant carriers were in no position, financially or otherwise, to exercise a good portion of those rights. The long-standing proposition that a motor common carrier had an obligation to serve the public over its authorized routes appeared to be a thing of the past.

A major effect of regulatory reform is the almost complete disappearance of the prohibitions of unjust discrimination in rates and fares which had built up over the years. The public is now able to observe airline fares from New York to Kansas City higher than those from New York to San Francisco, even though both are offered by the same airline. As freight rates are increasingly made by independent action, shippers are denied the opportunity successfully to charge discrimination in rate relationships, whether between competing commodities or competing hauls between origins and destinations. Rail contract rates are virtually unchallengeable. Carrier and shipper relations more and more come down to comparative bargaining power.

Effects of Deregulation. It is too early to evaluate the results of the 1980 revisions. Airline deregulation, however, has had several years to demonstrate its effects. One book-length study is already available. Interpretation is made difficult by the erratic performance of the economy during the period of adjustment and the sharp escalation of fuel prices that occurred roughly one year into the era of deregulation. The early proliferation of reduced fares, sharply increased passenger traffic, and enhanced load factors inevitably gave way to fare increases in many markets and in regular classes of passenger service as fuel costs mounted to 30% of airline operating expenses. Many airlines that had expanded route patterns in the initial phase of deregulation found it necessary to contract services to more compact configurations. Economic recession produced declines both in passenger and cargo traffic and reduced load factors in 1980 and into 1981. Operating losses of the scheduled airlines in 1980 ($225 million) had been the largest in history and 1981 showed little promise of improvement. The future of Braniff and Pan American in particular remained conjectural in the light of their heavy and continuing losses.

The adverse impact on airline earnings is not directly traceable to deregulation, though sharp price competition induced in major markets and shifts in operating patterns in the attempt to adjust to changing competitive circumstances bear some responsibility for the results. In general, certificated airlines have abandoned service at the smaller points. Hundreds of small commuter airlines have sprung up to service these points under the subsidy provisions of the Airline Deregulation Act. Hence few points have lost air service altogether, but the commuter airlines offer service in smaller aircraft, frequently with more daily departures but fewer available seats, and, generally, at higher fares. Medium-sized communities have suffered a loss of competitive service as certificated airlines concentrated their efforts in major markets and at principal hub airports. From July 1978 to July 1981, 326 communities lost the services of one or more certificated airlines. While sharp fare competition continued in major markets, fares at smaller points escalated rapidly. Aside from commuter lines, new entrants to the industry appeared principally in dense short-haul markets, e.g. New York Air, to the Washington-Boston corridor; Midway, out of Chicago; and People's Express, with service in a number of short-haul markets out of New York.

Both airline deregulation and motor carrier regulatory reform have put pressures on the labor unions and the carriers that employ union labor. New airlines begin service with nonunion personnel. This has been easy in a period when large numbers of pilots and other skilled personnel are on indefinite furlough from the major lines. Relatively low wages and fringes, as well as freedom from restrictive work rules, give the newcomers a distinct economic advantage in the markets they choose to enter. Unions involved in the first negotiations with a major airline (United) in 1981 recognized these pressures with significant concessions. In the motor carrier industry, too, new entrants are usually nonunion and often too small to attract organizing efforts. Freight rate discounts, which have become common following the 1980 act, were precipitated by a large established carrier that has maintained nonunion status. The expansion of private carrier operations, facilitated by the act, seems likely also to contribute to an increasing proportion of tonnage handled by nonunion labor. Financially ailing motor carriers and airlines alike are seeking concessions from their workers as a means to reduce red ink.

Railroad Developments. When the figures are compiled, 1981 should show a further growth in the railroad share of total freight ton miles. The rail share, which had been consistently declining since the end of World War II, climbed somewhat in 1980 as motor and water carriers felt the effects of recession more severely than did the railroads. Originated rail tonnage, however, was virtually the same in 1980 as in 1944 and declined somewhat in 1981. The increase in ton miles, therefore, represents a continuing increase in length of haul. The shift of short-haul business to trucks has continued and, since 1970, rail length of haul has been pushed rapidly upward by the increasing volume of Western low-sulfur coal, which moves over great distances.

Rate increases and surcharges, partly facilitated by the Staggers Act of 1980, acted favorably on rail earnings. Net railway operating income reached an all-time peak in 1980, which promised to be surpassed in 1981. Though an improvement over the 1970s, this performance loses much of its impressiveness when adjusted for inflation. The Rock Island continued in liquidation. Portions of its lines were taken over for rehabilitation and continued operation by other railroads, short lines and others. Most notable was the Tucumcari Line acquired by the Cotton Belt to provide a shorter route for its parent Southern Pacific into the Kansas City and St. Louis gateways. The possibility improved of a financial reorganization of the Milwaukee, now reduced to a core system, while negotiations continued for the sale of the westernmost portion of the system terminating at Miles City, MT. The Boston & Maine was on the verge of emerging from trusteeship following proposed acquisition by private parties, and the Delaware & Hudson may find a home in the same growing Mellon system.

Temporarily, at least, rail car shortages, which had been experienced in most years since the 1940s, appeared to be a thing of the past. Box cars and covered hoppers, in particular, were in surplus supply. Those car leasing companies that had developed sizable fleets of plain box in recent years of shortage found themselves in trouble as large portions of their ownership were idled. Railroad orders for new freight cars dried up and a shakeout in the car building industry appeared likely. Since ton miles were running about even with the prior year, it appeared that significant improvement in the utilization of the railroad car stock was finally being achieved. The mergers of recent years had reduced interchange delays, car information systems had been continually upgraded, and a revision of the car service rules in 1981 made most freight cars available for loading to any destination regardless of ownership.

A more than 40% increase in U.S. exports to Mexico had produced an unparalleled railroad congestion at the border crossings in 1980. The accumulation of U.S.-owned freight cars in Mexico surpassed acceptable limits and southward rail movements were embargoed. A permit system followed to enable the more urgently needed imports to move. Close cooperation between U.S. and Mexican rail officials produced gradual relief that enabled restoration of normal cross-border movements early in 1981. Meanwhile, several new steamship services were instituted between U.S. Gulf and Mexican ports.

The advent of the Reagan administration in Washington raised great uncertainty about the future of Conrail and Amtrak. The administration favored a breakup of Conrail and its sale to other railroads along with a major curtailment of Amtrak's passenger train services. Conrail continued to be more adversely affected than most other railroads by the low level of automobile production, the curtailment of steel production at several points on its lines, and the prolonged coal strike. Deferral of maintenance had begun again on the system as federal funds dried up. Amtrak passenger miles had fallen by more than 6% in 1980 and the burden of federal subsidy was growing. Congress took a more restrained approach than the administration had sought, providing $260 million in fiscal 1982 for Conrail and $735 million for Amtrak, a level of funding considered adequate to retain 85% of Amtrak's existing operations. Conrail was also relieved of the cost of Title V labor protection, the Congress appropriating $400 million for termination payments. As a result, Conrail should be able to reduce its work force by 4,600 by early 1983. By June 1, 1983, after commuter operations have been severed from Conrail and some light density lines disposed of, Conrail will be subject to sale in pieces unless the United States Railway Association finds it can operate at a profit during the ensuing five months. In that case it will be offered for sale as a whole. Thus the stage is set for disposal of Conrail to private parties provided that it can be made attractive. Meanwhile Conrail negotiated the folding of 285 separate labor agreements into 26, opening the prospect of more efficient utilization of workers.

Urban Transit. Progress continued on the rapid transit systems in Atlanta and Miami and the light rail systems in Buffalo and San Diego. Portland (OR) matured plans for a light rail system extending initially into the eastern suburbs. In all of these instances, well-tested technology is being employed and cost containment has been better than expected. In New York and a number of other cities, a new bus design produced by Grumman developed cracks in its frame and other defects which occasioned withdrawal from service and expensive retrofit.

The Reagan administration sought to alter federal mass transit programs. Most important was a reversal of the 1974 policy of extending operating subsidies for local transit; instead, designated local revenues will be employed for such purposes. In 1970, 84% of transit operating expenses had been covered by fare-box revenues. By 1980 the percentage had fallen to 42, while federal subsidies covered 15%. The Urban Mass Transit Administrator contended that 80% of operating expenses were payments to labor and that subsidies had resulted in loose bargaining with transit employees. In consequence their wages had, since 1974, increased far more rapidly than either the Consumer Price Index or wages of police and fire department personnel. Elimination of operating subsidies will, of course, pose serious problems for local transit administrators. Federal funding will continue to be available, however, for capital projects.

Transit and commuter rail systems in Chicago faced financial crises during the year. The Regional Transportation Authority found itself without funds to meet contractual payments to railroads for commuter services—several roads were without contracts. Some of the rail lines threatened to cease operations. The Chicago Transit Authority, too, was in difficulty. Transit fares were increased by 10 cents, while commuter fares were authorized a temporary increase of 52.5%. In the absence of effective state action, Mayor Jane Byrne secured passage of a package of city tax measures designed to provide funding.

The U.S. Department of Transportation, responsive to a Court of Appeals ruling, issued revised regulations concerning the access of handicapped persons to public transit facilities. The new rules permit considerable flexibility for the provision of alternate services rather than equipping all buses with wheelchair lifts and stations with elevators to platforms. Alternatives could include dial-a-bus service or the provision of taxicab vouchers.

Motor Carriers. The decline continued in freight tonnage carried by large, regulated intercity trucking companies, with traffic levels remaining below the depressed levels of 1980. The decline suggested that new entrants and expanded private hauling may have made increased inroads upon the large regulated carriers. There are no comprehensive statistics covering private, exempt, and regulated truck transportation, hence it is possible only to speculate on the total volume of business. In the face of economic and competitive uncertainties and

UPI

New York, a city with massive transit problems, experiments with the Japanese-made "Hino" bus.

continued high interest rates, new equipment orders remained depressed and only one manufacturer of heavy-duty tractors was able to show a profit. Nevertheless, many large carriers were extending their route patterns and opening new terminals.

Motor carriers employed the increased freedoms that the 1980 changes in the Interstate Commerce Act permitted to make rate changes. Of particular importance to the efficiency of the transport system is the ability, increasingly used, to quote reduced rates for multiple shipments tendered at one time and picked up by a single city vehicle. The opportunity to base general rate increases on prospective rather than actual costs promised to eliminate the regulatory lag that had plagued carriers during inflationary periods.

Air Transport. The significant development of the year was the strike by members of the Professional Air Traffic Controllers Organization (PATCO), which began on August 3. Some 13,000 controllers walked off the job in a strike which, since they were federal employees, was illegal. The president promptly ordered their dismissal, and the union was decertified in October. (*See also* TRAVEL.)

The General Accounting Office issued a report which detailed and criticized discriminatory practices by foreign governments against American-flag international air carriers and urged greater use by the Civil Aeronautics Board (CAB) of its powers to retaliate in the face of such discrimination.

ERNEST W. WILLIAMS, JR., *Columbia University*

TRAVEL

As 1981 neared its close, many facts and figures regarding U.S. domestic and international travel during the year remained unclear. No one could predict with certainty the results of the most dramatic happening, the walkout of some 13,000 members of the Professional Air Traffic Controllers Organization (PATCO) on August 3.

PATCO. Initially, union members and many industry officials predicted paralysis for tourism and business because of the public's fear of flying without PATCO members in U.S. airport towers. Several weeks after the strike, however, the chairman of the National Transportation Safety Board stated that despite public uncertainty, there was no "substantial indication" of hazards.

At year's end, the air lanes were being scanned by some 10,000 controllers, about 7,200 fewer than before the strike, of whom almost 6,000 were nonunion members or PATCO members who refused to walk out. Some 3,000 were supervisors; 850 were drafted from the military, and some 450 were newly hired controllers. The Federal Aviation Administration (FAA) estimated that it would take at least three years to being the system to proper staff levels and stated that about 3,000 controller jobs were probably "redundant."

An autumn price war by the airlines caused the traveler of late 1981 to search for the best bargain.

Michael Pfleger for "Business Week"

Economic results were severe. Thousands of airline employees were laid off and several small companies went out of business. In September, the Air Transport Association estimated that the industry was losing about $5 million a day, a figure sharply reduced from the $35 million daily losses when the walkout began.

For travelers, the strike meant fewer and more crowded flights as traffic was reduced substantially, particularly at the nation's 22 major airports. The aim of the FAA and the Transportation Department was to establish takeoffs at about 78% of the pre-strike levels.

Interestingly, in some senses the airlines that had been troubled financially earlier in the year were benefiting from the situation. Large aircraft began flying with fuller loads because of fewer departures, while general housecleaning resulted in mothballing of unneeded planes and employees and elimination of unprofitable routes. Analysts of the industry predicted that the airlines' earnings would soar from $75 million in 1980 to $400–600 million by the end of 1981.

Airfares. Flying in the tailwind of the controllers' strike came sharply reduced airfares as several trunk lines joined a price war started in the autumn by ailing Pan American World Airways. (Earlier, Pan Am had been forced to sell its huge headquarters building in New York City and its profitable Intercontinental Hotels subsidiary and to name a new chairman, C. Edward Acker, formerly boss of highly successful Air Florida.)

The slashing of ticket prices and such inducements as two-for-the-price-of-one coupons led to a startling upturn in the airline's passenger levels and was followed by similar actions by other major carriers. However, the bonanza for travelers was not expected to continue; when the battles ceased with the holiday and midwinter season, prices were expected to rise higher than before to make up for the temporary cuts.

At times, airline anxieties seemed to dominate all travel news during 1981, but there were other important economic and social stories.

U.S. Dollar. As the U.S. dollar strengthened against other major world currencies, travel overseas became much less expensive for Americans. Europe, in particular, was a major recipient of increased traffic. At one point the dollar bought more French francs than it had for a decade.

Packagers of "upscale" European tours were especially enthusiastic about the increase in business as compared with that of 1980. American Express claimed an 18.6% rise in bookings to Great Britain and Ireland, a 33% increase in Scandinavian business, and a 16% jump in tour sales to Greece and the Middle East. In general, tour operators reported that the dollar's continuing strength could mean very good travel years for 1982 and 1983.

Other Trends. Meanwhile, tourism inbound to the United States continued a trend that began in 1979 when, for the first time on record, the

UPI

Passengers on the first direct China-to-U.S. commercial flight arrive in New York in January.

number of overseas visitors exceeded the number of Americans going abroad. By the end of the year, California alone was to welcome more than 3.5 million international callers, who would have spent more than $1,000,000,000 on goods and services.

Again in 1981, the cruise business sailed on almost unruffled seas. As surveys indicated a yearly passenger growth of about 7%, 1,735 more berths went to sea in new or "stretched" ships.

While supertrains in Japan and Europe continued to accelerate in popularity and in speed—France's electric Paris-Lyon line set a world record of 238 mi (383 km) per hour—Amtrak was forced to cut back about 10% of its trains as well as the style of its meal service.

Travelers, like the stock market, despise uncertainty. Political upheavals abroad and economic ones in the United States thus turned what might have been a very good year into a nonvintage one.

GEORGIA I. HESSE
Travel Editor, "San Francisco Examiner"

TRINIDAD AND TOBAGO

On March 29, 1981, the oil-rich nation of Trinidad and Tobago lost its longtime political leader, Prime Minister Eric Williams, 69. Trained at Oxford University as a historian, Williams entered politics in 1956 by organizing the first island-wide political party, the People's National Movement. He led Trinidad and Tobago to independence from Great Britain in 1962 and proceeded to win every national election through the 1960s and 1970s.

Upon Williams' death, the People's National Movement was taken over by George Chambers, who had been minister of agriculture, industry, and commerce in the Williams government. Elections were delayed until the voting list could be prepared, but on November 9 approximately 732,000 citizens went to the polls.

The result of the election was a vote of confidence for Prime Minister Chambers and the governing People's National Movement. The party won 26 of the nation's 36 parliamentary seats, increasing its representation by two. Three political parties representing East Indian and other, black constituencies had banded together to form the National Alliance, but they were able to win only eight seats in parliament. The two re-

TRINIDAD AND TOBAGO • Information Highlights

Official Name: Republic of Trinidad and Tobago.
Location: Caribbean Islands.
Area: 1,980 sq mi (5 128 km^2).
Population (1981 est.): 1,200,000.
Chief Cities (1977 est.): Port of Spain, 120,000; San Fernando, 60,000; Arima, 20,000.
Government: *Head of state,* Ellis Clarke, president (took office Dec. 1976). *Head of government,* George Chambers, prime minister (took office Nov. 1981). *Legislature*—Parliament: Senate and House of Representatives.
Monetary Unit: Trinidad and Tobago dollar (2.41 TT dollars equal U.S.$1, July 1981).
Manufactures (major products): Petroleum, cement, cigarettes, rum, beer.
Agriculture (major products): Sugar, cocoa, coconuts, citrus fruits.

maining opposition seats went to another faction from the small satellite island of Tobago, whose inhabitants often protest the lack of attention paid to it by the larger island.

Even though about 90% of the government's income comes from taxes on private oil and gas companies, there was strong pressure on the new government to continue the trend, started by the late Prime Minister Williams, toward nationalization of private corporations. The new government also faced an ongoing strike by 52,000 public workers demanding higher pay.

In the first week of November, President Ronald Reagan nominated Dr. Melvin Herbert Evans as the U.S. ambassador to Trinidad and Tobago. A native of the island of St. Croix and a former governor of the Virgin Islands, Evans was one of the few Republicans who failed to win reelection to Congress in 1980.

THOMAS MATHEWS
University of Puerto Rico

TUNISIA

In 1981, President Habib Bourguiba demonstrated his support for the liberalization policies of Prime Minister Mohamed Mzali by agreeing to the first multiparty elections since independence in 1957. In an effort to neutralize opposition, Bourguiba legalized the Communist Party, arrested Muslim fundamentalists, and wooed the powerful trade unionists. Late in the year, after it was reported that Bourguiba was seriously ill, the issue of presidential succession became a concern. The strict socialist approach to the economy was relaxed to allow the introduction of more free market policies.

Politics. At a special congress of the ruling Destour Socialist Party (PSD) in April, President Bourguiba endorsed the liberalization policies undertaken by Prime Minister Mzali by announcing his readiness to permit a multiparty system of government in Tunisia. The PSD had been the country's only party since Bourguiba founded it 25 years earlier. A new 80-member central committee was also elected during the meeting.

The first multiparty legislative elections were held November 1. The previously banned Communist Party was legalized, as well as the Democratic Socialist Movement, and after initial hesitance, both parties entered candidates in the election. The PSD and its ally, the Tunisian labor union federation, won all the National Assembly seats.

In September, more than 100 members of the Mouvement de Tendance Islamique (MTI) were sentenced to jail terms of up to 11 years for a range of offenses, including illegal association, propagation of untruths, and affronts to the dignity of the head of state. The Islamic fundamentalists were arrested in July after a series of incidents, including violence on university campuses and an attack on a Mediterranean tourist resort. The MTI had applied to be recognized as a political party, but the government refused.

Labor Relations. Mzali's liberalizing trend also extended to the country's powerful labor organization, the General Union of Tunisian Workers (UGTT). Five union leaders, who were sentenced after the January 1978 unrest and released from prison in 1980, were pardoned in early 1981. Habib Achour, former UGTT secretary-general, as well as another UGTT official, Salah Brour, were still under house arrest and forbidden to participate in union responsibilities. The first UGTT conference since the 1978 riots was held in Gafsa in April, and Taieb Baccouche, a professor at Tunis University, was elected secretary-general.

Students, teachers, and transport workers went on strike in March in protest against a government plan to reorganize secondary schools. After a cabinet meeting, which included trade unionists, the school plan was scrapped and concessions to workers in the matters of salaries and working conditions averted a major confrontation.

Economy and Foreign Relations. Tunisia's sixth five-year plan, covering 1981–86 and totaling $14,000,000,000, focused on improving agricultural productivity and on the creation of 65,000 new jobs per year. A move away from socialist economics toward market policies also was undertaken.

Algerian Prime Minister Mohammed Ben Ahmed Abdelghani met with Mzali in Tunis in February to discuss the formation of a bilateral cooperation program to encompass all major sectors of the economies of both countries. The cooperation agreement includes the creation of a bank with $40 million in capital to develop joint projects in economic and financial areas. The collective operations were planned to strengthen the nations' positions relative to the European Community (EC), where most of Tunisia's exports are destined.

In July, the U.S. Pentagon announced that it would sell Tunisia M-60 tanks to help the country defend itself against Libya, part of an American policy to support Libyan opponents. Tunisia had blamed Libya for inspiring the 1980 dissident attack on the mining town of Gafsa.

MARGARET A. NOVICKI, *"Africa Report"*

TUNISIA • Information Highlights

Official Name: Republic of Tunisia.
Location: North Africa.
Area: 63,170 sq mi (163 610 km^2).
Population (1981 est.): 6,600,000.
Chief City (1975 census): Tunis, the capital, 550,404.
Government: *Head of state,* Habib Bourguiba, president-for-life (took office 1957). *Chief Minister,* Mohamed Mzali, prime minister (took office April 1980). *Legislature* (unicameral)—National Assembly.
Monetary Unit: Dinar (0.53 dinar equals U.S.$1, July 1981).
Manufactures (major products): Crude oil, phosphates, olive oil, textiles, construction materials.
Agriculture (major products): Wheat, olives, grapes, citrus fruits.

TURKEY

On May 19 and throughout 1981, Turkey celebrated the centennial of the birth of Mustafa Kemal Ataturk, the founder and first president of the modern Turkish republic. Ataturk bequeathed to Turkey a legacy of nationalism, reform, populism, secularism, etatism, and independence. Though his principles remain an inspiration to the Turkish people, formidable problems still faced the country in 1981.

Political Terrorism. The new military government, established in September 1980 by Chief of Staff Gen. Kenan Evren and five general officers of the National Security Council, set itself the task of suppressing terrorism as a prerequisite to writing a new constitution. Martial law was extended over the entire country. Political activity was banned and civil rights curtailed. Although the number of murders was reduced significantly, there was much uneasiness about the future. Trials of both leftist and rightist extremists of the Kurdish and Armenian minorities continued. Some 30 Communist cells were reportedly discovered in Kirkkale, near Ankara.

On May 13, Mehmet Ali Agca, a young Turk thought to have links with the right-wing National Movement Party, was arrested in Vatican City for his assassination attempt against Pope John Paul II. On May 24, members of a Marxist Turkish guerrilla group hijacked a Turkish airliner and forced it to land in Bulgaria, demanding the release of 47 prisoners from Turkish jails; the gunmen were overpowered by plane passengers the next day.

Economics and Finances. The Turkish economy did show some improvement during 1981. The military government managed to cut the inflation rate from 115% in 1980—the highest of all members of the Organization for Economic Cooperation and Development (OECD)—to 35%. The gross national product (GNP) remained about the same as in 1980, $49,000,000,000; the per capita GNP, $1,120, was the highest in the area. Exports for the first half of 1981 totaled approximately $1,630,000,000, an increase of 57%; the largest share, $842.1 million, went to OECD countries. As in previous years, many Turks—some 800,000—worked abroad, primarily in Germany; remittances to Turkey amounted to $2,071,000,000. Despite the economic improvements, the external debt remained high ($18,629,000,000), and it was essential for Turkey to continue receiving significant amounts of foreign aid.

Constitutional Changes. As chief of staff, General Evren was faced with the basic problems of constitutional and political reform. He reaffirmed that a constitution based on "democratic" principles would be drafted by a Constituent Assembly. That body would be composed of the five generals of the National Security Council and 160 other members, 120 chosen by the council from among candidates nominated by each of Turkey's 67 provinces and the remaining 40 appointed directly by the council. No politicians were permitted to participate in the pro-

TURKEY • Information Highlights

Official Name: Republic of Turkey.
Location: Southeastern Europe and southwestern Asia.
Area: 306,870 sq mi (794 793 km^2).
Population (1981 est.): 46,200,000.
Chief Cities (1980 est.): Ankara, the capital, 2,316,333; Istanbul, 3,033,810; Izmir, 776,954.
Government: *Head of state,* Gen. Kenan Evren, chairman of National Security Council (took power Sept. 1980). *Head of government,* Bülent Ulusu, prime minister (took office Sept. 1980). *Legislature*—Grand National Assembly: Senate and National Assembly.
Monetary Unit: Lira (129.08 liras equal U.S.$1, Nov. 1981).
Manufactures (major products): Textiles, processed foods, minerals.
Agriculture (major products): Cotton, tobacco, cereals, sugar beets, fruits, nuts.

Robin Laurence/New York Times Pictures

Gen. Kenan Evren (seated), chairman of Turkey's ruling National Security Council, is briefed by an aide at his office in Ankara. During his first year in power, Kenan faced the challenge of democratic reform in the midst of political and economic instability.

cess. Although critics of the military regime raised serious questions as to how a democratic instrument could be framed without the participation of politicians and intellectuals, it was acknowledged that General Evren had indeed made progress—by suppressing political terrorism and attempting to set the country on the road toward sound political, economic, and social policies. On October 16, the government ordered the dissolution of all political parties and the confiscation of their property for violating the ban on political activity. The Constituent Assembly convened on October 23 but was not expected to complete its work on a new constitution until late 1982.

Foreign Affairs. During 1981, there was no really basic change in Turkish foreign policy or interests. On August 15, Prime Minister Bülent Ulusu reaffirmed Turkey's commitment to NATO, emphasizing the alliance's importance to international peace and security. Turkey's ties to the United States remained firm. Its policy toward the USSR remained cautious, and its relations with Balkan and Arab neighbors were balanced. While Greco-Turkish relations did show some improvement, no solution was found to the problems of the Aegean islands and Cyprus.

HARRY N. HOWARD
Middle East Institute

UGANDA

The aftermath of a fraudulent election spoiling Uganda's return to democracy and an ever-greater state of social and economic disintegration were the disheartening highlights of the year in Uganda.

Politics. The long-awaited elections to choose a legitimate successor to the Amin regime were held on Dec. 10, 1980. However, the results produced only more anarchy and disruption, as the election of former president Milton Obote was accompanied by violence and charges of blatant fraud. Despite the presence of a Commonwealth observer team, it seems that the outcome was "fixed." The probable winner was the Democratic Party, led by Paul Ssemogerere, capturing about 63 of the 126 seats at stake for the new legislature, which was to choose the president. However, the interim military ruler, Paulo Muwanga, a close friend and political ally of Obote, suddenly suspended the vote counting on election night, and declared he would personally count the votes and declare the winner. Obote's Uganda People's Congress was then proclaimed the victor, and the former chief executive took the oath of office on December 15.

Even before the vote, Obote's party was awarded 17 seats through massive fraud and a virtual monopoly of the means to campaign. The fixing of the election, the gerrymandering of seats in the new legislature, and the clear anti-Ganda (a Bantu language of Uganda) bias of the new regime all led almost at once to armed violence and resistance to Obote's new government. Bombings became frequent, police and army patrols were ambushed, and a "Uganda Freedom Movement" declared virtual war on the new rulers. Obote responded with a severe crackdown on dissent, massive arrests, and a revival of Idi Amin's dreaded "State Research Bureau," which could detain and execute without warrant, cause, or warning.

Antigovernment attacks and reprisals by the new and almost undisciplined Uganda army led even Obote to admit that the nation lived in virtual anarchy. So violent was the situation that travel anywhere in Uganda became highly dangerous, and only a Tanzanian "Praetorian Guard" kept the president and his ministers and offices safe from attack. Whether the new regime could survive was open to doubt by year's end.

Social. The total disintegration of Ugandan society continued throughout 1981. Widespread random violence, as well as heavily armed gangs, made normal life impossible. No Ugandan dared to be out after dark, or in daylight if alone or unarmed. The new Ugandan police and army were ill-trained rabble, little better than the criminals they were chasing. Their combined forces numbered barely 4,000 and much of the country was given over to literal lawlessness. Every road had a roadblock where extortion or murder of any traveler was the rule. With the withdrawal of the 10,000 Tanzanian troops from Uganda in June 1981, there was no force left in the country that could stabilize the situation. A revived pro-Amin movement and raids by dissidents across the Zaire and Sudan borders added to the state of anarchy.

Economy. The Ugandan economy, for all intents, no longer existed. Production, transportation, and distribution were all impossible in the anarchic conditions prevailing. Robbery, in fact, became the main means of economic exchange. What little was produced ended up in the hands of smugglers, thus depriving the government of any sort of revenue or tax base. The black market flourished in spite of massive arrests and official price controls, and prices lost reality, such as $250 for a gallon of gasoline or $40 for one bunch of bananas. What little money the government had went to pay for oil imports costing $10 million a month. Even basic food crops were in short supply, and hunger, even starvation, were common. By the end of 1981, Uganda scarcely functioned as a modern, civilized society.

ROBERT GARFIELD, *DePaul University*

UGANDA • Information Highlights

Official Name: Republic of Uganda.
Location: Interior of East Africa.
Area: 91,134 sq mi (236 037 km^2).
Chief City: Kampala, the capital, 540,000.
Government: *Head of state,* Milton Obote, president (elected Dec. 1980). *Head of government,* Otema Alimadi, prime minister (appointed Dec. 1980). *Legislature* (unicameral)—Parliament, 126 members.
Monetary Unit: Uganda shilling (7.57 shillings equal U.S. $1, 1980).

UPI

Economic revitalization was the dominant theme at the 26th congress of the Soviet Communist party.

USSR

Grave internal and external difficulties troubled the Soviet government throughout 1981. For the third consecutive year bad weather caused a low grain harvest, necessitating large imports of wheat and corn. Also for the third year, Soviet industry remained in a production recession, with particularly low output of coal and steel. Because of these problems, the Five-Year Plan for 1981–1985 provided for smaller rates of growth in agriculture and industry than did the 1976–1980 plan. In a speech to the Communist Party's Central Committee on November 16, President Leonid I. Brezhnev said dwindling food supplies were the greatest problem facing the USSR.

Abroad the Soviet army was still unable to defeat the ill-armed Afghan nationalists rebelling against Kabul's Communist government. Though the Soviet press condemned Polish free trade unions as counterrevolutionary and large Soviet military maneuvers were held ominously near Polish frontiers, the USSR hesitated to invade Poland. Apparently the Kremlin realized that any invasion would end détente between Western Europe and the USSR and provoke U.S. reprisals. As it was, the declaration of martial law by the Polish regime in mid-December led U.S. President Ronald Reagan to impose harsh sanctions against Moscow.

FOREIGN AFFAIRS

United States. Throughout 1981 the USSR and United States waged a war of words, each accusing the other of planning a sneak nuclear attack. The U.S. State Department repeatedly asked the Kremlin to exercise restraint in foreign policy and particularly to cease aiding terrorist groups rebelling against Third World governments. Moscow replied that no foreign country can dictate Soviet foreign policy and urged that U.S.-Soviet negotiations for limitation of nuclear armaments be resumed. It also stated on several occasions that the USSR will match any increase in U.S. strategic armaments.

Several incidents disturbed Soviet-American relations during 1981. In January, a military attaché of the U.S. Embassy in Moscow was hurriedly sent home following Soviet attempts to recruit him as a spy. On May 12, U.S. customs officials delayed for three hours the departure of a Soviet airliner from Washington, DC, and removed from the plane "defense related" light electronic equipment being shipped to the USSR. Then it was discovered that U.S. export licenses had indeed been granted.

At least five times during 1981, Soviet reconnaissance planes operating from Cuban bases were sighted off the U.S. south Atlantic coast. In August, when two U.S. naval fighter planes from the aircraft carrier *Nimitz* shot down two Libyan fighter planes off the Libyan coast, the Soviet press condemned the U.S. action without mentioning that the downed planes were built in the USSR.

Though the Kremlin denounced the U.S. decisions to manufacture neutron bombs and to station medium-range nuclear missiles in Western Europe, Soviet-American relations did improve slightly compared with 1980. In April 1981, U.S. President Ronald Reagan removed the embargo, imposed by former President Jimmy Carter, on most U.S. grain sales to the USSR. On October 1, the Reagan administration authorized the sale of 25.3 million T (23 million t) of grain during the following 12 months. On November 18, President Reagan offered to stop the future deployment of 572 new U.S. medium-

UPI

In late September, Soviet Foreign Minister Andrei Gromyko (right) and U.S. Secretary of State Alexander Haig held the first meeting of high-level representatives of the two countries since the Reagan administration took office. Soviet-U.S. relations were a war of words throughout 1981.

range missiles in Western Europe if the Kremlin would dismantle its 600 medium missiles in European USSR aimed at Western Europe. Soviet President Brezhnev on November 23 rejected the offer, proposing that the deployment of new missiles in Europe be halted during negotiations on the reduction of all types of medium-range nuclear weapons in Europe. Those talks opened in Geneva on November 30.

In August, Arthur A. Hartman, a 55-year-old career diplomat who was previously ambassador to France, was appointed U.S. ambassador to the USSR.

Europe. Soviet relations with Western European nations were marred by several incidents. In April, Greece formally discontinued an agreement that provided for repair of noncombat vessels of the Soviet Mediterranean fleet. In August, a second secretary of the Soviet Embassy in London was expelled for undiplomatic activity. In retaliation, the Soviets expelled a cultural attaché of the British Embassy in Moscow. A note from the Soviet Union in September warned Spain that its adherence to NATO (North Atlantic Treaty Organization) would increase international tension. Spain rejected the warning as interference in Spanish affairs.

In late October, a Soviet diesel submarine armed with nuclear torpedo warheads ran aground in Sweden's territorial waters near a large Swedish naval base. Though the USSR apologized for the intrusion, Sweden angrily refused permission for Soviet ships to salvage the submarine. When questioned by Swedish officials, the submarine captain claimed that his navigational instruments had malfunctioned. Early in November, the Soviet ship was pulled free by Swedish tugboats and released to return home.

On a more peaceful note, Malta and the USSR in October concluded treaties concerning airline communication, trade, and recognition of Maltese neutrality.

Throughout 1981, while the independent trade union federation Solidarity struggled for power against Poland's Communist government, the USSR publicly threatened to intervene to restore governmental control. Supporting these threats were three large-scale Soviet army and navy maneuvers—in and around Poland during March–April, along the Soviet Baltic seacoast in August, and in the Baltic Sea and nearby Soviet areas during September. Yet, when Poland's economic difficulties were aggravated by numerous union strikes, the Kremlin in August postponed payment of Polish debts to the USSR until 1986–1990 and promised to supply Poland with more raw materials for consumer goods.

Middle East. In 1981, as before, the 85,000-man Soviet army in Afghanistan was unable to suppress the nationwide Islamic rebellion against Kabul's Communist government. Soviet troops could control only cities and major highways, while the countryside was ruled by Afghan nationalist guerrillas. Meanwhile, the USSR continued to develop the Afghan economy by building a copper smelter and oil refinery and opening coal mines and oil fields. By 1981, Soviet loans to Afghanistan amounted to $576 million.

The Soviet occupation of Afghanistan continued to be resented by most developing nations. A January summit meeting of 37 Islamic countries in Saudi Arabia concluded with a communiqué demanding that all foreign troops be withdrawn from Afghanistan. A similar demand was made by a conference of more than 90 nonaligned nations meeting in February in New Delhi.

On June 7, Israeli fighter-bombers destroyed an Iraqi nuclear reactor near Baghdad for fear it was being used to develop weapons. Though the USSR condemned the raid, no Soviet offer was made to help Iraq build a new reactor. As before, the USSR remained neutral in the Iraq-Iran war, rendering technical aid to both nations.

All together, nine Middle Eastern countries were receiving technical aid from the USSR, which was also openly arming the Palestine Liberation Organization (PLO). On October 20, the Soviet government granted embassy status to the PLO mission in Moscow.

Africa. In mid-September, Egypt expelled Soviet Ambassador Vladimir Polyakov, six members of his staff, two Soviet journalists, and more than 1,000 Soviet technical specialists. All were accused of subversion, espionage, and fomenting unrest. In response, the Soviet press angrily predicted that Egyptian President Anwar el-Sadat was "doomed."

After President Sadat was assassinated on October 6, the USSR sent no high-ranking representative to his funeral. When U.S. armed forces concentrated near Egypt to safeguard the presidential succession, the Kremlin accused the United States of interfering in internal Egyptian affairs. Then, on October 15, Soviet President Leonid Brezhnev sent a message to Egypt's new president, Hosni Mubarak, urging improved Egyptian-Soviet relations.

In June, Liberia expelled nine Soviet diplomats for undiplomatic behavior. During September, the Kremlin asked South Africa to return a Soviet warrant officer and the bodies of two military advisers and their wives. The latter four had been killed and the warrant officer captured in a brief South African invasion of southern Angola to destroy guerrilla bases of the South West Africa People's Organization (SWAPO).

In October, Morocco protested to the USSR that non-Africans were operating Soviet antiaircraft missiles in the possession of the Polisario Front, which was rebelling against Moroccan rule in the western Sahara.

Besides supporting SWAPO and the Polisario Front, the USSR rendered technical aid to 40 African countries, of which about half received Soviet arms.

During 1981 the Soviet government concluded cultural exchange and technical aid agreements with Libya, signed a 20-year treaty of friendship with the Congo, and established diplomatic relations with Zimbabwe.

Far East. Throughout 1981, Soviet leaders publicly expressed fear that Communist China and the United States might be allying against the USSR. Aggravating this worry were sporadic skirmishes along the Sino-Soviet frontier.

During June, a treaty between the USSR and Afghanistan altered their common frontier along the Wakhan Corridor, a small strip of territory in eastern Afghanistan bordered in the north by Soviet Central Asia, in the east by Communist China, and in the south by Pakistan. Peking protested that the treaty involved Chinese territory, but the Soviet Union summarily rejected the claim.

In July, two officers and an employee of the Soviet Embassy in Malaysia were expelled from that country for conducting espionage.

Latin America. Early in 1981, the USSR denied accusations by U.S. authorities that it was secretly supplying arms to leftwing rebels in El Salvador. The Kremlin admitted, however, that it had no control over the eventual use of Soviet weapons sold to Latin American countries.

In an effort to weaken U.S. influence, the USSR rendered technical aid to 13 Latin American nations. The chief recipient continued to be Cuba, with an estimated $2,900,000,000.

Canada. In April, the USSR finally paid the $3 million it owed to the Canadian government for its search for thousands of radioactive fragments from a Soviet spy satellite that disintegrated over northern Canada in 1978.

DOMESTIC AFFAIRS

Armed Forces. In 1981, the Soviet armed forces comprised about 4.2 million men. The USSR ranked first in the world in number of tanks, artillery, intercontinental ballistic missiles, submarine-based and medium-range missiles, medium-range bombers, and submarines. But the Soviet arsenal lagged behind that of the United States in number of aircraft carriers, long-range bombers, tactical atomic weapons, and total nuclear warheads.

The USSR maintained fleets of about 40 ships in the Mediterranean Sea and 25 vessels in the Indian Ocean. In July, marines from the Mediterranean fleet conducted a practice landing on the Syrian seacoast.

Space. By 1981, the Soviet Union had launched a total of 1,500 manned and unmanned space satellites. A series of space flights began on

A Soviet submarine run aground in Swedish waters embarrassed the Kremlin and angered the Swedes.

UPI

March 12, 1981, when Soyuz T-4 was launched in Kazakhstan with Col. Vladimir Kovalyonok and Viktor Savinykh on board. The next day, the craft docked with the Salyut-6 space station, where Kovalyonok and Savinykh stayed to receive four visitors from earth. The guests were Vladimir Dzhanibekov and Jugderdemidiyn Gurragcha of Mongolia, who were launched in Soyuz 39 on March 22 and returned to earth March 30; and Lt. Col. Leonid I. Popov, and Lt. Dumitru Prunariu of Rumania, who were launched in Soyuz 40 on May 14 and returned to earth May 22. The non-Soviet cosmonauts were the first from their countries to travel in space. On May 26, Kovalyonok and Savinykh returned safely to earth after spending 75 days in space.

During February and March, the USSR successfully tested two killer satellites, rockets to destroy enemy intercontinental ballistic missiles.

Population. In mid-1981, the total population of the USSR was 267.7 million. The total labor force numbered about 138 million, of which 51% were women. There were 49 million pensioners, of whom one fifth were still working.

Among the largest public organizations of the country were the Young Communist League, with 40 million members; sport societies, with 80 million; and trade unions, with 130 million.

Emigration was officially authorized for about 9,000 Soviet Jews, compared with 21,500 in 1980. Some 4,000 Soviet Germans were also permitted to emigrate permanently during 1981.

Dissidents. Many Soviet dissidents were imprisoned in 1981 for demanding freedom of religion, full political rights for non-Russian minorities, release of political prisoners from mental hospitals, or democracy in government.

In April, Maksim Shostakovich, 42, a Soviet conductor, and his son Dmitri, 19, a concert pianist, defected to the West while performing in West Germany. They are, respectively, the son and grandson of the deceased Soviet composer Dmitri Shostakovich.

Three Soviet writers pressured into emigrating to the West in 1980—Vasily Aksyonov, Lev Kopelev, and his wife, Raisa Orlova—were deprived of their Soviet citizenship and forbidden to return to the USSR.

Dissident physicist Andrei Sakharov, 60, and his wife were reported to have ended a 17-day hunger strike on December 8. The widely-publicized protest was made because of the government's refusal to grant Lisa Alekseya, the wife of Sakharov's stepson, Alexey Semyonov, an emigration visa to join her husband in the United States. The Sakharovs ended their hunger strike when the visa was granted.

Communist Party Congress. The 26th congress of the Soviet Communist party met in Moscow from February 23 to March 3. Few younger party members were promoted into the upper bureaucracy, predominantly staffed by men in their 60s and 70s. The entire Politburo was reelected, with no new members added. Also reelected were all ten top party secretaries, including 74-year-old Secretary-General Brezhnev. Of the 319 persons chosen to be full members of the party's central committee, 80% were holdovers.

According to congress statistics, the party had 17,480,000 members, of whom 44% were from the middle and upper classes, 43% were workers, and only 13% were peasants. About 27% of the party membership were women. By nationality, Russians were over-represented in the party and Asians greatly under-represented.

Most of the speakers at the congress either complained about or suggested remedies for Soviet economic difficulties. The main achievement of the congress was adoption of the Five-Year Plan for 1981–1985.

ECONOMY

New Five-Year Plan. Because of great underfulfillment of the 1976–1980 plan, the new Five-Year Plan for 1981–1985 has lower growth targets (1976–1980 goals in parentheses)—national income, 18–20% (24–28%); urban wages, 13–16% (16–18%); collective farm pay, 20–22% (24–27%); industry, 26–28% (35–39%); agriculture, 12–14% (14–17%); railway freight haulage, 14–15% (22%); and retail trade, 22–25% (27–29%). Production increases in coal, oil, cement, and finished steel had been so slow that 1985 targets were no larger than the original output goals for 1980. In contrast to previous five-year plans, the 1981–1985 plan stresses expansion of existing

A Kiev-class aircraft carrier, the USSR's largest class, entered the Baltic for the first time in July.

UPI

enterprises rather than large-scale new construction.

Agriculture. Because of a lengthy and widespread summer drought, the 1981 grain harvest of approximately 192 million T (175 million t) was even smaller than the poor 1980 crop of 208 million T (189 million t) and far below the 1981 goal of 260 million T (236 million t). As a result, the USSR had to purchase about 44 million T (40 million t) of foreign grain, with the United States and Argentina providing the most.

Agricultural efficiency suffered from a shortage of farm labor, primarily because many rural youths were migrating to cities to receive better pay. There was also a shortage of farm machinery, with two thirds of agricultural work having to be accomplished by hand labor.

All collective and state farm families and most rural residents have long had private gardens and some private livestock. In January 1981, Moscow issued a decree that permits, for the first time since the 1920s, garden land and private livestock to be increased above legal limits if the owners sell meat and milk to collective and state farms. To aid farm plot owners, state and collective farms will sell them young livestock and animal feed and provide pastures for their livestock. By encouraging small-scale private farming the government sought to overcome a shortage of animal products.

Industry. The industrial recession of 1979–1980 continued through 1981. Eighteen major industries were producing below 1980 levels.

A major cause of the industrial recession was a shortage of labor, resulting from two decades of a low national birthrate. During the 1981–1985 five-year plan, new workers are expected to total only one third the number that entered the labor force in 1976–1980. Aggravating industrial troubles is the continuing high degree of manual labor—40% in industrial production, 50% in construction, and 66% in loading and unloading.

One of the few Soviet industrial achievements of 1981 was the completion of the Leningrad nuclear power station. With a capacity of 4 million kilowatts, it is the world's largest producer of nuclear power.

USSR • Information Highlights

Official Name: Union of Soviet Socialist Republics.
Location: Eastern Europe and northern Asia.
Area: 8,649,540 sq mi (22 402 308 km^2).
Population (1981 est.): 267,700,000.
Chief Cities (Jan. 1980 est.): Moscow, the capital, 8,099,000; Leningrad, 4,638,000; Kiev, 2,192,000.
Government: *Head of state,* Leonid I. Brezhnev, president (took office June 1977). *Head of government,* Nikolai A. Tikhonov, premier (took office Oct. 1980). *Secretary-general of the Communist party,* Leonid I. Brezhnev (took office 1964). *Legislature*—Supreme Soviet: Soviet of the Union, Soviet of Nationalities.
Monetary Unit: Ruble (0.76 ruble equals U.S.$1, Aug. 1981—noncommercial rate).
Manufactures (major products): Iron and steel, steel products, building materials, electrical energy, textiles, domestic and industrial machinery.
Agriculture (major products): Wheat, rye, corn, oats, linseed, sugar beets, sunflower seeds, potatoes, cotton and flax, cattle, pigs, sheep.

UPI

Despite fragile health, President Leonid Brezhnev, 74, was reelected secretary-general of the party.

Standard of Living. The standard of living in the Soviet Union remained mediocre during 1981. There were admitted store shortages of meat, milk, eggs, fruit, and clothing. The government urged the public to cut back in consumption of bread. Housing was overcrowded, and there were not enough restaurants and stores.

In September, store prices were raised by 17–30% for alcoholic beverages, tobacco products, jewelry, china, carpets, furs, leather clothes, and quality furniture. Gasoline prices were doubled. The Soviet press explained that higher production costs necessitated higher prices.

Transportation. In 1981, the Armenian city of Yerevan began operating its first subway, and a 2,000-mi (3 200-km) oil pipeline from western Siberian oil fields to European USSR was completed. Aeroflot, the Soviet state-owned airline, commenced regular passenger flights to the African countries of Liberia and Sierra Leone. Because of intensive shipbuilding and purchase of foreign ships, the Soviet merchant marine in 1981 was larger than that of the United States.

Foreign Trade. In 1981, total Soviet foreign trade increased by about 15% over the 1980 level. Because of the lifting of the U.S. grain embargo, Soviet-American trade expanded by 30%.

Though the USSR was experiencing grave economic difficulties at home, its technical aid to developing nations was still extensive. In 1981, the Soviet Union was financing 550 economic projects in 77 Asian, African, and Latin American countries.

The USSR continued to be the world's largest exporter of raw materials and one of the biggest importers of grain.

ELLSWORTH RAYMOND, *New York University*

UNITED NATIONS

The most important decision taken by the United Nations in 1981 may well have been the choice of Javier Pérez de Cuellar, a 61-year-old Peruvian diplomat, to be its new secretary-general. The political and administrative powers of the $158,000-a-year post are limited by the charter and the evolution of the UN. Only the most intractable problems reach the secretary-general. He is often assigned unrealistic tasks by legislative bodies over which he has limited influence. His administrative authority is similarly circumscribed by the feudal fiefdoms of the UN divisions. Yet there remains the power to build or erode the usefulness of the institution. The secretary-general can speak out, acting as a catalyst or a conscience. And so each election becomes a watershed for the UN, and potentially for the world.

The contest initially pitted incumbent Kurt Waldheim of Austria, seeking an unprecedented third five-year term, against Tanzanian Foreign Minister Salim A. Salim. Waldheim was backed by the East and West, but the Third World majority felt it was time for one of their own to take the helm.

The battle began in the Security Council on October 27 and remained deadlocked over six weeks and 16 ballots. Waldheim was vetoed by China, while the United States blocked Salim. Only after both stepped aside did nine new candidates, all from the Third World, enter the race. On December 11, the Security Council chose Pérez de Cuellar on the first ballot by a 10–1 vote, with four abstentions. The USSR vetoed the only other candidate to win a majority, Prince Sadruddin Aga Khan of Iran, the former UN refugee commissioner. Three days later, the General Assembly ratified the council's choice.

Javier Pérez de Cuellar, 61, of Peru was elected secretary-general of the UN on December 11.

UPI

Pérez de Cuellar, a former ambassador to the UN and ranking member of the Secretariat, began his five-year term on Jan. 1, 1982, with a reputation as a cautious professional who could get along with all power blocs. What remained untested was his problem-solving ability and firmness against governmental pressures.

While the UN was preoccupied with its election, there was little movement in the traditional political issues before it—the Arab-Israeli dispute, disarmament, economic relations between rich and poor nations, the problems of Africa, and the Cyprus question. In his final report, Waldheim said 1981 had brought "new crises and few encouragements."

General Assembly. The 36th session of the General Assembly opened on September 15 with a record 134 items on the agenda. However, few of the resolutions adopted during the three-month session provided fresh impetus toward resolving the issues at hand.

An official in the Iraqi foreign ministry, Ismat Kittani, was chosen president of the assembly by lot (as provided in the rules) after he and Ambassador Kwaja Mohammed Kaiser of Bangladesh each had obtained 73 votes in the balloting.

Three newly-independent nations were admitted to the UN—Vanuatu, an island group in the Pacific; Belize, formerly British Honduras; and Antigua and Barbuda, islands in the Caribbean—bringing the total membership to 157.

On October 21, by a vote of 100 to 25 with 19 abstentions, the assembly reaffirmed its call for the withdrawal of Vietnamese troops from Cambodia. The resolution also endorsed the result of a UN conference in July, which called for a cease-fire, negotiations, and UN-supervised elections in Cambodia. The conference was boycotted by Vietnam and the Soviet bloc, but its chairman, Willibald Pahr of Austria, was invited to visit Hanoi early in 1982, sustaining hope of an eventual settlement of the dispute. In a further sign of protest against Hanoi's intervention, the Pol Pot regime, though internationally discredited and ousted by the Vietnamese troops, kept Cambodia's UN seat in a 77–37 vote on September 18.

The Soviet bloc suffered another setback on November 18, when the assembly—in a 116–23 vote, with 12 abstentions—again called on the USSR to remove its troops from Afghanistan.

The United States produced evidence on September 14 to back its charge that Soviet-made chemical agents, outlawed for a half-century, had been used against insurgents in Afghanistan, Laos, and Cambodia. A UN panel set up by a 1980 General Assembly resolution visited refugee camps in Thailand in October to

UPI

Ambassadors Jeane Kirkpatrick of the United States and Yehuda Blum of Israel discuss a Security Council resolution condemning Israel for its June 7 air attack on an Iraqi nuclear reactor. The resolution, negotiated by Kirkpatrick with Iraq, did not call for an arms embargo but was still bitterly denounced by Israel.

look into the charges. The four-man panel reported in November that it was "unable to reach a final conclusion as to whether or not chemical warfare agents had been used." On December 9, the assembly overrode Soviet objections and voted, 86–20, with 34 abstentions, to continue the probe for another year. The use of "yellow rain," the United States warned, has "growing implications for both present and future arms control arrangements."

Fifty-two other disarmament resolutions were adopted the same day, a number of them critical of U.S. arms policies, such as the development of a neutron bomb.

The most embarrassing U.S. setback came in a resolution calling for a negotiated settlement between the rival factions in El Salvador, a concept Washington staunchly opposed. Although 13 Latin American nations joined the United States in voting against the resolution, only one NATO ally (Turkey) did so.

The increased friction between the United States and the Third World was visible in a paper submitted by the nonaligned movement which was bitterly critical of American policy across the board but only obliquely chided the Soviet Union. U.S. Ambassador Jeane Kirkpatrick wrote back a harshly worded letter but admitted later that relations with the Third World had not improved.

The assembly once again adopted numerous resolutions condemning Israel and South Africa, but no new ground was broken.

The 36th session was suspended rather than adjourned, with action on three issues put off until 1982. One was Cyprus. The second was a controversial proposal that the $80 million deficit facing the UN relief agency for Palestine refugees—which depended on voluntary contributions—be funded out of the regular UN budget, for which all nations are assessed. Finally, the dialogue between rich and poor nations remained stalled despite a 22-nation summit meeting in Cancún, Mexico, at which the creation of a universal negotiating forum on the world economy was discussed.

Security Council. The major event in an otherwise quiet year for the Security Council was a week-long debate on Israel's startling June 7 raid that destroyed the Osirak nuclear reactor in Iraq. The resolution condemning the attack, adopted unanimously on June 19, was a compromise that emerged unexpectedly from intense negotiations between U.S. Ambassador Kirkpatrick and Iraqi Foreign Minister Saadoun Hammadi, mediated by Secretary-General Waldheim. It was viewed as a triumph for U.S. diplomacy but was bitterly denounced by Israel. The resolution recognized the right of all states to peaceful nuclear development, called on Israel to put its own nuclear facilities under inspection by the International Atomic Energy Agency (IAEA), and stated that Iraq was entitled to appropriate redress for the damages. The Israelis contended that Iraq was close to developing nuclear weapons, with the objective of destroying Israel. IAEA Director Sigvard Eklund told the council that Iraq had complied with agency safeguards and said the reactor could not have produced weapons. Israel insisted that there were loopholes in the inspection system.

Another Middle East debate took place in July, after an Israeli raid on Beirut. The council issued a unanimous appeal for a cease-fire throughout Lebanon.

In December, after the Israeli parliament passed a measure formally annexing the Golan Heights, the council unanimously declared the action "null and void." It agreed to meet again in January 1982 to "consider taking appropriate measures"—a hint at sanctions—if Israel refused to rescind the legislation.

ORGANIZATION OF THE UNITED NATIONS

THE SECRETARIAT

Secretary-General: Javier Pérez de Cuellar (until Dec. 31, 1986)

THE GENERAL ASSEMBLY (1981)

President: Ismat T. Kittani (Iraq) The 157 member nations were as follows:

Afghanistan
Albania
Algeria
Angola
Antigua and Barbuda
Argentina
Australia
Austria
Bahamas
Bahrain
Bangladesh
Barbados
Belgium
Belize
Belorussian SSR
Benin
Bhutan
Bolivia
Botswana
Brazil
Bulgaria
Burma
Burundi
Cambodia
Cameroon
Canada
Cape Verde
Central African Republic
Chad
Chile
China, People's Republic of
Colombia
Comoros
Congo
Costa Rica
Cuba
Cyprus
Czechoslovakia
Denmark
Djibouti
Dominica
Dominican Republic
Ecuador
Egypt
El Salvador
Equatorial Guinea
Ethiopia
Fiji
Finland
France
Gabon
Gambia
German Democratic Republic
Germany, Federal Republic of
Ghana
Greece
Grenada
Guatemala
Guinea
Guinea-Bissau
Guyana
Haiti
Honduras
Hungary
Iceland
India
Indonesia
Iran
Iraq
Ireland
Israel
Italy
Ivory Coast
Jamaica
Japan
Jordan
Kenya
Kuwait
Laos
Lebanon
Lesotho
Liberia
Libya
Luxembourg
Madagascar
Malawi
Malaysia
Maldives
Mali
Malta
Mauritania
Mauritius
Mexico
Mongolia
Morocco
Mozambique
Nepal
Netherlands
New Zealand
Nicaragua
Niger
Nigeria
Norway
Oman
Pakistan
Panama
Papua New Guinea
Paraguay
Peru
Philippines
Poland
Portugal
Qatar
Rumania
Rwanda
Saint Lucia
Saint Vincent and the Grenadines
São Tomé and Principe
Saudi Arabia
Senegal
Seychelles
Sierra Leone
Singapore
Solomon Islands
Somalia
South Africa
Spain
Sri Lanka
Sudan
Surinam
Swaziland
Sweden
Syria
Tanzania
Thailand
Togo
Trinidad and Tobago
Tunisia
Turkey
Uganda
Ukrainian SSR
USSR
United Arab Emirates
United Kingdom
United States
Upper Volta
Uruguay
Vanuatu
Venezuela
Vietnam
Western Samoa
Yemen
Yemen, Democratic
Yugoslavia
Zaire
Zambia
Zimbabwe

COMMITTEES

General. Composed of 29 members as follows: The General Assembly president; the 21 General Assembly vice presidents (heads of delegations or their deputies of Australia, Benin, Botswana, China, Cuba, Cyprus, France, Indonesia, Mexico, Morocco, Pakistan, Panama, Papua New Guinea, Rwanda, Seychelles, Sweden, Togo, Ukrainian SSR, USSR, United Kingdom, United States); and the chairmen of the following main committees, which are composed of all 154 member countries:

First (Political and Security): Ignac Golob (Yugoslavia)

Special Political: Nathan Irunba (Uganda)

Second (Economic and Financial): Leandro I. Verceles (Philippines)

Third (Social, Humanitarian and Cultural): Declan O'Donovan (Ireland)

Fourth (Decolonization): Jasim Yousif Jamal (Qatar)

Fifth (Administrative and Budgetary): Abdel-Rahman Abdalla (Sudan)

Sixth (Legal): Juan José Calle y Calle (Peru)

THE SECURITY COUNCIL

Membership ends on December 31 of the year noted; asterisks indicate permanent membership.

Japan (1982)
China*
France*
Guyana (1983)
Jordan (1983)
Panama (1982)
Poland (1983)
Ireland (1982)
Spain (1982)
Togo (1983)
USSR*
United Kingdom*
United States*
Uganda (1982)
Zaire (1983)

Military Staff Committee: Representatives of chief of staffs of permanent members.

Disarmament Commission: Representatives of all UN members.

THE ECONOMIC AND SOCIAL COUNCIL

President: Paul J. F. Lusaka (Zambia). Membership ends on December 31 of the year noted.

Argentina (1983)
Australia (1982)
Austria (1984)
Bahamas (1982)
Bangladesh (1983)
Belgium (1982)
Belorussian SSR (1983)
Benin (1984)
Brazil (1984)
Bulgaria (1982)
Burundi (1983)
Cameroon (1983)
Canada (1983)
Chile (1982)
China (1983)
Colombia (1984)
Denmark (1983)
Ethiopia (1982)
Fiji (1983)
France (1984)
Germany, Federal Republic of (1984)
Greece (1984)
India (1983)
Iraq (1982)
Italy (1982)
Japan (1984)
Jordan (1982)
Kenya (1983)
Liberia (1984)
Libya (1982)
Malawi (1982)
Mali (1984)
Mexico (1982)
Nepal (1982)
Nicaragua (1983)
Nigeria (1982)
Norway (1983)
Pakistan (1984)
Peru (1983)
Poland (1983)
Portugal (1984)
Qatar (1984)
Rumania (1984)
St. Lucia (1984)
Sudan (1983)
Swaziland (1984)
Thailand (1982)
Tunisia (1984)
USSR (1983)
United Kingdom (1983)
United States (1982)
Venezuela (1984)
Yugoslavia (1982)
Zaire (1982)

THE TRUSTEESHIP COUNCIL

President: Marrack Goulding (United Kingdom)

China[2]
France[2]
USSR[2]
United Kingdom[2]
United States[1]

[1] Administers Trust Territory. [2] Permanent member of Security Council not administering Trust Territory.

THE INTERNATIONAL COURT OF JUSTICE

Membership ends on February 5 of the year noted.

President: Sir Humphrey Waldock (United Kingdom, 1982)
Vice President: Taslim O. Elias (Nigeria, 1985)

Keba Mbaye (Senegal, 1991)
Guy Ladreit de La Charrière (France, 1991)
Manfred Lachs (Poland, 1985)
Platon Dmitrievich-Morozov (USSR, 1988)
José Maria Ruda (Argentina, 1991)
Hermann Mosler (Fed. Rep. of Germany, 1985)
Nagendra Singh (India, 1991)
Shigeru Oda (Japan, 1985)
Roberto Ago (Italy, 1988)
Abdullah Ali El-Erian (Egypt, 1988)
José Sette Câmara (Brazil, 1988)
Stephen M. Schwebel (United States, 1988)
Abdullah Fikri al-Khani (Syria, 1985)
Robert Y. Jennings (United Kingdom, 1991)

INTERGOVERNMENTAL AGENCIES

Food and Agricultural Organization (FAO); General Agreement on Tariffs and Trade (GATT); Intergovernmental Maritime Consultative Organization (IMCO); International Atomic Energy Agency (IAEA); International Bank for Reconstruction and Development (World Bank); International Civil Aviation Organization (ICAO); International Fund for Agricultural Development (IFAD); International Labor Organization (ILO); International Monetary Fund (IMF); International Telecommunication Union (ITU); United Nations Educational, Scientific and Cultural Organization (UNESCO); Universal Postal Union (UPU); World Health Organization (WHO); World Intellectual Property Organization (WIPO); World Meterological Organization (WMO).

The other major issue discussed in the Security Council was southern Africa. After a ten-day debate in April, a group of African nations put forward four resolutions imposing comprehensive sanctions against South Africa because of its refusal to grant independence to the territory of Namibia. All four were vetoed by Great Britain, France, and the United States on the ground that they would hurt the ongoing negotiations over Namibia.

In August, after a South African raid deep into Angola, the United States alone vetoed a resolution—modified sufficiently to win support from other Western nations—that would have condemned the incursion and demanded immediate South African withdrawal. The United States argued that the Cuban and Soviet troops and advisers in Angola should share the blame for regional tensions.

Secretariat. Secretary-General Waldheim was actively involved in mediating a number of disputes, among them Namibia, Afghanistan, Cyprus, Lebanon, and the Iran-Iraq war.

Waldheim's major success came in Lebanon, where a cease-fire was concluded on July 24 and held throughout the year. U.S. envoy Philip Habib led the peacemaking effort, but it was Waldheim who dealt directly with the PLO and to whom both Israel and the Palestinians made their commitments.

Waldheim's representative to Iran and Iraq, former Swedish Prime Minister Olof Palme, made several trips to the region in 1981 and offered peace proposals of his own but could not end the year-long hostilities.

UN Under Secretary Brian Urquhart presided over a Geneva conference on Namibia in January 1981, but the parties reached no agreement. Later in the year, the Namibia negotiations were taken over by five Western nations—the United States, Great Britain, Canada, France, and West Germany. At year's end they were hoping to launch the independence process before the end of 1982, with UN help.

Waldheim also mediated between Pakistan and Afghanistan, seeking a political solution that would permit the pullout of Soviet occupation troops. Little progress was made.

On October 22, the secretary-general submitted his own ideas for breaking the long deadlock between the Greek and Turkish communities on Cyprus, and the receptivity of both sides created new hope for a breakthrough.

After demands by major donor nations that the UN limit its expenditures, Waldheim submitted a budget proposal for 1982–83 based on the concept of "zero growth plus inflation." The budget called for $768 million for each of the two following years, an increase of 13.7%, "essentially" due to inflation.

In response to staff protests, Waldheim issued a report detailing violations of UN diplomatic immunity by Poland, Afghanistan, Syria, Ethiopia, East Germany, Jordan, and Israel. On Human Rights Day, December 10, staff members of the Secretariat held a candlelight vigil on behalf of 14 imprisoned colleagues. The next day, the General Assembly approved a resolution demanding the release of the UN employees and affirming their immunity from detention.

On October 14, the UN High Commissioner for Refugees was named the winner of the Nobel Peace Prize. It was the second such award for the UN agency.

Trusteeship and Decolonization. Self-determination for the last remaining UN trust territory, U.S.-ruled Micronesia, had been scheduled for 1981. The move was postponed indefinitely, however, pending a U.S. policy review.

The decolonization committee, meeting in August, called for the independence of Puerto Rico and—despite U.S. objections that the status of the commonwealth was no longer a UN concern—voted 11–2, with 11 abstentions, to ask that the General Assembly debate the issue in 1982. The assembly approved the committee's report, but its president ruled that the action did not constitute a decision to include Puerto Rico on the assembly's 1982 agenda.

Economic and Social Council. The council held three meetings in 1981. It called for a World Assembly on Aging to convene in Vienna in 1982 and designated 1983 as World Communications Year, 1985 as International Youth Year, and 1987 as International Year of Shelter for the Homeless. Numerous programs and observances around the world marked 1981 as International Year for the Disabled.

A council subsidiary, the Human Rights Commission, adopted resolutions in March condemning rights violations in Cambodia, Afghanistan, Chile, Israel, and South Africa and set up investigations into violations in Guatemala, Bolivia, and El Salvador. The report on El Salvador, issued in November, concluded that there has been "a consistent pattern of gross violations" for which "members of the state apparatus and violent groups of the extreme right apparently acting in collusion with them and armed groups of the extreme left are both responsible."

Legal Activities. The UN Conference on the Law of the Sea was another forum stalemated by a U.S. policy review. Just before the conference's first session of 1981, Washington submitted a request for more time to study the comprehensive sea-law treaty that was virtually complete after eight years of negotiation. The Americans indicated that they would want major changes in the provisions regulating mining on the deep-sea floor. The conference held two sessions in 1981, and the General Assembly endorsed plans for a "final decision-making session" to start on March 8, 1982. But by year's end Washington still had not announced what changes it would seek or whether it would participate in the treaty process at all.

MICHAEL J. BERLIN, *"New York Post"*

UPI

UNITED STATES

Conservatism on a scale unknown for half a century revisited the United States in 1981. Taking his mandate from the 1980 elections, President Ronald Reagan pressed for domestic retrenchment and reinforcement of U.S. military power. Taxes were slashed, government operations were pared, and social programs shrunk, while the defense budget rose. But inflation persisted and the year ended in business recession.

DOMESTIC AFFAIRS

The Administration. Ronald Reagan, at 69 the oldest man to become president, began his term with a call for "an era of national renewal." Domestically, the 40th president committed his administration to "curb the size and influence of the federal establishment." Globally, he proposed to "maintain sufficient strength to prevail if need be" and to make the United States "the exemplar of freedom and a beacon of hope for those who do not have freedom." Reagan clearly intended to redeem campaign pledges to turn both foreign and domestic policies hard right—and he had the support of a majority of the public that elected him.

The narrowly divided 97th Congress accepted and enacted Reagan's rightist economic program in the first seven months of the year. But the honeymoon cooled in the autumn air.

As the new president ended his inaugural address on January 20, Iran's revolutionary regime released 52 Americans it had held hostage for 444 days. Reagan assigned outgoing President Jimmy Carter to greet the returning hostages at Wiesbaden, West Germany. Later, Reagan welcomed the hostages at the White House in words that set the tone for his administration's foreign policy. "Let terrorists be aware," he said, "that when the rules of international behavior are violated, our policy will be one of swift and effective retribution. We hear it said that we live in an era of limits to our powers. Well, let it also be understood, there are limits to our patience."

Reagan's cabinet, all male and all white, with two exceptions, was on the president's ideological wavelength. At Senate confirmation proceedings, the focus was on the nominee for secretary of state, retired Army Gen. Alexander M. Haig, Jr., who had served both as chief of staff in the Nixon White House and as NATO's supreme commander. It took 30 hours of hearings to clear Haig for the post, in which he later found himself in repeated policy conflicts with the White House staff. Almost as controversial was Reagan's choice of Wyoming attorney James G. Watt to be interior secretary. Once Watt was installed, his readiness to relax curbs on land use and exploitation of resources aroused fervent protests from environmentalists.

Reagan told the first of the weekly cabinet meetings he built into his decision-making process, "We've got to get control of the federal budget." And the budget became his overriding concern. His goal was to fulfill pledges to balance the budget by 1984. His strategy was to halt growth of domestic programs and cut back federal regulation, to strengthen national defense and still carry out a pledge to cut taxes.

On March 30, as he left a Washington hotel after addressing a labor union audience on his economic program, President Reagan was shot in the chest by a lone gunman. Prompt, expert care saved him from permanent consequences. But three other men, including White House Press Secretary James S. Brady, were wounded. Brady sustained brain damage and was hospitalized until late November. The assailant, John W. Hinckley, Jr., 25, was arrested on the spot. His lawyers planned for him to plead not guilty for reasons of insanity.

Following a two-hour operation for removal of a bullet from his left lung, Reagan was back in the White House after 12 days of hospitalization. By April 28, he was able to appear before a joint session of Congress and sound a televised call for action on his fiscal plan. The warm response was a personal tribute to the president's courage as well as to his bold program. It presaged a string of administration victories.

By early August, Congress had enacted a three-year, 25% tax cut and lopped $35,200,000,000 off Carter's 1982 budget. Resistance to cuts was eased by a White House pledge not to slash seven programs it described as the "social safety net" against destitution. Reagan signed the budget and tax bills as he vacationed at his 688-acre (278-ha) mountain ranch near Santa Barbara, CA. He also signed legislation to boost military pay by an average of 17% at a yearly cost of $4,500,000,000.

When the president returned to the capital in early September, the economy was stagnant; there was bipartisan resistance in Congress to further budget-cutting; environmentalists assailed Interior Secretary Watt's moves to encourage exploitation of resources on public lands; and state and local governments warned of drastic social consequences from overzealous cuts in federal aid.

Polls showed Reagan retaining his popularity. The only electoral tests came in two gubernatorial races that put a Democrat in the Virginia statehouse for the first time since 1965 and replaced New Jersey's Democratic governor with a Republican by a whisker-thin 1,700 votes.

Reagan broke precedent by sending the three surviving former presidents—Carter and his two Republican predecessors, Gerald R. Ford and Richard M. Nixon—as heads of the U.S. delegation at the October 10 funeral in Cairo of Egypt's assassinated president Anwar el-Sadat.

Reagan picked fewer women than Carter for top posts, but he scored politically with his choice of Sandra Day O'Connor, 51, an Arizona state judge, to succeed retiring Associate Justice Potter Stewart on the Supreme Court. The nomination of the first woman ever named to the high bench breezed through the Senate 99-0 September 21 after hearings in which conservatives pressed her to reject the court's acceptance of abortion. Judge O'Connor declined, saying the issue would probably come again before the court.

On abortion, Reagan told his second news conference he believed that life begins at conception, which the Right to Life movement construed as support for its drive to win constitutional protection for unborn fetuses.

Attorney General William French Smith told a meeting of government lawyers October 29 that the administration would press for restraint in areas of past judicial activism that appeared to include abortion, school desegregation, and sexual and racial quotas.

The hush-hush Central Intelligence Agency spent most of the year in the news, starting with President Reagan's choice of William J. Casey, his 1980 campaign manager, to be CIA director. Casey, 68, was a businessman and former chairman of the Securities and Exchange Commission whose last known intelligence experience was in World War II. Critics grumbled when Casey picked Max Hugel, a New Hampshire businessman and former Reagan campaign organizer, as CIA's deputy director of operations—in fact the chief of clandestine operations.

Accused July 14 of improprieties in securities deals, Hugel called the charge "unfounded, un-

(*Continued on page 530.*)

UNITED STATES—SPECIAL REPORT:

THE TRANSITION OF PRESIDENTIAL POWER

On the afternoon of March 30, 1981, a tormented young man stood with a group of sightseers and newsmen outside the Washington Hilton Hotel waiting for a glimpse of President Ronald Reagan. As the President emerged, the man fired a gun in the President's direction.

Immediately thereafter, news accounts flashed a mixture of fact and fiction, recounting the event. A Secret Service agent and a Washington policeman had been shot. Presidential Press Secretary James Brady had taken one bullet in the forehead. It was reported erroneously that he died. The first account flashed the news that the President had escaped unharmed. Later, it was said that his rib had been broken as the Secret Service pushed him into his limousine. Finally, the truth: a bullet had found its mark and Ronald Reagan had narrowly escaped becoming the ninth President to die in office.

News accounts and events ricocheted in near hysterical fashion. The President was rushed to George Washington University Hospital where he collapsed in the emergency room prior to undergoing lengthy surgery. Secretary of State Alexander Haig held a press conference in the White House where he announced that he had everything under control. The Secretary's remarks led many to conclude that he was unaware of the nation's 1947 succession act that had placed both the Speaker of the House of Representatives and the President Pro Tempore of the Senate ahead of the Secretary of State in the line of succession following the President and the Vice-President. Top White House advisers Edwin Meese and James Baker attempted to allay suspicions that the President had been critically wounded. Vice-President George Bush, who had been in Texas, returned to the capital. Secretary of Defense Caspar Weinberger and Haig quibbled over who had what authority during the crisis.

People everywhere asked the same questions. Who was really running the store in Washington? Whose finger rested on that horrible black button of American nuclear response? Who was really performing the powers and duties of the President of the United States?

By Constitutional fiat, the Presidency was to be, and still is, a unique office. No other office in the world possesses such concise constitutional authority which is specifically designed to encompass the will of the governed. The Presidency was developed in a primitive, pioneer society. The nation was young. Life was comparatively simple and straightforward. So, too, was the Founding Fathers' establishment of the Presidency. Article II, Section 1 of the Constitution specifies: "The executive power shall be vested in a President of the United States of America."

Little attention was given to the human frailties that might beset the nation's highest official. In fact, the Vice-Presidency was included within the Constitution almost as an afterthought. Insufficient attention appears to have been given to the possession, disposition, and succession of presidential power.

The death of President William Henry Harrison in 1841 forced the nation to confront the succession question for the first time. Vice-President John Tyler claimed the office of President, despite significant evidence that the Constitutional Convention had intended that the Vice-President serve only as Acting President while a permanent successor was chosen. However, the Tyler precedent was not successfully contested and, thus, it established a foundation of authority for future Vice-Presidents to succeed to the Presidency.

The 25th Amendment. As the world tempo increased, uncertainties about presidential power could be disastrous at home and abroad. It was to minimize, if not completely remove, these uncertainties that Congress passed the 25th Amendment to the Constitution, which went into effect in February 1967.

Section one of the 25th Amendment lays to rest any doubts about the validity of the Tyler precedent. When the President dies, the Vice-President becomes President. The same is true if the President resigns or is removed from office. The Vice-President becomes President with all the powers and duties of the office.

Section two of the 25th Amendment provides a means to fill vacancies that occur in the office of Vice-President. Prior to the passage of the 25th Amendment, such vacancies had occurred on 16 occasions. Under the new procedure, vice-presidential vacancies are to be filled by the President nominating a new Vice-President who takes office after having been confirmed by a majority vote of both houses of Congress. The 25th Amendment has been utilized twice to fill vice-presidential vacancies. Gerald R. Ford became Vice-President on Dec. 6, 1973, following the resignation of Spiro Agnew. Nelson A. Rockefeller became Vice-President on Dec. 19, 1974, following Gerald R. Ford's succession to the Presidency upon the resignation of President Richard M. Nixon.

The 25th Amendment also provides for a means of dealing with a much more difficult and vexatious aspect of presidential power; namely, that of presidential disability or inability to perform the powers and duties of the office. The

Michael Evans, The White House

Leaving a Washington hotel, President Reagan waves to the crowd; seconds later he is shot.

Convention records contain only one reference to the problem of inability. On Aug. 28, 1787, John Dickinson asked, "What is the extent of the term 'disability' and who is to be the judge of it?" The question was not answered. However, the nation was thrice confronted with instances of serious presidential inability.

In 1881, President James Garfield lay for 80 days unable to perform after being struck by an assassin's bullet. The President's cabinet could not agree that Vice-President Chester Arthur should assume the powers and duties of the Presidency. There existed a strong body of legal opinion, which continued until the ratification of the 25th Amendment, that argued that once the Vice-President assumes the powers and duties of the Presidency he becomes, in fact, President. Thus, if Arthur had assumed the Presidency, Garfield could not have reclaimed the office if he had recovered.

Inability became a matter of pressing urgency again in 1919, when President Wilson suffered a severe stroke. During this period of more than a year, 28 bills became law without presidential signature. During the 1950s, President Dwight Eisenhower suffered three serious illnesses. President Eisenhower did attempt to reduce the dangers involved in the event of presidential inability by entering into an informal agreement with Vice-President Nixon. This agreement contained basic instructions under which the Vice-President could execute presidential duties. A similar agreement was entered into by President John Kennedy and Vice-President Lyndon Johnson and by President Johnson and Speaker John McCormack.

The 25th Amendment provides for the resolution of the presidential inability problem by three ways. First, the President may declare his own inability, whereupon his "powers and duties shall be discharged by the Vice-President as Acting President." In this instance, the President may reclaim the powers and duties of the office by merely stating his ability to perform.

Second, in the event the President cannot declare his own inability, the Vice-President and a majority of the Cabinet may declare that such an inability exists, whereupon "the Vice-President shall immediately assume the powers and duties of the office as Acting President."

Third, in the event that the Vice-President and a majority of the Cabinet conclude that the President is unable to perform the powers and duties of his office and the President disagrees with this conclusion, the matter will be decided by Congress. "If the Congress, within 21 days, . . . determines by two-thirds vote of both Houses that the President is unable to discharge the powers and duties of his office, the Vice-President shall . . . discharge the same as Acting President; otherwise, the President shall resume the powers and duties of his office."

The proper fulfillment of the powers and duties of the President is critical to the well-being of the nation. Thus, it is imperative that they be carried out by one of sound mind. In a democracy, it is equally important to ensure that, once these powers and duties have been given to a President by the will of the people, they cannot be taken from him against his will without justifiable cause. The 25th Amendment seeks to ensure this delicate balance.

It is clear that any President can quite properly delegate certain assignments to members of his administration. Those to whom the President had delegated these tasks could quite properly fulfill the President's orders even though the President was unconscious at the time the orders were being fulfilled. No declaration of inability would be required to permit such subordinates to carry out specific tasks.

BIRCH BAYH

proven, and untrue." His resignation was accepted, however, and John H. Stein, a CIA career man, was named to the deputy's slot. The Senate Select Committee on Intelligence conducted a four-month closed-door review of Casey's stewardship and reported December 3 that he may have been "inattentive to detail" but was not unfit for the post.

Intelligence committees of both Congressional houses questioned provisions of a revision of a Carter executive order governing intelligence practices. There was particular concern about a provision giving the CIA limited authority in the domestic intelligence field, hitherto the preserve of the Federal Bureau of Investigation.

Meanwhile, Congressional committees, Justice Department investigators, and the CIA itself probed disclosures that two rogue former CIA agents had sold their services to the bitterly anti-American government of oil-rich Libya. The men, Edwin P. Wilson and Francis E. Terpil, both fugitives in the Middle East, came under federal indictment in 1980 for alleged violations linked with exports of arms and training programs to Libya. But officials warned of broad gaps in applicable U.S. criminal laws and serious constitutional questions raised by efforts to control the activities of former agents.

Two key Reagan aides, David A. Stockman and Richard V. Allen, caused embarrassment for the administration late in the year. Stockman, who as director of the Office of Management and Budget (OMB) served as overseer of the federal budget cuts, revealed in a series of interviews published in the December issue of *Atlantic Monthly* that he had misgivings about the Reagan economic plan. The OMB director did not deny the remarks but said they were made off the record. The president refused his immediate offer to resign. At about the same time, the White House acknowledged that National Security Adviser Richard V. Allen had received $1,000 from a Japanese magazine for helping to arrange an interview with the first lady, Nancy Reagan. Allen then took an administrative leave, pending an investigation into the case.

The Economy. Reagan took over an economy bloated by double-digit inflation and soaring interest rates that squeezed all credit-dependent industries, notably farming, automobiles, and housing. To reverse these trends, he boldly applied "supply-side" doctrine, which holds that tax cuts generate savings and investment that will stimulate sufficient economic activity to produce new government revenues to offset the effects of the tax cuts. Reagan also cut nondefense spending.

The president got most of what he sought from Congress and long-term projections suggested that his policies might indeed succeed in wringing inflation out of the economy and eventually sparking the investment needed for economic growth. But "Reaganomics" presented short-term problems.

In October, the president admitted that "a slight recession" prevailed, and all the indexes bore him out. The November unemployment

In executing the office of president, Ronald Reagan relies heavily on his White House staff, especially (r-l) Edwin Meese III, James A. Baker III, and Michael K. Deaver.

UPI

rate was 8.4%, more than a full point above July and higher than it had been since the 1974–75 recession, when the rate hit 9%. Interest rates and inflation were both edging down, but slowly. With months of economic stagnation probable, shortfalls in tax revenues seemed certain and Reagan conceded that his campaign predictions of a balanced 1984 budget had gone glimmering. He promised to seek no new taxes in fiscal 1982, but big deficits seemed likely in later years without added revenues.

By midsummer, Congress had enacted tax cuts aggregating 25% over 33 months, along with slashes in Carter's spending plan totaling $130,600,000,000 over three years. But a $45,200,000,000 deficit was projected for fiscal 1982, mainly because the tax cuts' estimated cost—$37,700,000,000 in 1982 and a total of $280,300,000,000 through 1984—eclipsed the spending cuts.

Reagan went on national television September 24 to recruit support for an additional $13,000,000,000 in spending cuts, plus $3,000,000,000 in 1982 and $22,000,000,000 over three years in "revenue enhancement"—administration jargon for new taxes bearing mostly on business. These moves, he said, would help him hold the 1982 deficit close to a revised $43,000,000,000 target. As Congress dawdled in passing appropriation bills, Reagan warned that he was standing firm on his program and intended to veto "any bill that abuses the limited resources of the taxpayers."

In the first half of 1981, 70% of the nation's savings and loan institutions operated in the red. To help thrift institutions lure back deposits that had strayed to higher-yield investments, Congress authorized them to issue all-savers certificates through Dec. 31, 1982. Such certificates paid interest pegged at 70% of the rate on Treasury bills—with no U.S. tax on the first $1,000 of income for individuals. The industry hoped for $250,000,000,000 in deposits; the Treasury feared a $4,700,000,000 revenue loss.

The price of mailing a first-class letter rose to 20 cents on November 1. It was the second postal increase of 1981, which began with stamps costing 15 cents.

The largest merger in U.S. history—the $7,600,000,000 takeover of Conoco, Inc., by E. I. du Pont de Nemours & Co.—made du Pont the nation's seventh-largest industrial concern. At the Justice Department, Attorney General Smith said that free competition, not size, should be the criterion for antitrust enforcement and that "bigness in business does not necessarily mean badness."

Coolness between the White House and labor leadership became an open rupture after the administration effectively broke a strike called August 3 by some 13,000 members of the Professional Air Traffic Controller's Organization (PATCO). Most strikers were fired for violating both federal law and no-strike affidavits they signed when they were hired.

UPI

President Reagan prepares to address a session of Congress. Vice-President George Bush (top left) and House Speaker Tip O'Neill join in the welcome.

The strike reduced the roster of 17,000 controllers by two thirds. Faced with the slow job of recruiting enough trained specialists to keep U.S. airways safe, the Federal Aviation Administration cut back airline flights 20% and limited private flying. There was a five-fold increase in late commercial flights.

A "Solidarity Day" demonstration, sponsored by the AFL-CIO, attracted 250,000 persons to Washington on September 19 to protest the impact of Reagan's economic policies on social programs. There was next to no public support, meanwhile, for a 49-day strike by major league baseball players that ended July 31.

Congress. The conservative trend of the November 1980 elections carried over into the early months of the 97th Congress. Aided by the most favorable party divisions a Republican president had enjoyed since the Eisenhower sweep of 1952, President Reagan used expert lobbying, professional charm, and unpredictable fortune to establish an early rapport with Capitol Hill.

The administration had the edge in the Senate, where Republicans held 53 of 100 seats. In

Wally McNamee/"Newsweek"

During much of 1981, David Stockman, director of the Office of Management and Budget, was the new administration's chief spokesman for the doctrine of supply-side economics. However, a candid, late-in-the-year magazine interview left in doubt the question of his future influence with the Reagan team, Congress, and the American public.

the House, the Republican Party was officially behind 191 to 243 with one vacancy when the session began. But Republican ranks held solid while Democratic conservatives—mostly Southerners who labeled themselves "Boll Weevils"—gave Reagan programs enough votes to tip the balance on crucial midsummer roll calls that put the Reagan administration tax and budget programs in place.

Party unity was the name of the game in both chambers. House Speaker Thomas P. (Tip) O'Neill led a battered majority rattled by the 1980 elections and painfully aware that the next campaign was only a year away. Fragmentation of Democratic votes on Reagan's fiscal program pointed up O'Neill's problems with developing a majority consensus among the Southern conservatives, Northern liberals, Western populists, and champions of urban minorities who filled Democratic ranks.

Among Republicans, there was less ideological diversity, and there was the unity that attends victory. But the mood changed after Labor Day, when Congress returned from an August recess glumly aware that its votes for Reagan's tax and spending cuts had done little to alter the facts of inflation or to reverse the upward climb of interest rates, which depressed Wall Street and threatened to add $20,000,000,000 to federal interest costs in fiscal 1981. That increase figured in the economy-minded administration's request for legislation raising the federal debt ceiling to the milestone figure of $1 trillion—which equals a mind-boggling thousand billion dollars. The House and Senate went along and voted the boost, together with stopgap financing for the start of fiscal 1982.

Declaring the "the practice of loading the budget with unnecessary spending—and then waiting until the eleventh hour to pass a continuing resolution . . . has gone on much too long," President Reagan vetoed on November 23 a government spending bill and ordered a shutdown of all but essential government services. The authority for financing government operations had ended technically at 12:01 A.M. on November 21. Congress then approved and the president signed a measure calling for a continuation of current fiscal levels until Dec. 15, 1981, and the government resumed business. In turn, both houses of Congress approved a resolution establishing binding budget levels for fiscal year 1982.

UNITED STATES • Information Highlights

Official Name: United States of America.
Location: Central North America.
Area: 3,615,123 sq mi (9 363 169 km^2).
Population (1980 census): 226,504,825.
Chief Cities (1980 census): Washington, DC, the capital, 637,651; New York, 7,071,030; Chicago, 3,005,072; Los Angeles, 2,966,763; Philadelphia, 1,688,210; Houston, 1,594,086; Detroit, 1,203,339.
Government: *Head of state and government,* Ronald Reagan, president (took office Jan. 20, 1981). *Legislature*—Congress: Senate and House of Representatives.
Monetary Unit: Dollar.
Manufactures (major products): Motor vehicles, aircraft, ships and railroad equipment, industrial machinery, processed foods, chemicals, electrical equipment and supplies, fabricated metals.
Agriculture (major products): Wheat, rye, corn, barley, oats, soybeans, tobacco, cotton, cattle, fruits.

In the Senate, GOP leaders fretted about the political consequences of the further spending cuts Reagan requested and explored prospects for new revenue through added taxes. In the House, GOP leaders moved charily, fearful that Democrats would try to use any new tax legislation as a vehicle to reverse the fiscal program Congress set in place in July.

While GOP moderates questioned the depth of Reagan's cuts in social programs, conservative hard-liners took issue with aspects of a $180,000,000,000 plan to modernize strategic nuclear forces which the administration unveiled October 2. One controversy centered on Reagan's decision to meet advances in Soviet strategic weapons development by deploying 100 highly accurate MX intercontinental missiles in hardened silos built for older weapons. Reagan proposed the plan as an alternative to President Carter's "shell game" strategy, under which 200 MXs would be secretly shuttled among as many as 4,600 launching sites. The Air Force favored the sidetracked "shell game" approach, but it scored when President Reagan asked for production of the B-1 intercontinental bomber, which Carter shelved in 1977.

There were objections from both political parties to Reagan's decision to sell Saudi Arabia five supersophisticated AWACS (Airborne Warning and Control System) reconnaissance jets. The administration sought the deal primarily to protect prized Saudi oil reserves, but critics maintained that it could compromise both U.S. military secrets and the security of Israel. The Reagan plan was to take effect unless it was turned down by both chambers, but that seemed possible when the House rejected AWACS, 301-111, on October 14. Fifty senators, among them 18 Republicans, signed a letter of opposition before the matter was aired in a hard-fought debate. But meetings with uncommitted senators turned a potential setback into a triumph for Reagan. When the roll was called October 28, the tally was 52 to 48 for the AWACS deal.

Veterans' pensions were among the outlays protected by Reagan's "safety net." Most of the $24,200,000,000 allocated to the Veterans Administration (VA) in fiscal 1982 was earmarked to aid veterans of earlier wars, but there was increasing Congressional concern for the needs of the 2.9 million younger Americans who served in Southeast Asia in the 1960s and 1970s. Congress directed the VA to reverse prior policies and treat conditions that "may be associated with exposure" to Agent Orange, a chemical defoliant used in Vietnam that has been blamed for ailments that include cancer, liver and skin diseases, and nervous and psychological afflictions. The VA was further required to continue a network of "storefront" centers to aid the readjustment of Vietnam veterans even though the administration proposed elimination of the program. Congress also vetoed administration plans to reduce the number of beds in VA hospitals and nursing homes below 100,000 and to lay off up to 20,000 medical personnel.

(For a listing of major legislation enacted in 1981 see page 585.)

Congress passes the tax bill and it is time for a White House toast.

Michael Evans/The White House

Bruce Hoertel

Democratic senators (l-r) Ernest F. Hollings (SC), Robert Byrd (WV), and Patrick Leahy (VT) display a typical school lunch that would be offered as a result of Reagan administration budget cuts.

Race Relations. The autumn economic slump, like most of its predecessors, hit black employment hardest. In the July-October quarter, while the national unemployment rate was rising a full point to 8%, the jobless rate for blacks reached 16.7% and 46.3% for black teenagers.

The black community contributed little to Reagan's election and it received little special attention from the Reagan White House. "I did not come here today bearing the promise of government handouts," Reagan told a National Association for the Advancement of Colored People convention on June 29. Budget cuts, he said, were "much more equitable than the tremendous cuts in social programs made by inflation and a declining economy." The president said his program would "move us toward black economic freedom."

On November 6, Reagan announced qualified support for a ten-year extension of the Voting Rights Act of 1965. Such an extension had passed the House, but was not slated for Senate hearings until January 1982. Reagan indicated that he would approve a direct extension of the act, which was to expire in August 1982, but endorsed two possible amendments to the House bill. One, generally opposed by civil-rights spokesmen, would require plaintiffs who allege that voting rights have been denied to prove that the act of denial was intentional. The other would make it easier for the 22 affected states to win exemption from the law's requirement that they submit local election law changes for federal "pre-clearance."

Attorney General Smith failed in an effort to persuade the president to issue a more conservative statement. A stiffening of Justice Department attitudes toward civil-rights enforcement was evident. In September, the department reversed its prior position to support Washington state in defending before the Supreme Court its ban on the use of busing for school desegregation. The department also approved a desegregation plan for Chicago which it had previously rejected as incomplete; it abandoned its prior support for a Houston busing plan; and it waived long-held objections to settlement of a discrimination suit against Louisiana's state university system.

Reagan seemed more determined than his predecessors to halt the flow of illegal aliens, many of them blacks, from the Caribbean region, and to curtail admissions of refugees from Southeast Asia, where the turmoil of the 1970s showed signs of abating.

To stem the tide that bore about 5 million undocumented aliens to the United States in the 1970s, the Justice Department proposed revised regulations for Congressional review. Its program included plans to impose sanctions, with fines, on employers who knowingly hire illegal aliens; amnesty for resident "illegals" who meet certain conditions, and stepped-up enforcement in the field, including interdiction of vessels carrying aliens without entry permits. The latter provision was aimed primarily at Haiti, an impoverished dictatorship from which an estimated 90,000 refugees had fled illegally to the United States since 1971—half of them to be sent back by the U.S. Immigration and Naturalization Service. In September, Haiti agreed to permit the U.S. Coast Guard to search its vessels on the high seas and force those carrying "illegals" to turn back. On October 27, a 30-ft (9-m) sailboat carrying 67 Haitians foundered off Florida's east coast with 33 fatalities. Civil libertarians protested that many Haitians were fleeing political persecution, but the administration stood by its policy of deporting undocumented Haitians unable to prove eligibility for political asylum.

DON IRWIN
Washington Bureau, "Los Angeles Times"

THE NATION'S 20th CENSUS

The 1980 census was the 20th census in an unbroken series of complete population counts taken every ten years since 1790.

Every census attempts to count everyone, but in reality this goal is never quite reached. In the 1970 census an estimated 97.5% of the population was counted. The 2.5% missed is called the undercount. For the census of April 1, 1980, the Bureau of the Census hired more than 250,000 enumerators and spent $1,000,000,000 in an attempt to find every person. It found 226,504,825 persons, but the precise extent of the undercount, if any, had not been estimated by autumn 1981. However, the fact that the Census Bureau found approximately 5 million more people than expected indicates that the undercount is substantially less than in the previous census.

Taking the census balances the government's need to have statistical information against the citizen's right to privacy. The same law (Title 13, U.S. Code) that requires public cooperation with the census also protects the confidentiality of individual information.

Format. The 1980 questionnaire was similar to the one used in 1970 in that only a few basic questions were asked of every household and person. More information was asked of a sample of the population. The process was simpler for 1980, because only two forms of the questionnaire were used—a short form for about 78% of the households and the long form for the remaining 22%. For most areas of the country in 1980, a sample of one in every six households received the long form. In communities with populations below 2,500, the sampling was on a one-in-two basis, in order to obtain more reliable statistics.

The short questionnaire, which was two pages long, contained seven questions about population characteristics and 12 questions about housing. The long form contained these same questions plus an additional 20 housing and 26 population questions. The Census Bureau estimated that it took about 15 minutes to complete the short questionnaire and 45 minutes for the long form.

The first page of the short form asked population questions about household relationships, age, sex, race, marital status, and Spanish origin. The second page asked housing questions about the type and size of the dwelling unit, whether it is owned or rented or a condominium, and the monthly rent if rented or the estimated value if owned. The sample questionnaire asked housing questions concerning the type and cost of utilities, mortgage or insurance costs, and the number of motor vehicles at the household.

Sample population questions concerned ethnic origin or ancestry, languages spoken, veteran and disability status, employment status, place of work, means of transportation to work, type of industry and occupation of worker, and annual income.

The Census Results. The 1980 Census of Population and Housing found 226.5 million persons and 80 million households. The population had grown by 11.4% since 1970. That growth rate, slightly more than 1% per year, is the lowest since the Great Depression and reflects a very low U.S. birth rate during the 1970s.

The 1980 census revealed several "firsts." For the first time the majority of the U.S. population lives in the South and the West, the result

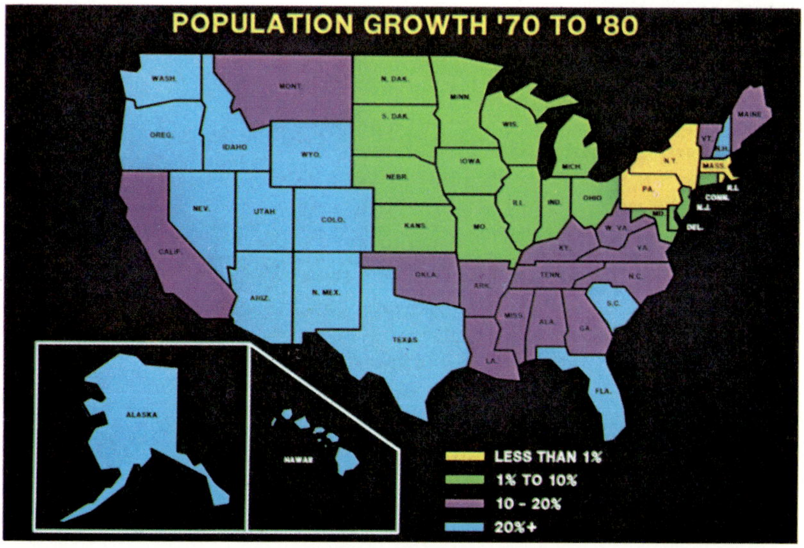

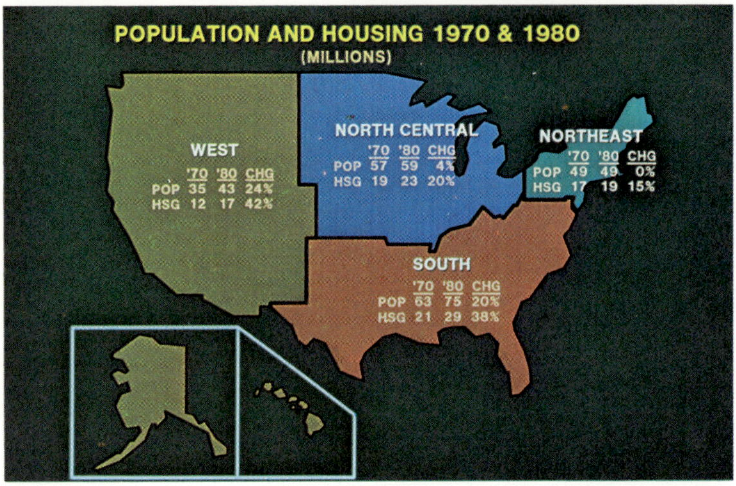

c 1981 "American Demographics"

The statistics on the map at left illustrate the change in population (pop) and in the number of households (housing, hsg) in the various regions of the United States between 1970 and 1980. The greatest growth was in the South and West.

of a 50-year migration trend toward warmer climates. Ninety percent of all population growth in the 1970s took place in the South and West. The Northeast region of nearly 50 million people had essentially zero population growth. New York State lost more population than any state in history. Only two other states, Rhode Island and the District of Columbia (which is considered a state for the census), lost population.

In the 1970s the most rapidly growing states in terms of percentage growth were Nevada, Arizona, and Florida, which increased by 63.5%, 53.1%, and 43.4%, respectively. California, Texas, and Florida gained the most population, each growing by about 3 million persons. Because of these shifts in population the South and West regions will gain 17 seats in the U.S. House of Representatives, giving them a majority of 227 out of 435.

The American population aged by two years since 1970; the median age of the population is now exactly 30 years. This rapid aging of the population is caused by the declining birth rate, the aging of the baby-boom population, and the longer life span of the elderly. The number of people 65 years old and older increased by nearly 28% in the last decade, more than twice the increase of people in general. Because women live longer than men there are now 6.5 million more women than men in the United States. The census counted 110 million men and 116.5 million women.

The population that identified themselves as Hispanic has increased 61% since 1970, partly due to a change in the census questionnaire but also because of higher birth rates among Hispanics and greatly increased immigration. The black population grew 17% during the decade and now numbers 26.5 million.

Since the Census Bureau enumerates both population and housing units, it found 88 million housing units of which a total of 80.4 million was occupied. Such occupied units, called households, had increased 27% since 1970. The fact that households grew so much faster than population is a result of the population per household declining from 3.11 to 2.75. For the first time in U.S. history there are fewer than three persons in the average American household. The number of persons per household has been declining because more people—both young and old—choose to live alone, because high divorce rates are fragmenting families, and finally because the modern American family has fewer children than in the past.

Purpose and Significance. Data from census questionnaires are used for statistical purposes only. Any information that can be linked to any individual is not given or sold to anyone.

Census statistics are vital not only to state and federal agencies but also to the general public. They determine the apportionment of seats in the House of Representatives and are the basis for drawing political boundaries for state legislatures as well as local election districts. In addition, they are used in U.S. federal programs to allocate funds annually to state and local governments. These allocations affect the level of services to people and, therefore, local and state taxes.

The extensive use of census statistics for fund allocation is a relatively recent phenomenon, having begun on a large scale with enactment of the federal revenue-sharing program in 1972. The major difficulty in tying fund allocation to the census is that generally when a community's population declines the money it gets declines and many American cities are losing population. New York City, for example, is the largest city in the United States and it had a loss of nearly 900,000 people (11%) in the 1970s.

A number of cities, New York included, faced with the loss of millions of dollars in federal assistance, sued the Bureau of the Census to try to have their populations adjusted upward by the amount of the undercount. If the undercount was estimated to be 2%, then these cities would want 2% added to their population. Several court suits were being litigated in late 1981.

PETER K. FRANCESE

THE ECONOMY

Not since the Great Depression of a half-century earlier had the economy so dominated the minds and emotions of Americans. It intruded into their dreams, it stirred up almost forgotten insecurities, it forced them to postpone or abandon long-held goals.

Every day there was news to threaten or, more rarely, to hearten. Inflation, high interest rates, taxes, unemployment, and big budget deficits led every newspaper and newscast. Feelings were intense; events were extreme. After three decades of the very good life, Americans had the feeling their economy no longer worked and that it would have to be changed. Change offered hope, and so their feelings were mixed. They were bidding farewell to a beneficent system of governance that had now become a burden to support.

The evidence abounded. As the year began the prime lending rate, publicized as the lowest rate to the best corporate customers, fluctuated around 20%, and prices were climbing at an annual rate of 14%. Wage increases trailed behind, and no less than 7.8 million people were jobless. The housing market was buried beneath 18% mortgages. A once-powerful automobile industry was now crushed by imports, high prices, high interest rates, and inefficiency. Budget deficits were being fought at every level of government from the local school board to the White House. Red ink, it appeared, was splashed everywhere, and no level of taxation or financial sleight of hand seemed able to erase the stains. They were, economists said, the stigmata of overindulgence, of too much consumption, year after year, at the expense of production.

The Reagan Program. It was on such issues that Ronald Reagan had won a landslide victory over President Jimmy Carter, and the new president quickly proclaimed his goals. He would, he said, offer tax incentives for business investment. He would cut federal spending and turn over many responsibilities to local and state governments. He would cut taxes and federal regulations. Military spending alone would not be reduced; it would be increased, the assumption being that military power and economic strength complemented and secured each other.

In his first week in office President Reagan imposed a federal hiring freeze, limited government travel and office refurbishing, and named Vice-President George Bush to study possible deregulations. The flurry of activity was more symbolic than substantial, but it portended fundamental changes to come.

"The taxing power of government must be used to provide revenues for legitimate government purposes," Reagan told Congress on February 18. "It must not bc used to regulate the economy or bring about social change. We've tried that and surely we must be able to see it doesn't work." Declaring that "we can no longer afford things simply because we think of them," he proposed that federal receipts be cut from 21.4% of the nation's output of goods and services to just 19.3% in 1984. The budget, he forecast, would be balanced in the latter fiscal year, by stimulating individual and business activity and by lowering taxes and spending less. He listed his plans in a 287-page volume, "America's New Beginning: A Program For Economic Recovery." The program sought spending of $695,-500,000,000 and revenues of $650,500,000,000.

For many people the most welcome proposals were those that would cut personal income taxes. Compared with fiscal 1981, income taxes overall would be 27% less in fiscal 1984. Capital gains taxes would be lowered. Business would be offered more liberal depreciation on plants and equipment. To accomplish this, government spending would be drastically lowered. In social programs, including medicaid, food stamps, and nutrition, the cuts would amount to more than $10,000,000,000. Job programs would be reduced more than $6,000,000,000. Foreign aid, student loans, renter subsidies, and the synthetic fuel program all would be slashed. But, the president declared, the truly needy would be protected by a "safety net" of benefits. If successful, the president's plan would raise annual output from 1.4% in 1981 to 5.2% in 1982, and at least 4% a year through 1986. Inflation, meanwhile, would tumble from 10.5% in 1981 to 7.2% in 1982 and to only 4.6% in 1985. The jobless rate would shrink to 7% in 1982 from its current 7.4% rate, and then

'I hope it's nothing serious.'

continue a slow but steady decline thereafter. Following much debate and complaints that the program was at the expense of the poor, and that it would undo decades of efforts to make government more humane, the president won most of his goals by early August. (*See also* TAXATION; UNITED STATES—*Domestic Affairs.*)

The price for this was high. The president pushed $35,000,000,000 in budget reductions through Congress in the fiscal year beginning October 1, amid a crescendo of denunciations that the poor were being victimized. States would lose $11,000,000,000 in federal aid over a year's time, and revenue sharing programs that benefited 39,000 localities were cut.

Wall Street, which had been expected to greet the new program with a burst of buying, was not impressed. Doubts were expressed that the combined tax and spending cuts would get the economy moving again, and as analysts dissected the budget documents their doubts increased. The Dow Jones industrial average peaked in April at close to 1,025 points and then began a long descent. In August alone it fell about 70 points, and in September it reached a 1981 low of 805 points. For the rest of the year it remained below 900.

Indicators. Ominous signs appeared everywhere, and doubts could not be fully assuaged by Reagan's assurances and by his explanation that before recovery began some pain must be endured. Loan rates remained near 20% into fall, a level that seemed to blunt the goal of greater business activity. Many small businesses were in deep trouble, unable to cover their costs with price increases. Savings banks were losing heavily, burdened with 7% mortgages on the books while they were forced to pay double that for new money. Still, the Federal Reserve stuck to its policy of high interest rates as the most effective way to control inflation, even though the housing and automotive industries had collapsed into a deep depression.

Nothing that automakers tried seemed to work, not rebates or deep discounts or any of the promotional tricks that once made it seem that big car companies made the market dance to their tune. With national unemployment rising and incomes falling behind price increases, Americans could not afford to pay $7,500 to $10,000 or more and then finance their car purchases with 18% loans. During November, domestic cars sold at an annual rate of only 5.3 million units, worse even than the devastating 6.4 million rate of the previous November. Adding to the woes, imports sold at a 2.3 million rate, increasing their share of the market to 26.5%. By late in the year 325,000 auto workers had lost their jobs since 1979. Including related industries, 655,000 jobs were lost in three years.

Designed by Frank Senyk

THE U.S. ECONOMY

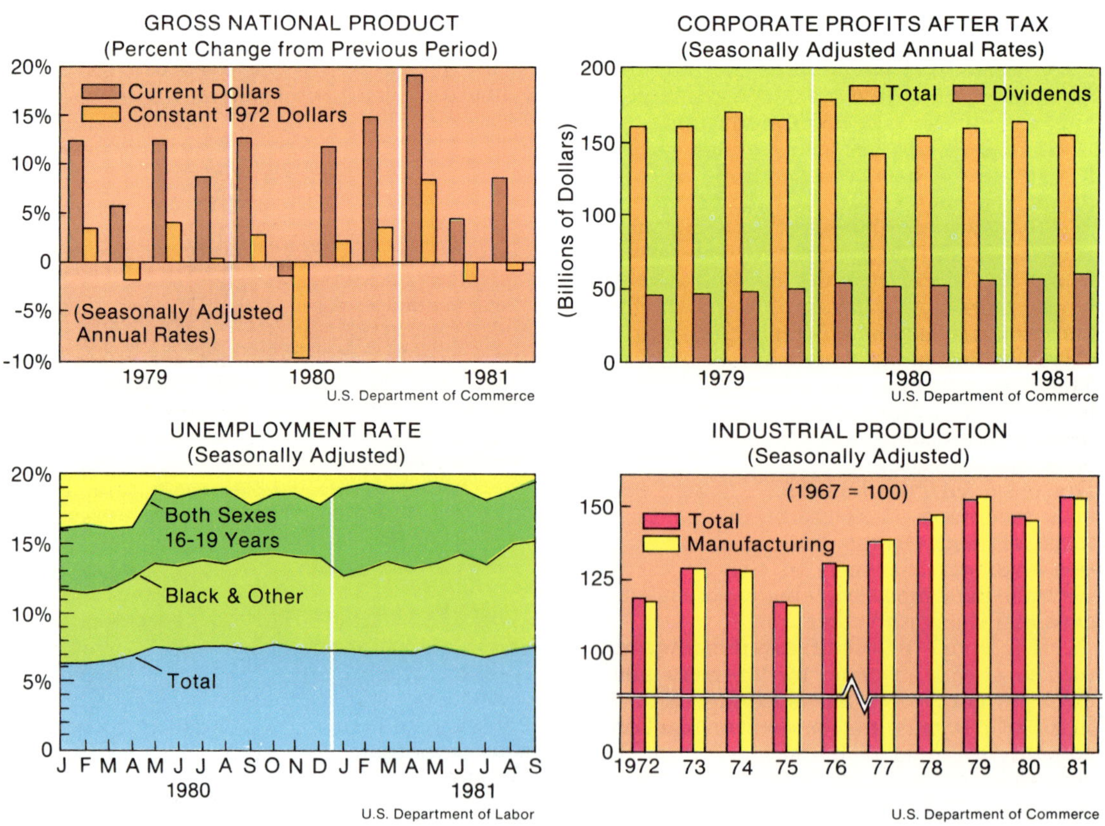

N.B. Third quarter 1981 GNP in constant dollars was revised to a 0.6% gain.

Unemployment was not confined to the automotive industry. By November, the national unemployment rate was up to 8.4%, with 9 million Americans out of work and with the administration forecasting monthly rates of 9% in 1982. But it was in the Midwest, muscle and sinew of industrial America, that the impact was most noticeable. Its plants had the same forlorn look that could be seen in New England textile mill towns five decades earlier. James Harbour, an analyst and consultant on automotive matters who had just completed a study of five Japanese and five American car assembly plants, concluded that unless U.S. management and labor improved their productivity, now at zero growth or worse, the entire industrial base of the country could be endangered. Japanese carmakers, he said, had average unit costs $1,700 below American producers on comparable models sold in the United States. Japanese auto workers, he found, averaged $12 an hour in wages and benefits, United States workers $19. Machine "uptime" in Japanese car plants was found to be 80%, but only 60% in the United States.

Words from Reagan's February address to Congress seemed especially appropriate. "We can no longer procrastinate and hope things will get better," the president had said. Now, in December, Douglas Fraser, United Automobile Workers (UAW) president, echoed the sentiment. The UAW, he said, would consider discussing wage concessions, a position he had rejected earlier. "Times have changed," he explained. In two years, UAW ranks had shrunk from 1.5 million to 1.2 million. Chrysler remained deep in the red and considered selling off its military tank subsidiary. American Motors asked its workers for a $150 million loan. Ford was in the midst of its second straight year of losses. Thanks in part to greater efficiency, General Motors had returned to profitability.

Great losses were suffered by other companies, too. Pan American World Airways was forced by creditors to sell its profitable hotel business. International Harvester, with a $636.7 million operating loss for the year, was also compelled to sell off a subsidiary and restructure $4,000,000,000 in credit. McLouth Steel, 11th largest in the industry, filed for protection under the U.S. bankruptcy code in December. Numerous smaller companies failed. In the week ending December 3, Dun & Bradstreet reported 443 business failures, bringing the total for the year to 15,982, compared with 11,030 in the like period a year earlier.

Mergers. Mergers became commonplace. On orders of the Federal Deposit Insurance Corp. (FDIC), Greenwich Savings Bank, for example, was merged with another New York institution, the Metropolitan Savings Bank at a cost to the FDIC of $465 million. That meant added insurance burdens for 14,000 other savings and commercial banks, some of the former on the brink of insolvency themselves. Mergers of industrial giants were for other reasons, one of which appeared to be a more lenient view of corporate marriages by the new administration. DuPont took over Conoco, an oil company, defeating Seagrams, the distiller, for the affection of shareholders, and Mobil Oil and U.S. Steel fought doggedly and expensively for Marathon Oil. Still another pattern of mergers evolved. Spurred by visions of a new world of finance in which banks, securities brokers, insurance agents, and others would be freed to sell each others' services, Prudential Insurance obtained control of Bache Group, a securities firm, and Sears, Roebuck & Co., acquired Dean Witter Reynolds, one of the biggest dealers in stocks and bonds.

Housing. While this was going on, sometimes with multi-billion-dollar credit lines, would-be homeowners could not get loans or could not afford payments. The median price of a new single-family home was close to $70,000 (figures varied). Herman Smith, president of the National Association of Home Builders, pointed out that at 17.5%, the payment on a $60,000 mortgage came to $880 a month, almost double the tab of two years earlier. It would require an annual income of nearly $40,000.

As the year ended, America's great production machine was growing dormant, and many forecasters said they expected that final figures would show a shrinkage in total output of 5–7% for the quarter. Moreover, most forecasters said that they expected the recession to continue well into 1982. The administration reduced its expectations greatly. Instead of a 5.2% gain in output for 1982, White House economist Murray Weidenbaum stated in December that "real growth is likely to average only 1% in 1981," although he foresaw a sharp pickup in the second half of the year. Almost at the same time came another shocker, an announcement that the 1982 budget deficit, which the White House had said in September would be $43,100,000,000, now was expected to reach $109,200,000,000, given current budget and economic trends.

Nevertheless, those who believed in the great economic experiment could provide some evidence to bolster their faith. Inflation was coming down, and the Consumer Price Index for the year seemed likely to drop below 10%. Interest rates tumbled. The prime rate, stuck at 19% in October, fell to under 16% in early December.

Whether it was this evidence of hope or, instead, faith in President Reagan, Americans seemed to understand and accept. They had heard him say over and over that it took years to produce the problems and it would take years to correct them. The stakes were enormous, they knew, because the president also had repeated another message again and again. Unless action were taken, said the president to Congress in February, "Inflation and the growing tax burden will put an end to everything we believe in and to our dreams for the future."

JOHN CUNNIFF, *The Associated Press*

UNITED STATES—SPECIAL REPORT:

Supply-Side Economics

The inauguration of Ronald Reagan brought to Washington a new theory of how to manage the U.S. economy. It is called "supply-side economics," a vague but descriptive term that suggests its major point of departure from the theory that had formed the basis of economic policy since the end of World War II. Keynesian economics, named after the British economist John Maynard Keynes (1883–1946), emphasizes the role of government in maintaining the proper level of aggregate demand. The new supply-side doctrine traces its roots to Jean Baptiste Say (1767–1832), the French economist whose famous law of markets held that demand is essentially self-regulating. It asserted that the proper role of government is to stimulate aggregate supply.

The debate between the two schools contains some obvious ideological overtones. Insisting that a large federal establishment and active intervention by government are necessary to the health of the private economy, Keynesianism had long been associated with liberal politics. Arguing not only that the private economy could take care of itself but that its growth was limited by the activities of government, supply-siders found a constituency among the conservatives who dominate the Republican Party.

In some important respects, however, supply-side theory represents a startling reversal of the traditional Republican position on economic policy. In the past, Republicans had tended to regard rapid economic expansion as almost automatically leading to inflation. But at a time when Democrats themselves had begun to share this belief, supply-siders taught that growth and price stability are perfectly compatible. Rep. Jack Kemp (R-NY), architect of the massive tax cut that became the centerpiece of President Reagan's economic policy, stated that "we must grow our way out of inflation."

The idea of cutting taxes in an era of inflation is, of course, sheer heresy to Keynesian economists. In their view, the 30% across-the-board tax cut that the Republicans favored would contribute to inflation by stimulating aggregate demand. But supporters of the tax cut countered that the most important effect would be to stimulate aggregate supply. The most politically popular form of this argument was the so-called "Laffer curve," invented by University of Southern California economist Arthur B. Laffer, a sometime Reagan adviser. This is essentially an updating of the traditional concept of the prohibitive tariff—the idea that if an impost is high enough to discourage trade it will reduce revenues rather than raise them. According to Laffer, the interaction between inflation and a progressive tax system had pushed rates so high over those of the previous decade that they had become a significant economic disincentive. Cutting them would encourage people to work longer and harder, and the resulting increase in economic activity would generate enough revenues for the tax cut eventually to pay for itself.

For those not convinced that the supply of labor would be so responsive to an increase in after-tax income, there was a second line of argument that involved the supply of capital. A cut in taxes would also increase the rate of return on investment, the supply-siders said, and thus induce people to save more. For one thing, this would mean that the Keynesian presumption of a large increase in consumer demand would not be realized. For another, it would mean that any increase in the federal deficit could be easily financed through the additional savings. And since the Federal Reserve System would not have to "monetarize" this debt, the tax would not be inflationary even if it did not pay for itself.

In this emphasis on the monetary aspects of inflation, supply-siders were allied with the monetarists, who believe that government exercises its major influence over the economy through the Federal Reserve's control over the money supply. Indeed, the economic program that evolved in the early days of the Reagan Administration was really the result of a coalition between supply-siders and monetarists.

But although they did not push for their monetary policy very hard while fighting for their tax cut, supply-siders differ significantly from their monetarist colleagues on how such policy should be conducted. They are skeptical as to whether inflation can be halted simply by the gradual reduction in the growth of the money supply. Their recommended solution is a return to the gold standard.

This recommendation is not based on any particular belief in the sanctity of gold but on the view that expectations play a decisive role in determining inflation. According to this view, the public has become so doubtful of the government's ability to avoid monetary excesses that the only practical anti-inflationary policy is to remove most discretion from monetary policy.

The tax bill passed by Congress during the summer of 1981 was close enough to the original Kemp-Roth tax proposal to make the subsequent period a test of supply-side fiscal policy. The future of that theory is probably going to be determined by the performance of the economy until the 1984 election. In many respects, the results depend on whether the public is convinced about the validity of the theory itself.

LEWIS BEMAN

FOREIGN AFFAIRS

During 1981, the United States dealt with new crises in Central America and Lebanon and with such continuing problems as instability in the Persian Gulf, the Arab-Israeli conflict, and foreign intervention in Asia and Africa. The Reagan administration launched a number of major policy shifts respecting foreign aid, human rights, international terrorism, and relations with Communist countries. Most Reagan changes were concerned primarily with emphasis and priorities.

Return of Hostages. Negotiations for the release of the 52 Americans held hostage by Iran were finally consummated at the end of the Carter administration. The United States unfroze $8,000,000,000 of impounded Iranian assets, and agreement was reached for arbitration of financial claims against Iran by an international commission.

The hostages boarded an airliner in Iran, minutes after Ronald Reagan was inaugurated as president. They were welcomed to a U.S. airbase in Wiesbaden, West Germany by former President Jimmy Carter, and returned to the United States on January 25 to be received in Washington by President Reagan. In February the new administration signed an executive order implementing the hostage agreements with Iran, but it decided not to supply $500 million of military equipment ordered but not shipped before the taking of the hostages.

General Policy. From the beginning, President Reagan sounded a strong position on several issues. For example, he accused the Soviets of reserving to themselves "the right to commit any crime, to lie, to cheat" in furthering their cause. Such expressions as renewing "American self-respect, pride, and confidence," superseding "excessive American introspection" by establishing a "national consensus" and reviving "the American spirit," reversing the U.S. reputation of "strategic passivity," restoring American leadership through "a steady accumulation" of prudent action, "negotiating from strength," promoting "peaceful change" rather than the status quo, and "quiet diplomacy" characterized the administration's foreign relations attitudes. The U.S. general objective, according to Secretary of State Alexander Haig, "remains simple and compelling: a world hospitable to our society and our ideals." The issue, he maintained, "is not whether we should defend our interests abroad but how vigorously to do so."

Substantively, the Reagan administration defined "four fundamental pillars" of American diplomacy: restraining the Soviet Union, including its terrorism and war by proxy; strengthening U.S. allies and friends; playing a more constructive role in dealing with the aspirations of developing countries; and revitalizing the U.S. econ-

AWACS planes played a major role in the foreign policy of the new Reagan administration.

UPI

omy and defense. The administration also expressed its desire to energize the American capacity to influence events in the pursuit of its interests, and to convince other nations that the United States acts in a manner befitting its responsibilities "as a trustee of freedom and peace."

Both the president and secretary of state spoke frequently of the linkage of such issues as Soviet adventurism abroad, East-West trade, American national security, and nuclear arms control rather than their dissociation and separate policy treatment. In response to media pressure for an overall policy statement, President Reagan rejected the notion that the absence of such a statement denotes the lack of policy. The president observed that he preferred to enunciate policy piecemeal by a combination of foreign relations actions and pronouncements.

Administration of Foreign Relations. To minimize conflict within his senior foreign relations team, the president made it clear that the secretary of state is his primary adviser and spokesman on foreign affairs. Secretary Haig defined this role as "vicar" for the framing and articulation of policy. To Haig's apparent annoyance, the president named Vice-President George Bush to head his national security crisis-management committee.

In addition to traveling to Mexico as president-elect January 5, President Reagan ventured abroad three times—to Canada on a state visit (March) and to attend the economic conference of major industrial powers (July), and to Cancún (Mexico) to attend the North-South economic conference (October). In October three former presidents—Richard Nixon, Gerald Ford, and Jimmy Carter—joined the U.S. delegation to attend the funeral of Egypt's President Anwar el-Sadat. When Soviet President Leonid Brezhnev suggested a summit meeting, the president regarded it as a ploy to put the United States on the defensive and he declared such a meeting to be premature.

Two new states—Belize (British Honduras) and Antigua and Barbuda—came into existence, increasing the community of nations to nearly 170. The United States maintained more than 150 diplomatic and 100 consular missions, and 141 foreign governments stationed embassies in Washington. Because of Libya's support of international terrorism, the United States ordered the North African nation to close its embassy in Washington and recall its staff.

Some 7,155 international treaties and agreements were in effect for the United States on Jan. 1, 1981, and during the year it became a party to an additional 10 treaties and 90 agreements. In

President Reagan welcomes West German Chancellor Schmidt to the White House.

UPI

Roch/Gamma-Liaison

Presidents Reagan and Mitterrand of France mark the 200th anniversary of the battle of Yorktown.

1981 the United States participated in approximately 900 international conferences and meetings, including UN conferences on aid to refugees (Geneva), assistance to the least developed countries (Paris), energy resources (Nairobi, Kenya), removing Vietnamese forces from Cambodia (New York), the law of the sea (10th session, New York and Geneva), and U.S.-USSR nuclear weapons talks (Geneva).

Foreign Aid and Development. The Reagan administration indicated that U.S. economic policy would be designed to advance American trade and security, to promote an open international economic system, to provide traditional assistance to the needy, and to support institutions and agreements devoted to global stability. Security assistance was given greater priority in regions of strategic importance, development aid was geared to benefit the U.S. economy, and humanitarian aid was monitored more carefully.

Secretary Haig stressed two basic guidelines: to show that the United States is receptive to problems attending development and that friends of the United States really benefit from such friendship. Tactically, under the linkage principle, the administration interrelated economic, political, and security policies.

Three policy shifts were made. A series of steps were taken to augment security assistance, such as providing aid to build Pakistan's defenses, to buttress Sudan against threats from Libya, and to provide for the sale of sophisticated weaponry—including AWACS (airborne warning and control system planes)—to Saudi Arabia. Second, in July Secretary Haig met at Nassau, the Bahamas, with the foreign ministers of Canada, Mexico, and Venezuela to plan a coordinated economic program for Caribbean and Central American countries—including direct investment, trade, and aid. Third, to deal with world hunger and poverty, the United States espoused the reduction of government restrictions and the promotion of free enterprise. At the Cancún conference, President Reagan urged governments to put their own economic houses in order; to make more development resources, trade, and private investment available to the poorer countries; and to encourage developing nations to rely more on their own food production.

Human Rights. While reaffirming the sanctity of human rights abroad, President Reagan criticized past selectivity of application, which penalized U.S. friends while the United States negotiated with some of the most blatant violators. The president and Secretary Haig also stressed the distinction between foreign "authoritarian" and "dictatorial" regimes, and reoriented American policy more against the violations of human rights by U.S. adversaries. The multipartite human rights treaties, submitted for approval by President Carter, continued to languish in the Senate. (*See also* HUMAN RIGHTS.)

F. Lochon/Gamma-Liaison

Cmdr. Henry M. Kleemann (extreme right), commanding officer of the squadron that shot down two Libyan jets over the Mediterranean in August, joins his Navy comrades in recounting their experience at a press conference.

Terrorism. The government adopted a hard line against international terrorism. On welcoming the Iranian hostages home, the president warned that "when the rules of international behavior are violated, our policy will be one of swift and effective retribution." Secretary Haig branded terrorism "a hemorrhaging phenomenon," the greatest threat to human rights today. He declared that governments—like those of Cuba, Libya, and the Soviet Union—that provide "funding, training, and philosophic underpinnings" for the use of force as their code of international behavior are equally responsible for terrorism, and he intimated that the United States regarded certain leftist guerrillas as terrorists rather than as liberationists.

To cope with the problem, the United States intensified its intelligence gathering function, increased security precautions in many of its diplomatic missions, and augmented the training of an antiterrorist military cadre. In the UN Human Rights Commission, the United States demanded tough sanctions against states that provide terrorists with assistance, and in May the United States joined the NATO powers in a unified "Declaration on Terrorism."

Crises and Other Problems. When Americans were killed in El Salvador, the United States intervened to assist in combating leftist guerrillas who were supported by arms supplied by Cuba through Nicaragua. American assistance to El Salvador consisted of military and economic aid and a few noncombatant technicians, and the United States suspended its aid program for Nicaragua. (*See also* CENTRAL AMERICA.)

Fighting between Lebanese Christians and Syrians erupted in Lebanon in the spring. Israeli forces came to the aid of the Lebanese and the Syrians introduced Soviet antiaircraft missiles. Special emissary Philip Habib was sent to help mediate the crisis, and he played a major role in negotiating a cease-fire in July.

Israel attacked and destroyed Iraq's nuclear reactor in June. The U.S. joined in a unanimous UN Security Council resolution condemning Israel and, because U.S.-made aircraft had been used by Israel, the United States suspended temporarily the shipment of more aircraft to Israel.

The principals reaffirmed support of the Camp David accords for settling the Arab-Israeli conflict. However, aside from agreement on the manning of an international peacekeeping force for the Sinai after Israel's withdrawal is completed (scheduled for April 1982), little progress was made. The issues of Jerusalem's status and self-rule for Palestinian Arabs in the West Bank and the Gaza Strip continued to fester.

A number of other territorial issues were unresolved: independence of Namibia (South-West Africa); the Vietnamese occupation of Cambodia; and Soviet intervention in Afghanistan and the Soviet threat to Poland, which the United States continued to oppose.

Other continuing problems faced by the United States included maintaining an active presence in the Persian Gulf to assure its stability and the free flow of oil; strengthening the Western balance in Europe and inducing European allies to bolster their NATO forces; restraining the proliferation of nuclear and conventional weapons; negotiating a revised strategic arms limitation treaty and agreements to limit European theater nuclear weapons; and rectifying an unfavorable international trade imbalance and improving the status of the dollar.

ELMER PLISCHKE

Uruguay's Minister of External Affairs Estanislao Valdes Otero outlines his government's views on the world scene before the newly convened UN General Assembly.

UPI

URUGUAY

The inauguration of a new president, the establishment of the new Council of State, and continued negotiations to reestablish a constitutional regime highlighted Uruguayan affairs in 1981.

Politics. On Dec. 3, 1980, President Aparicio Méndez and the commanders of the three armed forces announced their acceptance of a popular plebiscite the previous week, in which the regime's proposal for a new constitution was defeated. For the next several months, however, the country's military rulers seemed undecided as to what steps to take next.

In July 1981, consultations were begun between the military Political Affairs Commission and leaders of most factions of the Colorado Party, a minority group of the rival Blanco Party and the small Union Civica. The regime refused, however, to hold discussions with the majority Blanco faction or the leftist Frente Amplio.

At the same time, the military announced a new schedule for the return to constitutional government: the installation of a new president and the Council of State by September 1; the writing of a new constitution by the Council of State and a referendum on that document and general elections in November 1984; and a new constitutional government in March 1985. Virtually all civilian political groups rejected the plan, particularly a provision that the military would be guaranteed veto power in any new constitution.

Meanwhile, in late May, the military regime faced a major scandal over loans made to gamblers by several leading officials. As a result, there were forced resignations of the minister of interior, the commander of the Armed Services School, the chief of the Montevideo police, the ambassador to Paraguay, and a half dozen powerful colonels.

In March, the government permitted the publication of the first mildly oppositional periodical since 1973, *Opinar*. Its editor, Enrique Etarigo, became one of the country's most popular political figures, the only new one to emerge since the establishment of the military dictatorship in 1973.

On August 20, the Council of State was established, with 35 full members and 35 alternates. The nation's political parties refused to name members. On September 1, retired Gen. Gregorio Alvarez was sworn in as president, to succeed Aparicio Méndez. In his inaugural speech, Alvarez denounced "Marxism, Leninism, and other forms of extremism" and promised gradual liberalization of the regime and restoration of the right to strike.

Economy. Economic conditions were difficult, deteriorating markedly during the first half of the year. In July, however, the Administracion Nacional de Telecommunicaciones received a $40 million loan from the World Bank to modernize telephone service. Also in July, the Ronald Reagan administration announced that it was reversing its predecessor's policy of opposing loans to Uruguay by international agencies.

Foreign Affairs. The most notable foreign development of 1981 was the kidnapping of Gabriel Biurrum, Uruguayan honorary consul, by Basque terrorists in Pamplona in February. Throughout the year there were denunciations of the Uruguayan regime by such international human rights watchdog groups as Amnesty In-

URUGUAY • Information Highlights

Official Name: Eastern Republic of Uruguay.
Location: Southeastern coast of South America.
Area: 68,536 sq mi (177 508 km^2).
Population (1981 est.): 2,900,000.
Chief City (1975 census): Montevideo, the capital, 1,229,-748.
Government: *Head of state,* Gregorio Alvarez, president (took office Sept. 1981). *Head of government,* Lt. Gen. Luis Vicente Quevedo, head of the military junta. *Legislature*—Council of state.
Monetary Unit: Peso (11.20 pesos equal U.S.$1, Oct. 1981).
Manufactures (major products): Processed meat, textiles, wools and hides, shoes, handbags and leather wearing apparel, cement, fish, refined petroleum.
Agriculture (major products): Livestock, grains.

ternational and the UN Human Rights Commission.

In June, the International Labor Organization recognized the Convencion Nacional de Trabajadores as the authentic representative of organized labor in Uruguay; the body had been outlawed since 1973.

ROBERT J. ALEXANDER
Rutgers University

UTAH

U.S. defense policy, reapportionment, a race-related murder case, and higher education concerns drew the attention of Utah citizens in 1981.

The MX Missile System. The proposed deployment of a major mobile missile system (MX) by the U.S. Air Force in Utah and Nevada was a major issue in Utah in 1981. In October, President Ronald Reagan announced that his administration was revising the plan of the Carter administration and that Utah and Nevada had been eliminated from plans for basing the system. This news was generally well received in Utah. Following President Reagan's announcement, it was suggested by many that his decision was based on political motives since senators Jake Garn (Utah) and Paul Laxalt (Nevada), both close friends of the president, were vigorously outspoken opponents of the proposed missile deployment. This was strongly denied by both senators. Senator Garn held the view that no president would make a major strategic decision on the basis of political friendship. According to Senator Garn, the decision was made primarily because the proposed Carter system could not survive a massive Soviet attack.

Reapportionment. Congressional and legislative redistricting developed into a major political issue during 1981. Representation in the U.S. House of Representatives will be increased from two to three seats for the state of Utah beginning with the 1982 congressional elections. Further, redistricting of state legislative seats (House and Senate) is involved. Gov. Scott Matheson, a Democrat, appointed a Utah Advisory Commission on Reapportionment to study alternatives.

UTAH • Information Highlights

Area: 84,899 sq mi (219 888 km^2).
Population (1980 census): 1,461,037.
Chief Cities (1980 census): Salt Lake City, the capital, 163,033; Provo, 73,907; Ogden, 64,407; Orem, 52,399; Sandy City, 51,022; Bountiful, 32,877; Logan, 26,844; West Jordan, 26,794; Murray, 25,750; Layton, 22,862.
Government (1981): *Chief Officers*—governor, Scott M. Matheson (D); lt. gov., David S. Monson (R). *Legislature*—Senate, 29 members; House of Representatives, 75 members.
State Finances (fiscal year 1980): *Revenues*, $1,889,000,000; *expenditures*, $1,755,000,000.
Personal Income (1980): $11,203,000,000; per capita, $7,649.
Labor Force (July 1981): *Nonagricultural wage and salary earners*, 548,800; *unemployed*, 35,400 (5.8% of total force).

The report of the commission was challenged by the State Legislative Reapportionment Committee. Charges abounded that redistricting was being manipulated for partisan gain. The governor called the Utah legislature into special session in October to act on the issue. The Republican-dominated legislature passed a federal redistricting bill favoring the GOP. The governor allowed the bill to become law.

Crime. A 31-year old Alabama native, Joseph Paul Franklin, was convicted on March 4 in the U.S. District Court in Utah of violating the civil rights of Ted Fields, 20, and Dave Martin, 18, two black men who were gunned down while they jogged with two white women near a local public park in Salt Lake City. Franklin was sentenced by a federal judge to two consecutive life sentences. Subsequently, he was found guilty of first degree homicide in the slayings and was handed two more consecutive life sentences. The convicted killer, an avowed white supremacist, was then moved to a federal prison medical facility where he will remain pending resolution of other race-related murder charges in Oklahoma and Indiana.

Education. The Utah System of Higher Education, reflecting major concerns about the status of higher education, will ask the 1982 legislature for $266.1 million to run the state's nine public colleges and universities. This represents a $39.5 million (17.5%) increase, along with an 8% tuition raise. Salary increases in the 15% range were recommended for faculty and staff. Governor Matheson recommended a 10.5% salary increase. Education officials, however, stressed that salary increases were essential to allow Utah schools to catch up with average salaries at comparable schools outside Utah.

LORENZO K. KIMBALL, *University of Utah*

VENEZUELA

Increased diplomatic activity in Latin America; continued problems with Colombia, Cuba, and Guyana; and a sluggish economy which was affected by declining oil prices were concerns for Venezuela in 1981.

Foreign Affairs. President Luis Herrera Campins and Colombia's President Julio Cesar Turbay issued a joint September statement condemning as "intervention" a joint declaration by Mexico and France recognizing the Farabundo Martí National Liberation Front (FMLN) and the Democratic Revolutionary Front (FDR) as a "representative political force" with which the government of El Salvador ought to negotiate a political settlement. Seven other Latin American countries quickly indicated their support for the Venezuelan-Colombian position. Herrera Campin's continued support of President José Napoleón Duarte, a fellow Christian Democrat who heads El Salvador's civilian-military junta, generated some tension between Herrera and Mexico's Jose López Portillo. In April, the two presi-

Venezuela's President Luis Herrera Campins discusses trade matters with Simone Veil (left), the president of the European Community Parliament, in his Caracas office. The woman in the center is a translator.

UPI

dents agreed to coordinate their foreign policies to prevent Central America and the Caribbean area from becoming a focus of East-West tensions. The two leaders also agreed to sell oil to Haiti and Belize at the same favorable terms applying to nine other small nations in the region.

In May, representatives of 122 developing countries of the Group of 77 (Third World countries) met in Caracas to establish an agenda for the talks between developed (North) and developing (South) nations that took place in October at Cancún, Mexico.

Relations worsened with Guyana after President Forbes Burnham recalled Guyana's ambassador to Caracas following abortive talks between Burnham and Herrera Campins. Venezuela claims that the current boundary between the two nations, established by an 1899 International Tribunal, is flawed by a secret deal between Great Britain and the USSR at that time. Instead, Venezuela claims the equivalent of more than two thirds of Guyana's territory west of the Essequibo River.

Colombia hoped talks with Venezuela over disputed maritime boundaries would be resumed after Presidents Turbay Ayala and Herrera Campins met at the October 2 funeral of former Venezuelan President Romulo Betancourt.

President Herrera Campins made a state visit to the United States in mid-November. In Washington, he met with President Ronald Reagan, Secretary of State Alexander Haig, and Congressional leaders. The Venezuelan leader warned the United States that "it is urgent to stretch out our hands to the beleaguered democratic forces in Nicaragua." A Reagan administration plan to sell Venezuela 24 F-16 fighter planes was awaiting U.S. Congressional approval. The planes were sought as part of an overall defense buildup by Venezuela.

Oil Glut Affects Economy. Two consequences of the continued surplus of oil in the world market were 10% cuts in production in June by Venezuela's state-owned oil company and reduced government investments and spending in a revised Sixth National Development Plan announced August 29. Several projects, including a steel mill in Zulia state, were postponed or scaled down because the congress was not likely to approve much of the $13,200,000,000 in foreign borrowing envisaged by the plan. Venezuela also began calculating the impact on its foreign exchange earnings and government income of the unified price of $34 a barrel accepted by the Organization of Petroleum Exporting Countries (OPEC) on October 29 in a meeting in Geneva.

Efforts of the finance and state planning ministries to stimulate the economy were opposed by the Central Bank, which sought to reduce inflation to 15% in 1981 from a high of 23% in 1980 by holding interest rates 5–6% below international levels. Some members of the president's ruling Social Christian (COPEI) party feared that the loss of potential domestic investment capital to foreign banks paying higher interest rates would kill any chances of COPEI's being reelected in 1984 presidential elections.

In March, Venezuela awarded its first major contract to build a pilot plant to refine heavy viscous oil from the Orinoco Heavy Oil Belt. It is hoped that the project will help meet increased domestic demands estimated at more than one million barrels per day by the year 2000.

NEALE J. PEARSON, *Texas Tech University*

VENEZUELA • Information Highlights

Official Name: Republic of Venezuela.
Location: Northern coast of South America.
Area: 352,143 sq mi (912 050 km^2).
Population (1981 est.): 15,500,000.
Chief Cities (1976 est.): Caracas, the capital, 2,576,000; Maracaibo, 792,000; Valencia, 439,000.
Government: *Head of state and government,* Luis Herrera Campins, president (took office March 1979). *Legislature*—Congress: Senate and Chamber of Deputies.
Monetary Unit: Bolivar (4.294 bolivares equal U.S.$1, Dec. 7, 1981).
Manufactures (major products): Refined petroleum products, iron and steel, paper products, textiles, transport equipment, consumer goods.
Agriculture (major products): Coffee, bananas, sugar, rice, corn, livestock, dairy products.

VERMONT

The 1981 regular session of the Vermont legislature, under Republican leadership in both houses, was the longest since 1965. Deterred by uncertainty over the future of federal aid programs, the lawmakers put off action on most major issues, including revision of the formula for state aid to education. Gov. Richard Snelling (R) sought to reverse an impending deficit in the state highway fund (due to lowered gasoline consumption) by imposing an ad valorem tax, but the legislature permitted only a two-cent-per-gallon increase. A carry-over deficit in the general fund was paid off with funds from the 1979 surplus that had been held as a reserve for the state's program of property tax rebates to homeowners.

Minor bills acted on during the session included one to enforce the closing of large stores on Sunday, and another permitting banks to charge an annual credit card fee. Public opprobrium was directed toward a few legislators who accepted salary and expense money for time during the legislative session when they were on vacation out-of-state.

In July, a public petition campaign prompted Governor Snelling to call the legislature back into session in consequence of a brutal murder involving a juvenile defendant who would automatically go free at age 16. The legislature promptly passed an already-pending bill to allow youths as young as age 10 to be tried as adults and to extend state jurisdiction over juvenile delinquents from 16 to 21. However, Vermont's overall crime rate remained relatively low, and the state registered the lowest per capital jail population in the country.

Governor Snelling, a leading advocate of the "New Federalism," took office as chairman of the National Governors' Association in August. The same month, he called a state convocation in Montpelier to examine the federal system. In September, Vermont became the first state to apply for amalgamated federal funds under the block grant program. Meanwhile, Vermont's lone Congressman, James Jeffords, distinguished himself as the sole Republican to vote against the Reagan budget proposal.

VERMONT • Information Highlights

Area: 9,614 sq mi (24 900 km^2).
Population (1980 census): 511,456.
Chief Cities (1980 census): Montpelier, the capital, 8,241; Burlington, 37,712; Rutland, 18,436; Bennington, 15,815; Essex, 14,392; Brattleboro, 11,886; South Burlington, 10,679; Springfield, 10,190.
Government (1981): *Chief Officers*—governor, Richard A. Snelling (R); lt. gov., Madeleine M. Kunin (D). *General Assembly*—Senate, 30 members; House of Representatives, 150 members.
State Finances (fiscal year 1980): *Revenues*, $711,000,000; *expenditures*, $676,000,000.
Personal Income (1980): $4,013,000,000; per capita, $7,827.
Labor Force (July 1981): *Nonagricultural wage and salary earners*, 201,400; *unemployed*, 13,800 (5.4% of total force).

The year's most notable political upset was the narrow victory of self-proclaimed socialist Bernard Sanders as mayor of Burlington over a five-term Democratic incumbent. Sanders' administration began in April with a dispute with the board of aldermen over the mayor's appointment power and remained embroiled in controversy throughout the year.

Governor Snelling broke with tradition by appointing an assistant attorney general, instead of a Superior Court judge, to the Vermont Supreme Court. Snelling encouraged practicing attorneys as well as trial judges to apply for future Supreme Court nominations.

The issue of medical care costs was brought to a head in a test of Vermont's Certificate of Need Law, when the Medical Center Hospital in Montpelier, the state's largest medical complex, proposed a $60 million plant expansion. A slightly scaled-down version was approved.

SAMUEL B. HAND and ROBERT V. DANIELS
University of Vermont

VIETNAM

During 1981, the Vietnamese government groped for answers to the political and economic problems that have plagued the country since Hanoi's military victory over South Vietnam in 1975. Living standards were among the lowest in the world, due to a combination of bad management and unusual natural disasters. Because of its occupation of Cambodia, Vietnam found itself isolated from most potential foreign aid donors and trading partners outside the Soviet bloc. Hanoi's leaders seemed to be cornered. They were unwilling or unable to formulate a policy toward Cambodia that would end Vietnam's isolation. Yet the Vietnamese also seemed unable to get their economy on the tracks with Soviet aid.

Politics. Many of the top leaders of the Socialist Republic of Vietnam have held office for 30 years or more. Although several men in their fifties or early sixties were raised to key posts in 1980, the three top leaders, who are in their seventies, remained in office. The three were Le Duan, secretary-general of the Communist Party of Vietnam; Truong Chinh, who was named in 1981 chairman of the State Council, a committee that serves as a collective presidency; and Pham Van Dong, the premier. Dong agreed to remain in office after a long series of political conferences in early 1981 apparently failed to produce agreement on a successor. Dong is known to want to retire because of his age (75). A leading candidate to succeed him is To Huu (61). He was named first vice-chairman of the Council of Ministers in June. This meant that he would act for Pham Van Dong in the latter's absence.

Economics. The longevity in office of Vietnam's leaders may reflect a kind of political stability, but it also seems to represent a major obstacle to improving the economic management

Le Duan (left), the secretary-general of Vietnam's Communist Party, sought Soviet economic aid during talks with President Leonid Brezhnev in Moscow in March.

UPI

of the country. A 1980 World Bank report noted that Vietnam is one of the few countries in the world that has not made any major economic gains since the 1940s. The same report ranked Vietnam between India and Bangladesh in terms of living standards of the average person. By Asian standards, Vietnam is a very poor country. Even Cambodia, which has suffered a decade of war and destruction, has more goods, both necessities and luxuries, for sale in the market place. In Ho Chi Minh City (Saigon), the black market was flourishing more than in the northern capital city of Hanoi, but the authorities were allowing more free market exchange in the north in an effort to raise production. Though the authorities have tried to integrate the economies of the north and south since 1975, important differences and problems remain. The south produces a surplus of food, but transportation facilities are so poor that little of it reaches the food-deficient north. More of a free market has been allowed in Cambodia and Laos, in an effort to prevent hostility to Vietnamese rule.

Vietnam's economic recovery from the war has been badly disrupted by economic mismanagement, unusually bad weather conditions, and the withdrawal of almost all Western aid programs since the Vietnamese occupation of Cambodia in 1979. Foreign exchange reserves are almost nil, and Soviet bloc aid has not been adequate to finance the recovery of Vietnam's industry or transportation system. Soviet military aid is believed to run at a rate of $2 million per day. Though no exact figure is available, the amount of economic aid is much less. It is reliably estimated that at least half of the Vietnamese people, including many children, are undernourished. Vietnam is caught in a vicious circle in which its reliance on Soviet aid solves few problems but makes it pursue policies that antagonize the Western nations. This causes the West to refuse to help Vietnam, which only makes the Southeast Asian nation more reliant on Soviet aid.

Foreign Relations. In 1981, there were few changes in Vietnam's foreign relations. Relations with the Soviet Union, Hanoi's principal aid donor, were difficult because Moscow was providing far less than Vietnam needs to rebuild the economy and demanding far more in the way of military bases and other concessions than Vietnam would like to grant. The Vietnamese leaders tried to make the best of a bad situation by heaping public praise on the Soviet Union and its foreign policy. But the 6,000 or more Soviet technicians in Vietnam were unpopular, in part because they would seldom buy anything, and there were reports of attacks on the Soviets by Vietnamese mobs. Vietnam failed to gain any new international support for its occupation of Cambodia during the year, but it tried to exploit policy differences among other nations.

In December, four U.S. veterans of the Indochina War visited Vietnam to assess the impact of the herbicide Agent Orange and to investigate American soldiers still missing in Vietnam. During the visit, Vietnamese officials indicated that they were ready to open contacts with the United States.

PETER A. POOLE, *Old Dominion University*

VIETNAM • Information Highlights

Official Name: Socialist Republic of Vietnam.
Location: Southeast Asia.
Area: 127,246 sq mi (329 567 km^2).
Population (1981 est.): 54,900,000.
Chief Cities (1979 census): Hanoi, the capital, 2,570,905; Ho Chi Minh City, 3,419,067; Haiphong, 1,279,067.
Government: See text.
Monetary Unit: Dong (2.41 dongs equal U.S.$1, 1980).
Manufactures (major products): Phosphate fertilizer, cement, electric energy, processed foods.
Agriculture (major products): Rice, sugarcane, tea, sweet potatoes, cassava, rubber, corn, fruits.

VIRGINIA

Making a dramatic comeback, Virginia's Democratic Party saw the election of its candidates for governor, lieutenant-governor, and attorney general. Thus Charles (Chuck) Robb, the state's lieutenant-governor and son-in-law of former President Lyndon Johnson, became the first victorious Democratic gubernatorial nominee since 1965.

Attorney General Marshall Coleman, the Republican nominee, attempted to make the contest a referendum on President Ronald Reagan's national policies, but actually Coleman and Robb conducted basically similar campaigns attuned to the conservative climate of the state. The attorney general emphasized his full support of Reagan's national program and promised to extend it to Virginia by vetoing any state tax increase. Robb branded Coleman's tax stand as irresponsible, but cautiously endorsed Reagan's tax and budget cuts. Both candidates pledged a tougher attitude toward crime. Both opposed tampering with Virginia's right-to-work law.

By supporting postcard voter registration, minority hiring quotas, and the constitutional amendment giving the District of Columbia full voting representation in Congress, Robb attracted support from most Virginia blacks, but he also adroitly appealed to prominent conservatives identified with the old Byrd Democratic machine, a group that considered Coleman more liberal than Robb. In the election tally, Robb surpassed Coleman 53.5% to 46.4%. In elections for the House of Delegates, however, the Republicans picked up eight seats, reducing their previous three-to-one disadvantage. The new alignment is 66 Democrats, 33 Republicans, and one independent. The state Senate was not up for election.

Lt. Gov. Chuck Robb, 42, is the first Democrat to be elected governor of Virginia in 16 years.

UPI

Sen. Harry F. Byrd announced that he would not seek reelection in 1982

Redistricting. In legislative matters, the dominant issue was that of redistricting. From start to finish, the Democratic-led Assembly blundered badly, at one point triumphantly passing a plan discovered a day later to contain one seat too many for the House of Delegates. The final measure was designed to protect incumbents and ignored the maximum population variances previously permitted by the federal judiciary. Incredibly, when multiple court suits against the plan surfaced, the Assembly leadership tried to meet complaints from some localities by amending the plan via phone polling of legislators, a ploy rejected by the courts.

When the federal government, acting under the Voting Rights Act, rejected portions of the plan as racially discriminatory, a special session of the Assembly made the necessary adjustments, but this did not prevent a federal court from later overturning the House of Delegates apportionment on grounds of population disparity. Because of the electoral timetable, the court permitted the November House elections to be held on the basis of the faulted redistricting, but stipulated that winners serve only a one-year term and that a satisfactory plan be produced by February 1982.

Legislation. The Assembly passed a measure making medicaid funds available for abortions on grounds of incest, rape, or anticipated deformities. It also authorized creation of a state holiday in honor of Martin Luther King, Jr. Gov. John Dalton vetoed both bills. He rejected the King measure noting that even native Thomas Jefferson is not honored by a state holiday.

The Assembly rejected all proposals to alter the state tax system, including efforts to reduce the sales tax, to index the income tax to inflation, and to raise the personal income tax exemption from $600 to $1,000. By a surprisingly narrow margin, the House also rejected a radical proposal to tax all state incomes at a flat 4% and to establish a uniform $4,500 deduction for all state

VIRGINIA • Information Highlights

Area: 40,767 sq mi (105 587 km^2).
Population (1980 census): 5,346,279.
Chief Cities (1980 census): Richmond, the capital, 219,214; Norfolk, 266,979; Virginia Beach, 262,199; Newport News, 144,903; Hampton, 122,617; Chesapeake, 114,226; Portsmouth, 104,577; Alexandria, 103,217; Roanoke, 100,427; Lynchburg, 66,743.
Government (1981): *Chief Officers*—governor, John N. Dalton (R); lt. gov., Charles S. Robb (D). *General Assembly*—Senate, 40 members; House of Delegates, 100 members.
State Finances (fiscal year 1980): *Revenues*, $5,656,000,000; *expenditures*, $5,393,000,000.
Personal Income (1980): $50,333,000,000; per capita, $9,392.
Labor Force (July 1981): *Nonagricultural wage and salary earners*, 2,145,000; *unemployed*, 151,700 (5.9% of total force).

taxpayers, with no specific deductions permitted. The Assembly gave initial approval to a proposed constitutional amendment requiring a balanced budget.

A bill raising the minimum age from 18 to 19 for takeout beer purchases was passed. (The age had only recently been lowered to 18.) The legislature again refused to ratify the Equal Rights Amendment and enacted a bill permitting the death penalty for multiple murders. A proposal permitting the governor to succeed himself and bills establishing statewide initiative procedures and permitting localities to elect school boards were rejected.

WILLIAM LARSEN

VIRGIN ISLANDS

Economic matters dominated the affairs of the Virgin Islands during 1981.

Faced with the cutbacks in federal taxes announced by the Ronald Reagan administration, the territorial government sought to decrease its spending and intensify its search for other sources of income. One of the sources was a new agreement with the Hess Oil Refinery on the island of St. Croix. The corporation's agreement with the government of the Virgin Islands expired on Sept. 1, 1981, after being in operation for 16 years. The company was anxious to renew the agreement, which gave it substantial tax benefits, for another 16 years. The government, on its part, was anxious to increase the benefits for the people of the Virgin Islands in exchange for allowing one of the largest oil refineries in the world to operate on the small island of St. Croix. The agreement that was eventually worked out between Gov. Juan Luis and Leon Hess, the chief executive officer of the refinery, was approved almost unanimously by the legislature. It increased by about $20 million the income of the government but allowed the corporation to continue to enjoy substantially reduced tax rates. Other elements of the agreement included a guarantee that no aliens would be hired for work that Virgin Islanders could undertake; a guarantee that fuel prices for the Virgin Islands would be maintained at the level of costs; and a substantial monetary fine if the refinery were to cease operations.

Governor Luis submitted to the legislature a budget of $220 million, which included $12 million in subsidies requested from the U.S. government to avoid an illegal deficit. The legislature scaled down the proposal slightly, approving before the October 1 deadline a $215 million budget. In either case, the prospects for a subsidy from the Reagan administration were considered minimal. The islanders faced a bleak future, with cutbacks in federal programs driving up the unemployment rate, an inflation rate estimated to be 28% over the admittedly high level of Washington, DC, and the prospect of severe restrictions on an already reduced insular budget.

Increased activity in the private sector of the economy was doubtful, as the Virgin Islands anticipated that the Reagan administration's efforts to improve the economic plight of Jamaica would increase competition for the tourist dollar in the Caribbean. (*See* special report, page 154.) Specifically, professional conventions held in Jamaica were to be tax deductible, a privilege previously enjoyed in the Caribbean only by Puerto Rico and the Virgin Islands.

Early in 1981, the U.S. Congress approved a proposed constitution for the Virgin Islands, clearing the way for a popular referendum. But in the November 3 vote, the proposed constitution was defeated by a 3-to-2 margin.

THOMAS MATHEWS, *University of Puerto Rico*

WASHINGTON

On June 21, 1981, 11 mountain climbers were swept into a crevasse and to their deaths by an icefall on Mount Rainier. It was the worst mountain climbing accident in American history. The 11 climbers, from a party of 23 amateur climbers and 6 guides, were at about 11,000-ft (3 352-m) level on their way to the summit of the 14,408-ft (4 392-m) peak. The climbing party had paused at 5:30 A.M. while guides went forward to scout a safe route past Disappointment Cleaver when the icefall struck.

The tragic climbing accident did not daunt the members of Project Pelion. On July 3 nine handicapped mountain climbers reached the summit of Rainier; two other climbers, both blind and one a diabetic, had dropped out short of the summit. Project Pelion, a major event of the International Year of the Disabled, drew its name from a mountain in Greek mythology which the gods used as a stepping stone. The climbers who reached the summit included five who are blind, two who are deaf and mute, an amputee, and an epileptic.

Legislature. The 1981 legislature, under Republican control, honored pledges not to increase taxes, but by midyear this action, coupled with a steadily declining economy, caused state revenues to drop precipitously. On September 17 Gov. John Spellman ordered all state agencies

WASHINGTON • Information Highlights

Area: 68,139 sq mi (176 480 km^2).
Population (1980 census): 4,130,163.
Chief Cities (1980 census): Olympia, the capital, 27,447; Seattle, 493,846; Spokane, 171,300; Tacoma, 158,501; Bellevue, 73,903; Everett, 54,413; Yakima, 49,826; Bellingham, 45,794; Vancouver, 42,834; Bremerton, 36,208.
Government (1981): *Chief Officers*—governor, John Spellman (R); lt. gov., John A. Cherberg (D). *Legislature*—Senate, 49 members; House of Representatives, 98 members.
State Finances (fiscal year 1980): *Revenues*, $6,324,000,000; *expenditures*, $5,715,000,000.
Personal Income (1980): $42,677,000,000; per capita, $10,309.
Labor Force (July 1981) *Nonagricultural wage and salary earners*, 1,582,000; *unemployed*, 175,200 (9.1% of total force).

and departments to reduce their biennial budgets by 10.1% and to prepare for a 20% reduction. Three days later, as the dimensions of the state's fiscal problems became clearer, the governor announced that he would call a special session of the legislature in November to consider temporary and new taxes.

On February 13, during the legislative session, in which Democrats were working with a one-seat majority, state Sen. Peter von Reichbauer, who had served in the Senate as a Democrat for eight years, announced that he was becoming a Republican. This gave control of the Senate to Republicans and prompted a petition for Von Reichbauer's recall. Petitioners were sufficient to place the recall issue on the ballot of the primary election, where the senator survived the effort with about 55% of the ballots cast against recall. The event attracted national attention because the outcome could affect a congressional redistricting measure, expected to be acted upon by the legislature in 1982.

Other. On September 26 the Boeing Co. test flew the 767, the first all-new airplane to be developed by the company since the 747 was test flown in the 1960s. The 767, a medium-range twinjet plane, is designed to carry slightly more than 200 passengers. At flight time, Boeing had orders and options from 17 airlines for 311 of the new planes. First deliveries of the new plane will be in August 1982, about six months after the company's second new-generation plane, the smaller 757 twinjet, is scheduled for test flights.

Five nuclear energy plants, being constructed by the Washington Public Power Supply System (WPPSS) for a consortium of 88 utility districts and power companies, came under heavy attack for cost overruns. The five plants, three at Hanford near Richland and two at Satsop, were projected to cost about $24,000,000,000. Late in the year, a panel, appointed by the governors of Washington and Oregon, recommended deferring construction on one plant at each site.

WARREN W. ETCHESON
University of Washington

The August closing of "The Washington Star" left the U.S. capital with only one daily newspaper.

UPI

WASHINGTON, DC

The U.S. capital city hosted the quadrennial presidential inaugural ceremonies as Ronald Reagan took the oath of office to become the 40th president on Jan. 20, 1981. The event was marked by a major parade, fireworks, ten inaugural balls, and the release of the 52 U.S. citizens held hostage in Iran, who visited Washington one week later.

President Reagan survived an assassination attempt as he left a trade union meeting at a local hotel on March 31. John W. Hinckley, Jr., was accused of firing the shots that also felled White House Press Secretary James S. Brady, secret service agent Timothy J. McCarthy, and district policeman Thomas K. Delahanty.

Personnel. Eugene G. Kinlow, former head of the Anacostia community school board and an employee of the U.S. Census Bureau, was elected president of the Washington, DC, school board. Floretta D. McKenzie, who served as acting superintendent of the public school system for three months in 1973 and was the deputy assistant secretary of education for three years, was selected as the new school superintendent. McKenzie is the first superintendent to have attended the district's public schools and the second woman to hold the position. Maurice T. Turner, a native Washingtonian, became the new police chief. Turner began his career in the district police force as a foot patrolman and for two years was the assistant chief in charge of field operations.

Media. *The Washington Star,* the city's oldest afternoon newspaper, ceased publication on August 7, making Washington the largest U.S. city with just one daily newspaper. Founded on Dec. 16, 1852, the *Star* fell victim to declining circulation and advertisers.

Constitutional Amendment. Oregon became the tenth state to ratify the proposed constitutional amendment giving the district full voting representation in Congress.

Statehood. Voters elected 45 delegates to a convention to write a state constitution as the district continued its drive toward statehood.

Population. The Census Bureau reported that the city's population declined by almost 17% during the 1970s, from 756,510 to 637,651; the racial composition remained stable at just more than 70% black.

Metro. The city's subway system extended farther into Maryland, Virginia, and the district itself as six new stations and 6.1 mi (9.8 km) were opened for service.

MORRIS J. LEVITT, *Howard University*

WEST VIRGINIA

The state's legislators wrestled with a record number of proposed bills during their regular 60-day session as well as in two special meetings in May. They voted the taxpayers the biggest single boost in state history, yet disposed of only a few of the nagging financial issues that beset them. The consumer sales tax was raised from 3 to 5 cents, although the tax disappeared from food. Other tax increases were attached to drivers' licenses, automobile registration, liquor purchases, and hunting and fishing permits.

Gov. John D. (Jay) Rockefeller IV tried throughout all sessions—and threatened a third special one—to get approval of larger appropriations for road improvements. He finally succeeded in getting a major bond issue placed on a November ballot, but the voters rejected it by almost a two-to-one margin. It was the first time in the 20th century that such a road issue was rejected in the state. The governor also failed to get approval of a proposed levy on oil extraction and sales.

Enacted legislation included adoption of required proof of liability insurance for all car owners, harsher penalties for drunken driving, the establishment of a public defender system, and an across-the-board pay raise for teachers. The legislature overrode Governor Rockefeller's veto of a bill permitting the sale of wine in grocery stores. But it failed to resolve the perennial squabble over branch banking and fell far short of passing the governor's proposals regarding special care for the elderly, the blind, and the disabled.

The Economy. The state's economy repeated its unstable pattern of recent years, showing major gains in the oil and gas industries, which, however, did not offset the continuing depression of the steel industry or the major blow of a 72-day strike in bituminous coal mining, West Virginia's chief producer. Although the employment picture turned brighter in September with the gain of a full percentage point, it still was about 1% below the national average. The coal strike was the chief culprit in a late-spring slump that led the governor to order a spending and hiring freeze for all state agencies. The effects of this action were still being felt six months later, particularly in the Department of Highways, where layoffs ran into the thousands. By mid-October, fewer than half of the state's major economic indicators were showing improvement. A serious long-range blow to the economy fell when plans were dropped for a proposed liquid fuels installation on the Monongahela River.

Nine years after the Buffalo Creek earthen dam disaster of 1972, the state was still trying to sort out damages and responsibilities. Representatives of both the Rockefeller and Arch A. Moore, Jr., administrations testified before investigating committees in October.

DONOVAN H. BOND, *West Virginia University*

WEST VIRGINIA • Information Highlights

Area: 24,231 sq mi (62 758 km²).
Population (1980 census): 1,949,644.
Chief Cities (1980 census): Charleston, the capital, 63,968; Huntington, 63,684; Wheeling, 43,070; Parkersburg, 39,967; Morgantown, 27,605; Weirton, 24,736; Fairmont, 23,863; Clarksburg, 22,371; Beckley, 20,492; Bluefield, 16,060.
Government (1981): *Chief Officers*—governor, John D. Rockefeller IV (D); secy. of state, A. James Manchin (D). *Legislature*—Senate, 34 members; House of Delegates, 100 members.
State Finances (fiscal year 1980): *Revenues,* $2,640,000,000; *expenditures,* $2,679,000,000.
Personal Income (1980): $15,243,000,000; per capita, $7,800.
Labor Force (July 1981): *Nonagricultural wage and salary earners,* 641,300; *unemployed,* 71,700 (9.3% of total force.)

WINE

Nearly a half-century after the repeal of Prohibition, Americans in increasing numbers are recognizing wine as the beverage of moderation. In 1970, per capita consumption of wine in the United States was not yet one gallon (3.8 L), compared with more than 20 gal (76 L) per person in many European countries. Today, the American figure is 2.4 gal (9.1 L) and continues to grow at such a steady rate that some estimates predict it will top 10 gal (38 L) by the year 2000.

In 1960, dessert wines enjoyed a 54% share of the U.S. market, while table wines were at 32%. Over the next 20 years, the table wine share rose rapidly, while dessert wines dropped off. By 1980, table wines had grabbed a 75.3% share, and dessert wines had fallen to 9.5%. During the same period, special natural, vermouth, and sparkling wines remained static, with only sparkling wines showing improvement between 1978 and 1981. Table wine growth continues at an annual rate of about 11% and sparkling wines 8%, while all other types are decreasing.

A family vineyard in Augusta, MO. U.S. wine production has increased dramatically in recent years.

UPI

Recent figures show that 36 of the 50 states grow wine, compared with 20 in 1969. Since the early 1960s, California has led the United States in wine growing, followed by New York, Ohio, and Pennsylvania. New areas, such as the Northwest, are now expanding their vineyard acreage. Oregon, Washington, and Idaho are producing varietal wines (named for the major grape) which compete with the best of California. In 1981, Eastern vintners experienced healthy growth, especially in New York State. Young Eastern winemakers, recognizing that today's American wine drinker does not like the earthy character of wines made from such native grapes as Concord and Catawba, are planting more vinifera and hybrid grapes.

Import wines in 1980 had a 21% share of the U.S. market, compared with 10% in 1970. Certain legal restrictions on vineyard yield and wine production in most European countries accounted for the relatively small increase. Few of the same controls apply in the United States, where open land for new vineyards far exceeds that found in Europe.

In 1970, France held a 35% share of the U.S. import wine market; Italy and Portugal tied for second with a 20% share. Six years later, Italy had passed France and by the middle of 1981 was the undisputed leader with 60%.

Of the top ten imported brands in the U.S. market, six are from Italy, led by Lambrusco. Germany's Blue Nun, once the leader, dropped to seventh place, while Portugal's two rosés, Mateus and Lancers, languished in eighth and tenth places, respectively, at the end of 1980.

The American wine taste in 1981 began to favor wines lower in alcohol content and calories. By June, four of California's biggest wineries (Sebastiani, Paul Masson, Beringer/Los Hermanos, and Taylor California Cellars), had released a "light" wine to a receptive public.

American wine drinkers were also looking more seriously at California Chardonnay and Cabernet Sauvignon as the equals of any comparable French wines. Comparative tastings usually resulted in the California wines taking most of the laurels.

During 1981, the English and, to a lesser degree, the French and Germans, drank more California wine. London has become a hot market for California wines, and even the French are sipping a few wines from the Golden State. Germany, a producer of sweet white wines, has shown interest in California dry red table wines.

Vintage 1981 for the vineyards of Europe and the United States was mostly a mixed bag of quality and quantity. Because of high summer heat in California, picking began as early as four weeks ahead of schedule in Napa and Sonoma counties, while Mendocino had a normal growing year. The central coast, Monterey, and San Joaquin Valley all harvested ahead of schedule. Quantity in all growing areas appeared to be down from 1980's crop, while quality was expected to be good, though not great.

Hard, early spring frosts in New York's Finger Lakes district damaged some of the new vinifera vines, though the native labrusca grapes fared better. Quantity was lower than in 1980.

An early harvest of good quality was completed in France, though with lower yields than 1980. The province of Champagne, still suffering from a series of bad crops, harvested a small wine crop in 1981, but of very high quality.

Germany picked a normal crop in 1981. Italy harvested a smaller crop than the previous year, though of good quality. The quantity in Spain's Rioja district was normal to high, with very good quality expected.

GERALD D. BOYD, *"The Wine Spectator"*

WISCONSIN

A long stalemate over state aid to municipalities and charges of police brutality in Milwaukee highlighted the year in Wisconsin.

Budget Battle. Reflecting the national concern over the cost of government programs and the threat of higher taxes, Wisconsin waged its own battle as it tried to write a new budget for the 1981–83 biennium. It was a fight over finances, but also a political struggle, with Republican Gov. Lee S. Dreyfus defying the Democratic-controlled legislature.

UPI

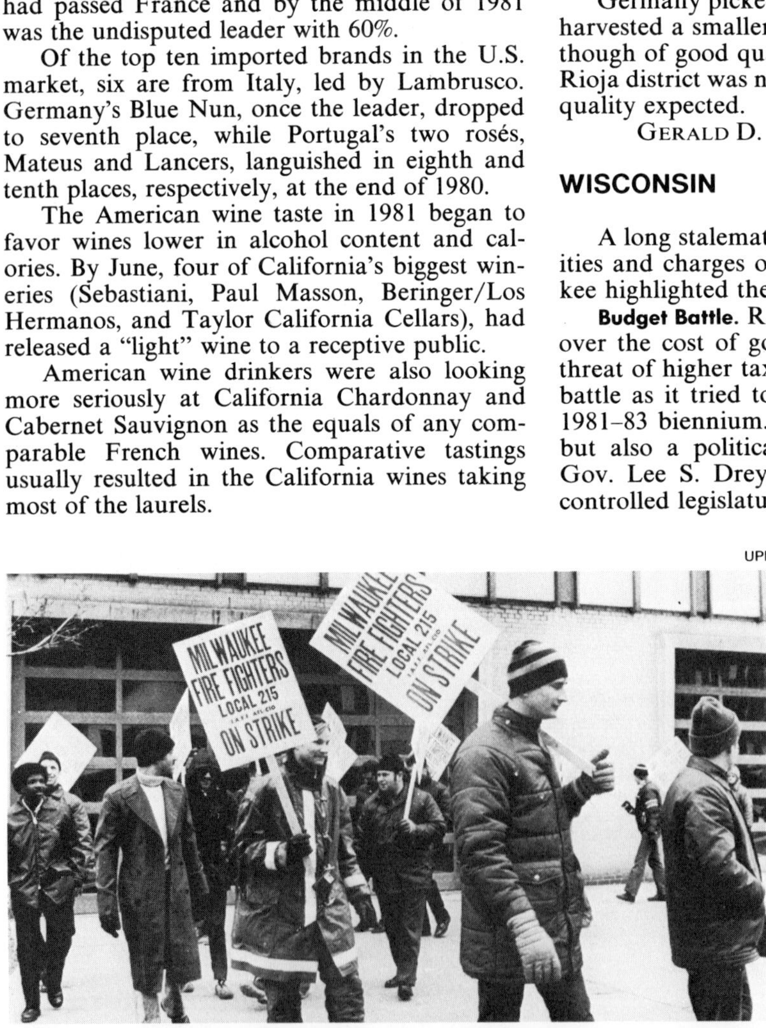

Firemen in Milwaukee, WI, went to the picket lines in early March following the breakdown of contract negotiations. National Guardsmen assisted supervisory personnel during the strike.

The main contest was over state financial aid to local units of government. Declining to use a partial veto, Dreyfus vetoed the entire appropriation of $695 million and instead offered a new budget bill calling for $620 million. The governor, who has sometimes been called a Republicrat, seemed to take a decided step to the right, refusing to raise taxes and telling local governments they had to restrain their spending. The Democrats and local mayors were furious and fought to have the money restored. The impasse went on for weeks until a state aid figure of $638 million was finally agreed upon.

State aid was not the only issue. The governor also cut some social service programs and scrapped about $117 million in building projects. Among them was practically all major new building for the University of Wisconsin and state agencies. He did, however, approve plans for a new medium-security prison near Oshkosh and the housing of prisoners in the State Office Building in downtown Milwaukee.

The only new tax increases involved gasoline, cigarettes, and liquor.

Police Case. A young black man who died while in the custody of white police officers became the focal point for charges of police brutality and led to tensions between blacks and the police in Milwaukee. Ernest Lacy, 23, had been arrested on July 9 as a suspect in a rape that had just been committed in downtown Milwaukee. The police said he resisted arrest and they were merely trying to restrain him. Minutes later, he was found dead in the police van, and shortly after that it was found that another man had committed the rape.

Blacks rallied to protest what they called police brutality and to call for the resignation of 70-year-old Police Chief Harold A. Breier, in office for life. After a four-week coroner's inquest, the jury called for charges of homicide by reckless conduct against the three arresting officers and of misconduct in public office against the three officers in the van. The action resulted in a swelling of white support for the officers as they awaited trial.

Schlitz Closing. The beer may have made Milwaukee famous, but sales slipped and there was a long strike, so it will not be brewed in Milwaukee anymore. The Joseph Schlitz Brewing Co. ended a tradition that began in 1849 when it said its beer would be brewed elsewhere. The brewery, which kept its headquarters in Milwaukee, also attempted to merge with the G. Heileman Brewing Co. of La Crosse, but the United States Justice Department blocked the move under antitrust laws.

Economy. Declining demand for durable goods resulted in substantial layoffs among manufacturing workers in Wisconsin in 1981. For some months, the unemployment rate was higher than the national average. Agricultural income remained high thanks to strong support prices for milk. Overall tourism volume held up well.

PAUL SALSINI, *"Milwaukee Journal"*

WISCONSIN • Information Highlights

Area: 56,153 sq mi (145 436 km²).
Population (1980 census): 4,705,335.
Chief Cities (1980 census): Madison, the capital, 170,616; Milwaukee, 636,212; Green Bay, 87,899; Racine, 85,725; Kenosha, 77,685; West Allis, 63,982; Appleton, 59,032; Eau Claire, 51,509; Wauwatosa, 51,308; Janesville, 51,071.
Government (1981): *Chief Officers*—governor, Lee S. Dreyfus (R); lt. gov., Russell A. Olson (R). *Legislature*—Senate, 33 members; Assembly, 99 members.
State Finances (fiscal year 1980): *Revenues*, $6,588,000,000; *expenditures*, $6,074,000,000.
Personal Income (1980): $44,095,000,000; per capita, $9,348.
Labor Force (July 1981): *Nonagricultural wage and salary earners*, 1,952,700; *unemployed*, 172,900 (7.0% of total force).

WOMEN

President Ronald Reagan made history July 7, 1981, when he announced the nomination of Sandra Day O'Connor, an Arizona appeals court judge, as the first woman Supreme Court justice. Mrs. O'Connor was sworn in September 25, four days after Senate confirmation. She replaced retiring Associate Justice Potter Stewart. At 51, she is the court's youngest member. The only real opposition to her appointment had come from anti-abortion groups and their supporters on Capitol Hill. O'Connor told the Senate Judiciary Committee that she found abortion personally offensive, but she refused to comment on the 1973 Supreme Court decision that legalized abortion.

Although O'Connor generally is regarded as a judicial conservative, her appointment was loudly cheered by women's rights advocates. They were not so happy with President Reagan's record in other areas, including his continued opposition to the Equal Rights Amendment (ERA).

Other Governmental Action. On August 12, Vice-President George Bush announced an administrative review of guidelines intended to protect women from sexual harassment on the job and from discrimination in college athletics.

Attorney General William French Smith said May 22 that the Justice Department had begun a reevaluation of affirmative action programs designed to prevent discrimination in the hiring and promotion of women and minorities. Women's groups charged that weakening of affirmative action requirements was unwarranted or, at best, premature. Affirmative action "is a necessary and effective means of changing ingrained patterns of discrimination which still plague our nation," said a report issued June 18 by Working Women, a national organization of office workers.

A June 8 ruling by the Supreme Court paved the way for new lawsuits by women facing pay discrimination. The court said women may file suit under the 1964 Civil Rights Act without

UPI

Actresses Esther Rolle (left) and Patty Duke Astin meet the press prior to an ERA rally in Springfield, IL, in June. To become part of the Constitution, the amendment must be ratified by 38 states by June 30, 1982. By 1981, 35 states had so acted.

having to prove they were denied "equal pay for equal work," as forbidden by the 1963 Equal Pay Act. All that is necessary, the court said, is for a woman to show that her sex was used against her in the determination of her pay scale.

In this ruling, the court specifically declined to address the argument that women are entitled to the same pay as men when their jobs, however different, are of "comparable worth" to society. Although many people still have not heard of the comparable worth concept, employers take the issue very seriously. Comparable worth was a crucial issue in a nine-day public employee strike in San Jose, CA. The strike ended July 14 with an agreement to bring women's pay up to men's pay for comparable work.

Opponents of the concept contend that raising salaries to comparable levels would be inflationary and that the free marketplace should determine the level of wages. They also argue that there is no existing method by which the value or worth of dissimilar jobs can be compared.

Supporters of the comparable worth idea argue that women do not necessarily gravitate toward low-paying, low status jobs, but rather that these positions generally pay less because they are held primarily by women. "The jobs that women do are often complicated and highly skilled," said Eleanor Smeal, president of the National Organization for Women.

In another ruling affecting women, the Supreme Court on June 25 upheld the constitutionality of the male-only draft. The court, in overturning a July 1980 ruling by a federal district court in Pennsylvania, said it was not a form of sex discrimination to require only young men to register for the draft.

Reaction to the court's ruling was mixed. Conservatives were elated, calling the decision a vindication of traditional values. ERA opponent Phyllis Schlafly said the ruling was "a tremendous victory for everything we've been fighting for." Feminists viewed the ruling as a setback.

The abortion issue received considerable attention in 1981. Early in the year the focus was on a bill, sponsored by Sen. Jesse Helms (R-NC) and Rep. Henry J. Hyde (R-IL), declaring that human life begins at conception and allowing states to pass anti-abortion laws. Many legal scholars questioned the constitutionality of the federal proposal, especially a section that would keep lower federal courts from considering the legality of state laws banning abortion. The bill was approved July 9 by the Senate Judiciary's Subcommittee on Separation of Powers, but further action was postponed when Sen. Orrin Hatch (R-Utah) demanded that his subcommittee first have a chance to hold hearings on proposed constitutional amendments to ban or restrict abortion. Hatch's own proposed amendment, which would give Congress and the states joint authority to regulate or prohibit abortions, was criticized by both supporters and opponents of abortion rights. Despite all the attention the anti-abortion movement received in 1981, public opposition to a constitutional amendment banning abortions remained strong.

International News. On February 4, Gro Harlem Brundtland became Norway's first woman prime minister. A physician and former environment minister, Brundtland was deputy chairman of the ruling Labor Party's parliamentary delegation when she was named to replace resigning Prime Minister Odvar Nordli. She lost the office seven months later when the Labor government was swept from power.

The Spanish parliament on June 22 lifted a ban on divorce that had been imposed since the establishment of the dictatorship of Gen. Francisco Franco in 1939.

Swiss voters on June 14 approved a constitutional amendment guaranteeing women equal rights. The major Swiss political parties, unions, and religious organizations endorsed the amendment.

SANDRA STENCEL, *Editorial Research Reports*

WYOMING

The state's economy, the legislative session, water resource problems, and various personalities made news in Wyoming in 1981.

The Economy. Fueled by a high level of energy-related activity, the state's overall economy expanded significantly. Demand for Wyoming coal, oil, and natural gas continued unabated. The state's mineral royalties increased by 24% over 1980. Its tourist industry witnessed record years in 1980 and 1981. Its labor force grew at an annual rate of 5.1% and totaled about 257,000. A July unemployment rate of 3.7% was second lowest in the nation and Wyoming's 1980 per capita income ($10,898) was fifth highest. An exception in this otherwise bright picture was the state's uranium industry, where a depressed market caused layoffs affecting some 5,000 mine and mill workers.

Legislation. The 46th session of the legislature convened in January with Republican majorities in both House and Senate. Significant new laws included a 2% increase in the state severance tax on oil and gas; an act making solar energy use a property right; inclusion of synthetic fuel plants under the state's industrial siting authority; state reapportionment based on 1980 census results; and a school finance equalization plan to be approved in a constitutional amendment. Proceeds from the new severance levy, estimated at $90 million for 1981, will be distributed among cities, towns, and counties, as well as among the highway, mineral trust, and water development funds.

Water Resources. A mild winter with subnormal snow pack and stream flow reminded residents that water remains Wyoming's most critical resource. The transfer of water rights to private energy companies planning coal slurry pipelines continued to generate controversy. One major pipeline would draw water from deep wells in northeastern Wyoming. An environmental impact statement on the project appeared in August but did not settle the objections of Gov. Ed Hershler and various citizen groups, who fear the long range effect of heavy pumping on the underground aquifer. In another slurry project, the 1981 legislature blocked plans for an energy company to use surface water from the Little Big Horn River. No less controversial was the Cheyenne Water Project. This aims to divert stream flow from west of the continental divide to Casper and Cheyenne, several hundred miles to the east. Partly financed by legislative funds, the plan hit a snag in August when Cheyenne voters rejected an $80 million bond issue needed for its completion.

Personalities. James Watt, a Wyoming native, became secretary of the interior in the Reagan cabinet (*see also* BIOGRAPHY). In Cheyenne, Kimerli Pring, Miss Wyoming of 1978, won a libel suit against *Penthouse* magazine and with it jury-awarded damages of $26.5 million. In 1979, the magazine had published a story depicting the exploits of a Miss Wyoming at a national beauty pageant. *Penthouse* claimed the work was fiction, but Miss Pring's lawyer asserted it was libelous in the extreme. A judge later reduced the damages to $14 million. At the University of Wyoming, president Edward Jennings resigned in June to take a similar post at The Ohio State University.

H. R. DIETERICH
University of Wyoming

WYOMING • Information Highlights

Area: 97,809 sq mi (253 325 km^2).
Population (1980 census): 470,816.
Chief Cities (1980 census): Cheyenne, the capital, 47,283; Casper, 51,016; Laramie, 24,410; Rock Springs, 19,458; Sheridan, 15,146; Green River, 12,807; Gillette, 12,134; Rawlins, 11,547.
Government (1981): *Chief Officers*—governor, Ed Herschler (D); secy. of state, Thyra Thomson (R). *Legislature*—Senate, 30 members; House of Representatives, 62 members.
State Finances (fiscal year 1980): *Revenues*, $937,000,000; *expenditures*, $797,000,000.
Personal Income (1980); $5,152,000,000; per capita, $10,898.
Labor Force (July 1981): *Nonagricultural wage and salary earners*, 213,300; *unemployed*, 9,700 (3.7% of total force).

THE YEMENS

The politics of the southern Arabian peninsula have for more than a decade been characterized by what one observer called "the equilibrium of chaos." Violence and disorder, uncertainty as to what events have actually occurred and what they mean, and bizarre happenings that seem in the end to change little continued to be the way of things in North Yemen and South Yemen for much of 1981.

North-South Relations. Relations between North and South Yemen are complex and curious. North Yemen's National Democratic Front (NDF) is a dissident group supported by South Yemen, comprising Marxists, Baathists, and socialists. It commands a small but effective army of some two or three thousand guerrillas. The NDF is said to control a band of territory along the southern border stretching northeast to Marib. Skirmishes between the North Yemen army and the NDF are more or less chronic.

Hostilities flared up in August 1981. Several hundred men on both sides were killed in three

NORTH YEMEN • Information Highlights

Official Name: Yemen Arab Republic.
Location: Arabian peninsula in southwest Asia.
Area: 75,000 sq mi (194 250 km^2).
Population (1981 est.): 5,400,000.
Chief City (1975 census): San'a, the capital, 447,898.
Government: *Head of state*, Ali Abdullah Saleh, president. *Head of government*, Abdel Karim al-Iryani, prime minister. *Legislature* (unicameral)—Constituent People's Assembly.
Monetary Unit: Rial (4.56 rials equal U.S.$1, July 1981).
Manufactures (major products): Textiles, aluminum, cement.
Agriculture (major products): Wheat, barley, maize, sorghum, potatoes.

major engagements before a cease-fire was arranged on August 10. The NDF threat led to an urgent meeting in mid-August, held in Taif, Saudi Arabia, between Foreign Minister Ali Lutf al-Thour of North Yemen and Prince Sultan Ibn-Abdel Aziz, the Saudi minister responsible for Yemeni affairs. At this meeting, Saudi Arabia reportedly agreed to arrange and finance increased U.S. arms for North Yemen.

These developments were sharply in contrast to another set of events. Moves toward a merger of the Yemens, initiated in 1979, had led to various high-level contacts between June and September 1980, but then came to a lull. Such contact was revived when North Yemen's President Ali Abdullah Saleh and South Yemen's President Ali Nasser Mohammed met at Taiz, North Yemen, on September 14. A joint communiqué expressed concern over the U.S. military presence in the Gulf of Aden, the Indian Ocean, and the Red Sea. Two further moves in the late summer that spoke of North-South cooperation, if not unification, were the creation of the joint Yemen Tourism Company and the launching of a joint program for water and geological research, to be financed by Kuwait and the United Nations.

North Yemen. Abdel Karim al-Iryani continued as premier throughout the year, having been appointed by President Saleh on Oct. 15, 1980, to replace Maj. Abdel Ghani. On Jan. 15, 1981, Minister of Local Government Khamis was shot dead by gunmen on the road from Hodeida to San'a. On April 20 three new appointments were made to the cabinet. Abdullah al-Asnag, a presidential adviser since 1979, was reported to have been executed for treason in April.

A continuation of the economic slowdown was blamed chiefly on a decline in expatriate remittances.

South Yemen. On June 28, President Mohammed announced the results of elections to local councils and some seats in the assembly. He claimed that 94.6% of the electorate had voted and had demonstrated "absolute support" for the government. Cabinet changes were made in May and August. Mohammad Sali Muti, a former cabinet member, was reported to have been executed in March.

In Aden on August 19, Libya, Ethiopia, and South Yemen—all having close relations with the Soviet Union—signed a treaty of cooperation and friendship aimed at reducing U.S. influence in the Middle East. On September 14, President Gustav Husák of Czechoslovakia signed a 20-year treaty of cooperation with South Yemen.

ARTHUR CAMPBELL TURNER
University of California, Riverside

SOUTH YEMEN • Information Highlights

Official Name: People's Democratic Republic of Yemen.
Location: Arabian peninsula in southwest Asia.
Area: 112,000 sq mi (290 080 km^2).
Population (1981 est.): 2,000,000.
Chief City: Aden, the capital, 271,590.
Government: *Head of state,* Ali Nasser Mohammed, president and secretary-general of the Yemeni Socialist Party. *Legislature* (unicameral)—People's Supreme Assembly.
Monetary Unit: Dinar (.3454 dinar equals U.S.$1, Jan. 1981).
Manufactures (major products): Fuel oils, processed foods.
Agriculture (major products): Millet, wheat, barley, sesame.

YUGOSLAVIA

On July 3, 1981, the Yugoslav parliament adopted seven constitutional amendments formalizing the system of collective leadership. The country's two key ruling bodies—the eight-member state presidency and the 23-member presidium of the central committee of the League of Communists of Yugoslavia (LCY), both with annual rotation of chairmen—maintained political cohesion in 1981 but were confronted with major difficulties and showed signs of internal strain.

Domestic Affairs. The country experienced its worst internal crisis since the end of World War II when violent demonstrations broke out in the autonomous province of Kosovo in March and April. Kosovo is formally part of the Republic of Serbia, but more than three quarters of its population are ethnic Albanians. Surprising government authorities, well-organized demonstrators demanded the establishment of a full-fledged Kosovo republic within or even outside Yugoslavia. Demonstrations turned into riots, with many persons killed or injured in clashes with local militia. Central authorities claimed that a Kosovo republic would foster separatist movements in other parts of the country and lead to the disintegration of Yugoslavia. It was also hinted that foreign powers were trying to use Kosovo to "destabilize" Yugoslavia.

An uneasy truce was finally reached, followed by a purge of state and LCY officials, as well as arrests, trials, and sentencing to jail of demonstration leaders. Public opinion was highly aroused, and government press polemics reached unprecedented proportions. Official explanations for the rioting, at first scarce and later contradictory, showed that LCY leaders were not of one mind as to whether the troubles were foreign-inspired or caused by domestic factors; nor was there unanimity on how to deal with the Kosovo dissenters.

Church-state relations showed unusual signs of tension. A statement by Croatian Catholic bishops, issued on April 30 in Zagreb, complained that basic church rights were being "appreciably restricted in practice." There were stirrings from other main religious groups—especially Muslims and the Serbian Orthodox—which the regime assailed as "clerical nationalism." Priests of several denominations were arrested and sentenced to jail for illegal acts.

While advocating greater democratization of public life, the regime dealt harshly with all op-

Two weeks of heavy rain in March caused considerable flood damage in towns and agricultural regions throughout Yugoslavia. In Belgrade, right, the Sava river overflowed, flooding major thoroughfares.

UPI

position, especially among intellectuals. Petitions to amend laws restricting freedom of the press were denied, and permits to launch nonofficial literary and political views were withheld. Prominent intellectuals, chiefly in Croatia, were arrested, accused of spreading hostile nationalist propaganda and maintaining contacts with emigré groups, and sentenced to jail terms.

Economy. The performance of the Yugoslav economy in 1981 was highly unsatisfactory. By early summer the inflation rate had reached 50%. On a per capita basis, the hard-currency debt—$17,700,000,000 at the end of June—was roughly equal to Poland's $27,000,000,000. The trade deficit in July exceeded $3,500,000,000, an increase of 8% over the same period in 1980. The year's wheat crop was 7% less than in 1980, requiring heavy imports. In August, sudden and high increases in the cost of some foodstuffs—sugar, oil, and milk—led to grumblings among the population.

At its meeting on September 30, the LCY's central committee drew attention to the gravity of the economic situation, criticizing "republican statism, localism, bureaucracy and regional autarchy." In a public speech the next day, the outgoing chairman of LCY's presidium, Lazar Mojsov, added to that list "deformations and disruptions of social values, erosion of morals, bribery, corruption, usurpation. . . ." More significantly, he described the central aim of Yugoslav economy—stabilization—as "merely a noisy slogan." In October, Mojsov was replaced by Dušan Dragosavac.

On the other hand, industrial growth was strong, especially in crude steel. In view of Yugoslavia's inability to compete in Western markets, it exports have been heavily reoriented to the East, especially the USSR. On June 15, an agreement on reciprocal delivery of goods for the period 1981–85 was signed in Moscow. The agreement calls for $32,000,000,000 in trade, an increase of some 80% over the previous five-year period.

Foreign Relations. The events in Kosovo led to a drastic deterioration in Yugoslav-Albanian relations. The Yugoslavs accused the Albanians of indirectly encouraging and even helping Kosovo insurgents; Tiranë blasted Belgrade for persecuting Kosovo Albanians. Relations with Bulgaria again grew strained, over the perennial Macedonian question and other issues, including a border shooting incident in September. The Socialist election victory in Greece in October was warmly greeted. And in Poland, a delegate of Yugoslav trade unions addressed the Solidarity congress in September in Gdansk; however, the official Yugoslav trade-union confederation took issue with Solidarity's call for workers in other Eastern European countries to establish their own free unions.

U.S. Secretary of State Alexander Haig visited Belgrade on September 12–13, stating that U.S. foreign policy would continue its traditional course of strongly supporting Yugoslavia's "independence, territorial integrity, and national unity."

The 20th anniversary of the first conference of nonaligned nations, which took place in Belgrade, was solemnly celebrated on September 1. State President Sergej Kraigher declared that nonalignment would continue to be the cornerstone of Yugoslavia's foreign policy and that it represented "not only the conscience but also the future of mankind."

MILORAD M. DRACHKOVITCH
The Hoover Institution
Stanford University

YUGOSLAVIA • Information Highlights

Official Name: Socialist Federal Republic of Yugoslavia.
Location: Southwestern Europe.
Area: 98,650 sq mi (255 504 km^2).
Population (1981 est.): 22,500,000.
Chief Cities (1974 est.): Belgrade, the capital, 845,000; Zagreb, 602,000; Skopje, 389,000.
Government: *Head of state,* collective state presidency, Sergej Kraigher, president (took office May 1981). *Head of government,* Veselin Djuranović, prime minister (took office March 1977). *Legislature*—Federal Assembly: Federal Chamber and Chamber of Republics and Provinces.
Monetary Unit: Dinar (36.37 dinars equal U.S.$1, July 1981).
Manufactures (major products): Processed food, machinery, textiles, nonferrous metals, wood.
Agriculture (major products): Corn, wheat, sugar beets, tobacco.

YUKON

Government and Politics. The most important step taken by the Yukon government in 1981 was the submission of its position paper on amendments to the Canadian constitution. The five major demands were a clear declaration in the Canada Act of the rights of Canada's original peoples; a provision in the Canada Act to establish a mechanism for the entry of new provinces into the Confederation, with a guarantee of the same rights and privileges as existing provinces; an amendment to ensure that future provinces would be given equal control over their resources; that the Yukon government be included in all future first ministers' conferences; and that a formula be established to permit the negotiation of preferential hiring and purchasing policies between the federal and provincial governments.

Two territorial by-elections saw the official opposition party change from the Liberal party to the New Democratic Party (NDP) and the opposition leader change from Ron Veale to Tony Penikett. Cabinet Minister Douglas Graham resigned in the face of an investigation by the Royal Canadian Mounted Police (RCMP) and was replaced by Howard Tracey. Yukon federal Member of Parliament (MP) Erik Neilsen was appointed official opposition House leader by Conservative Leader Joe Clark.

Economy. Yukon experienced a record year in tourism, with visitors and revenues up an estimated 35% over 1980.

The largest mine in the territory, Cyprus Anvil in Faro, was purchased by Hudson Bay Mining, which continued with a major mill expansion and the development of a new ore body, extending the projected life of the mine by 25 years. Mining exploration continued at an accelerated pace in the MacMillan Pass area on the Yukon-Northwest Territories (NWT) border, where three new mines are expected to be producing by 1985. Placer gold-mining continued to increase dramatically, with claim stakes surpassing the historic high set during the Klondike Gold Rush of 1898–99.

The start of construction on the Alaska Highway natural gas pipeline in the Yukon was again delayed, to 1983. However, Foothills Pipeline Ltd. completed a $4 million test section near the Yukon-Alaska border. Right-of-way clearing also continued.

ANDREW HUME, *Free-lance writer, Yukon*

YUKON • Information Highlights

Area: 207,076 sq mi (536 327 km²).
Population (April 1981 est.): 21,800.
Chief City (1981 est.): Whitehorse, the capital, 16,649.
Government (1981): *Chief Officers*—commissioner, vacant; administrator, Douglas Bell; government leader, Christopher Pearson; chief justice, Court of Appeal, and judge of the Supreme Court, H. C. B. Maddison. *Legislature*—16-member legislative assembly.
Education (1981–82 est.): *Enrollment*—elementary and secondary schools, 4,800 pupils.

ZAIRE

Zaire's recent economic woes moderated as copper production recovered slightly and foreign trade increased. The government continued its past practice of cabinet reshuffles while a rehabilitated opponent once again returned to the opposition.

Peace in Shaba. Not only was there no repetition of the 1978–79 rebel invasion from Angola into the southern province, but the previous instability and looting caused by armed gangs receded in Shaba. The Belgian-trained Zairian forces reasserted law and order in the countryside and discipline within military ranks.

Domestic Affairs. Although Zaire has attained a measure of stability in its southern region, partly as a result of an agreement with Angola not to harbor each other's dissidents, its northeastern corner has experienced a serious refugee problem as 150,000 Ugandans have fled the banditry and insurgency of the Kampala regime. (*See also* UGANDA.)

A cabinet reshuffle in February, the second in five months, saw the rehabilitation of Bomboko Lokumba to deputy prime minister and minister of foreign affairs and international cooperation. He had fallen from the favor of President Mobutu Sese Seko in 1969. Before his restoration he had been elected to the political bureau of the Popular Movement of the Revolution (MPR), the sole party. In April, Prime Minister Nguza Karl-I-Bond announced from Brussels that he had resigned his post and would oppose Mobutu. He had only been restored to high position for a year. An MPR leader and former interior minister, Nsinga Untube, became the prime minister.

Economy and Mining. Gécamines, the state-owned mining company, announced a stable copper production. But shortages in foreign investment capital threatened current levels because new machinery is needed. Fighting in Angola still blocked most mineral shipments on the Benguela rail to the Angolan seaport of Lobito. Slumping diamond sales caused a reduction in output to maintain prices. After seven years and many delays, a power line running 1,100 miles (1 770 km) from Inga Dam to Shaba's copper mines was completed. Inland oil prospecting

ZAIRE • Information Highlights

Official Name: Republic of Zaire.
Location: Central equatorial Africa.
Area: 905,365 sq mi (2 344 895 km²).
Population (1981 est.): 30,100,000.
Chief City (1980 est.): Kinshasa, the capital, 3,000,000.
Government: *Head of state and government,* Mobutu Sese Seko, president (took office 1965). *Legislature* (unicameral)—National Legislative Council.
Monetary Unit: Zaire (5.62 zaires equal U.S. $1, October 1981).
Manufactures (major products): Processed and unprocessed minerals, consumer products, processed food, cement.
Agriculture (major products): Coffee, palm oil, rubber, tea, cotton, cocoa, fruits, rice, vegetables.

began as the small offshore production offered hopes of greater yields in the interior.

Foreign Affairs. The resignation of Karl-I-Bond contributed to strained relations with Belgium as Kinshasa accused Brussels of abetting dissidents. The Mobutu government views favorably the new Reagan administration in the United States, for Zaire promotes itself as one of Africa's anti-Communist bastions. It hopes for increased financial aid and investment, and a friendly Washington could build up confidence in Western creditors to Zaire's benefit.

Zaire's relations with the Eastern bloc have also improved, and trade with Comecon countries has increased. Air connection between Moscow and Kinshasa is planned, and Yugoslavia has promised food projects. Exports to Rumania accounted for 2% of total exports, and Belgrade has invested sizably in Zaire's rural industries.

THOMAS K. HENRIKSEN
Hoover Institution on War, Revolution and Peace

ZIMBABWE

On April 17, 1981, Zimbabwe celebrated the first anniversary of its independence. By that time much of the euphoria surrounding the event had ended, and the government of Zimbabwe was immersed deeply in grappling with such key problems as the consolidation of power, military reorganization, the demobilization of the guerrillas who fought in the war, programs of rural development and resettlement, the position and importance of whites in the society, relations with South Africa, and programs of social and economic change.

Cabinet and Government Changes. In a Cabinet reshuffle in January 1981, Prime Minister Robert Mugabe dropped Edgar Tekere as minister of manpower, planning, and development, and in August he was dismissed as secretary-general of the Zimbabwe African National Union-Patriotic Front (ZANU-PF) Party. Also in January, Joshua Nkomo, Mugabe's partner in the coalition government, was moved from the home affairs ministry (from which his control of the police had already been removed) to the less powerful position of public service minister. This reduction in Nkomo's power threatened the viability of the ZANU-PF coalition and angered his Ndebele supporters, who form 18% of the nation's African population. Assessing the risks involved, Mugabe changed Nkomo's appointment to minister without portfolio (with some responsibility for defense and public service) and averted a crisis. Nkomo had found his demotion totally unacceptable even though in exchange the PF had been offered an additional cabinet seat, as well as a deputy ministerial appointment. Nkomo was satisfied with his new position and actively set about trying to reconcile Shona differences, particularly in Ndebele strongholds.

Military Reorganization. After independence in 1980, Prime Minister Mugabe called upon Lt. Gen. Peter Walls, former commander of the Rhodesian Combined Operations, to create a unified national army that would bring together the guerrilla armies and the former Rhodesian security forces. Walls was subsequently exiled from Zimbabwe because of comments he made, while on a visit to Britain, regarding the legitimacy of the 1980 election and the possibility of a white coup d'etat in the period immediately prior to independence.

In August 1981, Mugabe appointed a white general, Alexander Maclean, as supreme commander of Zimbabwe's military forces. Lt. Gen. Rex Nhongo, former commander of the Zimbabwe National Liberation Army (ZANLA), the military wing of ZANU, was named commander of the Army and Lt. Gen. Lookout Maksuku, who headed the Zimbabwe People's Republican Army of the Patriotic Front (ZIPRA), was ap-

Wide World Photos

In Tokyo in May 1981, Prime Minister Robert Mugabe seeks aid for his Zimbabwe from Japan's Prime Minister Zenko Suzuki. Following the meeting, Japan promised Zimbabwe $170 million in aid and equipment for rural development.

pointed his deputy. The appointment of Maclean allayed whites' fear to some extent, particularly since the former guerrilla leaders were in positions of lesser command.

Following Mugabe's state visit to North Korea, more than 100 North Korean soldiers arrived in Zimbabwe in August, presumably to train a special unit of between 4,000 and 5,000 men. The unit was to fight along the Mozambique border against the South African-backed National Resistance Movement (NRM), which was challenging the Samora Machel regime in Mozambique. Joshua Nkomo expressed the fear that this unit might become Mugabe's private army rather than a special force, but its primary purpose seemed to be to operate along the Mozambique border.

Guerrilla Conflict. During the November 1980 violence between ZANLA and ZIPRA guerrillas, one of the integrated national army battalions demonstrated no partisan bias and operated as a unit in an effort to reestablish order. Unfortunately, in the clashes that took place in February 1981, and which resulted in 375 deaths, this was not possible and order had to be restored by white officers and former Rhodesian African Rifles. Subsequently, all guerrillas were disarmed. Over the course of the year, the situation began to stabilize and the demobilization of a large number of guerrillas was completed. Mugabe's land policy and the resettlement of the guerrillas are connected issues, particularly since the maintenance of the guerrillas at $100 each a month takes 20% of the Zimbabwean budget. The allocation of parcels of land to some of the guerrillas has been one form of compensation and a number of the guerrillas will be guaranteed employment in the rural sector, working on farms, clearing land, or engaging in rural reconstruction or agricultural projects. Because some guerrillas are unwilling to go into the rural areas, a number will remain in the military.

Zimbabwe will eventually have an army of close to 40,000, and this will absorb at least one third of the guerrillas and 10,000 African soldiers from the former Rhodesian army. The formation of such an army will defuse much of the guerrilla problem and will generally help stabilize the country. A large number of the former white officers have now resigned or retired and white conscription has ended.

Whites. It is essential for Zimbabwe to keep its skilled white population from emigrating. Furthermore, the sudden loss of large numbers of whites would discourage foreign companies from investing in Zimbabwe, and the loss of business and investment would in turn lead to extensive African unemployment. Mugabe was relatively successful in encouraging whites to remain. In the first 14 months after independence, 26,000 whites left the country.

The government is particularly concerned about the monthly departure of skilled white emigrants. By late 1981, there were significant numbers of vacancies for skilled workers in mechanical, motor, electrical, and construction fields, and the government was trying to keep such workers from leaving the country. Africans were eligible for apprenticeship training and an international effort was to be made to hire replacements. Indian and Pakistani mechanics began to work in some skilled positions on the Zimbabwe railway.

Emigrants thus far mainly include blue-collar workers, those threatened by Africanization, and those with a limited stake in the future of the country. Many whites in the business sector and white commercial farmers decided to stay either because they had given a vote of confidence to Mugabe or because they did not wish to abandon their assets. As long as Mugabe remains prime minister and maintains his moderate and flexible stance, this vital sector of the white population will remain, particularly since the gov-

Bill Campbell/Sygma

Near Bulawayo, Zimbabwe, women mourn the loss of some 375 persons killed during clashes between elements of the new national Army and former guerrilla forces loyal to Joshua Nkomo.

ernment has made it more difficult for them to emigrate by placing restrictions on what they can take with them upon their departure.

White Political Organizations. In April 1981, Andre Holland, a former Rhodesian Front Cabinet minister, announced the formation of the Democratic Party. By 1987 the 20 seats reserved for whites in the Zimbabwean House of Assembly under the 1980 Lancaster House Agreement will no longer exist. The Democratic Party, therefore, urged whites to begin to identify with the dominant African political leadership. However, whites showed little interest in shifting their political loyalties from the Republican Front Party (formerly the Rhodesian Front Party) of Ian Smith.

The Riddell Commission. The Riddell Commission released its report in June 1981, suggesting fundamental changes in the Zimbabwean economy. It called for higher minimum wages over a three-year period, increased taxes on corporations and the rich, and more land and credit for peasant farmers. For Zimbabweans paid more than $29,000 a year, it suggested that there should be no further income increases but only cost of living adjustments. Ultimately some of the findings of the commission might become law, but by late 1981 its overall recommendations appeared to be too extreme for the government. A prime objective of the government is to attract foreign investment and hence, policies are being avoided which might frighten away international investors and corporations. It is unlikely that the government will take any radical expropriatory action, but it might seek some equity control and schemes for the sharing of profits with workers. Reforms included minimum wage legislation and a workers' charter specifying employment conditions. A free health service was introduced for those earning less than $100 per month. In 1981, secondary school enrollments increased from 70,000 to 90,000 students, and 100,000 primary schoolchildren were receiving free education.

The 1981–82 budget, presented by Minister of Finance Enos Nkala, increased taxation in order to support Zimbabwe's new social programs. Zimbabwe had a budget deficit of $700 million which had to be met by foreign borrowing. Zimbabwe also had a rapidly increasing inflation rate of 15% per annum.

International Assistance. In March 1981, the Zimbabwe Conference on Reconstruction and Development (ZIMCORD) occurred, with representatives from more than 30 countries and a dozen international organizations attending. Before the conference, Zimbabwe had received aid pledges of $500 million and a further $1,800,000,000 was promised during the conference. Half of the total of $1,900,000,000 was in the form of grants and the rest as loans. The United States promised to give a $50 million loan for housing development and pledged aid totaling $225 million over three years. The World Bank promised $459 million and the European Community (EC) $180 million. Because of ZIMCORD, Zimbabwe should be able to engage in rural development projects, land resettlement, and housing programs.

South African Pressure. By mid-1981, South Africa began to bring pressure on Zimbabwe in an effort to reassert its dominance over the region and to prevent the Mugabe government from giving tangible support to the South African liberation movements. Early in the year, South Africa announced termination of its long-standing preferential trade agreement (first established with Rhodesia) with Zimbabwe. In May 1981 South Africa withdrew 26 locomotives which had been on loan to Zimbabwe and this, coupled with shortages of diesel fuel caused by South Africa, led to significant problems. Agricultural exports and general imports and exports were stalled, which in turn adversely affected Zimbabwe's already precarious balance of payment situation. Zimbabwe will be taking delivery of new locomotives from the United States in 1982, and this should resolve at least part of the problem.

South Africa also refused to renew work permits on expiration for 20,000 Zimbabweans who have been working in South Africa since 1958. The loss of the remitted salaries of these workers, plus their potential unemployment once they return to Zimbabwe, will cause further dislocation to the economy.

South Africa appeared to have over-responded to the potential threat of guerrilla incursions from Zimbabwe and to the need to assert regional hegemony, and in so doing threatens the stability of Zimbabwe, which is so vital for the general security of the region.

Directions. The year saw considerable speculation in Zimbabwe about the creation of a one-party state. It is unlikely that Mugabe will make such a move in the immediate future because of white fears and his delicate coalition with Joshua Nkomo. In the long run, however, this is a very real possibility.

The new state of Zimbabwe faces significant challenges but continues to show considerable future promise.

PATRICK O'MEARA, *Director*
African Studies Program, Indiana University

ZIMBABWE • Information Highlights

Official Name: Zimbabwe.
Location: Southern Africa.
Area: 150,673 sq mi (390 243 km²).
Population (1981): 7,600,000.
Chief Cities (1979 est.): Salisbury, the capital, 650,000; Bulawayo, 350,000.
Government: *Head of state,* Canaan Banana, president (took office April 1980). *Head of government,* Robert Mugabe, prime minister (took office March 1980). *Legislature*—Parliament: Senate and House of Assembly.
Monetary Unit: Zimbabwe dollar (0.723 Z. dollar equals U.S.$1, July 1981).
Manufactures (major products): Textiles, machinery, fertilizers.
Agriculture (major products): Tobacco, corn, sorghum, wheat, sugar, cotton, cattle.

ZOOLOGY

The number of articles and books about animals continued to rise in 1981, with behavior, physiology, and evolution major areas of interest.

Behavior. Ants have been the subject of study for many years, but new findings are still being made. In 1981, B. Hölldobler and C.J. Lumsden of Harvard University reported on some of the territorial behavior patterns of ants. Harvester ants, for example, have territories that consist of a nest and various radiating paths from which feeding trips are made. The result is a series of interdigitating territories. In contrast, a colony of as many as 500,000 African weaver ants controls a territory that includes several different trees, in which the ants bind leaves to construct tents. Most of the leaf tents house workers, and there is only one queen in the territory. She moves from tent to tent, surrounded by guards and depositing eggs. The whole territory is patrolled by the colony members. Any infringement by members of an adjacent colony results in combat. A third type of territorial behavior is seen in various honey ants. They defend only the portion of their feeding area in which they happen to be feeding at a given moment.

T.S. Ray and C.C. Andrews of Harvard reported a complex interrelation among army ants, antbirds, and butterflies in Costa Rican tropical rain forests. Swarms of army ants moving through the leaf litter of the forest floor disturb large numbers of insects. The antbirds follow the ants and feed on the insects. As this occurs, the birds produce droppings, which are a nutrient source for the adult butterflies. Thus, the butterflies follow the birds. To make the relationship even more complicated, the butterflies lay their eggs on plants that have poisonous compounds. The larvae are able to thrive on the plant leaves and store the poisons in their bodies. The poisons remain there even after the larvae transform into adults, and so the antbirds cannot feed on the butterflies.

Among vertebrates, fish are notoriously diverse and adaptive in the ways they "make a living." Bottom feeding—be it in the ocean, shallow marine waters, tide pools, lakes, or rivers—is one variation in feeding. Other fish feed at intermediate depths, on the surface, and even, as in the case of angler fish, by knocking insects from above-stream vegetation in tropical jungles. In his new book *Diversity and Adaptation in Fish Behavior,* Miles H.A. Keenleyside adds a great deal to current knowledge of fish behavior, with special attention given to reproduction.

J.L. and E.R. Brown of the State University of New York at Albany reported on extended family organization in Mexican jays. For ten years the Browns banded and observed six different extended families of jays in the mountains of southeastern Arizona. The jays live all year in flocks. All members of a flock appear to be related, with parents, siblings, grandparents, aunts, uncles, and cousins all living together. Flock members cooperate in defending their territory from other flocks, and during nesting they all help in feeding the young.

Mutualism, whereby two species evolve habits or traits that help both to survive, was demonstrated in two sessile marine vertebrates. R.W. Osman and Julie Ann Haugsness of the University of California at Santa Barbara described how a bryozoan produces a protective skeletal material that protects tiny hydra-like animals that live on the bryozoan's shell. The hydroid, in turn, helps fend off predators with stinging cells.

Conservation. African elephants continued to suffer from poaching. With bulk ivory selling at $34 per pound (up from $2 ten years earlier), the number of illegally slaughtered elephants is thought to exceed one tenth the total population each year. With the population of Asian elephants also dwindling, the World Wildlife Fund launched a campaign to combat poaching.

Evolution. That birds serve as plant dispersers by eating the fruit surrounding an indigestible seed is well known. But H.F. Howe and G.A.

UPI

An 11-year-old hippopotamus in Prague, Czechoslovakia, gave birth to male twins in February. They were the first hippo twins born in captivity in Europe.

At the Bronx Zoo in New York, an 11-year-old Indian elephant gave birth to a 180-lb (82-kg) bull calf, said to be the first elephant born in the area since woolly mammoths.

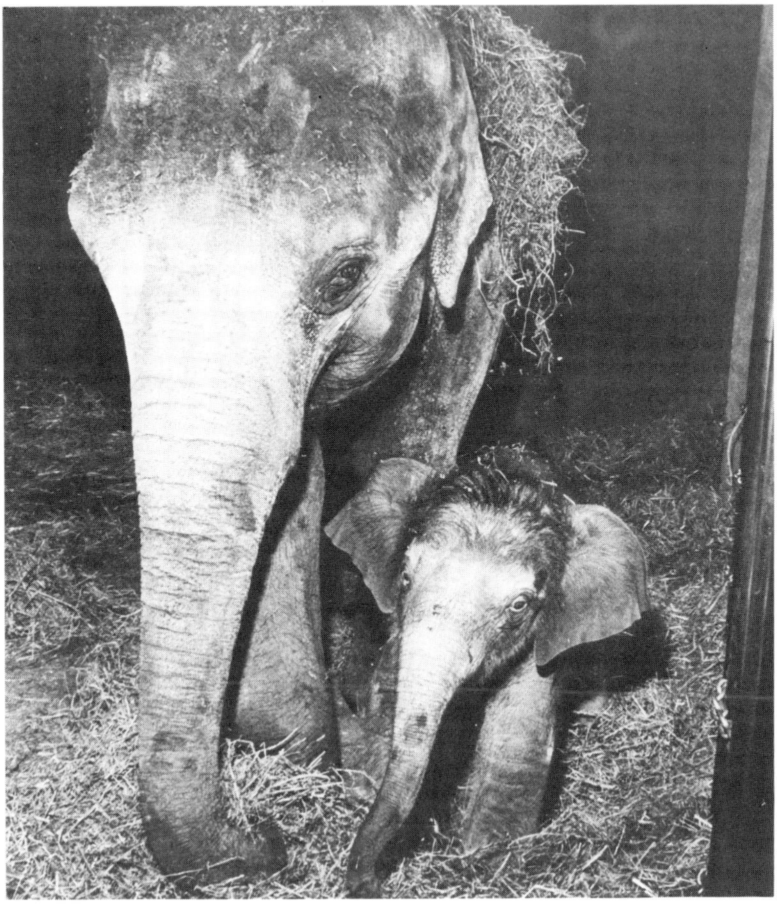

Edward Hausner, New York Times Pictures

Vande Kerckhove of the University of Iowa have demonstrated that birds actively select and eat those fruits with the largest amount of pulp and the least weight of indigestible seed. Over a long period of time, plants producing such seeds will become the most numerous, exemplifying the process of natural selection.

Primitive insects are wingless, and the origin of wings has been the subject of much speculation. Matthew W. Douglas of Boston University presented a convincing argument that temperature control was the driving force in wing origin. Because insects are cold-blooded, any increase in body surface, especially near the leg muscles, would permit faster warming and quicker reactions. Thus, large lateral body lobes above the leg attachments aided survival more than smaller lobes. Douglas' view is that the evolution of larger-sized lobes eventually resulted in gliding or flapping wings.

Physiology. Laurence E. Taplin and Gordon Grigg of the University of Sydney, Australia, finally solved the mystery of how various crocodiles can live in salt water (marine and salty marsh habitats). Food and water intakes are too salty for the proper operation of the metabolic system. To rid their bodies of the poisonous effects of excessive salt, reptiles, fish, and several birds evolved salt-secreting glands that extract sodium chloride from the blood and excrete it to the outside. Crocodile tears, first discovered by biologists at least 800 years ago, were thought to serve the same function. When investigations proved them to be relatively salt-free, however, the mystery deepened. The Australian zoologists discovered that glands in the tongue of the crocodiles secrete almost pure salt.

The extension of life as a result of long periods of hibernation has been the theme of many fictional stories, but little evidence has ever been published to support this thesis. C.P. Lyman and associates at Harvard Medical School, however, conducted a study of hibernation in laboratory colonies of Turkish hamsters, with interesting results. Their findings showed a correlation between life span and time spent in hibernation and suggested that the aging process is slowed during hibernation.

The lowering of body temperature in birds in hot weather is known to be accomplished by panting and evaporation of water from the upper respiratory tract. S.L.L. Gaunt of The Ohio State University discovered that doves have evolved a mechanism for inflating the esophagus (thus increasing the area available for heat loss), with a unique, underlying plexus of capillaries. The heat loss is greatly increased, enabling the doves to tolerate quite high temperatures.

E. LENDELL COCKRUM
University of Arizona

STATISTICAL AND TABULAR DATA

Table of Contents

NATIONS OF THE WORLD

A PROFILE AND SYNOPSIS OF MAJOR 1981 DEVELOPMENTS

Nation, Region	Population in millions[1]	Capital	Area Sq mi (km^2)	Head of State/Government[2]
Bahamas, Caribbean	0.3	Nassau	5,382 (13 939)	Sir Gerald Cash, governor general Lynden O. Pindling, prime minister
	More than three weeks after the deadline for illegal Haitian refugees to leave the country, Bahamian police arrested more than 390 on February 10. The Haitian consul filed for the release of 250, claiming that the arrests violated a 1978 agreement, and banned all travel between the two countries. Bahamian police authorities reported late in the year that the crime rate had risen to an all-time high; the increase in violent crime was said to be directly linked to a growing, multibillion-dollar drug trade.			
Bahrain, W. Asia	0.4	Manama	258 (668)	Isa ibn Salman, emir Khalifa ibn Salman, prime minister
	Bahrain joined with five other Arab nations of the Persian Gulf March 10 to form the Joint Council of Cooperation to ensure stability and security in the region. The bloc was strengthened during talks in May and formally inaugurated as the Gulf Cooperation Council. In July it was announced that Bahrain and Saudi Arabia had signed a contract for the construction of a chain of bridges linking the two countries. The 15.5-mi (25-km) causeway, to be built by a Dutch-Saudi firm, was expected to take five years to complete at a cost of $564 million, borne entirely by Saudi Arabia.			
Barbados, Caribbean	0.3	Bridgetown	166 (430)	Deighton Ward, governor general John M.G. Adams, prime minister
	In parliamentary elections on June 18, Prime Minister John M. G. Adams and his Barbados Labor Party captured 52% of the vote to defeat Errol Walton Barrow and his opposition Democratic Labor Party. Ronald Biggs, called the "Great Train Robber" for his $7 million heist of the London-Glasgow mail train in 1963, was released by a Barbados court April 23 and allowed to return to exile in Brazil, thus defeating an extradition claim by Great Britain. Biggs, who escaped from a British prison in 1965, had been kidnapped in March.			

* Independent nations not covered separately, or under Central America, in alphabetical section (pages 68–565).
1 Mid-1981 estimates.
2 As of Dec. 31, 1981.

<table>
<tr><th>Nation, Region</th><th>Population in millions[1]</th><th>Capital</th><th>Area Sq mi (km^2)</th><th>Head of State/Government[2]</th></tr>
<tr><td>Benin, W. Africa</td><td>3.8</td><td>Porto-Novo</td><td>43,484 (112 624)</td><td>Mathieu Kérékou, president</td></tr>
<tr><td></td><td colspan="4">According to reports in March, troops from Benin had occupied villages in the Nigerian state of Sokoto. President Kérékou visited Nigeria in April for talks on several issues, including the alleged "invasion." Kérékou and Nigerian President Shehu Shagari agreed to reactivate a joint border commission. In September, Kérékou made his first official visit to France since coming to power in 1972 and expressed "confidence" in future relations between the two countries.</td></tr>
<tr><td>Bhutan, S. Asia</td><td>1.3</td><td>Thimphu</td><td>18,000 (46 620)</td><td>Jigme Singhye Wangchuk, king</td></tr>
<tr><td>Botswana, S. Africa</td><td>0.8</td><td>Gaborones</td><td>224,711 (582 000)</td><td>Quett Masire, president</td></tr>
<tr><td></td><td colspan="4">The Botswana government granted the Shell Oil Co. a license to prospect for coal in central Mmamabula district. In a further attempt to increase the country's energy production, President Masire announced that a new power station, to be fueled by coal, would be built at Morupule, north of Gaborones.</td></tr>
<tr><td>Burundi, E. Africa</td><td>4.2</td><td>Bujumbura</td><td>10,747 (27 835)</td><td>Jean-Baptiste Bagaza, president</td></tr>
<tr><td></td><td colspan="4">The leaders of Burundi, Rwanda, Uganda, and Tanzania met in Bujumbura for the third summit of the Organization for the Development of the Kagera River Basin. Discussions centered on the problems of trade and transportation in Burundi and Rwanda, both of which are landlocked. Interest expressed by foreign concerns in Burundi's nickel and peat deposits increased the need and desire to improve transport.</td></tr>
<tr><td>Cameroon, Cen. Africa</td><td>8.7</td><td>Yaoundé</td><td>183,569 (475 444)</td><td>Amadou Ahidjo, president</td></tr>
<tr><td></td><td colspan="4">Continuing border tensions with Nigeria erupted again in May, when a Cameroon patrol fired upon and killed five Nigerian soldiers. Lagos warned that drastic action would be taken if an apology were not forthcoming, and within Nigeria there were calls for immediate retaliation. The Nigerian government was dissatisfied with Cameroon's expression of "regret," but the crisis was resolved when President Ahidjo agreed to pay reparations to the families of the dead soldiers; he also accepted an invitation to visit Lagos. Cameroon's first offshore oil discovery was made near the Kribi region, located in the southwestern part of the country, on the Gulf of Guinea. President Ahidjo warned, however, that the oil reserves were limited and emphasized that agriculture would remain the country's economic mainstay.</td></tr>
<tr><td>Cape Verde, W. Africa</td><td>0.3</td><td>Praia</td><td>1,557 (4 033)</td><td>Aristides Maria Pereira, president</td></tr>
<tr><td></td><td colspan="4">In late January 1981, President Pereira announced the creation of a new national party, the African Party for the Independence of Cape Verde (PAICV), replacing the former PAIGC. The latter had been the national party of both Guinea-Bissau and Cape Verde, pursuing a bilateral effort for eventual unification of the two nations. After creation of the PAICV, President Pereira was reelected by the national assembly, and a new constitution, formalizing the split with the PAIGC and with Guinea-Bissau, was approved.</td></tr>
<tr><td>Central African Republic, Cen. Africa</td><td>2.4</td><td>Bangui</td><td>240,535 (622 986)</td><td>André Kolingba, head of state and government</td></tr>
<tr><td></td><td colspan="4">In a referendum on February 6, voters overwhelmingly approved (by 97%) a new constitution calling for a multiparty system. Presidential elections were held March 19, with incumbent David Dacko being returned for a six-year term. Dacko captured more than 50% of the vote to defeat four other candidates, including former Premier Ange Patasse, the runner-up with 38%. When the results were announced, rioting broke out in Bangui. Most of the demonstrators were supporters of Patasse, who charged that the balloting was rigged with the help of France. More than 50 persons were injured in rioting the next day, and President Dacko declared a state of emergency. On April 3, Dacko was sworn in and ended the state of emergency. In his inaugural address, he called for an end to "hostile, partisan, and sterile actions." But the desperate state of the economy further fueled popular discontent and political opposition. President Dacko declared a state of siege again in July, banning all opposition parties and arresting opposition leaders. Finally, on September 1, after two years in office, President Dacko was ousted by the army. Commander-in-Chief Gen. André Kolingba took over the government and formed an all-military cabinet. He promised elections at some unspecified future date. Meanwhile, the political turmoil was having a damaging effect on an already-weak economy. Despite abundant natural resources, the republic suffered declining production in all sectors and average income fell steadily. Aid from France—some $90 million—was essential, nearly equaling the country's own budget.</td></tr>
<tr><td>Comoros, E. Africa</td><td>0.4</td><td>Moroni</td><td>838 (2 170)</td><td>Ahmed Abdallah, president</td></tr>
<tr><td></td><td colspan="4">A coup, to have been carried out by the presidential guard, was put down in February. Fifty alleged participants, many of them army personnel and civil servants, were arrested.</td></tr>
<tr><td>Congo, Cen. Africa</td><td>1.6</td><td>Brazzaville</td><td>132,047 (342 000)</td><td>Denis Sassou-Nguesso, president</td></tr>
<tr><td></td><td colspan="4">During a five-day visit to Moscow in mid-May, President Sassou-Nguesso signed a treaty of friendship and cooperation with the Soviet Union. The Congo People's Republic and USSR also issued a joint communiqué which accused the West of "exporting counter-revolution" to Africa.</td></tr>
<tr><td>Djibouti, E. Africa</td><td>0.5</td><td>Djibouti</td><td>8,494 (22 000)</td><td>Hassan Gouled Aptidon, president</td></tr>
<tr><td></td><td colspan="4">After two years of drought, spring floods left more than 100,000 persons homeless; according to the national radio service, more rain fell in one day—March 18—than in all of 1980. President Hassan Gouled visited Ethiopia in March, with the two countries signing a ten-year friendship and cooperation pact. Elections held on June 27 were the first in Djibouti since 1977, but President Gouled declared himself the sole candidate. The 65-year-old president won a six-year-term, receiving 85% of the vote (15% were abstentions). Prime Minister Barkat Gourad Hamadou tendered the resignation of his government on June 30, but a new cabinet without any significant changes was appointed July 7. Political opposition escalated after the single-candidate election. In August the government refused to legalize a formal opposition party, the Djibouti People's Party, and in September arrested two of its leading members.</td></tr>
<tr><td>Dominica, Caribbean</td><td>0.1</td><td>Roseau</td><td>289 (749)</td><td>Aurelius Marie, president
Mary Eugenia Charles, prime minister</td></tr>
<tr><td></td><td colspan="4">Prime Minister Charles declared a state of emergency February 13 after the father of the government press secretary was kidnapped by members of the Rastafarian sect known in Dominica as "Dreads." Security forces on March 7 discovered a plot to overthrow the government; five men were arrested. Meanwhile, the U.S. FBI assisted in investigating external involvement in the plot. On April 27, ten U.S. mercenaries were arrested near New Orleans, LA, for their alleged role in the scheme. Seven pleaded guilty in a plea-bargaining arrangement, and on June 20 a federal jury found two others, both with links to the Ku Klux Klan, guilty of conspiracy and violating the federal Neutrality Act. The state of emergency in Dominica was lifted in July, but by December another coup attempt—by Dominican soldiers, Rastafarians, and American mercenaries—had been staged. On December 19, two groups of gunmen stormed police headquarters and the main prison in Roseau. They in-</td></tr>
</table>

Nation, Region | **Population in millions**[1] | **Capital** | **Area Sq mi (km^2)** | **Head of State/Government**[2]

tended to seize a cache of weapons at the police station and to free former Prime Minister Patrick John from the prison, but both groups were repulsed. Among those arrested was the former head of the army. Dominica was a founding member of the new Organization of East Caribbean States.

Dominican Republic, Caribbean | 5.6 | Santo Domingo | 18,818 (48 739) | Antonio Guzmán, president

In a major reorganization of his cabinet in early January 1981, President Guzmán appointed three new ministers. On October 12, U.S. Vice-President George Bush addressed a joint session of the National Assembly. In subsequent discussions, the legislators emphasized to him that the Dominican Republic exports about 98% of its sugar crop to the United States and that proposed U.S. legislation to establish price supports for domestic sugar growers would have a disastrous effect on the Dominican Republic. (Later that month, the U.S. House of Representatives rejected the proposed price supports.)

Equatorial Guinea, Cen. Africa | 0.3 | Malabo | 10,831 (28 052) | Teodoro Obiang Mbasogo, president

President Mbasogo took several steps to demilitarize the government and establish rule of law. In February he announced the drafting of a constitution and a gradual reduction in the political role of the armed forces. The next month he decreed that anyone in the government with military duties would have to take a leave of absence from the armed forces. In March he also appointed the first civilian to his cabinet. But the government was not without radical opposition. In early April, security forces in Malabo foiled a violent coup attempt. Seventeen persons, including two members of the presidential guard and two soldiers, were killed in the fighting. Among the many alleged participants arrested were several ministers from the regime of Macias Nguema, overthrown by Mbasogo in 1979. In June, severe sentences were handed down against 31 army officers and four civil servants for their participation in the failed overthrow.

Fiji, Oceania | 0.7 | Suva | 7,095 (18 376) | Ratu Sir George Cakobau, governor general; Ratu Sir Kamisese Mara, prime minister

In mid-January 1981, the prime minister announced a reorganization of the government; six ministers were affected, and the new post of energy minister was created. A major issue during the year was a decision by the government to delay the introduction of television; the government maintained that the $20 million needed to bring TV to the country's 700,000 inhabitants would be better spent on economic development. Fiji was the first nation to pledge participation in a Sinai peacekeeping force to help patrol the peninsula after the final stage of Israeli withdrawal in April 1982.

Gabon, Cen. Africa | 0.7 | Libreville | 103,346 (267 666) | Omar Bongo, president; Leon Mébiame, prime minister

Joining with three other African members of OPEC—Libya, Algeria, and Nigeria—Gabon announced after a meeting in Algeria on June 23 that it would not cut the price of its oil despite the worldwide glut. "Africa Number One," the continent's most powerful radio station, was inaugurated in February, 300 mi (483 km) south of Libreville; the government has a 60% share in the $64 million project, with a French company owning the other 40%. In a major cabinet shuffle to implement his program of "democratization," President Bongo elevated Prime Minister Mêbiame to head of government. Mêbiame officially took over the functions exercised by Bongo, who was thereupon without ministerial portfolio. The new government, said Bongo, would have as its major tasks the implementation of an austere budget and more state involvement in commercial activity. In June, President Bongo became the first African head of state to meet with U.S. President Ronald Reagan.

Gambia, W. Africa | 0.6 | Banjul | 4,361 (11 295) | Sir Dawda K. Jawara, president

On July 30, while in London for the wedding of Prince Charles, President Dawda Jawara was ousted in a coup led by Kukli Samba Sanyang of the Socialist Revolutionary Party. In Dakar the next day, Dawda asked for Senegal's help, under a mutual defense pact, in putting down the rebellion. Senegalese troops surrounded the rebels in Banjul, and on August 2 Dawda returned to his home capital. By August 6, Senegalese troops had freed more than 100 hostages, including Dawda's eight children and one of his two wives. On August 21, President Dawda and Senegal's President Abdou Diouf announced their intention to confederate the two countries. The formal unification was declared on November 14. Under the agreement, the new confederation of Senegambia would be headed by Diouf of Senegal, with Dawda of Gambia as vice-president. Security and military forces, monetary and economic institutions, and foreign policy would all be integrated. Each state, however, would retain its separate independence and sovereignty.

Grenada, Caribbean | 0.1 | St. George's | 133 (344) | Sir Paul Scoon, governor general; Maurice Bishop, prime minister

Grenada became a member of the newly-established Organization of East Caribbean States.

Guinea, W. Africa | 5.1 | Conakry | 94,926 (245 858) | Sékou Touré, president

In February, President Touré reshuffled his cabinet to ensure "the maximum effectiveness in the realization of the objectives of the fourth economic and social development plan." That plan, introduced in December 1980 and covering the years 1981–85, emphasizes the growth of agriculture, industry, energy, fishing, and mining. International mining interests met in Conakry in March to discuss the exploitation of Guinea's uranium potential. Eight deposits had recently been discovered. In May, U.S. Steel agreed to join with Nigeria in an iron ore mining project in Guinea.

Guinea-Bissau, W. Africa | 0.8 | Bissau | 13,948 (36 125) | João Bernardo Vieira, leader, Council of the Revolution

Three months after taking power in a November 1980 coup, Vieira set up a provisional government composed of 16 ministers and two secretaries of state. In a crackdown on "corruption," the government in March arrested the director and deputy director of the state-run People's Stores and the former minister of commerce and industry. To halt serious food shortages (the country was expected to lose between 70 and 80% of its 1981 harvest), the new regime declared agricultural production as its top priority. Despite the advent of the revolutionary government, the World Food program sent 5,000 T (4 545 t) of maize as emergency food aid, and the International Development Association went ahead with a $6.8 million credit arrangement to finance oil exploration on the country's continental shelf.

Haiti, Caribbean | 6.0 | Port-au-Prince | 10,714 (27 750) | Jean-Claude Duvalier, president

Mexico and Venezuela, the two largest oil-producers in Latin America, agreed April 8 to include Haiti in their program to provide oil at low-interest credit to nations in the Caribbean. On August 26, opposition leader Sylvio Claude of the Social Democratic party, his daughter, and 20 supporters were arrested for opposing the Duvalier regime. The continuing problem of illegal Haitian immigrants caused increased friction with both the United States—which began expulsion hearings against 3,900 Haitians who had illegally entered the country since October 1980—and the Bahamas. (See REFUGEES AND IMMIGRATION; NATIONS OF THE WORLD—Bahamas.)

Nation, Region	Population in millions[1]	Capital	Area Sq mi (km^2)	Head of State/Government[2]
Ivory Coast, W. Africa	8.5	Abidjan	124,503 (322 463)	Félix-Houphouët-Boigny, president

In February, President Houphouët-Boigny formed a new, 36-member cabinet, larger than the previous body by six ministers. But he did not appoint a vice-president, who would have been his designated successor under a constitutional amendment enacted in late 1980. Houphouët-Boigny, 75, had been reelected to a five-year term in October 1980, before the constitution was changed. In March (1981), 46 Ghanians arrested in a government crackdown on crime died of asphyxiation in an overcrowded cell in Abidjan. Ghana lodged an official protest and refused to attend a meeting of the African Parliamentary Union in Abidjan. The tension was eased in early April in a meeting of the two presidents in Lomé, Togo. Early in the year, former French Foreign Minister Jean François-Poncet traveled to the Ivory Coast and promised military aid in the advent of a foreign threat. And in June, President Houphouët-Boigny became the first African head of state to be officially received by newly-elected French president François Mitterrand. On March 4, the International Monetary Fund (IMF) announced the granting of two loans, totaling $626 million, for economic stabilization in the Ivory Coast. The IMF also predicted that newly-discovered offshore oil held promise for the nation's economic future. In September, however, the ministry of planning and industry stated that coffee and tobacco would continue to be emphasized and that revenues from oil would be used mainly to finance agro-industry.

Nation, Region	Population in millions	Capital	Area Sq mi (km^2)	Head of State/Government
Kiribati, Oceania	.06	Bairiki	331 (857)	Ieremia T. Tabai, president
Kuwait, W. Asia	1.4	Al Kuwait	6,880 (17 819)	Jabir al-Ahmad al-Sabah, emir Saad al-Abdullah al-Sabah, prime minister

In the nation's first election since parliament was dissolved in 1976, conservative, pro-government candidates won an overwhelming majority in the 50-member National Assembly, February 23. Still the wealthiest nation in the world (highest gross national product per capita), Kuwait joined with other OPEC members in raising the price of crude oil in the first quarter of 1981. Kuwait also joined with five other Arab countries in the Persian Gulf to form the Gulf Cooperation Council (see NATIONS OF THE WORLD—Bahrain*), and with nine other states to form a banking and investment group, called the House of Islamic Funds (DMI), based on Islamic principles. On October 1, the oil gathering complex at Um Aleish was set ablaze in a bombing, which Kuwait blamed on Iran. Iran earlier had accused Kuwait of aiding Iraq in its war effort, but Iran denied having played any role in the bombing.*

Nation, Region	Population in millions	Capital	Area Sq mi (km^2)	Head of State/Government
Lesotho, S. Africa	1.4	Maseru	11,720 (30 355)	Moshoeshoe II, king Leabua Jonathan, prime minister

A series of bomb explosions rocked an electricity substation on the Caledon River in mid-March. The substation, which supplies electrical power throughout the country, was not seriously damaged. In September, another series of explosions caused extensive damage in the capital of Maseru. The Lesotho Liberation Army (LLA), military wing of the banned Basotho Congress Party (BCP), claimed responsibility. The LLA stepped up guerrilla activity to force Prime Minister Jonathan to hold the country's first open elections in 11 years. Meanwhile, several influential supporters of the opposition disappeared or were found murdered. Although the political turmoil might have been quieted by an open election, the poor economic picture—rising unemployment, growing foreign debt, declining foreign assistance, and a general failure of development—made it unlikely that the Jonathan government would be returned to power.

Nation, Region	Population in millions	Capital	Area Sq mi (km^2)	Head of State/Government
Liberia, W. Africa	1.9	Monrovia	43,000 (111 370)	Samuel K. Doe, chairman, People's Redemption Council

Togba-Nah Tipoteh, the minister of economic planning and a leading civilian member of the ruling People's Redemption Council (PRC), resigned in August, citing rivalry and suspicion in the government as "the old order slides right back again in some dressed-up form to fool the Liberian masses." Tipoteh was out of the country and had just heard of the executions of Maj. Gen. Thomas Weh Syen, the deputy head of state, and four other PRC members for allegedly plotting the overthrow of the Doe regime. In June, 13 soldiers had been executed for plotting a coup while Doe was attending a summit in Freetown, Sierra Leone. The International Monetary Fund in late August approved a $62 million economic stabilization loan. As part of its program to cut state spending and reduce the large foreign debt, the government decided to sell its only jet plane, a Boeing 737.

Nation, Region	Population in millions	Capital	Area Sq mi (km^2)	Head of State/Government
Liechtenstein, Cen. Europe	.03	Vaduz	62 (161)	Franz Josef II, prince Hans Brunhart, head of government

Voters on May 10 defeated a referendum on a constitutional amendment that would have altered the system of parliamentary representation. According to the amendment, any party gaining more than half the votes in a national election would have automatically received a majority of seats in the Landtag.

Nation, Region	Population in millions	Capital	Area Sq mi (km^2)	Head of State/Government
Madagascar, E. Africa	8.8	Antananarivo	226,656 (587 039)	Didier Ratsiraka, president

A march by several thousand students in the capital in February dissolved in violence; six persons were killed and 60 injured in skirmishes with police. The demonstrations were related to the nation's economic problems; unemployment rose rapidly, and job prospects for students dimmed. With almost no foreign exchange, Madagascar in December appealed to the International Monetary Fund (IMF) for help. The IMF balked. In June the organization had suspended a standby drawing program—by which Madagascar had borrowed 50%—because of the government's failure to enforce austerity measures.

Nation, Region	Population in millions	Capital	Area Sq mi (km^2)	Head of State/Government
Malawi, E. Africa	6.2	Lilongwe	45,747 (118 485)	Hastings Kamuzu Banda, president

Former minister Gwanda Chakuamba, considered the nation's most powerful political figure after President Banda, was found guilty of sedition and three related charges in late March; he was sentenced to 22 months in prison at hard labor. President Banda denied reports that Malawi, one of the world's poorest nations, was suffering an acute shortage of its major food, maize. He called for all discussion of food shortages to "cease forthwith." Newspapers in Tanzania and Zimbabwe reported that the lack of food had led to outbreaks of looting, assaults, and murders. Meanwhile, exile groups held a "unity congress" in Dar es Salaam, Tanzania, to form an alliance in opposition to the Banda regime.

Nation, Region	Population in millions	Capital	Area Sq mi (km^2)	Head of State/Government
Maldives, S. Asia	0.2	Malé	115 (298)	Maumoon Abdul Gayoom, president and prime minister
Mali, W. Africa	6.8	Bamako	478,767 (1 240 000)	Moussa Traoré, president

In February, President Traoré revealed that a plot to assassinate him and several military leaders on New Year's Eve was foiled only hours before it was to have been carried out. At a special congress of the Democratic Union of Malian People later in February, the government decided to abolish the quasi-public sector of the economy. The first steps in this "liberalization" process would be to dismantle the government agencies that controlled farm production and foreign trade. And in July, teachers and students arrested during unrest in 1980 were pardoned. President Traoré made an official visit to China in September to "further friendly cooperation."

Nation, Region	Population in millions[1]	Capital	Area Sq mi (km^2)	Head of State/Government[2]
Malta, S. Europe	0.3	Valletta	122 (316)	Anton Buttigieg, president Dominic Mintoff, prime minister

In late January 1981, Malta signed an agreement with the USSR whereby oil storage and refueling facilities on the island would be at the disposal of Soviet merchant ships. The Italian Chamber of Deputies on March 10 and the Senate on April 10 formally ratified an agreement, reached in September 1980, guaranteeing the future neutrality of Malta. Neutrality, the goal of socialist Prime Minister Dominic Mintoff, was a key issue in December 12 elections for the 65-seat House of Representatives. Mintoff's Labor Party retained its 34 seats to stave off a strong challenge from the Nationalist Party, which took the remaining 31 seats. Mintoff was elected to a third five-year term as prime minister.

Nation, Region	Population in millions[1]	Capital	Area Sq mi (km^2)	Head of State/Government[2]
Mauritania, W. Africa	1.7	Nouakchott	397,950 (1 030 691)	Mohammed Khouna Ould Haidala, president Maaouya Ould Sidi Taya, prime minister

On March 16, the government announced that it had defeated a coup attempt by military exiles who were supported by Morocco. The Mauritanian government claimed that Morocco had promoted the coup because Mauritania had withdrawn from the fighting against Polisario guerrillas in the Western Sahara. Days earlier, Morocco warned that it would launch a preemptive attack if the Polisario infiltrated northern Mauritania. Morocco denied any involvement in the coup, but Mauritania broke off diplomatic relations. By late June, reconciliation efforts launched by Saudi Arabia's King Khalid proved successful, and the two countries restored ties. For the stated purpose of "leading the country toward democracy"—but as a reversal of the trend toward civilian government—the ruling junta on April 26 installed Lt. Col. Maaouya Ould Sidi Taya as prime minister, replacing civilian Sidi Ahmed Ould Bneijara. A new 14-member cabinet, including five military officers, also was named. Libya's Muammar el-Qaddafi had visited earlier in April to propose a merger between Mauritania and Western Sahara, as well as an alliance among Mauritania, Libya, and Algeria. The government in late August denied a report by the London-based Anti-Slavery Society that as many as 100,000 people were still being held slaves; slavery was formally abolished in 1980.

Nation, Region	Population in millions[1]	Capital	Area Sq mi (km^2)	Head of State/Government[2]
Mauritius, E. Africa	1.0	Port Louis	790 (2 046)	Sir Dayendranath Burrenchobay, governor general Sir Seewoosagur Ramgoolam, prime minister

The government in March accepted a $187 million loan from South Africa to rebuild roads, housing, and fishing facilities damaged by a cyclone in March 1980. However, increasing trade ties with Pretoria were a sensitive political issue.

Nation, Region	Population in millions[1]	Capital	Area Sq mi (km^2)	Head of State/Government[2]
Monaco, S. Europe	.025	Monaco-Ville	0.7 (1.81)	Rainier III, prince
Mongolia, E. Asia	1.7	Ulan Bator	604,247 (1 565 000)	Yumjaagiyn Tsedenbal, president

At the 18th congress of the Mongolian People's Revolutionary Party (MPRP) in Ulan Bator, May 26–30, Yumjaagiyn Tsedenbal was reelected first secretary, a post which he has held since 1958, as well as from 1940 to 1954. The congress also voted in a new Central Committee, which in turn elected the Politburo; there were no significant changes. Mongolian cosmonaut Jugderdemidiyn Gurragcha was part of the two-man team launched March 22 in the Soviet spacecraft Soyuz 39.

Nation, Region	Population in millions[1]	Capital	Area Sq mi (km^2)	Head of State/Government[2]
Mozambique, E. Africa	10.7	Maputo	302,330 (783 035)	Samora Machel, president

In late January 1981, South African commando forces entered Mozambique and destroyed three guerrilla bases in Maputo. The next day, South Africa said it would continue to carry out such raids if necessary. In a speech at the Soviet Communist Party Congress on February 23, Soviet President Leonid Brezhnev hailed the USSR's friendship treaty with Mozambique and five other African and Middle Eastern countries; the same day, the USSR announced that it would come to the aid of Mozambique in the event of further invasions by South Africa. In late summer, the Mozambique Resistance Movement (MRM), a guerrilla group opposed to the Machel government and supported by South Africa, stepped up its activities. Heavy fighting was reported between MRM guerrillas and government forces in Manica and Chicualacuala provinces. In September, Mozambique accused South Africa of increasing its forces on the frontier, violating Mozambican airspace, and arming the MRM. Four U.S. embassy officials were accused of spying and expelled from Mozambique on March 4. In retaliation, the U.S. State Department suspended all food aid—wheat, rice, and corn—March 13. One week later, President Machel joined with several other African leaders in issuing a strong criticism of the Reagan policies in Africa.

Nation, Region	Population in millions[1]	Capital	Area Sq mi (km^2)	Head of State/Government[2]
Nauru, Oceania	.008	Nauru	8 (21)	Hammer DeRoburt, president
Nepal, S. Asia	14.4	Katmandu	55,304 (143 237)	Birendra Bir Bikram, king Surya Bahadur Thapa, prime minister

Under a constitutional amendment passed in December 1980, Nepal on May 9 held its first direct parliamentary elections since 1959. Nearly 1,100 candidates contested 112 seats in the 140-member Rashtriya Panchayat *(parliament); the remaining 28 members were appointed by King Birendra. None of the candidates was affiliated with a political party, however, as a multi-party system was rejected in a May 1980 referendum. Prime Minister Surya Bahadur Thapa was reelected under the new constitutional arrangements on June 14, appointing a cabinet two days later.*

Nation, Region	Population in millions[1]	Capital	Area Sq mi (km^2)	Head of State/Government[2]
Niger, W. Africa	5.7	Niamey	489,191 (1 267 005)	Seny Kountché, president and prime minister

President Kountché revealed April 15 that Niger had sold 450 t (495 T) of unenriched uranium to Libya; uranium sales to Pakistan and Iraq were also reported during the year. Niger is the fourth-leading producer of uranium in the world. In a major government shakeup in February, Kountché dismissed four high-ranking ministers and reshuffled his cabinet. The president's desire to "demilitarize" the government was reflected in the replacement of a military officer in his cabinet. Kountché made an official visit to France in July to discuss economic aid and development with the new leadership there.

Nation, Region	Population in millions[1]	Capital	Area Sq mi (km^2)	Head of State/Government[2]
Oman, W. Asia	0.9	Muscat	89,029 (230 585)	Qabus ibn Said, sultan

Oman joined the Gulf Cooperation Council (see NATIONS OF THE WORLD—*Bahrain**). Libyan leader Muammar el-Qaddafi disclosed March 23 that he had supported guerrilla forces in Oman and Somalia. British Prime Minister Margaret Thatcher visited April 23–24. Operation Bright Star—U.S. war games covering Egypt, Sudan, Somalia, and Oman—got under way November 14; it was the largest U.S. military exercise in the Middle East since World War II.*

Nation, Region	Population in millions[1]	Capital	Area Sq mi (km^2)	Head of State/Government[2]
Papua New Guinea, Oceania	3.3	Port Moresby	178,704 (462 843)	Sir Troe Lokoloko, governor general Sir Julius Chan, prime minister

In August, a syndicate of 19 foreign banks agreed to lend the tiny island state $100 million for ten years at favorable interest rates. The purpose of the loan was "to assist Papua New Guinea in meeting its development program and ongoing budgetary requirements."

Qatar, W. Africa	0.2	Doha	4,402 (11 400)	Khalifa ibn Hamad al-Thani, emir

Qatar joined in the formation of the Gulf Cooperation Council and the House of Islamic Funds (see Nations Of The World*—Bahrain; Kuwait). British Prime Minister Margaret Thatcher concluded a ten-day trip to India and the Persian Gulf with a two-day stop in Qatar, April 24–25. Qatar followed the basic pricing and production policies of OPEC.*

Rwanda, E. Africa	5.3	Kigali	10,169 (26 338)	Juvénal Habyarimana, president and prime minister

President Habyarimana dismissed three cabinet ministers in March and retained for himself the additional posts of prime minister and defense minister. Rwanda attended the third summit of the Organization for the Development of the Kagera River Basin (see Nations Of The World*—Burundi).*

Saint Lucia, Caribbean	0.1	Castries	238 (616)	Winston Cenac, prime minister

After a new outbreak in the longstanding dispute between centrist and leftist factions of the governing St. Lucia Labor Party (SLP), Allan F. L. Louisy resigned as prime minister April 30. Former Attorney General and Minister of Legal Affairs Winston Cenac was able to form a new government, which included Louisy as minister without portfolio. George Odlum, who had led the SLP's more radical wing, and four other former ministers created a new party, the Progressive Labor Party, to oppose the Cenac government. At a meeting of the Organization of American States (OAS) in Castries on December 4, U.S. Secretary of State Alexander Haig called for regional cooperation in halting the arms race and outlined a three-part economic assistance program for Latin America and the Caribbean. In mid-December, the newly-established Organization of East Caribbean States (comprising St. Lucia, Antigua and Barbuda, Grenada, St. Vincent and the Grenadines, Dominica, Montserrat, and St. Kitts-Nevis) established its secretariat in Castries.

Saint Vincent and the Grenadines, Caribbean	0.1	Kingstown	150 (389)	Sir Sydney Gun-Munro, governor general Robert Milton Cato, prime minister

Two bills proposed by the government to tighten police security led to popular protests against Prime Minister R. Milton Cato and to the resignation of several government officials. The government responded by announcing that it would not immediately proceed with the bills. In August, with Cato overseas, the acting prime minister reported that an alleged coup plot had been uncovered, but the lack of arrests led to speculation that the plot had been fabricated as a pretext for instituting stricter security measures. In March, the International Monetary Fund agreed to further aid assistance to overcome the damage caused by Hurricane Allen in August 1980.

San Marino, S. Europe	.021	San Marino	24 (62)	Co-regents selected semiannually
São Tomé and Príncipe, W. Africa	0.1	São Tomé	372 (964)	Mañuel Pinto da Costa, president and prime minister

On July 12, the sixth anniversary of independence from Portugal, former Prime Minister Miguel Trovoada was freed from prison. Trovoada had been held since December 1979 for his alleged role in a plot to overthrow the da Costa government.

Senegal, W. Africa	5.8	Dakar	75,955 (196 723)	Abdou Diouf, president Habib Thiam, prime minister

On Jan. 1, 1981, Prime Minister Abdou Diouf was sworn in as president, replacing the retired Léopold Senghor. Diouf named Habib Thiam as his own prime minister. After taking office, Diouf instituted a series of reforms to liberalize government, politics, the economy, and the society in general. In April the national assembly passed a constitutional amendment lifting the limit of four officially recognized political parties. Prime Minister Thiam said the government would "permit and guarantee the democratic expression of all the representative political currents." That month the legislature also granted amnesty for most political and press offenses between 1976 and 1980. In a speech marking the 21st anniversary of independence from France, Diouf announced programs to reform the educational system and increase literacy. In May, the government withdrew dismissal notices issued to 59 teachers after a strike in 1980 and canceled $88,000 in debts owed by farmers. A national oil company, Petrosan, was created to exploit newly-discovered light crude off the southern coast. But the most important development occurred on the foreign front. Senegalese troops helped put down a rebellion in Gambia during late July and early August, and three months later the two countries announced their unification into the confederation of "Senegambia." (See Nations Of The World*—Gambia.)*

Seychelles, E. Africa	0.1	Victoria	119 (308)	F. Albert René, president

The third coup attempt by foreign mercenaries since President René came to power in 1977 occurred November 25, when 50 armed mercenaries arrived at the Victoria international airport. The plot was revealed when customs officials discovered a gun in checked luggage. Fighting broke out immediately, and the gunfire lasted 20 hours. Forty-four of the mercenaries escaped by hijacking an Air India jet to South Africa; five others were captured and one killed. Pretoria quickly denied charges that it was involved in the coup. President René requested extradition, but on December 2 South Africa released 39 of the mercenaries without charges and the other five on bail. René believed that the release confirmed South Africa's role in the operation, but Pretoria insisted it had played no part. Because of a slump in tourism, long the economic mainstay, the government took major steps to diversify the economy. Expansion of farming and fishing were emphasized, and development projects on the small outer islands were begun.

Sierra Leone, W. Africa	3.6	Freetown	27,699 (71 740)	Siaka P. Stevens, president

The finance minister in February uncovered a political scandal, which became known as "Vouchergate," involving officials in his ministry and the treasury. Hundreds of thousands of dollars were paid out against false vouchers to fictitious companies. In subsequent weeks, three cabinet ministers, several prominent businessmen, and many other government employees were arrested and charged. For the first time in Sierra Leone history, union leaders called a strike August 14, protesting high consumer prices, high rent, and food shortages. After a second general strike in early September, President Stevens declared a state of emergency. Looting and some violence occurred as the government detained numerous labor and political opposition leaders. By late September, however, striking workers reportedly were back on the job and the country had returned to normal.

Nation, Region	Population in millions[1]	Capital	Area Sq mi (km^2)	Head of State/Government[2]
Solomon Islands, Oceania	0.2	Honiara	10,983 (28 446)	Baddeley Devesi, governor general Peter Kenilorea, prime minister
Somalia, E. Africa	3.8	Mogadishu	246,201 (637 661)	Mohammed Siad Barre, president

Muammar el-Qaddafi of Libya revealed in March that he had given aid to guerrillas in Somalia and Oman. President Mohammed Siad Barre announced June 29 that he was ready to engage in "peace negotiations" with Ethiopia over the contested Ogaden region. Somalia broke diplomatic relations with Libya when Qaddafi signed a friendship treaty with Ethiopia and South Yemen in mid-August. Meanwhile, a steady influx of refugees from Ogaden, which was plagued by shortages of food and fuel, aggravated Somalia's economic problems. Relief from the UN High Commission for Refugees was expected to be $200 million for the year, but the Somalian government pleaded for more international aid, claiming that there were 1.3 million refugees in the country. Late in the year, foreign relief workers charged that food intended for the refugees was being stolen by the army and government-supported guerrillas fighting in Ogaden. Because of the country's economic difficulties and the guerrilla war with Ethiopia, President Siad Barre's popularity reached an all-time low. In April, he dismissed ten cabinet members of the Supreme Revolutionary Council. In mid-May he made an unexpected trip to the United States, both to strengthen diplomatic ties and for "medical reasons."

Surinam, S. America	0.4	Paramaribo	63,037 (163 266)	Henk R. Chin-a-Sen, president

In its annual "Comparative Survey of Freedom," the human rights watchdog organization Freedom House named Surinam as the only nation in the world to have moved down the entire classification spectrum from "free" to "not free." On Jan. 6, 1981, André Haakmat, the nation's vice-president, foreign minister, defense minister, and justice minister was ousted by the military regime for creating dissension in the cabinet and military. On March 15, the army defeated a coup attempt some 40 mi (64 km) west of Paramaribo. It was the second attempted overthrow of the regime since army officers took control from an elected civilian government in February 1980.

Swaziland, S. Africa	0.6	Mbabane	6,704 (17 363)	Sobhuza II, king

On September 4, King Sobhuza II, 82, the world's longest-ruling head of state, celebrated the 60th year of his reign. Known as Ngwenyama, *or Lion, King Sobhuza continued to make the major decisions of government.*

Togo, W. Africa	2.6	Lomé	21,622 (56 000)	Gnassingbe Eyadéma, president

President Eyadéma helped ease a potentially explosive dispute between the Ivory Coast and Ghana by calling a meeting of their presidents in Lomé in April (see NATIONS OF THE WORLD—Ivory Coast*). An oasis of calm in an unsettled region, Togo pushed ahead in its effort to become a major center of tourism and international trade.*

Tonga, Oceania	0.1	Nuku'alofa	289 (749)	Taufa'ahau Tupou IV, king Prince Fatafehi Tu'ipelehake, prime minister
Tuvalu, Oceania	0.01	Funafuti	10 (26)	Toaripi Lauti, prime minister
United Arab Emirates, W. Asia	1.0	Abu Dhabi	32,278 (83 600)	Zaid ibn Sultan al-Nuhayan, president Rashid ibn Said al-Maktum, vice-president

The United Arab Emirates (UAE) joined in the formation of the Gulf Cooperation Council and the House of Islamic Funds (see NATIONS OF THE WORLD—Bahrain; Kuwait*). The strategic importance of the UAE was evidenced by visits from Prime Minister Margaret Thatcher of Great Britain on April 22 and by Chancellor Helmut Schmidt of West Germany one week later. Thatcher agreed to sell—for between $160 million and $200 million—30 training and attack planes, as well as a training system and instructors. Schmidt did not offer the sale of any arms or equipment, hoping the area would remain free of confrontation among the big powers. On September 6, Sheikh Humaid ibn Rashid was declared the new ruler of Ajman, succeeding his father, whose death was announced earlier in the day.*

Upper Volta, W. Africa	7.1	Ouagadougou	105,870 (274 203)	Saye Zerbo, president and prime minister

Upper Volta's trade unions, the most significant political force in the country after the military government, were at the center of domestic unrest in 1981. On May Day, President Zerbo called on them to accept constraints on freedom of speech and assembly. Later in the month, unionists who went on strike were placed on forced "sabbatical" without pay for three to six months. In mid-August, three of the four labor associations met and issued a condemnation of any attempts to limit union rights.

Vanuatu, Oceania	0.1	Vila	5,700 (14 763)	Walter Hayde Lini, prime minister Ati George Sokomanu, president
Vatican City, S. Europe	0.001	Vatican City	0.17 (0.44)	John Paul II, pope

In a rare public disclosure of finances, Vatican officials announced July 15 that they expected the government of the Roman Catholic Church to incur a deficit of about $26 million for the year. On September 29, Bishop Paul C. Marcinkus, 59, of the United States, was made an archbishop and named by Pope John Paul II as chief administrator of the Vatican city-state. While the position of president of the Pontifical Commission for the State of Vatican City was held by Agostino Cardinal Casaroli, also secretary of state, the actual running of the administration would be left to Bishop Marcinkus.

Western Samoa, Oceania	0.2	Apia	1,095 (2 836)	Malietoa Tanumafili II, head of state Tupuola Taisi Efi, prime minister
Zambia, E. Africa	6.0	Lusaka	290,585 (752 615)	Kenneth D. Kaunda, president

In the face of severe economic difficulties and in an effort to win assistance from the International Monetary Fund (IMF), President Kaunda in January ordered a series of strict austerity measures. On January 20, however, copper miners went on strike for nine days, protesting reforms in local government. Largely as a result, President Kaunda replaced the prime minister and the secretary-general of the ruling United National Independence Party (UNIP). After widespread crop failure, Zambia won approval of a $944 million aid loan from the IMF over three years. On June 22, two U.S. diplomats were expelled for an alleged CIA plan to overthrow the government. The U.S. State Department denied the charge and pointed out that Zambia's economic difficulties were responsible for a growing political opposition. President Kaunda admitted 17 trade union officials into his UNIP in April, but another miners' strike in mid-July halted production for the third time during the year. In what some regarded as Zambia's most serious political crisis to date, Kaunda ordered the arrest of Frederick Chiluba, chairman of the Zambian Congress of Trade Unions (ZCTU), and four colleagues.

POPULATION

Vital Statistics of Selected Countries

	Estimated Population mid-1981	Birthrate per 1,000 population[1]	Deathrate per 1,000 population[1]	Infant mortality[2]	Life expectancy at birth	Urban population (%)	Density[3]
World	4,492,000,000	28	11	97	62	41	98
Afghanistan	16,400,000	48	21	185	42	15	28
Albania	2,800,000	29	7	--	69	37	226
Algeria	19,300,000	46	14	127	56	61	44
Angola	6,700,000	48	23	192	41	21	22
Argentina	28,200,000	25	9	41	69	82	16
Australia	14,800,000	16	7	12	73	86	3
Austria	7,500,000	11	12	15	72	54	202
Bangladesh	92,800,000	46	20	139	47	11	954
Belgium	9,900,000	13	11	12	73	95	682
Bolivia	5,500,000	44	19	168	51	33	18
Brazil	121,400,000	32	8	84	64	61	58
Burma	35,200,000	39	14	140	53	27	340
Cambodia	5,500,000	33	15	150	45	14	152
Cameroon	8,700,000	42	19	157	45	35	55
Canada	24,100,000	15	7	12	74	76	35
Cen. Afr. Republic	2,400,000	42	19	190	46	41	40
Chile	11,200,000	22	7	38	67	81	63
China	985,000,000	18	6	56	68	25	309
Colombia	27,800,000	29	8	77	62	60	120
Cuba	9,800,000	15	6	19	72	65	185
Cyprus	600,000	21	8	16	73	53	121
Czechoslovakia	15,400,000	18	12	19	70	67	222
Denmark	5,100,000	12	11	9	74	84	175
Ecuador	8,200,000	42	10	70	60	43	159
Egypt	43,500,000	41	11	90	55	45	1,533
El Salvador	4,900,000	39	7	53	63	41	383
Ethiopia	33,500,000	50	25	178	39	13	43
Finland	4,800,000	13	9	8	72	62	185
France	53,900,000	14	10	10	73	78	169
Germany, East	16,700,000	14	14	13	72	77	267
Germany, West	61,300,000	10	12	15	72	92	465
Ghana	12,000,000	48	17	115	48	31	90
Greece	9,600,000	16	9	19	73	65	105
Guatemala	7,500,000	43	12	69	58	36	282
Haiti	6,000,000	42	16	130	51	25	425
Hungary	10,700,000	15	13	24	70	54	160
India	688,600,000	36	15	134	52	22	381
Indonesia	148,800,000	35	15	91	50	20	524
Iran	39,800,000	44	14	112	58	50	66
Iraq	13,600,000	47	13	92	55	72	145
Ireland	3,400,000	20	10	15	73	58	60
Israel	3,900,000	25	7	16	74	89	321
Italy	57,200,000	12	9	15	73	69	326
Japan	117,800,000	14	6	8	76	76	2,145
Jordan	3,300,000	46	13	97	56	42	223
Kenya	16,500,000	53	14	83	53	14	273
Korea, North	18,300,000	33	8	70	62	60	808
Korea, South	38,900,000	23	6	37	66	48	1,719
Laos	3,600,000	44	20	175	42	13	217
Lebanon	3,200,000	34	8	45	65	76	904
Liberia	1,900,000	50	17	148	48	33	315
Libya	3,100,000	47	13	130	55	52	33
Malaysia	14,300,000	31	8	44	61	29	220
Mexico	69,300,000	33	8	70	65	67	71
Morocco	21,800,000	43	14	133	55	40	107
Netherlands	14,200,000	12	8	8	75	88	694
New Zealand	3,100,000	17	8	14	73	85	22
Niger	5,700,000	51	22	200	42	13	46
Nigeria	79,700,000	50	18	157	48	20	178
Norway	4,100,000	13	10	9	75	44	455
Pakistan	88,900,000	44	16	142	52	28	356
Panama	1,900,000	28	6	47	70	51	109
Paraguay	3,300,000	34	7	58	64	40	20
Peru	18,100,000	39	12	92	56	67	59
Philippines	48,900,000	34	10	65	61	36	538
Poland	36,000,000	20	9	22	71	57	189
Portugal	10,000,000	15	8	39	70	30	244
Rumania	22,400,000	18	10	30	70	48	150
Saudi Arabia	10,400,000	49	18	118	48	67	12
South Africa	29,000,000	36	12	97	60	50	30
Spain	37,800,000	16	8	13	73	74	120
Sweden	8,300,000	12	11	7	75	83	223
Syria	9,300,000	42	9	81	62	50	66
Taiwan	18,200,000	25	5	25	72	77	--
Tanzania	19,200,000	46	16	125	50	12	38
Thailand	48,600,000	28	8	68	61	14	273
Tunisia	6,600,000	33	8	123	57	52	87
Turkey	46,200,000	32	10	125	61	47	83
Uganda	14,100,000	45	14	120	52	12	132
USSR	268,000,000	18	10	36	69	65	44
United Kingdom	55,900,000	13	12	13	73	76	304
United States	229,800,000	16	9	13	74	74	53
Uruguay	2,900,000	20	10	48	71	84	19
Venezuela	15,500,000	36	6	45	66	75	70
Vietnam	54,900,000	37	9	115	62	19	512
Yugoslavia	22,500,000	17	8	32	69	42	158
Zaire	30,100,000	46	19	171	46	30	97
Zambia	6,000,000	49	17	144	48	39	17
Zimbabwe	7,600,000	47	14	129	53	20	104

[1] 1978–79 data [2] Deaths under age one per 1,000 live births [3] persons per km^2 of arable land

Source: 1981 World Population Data Sheet, Population Reference Bureau, Inc., Washington, D.C.

WORLD ECONOMIC INDEXES

"Since the Venice summit [June 1980] the average rate of inflation in our countries [the seven principal industrial democracies] has fallen, although in four of them inflation remains in double figures. In many countries unemployment has risen sharply and is still rising. There is a prospect of moderate economic growth in the coming year but at present it promises little early relief from unemployment. The large payments deficits originating in the 1979–80 oil price increase have so far been financed without imposing intolerable adjustment burdens but are likely to persist for some time."

Declaration, Ottawa Economic Summit Conference
July 21, 1981

Name & Region	Consumer Price Index—1980 1970 = 100 All items	Consumer Price Index—1980 1970 = 100 Food	Wholesale Price Index—1980 1970 = 100	Industrial Production Index—1980 1975 = 100	Unemployment Rate %—1980	Foreign Trade 1980—Million U.S. Dollars Imports	Foreign Trade 1980—Million U.S. Dollars Exports	Estimated GNP 1980—Million U.S. Dollars	GNP Per Capita—1979 U.S. Dollars
AFGHANISTAN	112.6[1]	104.0[1]				686[2]	551	3,400[2]	170
ALGERIA	205.2[2]	254.0[2]				8,537[2]	12,409	40,680[16]	1,580
ANGOLA						720[10]	800[10]	2,660[4]	440
ANTIGUA	288.9[2]	337.6[2]				60[2]	11[2]	73[16,4]	
ARGENTINA	259,090.0	62,163.0	209,098.0	95		6,713[2]	7,810[2]	62,000[2]	2,280
AUSTRALIA	269.2	271.3	340.0	111[2]	6.1	20,332	22,048	120,400[2]	9,100
AUSTRIA	183.9	170.3	111.7	127	1.9	24,495	17,508	73,000	8,620
BAHAMAS	183.4[3]	202.2[3]				3,949[2]	3,495[2]	1,083[2]	2,780
BAHRAIN						2,481[2]	3,671	1,700[16,2]	5,460
BANGLADESH	401.6	383.4				2,438	761	9,100[2]	100
BARBADOS	377.9	406.8				521	219	644[16,2]	2,400
BELGIUM	203.5	178.8	166.3	115	11.8	71,185[14]	64,066[14]	112,300[2]	10,890
BELIZE						80[4]	106[4]	120[16,4]	1,030
BENIN						267[4]	26[4]	1,140	250
BHUTAN						1.4	1	90[12]	80
BOLIVIA	561.1	609.6	251.3			833	1,033	4,100[2]	550
BOTSWANA	156.9	167.5				380	383	401[4]	720
BRAZIL	1,321.2	1,502.7	2,331.7	142		25,000	20,131	215,000	1,690
BRUNEI						394[2]	2,649[2]	2,660[2]	10,680
BULGARIA				134		9,650	10,372	37,400	3,690
BURMA	274.2	289.5				319[2]	363[2]	5,060	160
BURUNDI	332.6	321.2				168	65	614[2]	180
CAMEROON	274.7	301.2				1,271[2]	1,129[2]	4,900	560
CANADA	216.7	263.5	247.2[5]	116	7.5	58,545	64,252	298,000[15]	9,650
CAPE VERDE	437.0[4]	435.8[4]				59	12	41[16,4]	270
CEN. AFR. REP.	134.4[2]	215.0[4]	410.9			70[2]	79[2]	535[16,4]	290
CHAD						118[12]	59[12]	924[16,4]	110
CHILE	419,601.0	500,946.0	1,316,052.0	142[17]	12.0	5,720	4,818	18,900[2]	1,690
CHINA						14,500	13,800	628,000	230
COLOMBIA	680.5	856.8	836.8			4,739	4,016	26,200[2]	1,010
CONGO	213.7[2]	158.0[12]				184[10]	180[10]	805[16,2]	630
COSTA RICA	279.4	303.9	408.4			1,528	963	4,000[16,2]	1,810
CUBA						4,687[4]	4,456[4]	18,400	1,410
CYPRUS	133.5	129.2	230.3	103	1.8[2]	1,202	525	1,970[2]	2,940
CZECHOSLOVAKIA	111.8	105.8		125		15,148	14,891	92,000	5,290
DENMARK	255.6	163.0[9]	250.9	120[17]	6.9	19,363	16,485	70,300	11,900
DOMINICA	299.8[2]	289.7[2]				24	8	34[2]	410
DOM. REP.	221.1[2,5]	205.2[2,5]	240.4			1,436	962	5,500[2]	990
ECUADOR	327.3	380.9				2,248	2,013[2]	8,600[2]	1,050
EGYPT	244.6	296.7	256.8			4,860	3,046	17,800[2]	460
EL SALVADOR	117.4[1]	119.7[1]	278.4[2]			966	966	3,500[2]	670
ETHIOPIA	247.2	271.0				567[2]	418[2]	3,000[2]	130
FIJI	260.8	271.4				562	350	811[2]	1,690
FINLAND	292.5	300.1	160.7[9]	127	4.8	15,580	14,155	47,800	8,260

Name & Region	Consumer Price Index—1980 1970 = 100 All items	Food	Wholesale Price Index—1980 1970 = 100	Industrial Production Index—1980 1975 = 100	Unemployment Rate %—1980	Foreign Trade 1980—Million U.S. Dollars Imports	Exports	Estimated GNP 1980—Million U.S. Dollars	GNP Per Capita—1979 U.S. Dollars
FRANCE	251.3	254.0		117	8[15]	134,912	111,251	535,000[2]	9,940
FRENCH GUIANA	260.4	252.3				255	25	100[7]	
GABON	258.7[2]	156.9[4]	219.8[10]			804[2]	1,477[2]	3,010[16,4]	3,280
GAMBIA	267.1	290.1				226	61	161[2]	260
GERMANY, E.				127	3.8	19,082	17,312	106,000	6,430
GERMANY, W.	164.3	153.3	173.6	118		188,001	192,930	766,100[2]	11,730
GHANA	2,950.0	3,737.1	350.9[6]			993[4]	1,096[4]	10,100[16,2]	400
GIBRALTAR	401.5	385.1				59[10]	25[10]		
GREECE	379.7	425.2	428.0	130		10,531	5,143	39,500[2]	3,890
GUADELOUPE	267.7	288.5				679	107	864[10]	3,260
GUATEMALA	166.1	156.1	264.3			1,351[2]	1,502	6,900[2]	1,020
GUINEA						272[4]	334[4]	1,200[4]	270
GUINEA-BISSAU						50[4]	11[4]	174[16,4]	170
GUYANA	264.0	326.2				317[2]	386	521[2]	570
HAITI	277.3	312.9				212[4]	185[2]	1,500[2]	260
HONDURAS	208.7	227.7				1,019	806	2,170[2]	530
HONG KONG	160.0	156.0			3.8	24,554	19,009	17,400[16,2]	4,000
HUNGARY	155.4	165.3		118		9,235	8,677	46,000	3,850
ICELAND	1,750.9	1,921.4				1,000	931	2,385[2]	10,490
INDIA	212.0	203.0	206.5[2]	126		12,858	5,911	116,000	190
INDONESIA	156.3[6]	152.8[6]	706.7			10,834	21,909	51,200[2]	380
IRAN	274.5[2]	242.0[4]	213.4[10]			9,738[2]	13,523	81,700[2]	
IRAQ	151.9[4]	153.4[4]	147.5[12]			4,213[4]	26,429	35,200[2]	2,410
IRELAND	360.0	367.1	189.1[9]	136	10.3	11,159	8,489	15,000[2]	4,230
ISRAEL	3,235.7	3,913.9		120	2.9	7,910	5,265	23,000	4,170
ITALY	369.1	355.6	417.0	130	7.6	99,452	77,667	384,000[16]	5,240
IVORY COAST	312.7	360.6				2,493[2]	2,515[2]	9,100[16,2]	1,060
JAMAICA	414.4[2]	459.4[2]			24.5[4]	1,178	942	2,900[2]	1,240
JAPAN	236.6	234.3	206.7	142	2.0	140,520	129,248	975,700	8,800
JORDAN	173.3	159.2	156.2[9]			1,949[2]	402[2]	2,690	1,180
KENYA	234.5	242.6				2,305	1,299	6,300[16,2]	380
KOREA, N.						1,300[2]	1,320[2]	14,100[2]	1,130
KOREA, S.	450.7	514.2	536.0	210	5.2	22,292	17,548	60,300	1,500
KUWAIT	188.5[3]	206.9[3]	175.6[2]			5,204[2]	19,945	23,500[2]	17,270
LAOS	457.3[7]	544.9[7]				80[2]	15[2]	260[4]	
LEBANON	130.4[7]	148.4[7]				1,701[10]	436[10]	2,900[10]	
LESOTHO	261.9	295.6				262[4]	35[4]	210[4]	340
LIBERIA	258.2	255.0				487[2]	601	810[16,4]	490
LIBYA	178.2[4]	120.0[4]				5,311[2]	16,085[2]	20,000[2]	8,210
LUXEMBOURG	190.2	180.8		108		71,185[14]	64,066[14]	4,400	12,820
MADAGASCAR	242.7	261.5				641[2]	394[2]	2,800[16,2]	290
MALAWI	243.9	269.9		124[17]		418	317	870[16,2]	200
MALAYSIA	177.2	190.0		161		8,658[2]	12,014[2]	19,600[2]	1,320
MALI		382.7				180[2]	177[2]	840[16,4]	140
MALTA	191.0	222.5				938	497	1,100	2,640
MARTINIQUE	277.0	234.4[2]				775	140	1,169[10]	4,680
MAURITANIA	135.3[4]	139.8[4]				259[2]	194	619[16,2]	320
MAURITIUS	388.5	402.4				609	429	877[4]	1,040
MEXICO	418.5[3]	422.9[3]	492.5	139		11,829[2]	8,768[2]	120,000[2]	1,590
MONGOLIA									780
MOROCCO	171.4	168.1		135		4,185	2,403	15,200[2]	740
MOZAMBIQUE						278[10]	129[10]	1,700[4]	250
NEPAL	146.5	141.1				241[2]	91[2]	1,760[2]	130
NETHERLANDS	202.9	124.1[1]		113	5.8	76,881	73,871	165,100	10,240
NETH. ANTILLES	238.2	333.5				3,128[10]	2,646[10]	652[12]	3,540
NEW ZEALAND	324.6	340.1				5,464	5,414	17,380[16]	5,940
NICARAGUA	258.2[8]	211.7[2,8]				360[2]	567[2]	1,341[2]	660
NIGER	285.2	318.4				127[12]	134[12]	2,100[16,2]	270
NIGERIA	186.3[2,9]	185.7[2,9]				12,399[2]	18,073[2]	46,500[16,2]	670
NORWAY	223.6	216.7	225.0	132	1.3	16,957	18,474	46,300[2]	10,710
OMAN						1,387[2]	3,202	2,600[4]	2,970

Name & Region	Consumer Price Index—1980 1970 = 100 All items	Food	Wholesale Price Index—1980 1970 = 100	Industrial Production Index—1980 1975 = 100	Unemployment Rate %—1980	Foreign Trade 1980—Million U.S. Dollars Imports	Exports	Estimated GNP 1980—Million U.S. Dollars	GNP Per Capita—1979 U.S. Dollars
PAKISTAN	305.1[5]	307.1[5]	316.7	122[2,17]		5,350	2,588	30,000	270
PANAMA	196.9	212.3	300.7			1,187[2]	349	2,850[2]	1,350
PAPUA N.G.	220.7[5]	230.4[5]				788[2]	1,049	2,050[2]	650
PARAGUAY	342.7	386.5	347.8[3]			494	310	2,000[2]	1,060
PERU	159.2[1]	158.8[1]	1,347.6[11]			2,090[2]	3,474[2]	11,100[2]	730
PHILIPPINES	294.7[3]	275.7[3]	345.5[3]	122[2]	5.3[4]	7,727	5,977	36,000	600
POLAND	134.1[4]	136.8[4]		125		18,871	16,998	155,000	3,830
PORTUGAL	225.0[13]	229.8[13]	486.9	142	7.8	9,410	4,628	24,900[2]	2,160
PUERTO RICO	197.3	229.3			17.1				2,970
QATAR						1,429	5,684	5,000[2]	16,590
RÉUNION	258.1	118.9				779[2]	140[2]		4,180
RUMANIA						13,200	12,230	104,000	1,900
RWANDA	202.0[10]	208.0[10]				190[2]	115[2]	959[16,2]	210
SAMOA, W.	246.6[11]	256.8[11]				90[2]	18[2]		
SAUDI ARABIA						30,177	109,111	94,600[2]	7,370
SENEGAL	240.7[2]	268.8[2]		90		888[2]	461[2]	2,500[16,2]	430
SEYCHELLES	142.8[6]	131.3[6]				51[4]	13[4]	89[16,10]	1,400
SIERRA LEONE	285.1	306.0				297[2]	205[2]	835[16,2]	250
SINGAPORE	112.9[1]	110.7[1]	152.7[8]	177[17]		24,008	19,376	9,400	3,820
SOMALIA	204.7[4]	236.2[4]				287[2]	111[2]	425[4]	
SOUTH AFRICA	277.1	314.5	291.4[2]	105[2,17]		8,336[2]	9,618[2]	54,300[2]	1,720
SPAIN	414.1	372.6	282.4[2]	117		34,080	20,721	197,000[2]	4,340
SRI LANKA	230.2	248.8	228.4[8]			2,029	924	3,200[2]	230
SUDAN	385.9[2]	398.3[2]				1,616	543	5,600[16,2]	370
SURINAM	255.1	247.4				411[2]	444[2]	822[16,4]	2,360
SWAZILAND	298.3	309.4				231[4]	305[4]	313[16,10]	650
SWEDEN	241.5	248.9		99	1.4	33,441	30,914	113,000	11,920
SWITZERLAND	162.5	162.8	139.7	108	2.0	36,356	29,634	99,000[2]	14,240
SYRIA	285.0[6]	310.0[6]	293.5			4,124	2,108	9,200[2]	1,070
TAIWAN						14,800[2]	16,100[2]	27,800	
TANZANIA	369.5	425.3				1,258	523[2]	3,900[2]	270
THAILAND	248.9	271.0	154.7[13]			9,212	6,509	27,300[2]	590
TOGO	233.7[2]	246.3[2]				518[2]	218[2]	960[16,2]	340
TONGA	295.2	312.4				29[2]	8[2]	34[12]	
TRIN. & TOB.	339.7	358.2			11.0[2]	3,178	4,077	4,500[16,2]	3,390
TUNISIA	124.9[6]	131.9[6]	198.1	147		3,536	2,201	7,000[2]	1,120
TURKEY	1,638.7	1,638.4	1,742.3			4,946[2]	2,261[2]	45,300[4]	1,330
UGANDA						167[2]	427[2]	931[16,4]	290
USSR	100.7[4]	101.9[4]		124		68,523	76,481	1,374,800[2]	4,110
UN. ARAB EM.						8,752	20,639	21,000[2]	15,590
UN. KINGDOM	360.8	395.8	493.6	107	7.4	120,095	115,350	488,700	6,340
USA	212.4	216.8	243.5	125	7.1	255,657	216,668	2,956,600[15]	10,820
UPPER VOLTA						300[2]	43[2]	869[2]	180
URUGUAY	13,007.0	13,620.0	13,030.0			1,642	1,059	7,000[2]	2,090
VANUATU						45[4]	33[4]		
VENEZUELA	226.8	313.0	244.4			9,618[2]	14,159[2]	47,900	3,130
VIETNAM						900[4]	300[4]	9,500	
YEMEN						1,492[2]	7[4]	3,800[2]	420
YEMEN, S.						393[2]	248[2]	500[4]	500
YUGOSLAVIA	558.7	592.3	415.0	139	11.9	14,029	8,367	64,400[2]	2,430
ZAIRE	1,339.0	1,313.3				725	1,639	2,300[4]	260
ZAMBIA	253.8[2]	265.1[2]	267.0[2]	96[2]		755[2]	1,377[2]	2,800[2]	510
ZIMBABWE	204.0	197.7		105		940[2]	1,194[2]	3,300[4]	470

[1] 1978–79 = 100. [2] 1979. [3] 1972 = 100. [4] 1978. [5] 1971 = 100. [6] 1977–78 = 100. [7] 1975. [8] 1974 = 100. [9] 1975 = 100. [10] 1977. [11] 1973 = 100. [12] 1976. [13] 1976 = 100. [14] Includes Belgium-Luxembourg. [15] 1981. [16] GDP (gross domestic product). [17] Manufacturing.

Sources of Information: Consumer and wholesale prices, industrial production, unemployment rate—The Monthly Bulletin of Statistics, United Nations; foreign trade—The Monthly Bulletin of Statistics and The World Factbook; GNP—The Military Balance 1981–82 and The World Factbook; GNP Per Capita—1981 World Population Data Sheet, Population Reference Bureau, Inc.

DEFENSE EXPENDITURE AND MILITARY MANPOWER 1975–81

Country	$ million 1975	$ million 1981	$ per head 1975	$ per head 1981	% of government spending[a] 1975	% of government spending[a] 1981	% of GNP[b] 1975	% of GNP[b] 1980	Numbers in armed forces (000) 1981
WARSAW PACT[c]									
Bulgaria	457	1,340	52	151	6.0	6.0	2.7	3.4	149.0
Czechoslovakia	1,706	3,520[h]	116	229[h]	7.3	7.6[h]	3.8	4.0	194.0
Germany, East	2,550	6,960	148	415	7.9	8.5	5.5	6.1	167.0
Hungary	506	1,240	48	115	3.5	3.9	2.4	2.3	101.0
Poland	2,011	4,670[h]	59	131[h]	7.0	6.0[h]	3.1	3.2	319.5
Rumania	707	1,350	33	61	3.7	2.3	1.7	1.3	184.5
Soviet Union[d]	124,000	n.a.	490	n.a.	n.a.	n.a.	12–14%		3,673.0
NATO[e]									
Belgium	1,971	3,560	200	359	10.0	9.0	3.0	3.3	89.5
Britain	11,118	28,660	198	512	11.6	12.3	4.9	5.1	343.6
Canada[f]	2,965	4,990	130	205	11.9	9.1	2.2	1.7	79.5
Denmark	939	1,520	185	295	7.3	7.1	2.2	2.4	32.6
France	13,984	26,008	264	483	20.2	20.5	3.9	3.9	504.6
Germany[g]	16,142	25,000	259	405	24.4	22.6	3.7	3.2	495.0
Greece	1,435	n.a.	159	n.a.	25.5	n.a.	6.9	5.1	193.5
Italy	4,700	8,887	84	155	9.7	5.1	2.6	2.4	366.0
Luxembourg	22	51	65	140	3.0	3.3	1.1	1.0	0.7
Netherlands	2,978	4,930	218	348	11.0	9.5	3.6	3.4	102.8
Norway	929	n.a.	232	n.a.	8.2	n.a.	3.1	2.9	37.0
Portugal	1,088[f]	944	124	94	35.2	10.9	6.0	3.8	70.9
Turkey[f]	2,200	3,106	55	67	26.6	19.0	9.0	4.2	569.0
United States	88,983	171,023	417	759	23.8	23.7	5.9	5.5	2,049.1
OTHER EUROPEAN									
Austria	410	870	54	116	3.7	3.8	1.0	1.2	50.3
Finland	388	713	83	149	5.0	5.1	1.4	1.5	39.9
Ireland	128	285[h]	41	86[h]	4.3	3.3[h]	1.6	n.a.	14.0
Spain	1,701	3,980	48	105	14.5	12.0	1.8	n.a.	342.0
Sweden	2,483	3,790	303	455	10.5	7.7	3.4	3.2	64.3
Switzerland	1,047	1,840	160	154	19.3	20.2	1.8	n.a.	20.5
Yugoslavia	1,705	3,470	80	154	49.9	56.9[h]	5.6	n.a.	252.5
MIDDLE EAST									
Algeria	285	914	17	47	4.7	5.3[h]	2.2	n.a.	101.0
Egypt	6,103	n.a.	163	n.a.	42.0	n.a.	50.4	n.a.	367.0
Iran	8,800	4,200[h]	268	110[h]	24.9	12.3[h]	17.4	n.a.	195.0
Iraq	1,064	2,700[h]	107	202[h]	43.7	24.0[h]	7.9	n.a.	252.3
Israel	3,552	7,340	1,045	1,835	50.1	30.6	35.9	23.2	172.0
Jordan	155	420	57	127	22.0	25.0	12.2	n.a.	67.5
Libya	203	n.a.	83	n.a.	13.7	n.a.	1.7	n.a.	55.0
Morocco	224	1,210	13	56	4.5	16.7	2.8	6.7	120.0
Saudi Arabia	6,771	27,695	1,153	2,664	20.0	31.0	18.0	n.a.	51.7
Sudan	120	245[h]	7	13[h]	15.1	12.7[h]	n.a.	n.a.	71.0
Syria	706	2,389	96	261	25.3	30.8	15.1	13.1	222.5
AFRICA									
Ethiopia	84	385[h]	3	17[h]	19.4	n.a.	2.9	n.a.	230.0
Nigeria	1,786	1,702[h]	28	22[h]	11.8	8.7[h]	7.1	n.a.	156.0
South Africa	1,332	2,556[h]	53	89[h]	18.5	18.1[h]	5.3	n.a.	92.7
Zimbabwe	102	444[h]	16	6[h]	12.3	22.0[h]	3.0	n.a.	34.0
ASIA									
Australia	2,492	3,900[h]	184	272[h]	8.6	9.7[h]	3.2	3.0	72.6
China	n.a.	56,941[h]	n.a.	56[h]	n.a.	n.a.	n.a.	n.a.	4,750.0
China (Taiwan)	1,007	n.a.	61	n.a.	n.a.	n.a.	6.9	n.a.	451.0
India	2,660	5,119	4	7	21.1	16.9	3.0	3.8	1,104.0
Indonesia	1,108	2,387	9	5	16.7	n.a.	3.8	n.a.	273.0
Japan	4,620	11,497	42	98	6.6	5.0	0.9	0.9	243.0
Korea, North	878	1,470	54	74	n.a.	14.7	n.a.	n.a.	782.0
Korea, South	943	4,400	28	113	29.2	n.a.	5.1	5.7	601.6
Malaysia	385	2,250	31	157	17.3	23.0	4.0	n.a.	102.0
New Zealand	243	426[h]	79	135[h]	4.3	3.9[h]	1.8	1.8	12.9
Pakistan	725	1,540[h]	10	17	12.3	n.a.	7.2	n.a.	450.6
Philippines	407	863	10	17	19.3	13.0[h]	2.6	2.0	112.8
Singapore	344	574[h]	152	239[h]	18.1	16.5[h]	5.3	6.1	42.0
Thailand	542	1,279	13	26	25.7	18.7	3.7	n.a.	238.1
LATIN AMERICA									
Argentina	1,031	3,380[h]	41	123[h]	9.7	15.1[h]	0.9	n.a.	185.5
Brazil	1,283	1,540[h]	12	13[h]	9.3	6.8[h]	1.3	0.7	272.6
Colombia	106	31[h]	4	12[h]	n.a.	9.3[h]	0.8	n.a.	70.0
Cuba	n.a.	1,100[h]	111[h]	n.a.	n.a.	n.a.	n.a.	8.5	227.0
Mexico	586	1,166	10	17	2.4	1.1[h]	0.7	n.a.	369.5
Peru	383	n.a.	24	n.a.	15.3	n.a.	3.1	n.a.	130.0
Venezuela	494	1,399	41	85	5.4	n.a.	1.7	2.3	40.8

[a] This series is designed to show national trends only; differences in the scope of the government sector invalidate international comparisons.
[b] Based on local currency. GNP estimated where official figures unavailable.
[c] The difficulty of calculating suitable exchange rates makes conversion to dollars imprecise.
[d] Estimated in rubles.
[e] Defense expenditures are based on the NATO definition.
[f] Expenditure and GNP figures estimated from nationally-defined data.
[g] Incl. aid to W. Berlin.
[h] 1980.

Source: "The Military Balance, 1981–1982," The International Institute for Strategic Studies.

WORLD MINERAL PRODUCTION

Aluminum, primary smelter (thousand metric tons)

	1979	1980
United States	4,557	4,650
USSR	1,750	1,790
Japan	1,010	1,091
Canada	860	1,068
West Germany	742	731
Norway	660	651
France	395	432
Spain	260	386
United Kingdom	359	374
China[e]	360	360
Venezuela	207	313
Other countries[a]	3,403	3,522
Total	14,563	15,368

Antimony, mine [b] (metric tons)

	1979	1980
Bolivia	13,019	15,465
South Africa	11,652	13,073
China[e]	10,000	10,000
USSR[e]	8,200	8,200
Mexico	2,872	[e]2,900
Thailand	2,935	[e]2,850
Canada	2,953	2,140
Morocco	1,973	[e]2,000
Turkey[e]	1,900	1,800
Australia	1,558	[e]1,560
Yugoslavia	2,036	1,540
Other countries[a]	6,159	5,663
Total	65,257	67,191

Asbestos[c] (thousand metric tons)

	1979	1980
USSR[e]	2,020	2,150
Canada	1,493	1,291
South Africa	249	[e]270
Zimbabwe	260	[e]251
China[e]	250	250
Other countries[a]	618	606
Total	4,890	4,818

Barite[c] (thousand metric tons)

	1979	1980
United States	1,916	2,037
China[e]	500	680
USSR[e]	500	500
Peru	436	450
India	387	346
Ireland	328	[e]330
Morocco	287	[e]318
Thailand	378	305
Mexico	151	269
Italy	215	[e]220
Other countries[a]	2,028	2,037
Total	7,126	7,492

Bauxite[d] (thousand metric tons)

	1979	1980
Australia	27,583	27,584
Guinea	13,700	13,780
Jamaica	11,505	12,261
USSR[d e]	6,180	6,180
Surinam	5,010	[e]4,696
Brazil	2,388	[e]3,970
Yugoslavia	3,012	3,138
Hungary	2,976	[e]3,020
Greece	2,915	[e]2,950
Guyana	2,312	[e]2,348
India	1,934	1,740
France	1,969	1,665
United States	1,821	1,559
Other countries[a]	5,951	6,522
Total	89,256	91,413

Cement,[c] (thousand metric tons)

	1979	1980
USSR	123,019	[e]125,000
Japan	87,804	88,128
China	73,900	81,400
United States	77,931	69,589
Italy	40,140	42,825
West Germany	37,036	35,798
France	28,824	29,104
Spain	27,912	28,458
Brazil	24,880	[e]26,490
Poland	19,176	18,443
India	18,264	[e]17,510
Mexico	15,178	[e]16,000
Rumania	15,598	15,600
Other countries[a]	284,154	292,542
Total	873,816	886,887

Coal, anthracite and bituminous (million metric tons)

	1979	1980
United States	670.6	709.3
China	635.0	620.0
USSR	554.0	552.0
Poland	201.0	193.1
United Kingdom	122.8	130.1
South Africa	103.8	112.2
India	103.8	[e]106.0
Australia	93.0	94.4
West Germany	86.3	87.1
North Korea[e]	43.8	44.8

Coal, anthracite and bituminous (cont'd.) (million metric tons)

	1979	1980
Canada	28.0	31.0
Other countries[a]	156.1	157.0
Total	2,798.2	2,837.0

Coal, lignite[f] (million metric tons)

	1979	1980
East Germany	256.1	258.4
USSR	164.8	[e]164.0
West Germany	130.5	129.8
Czechoslovakia	96.9	95.5
Yugoslavia	41.7	46.6
United States	38.0	43.4
Poland	38.1	36.9
Australia	32.6	32.9
Other countries[a]	143.7	161.1
Total	942.4	968.6

Copper, mine[b] (thousand metric tons)

	1979	1980
United States	1,444	1,168
Chile	1,061	1,068
USSR[e]	885	900
Canada	636	710
Zambia	588	596
Zaire	400	459
Peru	400	365
Poland	325	346
Philippines	301	[e]324
Australia	235	217
South Africa	191	[e]215
China[e]	200	200
Mexico	107	175
Papua New Guinea	171	147
Other countries[a]	731	727
Total	7,675	7,617

Copper, refined, primary and secondary (thousand metric tons)

	1979	1980
United States	2,014	1,726
USSR[e]	1,000	1,115
Japan	984	1,014
Chile	780	811
Zambia	564	607
Canada	397	505
West Germany	383	374
Belgium	369	374
Poland	336	357
China[e]	280	280
United Kingdom	122	162
Spain	144	158
Australia	138	145
Zaire	103	144
South Africa	151	141
Other countries[a]	1,147	1,129
Total	8,912	9,042

Diamond (thousand carats)

	1979	1980
USSR	10,700	10,850
Zaire	8,734	10,235
South Africa	8,384	8,522
Botswana	4,394	5,101
Namibia	1,653	1,560
Ghana	1,253	[e]1,200
Other countries[a]	3,895	4,125
Total	39,013	41,593

Fluorspar[g] (thousand metric tons)

	1979	1980
Mexico	965	920
USSR[e]	520	520
South Africa	451	[e]500
Mongolia[e]	450	450
China[e]	400	400
Spain	193	[e]340
France	291	[e]290
Thailand	234	[e]233
Italy	183	145
East Germany[e]	100	100
Kenya	100	100
Czechoslovakia[e]	96	96
Other countries[a]	606	556
Total	4,589	4,650

Gas, natural[h] (billion cubic feet)

	1979	1980
United States	20,373	19,992
USSR	14,359	15,362
Canada	3,271	3,320
Netherlands	3,292	3,211
United Kingdom	1,410	1,352
Rumania	1,161	[e]1,203
Mexico	915	1,129
Algeria	916	[e]1,000
Other countries[a]	8,803	8,981
Total	54,500	55,500

Gold, mine (thousand troy ounces)

	1979	1980
South Africa	22,617	21,669
USSR[e]	8,160	8,300
Canada	1,644	1,552
Brazil[e]	354	1,300

Gold, mine (cont'd.) (thousand troy ounces)

	1979	1980
United States	970	951
Philippines	561	701
Australia	597	557
Papua New Guinea	630	452
Dominican Republic	353	[e]370
Zimbabwe	386	[e]367
Other countries[a]	2,850	2,611
Total	38,802	38,830

Graphite[c] (thousand metric tons)

	1979	1980
China[e]	100	100
USSR[e]	100	100
South Korea	57	61
Mexico	51	[e]56
India	51	49
Czechoslovakia[e]	45	45
Austria	41	[e]40
Other countries[a]	91	91
Total	536	542

Gypsum[c] (thousand metric tons)

	1979	1980
United States	13,272	11,321
Canada	8,098	7,209
Iran[e]	7,000	6,800
France	5,900	[e]6,000
Spain	5,275	[e]5,500
USSR	5,400	5,400
United Kingdom	3,500	[e]3,500
West Germany	2,251	[e]2,250
Mexico	2,021	[e]2,000
China[e]	2,000	2,000
Italy	1,479	1,642
Poland	1,360	1,300
Other countries[a]	18,785	20,608
Total	76,341	74,230

Iron ore[c] (thousand metric tons)

	1979	1980
USSR	241,739	245,000
Brazil	104,083	[e]106,000
Australia	91,717	95,542
China[e]	75,000	75,000
United States	87,092	70,672
Canada	59,888	48,754
India	39,535	40,670
France	31,627	28,980
Sweden	26,619	27,184
South Africa	29,565	26,313
Liberia	18,344	[e]17,380
Venezuela	16,349	16,102
Other countries[a]	89,937	89,109
Total	911,495	886,706

Iron, steel ingots (thousand metric tons)

	1979	1980
USSR	149,099	148,000
Japan	111,748	111,408
United States	123,694	101,455
West Germany	46,040	43,840
China	34,430	36,100
Italy	24,250	26,509
France	23,264	23,165
Poland	19,218	19,484
Canada	16,078	15,901
Brazil	13,816	15,324
Czechoslovakia	14,817	14,225
Rumania	12,909	13,176
Belgium	13,442	12,320
Spain	12,304	[e]11,503
United Kingdom	21,476	11,304
India	9,996	[e]10,270
South Africa	8,875	[e]8,981
Australia	8,125	7,924
Other countries[a]	76,939	76,691
Total	740,520	707,580

Lead, mine output[b] (thousand metric tons)

	1979	1980
United States	526	550
USSR[e]	525	525
Australia	422	395
Canada	311	274
Peru	184	189
China[e]	155	155
Mexico	174	146
Morocco	116	[e]130
Yugoslavia	130	119
Other countries[a]	980	1,035
Total	3,523	3,518

Lead, refined, primary and secondary[i] (thousand metric tons)

	1979	1980
United States	1,226	1,150
USSR[e]	625	625
West Germany	373	350
United Kingdom	368	325
Japan	263	305
Canada	252	235
Australia	255	233
France	220	219
Mexico	225	185

	1979	1980
Lead, refined, primary and secondary[i] (cont'd.)		
(thousand metric tons)		
China[e]	170	175
Italy	126	134
Spain	127	121
Bulgaria	120	[e]118
Other countries[a]	1,088	1,279
Total	5,438	5,235
Magnesium, primary		
(thousand metric tons)		
United States	147	154
USSR[e]	72	75
Norway	44	[e]44
Canada	9	9
France	9	[e]9
Japan	11	9
Italy	9	[e]9
China[e]	6	7
Yugoslavia	2	2
Total	309	318
Manganese ore[c]		
(thousand metric tons)		
USSR	10,244	10,251
South Africa	5,182	5,695
Brazil	2,259	[e]2,180
Gabon	2,300	2,147
Australia	1,666	1,961
India	1,755	1,645
China	1,500	1,600
Other countries[a]	1,217	1,347
Total	26,123	26,826
Mercury[b]		
(76-pound flasks)		
USSR[e]	61,000	62,000
Spain	33,275	[e]33,000
United States	29,519	30,657
Algeria[e]	30,000	30,000
China[e]	20,000	20,000
Other countries[a]	16,245	15,412
Total	190,039	191,069
Molybdenum, mine[b]		
(metric tons)		
United States	65,302	68,212
Chile	13,559	13,341
Canada	11,175	12,198
USSR[e]	10,200	10,400
China[e]	2,000	2,000
Other countries[a]	1,811	1,712
Total	104,047	107,863
Natural gas liquids		
(million barrels)		
United States	611	[e]600
USSR[e]	120	130
Canada	102	118
Saudi Arabia[e]	100	105
Mexico	57	71
Algeria	34	[e]32
Other countries[a]	148	148
Total	1,172	1,204
Nickel, mine[b]		
(thousand metric tons)		
Canada	126	195
USSR[e]	152	154
New Caledonia	83	88
Australia	70	71
Philippines	29	38
Cuba	35	37
Indonesia	37	[e]37
Other countries[a]	151	151
Total	683	771
Nitrogen fertilizers[j]		
(thousand metric tons)		
United States	10,212	11,239
USSR[k]	9,220	9,074
China[e]	7,637	8,821
India	2,173	2,224
Rumania[k]	1,723	1,738
France	1,781	1,650
Canada	1,560	1,607
Netherlands	1,518	1,500
Italy	1,427	1,500
West Germany	1,781	1,476
Poland[k]	1,470	1,376
Other countries[a]	15,508	17,405
Total	56,010	59,610

	1979	1980
Petroleum, crude		
(million barrels)		
USSR	4,304	4,432
Saudi Arabia	3,479	[e]3,530
United States	3,114	3,146
Iraq	1,252	[e]961
Venezuela	860	793
China[e]	775	772
Nigeria	841	754
Mexico	533	708
Libya	754	654
United Arab Emirates	663	624
Kuwait	913	[e]602
United Kingdom	562	581
Iran	1,121	[e]550
Indonesia	601	[e]537
Algeria	421	398
Other countries[a]	2,723	2,729
Total	22,916	21,771
Phosphate rock[c]		
(thousand metric tons)		
United States	51,611	54,415
USSR	25,580	[e]26,000
Morocco	20,032	18,824
China[e]	5,500	5,500
Tunisia	4,154	4,582
Jordan	2,825	4,243
Senegal	3,221	3,185
Togo	2,920	2,933
Israel	2,216	2,610
Other countries[a]	12,112	12,596
Total	130,171	134,888
Potash, K_2O equivalent basis		
(thousand metric tons)		
USSR	6,635	[e]8,000
Canada	7,074	7,532
East Germany	3,395	3,422
West Germany	2,690	2,674
United States	2,225	2,239
France	1,920	1,939
Other countries[a]	1,994	2,065
Total	25,933	27,871
Salt[c]		
(thousand metric tons)		
United States	41,567	36,631
China	15,770	17,280
USSR[e]	14,300	14,500
West Germany	15,089	12,970
India	7,036	7,262
France	8,058	7,103
Canada	6,881	7,029
United Kingdom	7,819	6,586
Mexico	5,625	[e]5,985
Italy	4,762	5,267
Rumania	4,720	4,717
Poland	4,429	3,357
Other countries[a]	35,797	36,064
Total	171,853	164,751
Silver, mine[b]		
(thousand troy ounces)		
Mexico	49,310	49,408
Peru	43,415	[e]47,900
USSR[e]	46,000	46,000
Canada	36,874	33,340
United States	38,087	31,327
Australia	26,816	24,714
Poland[e]	22,600	23,100
Japan	8,680	[e]8,930
Chile	8,740	[e]8,500
Bolivia	5,742	6,099
South Africa	3,236	[e]5,500
Sweden	5,649	[e]5,000
Other countries[a]	50,809	51,552
Total	345,958	341,370
Sulfur, all forms[l]		
(thousand tons)		
United States	12,101	11,839
USSR[e]	10,550	10,900
Canada	7,027	7,405
Poland	5,195	[e]4,850
Japan	2,894	[e]2,900
Mexico	2,374	2,552
China[e]	2,282	2,300
France	2,190	[e]2,077
West Germany	1,811	[e]1,800
Spain	1,152	[e]1,240
Other countries[a]	7,631	8,214
Total	55,207	56,077

	1979	1980
Tin, mine[b]		
(thousand metric tons)		
Malaysia	63	61
USSR[e]	35	36
Thailand	34	34
Indonesia	30	33
Bolivia	28	27
China[e]	14	15
Other countries[a]	41	40
Total	245	246
Titanium materials[c m]		
(thousand metric tons)		
Ilmenite		
Australia	1,172	1,331
Norway	820	828
United States	580	498
USSR[e]	410	420
India	144	[e]180
Malaysia	200	160
Other countries[a]	186	195
Total	3,512	3,612
Rutile		
Australia	279	294
Other countries[a]	81	129
Total	360	423
Titaniferous slag		
Canada	477	875
South Africa	287	344
Total	764	1,219
Tungsten, mine[b]		
(metric tons)		
China[e]	10,000	15,000
USSR[e]	8,700	8,700
Canada	2,581	3,688
Bolivia	3,114	3,359
Australia	3,193	3,332
South Korea	2,713	2,737
United States	3,015	2,708
North Korea	2,150	2,200
Portugal	1,378	[e]1,700
Thailand	1,826	1,616
Austria	1,496	1,495
Other countries[a]	6,876	6,738
Total	47,042	53,273
Uranium Oxide (U_3O_8)[b n]		
(metric tons)		
United States	16,970	[e]17,000
Canada	7,701	7,509
South Africa	5,637	7,295
Namibia	4,980	5,250
Niger	3,740	[e]4,000
Other countries[a]	5,965	6,962
Total	44,993	48,016
Zinc, mine[b]		
(thousand metric tons)		
Canada	1,100	895
USSR[e]	770	785
Australia	532	494
Peru	491	487
United States	267	335
Mexico	246	238
Japan	243	238
Ireland	212	229
Poland	183	[e]180
Spain	143	168
Sweden	170	167
Other countries[a]	1,560	1,545
Total	5,917	5,761
Zinc, smelter		
(thousand metric tons)		
USSR[e]	850	865
Japan	816	782
Canada	580	592
United States	526	370
West Germany	356	365
Australia	310	306
Belgium	262	252
France	249	253
Italy	203	206
Poland	209	[e]205
Netherlands	154	170
Spain	183	162
China[e]	160	160
Finland	147	147
Other countries[a]	1,240	1,201
Total	6,245	6,036

[a] Estimated in part. [b] Content of ore. [c] Gross weight. [d] Includes calculated bauxite equivalent of estimated output of ores of aluminum other than bauxite (nepheline concentrates and alunite ores). [e] Estimate. [f] Includes coal classified in some countries as brown coal. [g] Marketable gross weight. [h] Marketed production (includes gas sold or used by producers, excludes gas reinjected to reservoirs for pressure maintenance and that flared or vented to the atmosphere which has no economic value and which does not represent a part of world energy consumption). [i] Excludes bullion produced for refining elsewhere. [j] Source: British Sulphur Corp.; except as individually noted, figures represent output for years ended June 30 of that stated. [k] Calendar year. [l] Includes (1) Frasch process sulfur, (2) elemental sulfur mined by conventional methods, (3) by-product recovered elemental sulfur, and (4) recovered sulfur content of pyrite and other sulfide ores. [m] Excludes output (if any) by China. [n] Excludes output (if any) by Albania, Bulgaria, China, Czechoslovakia, East Germany, Hungary, North Korea, Mongolia, Poland, Rumania, USSR, and Vietnam.

Compiled by Charles L. Kimbell, United States Bureau of Mines

THE UNITED STATES GOVERNMENT

EXECUTIVE BRANCH
(selected listing, as of Dec. 31, 1981)

President: Ronald Reagan

Vice-President: George Bush

Executive Office of the President
The White House

Counsellor to the President: Edwin Meese III
Chief of Staff and Assistant to the President: James A. Baker III
Deputy Chief of Staff and Assistant to the President: Michael K. Deaver
Assistant to the President for National Security Affairs: Richard V. Allen (resigned Jan. 4, 1982)
Assistant to the President for Policy Development: Martin Anderson
Assistant to the President and Press Secretary: James S. Brady
Assistant to the President for Public Liaison: Elizabeth H. Dole
Counsel to the President: Fred R. Fielding
Assistant to the President for Legislative Affairs: Max L. Friedersdorf (resigned effective Jan. 2, 1982)
Assistant to the President and Staff Director: David R. Gergen
Assistant to the President: Edwin L. Harper
Assistant to the President for Presidential Personnel: E. Pendleton James
Assistant to the President for Political Affairs: Edward J. Rollins, Jr.
Assistant to the President for Intergovernmental Affairs: Richard S. Williamson
Deputy Press Secretary: Larry Speakes
Office of Management and Budget, Director: David A. Stockman
Council of Economic Advisers, Chairman: Murray L. Weidenbaum
Office of United States Trade Representative, U.S. Trade Representative: William E. Brock
Council on Environmental Quality, Chairman: A. Alan Hill
Office of Science and Technology Policy, Director: George A. Keyworth II
Office of Administration, Director: John F. W. Rogers II

The Cabinet

Department of Agriculture
Secretary: John R. Block
Deputy Secretary: Richard E. Lyng

Department of Commerce
Secretary: Malcolm Baldrige
Deputy Secretary: Joseph R. Wright, Jr.
National Oceanic and Atmospheric Administrator: John V. Byrne
National Bureau of Standards, Director: Ernest Ambler
Bureau of the Census, Director: Bruce Chapman

Department of Defense
Secretary: Caspar W. Weinberger
Deputy Secretary: Frank C. Carlucci
Joint Chiefs of Staff
  Chairman: Gen. David C. Jones, USAF
  Chief of Staff, Army: Gen. Edward C. Meyer, USA
  Chief of Staff, Air Force: Gen. Lew Allen, Jr., USAF
  Chief of Naval Operations: Adm. T. B. Hayward, USN
  Commandant, Marine Corp: Gen. R. H. Barrow, USMC
Secretary of the Air Force: Verne Orr
Secretary of the Army: John O. Marsh, Jr.
Secretary of the Navy: John F. Lehman, Jr.

Department of Education
Secretary: Terrel H. Bell

Department of Energy
Secretary: James B. Edwards
Deputy Secretary: W. Kenneth Davis

Department of Health and Human Services
Secretary: Richard S. Schweiker
Undersecretary: David B. Swoap
Surgeon General: C. Everett Koop
Alcohol, Drug Abuse, and Mental Health Administrator: William E. Mayer
Centers for Disease Control, Director: William H. Foege
National Institutes of Health, Director: Donald S. Fredrickson
Social Security Administration, Commissioner: John A. Svahn

Department of Housing and Urban Development
Secretary: Samuel R. Pierce, Jr.
Undersecretary: Donald I. Hovde

Department of the Interior
Secretary: James G. Watt
Undersecretary: Donald P. Hodel
Assistant Secretary for Indian Affairs: John W. Fritz
Fish and Wildlife Service, Director: Robert A. Jantzen
National Park Service, Director: Russell E. Dickenson
Bureau of Mines, Director: Robert C. Horton

Department of Justice
Attorney General: William French Smith
Deputy Attorney General: Edward C. Schmultz
Solicitor General: Rex E. Lee
Federal Bureau of Investigation, Director: William H. Webster
Drug Enforcement Administrator: Peter B. Bensinger
Immigration and Naturalization Service, Commissioner: Norman Braman
Bureau of Prisons, Director: Norman A. Carlson

Department of Labor
Secretary: Raymond J. Donovan
Undersecretary: Malcolm R. Lovell, Jr.
Women's Bureau, Director: Lenora Cole-Alexander
Commissioner of Labor Statistics: Janet L. Norwood

Department of State
Secretary: Alexander M. Haig, Jr.
Chief of Protocol: Lenore Annenberg
Undersecretary for Political Affairs: W. J. Stoessel, Jr.
Undersecretary for Security Assistance, Science and Technology: James L. Buckley
Undersecretary for Management: Richard T. Kennedy
Assistant Secretary for Human Rights and Humanitarian Affairs: Elliott Abrams
Assistant Secretary for African Affairs: Chester A. Crocker
Assistant Secretary for East Asian and Pacific Affairs: John H. Holdridge
Assistant Secretary for European Affairs: Lawrence S. Eagleburger
Assistant Secretary for Inter-American Affairs: Thomas O. Enders
Assistant Secretary for Near Eastern and South Asian Affairs: Nicholas A. Veliotes
Assistant Secretary for Administration: Thomas M. Tracy
United Nations Representative: Jeane J. Kirkpatrick

Department of Transportation
Secretary: Andrew L. Lewis, Jr.
Deputy Secretary: Darrell M. Trent
U.S. Coast Guard, Commandant: Adm. John B. Hayes, USCG
Federal Aviation Administrator: J. Lynn Helms
Federal Highway Administrator: R. A. Barnhart
Federal Railroad Administrator: Robert W. Blanchette

Department of the Treasury
Secretary: Donald T. Regan
Deputy Secretary: R. T. McNamar
Undersecretary for Monetary Affairs: Beryl W. Sprinkel
Undersecretary for Tax and Economic Affairs: Norman B. Ture
Comptroller of the Currency: C. T. Conover
Internal Revenue Service, Commissioner: Roscoe L. Egger

Independent Agencies

ACTION, Director: Thomas W. Pauken
  Peace Corps, Director: Loret M. Ruppe
Appalachian Regional Commission, Federal cochairman: Albert P. Smith, Jr.
Central Intelligence Agency, Director: William J. Casey
Civil Aeronautics Board, Chairman: Clinton D. McKinnon
Commission on Civil Rights, Chairman: Clarence M. Pendleton, Jr.
Commission of Fine Arts, Chairman: J. Carter Brown
Consumer Product Safety Commission, Chairman: Nancy H. Steorts
Environmental Protection Agency, Administrator: Anne McGill Gorsuch
Equal Employment Opportunity Commissioner: William M. Bell
Export-Import Bank, President and Chairman: William H. Draper III
Federal Communications Commission, Chairman: Mark S. Fowler
Federal Deposit Insurance Corporation, Chairman: William M. Isaac
Federal Election Commission, Chairman: John Warren McGarry
Federal Emergency Management Agency, Director: Louis O. Giuffrida
Federal Farm Credit Board, Chairman: William Dale Nix
Federal Home Loan Bank Board, Chairman: Richard T. Pratt
Federal Labor Relations Authority, Chairman: Ronald W. Haughton
Federal Maritime Commission, Chairman: Alan Green, Jr.
Federal Mediation and Conciliation Service, Director: Kenneth E. Moffett, acting
Federal Reserve System, Chairman: Paul A. Volcker
Federal Trade Commission, Chairman: James C. Miller III
General Services Administrator: Gerald P. Carmen
International Communication Agency, Director: Charles Z. Wick
Interstate Commerce Commission, Chairman: Reese H. Taylor, Jr.
National Aeronautics and Space Administration, Administrator: James M. Beggs
National Foundation on the Arts and Humanities
  National Endowment for the Arts, Chairman: Francis S. M. Hodsoll
  National Endowment for the Humanities, Chairman: William J. Bennett
National Labor Relations Board, Chairman: John R. Van de Water
National Science Foundation, Director: John B. Slaughter
National Transportation Safety Board, Chairman: James B. King
Nuclear Regulatory Commission, Chairman: Nunzio J. Palladino
Postal Rate Commission, Chairman: Kieran O'Doherty
Securities and Exchange Commission, Chairman: John S. R. Shad
Selective Service System, Director, Maj. Gen. Thomas K. Turnage
Small Business Administrator: Michael Cardenas
Tennessee Valley Authority, Chairman: Charles H. Dean, Jr.
U.S. Arms Control and Disarmament Agency, Director: Eugene V. Rostow
U.S. International Development Cooperation Agency, Director: M. Peter McPherson
U.S. International Trade Commission, Chairman: Bill Alberger
U.S. Postal Service, Postmaster General: William F. Bolger
Veterans Administrator: Robert P. Nimmo

THE SUPREME COURT

Warren E. Burger, chief justice
William J. Brennan, Jr.
Byron R. White
Thurgood Marshall
Harry A. Blackmun
Lewis F. Powell, Jr.
William H. Rehnquist
John Paul Stevens
Sandra Day O'Connor

THE 97TH CONGRESS

Senate Committee Chairmen

Agriculture, Nutrition, and Forestry: Jesse Helms (NC)
Appropriations: Mark O. Hatfield (OR)
Armed Services: John Tower (TX)
Banking, Housing, and Urban Affairs: Jake Garn (UT)
Budget: Peter V. Domenici (NM)
Commerce, Science, and Transportation: Bob Packwood (OR)
Energy and Natural Resources: James A. McClure (ID)
Environment and Public Works: Robert T. Stafford (VT)
Finance: Bob Dole (KS)
Foreign Relations: Charles H. Percy (IL)
Government Affairs: William V. Roth, Jr. (DE)
Judiciary: Strom Thurmond (SC)
Labor and Human Resources: Orrin G. Hatch (UT)
Rules and Administration: Charles McC. Mathias, Jr. (MD)
Small Business: Lowell P. Weicker, Jr. (CT)
Veterans' Affairs: Alan K. Simpson (WY)

Select Senate Committee Chairmen

Aging: John Heinz (PA)
Ethics: Malcolm Wallop (WY)
Indian Affairs: William S. Cohen (ME)
Intelligence: Barry Goldwater (AZ)

House Committee Chairmen

Agriculture: E. de la Garza (TX)
Appropriations: Jamie L. Whitten (MS)
Armed Services: Melvin Price (IL)
Banking, Finance and Urban Affairs: Fernand J. St. Germain (RI)
Budget: James R. Jones (OK)
District of Columbia: Ronald V. Dellums (CA)
Education and Labor: Carl D. Perkins (KY)
Energy and Commerce: John D. Dingell (MI)
Foreign Affairs: Clement J. Zablocki (WI)
Government Operations: Jack Brooks (TX)
House Administration: Augustus F. Hawkins (CA)
Interior and Insular Affairs: Morris K. Udall (AZ)
Judiciary: Peter W. Rodino, Jr. (NJ)
Merchant Marine and Fisheries: Walter B. Jones (NC)
Post Office and Civil Service: William D. Ford (MI)
Public Works and Transportation: James J. Howard (NJ)
Rules: Richard Bolling (MO)
Science and Technology: Don Fugua (FL)
Small Business: Parren J. Mitchell (MD)
Standards of Official Conduct: Louis Stokes (OH)
Veterans' Affairs: G. V. Montgomery (MS)
Ways and Means: Dan Rostenkowski (IL)

Select House Committees

Aging: Claude Pepper (FL)
Intelligence: Edward P. Boland (MA)
Narcotics Abuse and Control: Leo C. Zeferetti (NY)

UNITED STATES: 97th CONGRESS
Second Session

SENATE MEMBERSHIP

(As of January 1982: 53 Republicans, 47 Democrats)

Letters after senators' names refer to party affiliation—D for Democrat, R for Republican. Single asterisk (*) denotes term expiring in January 1983; double asterisk (**), term expiring in January 1985; triple asterisk (***), term expiring in January 1987; (1) ran as independent; (2) appointed in 1980 to fill vacancy.

ALABAMA
**H. Heflin, D
***J. Denton, R

ALASKA
**T. Stevens, R
***F. H. Murkowski, R

ARIZONA
***B. Goldwater, R
*D. DeConcini, D

ARKANSAS
***D. Bumpers, D
**D. Pryor, D

CALIFORNIA
***A. Cranston, D
*S. I. Hayakawa, R

COLORADO
***G. Hart, D
**W. Armstrong, R

CONNECTICUT
*L. P. Weicker, Jr., R
***C. J. Dodd, D

DELAWARE
*W. V. Roth, Jr., R
**J. R. Biden, Jr., D

FLORIDA
*L. M. Chiles, Jr., D
***P. Hawkins, R

GEORGIA
**S. Nunn, D
***M. Mattingly, R

HAWAII
***D. K. Inouye, D
*S. M. Matsunaga, D

IDAHO
**J. A. McClure, R
***S. D. Symms, R

ILLINOIS
**C. H. Percy, R
***A. J. Dixon, D

INDIANA
*R. G. Lugar, R
***D. Quayle, R

IOWA
**R. Jepsen, R
***C. E. Grassley, R

KANSAS
***R. J. Dole, R
**N. Kassebaum, R

KENTUCKY
**W. Huddleston, D
***W. H. Ford, D

LOUISIANA
***R. B. Long, D
**J. B. Johnston, D

MAINE
**W. Cohen, R
*G. Mitchell, D (2)

MARYLAND
***C. M. Mathias, Jr., R
*P. S. Sarbanes, D

MASSACHUSETTS
*E. M. Kennedy, D
**P. Tsongas, D

MICHIGAN
*D. W. Riegle, Jr., D
**C. Levin, D

MINNESOTA
*D. Durenberger, R
**R. Boschwitz, R

MISSISSIPPI
*J. C. Stennis, D
**T. Cochran, R

MISSOURI
***T. F. Eagleton, D
*J. C. Danforth, R

MONTANA
*J. Melcher, D
**M. Baucus, D

NEBRASKA
*E. Zorinsky, D
**J. Exon, D

NEVADA
*H. W. Cannon, D
***P. Laxalt, R

NEW HAMPSHIRE
**G. Humphrey, R
***W. Rudman, R

NEW JERSEY
*H. A. Williams, Jr., D
**W. Bradley, D

NEW MEXICO
**P. V. Domenici, R
*H. Schmitt, R

NEW YORK
*D. P. Moynihan, D
***A. D'Amato, R

NORTH CAROLINA
**J. Helms, R
***J. P. East, R

NORTH DAKOTA
**Q. N. Burdick, D
***M. Andrews, R

OHIO
***J. H. Glenn, Jr., D
*H. M. Metzenbaum, D

OKLAHOMA
**D. Boren, D
***D. Nickles, R

OREGON
**M. O. Hatfield, R
***B. Packwood, R

PENNSYLVANIA
*H. J. Heinz, III, R
***A. Specter, R

RHODE ISLAND
**C. Pell, D
*J. H. Chafee, R

SOUTH CAROLINA
**S. Thurmond, R
***E. F. Hollings, D

SOUTH DAKOTA
**L. Pressler, R
***J. Abdnor, R

TENNESSEE
**H. H. Baker, Jr., R
*J. Sasser, D

TEXAS
**J. G. Tower, R
*L. M. Bentsen, D

UTAH
***J. Garn, R
*O. Hatch, R

VERMONT
**R. T. Stafford, R
***P. J. Leahy, D

VIRGINIA
*H. F. Byrd, Jr., D (1)
**J. Warner, R

WASHINGTON
*H. M. Jackson, D
***S. Gorton, R

WEST VIRGINIA
**J. Randolph, D
*R. C. Byrd, D

WISCONSIN
*W. Proximire, D
***R. W. Kasten, Jr., R

WYOMING
*M. Wallop, R
**A. Simpson, R

HOUSE MEMBERSHIP

(As of January 1982: 242 Democrats, 192 Republicans, 1 Vacant)

"At-L." in place of Congressional district number means "representative at large." *Indicates elected in special 1981 election; **special election scheduled Jan. 12, 1982.

ALABAMA
1. J. Edwards, R
2. W. L. Dickinson, R
3. W. Nichols, D
4. T. Bevill, D
5. R. Flippo, D
6. A. Smith, R
7. R. Shelby, D

ALASKA
At-L. D. Young, R

ARIZONA
1. J. J. Rhodes, R
2. M. K. Udall, D
3. B. Stump, D
4. E. Rudd, R

ARKANSAS
1. W. V. Alexander, Jr., D
2. E. Bethune, Jr., R
3. J. P. Hammerschmidt, R
4. B. Anthony, Jr., D

CALIFORNIA
1. E. Chappie, R
2. D. H. Clausen, R
3. R. Matsui, D
4. V. Fazio, D
5. J. L. Burton, D
6. P. Burton, D
7. G. Miller, D
8. R. V. Dellums, D
9. F. H. Stark, Jr., D
10. D. Edwards, D
11. T. Lantos, D
12. P. N. McCloskey, Jr., R
13. N. Y. Mineta, D
14. N. Shumway, R
15. T. Coelho, D
16. L. E. Panetta, D
17. C. Pashayan, R
18. W. Thomas, R
19. R. J. Lagomarsino, R
20. B. M. Goldwater, Jr., R
21. B. Fiedler, R
22. C. J. Moorhead, R
23. A. C. Beilenson, D
24. H. A. Waxman, D
25. E. R. Roybal, D
26. J. H. Rousselot, R
27. R. K. Dornan, R
28. J. Dixon, D
29. A. F. Hawkins, D
30. G. E. Danielson, D
31. M. Dymally, D
32. G. M. Anderson, D
33. W. Grisham, R
34. D. Lungren, R
35. D. Dreier, R
36. G. E. Brown, Jr., D
37. J. Lewis, R
38. J. M. Patterson, D
39. W. Dannemeyer, R
40. R. E. Badham, R
41. B. Lowery, R
42. D. Hunter R
43. C. W. Burgener, R

COLORADO
1. P. Schroeder, D
2. T. E. Wirth, D
3. R. Kogovsek, D
4. H. Brown, R
5. K. Kramer, R

CONNECTICUT
1. vacant**
2. S. Gejdenson, D
3. L. DeNardis, R
4. S. B. McKinney, R
5. W. Ratchford, D
6. T. Moffett, D

DELAWARE
At-L. T. B. Evans, Jr., R

FLORIDA
1. E. Hutto, D
2. D. Fuqua, D
3. C. E. Bennett, D
4. W. V. Chappell, Jr., D
5. B. McCollum, R
6. C. W. Young, R
7. S. M. Gibbons, D
8. A. P. Ireland, D
9. B. Nelson, D
10. L. A. Bafalis, R
11. D. Mica, D
12. C. Shaw, R
13. W. Lehman, D
14. C. D. Pepper, D
15. D. B. Fascell, D

GEORGIA
1. R. B. Ginn, D
2. C. Hatcher, D
3. J. Brinkley, D
4. E. H. Levitas, D
5. W. F. Fowler, Jr., D
6. N. Gingrich, R
7. L. P. McDonald, D
8. B. L. Evans, D
9. E. L. Jenkins, D
10. D. D. Barnard, Jr., D

HAWAII
1. C. Heftel, D
2. D. K. Akaka, D

IDAHO
1. L. Craig, R
2. G. V. Hansen, R

ILLINOIS
1. H. Washington, D
2. G. Savage, D
3. M. A. Russo, D
4. E. J. Derwinski, R
5. J. G. Fary, D
6. H. J. Hyde, R
7. C. Collins, D
8. D. Rostenkowski, D
9. S. R. Yates, D
10. J. Porter, R
11. F. Annunzio, D
12. P. M. Crane, R
13. R. McClory, R

14. J. N. Erlenborn, R
15. T. J. Corcoran, R
16. L. Martin, R
17. G. M. O'Brien, R
18. R. H. Michel, R
19. T. Railsback, R
20. P. Findley, R
21. E. R. Madigan, R
22. D. Crane, R
23. C. M. Price, D
24. P. Simon, D

INDIANA

1. A. Benjamin, Jr., D
2. F. J. Fithian, D
3. J. Hiler, R
4. D. Coats, R
5. E. H. Hillis, R
6. D. W. Evans, D
7. J. T. Myers, R
8. H. Deckard, R
9. L. H. Hamilton, D
10. P. R. Sharp, D
11. A. Jacobs, Jr., D

IOWA

1. J. A. S. Leach, R
2. T. Tauke, R
3. C. Evans, R
4. N. Smith, D
5. T. R. Harkin, D
6. B. W. Bedell, D

KANSAS

1. P. Roberts, R
2. J. Jeffries, R
3. L. Winn, Jr., R
4. D. Glickman, D
5. R. Whittaker, R

KENTUCKY

1. C. Hubbard, Jr., D
2. W. H. Natcher, D
3. R. L. Mazzoli, D
4. G. Snyder, R
5. H. Rogers, R
6. L. Hopkins, R
7. C. D. Perkins, D

LOUISIANA

1. R. L. Livingston, Jr., R
2. C. C. Boggs, D
3. W. J. Tauzin, D
4. C. Roemer, D
5. J. Huckaby, D
6. W. H. Moore, R
7. J. B. Breaux, D
8. G. W. Long, D

MAINE

1. D. F. Emery, R
2. O. Snowe, R

MARYLAND

1. R. Dyson, D
2. C. D. Long, D
3. B. A. Mikulski, D
4. M. S. Holt, R
5. S. Hoyer, D*
6. B. Byron, D
7. P. J. Mitchell, D
8. M. Barnes, D

MASSACHUSETTS

1. S. O. Conte, R
2. E. P. Boland, D
3. J. D. Early, D
4. B. Frank, D
5. J. Shannon, D
6. N. Mavroules, D
7. E. J. Markey, D
8. T. P. O'Neill, Jr., D
9. J. J. Moakley, D
10. M. M. Heckler, R
11. B. Donnelly, D
12. G. E. Studds, D

MICHIGAN

1. J. Conyers, Jr., D
2. C. D. Pursell, R
3. H. Wolpe, D
4. M. Siljander, R*
5. H. S. Sawyer, R
6. J. Dunn, R
7. D. E. Kildee, D
8. B. Traxler, D
9. G. A. Vander Jagt, R
10. D. Albosta, D
11. R. Davis, R
12. D. E. Bonior, D
13. G. Crockett, Jr., D
14. D. Hertel, D
15. W. D. Ford, D
16. J. D. Dingell, D
17. W. M. Brodhead, D
18. J. J. Blanchard, D
19. W. S. Broomfield, R

MINNESOTA

1. A. Erdahl, R
2. T. M. Hagedorn, R
3. B. Frenzel, R
4. B. F. Vento, D
5. M. Sabo, D
6. V. Weber, R
7. A. Stangeland, R
8. J. L. Oberstar, D

MISSISSIPPI

1. J. L. Whitten, D
2. D. R. Bowen, D
3. G. V. Montgomery, D
4. W. Dowdy, D*
5. T. Lott, R

MISSOURI

1. W. L. Clay, D
2. R. A. Young, D
3. R. A. Gephardt, D
4. I. Skelton, D
5. R. Bolling, D
6. E. T. Coleman, R
7. G. Taylor, R
8. W. Bailey, R
9. H. L. Volkmer, D
10. B. Emerson, R

MONTANA

1. P. Williams, D
2. R. Marlenee, R

NEBRASKA

1. D. Bereuter, R
2. H. Daub, R
3. V. Smith, R

NEVADA

At-L. J. D. Santini, D

NEW HAMPSHIRE

1. N. E. D'Amours, D
2. J. Gregg, R

NEW JERSEY

1. J. J. Florio, D
2. W. J. Hughes, D
3. J. J. Howard, D
4. C. Smith, R
5. M. Fenwick, R
6. E. B. Forsythe, R
7. M. Roukema, R
8. R. A. Roe, D
9. H. C. Hollenbeck, R
10. P. W. Rodino, Jr., D
11. J. G. Minish, D
12. M. J. Rinaldo, R
13. J. Courter, R
14. F. Guarini, D
15. B. Dwyer, D

NEW MEXICO

1. M. Lujan, Jr., R
2. J. Skeen, R

NEW YORK

1. W. Carney, R
2. T. J. Downey, D
3. G. Carman, R
4. N. F. Lent, R
5. R. McGrath, R
6. J. LeBoutillier, R
7. J. P. Addabbo, D
8. B. S. Rosenthal, D
9. G. Ferraro, D
10. M. Biaggi, D
11. J. H. Scheuer, D
12. S. A. Chisholm, D
13. S. J. Solarz, D
14. F. W. Richmond, D
15. L. C. Zeferetti, D
16. C. Schumer, D
17. G. Molinari, R
18. S. W. Green, R
19. C. B. Rangel, D
20. T. Weiss, D
21. R. Garcia, D
22. J. B. Bingham, D
23. P. Peyser, D
24. R. L. Ottinger, D
25. H. Fish, Jr., R
26. B. A. Gilman, R
27. M. F. McHugh, D
28. S. S. Stratton, D
29. G. Solomon, R
30. D. Martin, R
31. D. J. Mitchell, R
32. G. Wortley, R
33. G. Lee, R
34. F. Horton, R
35. B. B. Conable, Jr., R
36. J. J. LaFalce, D
37. H. J. Nowak, D
38. J. Kemp, R
39. S. N. Lundine, D

NORTH CAROLINA

1. W. B. Jones, D
2. L. H. Fountain, D
3. C. O. Whitley, Sr., D
4. I. F. Andrews, D
5. S. L. Neal, D
6. E. Johnston, R
7. C. Rose, D
8. W. G. Hefner, D
9. J. G. Martin, R
10. J. T. Broyhill, R
11. B. Hendon, R

NORTH DAKOTA

At-L. B. Dorgan, D

OHIO

1. W. D. Gradison, Jr., R
2. T. A. Luken, D
3. T. Hall, D
4. M. Oxley, R*
5. D. L. Latta, R
6. B. McEwen, R
7. C. J. Brown, R
8. T. N. Kindness, R
9. E. Weber, R
10. C. E. Miller, R
11. J. W. Stanton, R
12. B. Shamansky, D
13. D. J. Pease, D
14. J. F. Seiberling, D
15. C. P. Wylie, R
16. R. Regula, R
17. J. M. Ashbrook, R
18. D. Applegate, D
19. L. Williams, R
20. M. R. Oakar, D
21. L. Stokes, D
22. D. Eckart, D
23. R. M. Mottl, D

OKLAHOMA

1. J. R. Jones, D
2. M. Synar, D
3. W. W. Watkins, D
4. D. McCurdy, D
5. M. Edwards, R
6. G. English, D

OREGON

1. L. AuCoin, D
2. D. Smith, R
3. R. Wyden, D
4. J. Weaver, D

PENNSYLVANIA

1. T. Foglietta, D
2. W. Gray, D
3. J. F. Smith, R*
4. C. Dougherty, R
5. R. T. Schulze, R
6. G. Yatron, D
7. R. W. Edgar, D
8. J. Coyne, R
9. B. Shuster, R
10. J. M. McDade, R
11. J. Nelligan, R
12. J. P. Murtha, D
13. L. Coughlin, R
14. W. Coyne, D
15. D. Ritter, R
16. R. S. Walker, R
17. A. E. Ertel, D
18. D. Walgren, D
19. W. F. Goodling, R
20. J. M. Gaydos, D
21. D. Bailey, D
22. A. J. Murphy, D
23. W. Clinger, Jr., R
24. M. L. Marks, R
25. E. Atkinson, R

RHODE ISLAND

1. F. J. St Germain, D
2. C. Schneider, R

SOUTH CAROLINA

1. T. Hartnett, R
2. F. D. Spence, R
3. B. C. Derrick, Jr., D
4. C. Campbell, Jr., R
5. K. Holland, D
6. J. Napier, R

SOUTH DAKOTA

1. T. Daschle, D
2. C. Roberts, R

TENNESSEE

1. J. H. Quillen, R
2. J. J. Duncan, R
3. M. L. Bouquard, D
4. A. Gore, Jr., D
5. W. H. Boner, D
6. R. L. Beard, Jr., R
7. E. Jones, D
8. H. Ford, D

TEXAS

1. S. B. Hall, Jr., D
2. C. Wilson, D
3. J. M. Collins, R
4. R. Hall, D
5. J. A. Mattox, D
6. P. Gramm, D
7. B. Archer, R
8. J. Fields, R
9. J. Brooks, D
10. J. J. Pickle, D
11. J. M. Leath, D
12. J. C. Wright, Jr., D
13. J. E. Hightower, D
14. W. Patman, D
15. E. de la Garza, D
16. R. C. White, D
17. C. Stenholm, D
18. M. Leland, D
19. K. Hance, D
20. H. B. Gonzalez, D
21. T. Loeffler, R
22. R. Paul, R
23. A. Kazen, Jr., D
24. M. Frost, D

UTAH

1. J. Hansen, R
2. D. D. Marriott, R

VERMONT

At.-L. J. M. Jeffords, R

VIRGINIA

1. P. S. Trible, Jr., R
2. G. W. Whitehurst, R
3. T. Bliley, Jr., R
4. R. W. Daniel, Jr., R
5. D. Daniel, D
6. M. C. Butler, R
7. J. K. Robinson, R
8. S. Parris, R
9. W. C. Wampler, R
10. F. Wolf, R

WASHINGTON

1. J. M. Pritchard, R
2. A. Swift, D
3. D. L. Bonker, D
4. S. Morrison, R
5. T. S. Foley, D
6. N. D. Dicks, D
7. M. Lowry, D

WEST VIRGINIA

1. R. H. Mollohan, D
2. C. Benedict, R
3. M. Staton, R
4. N. J. Rahall, D

WISCONSIN

1. L. Aspin, D
2. R. W. Kastenmeier, D
3. S. Gunderson, R
4. C. J. Zablocki, D
5. H. S. Reuss, D
6. T. E. Petri, R
7. D. R. Obey, D
8. T. Roth, R
9. F. J. Sensenbrenner, Jr., R

WYOMING

At-L. R. Cheney, R

AMERICAN SAMOA

Delegate, Fofo Sunia

DISTRICT OF COLUMBIA

Delegate, W. E. Fauntroy, D

GUAM

Delegate, Antonio Borja Won Pat

PUERTO RICO

Resident Commissioner
B. Corrada

VIRGIN ISLANDS

Delegate, Ron de Lugo

AMBASSADORS AND ENVOYS[1]

From U.S.	Countries	To U.S.
(vacant)	AFGHANISTAN	Salem M. Spartak[2]
Michael H. Newlin	ALGERIA	Redha Malek
Milan D. Bish	ANTIGUA AND BARBUDA	(vacant)
H. W. Shlaudeman	ARGENTINA	Esteban Arpad Takacs
Robert D. Nesen	AUSTRALIA	Sir Nicholas F. Parkinson
Theodore E. Cummings	AUSTRIA	Karl Herbert Schober
William B. Schwartz, Jr.	BAHAMAS	Reginald L. Wood
P. A. Sutherland	BAHRAIN	Abdulaziz A. Buali
Jane Abell Coon	BANGLADESH	Tabarak Husain
Milan D. Bish	BARBADOS	Charles A. T. Skeete
Charles H. Price III	BELGIUM	J. Raoul Schoumaker
(vacant)	BENIN	Thomas Setondji Boya
Edwin G. Corr	BOLIVIA	Hernan Munoz-Reyes
Horace G. Dawson, Jr.	BOTSWANA	Moteane J. Melamu
Langhorne A. Motley	BRAZIL	Antonio F. Azeredo da Silveira
Robert L. Barry	BULGARIA	Stoyan I. Zhulev
Patricia M. Byrne	BURMA	Kyaw Khaing
Francis D. Cook	BURUNDI	Simon Sabimbona
J. Thompson[2]	CAMEROON	Benoit Bindzi
Paul H. Robinson, Jr.	CANADA	Allan Ezra Gotlieb
Peter Jon de Vos	CAPE VERDE	Jose Luis Fernandes Lopes
Andrew H. Woodruff	CENTRAL AFR. REP.	Jacques Topande Makombo
Donald R. Norland	CHAD	Mahamat Ali Adoum[2]
James D. Theberge	CHILE	Enrique Valenzuela
Arthur W. Hummel, Jr.	CHINA	Chai Zemin
Thomas D. Boyatt	COLOMBIA	Faernando Gaviria
Kenneth L. Brown[3]	CONGO	Nicolas Mondjo
Francis J. McNeil	COSTA RICA	José R. Echeverria
Raymond C. Ewing	CYPRUS	Andrew J. Jacovides
Jack F. Matlock, Jr.	CZECHOSLOVAKIA	Jaromir Johanes
J. L. Loeb, Jr.	DENMARK	Otto R. Borch
J. M. North	DJIBOUTI	Saleh Hadji Farah Dirih
Milan D. Bish	DOMINICA	(vacant)
Robert L. Yost	DOMINICAN REP.	Rafael Molina Morillo
Raymond E. González	ECUADOR	Ricardo Crespo Zaldumbide
Alfred L. Atherton, Jr.	EGYPT	Ashraf A. Ghorbal
Dean R. Hinton	EL SALVADOR	Ernesto Rivas-Gallont
Alan M. Hardy	EQUATORIAL GUINEA	Don Carmelo Nvono-Nca Memene Oluy
Frederick L. Chapin	ETHIOPIA	Tesfaye Demeke[2]
William Bodde, Jr.	FIJI	Filipe N. Bole
Keith Foote Nyborg	FINLAND	Jaakko O. Iloniemi
Evan Galbraith	FRANCE	François de Laboulaye
Francis T. McNamara[3]	GABON	Hubert Ondias Souna
Larry G. Piper	GAMBIA	Ousman A. Sallah
Herbert S. Okun	GERMANY (E)	Horst Grunert
Arthur F. Burns	GERMANY (W)	Peter Hermes
Thomas W. M. Smith	GHANA	Joseph K. Baffour-Senkyire
John J. Lewis	GREAT BRITAIN	Sir Nicholas Henderson
Monteagle Stearns	GREECE	John Tzounis
(vacant)	GRENADA	Bernard K. Radix
Frederic L. Chapin	GUATEMALA	Felipe D. Monterroso
Allen C. Davis	GUINEA	Mamady Lamine Conde
Peter Jon de Vos	GUINEA-BISSAU	Inacio Semedo, Jr.
Gerald E. Thomas	GUYANA	Laurence E. Mann
Ernest H. Preeg	HAITI	Georges N. Leger
John D. Negroponte	HONDURAS	Federico A. Poujol
Harry E. Bergold, Jr.	HUNGARY	Janos Petran
Marshall Brement	ICELAND	Hans G. Andersen
Harry G. Barnes, Jr.	INDIA	K. R. Narayanan
Edward E. Masters	INDONESIA	D. Ashari
(vacant)	IRELAND	Tadhg F. O'Sullivan
Samuel W. Lewis	ISRAEL	Ephraim Evron
Maxwell M. Robb	ITALY	Rinaldo Petrignani
Nancy V. Rawls	IVORY COAST	Timothée N'Guetta Ahoua
Loren E. Lawrence	JAMAICA	Keith Johnson
Michael J. Mansfield	JAPAN	Yoshio Okawara
Richard Noyes Viets	JORDAN	Abdul Hadi Majali
W. C. Harrop	KENYA	John P. Mbogua
William Bodde, Jr.	KIRIBATI	Atanraoi Baiteke
Richard L. Walker	KOREA (S)	Byong Hion Lew
François M. Dickman	KUWAIT	Shaikh Saud Nasir Al-Sabah
(vacant)	LAOS	Khamtan Ratanavong[2]
(vacant)	LATVIA	Anatol Dinbergs[2]
Robert S. Dillon	LEBANON	Khalil Itani
John R. Clingerman	LESOTHO	'M'alineo N. Tau
William L. Swing	LIBERIA	Joseph Saye Guannu
(vacant)	LITHUANIA	Stasys A. Backis[2]
John E. Dolibois	LUXEMBOURG	Adrien F. J. Meisch
F. E. Rondon	MADAGASCAR	
John A. Burroughs, Jr.	MALAWI	Nelson T. Mizere
Ronald DeWayne Palmer	MALAYSIA	Zain Azraai
John H. Reed[3]	MALDIVE IS.	(vacant)
Parker W. Borg	MALI	Maki K. A. Tall
(vacant)	MALTA	Leslie N. Agius
(vacant)	MAURITANIA	Abdellah Ould Dadda
Robert C. Gordon	MAURITIUS	Chitmansing Jesserar ing
John A. Gavin	MEXICO	Hugo B. Margain
Joseph Verner Reed, Jr.	MOROCCO	Ali Bengelloun
(vacant)	MOZAMBIQUE	(vacant)
Robert D. Nesen	NAURU	T. W. Star
Carleton S. Coon, Jr.	NEPAL	Bhekh Bahadur Thap
William J. Dyess	NETHERLANDS	Jan Hendrik Lubbers
H. Monroe Browne	NEW ZEALAND	Thomas Francis Gill
Lawrence A. Pezzullo	NICARAGUA	Arturo J. Cruz
William R. Casey, Jr.[3]	NIGER	André Wright
Thomas R. Pickering	NIGERIA	Abudu Yesufu Eke
Mark E. Austad[3]	NORWAY	Knut Hedemann
John R. Countryman	OMAN	Sadek Jawad Sulaim
Ronald I. Spiers	PAKISTAN	Ejaz Azim
Ambler H. Moss, Jr.	PANAMA	Juan José Amado III
M. Virginia Schafer	PAPUA NEW GUINEA	Kubulan Los
Lyle F. Lane	PARAGUAY	Mario Lopez Escobar
Frank V. Ortiz, Jr.	PERU	Fernando Schwalb
Michael H. Armacost[3]	PHILIPPINES	Eduardo Z. Romuald
Francis J. Meehan	POLAND	(vacant)
Richard J. Bloomfield	PORTUGAL	Vasco Futscher Pere
C. E. Marthinsen	QATAR	Abdelkader Braik Al-Ameri
David B. Funderburk	RUMANIA	Nicolae Ionescu
Harry R. Melone	RWANDA	Bonaventure Ubalijor
Milan D. Bish	ST. LUCIA	B. B. L. Auguste
Milan D. Bish	ST. VINCENT AND THE GRENADINES	Hudson Kemul Tannis
Francis T. McNamara	SÃO TOME AND PRÍNCIPE	(vacant)
Richard M. Murphy	SAUDI ARABIA	Sheikh Faisal Alhegel
Charles W. Bray III	SENEGAL	André Coulbary
W. C. Harrop	SEYCHELLES	(vacant)
T. A. Healy	SIERRA LEONE	Ahmed A. Seray-Wur
Harry Thayer	SINGAPORE	Punch Coomaraswam
M. Virginia Schafer	SOLOMON ISLANDS	Francis Bugotu
Donald K. Petterson	SOMALIA	Mohamud Haji Nur
William B. Edmondson	SOUTH AFRICA	Donald B. Sole
Terence A. Todman	SPAIN	José Llado
John H. Reed[3]	SRI LANKA	Ernest Corea
C. William Kontos	SUDAN	Omer Salih Eissa
John J. Crowley, Jr.	SURINAM	H. A. F. Heidweiller
Richard C. Matheron	SWAZILAND	Lawrence Mfama Mn
Franklin S. Forsberg	SWEDEN	Count Wilhelm Wacht meister
Faith Ryan Whittlesey	SWITZERLAND	Anton Hegner
Robert P. Paganelli	SYRIA	Rafic Jweijeti
David C. Miller, Jr.	TANZANIA	Paul L. Bomani
John Gunther Dean	THAILAND	Prok Amaranand
Howard K. Walker	TOGO	Yao Grunitzky
William Bodde, Jr.	TONGA	'Inoke Fotu Faletau
Melvin H. Evans	TRINIDAD AND TOBAGO	Victor McIntyre
Walter L. Cutler[3]	TUNISIA	Habib Ben Yahía
Robert Strausz-Hupé	TURKEY	Sukru Elekdag
William Bodde, Jr.	TUVALU	Ionatana Ionatana
Gordon R. Beyer	UGANDA	John W. Lwamafa
Arthur A. Hartman	USSR	A. F. Dobrynin
William D. Wolle	UNITED ARAB EMIRATES	Ahmad Salim Al-Mok
Julius W. Walker, Jr.	UPPER VOLTA	Tiemoko Marc Garan
Thomas Aranda, Jr.	URUGUAY	Jorge Pacheco Arecc
William H. Luers	VENEZUELA	Marcial Perez-Chiribc
H. Monroe Browne	WESTERN SAMOA	Maiava I. Toma
David E. Zweifel	YEMEN	Mohammad Abdallah Iryani
David Anderson	YUGOSLAVIA	Budimir Loncar
Robert B. Oakley	ZAIRE	Kasongo Mutuale
Frank G. Wisner II	ZAMBIA	Putteho M. Ngonda
Robert V. Keeley	ZIMBABWE	E. K. Mashingaidze

[1] As of December 1981. [2] Changé d'affaires. [3] Nominated but not continued.

UNITED STATES: Major Legislation Enacted During First Session of the 97th Congress

Working late into the night on several major pieces of legislation, the first session of the 97th Congress completed its legislative business on Dec. 16, 1981. The Senate adjourned *sine die* at 10:28 P.M., and the House, after rejecting an earlier motion to adjourn, followed suit at 11:22 P.M.

The session, which convened at noon on Jan. 5, 1981, lasted 346 days and tied with the first session of the 95th Congress and the second session of the 77th Congress as the 14th longest in history. The third session of the 76th Congress, from Jan. 3, 1940, to Jan. 3, 1941, is the longest on record.

The Senate met for 165 days during the year, the House for 163 days. There were 8,719 bills and resolutions (2,478 Senate and 6,241 House) introduced during the session, an increase of 4,296 from 1980 but fewer than the 10,171 bills and resolutions introduced during the first session of the 96th Congress.

Congressional Quarterly Weekly Report,
Dec. 19, 1981

SUBJECT	PURPOSE
The Hostages	Designates Jan. 29, 1981, as a "day of thanksgiving to honor our safely returned hostages" from Iran. Signed January 26. Public Law 97-1.
Virgin Islands	Approves a constitution for the U.S. Virgin Islands. Signed July 9. Public Law 97-21. Residents of the Virgin Islands later rejected the constitution in a referendum.
Cash Discounts	Permits merchants to offer unlimited discounts to cash-paying customers and extends the ban on credit-card surcharges until 1984. Signed July 27. Public Law 97-25.
Maritime Administration	Transfers the Maritime Administration from the U.S. Department of Commerce to the U.S. Department of Transportation. Signed August 6. Public Law 97-31.
Taxation	*See* page 492. Signed August 13. Public Law 97-34.
Budget	Authorizes $35,200,000,000 in cuts in the 1982 fiscal year budget. Signed August 13. Public Law 97-35.
Debt Ceiling	Increases the public debt ceiling to $1,079,800,000,000 through Sept. 30, 1982. Signed September 30. Public Law 97-49.
Military Pay	Authorizes $4,500,000,000 for military pay increases effective Oct. 1, 1981. Signed October 14. Public Law 97-60.
Tourism	Increases the federal role in encouraging tourism. Replaces the U.S. Travel Service with an upgraded U.S. Travel and Tourism Administration (USTTA). Signed October 16. Public Law 97-63.
Kansas–Missouri Boundary	Grants the consent of Congress to an agreement between the states of Kansas and Missouri establishing their mutual boundary. Signed October 16. Public Law 97-64.
Veterans	Increases the rate of disability compensation for disabled veterans and the rates of dependency and indemnity compensation for their survivors. Signed October 17. Public Law 97-66.
The Family	Designates the week of Nov. 22–28, 1981, as "National Family Week." Signed November 3. Public Law 97-75.
Energy	Encourages the production of oil from tar sands and other hydrocarbon deposits. Signed November 16. Public Law 97-78.
Budget	Provides by continuing resolution budget appropriations for most of the federal government for fiscal year 1982. Signed December 15. Public Law 97-92.
Alaska	Approves a waiver of law pursuant to the Alaska Natural Gas Transportation Act of 1976. (*See* ALASKA.) Signed December 15. Public Law 97-93.
Agriculture	Reauthorizes basic farm programs for four years with controversial provisions on peanuts, tobacco, dairy, and sugar. Signed December 22. Public Law 97-98.
Foreign Aid	Authorizes $5,900,000,000 for military and economic aid spending in fiscal 1982 and $5,960,000,000 for such spending in fiscal 1983. Signed December 29. Public Law 97-113.
Clean Water	Provides $10,000,000,000 over a four-year period for sewage treatment facilities. Signed December 29. Public Law 97-117.
Social Security	Restores minimum Social Security benefits that were eliminated by the August 1981 budget reduction act. Signed December 29. Public Law 97-123.
Middle East Peacekeeping Force	Allows the deployment of up to 1,200 American troops as part of the multinational peacekeeping force for the Sinai following Israel's withdrawal. Signed December 29. Public Law 97-132.

SOCIETIES AND ORGANIZATIONS

This article lists some of the most noteworthy associations, societies, foundations, and trusts of the United States and Canada. The information has been verified by the organization concerned.

Academy of Motion Picture Arts & Sciences. Membership: 4,341. Executive director, James M. Roberts. Headquarters: 8949 Wilshire Blvd., Beverly Hills, CA 90211.

Alcoholics Anonymous (The General Service Board of A.A., Inc.). Membership: more than 1,000,000 in more than 40,000 affiliated groups. Chairman, Milton Maxwell. Headquarters: 468 Park Ave. S., New York, NY. Mailing address: Box 459, Grand Central Station, New York, NY 10163.

American Academy and Institute of Arts and Letters. Membership: 250. Executive director, Margaret M. Mills. Headquarters: 633 W.155th St., New York, NY 10032.

American Academy of Political and Social Science. Membership: 10,500, including 5,500 libraries. President, Marvin E. Wolfgang. Headquarters: 3937 Chestnut St., Philadelphia, PA 19104.

American Anthropological Association. Membership: 10,268. Annual meeting: Washington, DC, Dec. 4–7, 1982. Executive director, Edward J. Lehman. Headquarters: 1703 New Hampshire Ave. NW, Washington, DC 20009.

American Association for the Advancement of Science. Membership: 135,000 and 285 affiliated groups. Meeting: Washington, DC, Jan. 3–8, 1982. President, D. Allen Bromley; executive officer, William D. Carey. Headquarters: 1515 Massachusetts Ave. NW, Washington, DC 20005.

American Association of Museums. Membership: 7,000. Annual meeting: Philadephia, June 1982. Director, Lawrence L. Reger. Headquarters: 1055 Thomas Jefferson St., Suite 428, Washington, DC 20007.

American Association of Retired Persons. Membership: 13,500,000. Convention: New Orleans, LA, May 19–22, 1982. Executive director, Cyril F. Brickfield. Headquarters: 1909 K St. NW, Washington, D.C. 20049.

American Association of University Professors. Membership: approximately 65,900. President, Henry T. Yost. Headquarters: One Dupont Circle NW, Washington, DC 20036.

American Association of University Women. Membership: 190,000. President, Mary Purcell. Headquarters: 2401 Virginia Ave. NW, Washington, DC 20037.

American Astronomical Society. Membership: 3,800. Meetings: Boulder, CO, Jan. 10–13, 1982; Troy, NY, June 6–9, 1982. Executive officer: Peter B. Boyce. Headquarters: 1816 Jefferson Place NW, Washington, DC 20036.

American Automobile Association. Membership: 21,500,000 in 190 affiliated clubs. Annual meeting: New Orleans, LA, Oct. 12–14, 1982. President, James B. Creal. Headquarters: 8111 Gatehouse Rd., Falls Church, VA 22047.

American Bankers Association. Membership: 13,537. Annual convention: Atlanta, GA, Oct. 16–20, 1982. President, Lee E. Gunderson. Headquarters: 1120 Connecticut Ave. NW, Washington, DC 20036.

American Bar Association. Membership: 283,419. Annual meeting: San Francisco, Aug. 5–12, 1982; Midyear meeting: Chicago, Jan. 20–27, 1982. President, David R. Brink; executive director, Thomas Gonser. Headquarters: 1155 E. 60th St., Chicago, IL 60637.

American Bible Society. 1980 United States distribution: 76,015,828 copies. Annual meeting: New York City, May 13, 1982. President, Edmund F. Wagner. Headquarters: 1865 Broadway, New York, NY 10023.

American Booksellers Association, Inc. Membership: 5,935. Convention: Anaheim, CA, May 29–June 1, 1982. President, Joan Ripley. Headquarters: 122 E. 42nd St., New York, NY 10168.

American Cancer Society, Inc. Membership: 194 voting members; 58 chartered divisions. Executive vice-president, Lane W. Adams. Headquarters: 777 Third Ave., New York, NY 10017.

American Chemical Society. Membership: 120,000. National meetings, 1982: Las Vegas, NV, March 28–April 2; Kansas City, MO, Sept. 12–17. President, Robert W. Parry. Headquarters: 1155 16th St. NW, Washington, DC 20036.

American Civil Liberties Union. Membership: 200,000. Board chairman, Norman Dorsen. Headquarters: 132 W. 43rd St., New York, NY 10036.

American Correctional Association. Membership: 10,000. Annual Congress of Correction: Toronto, Ont., Aug. 15–19, 1982. Executive director, Anthony P. Travisono. Headquarters: 4321 Hartwick Rd., College Park, MD 20740.

American Council of Learned Societies. Membership: 43 professional societies concerned with the humanities and the humanistic aspects of the social sciences. President, R. M. Lumiansky. Headquarters: 800 Third Ave., New York, NY 10022.

American Council on Education. Membership: 1,385 institutional members, 113 associated organizations, 63 constituent organizations, 61 affiliates, and 20 international affiliates. Annual meeting: Minneapolis, Oct. 13–15, 1982. President, Jack W. Peltason. Headquarters: One Dupont Circle NW, Washington, DC 20036.

American Dental Association. Membership: 136,000. President, John J. Houlihan, D.D.S.; president-elect, Robert H. Griffiths, D.D.S.; executive director, John M. Coady, D.D.S. Headquarters: 211 E. Chicago Ave., Chicago, IL 60611.

American Economic Association. Membership: 19,400 and 6,200 subscribers. Annual meeting: New York City, Dec. 28–30, 1982. President, Gardner Ackley. Headquarters: 1313 21st Ave. S., Nashville, TN 37212.

American Electroplaters' Society, Inc. Membership: 8,500 with 79 branches in the United States, Canada, Australia, South America, and Mexico. Annual meeting: San Francisco, CA, June 20–25, 1982. President, Harry J. Litsch. Headquarters: 1201 Louisiana Ave., Winter Park, FL 32789.

American Farm Bureau Federation. Membership: 3,076,867 families. President, Robert B. Delano. Headquarters: 225 Touhy Ave., Park Ridge, IL 60068.

American Geographical Society. Fellows and subscribers: 4,000. President, John E. Gould; director, Sarah Myers. Headquarters: Broadway at 156th St., New York, NY 10032.

American Geophysical Union. Membership: 13,000 individuals; 2,000 institutions. Meetings, 1982: San Antonio, TX, Feb. 16–19; Philadelphia, PA, May 31–June 4; San Francisco, CA, Dec. 6–10. President, J. Tuzo Wilson. Headquarters: 2000 Florida Ave. NW, Washington, DC 20009.

American Heart Association. Membership: 140,000 in 55 affiliates, 125 chapters, and approximately 1,000 local subdivisions. President, James A. Schoenberger, M.D. Headquarters: 7320 Greenville Ave., Dallas, TX 75231.

American Historical Association. Membership: 13,000. Annual meeting: Washington, DC, Dec. 28–30, 1982. President, Gordon Craig; executive director, Samuel Gammon. Headquarters: 400 A St. SE, Washington, DC 20003.

American Horticultural Society. Membership: 30,000 individuals, more than 400 organizations, institutions, and commercial establishments. National congress: Cincinnati, OH, Sept. 29–Oct. 2, 1982. Symposium, New Orleans, LA, March 10–14, 1982. President, Gilbert S. Daniels. Headquarters: Mt. Vernon, VA 22121.

American Hospital Association. Membership: 29,600 persons; 6,175 institutions. Annual meeting: Washington, DC, Jan. 31–Feb. 3, 1982; convention: Atlanta, GA, Aug. 30–Sept. 2, 1982. Chairman of the board, Stanley R. Nelson. Headquarters: 840 North Lake Shore Dr., Chicago, IL 60611.

American Hotel & Motel Association. Membership: 7,700. Annual convention: Vancouver, B.C., Oct. 11–14, 1982. Executive vice-president, Robert L. Richards. Headquarters: 888 Seventh Ave., New York, NY 10019.

American Institute of Aeronautics and Astronautics. Membership: 26,000, plus 4,705 student members. Executive secretary, James J. Harford. Headquarters: 1290 Avenue of the Americas, New York, NY 10109.

American Institute of Architects. Membership: 36,000. Convention 1982: Honolulu, HI. President, Robert M. Lawrence, FAIA. Headquarters: 1735 New York Ave. NW, Washington, DC 20006.

American Institute of Biological Sciences. Membership: 8,000 with 40 member societies and 7 affiliate organizations. Annual meeting: State College, PA, Aug. 9–13, 1982. President, Forest Stearns. Headquarters: 1401 Wilson Blvd., Arlington, VA 22209.

American Institute of Certified Public Accountants. Membership: 170,000. Annual meeting: Portland, OR, Oct. 3–5, 1982. Chairman: George D. Anderson. Headquarters: 1211 Avenue of the Americas, New York, NY 10036.

American Institute of Chemical Engineers. Membership: 52,000. President, R. R. Hughes. Headquarters: 345 E. 47th St., New York, NY 10017.

American Institute of Graphic Arts. Membership: 2,000. President, David Brown; executive director, Caroline Hightower. Headquarters: 1059 Third Ave., New York, NY 10021.

American Institute of Mining, Metallurgical and Petroleum Engineers, Inc. Membership: 81,733. Annual meeting: Dallas, TX, Feb. 14–18, 1982. President, Robert H. Merrill. Headquarters: 345 E. 47th St., New York, NY 10017.

American Institute of Nutrition. Membership: 2,000. Annual meeting: New Orleans, April 16–19, 1982. Executive officer, M. Milner. Headquarters: 9650 Rockville Pike, Bethesda, MD 20814.

American Legion, The. Membership: 2,700,000. Headquarters: 700 N. Pennsylvania St., Indianapolis, IN 46206.

American Library Association. Membership: 36,000. Meetings, 1982: Midwinter, Denver, Jan. 23–28; annual conference, Philadelphia, July 9–15. Executive director, Robert Wedgeworth. Headquarters: 50 E. Huron, Chicago, IL 60611.

American Lung Association. Membership: 175 affiliated groups. Annual meeting: Los Angeles, CA, May 1982. President, Edmund C.Casey, M.D. Headquarters: 1740 Broadway, New York, NY 10019.

American Management Associations. Membership: 84,000. Chairman of the board, Paul Elicker; president and chief executive officer, James Hayes. Headquarters: 135 W. 50th St., New York, NY 10020.

American Mathematical Society. Membership: 19,994. President, Andrew M. Gleason; secretary, Everett Pitcher. Headquarters: P.O. Box 6248, Providence, RI 02940.

American Medical Association. Membership: 230,700. Meeting: Chicago, June 13–17, 1982. President, Daniel T. Cloud, M.D. Headquarters: 535 N. Dearborn St., Chicago, IL 60610.

American Meteorological Society. Membership: 9,800 including 128 corporate members. President, Richard E. Hallgren. Headquarters: 45 Beacon St., Boston, MA 02108.

American Newspaper Publishers Association. Membership: 1,420. Annual convention: San Francisco, April 26–28, 1982. Chairman and president, Katharine Graham. Executive offices: The Newspaper Center, 11600 Sunrise Valley Dr., Reston, VA 22091. Mailing address: The Newspaper Center, Box 17407, Dulles International Airport, Washington, DC 20041.

American Nurses' Association. Membership: 180,000 in 53 state and territorial associations. National convention: Washington, DC, June 26–July 2, 1982. President, Barbara Nichols. Headquarters: 2420 Pershing Road, Kansas City, MO 64108.

American Physical Society. Membership: 31,664 American and foreign. Annual meeting: San Francisco, Jan. 25–28, 1982. President, Maurice Goldhaber; executive secretary, W. W. Havens, Jr. Headquarters: 335 E. 45th St., New York, NY 10017.

American Psychiatric Association. Membership: 25,400; 75 district branches. Annual meeting: Toronto, Ont., May 9–15, 1982. President, Daniel X. Freedman, M.D. Headquarters: 1700 18th St. NW, Washington, DC 20009.

American Psychological Association. Membership: 51,000. Annual meeting: Washington, DC, Aug. 23–27, 1982. President, William Bevan. Headquarters: 1200 17th St. NW, Washington, DC 20036.

American Red Cross. Divisions: 59; chapters: 3,052. National convention: St. Louis, MO, May 23–26, 1982. Chairman, Jerome H. Holland; president, George M. Elsey. Headquarters: 17th and D Sts. NW, Washington, DC 20006.

American Society of Civil Engineers. Membership: 78,243. Executive director, Eugene Zwoyer. Headquarters: 345 E. 47th St., New York, NY 10017.

American Society of Composers, Authors, and Publishers. Membership: 18,963 composers and authors; 6,495 publishers. President, Hal David; secretary, Morton Gould. Headquarters: One Lincoln Plaza, New York, NY 10023.

American Society of Mechanical Engineers. Membership: 105,101. President, Robert B. Gaither. Headquarters: 345 E. 47th St., New York, NY 10017.

American Society of Newspaper Editors. Membership: 875. National convention: Chicago, IL, May 1982. President, Thomas Winship. Headquarters: Box 551, 1350 Sullivan Trail, Easton, PA 18042.

American Sociological Association. Membership: 14,000. Annual meeting: San Francisco, CA, Sept. 6–10, 1982. President, Erving Goffman. Headquarters: 1722 N St. NW, Washington, DC 20036.

American Statistical Association. Membership: 14,200. President, Ralph A. Bradley. Meeting: Cincinnati, Aug. 16–19, 1982. Headquarters: 806 15th St. NW, Suite 640, Washington, DC 20005.

American Youth Hostels, Inc. Membership: 100,000; 31 councils in the United States. Executive director, Thomas L. Newman. Headquarters: 1332 I St. NW, Suite 800, Washington, DC 20005.

Archaeological Institute of America. Membership: 7,900; subscribers, 30,000. President, Machteld J. Mellink; executive director, Eugene L. Sterud. Headquarters: 53 Park Place, New York, NY 10017.

Arthritis Foundation. Membership: 71 chapters. Annual scientific meeting: Washington, DC , June 6–12, 1982. Chairman: Joseph N. Masci; president, Clifford M. Clarke. Headquarters: 3400 Peachtree Rd. NE, Atlanta, GA, 30326.

Association of American Publishers. Membership: approximately 340. Annual meeting: May 1982. Chairman of the board, Martin Levin; president, Townsend W. Hoopes; vice-president, Thomas McKee. Addresses: One Park Ave., New York, NY 10016 and 1707 L St. NW, Washington, DC 20036.

Association of Junior Leagues, Inc. Membership: 244 member leagues in U.S., Canada, and Mexico. Annual conference: San Francisco, CA, May 2–6, 1982. President, Margaret M. Graham. Headquarters: 825 Third Ave., New York, NY 10022.

Association of Operating Room Nurses, Inc. Membership: 28,500 with 292 local chapters. Convention: March 7–12, 1982. President, Margaret Huth; executive director, Jerry G. Peers. Headquarters: 10170 E. Mississippi Ave., Denver, CO 80231.

Benevolent and Protective Order of Elks. Membership: 1,644,496 in 2,264 lodges. Grand exalted ruler, Raymond V. Arnold; grand secretary, S. F. Kocur. Headquarters: 2750 Lake View Ave., Chicago, IL 60614.

Bide-A-Wee Home Association. Executive director, Richard F. L. Carlson. Headquarters: 410 E. 38th St., New York, NY 10016.

Big Brothers/Big Sisters of America. Membership: 400+ local affiliated agencies. National conference: St. Louis, MO, June 15–19, 1982. Executive vice-president, David W. Bahlmann. Headquarters: 117 South 17th St., Suite 1200, Philadelphia, PA 19103.

B'nai B'rith. Membership: 500,000 in approximately 3,000 men's, women's, and youth lodges, chapters, and units. President, Jack Spitzer; executive vice-president, Daniel Thursz. Headquarters: 1640 Rhode Island Ave. NW, Washington, DC 20036.

Boat Owners Association of the United States. Membership: 85,000. Executive director, Richard Schwartz. Headquarters: 880 S. Pickett St., Alexandria, VA 22304.

Boys Clubs of America. Youth served: 1,000,000 in 1,000 affiliated clubs. National conference: Washington, DC, June 4–8, 1982. President, John L. Burns; national director, William R. Bricker. Headquarters: 771 First Ave., New York, NY 10017.

Boy Scouts of America. Membership: total youth members and leaders—4,326,082 in 416 scouting councils. Biennial meeting: Atlanta, GA, May 20–22, 1982. President, Thomas C. MacAvoy; chief scout executive, J. L. Tarr. National office: 1325 Walnut Hill Lane, Irving, TX; P.O. Box 61030, Dallas/Fort Worth Airport, TX 75261.

Camp Fire, Inc. Membership: 500,000 boys and girls in more than 35,000 communities. President, Mrs. Jean Morgan. Headquarters: 4601 Madison Ave., Kansas City, MO 64112.

Canadian Library Association. Membership: 4,050 personal, 1,000 institutional, 5,050 total. Annual conference 1982: Saskatoon, Sask. Executive director, Paul Kitchen. Headquarters: 151 Sparks St., Ottawa, Ont. K1P 5E3.

Canadian Medical Association: Membership: 34,000. Annual meeting: Saskatoon, Sask., Sept. 19–24, 1982. Secretary general, R. G. Wilson, M.D. Headquarters: 1867 Alta Vista Dr., Ottawa, Ont. K1G OG8.

Chamber of Commerce of the United States of America. Membership: approximately 4,000 trade associations and local and state chambers, more than 120,000 business members. President, Richard Lesher; chairman of the board, Donald M. Kendall. Headquarters: 1615 H St. NW, Washington, DC 20062.

Common Cause. Membership: 220,000. Chairman, Archibald Cox. Headquarters: 2030 M St. NW, Washington, DC 20036.

Consumers Union of United States, Inc. Executive director, Rhoda H. Karpatkin. Headquarters: 256 Washington St., Mount Vernon, NY 10550.

Council of Better Business Bureaus. Membership: 1,000. Headquarters: 1515 Wilson Blvd., Suite 300, Arlington, VA 22209.

Council on Foreign Relations, Inc. Membership: 2,000. Annual meeting: New York City, fall 1982. President, Winston Lord. Headquarters: 58 E. 68th St., New York, NY 10021.

Daughters of the American Revolution (National Society). Membership: 208,518 in 3,125 chapters. Continental Congress: Washington, DC, April 20–24, 1982. President general (1980–83), Mrs. Richard Denny Shelby. Headquarters: 1776 D St. NW, Washington, DC 20006.

Esperanto League for North America. Membership: 750. Congress: July 1982. President, William R. Harmon. Headquarters: P.O. Box 1129, El Cerrito, CA 94530.

Foreign Policy Association. President, William E. Schaufele, Jr. Headquarters: 205 Lexington Ave., New York, NY 10016.

Freemasonry, Ancient Accepted Scottish Rite of (Northern Masonic Jurisdiction): Supreme Council, 33°. Membership: 505,379 in 112 valleys. Sovereign grand commander, Stanley F. Maxwell. Headquarters: 33 Marrett Rd., Lexington, MA 02173.

Freemasonry, Ancient and Accepted Scottish Rite of (Southern Jurisdiction): Supreme Council, 33°. Membership: 660,000 in 218 affiliated groups. Sovereign grand commander, Henry C. Clausen. Headquarters: 1733 16th St. NW, Washington, DC 20009.

Future Farmers of America. Membership: 482,000 in 50 state associations. Executive secretary, Coleman Harris. Headquarters: Box 15160, Alexandria, VA 22309.

Gamblers Anonymous. Membership: 6,500. National executive secretary, James J. Zeysing. Headquarters: 2703A W. Eighth St., Los Angeles, CA 90005.

Garden Club of America, The. Membership: 14,000 in 184 clubs. Annual meeting: Rochester, NY, June 14–16, 1982. President, Mrs. Samuel M. Beattie. Headquarters: 598 Madison Ave., New York, NY 10022.

General Federation of Women's Clubs. Membership: 600,000 in 12,000 U.S. clubs and 10,000,000 worldwide. National convention: Bismarck, ND, June 6–11, 1982. President, Mrs. Don L. Shide. Headquarters: 1734 N St. NW, Washington, DC 20036.

Geological Society of America. Membership: 12,500. Annual meeting: New Orleans, LA, Oct. 18–21, 1982. President, Digby J. McLaren; executive director, John C. Frye. Headquarters: P.O. Box 9140, 3300 Penrose Pl., Boulder, CO 80301.

Girl Scouts of the U.S.A. Membership: 2,784,000. National president, Mrs. Orville L. Freeman; national executive director, Frances R. Hesselbein. Headquarters: 830 Third Ave., New York, NY 10022.

Humane Society of the United States. Membership: 160,000. Annual convention: Boston, MA, Nov. 3–7, 1982. President, John A. Hoyt. Headquarters: 2100 L St. NW, Washington, DC 20037.

Institute of Electrical and Electronics Engineers, Inc. Membership: 213,812. President, Richard W. Damon. Headquarters: 345 E. 47th St., New York, NY 10017.

Jewish War Veterans of the U.S.A. Membership: 100,000 in 750 units. National commander, Irvin Steinberg; national executive director, Jerome Levinrad. Headquarters: 1712 New Hampshire Ave. NW, Washington, DC 20009.

Kiwanis International. Membership: 300,000 in 7,800 clubs in U.S. and abroad. President, Merald J. Enstad. Headquarters: 101 E. Erie St., Chicago, IL 60611.

Knights of Columbus. Membership: 1,342,978. Supreme knight, Virgil C. Dechant. Headquarters: Columbus Plaza, New Haven, CT 06507.

Knights of Pythias, Supreme Lodge. Membership: 124,000 in 1,248 subordinate lodges. Supreme chancellor, William E. Thomas. Office: 47 N. Grant St., Stockton, CA 95202.

League of Women Voters of the U.S. Membership: 120,000. President, Ruth J. Hinerfeld. Headquarters: 1730 M St. NW, Washington, DC 20036.

Lions International. Membership: 1,326,518 in 34,637 clubs in 152 countries and areas. Annual convention: Atlanta, GA, June 30–July 3, 1982. President, Kaoru "Kay" Murakami. Headquarters: 300 22nd St., Oak Brook, IL 60570.

March of Dimes Birth Defects Foundation. Membership: 763 chapters. President, Charles L. Massey. Headquarters: 1275 Mamaroneck Ave., White Plains, NY 10605.

Mental Health Association. Membership: 800 state and local organizations. Headquarters: 1800 N. Kent St., Arlington, VA 22209.

Modern Language Association of America. Membership: 26,000. Annual convention: Los Angeles, CA, Dec. 27–30, 1982. President, Wayne Booth. Headquarters: 62 Fifth Ave., New York, NY 10011.

National Academy of Sciences. Membership: approximately 1,250. Annual meeting: Washington, DC, April 1982. President, Frank Press. Headquarters: 2101 Constitution Ave. NW, Washington, DC 20418.

National Association for the Advancement of Colored People. Membership: 450,000 in 1,700 branches and 500 units. National convention: Boston, June 26–July 1, 1982. President, W. Montague Cobb, M.D.; board chairman, Margaret Bush Wilson; executive director, Benjamin L. Hooks. Headquarters: 1790 Broadway, New York, NY 10019.

National Association of Manufacturers. Membership: 12,000. President, Alexander B. Trowbridge. Headquarters: 1776 F St. NW, Washington, DC 20006.

National Audubon Society. Membership: 434,000. President, R. W. Peterson. Headquarters: 950 Third Ave., New York, NY 10022.

National Committee for the Prevention of Child Abuse. Executive director, Anne H, Cohn. Headquarters: 332 S. Michigan Ave., Suite 1250, Chicago, IL 60604.

National Conference of Christians and Jews, Inc. Membership: 82 regional offices. President, David Hyatt. Headquarters: 43 W. 57th St., New York, NY 10019.

National Council of the Churches of Christ in the U.S.A. Membership: 32 Protestant, Anglican, and Orthodox denominations. General secretary, Claire Randall. Headquarters: 475 Riverside Dr., New York, NY 10115.

National Council on the Aging, Inc. Membership: 5,000. Executive director, Jack Ossofsky. Headquarters: 600 Maryland Ave. SW, Washington, DC 20024.

National Easter Seal Society, Inc. President, Tom Cook, Jr. Headquarters: 2023 West Ogden Ave., Chicago, IL 60612.

National Education Association of the U.S. Membership: 1,687,-697, with units in every state, and 12,389 local affiliates. Annual convention: Los Angeles, CA, July 1982. President, Willard H. McGuire. Headquarters: 1201 16th St. NW, Washington, DC 20036.

National Federation of Business and Professional Women's Clubs, Inc. Membership: 160,000 in 3,700 clubs. President, Phyllis Harrison. Headquarters: 2012 Massachusetts Ave. NW, Washington, DC 20036.

National Federation of Independent Business, Inc. Membership: 582,000. President, Wilson S. Johnson. Headquarters: 150 W. 20th Ave., San Mateo, CA 94403.

National Federation of Music Clubs. Membership: 500,000 in 4,300 clubs and 12 national affiliates. President, Mrs. Jack C. Ward. Headquarters: 1336 North Delaware St., Indianapolis, IN 46202.

National Fire Protection Association, Membership: 31,500. Annual meetings, 1982: San Francisco, May 17–21 and Philadelphia, Nov. 15–17. President, Robert W. Grant. Headquarters: Batterymarch Park, Quincy, MA 02269.

National Organization for Women. Membership: 125,000 in 800 local groups. President, Eleanor Smeal. Headquarters: 425 13th St. NW, Suite 1048, Washington, DC 20004.

National PTA (National Parent-Teacher Association). Membership: 6,069,438 in 27,971 local units. National convention: Nashville, TN, June 6–9, 1982. President, Mrs. Mary Ann Leveridge. Headquarters: 700 N. Rush St., Chicago, IL 60611.

National Safety Council. Membership: 15,000. National Safety Congress and Exposition: Chicago, Oct. 18–21, 1982. President, Vincent L. Tofany. Headquarters: 444 N. Michigan Ave., Chicago, IL 60611.

National Urban League, Inc. President, Vernon E. Jordan, Jr. (resigned effective Dec. 31, 1981). Headquarters: 500 E. 62nd St., New York, NY 10021.

National Woman's Christian Temperance Union. Membership: approximately 250,000 in 6,000 local unions. National convention: Syracuse, NY, August 1982. President, Mrs. Kermit S. Edgar. Headquarters: 1730 Chicago Ave., Evanston, IL 60201.

Parents Without Partners. Membership: 200,000. International convention: Cleveland, OH, July 8–11, 1982. Executive director, Virginia L. Martin. International office: 7910 Woodmont Ave., No. 1000, Washington, DC 20014.

Phi Beta Kappa. Membership: 355,000. Secretary, Kenneth M. Greene. Headquarters: 1811 Q St. NW, Washington, DC 20009.

Photographic Society of America. Membership: 18,700. Executive director, Harold J. Vermes. Headquarters: 2005 Walnut St., Philadelphia, PA 19103.

Planned Parenthood Federation of America, Inc. (Planned Parenthood—World Population). Membership: 188 U.S. affiliates. President, Faye Wattleton; chairperson of the Federation, Jean Mahoney. Headquarters: 810 Seventh Ave., New York, NY 10019.

Rotary International. Membership: 883,250 in 19,099 clubs functioning in 156 countries and geographical regions. International convention: Dallas, TX, June 6–9, 1982. General secretary, Herbert A. Pigman. Headquarters: 1600 Ridge Ave., Evanston, IL 60201.

Salvation Army, The. Membership: 417,359. National commander: Ernest Holz. Headquarters: 120 W. 14th St., New York, NY 10011.

Special Libraries Association. Membership: 11,500. Annual conference: Detroit, MI, June 1982. President, George Ginader. Headquarters: 235 Park Ave. S., New York, NY 10003.

United Dairy Industry Association (including American Dairy Association, Dairy Research Inc., National Dairy Council). Annual convention: Orlando, FL, March 17–20, 1982. Executive vice-president, John W. Sliter. Headquarters: Dairy Center, 6300 N. River Rd., Rosemont, IL 60018.

United States Jaycees, The. Membership: 300,000 in 7,500 affiliated groups. Annual meeting: Phoenix, AZ, June 1982. President, Gene Honn. Headquarters: P.O. Box 7, Tulsa, OK 74121.

United Way of America. Service organization for more than 2,200 autonomous local United Way organizations. 1982 Volunteer Leaders Conference: Miami Beach, FL, April 18–20, 1982. Chairman of the board of governors, Donald V. Seibert. Headquarters: 801 N. Fairfax St., Alexandria, VA 22314.

U.S. Metric Association. Membership: 3,500. President, Valerie Antoine. Headquarters: 10245 Andasol Ave., Northridge, CA 91325.

Veterans of Foreign Wars of the United States. Membership: V.F.W. and Auxiliary 2,650,000. Commander-in-chief: Arthur J. Fellwock. Headquarters: V.F.W. Building, Broadway at 34th St., Kansas City, MO 64111.

World Council of Churches (U.S. Conference). Membership: 27 churches or denominations in U.S. Moderator, Cynthia Wedel. Headquarters: 150, route de Ferney, 1211 Geneva 20, Switzerland. New York Office: 475 Riverside Dr., Room 1062, New York, NY 10115.

Young Men's Christian Associations (National Council). Membership: 10,662,904 in 1,855 associations. Board chairman, Dale A. Vonderau. Headquarters: 101 North Wacker Dr., Chicago, IL 60606.

Young Women's Christian Association of the U.S.A. Members and participants: approximately 2,400,000. President, Jewel Freeman Graham. Headquarters: 600 Lexington Ave., New York, NY 10022.

Zionist Organization of America. Membership: 130,000 in 600 districts. President, Ivan J. Novick; national executive director, Paul Flacks. Headquarters: ZOA House, 4 E. 34th St., New York, NY 10016.

CONTRIBUTORS

ADRIAN, CHARLES R., Professor of Political Science, University of California, Riverside; Coauthor, *Governing Urban America:* CALIFORNIA; LOS ANGELES

ALEXANDER, ROBERT J., Professor of Economics and Political Science, Rutgers University: ECUADOR; GUYANA; URUGUAY

AMBRE, AGO, Economist, Bureau of Economic Analysis, U.S. Department of Commerce: INDUSTRIAL PRODUCTION

BAGDIKIAN, BEN H., Graduate School of Journalism, University of California; Author, *The Effete Conspiracy and Other Crimes of the Press:* PUBLISHING—*Investigative Reporting*

BATRA, PREM P., Professor, Biochemistry Department, Wright State University: BIOCHEMISTRY

BAYH, BIRCH, U.S. Senator (D-IN, 1963–81); Former Chairman, Senate Subcommittee on the Constitution: UNITED STATES—*The Transition of Presidential Powers*

BECK, KAY, School of Urban Life, Georgia State University: ATLANTA; GEORGIA

BEMAN, LEWIS, Free-lance Writer, former Economics Editor of *Business Week* and Associate Editor of *Fortune:* UNITED STATES—*Supply-Side Economics*

BERGEN, DANIEL P., Professor, Graduate Library School, University of Rhode Island, Kingston, RI: LIBRARIES

BERLIN, MICHAEL J., Diplomatic Correspondent, *New York Post:* BIOGRAPHY—*Jeane Kirkpatrick;* UNITED NATIONS

BEST, JOHN, Chief, *Canada World News,* Ottawa: NEW BRUNSWICK; PRINCE EDWARD ISLAND

BÖDVARSSON, HAUKUR, Coeditor, *News From Iceland:* ICELAND

BOLUS, JIM, Sportswriter, *The Louisville Times;* Author, *Run for the Roses:* SPORTS—*Horse Racing*

BOND, DONOVAN H., Professor of Journalism, West Virginia University: WEST VIRGINIA

BOULAY, HARVEY, Assistant Professor of Political Science, Boston University; Author, *The Twilight Cities:* BOSTON; MASSACHUSETTS

BOWERS, Q. DAVID, Vice-President, American Numismatic Association; member of the board of governors of the Professional Numismatists Guild; Chairman of the Board of Bowers & Ruddy Galleries, Inc.: COINS AND COIN COLLECTING

BOYD, GERALD D., Editor, *The Wine Spectator;* Author, American wine section, *Harvey's Pocket Guide to Wines:* WINES

BRAMMER, DANA B., Associate Director, Bureau of Governmental Research, University of Mississippi: MISSISSIPPI

BRANDHORST, L. CARL, Associate Professor of Geography, Western Oregon College, Monmouth, OR: OREGON

BURKS, ARDATH W., Professor Emeritus of Asian Studies, Rutgers University; Author, *Japan, Profile of a Postindustrial Power:* JAPAN

BUSH, GRAHAM W. A., Senior Lecturer in Political Studies, University of Auckland, New Zealand; Author, *Local Government & Politics in New Zealand:* NEW ZEALAND

BUTWELL, RICHARD, Vice-President for Academic Programs and Professor of Political Science, Murray State University, Murray, KY; Author, *Southeast Asia, a Political Introduction, U-Nu of Burma, Southeast Asia Today and Tomorrow,* and *Foreign Policy and the Developing State:* ASIA; BURMA; LAOS; PHILIPPINES

CALABRESE, MICHAEL A., Program Manager, National Aeronautics and Space Administration: BIOGRAPHY—*Robert L. Crippen, John W. Young;* SPACE EXPLORATION (articles written independent of NASA)

CALABRIA, PAT, Sports Department, *Newsday,* Long Island, NY: BIOGRAPHY—*Wayne Gretzky;* SPORTS—*Ice Hockey*

CAMMACK, PAUL, Lecturer in Government, University of Manchester, England: BOLIVIA

CANN, STANLEY, Consultant, *The Forum,* Fargo, ND: NORTH DAKOTA

CAREY, GARY, Free-lance Writer, Author, *Brando!, Katharine Hepburn,* and *All the Stars in Heaven:* MOTION PICTURES—*Katharine Hepburn*

CARLYLE-GORDGE, PETER, Manitoba Correspondent, *Maclean's* magazine and Contributing Writer to *The Financial Post, Montreal Gazette, Toronto Star:* MANITOBA

CHALMERS, JOHN W., Concordia College, Edmonton, Alberta; Editor, *Alberta Diamond Jubilee Anthology:* ALBERTA

CLARKE, JAMES W., Professor of Political Science, University of Arizona: ARIZONA

CLIFT, ELEANOR, Washington Bureau, *Newsweek:* BIOGRAPHY—*Edwin Meese, Robert H. Michel, David A. Stockman, James Watt*

COCKRUM, E. LENDELL, Professor and Head, Department of Ecology and Evolutionary Biology, University of Arizona: ZOOLOGY

COLE, GORDON H., Senior Staff Associate, George Meany Center for Labor Studies: LABOR

COLLINS, BOB, Sports Editor, *The Indianapolis Star:* SPORTS—*Auto Racing*

COMMANDAY, ROBERT, Music Critic, San Francisco Chronicle: MUSIC—*Classical*

CORLEW, ROBERT E., Dean, School of Liberal Arts, Middle Tennessee State University: TENNESSEE

CORNWELL, ELMER E., JR., Professor of Political Science, Brown University: RHODE ISLAND

CUNNIFF, JOHN, Business News Analyst, The Associated Press; Author, *How to Stretch Your Dollar:* UNITED STATES—*The Economy*

CUNNINGHAM, PEGGY, Staff Reporter, *The News American,* Baltimore: MARYLAND
CURRIER, CHET, Financial Writer, The Associated Press: STOCKS AND BONDS
CURTIS, L. PERRY, JR., Professor of History, Brown University: BIOGRAPHY—*Garrett FitzGerald;* IRELAND
DANIELS, ROBERT V., Professor of History, University of Vermont: VERMONT
DARBY, JOSEPH W., III, Reporter, *Times-Picayune,* New Orleans: LOUISIANA
DE GREGORIO, GEORGE, Sports Department, *The New York Times;* Author, *Joe DiMaggio, An Informal Biography:* BIOGRAPHY—*Tom Watson;* SPORTS—*Ice Skating, Skiing, Swimming, Track and Field*
DELZELL, CHARLES F., Professor of History, Vanderbilt University; Author, *Italy in the Twentieth Century:* ITALY
DENNIS, LARRY, Senior Editor, *Golf Digest;* Coauthor, *How to Become a Complete Golfer;* SPORTS—*Golf*
DIETERICH, H. R., Professor, History/American Studies, University of Wyoming, Laramie: WYOMING
DOBLER, CLIFFORD I., Professor Emeritus of Business Law, University of Idaho: IDAHO
DOLAN, PAUL, Professor of Political Science, University of Delaware; Coauthor, *Government of Delaware:* DELAWARE
DORPALEN, ANDREAS, Professor Emeritus of History, The Ohio State University: GERMANY
DRACHKOVITCH, MILORAD M., Senior Fellow, The Hoover Institute on War, Revolution, and Peace, Stanford University; Author, *U.S. Aid to Yugoslavia and Poland:* YUGOSLAVIA
DRIGGS, DON W., Chairman, Department of Political Science, University of Nevada; Coauthor, *The Nevada Constitution: Its Origin and Growth:* NEVADA
DUFF, ERNEST A., Professor of Political Science, Randolph-Macon Women's College; Author, *Agrarian Reform in Colombia:* COLOMBIA
DUFFY, HELEN, Art Critic, *Vie des Arts,* Montreal and *Artsmagazine,* Toronto: CANADA—*The Arts*
DUROSKA, LUD, *The New York Times;* Author/editor, *Football Rules in Pictures, Great Pro Quarterbacks,* and *Great Pro Running Backs:* SPORTS—*Football*
DURRENCE, J. LARRY, Department of History, Florida Southern College: FLORIDA
EADINGTON, WILLIAM R., Professor of Economics, University of Nevada, Reno; Organizer and Coordinator, First through Fifth National Conferences on Gambling, 1974–81; Author, *The Economics of Gambling Behavior;* Editor, *Gambling and Society:* GAMBLING
EINFRANK, AARON R., Free-lance Writer, Specialist in Middle East, Third World, and Soviet Affairs: IRAN; IRAQ; THIRD WORLD
ELGIN, RICHARD, Metro Desk, *The Patriot, The Evening News,* and *The Sunday Patriot-News,* Harrisburg, PA: PENNSYLVANIA
ELKINS, ANN M., Fashion Director, *Good Housekeeping Magazine:* BIOGRAPHY—*Bill Blass;* FASHION
ENSTAD, ROBERT H., Writer, *Chicago Tribune:* CHICAGO; ILLINOIS
ETCHESON, WARREN W., Graduate School of Business Administration, University of Washington: WASHINGTON
EWEGEN, BOB, Editorial Writer, *The Denver Post:* COLORADO
FAGEN, M. D., Bell Telephone Laboratories (retired); Editor, *A History of Engineering and Science in the Bell System,* Vols. I and II: COMMUNICATIONS TECHNOLOGY; TELEVISION AND RADIO—*Videodiscs*
FRANCESE, PETER K., Publisher, *American Demographics* magazine; member, Population Advisory Committee of the U.S. Bureau of Census; Author, *The 1980 Census—The Counting of America:* UNITED STATES—*The Nation's 20th Census*
FRANCIS, DAVID R., Business Editor, *The Christian Science Monitor:* INTERNATIONAL TRADE AND FINANCE
FRIIS, ERIK J., Editor-Publisher, *The Scandinavian-American Bulletin;* Author, *The American-Scandinavian Foundation 1910–1960: A Brief History:* DENMARK; FINLAND
GAILEY, HARRY A., Professor of History and Coordinator of African Studies, San Jose State University, California: CHAD; GHANA; NIGERIA
GARFIELD, ROBERT, Associate Professor of History, Co-Director, Afro-American Studies Program, De Paul University, Chicago, IL; Editor, *Readings in World Civilizations:* KENYA; TANZANIA; UGANDA
GEIS, GILBERT, Professor, Program in Social Ecology, University of California, Irvine; Author, *Man, Crime and Society:* CRIME; CRIME—*Protecting Public Figures*
GERBNER, GEORGE, Professor of Communications and Dean, The Annenberg School of Communications, University of Pennsylvania: LAW—*Television in the Courtroom*
GJESTER, THØR, Editor, *Økonomisk Revy,* Oslo: NORWAY
GOODMAN, DONALD, Associate Professor of Sociology, John Jay College of Criminal Justice, City University of New York: PRISONS
GORDON, MAYNARD M., Editor, *Motor News Analysis:* AUTOMOBILES; AUTOMOBILES—*Internationalization of the Industry*
GRAYSON, GEORGE W., Professor of Government, College of William and Mary: BIOGRAPHY—*Leopoldo Calvo Sotelo;* PORTUGAL; SPAIN
GREEN, MAUREEN, British Author and Journalist: BIOGRAPHY—*The Princess of Wales;* GREAT BRITAIN—*The Arts;* LONDON
GRENIER, FERNAND, Inter American Organization for Higher Education: QUEBEC
GROTH, ALEXANDER J., Professor of Political Science, University of California, Davis; Author, *People's Poland:* OBITUARIES—*Stefan Cardinal Wyszynski;* POLAND
GRUBERG, MARTIN, Professor of Political Science, University of Wisconsin, Oshkosh: HUMAN RIGHTS; LAW—*International*
HAKKARINEN, IDA, Research Meteorologist, General Electric Management and Technical Services Company, Beltsville, MD: METEOROLOGY—*The Weather Year*
HAND, SAMUEL B., Professor of History, University of Vermont: VERMONT
HARVEY, ROSS M., Assistant Director of Information, Government of the Northwest Territories: NORTHWEST TERRITORIES
HATHORN, RAMON, Professor of French Studies, University of Guelph, Guelph, Ontario: LITERATURE—*Canadian Literature in French*
HAYES, KIRBY M., Professor of Food Science and Nutrition, University of Massachusetts: FOOD
HEADY, EARL O., Charles F. Curtiss Distinguished Professor of Agriculture; Director, Center for Agricultural and Rural Development; Iowa State University; Author, *Economics of Agricultural Production and Resource* and *Agricultural Policies Under Economic Development:* AGRICULTURE
HECHINGER, FRED M., President, The New York Times Company Foundation, Inc.; Educational Columnist, *The New York Times;* Author, *The Big Red Schoolhouse;* Coauthor, *Teen-Age Tyranny* and *Growing Up in America:* EDUCATION—*U.S. Private Schools*
HELMREICH, E.C., Thomas B. Reed Professor of History and Political Science, Bowdoin College, Bowdoin, ME; Author, *The German Churches Under Hitler: Background, Struggle, and Epilogue:* AUSTRIA
HELMREICH, JONATHAN E., Professor of History, Allegheny College, Meadville, PA; Author, *Belgium and Europe: A Study in Small Power Diplomacy:* LUXEMBOURG
HELMREICH, PAUL C., Professor of History, Wheaton College, Norton, MA: SWITZERLAND
HELMS, ANDREA R. C., Associate Professor of Political Science, University of Alaska: ALASKA
HENDERSON, JIM, Sportswriter, *The Tampa Tribune,* Tampa, FL; Former Publisher, *Annual Soccer Guide:* SPORTS—*Soccer*
HENRIKSEN, THOMAS H., Research Fellow, Hoover Institution on War, Revolution, and Peace, Stanford, CA; Author, *Mozambique: A History;* Coauthor, *The Struggle for Zimbabwe: Battle in the Bush:* ANGOLA; ZAIRE
HESSE, GEORGIA I., Travel Editor, *San Francisco Examiner;* Author, *Going My Way, A Travel Editor's Guide to Getting More for Less* and *France:* TRAVEL
HOGGART, SIMON, Special Correspondent, *The Observer,* London; Author, *The Pact:* GREAT BRITAIN; GREAT BRITAIN—*Northern Ireland*
HOOVER, HERBERT T., Professor of History, University of South Dakota: SOUTH DAKOTA
HOPKO, THE REV. THOMAS, Assistant Professor, St. Vladimir's Orthodox Theological Seminary, Crestwood, NY: RELIGION—*Orthodox Eastern*
HOWARD, HARRY N., Board of Governors, Middle East Institute, Washington, DC; Author, *Turkey, the Straits and U.S. Policy:* TURKEY
HOYT, CHARLES K., Associate Editor, *Architectural Record;* Author, *Interior Spaces Designed by Architects, Public Municipal and Community Buildings,* and *Buildings for Commerce and Industry:* ARCHITECTURE
HULBERT, DAN, *The Dallas Times-Herald:* TELEVISION AND RADIO
HULL, RICHARD W., Associate Professor of African History, New York University; Author, *Southern Africa: Civilization in Turmoil, Modern Africa: Change and Continuity,* and *African Cities and Towns Before the European Conquest:* AFRICA
HUME, ANDREW, Free-lance Writer/Photographer, Former Reporter, *The Whitehorse* (Yukon) *Star;* Author, *The Yukon:* YUKON
HUTH, JOHN F., Reporter, Financial News Department, *The Plain Dealer,* Cleveland: OHIO
IRWIN, DON, Reporter, Washington Bureau, *Los Angeles Times:* UNITED STATES—*Domestic Affairs*
IVEY, WILLIAM, Director, The Country Music Foundation: MUSIC—*Country Music*
JACKSON, LIVIA E. BITTON, Professor of Judaic Studies, Herbert H. Lehman College, City University of New York; Author, *Elli: Coming of Age in the Holocaust:* ISRAEL; RELIGION—*Judaism*
JAFFE, HERMAN J., Department of Anthropology, Brooklyn College, City University of New York: ANTHROPOLOGY

JENNINGS, PETER, Chief Foreign Correspondent, ABC News: THE YEAR IN REVIEW
JEWELL, MALCOLM E., Professor of Political Science, University of Kentucky; Coauthor, *Kentucky Politics:* KENTUCKY
JOHNSON, JENNIFER, Librarian, Prairie History Room, Regina Public Library, Regina, Saskatchewan: SASKATCHEWAN
JOHNSTON, ROBERT L., Editor, *The Catholic Review,* newsweekly of the Baltimore Archdiocese: RELIGION—*Roman Catholicism*
JOHNSTONE, J. K., Professor of English, University of Saskatchewan; Fellow of the Royal Society of Literature; Author, *The Bloomsbury Group:* LITERATURE—*English*
JONES, H. G., Curator, North Carolina Collection, University of North Carolina Library: NORTH CAROLINA
JOSEPH, LOU, Scientific Information Chief, Bureau of Communications, American Dental Association: MEDICINE AND HEALTH—*Dentistry*
KARNES, THOMAS L., Chairman, Department of History, Arizona State University; Author, *Latin American Policy of the United States* and *Failure of Union: Central America 1824-1960:* BELIZE; BIOGRAPHY—*José Napoleón Duarte;* CENTRAL AMERICA; CENTRAL AMERICA—*El Salvador;* OBITUARIES—*Omar Torrijos Herrera*
KARSKI, JAN, Professor of Government, Georgetown University; Author, *Story of a Secret State:* BULGARIA; HUNGARY; RUMANIA
KASH, DON E., Professor, University of Oklahoma; Coauthor, *Our Energy Future: The Role of Research, Development, and Demonstration in Reaching a National Consensus on Energy Supply:* ENERGY
KEHR, ERNEST A., Stamp News Bureau; Author, *The Romance of Stamp Collecting:* STAMPS AND STAMP COLLECTING
KIMBALL, LORENZO K., Professor of Political Science, University of Utah: UTAH
KIMBELL, CHARLES L., Supervisory Physical Scientist, United States Bureau of Mines: MINING; STATISTICAL AND TABULAR DATA—*World Mineral Production*
KING, PETER J., Associate Professor of History; Carleton University, Ottawa: ONTARIO; OTTAWA
KISSELGOFF, ANNA, Chief Dance Critic, *The New York Times:* DANCE
KOSAKI, RICHARD H., Professor of Political Science, University of Hawaii: HAWAII
LAI, CHUEN-YAN DAVID, Associate Professor of Geography, University of Victoria, B.C.: HONG KONG
LANDSBERG, H. E., Professor Emeritus, University of Maryland; Author, *Physical Climatology, Weather and Health,* and *The Urban Climate:* METEOROLOGY
LARSEN, WILLIAM, Author, *Montague of Virginia, The Making of a Southern Progressive:* VIRGINIA
LAURENT, PIERRE-HENRI, Professor of History, Tufts University; Adjunct Professor of Diplomatic History, Fletcher School of Law and Diplomacy: BELGIUM
LAWRENCE, ROBERT M., Department of Political Science, Colorado State University; Author, *Arms Control and Disarmament: Practice and Promise* and *Nuclear Proliferation: Phase II:* MILITARY AFFAIRS; MILITARY AFFAIRS—*Nuclear Proliferation*
LEE, STEWART M., Professor and Chairman, Department of Economics and Business Administration, Geneva College, Beaver Falls, PA; Editor, *Newsletter,* American Council on Consumer Interests: CONSUMER AFFAIRS
LEVITT, MORRIS J., Professor, Department of Political Science, Howard University; Coauthor, *Of, By and For The People: State and Local Government and Politics:* WASHINGTON, DC
LIDDLE, R. WILLIAM, Professor of Political Science, The Ohio State University; Author, *Political Participation in Modern Indonesia:* INDONESIA
LINDAHL, MAC, Harvard University: SWEDEN
LIPSET, SEYMOUR MARTIN, Professor of Sociology and Political Science; Senior Fellow, The Hoover Institution on War, Revolution, and Peace, Stanford University: Author, *Political Man: The Social Bases of Politics:* U.S. POLITICAL CONSERVATISM—MEANINGS AND ORIGINS
LOBRON, BARBARA, Writer, Editor, Photographer; Copy Editor, *Camera Arts:* PHOTOGRAPHY
LORD, RODNEY, Economics Correspondent, *The Daily Telegraph,* London; GREAT BRITAIN—*The Economy*
LOWRY, W. McNEIL, Former Vice-President, The Ford Foundation; Editor, *The Performing Arts and American Society:* THE ECONOMICS OF THE ARTS
MABRY, DONALD J., Professor of History, Mississippi State University; Author, *Mexico's Acción Nacional:* MEXICO
McCORQUODALE, SUSAN, Associate Professor, Department of Political Science, Memorial University of Newfoundland: NEWFOUNDLAND
McDOUGALL, EDGAR J., JR., Vice-President, Stadler Development Corporation: HOUSING
McGILL, DAVID A., Professor of Ocean Science, U.S. Coast Guard Academy, New London, CT: OCEANOGRAPHY
MADIER, MONIQUE, French Writer and Editor; BIOGRAPHY—*François Mitterrand;* FRANCE
MARCOPOULOS, GEORGE J., Associate Professor of History, Tufts University, Medford, MA: CYPRUS; GREECE
MASOTTI, LOUIS H., Center for Urban Affairs & Policy Research, Northwestern University, Evanston, IL; Author, *The New Urban Politics* and *The City in Comparative Perspective:* CITIES AND URBAN AFFAIRS
MATHEWS, THOMAS G., Secretary-General of the Association of Caribbean Universities, University of Puerto Rico; Author, *Politics and Economics in the Caribbean* and *Puerto Rican Politics and the New Deal:* CARIBBEAN; CARIBBEAN—*Jamaica;* PUERTO RICO; TRINIDAD AND TOBAGO; VIRGIN ISLANDS
MEYER, EDWARD H., President and Chairman of the Board, Grey Advertising Inc.: ADVERTISING
MICHAELIS, PATRICIA A., Curator of Manuscripts, Kansas State Historical Society: KANSAS
MIRE, JOSEPH, Former Executive Director, National Institute for Labor Education: LABOR
MITCHELL, GARY, Professor of Physics, North Carolina State University, Raleigh: PHYSICS
MONTVILLE, LEIGH, Sports Columnist, *The Boston Globe;* Contributor, *The Sporting News:* BIOGRAPHY—*Bobby Knight;* SPORTS—*Basketball*
MORTON, DESMOND, Professor of History, Erindale College, University of Toronto; Author, *Ministers and Generals, The Canadian General, Social Democracy in Canada, Working People: An Illustrated History of Canadian Labour,* and *Canada and War:* CANADA
MULLINER, K., Southeast Asia Collection, Ohio University; Coeditor, *Southeast Asia, An Emerging Center of World Influence?:* MALAYSIA; SINGAPORE; THAILAND
MURPHY, ROBERT F., *The Hartford Courant:* CONNECTICUT; OBITUARIES—*Ella Grasso*
NADLER, PAUL S., Professor of Finance, Rutgers University; Author, *Commercial Banking in the Economy* and *Paul Nadler Writes About Banking:* BANKING
NAFTALIN, ARTHUR, Professor of Public Affairs, Hubert H. Humphrey Institute of Public Affairs, University of Minnesota: MINNESOTA
NATIONAL FIRE PROTECTION ASSOCIATION, Public Affairs Division: DISASTERS—*Fires and Fire Prevention in the United States*
NOLAN, WILLIAM C., Professor of Political Science, Southern Arkansas University: ARKANSAS
NORMAN, COLIN, Writer, *Science* magazine, former Senior Researcher, Worldwatch Institute: THE COMPUTER EXPLOSION
NOVICKI, MARGARET A., Assistant Editor, *Africa Report,* The African-American Institute: ALGERIA; MOROCCO; SUDAN; TUNISIA
OCHSENWALD, WILLIAM L., Associate Professor of History, Virginia Polytechnic Institute; Author, *The Hijaz Railroad:* SAUDI ARABIA
O'MEARA, PATRICK, Director, African Studies Program; Associate Professor, School of Public and Environmental Affairs; Associate Professor of Political Science, Indiana University, Bloomington, IN: SOUTH AFRICA; ZIMBABWE
OMENN, GILBERT S., Professor of Medicine, Division of Medical Genetics, University of Washington; Science and Public Policy Fellow, The Brookings Institution; Coeditor, *Genetics, Environment and Behavior: Implications for Educational Policy:* GENETICS
O'ROURKE, E. N., Professor of Horticulture, Louisiana State University: BOTANY; GARDENING AND HORTICULTURE
PALMER, NORMAN D., Professor of Political Science and South Asian Studies, University of Pennsylvania; Author, *Elections and Political Development: The South Asian Experience:* INDIA; SRI LANKA
PANO, NICHOLAS C., Professor of History, Western Illinois University; Author, *The People's Republic of Albania:* ALBANIA
PARDES, HERBERT, Director, National Institute of Mental Health: MEDICINE AND HEALTH—*Mental Health*
PARKER, FRANKLIN, Benedum Professor of Education, West Virginia University; Author, *Battle of the Books, British Schools and Ours,* and *U.S. Higher Education: A Guide to Education Sources:* EDUCATION
PARSONS, KAREN ELISE, Free-lance Writer, formerly with the Council of State Governments: FORESTRY
PEARSON, NEALE J., Associate Professor of Political Science, Texas Tech University, Lubbock, TX: CHILE; PERU; VENEZUELA
PERKINS, KENNETH J., Assistant Professor of History, University of South Carolina: BIOGRAPHY—*Muammar el-Qaddafi;* LIBYA; RELIGION—*Islam*
PIPPIN, LARRY L., Professor of Political Science, Elbert Covell College, University of the Pacific; Author, *The Remón Era:* ARGENTINA; BIOGRAPHY—*Roberto Eduardo Viola;* PARAGUAY
PLATT, HERMANN K., Professor of History, Saint Peter's College, Jersey City: NEW JERSEY
PLISCHKE, ELMER, Professor Emeritus, University of Maryland; Adjunct Professor, Gettysburg College; Adjunct Scholar, American Enterprise Institute; Author, *Microstates in World Affairs, Modern Diplomacy: The Art and the Artisans,* and *Con-*

duct of American Diplomacy: MICROSTATES AND THE COMMUNITY OF NATIONS; BIOGRAPHY—*Alexander Haig;* UNITED STATES—*Foreign Affairs*

POOLE, PETER A., Associate Professor, Old Dominion University, Norfolk, VA; Author, *The Vietnamese in Thailand:* CAMBODIA; VIETNAM

POPKIN, HENRY, Professor of English, State University of New York at Buffalo: THEATER

POULLADA, LEON B., Professor of Political Science, Northern Arizona University; Author, *Reform and Rebellion in Afghanistan:* AFGHANISTAN

PRITCHETT, C. HERMAN, Professor of Political Science, University of California, Santa Barbara; Author, *The Roosevelt Court* and *The American Constitution:* BIOGRAPHY—*Sandra Day O'Connor;* LAW—*The Supreme Court*

QUIRK, WILLIAM H., Construction Consultant; Former North American Editor, *Construction Industry International* magazine: ENGINEERING, CIVIL

RAGUSA, ISA, Research Art Historian, Department of Art and Archaeology, Princeton University: ART

RAYMOND, ELLSWORTH L. Professor of Politics (retired), New York University; Author, *Soviet Economic Progress* and *The Soviet State:* USSR

REUNING, WINIFRED, Writer, Polar Programs, National Science Foundation: POLAR RESEARCH

RICHTER, WILLIAM L., Director, South Asia Center, Kansas State University: BANGLADESH; PAKISTAN

RIGGAN, WILLIAM, Associate Editor, *World Literature Today,* University of Oklahoma; Author, *Picaros, Madmen, Naïfs, and Clowns: The Unreliable First-Person Narrator* and *Comparative Literature and Literary Theory:* LITERATURE—*World Literature*

ROBINSON, LEIF J., Editor, *Sky & Telescope:* ASTRONOMY

ROEDER, RICHARD B., Professor of History, Montana State University: MONTANA

ROSS, RUSSELL M., Professor of Political Science, University of Iowa; Author, *Iowa Government & Administration:* IOWA

ROTHSTEIN, MORTON, Professor of History, University of Wisconsin, Madison: SOCIAL WELFARE; SOCIAL WELFARE—*Social Security and Retirement Income*

ROWEN, HERBERT H., Professor, Rutgers University; Editor, *The Low Countries in Early Modern Times: A Documentary History:* THE NETHERLANDS

ROWLETT, RALPH M., Professor of Anthropology, University of Missouri; Coauthor, *Neolithic Levels on the Titelberg, Luxembourg:* ARCHAEOLOGY

RUFF, NORMAN J., Assistant Professor, University of Victoria: BRITISH COLUMBIA

SALSINI, PAUL, State Editor, *The Milwaukee Journal:* WISCONSIN

SAVAGE, DAVID, Lecturer, Department of English, Simon Fraser University: LITERATURE—*Canadian Literature in English*

SCHERER, RON, Business and Financial Correspondent, *The Christian Science Monitor:* BUSINESS AND CORPORATE AFFAIRS

SCHLOSSBERG, DAN, Contributing Editor, *Baseball World Magazine;* Author, *The Baseball Catalog, Barons of the Bullpen,* and *Hammerin' Hank: The Henry Aaron Story:* SPORTS—*Baseball*

SCHORR, THELMA M., President and Publisher, American Journal of Nursing Company: MEDICINE AND HEALTH—*The U.S. Nursing Profession*

SCHRIVER, EDWARD, University of Maine, Orono; Author, *Go Free: Antislavery, Maine 1833-1855:* MAINE

SCHROEDER, RICHARD C., Syndicated Writer on Foreign Affairs, Social Problems, and Legislation: BRAZIL; LATIN AMERICA; REFUGEES AND IMMIGRATION

SCHWAB, PETER, Professor of Political Science, State University of New York at Purchase; Author, *Decision-Making in Ethiopia* and *Haile Selassie I:* ETHIOPIA

SCOTT, EUGENE L., Publisher and Founder, *Tennis Week;* Author, *Björn Borg: My Life & Game, Tennis: Game of Motion,* and *The Tennis Experience:* SPORTS—*Tennis*

SELDEN, MARK, Professor, Department of Sociology, State University of New York at Binghamton; Coauthor, *North & South Korea: The Deepening Crisis:* KOREA

SETH, R. P., Professor of Economics, Mount Saint Vincent University, Halifax: NOVA SCOTIA

SEYBOLD, PAUL G., Associate Professor of Chemistry, Wright State University, Dayton, OH: CHEMISTRY

SIEGEL, STANLEY E., Professor of History, University of Houston: Author, *A Political History of the Texas Republic, 1836-1845:* TEXAS

SIMMONS, MARC, Author, *New Mexico, A Bicentennial History:* NEW MEXICO

SLOAN, HENRY S., Associate Editor, *Current Biography:* BIOGRAPHY—*Alan Alda, A. W. Clausen, Christopher Cross, Robert De Niro, Goldie Hawn, L. Bruce Laingen;* OBITUARIES—*Omar Bradley*

SPECTER, MICHAEL, *The New York Times:* NEW YORK; NEW YORK CITY

SPERA, DOMINIC, Associate Professor of Music, Indiana University; Author, *The Prestige Series—16 Original Compositions for Jazz Band:* MUSIC—*Jazz*

STENCEL, SANDRA, Managing Editor, *Editorial Research Reports:* BIOGRAPHY—*Nancy Reagan;* WOMEN

STERN, JEROME H., Associate Professor of English, Florida State University: BIOGRAPHY—*Walter Percy;* LITERATURE—*American*

STEWART, WILLIAM H., JR., Associate Professor of Political Science, The University of Alabama; Author, *The Alabama Constitutional Commission:* ALABAMA

STOKES, WILLIAM LEE, Professor, Department of Geology and Geophysics, University of Utah; Author, *Essentials of Earth History* and *Introduction to Geology:* GEOLOGY

STOUDEMIRE, ROBERT H., Professor of Government, University of South Carolina: SOUTH CAROLINA

SUGAR, BERT RANDOLPH, Editor and Publisher, *The Ring* magazine: OBITUARIES—*Joe Louis;* SPORTS—*Boxing*

SYLVESTER, LORNA LUTES, Associate Editor, *Indiana Magazine of History,* Indiana University: INDIANA

TABORSKY, EDWARD, Professor of Government, University of Texas, Austin; Author, *Communism in Czechoslovakia, 1948-1960* and *Communist Penetration of the Third World:* CZECHOSLOVAKIA

TAFT, WILLIAM H., Professor Emeritus of Journalism, University of Missouri, Columbia; Author, *American Journalism History:* PUBLISHING

TAN, CHESTER C., Department of History, New York University; Author, *Chinese Political Thought in the 20th Century:* CHINA; TAIWAN

TATTERSALL, IAN, Curator, Department of Anthropology, American Museum of Natural History; Author, *Man's Ancestors:* LUCY—A HUMAN ANCESTOR?

TAYLOR, WILLIAM L., Professor of History, Plymouth State College, Plymouth, NH: NEW HAMPSHIRE

TESAR, JENNY, Free-lance Science Writer: MEDICINE AND HEALTH; MICROBIOLOGY

THEISEN, CHARLES W., Assistant News Editor, *The Detroit News:* MICHIGAN

TOWNE, RUTH W., Professor of History, Northeast Missouri State University: MISSOURI

TURNER, ARTHUR CAMPBELL, Professor of Political Science, University of California, Riverside; Author, *Tension Areas in World Affairs;* Coauthor, *Control of Foreign Relations:* BIOGRAPHY—*Hosni Mubarak;* EGYPT; MIDDLE EAST; OBITUARIES—*Anwar el-Sadat, Moshe Dayan;* THE YEMENS

VAN RIPER, PAUL P., Professor and Head, Department of Political Science (retired), Texas A&M University; Author, *Handbook of Practical Politics:* POSTAL SERVICE

VOGT, BILL, Senior Editor, *National Wildlife* and *International Wildlife* magazines; Author, *How to Build a Better Outdoors:* ENVIRONMENT

VOLSKY, GEORGE, Center for Advanced International Studies, University of Miami: CUBA

WALL, JAMES M., Editor, *The Christian Century;* Author, *Church and Cinema: A Critical Methodology for Evaluating Film* and *Three European Directors:* RELIGION—*Protestantism*

WATTERS, ELSIE M., Director of Research, Tax Foundation, Inc.: TAXATION

WEEKS, JEANNE G., Member, American Society of Interior Designers; Coauthor, *Fabrics for Interiors:* INTERIOR DESIGN

WEISS, PAULETTE, Popular Music Editor, *Stereo Review Magazine:* MUSIC—*Popular;* RECORDINGS

WENTZ, RICHARD E., Professor of Religious Studies, Arizona State University; Author, *Saga of the American Soul:* RELIGION—*Survey, Far Eastern*

WHITTINGHAM, ANTHONY, Senior Writer, *Maclean's* magazine: CANADA—*The Economy*

WILLARD, F. NICHOLAS, Professor, Washington, DC: JORDAN; LEBANON; SYRIA

WILLIAMS, DENNIS, General Editor, *Newsweek:* ETHNIC GROUPS; OBITUARIES—*Roy Wilkins*

WILLIAMS, ERNEST W., JR., Professor of Transportation, Graduate School of Business, Columbia University; Coauthor, *Transportation and Logistics* and *Shipping Conferences in the Container Age:* TRANSPORTATION

WILLIS, F. ROY, Professor of History, University of California, Davis; Author, *Italy Chooses Europe* and *France, Germany and the New Europe:* EUROPE

WOLF, WILLIAM, Film Commentator, *New York* magazine; Author, *The Marx Brothers* and *The Landmark Films/The Cinema and our Century:* MOTION PICTURES

WOOD, JOHN, Professor of Political Science, University of Oklahoma: OKLAHOMA

WOODS, GEORGE A., Children's Book Editor, *The New York Times;* Author, *Vibrations* and *Catch a Killer:* LITERATURE—*Children's*

YOUNGER, R. M., Author, *Australia's Great River* and *Australia! Australia! March to Nationhood:* AUSTRALIA

ZABEL, ORVILLE H., Professor of History, Creighton University, Omaha: NEBRASKA

INDEX

Main article headings appear in this index as bold-faced capitals; subjects within articles appear as lower-case entries. Both the general references and the subentries should be consulted for maximum usefulness of this index. Illustrations are indexed herein. Cross references are to the entries in this index.

A

D

E

F

G

J

K

L

M

N

O

T

U